THE BANTAM GREAT OUTDOORS VACATION & LODGING GUIDE

Eastern United States • Western United States and Alaska • Canada

The Bantam Great Outdoors Guide, the first book of this trail-blazing series, was hailed from coast to coast as the most comprehensive, authoritative travel encyclopedia and wilderness guide ever published to the U.S. and Canada. A beautifully illustrated wilderness library in one fact-packed volume, it was selected by the Literary Guild Book Club, L.L. Bean and Montgomery Ward catalogs, Reader's Digest Books, and designated one of the "Outstanding Reference Books of the Year" by the American Library Association.

The new three-volume *Bantam Great Outdoors Vacation & Lodging Guide* was created for the family on the go as well as the lone nature lover. Its revolutionary format will provide you with the most useful and complete all-year-round vacation and lodging information ever published to the Eastern United States, Western United States and Alaska, and Canada.

No other guide offers the breadth and depth of coverage you'll get in *The Bantam Great Outdoors Vacation & Lodging Guide*. Here, finally, is all the hard-to-find information you'll ever need to make planning your next vacation or weekend trip easier than ever before. Organized in an easy-to-use A–Z format, it provides the indispensable details on all major vacation and outdoor recreation areas; gateway cities and towns; information sources, maps and access; accommodations, lodges and resorts; transportation and outfitting services.

The perfect gift for you and everyone who loves the great outdoors!

Book-of-the-Month Club Selection
Quality Paperback Book Club Selection

Bantam Books by Val Landi
Ask your bookseller for the books you have missed

THE BANTAM GREAT OUTDOORS GUIDE

THE BANTAM GREAT OUTDOORS VACATION AND LODGING GUIDE: Canada

THE BANTAM GREAT OUTDOORS VACATION AND LODGING GUIDE: Eastern U.S.

THE BANTAM GREAT OUTDOORS VACATION AND LODGING GUIDE: Western U.S. and Alaska

THE BANTAM

GREAT OUTDOORS VACATION & LODGING GUIDE

Western United States and Alaska

BY VAL LANDI

Illustrated by Gordon Allen

PHOTO CREDITS

We are grateful to the following United States government agencies, firms, lodge and resort operators for granting us permission to reproduce their photos: U.S. Dept. of Interior—National Park Service, U.S. Fish and Wildlife Service, U.S. Forest Service, U.S. Geological Survey, Yosemite Park & Curry Co., Yellowstone Park Company, Aspen Highlands Resort Group, 7-D Ranch—Frank Woods, Sun Valley Co., Purgatory Ski Resort, Golden Horn Lodge—Alaska, Sequoia & Kings Canyon Hospitality Service, Keystone—Colorado, Kirkwood Meadows Inc., Winter Park Recreational Assn.—Kristin Rud, Timberline Lodge—Oregon, Taos Ski Valley, Yes Bay Lodge—Alaska, Rocky Mountain River Tours—David Mills, Nine Quarter Circle Ranch—Montana, Grand Canyon National Park Lodges, Bristol Bay Lodge—Alaska, Sage Advertising, Afognak Wilderness Lodge—Alaska, Mountain Travel—California, Ski Heavenly, Boyne USA, Mt. Adams Wilderness Institute, Grand Teton Lodge Co., Glacier Bay Lodge Inc., Mt. Rainier Nat'l Park Hospitality Service, Wien Consolidated Airlines Inc., and the Breckenridge Resort Assn.—Colorado.

THE BANTAM GREAT OUTDOORS VACATION AND LODGING GUIDE:
WESTERN U.S. AND ALASKA
A Bantam Book / April 1980

Cover photos courtesy National Park Service, Sequoia & Kings Canyon Hospitality Service, 7-D Ranch, Grand Canyon National Park Lodges, Nine Quarter Circle Ranch, Grand Teton Lodge Co.

ISBN 0-553-01232-0

Published simultaneously in the United States and Canada

Bantam Books are published by Bantam Books, Inc. Its trademark, consisting of the words "Bantam Books" and the portrayal of a bantam, is Registered in U.S. Patent and Trademark Office and in other countries. Marca Registrada. Bantam Books, Inc., 666 Fifth Avenue, New York, New York 10019.

PRINTED IN THE UNITED STATES OF AMERICA

0 9 8 7 6 5 4 3 2 1

ACKNOWLEDGMENTS

I am deeply grateful to the hundreds of United States government travel, forestry, fish and wildlife, park and conservation authorities and their agencies (listed throughout the book) and the lodge, resort, hotel, and motel operators and local chambers of commerce and state travel officials who contributed their time and expertise, and provided much of the source material that made the compilation of *The Bantam Great Outdoors Vacation & Lodging Guide to the Western United States* possible. I also wish to acknowledge the kind assistance given by the members of the American Hotel & Motel Assn. and the useful *AHMA Redbook*.

Special thanks go to the members of the *Great Outdoors Vacation & Lodging Guide* Series editorial research and field staff—especially Jason Mackenzie, Marilyn Young, Anne Ashely, and Judy May—for their valuable contributions. For much of the fascinating local historical information found throughout the guide, we are indebted to the useful Federal Writers' Project guides to Alaska, Washington, Oregon, California, Nevada, Idaho, Utah, Arizona, Montana, Wyoming, Colorado, New Mexico, Oklahoma, Texas, Louisiana, Arkansas, Missouri, Kansas, Nebraska, South Dakota, and North Dakota.

My thanks go also to Beverly Susswein and Ken Leish of Bantam Books for their support and kind assistance; and to Gordon Allen, for his superb and powerful drawings of the great outdoors.

CONTENTS

INTRODUCTION

Lodging Symbols & Rates

The Western United States lodges, resorts, inns, ski centers, motels, and hotels described in the pages that follow have been listed, after rigorous evaluation, as a service for vacation travelers. Be sure to contact lodgings of interest directly for possible changes in conditions or rates, due to the constant cost increases caused by the rate of inflation. In most instances, we have provided summer and/or ski season rates.

Please note that rates have been included only as a guide to help you plan a trip to fit your budget. It's advisable to check references provided by the vacation lodges and resorts, and make your reservations at the earliest possible dates. Most of the outstanding lodges, resorts, and ski centers are booked up months in advance. In almost all cases, a deposit is required to hold your reservation.

The following rating symbols are used throughout the book:

★★★★—Outstanding
★★★—Excellent
★★—Very good
★—Good

In rating lodges, resorts, and guest ranches, we have given considerable weight to location and the quality of the outdoor recreation opportunities of the surrounding area, in addition to the quality of facilities and services.

Western United States Youth Hostels

American Youth Hostels, a non-profit youth service organization, sponsors a nationwide system of inexpensive overnight accommodations, many of which are located in major outdoor recreation areas, with responsible adult supervision, owned or chartered by one of the 50 national hosteling associations affiliated with the International Youth Hostel Federation. These inexpensive lodgings—in such outdoor meccas as Wyoming's Jackson Hole, Washington's Olympic Peninsula, and California's High Sierras—are ideally suited for young people on the go—backpacking, canoeing, skiing, sailing, bicycling, or bird watching.

A 192-page *American Youth Hostels Guide* ($1.75, plus 50¢ postage and handling) and information may be obtained from: American Youth Hostels, Inc., National Headquarters, Delaplane, VA 22025 (703)592–3271.

Maps & Trip Planning Information

The fabled outdoor recreation areas of the Western United States are shown on the full-color U.S. Geological Survey topographic maps, which may be ordered using the *Topographic Map Indexes*, available free for each state upon request from the Distribution Office at the following address: U.S. Geological Survey, Federal Center, Denver, CO 80225. These eminently useful maps show man-made and natural features, including contours, forests, lakes and streams, mountain ranges, roads, villages, trails, bogs, portages, rapids and falls, wilderness cabins, and much more.

If you're planning an extended backcountry vacation, it pays to get in top physical condition before you depart. Watch out for bad sunburns from the bright reflecting surfaces of lakes and rivers. To avoid exposure, wear a wide-brimmed hat and a pair of quality sunglasses, along with an effective sunscreen such as Almay Deep Tanning Oil, Sun Block Gel, Pabanol, Pre-Sun, and Bain de Soleil Suntan Foam—all of which contain a concentration of 5 percent para-aminobenzoic acid in 50–70 percent ethanol. A supply of salt tablets will help restore sodium lost through perspiration. Be sure to pack a good supply of bug dope and a head net and cotton gloves for travel during the black fly and mosquito season. Recommended insect repellents include Muskol, Mosquitone, Off!, and Cutters, all of which contain a 50 percent plus concentration of DEET—the most effective known repellent against insect pests.

For detailed travel information on the area you plan to visit contact the addresses and/or phone numbers listed under the "Information Sources, Maps & Access" sections found throughout the book. Listings and descriptions of all national forest and wilderness area maps, national park maps, state highway and road maps, and regional guidebooks are listed throughout the book. Perhaps the best source of information about the area you plan to visit are the local lodges and resorts, as well as outfitters.

Traveler's Field Guides to Wildlife and Flora

In addition to the proper maps, equipment, and accessories, no outdoor traveler is complete without a good set of field guides to the wildlife and flora of the major life zones he is likely to travel through. Among the classic, time-tested field guides are *Roger Tory Peterson's Field Guide Series*—to the Birds, Mammals, Pacific Coast Shells, Rocks and Minerals, Animal Tracks, Ferns, Trees and Shrubs, Reptiles and Amphibians, and Rocky Mountain Wildflowers—all published by Houghton Mifflin Co. The *Golden Field Guide to the Birds of North America* is thought by many to be the best bird guide ever published—its color paintings are without parallel for identification of field markings. The *Golden Field Guide Series* includes useful, full-color guides to Trees of North America, Rocks and Minerals, and Seashells.

The new all-photographic, full-color *Audubon Society Field Guides* to North American Birds—Western Region, North American Wildflowers—Western Region, and Rocks and Minerals, have set a new standard for field guides, with exclusive use of full-color photographs, new visual identification systems, fullness of textual data, and a handy, waterproof, pocket-sized format. Each guide has 864 pages, with between 650 and 700 color photographs which show the individual species as you would see them with the naked eye or through a pair of

binoculars. Radically new identification keys make it possible to identify birds, wildflowers, or rock specimens quickly and accurately without special knowledge or training. The breadth

of coverage is far greater than in competing guides, and the text provides scientific facts and background notes on habitat and environment, use, folklore, and more. The texts are supplemented with dozens of black and white drawings.

ALASKA—THE LAST FRONTIER

Introduction

Alaska, derived from the Eskimo word *Alayeska*, meaning "the great land," is one of the world's last great outdoor frontiers. Here, contained within an immense land area of 586,000 square miles, are historic gold rush boom towns, picturesque coastal fishing villages, and several of the world's greatest remaining fishing, hunting, and wild-river canoeing areas, set amongst a majestic wilderness of wave-swept coastal rain forests, towering glacier-studded snow-crowned mountain ranges and awesome volcanic highlands that reach up toward the clouds, eerie windswept sand dunes located north of the Arctic Circle, huge blue mountain-girded lakes, vast boreal forests and soft tundra barrens, wild torrential rivers, and seemingly endless mazes of mist-shrouded, evergreen-clad islands, inhabited by giant Alaskan brown bear, moose, Dall sheep, barren-ground grizzly, Roosevelt elk, wolves, caribou, and the nation's largest population of bald eagles. The remote, seldom fished lakes and streams hold record-sized rainbow and lake trout, salmon, huge northern pike, arctic grayling, and giant mysterious sheefish—the "tarpon of the Arctic."

Alaska has an enormous diversity and range of climate. The maritime climate of the Panhandle, warmed by the Japan Current, has mild winters, cool summers, and extremely heavy rainfall. In some areas of the Tongass Country, average annual precipitation exceeds 150 inches. In the high country of south central Alaska, snowstorms are likely to occur at all times of the year; bad weather conditions are the rule here. The inland valleys have moderate rainfall, short but rather warm summers, and winter temperatures not unlike those found in the northern prairie states. The rugged, mountainous terrain of southwestern Alaska is generally wet, with mild foggy summers and harsh winters. South of the Aleutian Islands is an area of low pressure with an east-west trend commonly known as the Aleutian Low. Many of the cyclonic disturbances of the Northern Hemisphere swirl through this low-pressure trough. The Great Interior is a land of intensely hot summers and harsh, frigid winters. The subarctic far-north regions have very short summers with little precipitation.

When fishing, hunting, or camping in the high country of southern Alaska, you should be alert for the violent and gusty wind known to the natives as the *williwaw*, which sweeps across the Bering Sea from Siberia, often reaching gale forces of up to 100 miles per hour on the high passes and leeward slopes of mountains. For protection against these fearsome winds, which have been known to flip over commercial salmon-fishing boats and bush planes and collapse tents, the smart woodsman will camp down low, pitching his tent in an isolated, protected stand of timber. Be sure in planning your trip to avoid the freeze-up, which lasts from the second week in October well into May, and even into mid-July in some high-country regions.

Alaska's grizzlies, both the barren-ground and giant Kodiak varieties, present potential hazards to the wilderness fisherman, hunter, backpacker, and paddler. Several unknowing backpackers have lost their lives or have been seriously maimed by foolishly camping along well-traveled bear trails.

The most ferocious beast of prey in this great land, however, is the voracious Alaskan mosquito. If you are planning a trip to Alaska, be sure to pack a good supply of Muskol, Mosquitone, Cutters, or Off! insect repellent. All of them contain concentrations of 50%–plus of DEET, the most effective known insect repellent. It's also advisable to take along a wide-brimmed hat, raingear, a light-colored heavy cotton or wool shirt, and sunglasses.

Accommodations & Travel Information

Alaska's major vacation lodges and sporting camps are described in the "Vacation/Lodging Guide." Important gateway hotels, motels, and inns are listed in the "Vacation/Lodging Guide" and also in this section under "Gateways." Detailed information and literature about vacation travel in Alaska may be obtained from: Alaska Division of Tourism, Pouch E, Juneau 99811 (907)465–2010.

If you plan to travel to Alaska through Canada, you'll have to pass through Canadian customs. For information write: Customs & Excise Branch, Dept. of National Revenue, Connaught Bldg., Mackenzie Ave., Ottawa, Ontario. If you plan on using a citizen band radio on your trip through Canada, a Canadian license is required. There is no charge for a license, however, and the application procedure is easy. Write: Regional Superintendent, Telecommunications Regulations Branch, Dept. of Communications, Room 320–25, 300 Financial Bldg., 10621 100th Ave., Edmonton, Alberta T5J 0B1, and request a license application form. Unless you have a Canadian permit, your CB set will be sealed at the border.

U.S. Forest Service Cabins. Forest Service wilderness cabins are located on remote lakes, streams, and coastal beaches throughout the Chugach, North Tongass, and South Tongass national forests. There are 150 cabins, accessible by floatplane, boat, or trail, and available for public use for a fee of $5 per party per night. Reservations can be made a maximum of 6 months in advance by writing: Information Officer, U.S. Forest Service, 121 E. Fireweed La., Suite 205, Anchorage 99501. No reservations are accepted without payment of fee. Permits are issued on a first-come-first-served basis for periods not exceeding 7 nights. Boats are usually available with cabins located on lakeshores. A Coast Guard-approved flotation device is required to be on board for each passenger. Many of these cabins are located in brown bear country; you are encouraged to carry a .30–06 or larger-caliber rifle. The cabins are equipped with oil- or wood-burning stoves, bunks, and outdoor sanitary facilities. Unauthorized use of these popular cabins is a violation of state and federal laws and regulations.

Alaska Magazine Travel Service, a travel firm sponsored by the acclaimed *Alaska* magazine, can arrange and handle all your north-country travel arrangements from the moment you leave your hometown. Their packaged and professionally guided trips include Alaska's Golden Circle through central Alaska, Arctic Alaska, Anchorage, Columbia Glacier Flightseeing, Mt. McKinley National Park, Kenai Peninsula Wilderness Flight, Columbia Glacier Cruise-Tour, Fairbanks, Glacier Bay National Monument, the Inside Passage Cruise, Katmai National Monument, Kodiak—Russian Alaska, the Pribilof Seal and Bird Islands, and Wilderness Alaska. For detailed information, rates, schedules, and a free *Alaska Trip Planner,* contact: Alaska Magazine Travel Service, 130 Second Ave. S., Edmonds, WA 98020 (206)775–4504.

Mountain Travel of California, one of the nation's outstanding wilderness travel firms, offers several professionally guided trips to the remote wilderness regions of Alaska, including its Arctic Dog Team Trek across the historic Iditarod Trail, a 1,049–mile cross-country path that was once the only land route between Anchorage and Nome; climbs of Mt. McKinley and Mt. Sanford (16,185 feet) in the proposed Wrangell-St. Elias National Park; canoeing and kayaking trips in Glacier Bay and Admiralty Island; St. Elias Range expedition; treks in Mt. McKinley National Park and hiking among the towering granite spires of the Arrigetch Peaks of the Brooks Range; wildlife safari in the tundra world of the Arctic National Wildlife Range; a gold rush trek along the historic Chilkoot Trail and Yukon River; and a grand trans-Alaska hiking tour of Glacier Bay, Chilkoot Pass, Mt. McKinley National Park, and Katmai National Monument. These all-inclusive trips range in cost from $1,100 to $2,590 per person. For detailed information, rates, trip schedules, and a free *Mountain Travel Catalog of Expeditions & Outings to Remote Wilderness Areas of the World,* contact: Mountain Travel, 1398 Solano Ave., Albany, CA 94706 (415)527–8100.

Airlines & Charter Fly-in Services

Several major airlines provide jet service and package wilderness hunting and fishing adventure trips to Alaska from the lower 48.

Write or call the following airlines or your local travel agent for rates, flight information, and free wilderness adventure tour folders. *Alaska Airlines*, City Ticket Office, 418 University St., Seattle, WA 98101, connects Seattle with Sitka, Anchorage, and Fairbanks and also serves Cordova, Yakutat, and southereastern Alaska fish and game points. *Pan American World Airways*, 332 White-Henry-Stuart Bldg., Seattle, WA 98101, has daily nonstop service between Fairbanks and Seattle and New York with connections to all principal U.S. cities. *Northwest Orient Airlines*, White-Henry-Stuart Bldg., Seattle, WA 98101, has daily Boeing 747 nonstop service connecting major cities across the U.S. with Anchorage. *Western Airlines*, Sea-Tas International Airport, Seattle, WA 98158, has service from Seattle and Minneapolis and major cities of the West to Ketchikan, Juneau, and Kodiak. *Wien Air Alaska*, 4100 International Airport Road, Anchorage 99502, and 6640 White-Henry-Stuart Bldg., Seattle, WA 98101, provides the only scheduled flights to Alaska's North Slope and serves over 150 outfitting centers and cities throughout the state, with B–737 jets to Anchorage, Bethel, Dillingham, Fairbanks, Homer, Juneau, Kenai, King Salmon, Kodiak, Kotzebue, Nome, and Point Barrow. In addition to scheduled airline service, there are close to 200 certified air charter bush pilots operating throughout Alaska to serve the fisherman, hunter, and wilderness paddler.

A listing of bush pilots who hold a valid air taxi certificate can be obtained by writing: Alaska Transportation Commission, 5410 International Airport, Anchorage 99510. A complete listing with descriptions of air taxis and air charter services, by city, is found in the 54–page travel guide *Worlds of Alaska*, available free from: Division of Tourism, Dept. of Commerce and Economic Development, Pouch E, Juneau 99811. Costs for fly-in services include the time required to fly to the designated hunting or fishing area and return flight to point of origin. Fly-in trips usually average $25–$40 a person. Larger charters, such as an 18–passenger De Havilland Twin Otter, can be chartered for about $150 per hour; the smaller 4–passenger Cessna 185 costs about $70 per hour. Often the size and bulk of your equipment, plus the number of passengers, determine the type of aircraft you will charter. Be sure to correspond with your pilot to determine how much weight the plane you will be flying will haul. It's best to pack your gear in several small bundles rather than in a few large ones. A first-aid kit and survival gear are essential for wilderness fly-in trips in case of accident or sickness. Hunters should arrange with their pilot for cold-room storage or freezing of game. Transporting the antlers of trophy moose, elk, and caribou can present a problem in small aircraft because of new federal regulations that prohibit the carrying of antlers and other large objects on the struts of the plane. (Note: It is illegal to use helicopters in any manner to hunt in Alaska.)

Alaska Air Guides, Inc., offers a number of flightseeing and fishing trips in addition to standard air-taxi and regional charter services. Scenic aerial tours of the Alaska wilderness range from 1½ to 3 hours and include the rocky grandeur of Mt. McKinley and the Alaska Range down to Ruth Glacier; Columbia Glacier and its surrounding fjords and barren islands; a Kenai Peninsula wildlife tour; and flights over the Portage Glacier and Lake George. Alaska Air Guides also features one-day fly-in fishing trips to tent camps on King Lake in the Kenai Peninsula and the Iliamna trophy fishing area. For longer adventures, try 3 to 5 days of river float fishing at the river of your choice; Alaska Air Guides will help you plan your journey, take you there, and pick you up at a prearranged time and place. For further information write: Alaska Air Guides, Inc., 327 E. Fireweed Lane, Anchorage 99503 (907)279–4842.

Alaska Marine Ferry System

Alaska Marine Ferry System operates its world-famous cruise service along the spectacular fjords and massive, glacier-studded mountains of the Inside Passage from Seattle, Washington; Vancouver, British Columbia; and Kelsey Bay on Vancouver Island to Prince Rupert, British Columbia; Ketchikan, Alaska, and other southeastern Alaskan ports of call. The marine ferry system serving southwestern Alaska connects the Kenai Peninsula, Kodiak Island, and Prince William Sound ports. Southeast Alaska Marine Highway System vessels operate between Prince Rupert and Skagway, stopping at Ketchikan, Wrangell, Petersburg, Sitka, Juneau, and Haines. Service is provided between Seattle and southeastern Alaska.

Access is provided at Prince Rupert to Highway 16 and the B.C. Ferry. Prince Rupert is also served by railroad, bus lines, and airlines. Access to the Alaska Highway is made at Haines via the 159–mile Haines Highway, and Skagway provides connections to the White Pass and Yukon Railway to Whitehorse. Currently under construction is a highway connecting Skagway and Whitehorse on the Alaska Highway. There is no land highway connection between any southeast Alaska ports.

Deluxe staterooms aboard the vessels accommodate 1 to 4 persons comfortably in upper and lower berths, and have shower, toilet, and washbasin. Semideluxe staterooms have upper and lower berths but no shower. Standard staterooms have upper and lower berths only.

On all stateroom vessels, public showers and washrooms are available for passengers. Ships with staterooms: *Columbia*, *Malaspina*, *Matanuska*, *Taku*, and *Tustumena*. Ships without staterooms: *Bartlett*, *Le Conte*, *Aurora*, and *Chilkat*. Food and beverages are available on all Alaska Marine Highway ships, and the choice of cuisine is as varied as you would find in a deluxe hotel.

The highlight of your Alaskan visit may well be the hours—or days—you choose to spend in the picturesque ports along the route of the Marine Highway. Since ferry time in each city is normally only enough to permit loading, you'll need to plan your stopovers in advance and make your reservations accordingly. There is no extra charge for stopover privileges. Off-season, you'll find accommodations easy to obtain. During the summer months, however, many hotels are completely booked, so be sure to make your reservations well in advance.

Alaska towns and villages along the Southeastern Marine Highway system include: Skagway, a historic frontier town, the site of the great Klondike gold rush of '98, with its wooden sidewalks and weather-beaten buildings; Juneau, Alaska's capital city, with excellent fishing, hunting, and sight-seeing nearby; Haines-Port Chilkoot; Sitka, on lake-dotted Baranof Island, one of the earliest Russian settlements in Alaska and site of the Russian Orthodox Church of St. Michael and Mt. Edgecumbe—often called the Mt. Fuji of the Western Hemisphere; Petersburg, a rustic fishing village, known as Little Norway; Ketchikan, the first Alaskan port of call along the Inside Passage, noted for its collection of totem poles (the largest in the world) and its year-round salmon fishing derby; and the picturesque pioneer fishing villages of Hoonah, Wrangell, Angoon, Kake, Hollis, and Metlakatla.

The South Central Marine Highway system serves Homer, at the tip of the Kenai Peninsula in a beautiful, mountainous region known as Land's End; Seward, the main port on the Kenai Peninsula, on picturesque Resurrection Bay; Valdez, the saltwater terminus of the 800–mile Alyeska pipeline on Prince William Sound and often referred to as America's Switzerland; Kodiak on wild Kodiak Island, the nation's third-largest fishing center, famed for its giant strain of Alaskan brown bear; and the coastal lumbering and fishing villages of Cordova, Whittier, and Seldovia.

Wildlife often sighted along the Marine Highway system includes whales, porpoises, sea lions, seals, swans, cranes, ducks, terns, bald eagles, Sitka blacktail deer, and black or brown bear. A good pair of binoculars will add hours of enjoyment to your cruise.

For additional information, rates, schedules, and reservations, contact: Alaska Marine Highway, Pouch R, Juneau, AK 99811; or phone Seattle (206)623–1970.

Railway Services & the White Pass-Yukon Route

The Alaska Railroad, sometimes called the Mt. McKinley National Park Route, offers scenic tours during summer months via the air-conditioned AuRoRa, a streamlined, fully equipped passenger train with large picture windows and vista-dome rail cars. Trains operate between Anchorage and Fairbanks through breathtaking wilderness country populated by moose, bear, mountain sheep and goats, and nesting wildfowl. Accommodations for the trip are available at McKinley Park Hotel Station. The Alaska Railroad also offers one-day sight-seeing jaunts and transport between Anchorage, Portage, and Whittier to connect with Alaska State ferries leaving Whittier for points of interest on neighboring Prince William Sound. For information on the Alaska Railroad and the Mt. McKinley Park Route, write: Traffic Division, The Alaska Railroad, Pouch 7–2111, Anchorage, AK 99510 (907)265–2494.

White Pass & Yukon Railroad. This privately owned narrow-gauge (36–inch) railroad links the coastal forests of Skagway, Alaska, with Whitehorse and the Klondike country of the Yukon. The route winds along one of the steepest railroad grades in North America on the eastern side of the Coast Range Mountains, climbing from sea level at Skagway to 2,885 feet at White Pass in only 20 miles of track. The railroad reaches its highest point at Log Cabin, British Columbia, where it climbs to an elevation of 2,916 feet. At Rocky Point, just out of Skagway, the railroad crosses the famous Trail of '98, visible 300 feet below on the floor of the Skagway River gorge. The train continues on past Black Cross Rock, where two men were buried under the rock by blasting operations during construction of the railroad, past the cataracts of Bridal Veil Falls and the ghost town of White Pass City, which boasted a population of 10,000 during the gold rush. On Inspiration Point, at an altitude of 2,400 feet, is a monument to the thousands of packhorses that died during the gold rush. The train climbs over White Pass at an elevation of 2,885 feet and winds on to Log Cabin, formerly the headquarters for the old North West Mounted Police and the Canada customs in the gold rush days and the jumping-off point for the Fan Tail Trail to the Atlin Lake country of British Columbia. From Log Cabin the train passes through scenic moose and caribou country to Lake Bennett, Carcross, and Whitehorse, where it ends its 110–mile journey. Today the mainstay of the route is the shipment of freight and mining concentrates and of summer tourists who wish to retrace the Trail of '98. The White Pass and Yukon has a one-day adventure tour out of Skagway to Lake Bennett and return. It also has

arrangements for travelers who want to take their car or camper from Skagway to Whitehorse, or vice versa. For information write: White Pass and Yukon Route, P.O. Box 2147, Seattle, WA 98111 (206)623–2510.

Information & Services

The Alaskan bush is a tough challenge for the outdoorsman. It's not a place for the weekend tenderfoot. The wilderness traveler should be prepared to encounter extremely rugged terrain, bears, moose in rut, brawling rivers, voracious mosquitoes, and devil's club. The hazards come part and parcel with the rewards. The fishing in Alaska ranks with the finest in the world, but as in any true wilderness, the fishing varies greatly from one watershed to another. This is especially true of the sea-run, or migratory, species. Southwest and central Alaska generally have the best fishing for a mixed bag of salmon, rainbow and lake trout, northern pike, arctic char, grayling, and Dolly Varden. Fly-in guides operate charter aircraft throughout southwest and central Alaska from the Lake Hood seaplane base in Anchorage. Southeast Alaska is a top-ranked region for cutthroat trout, silver and king salmon, and steelhead trout. The remote lakes and rivers of the Far North and the Brooks Range Wilderness hold lunker lake trout, grayling, sheefish, and great northern pike—often seen lined up along the shoals in the lakes like a fleet of submarines. A comprehensive guide to the fishing waters adjacent to Alaska's highway systems and fly-in waters, the *Alaska Sport Fishing Guide*, is available free from: Alaska Dept. of Fish & Game, Sportfish Division, Subport Bldg., Juneau 99801 (907)465–4100. The 96–page guide is packed with maps, and lists the lakes and streams, locations, and fish species present along the Alaska, Copper River, Taylor, Richardson, George Parks, Steese, Elliott, Denali, Glenn, Seward, Sterling, Slana-Tok Cutoff, and Palmer highways; along the Matanuska Valley, Skilak, and Nome-Solomon-Teller roads; and in the Brooks Range, Bristol Bay-Alaska Peninsula, Kotzebue-Kobuk, and Kodiak and Afognak Island fly-in waters. The Alaska-bound angler should also send for the *Alaska Sportfishing Seasons & Bag Limits*, a 69–page handbook published by the Dept. of Fish & Game. It describes and lists license fees and regulations, and contains a useful "Field Guide to Alaskan Game Species." The *Alaska Fishing Guide*, 171 pages, illustrated with maps, charts, and photos, is published by the Alaska Northwest Publishing Co., Box 4–EEE, Anchorage 99509, for $3.95, plus 50¢ handling and postage. This handy guide provides valuable info on planning an Alaskan fishing trip and describes the major fishing regions and 557 lakes and streams. The Dept. of Fish & Game provides daily prerecorded reports on sportfishing in central Alaska if you phone (907)344–0566 in Anchorage or (907)452–1525 in Fairbanks.

The big-game species of Alaska offer some of the finest hunting in North America. The *Alaska Hunter's Guidebook*, a useful and interesting 47–page guide, is a must for anyone planning an Alaskan

trip. It describes the seasons, feeding habits, hunting methods, and trophy hunting areas for Alaska's big-game species, with fascinating details on how to travel and select gear, and a section on trophy care and field handling of game. It is available free, along with the *Alaska Game Management Units Map*, *Alaska Hunting Regulations*, and *Upland Game Birds of Forest & Tundra*, from the Alaska Dept. of Fish & Game, Juneau 99801. The *Alaska Hunting Guide*, 170 pages, and *Fair Chase with Alaskan Guides*, 270 pages, are available for $3.95 each plus 50¢ postage and handling from: Alaska Northwest Publishing Co., Box 4–EEE, Anchorage 99509. All nonresident hunters are required to hire the services of a licensed guide. Alaska's largest moose trophies are taken in the Kenai and Alaska peninsulas. Moose with antler spreads exceeding 60 inches may be taken throughout southwest and interior Alaska if a hunter is lucky and persistent. Only a few of Alaska's caribou herds are accessible to the average hunter. The Nelchina herd, one of the most accessible, numbers more than 60,000 animals, generally sighted in an area bounded by the Alaska Range, the Talkeetna Mountains, and the Glenn and Richardson highways. Alaska's largest caribou are found on remote Adak Island, where bulls weighing up to 700 pounds have been reported. Large Roosevelt elk in excess of 1,200 pounds are found in the alpine meadows and dense forests of Afognak and Raspberry islands in the southwest. Sitka black-tailed deer inhabit the Panhandle, a few islands in Prince William Sound, and parts of the Kodiak island group. Deer country is often brown bear country, and experienced hunters will carry a rifle capable of stopping a "brownie." The Dall sheep, the white king of Alaska's high country, roams the towering peaks of the Wrangell, Chugach, and Talkeetna mountains, the Alaska Range, the Tanana Hills, the Brooks Range, and the Kenai Peninsula. Trophy Wrangell Mountain sheep are noted for their wide, flaring horns. Mountain goats dwell in the coastal mountains throughout the Panhandle to the Kenai Peninsula. The Alaska brown bear is found on Kodiak Island, Admiralty Island, and the Alaska Peninsula—where many blond-colored specimens are found. The grizzly is common throughout the Great Interior at or above timberline, particularly in the Alaska Range and the Talkeetna Mountains and on the south slope of the Brooks Range. Black bear range through the entire state, except for the Alaska Peninsula and the arctic coast. Pack-hunting wolves are found wherever there are moose or caribou.

Nonresident hunters and fishermen planning to travel into the Alaskan bush are well advised (and in certain instances required) to hire the services of a licensed registered guide. *The Guide Register*, a complete listing of the 400 master and registered Alaska guides, the species of game they hunt, and the type of transportation they offer, is availa-

ble from: Dept. of Commerce, Division of Occupational Licensing, State of Alaska, Pouch D, Juneau 99811. A comprehensive listing of Alaskan wilderness hunting, fishing, photography, and canoe outfitters and gear rentals is found in the 54–page travel guide *Worlds of Alaska*, available free from: Division of Tourism, Dept. of Commerce and Economic Development, Pouch E, Juneau 99811. Alaska's hunting regulations specify that a nonresident hunter be accompanied by a guide when hunting grizzly or brown bear, Dall sheep, or polar bear. The majority of Alaska's guides charge a minimum of $150 per day for their services and require from one-third to one-half the price of the time scheduled for your hunting or fishing journey. Always keep in mind that a competent, ethical guide sells his time and expertise, not big-game heads or trophy fish. Fish and game conditions vary from year to year and from place to place, even in the Alaskan wilderness. Most of Alaska's guides are certified bush pilots and hold air taxi certificates.

Before you hire a guide, ask him for half a dozen references and check them out thoroughly by correspondence or telephone (it's often easier to get an honest appraisal by phone than by letter; most people are busy and hesitate to put negative statements in cold print). Be sure to ask your guide for a list of recommended clothing and gear to bring. Also ask what kind of living accommodations (a well-heated tent camp should be the minimum shelter in Alaska's bush) and food you can expect. These conditions will be stipulated in the guide-client contract required by the Dept. of Fish & Game. Some guides will outfit you, if necessary, with sleeping bags, gear, and down clothing.

Alaska has hundreds of well-maintained campgrounds and wilderness cabins scattered throughout the mountains and alpine tundra, in the lake country, coastal and interior forests, and along the highway systems of the Panhandle, Kenai and Alaska peninsulas, and the Great Interior. Nonresidents may purchase a $10 annual camping permit for Alaska's state campgrounds. For information about camping and state campgrounds write: Alaska Division of Lands, 344 E. 6th Ave., Anchorage 99501. The 20–page *Outdoor Guide of Alaska* lists all campsites and can be obtained free from: Division of Tourism, Dept. of Commerce and Economic Development, Pouch E, Juneau 99811. The booklet *Alaska State Park System*, available free from the Dept. of Natural Resources, Division of Parks, 323 E. 4th Ave., Anchorage 99501, describes the recreational and wilderness campground facilities located in the Chugach and Denali state parks, Kachemak Bay State Wilderness Park, and the Captain Cook, Chena River, Harding Lake, and Nancy Lake state recreation areas. *Camps and Trails*, a guide to the campgrounds and public-use cabins located on the 283 million acres of national resource lands in Alaska, can be obtained free from: Bureau of Land Management, 555 Cordova St., Anchorage 99501, along with the *Alaska Recreation Guide Map*, which lists and describes all state, U.S. Fish & Wildlife Service, U.S. Forest Service, and National Park Service recreation areas and campgrounds. Write National Park Service, 334 E. 5th Ave., Suite 250, Anchorage 99501, for information on camping and hiking in Mt. McKinley National Park and Katmai and Glacier Bay national monuments. For campground and trail maps of the Chugach and Tongass national forests write: U.S. Forest Service, P.O. Box 1628, Juneau 99801. Two useful guidebooks, *55 Ways to the Wilderness in South Central Alaska* and *Discovering Southeast Alaska with Pack & Paddle*, are available for $7.95 each, plus 50¢ handling and postage, from: Alaska Northwest Publishing Co., Box 4–EEE, Anchorage 99509.

Alaska is blessed with many of the finest—and most dangerous—wilderness canoeing waters in North America. Generally speaking, canoe travel on Alaska's clearwater rivers is 3–4 miles per hour; on glacial rivers, 5–7 miles per hour; and on lakes, 2 miles per hour. Be sure to write for the useful *Alaska Recreation Guide Map* and *National Wild & Scenic Rivers* booklet, available free from: Bureau of Land Management, 555 Cordova St., Anchorage 99501. Proposed national wild and scenic rivers within Alaska include the Yukon-Charley National Rivers, 1.9 million acres near the eastern Yukon-Alaska border; Birch Creek National Wild River, a 135–mile stretch between Fairbanks and Circle; Fortymile National Wild & Scenic River, a 375–mile stretch along the Yukon-Alaska border; Beaver Creek National Wild River, a 135–mile stretch north of Fairbanks; and the Unalakleet National Wild River, a 60–mile stretch located 400 miles northwest of Anchorage on the Seward Peninsula. *Canoeing on the Kenai National Moose Range*, a detailed guide to the Swanson River route and Swan Lake route, is available free from: Superintendent, Kenai National Moose Range, Box 500, Kenai 99611. A fascinating guide to the remote wilderness canoe routes of scenic Admiralty Island in the Tongass National Forest, *Cross Admiralty Canoe Route*, is available free from: Supervisor, Tongass National Forest, Box 2278, Ketchikan 99901. Please note that Alaska's wilderness canoe routes travel through the heart of grizzly and brown bear country; they are extremely dangerous and should be attempted only by the experienced and well-prepared canoeist or with a registered Alaskan guide. Anyone planning an Alaska wilderness canoe trip is advised to read *Wild Rivers of Alaska*, a 176–page bible by Sepp Weber, published by Alaska Northwest Publishing Co., Box 4–EEE, Anchorage 99509 ($8.95, paperback). This handsome book contains more than 70 color photographs, maps, and charts and describes 53 wild rivers.

Guided wild river trips are provided by *Alaska Wilderness Expeditions, Inc.*, Box 882, Wrangell 99929; *Alaska Wilderness River Trips, Inc.*, Box 1143, Eagle River 99577; *Arctic Outfitters Ltd.*, Box 33, Kiana 99749 (Kobuk River); *Bear Bros. Whole Wilderness Experience*, Box 4–2969, Anchorage 99509 (kayak touring in Prince William Sound); *Wild Rivers North*, Box 151, McGrath 99627; and *Challenge Wilderness Adventure*, P.O. Box 4–2881, Anchorage 99509 (Yukon River).

Angler's Alaska operates wilderness fishing vacations in various Alaska locations, particularly for families or small groups of friends who want an exclusive and unique outing. These are not mass-produced tours, and hosts Bob and Lee Grogan guide only a few tours a year.

They do not rely on float planes to fly daily to the fishing spots; therefore, disappointments often caused by Alaska's poor flying weather are avoided. They provide the finest and safest outdoor equipment available. There are three basic types of vacations: Interior, Southeastern, and Southwestern.

Interior vacations begin in central Alaska near Mt. McKinley Park. The party is transported from Cantwell (reached by Alaska Railroad or Parks Highway from Fairbanks or Anchorage) and taken to Brushkana Creek. There the trip proceeds on horseback exploring lakes and streams in the scenic, high plateau region. These waters offer excellent grayling and lake trout fishing, with the emphasis on fly fishing. Besides fishing, participants can enjoy the wilderness and will usually see grizzly, caribou, moose and Dall sheep. Nights are spent in cabins and tented camps. The season for this trip is July 1 to September 1, with a minimum of five days and a normal duration of seven to fifteen days. Cost for a minimum of two persons is $100 per day per person.

The Southeastern vacation is in the panhandle area near Juneau. Anglers are met at the Juneau airport and flown by float plane to a remote campsite among the scenic islands of the Panhandle. Fishing is for red and coho salmon, cutthroat trout and Dolly Varden char, with wonderful streamer fly fishing in the estuary areas. Participants on this trip will enjoy the wildlife which includes seals, sea lions, whales, bald eagles and brown bear. They will also try their hands at digging clams, catching crab and smoking salmon. The season is July 1 to August 15 with a five-day minimum. Rates are $150 per day per person for two or more and include the air charter to and from Juneau.

Southwestern vacations are float trips on Alaskan rivers which allow serious fishermen to reach the inaccessible, virgin areas. Anglers fly from Anchorage to either Iliamna or Dillingham (approx. $80 and $105 respectively). There, they will be met and taken by float plane to the first fishing site. From this point on, they will float downstream in large, stable rubber rafts, fishing some of the finest waters along the way. Rainbow trout are especially abundant in these remote streams. Camp is made at a different spot each night. The season for this trip is August 15 through September 30 and is $200 per day per person with a five-day minimum.

For information on all trips or reservations write: Anglers' Alaska, Box 529, Douglas, Alaska 99824.

The Alaska Northwest Publishing Company, one of the most renowned institutions of the "Last Frontier," publishes *Alaska* magazine, a beautifully illustrated full-color monthly which contains useful articles of interest to the outdoor traveler ranging from fishing to backpacking, where-to-go, history and lore, Alaska's great fish and game areas, and bush pilots and guides. The subscription cost, $12 per year for 12 issues, is worth every dime. Write: Alaska Northwest Publishing Co., Box 4–EEE, Anchorage 99509. The *Alaska Magazine Travel Service* will provide specific trip-planning assistance and provide tickets and reservations for Alaska tours, sportfishing packages, and carriers, including the Alaska state ferries. Address all inquires to: Alaska Magazine Travel Service, 139 Second Ave. S., Edmonds, WA 98020 (206)774–4111. The firm also publishes the famous *Milepost*, and for $20 per year you can subscribe to Alaska Geographic, which publishes beautiful special issues on such subjects as *Southeast-Alaska's Panhandle* ($9.95), *Bristol Bay Basin* ($9.95) and *Alaska Whales & Whaling* ($9.95). In *Alaska Whales and Whaling*, the wonders of whales in Alaska—their life cycles, travels and travails—are examined, along with an authoritative history of commercial and subsistence whaling in the North . . . with special

focus on the issue of Eskimo bowhead whaling. Included are color photos and illustrations of 15 whales found in Alaskan waters, together with maps showing whale distribution. Introduction by Dr. Victor Scheffer, author of *Year of the Whale*.

Gateways

Anchorage—Gateway to Alaska's Wilderness Rim

(Pop. 48,000; zip code, see below; area code 907.) This flat, sprawling city in south central Alaska was founded as a tent camp in 1914 during the construction of the Alaska Railroad. Anchorage is on an alluvial plain in upper Cook Inlet, surrounded by the peaks of the Chugach Mountains and dense forests of spruce, birch, and aspen. Anchorage is Alaska's largest city and the gateway to the wilderness recreation areas in the Alaska and Kenai peninsulas, Bristol Bay, the south central coast, Mt. McKinley National Park, and the Great Interior. Area attractions include Earthquake Park, Chugach State Park, the Alaska Zoo, the Anchorage Historical and Fine Arts Museum, city sight-seeing tours, and the 8,600–acre Portage Glacier Recreation Area. Several of the state's foremost bush pilots, guides, and charter wilderness fishing and hunting fly-in services are headquartered here, including *Alaska Air Guides, Inc.*, 327 E. Fireweed La., 99503; *Alaska Bush Carrier*, 4801 Aircraft Road, 99502; *Alaska Travel Air*, Box 4–2646, 99509; *Alyeska Air Service*, Box 5154 Annex, 99502; *Central Northern Ltd.*, Air Service 161, 7800 De Barr St., 99504; *Charlie Allen Flying Service*, Box 5105, 99502; *Denali Air Service*, Box 4–2769, 99501; *Great Northern Airlines*, 3400 W. Airport Road, 99502; *Ketchum Air Service*, 2708 Aspen Drive, 99503; *Lee's Air Service, Inc.*, Box 4–2495, 99509; *Northwestern Air Service, Inc.*, 1704 E. 5th Ave., 99501; *Petco Aviation, Inc.*, Box 6358, 99502; *Rust's Flying Service*, Box 6301, 99502; *Spernak Airways, Inc.*, Box 2255, 99510; *Stoddard Aero Service, Inc.*, 2250 E. 5th Ave., 99501; and *Totem Airways, Inc.*, Box 4–2344, 99509. The city is reached by the major airlines, the George Parks and Glenn highways, and the Alaska Railroad.

Accommodations: (Airport area) *Anchorage International Inn* (rates: $45–50 double), 140 very good rooms and suites, with dining room, coffee shop, and limo service, 1 mile east of airport, 3333 International Airport Road, 99502 (907)243–2233; *Best Western Barratt Inn* (rates: $37–42 double), 1 mile east of airport, 100 units, restaurant and cocktail lounge, 4616 Spenard Road, 99503 (907)243–3131. (Downtown area) *Anchorage Westward Hilton* (rates: $60–70 double), 500 good to superb rooms and suites, with dining room, coffee

shop, cocktail lounge and entertainment, parking garage, at 3rd Ave. and E St., 99501 (907)272–7411; *Captain Cook Hotel* (rates: $68–76 double), one of Alaska's finest hotels, 650 excellent rooms and suites, the Crow's Nest Restaurant for rooftop dining with view of city and Cook Inlet, heated indoor pool, coffee shop, and cocktail lounge, at 4th Ave. and K St., 99510 (907)276–6000; *Holiday Inn of Anchorage* (rates: $57 double), 252 very good units, dining room, cocktail lounge, heated indoor pool and sauna, at 239 W. 4th Ave. and C St., 99501 (907)279–8671.

Fairbanks—Gateway to the Great Interior & Arctic Alaska

(Pop. 14,800; zip code 99701; area code 907.) This former gold-mining community, known as the Golden Heart of Alaska, is the state's second-largest city and a renowned outfitting center and jumping-off point for the remote fishing and big-game hunting areas of the Great Interior and the Far North. Fairbanks, located on a bend of the Chena River, is the northern terminus of the Alaska Highway and the meeting point of the Elliott, Steese, George Parks, and Richardson highways. An extremely flat city, Fairbanks is surrounded by the White Mountains to the north, the foothills of the Alaska Range to the south, and low, rolling hills to the east and west. The University of Alaska Museum houses one of the finest collections of Eskimo, Aleut, and Indian artifacts, pioneer relics, and specimens of northern wildlife in Alaska. Other area attractions include Alaskaland, a picturesque reconstruction of the old gold rush town; river cruises; sight-seeing tours; and the Creamer Field Wildlife Reserve. The city is home base for many of Alaska's great guides and bush pilots, and numerous air charter services serving the fisherman and hunter, including *Alaska Air Charter*, Box 80507, and *Al Wright Air Service, Inc.*, Box 60142, both College 99701; and *Elliott Air Service*, 5920 Airport Way, and *Great Northern Airlines, Inc.*, 3400 W. International Airport Road, both Anchorage 99502. *Alaska Riverways*, Box G, 99701, offers stern-wheeler cruises out of Fairbanks on the Tanana River. The *Itkillik Brooks Range Lodge*, 1206 Coppet St., 99701, has floatplane transportation from Fairbanks to lodges and cabins on the Itkillik River in the Brooks Range for arctic grayling, lake trout, and northern pike fishing. *Alaska Guide Service, Inc.*, Box 80929, College 99701, operates float trips for photography and fishing at the Chatanika River Camp, north of Fairbanks. Fairbanks is served by scheduled domestic and international airline service and by the Alaska Railroad.

Area Accommodations: Fairbanks Inn (rates: $52) 172 rooms and suites, dining room, cocktail lounge, at 723 1st Ave., 99701 (907)456–6602; *Golden Nugget Motel* (rates: $49 double), 36 motel units and suites, at 900 Noble St., 99701 (907)452–5141; *Travelers Inn* (rates: $55–65 double), 240 very good rooms and suites, the superb Bear and Seal Restaurant, coffee shop, and cocktail lounge, at 8th Ave. and Nobel St., 99701 (907)456–7722.

Juneau—the Capital City & Gateway to Alaska's Panhandle

(Pop. 13,600; zip code, see below; area code 907.) Alaska's capital is at the foot of 3,576–foot Mt. Juneau on the scenic Gastineau Channel, the former water route to Skagway and the Klondike goldfields. The town was founded in the summer of 1880, when Joe Juneau and his sidekick Dick Harris discovered rich gold deposits in Silver Bow Basin and launched the first gold rush in Alaska. Thirteen miles north of Juneau, off the recently completed Glacier Highway, is the Mendenhall Glacier, where the U.S. Forest Service maintains an observatory and hiking trails. Juneau is the jump-off point for trout and salmon fishing and big-game hunting trips throughout the Tongass National Forest, which encompasses the whole of southeast Alaska. Air charter and fly-in services are provided by *Capitol Air*, RR 5, Box 5112; *Channel Flying, Inc.*, RR 3, Box 3577; *L.A.B. Flying Service*, Terminal Bldg., Municipal Airport; and *Southeast Skyways, Inc.*, RR 5, Box 5112, all 99803. Juneau is served by major airlines and the Alaska Marine Highway System.

Area Accommodations: Baranof Hotel (rates: $42.50–48.50 double), 218 rooms and suites, the Latchstring Restaurant, sauna and exercise room, coffee shop, and entertainment, at North Franklin St. and 2nd St., 99801 (907)586–2660; *Juneau Hilton* (rates: $60 double), 104 excellent, spacious rooms and suites overlooking the Gastineau Channel, fine dining facilities and airport limo service, at 51 West Egan Drive, 99801 (907)586–6900; *The Prospector* (rates: $44.50 double) 60 rooms, dining room, cocktail lounge and entertainment, at 340 Whittier St., 99801 (907)586–3737.

Skagway—Gateway to Klondike National Park & the Chilcoot Trail

(Pop. 700; zip code 99840; area code 907.) This famous southeast Alaska town, originally known as Skaguay, "home of the north wind" in Tlingit dialect, is the state's oldest city and the site of the proposed Klondike National Park. It was the gateway to the White Pass Trail and the infamous Chilcoot Trail—the Trail of '98—which climbed over the Chilcoot pass to Lake Bennett and the Klondike goldfields. The journey from Skagway along the Chilcoot to Lake Bennett can also be made by the narrow-gauge White Pass & Yukon Railroad. The town still has a boom-town atmosphere with its boardwalks and weather-beaten false-front gold-rush saloons and hotels. Skagway's major attractions include the Trail of '98 Museum and the Gold-Rush Graveyard, where Soapy Smith, the notorious Klondike con artist, is buried. *Skagway Air Service*, Box 357, 99840, provides fly-in service for the outdoorsman and sight-seeing flights of the Chilcoot and White Pass trails.

Area Accommodations: The Klondike (rates: $52) is Skagway's finest hotel, with contemporary design and a panoramic view of the Lynn Canal and the Sawtooth Mountains; 130 spacious, comfortable rooms and luxury suites in gold rush decor, with the Chilkoot Dining Room and Bonanza Lounge, adjacent to the historic business district and close to cruise ship docks and ferry landing, P.O. Box 515, 99840 (907)983–2291.

Highways & Maps

Alaska is served by an excellent system of paved and gravel-top highways that provide access to the major fishing, big-game hunting, and camping areas and outfitting centers. The official *Highway Map*

of Alaska is available free from: Alaska Travel Division, Pouch E, Juneau 99801. This useful full-color map describes access routes from the U.S. and shows the major highway routes in Alaska, the Yukon Territory, and northern British Columbia as well as paved and gravel roads, marine ferry routes, railroads, glaciers, recreation areas, and other points of interest. It contains a recreation-areas chart that lists the camping units, boat-launching sites, shelter, drinking-water facilities, fishing, canoeing, and trails in each area. The Alaska Dept. of Highways, P.O. Box 1467, Juneau 99811, publishes free, periodic *Highway Conditions Bulletins*. The full-color *Alaska Recreation Guide Map* shows all highways and Bureau of Land Management, Alaska Division of Lands, U.S. Fish & Wildlife Service, U.S. Forest Service, and National Park recreation areas and campgrounds in the Panhandle, Interior, Anchorage-Palmer, and Kenai Peninsula regions. It may be obtained free from: Bureau of Land Management, 555 Cordova St., Anchorage 99501. A useful *Highway Guide to the Copper River* is available free from: Supervisor, Chugach National Forest, 121 E. Fireweed La., Suite 205, Anchorage 99503. A free travel information kit, *Touring the Prince of Wales Island Road System*, may be obtained by writing: Supervisor, U.S. Forest Service, Ketchikan Area, Box 2278, Ketchikan 99901. The kit contains detailed maps and nitty-gritty about key fishing sites, milepost attractions, forest development roads, campgrounds, trails and hiking, wildlife, and hunting. Avis, Hertz, and National Car Rental services have offices in Anchorage, Cordova, Fairbanks, Haines, Homer, Juneau, Kenai, Ketchikan, Kodiak, Mt. McKinley Park, Nome, Seward, Sitka, and Valdez. Campers may be rented at Winnebago Rentals, 2301 E. 5th Ave., Anchorage 99501. Listed below are brief descriptions of Alaska's great wilderness and scenic highways.

Alaska Highway (2)

The famous Alaska Highway is blacktopped from the Yukon border northwest to Fairbanks, with the usual number of bumps and dips caused by permafrost. This segment of the Alaska Highway passes through the great boreal forests and alpine tundra of the interior plateau past innumerable lakes and wild rivers. West of the Yukon border the highway passes through the Alaskan villages of Northway Junction, Tetlin Junction, Tok, Dot Lake, Delta Junction, Big Delta, Richardson, Salchaket, and North Pole to Fairbanks. The major features along the route include Tetlin, Dot, and Healy lakes, the Alaska Range mountains, the Gerstle and Little Delta rivers, Moose Slough, Craig Lakes, the Tanana and Goodpaster rivers, and George and Blair lakes. There are campgrounds at Big Delta and Harding Lake Recreation Area.

Denali Highway (8)

This highway, once the only road link to Mt. McKinley National Park, is a two-lane gravel road which leads the traveler to the cloud-shrouded twin peaks of Mt. McKinley. The highway winds through arctic tundra, sparsely wooded hills, and shallow lakes from its junction with the Anchorage-Fairbanks George Parks Highway 3. The region was once the home and hunting grounds of the seminomadic Athabascan Indians. Wildlife seen along the highway includes grizzly and black bear, caribou, bald eagle, moose, and

Dall sheep. Major features shown on the maps include the Susitna River, Windy Creek, the MacLaren River, the Amphitheater Mountains, the Reindeer Hills, and Mt. McKinley National Park. There is good fishing for grayling, whitefish, and lake trout in the remote lakes and along the Delta, Gulkana, and Upper Tangle Lakes wilderness canoe trails. A handy guide, *Recreation along Alaska's Denali Highway*, is available free from: Bureau of Land Management, 555 Cordova St., Anchorage 99501. The several roadhouses along the highway do not open until mid-June, and they close early in September. Travelers should fill their gas tanks at Paxson or Cantwell. There are campgrounds at Brushkana Creek, Denali, and Tangle Lakes.

Elliott Highway (2)

This highway winds northwest from Fairbanks 156 miles to Manley Hot Springs, which is on a short tributary of the Tanana River. The Elliott is a well-maintained gravel road, but you should exercise caution when pulling a trailer because of numerous steep hills and sharp turns. The highway provides access to the White Mountain Trail system. The summer trail is 23 miles long and traverses low marshy areas and high alpine tundra at Wickersham Dome. Access to the trail is at Mile 28. Three useful guides to the highway, *Alaska's White Mountain Trails, Recreation along Alaska's Steese and Elliott Highways*, and *Alaska's Steese and Elliott Highways*, are available free from: Bureau of Land Management, 1028 Aurora Drive, Fairbanks 99701. The White Mountain Trail terminates at the Borealis LeFevre Cabin, which is open to public use for $2 per day by reservation through the Fairbanks district office of the Bureau of Land Management. The cabin is on the scenic grayling waters of Beaver Creek. The highway winds through the heart of grizzly and black bear, caribou, and moose hunting country and provides access to northern pike, sheefish, whitefish, and arctic grayling fishing in the Tatalina and Tolovana rivers, Minto Flats, and Hot Springs Slough. There are campgrounds at Tolovana River and Manley Hot Springs.

George Parks Highway (3)

The George Parks Highway, also known as the Anchorage-Fairbanks Highway, is the paved direct-access route to Mt. McKinley National Park. It winds for 359 miles through some of the most scenic, rugged wilderness in Alaska, from Anchorage northward through the fishing and hunting outfitting centers of Wasilla, Willow, Talkeetna, Colorado, Summit, Cantwell, McKinley Park, and Nenana to its terminus at Fairbanks. Major features along the route include the majestic peaks of the Talkeetna and Alaska Range mountains, Mt. McKinley National Park, Broad Pass Lakes, and the Nenana, Chutitna, Talkeetna, and Sheep rivers. Campgrounds and recreation areas along the route include Rocky Lake, Big Lake, Willow Creek, Denali State Park, and Igloo Creek recreation areas and the Sanctuary River, Savage River, and Morina campgrounds. Advance campground reservations are required to drive past Savage River in Mt. McKinley National Park.

Glenn Highway (1)

This highway is the major access route from the Alaska Highway southwest to Anchorage and the Kenai Peninsula in south central Alaska. The Glenn winds from the village of Tok on the Alaska Highway through a mountainous wilderness of alpine tundra and boreal forests surrounding the big-game hunting and fishing areas at Tetlin Lake, Tok River, Cobb Lakes, the Mentasta and Wrangell mountains, the Gulkana and Copper rivers, the Tazlina River, the Talkeetna Mountains, and the Matanuska River. The wilderness lakes and rivers accessible from the highway hold grayling, lake trout, and whitefish. The hunting and fishing outfitting centers along the route include the villages of Chistochina, Gakona, Gulkana, Glennallen, Eureka Lodge, and Sheep Mountain Inn. The Nabesna Gold-Mine Road winds from the Slana Roadhouse past Tanana Lakes to the old Nabesna gold mines on the Nabesna River. There are campgrounds at Lake Louise and Finger Lakes.

Richardson (4) & Edgerton Highways

The blacktopped Richardson Highway runs north from Valdez on Prince William Sound through the 12,000–foot peaks and massive glaciers of the Chugach and Alaska Range mountains along the original route of the historic Abercrombie and Richardson trails to its junction with the Alaska Highway at Delta Junction. The highway passes through the villages of Tonsina, Copper Center, Glennallen, Gulkana, Sourdough, Paxson, Rapids, and Donnelly to Delta Junction. The major fish and game areas accessible from the highway include the Copper River, Chugach Mountains, Summit Lake, Alaska Range, and Gulkana and Delta River wilderness canoe trails. The Edgerton Highway, also known as the Edgerton Cutoff, runs for 33 miles from Milepost 82.6 of the Richardson Highway to the settlement of Chitina at the confluence of the Copper and Chitina rivers. The hundreds of lakes and rivers along the Richardson and Edgerton highways hold trophy grayling, northern pike, silver salmon, and lake and rainbow trout.

Steese Highway (6)

The Steese Highway runs from Fairbanks northeast to the picturesque village of Circle City, 50 miles south of the arctic circle on the Yukon River. The Steese, once used by prospectors freighting supplies by dogsled and wagon, is the gateway to the Circle Mining District of pre-Klondike fame. The area is famous for its grayling fishing, big-game hunting for grizzly and black bear, moose, and caribou, canoeing, hiking, wildlife, and alpine grandeur. Portions of the Steese-Fortymile caribou herd may be seen near Eagle Summit and Twelvemile Summit during their spring and fall migrations. The highway has two trailheads for the 24–mile-long Pinnell Mountain National Recreation Trail. The trail winds through alpine terrain along high ridges and through mountain passes offering views of the "midnight sun" and scenic panoramas of the White Mountains, the Yukon River Flats, the Brooks Range, and the Alaska Range mountains. The trail is above timberline, so carry water and a pocket stove. Three guides, *Alaska's Pinnell Mountain National Recreation Trail, Alaska's Steese and Elliott Highways*, and *Recreation along Alaska's Steese and Elliott Highways*, are available free from:

Bureau of Land Management, 1028 Aurora Drive, Fairbanks 99701. The Steese provides access to the Chatanika and Birch Creek wilderness canoe trails. Facilities are limited along the highway; extra gasoline and tools should be carried. The Steese is paved for the first 40 miles; the remainder is gravel-surfaced all the way to Circle City. There are campgrounds at Cripple Creek, Chatanika River, Ketchem Creek, Circle City, and Bedrock Creek.

Sterling & Seward-Anchorage Highways (1 & 9)

The Sterling Highway passes through the Kenai Peninsula from Homer northeast through the famous fish and game wilderness areas of the Chugach National Forest and the majestic Chugach Mountains to its junction with the Seward-Anchorage Highway at Sterling. The highway provides access to the Kenai River, Quartz Creek Campground, Kenai Lake, Resurrection Pass Hiking Trail, Russian Lakes and River, Juneau and Swan lakes, Kenai National Moose Range, Forest Lakes, Hidden Lake and Petersen Lake campgrounds, Swanson and Moose rivers, Lake Tustumena, and Cook Inlet. Herds of white beluga whale can often be seen feeding on salmon and hooligan during incoming tides at the mouth of the Kenai River on Cook Inlet. The Seward-Anchorage Highway runs through the eastern section of the Kenai from Seward, northward past its junction with the Sterling Highway to Anchorage. The highway travels through the Chugach National Forest and provides access to the scenic Portage Glacier Wilderness. There are campgrounds along the route at Bertha Creek, Granite Creek, Beaver Pond, Williwaw, Tenderfoot Creek, Trail River, Ptarmigan Creek, Primrose Landing, First Lake, Caines Head Recreation Area, Tern Lake, Quartz Creek, and Crescent Creek.

Taylor Highway (5)

This scenic highway extends for 162 miles northward along a narrow and winding route from Tetlin Junction on the Alaska Highway to the village of Eagle on the Yukon River near the Yukon-Alaska border. At Jack Wade Junction the Taylor connects with the Canadian Dawson Road. If you plan to drive into Canada, check on which hours the Alaskan-Canadian border is open before leaving Tok. There is no telephone service along the route or in Eagle. From Tetlin Junction the highway passes through low, wooded hills and then crosses the high divide that separates the Tanana River drainage to the south from the Fortymile River drainage to the north. The Taylor provides access to the famous Fortymile River country, so named because the mouth of the stream is about 40 miles below the site of Fort Reliance, a former trading post on the Yukon River. Gold was discovered along the Fortymile in 1886, and old cabins, gold dredges, and sluice boxes are still found along its banks. Place-names like Nugget Gulch, Discovery Creek, and Deadman Riffle are reminders of the romantic gold-rush days. The highway provides three major access points to the Fortymile River wilderness canoe trail. Canoeists attempting this trip should use extreme caution due to the river's complete isolation and long stretches of severe rapids. The *Alaska's Historic Eagle & Taylor Highway* guide is available free from: Bureau of Land Management, 555 Cordova St., Anchorage 99501. There are campgrounds along the highway at Walker Fork, Liberty, and Eagle.

VACATION/ LODGING GUIDE

Alaska Panhandle & Tongass National Forest

Southeastern Alaska, the ancient home and hunting grounds of the once powerful Tlingit Indians, known as the Panhandle, is encompassed within the vast boundaries of the Tongass National Forest. It includes a narrow strip of mainland and the adjacent labyrinth of picturesque, wave-lapped islands known as the Alexander Archipelago—including the prolific wilderness fish and game lands of the Admiralty, Baranof, Chichagof, Kupreanof, Wrangell, Revillagigedo, and Prince of Wales islands, whose scenic shores are dotted with rustic fishing and logging villages—both of which stretch for 400 miles from the Alaskan mainland and the massive 16,000–foot peaks of the St. Elias Range southeastward along the beautiful Coast Range Mountains and the western boundary of British Columbia. The Panhandle is one of the scenic wonders of the modern world with its great glaciers, wild salmon and steelhead streams, awesome sheer-walled fjords, lush rain forests of western hemlock and towering Sitka spruce, and high mountains rising above a rocky, moss-covered, log-strewn coast, with dense alder thickets and alpine tundra meadows laced by an intricate network of deep mountain valleys and torrential whitewater streams. The coastal rain forests contain an almost impenetrable undergrowth of moss-carpeted down timber, giant ferns, spiny devil's club, salmonberry, salal, copperbush, Sitka willow, Alaska and dwarf blueberry, Nootka rose, Pacific red elder, alpine bearberry, dwarf arctic birch, mountain cranberry, sweetgale, silverberry, mountain ash, and buffaloberry.

Information Sources, Maps & Access

For travel information on Alaska's Panhandle, contact the Alaska Division of Tourism, Pouch E, Juneau 99811 (907)465–2010. For two full-color *Tongass National Forest Maps* (50¢ each) and a *Recreational Facilities Guide*, write: Supervisor, North Unit, P.O. Box 1049, Juneau 99801 (907)586–7263; and Supervisor, South Unit, P.O. Box 2278, Ketchikan 99901 (907)225–3101. For vacation travel information about the Glacier Bay National Monument and a free *Glacier Bay Map/Brochure*, write: Superintendent, Box 1089, Juneau 99801 (907)586–7127. The free guide *Bald Eagles in Alaska* may be obtained from: Bureau of Sport Fishing & Wildlife, 813 D St., Anchorage 99501. The following useful guides may be ordered from Alaska Northwest Publishing Co., 139 Second Ave., Edmonds, WA 98020. *Southeast: Alaska's Panhandle.* Most colorful edition to date, exploring Southeastern Alaska's maze of fjords and islands,

mossy forests and glacier-draped mountains—from Dixon Entrance to Icy Bay, including all of the state's fabled Inside Passage. Along the way are profiles of every town, together with a look at the region's history, economy, people, attractions and future. Includes large fold-out map and seven area maps. 192 pages, $9.95. *Admiralty . . . Island in Contention*. An intimate and multifaceted view of Admiralty: its geological and historical past, its present-day geography, wildlife and sparse human population. Discusses the views of factions "in contention" for the island. Color photos. 78 pages, $5.00. *Glacier Bay: Old Ice, New Land*. The expansive wilderness of Southeastern Alaska's Glacier Bay National Monument unfolds in crisp text and color photographs. Records the flora and fauna of the area, its natural history, hike and cruise information for visitors. Glossary of plants and animals, large-scale color map included. 132 pages, $9.95. The Tongass National Forest and the Panhandle are reached by the Alaska Marine Highway System and scheduled airline and charter fly-in service from Prince Rupert, Ketchikan, Wrangell, Petersburg, Kake, Sitka, Hoonah, Juneau, Haines, Skagway, and Yakutat.

Recreation Areas

Admiralty Island

Admiralty, with its 678–mile coastline, is the second-largest island in the massive Alexander Archipelago and the most productive bald eagle habitat in the world. The eagle and the raven represented the two main clans of the Tlingit Indians, who lived in this region. More eagles nest on this majestic island than live in the lower 48 states. Admiralty's eagles nest in the tops of old-growth Sitka spruce or hemlock trees within a few hundred yards of the seacoast. The tall Sitka spruce, sometimes 300 years old, with their damaged, flattened tops, serve as natural platforms for the eagles' massive nests. The island has an estimated total of 1,000 of these great nests, averaging about two nests per mile; they attain tremendous size and weight and often survive the winter and are used again and again, for as long as 65 years. In order to reserve a sample of undisturbed eagle-nesting area where the bird can be studied and observed in its natural setting, several islands in the Seymour Canal on Admiralty Island have been designated as the Seymour Eagle Management Area. Spectacular concentrations of eagles can be seen feeding on the spring smelt runs in the Stikine River near Wrangell, the rivers of Berners Bay near Juneau, along the rivers entering Prince William Sound and Cook Inlet near Anchorage, and in the Chilkat Valley near Haines at the end of the Lynn Canal. Admiralty's scenic wilderness, incredibly rich in fish and marine life, also has Alaska's highest-density population of brown bears. The Angoon Tlingit tribe's name for Admiralty was *Hutsnuwu*, meaning "Brown Bear Fort Island." The Tlingits had a great fear of the supernatural powers of the island's thick interior forests—the territory of the great bear.

Glacier Bay National Monument

This is a 400–square-mile icy wilderness of scenic glaciers, deep fjords, and lush coastal rain forests. Several glaciers, such as the Muir and John Hopkins, discharge massive icebergs, so it is impossible to get within a 2–mile range of them. Mt. Fairweather and surrounding peaks soar to over 12,000 feet and are surrounded by coastal highlands inhabited by the rare blue, or glacier, bear, wolf, moose, Sitka deer, and wolverine. Campers and hikers should be prepared for cool, damp weather, with temperatures seldom rising above 72°F.

Tongass National Forest Wilderness Areas

Tongass's 16 million acres encompass the Mendenhall Glacier Recreation Area, the rugged cliffs and fjords of Rudyard Bay-Walker Cove Scenic Area, the iceberg-filled fjord of the Tracy Arm-Fjord's Terror Scenic Area, and the remote wilderness of bald eagle, salmon, and brown bear country surrounding the Admiralty Lakes Recreation Area. The crazy-quilt maze of islands in the Tongass contains several proposed wilderness areas. The King Salmon Wilderness Area takes in 120,000 acres of ocean islands with scenic cliffs, capes, log-strewn beaches, and dense spruce and hemlock forests that are the home of wolf, deer, black bear, and thousands of seals and sea lions. The beautiful Granite Fjords Wilderness is characterized by rugged highlands cut by U-shaped glacial valleys, ancient stands of lichen-hung lodgepole pine, Sitka spruce, hemlock, and cedar, ice fields, glaciers, and muskeg bogs. Big Goat Lake is a top fly-in spot for goat hunting, and fishermen stalk the aristocratic steelhead in the deep pools and riffles of the wild Chickamin River.

Gateways & Accommodations

Ketchikan

(Pop. 7,000; zip code 99901; area code 907.) Known as the Salmon Capital of Alaska, Ketchikan is a picturesque fishing and forest products town on Revillagigedo Island on the Tongass Narrows, 235 miles south of Juneau. Ketchikan is Alaska's southernmost city and is the first port of call for Inside Passage cruise ships and Alaska Marine Highway ferries. Area attractions include the Tongass Historical Society Museum, the Totem Bight Community House and Totem Park overlooking Tongass Narrows, Fort Tongass, and the famous Saxman Totem Park. Daily sight-seeing tours of area attractions are provided by *Ketchikan Sightseeing*, Box 5440 (225–4440). Area accommodations are provided by: *Hilltop Motel* (rates: $34 double), 46 very good rooms, coffee shop, and cocktail lounge, at 3434 Tongass Ave. (225–5166); *Ingersoll Hotel* (rates: $30–31 double), 59 rooms, restaurant, and cocktail lounge, at Front & Mission Sts. (225–2124); *Yes Bay Lodge*, on the picturesque Behm Canal, 45 miles northwest of Ketchikan, with modern lodge rooms, fresh Alaskan seafood, cocktail lounge, and excellent fishing, hiking, wildlife photography, wild-river trips, and beachcombing, rates on request, Yes Bay 99950.

Petersburg

(Pop. 2,000; zip code 99833; area code 907.) Known as Alaska's Little Norway, the town is famous for the largest halibut fleet in the world and a picturesque fishing village atmosphere on Mitkof Island at the northern tip of the scenic Wrangell Narrows. Area attractions include the Le Conte Glacier, charter fishing, the Petersburg Museum and the world-record 126½–pound Chinook salmon, the fish hatchery, and the Little Norway Festival. Le Conte Bay iceberg cruises are provided by *Blue Star Cruises*, Box 37 (772–4774). Area accommodations: *Beachcomber Inn* (rates on request), charming modern rooms and dining featuring local seafood and steak, cocktails, floatplane facilities, at Mile 4, Mitkof Hwy., Box 1027 (772–3888); *Tides Inn Motel* (rates: $36 double), downtown, beautiful view from rooms, free coffee and rolls, First St. (772–4288).

Sitka

(Pop. 3,400; zip code 99835; area code 907.) Established as a Russian fur-trading outpost in 1799, Sitka subsequently became the headquarters of the Russian-American fur company and the capital of Russia's American territory, which stretched from California to the Alaska Peninsula. The town is located southwest of Juneau on the west side of mountainous Baranof Island, named after the great Russian explorer. The old section of this incredibly scenic coastal village, flanked by snowcapped volcanic peaks and a maze of evergreen-clad islands, is a national historic park. The site of the Russian defeat of the powerful Tlingit Indians in 1804, the park has excellent exhibits of Tlingit totem poles and carvings, and a self-guiding trail. Area attractions include the Sheldon Jackson Museum of native arts and crafts, hiking trails, beautiful Silver Bay, and the all-Alaska Logging Championships, held each Fourth of July weekend. Accommodations are available at: *Shee Atika Lodge* (rates on request), 107 excellent rooms and suites, dining room, and cocktail lounge, 2 blocks east of ferry terminal (747–6241); *Sheffield House* (rates on request), 80 new rooms and suites, dining room and cocktail lounge, downtown at 202 Katlean (747–6616); *Sitka Hotel* (rates on request), 60 rooms in downtown central location (747–3288).

Wrangell

(Pop. 2,000; zip code 99929; area code 907.) Located at the northwest tip of scenic Wrangell Island, Wrangell is the only Alaskan settlement to have existed under three flags—Russian, British, and American. By turns it has been a fur-trading center, gold rush town, and lumber and fishing port. Area attractions include the historic totem poles and tribal Chilkat Indian house on Chief Shakes Island just offshore from the busy harbor, and numerous Indian petroglyphs. Area accommodations: *The Roadhouse* (rates on request), excellent rooms and suites with balconies and view, dining room and dancing (874–2335); *Stikine Inn* (rates on request), 18 spacious, modern rooms, Aunt Winnie's Restaurant & Dining Room, cocktail lounge, downtown, one block from ferry terminal (874–3388).

Lodges & Sporting Camps

★★★*Bell Island Fishing Resort* is located 45 miles north of Ketchikan in a region famous for its natural hot springs bordering superb king salmon fishing grounds. There's also good trout fishing at the end of a short air-taxi ride, plus nearby salt waters teeming with halibut, cod, red snapper, coho salmon, and other game species native to Alaska. The resort itself consists of attractive, modern cabins, each with a huge tub for bathing in the hot mineral water, a central lodge with a rustic bar and dining room, and a large, heated swimming pool. Rates: $537 per person (based on double occupancy) for 4 days and 3 nights, or $924 per person for 7 days and 6 nights. Prices cover lodgings, all meals, boats, motor, bait, fishing gear, and

cleaning and packaging of your fish. Direct connections to Bell Island leave at scheduled intervals from Ketchikan International Airport. For additional information write: Bell Island Hot Springs, Inc., 131 3rd Ave. N., Edmonds, WA 98020 (206)776–7100.

★★★*Clover Pass Resort*, 15 miles from downtown Ketchikan, is located on a protected waterway flanked by the "Little Alps" of Revilla Island and the Cleveland Peninsula. Nearby waters abound in fighting king and coho salmon, plus monster halibut up to 200 pounds. The resort offers roomy modern cabins, a fleet of 17–foot Starcrafts or modern cabin cruisers, a complete sport shop, and a restaurant on the premises specializing in succulent local lobsters and seafood, steaks, and weekend smorgasbords. Rates: $210 per person for 3 days, $290 for 4 days, including cabin accommodations, transfer from Ketchikan and back, 2 meals a day, boat, motor, fuel, bait, and fishing gear. Rooms may be rented on a daily basis at $35 double occupancy exclusive of meals, boats, tackle, etc. For complete information write: Clover Pass Resort, P.O. Box 7322, Ketchikan, AK 99901 (907)247–2234.

★★★★*Glacier Bay Lodge* is located at Bartlett Cove in the Glacier Bay National Monument with its awesome glaciers, deep fjords, and soaring snowcapped mountains only 20 minutes from Juneau. This beautiful, rustic resort offers deluxe accommodations, fresh seafoods, hiking, wildlife photography, nature tours, bird-watching, and fishing for salmon, halibut, and trout. Cruises depart daily from the lodge to the faces of nearby active glaciers. Daily rates: $51 per person, double occupancy. Juneau airport transportation service is available. For additional information, contact: (May 23–Sept. 16) Glacier Bay Lodge, Gustavus, AK 99826 (907)697–3221; or year-round at Suite 312, Park Place Bldg., Seattle, WA 98101 (phone toll-free (800) 426–0600).

★★★*The Gustavus Inn*, built in 1928 as a homestead for a family of nine hardy pioneers, has been converted into a handsome, comfortable lodge adjacent to an active farm. Surrounding the inn is Glacier Bay National Monument, a major attraction spring through fall. Boat tours and guided nature walks are offered through this magnificent, glacier-studded park. The flatness of the Gustavus terrain affords a sharp contrast with the rest of mountainous southeast Alaska and offers ideal opportunities for walking and hiking along scenic country roads. Fishing is another popular activity with guests of the inn; charters are available at Bartlett Cove, or you can try your luck for king and silver salmon in Icy Straits, the Gustavus waterfront. Daily rates: $38 for adults, $28 for children, including lodging and all meals. Rooms are cozy and quiet, with twin beds in each. Only 16 guests are on hand at any one time, so you are guaranteed a maximum of personalized attention. Meals are served family-style in the inn dining room. Fresh seafood, home-grown fruits and vegetables, and wild berries are some of the house specialties. Alaska Airlines offers regularly scheduled service to Gustavus from Juneau, May through September, or you can arrange for charter service from most southeastern Alaska cities and towns. For more details write: The Gustavus Inn, P.O. Box 31, Gustavus, AK 99826 (907)697–3311.

★★*Prince of Wales Lodge*, tucked away in the wilderness of southeast Alaska, overlooks sparkling Klawock Bay and offers handsome accommodations in carpeted rooms with private baths. Trolling is excellent for king and silver salmon in the bay itself, or you can test your skill casting for Dolly Varden, steelhead, and rainbow trout. The 5–day fishing package includes a fly-out trip to hot spots. Package trips include airfare from Ketchikan, Seattle, or Anchorage and begin at $453 for 4 days and 3 nights per person. Season runs April 16 to September 15. Write: Prince of Wales Lodge, Klawock, AK 99925.

★★*Thayer Lake Lodge*, on the shores of 9–mile-long Thayer Lake, lies in the heart of the Tongass National Forest on Admiralty Island. Just 60 air miles from Juneau, the lodge offers a true wilderness setting among stands of virgin timber bordered by a sandy beach. From June through September there is excellent fishing for cutthroat trout, taken on a fly or with your favorite lure and spin tackle. You can also pursue stream fishing just a short walk from the lodge.

Boats and motors are included in the daily rates. The lodge offers modern accommodations in guest cabins with comfortable beds for 4, cooking facilities, bathrooms, and fireplaces. Electricity is provided by an old-fashioned overshot water wheel on a creek directly behind the lodge. American-plan rates, including family-style meals in the dining room: $40 per person per day. Two housekeeping cabins offer greater privacy and full kitchens ($35–$55 daily for 2; $45–$55 daily for 4). Groceries should be purchased before arrival. Guide services may be arranged through the lodge. For more information write: (winter) Bob Nelson, Box 5416, Ketchikan, AK 99901; (May 30–Sept. 15) phone or wire Bob Nelson, Thayer Lake Lodge, Radio KWA78, via RCA Communications, Juneau. Ketchikan phone: (907)255–3343.

Travel Services

Alaska Discovery sponsors a broad range of wilderness adventure trips through Alaska and the Northwest Territories. Among the adventures offered are 7–day kayak and hiking trips in the breathtaking Glacier Bay area; 7–day hiking and canoeing trips on Admiralty Island, home of the bald eagle and Alaskan brown bear; 6–day canoe trips through the historic lakes that form the headwaters of the mighty Yukon River system; and 10–day canoeing and camping excursions on the Yukon itself from Whitehorse through Lake Laberge. Other trips explore the fast-moving Hubbard Glacier and remote Russell Fjord, the Indian village of Hoonah, and Tenakee Hot Springs. Trips originate in Juneau or Skagway, and are guided by experienced outdoorsmen with advanced first-aid training. Basic equipment and instruction are provided. Complete costs vary from $350 for 7–day adventures to $600 for the 10–day Yukon River expedition. Alaska Discovery also offers guide and outfitting services for custom trips and cross-country ski tours in the winter and spring. For complete descriptions write: Alaska Discovery, P.O. Box 337, Juneau, AK 99802.

Glacier Bay Airways provides air charter service to all points in southeast Alaska, with frequent flights between Gustavus or Glacier Bay and Juneau, Skagway, Sitka, and Haines. Special aerial tours of Glacier Bay National Monument are offered. Veteran bush pilots are available to take you to remote wilderness hot spots for a day of fishing. Open year-round, Glacier Bay Airways is located at the Gustavus Airfield and at Glacier Bay, where they maintain a 5–passenger Cessna 206 landplane and a 7–passenger De Havilland Beaver. Charter costs are based on an hourly rate, which varies according to aircraft and destination. For information write: Glacier Bay Airways, P.O. Box 1, Gustavus, AK 99826 (907)697–3331.

Glacier Bay Yacht Tours offer 1–3-day tours of the magnificent inlets and fjords, rain forests, snowcapped mountains, icebergs, and active glaciers of Alaska's spectacular Glacier Bay. Boats are expertly guided for close-up views of area wildlife—whales, seals, sea lions, porpoises, bears, and mountain goats—and there are ample opportunities to go ashore and explore for yourself. Four weekly departures are scheduled from Juneau, with rates varying from $100 per person for 1 day to $175 for 2 nights and 3 days. These rates include meals, berths, and lodge rooms for overnight stays. Glacier Bay will also arrange for charters through the channels and bays of southeast Alaska for one or several days of fishing, big-game hunting, camping, photography, sight-seeing—you name it. Fishing trips start at $125 for part of a day with little running time and up to 4 passengers. Full-day trips are $200 to $300. For further information write: Glacier Bay Yacht Tours, Box 424, Juneau, AK 99802 (907)586–6835; evenings and holidays (907)789–7429.

Glacier Guides, Inc., sponsors spring and fall hunting expeditions for Alaskan brown, grizzly, and black bear, mountain goat, Sitka deer, wolf, wolverine, waterfowl, and game birds. Glacier Guides' "mobile camp," a new 50–foot custom-built cruiser, features 3 private staterooms, extra crew quarters, showers, and other amenities, and provides all your transportation in and around the sportsman's mecca of southeast Alaska. On board the *Chaik*, you'll have plenty of opportunities for fishing, photography, and close-up sight-seeing of wildlife, massive glaciers, and breathtaking fjords. Each day you will hunt a separate bay alone with your guide in some of Alaska's most productive and unspoiled wilderness. In past years, Glacier Guides realized a 97% hunter success ratio for Alaskan browns and grizzlies. Fall hunts for Dall sheep, Alaskan moose, or barren-ground caribou in the Wrangell and Alaska ranges are also booked, and fishing charters are available June through August. Rates: $4,000, all-inclusive, for bear hunts, with your personal guide. Exclusive use of the *Chaik* may be booked for $7,500 total for the hunt. For references, complete information, and rates, write: Glacier Guides, Inc., P.O. Box 66, Gustavus, AK 99826 (907)697–3391. In winter write: 275 West 200 South, St. George, UT 84770 (801)628–0973.

Ketchikan Air Service, Inc., offers fishing, hunting, photography, and sight-seeing trips to all parts of southeastern Alaska and British Columbia via amphibian, single-engine, and multi-engine aircraft. Rates are by the hour or by the trip or per passenger. Located at Ketchikan International Airport. For further information write: Ketchikan Air Service, Inc., P.O. Box 6900, Ketchikan, AK 99901.

Stikine Air Service specializes in year-round charter flights within a 200–mile radius of Wrangell. "Flightseeing" trips are guided over the beautiful and fast-moving Le Conte Glacier, the lower Stikine River, and up Shakes Glacier. Charter aircraft available for lake, river, and airport landings include 3 single-engine amphibians, 2 Cessna 185s, and 1 De Havilland Beaver with 6 passenger seats. Seat fares are available between registered points. No package trips are available. In operation since 1962, Stikine offers experienced bush pilots and the finest equipment. For information write: Stikine Air Service, Box 631, Wrangell, AK 99929 (907)844–3327.

Alaska Peninsula & Bristol Bay Region

The Bristol Bay area and the Alaska Peninsula offer some of the finest trophy fishing, big-game hunting, and wilderness adventure in North America. The narrow, mountainous peninsula stretches for 500 miles from the southwestern corner of Alaska into the northern Pacific along the volcanic snowcapped peaks of the Aleutian Range mountains and the stepping-stones of the remote Aleutian Islands. The world-famous grayling, rainbow trout, and salmon waters of the Bristol Bay uplands encompass the northwestern portions of the Alaska Peninsula, where it joins the mainland.

The Bristol Bay area is dominated by the craggy, glacier-studded peaks of the Aklun Mountains to the north and west and by the scenic Wood River-Tikchik Lakes country. This majestic chain consists of hundreds of cold, clear lakes connected by wild rivers and streams surrounded by boreal forests, muskeg, and alpine tundra. The 2 million acres of mountains, forests, streams, lakes, and fjords of the Wood River-Tikchik Lakes region offer what is considered by many to be the world's finest fishing for record rainbow trout to 10 pounds, arctic char, grayling, steelhead, lake trout, northern pike, Dolly Varden, sheefish, and five species of salmon.

Information Sources, Maps & Access

For detailed information on the Bristol Bay area and the Alaska Peninsula, write to the area lodges and sporting camps or the Alaska

Division of Tourism, Pouch E, Juneau 99811 (907)465–2010. For detailed info on Katmai National Monument, the free *Katmai Map/Brochure*, and the free pamphlets *Brooks River Area* and *Hiking the Katmai Backcountry*, write: Superintendent, Katmai National Monument, P.O. Box 7, King Salmon, AK 99613 (907)246–3305. The free brochure *Kodiak National Wildlife Refuge* is available from: Supervisor, Alaskan National Wildlife Refuges, Box 280, Anchorage 99510. *Kodiak: Island of Change*. Although half the size of New Jersey, and once the administrative center of Russian Alaska, the 3,588–square-mile island of Kodiak remains well off the beaten path. Past, present and future—everything from Russian exploration to the present-day quest for oil. Maps, color photos. 96 pages, $7.95 from Alaska Northwest Publishing Co., 139 Second Ave., Edmonds, WA 98020.

The Bristol Bay Area and Alaska Peninsula are reached by air from Anchorage via Wien Air Alaska to Dillingham and King Salmon. Charter fly-in air service is provided by Peninsula Airways, Kodiak Western Alaska Airlines, Katmai Air Taxi, and Wien Air Alaska to wilderness fishing and big-game hunting areas. Outfitting and supply services are located at Dillingham, Iliamna, and King Salmon.

Recreation Areas

Aleutian National Wildlife Refuge

This 2.7–million-acre refuge is the third-largest unit in the National Wildlife Refuge System. The Aleutian Islands, commonly called the chain, are emergent peaks of a submarine mountain range. The often fog-shrouded archipelago includes 200 mountainous, volcanic islands dotted by thousands of lakes and crisscrossed by wild streams. The islands are a largely uninhabited wilderness, except for the Aleut villages of Atka and False Pass and a few active military installations. A high percentage of the world's emperor geese winter on the refuge. Bridging the north Pacific to Asia, the western Aleutians offer refuge to whooper swans, tufted ducks, and the Aleutian race of green teal. At the eastern end of the refuge, whistling swans, black brant, and the North American race of green-winged teal are found. Seabirds, including fulmars, storm petrels, cormorants, gulls, kittiwakes, murres, guillemots, murrelets, auklets, and puffins, nest in noisy colonies on the islands' cliffs and heather-covered hillsides. The once abundant Canada goose is dangerously near extinction as a result of blue fox introductions during the early fur-farming enterprises. The short-tailed albatross is almost extinct. Black-footed and Layson albatrosses, however, still soar offshore on motionless wings. The bald eagle and peregrine falcon are commonly sighted, and some gyrfalcons are also present. Sea otters have increased from near extinction to a population estimated at 20,000, and the northern sea lion is common. Unimak Island, an ecological extension of the Alaska Peninsula, is a stronghold of the Alaskan brown bear. The island has over 1,000 caribou, and wolf and wolverine are common. Portions of the refuge are open to hunting of migratory and upland birds and big game.

Katmai National Monument & the Valley of 10,000 Smokes

Katmai National Monument, a tranquil 4–million-acre wilderness of unmatched natural beauty which was rocked in 1912 by one of the most violent volcanic eruptions in modern history, lies to the south of Lake Iliamna. It encompasses the great peaks of the Aleutian Range; a segment of the Pacific ring of fire, one of the most active volcanic regions in the world, which forms the mountainous backbone of the Alaska Peninsula; bowl-shaped calderas with crater lakes—depressions caused by the collapse of crater walls by erosion; novaruptas—newly erupted volcanic domes; massive glaciers; the steaming fumaroles of the awesome Valley of Ten Thousand Smokes; island-studded lakes fringed with coniferous forests, alpine streams, and braided rivers; a rugged coastline of fjords, bays, and surf-pounded beaches; and haunting "ghost forests" caused by the blasts of hot wind and gas of the cataclysm of 1912, which buried 40 square miles of lush green forests under as much as 700 feet of volcanic ash and darkened the sky over most of the Northern Hemisphere with a haze of fine ash.

The boreal forests, valleys, mountain chains, alpine tundra, and rugged coastal regions of Katmai are inhabited by soaring bald eagles, which frequent the islands and coast of the Shelikof Strait, as well as petrels and eiders, auks, murres, moose, caribou, wolves, lynx, arctic hare, wolverine, beaver, and otter. The wilderness traveler should be alert at all times in Katmai country for brown bears. Their coloration serves as a natural camouflage, often difficult to spot. To avoid the potentially tragic mistake of jumping a bear, always make lots of noise and avoid dense alder patches and forests.

Further down the peninsula are the Ugashik Lakes, which consistently produce char and record grayling up to 5 pounds, and the Meshik River, which is outstanding for bull Dolly Varden. The central region of the peninsula is renowned for its salmon streams and Alaskan moose, Dall sheep, and brown bear hunting. The Aniakchak flows through the 440,000–acre Aniakchak Caldera National Monument, noted for boiling sulfur pools, hot springs, and steam vents. At the tip of the peninsula is the 320,000–acre estuary of the Izembek National Wildlife Range. It is a good area for camping and has many rivers, lakes, lagoons, mountains, and heaths. It's also the only breeding ground in North America for the black brant.

Kodiak Island National Wildlife Refuge

The Kodiak National Wildlife Refuge is a 1.8–million-acre reserve in the Gulf of Alaska, due east of the Alaska Peninsula. The refuge provides a natural habitat for the great Kodiak brown bear. Hundreds of miles of brawling, wild rivers and streams are traveled by spawning salmon and support the important Kodiak commercial salmon industry. The refuge provides top-ranked hunting for trophy brown bear and often phenomenal fishing for salmon and rainbow trout. Chartered flights to the interior of the island for brown bear photography can be arranged through Wien Air Alaska with local bush pilots. Guiding service for hunting and photography, available in and around Kodiak, is required for nonresidents.

Lake Clark National Park

The proposed Lake Clark National Park takes in 2.6 million acres of high country wilderness, varying from alpine tundra to Sitka spruce forests at the southernmost part of the Alaska Range and the northernmost portion of the Aleutian Range. This is a top wilderness fishing area for rainbow, grayling, and lake trout to 30 pounds. Wildlife in the Iliamna-Lake Clark region includes wolf, black and brown bear, grizzly, moose, caribou, and the majestic golden-horned Dall sheep. The wilderness traveler may come upon several of the Eskimo-Athabascan Indian archaeological and prehistoric fossil sites that exist around Lakes Clark and Iliamna and along the Newhalen and Kvichak rivers.

Lake Iliamna National Resource Range

The rainbow trout waters of the Lake Iliamna National Resource Range, a proposed 2¾–million-acre wilderness located in the northernmost part of the Alaska Peninsula due east of the Wood River-Tikchik Lakes region, are world-renowned. Lake Iliamna, Alaska's largest at 75 miles long and 20 miles wide and the seventh-largest lake in the United States, dominates the region. The lake and the surrounding network of lakes and wild rivers hold trophy-size pink, king, and silver salmon, Dolly Varden, lake and rainbow trout, arctic char, grayling, steelhead, and northern pike. Lake Iliamna has been rumored to contain in its cold, clear depths a mysterious monster fish, believed to be a world's record lake trout, a prehistoric fish species that has somehow survived through the ages, or a beluga, a whale known to live in fresh water. The validity of these rumors, however, is doubtful. The Indians of Iliamna, who are usually the first to tell tall tales, have never reported seeing the giant mystery fish.

Gateways & Accommodations

Kodiak

(Pop. 3,800; zip code 99615; area code 907.) The town is located on Kodiak Island south of the Kenai Peninsula in the Gulf of Alaska. The island, first discovered in 1763 by Russian explorers, is the oldest permanent European settlement in Alaska. Area attractions include the old Russian Orthodox churches; Baranof House Museum, an 18th-century fur warehouse; Fort Abercrombie State Park; and the world-famous brown bear habitat of Kodiak National Wildlife Refuge. Accommodations are available at: *Kodiak Travelodge* (rates: $48 double), rooms and suites, dining room, and cocktail lounge, at Benson St., (486–5712); *Shelikof Lodge* (rates: $40–50), rooms and family units, restaurant, and cocktail lounge, at 211 Thorsheim Ave., (486–4141).

Lodges & Sporting Camps

★★★*Afognak Wilderness Lodge*, on a densely forested and mountainous island in the Kodiak Island group, is a comfortable, inviting log structure with accommodations for 10 guests at a time. Family-style meals, snug guest rooms, and indoor plumbing give the lodge a fine reputation for wilderness hospitality. One of the area's greatest attractions is the abundance of protected wildlife, including sea lions, seals, killer whales, porpoises, bald eagles, wapiti, otter, elk, black-tailed deer, and many other species. There is also excellent fishing for trout and salmon, plus superb saltwater angling for North Pacific game fish. Other activities at the lodge include hiking, octopus hunting, beachcombing, visits to archaeological sites, and swimming in a natural rock-bottomed pool at the top of a small mountain. Rates are $100 per person daily and cover lodging, all meals, and boat travel. Charter bush flights are available between Kodiak and Seal Bay. For more information write: Afognak Wilderness Lodge, Seal Bay, AK 99697.

★★★★*Bristol Bay Lodge*, accessible by plane from Dillingham, offers

superlative fishing on Alaska's Wood River-Tikchik Lakes system, which consists of nearly 2 million acres and 14 lakes connected by short, swift rivers. Private air and water transportation allows guests to fish remote corners of this magnificent watershed for rainbows, arctic char, northern pike, Dolly Varden, and lake trout, plus fighting members of the salmon family—king, sockeye, coho, and chum. This is a small camp specializing in personalized vacations with accommodations for 12 guests at a time in roomy, attractive sleeping quarters with private baths and hot showers. The beautiful main lodge with its panoramic views houses a lounge, dining room, and guest rooms. Also on the premises are an outcabin, Eskimo steam bath, angling library, and aquatic insect aquarium. Bristol Bay's fishing fleet includes floatplanes, versatile Zodiac rubber boats and rafts, river jet boats, and canoes. Weekly rates of $1,250 per person cover 7 nights and 6 full days of fishing, meals, lodging, guide services, daily fly-out and boat trips, and maid and laundry services. For additional information write: Fishing International, 2310 4th St., P.O. Box 2132, Santa Rosa, CA 95405 (707)542–4242.

★★★*Enchanted Lake Lodge* is strategically centered in the Alaska Peninsula around some of the state's finest sportfishing waters. There is superlative fly casting, spinning, and trolling in Enchanted Lake, right at the lodge doorstep, plus fly-out fishing via amphibian and float craft to remote streams and lakes in western Alaska. These daily jaunts also give guests an opportunity to photograph and observe Alaska's awesome landscape and abundant wildlife in such spots as the Katmai National Monument, the Valley of 10,000 Smokes, McNeil River Brown Bear Refuge, and Tikchik and Wood River lakes. Lodge accommodations are in big, comfortably furnished double bedrooms separated by a common sitting room. Each bedroom has a private bath with shower, comfortable twin beds, and big picture windows. Meals are served in the main lodge building, and delicious picnic lunches are provided for fishing jaunts. The lodge has central heating, electricity, a big open fireplace, and a deep freeze and facilities for packing fish. Rates: $250 per person daily based upon a minimum party of 4. All bush flying, guide service, transport between the lodge and King Salmon airport, lodging, meals, boats, and motors are included. For further information write: (May 1–Oct. 15) Enchanted Lake Lodge, c/o E. W. Seiler, P.O. Box 197, King Salmon, AK 99613 (radio call sign KRV59); (Oct. 16–Apr. 30) E. W. Seiler, 1270 Dove Meadow Road, Solvang, CA 93463 (805)688–6265.

★★★★*Golden Horn Lodge* is located in the heart of the spectacular Wood River-Tikchik Lakes region, surrounded by long, fjord-like lakes, mountains and wild rivers. This rustic, yet fully modern fly-in lodge, offers first-rate accommodations, services, and trophy fishing for rainbow trout, arctic char, grayling, lake trout and salmon on day-long float trips or fly-in trips to the headwaters of remote, seldom-fished wild rivers with chance opportunities to photograph moose, waterfowl, eagles, and grizzly. The Golden Horn is a beautiful hand-hewn log lodge with attractive heated guest rooms and

private baths, a comfortable living room with a wood burning fireplace, and a lakeside sauna. Hearty meals with home-baked breads and pastries are served family-style in the lodge dining room. Guests are limited to 16 at a time to insure full personal attention by the Golden Horn staff and guides. The daily schedule is based on your personal fishing desires. You can take a day-long float and fishing trip, wade and fly fish in some of Alaska's finest rainbow streams, fish for salmon from a 41–foot river boat, or take leisurely cross country flights with the aircraft and stop to fish wherever it looks tempting. Daytime temperatures average in the high 50's to high 70's during June, July, and August, and in the high 40's to low 60's in September. There is generally little or no humidity, and most guests find shirt sleeves or a light jacket comfortable during the day. Lodge rates are $1,500/person per 7–day week, all-inclusive. For additional information, contact: Golden Horn Lodge, P.O. Box 546, Anchorage, AK 99510 (907)337–5113.

★★★★*Iliaska Lodge* is a small family sporting lodge nestled on the north shore of Lake Iliamna. Owner and host Ted Gerken, an avid fly fisherman and Alaskan bush pilot will guide you to the outstanding fishing spots in the myriad of fast-running, clear mountain streams surrounding the lodge and the nearby Bristol Bay Wild Trout Area. Float equipped aircraft carry guests to remote rivers chocked with spawning salmon. The lodge operates outboards on rivers requiring travel to the outstanding fishing waters, and other streams and mountain tarns are easily wadeable wearing hip boots. The lodge offers all modern conveniences in a rustic setting of incomparable beauty. Hot, home-baked breads and pies baked by hostess Mary Gerken highlight each evening menu. Rates are $55 per person daily, $90 per person including Newhalen River fishing, and $190 daily for fly-out river fishing in the remote wilderness areas. Iliaska Lodge also operates a small hunting camp in mid-August following the local caribou herd north of Iliamna, and in mid-September opens a cabin directly in the migration route of wandering caribou herds. Iliaska Lodge also operates a small hunting lodge on one of the several alpine lakes in the area having a known bull moose population. For more information write: Ted and Mary Gerken, Iliaska Lodge, P.O. Box 28, Iliamna, Alaska 99606 (907)571–1221.

Katmai National Monument Lodges & Sporting Camps:

★★★★*"Angler's Paradise" Lodges:* In the heart of the Bristol Bay fishing region, an area embracing hundreds of miles of streams, rivers, lakes, lagoons, and the world's largest sockeye salmon spawning grounds, are three excellent wilderness lodges operated through the state's premier airline, Wien Air Alaska. Some of the species available in this unspoiled trophy region include rainbow trout, Dolly

Varden, arctic char, grayling, pike, and king, red, and silver salmon. Wien Air Alaska lodges follow a hook-and-release policy, requesting that fishermen keep only fish that are mishooked and take home only trophy mounts, thereby ensuring a sane balance of the native fish population and a high standard of good angling year after year.

Brooks Lodge, on the beautiful Brooks River, offers 16 guest cabins accommodating a maximum of 60 persons at any one time. The central lodge building houses a dining area with a big fireplace and men's and women's bathhouses. The river has a superb run of red salmon from July 4 to July 25 and provides easily accessible fishing. Rates: $33 per person per night, not including meals. Also offered through the lodge is an all-day guided bus tour to the Valley of 10,000 Smokes.

Grosvenor Camp is a small facility in a very secluded lakeside location, ideal for families or small parties. There are 2 cabins accommodating a maximum of 8 guests, a lodge building, a cookhouse, and a bathhouse. You can fish just a few steps from your front door or take a boat to other spots in the area. Charter side trips via air taxi are available to more remote locations. Rates for 3 nights or more: $130 per person per day; $115 per person for parties of 2 to 4; or $100 per person for parties of 5 to 8. The lodge is open from approximately June 10 to July 15.

Kulik Lodge is a medium-sized camp (29 guests at a time) with a worldwide reputation for hospitality and spectacular fishing. Surrounding the comfortable central lodge are 9 cabins with heat, electric lights, screened windows and doors, hot and cold running water, and modern plumbing. Showers are located adjacent to the cabins. Meals are served family-style in the lodge dining room. Fishing in the Kulik area is readily available from the lodge, and the cost of your stay includes a fly-out trip to nearby hot spots determined by the lodge as the most productive areas for that period of time. Rates begin at $390 per person for 4 days and 3 nights and include lodging, all meals, freezing and care of your fish, guide and boat service, and fly-out trips.

Airfare to the above lodges via Wien Air Alaska averages $135–$140 round trip from Anchorage. For information on any of the Angler's Paradise lodges, contact: Fishing International, P.O. Box 2132, 2310 4th St., Santa Rosa, CA 95405 (707)542–4242.

★★★*Koksetna Camp*, in the heart of Alaska's beautiful Lake Clark wilderness, offers comfortable log cabin accommodations, river float

trips, sight-seeing by boat or on foot, and great sportfishing for big pike, grayling, char, lake trout, and Dolly Varden. Lake Clark is 60 miles long and 6–10 miles wide, glacier-fed, and surrounded by mountains of incomparable beauty. The area abounds in native wildlife, including moose, bald eagles, falcons, owls, and a vast array of bird life. Koksetna Camp specializes in wilderness vacations with an emphasis on getting to know the area; hence both boat and "flightseeing" tours can be easily arranged through the camp. Comfortable cabins have 2 bedrooms and a sitting room in each; there is a central bathhouse with hot and cold running water. Electricity is wind-generated. Excellent home-cooked meals are served family-style, with vegetables fresh from the garden. Rates of $95 per day per person cover lodging, meals, and guided fishing or sight-seeing trips. A remote wilderness cabin on Portage Creek, accessible by boat or floatplane, is available for $30 per day or $175 per week. The camp is reached via charter flights from Anchorage or Iliamna. For additional information write: Koksetna Camp, Box 69, Iliamna, AK 99606.

★*Kvichak Lodge*, located approximately 100 miles north of King Salmon and ½ mile south of Lake Iliamna, offers superb fishing for rainbow and steelhead trout, arctic grayling, Dolly Varden, and sockeye salmon. Each day your guide takes you to various parts of the lake and Kvichak River—which runs right by the lodge—so that you are guaranteed the best possible chance at the big ones. All lures, hooks, and salmon clusters are provided. At the lodge your trophies are cleaned, frozen, and carefully packed for shipment. Kvichak offers many conveniences that are often missing from wilderness lodges: electric lights, hot and cold running water, baths, oil heat, bedding, and sleeping bags. All-inclusive rates: $140 per person daily. Flight arrangements from King Salmon to the lodge may be made through Peninsula Airways (907)246–3712. For additional details write: Kvichak Lodge, Box 37, Naknek, AK 99633 (907)268–4276. The California representative for Kvichak Lodge is Carl Schoeller, 267 Orlando St., El Cajon, CA 92021 (714)440–3733.

★★★★*Ray Loesche's Rainbow King Lodge* offers a complete and all-inclusive package for the fisherman who wants to enjoy exceptional fishing, scenic flights, camping out, float trips and daily expeditions for the fish of his choice. The resort is located at Iliamna, 190 miles southwest of Anchorage. Guests pay transportation to Iliamna, but from the time they are met at the Iliamna airport, everything is included. Trips are for a full week, from Monday to Monday. Each day, guests can choose their own activities. The lodge has two new Cessna 185 floatplanes and a specially-equipped wheel plane to get anglers onto the gravel bars up the rivers and on the beaches. Guests can choose to be flown to the best areas for the fish of their choice, or use the 22–foot cabin cruiser, one of the

19–foot Grumman square-stern canoes with motors, an Avon raft with motor for a one-, two- or three-day drift trip or plan an overnight camp-out. Since there are only ten rooms, accommodating a maximum of 20 fishing guests, anglers get personal treatment, with a personal guide who will find the best fishing, fry your catch and prepare a hot shore lunch. Guests can also enjoy a scenic flight over Katmai National Monument to view the active volcanoes, glacial ice fields and crater lakes. They can fish for the famous Ugashik Lake Grayling, dig razor clams on Pacific beaches or see the Red Salmon Run in Bristol Bay. The season is from June 15 through October 1st. There is at least one species of salmon available at all times, and the rainbow trout are caught all season with the largest hooked in August and September. The food at Rainbow King Lodge is excellent with dinners of Alaska king crab, filet mignon, prime rib and cornish game hens—all at no extra charge. The Lodge does not sell liquor, but guests can bring their own bottles and mix is provided free. The dining room and the lodge room both have large fireplaces, offering a place to gather in the evening. Accommodations are ten lodge rooms with private full bath, two double beds, carpeting, thermostatically controlled heat and a view of Iliamna Lake and the snow-capped peaks across the lake. The all-inclusive rate for one week is $1495 per person. Children under 12 are $800 and can use the equipment and fish with their parents. Non-fishing guests are also $800, but they are not flown out with the fishing clients. For reservations and information write or call: Ray Loesche's Rainbow King Lodge, Iliamna Lake, Alaska 99606 (907)571–1277. During the off season write or phone P.O. Box 3446, Spokane, Wash. 99220 (507)924–8077.

★★★*Red Quill Lodge*, 250 miles southwest of Anchorage, overlooks 80–mile-long Lake Iliamna. Fishing in the lake and dozens of nearby streams and rivers is superb for king salmon in the 40–50 pound range, elusive arctic grayling, huge arctic char, and powerful, fighting rainbow trout. Fly-out fishing trips are arranged each day according to guest preferences; some of the rivers explored include the Tularek, Nushagak, and Newhalen. Lodge accommodations are friendly and comfortable, with a limited guest list often booked well in advance. Rates: $1,150 per person, all-inclusive, for 7 days of fishing, with additional days at a rate of $165 per day. Transporation from Anchorage to Red Quill Lodge is arranged through Wien Air Alaska. For more information write: Red Quill Lodge, P.O. Box 49, Iliamna, AK 99606 (907)571–2215.

★★★*The Royal Coachman Lodge* is located at the outlet of Tikchik Lakes on the Nuyakuk River, 375 miles southwest of Anchorage and 60 miles north of Dillingham. Guests are flown in float-equipped aircraft to surrounding lakes and streams to hit the hot spots for grayling, lake trout, arctic char, rainbows, king salmon, sockeye, and other species of sport fish. Good fishing is also available within 150 feet of the lodge, so there are no "bad days" if weather prevents flying. The modern lodge building has a lounge area, wet bar, and comfortable dining area. All meals are home-cooked and served family-style. Guest cabins offer all the amenities, including electricity and modern plumbing. Season runs from early June to mid-October. Per person rates are $1,200, Tuesday through Tuesday, including personalized guide service, meals, lodging, fly-out trips from lodge, boats, motors, and fish smoking and preparation. For more information write: The Royal Coachman Lodge, Bill Martin's Fish Alaska, P.O. Box 1871, Anchorage, AK 99510 (907)243–7645. Seattle contact: (206)783–4976.

★★★*Tikchik Narrows* operates two fly-out fishing camps, one on the narrows and the other on Wood River, in a lake-studded region of southwestern Alaska surrounded by the rugged Kilbuck Mountains. The area encompasses 14 lakes connected by fast, clear streams draining into the Nuyakuk and Wood rivers. Each morning after breakfast, fishermen are flown from the lodge to a variety of productive spots for a day's angling. There are 14 different species available in Tikchik's fishing area and almost as many methods for catching them—spinning, fly casting, trolling, wading, boating, lake fishing, or stream fishing. The choice is up to you. In case weather prevents daily fly-out trips, the lodge maintains a fleet of boats, canoes, and fishing platforms. Accommodations at the two camps are modern and comfortable. Each cabin has carpeting, a heater or fireplace, and private bath with hot showers and modern plumbing. Excellent meals, including freshly baked breads and pastries, are served in the lodge dining room. A shore or box lunch is prepared for your enjoyment in the wilderness. Bookings at Tikchik Narrows are kept small to insure the finest personal service. Season runs from approximately mid-June to mid-October, with some geese and duck shooting available in early October. Total price for 8 days and 7 nights is $1,300 per person, including all meals, lodgings, guide services, boats, flying from main lodge, light laundry, and tackle box. The lodge is reached via Wien Air Alaska from Anchorage to Dillingham and via floatplane from Dillingham to the lodge. For more information write: (winter) Tikchik Narrows, P.O. Box 1631, Anchorage, AK 99510 (907)277–8426; (June through September) General Delivery, Dillingham, AK 99576.

★★★*Ugashik Lake Lodge*, in the rugged lake country of the Arctic peninsula, offers superlative fishing for 2–3–pound arctic grayling, fighting sockeye salmon, silver and pink salmon, northern pike, and both sea-run and landlocked Dolly Varden. The permanent "bush camp" lodge is replete with all the comforts of home (kitchen

facilities, hot and cold running water, heat, showers, full electric power) and surrounded by some of the most awesome country on the continent, where everyday sights are exotic wildlife and still-active volcanoes surrounded by tundra. Hunting trips are offered in season for the region's abundant waterfowl, or you can arrange a combined fishing and hunting trip. Package rates of $850 per person include 7 nights and 8 days, lodging, food, and use of boats. Transportation from King Salmon to the lodge is provided by a chartered twin-engine seaplane. Bookings are Saturday to Saturday, starting in July and running through October. For more information on Ugashik Lodge, write: Fishing International, Box 2132, 2310 4th St., Santa Rosa, CA 95405 (707)542–4242.

★*Walker's Copper River Lodge* is located at the river's outlet on beautiful Lake Iliamna. The wadable waters of the Copper River, its gravel bars, winding deep pools, swift runs, and rock-studded rapids all make for superior fly-fishing for rainbows averaging 3 pounds, Dolly Varden, and grayling. Numerous trails have been established around the lodge for wildlife and photography buffs. Alaskan brown bear are frequently sighted during salmon season in the late fall. A canoe, 2 river skiffs, and an 18–foot lake boat are on hand for fishing and exploring Intricate Bay of Lake Iliamna, so called for its complex maze of islands. Rafts are available for guests who want to run up the river by jet boat and drift down, fishing at a leisurely pace. Sleeping quarters are large, comfortable tent-houses, furnished with sleeping bags and kerosine lamps. Rates: $85 per person daily, including all meals. For information write: (before June 1) Bob R. Walker, RR 1, Box 260, N. Kenai, AK 99611; (after July 1) Walker's Copper River Lodge, c/o Pope-Vannoy Landing, Iliamna, AK 99606.

Travel Services

Alaska Wilderness River Trips, Inc., explore Alaska's vast, open stretches of untouched wilderness in 16–foot inflatable rubber boats guided by rivermen with many years of experience. Among the waterways floated are the Chilikadrotna-Mulchatna river system, a 275–mile run from the rugged Alaska Range to Bristol Bay with fishing for salmon and pike along the way; the Kobuk River, which flows out of Walker Lake and is one of the most beautiful streams in arctic Alaska; the Talchulitna River, just north of Anchorage, teeming with rainbows and salmon; and Lake Creek on the south side of the Alaska Range. Trips range from 7 to 14 days, and all are fly-in via bush aircraft. Rates average $610 for 7 days and $1,190 for 14 days and include excellent meals prepared by your guides, all flying to and from Anchorage, tents, and all camp equipment. Each trip is limited to a maximum of 16 people. For more details write: Alaska Wilderness River Trips, Box 1143, Eagle River, AK 99577 (907) 694–2194.

Branham Adventures sponsors hunting and fishing expeditions in the rugged wilds of Alaska. Experienced guides take the hunter into the Alaska Peninsula, the Alaska Range, the Holitna River, and the Kuskokwim Mountains. Sheep, moose, caribou, and black and brown bear are among the game commonly bagged on guided trips to remote fly-in areas. Branham's base of operations is a modern hunting lodge 90 miles northwest of Anchorage on a lake surrounded by rivers, mountains, and snowfields. They also sponsor polar bear hunting in April and walrus hunts in St. Lawrence Island in late May and early June. Hunts of 7–10 days start at $2,450. Branham's fishing trips concentrate on three prime locations: the Susitna Valley near Anchorage, the Iliamna-Bristol Bay drainages, and the Kuskokwim River, all of which boast a reputation for fine steelhead, salmon, grayling, and trout waters. Each party of fishermen is provided with a personal guide and/or professional pilot for maximum fishing success in fly-in hot spots. A fishing lodge situated on the slopes of the Alaska Range 100 miles northwest of Anchorage offers modern facilities and private rooms. Trips of 7–10 days for a party of 2 or 3 begin at $1,295 per person, all-inclusive. For detailed information and rates, write: Alaska's Branham Adventures, Box 6184–Annex, Anchorage, AK 99502 (907)277–9403.

Far North Guide and Outfitter offers hunting and fishing expeditions based on the Battle River Wilderness Camp in the heart of the Alaska Peninsula, a setting flanked on three sides by awesome mountains and complemented by the clear blue waters of the Battle River. Some of the readily available trophy species include steelhead, arctic char, Dolly Varden, mackinaw trout, and northern pike. There's also unsurpassed angling for rainbow trout and grayling. The hunting season at Battle River Camp brings its fair share of trophies too, with guided trips for the peninsula's famed caribou, grizzly, and moose. Camp accommodations are rustic but comfortable, and the limited number of guests guarantees personalized service. Rates vary according to length of stay and type of hunting desired: 7 days of moose hunting averages $2,000 per person; 5 days of fishing is $950 per person. These prices include lodging, meals, guide service, boats, and motors. For complete rates and more information, write: Far North Guide and Outfitter, 1513 F St., Anchorage, AK 99501 (907)272–0903.

Griechen Air Taxi, serving Bristol Bay and the Alaska Peninsula, offers sportfishing trips to six scenic river areas, including Naknek, Kvichack, and King Salmon rivers and Ugashik Lakes, with or without an experienced guide. Two river float trips with a guide and daily fly-out fishing charters are also available. Sportfishing runs from June 10 through September, but some winter fishing trips in trophy areas are sponsored. Unguided fly-in services for stalking caribou, brown bear, and moose, private hunting cabins, and boat rentals can be arranged through Griechen, which takes pride in its superb safety record and 98% hunter and fisherman success. Aircraft include a Cessna 185 and a Maule M-5. For estimates on charter time and rates, write: Griechen Air Taxi, P.O. Box 161, Naknek, AK 99633. Griechen will also provide estimates on request for specific areas you wish to hunt or fish.

Munsey's Kodiak Island Bear Camp offers photographic expeditions for Alaskan brown bear led by Bill Munsey, a registered Alaskan guide. For information write: Box 1186, Kodiak, AK 99615.

Totem Airways, Inc., based in Anchorage, specializes in hunting, fishing, "flightseeing," river float trips, and other custom air charters on a year-round basis. Enjoy air photography safaris over the Columbia Glacier and Lake Hood; fishing trips from June through October in remote Alaskan streams; hunting for grizzly and Dall sheep with experienced, registered guides. Fully equipped camps and a 3–day duck camp package trip in southern Alaska are available. For further information on fishing and hunting packages and personalized rates, write: Totem Airways, Inc., P.O. Box 4–2344, Anchorage, AK 99509 (907)277–8001.

Alaska Range & Mt. McKinley National Park

The snowcapped peaks of the Alaska Range, the highest in North America, form a sweeping 580–mile arc from the Yukon border across to the Alaska Peninsula, where they merge with the Aleutian Range. It is a high-country wilderness of craggy summits, massive glaciers and ice fields, dense taiga forests and alpine tundra carpeted by white mountain avens, red and blue mountain heath, Labrador tea, crowberry, dwarf birch, and willows. This world-famous region

is dominated by the spectacular peaks and wildlands of Mt. McKinley National Park. The high-country lakes, streams, and wild rivers hold arctic grayling, whitefish, lake trout, northern pike, Dolly Varden, and rainbow trout. Don't forget that in some areas it is not safe to fish without carrying a rifle, and the Alaska Range is one of them. The range is one of Alaska's finest hunting regions for grizzly and black bear, caribou (found along the southeastern side of the range), moose, trophy Dall sheep, and wolf. Hunting the Dall sheep, the white king of Alaska's mountains, is usually hard work and requires a great deal of climbing. It pays to be in top physical condition before embarking on a sheep-hunting expedition.

To the ancient Athabascan Indians, Mt. McKinley was known as *Denali*, "the great one." Its summit soars to an altitude of 20,320 feet in Mt. McKinley National Park and forms a natural barrier between the coastal lowlands to the south and the Great Interior to the north. The mountain dominates a wilderness of taiga, "the land of little sticks," a term of Russian origin that describes the scant forest growth near the Arctic Circle, found in narrow swaths that follow the winding course of rivers in the park. Above timberline at 2,700 feet on the windswept slopes are dwarf willows, birch, mountain cranberry and heaths, white mountain avens, and alpine bearberry. The taiga is mostly a land of white and black spruce, quaking aspen, paper birch, and balsam poplar, carpeted with a thick, springy mat of mosses and lichens. The Denali Fault, the largest crustal break in North America, stretches for 1,300 miles across Alaska and passes through this wilderness of contrasting lowlands, braided rivers, somber mountains, brightly colored peaks, and sheer granite domes.

McKinley Park is a naturalist's paradise. Caribou herds still follow their ancient migration patterns across the open tundra and through mountain passes. Dall sheep are found in the rugged high country, and moose in the pastures and willow thickets near the spruce forests, as well as wolves, grizzly, beaver, red squirrel, and bald eagle. The Sable Pass wildlife protection zone is prime grizzly bear habitat for the wildlife photographer.

There are few trails in the park. Wilderness travel is generally along river bars, gravel-covered ridges, or animal trails. Try to avoid, when possible, traveling through thick brush, low-lying tundra flats, tussocks and alder thickets on hillsides, and willows along riverbanks. The best time to hike depends on snow melt. General travel conditions tend to improve in July and are best in August. The mosquito is king between late June and mid-August. Even the caribou head for the snow patches of the high country during this time of the year to avoid the voracious warble and nostril flies. The last two weeks of August and the early weeks of September are prime time for cross-country hikes. Snowstorms may occur at any time of the year in the high country. Hunting is prohibited and there is little fishing, because most of the rivers contain a milky suspension of glacial silt, or rock flour, which makes them uninhabitable. Wonder Lake, however, holds large lake trout.

Information Sources, Maps & Access

For information on the Alaska Range, contact the Alaska Division of Tourism, Pouch E, Juneau, AK 99811 (907)465–2010. For detailed info on Mt. McKinley National Park and free travel brochures and the free *Mount McKinley National Park Map/Brochure,* write Park Superintendent, P.O. Box 9, McKinley Park, AK 99755 (907)683–2294. A beautiful full-color 25–by 32–inch *Mount McKinley National Park Map* at a scale of 1:250,000 covering 8,634 square miles may be obtained for $2 (add 50¢ for postage) from: U.S. Geological Survey, Federal Center, Denver, CO 80225. The map is available in either a topographic or a shaded-relief edition suitable for framing. The Alaska Range and Mt. McKinley National Park are reached by charter fly-in service, the Alaska Railroad, and the Denali Alaska and Anchorage-Fairbanks highways. Outfitting and supplies are located at Talkeetna, Farewell, Skwentna, McKinley Park, Healy, Delta Junction, Dot Lake, Parson, Tanacross, and Fairbanks.

Lodges & Sporting Camps

★★★*Arctic Tern Lodge,* just north of Mt. McKinley, is situated on a high bluff overlooking Lake Wien. A rustic resort with activities for the whole family, the lodge is open year-round and features a complete canoe-outfitting service for floating Alaska's renowned rivers. Popular summer activities include fishing for northern pike, sheefish, and grayling, swimming, "flightseeing," hiking, and a variety of other outdoor pleasures. Winter and fall are the prime seasons for moose hunting, ice fishing, and cross-country skiing. The main lodge is a hand-built log structure with carpeting, a big fireplace, and tremendous views of Mt. McKinley. Cabins around the lodge feature twin beds, fireplaces, and good views of the lake. Meals are home-cooked and appetizing, with an emphasis on famous "sourdough" recipes. American-plan rates: $125 per person per day, including meals, lodging, equipment, and fly-in transportation. For information write: Arctic Tern Lodge, Box 425, Nenana, AK 99760.

★★★*Camp Denali,* a wilderness vacation retreat on the north boundary of Mt. McKinley National Park, offers the finest in rustic bush-country hospitality, with special emphasis on an "experience away from the hectic mechanized tempo of modern living." Situated a mile off the main road, the camp sprawls over 55 acres of tundra and spruce woods dominated by the massive shape of Mt. McKinley, easily visible from almost all parts of the camp. Activities include hiking, fishing, wildlife photography, and exploring the vast natural wonderland of McKinley Park. Overnight camping in the backcountry is also popular with guests at Denali Camp. Accommodations are in comfortable cabins for 2–7 persons, with cold, pure stream water piped to each unit and a Yukon stove for heat. Tasty meals are served family-style in the lodge, which features a library and herbarium. All buildings are scattered along a ridge and around a tundra pond, spaced wide apart for maximum privacy. Cabin rentals exclusive of meals, guide service, and transportation, are $35 (double) to $75 (6 guests) per night. All-inclusive vacation packages are also available, beginning at $240 per person for 4 days and 3 nights; $288 for 5 days and 4 nights; and $504 for 8 days and 7 nights. For complete information write: Camp Denali, McKinley Park, AK 99755 (907)683–2290 summer; (907)683–2302 winter.

★★*Chulitna River Lodge,* 40 miles from Mt. McKinley in the heart of Denali State Park, specializes in sight-seeing trips around the Ruth Gorge ("the Grand Canyon of Alaska") and remote fishing camps accessible only by floatplane. Rainbow, lake trout, Dolly Varden, grayling, and salmon are caught in season. Most of Chulitna's fishing camps offer comfortable cabins, boats, and motors. Chulitna also operates a fully certified air taxi service into the Alaskan wilderness. Two-, three-, and seven-day fishing trips are offered, starting at $75 per person per day. Write: Chulitna River Lodge, Star Route B, Box 374A, Willow, AK 99688.

Mt. McKinley National Park Hotels & Lodges:

★★★*The McKinley Park Station Hotel,* located 2 miles within the park from the main entrance, is built around the theme of a pioneer railroad station with train cars on tracks housing the saloon, gift shop, snack bar, and Pullman sleeping accommodations. In addition there are 100 handsomely appointed modern hotel rooms, a full dining room, and a spacious lobby. Rates: $19–23 daily for Pullman sleepers (showers and restroom facilities in each car), $13 for a roomette with one single bed, and $42 (single) or $49 (double) for hotel rooms with private baths. The hotel is open from mid-May to late September.

Carlo Creek Lodge, open June 16 through Labor Day, is located outside the park, 12 miles south on Alaska Highway #3 (Milepost 224). Accommodations are available in modern log cabins and vacation trailers, all with private bath. Free transportation to and from the lodge coincides with the Anchorage-Fairbanks bus and train schedules and the Tundra Wildlife Tour, a guided 8–hour bus safari through the interior of McKinley Park. Rates: $30 daily for a single, $35 daily for a twin or double, and $2 for each additional guest.

The McKinley Chalet, 1 mile north of the park entrance on the banks of the Nenana River, offers 8 deluxe suites. Rates: $45 single, $50 twin, and $5 for each additional guest. Transportation is available for guests arriving by train, bus, or plane. The chalet is open July 1 through mid-September.

The Hostel is located just south of the McKinley depot and provides overnight accommodations for guests of all ages. The charge is $1 per night, and guests must provide their own bedding. Ideal as a base for backpackers and climbers.

For more information write: Mount McKinley National Park Co., McKinley Park, AK 99755 (907)683–2295.

★★★*Mt. McKinley Village,* at the southern entrance to Alaska's awesome Mt. McKinley National Park, offers an excellent base from which to explore this 3,000–square-mile wilderness of sweeping tundra and cloud-ringed peaks. Rooms are carpeted, clean, and handsomely appointed with private baths and comfortable beds. Rates: $47 daily for single rooms; $67 for rooms that sleep 4. Off-season rates are somewhat lower. For dining there is a coffee shop, the Grub Steak Room offering Alaskan fare, and the Village Pub cocktail lounge. Visitors to Mt. McKinley Village may want to take advantage of the special overnight trips to North Face Lodge, reached via air-conditioned bus through 100 miles of spectacular scenery. The village is 130 miles from Fairbanks and is served by the

Alaska Railroad from both Anchorage and Fairbanks. For information write: Mt. McKinley Village, P.O. Box 66, McKinley Park, AK 99755 (907)683–2265.

North Face Lodge, located near Wonder Lake in Mt. McKinley National Park, offers modern accommodations and delicious meals (American plan) with a view of Mt. McKinley. Wildlife includes moose, caribou, Dall sheep, bear, and wolverine. The lodge accommodates up to 14 people per day. Glacier tours are available. Season—all year round. A 2–day tour to North Face Lodge, round trip from Anchorage, is $184. Rates include round-trip travel through valleys and foothills of the Alaska Range to Mt. McKinley National Park, a guided drive through alpine wilderness, sight-seeing, hiking, fishing, comfortable rooms, private bath and toilet, and meals. For information, contact: 720 W. .5th Ave., Anchorage, AK 99501 (907)274–8539.

★★★★*Silvertip* operates three top-quality fishing lodges on some of Alaska's most beautiful and productive waterways. The Silvertip Lodge at *Judd Lake*, approximately 80 miles west of Anchorage, is a handsome, contemporary structure on an elevated point of land overlooking the headwaters of the Talachulitna River on one side and the calm azure blue waters of Judd Lake on the other. In the distance are the towering silver peaks and glaciers of the Alaska Range. Fishing here is both varied and superb for rainbows, Dolly Varden, and arctic grayling from June through October, and for salmon runs beginning in July. Lake fishing yields lake trout, burbot, and whitefish. There are also overnight trips to an untouched spawning stream and abundant opportunities to explore and photograph unusual flora and fauna. The comfortable, two-story lodge has an inviting living-dining-bar area set off by big picture windows. Meals are served family-style and enhanced by complimentary wine. There are 6 guest rooms with a pair of single beds in each, modern indoor toilet facilities, and 2 new private cabins with accommodations for 4 in each. The lodge is only 45 minutes by floatplane from Anchorage. Rates: from $180 per person for 2 days and 1 night to $500 per person for 7 days and 6 nights. Base price includes lodging, guide service, fishing equipment, canoes and boats, and transportation between the lodge and Anchorage.

Silvertip's *Talachulitna River Lodge* is located 55 miles from the headwaters at the river's mouth on a wooded bluff 40 feet above the Talachulitna's blue green waters. Though somewhat more rustic than the Judd Lake facility, the one-story lodge preserves its natural charm without sacrificing comfort. The living-dining area has a big stone fireplace and fine vistas of the surrounding forest. There's also a bar-lounge with hand-hewn stools and comfortable chairs. Three guest rooms in the main lodge accommodate 2 persons each. The plumbing is up-to-date and indoors, with lots of hot water for showers. A separate log cabin with its own fireplace and porch sleeps 4 additional guests in snug comfort. To complete your wilderness experience, try the wood-burning Finnish sauna followed by an icy plunge. For fishing, the lodge offers 20–foot jet boats to explore the many tributaries of the Skivetna and Talachulitna rivers, streams teeming with Dolly Varden, grayling, and all five species of salmon. For greater variety, a 2–day trip to remote Canyon Creek guarantees secluded fishing on an unpressured stream. Rates for Silvertip's Talachulitna Lodge are all-inclusive and identical with those for Judd Lake Lodge, described above.

The lodge on the remote *Unakleet River*, near the Bering Sea 400 miles from Anchorage, is Silvertip's newest fishing resort, set on a hill overlooking a vast river valley and the sea beyond. Guests are transported by jet river boat from the Eskimo village of Unakleet

(accessible via commercial airlines) to a modern lodge fashioned from native logs with huge picture windows and a sunken lounge area. An open bar, delicious family-style meals, and all the modern conveniences make the lodge a welcome respite after a day's fishing. The Unakleet River and neighboring waters promise unexcelled fishing for silver salmon and trophy arctic char and grayling. From September 1 to October 15 the lodge offers some of the best shooting in North America for goose and duck. Rates at Unakleet Lodge are $200 per person per day, including lodgings, guides, all meals, fishing equipment and licenses, open bar at no cost, boats, and transportation between the lodge and Unakleet.

For information on any or all of the above Alaskan lodges, write: Fishing International, P.O. Box 2132, 2310 4th St., Santa Rosa, CA 95405 (707)542–4242.

Travel Services

Alaskan Adventure has sponsored big-game hunts and trail-riding expeditions for over 20 years. Trips begin at Brushkana Creek headquarters on the Denali Highway, where rustic cabin accommodations are offered, and proceed to remote cabin or tent camps in small groups of 6–8 persons. Along the way there is outstanding fly-fishing for grayling and lake trout, plus hiking, climbing, and wilderness side trips, including a trek to the Nenana Glacier. Package-plan rates of $595 per person per week include horses, meals, lodging, and transportation to Brushkana Creek from Cantwell. For information write: Alaskan Adventure, Hope, AK 99605.

Genet Expeditions sponsors mountain-climbing adventures of varying levels of difficulty. Three climbs up Mt. McKinley (20,320 ft.) are offered: the West Buttress, via Windy Corner and Denali Pass to the south peak; the Kahiltna-Muldrow Traverse, with a descent via Muldrow Glacier to Wonder Lake; and the South Buttress, via the west fork of Ruth Glacier. Experienced climbers in top physical condition may also join the climbs up Mt. Hunter (14,470 feet), Mt. Foraker (17,400 ft.—second-highest peak in the Alaska Range), and Mt. Aconcagua (22,831 ft.—highest summit in the Americas). Genet Expeditions supplies leadership, food, general climbing gear, and transportation between Talkeetna and starting points. Expeditions take anywhere from 12 to 30 or more days and cost between $900 and $1,800 per person, depending on the climb chosen. For complete information, an equipment checklist, and an application, write: Genet Expeditions, Talkeetna, AK 99676 (907)733–2306.

Golden North Air Service, just outside McKinley National Park, offers charter services for campers, fishermen, photographers, skiers, and backpackers headed toward the magnificent Alaska and Talkeetna ranges. Flightseeing trips in and around the park, over living glaciers and deep-flowing rivers, are especially noteworthy and are available all year round. Golden North also maintains a roomy, fully equipped cabin at Soule Lake, high in the Talkeetna Mountains, and a large tent/frame camp in the valley at Bull Lakes, also completely outfitted. (Your first night at either camp is on the house.) Whatever your interest, Golden North will be glad to help you plan your trip and see it to completion with expert advice and skilled pilots. For information and rates, write: Golden North Air Service, Mile 131½ Denali Highway, Cantwell, AK 99729 (907)768–2434.

Far North Region & The Brooks Range

The great wilderness of Alaska's Far North is bounded on the south by the Brooks Range Mountains, on the east by the Yukon border and the Porcupine Plain, and on the west by the Chukchi Sea. This rugged wilderness is dominated by the countless mountains, deep canyons, primeval valleys, and hundreds of height-of-land headwater lakes and wild rivers formed by the little-explored Brooks Range, which sweeps for 600 miles across Alaska's Arctic from the Philip Smith, Davidson, and Romanzof mountains on the east to the De Long, Baird, and Waring mountains on the west. When the renowned explorer and conservationist Robert Marshall came upon the Arctic Divide and the massive Gates of the Arctic during his explorations of the Central Brooks Range in 1930, he observed the magnificence of a wild, timeless world filled with untold thousands of jagged spires, alpine valleys, lakes, and wild rivers teeming with arctic char and grayling, giant lake trout, and northern pike, previously unmapped, unnamed, and unknown. Today the great caribou, grizzly, and Dall sheep habitat of this magnificent central Brooks Range Wilderness has been irrevocably disrupted by the construction of the Alaska pipeline and the North Slope oil boom.

Information Sources, Maps & Access

For information on the Far North Region, write: Alaska Division of Tourism, Pouch E, Juneau, AK 99811 (907)465–2010. A descriptive *Map of the Proposed Gates of the Arctic National Park* is available free from: National Park Service, 334 W. 5th Ave., Suite 250, Anchorage, AK 99501. An *Arctic National Wildlife Range Map/Brochure* may be obtained free from: Bureau of Sport Fishery & Wildlife, 813 D St., Anchorage 99501. *The Brooks Range: Environmental Watershed* looks at early exploration by white men through journals, at historic periods that rival present interest in the area's natural wealth, and at controversy over uses for it: Native land claims, recreation, proposed national parks and development of resources. Maps, color photos. 112 pages, $9.95 from Alaska Northwest Publishing Co., 139 Second Ave., Edmonds, WA 98020. The Far North and Brooks Range are reached by scheduled and charter aircraft from Fairbanks and the arctic bush villages of Chandalar, Arctic Village, Fort Yukon, Bettles, Allakaket, Anaktuvik Pass, Deadhorse, Kiana, Ambler, and Kotzebue.

Recreation Areas

Arctic National Wildlife Range

The mountains of the Eastern Brooks Range, which joins the central and western portions of the range to form a continental divide between the arctic coastal plain and the Great Interior of the Yukon River system, form a great swath over 100 miles wide rising to a series of rugged, glacially eroded peaks 5,000–8,000 feet high from the Yukon border westward to the Sagavanirktok River. This land of permafrost, broad, colorful valleys, rock and alpine tundra, isolated stands of white spruce and poplar brush, muskeg bogs, lakes, and meadows dominated by sedges, scattered willows, and dwarf birch, is encompassed within the 8.9–million-acre Arctic National Wildlife Range. The southern portion of the wildlife range contains fertile valleys, warmed by summer winds that flow from the Yukon River basin, and carpeted by yellow snow buttercup, tundra rose, red shooting star, fireweed, blue Siberian aster, and monkshood. Old Woman Creek and the Sheenjek River flow southward out of the mountains, winding through a valley floor of rich lakes, oxbow sloughs, and groves of spruce and cottonwood into the vast, densely forested plain of the Yukon River. In the north is the rolling tundra of the great treeless arctic plain. In the western part of the wildlife range lie Peters and Schroder lakes at the foot of Mt. Chamberain, each 5 miles long. The lakes contain grayling and large lake trout, and you can easily see white Dall sheep, caribou, and moose from the shores. In the eastern part of the range, the clear, cold Firth River flows past towering limestone ramparts and groves of cottonwood and white spruce.

The range is one of the finest caribou-hunting zones in Alaska. The great porcupine caribou herd migrates through the region along deeply worn trails in the river valleys and mountain passes and on high slopes, similar to the buffalo trails on the Great Plains 100 years ago. Moose herds are found scattered in the willow and poplar stands along valley bottoms and lakes of the southern portion of the range and to within 25 miles of the Arctic Ocean on the north side. A few barren-ground grizzly in color phases from dark brown to blond roam the high country along with Dall sheep. Other wildlife in the range includes large populations of hawks, eagles, and falcons, wolves, black bear, wolverine, lynx, fox, beaver, mink, marten, weasel, and snowshoe and arctic hares. Good hiking routes are found along the lichen-and-heath-carpeted uplands of the Brooks Range and along the headwaters of the Chandalar River and the Hulahula River. Warm clothing, raingear, and plenty of insect repellent are a must. No campgrounds are available.

Gates of the Arctic National Park

The Central Brooks Range wilderness, explored and mapped by Marshall during his journey to the headwaters of the upper Koyukuk River and across the Arctic Divide in the Endicott Mountains during the decade 1929–39, is encompassed within the proposed 8.36–million-acre Gates of the Arctic National Park with its massive spires and pinnacles. Due east of the Arctic Divide and the Gates of the

Arctic is the Trans-Alaska Pipeline corridor. The major features of the central and western park regions, an outstanding example of tundra country and taiga famous for the stark, scenic grandeur of its vast open valleys and great sweeps of mountain slopes, include the Alatna, Killik, Noatak, Tinayguk, Upper Kobuk, and John rivers; the jagged, dark spires of the Arrigetch Peaks, Mount Igikpak—the highest peak in the Central and Western Brooks Range—Alatna Hills, Anaktuvuk Pass; the lunker lake trout and great northern pike waters of Walker, Chandler, Nutuvukti, Iniakuk, Minakokosa, Selby, and Narvak lakes; and the arctic foothills to the north. The Central Brooks Range and the Gates of the Arctic region still comprise one of the finest big-game hunting regions left in North America for barren-ground grizzly, Dall sheep, moose, and wolves. The biological resources of the region are of high scientific importance and value for wilderness recreation. It is located 200 air miles from Fairbanks.

Kobuk National Monument & the Great Sand Dunes

The Western Brooks Range takes in the De Long, Baird, and Waring mountains and the vast wild country of scenic foothills, broad valleys, clear lakes and rivers, boreal forests and tundra, and prehistoric archaeological features surrounding the Noatak and Kobuk rivers. The Grand Canyon section of the Noatak River is the nesting and hunting grounds for golden eagles, rough-legged hawks, gyrfalcons, and peregrine falcons. Black bear are found throughout the region, and grizzlies roam the highlands and valleys of salmon streams; a few polar bear are occasionally sighted along the ice floes of Kotzebue Sound. Portions of the arctic caribou herd winter in the lower stretch of the Noatak, the upper Kobuk, and along the Selawik Hills and Selawik River west of Inland Lake. Moose inhabit the river valleys and lowlands, and Dall sheep are found among the peaks and alpine meadows.

The scenic wetlands, open tundra, barren jagged peaks, forested rolling hills, and the Great Kobuk Sand Dunes covering 25 square miles of the central Kobuk River Valley are encompassed by the proposed 1.85–million-acre Kobuk Valley National Monument. The proposed national monument is located north of the Arctic Circle

between the Eskimo villages of Kiana and Ambler, about 100 miles east of Kotzebue. The famous Onion Portage Archaeological District—one of the most important sites in arctic North America to the understanding of the culture of early man in the New World and his relationship to Asia—lies just outside the eastern boundary of the proposed monument. Along the Chukchi Sea coast to the west lie the famous tundra lowlands, lava fields, and volcanic crater lakes of the proposed Chukchi-Imuruk National Reserve and the Cape Krusenstern National Monument, which embrace an ancient relic of the Bering land bridge. About 40,000 years ago, the sea level dropped during the last of the Pleistocene's great ice ages, and Alaska became linked to Asia by a 1,000-mile-wide land bridge across which prehistoric hunters are believed to have entered America.

Travel Services & Lodges

Alatna Guide Service, headquartered in Fairbanks, specializes in guided hunting and fishing excursions, float trips, backpacking, wildlife photography, and sight-seeing trips into some of the most scenic regions of the Arctic. Alatna maintains several privately owned camps in the Brooks Range, including the handsome and rustic Iniakuk Lodge. All camps are accessible by air only; there are no roads within 100 miles. This is an exclusive service, catering to a limited clientele. Hence, rates vary according to your specifications on the type of trip desired, length of stay, and number of participants. All inquiries will be answered personally. Just give Alatna a few details on what you have in mind. Write: Alatna Guide Service, P.O. Box 80424, Fairbanks, AK 99708 (907)479–6354.

Arctic Outfitters, based in Kiana, Alaska, offer unguided river float trips of several unspoiled and beautiful rivers above the Arctic Circle, including the Kobuk, Noatak, Grand Canyon, Eli, Squirrel, and Kelly rivers. For each trip of 10 days (itineraries carefully plotted in advance), Arctic Outfitters provide 3–man inflatable Matyeler boats, motor and fuel for the Kobuk-Kiana trip, 4–man tents, cook stove and fuel, camp equipment, portable CB radio, and first-aid kit. Your progress will be checked once during the 10–day period. Travel is through Anchorage or Fairbanks via Kotzebue. Travel from Kiana to the float-trip site and back is included in the package price. Both Wien Air Alaska and Great Northern Airlines serve Kotzebue from Anchorage and Fairbanks. Rates vary according to your route, ranging from $500 to $1,400 for a party of 3. For full details write: Arctic Outfitters, Ltd., Box 33, Kiana, AK 99749.

★★★*Midnight Sun Lodge* is located 130 miles north of the Arctic Circle, 90 air miles northwest of Kotzebue, in an area as uncrowded as it is remote. Fishing here is excellent for arctic char and grayling in the Wulik River from late June through October 1. If it's trophy game you're after, the area abounds in moose and arctic caribou. Dall sheep and grizzly are also available, along with wolf, wolverine, and walrus. Photography buffs will have a field day in the cliffs of Cape Thompson, the De Long Mountains, and the virgin wilderness of the Noatak Valley. Though by no means plush, the lodge and facilities are modern and comfortable by Arctic standards. Cabins have heat and electricity; excellent meals, with beer and wine, are served in the dining room; and there are modern bathrooms and laundry facilities. Rates include everything but personal items, guns, and fishing tackle. A 6–day fishing trip is $180 per person per day; rates vary from $2,000 to $4,000 per week, depending on your choice of game. License and trophy fees are extra. Small aircraft (included in package price) are used for transportation between fishing holes and hunting camps. For full details write: Phil Driver, Midnight Sun Adventures, 1306 E. 26th Ave., Anchorage, AK 99504 (907)277–8829.

Great Interior & The Yukon Country

The Great Interior, or central region, of Alaska stretches from the northern slope of the Alaska Range north beyond the Arctic Circle to the southern slopes of the massive Brooks Range, named in honor of Alfred Brooks, who served as chief Alaska geologist for the U.S. Geological Survey from 1903 to his death in 1924. This relatively low, rolling interior belt, dominated by taiga of white and black spruce, quaking aspen, paper birch, and balsam poplar, extends from the Yukon Territory border west almost to the Bering Sea, slashed by the mighty Yukon and Kuskokwim rivers and the wild Yukon tributaries, including the Nation, Fortymile, Charley, Birch Creek, Koyukuk, and Beaver Creek rivers. The forests of the interior belt, which stretch in places for more than 300 miles from north to south and for 1,000 miles from east to west, have an understory of Labrador tea, crowberry, stunted willows, bearberry, bog and dwarf blueberry, mountain cranberry, and prickly rose, inhabited by moose, barren-ground grizzly, and caribou.

Information Sources, Maps & Access

Detailed information on the Yukon River region and a free *National Wild & Scenic Rivers* booklet and canoeing information may be obtained from: Bureau of Land Management, 555 Cordova St.,

Anchorage 99501. The Yukon country of the interior is reached by scheduled air service, the Elliott and Steese highways, and charter fly-in service from Fairbanks. Outfitting and supplies are found at Eagle, Chatanika River, Circle Hot Springs, Circle, Fort Yukon, Livengood, Manley Hot Springs, Minto, Stevens Village, Beaver, Rampart, Tanana, Ruby, Galena, Koyukuk, Nulato, Kaltag, Grayling, Anvik, Holy Cross, Russian Mission, Marshall, St. Marys (Andreafsky), and Alakanuk.

Recreation Areas

Porcupine National Forest

The great lake-dotted lowlands of the Yukon Flats and the Porcupine wetlands, encompassed within the remote 5.5 million acres of the porposed Porcupine National Forest, surround the confluence of the Porcupine and Yukon rivers at the historic Hudson's Bay Company trading post of Fort Yukon, northwest of Circle and the upper Yukon region. The Yukon-Porcupine Flats are Alaska's most productive waterfowl area. Ducks in untold thousands nest in the flats, including lesser scaup, widgeon, pintail, white-winged scoter, green-winged teal, mallard, and one-fourth of the world's population of canvasbacks. The upper Porcupine River is an important area for the endangered peregrine falcon, gyrfalcon, and golden eagle. Moose, wolves, grizzlies, and the Fortymile and Porcupine caribou herds are found through the lowlands and in the Hodzana Highlands.

Yukon-Kuskokwim National Forest

Westward of Fort Yukon and the flatlands, the Yukon winds through its broad, densely forested valley, past the outposts of Beaver and Stevens Village, Mt. Tozi, and the Ray Mountains to its confluence with the Tanana River, flowing on past the Kokrines Hills on the north and the Kaiyuh Mountains on the south to its confluence with the Koyukuk River and Koyukuk Flats and the Nogahabare Sand Dunes, where it bends sharply and flows southwest through the wilderness of the proposed 7.3–million-acre Yukon-Kuskokwim National Forest and the lake-dotted "pothole country" of the Yukon Delta, to its mouth on the Bering Sea.

Yukon Wild & Scenic Rivers

The Yukon, known to the Athabascan Indians as the great river flows for 1,200 miles through Alaska from the Yukon border to the Bering Sea and has three major tributaries, the Porcupine, Tanana, and Koyukuk. The upper Yukon region includes the scenic section of the river and the surrounding wildlands between the Yukon-Alaska border at Eagle and Circle (the town, established as a trading post in 1887, owes its name to early traders and Klondike prospectors who mistakenly thought it was on the Arctic Circle). The upper Yukon is bordered by hills and the Crazy Mountains, colorful bluffs, and bottomland forest, and is the principal segment of a network of wild and scenic rivers that includes the Charley, Kandik, Tatonduk, and the renowned Nation rivers—the latter a wild, deep-flowing stream that offers some of the finest arctic grayling fishing in North America. Other wild and scenic streams and wilderness canoe routes in the region are the historic Fortymile River and the Birch and Beaver Creek, which rise in the alpine uplands of the White Mountains. The entire Charley River basin lies within the 1.97 million acres of the proposed Yukon-Charley National Wild and Scenic Rivers area. The wild Charley River, one of Alaska's clearest and a top-ranked wilderness canoe route, has its headwaters in the primitive uplands area of the Tanana Hills. Moose congregate along the river lowlands from late fall to spring. The Steese-Fortymile caribou herd roams the wildlands along the Taylor Highway. A small population of white Dall sheep inhabits the rugged glacier peaks between the Charley and Fortymile rivers. The peaks are designated a walk-in area where no vehicles or pack animals are allowed for hunting

purposes. Wolves, wolverine, and black bear are common to the area, and grizzlies are found in the uplands. The remote headwater lakes and crystal-clear tributaries of the "great river" are accessible by floatplane and canoe, and hold record grayling, sheefish, northern pike, and king, silver, and sockeye salmon. The upper Yukon area is also considered to be the finest peregrine falcon habitat in Alaska, with one nest per 8 miles of river.

Travel Services & Lodges

Alaskan Adventures, based at Snowshoe Lake on Glenn Highway connecting Anchorage and the Canadian border, specializes in guided photography tours, glacier flying for skiing and climbing parties, fly-in fishing, resident hunting, and bush outings. A 3–place aircraft operates year-round on skis or wheels and charters for approximately $60 an hour; there is also a 4–place craft available on floats and skis for $90 an hour. Bush pilots provide the best in personalized service and have a firsthand knowledge of this vast, lake-dotted plateau surrounded by four major mountain ranges. Parties are requested to bring their own outing equipment, but some furnished cabins are available. For additional details write: Alaskan Adventures, Snowshoe Lake, Star Route C, Box 212, via Palmer, AK 99645.

★★*Circle Hot Springs, Inc.*, operates a hotel and restaurant 137 miles from Fairbanks in an area renowned for its natural, warm mineral springs. Basically unchanged since its opening in 1932, the 24–room hotel features an Olympic-sized pool and a small museum highlighting the region's colorful history. Activities at Circle Hot Springs include helicopter flights of the area, horseback riding tours, and panning for gold during the summer months. Rates: $32 daily, double occupancy ($24 in winter), or $40 daily, triple occupancy ($32 in winter). The hotel and pool are open year-round. Air North has 3 scheduled flights per week to Circle Hot Springs, or you can arrange for charter flights through the hotel. If you fly your own craft, there's also a 4,400–foot airstrip maintained year-round. For further information write: Circle Hot Springs, Inc., Circle Springs, AK 99730 (907)479–4641.

Gulf Coast & The Kenai Peninsula

This south central region of Alaska lies to the northwest of the Panhandle. It includes Prince Edward Sound, the Kenai Peninsula and Cook Inlet regions of the southern coast, and adjacent wilderness

areas and waterways that extend inland from the Gulf of Alaska through the Chugach National Forest to the soaring 14,000–foot peaks of the massive Alaska Range in central Alaska.

Information Sources, Maps & Access

For information on the Gulf Coast Region and the Kenai Peninsula, contact: Alaska Division of Tourism, Pouch E, Juneau, AK 99811 (907)465–2010. A full-color *Chugach National Forest Map* (50¢) is available from: Forest Supervisor, 121 W. Fireweed Lane, Suite 205, Anchorage, AK 99503 (907)272–4485, along with the free booklet *Recreation Cabins in the Chugach National Forest*. The free *Kenai National Moose Range Map/Brochure* and the free booklet *Canoeing on the Kenai National Moose Range* and wilderness travel info may be obtained from: Kenai National Moose Range, P.O. Box 500, Kenai, AK 99611 (907)283–4877. *Cook Inlet Country*. A very special tour of the Cook Inlet region—its communities, big and small, and its countryside. Begins at the southern tip of the Kenai Peninsula, circles Turnagain Arm and Knik Arm for a close-up view of Anchorage, and visits the Matanuska and Susitna valleys and the wild, west side of the inlet. 144 pages; 230 color photos, separate map. $9.95 from Alaska Northwest Publishing Co., 139 Second Ave., Edmonds, WA 98020.

The Kenai Peninsula-Gulf Coast region is reached via scheduled airline service, charter aircraft, the Alaska Marine Highway System, and the Sterling, Seward-Anchorage, George Parks, Glenn, Edgerton, and Richardson highways. Outfitting and supply services are located at Kenai, Soldotna, Seward, Anchorage, Valdez, and Cordova.

Recreation Areas

Chugach National Forest

The Chugach National Forest is one of Alaska's most scenic and popular areas for fishing, wilderness canoeing, cross-country hiking, and big-game hunting. Named for the Chugach Eskimos of Prince William Sound, the forest takes in 4¾ million acres of the mountainous, lake-studded Kenai Peninsula and a narrow strip of shoreline along the Prince William Sound and Boswell Bay of Alaska's Gulf Coast. It also includes the cluster of densely forested islands in Prince William Sound, including Afognak and Montague islands, which are covered with magnificent conifers, scenic fjords, log-strewn beaches, and quiet lagoons and spits, located between the peninsula and the mouth of the Cooper River. Wildlife seen along the rugged coastal areas includes the majestic bald eagle and the legendary killer whale (actually a dolphin), the Minke whale, humpback and gray whale, sea lion, sea otter, harbor seal, and porpoise. The notorious killer whale, which has been observed at Chugach, is identified by conspicuous white markings on a black background and the triangular dorsal fin, up to 6 feet high on the male.

Kenai National Moose Range

The famous Kenai National Moose Range encompasses the major portion of the Kenai Peninsula wilderness to the south and west of the Chugach National Forest. The 1,730,000–acre refuge was established in 1941 by the U.S. Fish and Wildlife Service to protect the natural breeding and feeding range of the great Kenai moose, renowned for their palmated antlers in excess of 6 feet, and other native wildlife. The moose range is divided into two natural zones, a scenic mountain country with hundreds of lakes and glaciers, dominated by the huge Tustumena and Skilak lakes known as the Andy Simons Natural Area, and a lowland area dotted with over 1,200 lakes and dense forests of spruce, birch, and aspen.

Nearly 500,000 outdoorsmen visit the moose range each year to fish, hunt in the high country and lowlands, and canoe the wilderness water trails. The region provides excellent fishing in the Kenai and Russian rivers for record red salmon, silver salmon, and king salmon, running as large as 100 pounds. The wilderness lakes and rivers hold arctic char, Dolly Varden, lake trout, steelhead, and kokanee. The range also offers opportunities for alpine camping, wildlife photography, and canoeing on Kenai and Swan lakes and the Swanson and Moose rivers. There are over 100 miles of well-marked hiking trails. Much of the lowland area is wet and swampy and requires waterproof footwear. The moose range has 14 established campsites, varying from small, rustic overnight access camps to larger individual units with parking spurs, boat ramps, and water and sanitary facilities, located at various scenic and popular fishing areas.

The refuge is the habitat of more than 146 species of birds, including grebes, loons, terns, and the graceful white trumpeter swan, which reaches weights up to 33 pounds, has a wingspan of almost 8 feet, and has been known to live for over 32 years. Bald eagles, hawks, owls, and marsh and water birds are found throughout the moose range. Thousands of pintails, mallards, and lesser Canadian snow geese use the tidal waters of the Chickaloon Flats during migrations.

Wildlife populations include approximately 9,000 moose at lower elevations and about 1,000 Dall sheep, as well as black bear, wolves, wolverine, brown bear, mountain goat, coyotes, and caribou. Furbearers include beaver, muskrat, fox, otter, mink, and lynx.

Wrangell National Forest & St. Elias National Park

Due east of the Copper River lie the world-famous big-game hunting ranges of the Wrangell-Mentasta-Nutzotin mountains. This high-country region is the premier Dall sheep-hunting area in Alaska. Part of the wintering range for the Nelchina caribou herd, the most important in the state for the hunter, is located on the northwestern flank of the Wrangell Mountains. The boreal forests, lowlands, and alpine tundra of this high country are the habitat of brown, grizzly, and black bear, moose, wolves, wolverine, and mountain goats. There are also two small herds of wild bison. The Wrangell Mountains encompass the interior and coastal forests of the proposed Wrangell Mountains National Forest and the Wrangell-St. Elias National Park, which together form 14 million acres of the greatest concentration of peaks over 14,500 feet in North America, including Mt. St. Elias (18,008 ft.), Mt. Blackburn (16,390 ft.), and Mt. Sanford (16,237 ft.). The rugged coastline from Yakutat Bay to

Prince William Sound, south of the Wrangell Mountains, is a prime habitat for bald eagles, harbor seals, sea otters, sea lions, and the endangered peregrine falcon.

Gateways & Accommodations

Kenai

(Pop. 3,500; zip code 99611; area code 907.) Known as the oil capital of Cook Inlet, this is the largest town on the Kenai Peninsula. Area atractions of the historic Russian fur-trading center, located on the western portion of the peninsula, include the old Russian Orthodox church on the original site of Fort St. Nicholas, built in 1791, the Fort Kensy Museum, the Kenai Fine Arts Center, salmon canneries, and the active Mt. Redoubt and Mt. Iliamna volcanoes across Cook Inlet. Herds of beluga whales are often sighted offshore during early summer. The town is the administrative headquarters of the Kenai National Moose Range. Area accommodations: *Katmai Motel* (rates on request), 34 modern units, dining room, and cocktail lounge (283–4846); *Kenai Sheffield House* (rates: $36–42 double), 60 units, dining room, coffee shop, and cocktail lounge, in center of town at Willow St. (283–7566).

Seward

(Pop. 1,600; zip code 99664; area code 907.) On Resurrection Bay, this picturesque coastal fish-processing center on the eastern side of the Kenai Peninsula near the Chugach National Forest boundary and the Kenai National Moose Range is nestled between rugged mountain ranges. The town is the southern terminus of the Alaska Railroad and a major Alaska Marine Highway port of call. Attractions include the Seward Museum, a movie depicting the 1964 earthquake shown daily at the community library, the 868–square-mile Harding Ice Field 18 miles west of town, and charter boat fishing and nature hikes. Accommodations: *Merle's Marina Motel* (rates: on request), 11 units, airport and ferry terminal transportation service, just north of town on the Seward-Anchorage Hwy. (224–5518); *Murphy's Motel* (rates: on request), 11 units overlooking beautiful Resurrection Bay, airport courtesy car, 4th and D St. (224–5650).

Soldotna

(Pop. 1,200; zip code 99669; area code 907.) A major jumping-off point for trips into the Kenai National Moose Range, Soldotna is located on the western side of the Kenai Peninsula, 147 miles from Anchorage. Area accommodations: *International Hotel* (rates: on request), 26 good units, dining room, cocktail lounge, and coffee shop, at Mile 95 of the Sterling Hwy. (262–4451); *Soldotna Inn* (rates: on request), good rooms and restaurant in the center of town, on the Kenai Spur Rd. (262–9169).

Valdez

(Pop. 1,000; zip code 99686; area code 907.) Once a gold-rush boom town, today a modern port city on beautiful Prince William Sound, Valdez is the terminal of the Trans-Alaska oil pipeline. It is served by regularly scheduled air service and the Alaska Marine Highway system. Area attractions include the oil pipeline terminus, Old Valdez, Gold Rush Days in August, the Valdez Heritage Center, and the massive Columbia Glacier. Daily tours of the glacier and its wildlife, including harbor seals, whales, porpoises, and seabird rookeries, are available at the Valdez dock. Area accommodations: *Sheffield House* (rates on request), 99 very good rooms and suites, restaurant, cocktail lounge, courtesy car service from the ferry terminal (835–4381); *Totem Inn Motel* (rates on request), modern rooms, dining room, cocktail lounge, and one of the largest mounted animal collections in Alaska (835–4443).

Lodges & Sporting Camps

★★*Alexander Lake Lodge*, a rustic fly-in resort in lowland lake country 50 miles northwest of Anchorage, offers unspoiled fishing in over 200 miles of spring-fed wilderness streams, 1–4-day river float trips, trophy hunting for moose and grizzly, brown, and black bear, wilderness hiking, and boating on Alexander Lake. Comfortable heated cabins sleep 2–4 people. The main lodge offers a congenial bar and family-style living-dining room where home-cooked meals are served. Rates: $75 per person per day including all meals, lodging, and boat service. For details write: Alexander Lake Lodge, c/o Ken Clark, P.O. Box 4–212, Anchorage, AK 99509.

★★★★*Alyeska Resort*, a luxurious year-round resort in the state's largest ski area, is framed by lofty mountains and nestled in south central Alaska's beautiful Glacier Valley, just 40 miles southeast of Anchorage. Powder hounds will appreciate the ski facilities—4 double chair lifts, a Poma lift, 2 rope tows, and miles of trails for every level of expertise. Since the introduction of skiing at Mt. Alyeska in the early 1950s, the resort has played host to numerous major ski events, including the Olympic Trails and coveted World Cup alpine events. Cross-country skiing is also available on a variety of nearby

trails and meadows. In warmer weather, the resort's scenic chair-lift ride, slowed to half its winter speed, takes visitors on a leisurely and breathtaking tour 2,000 feet above the valley. The long Alaskan summer days are also perfect for sight-seeing jaunts to Portage Glacier and Erickson's Gold Mine and around the region's fabulous landscapes. Alyeska Air Service offers flightseeing trips to Lake George, the Matanuska Valley, Mt. McKinley, and other areas abounding in native wildlife. Resort facilities include the Skyride Restaurant, a glass-enclosed dining room reached via chair lift; the Mt. Alyeska Nugget Inn, which specializes in steaks and native seafood; a day lodge with cafeteria; the Sitzmark Lounge for après-ski refreshments and cocktails; a disco-bar; extensive conference facilities; and many other amenities. The central inn has 32 deluxe hotel rooms. A second wing of the hotel houses 43 condominium suites, and 2 additional condominium hotels contain 70 units. All told, the Alyeska resort has fine accommodations for over 250 guests. Rates are $33–$45 daily, double occupancy, with the lowest tariff on weekdays. Special skiers' packages, season passes, group instruction, and learn-to-ski holidays are available. For full details write: Alyeska Resort, Girdwood, AK 99587 (907)783–6000.

★★*Evergreen Lodge*, on Lake Louise, is located at the southern end of a series of spectacular lakes that connect end to end and allow you to travel 27 miles in one direction or explore some 100 miles of pine-rimmed shoreline. The lakes also connect to a number of eminently canoeable rivers. Lake Louise boasts big lake trout up to 44 pounds, plus arctic grayling, burbot, and whitefish. You can also fly to wilderness fishing camps or drive to smaller lakes in the immediate area for a leisurely day of fishing. Hunting by boat, aircraft, or snowmobiles for the caribou, sheep, and moose that abound in this region is also a popular activity at Evergreen Lodge. Comfortable sleeping cabins are propane-heated and accommodate up to six guests. The main lodge offers a lounge area, a dining room, central washroom facilities, a small grocery and tackle shop, and a liquor store. Rates: $28 per night for two persons. Meals, boat and canoe rentals, and boat launching are extra. For information write: Evergreen Lodge, Box 264, Star Route C, Palmer, Alaska.

★★★*Gwin's Lodge* is a small family guest lodge nestled in the Chugach National Forest near the clear, free-running Kenai and Russian Rivers. The lodge, built of hand-hewn logs and fieldstone and dwarfed by the stunning Chugach mountains, offers rustic lodging, delicious home cooked meals, and guided fishing trips into the fast running salmon country. Rates are $36 daily, for a double room. For more information write: Gwin's Lodge, Mile 52, Sterling Highway, Cooper Landing, Alaska.

★★★★*Kachemak Bay Wilderness Lodge* is a small, family-operated lodge tucked away at the head of a lovely cove across Kachemak Bay at the end of the Kenai Peninsula, 100 air miles from Anchorage. This incredibly scenic area of snowcapped mountains and narrow fjords supports a variety of rare, native wildlife—Kenai moose, bald eagles, Alaskan brown bear, sea lions, caribou, Dall sheep, and many other species. Activities at the lodge revolve around the seldom-visited wilderness. Backpacking, photography, deep-sea fishing from a boat or the shoreline, visiting archaeological sites, hiking, and sight-seeing are just some of the possibilities. The lodge also maintains a remote fly-in camp with rustic tent cabins in Kachemak Bay Wilderness Park. In summer there are fine opportunities for climbing high ridges, hiking the many trails, and lake fishing. The main lodge is open year-round and offers accommodations for no more than 12 guests at a time. The hand-hewn log structure has an enormous fireplace, dining room, guest bedroom, living room, and kitchen, with superb views all around. Separate private accommodations are in rustic guest cabins and a large guesthouse-chalet. Excellent meals, cooked over a wood stove, are served family-style in the lodge dining room. Host Mike McBride is a licensed pilot and registered guide and will be glad to arrange big-game hunts for guests. Duck hunting is also popular at the lodge from September 1 through mid-October.

The region attracts a large variety of species and excellent duck marshes are just a short walk from the lodge. For more information write: Kachemak Bay Wilderness Lodge, China Poot Bay via Homer, AK 99603 (907)235–8910.

Travel Services

Alaska Pioneer Canoers Association offers planning and guide services for group canoe trips on the Swanson River and Swan Lake in the heart of the Kenai National Moose Range. "Pioneer" trips are the specialty of this association: all meals are prepared over an open fire, and sleeping accommodations are in lean-to shelters under the open skies. Everyone has an opportunity to cook, portage, set up camp, fish, swim, prospect, or whatever your group desires. For your trip, Alaska Pioneer provides canoes, one guide, packboards, food, and shelter. You just set the date and the number of days you wish to travel. Individuals with no group affiliation may coordinate through this association to join up with others for canoe outings in the Kenai Range. Canoe rentals are also available. Rates for group trips depend on the number of participants, length of trip, and itinerary. For full information write: Alaska Pioneer Canoers Association, Box 931, Soldotna, AK 99669 (907)262–4003.

Kenai Lake Air Taxi, Inc., provides unguided fly-in hunting and fishing services to the Kenai Peninsula from Cooper Landing. Flying rates start at $45 per person round trip (minimum of 2 to a party) to the areas's great fishing lakes, where tent camps, boats, and motors are also available on a rental basis. Hunting rates for resident hunters begin at $50 per person round trip (minimum of 2 hunters). Within Cooper Landing itself are a number of roadside inns and lodges offering overnight accommodations for incoming sportsmen and their families. For details write: Kenai Lake Air Taxi, P.O. Box 800, Cooper Landing, AK 99572 (907)595–1213.

ARIZONA

Introduction

The great open spaces, rugged mountains, eerie wind-tortured deserts and rolling sagebrush flats, evergreen-clad highlands, awesome canyons, and huge reservoirs of the American Southwest offer a wide variety of outdoor recreation opportunities, including fishing, hunting, wilderness camping, and wild-river touring. Arizona, known as the Apache, or Grand Canyon, State, is divided into three distinct regions: the first is the Colorado Plateau region, which occupies some 45,000 square miles in the northern area of the state, including the high prairie and conifer forests north of the Mogollon Rim and the densely forested, mountainous country of the Kaibab Plateau, which stretches north from the rim of the Grand Canyon of the Colorado; the second region is a broad zone of greatly eroded ranges and gently sloping valleys with crests rising to 5,000 feet above the plains; the third, or desert, region occupies the southwestern quarter of the state. Arizona's wild country, portrayed in the rough-'n'-ready tales of Zane Grey, and famed recreation areas include the spruce-and-alpine-meadow God's Country of the Apache National Forest and the trout lakes of the White Mountains; the Grand Canyon Game Preserve established by Theodore Roosevelt and the backpacking and big-game hunting lands of the Kaibab National Forest; the Tonto National Forest fish and game lands; and the trophy bass waters of the Lake Mead National Recreation Area and the fire-red Grand Wash Cliffs, Buckskin Mountains, Topock Swamp area, and lakes Mohave and Havasu in the vast 1.5–million-acre Kingman Resource Area.

Accommodations & Travel Information

Arizona's major guest ranches, lodges, inns, and motels are listed and described in the "Vacation/Lodging Guide" which follows. For detailed information on all aspects of travel in the state, write or call: Arizona Office of Tourism, 1700 W. Washington, Phoenix 85007 (602)271–3618.

Information & Services

Arizona fishing and hunting regulations, permits, hunting-zone species maps, and information may be obtained by writing: Game & Fish Dept., 2222 West Greenway Road, P.O. Box 9099, Phoenix 85068. The department also publishes the following free guides: *Arizona Fishing Holes* gives the locations and facilities of important fishing areas managed by the department; *Arizona Game Bulletins* provides information sheets describing the state's important wildlife species and groups; *Emergency Code Card* gives ground-to-air emergency code symbols; *Hunting and Fishing in Arizona* provides information about the state's wildlife resources.

Arizona's mountain forests, sweeping canyons, and expansive desert country offer many different kinds of camping opportunities. Visitors can find themselves thousands of feet above sea level, deep in the plunging gorges, or flat on the hot desert sand. *National Forest Camp and Picnic Grounds*, a free booklet available from the U.S. Forest Service, Southwestern Region, Albuquerque, NM 87101, lists and describes every recreation site in each of the great national forests of the area. It includes an index of facilities for each forest, and a map of each forest showing major roads, campsites, streams, and ranger stations. *Amazing Arizona: Camping & Campgrounds* is another very useful and compact guide. It is also available free, from the Arizona Office of Tourism, 1700 W. Washington, Phoenix 85007. It divides Arizona into five major recreation areas, listing sites and their facilities under each area. All the sites are shown on a large map of the state that also indicates roads and cities.

Highways & Maps

Arizona's magnificent landscape makes driving a pleasant experience throughout this land of contrasts. Indian ruins, historic sites, recreational areas, and astounding terrain are never very far away. *Explore Arizona*, a map guide of the state, is available free from the Office of Economic Planning and Development, 1645 W. Jefferson, Phoenix 85007. It divides the state into five regions, providing a highway map and description of each one. *County Road Maps*, showing highways, campgrounds, and recreation areas, are available free from the Arizona State Highway Dept., Administrative Services, 206 S. 17th Ave., Phoenix 85007.

The *Arizona State Highway Map*, showing all highways and roads, national forests, recreation areas, towns and settlements, lakes and streams, and airfields and railroads, is also available free from the Arizona State Highway Dept. (address above).

VACATION/ LODGING GUIDE

Apache-Sitgreaves National Forest

This region, known as God's Country, encompasses 1,808,000 acres of cool fir and spruce forests, mountains, and meadows in eastern Arizona and extends partway into New Mexico. The headwaters of the Black, Little Colorado, Blue, and San Francisco rivers rise in the Apache. Forest roads and trails lead to the renowned fishing waters of the White Mountains, Big Lake, Crescent Lake, Luna Lake, Mangas Mountains, Gallo Mountains, Mexican Hay Lake, Blue Range Mountains, Greer Lakes, San Francisco Mountains, and the Mt. Baldy Wilderness. This region was once the hunting grounds of Ben Lilly, the legendary lone hunter who killed bears with his knife and, according to local lore, treed over 50 mountain lions in one season.

Information Sources, Maps & Access

For vacation travel and recreation information, a full-color *Apache-Sitgreaves National Forest Map* (50¢), and a free *Mt. Baldy Wilderness Map/Brochure*, contact: Supervisor, Apache-Sitgreaves National Forest, P.O. Box 640, Springerville, AZ 85938. For a free *Fort Apache Indian Reservation Map/Brochure;* and fishing, camping, and boating regulations, write: White Mountain Recreation Enterprise, P.O. Box 218, Whiteriver, AZ 85941. The Apache National Forest is reached via U.S. Highways 60, 180, and 666, and Arizona State Highway 73. Lodging, supplies, guides, and outfitting services are available at Alpine, Springerville, Greer, Clifton, Morenci, and Nutrioso. The Sitgreaves National Forest is reached via Arizona State Highways 377, 277, 173, and 87, and U.S. Highway 60. The Petrified Forest National Forest is reached via Interstate 40 and U.S. 80. For detailed information and a free *Petrified Forest National Park-Painted Desert Map/Brochure*, contact: Superintendent, Petrified Forest National Park, Holbrook 86025 (602)524–6228.

Recreation Areas

Giant Meteor Crater

The Giant Meteor Crater, 25 miles west of Winslow off Interstate 40, is approximately one mile in diameter and 600 feet deep. Scientists estimate that the meteor struck here from outer space about 50,000 years ago, displacing about six million tons of rocky desert. Test drillings indicate that the meteor's core is lodged at a depth of 1,400 feet below the earth's surface. This sheer-sided crater served as a training site for NASA astronauts. A museum with displays and lectures is open daily from 8 A.M. to sundown for a small fee.

Mt. Baldy Wilderness & The Blue Range

Fishing and hunting are good in the headwaters area on the West Fork of the Little Colorado in the Mt. Baldy Wilderness. Elevations in the wilderness vary from 8,700 feet to 11,000 feet, from gently

sloping timbered benches to extremely steep, rock-strewn mountainsides cut by deep canyons. Volcanic Mt. Baldy (11,590 ft.) dominates this 7,000–acre blend of remote mountains, forests, valleys, and streams located on the border between the Apache Forest and the Fort Apache Indian Reservation. Two main trails lead to the summit of Mt. Baldy, passing through forests of Douglas, white, and corkbark fir, blue and Engelmann spruce, and white and ponderosa pine, and along meadows ringed with quaking aspen. Another outstanding hiking and hunting region is the Blue Range Primitive Area, encompassing 173,713 acres along the southern edge of the Colorado Plateau. Old Apache Indian trails lead past the barren lava pinnacles, timbered ridges, gray cliffs, and deep canyons found along the Mogollon Rim, to the spectacular Blue River canyon, Saddle Mountain, Whiterocks Mountain, and the Bear and Alder mountains.

Petrified Forest National Park & the Painted Desert

The Petrified Forest is a fascinating 92,000–acre reserve containing five separate forests of petrified wood, Indian ruins, and points of geological interest. Scientists believe the area to have been part of a vast valley that stretched from Texas to Utah over 150 million years ago. The major features of the forest include the Tepees, mounds of blue, white, and purple banded clay; Blue Forest, a colorful badlands with numerous petrified logs; Newspaper Rock, a massive boulder with ancient petroglyphs and designs, etched on both sides; Puerco River Indian Ruin; the 111–foot-long Agate Bridge petrified log; First, Second, and Third forests and the Agate House, an Indian ruin believed to have been built in 1100 A.D.; the brilliant Rainbow Forest; and the Black Forest, which includes a portion of the Painted Desert, some 3 miles north of the Painted Desert Rim Drive. The Rainbow Forest and Painted Desert visitor centers house museums. Overnight camping with permits is available in the Rainbow Forest and Painted Desert wilderness areas. There are no overnight accommodations in the park (see Holbrook for listings).

The vivid yellow, red, blue, lilac, and mauve sands of the Painted Desert extend for 300 miles along the north bank of the Little Colorado River. The rainbow-splashed colors of the shale mesas, hills, terraces, and ledges of the desert were exposed and eroded by millions of years of winds and rains. The Painted Desert Rim Drive skirts the most brilliant section of the area.

Sitgreaves National Forest Region

This region contains 800,000 acres of green meadows and pine forests at elevations ranging from 5,500 feet to 9,000 feet on the Mogollon Plateau in north central Arizona. The spectacular 1,000–foot vertical cliffs on the Mogollon Rim (or Tonto Rim) have figured in many a tale by Zane Grey. The lakes along the Mogollon Rim provide some of the finest fishing in the state. There is a goodly amount of trout fishing in this region, much of it requiring a pack trip or a day-long hike into the remote areas. Clear Creek is an ideal fly stream and is well known for its big rainbows. Fool's Hollow, Show, Whipple, Sponseller, Rainbow, and Woodland lakes and Lake-of-the-Woods all have fishing for rainbows. Grayling can be found in Bear Canyon Lake. Fishing is best in the early spring and autumn, when the forest surrounding the lake country is ablaze with the brilliant shades of red, yellow, and brown.

The Merriam elk, once native to the forest, was killed off by the early pioneers, and was replaced in the 1920s by the introduction of Rocky Mountain elk from Yellowstone. Today the forest is a major elk range. Hunting is also good for mule deer, whitetail deer, antelope, and wild turkey. In season, wing-shooting is excellent for mourning dove, band-tailed pigeon, and duck. For camping information, write to the Supervisor, Sitgreaves National Forest, Holbrook 86025.

White Mountains

The White Mountain region, located in the cool spruce and fir forests at the eastern edge of the state boundary, is perhaps the most important trout-fishing area in Arizona. The White Mountains embrace more than 24 major trout lakes and over 600 miles of streams. The lakes in the eastern portion of the White Mountains, including Rainbow Lake, Show Low Lake, and Fool's Hollow Lake, have first-rate fishing for large rainbow trout. Good populations of cutthroat and rainbow trout are found in Becker, Lyman, Mexican Hay, Luna, Lee Valley, Greer, Big, and Crescent lakes. Along the western section of the White Mountains are the trout streams and lakes of the Fort Apache Indian Reservation. The Apache tribe, with the assistance of the U.S. Fish and Wildlife Service, keeps the streams and lakes well stocked with fat rainbow and brown trout. The White River flows through a major portion of the reservation, and provides good fly-fishing for cutthroats and rainbows. Reservation permits and the regular Arizona fishing licenses are required to fish the Apache waters.

Gateways & Accommodations

Greer

(Pop. 100; zip code 85927; area code 602.) Greer is nestled in the heart of the White Mountains country of the Apache-Sitgreaves National Forest on scenic Arizona Highway 373. Accommodations: *Greer Lodge* (rates: $21 double), 11 rooms, fireplace lounge and family-style dining room in rustic lodge overlooking the Little Colorado River (735–7515).

Holbrook—Gateway to Petrified Forest National Park

(Pop. 4,800; zip code 86025; area code 602.) Once a rough and ready little cow town and haunt of the cowboys of the great Aztic Land & Cattle Co., known as the Hash Knife men from the design of their brand, Holbrook is located at the junction of U.S. 180 and Interstate 40, south of the Navajo Indian Reservation. Accommodations: *Best Western City Center Motel* (rates: $26–30 double), 41 rooms and heated pool next to restaurant at 615 W. Hopi Drive on U.S. 66/180 (524–3948); *Sun'n Sand Motel—A Friendship Inn* (rates: $21–24 double), 45 rooms and family units, heated pool, across from restaurant at 902 W. Hopi Drive on U.S. 66/180 (524–6205).

McNary—Gateway to Fort Apache Indian Reservation

(Pop. 1,000; zip code 85930; area code 602.) McNary is located in the northeast corner of the Indian reservation on Arizona Highway 260 in the heart of the White Mountains. The Sunrise Ski Area is located 17 miles east of the village on 260 and offers good alpine skiing, instruction, and rentals (call 334–2122 for info). Area accommodations: *Sunrise Lodge* (seasonal rates: $28 double), in the Sunrise Ski Area in the Fort Apache Reservation, 100 rooms and family units, restaurant, cocktail lounge, outdoor sports, boat rentals, 20 miles east of town on Arizona 273 (334–2144).

Pinetop

(Pop. 1,000; zip code 85935; area code 602.) This attractive recreation gateway lies at 7,000–feet elevation on Arizona Highway 260 near the northern boundary of the vast Fort Apache Indian Reservation, flanked on the north by the Apache-Sitgreaves National Forest. The state fish hatchery located here raises brown, rainbow, and Eastern brook trout. Area accommodations: *Brandy's Whispering Pines Re-*

sort (rates: $28–36 double), 15 rustic guest cabins with fireplaces and kitchens, among stands of pine on Arizona 260, 1½ miles northwest of town (336–4386); *Moonridge Lodge* (rates: $22–35 double), 17 guest cabins with fireplaces and kitchens, horseback riding, fishing and other outdoor sports, on Arizona 260 at Lakeside, 3 miles northwest of town (336–4580); *Pine Gables Lodge* (rates: $24.50 double), 8 rooms at Mountain Pond on Arizona 173 (336–4316); *Timber Lodge Motel* (rates: $22–24 double), 15 good rooms in scenic location on Arizona 260, just northwest of town (336–4463).

Show Low

(Pop. 2,100; zip code 85901; area code 602.) This town is a major gateway to the Lone Pine, White Mountain, Show Low, and Fool's Hollow lakes country of the Sitgreaves National Forest. Accommodations: *Best Western Maxwell House* (rates: $29–31 double), 81 excellent rooms, restaurant, coffee shop, cocktail lounge, heated pool, 1 mile southwest of town on U.S. 60 and Arizona 260 (537–4356); *Best Western Paint Pony Lodge & Steak House* (rates: $31 double), 32 good rooms, located 1¼ miles southwest of town on U.S. 60 and Arizona 260 (537–5773).

Springerville—Gateway to Apache National Forest & Mt. Baldy Area

(Pop.1,200; zip code 85938; area code 602.) On U.S. 180/666, this is the headquarters of the Apache-Sitgreaves National Forest, surrounded by the lakes, streams, and forests of the beautiful White Mountains. Accommodations: *Ramada Inn* (rates: $23.50–27 double), 60 rooms, coffee shop, cocktail lounge, on U.S. 180/666 (333–4365); *Reed's Motor Lodge* (rates: $21–23 double), 39 excellent rooms and family units, heated pool, across from restaurant on U.S. 180/666 (333–4323).

Winslow—Gateway to the Giant Meteor Crater

(Pop. 8,100; zip code 86047; area code 602.) Located off Interstate 40 on U.S. 66/180. Accommodations: *Best Western Town House Motor Inn* (rates: $31–33 double), 67 rooms and family units, restaurant, coffee shop, cocktail lounge, heated pool, 1½ miles west of town on U.S. 66/180 (289–4611).

Lodges & Guest Ranches

★*Canyon Cove*, in the heart of the White Mountains, offers modern housekeeping cabins near miles of beautiful trout streams, including the South Fork of the Little Colorado. Cabins have hot and cold running water, showers, lavatories, gas for cooking, and electric refrigerators. Canyon Cove supplies linen, cooking utensils, and dishes. Ponds are stocked with trout, and Big and Crescent lakes are nearby attractions. Rates begin at $15 per person per night. Write: Jack L. Davis, Canyon Cove, Box 263, Springerville, AZ 85224.

★★*Hogan's Lake of the Woods Resort* is an all-year-round log cabin retreat on a private lake, surrounded by cool pines. The lake offers fishing for trout, bass, and panfish, plus outings with boats and canoes rented from the resort. There is a recreation room on the premises, featuring pinball machines, ping pong and pool tables. And there is a children's playground. Restaurants, stores, golf courses all available in nearby towns. There is also the Sunrise ski area just thirty miles away. Special events at Lake of the Woods include scouting for Christmas trees during the holiday season, local Fall Festivals with a variety of activities from bicycle races to arts and crafts fairs, and Spring skiing without the crowds. Cabin rates for two range from about $24–30/day, $156–195/week. Cabins come fully equipped with dishes, silverware, pots and pans, and all linens. For details, contact: Hogan's Lake of the Woods, Box 777, Lakeside, Ariz. 85929 (602)336–2323.

★★*South Fork Guest Ranch*, high in the cool White Mountains, is located on the banks of two sparkling trout streams, surrounded by dense green forests. Completely furnished modern cottages, a large heated swimming pool, hiking trails, and nearby horseback riding are some of the attractions here. Open year-round, South Fork is close to Arizona's newest ski area, the Sunrise Park ski run on Sunrise Lake. Rates range from $14 per night in 1–room cottages to $35 per night in deluxe 2–bedroom cottages. Write: South Fork Guest Ranch, P.O. Box 627, Springerville, AZ 85938 (602)333–4455.

Coconino National Forest

This 1.8–million-acre reserve stretches from the desert country near Camp Verde up over the Mogollon Rim to the San Francisco Peaks and from the wild Sycamore Canyon on the west to the cool, tall-timbered lake country above Mormon Lake. Major features include Lake Mary, Kinnikinick Lake, Beaver Creek, Blue Ridge Reservoir, Stoneman Lake, and the Elden Mountains. Wildlife includes Rocky Mountain mule deer, antelope, turkey, a few black bears, and, in the lower elevations, javelina.

Coconino is a Hopi word for "piñon-nut people." The Hopis used it to describe their neighbors, the Havasupai. Much of the Coconino lies on the Colorado Plateau, part of the massive geologic uplift through which the mighty Colorado has cut its course. The region occupies a section of the plateau that is an irregular tableland of pine forest. The Mogollon Rim to the south is part of a great fault that runs for 200 miles across Arizona from the southeast to the northwest. The San Francisco Peaks, the tallest of Arizona's mountains, rise from the vast Colorado Plateau; they are remnants of an ancient volcano that may well have reached 15,000 feet at the peak of its activity. The beautiful lake country, a remnant of ancient lake beds, is located southeast of Flagstaff and has good bass fishing in Mary and Mormon lakes. Kinnikinick Lake, to the south, has fishing for cutthroat trout. Oak Creek, about 15 miles farther south, holds rainbows and browns. Forest roads and trails provide access to the backcountry areas along Beaver Creek, Blue Ridge Reservoir, Stoneman Lake, Sycamore Canyon, and the Elden Mountains.

The Sycamore Canyon Wilderness is reached by a gravel road 12 miles north of Clarkdale. This 49,575–acre region winds for 20 miles along the red-rock canyon of Sycamore Creek, which cuts through the sothern edge of the Colorado Plateau. Numerous trails lead through forests of ponderosa pine and alligator juniper and along red, white, and yellow rock formations.

Information Sources & Access

Vacation travel and recreation information and a full-color *Coconino National Forest Map* (50¢) may be obtained from: Supervisor, Coconino National Forest, Flagstaff, AZ 86001 (602)779–3311. The Coconino National Forest is reached via U.S. Highways 89, 66, and 180, and Arizona Highways 87, 209, and 79. Lodging, supplies, guides, and outfitting services are available at Flagstaff, Cosnino, Winona, Angell, Mountainaire, Bellemont, Sedona, Cornville, Bridgeport, Happy Jack, and Camp Verde.

Gateways & Accommodations

Flagstaff

(Pop. 26,100; zip code 86001; area code 602.) The city is located on the Coconino Plateau, flanked on the south by the painted mesas and canyons of Oak Creek, on the east by colorful deserts, and on the north by the San Francisco Mountains. Scenic auto routes provide access to Sunset Crater National Monument, Wupatki National Monument, Walnut Canyon National Monument, and Oak Creek Canyon. Area attractions of the popular tourist center include the famous Lowell Observatory, 1 mile west off Santa Fe Avenue, with 1–hour guided tours on weekdays (774–3358); Arizona Snow Bowl winter sports area in the San Francisco Mountains, 15 miles northwest of town on U.S. 180 in Coconino National Forest, with panoramic views of the Grand Canyon country from the summit, which is reached by the chair lift (774–0562); Museum of Northern Arizona, 3 miles northwest of town on U.S. 180; Schuly Pass Scenic Route, off U.S. 180 to U.S. 89. Accommodations: *Best Western King's House Motel* (rates: $38–40 double) 57 excellent rooms, heated pool, next to restaurant at 1560 E. Santa Fe Ave., 1 mile east of town on U.S. 66/89/180 (774–7186); *Best Western Little America* (rates: $47 double), 248 luxurious rooms and family units, on 400 pine-fringed acres, Western Gold Dining Room and coffee shop, cocktail lounge, heated pool, off 1-40, Exit 198, at 2515 E. Butler Ave. (779–2741); *Best Western Pony Soldier Motel* (rates: $32–36 double), 90 excellent rooms, heated pool, next to restaurant at 3030 E. Santa Fe Ave., 3 miles east of town on U.S. 66/89/180 (526–2388); *Holiday Inn* (rates: $35 double), 157 excellent rooms, restaurant, coffee shop, cocktail lounge, heated pool, at 1000 W. U.S. 66, 1 mile west of town (774–5221).

Sedona, Gateway to Oak Creek Canyon

(Pop. 2,000; zip code 86336; area code 602.) An attractive vacation resort center south of Flagstaff on U.S. 89A, the town is a major gateway to the scenic cliffs, mesas, and gorges of huge Oak Creek Canyon in the Coconino National Forest. This spectacular red-walled canyon with its miles of thick pine and wild blue cypress forests is said to have been the setting for Zane Grey's *Call of the Canyon*. Oak Creek is noted for its trout fishing. U.S. Forest Service campgrounds and picnic areas are located along the canyon floor. Several hiking trails provide access to remote scenic areas with red cliffs, orange-yellow ledges, cathedrallike rocks, natural bridges, old orchards, and a red limestone box canyon. Maps of the Oak Creek Canyon area are available at the Chamber of Commerce Office in Sedona. Jeep tours are available from Pink Jeep Tours (282–5000). The Page Springs State Fish Hatchery, located 12 miles west of Sedona on Page Springs Road, is open to visitors daily, free of charge. Area accommodations: *Best Western Randee Motor Inn* (rates: $36 double), in Oak Creek Canyon, 39 excellent rooms, the Turtle Restaurant, cocktail lounge, heated pool, on U.S. 89A (282–7131); *King's Ransom Quality Inn Motor Hotel* (rates: $32–36 double), 52 rooms and family units, restaurant, coffee shop, heated pool, balconies and private patios with scenic views, ½ mile south of town on Arizona Hwy. 179 (282–7151); *Matterhorn Motor Lodge—A Friendship Inn* (rates: $30 double), 20 rooms, heated pool, overlooking Oak Creek Canyon on U.S. 89A (282–7176).

Lodges

★★*Garland's Oak Creek Lodge* is located in the heart of Oak Creek Canyon, surrounded by stunning red rock mountains. The lodge is nestled amid two mountain fruit orchards with some 300 peach, apple, pear, apricot, plum and cherry trees all around. Chickens, rabbits and squirrels run loose in the orchards, giving it all a relaxed farm-like atmosphere. Oak Creek is well known as a good mountain fishing stream and there are many trout lakes within a 30 mile radius. There are hiking trails in the area, a golf course at nearby Oak Creek Village, and six tennis courts in the town of Sedona. Numerous national monuments, the Painted Desert, the Petrified Forest, Hopi Indian Country and Grand Canyon National Park are all one day car trips from the lodge. Accommodations are in rustic log cabins. Rates, including breakfast, dinner and lodging are $58 per couple per night in the larger cabins (two queen sized beds) and $48 per couple per night in the smaller cabins (one double bed). For more information, contact: Garland's Oak Creek Lodge, P.O. Box 152, Sedona, Ariz. 86336 (602)282–3343.

★★*Mormon Lake Lodge and Ski Touring Center*, 30 miles southeast of Flagstaff, is nestled in a 7,200–foot lake basin surrounded by beautiful mountain scenery. There are over 500 square miles of untraveled terrain and more than 50 miles of marked trails for cross-country ski touring, including alpine meadows, old logging roads, and gentle slopes. The ski-touring center offers a complete line of sales and rentals, basic touring instruction, 1– and 2–day package tours, ski-camping trips, and moonlight and afternoon guided tours. The Mormon Lake Lodge, with its massive stone fireplace and western-style steak house, is a fine place to unwind after a day of ski touring. In warm weather, the Mormon Lake area offers abundant fishing, hunting, horseback riding, and hiking through magnificent scenery, including the world's largest stand of ponderosa pine. The lodge has cocktail lounge, a general store, campgrounds, and fishing and hunting supplies. Accommodations are in heated motel units ($24 per night) with sleeping quarters for four, housekeeping cabins ($16 per night) with cooking facilities and two beds, or rustic backpacker log cabins ($10 per night) heated by wood stoves. For more information write: Mormon Lake Lodge, Mormon Lake, AZ 86001 (602)774–0462; or Mormon Lake Ski Touring Center, Mormon Lake, AZ 86038 (602)354–2240.

Coronado National Forest Guest Ranch Country

This 1,791,000–acre tract is located in south-central Arizona and embraces the Santa Catalina Mountains, Sonora Desert, Sabino

Canyon, and a portion of the Chiricahua Mountains. The old Swift Trail winds along the crest of the Grahams Range, the highest of the Coronado Mountains, reaching 11,000 feet at Mt. Graham. Heliograph Peak is one of a chain of mountaintop sun-signal stations used by the army during the years of the Apache wars. Other features include the Whetstone Mountains, Tumacacori Mountains, Chiricahua Wilderness, Galiuro Wilderness, and the Rincon Mountains.

Madera Canyon provides conditions that are unique in the United States. The combination of climate, moisture, and elevation creates an atmosphere that harbors such creatures as the trogon, a colorful, red-breasted, parrotlike bird that is more commonly seen in Mexico. There are more than 200 species of birds in the canyon. The Spaniards named the canyon Madera for its heavy timber supply. Cactus and other low desert vegetation give way to ponderosa pine on the upper elevations. A few abandoned frontier army posts remain nearby. They were built to ward off attacks from the Apaches, but were destroyed by Confederate troops during the Civil War.

The Santa Catalinas are an excellent recreation area, with 12 camp and picnic grounds. They are close to Tucson and are very popular with families in the summer months.

Tantalizing bits of history are present at Cochise Stronghold Canyon, located in the heart of the Dragoon Mountains. It is a rugged natural fortress, bordered by granite domes and sheer cliffs, and covered with beautiful natural forestland. Cochise, the Apache chief, lived here with his clan and was never conquered or captured by white men. He is buried somewhere in or near his impregnable fortress, but no one knows the exact spot. The area contains several ghost towns that were once livestock and mining centers. The only one left is Tombstone, with its famous Boot Hill Cemetery. Camp-

grounds and trails provide recreational opportunities, and the ruins of the Dragoon Springs station, a favorite target of the Apaches, can still be seen.

The Coronado Trail, a scenic portion of U.S. Highway 666, begins at Clifton and winds north up from the Mogollon Rim through high country of the Apache-Sitgreaves National Forest along the historic route followed by Coronado during his search for the Seven Cities of Gold. The route is hemmed in by thick forests of spruce, Douglas fir, mountain fern, and quaking aspen and flanked here and there by green valleys and mountain vistas, which can be viewed from the U.S. Forest Service lookout near Rose Peak. The Coronado Trail ends at the village of Alpine at 8,000–feet elevation, surrounded by pine-clad ranges. U.S. 666 continues north to its junction with U.S. 60 at Springerville.

Information Sources, Maps & Access

Vacation travel and recreation information, a full-color *Coronado National Forest Map* (50¢), and a *Madera Canyon Recreation Area Map* may be obtained from: Supervisor, Coronado National Forest, Federal Bldg., 301 Congress St. W., Tucson 85701 (602)792–6483. The Coronado National Forest is reached via U.S. Highways 80, 666, 89, 70, and 10. Lodging, supplies, guides, and outfitting services are available at Safford, Tucson, Douglas, Nogales, Dragoon, Sonoita, Patagonia, Lochiel, Arivaca, Tubac, Amado, Greaterville, Rosemont, Bonita, Oracle, Klondyke, and Aravaipa.

Gateways & Accommodations

Douglas

(Pop. 12,500; zip code 85607; area code 602.) Douglas is located near the border of Mexico in the southeastern corner of the state. The town has a district ranger's office of the Coronado National Forest. Accommodations: *Douglas Travelodge* (rates: $21–23 double), 29 rooms, heated pool, and coffee shop, at 1030 19th St., 1 mile east of town on U.S. 80 (364–8434); *Gadsden Hotel* (rates: $15.50–25 double), a national historic monument built in 1907 with an ornate lobby, Tiffany skylights, dining room, 160 rooms and suites, at 1046 G. Ave. on U.S. 80 (364–2411).

Sierra Vista

(Pop. 6,700; zip code 85635; area code 602.) This Coronado National Forest gateway is located in the southeast portion of the state on Arizona Highway 90 near the Coronado National Monument and Fort Huachuca Historical Museum, just west of town at Boyd and Grierson Avenues in Bldg. 41401. The fort was established as a camp in 1877 to protect pioneers and travelers from Apache raids led by Geronimo. Today the fort houses the U.S. Army Communications Command. Accommodations: *Thunder Mountain Inn* (rates: $25–28 double) 105 rooms, restaurant, coffee shop, cocktail lounge, heated pool, at 1631 S. Arizona Hwy. 82 (458–7900).

Tombstone—National Historic Site

(Pop. 1,200; zip code 85638; area code 602.) In the desert hills between the San Pedro Valley and the Dragoon Mountains, this historic mining camp was once called Graveyard by its prospector founders because it was here that they buried their hopes of fortune. Also known as the town too tough to die and as Helldorado, it boomed to a population of 7,000 miners, tinhorn gamblers, and outlaws, and was the site of the Wyatt Earp clan shootout at the OK Corral in 1881. By 1890 Tombstone, cleaned out of hard characters by Sheriff John Slaughter, dwindled to a population of about 1,800. Attractions of this popular resort and tourist center include the Bird Cage Theater at 6th and Allen Sts., built in 1881, which served as old Tombstone's saloon, gambling house, and brothel; the Crystal Palace Saloon, at the corner of 5th & Allen Sts., one of the most luxurious and famous of the town's early saloons and gambling houses; the office of the Tombstone *Epitaph*, 5th St. between Fremont and Allen Sts., which publishes the town's only newspaper, the oldest weekly continuously published in Arizona; the Wyatt Earp Marker on Allen St., between 4th and 5th Sts., where Wyatt Earp single-handedly fought off a mob of 300 would-be lynchers of the killer Johnny-behind-the-Deuce; Boot Hill Graveyard at the northwest city limits adjoining U.S. 80; and the Tombstone Courthouse at 3rd and Toughnut Sts., a two-story, red brick building built in 1882. Accommodations: *Best Western Lookout Lodge* (rates: $20 double), 40 rooms with views of the Dragoon Mountains, heated pool, 1 mile north of Tombstone on U.S. 80 (457–2223).

Tucson

(Pop. 262,900; zip code, see below; area code 602.) Famous as a health and winter resort, commonly called Old Pueblo, Tucson has grown up around one of the oldest Spanish settlements in the Southwest, founded in 1776. Area attractions include the Arizona Sonora Desert Museum in Tucson Mountain Park; "Old Tucson," a replica of Tucson in the 1860s built in 1940 for the filming of *Arizona* by Columbia Pictures, 12 miles west of town in Tucson Mountain Park; and the Arizona State Museum and the Grace H. Flandreau Planetarium at the University of Arizona at Park Ave. and University Blvd. Accommodations: *Arizona Inn* (rates: $41–55 double), 85 excellent rooms, family units, and cottages, dining room, cocktail lounge, heated pool, tennis, in beautiful setting at 2200 E. Elm St., 85719 (325–1541); *Best Western Aztec Inn* (rates: $39.50 double), 158 excellent rooms and family units, restaurant, cocktail lounge, heated pool, sauna, at 102 N. Alvernon Way, 85711, 4½ miles east of town (795–0330); *Best Western Ghost Ranch Lodge* (rates: $23–30 double), 75 excellent rooms, family units, and cottages, dining room, cocktail lounge, two heated pools, in scenic setting at 801 W. Miracle Mile off 1-10, Miracle Mile Exit, 3½ miles north of town on Arizona 93 (791–7565); *Doubletree Inn* (rates: $40–57 double), 300 superb rooms and suites, restaurant, coffee shop, cocktail lounge, heated pool, tennis, at 445 S. Alvernon Way, 85711, 4 miles east of town (881–4200); *Hilton Inn* (rates: $32–38 double), 200 excellent rooms and suites, restaurant, coffee shop, cocktail lounge, heated pool, at 1601 Miracle Mile, 85705, 1¾ miles north of town on U.S. 80/89 (624–8541); *Holiday Inn North* (rates: $32–34 double), 144 excellent rooms, restaurant, cocktail lounge, heated pool, off 1-10 at 1365 W. Grant Road, 85705, 2 miles north of town (622–7791); *Holiday Inn South* (rates: $32–34 double), 146 excellent rooms, restaurant, cocktail lounge, heated pool, 1 mile south of town off 1-10, 22nd St. Exit, at 1010 S. Freeway, 85705 (622–5871); *Howard Johnson's Motor Lodge* (rates: $25.50–28.50 double), 136 excellent rooms, restaurant, cocktail lounge, heated pool, sauna, 3½ miles south of town off 1-10, Park Ave. Exit, at 1025 Benson Hwy., 85725 (623–7792); *Lodge on the Desert* (rates: $35–67 double), 37 excellent rooms with fireplaces, dining room, cocktail lounge, heated pool, on beautiful landscaped grounds at 306 N. Alvernon Way, 85733, 4½ miles east of town (325–3366); *Marriott Hotel* (rates: $30–45 double), 312 excellent rooms and suites, restaurant, cocktail lounge, heated pool, at 180 W. Broadway, 85701, downtown off 1-10, Congress St. Exit (624–8711); *Ramada Inn* (rates: $24–32 double), 302 excellent rooms and family units, restaurant, coffee shop, cocktail lounge, heated pool, at 404 N. Freeway, 85705, off 1-10, St. Mary's Exit (624–8341); *Tanque Verde Guest Ranch* (rates: $75–110 double), 60 superb western resort units, dining room, fireplaces, two heated pools, mountain riding trails, saunas, tennis, photography and bird-watching, on 500 acres at the foot of the Rincon Mountains at the end of Speedway Road, 19 miles east of Tucson, reservations required, Box 66, 85710 (296–6275); *Westward Look Resort* (rates: $40–75 double), 92 excellent rooms and family units, dining room, cocktail lounge, heated pool, tennis, in scenic desert location at 245 E. Ina Road, 85704 (297–1151).

Guest Ranches

★★★*Hacienda del Sol*, a gracious and sunny resort on the gentle slopes of the Catalina foothills, offers handsome accommodations in the heart of Arizona's dust-free thermal belt. Individual rooms and suites are beautifully decorated in the warm colors and distinctive furniture of the old Spanish Southwest. All have private baths with tub-shower combinations and are scrupulously maintained by a solicitous staff. The surrounding landscaped grounds feature lush desert gardens, spacious patios, and sprawling lawns. Activities include horseback riding, tennis, and swimming in two sparkling pools warmed by sunshine all winter long. The resort is open November 1–May 1. Rates: $45–65 daily single and $80–95 double occupancy, including all meals chosen from a gourmet menu and served in a beautiful dining room, plus use of tennis courts, swimming pools, exercise room, and health center. For more information write: Robert E. Hartman, Hacienda del Sol, Hacienda del Sol Road, Tucson, AZ 85718 (602)299–1501.

★★★*Lazy K Bar Ranch*, nestled at the base of the rugged Tucson Mountains, has modern resort accommodations in an awesome desert setting warmed by sunshine all year round. The ranch has its own corral of surefooted horses for long or short rides on beautiful trails winding through the mountains and across varied desert terrain. The resort's swimming pool, surrounded by a spacious deck and patio, is heated to a constant 80°. There are also excellent tennis courts a few yards from your door and several nearby golf courses. Meals are served in the bright and cheery dining room or on the patio under an umbrella. A comfortable TV lounge and bar complete the facilities in the central ranch house. All rooms are attractively furnished with air conditioning, private baths, and comfortable twin, king, or queen-size beds. Rates, including meals and all ranch facilities: $35–40 per person, double occupancy, for a single room; $40–45 double occupancy for a deluxe room or 2–room suite. For additional information write: Lazy K Bar Guest Ranch, Box 560, Tucson, AZ (602)297–0702.

★★*Price Canyon Ranch* is a working cattle ranch surrounded by the Chiricahua Mountains 42 miles north of Douglas. The ranch takes only a few guests at a time, thus insuring an intimate experience of general ranch life. Activities include horseback riding, hiking, rockhounding, swimming, and fishing for catfish in a pond right at the ranch house doorstep. Accommodations are in 1– or 2–room bunkhouses with bath. The main ranch building, a rambling structure built in 1880, has a comfortable living room and dining area, where hearty western meals are served buffet-style. Rates: $35 per day for one person; $60–65 per day double occupancy; and $10–20 for children accompanied by their parents. Rates include meals, lodgings, and horseback riding. The ranch welcomes singles, couples, families, children with or without their parents, and groups up to 25. Each inquiry will be answered individually. Write: Price Canyon Ranch, P.O. Box 1065, Douglas, AZ 85607 (602)558–2383.

★★★*Rancho Santa Cruz* is a deluxe family vacation resort located in the Santa Cruz Valley, flanked by the mountain ranges of the Coronado National Forest. The ranch features all-day trail rides and cookouts and numerous area attractions including Old Mexico, working cattle ranches, abandoned mines, Tumacacori Mission, Box Canyon, Geronimo's cave, and the historic Josephine Canyon. Ranch accommodations consist of comfortable, spacious rooms and suites with fireplaces. Gourmet meals are served western-style in the attractive main dining room. Western riding instruction is available at no extra cost; so are swimming and golf. American-plan weekly rates (double occupancy): $357–441, with two-thirds rate for children 12 and under. For info, contact: Rancho Santa Cruz, P.O. Box 8, Tumacacori, AZ 85640 (602)398–2261.

★★★*Sahuaro Vista Guest Ranch* is adjacent to a 70,000–acre State and National Park, the thickest growth of majestic Sahuaro cacti in the world. The ranch is situated in a forest of these great plants in the rolling foothills of the Tucson Mountains, just 13 miles northwest of Tucson. Activities on the ranch include horseback riding on beautiful trails through mountain canyons and cacti-studded desert, swimming in a heated pool, tennis, recreation room games, moonlight steak fries, and golfing on nearby courses less than 10 minutes from the ranch. The city of Tucson offers plenty of sightseeing and entertainment facilities. Accommodations include comfortable hotel rooms as well as studio apartments and individual cottages, some with kitchens. Rates per person, including lodging, all meals, and use of all ranch facilities $30–40/day, double occupancy, depending on the season. The ranch also offers a selected health-food menu for those on special diets. For more information, write: Sahuaro Vista Guest Ranch, P.O. Box 554, Rt. 14, Tucson, AZ. 85704 (602) 297–0502.

★★★★*Sundancer Saddle & Surrey Ranch Resort*, flanked by the Tucson Mountains, is one of the old Southwest's finest ranch resorts. In operation for the past 26 years, the ranch offers first-class, deluxe services, accommodations, and facilities, including a sky-blue tournament-grade tennis court, swimming pool in beautifully landscaped area, sunbathing tower with a spectacular view of the surrounding area, elevated seven-hole putting green, sunny casitas with Mexican and Southwestern flavor, billiards in the foliage-filled pool table room, championship golf courses within minutes of the ranch, and a stable of responsive and well-trained horses on which to explore the desert foothills and miles of riding trails. Sundancer guests may enjoy sight-seeing trips to nearby attractions such as Old Tucson, the Arizona-Sonora Desert Museum, and Tombstone. Guests arriving by air are met at the Tucson International Airport. The ranch also offers guided hunts throughout the season for deer, duck, dove, turkey, pheasant, quail, and javelina. Delicious cuisine is served family-style in the attractive ranch dining room. Cocktails are available at the Sundowner Barroom. Dress is casual. The ranch season begins November 1 and ends May 1 and is limited to approximately 28 guests. All-inclusive American-plan daily rates: $92 (double) in 1–bedroom casita with twin beds, bath, and shower; $164 for a casita suite with 2 bedrooms. Contact: Sundancer Saddle & Surrey Ranch Resort, 4110 Sweetwater Drive, Tucson, AZ 85705 (602)743–0411.

★★★*White Stallion Ranch*, just 17 miles from downtown Tucson, is a sprawling, full-service guest resort surrounded by 4,000 acres of rugged hills and colorful desert. The quarter horses raised and trained here include gentle mounts for trail rides and show ponies eager to perform in the twice-weekly rodeos that are a special feature of the ranch. Spacious cottages facing the desert are attractively furnished with wall-to-wall carpeting, pine paneling, and comfortable beds. Outdoor activities center on the tennis courts, heated pool, and miles of primitive terrain perfect for wildlife photography and rock-hounding. Indoor attractions include pocket billiards, Ping-Pong, an old-time saloon, and excellent native cuisine served in a big Spanish-style dining room. Rates are $44–55 daily per person

($315–385 weekly) and include all meals, horseback riding, barbecues, and use of ranch facilities. High season rates (Dec. 16–Jan. 5 and Feb. 3–Apr. 21) are slightly higher. For further information write: White Stallion Ranch, Route 9, Box 567, Tucson, AZ 85704 (602)297–0252.

★★★*Wild Horse Ranch Club*, a distinguished ranch resort, lies on 50 landscaped acres just northwest of Tucson in the center of an unspoiled 150,000–acre desert wildlife area. Audubon Society members have identified over 250 species of birds on the ranch lands. Ranch activities include horseback riding, tennis on two tournament-level courts, hiking on nature trails, outdoor barbecues, photography, and swimming in a heated pool with a spacious sundeck. Accommodations are in private ranch cottages with carpeted rooms, twin beds, private baths, and shower. All rooms have a telephone and color television. Side trips from the ranch may be taken to nearby caves, old silver and copper mines, ancient Indian hieroglyphics and campsites, the famous Arizona Desert Museum, and the Old Tucson movie set. Rental cars are available at the ranch. American-plan rates with excellent cuisine: $65–99 per day (double) Dec. 16–May 1; $60–85 per day (double) Oct. 15–Dec. 15. For additional information write: Wild Horse Ranch Club, P.O. Box 5505, Tucson, AZ 85703 (602)297–2266.

Glen Canyon National Recreation Area

For a complete description, gateways, and accommodations, see the "Vacation/Lodging Guide."

Grand Canyon National Park & Kaibab National Forest

The Grand Canyon is one of the world's most awesome and spectacular natural structures. It provides unforgettable river trips, hiking trips, mule rides, and dazzling views. The dark pines of the Kaibab National Forest conceal the Grand Canyon until the rim is reached. There, spread out for miles and miles, is an ocean of color. From misty blue depths rise gigantic islands of crimson sandstone, with undulating bands of reds and purples growing softer in color and outline toward the horizon. The immensity is staggering, the boldness of its contours overwhelming. Colors change continually as the sun moves across the sky, creating new shadows and illuminating new contours.

The Grand Canyon is more than 1½ billion years old. The many ancient layers of rock were pushed into high mountains by move-

ments of the earth's crust and contain fossils and remnants of early plant and animal life. Compared to the age of its rocks, man's advent in the canyon is very recent. The earliest ruins are those of the Pueblo Indians, from about A.D. 1200. The first explorers to see the canyon were the Spaniards. Coronado and his men tried to climb down, but they wisely abandoned the effort. The Colorado River was finally navigated in 1869 by John Wesley Powell, a one-armed veteran of the Civil War. Powell and his expedition of 10 men set off from Green River City, Wyoming, on May 24, 1869, in three small rowboats 21 feet long and one 16–foot boat.

The Grand Canyon is generally referred to in terms of the North Rim and the South Rim. The road to the North Rim winds through forests of ponderosa pine, spruce, and aspen and occasional mountain meadows. A hike to the canyon bottom will take you through as many life zones as there are between Canada and Mexico. The North Rim is generally cooler than the South Rim, because the elevations are higher. However, it is closed during the winter. The South Rim includes many overlooks and rim trails. The Grand Canyon is one mile deep, and while its size can readily be measured, its impact on the human spirit cannot. People standing on the rim can look down to the tops of mountains that are thousands of feet high. The Colorado River was the chief architect of the canyon, and remains a staggering living example of the power of moving water. Each layer of the canyon was revealed by the insistent flow of the river, recording the evolution of life forms. Nowhere else on earth is such a complete geological record exposed. Each layer and climate supports its own distinct groups of plant and animal life. The gorges are desert regions, but the rims are covered with forests. It's the elevation that makes the difference. Many day hikes can be taken from the rims, but hikers should remember that the canyon is an upside-down mountain—the second half of the trip will be more strenuous than the first.

The two most popular hiking trails on the canyon are the Bright Angel Trail and the Kaibab Trail. The Bright Angel Trail, originally used by Havasupai Indians of the South Rim, has two campgrounds and several rest houses with water. The Kaibab Trail links the north and south ends of the canyon. The South Kaibab Trail has no campgrounds, no water, and little shade. It descends down into Bright Angel Campground and Phantom Ranch, where it meets the North Kaibab Trail. This trail is a little more receptive, with campgrounds and water at two locations.

A wide range of plant and animal life complements the beauty of the canyon. Desert cacti flourish along the river, and blue spruce and Douglas fir grow along the rim. Many flowers are present, including delphinium, white sego lily, white thistle poppy, scarlet bugle, blue locoweed, prickly pear, and the yucca plant. Wildlife includes the Kaibab squirrel, a dark animal with a plumy white tail and tufted ears, whose habitat is limited to the North Rim. There are also beaver, deer, mountain sheep, porcupine, a few mountain lions, some beautifully colored lizards and snakes, meadowlarks, mockingbirds, long-tailed chats, spurred towhees, water ouzels, and roadrunners.

Kaibab Plateau and National Forest, a 1.7–million-acre reserve, is located in northwestern Arizona and is divided into northern and southern sections by the Grand Canyon. The Kaibab Plateau, north of the Grand Canyon, was established as the Grand Canyon Game Preserve by Theodore Roosevelt. Hunting is regulated by special permit for elk, bear, and deer. Hundreds of miles of hiking trails wind through the forests and canyons. Since primitive times, the

Kaibab Plateau has been a choice hunting ground. Indian legends tell of hunting seasons in which more than a thousand deer were shot. Wilderness trails provide access to the deep canyons along the low desert country near the Colorado River. Because of heavy precipitation, the Kaibab Plateau region is a verdant island within the desert, a stark contrast to the more arid region along the South Rim of the Grand Canyon. The Paiutes called it a "mountain lying down," and it is indeed an oasis that harbors its own flourishing greenery. The remote tributary streams in the Grand Canyon area, located in the Kaibab National Forest, offer exciting fishing for pan-sized rainbows. The wilderness fly-fisherman may reach these streams only by a long hike or packhorse trip. The most productive of these scenic, wild streams are North Canyon Creek, Clear and Bright Angel creeks, Thunder River, and Tapeats Creek.

Information Sources, Maps & Access

For detailed vacation travel and recreation information and a free *Grand Canyon National Park Map/Brochure*, contact: Superintendent, Grand Canyon National Park, Grand Canyon, AZ 86023 (602) 638–2411. For forest recreation information and full-color *Kaibab National Forest Maps* (north and south sections, 50¢ each), contact: Supervisor, Kaibab National Forest, P.O. Box 817, Williams, AZ 86046 (602)635–2681. An excellent selection of topographic and shaded relief maps is available from the U.S. Geological Survey, Federal Center, Denver, CO 80225. *The Grand Canyon National Monument Map* shows the monument and adjacent area. The scale is 1:48,000, or 1 inch to 4,000 feet. Size is 33 by 42 inches. It is available for $2. The *Grand Canyon National Park and Vicinity Map* shows the entire park and the adjacent area. The scale is 1:62,500, or about 1 inch to 1 mile. Size is 38 by 60 inches. The topographic and shaded-relief edition is $2. A *Map of the Bright Angel Area* is also available, with a brief geologic history on the back. The scale is 1:62,500, or about 1 inch to 1 mile. Size is 17 by 21 inches. Both a topographic and shaded-relief edition are available for $1.25 each. The *Inner Canyon Hiking Booklet* (90¢), a guide to the abandoned trails of Grand Canyon National Park and Monument, and *Grand Canyon Wildflowers* ($2.50, an annotated checklist with key; illustrated in color and black and white) may be obtained from: Grand Canyon Natural History Assn., Box 219, Grand Canyon 86023 (include 20¢ for postage). *Guidebook to the Colorado River*, Part I, Lee's Ferry to Phantom Ranch ($1.75), and Part II, Phantom R Ranch to Temple Bar ($2.25), may also be obtained from the same address. The beautiful *Grand Canyon Scroll Map*, Lee's Ferry to Temple Bar ($3.50), is available from Leslie A. Jones, Star Route, Box 13A, Heber, UT 84032. *Maps & Profiles of the Colorado River*, Lee's Ferry to Temple Bar ($5), is available from the American River Touring Assn., 1016 Jackson St., Oakland, CA 94607.

The Grand Canyon and Kaibab National Forest can be reached via U.S. Highways 89 and 66, and Arizona Highways 67 and 64. Lodging, supplies, guides, and outfitting services are available at Fredonia, Jacob Lake, and the town of Grand Canyon.

Gateways & Accommodations

Seligman—Gateway to the Grand Canyon Caverns

(Pop. 1,000; zip code 86337; area code 602.) Seligman is just off Interstate 40 on U.S. 66, south of the Hualapai Indian Reservation. The Grand Canyon Caverns, open year-round (small fee), are reached by an underground 21–story elevator. The area has self-guiding trails and the Chapel of Ages. The caverns are located 25 miles west of town on U.S. 66.

Williams—Kaibab National Forest & Grand Canyon Gateway

(Pop. 2,400; zip code 86046; area code 602.) The town is headquarters of the Kaibab National Forest, located at the junction of Interstate 40 and Arizona Highway 64 north to the Grand Canyon. The town is a popular tourist center named after old Bill Williams, a wily trapper and guide who died at the hands of the Ute Indians in 1849. Area attractions include the Bill Williams Winter Sports Area and the Sycamore Canyon Wilderness Area. Accommodations: *Best Western Ponderosa Inn* (rates: $30–34 double), 69 rooms, restaurant, coffee shop, cocktail lounge, heated pool, 8 miles east of town on 1-40 (635–2625); *Williams Travelodge* (rates: $32 double), 39 rooms and family units, heated pool, at 430 E. Bill Williams Ave. on U.S. 66/89 eastbound (635–2651).

Grand Canyon National Park North Rim Lodging

★★★*Grand Canyon North Rim Lodge* offers rustic cabin and motel accommodations and dining facilities. The lodge provides views across the canyon of the Painted Desert and San Francisco Peaks near Flagstaff as well as spectacular views of the canyon itself from the sun room, dining room, and open-air patios. The lodge is flanked on the east by the Bright Angel area and on the west by Transept Canyon. The North Rim Lodge, built of native stone and massive timbers from the Kaibab National Forest, provides rustic accommodations in Frontier Cabins, with double and single bed, carpeting, individual heating and shower; Pioneer Cabins, each with four single beds, heating units, and shower; Western Cabins, each with two double beds, carpeting, fireplace, bath, shower, telephone, and high-pitched roofs; motel units, with two double beds, carpeting, shower, and oak furniture. Daily rates: $21–30. The lodge also offers a Western-style saloon, a patio lounge, service station facilities, and a camper store at the campground with food provisions and hiking and camping supplies. Park rangers give lectures at the lodge and lead nature hikes and campfire programs. Contact: TWA Services, Inc., 4045 S. Spenser St., Suite A-43, Las Vegas, NV 89109 (602)638–2611 or call toll-free (1–800)634–6951.

★★*Jacob Lake Inn* has 49 rustic cabins and modern motel units 44 miles north of North Rim on Arizona Highway 67. Facilities include dining room, coffee shop, and playground. Daily rates (double): $18–24. Contact: Jacob Lake Inn, Jacob Lake, AZ 86022 (602)643–5532.

Marble Canyon Lodge has 18 rooms, and a restaurant at the head of the awesome Marble Canyon of the Colorado on U.S. 89 in Grand Canyon National Park at Navajo Bridge (616 ft. long and 467 ft. above the river) rates: $27 double. Phone (602)355–2225.

Grand Canyon National Park South Rim Lodging

Bright Angel Lodge and Cabins offer a wide range of comfortable and moderately priced accommodations. This complex of buildings, stretching along the canyon rim, offers a combination of rustic simplicity and modern convenience. Within the main lodge at Bright Angel, guests will find a gift shop, a newsstand, and barber and beauty shops. The Arizona Room at Bright Angel offers western dining. A la carte meals in the Bright Angel Coffee Shop and Snack Bar are moderately priced. Garage and coin laundry are available. Fred Harvey Transportation Desk is in the main lobby for mule-trip and bus-tour information and reservations. Rates range from $20 in Bright Angel Lodge to $65 for suites with fireplace, double occupancy.

★★★*El Tovar Hotel*, standing in silhouette at the brink of the Grand Canyon, is one of the great resort hotels in America. The newly renovated El Tovar is spaciously built of native boulders and rustic pine logs. For over 71 years, El Tovar has been deservedly known for its unobtrusive hospitality and excellent cuisine. Breakfast, lunch, and dinner are served daily in the El Tovar dining room. Your favorite beverages are offered in El Tovar's Lounge. A gift shop and newsstand are located within the hotel. Garage and coin laundry are available. A Fred Harvey information desk is located in the hotel's main lobby for mule-trip and bus-tour information and reservations. Rates: $33–75 double.

★*Grand Canyon Motor Lodge* is located a short distance from the rim. The lodge motel offers comfortable and reasonable family accommodations. A cafeteria, curio shop, and newsstand are in the main lodge. Motor lodge rates (double): $20–27.

★*Moqui Lodge*, at the entrance to the park, is now operated by Fred Harvey. Moqui Lodge has 135 comfortable and modern rooms, as well as dining and beverage facilities, horseback riding, and entertainment most evenings. Rates on request.

Phantom Ranch, located on Bright Angel Creek near the Colorado River, lies almost a mile below the canyon rim. Accessible only via hiking and daily mule trains that descend by inner canyon trails, the ranch offers a grouping of rustic cabins. Phantom Ranch is open year-round. Overnight trail trips are available daily. Many times reservations are required six months in advance. Rates on request.

★★*Thunderbird and Kachina Lodges*, some rooms with views of the Grand Canyon, provide comfortable modern accommodations for couples and families. All rooms are individually temperature-controlled. Each has bath and shower. Parking is provided. Garage and coin laundry are available. Thunderbird Lodge's registration is at Bright Angel Lodge. Registration for the Kachina is at the El Tovar Hotel. Double occupancy rates range from $32 for standard room to $60 for luxury suite.

★★*Yavapai Lodge*, midway between Yavapai Point and El Tovar, in pine and juniper woodlands, offers 355 modern, comfortable accommodations minutes from the rim. Accommodations are in individual motel structures and lodges. All rooms with bath and shower. Other guest facilities include a cafeteria, snack bar, cocktail lounge and curio shop. Double occupancy rates range from $24–29.

Day Visitors to the Grand Canyon are welcome at all the Fred Harvey restaurants, shops and public facilities at the canyon rim. Among the points of particular interest are Hopi House across from El Tovar, Hermit's Rest, and the Watchtower at Desert View on the East Rim Drive. All tours and trail trips are available to day visitors.

For hotel and lodge reservations at any of the Grand Canyon's facilities, contact your travel agent or the Grand Canyon National Park Lodges Reservations Office at the Grand Canyon. Call (602)638–2401 or write Grand Canyon National Park Lodges Reservations, Grand Canyon, AZ 86023. Reservations office hours, 8 A.M. to 5 P.M. Mountain Standard Time, Monday through Saturday. Lodges to the south of Grand Canyon Village on Arizona Highway 64 include:

★★★*Best Western Canyon Squire Inn* has 153 good-to-outstanding units 9 miles south of Grand Canyon Village on Highway 64. Inn facilities include a swimming pool, dining room, coffee shop, sauna, tennis court, playground for children, cocktail lounge, health spa, and air sight-seeing tours of the Grand Canyon. Daily summer season rates (double): $38. Contact: Box 130, South Rim 86023 (602)638–2681.

★★*Red Feather Lodge* has 110 fine motor inn units on Highway 64, 9 miles south of Grand Canyon Village. Facilities and services include restaurant and fireside dining room, coffee shop, Indian arts and crafts, courtesy transportation to and from Grand Canyon. Daily summer season rates (double): $33–35. Contact: Box 520, South Rim 86023 (602)638–2673.

Travel Services

Canyoneers, Inc., offers expertly guided river float trips, jeep tours, and backpacking trips in the Grand Canyon. For detailed information, rates, and schedules, contact: P.O. Box 2997, East Flagstaff, AZ 86003 (602)526–0924.

Grand Canyon Airlines Tours, based at Grand Canyon National Park Airport on the South Rim, offers fully narrated 130–mile tours (approximately 1 hour) of the area's scenic wonders, including Mooney Falls, Havasupai Indian Village, Phantom Ranch, and, of course, the canyon itself ($30 per adult). Other regularly scheduled air tours take in Zion National Park, Lake Powell, the Painted Desert, and Bryce Canyon ($68 per person, 350 mi., 2 hours), or the North Rim Plateau, Glen Canyon Dam, and Monument Valley ($68 per person, 350 mi., 2 hours). A fly/drive trip including an air tour of the Canyon and a 150–mile guided coach tour through Hopi Indian reservations is offered twice daily all year round ($80 per person). There's also a 1–day Colorado River rafting adventure ($80 per person) which starts with a flight to the North Rim and proceeds by bus through Kaibab National Forest to the river with a stop for lunch on a lovely beach. All air tours include a window seat for every passenger and complete narration en route. Many trips are offered year-round and feature special children's rates. For details write: Grand Canyon Airlines, P.O. Box 186, Grand Canyon, AZ 86023 (602)638–2407.

Grand Canyon Helicopters offers scenic flights across the canyon from its north to south rim and bird's-eye views of such legendary sights as the Little Colorado Painted Desert, Vishnu Temple, Phantom Ranch, Havasu and Mooney waterfalls, Granite Gorge, and portions of the Kaibab National Forest, the largest ponderosa pine forest in the world. Four different, regularly scheduled tours are available, ranging in distance from 32 to 110 miles. By far the most popular is the Havasupai flight, which includes a half-hour stop at the magnificent falls at the bottom of the canyon. All scenic helicopter tours cover carefully planned routes, including many remote areas accessible only by chopper. Big clear picture windows in each helicopter provide maximum scenic enjoyment and excellent opportunities for photography. All flights originate and terminate at the Grand Canyon Heliport, located 7 miles south of Grand Canyon Village on Highway 64. For more information, write: Grand Canyon Helicopters, P.O. Box 455, Grand Canyon, AZ 86023 (602)638–2419.

Grand Canyon National Park Tours & Trail Trips

Free nature walks, lectures, and films are provided by the National Park Service at the Grand Canyon. Information concerning schedules is available at the National Park Visitors' Center or from the transportation desks at the Fred Harvey hotels at the Grand Canyon. Courteous National Park Rangers will be pleased to answer your specific questions.

Trips into the surrounding country by private or chartered car can be particularly rewarding. Nearby lie the Navajo Indian Reservation, Old Moencopi, Glen Canyon Dam, Lake Powell, the Hopi villages, the prehistoric ruins of Wupatki and Walnut Canyon National Monuments, Sunset Crater National Monument Meteor Crater, the

Painted Desert, Cameron Trading Post, and the natural wonders of the high Arizona plateau. Motor Coach Tours of the Grand Canyon Rim are conducted year round.

The Desert View Drive begins at El Tovar Hotel and Bright Angel Lodge and continues eastward along the rim road. Stops include Yavapai Point Museum and Moran and Lipan points. The high point of the trip is the stop at Desert View Watch Tower. This structure, a reconstruction of the ancient Indian watchtowers, offers a magnificent view of the Grand Canyon, the Kaibab National Forest, the Painted Desert, and the Navajo country. A Fred Harvey Trading Post and luncheonette are located near the tower. The tour is available year-round.

The Hermit's Rest Drive begins at the El Tovar and Bright Angel Lodge and continues westward along the canyon rim to Hermit's Rest. Along the way, stops are made at Trail View and Hopi and Pima points, natural rim points which provide superb views of the Grand Canyon. Midway in the tour is Hermit's Rest, a unique cliff house of native boulder with a rustic lounge, a great fireplace, and an observation porch commanding a sweeping view of the canyon. Free shuttle during the summer months.

Canyon Mule Trips leave the South Rim to wind their way miles down into the canyon. Led by experienced guides, these trips cover trails cut directly into the canyon walls by government engineers. For anyone with even moderate horseback-riding experience, the mule trip into the inner canyon is an unforgettable experience. And only the descent into the canyon reveals many of the most spectacular aspects of its geology. Trips depart from the rim each morning, weather permitting.

Management restricts trail trips to persons physically fit, weighing not more than 200 pounds fully clothed, persons not too advanced in years, and to children 12 years of age or older. Previous riding experience is recommended. It is suggested that reservations be made six months in advance. All trail-trip tickets must be claimed before 7:45 A.M. on the day of the trip. Cost is $20 per person and includes a box lunch.

Two-Day Trips to Phantom Ranch, nearly a mile below the canyon rim, are available year-round. Mule trains leave the rim each morning and proceed down to the Colorado River. A suspension bridge across the Colorado provides access to Bright Angel Canyon and the Phantom Ranch. After an overnight stay in the comfortable accommodations at Phantom Ranch, the trip returns to the South Rim, arriving early in the afternoon. Reservations six months in advance are recommended. Rates range from $89.49 for one person to $295.13 for a party of four and include cabin accommodations, box lunch, dinner, and breakfast. For additional information, contact Grand Canyon National Park Lodges, Grand Canyon, AZ 86023 (602)638–2401.

Grand Canyon Youth Expeditions offers superb, professionally guided family float trips, backpacking and ski-touring trips, and youth expeditions in the Grand Canyon country. For complete details, rates, and trip schedules, contact: Grand Canyon Youth Expeditions, RR 4, Box 755, Flagstaff, AZ 86001 (602)774–8176.

Sanderson River Expeditions offers guided raft trips down the Grand Canyon in 33–foot motorized or 22–foot oar-powered rubber boats. For info, rates, and schedules, contact: Sanderson River Expeditions, 148 Sixth Ave., P.O. Box 1535, Page, AZ 86040 (602)647–2587.

Lake Mead National Recreation Area & Vicinity

This outstanding recreation area lies along the spectacular Grand Wash Cliffs, surrounded by stark, colorful desert landscapes. Lake Mead stretches 115 miles up the old course of the Colorado River from Hoover Dam to the Grand Canyon. Its 550–mile shoreline has wide, sandy beaches, shaded coves, and steep canyon walls, providing opportunities for fishing and beach camping. The famous rainbow trout waters of Lake Mohave reach northward 67 miles to the base of Hoover Dam. The whole area is surrounded by rugged desert country that provides scenic views and excellent hiking. Desert animals and plants include creosote bush, yucca, Joshua tree, and of course cactus, and kit fox, kangaroo rats, bighorn sheep, and a variety of reptiles and birds. Mule deer are common on the plateaus. Juniper, piñon pine, and Gambel oak populate the woodland regions. Ducks, gulls, and grebes feed on the surface of the water, and largemouth black bass, rainbow trout, and black crappie are caught around the submerged cliffs. Rainbow trout make up the majority of the catch in Lake Mohave, along with coho salmon, catfish, bluegill sunfish, and threadfin shad. There are several recreation areas and campsites in this area, accommodating fishermen and families.

The Lake Mead–Mohave region was first explored in 1826 by Jedediah Smith on his first southwest expedition in search of beaver. Smith was followed by a long list of explorers, including John C. Frémont and Maj. John Wesley Powell. The ancient Lost City Pueblo and the Virgin River salt quarries of the once great Pueblo Indian culture lie submerged at the bottom of the reservoirs.

The great Colorado River impoundments, including Lakes Mead, Mohave, Havasu, Cibola, Mittry, and Martinez, offer often excellent fishing for largemouth and striped bass up to world-record weights, crappie, and catfish. The famed sloughs of the Topock Swamp, between lakes Mohave and Havasu, produce outstanding fishing for bass and crappie. The frigid, turbulent tailrace waters below the giant dams offer some of the country's finest early-season drift-boat fishing for large, hard-hitting rainbow trout up to 20 pounds. Campgrounds, boat-launching sites, and rentals are available along the Colorado River lakes.

Information Sources, Maps & Access

For vacation travel and recreation information and a *Lake Meade National Recreation Area Map/Brochure*, contact: Superintendent, Lake Mead National Recreation Area, 601 Nevada Hwy., Boulder City, NV 89005 (702)293–4041. *Angler's Guide*, with information about fishing and the kinds of fish available, as well as maps and descriptions of facilities, can be obtained for 25¢ from the Nevada Dept. of Fish & Game, P.O. Box 10678, Reno, NV 89510. Complete fishing information, including Davis Dam, Willow Beach, Eldorado Canyon, and Cottonwood Cove, is provided in *Boating Guide to Lake Mohave*, available for 50¢ from the Southwest Parks and Monuments Association, Box 1562, Globe, AZ 85501. *Indians of the Lake Mead Country* can be obtained for 50¢ from the same organization. It provides an unusual insight into the earliest history of the area. It begins with cavemen and ends with the arrival of the white explorers. *Nautical Charts* are also available for $3.25, and the *Recreational Boating Guide* is available for $1.20. The Lake Mead Recreation Area is reached via U.S. 93 and U.S. 95 off Interstate 40 and via Interstate 50.

Gateways & Accommodations

Bullhead City—Gateway to Lake Mohave

(Pop. 900; sip code 86430; area code 602.) This is a major resort center and gateway to the Lake Mohave portion of the Lake Mead National Recreation Area. Davis Dam, which impounds the Colorado River to form Lake Mohave, is 4 miles north. Area accommodations: *Best Western Riverside Resort* (rates: $32–36 double), 48 excellent rooms, restaurant, cocktail lounge, and dock, 6 miles northwest of town off Arizona Hwy. 68 (Nevada (702)298–2535); *Lake Mohave Resort* (rates: $34–39 double), 51 excellent rooms and family units, in beautiful setting on the lake with dining room, cocktail lounge, fishing, boat rentals, north of Davis Dam at Katherine Landing (754–3245).

Kingman—Gateway to Lake Mead & the Kingman Resource Area

(Pop. 7,300; zip code 86401; area code 602.) The major business and tourist center of Mohave County and a popular jumping-off point to the Lake Mead National Recreation Area and Hoover Dam. The sprawling, 1.5–million-acre Kingman Resource Area contains the spectacular peaks of the Hualapai Mountains, Lake Mead, the fire-red Grand Wash Cliffs, the scenic Buckskin Mountains and the Needles, Cerbat Mountains, Lake Mohave, Bill Williams River, Topock Swamp Area, Lake Havasu, the Black. Big Sandy, and Aquarius mountains, Mohave Canyon, Kofa Game Range (a

660,000–acre preserve for the desert bighorn sheep), and the Imperial National Wildlife Refuge, which stretches along both sides of the Colorado River for some 30 miles above Imperial Dam. *The Kingman Resource Area Recreation Map* is available free from the Kingman Resource Area Office, Box 386, Kingman 86401. It shows all public and Indian lands, roads, towns, springs and wells, mines, points of interest, recreation sites, airfields, and railroads. It also includes a close-up map of the Hualapai Mountains. Accommodations: *Best Western Holiday House Motel*, (rates: $24–26 double), 36 good rooms, restaurant, cocktail lounge, heated pool, at 1225 W. Beale St., 1 mile northwest of town on U.S. 93 (753–2153); *Best Western King's Inn Motel* (rates: $29–32 double), 53 excellent rooms and family units, heated pool, next to restaurant at 2930 E. Andy Devine Ave., 2 miles east of town on U.S. 66/93 (753–6101); *Best Western Wayfarer's Inn*, (rates: $27–32 double), 100 excellent rooms and family units, coffee shop, heated pool, at 2815 E. Andy Devine Ave., 2 miles east on U.S. 66/93 (753–6271); *Holiday Inn* (rates: $34–36 double), 160 excellent rooms, restaurant, cocktail lounge, heated pool, at 3100 E. Andy Devine Ave., 3 miles east of town on U.S. 66/93 (753–6262); *Ramada Inn* (rates: $30–32 double), 100 excellent rooms and family units, restaurant, cocktail lounge, heated pool, at 1400 E. Andy Devine Ave., 1½ miles east of town on U.S. 66/93 (753–5531).

Lake Havasu City—Gateway to Lake Havasu & the National Wildlife Refuge

(Pop. 2,700; zip code 86403; area code 602.) This popular resort center is on beautiful 45–mile-long Lake Havasu, one of the West's top bass fisheries. Area attractions include the 41,494–acre Havasu National Wildlife Refuge, inhabited by migratory waterfowl, bighorn sheep, herons, wild burros, cormorants, and, in the Topock Marsh Area, by the rare Yuma clapper rail; an international resort complex, which is based around a small English village and the famous London Bridge, transported from London where it was built in 1824–31, and now spanning a channel of the Colorado River; the London Arms Restaurant (855–4081) in an English Village at the foot of London Bridge; and the 13,000–acre Lake Havasu State Park recreation area. Accommodations: *Best Western Wings Motor Hotel* (rates: $26–28 double), 40 rooms, coffee shop, heated pool, at 33 Pima Drive, (855–2146); *Ramada Inn* (rates: $25–27 double), 100 excellent rooms, restaurant, cocktail lounge, heated pool, 2 miles southeast of town at 470 S. Acoma Blvd. (855–3021).

Lodges & Resorts

★★★★*Cottonwood Cove on Lake Mohave* is a complete recreation resort with excellent motel rooms and family units, marina, boat rentals, modern trailer park, sailing, waterskiing, and superb fishing on Lake Mohave, within the Lake Mead National Recreation Area. Many years ago the old river crossing near Cottonwood Cove was known as the Searchlight Ferry. Wagonloads of gold ore mined from the beautiful mountains of Searchlight, Nevada, were shipped to Kingman, Arizona, by way of Searchlight Ferry. For the hiker the old mines are still available but still privately owned—and dangerous, to explore and photograph. Today Cottonwood Cove may be reached by an all-weather road or a 3,000–foot airstrip. Davis Dam, completed in 1948, backs the water of the Colorado River 67 miles to the foot of Hoover Dam. This gives the boatman hundreds of miles of shoreline along which to explore the bays and inlets. For additional information and seasonal rates, contact: Cottonwood Cove on Lake Mohave, P.O. Box 1000, Cottonwood Cove, NV 89046 (702)297–1464.

★★★*Nautical Inn*, on 45–mile-long Lake Havasu, is a handsome beachfront resort in an oasislike setting surrounded by rugged, red-hued mountains. Fishing, sailing, and waterskiing start right at the inn's own dock; both the heated pool and sandy beach are ideal for swimming and sunbathing. Also on hand are two all-weather tennis courts lighted for night play and a challenging nine-hole, par-3 golf course. A championship 27–hole course is just a short drive away. For dining, the inn offers a fine restaurant, a terraced, lakeside dining room for lunch and cocktails, and the Bo's'n's Locker featuring nightly entertainment. Accommodations are available in two different locations: beachfront units have private baths, balconies, and color TV; bay-view rooms offer the same amenities plus a selection of living room–bedroom suites. All rooms are air-conditioned and within easy walking distance of resort facilities. Rates vary from $19 for single rooms ($26–55 double) to $75 daily for a deluxe suite with kitchen. A package plan of 7 days and 6 nights with 2 meals daily is available for $165 per person. For more information write: The Nautical Inn, P.O. Box 1885, Lake Havasu City, AZ 86403 (602)855–2141.

★★*Palo Verde Vista* offers vacation apartments in Lake Havasu City's sunny resort area, just a few minutes from the mountain-rimmed lake that gives the city its name. Activities include golf on a 100% zoysia grass course, tennis, scuba diving, fishing for striped bass and bluegill, shopping in London Village, and horseback riding. Palo Verde also has its own private pool and sundeck. Apartments are nicely furnished and roomy, with complete kitchens, large living rooms, 2 full baths, and king-size beds. For complete details and rates write: Palo Verde Vista Apartments, Paloverde Blvd., Box 2170, Lake Havasu City, AZ 86403 (602)855–6335.

Travel Services

Colorado River Houseboats offer a unique means of vacation transport on 50 miles of the Colorado River and the entire expanse of Lake Havasu. Along the way, there are numerous opportunities for sightseeing, fishing, waterskiing, swimming, and sunbathing beneath clear Arizona skies. Boats range from 30 feet (sleeps four) to 43 feet in size, and all are equipped with bunks or convertible couches, kitchenettes and convertible dining areas, large railed sundecks, vanities, and marine heads. The larger, more luxurious craft have carpeting throughout, walnut paneling, showers, and air conditioning. Rentals vary from $485 for 6 days on smaller boats to $755 for 6 days on a 43-foot craft. Minimum rental is for 2 nights. Off-season rates are in effect Oct. 16–Mar. 4. Even if you've never set foot on deck before, Colorado River Houseboats will give you detailed instructions on operation and safety before your departure from Park Moabi Marina near the Arizona-California border. For full information and houseboat floor plans, write: Colorado River Houseboats, P.O. Box 915, Needles, CA 92363 (714)326–4777.

Lake Mead Yacht Tours offers daily cruises on Lake Mead to Hoover Dam, departing from the Lake Mead Marina, approximately 7 miles east of Boulder City on Nevada Hwy. 41. Cruises depart at 10:30 A.M. and 12, 1:30 and 3 P.M. For additional information and rates, call (702)736–6180 or write: Lake Mead Yacht Tours, 5030 Paradise Road, Las Vegas, NV 89119.

Navajo & Hopi Indian Country

The vast Navajo Indian Reservation occupies the windswept 11,500,000–acre northeast corner of Arizona. The 1,560,000–acre Hopi Indian Reservation is within and completely surrounded by the territory of the Navajos, their traditional enemies. Within this vast, colorful expanse of mesas, buttes, towering pinnacles, spires, valleys, and canyons are some of the most fascinating archaeological and scenic wonders of the American Southwest, including awesome Monument Valley, the ancient Indian ruins of the Navajo and Canyon de Chelly national monuments, White Mesa Natural Bridge, Hubbell Trading Post National Historic Site, and the Navajo Indian Capitol at Window Rock.

Information Sources, Maps & Access

For vacation travel information for the Navajo and Hopi country, contact: Arizona Office of Tourism, 1700 W. Washington, Phoenix, AZ 85007 (602)271–3618. The major auto access routes within the Navajo country are U.S. 160 and 163, Arizona Highways 264, 77, and 63, and Interstate 40. For information and a *Canyon de Chelly National Monument Map/Brochure*, contact: Superintendent, Canyon de Chelly National Monument, Chinle, AZ 86503 (602) 674–5136. For detailed information on the Navajo National Monument, contact: Superintendent, Navajo National Monument, Shonto AZ 86044 (602)672–2366. Motorists should keep in mind that many of the spur routes during the August and September rainy season in Navajo country become nearly impassable. Be sure to check with the local authorities and traders on road conditions.

Scenic & Historic Areas

Canyon de Chelly National Monument

The ancient, prehistoric ruins of Canyon de Chelly National Monument, dating from A.D. 348 to 1300, are located in three long, deep canyons cut in the red sandstone of the Defiance Plateau in the northeast corner of the Navajo Indian Reservation. These fascinating Indian dwellings are found in niches in the steep canyon walls. The major ruins of the area, representing the early Basketmakers through Pueblo Indian culture, are the White House, Antelope House, Mummy Cave, and Standing Cow ruins. The Canyon de Chelly contains more than 300 prehistoric sites and 138 major ruins. Most of them are perched high on the north wall of the canyon and are inaccessible. The White House is one of the largest and best-preserved ruins. It flourished during the great Pueblo period from A.D. 1050 to 1300. The abandonment of this site by the pueblo dwellers is believed to have marked the arrival of the Navajos. The Antelope House, the Standing Cow with its Indian pictographs showing mounted Spanish soldiers and priests carrying crosses, and the Mummy Cave are located within the sheer-walled Canyon del Muerto. The Mummy Cave is located 300 feet above the canyon floor. Upstream from the Mummy Cave is Massacre Cave, named after the slaughter of Navajo men, women, and children by Spanish soldiers. The White House is the only ruin open to the public, who must be accompanied by a park ranger or authorized Navajo guide.

During 1863–64 Kit Carson's men invaded the canyon and herded 7,000 Navajos for their infamous "Long Walk" to the Bosque Redondo in New Mexico. During the summer, the 26–mile-long floor of Canyon de Chelly is used by the Navajos for livestock grazing and farming. The monument headquarters and visitor center (open 8 A.M. to 7 P.M. in the summer) is located at Chinle. Justin's Thunderbird Lodge (see below) conducts guided jeep tours into the canyon daily from mid-April through October. U.S. National Park ranger and Navajo Indian guide services are available at the monument headquarters. The park rangers are on duty from eight to five daily. A self-guiding tour winds from the White House Overlook

to the fascinating White House Ruin. Fees are charged for all guide service within the monument.

Fort Defiance

Fort Defiance, located at the mouth of sheer-walled Bonito Canyon due north of Window Rock near the New Mexico border, established in 1851, served for years as a military post used in warfare to subdue the Navajo tribes during the uprisings of the 1860s. It later served as an army headquarters and the Indian Bureau headquarters of the Southern Navajo Reservation. Today, Fort Defiance is the site of an Indian hospital. The surrounding country at nearby Window Rock is dotted by Navajo log and earth huts and hogans. During the fall and winter, visitors may witness the ancient Fire Dance and Yei-bi-chi Dance.

Hubbell Trading Post National Historic Site

The famous Hubbell Trading Post, located near the junction of Arizona Highways 264, and 63, was one of the most noted posts in the Navajo country, established about 1890. It houses a collection of paintings, many of Navajo and Hopi scenes, given by artists who stayed at the post when it was operated by Lorenzo Hubbell. Hubbell was one of the first traders to see and encourage the commercial possibilities of Navajo weavers and silversmiths. Guided tours of this still-active post are conducted daily.

Monument Valley

This spectacular valley is noted for its red sandstone mesas, pillars, and rose-colored spires that soar up to 1,000 feet in height and resemble the ruins of ancient Greek temples when viewed from a distance. For additional information, see the "Colorado River Canyonlands Country" in the Utah chapter.

Navajo National Monument

The Keet Seel, Betatakin, and Inscription House Indian ruins are in the Navajo National Monument. These complex 13th–century ruins, noted for their circular kivas, ceremonial chambers, and mazes of rooms, are set among some of the most awesome scenery in the Southwest. Access to the Betatakin Ruin is via a 3–hour guided tour from the visitors' center. The Keet Seel River is reached via a rugged 8–mile hiking and horse trail. Guided horseback trips to this large, spectacular ruin depart from the visitors' center at 8:30. Reservations must be in advance. Hiking permits are available at the visitors' center, which also offers exhibits and summer campfire programs. The monument is reached via a paved road from U.S. 160.

Gateways & Accommodations

Chinle—Gateway to Canyon de Chelly National Monument

(Pop. 500; zip code 86503; area code 602.) Chinle is a Navajo administrative headquarters. Accommodations: *Canyon de Chelly Motel* (rates: $28 double), 50 rooms and services, 3 miles west of Canyon de Chelly National Monument (674–5288); *Justin's Thunderbird Lodge* (see "Lodges" below).

Kayenta—Gateway to Navajo National Monument & Monument Valley

(Pop. 500; zip code 86033; area code 602.) The town is located at the junction of U.S. 160 and 163 in the northeast corner of the state in Monument Valley north of the vast Hopi Indian Reservation. Accommodations: *Holiday Inn*, (rates: $42 double), 100 excellent rooms and family units, restaurant, pool, jeep tours of Monument Valley, at junction of U.S. 160 and 163 (697–3221).

Second Mesa of the Hopi Indian Reservation

(Pop. 500; zip code 86043; area code 602.) This includes the Hopi Indian villages of Nishnognovi, Shilaulovi, and Shongopovi. The other Hopi villages are located on the first and third mesas of the reservation. The Hopi Cultural Center on the Second Mesa includes a museum, arts and crafts center, and campground. Accommodations: *Hopi Cultural Center Motel* (rates: $26 double), 33 good rooms in unique pueblo architecture and design, restaurant, next to the Hopi Indian Arts and Crafts Center on Arizona 264 (734–2401).

Window Rock—Headquarters of the Navajo Indian Reservation

(Pop. 600; zip code 86515; area code 602.) Located off Arizona 264, the town is surrounded by a wide-open country of eroded sandstone cliffs and hills, known as haystacks. Area attractions include the Navajo Indian Arts & Crafts Guild, with exhibits of craft work, located east of the junction of Navajo Route 12 and Arizona 264, and the Navajo Tribal Museum at the tribal fairgrounds on Arizona 264. Accommodations: *Window Rock Motor Inn* (rates: $28 double), 44 good rooms, restaurant, 1 mile south of town on Arizona 264 (871–4108).

Lodges & Travel Services

★★★*Justin's Thunderbird Lodge & Canyon de Chelly Tours* occupies an oasis of ancient cottonwood trees, flower gardens, and green lawns at the entrance to the Canyon de Chelly National Monument. The Old Thunderbird Trading Post, which served the Navajos from 1896 to 1969, is the lodge cafeteria today, and many rock and adobe lodge rooms built in the 1920s have been modernized within to accommodate visitors to Arizona's fabulous canyonlands. There are also contemporary motel units with air conditioning and private baths that have been added to the original complex of buildings. Rates: $18–28 daily, double occupancy; $30 daily for 3 persons, and $32 for 4 persons. The lodge offers jeep tours of the region's many spectacular sights: Navajo and Anasazi ruins, rock paintings of the Conquistadores, and the Mummy Cave, a 1,000–year-old village of pit houses, rock dwellings, and burial grounds, reputed to be the oldest continuously occupied place in North America. The climax of the trip is an 800–foot sandstone monolith called Spider Rock. For information on the lodge and tours of the canyons, write: Justin's Thunderbird Lodge, Box 548, Chinle, AZ 86503 (602)674–5443 or 674–5265.

Prescott National Forest & The Pine Mountain Wilderness

This forest, high but somewhat drier than the other areas along the Mogollon Rim, encompasses 1,250,000 acres of top-rate mule-deer country in central Arizona. The forest includes the western edge of a stand of ponderosa pine that stretches 350 miles across central Arizona and into New Mexico. Other trees include Douglas fir, white fir, and limber pine, found at elevations from 3,000 to 8,000 feet. Rocky Mountain mule deer are plentiful and widely distributed. The forest is also inhabited by antelope, javelina, whitetail deer, and black bear. Forest roads and trails lead to the more remote hunting and camping areas around Pine Mountain, Sycamore Canyon, Agua Fria River, Lyn Lake, Longfellow Ridge, Connell Mountains, Limestone Canyon, and Hassayampa Lake. Upland game-bird shooting is good for wild turkey, band-tailed pigeon, dove, and quail. Pine Mountain wilderness area lies along the high Verde River Rim. It stands as an island of tall, green timber, surrounded by desert mountains with hot, dry mesas and deep canyons. Major features include Mocking Bird Pass, Pine Mountain, and Turret Peak.

Information Sources, Maps & Access

For vacation travel and recreation information and a full-color *Prescott National Forest Map* (50¢), contact: Supervisor, Prescott National Forest, Box 2549, Prescott, AZ 86301 (602)445–1762. The forest is reached via U.S. Highway 89 and Arizona State Highways 279, 69, 79, and 255. Lodging, supplies, and outfitting services are available at Whipple, Humboldt, Dewey, Cordes, Bumble Bee, Paulden, Iron Springs, Walker, Groom Creek, Prescott, Crown King, Walnut Grove, Cherry, Jerome, Drake, and Simmons.

Gateways & Accommodations

Prescott

(Pop. 13,100; zip code 86301; area code 602.) Headquarters of the Prescott National Forest, Prescott lies northwest of Phoenix on U.S. 89A in the mountainous section of west-central Arizona. The town was the onetime capital of the Arizona Territory, founded in 1864 because of its abundance of pine timber and wild game and the lure of gold. In 1867 the territorial capital was moved to Tucson, where it remained for only ten years. Then it was temporarily moved back to Prescott until 1889, when it secured its permanent position at Phoenix. Area attractions include the Smoki Museum with its Indian artifacts on Arizona Ave.; Sharlot Hall Museum and the Territorial Governor's Mansion built by Richard McCormick in the 1860's and restored in 1927 by the poet and historian Sharlot Hall at 415 W. Gurley St.; and the nature trails at the 20–acre Prescott Nature Center on Williamson Valley Road. Accommodations: *Best Western Prescottonian Motel* (rates: $38–46 double), 94 excellent rooms and family units, next to coffee shop, 1¼ miles east of town on U.S. 89 at 1317 E. Gurley St. (445–3096); *Loba Lodge* (rates:$26.50 double), 14 motel rooms and family housekeeping cabins among stands of ponderosa pine, south of town on the Senator Hwy. (445–1987).

Lodges & Guest Ranches

★★★*Rancho de los Caballeros* is an elegant working ranch/guest resort set amid 20,000 acres of rolling hillsides and flowering Arizona desert. It is open from early Fall to late Spring and offers a wide variety of recreations and amenities. They have a corral of 75 horses, a skeet range, four acrylic tennis courts with lessons available, an unusual pearl-shaped swimming pool, counselors for the children and evening activities including square dancing, movies, games, and barbeques. You can join the wranglers on a cattle round-up or just take a leisurely stroll around the beautiful grounds. And there is golf at nearby Wickenburg Country Club. Accommodations are spacious and comfortable, with traditional Southwest decor. Rates on the American Plan (all meals included) for two run from about $78–108/day, depending on season and room size. For more information, contact: Rancho de los Caballeros, Wickenburg, Ariz. 85358 (602)684–5484.

★★★★*The Wickenburg Inn Tennis and Guest Ranch* is a uniquely inviting combination of sports resort and desert hideaway. It is one of the Southwest's most outstanding tennis ranches, and as such features 11 acrylic courts, professionally led tennis clinics and private lessons, rebound nets, stroke developers and automatic ball machines. For the horseman, the Inn has about 55 saddle horses suitable for beginners and experienced riders. Trails cover scenic and unspoiled miles. For the nature lover, the Inn's 2,295 acre Wildlife Preserve is open to all guests and includes marked nature paths, riding or hiking trails and water holes with viewing blinds. And for the artistic in temperament, the Inn offers a complete Arts and Crafts Center for pottery making, weaving, macrame and many other creative endeavors. There is also a heated swimming pool, a 9–hole golf course just 15 minutes away, and special evening activities including games, cookouts, professional rodeo performances and much more. At the Wickenburg Inn you can stay at one of the Spanish ranch-style Casitas or in the Ranch Lodge. The Casitas are of Mexican adobe brick with massive wooden beams, hand-painted Spanish tiles, and individual fireplaces. Some of the Deluxe Suites have private sundecks and Jacuzzi bathtubs. Rates per person, double occupancy, with all meals and use of facilities included run $33–53 for the Lodge (depending on the season) and $37–75 for Casitas. For more information, contact: The Wickenburg Inn Tennis and Guest Ranch, P.O. Box P, Wickenburg, Ariz. 85358 (602)684–7811.

Tonto National Forest & Superstition Mountains

The Tonto National Forest is a 1.5–million-acre reserve that embraces the Mazatzal Mountains Wilderness and Cave Creek area, Verde River, Camp Creek, Bartlett Reservoir, Salt River, Apache Lake, Saguaro Lake, Tonto Basin, the Gorge, and the New River Mountains. The forest contains some of the most outstanding wilderness areas in Arizona, ranging in terrain from semidesert to the cool pine forests beneath the Mogollon Rim.

The Superstition Mountains Wilderness, encompassing 124,117 acres of the Superstition Mountains, offers 140 miles of trails winding through rugged land. According to an Indian legend, a group of Indians once sought shelter on the mountaintop during a great flood and were warned not to make a sound until the waters receded. They disobeyed and were turned to stone.

The most frequently used trail heads are at Peralta and First Water. Across the Tonto Basin, about 35 miles southeast of the Mazatzal Mountains, is the exceptionally rough, scenic, and often inaccessible country of the Sierra Ancha Wilderness. This 20,850–acre reserve is a land of precipitous box canyons, high vertical cliffs, prehistoric cliff dwellings, and rugged trails leading to Devil's Chasm, Deep Creek, Center Mountain, Aztec Peak, and Cherry Creek.

The Lost Dutchman Gold Mine, reputedly located near Weaver's Needle, is the subject of a brutal and frightening legend. A young Mexican, fleeing the wrath of his sweetheart's father, discovered a

gold mine in the Superstition Mountains, and his entire community made the treck into the wilderness to mine as much gold as they could. On their way home, they were attacked by Apaches, and the whole party—400 men—was killed, except for two boys who hid safely under a bush. These two children found their way back to Mexico, but returned to claim their heritage many years later. While they were digging, the Dutchman came along. He was Jacob Wolz, or Walz; after befriending the Mexicans, he murdered them and jealously guarded the stolen property from 1870 until his death. On his deathbed, he gave directions for finding the mine to a neighbor. Unfortunately, one of the landmarks could not be found, and thousands of would-be prospectors have been looking for it ever since. Some have never returned, some have come back with pieces of human skeletons, and some have been mysteriously shot in the wild canyons.

The Apache Trail, a scenic 76-mile-long auto route, Arizona Highway 88, built in 1905, begins at Apache Junction and winds through the Superstition Mountains and above the awesome, 2,000-foot sheer walls of the Salt River and Fish Creek canyons through the Tonto National Forest. It skirts several lakes before its terminus at Globe. The 25-mile gravel stretch between Roosevelt and Tortilla

Flat contains many hairpin curves. This scenic route, not for the fainthearted or inexperienced mountain driver, is bordered by colorful stands of mesquite, palo verdes, and ironwood trees—noted for their beautiful lavender blossoms in May and June. This historic trail, built to transport supplies for the construction of the Hoover Dam, is crisscrossed by ancient Apache trails.

Information Sources, Maps & Access

For vacation travel and recreation information, a full-color *Tonto National Forest Map* (50¢), *Superstition Wilderness Map* (50¢), and *Cave Creek–Mazatzal Mountains Area Map* (50¢), contact: Supervisor, Tonto National Forest, 102 S. 28th St., Phoenix, AZ 85034 (602)261–3205. The Tonto National Forest is reached via Arizona State Highways 288, 260, 188, 87, and 205. Lodging, supplies, and outfitting services are available at Pleasant Valley, Payson, Pine, Strawberry, and Punkin Center.

Gateways & Accommodations

Carefree

(Pop. 400; zip code 85331; area code 602.) This gateway to Tonto National Forest is located due north of Phoenix, off Interstate 17. Area attractions include Horseshoe and Bartlett reservoirs and the New River Mountains. A Tonto National Forest District Rangers Office is located here. Accommodations: *Carefree Inn* (rates: on request), 197 superb rooms and family resort units, restaurant, two swimming pools and a wide variety of recreational activities, including riding, tennis, and golf, in beautiful mountain and desert area on Mule Train Road. (488–3551).

Globe—Gateway to the Apache Trail & Tonto National Monument

(Pop. 7,300; zip code 85501; area code 602.) This old frontier mining town is set against the background of the Apache Mountains at the junction of U.S. 70 and Arizona Highway 77. Area attractions include the Indian ruins at the Tonto National Monument, with a visitors' center, musuem, and self-guiding trails to the cliff dwellings; San Carlos Lake, Apache Lake, and Roosevelt Lake, which is skirted by a segment of the scenic Apache Trail. Accommodations: *Friendship Inn Ember Motel* (rates: $18–22 double), 24 rooms and family units, heated pool, at 1105 N. Broad St. on U.S. 60, 1 mile northwest of town (425–5736).

Mesa—Tonto National Forest Gateway

(Pop. 62,900; zip code, 85208; area code 602.) Site of Ancient Indian irrigation ditches dug about 500 A.D. in the Salt River valley. Accommodations: *Best Western Mezona Motor Hotel* (rates: $24–33 double), 136 excellent rooms, restaurant, coffee shop, cocktail lounge, heated pool, at 250 W. Main St. on U.S. 60/80/89 (834–9233); *Golden Hills Country Club Resort*, (seasonal rates: $24–32 double), 96 excellent rooms and family units, dining room, coffee shop, cocktail lounge, heated pool, tennis courts, golf, 8 miles east of town at 6901 E. Broadway and Powder Road, 85208 (832–3202); *Royal Inn of Mesa* (rates: $20–32 double), 100 excellent rooms and family units, restaurant, cocktail lounge, heated pool, 1 mile west of town on U.S. 60/80/89 at 951 W. Main St. (833–1231).

Payson—Gateway to the Lost Dutchman Gold Mine & Mazatzal Mountains

(Pop. 1,500; zip code 85541; area code 602.) This popular Old West recreation gateway is in the heart of the sprawling Tonto National Forest. A U.S. Forest Service District Ranger's Office is located here. Area attractions include the spectacular Tonto Natural Bridge, which arches 183 feet above Pine Creek Canyon; Zane Grey's cabins; the famous Four Peaks of the Mazatzal Mountains; Tonto Basin, also known as Punkin Center, in the center of the Tonto Creek area, 3,000 feet below the Mogollon Rim, Sierra Ancha, and Mazatzal Mountains; Sieber Monument on Sieber Mountain, in honor of Al Sieber, one of Arizona's greatest scouts, who commanded the Apache Kid and Tom Horn in pursuit of Geronimo. Accommodations: *Swiss Village Lodge* (rates: $36 double), 75 excellent rooms with private patios and balconies, dining room, coffee shop, just north of town on Arizona 87 at junction of Arizona 260(474–3241).

Phoenix

(Pop. 581,600; zip code, see below; area code 602.) Arizona's capital city and a booming desert metropolis, Phoenix is flanked far to the north by Squaw Peak and the Camelback Mountains and on the east by the Four Peaks, a famous landmark which blends into the yellows and browns of the desert floor. The city is one of the Southwest's most popular tourist gateways. Area attractions include the Capitol Building at W. Washington St. & 17th Ave.; Desert Botanical Garden in Papago Park, 8 miles east of town on U.S. 60/80/89; Heard Museum of Anthropology & Primitive Arts at 22 E. Monte Vista Road; Pueblo Grande Museum, an ancient Indian ruin at 4617 E. Washington St., 6 miles east of town; Arizona Mineral Museum, 2 miles northwest of the city on U.S. 60/89 at 1826 W. McDowell Road; Phoenix Zoo at 5800 E. Van Buren St.; Bayless Cracker Barrel Museum, a replica of an Old West general store of the 1890s at 118 W. Indian School Road; North Mountain Park, with nature trails and 275 acres of scenic desert and mountain life zones 9 miles north of the city at 10600 N. 7th St.; South Mountain Park, 14,817 acres of mountain and desert scenery and flora, 8 miles south of the city on S. Central Ave.; Thunderbird Park, 720 acres of colorful desert topography, flora, and nature trails, at 59th Ave. and Deer Valley Drive. Area accommodations: *Adams Hotel* (rates $34–60 double), 538 excellent rooms and suites, restaurant, coffee shop, heated pool, health club, at Central and Adams Sts., 85001 (257–1525); *Arizona Ranch House Motel* (rates: $22–26 double), 54 excellent motel and cottage units, heated pool, patios, on spacious, landscaped grounds 6 miles north of town at 5600 N. Central Ave., 85012 (279–3221); *Best Western Country Village* (rates: $29–31 double), 114 excellent rooms and family units, restaurant, cocktail lounge, heated pool, tennis, racketball, off 1–10, Exit 24th St., at 2425 S. 24th St., 85034 (273–7251); *Del Webb's Townehouse* (rates: $35–52 double), 397 superb, spacious rooms and family units, restaurant, cocktail lounge, heated pool, 3 miles north of town at 100 W. Clarendon Ave., 85013 (279–9811); *Doubletree Inn* (rates: $40–48 double), 139 excellent rooms and family units, restaurant, cocktail lounge, heated pool, 4½ miles north of town at 212 W. Osborn St. 85013 (248–0222); *Holiday Inn—Airport* (rates: $32–34 double), 144 excellent rooms, restaurant, cocktail lounge, heated pool, kennel, 2 miles southeast off 1–10, Sky Harbor/24th St. Exit, at 2201 S. 24th St., 85034 (267–0611); *Holiday Inn—Central* (rates: $32–34 double), 159 excellent rooms, restaurant, cocktail lounge, heated pool, kennel, 1½ miles east on U.S. 60/80/89 at 2247 E. Van Buren St., 85006 (244–9341); *Jokake Inn* (rates: on request) 100 resort rooms and cottage units at the base of Camelback Mountain on beautiful landscaped grounds, with dining room, cocktail lounge, heated pool, tennis, golf, horseback riding, chuck-wagon dinners, 10 miles northeast of Phoenix at 6000 E. Camelback Road, 85018 (945–6301); *Paradise Inn* (rates: on request) 78 superb winter lodge rooms and guest cottages with fireplaces and private patios, dining room, cocktail lounge, heated pool, horseback riding and instruction, golf, tennis, on beautiful grounds on Camelback Mountain, 10 miles northeast of town at 6150 Camelback Road, 85018 (945–8491); *The Pointe Resort* (rates: on request), 227 superb rooms and family units, dining room, restaurant, cocktail lounge, 2 heated pools, tennis, golf, horseback riding and instruction, 8 miles northeast of Phoenix at 7677 N. 16th St., 85020 (997–2626).

Scottsdale

(Pop. 67,800; zip code, see below; area code 602.) A resort suburb of Phoenix surrounded by the Paradise Valley resort mecca, the town is noted for its Old West frontier atmosphere, with false-front buildings and hitching posts, arts and crafts shops. Scenic air tours of the state are offered by Southwest Airlines from the Municipal Airport (call (948–2400). Area accommodations: *Best Western Papago Inn & Resort* (rates: $28–38 double), 58 excellent rooms, restaurant, cocktail lounge, heated pool, sauna, 2½ miles south of town at 7017 E. McDowell Road, 85257 (947–7335); *Del Webb's Mountain Shadows* (rates: $32–60 double), 235 superb rooms and family units, restaurant, cocktail lounge, 2 heated pools, sauna, tennis, golf on beautiful grounds, 4½ miles northwest of town at 5641 E. Lincoln Drive, 85253 (948–7111); *Doubletree Inn at Fashion Square* (rates: $33–62 double), 168 excellent rooms, restaurant, cocktail lounge, heated pool, tennis on landscaped grounds, at 4710 N. Scottsdale Road, 85251 (947–5411); *Doubletree Inn at Scottsdale Mall* (rates: $36–74 double), 206 excellent rooms, restaurant, cocktail lounge, heated pool, tennis, at 7353 E. Indian School Road, 85251 (994–9203); *Holiday Inn* (rates $28–39 double), 216 excellent rooms, restaurant, coffee shop, cocktail lounge, heated pool, 1¼ miles north of town at 5101 N. Scottsdale Road, 85253 (945–4392); *Inn at McCormick Ranch* (rates: $25–72 double), 126 outstanding rooms and family units, dining room, cocktail lounge, heated pool, tennis, golf, horseback riding, boat rentals in beautiful location on Camelback Lake, at 7401 N. Scottsdale Road, 2½ miles north of town (948–5050); *Marriott's Camelback Inn* (rates: $35–85 double), 420 superb rooms and family deluxe units with patios, sundecks, some fireplaces, restaurants, cocktail lounges, 2 heated pools, tennis courts, golf on spacious, scenic grounds, 2½ miles north of town at 5402 E. Lincoln Drive, 85252 (948–1700); *Paradise Valley Guest Ranch* (rates: on request), 37 excellent rooms and family units, heated pool, tennis, golf, next to dining room and coffee shop, on 10 acres with beautiful mountain views, 1¼ miles north of town at 5001 N. Scottsdale Road (949–1414); *Ramada's Valley Ho Resort* (rates: $24–60 double), 296 excellent rooms and family units, restaurant, coffee shop, cocktail lounge, 3 heated pools, tennis, in attractive location at 6850 Main St., 85251 (945–6321); *Safari Hotel & Paul Shank's Gracious Dining* (rates $32–74 double), 194 excellent rooms and family units, coffee shop, cocktail lounge, 2 heated pools, tennis on landscaped grounds, at 4611 N. Scottsdale Road, 85252 (945–0721); *Scottsdale Hilton* (rates $36–75 double), 183 excellent rooms and suites, restaurant, cocktail lounge, heated pool, tennis, 2½ miles north of town at 6333 N. Scottsdale Road, 85253 (948–7750); *Sheraton Scottsdale Inn* (rates: $36–52 double), 258 excellent rooms, restaurant, cocktail lounge, 3 heated pools, sauna, tennis, 3 miles north of town at 7200 N. Scottsdale Road, 85253 (948–5000); *Sunburst Hotel* (rates: $25–55 double), 212 excellent rooms and family units, restaurant, coffee shop, heated pool, tennis, on landscaped grounds at 4925 N. Scottsdale Road, 85251 (945–7666).

Guest Ranches & Resorts

★★*Kohl's Ranch*, located on the pine-studded banks of Tonto Creek in the dense forest of the Mogollon Rim, is a family guest resort offering varied accommodations and a wealth of activities. Fishing for elusive mountain trout is popular in Tonto Creek, the largest of the rim streams. For those who like their vacations on horseback, the ranch maintains a stable of 30 horses, a wrangler, and a guide. Expert guides and horses are available for seasonal hunting on 4 million acres of rugged country, prime habitat for deer, elk, antelope, mountain lion, bear, and wild turkey. Also on hand are an authentic old-fashioned stagecoach and covered wagon for children. Facilities include a heated pool, sauna, exercise room, a big family dining room, well-stocked bar and lounge, coffee shop, and soda fountain. Accommodations are in new and modern lodge rooms or in rustic cabins with kitchenettes. Many of the cabins also feature fireplaces. European-plan rates: $18–25 for two; $24–30 for four; $30–45 for six. A grocery store on the premises stocks supplies for housekeeping guests. For additional information write: Kohl's Ranch, Payson, Arizona (478–4444; from the Phoenix area call toll-free 271–9731).

★*Saguaro Lake Ranch Resort*, a family vacation resort between Stewart Mountain and Saguaro Lake—one of Arizona's most magnificent areas—offers guest accommodations in modern ranchettes, riding stables, hiking trails, a swimming pool, and a 10–mile-long recreational lake only minutes away. Panoramic views from the ranch take in the Bulldog and Superstition mountains, the Salt River, and acres of unspoiled wilderness. The climate is clear, dry, and invigorating. Season is December 15 to May 1 for winter vacations, and all other months (except July, August, and September) for groups, conventions, and special parties. Daily rates (American plan) are $40–50 per person (Dec. 15–Jan. 5 and Feb. 1–May 1), or $60–80 double occupancy (Dec. 15–Jan. 5 and Feb. 1–May 1). For information, write Saguaro Lake Ranch Resort, P.O. Box 4066, Mesa, AZ 85201 (602)985–1330.

★★★★*The Wigwam* is a luxury vacation resort built along the lines of a sumptuous, full-service country club. There are three championship 18–hole golf courses as beautiful to look at as they are to play on. For tennis buffs, the resort offers eight excellent courts, six of which are lighted for night play, plus a tennis center, lounge, and patio adjacent to the courts. The Goodyear Golf and Country Club, owned and operated by the Wigwam for members and guests, has a complete golf shop, locker rooms, lounge and dining rooms, and a professional staff to offer pointers and arrange foursomes. Other amenities of this outstanding retreat include a pool surrounded by a spacious sundeck, horseback riding and sight-seeing trips, a cocktail lounge, a terrace dining room for dinner and dancing, weekly movies, poolside buffet luncheons, and numerous private meeting rooms for business conventions and catered parties. Full American-plan accommodations are air-conditioned with private baths, TV, and patios. Daily per person rates: $43–55 for twin-bedded rooms; $55–96 for 1–3-bedroom suites and bungalows; $95–110 for 2–bedroom executive suites; and $82–96 for 4–bedroom privates casas. The above prices, with the exception of the 4–bedroom casas, are quoted on a double-occupancy basis. Children's rates and special golf and tennis holiday package plans are also available. For further information write: The Wigwam, Litchfield Park, AZ 85340 (602)935–3811.

ARKANSAS

Introduction

Arkansas, the "Land of Opportunity," takes in the scenic pine, oak, and beech forests, deep, clear river, and spectacular bluffs and highlands of the Ouachita and Ozark national forests. Here, flowing through the beautiful highlands, are the renowned float fishing waters of the Buffalo, the Ouachita, and the crystal-clear White River, which offers nationally renowned fishing for giant rainbow trout in the frigid water below Bull Shoals Dam. Arkansas's great sprawling lakes and reservoirs, among them Bull Shoals, Beaver, and Ouachita, offer top-ranked fishing for trophy largemouth bass and trout. Rugged hiking trails and old forest roads provide access to wild forests inhabited by whitetail deer, bobwhite quail, wild turkey, raccoon, and red fox.

Accommodations & Travel Information

The state's major vacation lodges and resorts are described in the "Vacation/Lodging Guide" which follows. The *Arkansas Tour Guide*, a 112–page booklet, is available free from: Dept. of Parks & Tourism, State Capitol, Little Rock 72201 (501)371–7777. It gives information on specific attractions and areas of interest in the state, listing local Chambers of Commerce, and state park facilities. It features maps for each recreational region, and describes local points of interest, as well as hotels and inns. The department also offers free booklets on specific vacation areas: *Greater Beaver Lake Area: Queen of the White River Lakes, Hot Springs National Park: Diamond Lakes Country, The Lake Dardanelle Recreation Area, Greers Ferry Lake & Little Red River, Delta Highlands.* The 44–page *Ozark Mountain Region* booklet is available free from Ozark Mountain Region, Inc., P.O. Box 122, Mountain Home 72653.

Arkansas fishing and hunting regulations, license and seasons information, and the free booklet *Public Owned Fishing Lakes* may be obtained from: Game & Fish Commission, State Capitol Mall, Little Rock 72201. Many of the state's old logging roads and deserted railroad beds which provide access to the remote fishing and hunting areas are shown on *Arkansas County Maps*, available for 50¢ each from: Highway Dept., Little Rock 72201. Arkansas's 18 million acres of forest lands, two mountain ranges, and the remote country surrounding its wild and scenic rivers provide unlimited opportunities for camping and backpacking. The vast high country forest regions are crisscrossed by old logging roads, firebreaks, and abandoned railroad beds that make excellent paths into seldom explored areas. The state's public camping areas are in the state parks, Buffalo River and Hot Springs national parks, Ozark and Ouachita national forests, and Corps of Engineers recreation areas, including the Arkansas River Development Project, Beaver Lake, Blue Mountain Lake, Bull Shoals Lake, Greers Ferry Lake, Nimrod Lake, Lake Ouachita, Norfork Lake, and DeGray, Millwood, and Talbe Rock lakes. The camping areas are listed and described in the 32–page *Arkansas Camper's Guide*, available free upon request along with detailed camping information from: Travel Division, Dept. of Parks & Tourism, State Capitol, Little Rock 72201. For additional information about Arkansas's Ozark wild and scenic float streams, write for the following publications. *The Float Streams of Arkansas* is available free from: Dept. of Parks & Tourism, State Capitol, Little Rock 72201. *Buffalo River Canoeing Guide* ($1), *Buffalo River Country* ($4.95), *Mulberry River Canoeing Guide* ($1), and reprints of guides to other Arkansas streams ($2.50) are available from: Ozark Society Book Service Box 725, Hot Springs 71901. *Buffalo National River* (50¢), an illustrated booklet with a useful river map, is available from: Superintendent, Buffalo National River, P.O. Box 1008, Harrison 72601. Maps of the *Spring River & South Fork, Little Red River, White River Trout Fishing*, and *Buffalo River*,

showing public access, boat dock and fishing services, portage points, graveled roads, and trout areas, are available free upon request from: Game & Fish Commission, State Capitol Mall, Little Rock 72201. The commission also publishes a free *Guide to the Smallmouth Bass Streams of Arkansas.*

Highways & Maps

The free *Arkansas State Highway Map* includes all major and minor roads, cities and towns, railroads, colleges and universities, roadside tables, campsites, national forests, wildlife management areas, and estimated mileage between major points. It also features detail maps of Little Rock and North Little Rock, Jonesboro, West Memphis, Pine Bluff, El Dorado, Fort Smith, Blytheville, Texarkana, Springdale, Hot Springs National Park, Fayetteville, Camden, and Conway, Write: Dept. of Parks and Tourism, State Capitol, Little Rock 72201.

Ouachita Mountains & National Forest

The 1.5–million-acre Ouachita National Forest is located due west of Little Rock, encompassing the rugged mountainous backcountry surrounding the headwaters of the Little Missouri, Cossatot, Fourche la Fave, and Caddo rivers. The Choctaw district of the forest sprawls across the Arkansas boundary into Oklahoma. The major features of this outstanding camping, fishing, and hunting region include the Ouachita, Kiamichi, and Winding Stair mountains, the renowned smallmouth bass and crappie waters of beautiful Ouachita, Nimrod, Winona, and Hamilton lakes, Blue Mountain Lake, and the Caney Creek and Muddy Creek wildlife management areas. The 14,433–acre Caney Creek Wilderness is the largest roadless mountain area in the central United States. There are several rugged hiking trails and old forest roads which provide access to the remote interior wildlife management areas where the hunting is excellent for bobwhite, wild turkey, deer, raccoon, red fox, and opossum. Lake Ouachita is nationally renowned for its striped bass to 17 pounds and rainbows to 10 pounds.

The major warmwater fisheries located south of the Ozark highlands include beautiful blue mountain lakes on the Petit Jean River, huge Lake Ouachita encircled by the craggy bluffs and dense green forests of the million-acre Ouachita National Forest, De Gray Reservoir on the Caddo River, Lake Greerson on the Little Missouri, Lake Dardanelle and the historic Arkansas River—surrounded by the plain of the Arkansas River Valley, and the oxbows of the meandering Mississippi on the eastern boundary, and the Spanish–moss-lined sloughs and bayous of the southern forests, bysected by the Ouachita River. Trophy rainbows and browns are found in the cold tailrace waters below the Greerson Reservoir and Lake Ouachita dams. Huge alligator gars up to 200 pounds are caught and sometimes landed on the lower White River, Red River, and the lower sluggish stretches of the Ouachita.

VACATION/ LODGING GUIDE

Information Sources, Maps & Access

For detailed vacation travel and recreation information, and a full-color *Ouachita National Forest Map* (50¢), contact: Supervisor, Ouachita National Forest, Hot Springs, AR 71901 (501)321–5202. The waterproof *Lake Ouachita Contour Map* ($3), *Greers Ferry Lake Contour Map*, ($3), *De Gray Contour Map* ($3), and *Lake Greeson Contour Map*, showing man-made and natural features, and hydrographics may be ordered from: Lakes Illustrated, Box 4854 GS, Springfield, MO 65804. For information on Hot Springs National Park, contact: Superintendent, Hot Springs National Park, Hot Springs, AR 71901 (501)624–3383. The forest is reached via US 71, 270, 64, and 70, and Interstate Routes 40 and 30. Overnight accommodations, supplies, guides, and boat rentals are available at Mountain Pine, Mena, Hartford, Hot Springs, Mansfield, and Hartfield (Arkansas), and Heavener (Oklahoma). Hot Springs National Park is reached by US 70 and Arkansas 7 off Interstate 30.

Gateways & Accommodations

Arkadelphia

(Pop. 10,000; zip code 71923; area code 501), situated along the bluffs of the Ouachita Valley, overlooking the Ouachita River, was an important port during steamboat days. Today, this pleasant community has much to offer for recreation. There is fishing in the Caddo and Ouachita Rivers, and De Gray Lake, a 13,400–acre lake formed by a dam across the Caddo with 207 miles of shoreline. De Gray State Park has a marina, restaurant and lodge and offers camping, picnicking, tennis and golf. Accommodations: *Best Western Continental Motor Inn* (rates: $23–25 double), with 57 excellent

rooms, restaurant, swimming pool, five miles north of town at the junction of Interstate 30 and Arkansas Highway 7 (246–5592).

Ft. Smith

(Pop. 65,000 zip code 72901; area code 501) has a rich history which dates back to 1817 as a frontier post on the Arkansas River. It was originally founded to keep peace between the Osage Indians upstream and the Cherokees downstream and to give protection to the trappers, traders and hunters and explorers of the early West. The fort, located on a rising ground of 50 feet, afforded a commanding and picturesque view of the entire area. During the gold rush days, Ft. Smith became an important junction to California and the site of outlaw activity, until Judge Parker "The infamous hanging judge" was sent to restore law and order. There is much to see in the way of historical sights—museums, forts, etc. Each year the city stages a wild west festival and rodeo. Located near the Ozark, Ouachita, Kiamichi Mountains, and Cookson Hills, the area offers hunting in the Boston Mountain area of the Ozarks, as well as nature and riding trails. Accommodations: *Best Western Peddler's Motor Inn* (rates: $23 double), with 135 excellent rooms and family units, restaurant, swimming pool, tennis, kennel, at 2301 Touson Ave. on US Highway 71–S (785–1401); *Best Western Trade Winds Inn* (rates: $24–28 double), with 134 excellent rooms and family units, heated pool, restaurant, coffeeshop at 101 North 11th St. in center of town on US 64 and 71 (785–4121); *Ramada Inn* (rates: $34 double), with 157 excellent rooms and family units, restaurant, coffeeshop, heated pool and sauna at 5101 Towson Ave. on US Highways 64–71 (646–2931); *Sheraton Inn* (rates $30–36.50 double), with 150 excellent rooms, restaurant, swimming pool at 5711 Rogers Ave., three miles east of town on Arkansas Highway 22 (452–4110).

Hot Springs & Hot Springs National Park

(Pop. 36,000; zip 71901; area code 501) noted particularly as a famous spa, the city itself offers much in the way of year-round resort activity, museums and historical sites, shopping, parks, boat trips, area tours, and animal farms and zoos as well as the typical sports activities available in the National Park. The city surrounds the 4500–acre park which is situated amidst the slopes and ridges of six mountains. The famous hot springs rise from the west slope of Hot Springs Mountain. Supposedly discovered by DeSoto in 1541, the springs' healing properties were known to the Indians before he arrived. They had declared this area neutral ground so that all could take advantage of the water's recuperative powers. There are 47 springs, with a water temperature of 143 degrees F. This water is cooled to a bath temperature of 92°F and piped to a variety of bathhouses for enjoyment by visitors. The Ouachita National Forest, also nearby, offers many recreational activities as well as lodging. Accommodations: *Avanelle Motor Lodge* (rates $26–45 double), with 88 excellent rooms and family units, restaurant, cocktail lounge, heated pool at Central and Grand (624–2521); *Best Western Hot Springs Inn* (rates: $26–29 double), with 50 excellent rooms, restaurant, swimming pool, east of town on US Highway 70 (624–4436); *Holiday Inn East* (rates $28 double), with 136 rooms, restaurant, cocktail lounge, heated pool, at 1125 East Grand (624–3321); *Majestic Hotel & Apartments* (rates: $24–33 double), with 348 good rooms and family units, dining room, cocktail lounge, heated pool, hot mineral baths, at Park and Central (623–5511); *Royale Vista Inn* (rates $27–32 double), with 210 excellent rooms and family units, dining room, cocktail lounge, heated pool, at 2204 Central Ave. (624–5551); *Velda Rose Towers* (rates: $30 double) with 200 excellent rooms and family units, restaurant, cocktail lounge, heated pool and saunas, tennis, at 309 Park Ave. (623–3311).

Lodges & Resorts

★★★*Buena Vista Resort at Hot Springs National Park*, is located on the shore of Lake Hamilton, surrounded by dense pine groves and with the Ouachita Mountains in view. Buena Vista has a heated pool, and paddleboats, pontoon boats, fishing boats, ski boats and water skis to rent on the waterfront. There is also a recreation room and a children's playground. Buena Vista has modern motel rooms for $19.50–24.50, (double occupancy), and living room/bedroom cabins for $19.50–21.50. One bedroom cottages are $20–30, two bedroom cottages are $27–39, and three bedroom cottages are $35–52. Cottages have the option of kitchenettes. There is a laundromat, and limited groceries are sold in the office. For more information write: Buena Vista Resort, Route 3, Box 175, Hot Springs National Park, Arkansas 71901 (501)525–1321.

★★★*DeGray State Park Lodgings* are situated on an island on Lake DeGray, in picturesque wooded mountain setting. The resort is near Hot Springs. DeGray State Park has a championship 18–hole golf course, two tennis courts, lake and pool swimming, scenic areas for hiking and bicycling, a gift shop, sailboats, houseboats, and a 132–slip marina with fishing boats. Fishing guide packages are available. The park has lodge accommodations in a rustic 96 room wilderness lodge, fashioned from redwood and stone. Meals, not included in rates, are available at the park's restaurant. Rates: (double occupancy) $24–29, depending on view. Children under 12 free. For further information contact: DeGray State Park Lodge, P.O. Box 375, Arkadelphia, AR 71923 (501)865–4591.

★★★*Mather Lodge at Petit Jean State Park*, is nestled between the Ozark and Ouachita Mountain Ranges. Hiking trails wind through 4,000 acres of woods, deep ravines, clear streams, springs, caves, and panoramic points. The park has 127 campsites, with water and electric hookups, and bath houses with hot and cold running water. There is a large picnic area, a fishing lake with a boat dock and paddle boats to rent, tennis courts, a swimming pool, and a children's playground. In the summer, there is an interpretive naturalists' program of guided nature walks, and evening programs, with slides and movies in the outdoor amphitheater. The lodge has 24 spacious guest rooms, 6 doubles with two double beds for $18 daily, and 18 single rooms for $16 daily. The Lodge restaurant serves generous country style meals to all park visitors. Private cabins, some with stone fireplaces are $17 daily and $102 weekly. Housekeeping cabins, air-conditioned with fully equipped kitchens are $22 daily and $132 weekly. Many of these have stone fireplaces. For more information write: Mather Lodge, Petit Jean State Park, Morrilton, AR 72110 (501)727–5431.

★★*Shorecrest Resort at Hot Springs National Park* on beautiful Lake Hamilton, has 25 modern air-conditioned cottages completely furnished with kitchenettes, on the lake front. The resort is situated on 5 acres of lakefront property, and has an open sandy beach, sheltered boat stalls, boat rentals, and outdoor pool. Cottage rates are $20 daily for an efficiency cottage during the summer season, and $14 off-season. Weekly rates are $120 summer season, and $80 past Labor Day. One bedroom cottages are $24 daily and $144 weekly in the summer, and $18 daily and $98 weekly after Labor Day. Two bedroom cottages are $35 daily and $120 weekly in the summer, and $25 daily and $150 weekly off season. For more information write: Shorecrest Resort, 230 Lakeland Drive, Hot Springs, AR 71901 (501)525–8113.

Ozark Mountains & National Forest

The Ozark National Forest embraces 1,103,000 acres of scenic mixed hardwood and pine forests, rivers, and spectacular limestone bluffs in the Ozark Highlands in northwestern Arkansas. Rugged backcountry trails and forest roads provide access to the major recreation areas and fish and game lands, including the Ozark and Boston mountains; Hurricane Creek Scenic Area; Illinois Bayou Bluffs; the streams, caves, lakes, and picturesque bluffs of the Blanchard Springs Recreation Area; the rugged Magazine Mountain Recreation Area; Upper Buffalo Wilderness at the headwaters of the river, surrounded by high rocky bluffs and canyons; and the renowned smallmouth bass waters of the Upper Buffalo, White, Mulberry, War Eagle, Big Piney, and Illinois rivers. The forest is a top-ranked hunting area for deer, wild turkey, red fox, raccoon, and squirrel.

Information Sources, Maps & Access

For detailed vacation travel and recreation information and a full-color *Ozark National Forest Map* (50¢) contact: Supervisor, Ozark National Forest, Box 340, Russellville, AR 72801 (501)968–2354. For information on the Buffalo National River, contact: Superintendent, Buffalo National River, P.O. Box 1173, Harrison, AR 72601 (501)741–5443. Guided backpacking and canoe trips on the river are provided by the Buffalo Outdoor Center, at Ponca (501)861–5590 and at Hasty (501)429–6433. A free *White River Trout Fishing Map* may be obtained from the Game & Fish Commission, State Capitol Mall, Little Rock, AR 72201. The waterproof *Bull Shoals Lake Contour Maps* (3 maps, $9), *Beaver Lake Contour Map* ($3), and *Norfork Lake Contour Map* ($3), showing hydrographics, man-made and national features, may be ordered from: Lakes Illustrated, Box 4854 GS, Springfield, MO 65804. The Ozark region is reached via US 65, 64, 62, and 71, and Interstate 40. Accommodations, supplies, guides, and outfitters are available at Ozark, Clarksville, Russellville, Harrison, Van Buren, Norfork, and Fayetteville.

Recreation Areas

Beaver Lake

The headwaters of the Upper White River rise in the Ozark National Forest and flow northward where the river's impounded waters form the

massive, sprawling Beaver Lake. The White flows out of Beaver Lake into Missouri, where it swings east through Table Rock Lake and then south back into Arkansas and Bull Shoals Lake. The clear, deep waters of 28,000–acre Beaver Lake, also fed by the top-ranked smallmouth bass waters of War Eagle Creek, hold trophy–sized largemouth bass, walleye, crappie, and landlocked striped bass in the 20–pound-and-over class. This beautiful lake, lined with sheer, towering limestone bluffs, has been the site of several major bass tournaments and has been a regular stop on the B.A.S.S. pro tour for several years. Beaver Lake also holds northern pike and giant rainbows in the frigid tail waters beneath the dam. Boat rentals, guides, and gear are available along the shoreline at Lost Bridge, Starkey, Rocky Branch, Prairie Creek, Horseshoe Bend, Hickory Creek, and War Eagle.

Buffalo National River

Arkansas's magnificent wild and scenic rivers offer some of the nation's finest canoeing and float fishing for smallmouth bass and trophy rainbow and brown trout. The famed Buffalo, a national wild and scenic river, is one of North America's great canoe routes; it flows east from its headwaters in the Ozark Mountains for 150 miles through lush forests, past towering spectacular 700–foot multicolored limestone bluffs, in a serpentine course characterized by numerous rapids, gravel bars, and gin-clear pools, to its confluence with the White River in the Sylamore district of the Ozark National Forest. The Buffalo offers top-ranked float fishing in a setting of great wilderness beauty for hard-hitting smallmouth bass up to trophy weights. Several primitive campsites are located along gravel bars on the river's twisting course, and maintained campgrounds, hiking trails, and rustic cabins, situated on high bluffs overlooking the river, are available at the Buffalo Point recreation area. Wilderness paddlers who plan to camp along the banks of the Buffalo should keep in mind that a heavy overnight rainfall can transform the river into a raging torrent. The headwaters of several other wildwater float streams are found in the Boston Mountains at 2,400 feet elevations in the Ozark National Forest in northwestern Arkansas, including the Big Piney (a 25–mile float), Illinois Bayou, and the Mulberry (a 55–mile float), which flow southward to their confluences with the mighty Arkansas River. These rugged, remote wilderness streams have an average gradient of 20 feet-per-mile and should be attempted only by experienced canoeists familiar with the challenges and joys of wilderness camping. Several renowned canoeing and float fishing streams flow northward from the Boston Divide, including the Upper White River (a 30–mile float) and the King (a 28–mile float); they all provide often spectacular fishing for explosive smallmouth bass. Crooked Creek, one of the South's top-ranked smallmouth streams, is a tributary of the White River and flows for 30 miles before coursing into underground caves along its lower reaches.

Norfork Lake & Little Red River

Famous Norfork Lake—located to the southeast of Bull Shoals on the North Fork River, a major tributary of the White, in the Ozark highlands—is considered by many fishermen as the nation's top largemouth bass lake. Norfork, with its 500 miles of shoreline surrounded by scenic wooded hills inhabited by deer and wild turkey, produces largemouth bass up to 12 pounds, smallmouths up to 6 pounds, and trophy-sized walleye, white bass, and crappie. The frigid, turbulent North Fork River below the dam holds rainbows in the 8– to 15–pound class. The U.S. Bureau of Sport, Fisheries, & Wildlife Federal Trout Hatchery—the largest in the U.S.—is located below the dam, and is responsible, along with the Arkansas Game & Fish Commission, for the excellence of White River country trout fishing. The bureau also operates a trout hatchery on the Little Red River, another tributary of the White, located just below the Greers Ferry Lake Dam. The turbulent, 30–mile, island-dotted, shoal-lined stretch of the Little Red below the dam is nationally renowned for its float fishing for trophy rainbow trout up to 15½ pounds. The major features of the river, including boat docks and fishing services, public access areas, roads, and the Cow, Ritchey, Winkley, Moss Dam, Scroncher, Mossy, and Dunham shoals are shown on the *Little Red River Map*, available free from the Game & Fish Commission (address above). The crystal-clear waters of the 40,000–acre Grass Ferry Lake provide excellent fishing for largemouth and smallmouth bass, walleye, and crappie. Lodging is available at luxurious lakeside resorts, or you can pitch your tent at one of the many campgrounds provided by the Corps of Engineers.

White River & Bull Shoals Lake

The White River, once famous for the quality of smallmouth bass fishing, has gained worldwide fame for its float fishing for giant rainbows and browns in the 70–mile stretch of cold, clear water below Bull Shoals Dam. The trophy waters of the White annually yield thousands of rainbows from 4 to 19 pounds and buckskin-flanked browns in the 4–to-25–pound range. The White, framed on the east from Buffalo Shoals to Sylamore by the beautiful Ozark National Forest lands, is best fished by floating using a johnboat equipped with a 9– or 10–horsepower motor. Camping in White River country is permitted in the largely undeveloped public access areas and along the scenic gravel bars. Be sure to guard against quick river rises and to check locally for the power-generating schedule of the Bull Shoals Dam. When the dam is not generating, the water level drops rapidly, making it difficult to get boats upstream over shoals, where the current is deceptively swift. Wading on the White is limited and can be extremely dangerous on this deep "big-water" river. The crystal-clear waters of massive Bull Shoals Lake, with its sprawling cove-indented 1,000 miles of shoreline surrounded by the hardwood and pine-clad hills of the Arkansas-Missouri Ozarks, is one of the nation's top-ranked trophy largemouth bass waters. Bull Shoals annually produces thousands of lunker "bucketmouth" bass in the 4–to-11–pound class, and holds rainbows up to 8 pounds, and smallmouth bass, walleye, crappie, and spotted bass up to record weights. The lake reaches depths of 200 feet near the Bull Shoals Dam—the fifth-largest concrete dam in the United States. Specific information about boat rentals, and fishing guides may be obtained by writing: Bull Shoals Lake, White River Assn., P.O. Box 311, Bull Shoals 72619.

Gateways & Accommodations

Fayetteville

(Pop. 31,000, zip 72701; area code 501) noted for its spring and fall scenery, is a famous resort area in the Ozarks. The healthful climate and proximity to the mountains provides much in the way of recreational activities. There are several lakes and streams for boating, fishing, swimming—Lake Wedington, Lake Sequoyah, and Beaver Lake among them—as well as grounds for picnicking, cabins, and lodges. An important location during the Civil War and an educational center today, there is also much in the way of museums and cultural activities. Accommodations: *Holiday Inn* (rates: $24–28 double), with 165 excellent rooms and family units, restaurant and coffeeshop, kennel, putting green, at 2402 North College Ave. (443–4323); *Ramada Inn* (rates: $28–32), with 120 excellent rooms, restaurant, cocktail lounge, heated pool, putting green, at 3901 North College Ave. (443–3431).

Harrison

(Pop. 7,000; zip 72601; area code 501) is located in one of the most scenic areas in Arkansas. It is the site of a magnificent, rustic, wild and beautiful resort area—and the highway, running south of the town and crossing two national forests, is especially noted for its outstanding views. An historical railroad town for the Missouri and Arkansas Railroads in the late 1800s, it is now the site of Dogpatch, USA—recreating Al Capp's comic strip about life in the Ozarks. The tourist village offers railroad and stagecoach rides, and a tour of an underground cave with crystal formations. There are two other such caves in the area—Hurricane River and Diamond Cave—both with unusual formations, and an underground river. The Bull Shoals Lake area offers superb fishing, boating, and swimming. The Northwest Arkansas Bluegrass Music Festival is held here, as well as an annual rodeo, fair and livestock show. There are also historical museums and a Heritage Center—a reconstructed village depicting frontier life. Accommodations: *Holiday Inn* (rates: $30 double), with 120 excellent rooms and family units, restaurant, indoor heated pool and sauna, just north of town on US Highway 65B (741–2391); *Ramada Inn* (rates $27–32 double), with 100 excellent rooms and family units, restaurant and coffeeshop, heated pool, one mile north of town on US Highway 65B (741–7611).

Mountain Home

(Pop. 5,000; zip 72653; area code 501) is situated on a high plateau between the North Fork and White Rivers and between Bull Shoals Lake and Lake Norfork—two of Arkansas' largest lakes. The famous Norfork National Fish Hatchery is located nearby on Arkansas Highway 177. It serves as an outfitting center for week-long float trips and excellent facilities are available for all water sports. Accommodations: *Best Western Carriage Inn* (rates: $25–26 double), with 82 good rooms, restaurant and heated pool, east of town on US Highway 62 (425–6001); *Holiday Inn* (rates: $25–27 double), with 100 excellent rooms, restaurant, cocktail lounge, swimming pool, south of town on US Highway 62 (425–5101).

Russellville

(Pop. 12,000; zip 72801; area code 501), the headquarters for the Ozark National Forest, is located on Arkansas Highway 7—the winding scenic route which is considered to be the most beautiful

drive in the state. Mt. Nebo State Park offers camping, tennis, swimming, cabins, and miles of scenic views. Dardanelle Lake has fishing, boating, hunting grounds as well as picnicking and camping. There is a wildlife refuge in the area and national forest hiking and nature trails—with rock formations, underground caverns, natural bridges and gorges and waterfalls. There are five lakes in the forest itself and facilities for camping. Nimrod Lake, nearby, also offers water activities. Accommodations: *Holiday Inn* (rates: $28 double), with 120 excellent rooms, restaurant, cocktail lounge, heated pool north of town on Arkansas Highway 7 at the junction of Interstate 40 (968–4300).

Lodges & Resorts

★★★*Bay Breeze Resort at Bull Shoals Lake* will arrange guided fishing trips for guests, and float trips down the White River, canoe trips, and night fishing on pontoon boats by lantern light. Bay Breeze has a large pool, patio, and picnic areas with barbecue grills. Kids will enjoy the large outdoor playground, and free pony rides and horseback riding. Nearby are the breathtaking Blanchard Springs Caverns, Mountain Village recreated from the 1890's, and the Ozark Tower, offering unparalleled views of the limestone bluffs and green valleys of the ancient Ozark mountain range. Spacious, modern motel rooms are available for $20 per day, $28 with three double beds, and $29 with three double beds and refrigerator. All have wall-to-wall carpeting and color TV. Family housekeeping units with kitchens are $24, two units with shared kitchen is $43 per day, and suites with three double beds, and kitchen is $32 per day. Bay Breeze also offers a special guided fishing weekend on the White River in July and August. The rate for two is $154 and includes expert guide, boat, motor gas, lunch, and three nights' lodging. For more information write: Bay Breeze Resort Motel, Box 185, Lakeview, AR (501)431–5261.

★★★*Blue Paradise Resort on Lake Norfork* is secluded among 35 acres of tall pines and cedars. Nearby are three of the most scenic float rivers in the nation: the White River, Crooked Creek, and the Buffalo National River. Blue Paradise will arrange float trips and professional fishing guides at guests' request. The Blue Paradise Marina rents outboards and pleasure boats. There is also an open sand beach for swimming, waterskiing and scuba-diving, a covered and lighted boat dock, a complete bait and tackle shop, guest laundromat, and recreation room. The resort also has a large outdoor pool with spacious sundecks. Deluxe cottages, with air-conditioning, TV's, private baths and fully equipped kitchens dot the lakeshore. Rates include the use of a 14′ aluminum boat or a covered stall for private boats. Rates are $20–45 daily, depending on the size of the cottage. The Blue Paradise Restaurant specializes in southern country cooking in a pleasant informal atmosphere. The resort offers a variety of fishing packages, weekend outings and mid-week specials. For details, write: Ralph and Norma Kubik, Blue Paradise Resort, P.O. Box 658, Mountain Home, Arkansas 72653; (501)492–5113.

★★★*Crow-Barnes Resort* overlooks Bull Shoals Lake in the heart of the Ozark Mountains. In addition to the beautiful scenery the lake and river make almost any water activity possible here. Enjoy lake fishing for rainbow trout, bass, walleye, pike, channel catfish, crappie. Trophy-size trout can be caught in the nearby White River. Bull Shoals Lake offers swimming, scuba diving and water skiing. There's floating on the exciting Buffalo National River. Crow–Barnes will happily make arrangements for your fishing or float trip on the White River. Party barges and pontoon boats are also available. On shore enjoy the resort's tennis court and swimming pool. Accommodations include rooms with phones, color TV and wall-to-wall carpeting. There are also housekeeping units and sleeping rooms and suites available. Meals are available in the family style dining room. Rates: rooms without kitchenettes $20–47.50 per day, with kitchenette $23–33 daily. Suites with lakeview, two baths and living room $105 per day. For further information contact: Crow-Barnes Resort, Bull Shoals, AR 72619 (501)445–4242.

★★★*Gaston's White River Resort* is a superb year-round resort tucked into the Arkansas Ozarks, along the beautiful White River. The main pastime at Gaston's is fishing and the resort has boats, motors and licensed guides. There are also bass fishing trips on Bull Shoals Lake. Gaston's will handle all arrangements for float trips down the White River, Buffalo River, or Crooked Creek. You can schedule trips for half or full day, or overnight excursions with camping along the river. The resort also has a swimming pool, tennis courts, playground for the youngsters, and a nearby golf course. And Gaston's Restaurant overlooking the river is one of the largest in the area. Accommodations include cottages, many with wood-burning fireplaces, some of which have kitchens furnished for housekeeping and some with beverage refrigerators. Rates for double occupancy, about $30 per day for cottage with two double beds. All cottages are air-conditioned, modern and comfortably furnished. For more information, contact: Gaston's White River Resort, Lakeview, AR 72642 (501)421–5202.

★★★*Indian Rock Resort* is a year-round resort, located on 40,000–acre Greers Ferry Lake, which meanders through the Ozark mountains. The lake has a large marina open year-round offering rental for skiing, sailing, fishing boats, and party barges. All water sports can be enjoyed on the lake. Nature enthusiasts flock to the area to enjoy the fresh air, Sugar Loaf Mountain, 400 miles of shoreline, and fascinating Indian Rock Cave. The resort has a health spa under way, with an indoor swimming pool and professional staff. There are ten, lighted, all weather tennis courts with a pro shop and instruction. There's an 18–hole championship golf course encompassing four lakes, bubbling mountain streams, and tall pines. There is a pro shop and professional instruction available. In addition, the resort has horseback riding, hiking trails, archery-skeet-pistol ranges, a youth recreation center, two swimming pools and organized sports. Accommodations are two bedroom condominums, one and two bedroom villas and single motel type units. Condominiums and villas have spacious living and dining areas with fully equipped kitchens. The resort operates on the European plan, and meals are available at the resort's Wild Boar restaurant. There is a mall complete with supermarket featuring fresh pastries, meats and produce. Dancing and seasonal entertainment are provided in the resort's Racquet Club. Rates: Guest house, for 4 people $60, for 6 people $85. Lakewood Villa for 2 people $38–63, for 4 people in a two–bedroom suite $111. Condominiums $55–69 per night. Special group rates are available. For further information contact: Director of Marketing, Indian Rock Resort at Fairfield Bay, P.O. Box 3375, Little Rock, Arkansas 72203 or call collect in Arkansas (501)664–6108), outside of Arkansas call toll free (1–800)643–8826.

★★★*Lakefront Lodge* overlooks spectacular Greers Ferry Lake in the Ozarks. Situated between Devil's Fork and Middle Fork in prime fishing country, Lakefront Lodge has a modern boat launching ramp, boats and motors to rent, and a complete guide service to show anglers the best fishing spots on the lake. The Lakefront Restaurant serves fresh seafood, hearty steaks and a variety of home-made Italian dishes in a spectacular setting overlooking the lake. All the modern motel rooms are spacious, with air-conditioning, TV, and electric heat. Rates are $16.50–18.50 daily and $99–111 weekly. Many rooms are also available with kitchenetts for $19 daily, $114

weekly. Efficiency rooms with full kitchens, are $22 daily and $132 weekly. Rates are slightly lower for October 1–February 28. For more information write: Lakefront Lodge and Restaurant, P.O. Box 5, Edgemont, AR 72044; (501)723–4243.

★★★*Narrows Inn & Marina at Greers Ferry Lake* is nestled on both shores of the narrows, a slim body of water connecting the east, north and south ends of this vast lake. Narrows marina has a fully equipped waterski and scuba shop, and a complete line of pontoon boats, ski boats, fishing boats and high performance jet ski boats. Fishermen will appreciate the variety of bait and tackle sold at the dock shop, and Narrows marina offers professional guide service. In addition, there are three hotels providing a variety of accommodations, a large campground, sundecks, a swimming pool, and a private Yacht Club with evening entertainment. The Narrows family style restaurant specializes in southern home cooking. The Narrows Inn and Restaurant is nestled just below the Narrows bridge and offers 40 spacious rooms with or without kitchenettes. Rates are $20–26.50 for a double room. On the other shore, the Narrows Motel opens from April 1 through Labor Day. Motel rooms are $15–18 for a double room. Double rooms with kitchenettes are $17.50–19.50. The Dollar Motel is more secluded, nestled on a quiet bank between the Narrows and Edgemont Bridges. Motel rooms are available for $17–20 double. Double rooms with kitchenettes are 19.50–22. Two bedroom cottages with fully-equipped modern kitchens are $26.50 for two people. For more information write: Narrows Motels, Inc., P.O. Box 337, Greers Ferry, AR 72067 (501)825–6246.

★★★*The Ozark Folk Center,* is a living museum of Ozark folk culture, where the pioneer crafts, lore and music of the people are displayed in a natural setting. The Ozark Folk Center is composed of 50 buildings of native stone and cedar, spread over 915 mountainous acres. The Craft Forum displays twenty-four cabin crafts such as wood carving, basket making, pottery, musical instrument making, spinning, weaving, dying, and blacksmithing. Crafts demonstrated and other authentic Ozark crafts are sold in the center's gift shop. The Ozark Folk Center includes a 1,050 seat auditorium, presenting mountain music at its finest, where Stone County musicians celebrate the Ozarks in tunes that are native to the hills on dulcimers, auto harps, banjos, fiddles, guitars and mandolins. The Annual Arkansas Folk Festival, old time guitar picking contests, fiddlers' jamborees, and the southern music banjo contest highlight the year. The Ozark Center Restaurant serves traditional specialties such as catfish, ham and beans, hot homemade breads and red-eye gravy, with mountain hospitality. Lodging, in 30 octagon shaped duplex units, is near the crafts and music centers. The lodge features a swimming pool, recreation room, and 160-seat conference center, with folk lore library. For rates and information write: Ozark Folk Center Lodge, Mountain View, AR 72560 (501)269–3871.

★★★*Red Apple Inn at Greers Ferry Lake* offers golf, fishing, swimming, sailing, waterskiing, and tennis, on a terraced mountain slope overlooking the lake. Private rooms are available, some with fireplaces. Luxurious suites, and plush two-and-three-bedroom condominiums with fully equipped modern kitchens and private baths overlook the Country Club. There is a complete golf pro-shop on the championship course, kennel, poolside pavilion and cocktail lounge, and two spacious dining rooms in the country club serving a variety of steaks and fresh seafood daily. Private rooms are $32–55 daily. Two bedroom condominiums are $65 daily, three bedroom condominiums are $85 daily. For more information write The Red Apple Inn, Eden Isle, Heber Springs, AR 72543 (501)362–3111.

★★★★*Stetson's Fishing Resort on the White River* offers excellent trout fishing year-round (closed Dec. 1–March 1). They'll provide a professional guide who will help navigate the boat, guide you to the best areas, and even prepare the tackle, bait, and clean the fish. Licenses are available at the tackle shop, along with the rest of the gear. Trout over 19 lbs. have been caught in this area. But that's not the only thing to do—there's a large pool with lots of deck space for sunning, well lighted at night for a midnight dip. The area offers the beauty of the Ozarks, as well as spots like Bull Shoals Dam and Caverns, Dogpatch USA, Federal Trout Hatchery, and the Ozark Folk Center. The cottages at the resort are comfortable, completely furnished, with heat and air-conditioning, a TV and complete kitchenette. Meals are also provided at the lodge. Cottages accommodate up to eight people and start at $16 per day up to $35. No pets please. Your hosts are Stu and Audrey Stetson and you can reach them at (501)453–2523 or by writing Stetson's Fishing Resort, Route A, Flippin, AR 72634.

Travel Services

Miller's Float Service organizes fishing trips, camping trips, and boat outings along the White River. Boat trips are in flat-bottom john boats, with guides for fishermen. Overnight camp trips last anywhere from 2–8 days and involve boating down the river during the day, and camping out in tents, tarps, cots, sleeping bags and mattresses provided by Miller's Service. All outdoor cooking equipment also provided. They also have trips on the rugged Buffalo River. Rates: one-day float trip for two, $90; overnight camp trips for two, $155 per day. For more information, contact: Miller's Float & Fishing Service, P.O. Box 277, Cotter, AR (501)435–6313.

CALIFORNIA

Introduction

California, bordered on the north by Oregon, on the east by Nevada and the Colorado River, on the south by Mexico's Baja Peninsula, and on the west by the warm currents of the Pacific and giant redwood forests, is a land of great contrasts, with the highest and lowest areas in the contiguous United States: Mt. Whitney rises to 14,494 feet, and a few miles away Death Valley drops to 282 feet below sea level. Within the state can be found all of the world's climatic zones but one—the tropical. Southern California is a vast desert panorama framed by rugged, sparsely vegetated mountains. To the northeast the great arc of the High Sierra Crest forms a continuous strip of sparkling blue alpine lakes, towering snowcapped peaks, granite pinnacles, and volcanic domes, traversed by the John Muir Trail, which stretches through some of the most stunning wilderness camping and alpine fishing country in North America, from Yosemite Valley south to the massive group of 14,000–foot peaks dominated by Mt. Whitney at the headwaters of the Kings and Kern rivers. The eastern slopes of the Sierras, among the most precipitous in the country, plunge into beautiful valleys, where some of the nation's top trout streams, including the Owens River and Hot Creek, are fed by the high snowfields. The famous Mother Lode gold rush country of the Sierra foothills, dotted by ghost towns and abandoned mines, was immortalized by the forty-niners and Mark Twain's *Roughing It*.

Several of the nation's legendary fishing, hunting, and wilderness camping areas are found within the Golden State's 158,693 square miles, including beautiful Lake Tahoe at 6,225–feet elevation, Desolation Valley, the ancient Bristlecone Pine Forest, John Muir Wilderness, the steelhead waters of the Klamath River, the Yosemite Valley and backcountry, Lassen Volcanic Highlands and the Caribou and Thousand Lakes wilderness areas, Hat Creek trophy trout waters, huge Lake Shasta, the classic fly-fishing waters of the McCloud River, the scenic Salmon-Trinity Alps, the Wild Middle Fork of the Feather River, and Eagle Lake, the "lake that time forgot." The virgin California wilderness and the High Sierras—the "Range of Light"—were first explored in 1845 by Captain John C. Frémont, followed by the fur trader and explorer Jedediah Smith and the Walker Expedition.

Accommodations & Travel Information

Major California vacation lodges, alpine ski resorts, guest ranches, inns, and motels are listed and described in the "Vacation/Lodging Guide" which follows. For detailed information on vacation travel and outdoor recreation, write or call the information offices of the national park and forest headquarters listed in the following section.

Information & Services

For fishing and hunting information, regulations, license and permit information, and hunting and wildlife management area maps, write: California Dept. of Fish & Game, Resources Bldg., 1416 Ninth Street, Sacramento 95814. The high-country wilderness fisherman will find the free publication *Where to Find California's Golden Trout* of interest. To obtain a copy, write to the Fish & Game Dept. and be sure to enclose a self-addressed, stamped, legal-size envelope. A wealth of useful Dept. of Fish & Game guides and maps may be obtained from: Office of Procurement, Documents Section, P.O. Box 20191, Sacramento 95820. The informative booklets *Offshore Fishes* and *Inshore Fishes* are available from the Documents Section for 70¢ each. Angler's Guides to *Striped Bass, Klamath River* and *Salmon and Steelhead* and Ocean Fishing

Maps for *Del Norte, Humboldt and Mendocino Counties, Marin and Sonoma Counties, San Francisco, San Mateo and Santa Cruz Counties,* and *Monterey and San Luis Obispo Counties* may be obtained from the Documents Section for 40¢ each. The following wildlife leaflets are available from the Documents Section free upon request: *Antelope, Bear, Bighorn Sheep, Canada Goose, Golden Trout, Striped Bass, Condor, Deer, Elk, Golden Eagle, Wolverine, Yellowtail, Wild Turkey, and Wood Duck.* Write to Chronicle Books, 54 Mint St., San Francisco 94119, for the following California Fishing Guides: *Trinity River, Klamath River, Shasta Lake, California Steelhead, California Trout, Lake Berryessa, San Diego Bass Lakes,* and *North Sierra Trout,* $1.95 each.

A complete guide to the *Anadromous Fishes of California* is available for 70¢ from: Office of Procurement, Documents Section, General Services Agency, P.O. Box 20191, Sacramento 95820. The 109–page book describes the steelhead trout and the various families and species of fish in California that migrate from salt or brackish water upstream to fresh water to spawn. It includes pictures of the individual species and descriptions of distinguishing characteristics, distribution, habits, and importance, as well as small distribution maps for each fish.

Another very helpful source of information is the *Salmon and Steelhead Fishing Map* (40¢) available from the same address. The large map is on a scale of 20 miles to 1 inch and shows streams that are open to steelhead fishing in the winter and a very few others where the runs start before the end of summer trout season (October 31). It also shows areas of ocean fishing for salmon. Information with the map describes the times of runs on the various rivers throughout the state and the areas where fishing is most successful. It describes the main species taken in the state and tells how to distinguish them.

Useful descriptions of golden trout areas are provided in the leaflet *Golden Trout,* available free from: Office of Procurement, Documents Section, P.O. Box 20191, Sacramento 95820. For detailed lake and fishing info, write: Dept. of Fish & Game, 9th & 0 Streets, Sacramento 95814, and ask for the free booklet *Golden Trout of the High Sierra.*

Detailed *Angler's Guides* with maps showing established horse trails, unmarked trails, major lakes and streams, and elevations are available for 40¢ each for Upper Bishop Creek, French Canyon, Humphreys Basin, Bear Creek Area, Granite Creek Area, and Mono Creek Area. Write: Office of Procurement, Documents Section, P.O. Box 20191, Sacramento 95820.

The indispensable *Starr's Guide to the John Muir Trail and the High Sierra Region* ($3.95, 156 pp.) published by Sierra Club Books, 530 Bush St., San Francisco 94108, contains detailed descriptions of the High Sierra trails and wild areas.

A useful *List of Licensed Fishing & Big-Game Hunting Guides* may be obtained by writing: Dept. of Fish & Game, 1416 Ninth St., Sacramento 95814. For listings of pack trip and saddle stock outfitters, write: *High Sierra Packers Association, Eastern Unit,* Box 147, Bishop 93514 or *High Sierra Packers Association, Western Unit,* P.O. Box 123, Madera 93637.

O.A.R.S., Inc., P.O. Box 67, Angels Camp 95222, is a top-notched outfitter offering a full line of wild-river trips in California and the western United States, including such widely diverse rivers as the San Juan, Dolores, Salmon, Rogue, and Tuolumne, in addition to the Colorado River trip it runs in cooperation with Mountain Travel Inc. Write for their free brochure and trip schedule. *Outdoors Unlimited,* 2500 5th Ave., Sacramento 95818, runs a number of rivers in the state. *River Adventures West,* P.O. Box 5219, Santa

Monica 90405, leads float trips on the Stanislaus, Tuolumne, American, and East Carson rivers. *Martin's River Expeditions*, 1127 Rock Springs Hollow, Escondido 92026, include a run down Kings River in Kings Canyon and Sierra National forests. *River Rat Raft Rentals*, 5929 Fair Oaks Blvd., Carmichael 95608, runs the American River exclusively. *Outdoor Adventures* include paddle trips on the American, Stanislaus, East Carson, Klamath, and Eel rivers. Write to 21666 Arbor Ct., Hayward 94541. *Wilderness Water Ways, Inc.*, 33 Canyon Lake Dr., Port Costs 94569, offers float trips on a variety of California's rivers. *Wilderness World*, 1342 Jewell Ave., Pacific Grove 93950, offers float trips on California waterways, as well as a 5–day boatman's training course on the Stanislaus or the Rogue. *Wilderness Expeditions Inc.*, 1127 Rock Springs Hollow, Escondido 92026, offers guided trips on the Kings River and the Lower Colorado.

The Pacific Crest National Scenic Trail, California is a free brochure and map of the trail available from: U.S. Forest Service, Division of Information and Education, Room 531, 630 Sansome St., San Francisco 94111. The map describes the trail briefly, gives information on permits and preparation, and includes addresses for a number of sources of more detailed information. Those who plan to hike portions of the trail in California may be interested in *The Pacific Crest Trail Volume 1: California*, a detailed 287–page guide to the trail with a 16–page supplement, 26 photos, and 127 two-color topographic maps ($4.95) published by Wilderness Press, 2440 Bancroft Way, Berkeley 94704. A similar book describing the trail through Washington and Oregon, *The Pacific Crest Trail Volume 2: Oregon & Washington*, is available from the same address. To gain a historical perspective of the trail, write for the free book *Journey: Being an Historical Adventure through the Lands of the Pacific Crest Trail* from: U.S. Forest Service Office, California Region, 630 Sansome St., San Francisco 94111. A free 68-page booklet, *Pacific Crest National Scenic Trail*, which contains a set of maps showing the California portion of the trail and an index sheet to U.S. Geological Survey quadrangle maps of the route, is available at the same address.

A *Guide to the California State Park System* is available from: California Dept. of Parks & Recreation, P.O. Box 2390, Sacramento 95811.

To the Wilderness Traveler is another useful free publication of the California Region Office, U.S. Forest Service, Information Office, 630 Sansome St., San Francisco, CA 94111. This brochure describes the 4,500 miles of roadless areas in the state wilderness areas and the trails through them, gives information on backpacking and traveling with stock, and lists regulations for these areas. The map in the brochure marks the wilderness areas in national parks and forests and keys the location of ranger stations throughout the state, as well as national forest and national park headquarters. It also keys the U.S. Geological Survey topographic quadrangle maps in backcountry areas. A shorter pamphlet from the same office, entitled the *Wilderness Traveler*, gives travel advice, horse and pack stock information, and specific suggestions for waste disposal and firebuilding in the wilderness, along with information about getting a wilderness permit. A separate pamphlet (also free), *California Campfire Rules*, is also available from the California Region Office.

Highways & Maps

A free *California Highway Map* showing the Golden State's recreation and scenic highways, interstate and federal highways, points of interest, recreation area campgrounds, scheduled airline stops, ski areas, boat ramps, time-zone boundaries, major mountain roads, national forests and parks, and cities and towns may be obtained by writing: California Chamber of Commerce, 455 Capitol Mall, Sacramento 94814.

Death Valley National Monument

The pale, brush-spotted floor of Death Valley, flanked on the west by the tawny Panamint Range and on the east by the Grapevine, Funeral and Black mountains, presents a harsh and awesome environment to the wilderness traveler. The plants of this desert land are unique; they have evolved specialized means of obtaining and preserving precious water, because less than 2 inches of rain fall here yearly and daytime temperatures reach 120 degrees. The small animals of the area have adapted to a life with little water, while the larger ones seek it out or obtain it from the bodies of the animals on which they prey.

Strangely, many men inhabited this wilderness before our time and left their mark on it. Prehistoric hunters and gatherers roamed the desert and left trails, rock drawings, and campsites. The Panamint Indians lived here when the forty-niners arrived in search of precious metals. But the settlements were short-lived, and today the permanent population is negligible.

Death Valley National Monument covers about 3,000 square miles along the central portion of the state's eastern border. The monument encompasses dunes, salt flats, colorful canyons, and desert mountains that vary from 200 feet below sea level to 11,329 feet. The four campgrounds in the monument are Furnace Creek, Grapevine, Stovepipe Wells, and Wildrose Canyon.

If you decide to camp here, remember that the desert is an untamed wilderness. Never travel alone, and always tell someone where you are going and when you expect to return. Watch for flash floods when storms threaten. Carry water for you and your car. The extremely hot months—May through October—are only for the hardy. The monument is especially beautiful in early spring, when colorful desert flowers burst into bloom.

Within Death Valley are the ruins of the old Harmony Borax works, founded in 1802. The refined borax was hauled by the famous mule teams, each of 12 to 20 mules guided by a check line 125 feet long, through Wingate Pass to Mojave, some 160 miles distant.

The Death Valley Visitor Center is at Furnace Creek and offers exhibits, guided walks, and self-guided auto tours.

VACATION/ LODGING GUIDE

Information Sources, Maps & Access

A *Death Valley National Monument* brochure describing its major features, accommodations and services, access, regulations, and trips through it is available free from: Supervisor, Death Valley Monument, Death Valley 92328 (714)786–2331. The brochure includes a map on a scale of 10 miles to 1 inch which keys the locations of campgrounds, secondary campgrounds, roads, jeep trails, and foot trails. Another brochure, *Camping in Death Valley*, describes bus service from Las Vegas to the monument, periods of heavy visitations, commercial services, and facilities, elevation, and location of campsites. It is available from: Death Valley Natural History Association, Inc., P.O. Box 188, Death Valley 92328. This ogranization also publishes a complete bibliography of books and maps about the area. Ask for its free list of publications. The U.S. Geological Survey publishes a full-color *Death Valley National Monument & Vicinity Topographic Map*. It is 24 × 37 inches with a scale of 1:250,000, costs $2, and may be ordered from: Distribution Branch, U.S. Geological Survey, Federal Center, Denver, CO 80225.

Death Valley is reached via U.S. 95 and California 190 and 127 off Interstate 15.

Lodges & Inns

★★★★*Furnace Creek Inn and Ranch Resort* is a luxurious, sprawling Spanish-style villa located atop a mesa in Death Valley. A green and spacious oasis surrounded by desert landmarks, the resort offers a full gamut of outdoor activities, including tennis on professional courts (floodlit for night games), guided horseback trips through the valley, golf on a beautiful 18–hole course, and swimming in the enormous spring-fed pool. Accommodations range from handsome, rustic cabins to elegant rooms at the inn, many with spectacular desert views. All guest accommodations are air-conditioned. For dining and entertainment, there are the Oasis Supper Club, a patio steak house, cafeteria, coffee shop, and cocktail lounge. Daily rates for cabins: $28–42, depending on the location. Furnace Creek Inn rooms are $80–98 daily, including breakfast and dinner. The inn is open from November 1 to April 30. During the summer months, limited cabin accommodations are available at reduced rates. For further information write: Furnace Creek Inn and Ranch, Death Valley, CA 92328 (phone toll-free (800)227–4700 or within California (800)662–0838).

★★★*Stove Pipe Wells Village*, an attractive resort exactly at sea level in the heart of Death Valley, is surrounded by unusual desert scenery and natural marvels of the Death Valley National Monument. Winter is the preferred season here, when lots of sunshine, pleasantly warm temperature, and low humidity provide an ideal climate for sight-seeing or resort living. The village has a total of 79 guest units, ranging from luxury suites to modern motel units. The Old West–style Badwater Saloon and three dining rooms offer draft beer, cocktails, and fine cuisine in warm and inviting settings. A reconstructed mine shaft, lighted by lanterns, connects the saloon and dining areas. Other creature comforts include a well-stocked general store and service station, a landing strip adjacent to the village, a heated mineral-water swimming pool, and evening entertainment, such as movies and illustrated talks by park rangers. Close at hand are Mosaic Canyon, the Devil's Cornfield, and the original Stovepipe Well, a water hole some 20 miles from the nearest water supply. Other Death Valley points of interest are easily accessible by car. For complete information and rates write: Stove Pipe Wells Village, Death Valley, CA 92328 (phone—ask operator for Stove Pipe Wells toll station #1 through San Bernardino).

High Sierras—Eldorado National Forest & the Gold Rush Country

The Eldorado National Forest encompasses 700,000 acres, from the upper foothill country near Georgetown, extending through the dense sugar pine and white and red fir forests of the Crystal Basin, to the rugged granite slopes and snowcapped peaks of the Sierra Crest and Lake Tahoe. The Eldorado territory (Eldorado means "gilded one") was explored in 1827 by Jedediah Smith, who camped along the banks of the American River. The area encompassed within the Lake Tahoe basin was explored in the winter of 1843–44, when John Frémont and Kit Carson crossed the Sierra and were the first white men to see Lake Tahoe, described, years later by Mark Twain in *Roughing It*, as ". . . a noble sheet of blue water . . . walled in by a rim of snow-clad peaks that towered aloft full 3,000 feet higher still. As it lay there with the shadows of the mountains brilliantly photographed upon its still surface . . . down through . . . these great depths, the water was not merely transparent, but dazzling, brilliantly so; we could see trout by the thousands winging about in the emptiness under us." The forest embraces a major portion of the legendary Mother Lode—a long narrow strip seamed and laced with gold stretching for 120 miles in the Sierra foothills. Ghost towns, abandoned mines, and romantic place-names such as Placerville, Rough and Ready, Sutter Creek, Shirt Tail Canyon, Angels Camp, Sailors' Slide, Spanish Dry Diggins, and Dutch Flat are the legacy

of the great gold rush and the hundreds of mining camps and thousands of adventurers and prospectors who invaded the territory in 1849, preserved in the stories of Bret Harte and Mark Twain.

Information Sources, Maps & Access

Additional information and a full-color *Eldorado National Forest Recreation Map* (50¢) may be obtained by writing: Forest Supervisor, Eldorado National Forest, 100 Forni Road, Placerville 95667 (916)622–5061.

Fishing, packhorse, and trail information, wilderness permits, and a free *Desolation Wilderness Map* can be obtained by writing: Pacific Ranger Station, Pollock Pines 95726 (916)644–2348 or Lake Tahoe Basin Management Unit, Box 8465, 1052 Tata Lane, South Lake Tahoe 95731 (916)541–1130. The free map shows all natural features, trails, pack stations, recreation sites, boat-launching ramps, ski areas, and resorts. *Desolation Wilderness* ($3.95, 256 pp., with 26 photos, 19 drawings, and 23 maps) by Robert S. Wood describes over 200 miles of trail and 140 trout streams and lakes. This indispensable quide, published by Wilderness Press, 2440 Bancroft Way, Berkeley 94704, contains an up-to-date index of overused and underused places and an Angling Index that helps the backpacker to plan his trip. Wilderness Press also publishes a *Desolation Wilderness Trail Map* (75¢, 19¼ × 22¼ inches), which includes a trip-planning guide with specifics and remarks on the area's 27 major trails. Guided ski tours, orienteering, camping, and survival courses in the Desolation Wilderness are conducted by *Sugar House West*, Box 8135, South Lake Tahoe 95731 (916)541–6811.

Information concerning wilderness permits, trails, and packers and a free *Mokelumne Wilderness Map* showing trails, camps, recreation sites, trailpoints, ranger stations, and pack stations may be obtained by writing: Amador Ranger Station, P.O. Box 1327, Jackson 95642 (209)223–1623; Lumberyard Ranger Station, Highway 88, Pioneer 95666; Arnold Ranger Station, Highway 4, Arnold 95223; Alpine Station, Bear Valley (209)753–2811. The *Silver Lake Guide* by J. R. Groden describes the Mokelumne Wilderness area, the least-used portion of the Tahoe-Yosemite Trail, where it runs along the giant 3,000–foot-deep canyon of the North Fork of the Mokelumne River. This guidebook costs $2.95 from Wilderness Press, 2440 Bancroft Way, Berkeley 94704.

Wilderness Press also publishes two useful guides to the region: *Sierra North* ($4.95) covers the Sierra from Desolation Wilderness south to the Mono Divide, and *The Tahoe-Yosemite Trail* ($4.95) covers this 180–mile mountain route from Meeks Bay at Lake Tahoe to Tuolumne Meadows in Yosemite National Park.

Major Routes to the Eldorado National Forest include Interstate 80 and U.S. Highways 50 and 395 and the scenic Carson Pass Highway 88—the route of the Frémont expedition of 1844. Lodging, supplies, boat rentals, guides, and outfitters are available at Placerville, Pollock Pines, Markleeville, South Lake Tahoe, Camino, Eldorado, Coloma, Georgetown, Foresthill, Silver Lake, Caples Lake, Fallen Leaf, Meeks Bay, and Loon Lake.

Recreation Areas

Desolation Wilderness

The Desolation Wilderness is the northernmost of the High Sierra wilderness areas, embracing 63,469 acres due west of Lake Tahoe. Hundreds of forest lakes lie beneath the high glaciated peaks in the Tahoe Basin, at elevations ranging from 6,500 to 10,000 feet, at the headwaters of the picturesque Rubicon River, a top-ranked fly-fishing trout stream. Rockbound and Desolation valleys lie between the main crest of the Sierra Range to the east and the summits of the Crystal Range to the west. Pyramid Peak dominates a group of four high summits to the south. Over 75 miles of trails provide access through the forests, valleys, and alpine meadows and over high mountain passes to the lake country. The major trails are the Rockbound National Scenic Trail and the Tahoe-Yosemite segment of the Pacific Crest Trail, which passes Lake Aloha, Pyramid Peak, Echo Lake, and on to Carson Pass, through the lake country, and into the Mokelumne Wilderness.

Kirkwood Meadows & Lake Tahoe Area

Eldorado has 5 campgrounds exclusively for groups, over 1,260 improved single-family camp units, and 6 boat-launching ramps. The Crystal Basin, located just west of Desolation Valley, and Lake Tahoe areas receive heavy use. The forest is host to almost half a million skiers annually in the Freel Peak, Stevens Peak, Round Top, Thimble Peak, and Kirkwood Meadows areas.

Mokelumne Wilderness

The 50,400–acre Mokelumne Wilderness is located in the Eldorado and Stanislaus national forests near the crest of the Sierra Nevada Range, bisected by the North Fork of the Mokelumne River and surrounded by dense forests, the towering peaks of the Mokelumne Tetons dominated by Mokelumne Peak (9,332 ft.), deep mountain valleys, and alpine lakes. The word *mokelumne* is thought to be a derivation of *Muquelemnes*, the name of a tribe of Indians who occupied a Miwok Indian village formerly situated along the Mokelumne River near what is now Lockeford. Numerous foot and horse trails wind through the interior high country and provide access to the scenic Double Falls on the Mokelumne River, Camp Irene, Lake Valley, Munson Meadow, and primitive campsites developed over the years by fishermen, packers, and hunters. Rainbow and eastern brook trout are found in most of the alpine lakes and streams.

Pacific Crest Trail

The forest is a famed backpacking, fishing, hunting, and wilderness camping region. Hundreds of miles of forest roads and trails, including the Pacific Crest Trail, wind through the forest at elevations ranging from 3,000 to 10,000 feet and provide access to the North Fork of the Mokelumne River, Camp Creek, Crystal Range, Horneblende Mountains, the Cosumnes and Rubicon rivers, and

the high peaks, meadows, jagged spires, and hundreds of remote alpine lakes in the Mokelumne and Desolation Valley wilderness areas.

Gateways & Accommodations

Jackson & the Sutter Creek Inn

(Pop. 1,900; zip code 95642; area code 209.) Jackson is bordered on the north by some of the deepest mines on the North American continent; one shaft extends over a mile below the ground and is still active after a century of production. Before the gold boom, the town was important as a stopping point on a branch of the Carson Pass Emigrant Trail. In its heyday, Jackson was notorious for its rough-and-tumble frontier justice; wrongdoers were strung up from a great oak that stood on Main St. Many old buildings with iron shutters and overhanging balconies still stand along this narrow and winding thoroughfare. The Amador County Museum, on Church St., dates from the 1850s and contains numerous displays relevant to the gold rush. Jackson is also a gateway to the Eldorado National Forest; a district ranger's office is located here. Accommodations: *Jackson Holiday Lodge* (rates: $20–24 double), 37 excellent rooms, studio units, housekeeping cottages, color TV, pool, large lobby with stone fireplace, ½ mile west of town on California Hwy. 49, (223–0486); *Sutter Creek Inn* (rates: $28–65 double), 17 excellent air-conditioned rooms in handsomely decorated 1857 house, oversize beds, fireplaces, antiques, beautiful grounds, free breakfast, at 75 Main St. in Sutter Creek 95685, 4 miles north of Jackson on California Hwy. 49 (267–5606).

Placerville

(Pop. 5,400, zip code 95667; area code 916.) A former gold-rush boom town, Placerville has been known by a variety of colorful names, including Old Dry Diggins and Ravine City. In its heyday the community was also called Hangtown because of the swift punishment meted out to wrongdoers; after a speedy trial, criminals were sometimes hanged in pairs from the great oak tree that stood at the corner of Main and Coloma Sts. Placerville has spawned several noteworthy native sons, including Philip D. Armour of meat-packing fame and John Studebaker, the automobile magnate. Area attractions include the Gold Bug Mine in Bedford Park, a double-shaft mine with an exposed vein and restored gold stamp mill, and Marshall Gold Discovery State Park, marking the place where James Marshall found flecks of gold in the tailrace of Sutters Mill in 1848, 8 miles northwest of town on California Hwy. 49. Placerville is also a gateway to the Eldorado National Forest; the forest headquarters is in town at 100 Forine Road. Accommodations: *Best Western Cameron Park Inn* (rates: $24–26 double), 61 excellent air-conditioned rooms and suites, 10 with kitchens, color TV, restaurant adjacent, 12 miles west of town, just off U.S. Hwy. 50, Cameron Park Dr. Exit, in Shingle Springs (933–1164); *El Dorado Motel* (rates: $21–24 double), 24 fine air-conditioned rooms, color TV, oversize beds, patio overlooking creek, nearby restaurant, at 1244 Broadway, 1 mile east of town, just off U.S. Hwy. 50 (622–3884); *Gold Trail Motel* (rates: $20–22 double), 32 air-conditioned rooms, spacious tree-shaded grounds, color TV, swimming pool, at 1970 Broadway, 2 miles east of town via U.S. Hwy. 50, Point View Drive or Smith Flat Exit (622–2906); *Mother Lode Motel* (rates: $27 double), 21 comfortable rooms, color TV, pool, at 1940 Broadway, 2 miles east via U.S. Hwy. 50, Point View Drive Exit (622–0895).

South Lake Tahoe

(Pop. 12,900; zip code, see below; area code 916.) Accommodations: *Best Western Lake Tahoe Inn* (rates: $42 double), 400 excellent rooms and suites on 6 acres of landscaped grounds, adjacent to casinos, 3 heated pools, color TV, restaurant, cocktail lounge, on U.S. 50, 95729; (541–2010); *Best Western Timber Cove Lodge* (rates: $42 double), 260 excellent rooms and suites, spacious lakefront grounds, sand beach, heated pool, marina, restaurant, cocktail lounge, ½ mile west of Ski Run Blvd., 1½ miles west of casinos on U.S. Hwy. 50, 95705 (541–6722); *Flamingo Lodge* (rates: $33–42 double), 90 fine rooms, 17 with kitchens, swimming pool, sauna, color TV, recreation room with fireplace, 4 blocks west of casino center on U.S. Hwy. 50, 95729 (544–5288); *Forest Inn* (rates: $35–42.50 double), 125 excellent motel rooms and 1– or 2–bedroom units, 2 heated swimming pools, saunas, 108 kitchens, adults only, adjacent to casinos on Park Ave., 95729; (541–6655); *Harrah's Tahoe Hotel* (rates: $34–80 double), 540 superlative rooms and suites, elegant decor, 2 baths in each room, oversize beds, 5 fine restaurants, theater, health club, casino, entertainment and dancing, on U.S. 50 in the casino area near the California-Nevada state line (702)588–6611; *Harvey's Resort* (rates: $44–54 double), 200 excellent rooms and suites, most with balconies and oversize beds, two 2–bedroom units, pool, casino, 4 restaurants, entertainment and dancing, on U.S. 50, 1 mile north of state line, 89449 (702)588–2411; *Lakeland Village* (rates: $44–135 double), 170 excellent apartments with kitchens and 1–5 bedrooms, fireplaces, oversize beds, balconies, 2 pools, private sand beach, tennis courts, boating, fishing, waterskiing, maid service, restaurant adjacent, on U.S. 50, 1¼ miles west of casino center, 95705; (541–7711); *Royal Valhalla Motor Lodge* (rates: $41 double), 80 excellent units, 30 with kitchens, many balconies, swimming pool, private beach, at Lakeshore and Stateline Aves., 95729 (544–2233); *Sahara-Tahoe Hotel* (rates: $55 double), 550 superlative rooms and suites, some with balconies, oversize beds, swimming pool, casino, sauna, golf course adjacent, 24–hour dining room and coffee shop, entertainment, off U.S. 50, 1 block northeast in casino area, Stateline, NV 89449 (702)588–6211; *Sierra House Inn* (rates: $36–40 double), 59 excellent rooms, three 2–room units, small swimming pool, sauna, whirlpool, nearby 24–hour restaurant, ski package plans available, 1 block north off U.S. 50, near lake at Park and Cedar Aves., 95729 (541–4800); *Tahoe Marina Inn* (rates: $35–40 double), 75 fine rooms and apartments with kitchens, some with

balconies, on the lake, private beach, swimming pool, sauna, restaurant adjacent, 1½ miles west of casino center, 1 block west of U.S. 50, 95705 (541–2180); *Trade Winds Motel* (rates $32–34 double), 70 excellent rooms, 3 with kitchens, color TV, oversize beds, 2 pools, beach privileges, coffee shop opposite, at Cedar and Friday Aves., 3½ blocks from casino center, 95729 (544–6459); *The Waystation* (rates: $48–60 double), 231 superlative rooms and suites, many with balconies and oversize beds, attractively landscaped grounds, swimming pool, private beach, sauna, marina adjacent, restaurant, coffeeshop, on the lake, 1 block west of Ski Run Blvd., 95705 (541–6220).

Travel Services & Ski Areas

Alpine Meadows Ski Area, just west of Lake Tahoe, encompasses 2,000 acres of excellent, diversified ski terrain including open bowls, mountain meadows, and spacious runs for all levels of expertise. The area rises from a base elevation of 7,000 feet to the summit at 8,700 feet, from which splendid views of Lake Tahoe can be had. There are 9 chair lifts, 4 surface lifts, snow-making over 30 acres of terrain, and a fine ski school staffed by professional instructors (day-long lessons are especially popular). Skiing begins in November and extends through May, with a mean midwinter temperature of 29°F and 400 inches of average annual snowfall creating a long and rewarding season. The Alpine Meadows day lodge has a complete cafeteria and bar, day lockers, and a check room. Those who want to stay on the mountain will find attractively priced food and drink at the Sitymark Restaurant, accessible on skis or by chair lift. Other amenities include free daily shuttle service to local hotels and resorts, 5–day clinics for intermediate and advanced skiers, learn-to-ski weeks, and full ski vacation package plans. For more information write: Alpine Meadows, P.O. Box AM, Tahoe City, CA 95730 (916)583–4332.

Heavenly Valley Ski Area encompasses 20 square miles of the magnificent High Sierras, stretching from Lake Tahoe to 10,000–foot peaks before it plunges in a 5,000–foot vertical drop to the floor of Nevada's Carson Valley. The area provides an amazing variety of terrain, including open bowls, vast timbered areas of untracked powder snow, and well-groomed slopes and runs up to 7 miles long. Facilities and services at the nation's largest ski area include an excellent ski school, equipment rentals, 3 lodges, 5 restaurants, 4 on-hill snack facilities, 6 bars, and quick access to the world-famous après-ski gaming casinos and entertainment in South Lake Tahoe. The Heavenly Valley season extends from mid-November to May. Rental cars are available at the Reno International Airport and South Lake Tahoe Airport, and a ski shuttle bus service operates between South Lake Tahoe and the ski area, 15 minutes away. For additional information, contact: Heavenly Valley, P.O. Box AT, South Lake Tahoe, CA 95705 (916)541–1330.

Kirkwood Ski Touring Center, just south of Lake Tahoe at the top of the Sierras, is a full-service cross-country ski school and tour base with extensive equipment rentals, a lounge area with a big wood stove, lockers, and rest rooms. Classes are available in beginning and intermediate ski touring, advanced racing, and Nordic downhill skiing. All-day and moonlight guided tours and conducted for groups of 4 or more along the miles of trails around Kirkwood Meadows, Caples Creek, and Kirkwood, Caples, and Emigrant lakes. Some of the special events sponsored by the center include races, mixed-doubles relays, and the Echo Summit-to-Kirkwood competition, one of the longest cross-country races in the country. For hungry ski buffs, the Kirkwood Inn, adjacent to the touring center, offers hearty food and drink in warm surroundings. For more information write: Kirkwood Ski Touring Center, P.O. Box 77, Kirkwood, CA 95646 (209)258–8864.

Sugar House West Ski Touring Center at South Lake Tahoe is a comprehensive ski-touring center dedicated to providing the finest in

backcountry ski trips, instruction, rentals, and annual competitions. Among the firm's most popular activities are overnight cabin tours in beautiful Meiss Meadow ($40 per person, including meals, equipment, skis, and guide); special classes in downhill skinny skiing; 2–day winter orienteering courses with instruction in land navigation ($25 per person, including equipment and lunch each day); and extended 3–day tours of the Echo Lakes area, Mokelumne Wilderness, and Pacific Crest South ($95–125 per person, including meals, guides, and equipment). Day tours, individually tailored to the skills of each guest, are sponsored to a variety of destinations in the Sierra backcountry ($15 per person, including skis, boots, poles, and lunch). Other offerings include evening tours culminating in a steak dinner over a roaring campfire, all-inclusive ski packages, and nature photography workshops throughout the ski season. For complete rates and information write: Sugar House West, P.O. Box 8135, South Lake Tahoe, CA 95731 (916)541–6811.

High Sierras—Inyo National Forest

The vast 1.8 million-acre Inyo National Forest lies east of Yosemite National Park and stretches south for about 160 miles along the eastern slope of the Sierra Nevada to the Nevada border in the eastern part of central California. The forest contains some of the most stunning alpine and camping and fishing areas in the West, including portions of the John Muir, Hoover, Minarets High Sierra wilderness areas. Hundreds of miles of trails and Forest Service roads provide access to the famous trout waters of the Owens River, Hot Creek, Crowley Lake, and Cottonwood Creek, and to the remote alpine lakes and streams in the Hall Natural Area, Inconsolable Range, Little Valley, and Mammoth Lakes area. The native home of the golden trout is in the headwater lakes and streams of the Kern Plateau in the forest, southwest of Lone Pine. The John Muir Trail segment of the Pacific Crest National Scenic Trail winds along the windswept peaks of the High Sierra Crest in the John Muir Wilderness along the forest's western boundary. East of Owens Valley lie the White Mountains, the famous Ancient Bristlecone Pine Forest, and portions of the Inyo Mountains. Access to a large portion of the Sequoia-Kings Canyon and Yosemite national parks is through the west side of the Inyo National Forest.

Information Sources, Maps & Access

The forest's natural features, trails, roads, recreation sites and campgrounds, pack stations, ranger stations, and lookout towers are shown on the full-color *Inyo National Forest Map* (50¢). The map and detailed fishing, camping, hiking, cross-country skiing, and hunting, information may be obtained by writing: Forest Supervisor, Inyo National Forest, 2957 Birth Street, Bishop 93514 (714)873–5841.

Fishing guide service and specific fishing, hunting, and High Sierra backpacking info are available at *Doug Kittredge Sport Shop*, Mammoth Lakes Village 93546 (714)934–2423.

The major automobile routes to the forest are U.S. Highways 395 and 6 and State Route 120 (east). Lodging, guides, supplies, boat rentals, and outfitters, are available at Bridgeport, Lee Vining (Mono Lake), June Lake, Mammoth Lakes, Convict Lake, Rock Creek, Bishop, Bishop Creek Basin, Big Pine, Independence, and Lone Pine.

Recreation Areas

Ancient Bristlecone Pine Forest

The White Mountains rise to the east of Bishop and Owens Valley and contain the site of the world's oldest trees—the Ancient Bristlecone Pine Forest. It was thought for years that the world's oldest tree was the General Sherman sequoia in Sequoia National Forest. However, in 1956 Dr. Edmund Schulman established that the Pine Alpha bristlecone was indeed older than the ancient sequoias. A year later, an even older tree, named Methuselah, was dated at 4,600 years old. The wild, rugged 28,000–acre Ancient Bristlecone Pine Forest was established in 1958. The area has two hiking trails, the Pine Alpha Trail, which winds through living driftwoodlike stumps bleached and gnarled from centuries of wind, rain, and blowing sand to the famous Pine Alpha tree; and the two-mile-long Methuselah Trail. The Patriarch Grove, named for the world's largest bristlecone tree, over 25 feet in height and 37 feet in diameter, is located at the north end of the forest. The forest lies at the crest of the White Mountains between 10,000 and 12,000 feet elevation, between Bishop and the California-Nevada border. A campground and the Sierra Viewpoint, which provides a spectacular view of the Eastern Sierra Nevada Range across Owens Valley, are located just south of the forest entrance. Piute, golden, and eastern brook trout are found in Cottonwood Creek, located at the northern edge of the forest, and Wyman Creek, which flows through the heart of the forest. The forest is reached by the Westguard Pass Road, which branches northeast from U.S. 395 at Big Pine.

Devils Postpile National Monument

The Devils Postpile National Monument, in the eastern Sierra Nevada near Mammoth Lakes, occupies a rectangular area about 2½ miles long by ½ mile wide, which extends along both sides of the Middle Fork of the San Joaquin River. Thousands of blue-gray

basaltic columns, 40 to 60 feet high, rise above the turbulent water and form a wall of nearly perfect prisms. An easy trail leads to the top of the columns where glacial action has polished the surface to resemble tile inlays arranged in a honeycomb pattern. Also within the national monument, 2 miles down the river trail from the Devils Postpile, are the lovely Rainbow Falls. Here the Middle Fork of the San Joaquin River drops 140 feet, its foamy white waters contrasting dramatically with the dark basaltic cliffs. The name of the falls stems from the rainbows that appear around noon on a clear day. The monument is reached via California Hwy. 203, which leads west from U.S. 395 and the Mammoth Lakes Ranger Station. A campground and picnic areas are maintained from June through mid-October (ranger station open daily 8 A.M. to 5 P.M.; phone (714)934–2289. For area accommodations, see Mammoth Lakes under "Gateways" below.

Mono Lake

The scenic northern district of the forest, located due east of Yosemite National Park, embraces several renowned fishing, backpacking, and wilderness camping and historic areas reached from trailheads and spur routes off U.S. Highway 359. Bodie Ghost Town is 20 miles north of Bridgeport via U.S. 395. From 1876 to 1880 this gold-rush town had a population of 12,000 and a reputation as one of the toughest and most lawless gold-mining camps in the West. It is surrounded by meager bunch grass, desert sage, and needle grass. Gold was first discovered in the Mono region in 1852, and the Mono Trail was blazed from Big Oak Flat through the present Yosemite National Park to Bodie and the Mono region. To the south at 6,409–feet elevation lies Mono Lake, covering 87 square miles. The lake is the third-largest natural body of water in California, formed more than 20,000 years ago by descending Sierra Nevada glaciers. Its blue waters are so impregnated with alkaline materials that nothing lives in its briny depths but one small species of saltwater shrimp and tiny black fly larvae. Two large volcanic islands dot the lake's surface: Paoha, the larger, with its hot spring; and Negit, an old volcanic crater, with a rookery for sea gulls, or "mono pigeons," that have flown inland from the Pacific. South of the lake are the 20 Mono Craters, forming a crescent-shaped range and resembling gigantic ash heaps. Two campgrounds are located on the shores.

Pacific Crest Trail

The Pacific Crest Trail winds through the snowcapped peaks and alpine meadows of the Minarets Wilderness (see "High Sierras—Sierra National Forest & John Muir Wilderness" page 89) and past the sparkling, island-studded Thousand Island and Garnet lakes, which at 9,000–feet elevation are surrounded by rocky islets, grassy shores carpeted with wild flowers in season, and rugged barren peaks, and which form the headwaters of the San Joaquin and Owens rivers. The trail winds out from the Minarets Wilderness and parallels the scenic rainbow and brook trout waters of the Middle Fork of the San Joaquin through the spectacular Devils Postpile National Monument.

Palisades Glacier Area

The High Sierra alpine lake basins surrounding the south and north forks headwaters of Big Pine Creek in the John Muir Wilderness form one of the most majestic areas along the eastern slope of the Sierra Crest. The two lake basins are walled in on the west by the towering, jagged Palisades Crest, dominated by three peaks over 14,000 feet, and are separated by a giant ridge dominated by Temple Crag at 12,999 feet. The massive Palisades Glacier at the upper end of the North Fork Basin is the southernmost glacier in the United

States and the largest in the High Sierras. Several foot, horse, and jeep trails provide access to the remote blue high-country lakes located above 10,000 feet in the two basins.

Gateways & Accommodations

Big Pine

(Pop. 1,000; zip code 93513; area code 714.) This small town shaded by giant oaks and maples is a key gateway to the Inyo National Forest. Within the immediate vicinity of Big Pine is the Ancient Bristlecone Pine Forest (open June through October), a preserve of venerable trees, many of them older than the famous California redwoods. The forest is reached via the Westgard Pass Road (California Hwy. 168) and a paved road to the Schulman Memorial Grove. Accommodations: *Big Pine Motel* (rates: $22 double), 15 rooms on shaded grounds, coffee shop adjacent, at 370 South Main St. near U.S. Hwy. 395 (938–2282); *Starlight Motel* (rates: $18 double), 9 air-conditioned rooms, TV, nearby coffee shop, open 24 hours, 2 blocks south of town on U.S. 395 (938–2369).

Bishop

(Pop. 3,500; zip code 93514; area code 714.) Bishop is an important gateway and outfitting center for visitors to the Inyo National Forest and High Sierra recreation points. The White Mountain Ranger District Office of the national forest is located here. Other area attractions include Bishop Creek Canyon, with its 1,000–foot cliffs, just west of town on Hwy. 168 (Bishop Creek Road), and the mysterious Indian petroglyphs of unknown origin north of Bishop on Fish Slough Road. Laws Railroad Museum, 5 miles northeast of town on U.S. 6, encompasses 11 acres of restored buildings, locomotives, and equipment from the once-active community of Laws (open daily Mar. 1 to Thanksgiving and weekends the rest of the

year). Accommodations: *Best Western Bishop Westerner* (rates: $28–30 double), 55 rooms, color TV, swimming pool, queen-size beds, at 150 Elm St., ½ block east of U.S. 6 (873–3564); *Bishop Thunderbird Motel* (rates: $20–22 double), 23 comfortable rooms in town, color TV, nearby coffee shop, at 190 W. Pine St., ½ block west of U.S. 395 (873–4215); *Bishop Travelodge* (rates: $25–30 double), 50 rooms (some with queen-size beds), color TV, heated pool, at 606 N. Main St., 1 block east of U.S. 395 (873–3548); *Holiday Lodge* (rates: $26–29 double), 60 excellent rooms, color TV, heated pool and whirlpool, adjacent coffee shop, at 1025 N. Main St., ½ mile north of town on U.S. 395 (873–3543); *Inn of Bishop* (rates: $24–26 double), 40 excellent rooms with oversize beds, heated pool and whirlpool, sauna, recreation room, deep-freeze facilities for fish, at 805 N. Main St., 5 blocks north of town on U.S. 6 (873–4284); *Sportsman's Inn* (rates: $20–26 double), 30 fine rooms, color TV, swimming pool and poolside service, coffee shop, room service, free airport bus, fish and game cleaning facilities, boat and trailer parking, at 636 N. Main St., 3 blocks north of Bishop on U.S. 6(873–5833).

Bridgeport

(Pop. 500; zip code 93517; area code 714.) The town lies in a valley ringed by the snow-crested Sierras and low, rolling hills. Southeast of town is the Bodie State Historic Park, site of an unrestored ghost town from the late 19th century. A church, 2–room schoolhouse, museum, jail, and hillside cemetery are all that remain in this onetime boom town (open year-round; admission free). Accommodations: *Best Western Bridgeport* (rates: $24–28 double), 30 comfortable rooms, open year-round, queen-size beds, free coffee in rooms, fish freezer, 2 blocks north of town on U.S. 395 (932–7241); *Walker River Lodge* (rates: $28–32 double), 34 rooms, open year-round, small heated pool, spa, free coffee in rooms, restaurant opposite, deep-freeze facilities for fish, 2 blocks south of Bridgeport on U.S. 395 (932–7021).

June Lake

(Pop. 400; zip code 93529; area code 714.) This is a popular 4–season High Sierras recreation center and gateway to the Inyo National Forest. The June Mountain Ski Area, west of U.S. Hwy. 395, has four double chair lifts, a T-bar, ski school, cafeteria, and bar. Accommodations: *Boulder Lodge* (rates: $25–50 double), 60 excellent rooms, housekeeping cabins, family suites, some with fireplaces and kitchens, on 5 acres of lakefront grounds, indoor pool, sauna, whirlpool, tennis, guide service for fishing and hunting, 4–day minimum stay for units with kitchens during summer and holidays, ¼ mile northeast of town on California Hwy. 158, Box 68; (648–7533); *Four Seasons Resort* (rates: $28 double), five 2–bedroom housekeeping cottages, attractive A–frame design, near ski area, queen-size beds, fireplaces, balconies, playground, 2–3-day minimum stay, off-season rates May–October, on California Hwy. 158, 4 miles west of U.S. 395, (648–7476); *June Lake Motel,* (rates: $26–28 double), 17 rooms, 15 with kitchens, sauna, whirlpool, coffee shop adjacent, in village center on California Hwy. 158, (648–7547); *June Lake Villager Motel* (rates: $22–24 double), 22 rooms, efficiencies, housekeeping apartments, some with fireplaces, color TV, in village center on Hwy. 158, (648–7529); *Whispering Pines* (rates: $24–50 double), 24 motel rooms and cottages with kitchens, excellent mountain views, closed in winter, weekly rates available, 3 miles northwest of the village on Hwy. 158, 5 miles west of U.S. 395 (648–7762).

Lee Vining—Eastern Gateway to Yosemite

(Pop. 400; zip code 93541; area code 714.) This gateway to the Inyo National Forest derives its name from the leader of a group of prospectors who found gold in the area in 1852. Nearby Mono Lake, 87 square miles in area, is almost twice as salty as the sea. In the center of the lake, 1,400–acre volcanic Paoha Island is a refuge for the thousands of gulls that feed on tiny brine shrimp. Another extinct crater, 700–acre Negit Island, contains many vents and crevasses from which steam pours forth. Those who wish to try the waters will find a marina on the west shore of the lake. A district ranger's office of the Inyo National Forest is located in Lee Vining. Accommodations: *Best Western Lake View Motel* (rates: $28–34 double), 35 rooms, some with kitchens, color TV, free coffee, trailer parking, on U.S. Hwy. 395, Box 345 (647–6543); *Gateway Motel* (rates: $22–24 double), 12 rooms overlooking Mono Lake, sundeck, TV, riding, restaurant opposite, on U.S. 395, Box 100 (647–6467); *Murphey's Motel* (rates: $22–24 double), 15 comfortable rooms, 3 with kitchens, heated pool, fish freezing facilities, near June Mountain Ski Area, open year-round, on U.S. 395, Box 57 (647–6316).

Lone Pine

(Pop. 1,800; zip code 93545; area code 714.) An outfitting point for visitors to Mt. Whitney and Inyo National Forest, Lone Pine is bordered by the rugged Alabama Hills, a mass of weather-beaten rock which has provided local color for many western movies. A drive due west leads to Mt. Whitney (14,494 ft.), highest mountain in the contiguous United States. At the summit is a perpetual snowfield. A 10.7–mile trail leads to the top from the end of Whitney Postal Road. In Lone Pine is a district ranger's office of the Inyo National Forest. Just south of town is an Interagency Visitors

Center, at the junction of U.S. 395 and California Hwy. 136. Accommodations: *Best Western Frontier Motel* (rates: $20 double), 46 comfortable air-conditioned rooms, color TV, heated pool, free airport bus, ½ mile south of town on U.S. 395, at 1008 S. Main St. (876–5571); *Dow Villa Motel* (rates: $26 double), 39 fine rooms, color TV, pool, coffee shop, open year-round, in town at 310 S. Main St. (876–5521); *Trails Motel* (rates: $24 double), 17 air-conditioned rooms, heated pool, nearby coffee shop, free airport bus, ¼ mile south of Lone Pine on U.S. 395, 633 S. Main St. (876–5555).

Mammoth Lakes

(Pop. 900; zip code 93546; area code 714.) The town is a gateway to the Inyo National Forest and to a vast region of resorts and lakes. The Mammoth Lakes Recreation Area encompasses some 200,000 acres and includes portions of the John Muir Trail, Pacific Crest Trail, the Earthquake Fault, Devils Postpile National Monument, and Mammoth Winter Sports Area. The National Forest Service Visitor Information Center, in town, sponsors guided naturalist hikes, ski tours, and nightly campfire programs. (For information, contact: District Ranger, Box 148; 934–2505). Accommodations: *Alpenhof Lodge* (rates: $25–40 double), 40 fine rooms, some with fireplaces, color TV, sauna, whirlpool, restaurant, cocktail lounge, open all year (on weekends only November–mid-May), 1 mile west of town on California Hwy. 203, (934–6330); *Edelweiss Lodge* (rates: $26 double), 12 units, most with kitchenettes and fireplaces, quiet forest setting, off-season rates May–October, 2 miles south of town, 6 miles southwest of U.S. 395 on Old Mammoth Road, (934–2445); *International Inn* (rates: $25–35 double), 25 comfortable rooms, 13 with kitchens, color TV, swimming pool, whirlpool, free airport bus, lounge with fireplace, coffee shop adjacent, ¼ mile west of town on California Hwy. 203, (934–2542); *Jagerhof Lodge* (rates: $22–26 double), 23 rooms, recreation room, sauna, whirlpool, many queen-size beds, coffee shop opposite, 1 mile southwest of town, 3½ miles west of U.S. 395 on Old Mammoth Road, (934–6162); *Swiss Chalet* (rates: $19–26 double), 22 comfortable rooms, with kitchens, color TV, excellent views, coffee shop opposite, ½ mile west of town on California Hwy. 203, (934–2403); *White Stag Inn* (rates: $20–32 double), 21 rooms, 5 with kitchens, color TV, sauna, airport transportation, ¾ mile west of town on California Hwy. 203, (934–2746); *Woods Lodge* (rates: $25–30 double), 22 housekeeping cabins (1–3 bedrooms), 2 lodge rooms, queen-size beds, porches, lounge and sundeck overlooking lake, beautiful mountain views, boats, and fishing tackle available, 1 mile west of Mammoth Lakes Road on Lake George Road, (934–2261).

Lodges & Alpine Resorts

★★*Cardinal Village Resort*, set in a grove of aspen trees on the edge of Bishop Creek in the Sierras, has modern, all-electric housekeeping cottages with sleeping quarters for 2–10 guests in each. Good fishing is available right on the resort grounds for rainbow trout. Lake fishing, both bait and fly, is generally excellent in the numerous lakes of the backcountry, with boat rentals available at nearby Sabrina and South lakes. Hiking and hunting in season are also popular in this wild and scenic area. All cottages at Cardinal Village have a full bath, electric heat, all dishes, utensils, and bedding. The local store carries a full line of grocery staples, plus bait and tackle. The central lodge building features a cocktail lounge, shading porch, and living room. Rates: $19–27 double occupancy; $25–37 for 4 guests. Add $3 for each additional person sharing the cabin. For more information write: Cardinal Village Resort, Box A3, Bishop, CA 93514 (714)873–4789.

★★★*Convict Lake Resort* is situated in California's East High Sierras on the unusually named Lake Convict. The lake received its name in 1871 when a group of escaped prisoners used the Lake as a temporary camp before being apprehended. The Lake is surrounded by rugged mountains, evergreens and its still waters provide beautiful mirror images. The Lake is known for its fishing, either from the shore or by trolling or still-fishing from boats. Trout, as large as 20 lbs. can also be caught. The resort has boats and motors for rent and there are nine additional Sierra Lakes to visit in the Convict canyon. The scenic area, with its many unique geological formations and vegetation provides the nature enthusiasts with a whole world of intrigue. Trips into Convict Canyon backcountry and hiking can unfold much of the area's natural beauty. Horseback and mule rides take guests into the John Muir Wilderness with stops at high-country lakes providing easy trout fishing. There is also fine deer hunting in the Convict Canyon area. U.S. Forest Service campgrounds provide running water throughout the camping area and new restrooms. The resort's cabins are centrally located, comfortable units nestled among the quaking aspen. They are completely furnished including linens. There is a restaurant, cocktail lounge and snack bar at the resort. A general store is also located on the resort's premises. Rates: Single cabins $19–23 nightly, $114–138 weekly. Double cabins $23–28 nightly, $138–168 weekly. For further information contact: Convict Lake Resort, Route 3, Box 204, Bishop, CA 93514 (714)935–4213.

★*Glacier Lodge* is a true wilderness outpost with comforts of a modern resort at 7,900–feet elevation on Big Pine Creek in the eastern High Sierras of the Inyo National Forest. Glacier Lodge is a few minutes' hike from John Muir Wilderness Area and provides trail access to 5 of the 10 highest peaks in the Sierras, a dozen high alpine lakes of the Big Pine Lakes backcountry, and to Palisade Glacier, the most southerly glacier in the U.S.A. and the High Sierras' largest active glacier. Accommodations include lodge rooms or modern housekeeping cabins scattered among the pines, secluded yet convenient to the main lodge. Completely furnished, each cabin has its own kitchen, fully equipped with dishes and utensils, a bath with shower, and all necessary linens provided. Cabins will accommodate up to 9 persons. The lodge has a main lounge, a well-stocked store, and a guest dining room known for its exceptional meals. Form the lodge, you can look up the south fork of Big Pine Canyon to the towering, cathedrallike peaks of the Middle Palisade rising to an elevation of 14,000 feet. The Glacier Pack Station is situated nearby for day rides or packhorse trips up into the backcountry. Lodge rooms are $27.50 (double occupancy) daily and a housekeeping cabin is $30. Hearty ranch-style dinners cost $7.50. For additional info, contact: Glacier Lodge, P.O. Box 327, Big Pine, CA 93513.

Mammoth Lakes Village & Ski Center is nestled at the foot of Mammoth Mountain in the High Sierras of the Inyo National Forest, 50 miles north of Bishop. This nationally renowned ski and summer resort complex offers outstanding alpine and cross-country skiing, fishing, backpacking, canoeing, horseback riding, and tennis. Most of the skiing at Mammoth Lakes is done between 9,000 and 11,000 feet. The ski season usually begins in October or November and continues through May or June. Mammoth Mountain has a vertical drop of 3,100 feet, with 22 lifts and over 60 runs of varying degrees of difficulty. Facilities and services include warming huts, the Mammoth Ski School and Children's Ski School, advanced ski clinics, a chalet with food services, and two ski-touring centers offering professional instruction, winter survival classes, guided day tours, and expedition tours to the Yosemite backcountry. The guided Nordic day tours provide an introduction to Mammoth history and wildlife. First-class accommodations, services, and dining are avail-

able at Mammoth Village. Popular dining spots include the St. Moritz Dining Room at the Mammoth Mountain Inn for a great buffet breakfast, lunch, and dinner; Mogul Steakhouse; Mill City Country Restaurant; Moostachio Pete's for Italian cuisine; Pea Soup Anderson's; and the casual Whiskey Creek Restaurant. For detailed info, contact: Mammoth Mountain Ski Area, P.O. Box 24, Mammoth Lakes, CA 93546 (714)934–2571; or Mammoth Lakes Ski Touring Center, P.O. Box 102, Mammoth Lakes 93546 (714)934–6955. Four-season accommodations are available at the following alpine lodges and inns:

★★*Alpenhof Lodge* with 40 comfortable, attractive rooms, some with fireplaces. Facilities include sauna, recreation room, whirlpool, the Clocktower Restaurant, and cocktail lounge. Daily rates (double): $26–40. Contact: Box 1157, Mammoth Lakes 93546 (714)934–6330.

★★★*Mammoth Mountain Chalets*, situated across from the ski-lift complex have a dramatic view of Mammoth Mountain in front and of the Minarets Wilderness Area behind. The 20 rustic A-frame alpine chalets will accommodate 4–12 people, with 2–3 bedrooms and 2 baths. Most have wood-burning fireplaces, sundecks, and expansive views of ski slopes as well as a living room, dining area, and fully equipped kitchen. The chalets rent for $65–80 per night during the ski season and for $40 per night during the summer season. Contact: P.O. Box 513, Mammoth Lakes, CA 93546 (714)934–8518.

★★*Minaret Lodge* is located in the upper village on the main road to the ski area and Devils Postpile. Lodging is available to suit your individual requirements in motel units or rustic housekeeping apartments with kitchen facilities which sleep 2–7 people. All units have individually controlled heat. Daily motel rates: $18–27; housekeeping apartments $22–42 per day. Contact: Box 23, Mammoth Lakes, CA 93546 (714)934–2416.

★★★*St. Anthony Condominium* at the ski-lift complex offers deluxe alpine accommodations with completely furnished 1– and 2–bedroom units with beautiful views, furnished kitchens, carpeting and fireplaces. Other facilities include a Finnish sauna, 2 Jacuzzis, swimming pool, game room, ski lockers, and underground parking. Winter rates (double occupancy): $40–50 per night; family summer rates start at $105 per week. Contact: P.O. Box 427, Mammoth Lakes, CA 93546 (714)934–6005.

★★★*Timber Ridge* offers deluxe condominium rentals with a view unmatched in the Mammoth area. This great resort complex, surrounded by national forests, offers beautiful 1– and 2–bedroom and loft units with award-winning interior design, wood-burning fireplaces, and fully equipped kitches. The Timber Ridge recreation center has a sauna, indoor Jacuzzi, pool, and game room. Summer activities include tennis, fishing, and backpacking. Winter rates: $45–75 per day; summer rates: $30–45 per day. Contact: P.O. Box 8623, Mammoth Lakes, CA 93546 (714)934–8102.

★★*Wild Wood Inn* (Best Western) on Highway 203 offers 32 motel units with a heated pool, sauna, and Jacuzzi. Daily rates (double): $30–36. Contact: Box 568, Mammoth Lakes, CA 93546 (714)934–6855 or call toll-free (800)528–1234.

Parchers Rainbow Village is located at South Lake, 20 miles west of Bishop on the eastern slope of the High Sierras in the Inyo National Forest, adjacent to the Kings Canyon National Park boundary. The village offers carpeted modern housekeeping cabins, store and coffee shop, packhorse rides, boat rentals, and hikes into the high country and over Bishop Pass into Kings Canyon. Pack outfits are available for overnight trips into the High Sierras. Daily rates (single or double occupancy): $30. For additional information, contact: P.O. Box 1658, Bishop, CA 93514 (714)873–4177 summer; October–May, (805)647–2578.

★★★*Tamarack Lodge* is located on the shores of beautiful Twin Lakes and surrounded by the spectacular alpine scenery of the Inyo National Forest. Within a radius of 4 miles are some 20 pine-rimmed lakes well stocked with rainbow, steelhead, golden, cutthroat, Lochleven, and Eastern brook trout. In addition to superlative fishing, the lodge offers horseback riding and pack trips arranged through the nearby Mammoth Pack Outfit. In winter there is fine downhill sport at the Mammoth Ski Area, with its 16 chair lifts and miles of varied terrain. The lodge is also the home of the Mammoth Ski Touring Center (see above). Cross-country buffs will find over 30 miles of well-maintained trails starting right at the door. Guest accommodations are in 40 cabins, most of them equipped with private baths and all with private toilets, near the lakeshore and completely furnished for light housekeeping. Cabins range in size from 1 to 4 bedrooms, with sleeping quarters for up to 10 guests. Summer rates are $25–60 nightly (for 2–10); winter rates are $26–36 nightly (for 2–4). Lodge rooms with private baths are $18–22 nightly (double occupancy). Weekly discounts are available. Other amenities of the lodge include a comfortable lounge, tackle and grocery store, boat rentals, weekly movies, and a restaurant and snack bar. For further information write: Tamarack Lodge, P.O. Box 69, Mammoth Lakes, CA 93546 (714)934–2442 or (714)934–3260.

Travel Services

Agnew Meadows Pack Train. Pack trips of all types to Shadow, Ediza, Garnet, and Thousand Island lakes. Excellent area for the novice. Spectacular scenic loop trips in the Minaret Wilderness area. Write for map and brochure. Open group riding and hiking trips. Packing school offered. Contact: Bob Tanner, Box 395, Mammoth Lakes, CA 93546 (714)934–2345.

Convict Lake Pack Station. Pack trips into Convict Lake Basin area. Beautiful lakes and streams. Fish for rainbow, Eastern brook, and the elusive golden. Hour rides and day rides for excellent fishing and sight-seeing up scenic Convict Canyon. Contact: Convict Lake Resort, Rte. 3, Box 204, Bishop, CA 93514 (714)935–4213.

Cottonwood Pack Station. Trips to Cottonwood Lakes—South Fork, Rock Creek, and Whitney District. And 28 exclusive golden trout lakes. Now located 6 miles from Cottonwood and South Fork lakes. Contact: Box 43, Olancha, CA 93549 (714)764–2225.

Frontier Pack Station. Easy access on scenic June Lake Loop, serving over 35 lakes in Minaret Wilderness, including Alger and Thousand Island lakes. Fishing for rainbow, brook, and trophy

goldens. Uncrowded deer hunting. They welcome all types of pack trips. Contact: Dink Getty, Box 18, Star Rt. 3, June Lake, CA 93521 (714)648–7701.

Glacier Pack Outfit, located 10 miles west of Big Pine on a good paved road—elevation 8,000 feet. Entrance to Palisade Glacier area in the John Muir Wilderness. Spectacular high-country scenery. Trips to Big Pine Lakes, Baker Lakes, and South Fork Big Pine Creek. Excellent stream and lake fishing in timbered campsites. Extended trips to Kings Canyon National Park via Taboose Pass Trail. Deer season station of McMurry Meadows. Dependable and early service. Contact: M.A. Stewart, Box 321, Big Pine, CA 93513 (714)938–2648.

Kennedy Meadows Pack Trains. Pack trips for fishermen, hunters, families, Scouts, and organizational groups. First to open for golden trout. Open for a full season of deer hunting. Contact: Box 966, Weldon, CA 93283 (714)378–2232.

Leavitt Meadows Pack Station, located 27 miles from Bridgeport on the Sonora Pass Highway 108. All kinds of pack trips into the headwaters of the West Walker River, Yosemite Park, and the Emigrant Basin. There are 26 lakes, and 18 without going over a mountain pass. Good deer hunting. Contact: Leavitt Meadows Pack Station, Bridgeport, CA 93517.

Little Antelope Pack Station & Lodge, located 2 miles south of Coleville, serving many lakes, the Silver King Creek, and Carson River. All of which provide excellent fishing, many within a half day from the lodge. All types of pack trips are available, also horses for rent by the day or hour. This area is known for its excellent deer hunting. The solitude of this country is unequaled. Contact: Larry and Marilyn Mitchell, Box 105, Coleville, CA 96107 (213)963–2774.

Mammoth Lakes Pack Outfit. Pack into the magnificent Mammoth Lakes Sierra for some of the finest stream and lake fishing. Deer-hunting trips available. Over 100 lakes can be reached by a day's horseback ride from the pack station. Picturesque campsites include Duck, Purple, Virginia, Jackson, and Ram lakes, Fish Creek, Deer Creek, and Cascade Valley. Contact: Lou Rolser, Box 61, Mammoth Lakes, CA 93546 (714)934–2434.

McGee Creek Pack Station. Personalized help to golden, rainbow, and brookie fishing, hunting, and scenic trips to the streams and lakes of colorful McGee Canyon and fabulous Fish Creek. While they specialize in all-expense trips, the spot trip is the most popular along with dunnage packs and the fun-filled day rides. Catering to families and first-trippers. Contact: The MacRoberts, Box 1054, Bishop, CA 93514 (714)935–4324.

Pine Creek Saddle & Pack Train. High Sierra scenery and fishing at its best with golden, Eastern brook, and rainbow trout at your disposal. Located 20 miles northwest of Bishop. Trips available to Pine Lakes, Honeymoon Lake, Granite Park, French Canyon, Gable Lakes, and Morgan Lakes. Contact: Wm. A. Cole, Box 968, Bishop, CA 93514 (714)933–2324.

Rainbow Pack Outfit is located on South Fork at Bishop Creek, packing up through the beautiful South Lake Basin, over Bishop Pass, Dusey Basin, Middle Fork of the King's River, King's Canyon National Park, John Muir Trail. Golden, rainbow, and Eastern brook Trout. Unsurpassed scenery. All kinds of trips. Contact: Jim & Donna Howell, Rt. 1, Box 26, Bishop, CA 93514 (714)873–4485.

Red's Meadow Pack Train, located near Devils Postpile National Monument on the Middle Fork of the San Joaquin River. Gateway to the John Muir and Minaret Wilderness areas. Over 100 lakes. Fishing, hunting, and scenic trips of all types and duration to fabulous Fish Creek, Minaret, Beck, Margaret, Bettlebug, and Lone Indian lakes. Open group riding and hiking trips. Packing school offered. Contact: Box 395, Mammoth Lakes, CA 93546 (714)934–2345.

Rock Creek Pack Station. Owens Valley trail ride and horse drive and High Sierra trail rides. Easiest access to lakes and streams of Pioneer Basin and Hopkins Basin. The Recesses, Mono Creek, Hilton Lakes, Little Lakes Valley. All types of pack trips, complete outfitting, day and excursion rides. Golden trout. Contact: Herbert London, Box 248, Bishop, CA 93514 (714)872–8331.

Schober Pack Station, located North Fork of Bishop Creek. Packs into Lake Sabrina, Humphrey Basin, and French Canyon. Circle trip via Piute, Muir, and Bishop passes. Fifty lakes are within a 1–day pack. Contact: Art Schober, Bishop, CA 93514 (714)873–4785.

Sierra Ski Touring offers guided ski tours throughout the High Sierra wilderness areas and maintains several ski-touring huts near Rainbow Falls on the San Joaquin River and Devils Postpile National Monument. In addition, Sierra Ski Touring offers expert instruction on new skiing techniques, orienteering, natural history, and winter travel safety, as well as special avalanche courses. Hut skiing courses cost $60 for 2 days; $30 for each additional day. Overnight tours in the Mammoth and June lake areas cost $50. The firm also offers a Trans-Sierra Tour from Mammoth to Yosemite Valley via Donohue Pass and Tuolumne Meadows (cost: $250); Trans-Sierra California Haute Route tour from the high desert, across the Great Divide to the Sequoia groves in Sequoia National Park (cost: $250); and the Bighorn Plateau Loop tour which offers spectacular Nordic skiing among the foxtail pine forests on the Bighorn and Kern plateaus and above timberline surrounded by Mt. Whitney, the jagged Kaweah Range, and the Great Western Divide (cost: $200). Sierra Ski Touring also offers guided tours of the White Mountains and the Bristlecone Pine Forest (cost: $200) and Yellowstone National Park. Sierra Ski Touring is owned and directed by David and Susan Beck. David worked four winters on avalanche crews at various California ski resorts and has conducted avalanche schools both for the National Park Service and the Professional Ski Instructors of America. He has written a ski-touring guide book, *Ski Tours in California*. For the past four years he has taught a winter natural history course for the University of California Extension Service. Sierra Ski Touring is a member of the National Ski Touring Operators Association and the Professional Ski Instructors of America. It operates under permits to Inyo National Forest and Sequoia, Kings Canyon, Yosemite, and Yellowstone national parks. For additional information, contact: Sierra Ski Touring, P.O. Box C–9, Mammoth Lakes, CA 93546 (714)934–4495.

High Sierras—Sequoia & Kings Canyon National Parks

Sequoia and Kings Canyon national parks cover the most spectacular wilderness fishing, camping, and mountaineering country on the western slopes of the High Sierra. Sequoia covers 386,863 acres, stretching from the headwaters of the Kings River on the north to the headwaters of the Tule River on the south. A majestic arc of cloud-weathered High Sierra peaks—dominated by Mt. Whitney

(14,494 ft.), the highest point in the contiguous United States—bounds the park on the east, sloping down to the foothills of the Sierras on the west. The Great Western Divide, a jagged granite ridge, bisects the park from north to south. Situated between the divide and the High Sierra crest are hundreds of remote blue alpine trout lakes and streams, the awesome Kaweah Peaks, the 3,000–foot walls of the Kern River Canyon (which parallel the divide for 25 miles), and the Chagoopa, Bighorn, and Boreal plateaus, formed in the Ice Age thousands of years ago. West of the Great Western Divide in the 4,000 to 8,000 feet elevations of the foothills are the park's major accommodations and the groves of giant redwoods, *Sequoia gigantea*.

Adjoining Sequoia on the north is Kings Canyon National Park, whose 460,331 acres embrace the renowned wilderness trout-fishing waters and camping areas of the rugged Kings-Kern Divide, Kearsarge Pinnacles, Painted Lady High Country, Sixty Lakes Basin, Kings Canyon, Cirque Crest, Upper and Lake basins, the Enchanted Gorge, the lake-dotted high country of the Goddard Divide and Evolution Basin, the Gorge of Despair, and hundreds of lush green alpine meadows, spurs, cascades, and valleys. The wild Middle Fork and South Fork of the Kings River and the South Fork of the San Joaquin River cut sheer-walled canyons on their journeys through the glacial high country of the park and provide top-ranked fishing for brook, brown, and rainbow trout.

The Sequoia-Kings Canyon country was once the hunting grounds of the Mono and Paiute Indians, who during their many crossings of the High Sierra mountain passes established many of the trails used today by backpackers and fishermen. Many of these trails, including the John Muir, Knapsack Pass, Cartridge Pass, Lost Canyon, Giant Forest, Indian Basin, and Sawtooth Pass trails, lead past old Indian campsites and archaeological remains in Evolution Valley, Palisade Basin, Upper Basin, Quail Flat, and Five Lakes. The abundant game and beaver found in the area were first discovered in 1826 by Jedediah Smith. In 1858 Hale Tharp, a cattle rancher who lived on the Kaweah River near the present town of Three Rivers, traveled up the Middle Fork of the Kaweah guided by two Indians and became the first white man to discover the magnificent sequoias of the Giant Forest. In 1869 Tharp mapped out a route along an old Indian trail in the Log Meadow area of the Giant Forest to serve as a summer trail and pasture for his herd of cattle, and built a summer home in a giant hollow log!

The first significant exploration of the Sierra high country and Kings Canyon was accomplished by the Whitney Survey of 1864, led by William H. Brewer. The Brewer party headed east from Big Meadows to the summit of a peak they named Mt. Brewer at the northern end of the Great Western Divide. For the first time, the spectacular upper Kern River canyon and numerous other canyons 2,000 to 5,000 feet deep, seemingly endless series of ridges with sharp needlelike pinnacles; hundreds upon hundreds of sparkling blue cloud-high lakes and glacial cirques; sweeping snowfields, glaciers, and barren, boulder-strewn meadows; giant, craterlike amphitheaters; and the soaring snowcapped 14,000–foot summits of the Southern Sierra Crest, were scientifically observed, and opened the way for further exploration and mapping of the Kings-Kern-Kaweah watersheds.

As the news of the Whitney expedition spread, hunters, fishermen, mountaineers, and naturalists were lured into the majestic Kings Canyon country on the South Fork. In the summer of 1873 John Muir, accompanied by his mule, Brownie, explored the "Range of Light" and Kings Canyon country, and crossed the Middle and North forks of the Kaweah River into the giant sequoia country, which he aptly named the Giant Forest. Muir further explored the

South and Middle forks of the Kings River in 1875 and 1877. The northernmost reaches of the region that was to become Kings Canyon National Park remained isolated and unexplored until Theodore Solomons discovered the alpine lakes and peaks surrounding the beautiful meadows of Evolution Valley in the mid–1890s.

Information Sources, Maps & Access

For additional vacation travel and recreation information and a free *Sequoia & Kings Canyon Map/Brochure*, contact: Superintendent, Sequoia & Kings Canyon National Park, Lodgepole 93262 (209)565–3341. The rugged grandeur of this country is shown on the full-color U.S. Geological Survey *Sequoia-Kings Canyon National Park Map* ($2, available in either a topographic or shaded-relief edition). This map, 30 × 41 inches with a scale of 1 inch to 2 miles, shows trails (including the John Muir and High Sierra trails), campgrounds, ranger stations, shelters, contours, and natural features. It may be ordered from: Distribution Branch, U.S. Geological Survey, Federal Center, Denver, CO 80225.

A complete listing of Sequoia-Kings Canyon publications may be obtained free from: Sequoia Natural History Association, Ash Mountain, Three Rivers 93271.

Major routes to Sequoia and Kings Canyon national parks are Interstate 5 to State Routes 198 and 180, and U.S. 395. Lodging, supplies, and equipment outfitters are available at Three Rivers, Silver City, Mineral King, Sequoia, Visalia, Badger, Pinehurst, Big Pine, and Independence. Generals Highway is the main road that connects the two. This all-weather road winds through the sequoia belt and covers 46 miles—a 2–hour drive from the Ash Mountain Entrance to Grant Grove. Branch roads provide access to recreation areas and trailheads. From Grant Grove, you travel 30 miles on California 180 through Sequoia National Forest and along the South Fork of the Kings River to Cedar Grove. The road then continues for 6 miles through the solid granite walls of Kings Canyon, which tower thousands of feet above the river floor. The road to Cedar Grove is closed from November 1 to May 1. Ski equipment and snowshoes may be rented in Sequoia at Wolverton.

Gateways & Accommodations

Three Rivers

(Pop. 900; zip code 93271; area code 209.) This gateway to the Sequoia National Park marks the point where the north and south forks of the Kaweah River unite. Accommodations: *Best Western Holiday Lodge* (rates: $23–28 double), 38 rooms, color TV, heated pool, 8 miles west of park entrance on California Hwy. 198, at

40105 Sierra Drive (561–4119); *Mountainaire Motel* (rates: $18–25 double), 21 rooms, 3 efficiency suites, air-conditioned, some fireplaces, swimming pool, at 43175 Sierra Drive, 2 miles northeast of town on Hwy. 198 (561–4379).

Lodges

Kings Canyon National Park Lodgings:

★*Grant Grove Lodge* is located near the big trees and Grant Grove Village at an altitude of 6,600 feet. The accommodations and daily rates are as follows: Standard cabins with modern facilities, tub bath, electric lights, Safe-Aire heaters, open late May to mid-October, single or double occupancy $23.50, each additional person $4. Sleeping cabins without bath, no electric lights, wood-burning stoves for heat, free showers in central bath, open late May to mid-October, single or double occupancy $11.75, each additional person $2. Semi-housekeeping cabins without bath, no electricity, free showers in central bath, patio kitchen with wood-burning cookstove, no cook or tableware provided, open late May to mid-October, single or double occupancy $13, each additional person $2.

Cedar Grove Camp is located near the terminus of the scenic highway into the spectacular Kings River Canyon, at an altitude of 4,600 feet. It offers a limited number of accommodations in sleeping cabins without bath, heated by wood-burning stoves (advance reservations accepted). There is also a snack bar, a well-stocked market, a camper's supply store, a service station, and a Park Service information center. The lodging accommodations and market and service station are open from early June to Labor Day. Rates on request. Additional information and reservation forms may be obtained by contacting: Sequoia & Kings Canyon Hospitality Service, Sequoia National Park, CA 93262 (209)565–3373).

★★*Wilsonia Lodge—Kings Canyon National Park*, located at 6,700 feet, offers rustic, yet modern lodge and cottage accommodations. Each room in the main lodge has a private bath and opens onto a balcony overlooking the countryside. The lodge contains a restaurant and lounge with a huge open fireplace. The lodge also has 4 one-bedroom sleeping cottages and 3 family units, each consisting of 2 large bedrooms that will sleep up to 6 per unit. All cottages are equipped with private baths. The lodge is centrally located for fishing, backpacking, and horseback trips into the surrounding high country and for auto tours of beautiful Kings Canyon, Grizzly Falls, Roaring River Falls, Boyden's Cave, and Cedar Grove. Scenic and educational tours are conducted daily under the supervision of park rangers. Lodge rates range from $23 (double) to $60 for a 3–bedroom housekeeping cottage with bath, kitchen, and living room with fireplace. For additional info, contact: Wilsonia Lodge, P.O. Box 808, Kings Canyon National Park, CA 93633 (209)335–2310.

★★★*Montecito—Sequoia Ski Lodge*, set amid towering fir and pine trees at 7,350–foot elevations in the Sequoia National Forest, offers spectacular views of the Great Western Divide, superb cross-country skiing, and fine American-plan accommodations. The cross-country ski program includes instruction as well as guided and unguided skiing on more than 16 loop and return ski trails (about 44 miles all together) surrounding the lodge in the Chimney Rock, Mt. Baldy, and Big Meadows areas. Trails range from an easy 2½ miles to nearly 20 miles, many leading to beautiful vistas. There's also a lighted outdoor skating rink on Lake Homavalo; professional skating instruction is available from the lodge staff. Other winter pursuits include sledding, snowshoeing, and tobogganing, plus a variety of games in the indoor recreation rooms. The lodge has 22 attractive, rustic guest rooms accommodating up to 110 persons. All have private baths, generous beds, electric blankets, picture windows, and individually controlled heat. Other amenities include 2 big recreation/lounge areas with oversized fireplaces, a refreshment center for snacks and cocktails, and a family-style dining room where buffet breakfasts and home-cooked meals are served. Rates for a 2–day weekend package, including 6 meals and 2 nights' lodging, are $55 per person for 3; $67 per person for 2. Daily rates, children and youth discounts, and group packages are available. Nearby residents may enjoy day-use privileges of the lodge, trails, and instruction on an annual basis ($50 per year for families and couples, $30 for singles). For full information write: Sequoia-Montecito Lodge, 1485 Redwood Drive, Los Altos, CA 94022 (415)967–8612.

Sequoia National Park Lodgings:

★*Giant Forest Lodge* consists of a main lodge and cottages in the heart of the Giant Forest near Giant Forest Village at an altitude of 6,500 feet. Accommodations and daily rates are as follows (please note that pets are not allowed): Superior motels and cabins, all with electric heat, most with tub and shower, a few with shower only, fully carpeted, comfortable, and roomy, sleep 4–6, open all year, single or double occupancy $25.75, winter midweek $17.75, each additional person $4. Standard cabins with modern facilities, tub or shower, propane Safe-Aire heat, sleep 2–5, open late May to mid-October, weather permitting, single or double occupancy $23.50, each additional person $4. Family cabins, 2–room cottages with connecting bath, most will accommodate 6, a few will accommodate 8, open late May to mid-October, weather permitting, single or double occupancy $25.50, each additional person $4. A limited number of motel units, all with tub/shower, electric heat, carpet, balcony, sleep 4–6, open all year, single or double occupancy $27.75, no reduction during winter midweek, each additional per-

son $4. Sleeping cabins without bath, most with electric lights, wood-burning stove, free showers in central bath house, mid-May to mid-October, single or double occupancy $11.75, each additional person $2. Semi-housekeeping cabins, same as sleeping cabins without bath, but have patio-kitchen with wood-burning stove, no cook or tableware provided, single or double occupancy $13, each additional person $2.

Bearpaw Meadow Camp is a trail camp for hikers and saddle-horse parties. Located on the High Sierra Trail at an altitude of 7,800 feet, Bearpaw Meadow Camp serves as base for trips to Kern Canyon and Mt. Whitney; it is surrounded by spectacular scenery. Accommodations are plain but comfortable, in tents. Open from approximately late June to Labor Day. The camp has tent dining facilities and hot showers. The cost per bed is $9.75, or $19.50 per tent. Meals not included.

For additional information and reservation forms, contact: Sequoia & Kings Canyon Hospitality Service, Sequoia National Park, CA 93262 (209)565–3373.

Travel Services

Mt. Whitney Guide Service School of Mountaineering is located at the town of Lone Pine in the Owens Valley of eastern California. The school offers a 4–day general mountaineering seminar, a 4–day seminar in the Whitney Portal area at an elevation of 9,000 feet, and a 4–day Mt. Whitney Park bagging seminar. The guide service offers guided ascents on the east face of Mt. Whitney and on other peaks of the southern Sierra Nevadas as well as hiking, backpacking and fishing. The Mt. Whitney Guide Service is operational throughout the year, the traditional climatic stability of the southern Sierra Nevada making it a preferred area for winter mountaineering. Conditions are usually most favorable for general snow-climbing between the months of March and May. And the southern peaks are often largely clear of snow as late as November. Dates for guided services are best secured through reservation in advance. For rates and information, contact: Box 659, Lone Pine, CA 93545 (714)876–4500.

Mt. Whitney Pack Trains. Serving the southern High Sierra including Sequoia-Kings National Park and upper Kern areas. Specializing in all-inclusive and traveling-type pack trips. Contact: Box 459, Lone Pine, CA 93545.

Sequoia National Park Nordic Ski Center is located in the Giant Forest within walking distance of lodgings and the cafeteria. The Nordic ski school, directed by Bob Lingard, provides a range of instruction, rentals, and guide services—with special services for families and children. Instruction is available from beginner to advanced levels, and weekly classes on downhill cross-country skiing are very popular. In addition to regularly scheduled classes, they provide guided tours for all levels of ability. There are day-long tours which often follow one of the marked trails. Easy trails wind through the stately Giant Sequoias, while advanced trails lead into the backcountry. Winter travel courses are designed for those who want to ski in the backcountry and must know about route finding, avalanches, and other winter survival skills. Trans-Sierra tours, held every spring, pass through the most spectacular regions of the High Sierras. Overnight accommodations are available at reasonable rates to fit your travel budget. Special midweek rates are available during nonholiday periods. They offer cafeteria service for dining and there is a cocktail lounge with a warm fireplace for cold winter evenings. All-day beginner, novice, and advanced lessons cost $10; half-day courses, $6. Winter travel courses range in cost from $15 for 1 day to $80 for 4 days. The overnight tours are $32 and the Trans-Sierra Tour costs $150; they include all food and group equipment. For additional information, contact: Sequoia Ski Touring, Sequoia & Kings Canyon Hospitality Service, Sequoia National Park, CA 93262 (209)565–3373.

High Sierras—Sequoia National Forest

The Sequoia National Forest encompasses 2 million acres of fishing, camping, backpacking, and hunting country along the southern Sierras in central California. It extends from the Kings River on the north to the Kern River Plateau on the south. The eastern boundary is on the Sierra Nevada Crest, where it joins the Inyo National Forest and portions of the Mojave Desert. The forest stretches westward to the brush-covered foothills along the San Joaquin Valley and is laced by a network of Forest Service roads and trails, including a segment of the Pacific Crest Trail, that provides access to the rugged 12,000–foot peaks of the High Sierra country on the north along the scenic South Fork of the Kings, to the remote grandeur of the High Sierra Primitive Area along the Monarch Divide, to Hume Lake and Logger Flat, and to the renowned rainbow trout waters of the Kern River Plateau, Greenhorn Mountains, Dome Land Wilderness, and the headwaters of the Tule-Quaking Aspen area on the south. The forest contains several groves of the majestic giant sequoia redwoods, varying from a hundred trees or less to groves containing thousands of awesome specimens. Among the larger of the trees is the Boole sequoia, located northwest of Hume Lake on Converse Mountain, with a base circumference of 90 feet and a height of 268 feet.

The Dome Land Wilderness takes in 62,206 acres at the southern end of the Kern Plateau between the South Fork and the main Kern River. Erosion and weathering have left the area strewn with oddly shaped rock outcroppings, giving the appearance of a "dome land." Backcountry trails lead to the "roughs" of the South Fork of the Kern River, Manter Meadows, Rockhouse Meadow, White Dome, Church Dome, Pilot Knob, and Trout Creek. The vegetation on the lower slopes is light, consisting mostly of piñon pine, mixed conifer, sagebrush, and rabbit brush. Access is by several spur trails off the Pacific Crest Trail, which winds south near the area's western boundary.

The remote High Sierra Primitive Area, a part of the proposed Monarch Wilderness, is in the northeasternmost section of the district. The Primitive Area lies astride a portion of the Monarch Divide, a great mountain mass that separates the Sequoia and Sierra national forests and the South Fork and Middle Fork of the Kings River. This seldom visited area is a land of high barren ridges and peaks, which fall in steep, unbroken slopes to the river canyons far below, with scattered stands of mixed conifers. The area is a summer range for mule deer, black bear, mountain lion, and a wide variety of birds and small mammals. Rainbow and brook trout are found in Grizzly Lake and Creek, while the Middle and South forks of the Kings River, to the north and south, offer trout fishing of a quality rarely found today.

The rugged Kings River from Pine Flat Lake upstream 18 miles to the confluence with the South and Middle forks is managed as part of the state's wild trout program, and provides excellent, but often frustrating, fly-fishing for spooky, hook-jawed browns and pink-flanked rainbows. The scenic South Fork of the Kings from its confluence with the Middle Fork upstream to the western boundary of Kings Canyon National Park is also a top-ranked rainbow and brown trout fly-fishing stream, included in the California Wild Trout Program.

Information Sources, Maps & Access

The U.S. Forest Service full-color *Sequoia National Forest Map* (50¢) shows all natural and man-made features, including campgrounds, roads, trails, ranger stations, cabins, lookout towers, and pack stations. The map and additional information about fishing, camping, hunting, backpacking, cross-country skiing, wilderness-use permits, and backcountry campgrounds may be obtained by writing: Forest Supervisor, Sequoia National Forest, P.O. Box 391, 300 W. Grand Avenue, Porterville 93257 (209)784–1507. *Mineral King*, an informative, useful guide to the endangered Mineral King wilderness and the spectacular Great Western Divide, may be obtained for $2.95 from Wilderness Press, 2440 Bancroft Way, Berkeley 94704. Wilderness pack trips in the area are provided by the *Mineral King Pack Station*, Box 61, Three Rivers 93271 (winter: Creston Star Rt., Paso Robles 93446). Packhorses and backcountry pack trips are provided by *Golden Trout Pack Trains, Inc.* P.O. Box 407, Springville 93265 (at Quaking Aspen and Mountain Home State Forest); *Wishon Resort*, P.O. Box 664, Springville 93265 (Tule River); *Quaking Aspen Pack Station*, P.O. Box 756, Springville 93265 (winter: 1030 Superba Ave., Venice 90291); *Kennedy Meadow Pack Station*, P.O. Box 966, Weldon 93283 (Troy Meadows); *Fairview Pack Station*, P.O. Box 81, Kernville 93238 (Weldon); *Jordon Hot Springs*, P.O. Box 31, Inyokern 93527 (Cannell Meadow); *Roads End Resort*, Star Rt., Kernville 93238 (lodging). For additional fishing, hunting, camping, and backpacking information, write: *Cannell Meadow Ranger District*, P.O. Box 6, Kernville 93238. Vacation accommodations in the Camp Nelson area are provided by *Camp Nelson Resort*, Camp Nelson 93208.

The major auto routes to the forest are U.S. 395 on the east and Interstate 5 on the west. State Route 178 bisects the southern portion of the forest, and hundreds of miles of secondary roads and Forest Service roads provide access to the interior recreation areas.

Gateways & Accommodations

Bakersfield

(Pop. 69,500; zip code, see below; area code 805.) Surrounded by oil wells and fields of cotton and grain, Bakersfield spreads along the south bank of the Kern River in the narrow southern end of the San Joaquin Valley. The discovery of gold in the Kern River Canyon in 1885 transformed a placid farm community into a wild mining town almost overnight. In 1889, fire destroyed most of the old buildings and led to an extensive face-lift for Bakersfield. The discovery of oil 10 years later rekindled the boom days of the gold rush. Today oil remains an important aspect of the city's economy. There are also vineyards nearby, which produce about one quarter of California's wine. Bakersfield is a key gateway to the Sequoia National Forest. Area attractions include the Kern County Museum and Pioneer Village (3801 Chester Ave.), a group of beautifully restored late–19th-century buildings, and the Cunningham Memorial Art Gallery (1930 R St.), housing a collection of portraits and rare Oriental stencils. The Tule Elk State Reserve, 8 miles south of town on California Hwy. 99, then 16 miles west on California Hwy. 119, is home to a small herd of elk native to this area. Accommodations: *Bakersfield Inn* (rates: $25 double), 178 excellent rooms, meeting facilities, cocktail lounge, dancing and entertainment, at 1101 Union Ave., 2½ miles south on Hwy. 99 (322–5931); *Bakersfield Lodge* (rates: $20–22 double), 50 fine rooms, swimming pool, cafe, at 1219 S. Union Ave. (zip code 93307), in the business district (327–7901); *Bakersfield Travelodge* (rates: $23 double), 56 rooms, sundeck and pool, free coffee in rooms, at 525 Union Ave. (zip code 93307), south on Hwy. 99 (324–4593); *Best Western Casa Royale Motor Inn*

(rates: $30 double), 120 excellent rooms and suites with air conditioning and color TV, coffee shop, room service, cocktail lounge, convention facilities, at 251 S. Union Ave. (zip code 93307), 2 miles south on Hwy. 99 (327–3333); *Best Western Oak Inn* (rates: $30 double), 42 comfortable rooms, swimming pool, adjacent to Hwy. 99 at 889 Oak St. (zip code 93304) (324–9686); *Hill House* (rates: $24–30 double), 100 first-rate rooms, swimming pool, coffee shop, dining room, quiet location 3 blocks west of Hwy. 99 at 700 Truxtun Ave. (zip code 93301) (327–4064); *Hilton Inn* (rates: $29–35 double), 200 air-conditioned rooms and luxury suites, color TV, swimming pool, 24–hour coffee shop, entertainment and dancing, free airport bus service, some private patios and balconies, 3535 Rosedale Hwy. (zip code 93308), at 24 St. Exit off Hwy. 99 (327–0681); *Holiday Inn* (rates: $28 double), 150 rooms and family suites, swimming pool, cocktail lounge, room service, free airport shuttle, at 2700 White Lane (zip code 93304), White Lane Exit, 3½ miles south on Hwy. 99 (832–3111); *Ramada Inn* (rates: $31–33 double), 200 rooms with air conditioning and color TV, swimming pool, coffee shop, dining room, some private balconies, at 2620 Pierce Road (zip code 93308), adjacent to Hwy. 99, Exit 24 St. or Rosedale Hwy. (327–9651); *Rodeway Inn* (rates: $34 double), 200 excellent rooms, cocktail lounge, 24–hour cafe, dining room, swimming pool, 818 Real Road (zip code 93309), at California Ave. Exit off California Hwy. 99; (322–1911); *Royal Inn* (rates: $27 double), 75 excellent rooms, therapy pool and saunas, heated swimming pool, 24–hour coffee shop, cocktail lounge, at 1011 Oak St. (zip code 93308), adjacent to Hwy. 99 at California Ave. Exit (325–0772); *Skyway House* (rates: $24–30 double), 75 fine rooms, some with balconies and patios, swimming pool, cocktail lounge, near airport on Airport Drive at Meadows Field (zip code 93308); (399–9321).

Porterville

(Pop. 12,600; zip code 93257; area code 209.) The city is the headquarters for the Sequoia National Forest. The forest supervisor's office is at 900 W. Grand Ave. Accommodations: *Paul Bunyan Lodge* (rates: $23–28 double), 100 fine air-conditioned rooms, swimming pool, playground, restaurant, coffee shop, lighted tennis court, adjacent to California Hwy. 65 at Henderson St. Exit, 940 W. Morton St. (784–3150).

Visalia

(Pop. 27,300; zip code 83277; area code 209.) Visalia is a gateway to Sequoia and Kings Canyon national parks. Mooney Grove Park, 5 miles south of town, encompasses 155 acres of valley oaks, a small lake, and the Tulare County Museum, which houses exhibits of local historical interest. Accommodations: *Holiday Inn* (rates: $34 double), 160 excellent rooms and suites, color TV, heated indoor pool, sauna, whirlpool, putting green, dining room, coffee shop, free airport bus, adjacent to Visalia Airport, 9000 W. Airport Drive, off Hwy. 99 (733–9000); *Lampliter Inn* (rates: $28 double), 100 excellent rooms, four 2–room cottages, on attractively landscaped grounds, color TV, pool, restaurant, coffee shop, free airport bus, at 3300 W. Mineral Ave., on Hwy. 198, ½ mile west of junction with Hwy. 63 (732–4511); *Visalia Travelodge* (rates: $24–26 double), 78 air-conditioned rooms, 3 with kitchens, color TV, swimming pool, playground, at 4645 W. Mineral King Ave., 2 miles west of town on Hwy. 198 (732–5611).

Lodges

★★★*Lazy River Lodge* commands 10 acres on the Upper Kern River, an area surrounded by the mighty redwoods of Sequoia National Forest. For the boat fisherman, there is year-round angling in the productive pools and riffles of the Kern River, with good fishing just a few steps from the lodge. The Lazy River Lodge Riding Stable offers saddle horses, competent guides, lessons, and regularly scheduled breakfast rides. Hunting is available in season for pheasant, quail, chukar, deer, bear, mountain lion, and other local game; both fishing and hunting licenses are sold at the lodge. Other activities run the gamut from swimming in a big outdoor pool to winter sports in the Greenhorn Mountains and boating on Lake Isabella, a 10–minute drive away. Also in the immediate vicinity, the Kern Valley Golf Course offers a 72–par course with spacious greens and two artificial lakes. Suites at the lodge accommodate 2–6 guests and feature air conditioning, wall-to-wall carpeting, fireplaces, beamed ceilings, all-electric kitchenettes, and private patios with brick barbecues for outdoor dining. Rates range from $22.50 daily (double occupancy) for a deluxe river-view suite. Seasonal discounts are offered Sunday through Thursday, November through April. For more information write: Lazy River Lodge, Kernville, CA 93238 (714)376–2242.

High Sierras—Sierra National Forest & John Muir Wilderness

The vast Sierra National Forest encompasses some of the West's most spectacular wilderness camping and fishing areas. The forest lies east of Fresno in central California, west of the High Sierra Crest between Yosemite and Sequoia and Kings Canyon national parks. Hundreds of miles of trails, including the John Muir segment of the Pacific Crest Trail, and old mining and logging roads wind through the region from brushy front country to dense forests and barren alpine peaks and valleys, and provide access to the Minarets and John Muir wilderness areas, Silver Divide Lake Basin, Mono Divide Area, the Pinnacles, Humphreys Basin, Dinkey Lakes, Blackcap Basin, Woodchuck Country, North Fork of the Kings River, and the Monarch Divide wildlands. During the 1850s the Mariposa section of the forest was the center of gold-mining activity, and it later became important as a way station to Yosemite. Old logging-camp buildings can be seen at Sugar Pine and Central Camp.

Information Sources, Maps & Access

All campgrounds, trails, ranger stations, lookout towers, boat-launching ramps, and pack stations are shown on the *Sierra National Forest Map* (50¢). The map also shows the John Muir Trail segment of the Pacific Crest Trail, the Minarets Wilderness, and John Muir Wilderness. The map and detailed fishing, camping, hunting, and wilderness travel info may be obtained by writing: Forest Supervisor, Sierra National Forest, 1130 O St., Fresno 93721 (209)487–5155. Several useful guidebooks and maps have been published to aid the wilderness fisherman, backpacker, and hunter planning to travel in the John Muir and Minarets wilderness areas. *Angler's Guides*, containing detailed maps, are published for *Granite Creek Area*, *Fish Creek Area*, *Bear Creek Area*, *Humphreys Basin-French Canyon Area*, and *Crown Valley-Blackcap Basin Area*. They are available for 40¢ each from: Dept. of Fish & Game, Documents Section, P.O. Box 20191, Sacramento 95820.

Packhorse stations and outfitters in the forest are located at Wishon Village, Dinkey Creek, Badger Flat, Mono Hot Springs, Blayney Meadows-Muir Trail Ranch, Florence Lake, and Warm Creek Meadow-Vermillion Recreation Area. High Sierra wilderness pack-trip service in the region is provided by the *High Sierra Pack Station*, Mono Hot Springs 93642 (winter: Box 396, North Fork 93643); *D & F Pack Station*, P.O. Box 156, Lakeshore 93634 (winter: Box 82, Raymond 93653); *Dean & Dave's Pack Train*, Dinkey Creek 93617

(winter: Box 383, Raymond 93653); *Minarets Pack Station*, 3218 N. Zediker, Sanger 93657; *Yosemite Trails Pack Station*, Fish Camp 93623 (winter: 8314 Santa Fe Drive, Chowchilla 93610).

Major routes to the forest are U.S. Highway 395 and state highways 120, 108, 140, 41, 180, and 168. Lodging, supplies, boat rentals, guides, and outfitters are available at Dinkey Creek, Lakeshore, North Fork, Oakhurst, Mariposa, and Mammoth Lakes.

Recreation Areas

John Muir Trail

The John Muir Trail winds for most of its 212–mile length along the western slope of the High Sierras through some of the most stunning wilderness camping and alpine fishing country on the continent. The great arc of the High Sierra Crest forms a continuous strip of remote, sparkling, jewellike lakes and soaring snowcapped peaks, extending from Yosemite Valley to the massive 14,000–foot peaks dominated by Mt. Whitney at the headwaters of the Kings and Kern rivers. From Yosemite, the trail passes through the Minarets Wilderness, winds on past the Devils Postpile National Monument and through the vast John Muir Wilderness in the Sierra National Forest, and enters the Sequoia National Park area, dominated by the Great Western Divide. The trail and numerous spur trails provide access to literally thousands of trout lakes, many of which hold thriving populations of prized golden trout, that lie in remote lake basins on both slopes of the High Sierra, including the Granite area in the Minarets Wilderness of the Sierra National Forest, the Upper Bishop Creek area in the John Muir Wilderness Area of the Inyo National Forest, and the Mono Creek area, French Canyon and Humphreys Basin area, and Bear Creek area—all situated in the John Muir Wilderness in the Sierra National Forest. Wildlife seen by the sharp-eyed wilderness traveler includes deer, the shrill-voiced coney, coyotes and weasels, and the tracks of the trout-loving pine marten. A few bands of bighorn sheep are occasionally sighted along the east slope of the Sierra Crest from Convict Lake to Mt. Whitney. Grouse and mountain quail are found throughout the timbered areas.

John Muir Wilderness

The famous John Muir Wilderness covers 503,000 acres of the High Sierra, extending along the western slope of the Sierra Crest from Mammoth Lakes, south of the Devils Postpile National Monument, southeast for 30 miles, then around the boundary of Kings Canyon National Park to the Crown Valley and Mt. Whitney region. This

majestic land of snowcapped peaks contains literally thousands of trout lakes and streams, the headwaters of the San Joaquin River, Kern River, and the North Fork of the Kings River, and numerous creeks that drain from the eastern slope into Owens Valley. Fishing ranges from fair to excellent for rainbow, golden, and Eastern brook trout in the Fish Creek area, Silver Divide area, Cascade Valley, Margaret Lakes, Mono Recesses area, Bear Creek, Seven Gables Peak area, French Canyon, Humphreys Basin, Mono Creek, Glacier Divide area, the Palisades group, Red Mountain Basin, and the Blackcap Basin. The wilderness is the summer range for over 50,000 mule deer, and grouse and mountain quail are common. Many of the least-known lakes of the wilderness have populations of trout and should not be overlooked. Most of the lakes below timberline have good camps built up over the years by packers, fishermen, and hunters.

Minarets Wilderness

In the northernmost section of the Sierra National Forest lies the famed Minarets Wilderness, a magnificent High Sierra hiking, camping, and fishing area that preserves 109,500 acres due northwest of the John Muir Wilderness. The northern portion of the Minarets extends into the Inyo National Forest. The wilderness has some excellent high-country fishing for rainbow, golden, and brook trout in the headwater lakes area of the Middle Fork and North Fork of the San Joaquin River. The largest lakes—Thousand Island, Garnet, and Shadow—and the Granite Creek Lakes lie on the eastern slope of the precipitous Ritter Range formed by the summits of Mt. Davis (12,306 ft.), Banner Peak (12,957 ft.), and the Minarets (12,255 ft.). At its higher elevations, much of the area is barren, with rock outcroppings and red fir and some Jeffrey pine along the upper reaches of the San Joaquin River. Other sections of the wilderness are more alpine in character, with scattered stands of lodgepole pine, mountain hemlock, and quaking aspen along the slopes and meadow edges. Both Inyo and California mule deer use the region as their summer range.

Gateways & Accommodations

Fresno

(Pop. 166,000; zip code, see below; area code 209.) Fresno lies in the geographic center of the state and is the heart of the lush and fertile San Joaquin Valley. In terms of agricultural wealth, Fresno and Fresno County claim the largest annual production of fruit and produce of any county in the United States. The downtown area, with its tall modern buildings rising abruptly from the flat valley floor, boasts a new 9–block, traffic-free shopping mall. Among the many points of interest are the Forestiere Underground Gardens at 5021 W. Shaw Ave., a subterranean maze of gardens and grottoes patterned after the Roman catacombs; and Roeding Park at W. Belmont Ave. and California Hwy. 99, encompassing varied botanical gardens, a zoo, and a children's storyland. Fresno is also a gateway to the Sierra National Forest (forest supervisor's office in town at 1130 O St., 93721, phone 487–5456), Sequoia and Kings Canyon national parks (54 miles east on Hwy. 180), and Yosemite National Park (60 miles northeast on Hwy. 41). Visitors to Fresno also enjoy the guided tours and wine tasting at the Gribari Winery at 3223 E. Church Ave. (485–3083). Restaurants worth exploring include *Estrada's Spanish Kitchen* (370 Blackstone Ave., 233–1248) for tasty Mexican specialities, and *Charlie's Sunnyside* (827 S. Clovis Ave., 251–8228), a popular spot for fresh seafood and Sunday brunch. Accommodations: *Best Western Parkside Inn* (rates: $26–30 double), 46 excellent rooms, swimming and wading pools, color TV, 24–hour coffee shop, cocktail lounge, opposite Roeding Park at 1415 W. Olive Ave., 93728 (237–2086); *Fresno Downtown Travelodge* (rates: $26–28 double), 110 fine rooms, swimming pool, coffee shop, free coffee in rooms, at 888 Broadway, 93721, Fresno St. Exit, ½ mile north on Hwy. 99 (485–7550); *Fresno Hilton* (rates: $35–43 double), 205 superlative rooms and suites, swimming pool, garage, dining room, cocktail lounge, coffee shop, airport transportation, at 1055 Van Ness Ave., 93721, in town on the mall (485–9000); *Hill House Motel* (rates: $28–30 double), 99 excellent rooms and family suites, pool, playground, coffee shop, at 1101 Parkway Drive, 93728, opposite Roeding Park (268–6211); *Holiday Inn—Airport* (rates: $33–36 double), 210 fine rooms, 2 swimming pools, whirlpool, putting green and recreation room, restaurants, cocktail lounge, next to airport at 5090 E. Clinton Ave., 93727 (252–3611); *Tradewinds Best Western* (rates: $27–30 double), 112 fine rooms with queen-size beds, color TV, swimming pool, restaurant, piano bar, attractive landscaped grounds, at 2141 N. Parkway Drive, 93705, 3 miles north of town on Hwy. 99, Clinton Ave. Exit (237–1881); *Piccadilly Inn* (rates: $38 double), one of the area's finest, with 203 large air-conditioned rooms, on spacious quiet grounds, swimming pool, restaurant, coffee shop, entertainment and dancing, free bus to airport, at 2305 W. Shaw Ave., 93711, 5 miles northwest of Fresno, then 3 miles east on Hwy. 99, Shaw Ave. Exit (226–3850); *Ramada Inn* (rates: $30–34 double), 170 rooms and family suites, some studio units, swimming pool, restaurant, coffee shop, free airport bus, at 324 E. Shaw Ave., 93710, 4½ miles north on Hwy. 99, Shaw Ave. Exit (224–4040); *Sheraton Inn* (rates: $31 double), 350 excellent rooms and suites, 2 swimming pools, whirlpool, 24–hour coffee shop, dining room, bar, discotheque, airport transportation, 3 miles north of town on Hwy. 99, Clinton Ave. Exit, 2550 W. Clinton Ave., 93728 (486–3000); *Smuggler's Inn* (rates: $38 double), 210 superlative rooms and family suites, some with patios, landscaped grounds, swimming pool, airport transportation, restaurant and bar, at 3737 N. Blackstone Ave., 93726, 3½ miles north on Hwy. 41, Clinton Ave. Exit (226–2200); *The Village Inn* (rates: $26–28 double), 154 excellent rooms with queen-size beds, swimming pool, restaurant adjacent, at 3110 N. Blackstone Ave., 93703, 3 miles north on Hwy. 41 (226–2110); *The Water Tree Best Western Inn* (rates: $32 double), 140 excellent rooms, some with private steam baths and oversize beds, pool, 24–hour coffee shop, bar, entertainment and dancing, free airport bus, at 4141 N. Blackstone Ave., 93726, 3 miles north on Hwy. 99 (222–4445).

Lodges & Guest Ranches

★*Lakeshore Village* offers excellent cross-country skiing in the Sierras plus open country and pine forest ski-touring in the breathtaking winter setting around Huntington Lake. If downhill skiing's your preference, China Peak has 3 double chair-lifts and fine ski terrain just a short drive away. Or take advantage of the shuttle service connecting the two facilities. Accommodations at Lakeshore Village are in pleasant, modern hotel rooms ($20 daily on weekends, double occupancy) and cabins with kitchens ($24–52 daily on weekends, for 2–8 guests in each). Other amenities include a full-service restaurant, large recreation hall, a cross-country mountain shop, equipment rentals, and general store. Après-ski entertainment runs the gamut from bluegrass to dance bands. Lakeshore Village is open summers too. Special midweek and package rates are available. For more information write: Lakeshore Village, Lakeshore, CA 93634 (209)893–3222 or (213)426–3545.

★*Muir Trail Ranch* is a remote High Sierra Wilderness ranch located midway along the John Muir Trail, accessible only by boat, horseback, or helicopter. The ranch is the only outpost on the Muir Trail between the Devils Postpile National Monument and Mt.

Whitney. The ranch is in the heart of the Sierra National Forest, nestled among peaks rising over 12,000 feet in the Blayney Meadows on the South Fork of the San Joaquin River, within 3 miles of the northwest boundary of Kings Canyon National Park. The ranch offers housekeeping log-cabin and tent-cabin accommodations, hot spring baths and a thoroughly trained string of trail horses. Guests reach the ranch by boat and pack trip to and from Florence Lake boathouse (accessible by auto). The ranch serves as an excellent base for pack trips, fishing, and backpacking in the surrounding High Sierra Wilderness. Daily rates: $50 per week for a log cabin (double occupancy) and $35–37.50 per adult for tent-cabin accommodations. For additional information, contact: Muir Trail Ranch, Box 176, Lakeshore, CA 93634 (no phone).

High Sierras—Stanislaus National Forest & Emigrant Basin

This 1.1 million-acre central High Sierra forest, once the hunting grounds of the Maidu Indians, is famous for its wilderness fishing, hunting, and camping areas. The region is primarily rugged mountainous forest along the west slope of the Sierras, traversed by the deep canyons of the Merced, Tuolumne, Stanislaus, and Mokelumne rivers. Elevations vary from 1,100 feet at the western edge to 11,570 feet at Leavitt Peak. The famous Mother Lode gold belt, formed by older metamorphic rocks, runs along the western edge of the forest. Scenic trails provide access to the remote Dardanelles Cone and the Columns of the Giants, Jawbone Ridge, Cherry Lake, Highland Lakes, and Iceberg Reservoir. Fishing is good in most of the high-country lakes for golden, rainbow, and brook trout. The Pacific Crest Trail enters the region at Carson Pass and descends through the beautiful lake country around Blue and Meadow lakes, passes Grover Hot Springs near the Mokelumne Wilderness, and climbs over Ebbetts Pass. The trail winds on past Highland Peak and Sonora Peak, over Sonora Pass, and skirts the Emigrant Basin Wilderness, entering Yosemite near Tower Peak.

Much of the Stanislaus gold-rush country is rich in early California history, particularly in the Emigrant Basin, Sonora Pass, and Ebbetts Pass areas. The old gold-rush ghost town at Columbia was once the home of 15,000 prospectors, 143 faro games, 30 saloons, 4 banks, 27 produce stores, 3 express offices, and an arena for bull-and-bear fights, which were described by Horace Greeley in the old New York *Tribune* and were said to have given Wall Street one of its best-known phrases. The Sierra Nevada Mountains were first crossed in 1827 by Jedediah Smith, about 8 miles south of Sonora Pass. Other explorers, including Frinnt, Ebbetts, and Goddard, followed, looking for easy routes for wagon trains and railroads, but moved north to the less arduous routes through the Lake Tahoe country. The pink volcanic ridges of the Sierra Crest at Sonora Pass marked the Emigrant Trail along the Walker River, across Emigrant Pass, and down rocky Dodge Ridge to the Mother Lode gold mines. It has been said that the Emigrant Trail was easy to follow, being well marked by broken wagons and the skeletons of dead animals.

Crossed by the Tahoe-Yosemite Trail, the 98,000–acre Emigrant Basin Primitive Area is located in the forest, bordered by the High Sierras to the east, Yosemite to the south, and high ridges to the west and north. The region is a favorite haunt of hunters seeking deer and bear and fishermen after trout in the headwaters area of the Tuolumne and Stanislaus rivers. Numerous trails cross the soft meadows, forests of pine and aspen, and patches of dark volcanic rock. The Emigrant Meadow area was used by travelers on the Trans-Sierra Trail seeking gold in the mountains beyond. The high mountain lakes are well stocked with trout, but they are often very difficult to catch. Packhorse stations and outfitters are located at Leavitt Meadows, northeast of the Primitive Area in the Toiyabe National Forest and the Stanislaus National Forest at Kennedy Meadow Resort to the north, Strawberry and Kerrick Corral in Aspen Valley to the west, and Cherry Valley to the south.

Information Sources, Maps & Access

Additional information and a full-color *Stanislaus National Forest Map* and a free *Sonora Pass Area Map*, may be obtained from the Supervisor, Stanislaus National Forest, 175 S. Fairview Lane, Sonora, CA 95370 (209)965–3435. Vacation lodging, guides, and wilderness pack trips are available at *Kennedy Meadows Resort*, Star Rt., Box 1490, Sonora 95370 (winter: Box 401, Sonora 95370); *Mather Pack Station*, Camp Mather via Groveland 95321 (winter: 12930 Lancaster Rd., Oakdale 95321); *Alpine Lake Lodge*, Lake Alpine 95235; *Tamarack Lodge*, Box 67, Bear Valley 95223. Guided cross-country ski tours, instruction, winter camping and survival courses are provided by *Bear Valley Nordic Ski School & Touring Center*, Box 5, Bear Valley 95223 (209)753–2844; and *Ebbetts Pass Ski Touring Center*, Tamarack Lodge, Box 67, Bear Valley 95223 (209)753–2121. Scenic air tours of the High Sierra gold-rush country are provided by *Yosemite Airlines*, Box 330, Columbia 94310 (209)532–6946.

Major routes to the forest include U.S. 395, 99, and 50 and state highways 49, 120, 4, 108, 89, 88, and 104. State Highway 4, once known as the Big Trees Road, passes east from Angels Camp through the historic gold-rush communities of Vallecito and Murphys before entering the forest near Red Apple at an elevation of 3,200 feet. Designated by the state as a Scenic Highway from Arnold eastward, the road winds through dense forests and alpine meadows and peaks, offering sweeping vistas of the Stanislaus River Canyon and beyond to the Dardanelles and distant snowcapped peaks of the High Sierra Crest. As far as Lake Alpine, the road is a two-lane highway. Proceeding eastward, it becomes increasingly narrow and winding, with steep grades, and is inadequate for autos towing large trailers. The highway also passes through Calaveras Big Trees State Park, famous since its discovery in 1852 for its magnificent stands of *Sequoia gigantea*. Angels Camp was the scene of Mark Twain's story "The Celebrated Jumping Frog of Calaveras County," based on a tale heard one winter's night in the old Hotel Angels barroom. Today the village holds an annual Jumping Frog Jubilee. Highway 120, a historic route better known as the Big Oak Flat Road, was a pack trail from Stockton in 1849, and by 1874 it was a wagon road which reached Yosemite Valley. Historic Highway 108 follows the old Sonora and Mono Toll Road. Lodging, supplies, boat rentals, guides, and outfitters in the forest region are available at Arnold, Sonora, Mi-Wuk Village, Groveland, Pinecrest, Dardanelles, Pioneer, Coulterville, and Lake Alpine.

Gateways & Accommodations

Angels Camp

(Pop. 1,800; zip code 95222; area code 209.) The town is named, not for a temporary outpost of the heavenly host, but for a man called Angel, who found gold in the creek running through town in the summer of 1848. Several years later Mark Twain first gathered information in the barroom of the Hotel Angels for his first published success, "The Celebrated Jumping Frog of Calaveras County." Every year in May the town holds a Jumping Frog Jubilee to commemorate the event. The Angels Camp Museum, 2 blocks north of Angels Creek, contains souvenirs and equipment from the town's prosperous mining days. Accommodations: *Gold County Inn* (rates: $23–25

double), 28 air-conditioned rooms, color TV, 1 mile north on Hwy. 49 (736–4611).

Sonora

Pop. 3,100; zip code 95370; area code 209.) Originally settled by Mexicans from the state of Sonora, this onetime gold-rush town stretches across seven small hills just west of the Stanislaus National Forest. The Big Bonanza on Piety Hill, richest pocket mine in the Mother Lode, yielded close to $500,000 within a week after its discovery. All told, over $40 million in gold was taken from gulches, rivers, and creeks around Sonora. The town served as a setting for stories by both Mark Twain and Bret Harte. Area attractions include Columbia State Historic Park, 4 miles north via Hwy. 49, where extensive renovation of this early gold town is under way; Mercer Caverns, 10 miles north on Hwy. 49, then 5 miles northeast on Hwy. 4, an unusual series of underground rock formations visible from lighted walkways; Railway Town 1897, 3 miles southwest of Sonora in Jamestown, a reconstruction of a 19th-century railroad and depot (984–3953); and the Tuolumne County Museum, at 158 W. Bradford Ave., which houses items from the gold-rush days. Accommodations: *Gunn House* (rates: $23–34 double), 27 fine rooms, originally built in 1850 and restored to period decor, swimming pool, recreation room, restaurant opposite, at 286 S. Washington St. (532–3421); *Modern Manor Motel* (rates: $26–27 double), 50 comfortable rooms on hillside location, color TV, swimming pool, restaurant opposite, at 300 S. Washington St. (532–3647); *Sonora Towne House* (rates: $27 double), 60 fine air-conditioned rooms, color TV, swimming pool, restaurant adjacent, at 350 S. Washington St. (532–3633).

Lodges & Resorts

★★*Kennedy Meadows Resort* offers rustic cabin accommodations and organizes and outfits pack trips into the Emigrant Basin Primitive area. On extended pack trips into this area the packer and stock stay with the party for the entire time, thus making it possible to move camp and fish or hunt in many different areas. Pack mules are limited to 150 pounds so that you can pack up for a short or extended trip; saddle horse or pack animals are available at $15/ day for 1–3 days and at $12.50 per day for 6 days or more. This area is the ideal vacation spot for the whole family. Housekeeping cabins furnished with cooking utensils, dishes and linens, are available for groups of 2 to 10. Sleeper cabins with baths are offered as well as single and double occupancy rooms in the lodge. The dining room is open early for breakfast, lunch, and dinner and a grocery store will outfit you for travel food or simply snacks. A sport shop offers a complete line of tackle and supplies. The club house offers music and dancing as well as a well-stocked bar. Short pack trips are recommended if there are small children in the party. For room

rates and further information, contact. Kennedy Meadow Resort, Star Route, Box 1490, Sonora, CA 95370 or call Kennedy Meadows 1, via Sonora. Winter address: P.O. Box 401, Sonora, CA 95370.

Travel Services

Sonora Mountaineering offers guided cross-country skiing tours and winter camping tours in the Stanislaus National Forest and Emigrant Basin Wilderness Area. In addition, the shop offers avalanche, survival, and Nordic downhill clinics as well as winter and summer equipment rentals for ski touring, backpacking, and camping. The Trans-Sierra ski tour across the high mountain passes, over frozen lakes, and down miles of unbroken snow surrounded by spectacular views of the High Sierras in the Emigrant Basin Wilderness Area is one of Sonora Mountaineering's premier trips. A large portion of the Yosemite National Park backcountry is nearby. Lodging is available at nearby Pine Crest and Sonora. For rates and info, contact: Sonora Mountaineering, 171 N. Washington, Sonora, CA 95370 (209)532–5621.

High Sierras—Tahoe National Forest & Squaw Valley

The Tahoe National Forest encompasses 698,000 acres northeast of Sacramento, in the central portion of the Sierra Nevada Mountains, and extends from Lake Tahoe to north of the massive and spectacular Sierra Buttes. The forest's name, taken from the famed Lake Tahoe, is thought to derive from a Washo Indian word meaning "big water." The Tahoe region was once the home and hunting grounds of the Maidu and Washo Indians and today offers renowned fishing, alpine and cross-country skiing, backpacking, and wild-river canoeing.

The Steven-Townsend-Murphy party, the first white men to explore the area, opened the Overland Emigrant Route through the forest in 1844. In 1846, the doomed Donner Party passed into the area. Their final campsite is located in the Donner Camp historical area near Truckee. Many abandoned mining camps, mines, and trails left from the gold-rush era may be seen scattered throughout the remote backcountry area. Hundreds of miles of forest roads and trails provide access to the remote backcountry areas near the Rubicon River, Grouse Lakes, Sagehen Valley, French Meadows, Bullards Bar, Fall Creek Mountain Lakes, Granite Chief, Royal Gorge, Desolation Valley, Yuba River, Jackson Meadow Reservoir, Old Man Mountain, and the Sierra Buttes lake basin (8,587 ft.) north of the Wild Plum Guard Station. The Pacific Crest Trail enters the Tahoe region as it winds south from the Feather River country and passes into the scenic lake region along the Milton and Jackson Meadow reservoirs, Bowman Lake, Weber Lake, and Summit Lake. It continues south through Emigrant Gap into the Lake Tahoe area along the French Meadows Reservoir, past Squaw Valley, through Alpine Meadows, along Wentworth Springs and Loon Lake, and into the Eldorado National Forest and the Desolation Wilderness.

Clear blue Lake Tahoe, the original home of the giant Lahontan cutthroat, is an extinct volcano 1,600 feet deep lying at an altitude of 6,229 feet. Tahoe's water is so crystal-clear that you can see small pebbles on the bottom at depths down to 50 feet. A stocking program was developed in 1949, and the quality of the fishing has improved almost to its peak in the "old days." Lake Tahoe has produced the California record cutthroat (31 lb. 8 oz.), kokanee salmon (4 lb. 13 oz.), and lake trout (37 lb. 6 oz.) During the early spring months, top-lining close to shore and along the shoals provides some exciting fishing for cruising lake trout, rainbows, and browns. The *Angler's Guide to Lake Tahoe* provides a complete description of the lake and its fish species as well as a useful lake contour map. It may be purchased for 50¢ by writing: Office of Procurement, Documents Section, P.O. Box L0191, Sacramento 95820. Donner Lake to the northwest has some good early-season fishing for lake trout and rainbows and browns up to 10 pounds.

The major trout-fishing waters in the interior areas of the forest for brook, rainbow, and browns are the wild North Fork of the American River, Middle Fork of the American River including the French Meadows Reservoir, and the Middle, North, and South forks of the Yuba River. The wilderness traveler will find excellent fly-fishing for large rainbows and browns in the spectacular Royal Gorge of the North Fork of the American River.

Information Sources, Maps & Access

The *Tahoe National Forest Map* (50¢) and hunting, fishing, hiking, camping, and wilderness travel information may be obtained by writing: Tahoe National Forest Headquarters, Highway 49, Nevada City 95959 (916)265–4531; or by writing to the District Ranger Offices at Foresthill 95631, Sierraville 96126, Downieville 95936, and Truckee 95734. The full-color Forest Service map shows all natural features, trails, roads, campgrounds, ranger stations, and recreation sites. The following Forest Service publications may be obtained free from the Forest Headquarters: *French Meadows-Hill Hole Recreation Areas, Jackson Meadow Recreation Area, Woodcamp Creek Interpretive Trail, Washo Snowmobile Area, Washo—Indian Peoples of the Washo Territory, Bullards Bar Recreation Area,*

Glacier Meadow Loop Trail, Rock Creek Nature Study Area, Birds of the Tahoe National Forest & Vicinity, and the *Tahoe National Forest Camping Guide*.

The Granite Chief Area (Foresthill and Truckee ranger districts), which embraces the headwaters of the North Fork of the American River and the Grouse Lakes Area (Nevada Ranger District) have been closed to all types of motorized vehicles. Information and the free *Granite Chief Area Map* and *Grouse Lakes Area Map* may be obtained from the district ranger stations and from the Forest Supervisor's Office in Nevada City. The *Squaw Valley Mountaineering Center*, Box 2288, Olympic Valley 95730, offers 5-day outings in the Granite Chief Wilderness Area, fly-fishing excursions, and nature hikes. The center also sells backpacking and climbing gear and topo maps and provides backcountry info. The Squaw Valley Center also runs *Alpine Meadows* and *Tahoe Nordic Ski Center*. For information, call (916)583-4316.

The major routes to the Tahoe National Forest are Interstate 80, U.S. Highway 50, and California Routes 28, 20, 49, and 89. Resorts, lodges, supplies, boat and canoe rentals, guides, and outfitters are available at Nevada City, Emigrant Gap, Cisco, Norden, Truckee, Boca, Graniteville, Sierra City, Meeks Bay, Tahoe City, Emerald Bay, South Lake Tahoe, Sierraville, and Downieville.

Gateways & Accommodations

Downieville

(Pop. 400; zip code 95936; area code 916.) The town lies in a small basin walled by sheer mountainsides. Once the site of incredibly rich gold-mining activity (a boiled trout taken from local waters reportedly left flakes of gold in the bottom of the pot), the town retains much of its 19th-century charm. Old brick and stone buildings, some of them key landmarks from Downieville's boom days, flank the narrow, tree-lined main street, and the sidewalks in certain parts of town are still made from planks. Downieville is also a gateway to the Tahoe National Forest; a district ranger's office is located here. Accommodations: *Downieville Motor Inn* (rates: $17 double), 12 rooms, many with queen-size beds, free coffee in rooms, restaurant opposite, 2 blocks west of town on Hwy. 49 (289-3243); *Herrington's Sierra Pines* (rates: $23-30 double), 15 fine rooms near a trout pond, most with king-size beds and TV, restaurant, in Sierra City (Box 235, zip code 96125), 12½ miles east of town on Hwy. 49 (862-1151); *Snider's Resort* (rates: $20-25 double), 13 rooms, 8 with kitchens, rustic decor, pool, restaurant, fish-freezing facilities, 1 block southeast on Hwy. 49 (289-3308).

Grass Valley

(Pop. 5,100; zip code 95945; area code 916.) Located on the edge of the Tahoe National Forest, the town was once the heart of California's richest gold-mining region, the legendary Mother Lode country. The Empire Mine, now part of a state historic park with over 200 miles of passageways, alone produced $960 million in gold during its operation. The celebrated beauty and favorite of royalty, Lola Montez, made her home for a time in Grass Valley, as did Lotta Crabtree, a popular 19th-century actress who came to prominence playing Little Nell. Just outside of town, 4½ miles west on Hwy. 20, is Rough and Ready, a gold strike named for Gen. Zachary "Rough and Ready" Taylor. In 1850 the miners who settled here attempted to secede from the Union and form an independent republic with its own laws and constitution. Another reminder of Grass Valley's past is the Pelton Wheel Mining Exhibit, on Allison Ranch Road, where early mining equipment and artifacts are on display. Accommodations: *Gold Country Inn* (rates: $19-26 double) 52 air-conditioned rooms, 12 units with kitchens, swimming pool, free continental breakfast, open year-round, at 11972 Sutton Way, 2½ miles northeast on Hwy. 20 (273-1393); *Golden Chain Motel* (rates: $26-28 double), 21 air-conditioned rooms on attractive grounds, swimming pool, putting green, coffee shop, open year-round, at 13363 Hwy. 49, 2½ miles south of Grass Valley (273-7279); *Holiday Lodge* (rates: $20-22 double), 31 rooms, swimming pool, coffee shop, at 1221 E. Main St., 1¼ miles east on Hwy. 49 at Idaho and Maryland Road exits (273-4406); *Wolf Creek Inn* (rates: $25-27 double), 11 fine air-conditioned rooms in the Alta Sierra Country Club, balconies overlooking several small lakes, attractive rustic decor, golf course, and driving range, at 135 Tammy Way, 6 miles south of town, then ¼ mile east of Hwy. 49 (273-9102).

Lake Tahoe Accommodations:

Kings Beach—North Lake Tahoe (Pop. 2,000; zip code 95719; area code 916.) *Crown Motel* (rates: 30-40 double) 36 rooms, many on the lakefront with electric fireplaces, 19 units with kitchens, color TV, private beach, sundeck, restaurant opposite, at 8200 North Lake Blvd., 2½ blocks west of town on Hwy. 28 (546-3388); *Falcon Motor Lodge* (rates: $20-40 double), 32 rooms, 2 with kitchens, some with balconies and king-size beds, private beach, sundeck, swimming pool, at 8258 N. Lake Blvd., 2 blocks west of town on Hwy. 28 (546-2236); *Stevenson's Holliday Inn* (rates: $25-27 double), 30 rooms in motel and cottages, some with lake view and king-size beds, 3 with kitchens, restaurant nearby, at 8742 North Lake Blvd., 4 blocks east of town on Hwy. 28 (546-3845); *Thornley Lodge* (rates: $28-34 double), 26 rooms and 1 or 2 bedroom units with kitchens, swimming pool, private beach, kayaks, boat ramp, at 7630 N. Lake Blvd., ¾ mile west of town on Hwy. 28 (546-3952).

Tahoe Vista—North Lake Tahoe (Pop. 250; zip code 95732; area code 916.) *Charmey Chalet* (rates: $22-45 double), 22 excellent rooms, most with lake view, attractive grounds, private beach, swimming pool, sauna, at 6549 N. Lake Blvd., 5 blocks west of town on Hwy. 28, register at Silver Sands Motel—below (546-2529); *Cottonwood Lodge* (rates: $30-35 double), 17 lakeside cottages, 13 with kitchens, private beach, waterskiing, fishing, pier, ski package plans available, at 6542 Lake Blvd., 5 blocks west of town on Hwy. 28 (546-2220); *Silver Sands Resort* (rates: $23-39 double), 60 fine motel rooms and rustic cottages with kitchens, attractive lakefront grounds, 2 swimming pools, private beach, fishing, waterskiing, playground, putting green, at 6610 N. Lake Blvd., 5 blocks west of town on Hwy. 28 (546-2592).

Nevada City

(Pop. 2,300; zip code 95959; area code 916.) In the foothills of the High Sierras, Nevada City has been a gold-mining center since the 1850s, when a reported 10,000 miners worked every foot of ground within a radius of 3 miles. The county's mines have yielded more than half of the state's total gold production; the gravel banks alone are said to have produced some $8 million in gold dust and nuggets over a 2-year period during the town's boom days. The mines were closed in 1942, but Nevada City still retains the picturesque charm of a prosperous small town, with multigabled frame houses in the residential sections and the Old Nevada Theater and South Yuba Canal Building gracing the downtown area. Information on walking tours of this picturesque town may be obtained from the Chamber of Commerce at 132 Main St. (265-2692). Nevada City is also a principal gateway to the Tahoe National Forest. Accommodations: *National Hotel* (rates: $25-37 double), 50 fine air-conditioned rooms in the state's oldest hotel, in continuous operation since 1854, lovely Victorian decor, antique furnishings, swimming pool, restaurant and bar, weekend entertainment, at 211 Broad St., just west of Hwy. 20 (265–4551).

Truckee

(Pop. 1,400; zip code 95734; area code 916.) Truckee is the gateway to some of California's finest ski country. Since the establishment of the first ski club here in 1913, the area has blossomed into a vast winter playground, with facilities for downhill and cross-country skiing, ice skating, tobogganing, and après-ski activities (see below). The town is surrounded by the Tahoe National Forest. Donner Memorial State Park, 2 miles west of Truckee on U.S. 40, is a monument to the ill-fated Donner Party, stranded here in October 1846 by fierce blizzards. Of the 89 in the party, only 47 survived after resorting to cannibalism. The park covers 353 acres and is open year-round (campsites, fishing, swimming, hiking, picnicking, and nature programs). Just west of town is lovely Donner Lake, framed by the evergreen-clad slopes of the Sierras. Accommodations: *Gateway Motel* (rates: $25 double), 27 guest cottages, 12 with kitchens, some oversize beds, rustic decor, nearby restaurant, 1 mile west on old U.S. Hwy. 40, at junction with Hwy. 89 (587–3183).

Lodges & Ski Resorts

★★★*Big Chief Nordic Ski Resort* on the banks of the Truckee River has been in operation for almost 60 years. This rustic alpine lodge offers expert instruction by certified Nordic instructors and guided tours to such scenic locations as Pole Creek, Big Meadow, Castle Pass, and Bullshead, as well as avalanche courses, a snow survival seminar, and overnight hut skiing. Big Chief accommodations are in 4 stone cabins, a cedar cabin, and a loft-dorm. The stone cabins have 2 double beds, equipped kitchens and baths. The cedar cabin has 2 bedrooms, bath, living room, and kitchen, and sleeps 6. The loft-dorm will sleep 8 and has 2 bathrooms and showers. Big Chief Lodge features hearty omelettes, home fries, and hot coffee, and for lunch offers homemade soup and hot sandwiches, beer and wine. Box lunches are made on request. Dinner is served family-style in the lodge, which has a big stone fireplace. Daily rates: $22 (double) in the stone cabins; $32 (4) in the cedar cabin; and $6 per person in the loft-dorm. Ski lessons for a full day are $12, as are guided tours. The lodge is reached off Interstate 80. For additional info, contact: Big Chief Guides & Nordic Ski Resort, P.O. Box 2427, Truckee, CA 95734 (916)587–3635.

★★★*Boreal Ski Area & Lodge*, on the west side of Donner Summit, offers excellent skiing and a full range of facilities, including a big selection of rentals, night skiing all week long, and 7 chairlifts, 2 of which are lighted at night and serviced by a 131,000–cubic-foot-capacity snow-making machine for early-season skiing. Most of Boreal's terrain is ideal for beginning and intermediate skiers, though even pros will find some exciting challenges. The ski school boasts a staff of 60 instructors, private and group lessons, children's classes, and expert American-method teaching. A recently expanded day lodge has a bar-lounge on the mezzanine with bird's-eye views of the slopes. There are also plenty of lockers, ski racks, and uncrowded lounging areas. The modern Boreal Hotel, within easy walking distance of the slopes, has attractive, spacious rooms, each with 2 queen-size beds. The lounge at the hotel has a pool table and color TV for après-ski relaxing. Daily rates: $21–25 double occupancy, $25–30 for 3 or 4. Ski packages and group discounts are available. For more information write: Boreal, Box 39, Truckee, CA 95734 (916)426–3666.

★★*Donner Ski Ranch* is a full-service ski facility in the Donner Summit Recreation Area of California's majestic Sierra Range. The ranch has its own double chair-lift rising from the lodge porch to high atop Signal Hill, 2 Poma lifts for beginners and intermediate skiers, a variety of trails, equipment rentals, and a ski school offering two 1½–hour lessons daily for all levels of skill. Both private and class sessions are available. The ranch has a wide range of reasonably priced lodgings: sleeping-bag dorms ($7 per person first night, $4 each additional night); family dorms and private rooms ($16 for the first night, $12 each additional night, $4–7 per night for each additional person in room). All accommodations include bath and shower facilities. There are also special group weekend packages, midweek budget rates, and midweek group discounts. The central lodge building houses a cafeteria, dining room, and cocktail lounge. Season runs from mid-December to mid-April. For more information write: Donner Ski Ranch, P.O. Box 66, Norden, CA 95724 (916)426–3578.

★★★★*Northstar-at-Tahoe Ski Area & Resort* offers deluxe, year-round accommodations and recreational facilities for hiking, downhill and cross-country skiing, golfing, and horseback riding surrounded by alpine meadows, mountain peaks, and valleys due north of Lake Tahoe. The terrain is long and varied, with 2,200 vertical feet and seemingly endless runs through stands of evergreens. The mountain is rated 33% beginner/novice, 50% intermediate, and 17% advanced terrain, with a total of 39 trails. Rustic alpine accommodations are available at the end of the runs at the Big Springs Day Lodge or Northstar Village. Spanning the mountain are 6 double chair-lifts and a new triple chair. The famous Sierra sunshine and an average annual snowfall of 300 inches, plus the Northstar snow-making system, make for ideal conditions.

The *Northstar Village* facilities and services include the lodgings, Northstar Alpine Ski School and Nordic Ski Touring Center, ski rentals, Schaffers Mill restaurant and lounge, deli, ski shop, and a recreation center with saunas, a universal gym, and a 25–foot outdoor Jacuzzi.

Big Springs Day Lodge up the hill from the village offers first-class accommodations with cafeteria, bar, ice cream parlor, wine & cheese shop, accessories and ski-repair shop, ski school, and professional ski patrol.

Northstar lodging rates range from $45 per night for a lodgette (up to 4 persons) to $60 per night for a penthouse, $60 per night for a 1–bedroom studio, and $100 per night for a 4–bedroom studio. For a free *Northstar Ski Trail Map*, detailed rates, and information on special ski package vacations, contact: Northstar-at-Tahoe, P.O. Box 129, Truckee, CA 95734 (916)562–1010. For Northstar ski condition reports, call (916)562–1330.

★★★★*Royal Gorge Nordic Ski Resort*, in the historic Donner Pass area of Soda Springs, offers fine accommodations in the rustic Royal Gorge Lodge and some 170 kilometers of double-track trails, constantly maintained by snocats and a special grooming cat to insure superlative ski conditions. The most popular ski package at Royal Gorge is the early weekend ($95, Nov. 17–Dec. 10). Guests are brought to the lodge in covered sleighs and greeted with fondue hors-d'oeuvres and mulled wine on arrival. Also on hand are a sauna, cross-country ski school offering expert instruction, complete ski shop with a comprehensive rental system, warming huts along the trails, and a cafe. Royal Gorge sponsors tandem ski championships and cross-country races, plus ski vacations on some of the most exciting slopes in the world: the French Alps, Norway's Lillehammer, the Tonquin Valley north of Banff, Mt. Cook in New Zealand, the Argentine Andes, and Yellowstone Park.

In addition, Royal Gorge offers their unique Deer Lake Hut Program. Deer Lake is the first of the Royal Gorge Overnight Huts

in the midst of our ever-expanding track system. This is a new program designed along the lines of the huts of the Alps; but where the Alpine retreats incline to be Spartan, Deer Lake offers many comforts as well as a beautiful setting between two lakes. Guests carrying their packs ski the 3½ miles in along our marked and groomed trails and are greeted by the amiable folk who look after the premises and cook for you. The days are spent skiing, and the evenings may be spent beside a pinewood fire recounting the tales of the day.

Arrive Saturday morning—check in at Royal Gorge Office in Soda Springs. Ski the 3½ miles out to Deer Lake Hut on the marked trails via the Royal Gorge Lodge, eating your lunch along the way or stopping at the Lodge Cafe. Dinner is served to you at 6 P.M. *Sunday*, cooked breakfast and trail lunch are provided, with the day free for skiing the tracks and surrounding area. Ski back to Trailhead in the afternoon. Program runs from Saturday morning to Sunday afternoon, save on holidays by prior arrangement. *No Friday night accommodations at any time*. The program, which costs $55 per person, includes 3 meals, lodging, hot and cold drinks, wine with dinner, 2 days' trail passes, skiing, and moonlight tours. For additional information contact: Royal Gorge Nordic, P.O. Box 178, Soda Springs, CA 95728 (916)426–3793.

★★★*Soda Springs Hotel* is a charming, old-fashioned stone and timber inn with a colorful history as a onetime speakeasy and posh casino. It was also one of the first ski resorts in the Sierras and still boasts superlative skiing at nearby Boreal Ridge and Sugar Bowl, plus a ski hill directly behind the hotel with two J-bars and a chair lift. Royal Gorge Ski Touring (see above) is located at the hotel for cross-country touring, instruction, and rentals. During the summer months, swimming and boating are popular on Lake Van Norden, half a block from the hotel. Within a 5–mile radius of the hotel are lakes and streams, riding stables, and hiking trails. The accent here is on warmth and graciousness—dinner by the glow of kerosene lanterns, cocktails beside a crackling potbellied stove, and big beds of hand-carved oak. The Soda Springs Restaurant enjoys a fine reputation for continental cuisine and homemade pastries, and is open for breakfast, lunch, and dinner. There's also a bar for après-ski relaxation and weekend entertainment. A sauna and hot tub are on hand to soothe tired muscles. Rates: $24–38, double occupancy; $12 per person for dormitory accommodations. For information write: Soda Springs Hotel, P.O. Box 36, Soda Springs, CA 95728 (916)426–3681.

★★★★*Squaw Valley U.S.A. Lodge & Ski Center* in the High Sierras, site of the 1960 Winter Olympics, is one of the nation's largest ski areas, with 25 ski lifts. The ski area encompasses 5 high Sierra peaks. The famous Squaw Valley terrain is suited for beginning, intermediate, and advanced skiers. The area's vertical drop is 2,700 feet. The longest run is 3 miles. Professional instructions are available at the Squaw Valley Ski School for both alpine and cross-country, with guided Nordic tours. Area facilities include bars, restaurants, churches, nursery school, ice skating at the Olympia Arena, ski-rental shops for both alpine and Nordic equipment. This popular family ski center offers free skiing for children under 11 years of age when accompanied by a skiing parent with a full-day ticket. Squaw Valley is located 5 miles north of Tahoe City on State

Highway 89. The season runs from mid-November to May 15. For additional information, reservations, and a 24–hour Sno-phone, call (916)583–6966.

Squaw Valley Lodge is located at the base of Granite Chief peak between the gondola and the tram base stations and offers excellent rooms and suites, dining, cocktails, ski shops, and services. Ski packages of 5 and 7 days are available from $120–150, including lodging, lift tickets, and the redwood hot tubs on Squaw Peak. Squaw Valley is a 50–minute drive from the Reno International Airport. For additional info write: Squaw Valley Lodge, P.O. Box 2393, Olympic Valley, CA 95730.

★★★*Tahoe Donner Resort* is a sprawling, 4–season family resort complex just north of Lake Tahoe in the awesome High Sierras. Skiing is the big attraction here—the Tahoe Donner ski bowl offers trails for all degrees of expertise, 2 double chair-lifts, and a surface tow. Other facilities include alpine and Nordic instruction, complete rentals, and a day lodge with a bar and cafeteria. Regularly scheduled events cover everything from torchlight parades and ski movies to "screaming eagle" championship races. The resort's Nordic Center caters to cross-country buffs and offers rentals, scheduled activities, guided tours, and moonlight and overnight jaunts. Accommodations are in modern condominiums and homes, all fully furnished with outside decks, fireplaces, new appliances, dishes, glassware, and linens. Some units also have washers and dryers. Weekly rentals are $265–395 for 1–3-bedroom units (rates are higher during the holiday season, Dec. 15–Jan. 1). Special midweek mini-vacations, 4–day ski packages, and 2–night rates are also available. Restaurants and cocktail lounges are available at Tahoe Donner; there are also numerous fine restaurants and entertainment facilities in nearby Truckee. For complete details write: Tahoe Donner Resort, P.O. Drawer G, Truckee, CA 95734 (916)587–2551.

Travel Services & Ski Areas

Tahoe Donner Ski Touring Center offers a complete cross-country program, including rentals, instruction (with an emphasis on beginning and intermediate levels), orienteering, and outdoor survival clinics. Among the tours regularly scheduled are afternoon guided trips with an instructor-naturalist covering various scenic routes in and around Tahoe-Donner; picnic tours, including lunch; overnight trips to snug wilderness cabins with meals provided; moonlight tours; and an annual tour of the historic Donner Trail. In addition, the

touring center has a full calendar of special winter events, December through April, such as lectures on subjects of interest to skiers, a 3–day Christmas vacation clinic, overnight tours of the Euer Valley, and "Nordic night" dinners and wilderness travel clinics. For full details write: Tahoe Donner Ski Touring Center, P.O. Box 2462, Truckee, CA 95734 (916)587–9821 or (916)587–2496.

High Sierras—Yosemite National Park

This 1,189–square-mile national park lies on the western slope of the Sierra Nevada in east and central California and contains the greatest concentration of natural grandeur along the entire 400–mile length of the Sierras. During the fall, Yosemite is a backpacker's paradise with its brilliant colors, granite domes and monoliths, trout streams, glaciers, great waterfalls that plunge over perpendicular cliffs as high as 1,612 feet, mountain chains soaring to over 10,000, and extensive forests of pine, fir, and oak. The park is bisected from east to west by Yosemite Valley to the south and the Grand Canyon of the Tuolumne to the north—both gouged down thousands of feet into solid rock when great rivers of ice advanced through Yosemite during the Ice Age.

The spectacular U-shaped trough of Yosemite Valley was first explored, accidentally, on March 25, 1851, by Maj. James D. Savage and Dr. L. H. Bunnell when, leading the Mariposa Battalion in an expedition to capture the warring Miwok Indians, they stumbled out of the forest at Inspiration Point, where the primeval valley lay spread out before them, cut by the winding blue waters of the Merced River. Bunnell was so entranced by the beauty of the valley that he gave up his chase. While camping on the banks of the Merced that night, he named the valley Yosemite, from the Miwok Indian word for grizzly bear, *Uzumati*, one of the tribal divisions, or totems. Afterward, Bunnell's book *Discovery of Yosemite* spread the fame of the valley's natural wonders far and wide.

Yosemite Valley lies at 3,985–feet altitude and is 7 miles long, with an average width of 1 mile, carved out of the granite slopes of the High Sierra by stream erosion and massive glacial action. The level, parklike floor is sunk 3,000 feet below the rim of the park, and the once famed trout waters of the Merced River meander through the green meadows and forests, dominated by immense domes and rock masses which form a sheer wall surrounding the valley. The valley was once the home of the Miwok Indians, who called it *Ahwahnee*, meaning "deep grassy valley."

The wild Yosemite North Country is a hiker's paradise, offering sculptured peaks and domes, waterfalls, valleys, meadows, groves of giant 3,000–year-old sequoias, alpine lakes and streams, and extensive forests of pine, fir, cedar, hemlock, oak, maple, western yellow pine, Jeffrey pine, and black oak. Glacial action has carved broad, U-shaped valleys and hundreds of lake basins along the crest of the High Sierras at elevations up to 13,000 feet. The Pacific Crest Trail enters the Yosemite region near Tower Peak (11,704 ft.), to the north of Stubblefield Canyon, and winds along the crest past Buckeye Pass, Kerrick Meadow, Burro Pass, and Fingers Peak, through the Matterhorn Canyon, to the grassy floor of Tuolumne Meadows at 8,600 feet—the largest subalpine meadow in the High Sierras and the jumping-off point for trips by foot or horse down the Grand Canyon of the Tuolumne by way of the old Glen Aulin High Sierra Camp to Waterwheel Falls and the High Sierras. The Tuolumne Grove of Giant Sequoias, near the headwaters of Crane Creek, was discovered in 1833 by Joseph Walker's expedition. At Tuolumne Meadows the Pacific Crest Trail merges with the John Muir Trail and begins the 150–mile route along the grand crescendo of the High Sierras to the headwaters of the Kern River and the towering summit of Mt. Whitney. To the west of the meadows, the Tuolumne River makes its wild and tumultuous descent through the Grand Canyon of the Tuolumne and through Muir Gorge.

There is fishing along the way for golden, cutthroat, and brook trout. Camping is permitted only in areas designated by the Park Service. Supplies, saddle horses, and guides are available at Wawona, White Wolf, Yosemite Valley, Tuolumne Meadows, and Mather ranger stations. The Curry Company provides corral and feed at its stables a mile downstream from Happy Isles at the upper end of Yosemite Valley on the Merced River. At all times, practice minimum-impact traveling and camping. Try to schedule your visit during the fall and spring to avoid the summer crowds.

Backpackers and fishermen planning a cross-country or wilderness trip through the remote interior areas may obtain a free wilderness permit at one of the following locations: Valley Visitor Center, Happy Isles Trail Center, Tuolumne Meadows Ranger Station, Lee Vining Ranger Station, Glacier Point Ranger Station, White Wolf Ranger Station, Wawona Ranger Station, or Big Oak Flat Entrance Station. Reservations for backcountry trips may be made between February 1 and May 31 by writing: Superintendent, Yosemite National Park, Yosemite 95389. Some of the state's finest fly-fishing is along the 15–mile stretch of the South Fork of the Merced River from its confluence with the main stem of the Merced upstream to the western boundary of Yosemite. Fishing is for wild rainbow and brown trout. Please note that bears are numerous at the following areas: all High Sierra camps, Little Yosemite Valley, Cathedral Lakes, Lyell Canyon, Pate Valley, Rancheria Falls, Pleasant Valley, Ten Lakes, and Laurel Lake. Backcountry use regulations and the free publication *The Yosemite Backcountry* may be obtained by writing: Superintendent, Yosemite National Park 95389.

Information Sources, Maps & Access

For information and bulletins about skiing (downhill and cross-country), fishing regulations, campgrounds, wilderness use permits, backpacking, geology, weather, an equipment check-list for summer backpacking, fees, and the free *Cycle Guide to Yosemite Valley* and *Yosemite National Park Map/Brochure*, write: Superintendent, Yosemite National Park 95389 (209)372–4532. For Yosemite weather, road conditions, etc., call (209)372–4222.

The invaluable U.S. Geological Survey *Yosemite National Park &*

Vicinity Topographic Map (also available in a beautiful shaded-relief edition) is 29 × 31 inches, with a scale of 1:125,000, or 2 miles to 1 inch, and shows all contours, natural features, campgrounds, ranger stations, wilderness shelters, trails, footbridges, and roads. The U.S. Geological Survey *Yosemite Valley Topographic Map* (also available in shaded-relief) is 19 × 42 inches, with a scale of 1:24,000, or 2,000 feet to 1 inch, and shows all natural and man-made features. A text on the reverse side of the map contains an illustrated description of the natural features of the valley. These beautiful, full-color maps are available for $2 each from: Distribution Branch, U.S. Geological Survey, Federal Center, Denver, CO 80225.

The major auto routes to the park are California Highways 140 and 120 and U.S. 395. Yosemite has more than 200 miles of historic, scenic roads that wind through the remote backcountry and the heart of the High Sierra. The Big Oak Flat Road (Route 120 West), named for an old gold-mining settlement, begins its winding mountain journey at the lower end of Yosemite Valley, 6 miles west of Yosemite Village, and provides spectacular views of the 620–foot-high Bridal Veil Falls, Big Meadow (remnant of an ancient glacial lake), Clark Range, San Joaquin Valley, and the wildlands and conifer forests of the Yosemite North Country. This mountain route provides access to Crane Flat, a High Sierra meadow, with a ranger station and public campground; Merced Grove of Giant Sequoias; Hodgdon Meadow Campground; and the "49er Route," Highway 49, which leads to many of the historic mining camps and towns of Mother Lode country. The Glacier Point Road winds for 16 miles from Chinquapin to Glacier and provides access to the 4,500–foot-deep gorge of the Merced River, Badger Pass Ski Area, Bridal Veil Creek Campground, Pothole Meadows, and the spectacular vistas of the High Sierra from Glacier Point at 7,214 feet. The Hetch Hetchy Road, or Mather Road, winds for 16 miles to Hetch Hetchy Reservoir and provides access to the South Fork of the Tuolumne River, Middle Fork of the Tuolumne Campground, and Mather Ranger Station. The Merced Road (Route 140) winds down from Yosemite Valley along the beautiful Merced River past Cascade Falls to the park boundary at El Portal. The scenic Tioga Road (Route 120 East) climbs through the wildlands of Yosemite's High Sierra to Tioga Pass at 9,941 feet—the highest auto pass in the Sierra Nevada. The Tioga Road provides access to the Old Big Oak Flat Road and the Tuolumne Grove of Big Trees, Smoky Jack Campsite (named for a man for whom John Muir herded sheep), Red Fir Forest, White Wolf Campground (named by a sheepherder who claimed to have seen a white wolf there), Yosemite Creek, Porcupine Flat Primitive Campground, May Lake Junction and High Sierra Camp, Tenaya Lake and the Tenaya Branch of the Tuolumne River, the Ghost Forest, Tuolumne Meadows and High Sierra Camp, old Mono Indian Trail, Dana Meadows, and Lee Vining Canyon. The Wawona (thought to be the Indian word for "big tree"), or Fresno (Spanish for "ash tree"), Road (Route 41) follows the route of the Mariposa Battalion when, in pursuit of the Miwok Indians in 1851, it entered Yosemite Valley. This route provides access to Bridal Veil Falls, the South Fork Canyon of the Merced River, Wawona Campground, and Wawona. Detailed descriptions of the routes discussed above are contained in the 77–page *Yosemite Road Guide*, available for $1.25 from the Yosemite Natural History Association, Yosemite 95389.

Gateways & Accommodations

Yosemite National Park Accommodations

(Area code 209): *Manzanita Lodge* (rates: $22–25 double), 10 air-conditioned rooms, 2 with kitchens, some oversized beds, nearby restaurant, on Hwy. 140, 2 miles from west entrance to park (379–2222); *Muir Lodge* (rates: $22–32 double), 14 air-cooled rooms, some with queen-size beds, 1 kitchen unit, picnic tables and grill, 27 miles southwest of west entrance to park (966–2468); *Narrow Gauge Inn* (rates: $30–36 double), 26 rooms in a chalet-type hotel, each with balcony, some queen-size beds, swimming pool, playground, 2 miles south of Fish Camp on Hwy. 41, 4 miles from south entrance to park (683–7720); *Yosemite View Lodge* (rates: $18–32 double), 27 fine air-conditioned rooms, 2 with kitchens, many oversize beds, some units have views of Merced River rapids, restaurant nearby, open mid-March through September, on Hwy. 140, 12 miles west of Park Headquarters, 2 miles from west entrance (379–2681)

Merced

(Pop. 22,700; zip code 95340; area code 209.) This major gateway to Yosemite National Park is surrounded by the rich agricultural country of the San Joaquin Valley. A national wildlife refuge is 16 miles southwest of town; 5 miles northeast is Lake Yosemite Park, a popular spot for water sports and picknicking. Accommodations: *Best Western Carousel* (rates: $22–24 double), 42 fine rooms and family suites, queen-size beds, swimming pool, at 1033 Motel Drive, 1½ miles south of town off Hwy. 99 near junction with Yosemite Hwy. (723–2163); *Best Western Pine Cone Inn* (rates: $25–30 double), 75 spacious air-conditioned rooms, many with oversize beds, color TV, swimming pool, restaurant, ½ mile north of Merced on Hwy. 99, off Gustine-Sonora Exit at 1213 V St. (723–3711); *Merced Travelodge* (rates: $26–40 double), 63 fine air-conditioned rooms, color TV, swimming pool, restaurant adjacent, bar, at 2000 E. Childs Ave., 2 miles south of town off Hwy. 99 (723–3121); *Sierra Lodge* (rates: $18–24 double), 25 air-conditioned rooms, 2 with kitchens, color TV, pool, free airport bus, coffee shop opposite, 1¼ miles south of Merced on Hwy. 99, near junction with Hwy. 140 (722–3926).

Lodges, Hotels & High Sierra Camps

★★*Tioga Pass Resort*, near one of the highest and most spectacular highways across the Sierras at 9,600–foot altitudes, has been a popular retreat with fishermen and outdoor lovers since its establishment in the 1920s. There are 50 lakes within a 5–mile radius of the resort, many of them continuously stocked with rainbow, brook, brown, and California golden trout. Boats and motors are available for trolling on Tioga and Ellery Lakes, or you can follow a high

mountain stream for truly secluded angling. For hikers and sightseers, Yosemite National Park and the beautiful Tuolumne Meadows are just a few miles away. A nearby riding stable offers guided day rides and pack trips. In the fall, there's excellent deer hunting in high mountain meadows. Housekeeping cabins at the resort have fully equipped kitchens, modern baths, electric heating, comfortable furnishings, all linen, and cooking and eating utensils. The main lodge building has a nice cafe serving three meals a day and a lounge with fireplace. Also on hand are a bait and tackle shop and a fully stocked general store. Season runs from late May to mid-October. Rates: $18–32 daily for a 1–2-bedroom cabin. There are also motel-type units at $14–16 daily. Weekly rates are lower. For more information write: (summer) Tioga Pass Resort, P.O. Box 7, Lee Vining, CA 93540; (winter) 15748 Condor Ridge Road, Canyon Country, CA 91351 (805)252–4607.

Yosemite National Park High Sierra Camps. Arranged roughly in a circle are 5 permanent summer High Sierra Camps and 2 lodges. On the average, they are located about 9 miles apart. Each is in an area of outstanding beauty and interest. Camps provide accommodations in tents, beds with springs and mattresses, linen, and ample blankets (nights are cold!). Breakfast and dinner are served in a central dining tent, and, though simple, the quality and preparation are excellent and quantities are ample. There are hot showers at each camp, which are a welcome luxury in the wilderness, especially at the end of a day on the trail.

White Wolf Lodge (8,000 ft.) is Yosemite's almost unknown high-country hideaway. The small, peaceful White Wolf area is separate from the High Sierra Loop, just 1 mile off Hwy. 120, about midway between Yosemite Valley and Tuolumne Meadows. White Wolf offers quiet and solitude, fabulous hiking in the nearby Pate Valley area of Yosemite, horseback riding, and fishing. White Wolf's springtime is the summer—wild flowers and snow-fed streams. Hearty family-style meals to furnish fuel for high-country hiking. No wolves (except in legend) despite the name—but a helpful contingent of friendly staff. Daily rates for rustic cabins: $16 double.

Glen Aulin Camp (7,800 ft.) is at the foot of the White Cascade on the Tuolumne River and on the fringe of one of the Sierra's finest stands of mountain hemlock. The camp is 4 miles from magnificent Waterwheel Falls.

May Lake Camp (9,270 ft.) is located beneath the eastern wall of Mt. Hoffman (10,850 ft.) and on the shore of May Lake. From Hoffman's summit (a not-too-difficult hike) are outstanding views of the park.

Sunrise Camp (9,400 ft.) is located on a long, rather narrow shelf 30–40 feet above Long Meadow. The careful arrangement of sleeping tents and main buildings makes it most attractive as the wilderness feeling has been only slightly disturbed. Inspiring view across Long Meadow to magnificent peaks.

Merced Lake Camp (7,150 ft.), at a somewhat lower elevation than the other camps, is restful rather than stimulating. The weather is warmer, and the atmosphere invites long, lazy stays. There is dependable fishing at Merced Lake within a few yards of the camp and on the Merced River.

Vogelsang Camp (10,300 ft.) is the highest and, to some, the most dramatic of the camps. Situated above timberline, it has an alpine character, with Fletcher Creek gurgling and slashing through camp and craggy Vogelsang Peak on the southern horizon. Near Fletcher, Booth, Vogelsang, Hanging Basket, and Townsley lakes, Vogelsang Camp is a favorite of fishermen.

Tuolumne Meadows Lodge (8,600 ft.), located near the confluence of the Dana and Lyell forks of the Tuolumne River, is accessible by auto, being 55 miles from Yosemite Valley and 20 miles from Lee Vining on Highway 395. It serves well as a starting point for High Sierra trips. Daily rates: $11 for 1 or 2 persons.

Daily rates for the High Sierra camps listed above are $25.50 per person and include dormitory tents, bedding, and meals (breakfast and dinner). Reservations should be made well in advance. For additional information and reservation, contact: High Sierra Camps, Yosemite National Park, CA 95389 (209)373–4171.

Yosemite National Park Lodges & Hotels offer a wide variety of accommodations within every price range—from rustic alpine cabins to elegant inns, renowned for their warmth and hospitality.

★★★★*Ahavahnee Hotel,* one of the world's most famous resort hotels, has been in operation since 1927. Situated in Yosemite Valley, this magnificent vacation retreat has a spectacular log-beamed dining room with tall windows, open to the public for all meals, including buffet suppers for skiers. Accommodations include large, rustic rooms with fireplace and picturesque views in the main hotel and cottages in the valley. All accommodations are available on a year-round basis. Pets not allowed. Rates: $46 double, daily.

★★★*Curry Village* offers picturesque, log-beamed cabins, rooms, cottages, and rustic tent-cabin accommodations near the east end of Yosemite Valley. This renowned hostelry was established by the Curry family at the turn of the century. Their tradition of warm hospitality still remains. Curry Village facilities include a swimming pool, cafeteria, lounge, children's playground, and bicycle rentals. No pets permitted. Rates: $8.50–24.00 daily for 1 or 2 persons in a room. Curry housekeeping cabins: $12.50 daily and $75 weekly (1–4 persons).

★★*Wawona Hotel*, an elegant Victorian hotel established in 1856, is one of California's oldest classic hotels. Situated near the south entrance of the park, the hotel offers spacious accommodations and first-class services from mid-May to early September. It is ideal for extended vacations in Yosemite, and special rentals with cooking facilities are available near Wawona for stays of 2 weeks or longer. Swimming, tennis, and a beautiful 9–hole golf course are available on the grounds. Rates range from $14.50 daily (without bath) to $25.50 (with private bath) for 1 or 2 persons.

★★★*Yosemite Lodge*, within sight of spectacular Yosemite Falls, offers rustic, modern accommodations consisting of rooms with patios or balconies as well as cabins with or without baths. The main lodge has a spacious lounge and fireplace, cafeteria, and restaurant dining at the Four Seasons and Mountain Room Broiler for steaks and chops. Other facilities include a cocktail lounge, swimming pool, gift shop, and bicycle rentals. Pets not allowed. Daily rates: $13.50–30.00 double.

For detailed information and reservations, contact: Yosemite Park & Curry Co., Yosemite National Park, CA 95389. Call toll-free in California (800)692–5811; out of state call (209)372–4671.

Travel Services

Yosemite Mountaineering & Ski Touring trips in the high Yosemite backcountry, instruction, and guide service are available in the park at the Mountain Shop in Yosemite Valley and the Mountain Sports Center in Tuolumne Meadows. You will find complete lines of high-quality climbing, backpacking, winter-camping, and ski-touring equipment there, as well as freeze-dried food and trail supplies. There is a stock of rental boots, day packs, ice axes, crampons, and other items at reasonable rates. In winter, ski-touring equipment may be rented. Overnight guided ski-touring trips are available to the Mariposa Grove of Giant Sequoias; Glacier Point, on the rim of Yosemite Valley, with a full view of the entire valley 3,000 feet below and a warm shelter; Ostrander Lake ski hut, a classic ski tour to a Scandinavian-style stone mountain house near timberline about 8 miles from Badger Pass, with emphasis on natural history, good food, and fine skiing; and advanced-level trips to 10,850–foot Mt. Hoffman for ski mountaineering and the 7–day High Sierra Tour—the ultimate winter-camping cross-country ski trip into the heart of the Sierra-Tuolumne Meadows. Dinner and breakfast are supplied on all overnight trips. In addition to summer alpencraft and alpine survival seminars, Yosemite Mountaineering offers guided natural history backpacking trips, designed for both experienced and inexperienced backpackers who want to learn more about the plants and animals of the Sierra, as well as cross-country backpacking seminars and custom guided trips. Overnight trips range from $29 to $140 per person. For detailed info and rates, contact: Yosemite Mountaineering, Yosemite National Park, CA 95389 (209)372–4611, ext. 244.

Yosemite National Park Backcountry Trips:

7–Day Hiking Trip. For those who wish to hike the Yosemite "loop" trail, 7–day hiking trips make the circle of camps each week.

Twenty persons is the maximum on each trip, and a ranger-naturalist guide is in charge. He points out and explains the flowers, trees, birds, and geology so that hikers come to know intimately the area. The trip begins each Monday from Tuolumne Meadows Lodge. Because hiking 9 miles daily on an average at elevations of 7,000–10,000 feet is quite demanding, it is advised that hiking party members be in good physical condition and spend about a day at Tuolumne Meadows to become accustomed to the rarefied air. From Tuolumne, the party stays at each camp in the following order: 1 night each at Glen Aulin Camp, May Lake Camp, and Sunrise Camp; 2 nights at Merced Lake Camp; and 1 night at Vogelsang Camp, returning to Tuolumne Meadows on the seventh day. Includes 6 nights' lodging in dormitory tent, breakfast, lunch, and dinner. In consideration of the typical ages of the entire party, children must be at least 12 years of age, and those under 18 must be accompanied by an adult. Rates: $156 per person.

6–Day Saddle Trip. Twice weekly (Saturday and Sunday) during the summer season, 6–day saddle trips start and end at Tuolumne Meadows. These trips are limited to 10 persons, and an experienced guide accompanies each group. Mules provide transportation, having been found trail-wise, surefooted, and somewhat more comfortable to sit astride than horses. Personal necessities are limited to 10 pounds per person and are carried on a pack mule. The saddle trip is arranged on an all-expense basis and covers all meals, dormitory tent accommodations, showers, saddle animal, and guide service. Minimum age limit is 7 years, and children under 12 must have had previous riding experience. Rates: $208 per person.

4–Day Saddle Trip. For those with too little time to take the 6–day trip, a 4–day trip departs twice weekly (Tuesday and Friday) from Tuolumne Meadows, stopping a night each at Glen Aulin, May Lake, and Sunrise camps, returning to the Meadows on the fourth day. On the first day's 7.3–mile trip, a lunch stop is made along the Tuolumne River, and camp is reached in time for a side trip to the unusual Waterwheel Falls. The second day's trip, 8.2 miles, brings the party to May Lake Camp on the shores of May Lake at the foot of Mt. Hoffman. From May Lake the trail descends sharply over the granite and then rises through heavy timber, past lakes and meadows, to Sunrise Camp. The fourth day is spent on 11.6 miles of the beautiful Sunrise Trail to Tuolumne, reached by midafternoon. This trip includes meals, dormitory tent accommodations, showers, guide service, and saddle animal. Minimum age limit is 7 years, and children under 12 must have had previous riding experience. Rates: $130 per person.

For reservations and information write or call: Yosemite Park and Curry Co., Yosemite National Park, CA 95389 (209)373–4171.

Yosemite Airlines offers scheduled flights and air tours of the High Sierra gold-rush country and the Yosemite National Park high country with departures from San Francisco International Airport. The Yosemite National Park Air Tours cover the Emigrant Basin Wilderness, Hetch Hetchy, Tuolumne Meadows, Yosemite Valley and Half Dome, El Capitan, and Bridal Veil Falls. For information and reservations, contact: Yosemite Airlines, P.O. Box 330, Columbia, CA 95310 (209)532–6946; in the San Francisco Bay Area call (415)441–5270.

Klamath National Forest & the Salmon-Trinity Alps

The 1.7 million acres of this large, rugged "big timber" forest contain some of the finest fishing, hunting, backpacking, and

wilderness-camping areas in the United States. The forest is located within the legendary Bigfoot country near Yreka in northwest California, due south of the Rogue River and Siskiyou National Forest in Oregon. Hundreds of miles of old logging and mining roads and scenic hiking trails wind from elevations ranging from 600 to 6,600 feet through forests of ponderosa pine, sugar pine, western white and Jeffrey pine, Douglas fir, white and red fir, incense cedar, mountain hemlock, the rare white-barked Brewer spruce, and lodgepole and knobcone pine, and provide access to the remote alpine camping areas in the Goosenest Range (a spur of the Cascades in the eastern part of the forest) and Klamath, Salmon, Siskiyou, Marble, and Scott mountains—all parts of the Coast Range system—and to the Red Buttes Wild Area and Seiad Valley, Sleepy Ridge Hunting Area, Indian Tom Lake Hunting Area, and some of the world's most beautiful salmon, trout, and steelhead fishing, canoeing, and kayaking waters.

Information Sources, Maps & Access

For additional vacation travel and recreation information, a full-color *Klamath National Forest Map* (50¢), and the free *Marble Mountains Wilderness Map/Brochure*, contact: Supervisor, Klamath National Forest, 1215 S. Main St., Yreka, CA 96097 (916)842–2741. Both the High Siskiyou and Red Buttes wildlands are described in fascinating detail in *Hiking the Bigfoot Country*, a 398–page totebook by John Hart, available from Sierra Club Books, Box 7959, Rincon Annex, San Francisco 94104, for $7.95. The book contains topo maps of each area and useful info about weather, hazards and problems, following faint trails, walking light in Bigfoot country, geology, forests, flowers, wildlife, and much more.

The major routes to Klamath National Forest are Interstate 5, U.S. Highway 97 from Oregon, and California Highways 89, 299, 96, and 3. Lodging, supplies, canoe and boat rentals, guides, and outfitters are available at Seiad Valley, Horse Creek, Yreka, Scott Bar, Hamburg, Happy Camp, Clear Creek, Somes Bar, Forks of Salmon, Sawyers Bar, Etna, and Cecilville.

Recreation Areas

High Siskiyou Mountains—The Bigfoot Country

North of the Salmon-Trinity Alps and Marble Mountains wilderness areas are two of northern California's most remote, scenic wild areas—the High Siskiyou Mountains and the Red Buttes. The High Siskiyou Wildlands encompass some 200,000 roadless acres along the western reach of the Siskiyous. Numerous old Indian and hiking trails wind through a rugged glaciated landscape; through one of the richest coniferous forest areas in the United States, including dense montane forests and lovely stands of white and noble fir, several kinds of pines, the elegant white-barked Brewer spruce, and Alaska cedar at the higher elevations; and through lush forests of Douglas fir, western hemlock, cedars, and yew. They provide access to Youngs Valley, the East Fork of the Illinois River, Indian Creek, Clear Creek, Preston Peak, Devils Punchbowl, and Raspberry and Island lakes. This wilderness traveler's paradise was the ancient hunting grounds of the Totawa, Karok, and Yurok Indians and is the home of the mythical Bigfoot. The trails of this alpine area are bordered by great drifts of rhododendron, lush fields of lilies, Pacific dogwood, pitcher plant beds, green-petaled coneflower, and pink deershead orchid, among others. The High Siskiyous are also inhabited by the wolverine—the "Indian devil" of the Far North—once believed to be extinct in California.

East of the High Siskiyous are the alplike highlands, broad high-country, barren red desert, snowcapped crags, and densely forested valleys of the 90,000–acre roadless area known as the "Red Buttes"—named after a red, two-horned mountain.

Klamath River Country

The famed Klamath River and its tributaries, the Shasta, Scott, Salmon, and Trinity, provide some of the state's finest salmon and steelhead fishing in a classic forest setting. The Klamath, a former fishing haunt of Zane Grey, and known during the fur trade and exploration era as the Clamitte, Klamet, or Indian Scalp, is a big turbulent stream with headwaters in Lake Ewauna near Klamath Falls; it flows through high mountains, valleys, and rugged canyons for 180 miles to its mouth at the Pacific Ocean. For much of its length, the Klamath flows through conifer forests and the rugged wildlands of the Klamath Mountains. It has three runs of steelhead—the popular fall run, the winter run, and the spring or summer run. The upper Klamath, between the Copco Reservoir and the Oregon border, is managed as part of the state wild trout program and is the home of the famous fighting Klamath River rainbow. Brook trout are abundant in the high-country headwater lakes and streams. Several historic outfitting and fishing centers are located along the banks of the Klamath and its tributaries. Scott Bar is located in the deep gorge of the Scott River, which enters the Klamath about 2 miles upstream from the village of Hamburg and is an important spawning and nursery stream for salmon and steelhead. Once a center of feverish gold mining, Scott Bar is a popular jumping-off point for fishing trips up the steep 15–mile-long canyon for steelhead and an occasional large, buckskin-flanked brown trout. Famous Happy Camp, known to fly-fishermen and steelheaders the world round, is popular for year-round fishing and as an outfitting center and jumping-off point for trips into the Salmon-Trinity Alps Wilderness. Downstream from Happy Camp is Somes Bar, where the Salmon River joins the Klamath. Somes Bar, which began as a mining town, is a popular year-round salmon and steelhead fishing spot and departure point for trails heading into the western part of the Marble Mountains Wilderness.

Marble Mountains Wilderness

The famous Marble Mountains Wilderness encompasses 213,363 acres of top-ranked fly-fishing, backpacking, and hunting country north of the Salmon-Trinity Alps. Its dominant feature is the snow-white marble cap 700 to 1,000 feet thick at the top of Marble Mountain. The cap was formed from the bodies of sea organisms deposited when the peneplain formed the bottom of an ocean. This region is a mild and thickly forested country with gently rising trails. Numerous hiking and packhorse trails wind through this colorful wilderness, passing the majestic white of Marble Mountain, the lush green of Morehouse Mountain, and the deep blue of Cliff Lake, interspersed with various hues of sheer rock cliffs and dense stands of evergreens. Hundreds of lakes lie in the glaciated pockets forming the headwaters of many small trout streams. Most of the lakes in the wilderness hold either brook or rainbow trout. Wooley Creek is known for its excellent summer run of king salmon and steelhead. The district ranger will give advice regarding trail conditions, licensed packers, campsites, and grazing pastures for saddle stock. Fire permits are required of all campers.

Salmon-Trinity Alps Primitive Area

The scenic Salmon-Trinity Alps Primitive Area contains 225,000 acres of some of the most rugged terrain in California north of the High Sierra. The alps include the high, rough mountain ridges and deep glacial canyons along the Salmon-Trinity Divide in sections of the Trinity, Shasta, and Klamath national forests. The region contains the headwaters of a number of large streams, such as the South Fork of the Salmon River, Coffee Creek, Swift Creek, Stuarts Fork, Canyon Creek, New River, and the North Fork tributaries of the Trinity River. Huge talus boulders and steep, jagged peaks character-

ize much of the area above the timberline. Fly–fishing enthusiasts will find numerous possibilities in the hundreds of alpine lakes for rainbow, brown, brook, and golden trout and a few grayling.

The district rangers will be glad to help you plan a trip through the Primitive Area and to help answer questions you may have. The district rangers are located at: Big Bar Ranger District, Big Bar; Weaverville Ranger District, Weaverville; Callahan Ranger District, Callahan; and Salmon River Ranger District, Sawyers Bar.

Gateways & Accommodations

Klamath

(Pop. 500; zip code 95548; area code 707.) Located in the northwestern corner of the state, this is a popular gateway to Redwood National Park and the Klamath National Forest. Jet-boat cruises of the Klamath River between Klamath and Roach Creek are offered daily, June 1–September 30, from the dock 1 mile north of the Douglas Memorial Bridge. Mystery Park, 4 miles north of town on U.S. Hwy. 101, is a forest of ancient redwoods carved in unusual animal shapes (open year-round; $2 entrance fee for adults, $1 for children). Accommodations: *Jack's Motel* (rates: $22–28 double), 20 rooms, coffee shop, and coin laundry opposite, open year-round, off-season rates October-June, on Hwy. 101, Box 99 (482–5911).

Weaverville

(Pop. 1,500; zip code 96093; area code 916.) A prosperous mining town during the gold-rush era, Weaverville has lost little of its rough charm and color since Bret Harte first described it in his stories. The J. J. Jackson Museum on Main St. houses Indian artifacts, Chinese weapons, and an unusual exhibit of old jail cells. At the corner of Main and Oregon streets is the Joss House State Historic Park, encompassing the oldest Chinese temple in the state still in use, as well as exhibits of tapestries and gilded scrollwork. Weaverville is a gateway to the Shasta-Trinity National Forest and the Salmon-Trinity Alps Primitive Area; a district ranger's office is located here. Accommodations: *Red Hill Motel* (rates: $20–22 double), 14 air-conditioned rooms, rustic single and duplex cottages, many queen-size beds, color TV, restaurant nearby, in pleasant setting among pine trees, 1 block northwest of Hwy. 299, (623–4331).

Yreka

(Pop. 5,400; zip code 95991; area code 916.) The name is from an Indian word, *Wai-ri-ka*, meaning "mountain." Many stately old buildings from Yreka's boom days have been restored and are protected by the town's Historic Preservation District, in the vicinity of Third and Miner streets. The County Courthouse contains displays of gold in all its forms, and the Siskiyou County Museum, at 910 S. Main St., houses pioneer and Indian exhibits. Yreka is also the headquarters for the Klamath National Forest, at 1215 S. Main St. Accommodations: *Best Western Miner's Inn* (rates: $27–30 double), 91 excellent rooms, some with private patios or balconies, queen-size beds, color TV, small swimming pool, restaurant and bar, at 122

E. Miner St., in town, 1 block west of Interstate 5 exit (842–4355); *Thunderbird Lodge* (rates: $20–21 double), 45 air-conditioned rooms, color TV, swimming pool, restaurant adjacent, 526 S. Main St., 3 blocks south on Interstate 5 business route (842–4404); *Yreka Travelodge* (rates: $21–25 double), 65 fine rooms, some with queen-size beds, color TV, swimming pool; restaurant opposite, at 136 Montague Rd., 1 mile north on Interstate 5, Montague Road Exit (842–5781).

Lodges & Guest Ranches

★★*Bonanza King*, on the banks of Coffee Creek in the Trinity Alps, is a small, secluded, year-round vacation resort offering modern housekeeping cabins in a superb wilderness setting. Fishing for rainbow and brown trout is one of the favorite activities here, but Bonanza King also makes an ideal base for cross-country skiing and snowshoeing in winter, and hiking, backpacking, and mountain climbing during the summer months. A grocery store, gas, boat rentals, dining-out facilities, and a pack station are located nearby. Daily rates for 2 guests begin at $24 or $41 per week. For information write: Bonanza King, Coffee Creek Route, P.O. Trinity Center, CA 96091 (916)266–3305.

★★*Coffee Creek*, a fine guest ranch near Trinity Lake in northern California, offers horseback riding, trout fishing, hiking, deer hunting, and a broad spectrum of other outdoor activities. Accommodations are handsome and inviting: 1– and 2–bedroom cabins and a ranch house feature modern conveniences, gas heaters, fireplaces, and secluded settings. Entertainment, fine food, a private pond, and heated swimming pool are additional drawing cards. Weekly summer rates range from $185 per adult for 1 bedroom to $205 for a 2–bedroom cabin. In the spring, rates vary from $165 per adult to $185. Trinity Center Airport, 13 miles from the ranch, accommodates twin-engine craft. For a brochure and rates write: Coffee Creek, Trinity Center, CA 96091 (916)266–3343.

★★*Seymour's Ranch*, on Coffee Creek in northwestern California's Trinity Alps area, offers sturdy housekeeping cabins for parties of 2–6. Each cabin features modern kitchens with all utensils, plenty of hot water, bathrooms with showers, fresh bed linens, and fireplaces with a generous supply of firewood. The ranch grounds include broad, tree-shaded lawns, wide meadows, and a private pond fed by a stream of pure mountain water and bordered by a sandy beach. There are no planned activities here, but the surrounding forests and streams offer unlimited outdoor recreation: hiking, backpacking, fishing, and swimming, to name just a few. Numerous mountain lakes are within easy walking distance along well-marked trails. At Trinity Center, a 10–minute drive from the ranch, there is a marina with excellent facilities for boating and fishing. Cabin rates at Seymour's Ranch vary according to size, from $150 per week for a spacious 1–room cabin with kitchen and bath to $235 per week for 2–bedroom, 2–bath cabins with a large front porch. Daily rates are available. For additional information write: Seymour's Ranch, Trinity Center, CA 96091 (916)266–3311.

★★*Somes Bar Lodge*, owned and operated by the principals of the famous Somes Bar guide service, is situated on the historic steelhead waters of the beautiful Klamath River. Lodge activities include rafting and kayaking, pack-in fishing trips to the Marble Mountain Wilderness, fly-fishing instruction, and gold-panning and mining expeditions. Rustic lodge accommodations and family-style meals with breakfast and dinner and a packed streamside lunch cost $25

per day per person. Rates for 2 fishermen with McKenzie River drift boat, guide, and gear are $90 per day. For additional information, contact: Somes Bar Lodge, Somes Bar, CA 95568 (916)469–3399.

★★*Trinity Alps Resort* is a family-centered resort bisected by the sparkling waters of Stuart's Fork in the magnificent high country of northern California. Completely furnished, rustic housekeeping cabins line the tree-shaded banks of the river, each with a veranda and view of the scenic Trinity Alps. Activities include fishing in nearby Trinity Lake, swimming, horseback riding, tennis, canoeing, hiking, and a wealth of other outdoor pursuits, such as snowshoeing and skiing in season. Riding clubs welcome. For information and rates write: Trinity Alps Resort, Star Route, Box 56, Lewiston, CA 96052 (916–Minersville 332).

★★*Trinity Mountain Meadow Resort* is located high in the Trinity Alps wilderness area of the Klamath National Forest. The surrounding high country offers excellent opportunities for hiking, fishing, backpacking, wildlife photography, and trail riding. Old gold mines are within walking distance. Trinity Mountain facilities include 10 deluxe cabins with private bath and heaters for 2–6 persons each, as well as cabins with centrally located bath house and lodge rooms with detached bath. The lodge contains a lounge and dining facilities, with views of the Alps. Saddle horses are available for rental. Daily cabin rates (double): $56 per deluxe cabin and $50 per economy cabin, including all meals and lodging. American-plan lodge rates: $45 double. For additional information contact: (Oct.-May) 24225 Summit Woods Drive, Los Gatos, CA 95030 (408)353–1663); (June-Sept.) Trinity Center, CA 96091.

Travel Services

Klamath River Steelhead Fishing & Marble Mountain Wilderness Pack Trip Service is offered by the nationally renowned Somes Bar Guide Service, operated by Jeff and Brad Throgmorton. Professionally guided steelhead fishing trips in McKenzie River drift boats are offered on the historic Klamath River—considered to be one of the top steelhead fisheries on the West Coast. Overnight accommodations are available at the Somes Bar Lodge. The Oakbottom Forest Service Campground is located nearby, 2 miles up the Salmon River, which flows into the Klamath about ¼ mile below the lodge. Some Bar Guide Service also offers 5–7–day pack-in fishing trips to remote high-country lakes in the Marble Mountain Wilderness for rainbow and brook trout. All food is supplied and prepared by your guides. These July-August trips are for parties of 6–10. For detailed information and rates, contact: Somes Bar Guide Service, Somes Bar, CA 95568 (916)469–3399.

Lassen National Forest & Volcanic Park

The Lassen National Forest contains 1.2 million acres of renowned fishing, hunting, cross-country skiing, and wilderness camping country surrounding Lassen Volcanic National Park west of Susanville in northeastern California. The forest, which straddles the beautiful Cascade Range, is named after Peter Lassen, a frontiersman, trapper, miner, rancher, and trail guide who blazed a northwest route called the Lassen Road to lure settlers north to virgin goldfields and to the hoped-for settlement of Shasta County. The forest terrain consists of gently rolling mountains, dense forests of pine and fir, volcanically formed lakes, and meadows ranging in elevation from 1,200 to 10,000 feet. The sagebrush-covered Great Basin High Desert, east of the forest, is the winter range of antelope and Columbian blacktail and mule deer that live throughout the summer in the forest's deep valleys. The Pacific Crest Trail and hundreds of miles of spur trails and winding forest roads provide access to the volcanic spring-fed waters of Hat Creek, Eagle and Almanor lakes, Painted Dunes, Rising River, the Susan River, and Willow Creek (a brush-lined gem that holds brown trout up to 5 pounds), and to the Caribou and Thousand Lakes wilderness areas.

Information Sources, Maps & Access

Detailed vacation travel and recreation information, a full-color *Lassen National Forest Map* (50¢), and the free *Caribou Wilderness* and *Thousand Lakes Wilderness* map/brochures, may be obtained by contacting: Supervisor, Lassen National Forest, 707 Nevada St., Susanville, CA 96130 (916)257–2151.

A full-color U.S. Geological Survey *Lassen National Volcanic Park Topographic Map*, 24 × 30 inches, shows the park and adjacent area, trails, contours, campgrounds, and all natural and man-made features. This map, also available in a shaded-relief edition, costs $2 and may be ordered from: Distribution Branch, U.S. Geological Survey, Federal Center, Denver, CO 80225. Detailed information, a free *Lassen Volcanic National Park Map-Brochure*, and information bulletins on fishing regulations, backcountry travel, campgrounds, and recreation fees may be obtained by writing: Superintendent, Lassen Volcanic National Park, Mineral 96063 (916)595–4444. The Loomis Museum Association, Mineral 96063, publishes several useful guidebooks to the park.

The Lassen National Forest and Volcanic Park is reached via Interstate 5, U.S. Highway 395, and state routes 89, 139, 299, 44, 36, 99, and 32. Lodging, supplies, guides, and outfitters are available at Chester, Greenville, Quincy, Mineral, Red Bluff, Redding, Susanville, Westwood, Hat Creek, Burney, and Fall River Mills.

Recreation Areas

Caribou Wilderness Area

The gentle, rolling, forested plateau of the Caribou Wilderness Area embraces some 19,080 acres of the forest along the eastern boundary of Lassen Volcanic National Park. The area's volcanic terrain is dominated by the Caribou Peaks and the Red Cinder Cone at 8,370 feet. A forest of Jeffrey and lodgepole pine mixed with white and red fir, western white pine, and hemlock at lower elevations provides cover for deer, black bear, and the rare pine marten. Alpine fishing

is good for rainbow and brook trout in Beauty, Long, Pasey, Triangle, Gem, Divide, Hidden, and Cypress lakes. Access to the remote interior lake basins is by hiking trail.

Eagle Lake Country

Eagle Lake, 18 miles northwest of Susanville at 5,000–feet elevation, is the second-largest natural lake in California. It was formed by the receding alkaline waters of a primeval lake that was larger than Lake Erie. This nationally renowned trout lake, over 13 miles long, is often called the lake that time forgot. The lake is the home of a unique species of rainbow trout that grows to lunker size in a period of about 3 years. The Eagle Lake rainbow was once near extinction, but has returned to its former abundance. Limit catches of rainbows averaging 2–3 pounds are common, and trout up to 11 pounds are caught each year from the lake's deep alkaline waters. The northern and middle sections of the lake are bordered by sagebrush-covered hills, and along the southern shoreline is a beautiful forest of pine and fir. Three campgrounds have been developed along the shoreline by the Forest Service and the Bureau of Land Management. Indian ruins, temporary shelters they used while catching and drying fish that were migrating upstream to spawn, may be seen on Pine Creek near the Spaulding tract.

Hat Creek Recreation Area

The famous rainbow and brown trout waters of Hat Creek, managed under the state's wild trout program, are thought to have been named for Hat-te-we-we of the Pit River Indians, or for an actual hat lost in the stream by a member of the Noble party, blazing trails in 1852. Hat Creek rises high in the volcanic crags of Lassen Park and flows northwest through the forest to its confluence with the Pit River. The Hat Creek Recreation Area offers camping facilities, fishing, and hiking. An archaeological site, the Subway Cave, lies in the Hat Creek area. This lava tube, 4–17 feet high, winds 1,300 feet through the lava flow that covered the Hat Creek Valley less than 2,000 years ago. A self-guided trail interprets the features of Subway Cave. A reliable lantern or flashlight must be carried.

Lassen Volcanic National Park

Within the forest lies Lassen Volcanic National Park, known as the "sweathouse of the gods," encompassing 100,000 acres of rugged coniferous forest surrounding lava-devastated acres of sheer, jagged cliffs, fumaroles, boiling lakes, great weirdly shaped rocks, and bubbling mud pots. The park is dominated by 10,487–foot Mt. Lassen, a plug-dome volcano situated at the southern tip of the Cascade Range. Mt. Lassen is one of the most recently active volcanoes in the contiguous United States. Beginning in May 1914, eruptions occurred intermittently for more than 7 years. Evidence of the activity is visible in the beautifully symmetrical cinder cone, active hot springs, steaming fumaroles, and sulfurous vents. Other major features include the other-worldly scenery of Chaos Crags, a wild disarray of magnificent piles of pointed blocks surrounded by enormous banks of pointed talus reaching 1,000 feet high. Lake Helen, named for Helen Tanner Brodt, the first white woman to climb Lassen Peak, lies within the crater rim of ancestral Mt. Tehama, once the dominant volcano of the region. The park has

more than 150 miles of trails, including the Pacific Crest Trail, which wind through remote forests of pine, fir, cedar, and aspen and along waterfalls, alpine meadows, and lava flows. Wilderness permits are required for all backcountry travel and camping. Beautiful Manzanita Lake has recently been closed to the public due to possible large-scale eruptions or a rockfall avalanche. Fishing in the park is good for rainbow, brook, and brown trout in Hat Creek, Lost Creek, Chester Lakes, Cliff Lake, and Big Bear and Widow Lakes.

The scenic Lassen Park Road, a 30–mile route between the Sulphur Works Entrance and Manzanita Lake, provides access to Bumpass Hell, Kings Creek Meadows, Lassen Peak Trail, and the summit of the park road.

Thousand Lakes Wilderness Area

The beautiful Thousand Lakes Wilderness is situated in the forest northwest of Lassen Volcanic National Park. It is dominated by the sparkling blue trout lakes of Thousand Lakes Valley, which is surrounded by towering peaks that reach their greatest heights at Magee Peak (8,550 ft.) and Crater Peak (8,677 ft.). This glacial valley is dotted by numerous small lakes and ponds surrounded by forests of ponderosa pine, white and red fir, and mountain hemlock and white bark pine above 8,000 feet. The Pacific Crest Trail and numerous spur trails wind through the wilderness and provide excellent opportunities for cross-country travel with the aid of a good map and compass.

Gateways & Accommodations

Almanor

(Pop. 100; zip code 95947; area code 916.) Accommodations: *Crawford's Lakeside* (rates: $16–20 double), 23 rooms, 18 with efficiency kitchens, on Lake Almanor, fishing boats and motors available, free airport pickup, closed November-April, on Hwy. 147, 3 miles north of Hwy. 89 (284–7525); *De Las Plumas* (rates: $20–24 double), 14 rooms, some with color TV, cafe, free coffee in rooms, ½ block south of Canyondam on Hwy. 89 (284–7390).

Chester

(Pop. 1,500; zip code 96020; area code 916.) The town is a major gateway to the Lake Almanor recreation area. Despite its Spanish sound, the 45–square-mile lake actually takes its name from the daughters of the Earl family—Alice, Martha, and Elinore—whose father was president of the Great Western Power Company. Good fishing is available in the lakes and neighboring streams, and boat landings and ramps are numerous. Hunting is also popular in season. Located on the northwestern shore of the lake, Chester is the home of one of the largest sawmills in the state. A district ranger's office of the Lassen National Forest is situated here. Accommodations: *Chester Manor* (rates: $18–23 double), 18 comfortable rooms, 10 with kitchens, adjacent restaurant, coin laundry, picnic tables and grills, on Main St., Box 624, 2 blocks southwest of town on Hwy. 36 (258–2441).

Red Bluff

(Pop. 7,700; zip code 96080; area code 916.) Named for the reddish sand and gravel banks in the area, the town spreads along low bluffs above the Sacramento River. Once an important center for steamboat traffic on the river, the town's chief industries today are lumbering and agriculture. Of special interest are the Kelly-Griggs House Museum, at 311 Washington St., a renovated Victorian home containing displays of Chinese art and Indian artifacts, and the William B. Ide Adobe State Historic Park, 2 miles northeast on Interstate Hwy. 1–5, encompassing the adobe home of the only president of the California Republic. Fishing for steelhead and salmon is popular year-round in the Sacramento River. An 11–acre island in the river near Red Bluff has picnic grounds and a hiking trail. Accommodations: *Best Western Lamplighter Lodge* (rates: $26–28 double), 50 excellent rooms, queen-size beds, color TV, small swimming pool, free airport pickup at 210 S. Main St., at 1–5 traffic exit via business loop 527–1150); *Cinderella Riverview Motel* (rates: 19–21 double), 40 fine air-conditioned rooms, some with balconies overlooking river, swimming pool, fishing, at 600 Rio St. (527–5490); *Hyatt Lodge* (rates: 20–22 double), 40 air-conditioned rooms, private patios, overlooking Sacramento River, swimming pool, adjacent coffee shop, free airport bus, at 38 Antelope Blvd., 2 blocks east on California Hwy. 99, just east of 1–5 (527–6020); *Red Bluff Travelodge*, (rates: $18–22 double), 30 air-conditioned rooms, swimming pool, queen-size beds, at 1142 N. Main St., 5 blocks north on 1–5, business loop (527–3711).

Susanville

(Pop. 6,600, zip code 96130; area code 916.) The town was once the capital of the short-lived Republic of Nataqua (an Indian word for woman), an area some 50,000 square miles in area. Its first settler, Isaac Roop, helped establish the republic in 1856, naming its capital after his only daughter. Nataqua later joined the Nevada Territory and Roop was elected first provisional governor and later senator of Nevada. Following a 5–hour skirmish known as the Sagebrush War, the territory was returned to California in 1864. Area attractions include Eagle Lake, 18 miles northwest of town, the second-largest natural lake in California, and Roops Fort, at 75 N. Weatherlow St., the first log cabin in the county and the chief stronghold during the Sagebrush War. Headquarters for the Lassen National Forest is located in town at 707 Nevada St. (257–2151). Accommodations: *Best Western Trailside Inn* (rates: $23–25 double), 40 comfortable air-conditioned rooms, color TV, swimming pool, coffee shop adjacent, at 2785 Main St., 1 mile east of town on Hwy. 36 (257–4123); *River Inn Motel* (rates: $23–25 double), 38 rooms, color TV, swimming pool, restaurant, cocktail lounge, at 1710 Main St., ½ mile east of town on Hwy. 36 (257–6051).

Lodges & Guest Ranches

★★★★*Childs Meadows Resort & Ski Touring Center*, in Lassen National Forest, 9 miles from the southwest entrance to Lassen Volcanic National Park, offers a full gamut of family activities including fishing in backcountry lakes and streams, hiking around the park's many thermal wonders, horseback riding, cross-country skiing, tennis, or lounging around the resort's big swimming pool. Famous Mill Creek, ¼–mile distant, and countless other trout streams and backcountry lakes are popular for fishing. The resort is located in Lassen National Forest, and a variety of hikes are available from the trailhead linking up to the Lassen Park and Pacific Crest Trail systems. The Ski Touring Center offers a network of prepared track trails. The center is known for its instruction and specializes in teaching beginners. Top-quality rentals and group programs are available. The resort is also convenient for visitors to Lassen Park Ski Area. Accommodations are available in handsome modern motel rooms ($26–32 double per night), 2–bedroom bungalows equipped for light housekeeping ($195 per week), or 2–bedroom rustic cabins ($110 per week). The Childs Meadow Restaurant has a long-established reputation for fine food and overlooks a beautiful mountain meadow. There's also a coffee shop and grocery store with a complete selection of camping supplies. For more details write: Childs Meadows Resort, Highways 36E and 89, Mill Creek, CA 96061 (916)595–4411 or 595–3391.

★★★*The Drakesbad Guest Ranch*, nestled in a scenic mountain valley near Lassen Volcanic National Park, has been in operation for over 100 years and still retains much of the rustic charm that made it a popular resort back in the 1860s. Warm-water baths and a pool filled by hot springs are big drawing cards at the ranch; for those who prefer more strenuous activity there are a good trout stream and several lakes within easy hiking distance, horseback riding, and pack trips through the various national park attractions. Accommodations are modest—lodge bedrooms and cabins are lighted by kerosene lamps—but the ranch prides itself on high standards of comfort and cleanliness. Drakesbad operates on the American plan ($23–35 per person daily), and the menu is always varied and delicious. Saddle horses and guides are available at additional cost. For full information write: Drakesbad Guest Ranch, Chester, CA 96020 (916–Drakesbad 2 via Susanville operator).

★★*Fire Mountain Lodge* offers secluded family accommodations in the lush evergreen forests of Lassen Volcanic National Park, just a few minutes away from Lake Almanor. Guests of the lodge have access to a private trout stream studded with deep pools and beaver dams and teeming with German browns and rainbows. In the fall, the lodge provides a fine base of operations for blacktail deer hunting. Nearby Lassen Park, with its warming huts, rope tows, and chair lifts, is an ideal spot for winter skiing. Cross-country touring is also popular right through the spring. For hikers and horseback riders, there are more than 100 miles of trails winding through mountain meadows, past colorful hot springs, and up Lassen Peak. Lodge accommodations are rustic and comfortable: 1–bedroom housekeeping cabins are approximately $25 daily; hotel rooms above the general store are $15 daily, and modern motel rooms are $20 daily, double occupancy. A coffee shop, old-time saloon, and fireside lounge are also on hand. For more details write: Fire Mountain Lodge, Mill Creek, CA 96061 (916)258–2938.

★★★*The Lassen Mineral Lodge* is a peaceful haven among the pines, nestled in a mountain meadow at an elevation of 5,000 feet. The scenery is awesome, the accommodations comfortable, and the climate mild and invigorating. The Lassen Mineral Lodge Complex includes modern motel and cottages, restaurant and saloon, general store, gift and antique shop, service station, and trailer park. Leisure facilities include heated swimming pool, tennis courts, fishing at nearby Battle Creek (one of northern California's most famous trout streams), deer-hunting, sightseeing, hiking and backpacking, and cross-country skiing (equipment rental on premises). The lodge will arrange easy hikes, rides or short trips in and around famous Lassen Volcanic National Park, the Lassen National Forest and the Lake Almanor area. Motel rates, $14–26 per night, double occupancy. Housekeeping cabins, which include bedding and linens but not cooking utensils and dishes, $20–22 per day for two. For more information, write: The Lassen Mineral Lodge, Mineral, Cal. 96063 (916)595–4422.

Modoc National Forest & Lava Beds Monument

The 1.7 million-acre Modoc National Forest, a renowned big-game and waterfowl hunting and backpacking area, is located in the northeast corner of California and includes the South Warner Wilderness, the Warner Mountains, Goose Lake, and Clear Lake National Wildlife Refuge. The setting of the forest is a complex

geological region of recent volcanic activity. At the eastern border of the forest are the Warner Mountains, a spur of the Cascade Range to the north. The topography ranges from the alpine peaks, canyons, glades, and lush green meadows in the South Warner Wilderness to the rugged obsidian mountains, lava caves, and craters in the Medicine Lake Highlands, located along the west boundary of the forest, directly southwest of the Lava Beds National Monument. The sagebrush-covered grasslands and thick forests of ponderosa pine, red and white fir, and incense cedar were the ancient home and hunting grounds of the Modoc, Paiute, and Pit Indians. Fierce Indian wars took place between 1848 and 1911 against the invading white man, and the region became known as the bloody ground of the Pacific. The Modoc War of 1872–73 was the largest Indian war in California.

Lava Beds National Monument encompasses 72 square miles of volcanic formations—cinder cones, collapsed tunnels, caves, and deep chasms—in the extreme northeast part of the state. Centuries ago active volcanoes produced the rivers of molten lava that carved this strange region. Some caves contain rivers of solid ice; others are decorated with Indian pictographs. Outstanding sights include Merrill Cave, containing a frozen waterfall, Catacombs Cave, Sentinel Cave, and Skull Cave, with its impressive dome rising 80 feet above the floor. Petroglyphs are carved on the bluffs of Tule Lake, in the northeastern section of the monument, which also features a wildlife refuge. The area provided natural trenches and defensive fortifications for the Modoc Indians during their battles with U.S. troops in the Indian War of 1872–73. A museum at the monument headquarters traces the history and geology of the area. In the summer, guided walks and campfire programs are sponsored. There is a campground at Indian Well, but no other lodgings or supplies are available in the immediate area. The monument is open daily (phone (916)667–2601 for information). For accommodations, see Alturas below.

The Medicine Lake Highlands, to the south of the lava beds, is an area of moderately sloping to steep mountains with numerous glass flows, lava caves, tubes, chimneys, cones, and craters and forests of sugar pine and red and white fir with an understory of bitterbrush, manzanita, and snowbrush. Medicine Lake has the forest's largest campground, which provides 88 family camping units. The cool, clear waters of the lake, situated at 6,676–feet elevation, hold rainbow and brook trout. The lake has 500 surface acres, a beach, and a new boat-launching ramp. Accommodations, supplies, and boat rentals are available at Medicine Lake Lodge. The Burnt Lava Flow Virgin Area is on the southern flanks of the highlands. This 9,000–acre

area is a spectacular flow of jumbled black lava surrounding islands of 10 to 60 acres each on three old cinder cones cloaked by virgin stands of pine and fir.

The South Warner Wilderness encompasses 68,507 acres along the southern Warner Mountains. Eagle Peak (9,906 ft.) and Warren Peak (8,875 ft.) dominate the area. The wilderness has a fairly extensive trail system for both the backpacker and horseman. Summit Trail follows the backbone of the wilderness crest for 27 miles from Patterson Meadow, near the southern border, following the 9,000–foot contour for more than 15 miles north along a steep ridge. Numerous spur trails provide access to the forest's peaks, canyons, glacial lakes, and alpine meadows.

The divide along the western edge of the forest is formed by a chain of volcanic peaks and cones extending southward along the southern tip of the Cascade Range to Mount Shasta. To the northeast, the blue waters of Clear Lake National Wildlife Refuge hold huge but extremely wary brown trout. The Clear Lake and Goose Lake areas also offer some of the state's finest waterfowl shooting. Upland bird hunting is good throughout the forest for the handsome mountain quail, chukar partridge, sage grouse, and mourning dove.

Information Sources, Maps & Access

The full-color *Modoc National Forest Recreation Map* (50¢) and the free *Modoc National Forest Camping Guide* and *South Warner Wilderness Map* may be obtained by writing to: Forest Supervisor, Modoc National Forest, 441 N. Main St., Alturas 96101 (916)233–3521.

The major routes to the forest include U.S. Highway 395 and state highways 139 and 299. Lodging, supplies, guides, and packhorses are available at Eagleville, Cedarville, Fort Bidwell, Davis Creek, Alturas, and Canby.

Gateways & Accommodations

Alturas

(Pop. 2,800; zip code 96101; area code 916.) Once the scene of violent warfare with the Modoc Indians, Alturas today is the principal commercial center for surrounding ranchers and the main gateway to the Modoc National Forest. The tribe for which the county and forest are named was originally called Moa Docks, meaning "near southerners," by their hereditary enemies, the Klamath Indians of the northwest coast. The Modoc War of 1872–73, during which a band of no more than 60 held off 1,200 soldiers for 5 months, proved to be the nation's costliest conflict with native Indian tribes. The Modoc Historical Museum (508 S. Main St.) houses artifacts and Indian handicrafts from this period, as well as a collection of antique guns. Also worth a visit is the Modoc National Wildlife Refuge (7 miles south on U.S. 395), a nesting habitat for Canada geese, ducks, and sandhill cranes. Accommodations: *Best Western Trailside Inn* (rates: $22–24 double), 39 air-conditioned rooms, 4 efficiencies, color TV, a small swimming pool, open year-round, at 343 N. Main St. (233–4111); *The Dunes Motel* (rates: $22–24 double), 50 rooms with air conditioning and color TV, adjacent coffee shop, at 511 N. Main St. (233–3545); *The Hacienda* (rates: $18 double), 20 air conditioned rooms, 2 with kitchens, TV, free coffee in rooms, ½ mile northeast on Hwy. 299 (233–3459).

Pacific Coast Recreation Areas & The Big Sur

Several national forests and wilderness areas stretch inland from California's scenic, frequently fog-bound coastal areas, from the majestic redwood forests of the north to the fabled Big Sur country and beyond to the south. The Yolla Bolly-Middle Eel Wilderness contains 111,000 acres in the Mendocino National Forest in the northwest region of the state. It contains the headwaters of the famed Eel River, South Fork Trinity River, and Stuart Gap (the main trailhead into the wilderness).

The King Range Natural Conservation Area runs from the Mattole River 35 miles south to Whale Gulch, about 70 miles south of Eureka on California's northern coast. This rugged area is known as California's lost coast. The range juts up from the sea to an altitude of 4,087 feet at the summit less than 3 miles inland. Streams plunge down to ocean over the steep craggy slopes. On the eastern side of the range streams flow less abruptly down to the Mattole River. The northern portion of the conservation area is grassy, while coastal chaparral and Douglas fir carpet the inland and southern areas.

Offshore, seals, sea lions, and a variety of marine birds inhabit the tidal areas and kelp beds. Black-tailed deer, black bear, quail and grouse, otter and mink live among the fir trees and brush of the slopes. Such rare species as the brown pelican, the bald eagle, the spotted owl, and peregrine falcons also inhabit the area.

The range's Shelter Cove is one of the few protected inlets along the northernmost coast of the state. It provides fishing for salmon,

bottom fish, and rock fish. The cove has boat-launching, restaurant, and motel facilities.

The Mattole River offers some of the finest salmon and steelhead fishing of the northern coast. Rainbow trout are among the species caught in the many streams that lace the area. The deer, bear, and upland game of the area offer hunting in season.

To reach the King Range Natural Conservation Area, follow the Redwood Highway, U.S. 101, to one of the paved access routes that lead to the area from Ferndale, Humboldt Redwoods State Park, or Redway. Paved, gravel, and dirt roads provide motorized travel through the conservation area. Mountain trails wind through the mountains and to the beach for foot travelers. If you plan to hike along the beach, however, consult tide tables, as the beach may be impassable at some points during high tide. Be alert for rattlesnakes in driftwood and rocky areas.

The Bureau of Land Management has four recreation sites in the southern end of the area—Wailaki, Nadelos, Tolkan, and Horse Mountain—all of which have tables, fire grills, and sanitary facilities.

The beautiful 98,112–acre Ventana Wilderness is situated in the Los Padres National Forest, stretching from the Big Sur River to the crest of the Coast Range. This backpacker's paradise, inhabited by bear, deer, and quail, embraces the Little and Big Sur river canyons and the Ventana Double Cone. The San Rafael Wilderness is also located in the forest and takes in the rugged Sisquoc River valley and the Sisquoc Condor Sanctuary.

The Cleveland National Forest encompasses the Agua Tibia Primitive Area, the world's largest telescope at Palomar Observatory on Mt. Palomar, and the historic Mexico-to-Oregon trail. The San Bernardino National Forest takes in the scenic San Gorgonio Wilderness, the 21,955–acre San Jacinto Wilderness, and the southernmost segment of the Pacific Crest Trail. For additional information, see "Redwood National Park."

Information Sources, Maps & Access

For detailed info and a *Mendocino National Forest Map* (50¢), write: Forest Supervisor, 420 E. Laurel St., Willows 95988. For free wilderness maps, trail info, and the *Los Padres National Forest Map* (50¢), write: Forest Supervisor, 42 Aero Camino St., Goleta 93017. The 25,995–acre Aqua Tibia Primitive Area near the Mt. Palomar Observatory is shown on the *Cleveland National Forest Map* (50¢) available from: Forest Supervisor, 3211 Fifth Ave., San Diego 92103. The 36,137–acre San Gabriel Wilderness is shown on the *Angeles National Forest Map* (50¢) available from: Forest Supervisor, 150 S. Los Robles, Pasadena 91101. The tiny Cucamonga Wilderness and the scenic San Gorgonio Wilderness, the San Jacinto Wilderness, and the southernmost segment of the Pacific Crest Trail in the rugged San Bernardino Mountains are shown on the *San Bernardino National Forest Map* (50¢), available from: Forest Supervisor, 144 N. Mountain View Ave., San Bernardino 92408.

The following maps and guides are available from Wilderness Press, 2440 Bancroft Way, Berkeley 94704: *An Outdoor Guide to the San Francisco Bay Area* ($6.95); *Trails of the Angeles Trail Map* (75¢); and *San Bernardino Mountain Trails Map* (75¢).

The major auto route to the Pacific Coast forests and recreation areas is U.S. 101. A map and brochure describing the King Range Natural Conservation Area, its accommodations and facilities, trails, camps, wildlife, and history, is available free from the District Manager, U.S. Bureau of Land Management, 555 Leslie Street, Ukiah, CA 95482. The map keys the locations of roads, primitive roads, jeep roads, BLM trails, BLM campgrounds, and water sources within the area. The map is on a scale of 1 inch to 1 mile. Smaller vicinity maps show the location of the conservation area on the northern coast.

Gateways & Accommodations

Big Bear Lake

(Pop. 5,300; zip code 92315; area code 714.) Located about 30 miles east of San Bernardino in the eastern San Bernardino Mountains, this popular year-round vacation spot is convenient to several winter sports centers, campgrounds, riding stables, and to Big Bear Lake itself. Ski areas include Goldmine (2 miles east of town off Hwy. 18) and Snow Summit (1 mile east of town off Hwy. 18). Accommodations: *Escape for All Seasons* (rates: $50–60 double), 2– and 3–bedroom town houses with patios and fireplaces in a quiet, shady setting, open year-round, at 41935 Switzerland Drive, ¼ mile south of Hwy. 18 (866–7504); *Robinhood Inn and Lodge* (rates: $25–37 double), 20 rooms, many with fireplaces, 4 efficiencies, color TV, cocktail lounge, dancing and entertainment, on Lakeview Drive, in the village on Hwy. 18 (866–4643); *Shore Acres Lodge* (rates: $25–55 double), 11 cabins with kitchens and shower or combination baths, lakefront location, heated pool, dock, rental boats, ¾ mile west of village on Lakeview Drive (866–4386); *Thunder Cloud Lodge* (rates: $25–40 double), 63 rooms in 2 lodges, heated pool, saunas, sundecks, on Lakeview Drive, 1 block north of Hwy. 18 (866–4543).

Big Sur

(Pop. 200; zip code 93920; area code 408.) About 30 miles south of Monterey on California Hwy. 1, Big Sur is framed by the crashing waters of the Pacific on the west and the Santa Lucia Mountains on the east. The Pfeiffer-Big Sur State Park covers more than 800 acres of redwood forest and coastal lands on the Big Sur River. The region has earned its place in literature as the background for many poems by Robinson Jeffers. (Contact the Big Sur Information Center for information on the area: 667–2353). Accommodations: *Big Sur Lodge* (rates: $29–32 double), 61 fine rooms, 1– and 2–bedroom cottages, some with fireplaces and kitchens, in the state park, coffee shop, sauna, pool, 28 miles south of Carmel on Hwy. 1 (667–2171); *Ventana Big Sur Lodge* (rates: $72–95 double), 24 rooms and suites, superb hilltop location overlooking the coast, large swimming pool, sauna, free continental breakfast, and a fine restaurant specializing in seafood and home-baked treats (667–2331).

Fort Bragg

(Pop. 4,500, zip code 95437; area code 707.) The town is situated on a sloping coastal shelf at the edge of a wild and rocky coastline. From 1857 to 1867, Fort Bragg was a military post, named for Gen. Braxton Bragg, a hero of the Mexican War. The post occupied a 10–acre clearing within the Mendocino Indian Reservation. In 1867 the land was opened for purchase, when the reservation was abandoned, and a lumber town sprang up. Area attractions include the gorgeous Mendocino Coast Botanical Gardens (2 miles south on Hwy. 1), 47 acres of exotic blooms and a cliff house overlooking the Pacific, and the California Western Railroad tour, which departs from the foot of Laurel St. and travels through beautiful redwood groves on a 40–mile journey along the Noyo River to Willits (round trip takes about 6 hours; half-day trips available in the summer; for info, contact: California Western Railroad, P.O. Box 907, Fort Bragg; phone 964–6371; rates approximately $4–10). Within a radius of 14 miles are three fine state parks. MacKerricher State Park, 3 miles north on Hwy. 1, features a group of harbor seals off the coast. Russian Gulch, 9 miles south on Hwy. 1, has hiking and nature trails. Van Damme State Park, 14 miles south on Hwy. 1, encompasses an unusual pygmy forest of stunted trees, some with trunks no more than ½ inch in diameter. Surf casting for cod and trout fishing in the Little River are also popular here. Area restaurants of note include the *Cafe Beaujolais* (in Mendocino at 861 E. Ukiah St., 937–5614, renowned for fine French specialties and a charming Victorian atmosphere) and the *Ledford House* (in Little River, 16 miles south of Fort Bragg on Hwy. 1, 937–0282, a good bet for fresh seafood, served in a 100–year-old house overlooking the Pacific). Accommodations: *Best Western Vista Manor* (rates: $28 double), 78 fine rooms and family suites, heated indoor pool, open year-round, 12 steam baths, hilltop location with beach opposite, at 1100 North Main St., 1 mile north of town on Hwy. 1 (964–4776); *City Motel* (rates: $26–28 double), 31 rooms, one 2–bedroom apartment, color TV, attractive garden, near California Western R.R. Station, at 250 S. Main St. (964–5321); *Harbor Lite Lodge* (rates: $28–32 double), 70 excellent rooms and family units, many with balconies overlooking Noyo Harbor, sauna, putting green, coffee shop, near beach, at 120 N. Harbor Drive, 1 mile south of Fort Bragg on Hwy. 1, open year-round (964–0221); *Heritage House* (rates: $64–105 double, including 3 meals), 50 rooms in attractively decorated cottages, many with antiques and fireplaces, on a lofty bluff overlooking the ocean, restaurant and bar, original inn building dates from 1875, outside town of Little River, 17 miles south of Fort Bragg (937–5885); *Pine Beach Inn* (rates: $28–50 double), 50 excellent rooms and suites on spacious grounds overlooking the ocean, private beach, tennis courts, restaurant, cocktail lounge, 4 miles south of town on Hwy. 1, (964–5603); *Tradewinds Lodge* (rates: $28–30 double), 52 large rooms, swimming pool, restaurant, open year-round, at 400 S. Main St., 6 blocks south of Fort Bragg on Hwy. 1 (964–4761).

Garberville—Gateway to Redwood Country & the King Range

(Pop. 900; zip code 95440; area code 707.) This town is a popular summer recreation center and gateway to the spectacular redwoods in the Richardson Grove State Park on the Redwood Highway 101, King Range Conservation Area, and the famous trout and steelhead waters of the South Fork of the Eel River. Accommodations: *Benbow Inn* (rates: $24–42 double), 70 excellent rooms in superb Tudor English inn in the heart of Redwood country, fine dining, across from the Benbow Lake State Recreation Area on the South Fork of the Eel River, 2 miles south of town on U.S. 101 (923–2124); *Hartsook Inn* (rates: $24–32 double), a famous resort in scenic redwood groves adjacent to Richardson Grove State Park, on 30 acres, rustic guest cottages and dining room on the Redwood Highway 101, 8 miles south of town (247–3305).

Idyllwild

(Pop. 900; zip code 92349; area code 714.) Site of a 250–acre campus of the University of Southern California, Idyllwild is a mountain resort town dominated by lofty San Jacinto Peak (10,300 ft.). The Indians believed that a powerful demon named Tahquity, who lived on the mountaintop, periodically stalked the canyons, howling and screaming and bringing bad weather in his wake. Area attractions include a summer arts festival, 2 pleasant county parks, the San Jacinto Wilderness State Park, and an aerial tramway at nearby Palm Springs. A district ranger's office of the San Bernardino National Forest is located in town. Accommodations: *Bluebird Motel* (rates: $20–42 double), 26 rooms and housekeeping cabins in secluded forest setting, some 1– and 2–bedroom motel rooms, TV, weekly rates available, ¾ mile south of town on Hwy. 243, (659–2696); *Woodland Park Manor* (rates: $20–28 double), 11 fine rooms, units with kitchenettes, fireplaces, and sundecks, color TV, pool, playground, at 55350 S. Circle Drive, 1 mile northeast of Idyllwild off Hwy. 243 (659–2657).

Lake Arrowhead

(Pop. 2,700; zip code 92352; area code 714.) One of the prettiest spots along the scenic Rim of the World Drive from San Bernardino, Lake Arrowhead is a village of rustic Norman-style cafes, shops, and houses protected by strict zoning laws. Roads and footpaths lead to the numerous resorts on the forested shore of the lake, which is about 2½ miles long and 1 mile wide. The lake and surrounding San Bernardino National Forest offer opportunities for both summer and winter recreation. Accommodations: *Tree Top Lodge* (rates: $27–37 double), 19 fine rooms and family units in a lovely forest setting, oversize beds, heated pool, picnic tables and grill, ½ mile south of village on Hwy. 173, Box 186 (337–2311).

Ojai

(Pop. 5,600; zip code 93023; area code 805.) Bounded by the Topatopa Mountains on the north and Sulphur Mountains on the south, Ojai is a popular resort spot and gateway to the Los Padres National Forest. A district ranger's office is located here. The best bet in local restaurants is the *Ranch House* (102 Besant Road 646–2360), an excellent chef-owned establishment specializing in crab and vegetarian dishes. Accommodations: *Ojai Valley Inn* (rates: $85–120 double, including 3 meals), a year-round resort complex on several acres of beautifully landscaped grounds, 41 air-conditioned rooms, 72 air-conditioned cottages, golf course, heated pool, horseback riding, tennis courts, dining room, cocktail lounge, weekend entertainment, convention facilities, 1 mile west of town, just off Hwy. 150 (646–5511).

Pine Valley

(Pop. 300; zip code 92062; area code 714.) The town is surrounded by the Cleveland National Forest, which encompasses the Laguna Mountains Recreation Area, 16 miles east on County Road S1. Accommodations: *Pine Valley Lodge* (rates: $35 double), 40 air-conditioned rooms, TV, swimming pool, private patios, recreation room, located in a quiet forest setting, on Hwy. 80, just off 1–8, (473–8711).

Ukiah

(Pop. 10,100; zip code 95482; area code 707.) The seat of Mendocino County lies in a long and narrow valley flanked by mountains. The town's name derives from the Indian word *Yo-ka-Ya*, meaning "deep valley." Just east of Ukiah is the Mendocino National Forest. Lake

Mendocino, 6 miles northeast, is an artificial lake with excellent facilities for boating, swimming, waterskiing, fishing, and camping (open daily April-September; phone 462–7581 for information). Southeast of Lake Mendocino, the Cow Mountain Recreation Area encompasses a 50,000–acre preserve. Accommodations: *Best Western Inn* (rates: $24–26 double), 40 excellent rooms, small swimming pool, airport pickup, putting green, at 601 Talmadge Road, east of U.S. 101 bypass (462–8868); *Best Western Satellite Lodge* (rates: $26–28 double), 40 air-conditioned rooms, color TV, swimming pool, at 406 S St., ½ mile west of U.S. 101, Perkins St. or Central Exit (462–8611); *Lu-Ann Motel*, (rates: $18–30 double) 56 excellent rooms, 5 with kitchens, queen-size beds, color TV, pool, sauna, 24–hour restaurant, sundeck, at 1340 N. State St., 1½ miles north on U.S. 101 business route (462–8873); *Ukiah Travelodge* (rates: $26–28 double), 32 fine air-conditioned rooms, some queen-size beds, color TV, pool, restaurant and bar, free airport bus, at 1070 S. State St., 1 mile south of town, ½ mile west of U.S. 101 at Talmadge Road Exit (462–6657).

Ventura

(Pop. 55,800; zip code, see below; area code 805.) Site of the ninth and last mission founded by the energetic Fray Junepero Serra, Ventura is a bustling city framed by low foothills on the east and the Pacific coast on the west. The restored mission, with its massive striped rib dome and tranquil garden, is located at Main and Figueroa Sts. Also of interest are the Ventura County Historical Museum, at 100 E. Main St., containing exhibits relevant to the area's history; the Olivas Adobe, at 4200 Olivas Park Drive, a beautifully restored hacienda originally built in 1841; and the Padre Serra Cross on Mission Hill, from which impressive views of the surrounding country are available. Sight-seeing cruises of the Channel Islands National Monument leave the Ventura Marina daily during the summer months (write Box 993 or phone 642–3370 for information). Ventura is a major gateway to the Los Padres National Forest. For maps and auto tours, contact the Visitor Information Center at 785 S. Seaward Ave. Accommodations: *Best Western Ventura Motor Lodge* (rates: $26 double), 75 fine rooms, 1 block from ocean beach, color TV, pool, 24–hour restaurant, at 708 E. Thompson Blvd., 93001, 3 blocks southeast of town on U.S. 101 business route (648–3101); *Holiday Inn of Ventura* (rates: $40 double), 260 excellent rooms and suites, balconies with ocean view, beachfront location, heated pool, color TV, free airport bus, coffee shop, cocktail lounge, revolving rooftop dining room, at 450 E. Harbor Blvd., 93001, adjacent to U.S. 101, California St. Exit (648–7731); *Pierpont Inn* (rates: $25–52 double), 80 excellent rooms and suites, most with balconies and ocean views, elegant decor, heated pool, lighted tennis courts, fine restaurant with views of Pierpont Bay, at 550 Sanjon Road, 93003, adjacent to U.S. 101, Sanjon Rd. or Seaward Ave. Exit (643–6144); *Vagabond Motor Hotel* (rates: $29–32 double), 82 fine rooms, color TV, heated pool, 24–hour coffee shop, playground, 1 block from beach, at 756 E. Thompson Blvd., 93001, ½ mile east on U.S. 101 business route, Ventura Ave. or California St. Exit (648–5371).

Plumas National Forest— The Feather River Country

Plumas National Forest encompasses 1,146,900 acres in the transition zone between the Sierra Nevada and the Cascade Mountains surrounding Quincy in northeastern California, and includes nearly the entire Feather River system. The terrain is mountainous, rugged, and exceedingly steep in some areas. The mountains, ranging in elevation from 1,000 to 8,372 feet, are cut by deep canyons, interspersed with large grassy valleys. Hundreds of miles of scenic trails, including the Pacific Crest Trail, and forest roads wind through colorful stands of sugar, ponderosa, and Jeffrey pine, white and red fir, Douglas fir, and incense cedar, and provide access to the remote Lakes Basin, Upper Canyon of the Middle Fork of the Feather River, Little Grass Valley, and Antelope, Bucks, Frenchman, and Davis lakes.

Remnants of the gold rush days, including old machinery, abandoned water ditches, and trails, are found in the remote backcountry areas near the Middle Fork. The beautiful Middle Fork of the Feather, a national recreation area and wild and scenic river, flows

southwesterly for 108 miles from the northeastern corner of Sierra Valley. It is joined by Last Chance Creek in a gentle valley, then switches into mountainous terrain, and finally plunges into the rugged canyons above Lake Oroville. Rainbow trout fishing is good along the entire length of the Middle Fork. The recreational zone of the Middle Fork flows for 65 miles from Last Chance Creek through small rocky canyons, timbered flats, and meadow lands to the quiet forest of the English Bar zone, where the river flows for 6 miles to the rugged, steep-banked Upper Canyon Wild River. Access to this section of the Middle Fork is by old mining and deer trails that skirt the break made by the river channel. The trail bridge and camp at Hartman Bar are on the crossing for the Pacific Crest Trail. The Middle Fork flows through the Upper Canyon zone for 27 miles into the forest of the Milsap Bar zone, where it flows over Seven Falls and continues on through the Bald Rock Canyon wild zone and pours into Lake Oroville. The Bald Rock Canyon area is dominated by huge boulders, rock cliffs, and sheer canyon walls; nearby is Feather Falls.

The Feather Falls Scenic Area includes portions of the Middle Fork and three of its tributaries—Fall River, the Little North Fork, and the South Branch Middle Fork Feather River. This 15,000–acre scenic area embraces spectacular granite domes and Feather Falls on the Fall River, the sixth-highest waterfall in the United States, which plummets 640 feet over a sheer granite cliff during its rush to meet the Middle Fork and Lake Oroville. Feather Falls was formed several million years ago when the Sierra Nevada tilted westward and erosion exposed a huge granite batholith that had fractured as it cooled. The Fall River eroded the soft fractured area back from the deep Bald Rock Canyon to hard solid rock at the brink of the falls. During March, April, and May, the water is at its highest flow and the falls are most spectacular. A foot trail provides easy access, and an overlook across from the falls provides an excellent view of one of the greatest scenic wonders in California. Another attraction in the scenic area is the South Branch Falls, a series of nine waterfalls varying in height from 30 to 150 feet, noted for their huge rock domes, boulders, and deep green pools. Hiking and riding trails wind throughout the scenic area and provide access to more than 22 miles of good rainbow trout streams, including the Little North Fork, a beautiful cascading stream that enters the Middle Fork near the Milsap Bar campground. Maidu Indian mortars and artifacts can be seen at Wagner Valley and Bald Rock Dome and along the Fall River.

The Pacific Crest Trail winds through the forest from Lassen National Forest on the north, crossing the North Fork near Belden and Lake Almanor to the east. The trail passes by Bucks Lake and across the Middle Fork of the Feather, veers southeast through the Lakes Basin area, and winds on into Tahoe National Forest on the south. Of the 67 miles of the Pacific Crest Trail in Plumas Forest, only 13 miles have been constructed and marked to date. The temporary route is marked by signs.

Information Sources, Maps & Access

Additional information, a full-color *Plumas National Forest Map* (50¢), and the free map/brochures *Middle Fork Feather River, Feather Falls Scenic Area, Antelope Lake Recreation Area, Bucks Lake Recreation Area, Grass Valley Recreation Area,* and *Frenchman Recreation Area* may be obtained from: Supervisor, Plumas National Forest, P.O. Box 1500, Quincy, CA 95971 (916)283–2050.

Major routes to the Plumas National Forest include Interstate Highway 5, U.S. Highway 395, and state routes 49, 70, 99, 36, 139, 44, and 89. Accommodations, boat rentals, supplies, guides, and outfitters are available at the towns of Quincy, Challenge, Sierra City, Blairsden, Greenville, Crescent Mills, Oroville, Chico, Paradise, and Westwood.

Gateways & Accommodations

Chico

(Pop. 19,600; zip code 95926; area code 916.) Chico was founded in the late 1840s when Gen. John Bidwell, a member of the first overland party to cross the Sierras, combined two prosperous ranches

to form the Rancho Chico, renowned for its orchards and miles of tree-shaded avenues. A strong force in the area's agricultural development, Bidwell ran for president on the Prohibition party ticket in 1892. The Bidwell Mansion State Historic Park, at 525 Esplanade Ave., surrounds the lavish 26–room Victorian home of Chico's founder. Bidwell Park, at the east end of Fourth St., winds along Big Chico Creek for 10 miles. This lush strip of greenery served as the setting for Sherwood Forest in the 1937 movie *The Adventures of Robin Hood*. Accommodations: *Holiday Inn* (rates: $31–32 double), 123 excellent rooms and family suites, swimming and wading pools, room service, cafe, cocktail lounge, restaurant, dancing and entertainment, at 685 Manganita Court, 1 mile east of town on Hwy. 99, Cohasset Exit (345–2491); *Imperial '400* (rates: $22–25 double), 42 fine rooms, free continental breakfast, pool, nearby coffee shop, at 630 Main St. (895–1323); *Safari Garden* (rates: $20–22 double), 50 comfortable rooms on lovely tree-shaded grounds, pool, 5 kitchen units, at 2352 Esplanade, 2 miles north of Chico on Hwy. 99 (343–3201).

Marysville

(Pop. 9,400; zip code 95901; area code 916.) The town lies at the confluence of the Yuba and Feather rivers and is named for Mary Murphy Covilland, a survivor of the ill-fated Donner Party and wife of one of the town's early settlers. In the late 19th century, the Yuba River bed was raised 70 feet above the town and is now contained by huge levees. Once the prosperous head of river navigation and third-largest community in California, Marysville today is a pleasant town of shady parks and old brick buildings. Area attractions include the Bok Kai Temple at 1st and D Sts., a Chinese temple built more than 100 years ago to honor the river god, Bok Kai, and the Mary Aaron Museum, at 704 D Street, which contains memorabilia of the gold-rush days in the restored rooms of an 1854 house. Accommodations: *Imperial 400 Motel* (rates: $22–24 double), 43 fine air-conditioned rooms, color TV, swimming pool, some studios with kitchens, on Hwy. 20 at 721 10th St. (742–8586); *Marysville Travelodge* (rates: $20–23 double), 43 air-conditioned rooms, some with oversize beds, swimming pool, adjacent to city park, at 904 E. Street (743–1531).

Oroville

(Pop. 7,500; zip code 95965; area code 805.) Located at the base of the Sierra foothills, Oroville is a jumping-off point for visitors to the Lake Oroville State Recreation Area and Plumas National Forest. Of special interest: the Chinese Temple, at the corner of Elma and Broderick Sts., built in 1861 and the largest of California's authentic temples; Sank Park-Historic Lott Home, at 1067 Montgomery St., a beautifully restored 1856 house furnished in period style; Table Mountain, 6 miles north of town via Table Mountain Blvd., with a ghost town, abandoned mines, and picnic grounds at the summit. Just east of town on California Hwy. 162 is the Oroville Reservoir, 167 miles long, a key part of the Feather River Project surrounded by three recreation areas (boating, swimming, camping, and hiking trails). Accommodations: *The Villa Motel* (rates: $26–28 double), 20 comfortable rooms, most with queen-size beds, small swimming pool, color TV, at 1527 Feather River Blvd., ¼ mile east off Hwy. 70 (533–3930).

Quincy

(Pop. 3,300; zip code 95971; area code 916.) A pleasant town resembling a New England village, Quincy is a key gateway to the Plumas National Forest. A district ranger's office is located here. From Quincy a trail leads to spectacular Feather Falls, plummeting 640 feet into the canyon of the Middle Fork of the Feather River. An old-time county fair is held annually, the 2nd week in August, at the Plumas County Fairgrounds. Accommodations: *Lariat Lodge* (rates: $22–24 double), 20 comfortable rooms, color TV, swimming pool, restaurant nearby, at 2370 E. Main St., 2½ miles east of town on Hwy. 70 (283–1000); *Ranchito Motel* (rates: $22–24 double) 18 excellent rooms, some units with kitchens, attractive Spanish decor, on 4 wooded acres with shaded gardens, restaurant opposite, off-season rates, at 2020 E. Main St., 2 miles east of Quincy on Hwy. 70 (283–2265).

Sacramento

(Pop. 254,400; zip code, see below; area code 916.) California's capital got its start in 1839, when Capt. John A. Sutter established New Helvetia, a colony for Swiss émigrés. The discovery of gold in the area 11 years later brought ruin to Sutter's Fort but boosted Sacramento's population to 10,000 within a few months. In 1854 the city was chosen as the state capital. The building of the Central Pacific Railroad and fine port facilities encouraged further growth and expansion during the 19th century. In recent years, nearby air force bases and missile development industries have bolstered the city's economy; restoration and redevelopment programs are in progress in the downtown area. Area attractions: Sutter's Fort State Historic Park, at 2701 L St., with the original adobe house, extensive displays, and the State Indian Museum; State Capitol, between 10th and 12th Sts. at the Capitol Mall, an impressive structure with a 237–foot-high dome, historical and fine arts exhibits, surrounded by 40 acres of parkland and stunning gardens; Governor's Mansion, at 16 and H Sts., restoration of the 19th–century building, the governor's official residence from 1903 to 1968; Old Sacramento Historic District, a 10–block section along the Sacramento River adjoining the central business district, with buildings restored to period 1850–80, shops, restaurants, and the Visitor Center at 2 and K Sts., which has maps and information; Sacramento Science Center and Junior Museum, at 3615 Auburn Blvd. in Del Paso Park, exhibits, films, and live animals; E.B. Crocker Art Gallery, 216 O St., European and American paintings, tapestries, Oriental art objects, changing exhibitions and concerts. Area accommodations: *Best Western Ponderosa Motor Inn* (rates: $32–34 double), 100 excellent rooms, color TV, pool, sauna, restaurant, cocktail lounge, entertainment, at 100 H St., 95814, 3 blocks from Capitol (441–1314); *Best Western Sandman Motel* (rates: $28–32 double), 112 fine rooms, color TV, swimming pool, whirlpool, airport transportation, restaurant, cocktail lounge, at 236 Jibboom St., 95814, north of town at Richards Blvd. Exit off Interstate 5 (443–6515); *Holiday Inn North* (rates: $29.50–32.50

double), 150 excellent rooms and family suites, color TV, swimming pool, restaurants and cocktail lounge, free airport bus, entertainment and dancing, at 1900 Canterbury Road, 95815, 3 miles northeast of town via Hwy. 160 (927–3492); *Host International Hotel* (rates: $40 double), 90 excellent rooms and suites, pool, restaurant, large rooms, direct underground concourse to airport terminal, at 6945 Airport Blvd., 95837, adjacent to Sacramento Metropolitan Airport (922–8071); *Mansion Inn* (rates: $33–39 double), 182 very attractive rooms, many with balconies and oversize beds, swimming pool, lovely courtyard and terrace, fine restaurant, at 16 and H Sts., 95814, opposite the Governor's Mansion (444–8000); *Red Lion Motor Inn* (rates: $46–48 double), 360 superlative rooms and suites, swimming pool, spacious grounds, restaurant and bar, free airport pickup, at 2001 Point West Way, 95815, 4½ miles northeast of town via I–80 (929–8855); *Sacramento Inn* (rates: $42–45 double), 325 excellent rooms, pool, steam baths, restaurant and cocktail lounge, at 1401 Arden Way, 95815, 4 miles east of town via I–80 (922–8041); *Vagabond Motor Hotel* (rates: $33–38 double), 109 excellent rooms, oversize beds, swimming pool, restaurant and bar, free airport pick-up, at 909 3rd St., 95814, 8 blocks west of Capitol, adjacent to Old Sacramento restoration (446–1481); *Woodlake Inn* (rates: $34–40 double), 340 excellent rooms and suites, oversize beds and balconies, resort facilities, swimming pool, tennis, putting green, playground, recreation room, restaurant and bar, dancing and entertainment, at 500 Leisure Lane, 95815, 3 miles northeast of town via Hwy. 160, Canterbury Road Exit (922–6251).

Lodges & Guest Ranches

★★*Elwell Lakes Lodge*, in the Feather River Lakes basin, is conveniently situated within easy walking distance of over 20 lakes, most of them ideal for swimming and boating. Fishing for trout is excellent in clear mountain streams and lakes, and there is shore fishing on all of the lakes for rainbows, browns, and brookies. Miles of well-graded, uncluttered trails, including the famous Sierra Crest Trail, afford unlimited hiking opportunities. For the golfer there are three courses in the vicinity, plus pro shops and a driving range nearby. Each of the rustic, fully equipped cabins has a bath, kitchenette, and barbecue, and will accommodate 3–6 guests. Rates, including lodgings and use of boats on nearby Long Lake: $18–20 daily for up to 3 persons; $25 daily for 4; and $30 daily for 6. Discounts are offered to guests staying a minimum of 3–7 days. For additional details write: (summer) Elwell Lakes Lodge, P.O. Box 68, Blairsden, CA 96103 (916)836–2347; (summer) 2011 Oakland Ave., Piedmont, CA 94611 (916)836–2347.

★★★*Greenhorn Creek Guest Ranch*, in the heart of California's Feather River country, is surrounded by hundreds of lakes and streams alive with big rainbows and kokanee salmon. For water enthusiasts there's a heated outdoor pool plus an old-fashioned swimming hole and many opportunities in the area for boating and waterskiing. A stable of good-natured horses is available for rides through Plumas National Park, and there's a pine-fringed fairway down the road at the Feather River Inn. Fully modern cabins are all attractively furnished and shaded by tall trees. Hearty ranch-style meals are served to the accompaniment of a crackling fire, with barbecues and candlelit dinners for a change of pace. Rates range from approximately $150 to $250 per person per week, depending on the season, and include lodging, all meals, use of recreational facilities, and daily maid service. For information write: Greenhorn Creek Guest Ranch, P.O. Box 11, Spring Garden, CA 95971 (916)283–0930.

★*Lakeshore Resort*, on Buck's Lake in the Sierra Mountains, has 17 fully equipped housekeeping cabins available May through October. The evergreen-fringed lake is ideal for swimming, waterskiing, boating, and fishing for native German brown trout. There are also facilities for boat launching, dockage, camping, and fishing boat rentals. A restaurant and lakeview cocktail lounge offer fine food and drink in a relaxing atmosphere. For additional information and rates write: Lakeshore Resort, P.O. Box 266, Quincy, CA 95971 (916)283–2333.

★*Plumas Pines Village* is located on placid Lake Almanor high in the Sierra Nevadas at 4,500–foot elevations. The lake is noted for fat rainbows in the 2–12-pound category, coho salmon, kokanee, and catfish. This is also prime mule and blacktail deer country, with excellent hunting in season available a short walk from your door. There's a large boat dock with ramp facilities for launching your craft, plus a complete selection of rentals: sailboats, canoes, fishing boats, and speedboats for waterskiing. All cottages are fully furnished, with private baths, electric kitchens, heat, and fresh linens. Twin, double, and 2–bedroom motel units are also available. Cottages are $22 per day ($135 weekly); motel units are $16–20 daily (double occupancy). Plumas Pines Village has its own dining room and cocktail lounge, both with panoramic views of the lake and surrounding countryside. For more information, write: Plumas Pines Village, Almanor, CA 95911 (916)258–2281.

Travel Services

★★*Mountain Base Camps* is a family vacation camping area, fully staffed with experienced personnel ready to provide you with the equipment and guidance for almost any outdoor activity of your choosing. It is located on the tip of Gold Lake, the largest of over 25 natural lakes in the spectacular Lakes Basin Recreation area. The Lakes Basin area is well known for its outstanding trout fishing, boating, hiking and backpacking. But the Mountain Base Camps also provides instructors and guides for riding, sailing, swimming, crafts, and other vacation interests. Facilities include tent and wood cabins, a dining hall and kitchen, spacious recreation hall, shower and bathroom facilities and craft shop. Golf and tennis courts within a 25–minute drive. Rates, all meals and linen included, are about $416.50/week for two. For more information, contact: Mountain Base Camps, P.O. Box 402, Graeagle, CA 96103 (916)836–2491.

Redwood National Park

Redwood National Park encompasses 58,000 acres along the northern coast of California just south of the state's boundary with Oregon. A network of trails winds along the 40 miles of primitive and rocky coastline; there is also a coastal drive, about 8 miles long, stretching past some of the area's outstanding scenery. Although the park's beaches are open year-round, visitors are cautioned against swimming and surfing in the rough waters of the Pacific. A heavy undertow and dangerous, rocky schoals prohibit most water sports, with the exception of surf casting. Wildlife observation is especially rewarding here. Waterfowl migrations and the birds that inhabit the region's bluffs and lagoons attract scores of bird-watchers. Sea lion colonies are found near the craggy promontories, and migrating whales are often sighted offshore. In addition to the giant trees for which the park is named, memorable natural landmarks include sweeping dunes, high cliffs, and scenic salt marshes. The park embraces three state parks—Del Norte Coast, Prairie Creek, and Jedediah Smith; each contains its own campgrounds, picnic areas, and other visitor facilities.

Information Sources, Maps & Access

For detailed vacation travel information and a free *Redwood National Park Map/Brochure*, contact: Superintendent, Redwood National Park, Drawer N, Crescent City, CA 95531 (707)458–3134 or 464–6101. Access is via the scenic Redwood Highway.

The Redwood Highway (U.S. 101), a major thoroughfare 4 lanes wide at many points, stretches for 300 miles, roughly southeast to northwest a few miles inland from the California coast, and traverses some of the state's most scenic countryside, including spectacular

groves of giant sequoias. The greatest concentration of redwoods occurs from Cummings north to Crescent City. Between Miranda and Red Crest, the highway intersects Humboldt Redwoods State Park, home of the 365-foot Rockefeller Tree and the awesome Avenue of the Giants. North of Trinidad, Redwood National Park runs on both sides of the road as far as Crescent City. The Redwood Highway is often heavily trafficked during the summer months; reservations for lodging along the route should be made in advance.

Gateways & Accommodations

Crescent City

(Pop. 2,600; zip code 95531; area code 707.) The town faces a shallow harbor edged by arc-shaped Crescent Beach, from which it derives its name. The harbor was discovered by a group of treasure-hunters seeking gold hidden by an old prospector; no gold was found, but the city was laid out a year later, in 1852, and grew rapidly during the second part of the century. Just north of Crescent City is Point St. George, scene of a disastrous shipwreck in 1865. Many of the 200 victims were buried in Brother Johnathan Cemetery, on 9th St. and Taylor Road. The old lighthouse on Battery Point, accessible only at low tide, houses a museum of memorabilia from the wreck, as well as antique clocks and old log books. East of town is the Redwood National Park, which encompasses 30 miles of picturesque coastline, scenic drives, dense redwood groves, campgrounds, and picnic sites. Also worth a visit are the Undersea Gardens, south on U.S. 101, with sea plants, animals, and scuba-diving shows. Accommodations: *Best Western Curly Redwood Lodge* (rates: $27–29 double), constructed of wood from a single redwood tree, 36 fine rooms and family suites, color TV, free coffee, restaurant opposite, at 701 Redwood Hwy. S., 1 mile south of town on U.S. 101 (464–2137); *Pacific Motor Hotel* (rates: $28–32 double), 63 comfortable rooms, color TV, restaurant adjacent, ¾ mile north of town on U.S. 101 (464–4141); *Royal Inn* (rates: $26–32 double), 30 rooms, many with queen-size beds, bay views, park opposite, 102 L St. at Front St. (464–4113); *The Town House* (rates: $22–24 double), 24 rooms, color TV, some queen-size beds, nearby restaurants, at 444 Redwood Hwy., ½ mile south on U.S. 101 (464–4176).

Eureka

(Pop. 24,300; zip code 95501; area code 707.) The city owes its name to surveyor James Ryan, who in 1850 drove his cart onto the mud flats shouting "Eureka! I have found it!" Spread along the shores of Humboldt Bay, Eureka is an important lumbering center and the chief port between San Francisco and the Columbia River. The city's past is commemorated by such landmarks as the ornate Victorian mansion of a local lumber baron (the Carson Mansion, 2nd and M Sts.) and Fort Humboldt, headquarters of Gen. Ulysses Grant in 1853, whose museum houses logging and military exhibits. The Sequoia Park and Zoo (entrance at Glatt and W Sts.) encompasses 46 acres of redwoods, a duck pond, picnic facilities, gardens, and a fine zoo. Eureka is the gateway to Six Rivers National Forest, reached via U.S. 101 or 199, where 1,120,000 acres slashed by numerous rivers provide excellent fishing, hunting, and camping. Also at the foot of C St. is one of the area's finest restaurants, *Lazio's Seafood*, a family-owned and -operated establishment serving ultrafresh seafood and home-baked sourdough bread (442–5772). Accommodations: *Best Western Thunderbird Lodge* (rates: $32–35 double), 100 excellent rooms and family suites, swimming pool, color TV, cocktail lounge, 24-hour coffee shop, at 5th St. & Broadway (443–2234); *Carson House Inn* (rates: $28–32 double), 45 rooms, color TV, swimming and wading pools, many oversize beds, 1 block from the Carson Mansion at 4th and M Sts. (443–1601); *The Downtowner Motel* (rates: $28–32 double), 70 excellent rooms, swimming pool, cocktail lounge, restaurant opposite, at 424 8th St., 3 blocks east of Hwy. 101; (443–5061); *Eureka Inn Motor Lodge* (rates: $36–46 double), 150 excellent rooms and suites, handsome English Tudor decor, fine dining room, coffee shop, cocktail lounge, room service, swimming pool, top-quality service and facilities, at 7th and F Sts., 2 blocks east of Hwy. 101 (442–6441); *Ramada Inn* (rates: $33–37 double), 80 comfortable rooms, color TV, pool, restaurant, room service, entertainment and dancing, free air airport bus, saunas and excercise room, 9 miles north of town, off U.S. 101, Guintoli Lane Exit (822–4861); *Red Lion Motor Inn* (rates: $34–39 double), 136 excellent rooms and family suites, small swimming pool, first-rate service and facilities, dining room, coffee shop, cocktail lounge, airport shuttle service, at 1428 4th St. (445–0844); *Royal Pacific Lodge* (rates: $29–32 double), 50 fine rooms, heated indoor pool, sauna, restaurant opposite, cocktail lounge, at 1304 4th St. (443–3193).

Shasta-Trinity National Forest

The Shasta-Trinity National Forest, once the home and hunting grounds of the Hoopa, Chilula, Whilkut, Nongathl, Wailaki, and Chimariko Indians, is located a few miles north of Redding in northern California. The forest overlaps into six counties. Its numerous old logging roads and trails, including over 150 miles of the Pacific Crest Trail, wind through grass and oak woodlands and heavily forested evergreen slopes, past soaring granite peaks, towering limestone bluffs, lakes, wild rivers, small mountain ranges near Shasta Lake, and deep, steep-sided canyons, and through gently rolling plateaus to the interior fishing, hunting, hiking, and wilderness camping areas.

The Shasta Division encompasses 1 million acres east of the Trinity Forest in northern California and contains some of the state's most outstanding hunting, fishing, and wilderness camping areas. The Shasta area is comprised of geological formations related to the southern section of the Cascade Range, varying from the snowcap and perpetual glaciers of Mt. Shasta to the colorful volcanic formations of the Medicine Lake Highlands to the east. Forest roads and trails provide access to the backcountry areas near Shasta Lake, Seven Lakes Basin at the Trinity Divide, Box Canyon Reservoir, Lake McCloud, Upper Sacramento River, and the Pit River.

Information Sources, Maps & Access

For additional information and a full-color *Shasta-Trinity National Forest Map* (50¢), contact: Supervisor, Shasta-Trinity National Forest, 1615 Continental St., Redding, CA 96001 (916)241–7100. See also "Klamath National Forest & the Salmon-Trinity Alps" above. Fishing information and guide service for the Upper Sacramento, McCloud, and Pit rivers are provided by *Ted Fay's Fly Casting Shop*, 4154 Dunsmuir Ave., Dunsmuir 96025 (916)235–2969.

The forest is reached via Interstate 5, U.S. Highway 97, and California routes 96, 3, 89, and 299. Lodging, supplies, boat and canoe rentals, guides, packers, and outfitters are available at Trinity Center, Big Bar, Junction City, Hayfork, Weaverville, Redding, Burney, Fall River Mills, Dunsmuir, McCloud, Weed and Mt. Shasta.

Recreation Areas

Mount Shasta Area

Mt. Shasta dominates the skyline in the north central part of the forest, due west of the Volcanic Highlands. This great mountain was discovered by the Spanish explorer Fray Norcisco Duran, who first sighted it in May 1817. Peter Skene Ogden, a trapper and fur trader, saw it in 1827 and gave it the name Sastie. About 14 years later, Lieutenant Emmons of the Wildes expedition showed it on his maps as

Mt. Shasta. The beautiful double cone of Mt. Shasta is the largest of the Cascade volcanoes, composed of Shastina (12,330 ft.) on the west and Shasta (14,162 ft.), the main peak, on the east. This majestic mountain rests on a base 17 miles in diameter and is shrouded at its upper levels by unusual cloud formations, rapid and violent storms, dazzling light displays, and the rare and transient alpine glow of winter evenings. Mt. Shasta has long been an object of awe and study by hikers, photographers, and mountaineers. Five perennial glaciers, Whitney, Bolam, Hotlum, Wintun, and Konwakiton, lie on the slopes above 8,500 feet. The glaciers form the headwaters of the McCloud, Shasta, and Sacramento rivers. To the north of Dunsmuir, the exposed gravel beds gush large volumes of water, creating the beautiful Mossbrae Falls. On the lower slopes of Mt. Shasta, plant life common to the High Sierra overlaps with plants common to the North Cascades, creating unique subspecies such as the beautiful and fragrant Shasta lily, Shasta daisy, and Shasta red fir. Manzanita and snowbrush have covered the old scars from the logging days.

To the west of Mt. Shasta lies the Trinity Divide, a maze of canyons, rivers, lakes, and peaks overlooked by Mt. Eddy. The Sacramento River canyon area to the south is dominated by the Castle Crags. To the north, the Black Butte cinder cone pierces the skyline, forming a miniature silhouette of Mt. Shasta. If you are interested in climbing Mt. Shasta, contact the district ranger at Mt. Shasta City.

Pacific Crest Trail

The Pacific Crest Trail winds through the region from the Salmon-Trinity Alps area, along the beautiful Scott Mountains, past the alpine trout lakes in the Eddy Mountains at the headwaters of the Sacramento River and the Seven Lakes Basin at the Trinity Divide. At Castle Crags near the town of Dunsmuir, the trail follows a route that passes along the lovely McCloud River, Grizzly Peak, and on to Lake Britton and into the Thousand Lakes Wilderness in the Lassen Forest.

Shasta Lake

The four great fingers of Shasta Lake lie at the junction of the Klamath and Cascade ranges in the northern part of the Sacramento Valley. This largest of the man-made lakes in California has over 370 miles of shoreline sprawling across a land of ancient lava flows, dormant volcanoes, ice caves, and spectacular limestone caverns. The start of the famous Oregon Trail up the Sacramento River canyon lies some 400 feet below the lake's surface. The trail was originally pioneered by the trapper La Framboise in 1834 for the Hudson's Bay Company. The Sacramento, Pit, and McCloud rivers and Squaw Creek feed the lake and form its four great fingers. Fishing has improved tremendously since the introduction of threadfin shad in 1960. The fishing varies from good to excellent, depending on the season, for Kamloops, native rainbow and brown trout, kokanee salmon, and largemouth and smallmouth bass. Kamloops are frequently caught in the 10–pound class, and brown are often reported in excess of 15 pounds.

Trinity Lake Country

The renowned hunting and fishing areas of the Trinity Forest Division encompass about 1 million acres in north central California adjacent to the western boundary of Shasta Forest. In the forest are the Klamath Mountains, Coast Range Mountains, Trinity (Clair Engel) Lake, the Big Bar area, and the Yolla-Bolly Mountains in the southernmost section and the Whiskeytown-Shasta-Trinity National Recreation Area, surrounding Whiskeytown Reservoir. To the south of the Salmon Mountains lies the famed Big Bar area, which includes the western section of the scenic Trinity River and its tributaries, the New River, Canyon Creek, and the North Fork of the Trinity. The Trinity produces some of the country's finest steelhead trout fishing. Lewiston Lake, formed by the damming of the upper Trinity, is one of the finest trout lakes in the West. Located in the northeastern part of the forest, this large lake has cold clear waters regularly producing early and late-season limit catches of fat rainbows and browns of 5 pounds and more. Trinity Lake lies due north of Lewiston, and has some fine fishing for rainbows, kokanee salmon, and largemouth bass, particularly near the mouths of its feeder streams such as Stuarts Fork and Coffee and Papoose creeks, which rise high in the Salmon Trinity Alps. These gin-clear streams provide exciting fly-fishing for small rainbow and brook trout.

Gateways & Accommodations

Dunsmuir

(Pop. 2,200; zip code 96025; area code 916.) Perched on a narrow shelf along the winding canyon bed of the Sacramento River, Dunsmuir is a popular jumping-off point for visitors to northern California's recreation areas. Castle Crags State Park, 6 miles southwest of town off Hwy. I–5, encompasses almost 6,200 acres and is named for the gigantic pile of gray-white granite spires rising 6,000 feet above the forested slopes above the Sacramento River. Accommodations: *Best Western Oak—Lo* (rates: $26 double), 27 air-conditioned rooms, color TV, swimming pool, free Mott Airport Bus, fine views of Mt. Shasta from most rooms, at 4221 Dwight Way, take Siskiyou Ave. Exit off Hwy. I–5, 1½ miles north of town (235–4802); *Cedar Lodge Motel* (rates: $21–24 double), 14 rooms, attractive tree-shaded

grounds, color TV, 2 kitchen efficiencies, free coffee in rooms, at 4201 Dunsmuir Ave., 1 mile north of Sacramento Bridge on Hwy. I–5 business loop (235–2836); *Dunsmuir Travelodge* (rates: $21–24 double), 18 rooms with oversize beds, color TV, free coffee in rooms, at 5400 Dunsmuir Ave., 2 blocks east of Hwy. I–5, Central Exit (235–4395); *Garden Motel* (rates: $23 double), 16 fine rooms, open year-round, on pleasantly landscaped grounds, playground, small pool, airport bus, at 4310 Dunsmuir Ave., 1 mile north of Sacramento Bridge on Hwy. I–5, N. Dunsmuir Exit (235–4805).

Mount Shasta

(Pop. 2,200; zip code 96067; area code 916.) Nestled at the base of the immense peak for which it is named, the town is the northern gateway to the Whiskeytown-Shasta-Trinity National Recreation Area, nearby Lake Siskiyou, and the Shasta-Trinity National Forest. Accommodations: *Alpine Lodge* (rates: $22–24 double), 20 air-conditioned rooms, 4 with kitchens, views of Mt. Shasta from some units, small heated swimming pool, color TV, ½ mile south of town on Hwy. I–5 business loop, 908 S. Mt. Shasta Road (926–3145); *Best Western Tree House*, (rates: $27–33 double) 70 excellent rooms and suites, attractive rustic decor, views of Mt. Shasta, indoor pool, sauna, dining room and cocktail lounge, on Lake St., just east of Hwy. I–5, Central Mt. Shasta Exit (926–3101).

Redding

(Pop. 16,700; zip code 96001; area code 916.) Located in the shadow of Mt. Shasta at the top of the Sacramento Valley, Redding is a major gateway to the surrounding Whiskeytown-Shasta-Trinity National Recreation Area and the Shasta-Trinity National Forest. North of town are the Lake Shasta Caverns, containing unusual stalactites, stalagmites, and flowstone deposits. A 2–hour guided tour includes a boat ride across McCloud Arm of Shasta Lake and a bus ride up the mountain to the well-lighted caves (May-Sept., every hour; Oct.-May, at 10 A.M., noon, and 2 P.M.). Also of interest is the Redding Museum in Caldwell Park, which houses Indian artifacts, exhibit of Pre-Columbian art, and changing art shows (at Rio Drive, on the north shore of the Sacramento River). Shasta State Historic Park, 6 miles west of Redding on Hwy. 299, encompasses several original buildings of a former gold-rush town. Accommodations: *Best Western Hospitality House* (rates: $26–28 double), 65 excellent air-conditioned rooms, color TV, swimming pool, oversize beds, 24–hour coffee shop, at 532 Market St., 1 block north on I–5 business loop, 6 blocks north of Hwy. 299; (241–6464); *Best Western Inn* (rates: $33–34 double), 115 excellent rooms and suites, swimming pool, color TV, free in-room movies, airport transportation, dining room, coffee shop, at 2300 Hilltop Drive, 1 block east of Hwy. I–5, Cypress Ave. Exit; (246–1000); *Best Western Ponderosa Inn* (rates: $24–26 double), 70 air-conditioned rooms, oversize beds, color TV, swimming pool, dining room, coffee shop, at 2220 Pine St., ¾ mile south of town, off Hwy. I–5, Cypress Ave. Exit (241–6300); *Holiday Inn* (rates: $33.50 double), 163 excellent rooms, some studio units, color TV, heated indoor pool, sauna, recreation room, putting green, free airport pickup, 2 restaurants, bar, entertainment and dancing, at 1900 Hilltop Drive, 2 miles east of town, 2 blocks east of I–5 Hilltop Drive Exit (246–1500); *Red Lion Motor Inn* (rates: $32–38 double), 195 attractive rooms and suites, many with balconies and patios, swimming pool, wading pool, dining room, coffee shop, bar, free airport pickup, at 1830 Hilltop Drive, 2 miles east of town, 1 block east of I–5 Hilltop Drive Exit (241–8700); *River Inn* (rates: $24–26.50 double), 60 fine air-conditioned rooms, some balconies and patios, swimming pool, sauna, whirlpool, sundeck, coffee shop, bar, at 1835 Marina Park Drive, ¾ mile east on Hwy. 299 (241–9500); *Shasta Inn* (rates: $31–33 double), 140 superlative rooms and suites, color TV, swimming pool, oversize beds, restaurant, cocktail lounge, entertainment and dancing, at 2180 Hilltop Drive, 2 miles east of Redding, 1 block east of Hilltop Drive Exit (241–8200); *Vagabond Motor Hotel* (rates: $30–34 double), 72 excellent rooms, swimming pool, coffee shop adjacent, at 536 Cypress Ave., 1 block west of I–5 Cypress Ave. Exit (243–9415).

Lodges

★*Corby's Steelhead Cottages* at Big Flat in the heart of Trinity County offers fishing in season for salmon, steelhead, and trout, hunting, swimming, rock-hounding and hiking. Furnished housekeeping cottages, with air conditioning and heating, are available at daily rates from $13 to $20 (weekly discounts). For details write: John & Martha Corby, P.O. Box 709, Big Bar, CA 96010 (916)623–6325.

★*Indian Creek Lodge* in scenic northern California boasts almost 9 acres of frontage on the salmon, trout, and steelhead waters of Trinity River. In addition to fine fishing, this family-type lodge offers canoeing, rafting, picnicking, and boating on finger-shaped Trinity Lake. Deer and bear hunting in the Trinity Alps is a popular fall activity. One- and 2–bedroom air-conditioned family units have kitchens, patios, and barbecues. For fishermen and hunters, freezers and a smokehouse are available. Fly-in at Weaverville Airport. For information and rates write: Indian Creek Lodge, P.O. Box 373, Douglas City, CA 96024 (916)623–6294.

★*Wyntoon Park Resort*, on 25–mile-long Trinity Lake, has 20 modern housekeeping cottages with fully equipped kitchens and comfortable furnishings. Activities at the resort include horseback riding at the Wyntoon Stables, swimming in the lake or Tom Sawyer Pond, bike riding, square dances, hayrides, boating, and fishing. Rentals are available for boats, motors, bicycles, and rods and reels. A generously stocked store on the premises offers groceries, fresh produce, film, fishing tackle, camping supplies, and other vacation necessities. Cottage rates: $30 daily for a family of 4, or $180 by the week. For more information write: Wyntoon Park Resort, P.O. Box 70, Trinity Center, CA 96091 (916)266–3411.

Six Rivers National Forest

The 960,000–acre Six Rivers National Forest is located along the western slope of the Coast Range Mountains down to the Pacific Coast from the Oregon border southward for 130 miles. The six major salmon and steelhead streams that flow from the mountain valleys through dense cool forests of fir and giant coastal redwoods into the Pacific are the Smith, Klamath, Trinity, Mad, Van Duzen, and North Fork of the Eel River. U.S. 101, the famed Redwood Highway, parallels the inland forest in a north-south direction on the coast side. The forest is just east of Redwood National Park. Hunting in Six Rivers country is good in the remote backcountry areas near the Hoopa Valley Indian Reservation, the Peaks, Mount Lassic, South Fork Mountain, Spike Buck Mountain, and Last Chance Ridge for black-tailed deer, black bear, blue grouse, and valley and mountain quail. The forest terrain is generally mountainous in the north and moderately rolling in the south, with elevations ranging from 500 to 7,000 feet.

Other attractions to the forest are floating the Klamath and Trinity rivers, the meadows of beautiful wild flowers in late April and May, water sports at Ruth Reservoir, and the perennial search for the elusive, legendary Bigfoot. There are 372 camping units in 15 Forest Service campgrounds. Many more primitive campsites are scattered throughout the remote backcountry areas. The local district ranger

should be contacted for information on the locations of such wilderness camps.

Information Sources, Maps & Access

The major features of the forest are shown on the full-color *Six Rivers National Forest Map*, available for 50¢, along with additional information, from: Forest Supervisor, Six Rivers National Forest, 710 E. St., Eureka 95501 (707)442–1721. The free *Six Rivers National Forest Camping Guide* may also be obtained from the Forest Supervisor's Office. This guide contains listings and descriptions of all Forest Service campgrounds, and maps. For steelhead and salmon fishing info write: Del Norte County Chamber of Commerce, Crescent City 95531.

Drawing 8 page 416

Major access routes to the forest include the spectacular "Redwood Highway" U.S. 101, U.S. 199 from Oregon, and state highways 299 and 96. Lodging, supplies, boat and canoe rentals, guides, and outfitters are available at Smith River, Gasquet, Fort Dick, Klamath, Crescent City, Requa, Orick, Orleans, and Weitchpec.

Gateways & Accommodations

See "Redwood National Park" for information on gateways and accommodations and the Redwood Highway.

Lodges & Resorts

★★*Six Rivers Lodge & Resort*, on the Mad River just south of the Trinity Alps, is a small, family-oriented vacation spot specializing in personal attention. Accommodations are available in centrally heated motel rooms or in "deluxe" log cabin units opposite the heated swimming pool. The Six Rivers Restaurant features excellent cuisine, including steaks, lobster, and prime ribs. In addition, there's a large redwood lodge with fireplace and an inviting cocktail lounge. The Six Rivers National Forest offers a number of things to see and do, from hiking to trout fishing at Mad River or bass fishing on nearby Ruth Lake. Rates: $14–18 for single rooms; $18–22 for double rooms accommodating 2 people. Off-season and group rates are available. For information write: Six Rivers Lodge and Resort, Mad River, CA 95552 (707)574–6222.

★★★*The Ship Ashore Resort*, at the mouth of the Smith River in northern California's Del Norte County, enjoys a handsome site overlooking the Pacific Ocean and a temperate climate year-round. Some of the country's best salmon and steelhead fishing are right at your doorstep, and there are unlimited opportunities for boating and side trips to nearby Jedediah Smith State Park, giant redwood groves, and miles of clean-swept beaches. A new 32–unit motel offers a variety of accommodations, ranging from private rooms with double bed to deluxe penthouse apartments with 2 bedrooms, kitchen, fireplace, and 1½ baths. Each unit has a sweeping view of the Pacific and its own private balcony. Completely equipped beach cottages are also available. Rates vary from $24 daily (double occupancy) to $75 daily (4–6 guests). Off-season rates are slightly lower. On the premises are a marina with boat rentals and dock space, a cocktail lounge, and the Ship Ashore Galley Dining Room. For more information write: Ship Ashore Resort, Smith River, CA 95567 (707)487–3141.

Travel Services

Wilderness Water Ways, in operation since 1962, pioneered the first raft trips on California's Stanislaus, Tuolumne, Eel, South Fork American, Klamath, and East Carson rivers. Today this firm offers 2– and 3–day trips on these beautiful, unspoiled streams, plus longer adventures on Oregon's famous Rogue and Illinois rivers. The Rogue

trip is undoubtedly the most plush of all, with overnight accommodations at lovely lodges. Or if you prefer to rough it, there's a 2–night, 3–day camping trip on the Rogue through the heart of a wilderness canyon. Camp is set up each night near a sandy beach with a side stream for fishing and swimming. Rafts are "Huck Finn" style, a maneuverable and comfortable design developed exclusively for these trips. Wilderness Water Ways supplies everything but your sleeping bag, personal gear, and eating utensils. Trip costs average $70 per person for 2 days, $90 for 3 days, and $140–150 for Rogue River camping and lodge trips. For additional details write: Wilderness Water Ways, 33 Canyon Lake Drive, Port Costa, CA 94569 (415)787–2820.

COLORADO

Introduction

Colorado contains 46 snowcapped peaks exceeding 14,000 feet, culminating at Mt. Elbert (14,431 ft.), the second-highest peak in the United States. The state's 104,247 square miles are bordered on the north by Wyoming and the Central Rockies, on the east by the Great Plains of Nebraska and Kansas, on the south by New Mexico, and on the west by Arizona and Utah. The Centennial State contains the Rocky Mountain headwaters of the historic Colorado, the "River of the Shining Mountains"; the beautiful Sangre de Cristo Range; the nationally renowned trophy trout waters of the upper North Platte, Yampa, Blue, Gunnison, Elk, South Platte, Animas, Michigan, Canadian, and Cache la Poudre rivers and creeks and the headwaters of the Rio Grande; the beautiful Indian Peaks wild country and Never Summer Range in Rocky Mountain National Park; the famous fishing, backpacking, and elk-hunting areas of the Grand Mesa high country and Flattops Primitive Area; and the remote fish and game lands of the Rocky Mountain high wilderness areas. The Colorado territory was first penetrated by Coronado in 1540, during his search for the fabled Seven Cities of Cibola. Fur traders and a host of explorers and surveyors followed, including Zebulon Pike, who in 1806 discovered the famous peak bearing his name while mapping the headwaters of the Arkansas River.

Accommodations & Travel Information

Colorado offers an incredibly wide range of vacation accommodations, from rustic Old West guest ranches and lodges to deluxe alpine ski chalets, hotels, motels, and inns. For complete descriptions of the state's major travel accommodations, lodges, and guest ranches, see the "Vacation/Lodging Guide" which follows.

Information & Services

For detailed fishing and hunting information and the free *Colorado Land & Water Use Information, Colorado Fishing Regulations & Statutes,* and *Licensed Outfitters & Guides* booklets, contact: Colorado Division of Wildlife, 6060 Broadway, Denver 80216 (303)473–2945.

For general information on ski touring in Colorado, write to: *Colorado Ski Country,* 1461 Larimer Sq., Denver 80202; or *Colorado Ranch & Ski Tours,* 3113 E. Third Ave., Denver 80206. For information on snow conditions throughout the state, call (303)893–2201.

Much of the remote mountain high country is best seen with an experienced guide and outfitter. Scores of professional guides are available throughout the state; for detailed information on individual guides, see the "Vacation/Lodging Guide" section. In addition to the guides and outfitters mentioned there, special wilderness outings and trips are conducted by the following individuals and organizations: *Rocky Mountain Expeditions, Inc.,* P.O. Box CC, Buena Vista 81211 (backpacking, fishing, ski touring, and river float trips in the Rocky Mountains); *Telluride Mountaineering School,* Box 4, Aspen 81611 (skills are taught on backpacking trips into Colorado's high mountain country and on float trips through the wild-river canyons of the state); *Wilderness Adventures, Inc.,* Box 265, South Fork 81154 (horsepacking, backpacking, hunting, fishing, and snow-camping trips in the Rio Grande National Forest; Rio Grande River float trips; and wilderness workshops); *The Mountain Men,* 11100 East Dartmouth 219, Denver 80232 (4–wheel-drive mountain wilderness tours, camping trips, fishing and hunting expeditions in the Colorado high country); *American Wilderness Experience,* Rt. 2, Nebraska Way, Longmont 80501 (horsepack and river expeditions through the mountains and rivers of the San Juan Wilderness,

Colorado, as well as in two other states); *The Bob Culp Climbing School*, 1329 Broadway, Boulder 80302 (climbing in the Flatiron Range near Boulder); *Colorado Wilderness Experience Trips*, 2912 Aspen Drive, Durango 81301 (camping and climbing trips in the San Juan Wilderness); *Adventure Bound, Inc.*, 6179 So. Adams Drive, Littleton 80121 (float trips throughout the wilderness waters of the Green, Yampa, and Colorado rivers); and *Rocky Mountain Ski Tours & Backpack Adventures*, P.O. Box 413, 172 E. Elkhorn Ave., Estes Park 80517 (backpacking and ski touring in the Rocky Mountain National Park and Routt and Roosevelt national forests).

The Colorado Dept. of Natural Resources (Division of Parks and Outdoor Recreation, 1845 Sherman, Denver 80203) publishes a free *Guide to Colorado's State Park & Recreation Areas*. The guide lists campsites, facilities and services, recreational opportunities, size, elevation, and location of each of the state parks and recreation areas, and shows the locations on a map. The guide also includes information on fees and lists regulations for the areas.

Wild and scenic river float trips are offered by the following Colorado-based firms: *Adventure Bound, Inc.*, 6179 South Adams Drive, Littleton, CO 80121 (303)771–3752. Rivers run: Colorado, Green, Yampa, North Platte. Oar and paddle trips. May thru September. *Anderson River Expeditions*, Gypsum, /CO 81637 (303)524–9525 or 524–7766. River run: Colorado. Oar and sportyak trips. Mid-May thru mid-September. *Aspen Whitewater Adventures*, P.O. Box 951, Aspen, CO 81611 (303)925–5730. Rivers run: Arkansas, Colorado, Dolores, Roaring Fork. Oar, paddle, and inflatable kayak trips. May thru September. *Blazing Paddles*, Box 2127A, Aspen, CO 81611 (303)925–5652. Rivers run: Arkansas, Colorado, Roaring Fork, Dolores. Individual sportyaks, oar and paddle trips. May thru September. *Colorado Adventures*, P.O. Box 851, Steamboat Springs, CO 80477 (303)879–2039 or toll-free in Colorado (1–800) 332–3200. River run: Colorado. Oar and paddle trips. May 15 thru October 15. *Colorado Outward Bound School*, 945 Pennsylvania St., Denver, CO 80203 (303)837–0880. Rivers run: Green, Yampa. Paddle trips. May thru August. *Colorado Rivers—Tours*, P.O. Box 1386, Durango, CO 81301 (303)259–0708. Rivers run: Animas, San Juan, Dolores. Oar, paddle, and inflatable kayak trips. May thru September. *Fastwater Expeditions*, Box 365, Boulder City, NV 89005 (702)293–1406. River run: Dolores. Mid-April thru mid-June. *Four Corners Expeditions*, P.O. Box 1032–C, Buena Vista, CO 81211 (303)395–8949. Rivers run: Arkansas, Dolores, Colorado, Roaring Fork, Animas, San Juan. Oar and paddle trips. April 26 thru August. *Don Hatch River Expeditions, North*, Box C, Vernal, UT 84078 (801)789–4316. Rivers run: Green, Yampa. Oar trips. May thru September. *Holiday River Expeditions*, 519 Malibu Drive, Salt Lake City, UT 84107 (801)266–2087. Rivers run: Yampa, Green, Dolores, Colorado. Oar and charter paddle trips. April thru October. *International Aquatic Adventures, Inc.*, 2047 Broadway, Boulder, CO 80302 (303)449–4620, Boulder, or (303)482–7395, Fort Collins. Rivers run: Colorado, Arkansas, North Platte, Dolores, Cache la Poudre. Oar and paddle trips. April thru September. *North American River Expeditions*, P.O. Box 9302, Aspen, CO 81611 (303)925–9490. Rivers run: Colorado, Roaring Fork. Oar and paddle trips. May thru September. *O.A.R.S., Inc.*, P.O. Box 67, Angels Camp, CA 95222 (209)736–2924. River run: Dolores. Oar, paddle, and inflatable kayak trips. *Outdoor Leadership Training Seminars* (Arkansas River Tours), 2220 Birch, Denver, CO 80207 (303)333–7831. Rivers run: Arkansas, Colorado, Dolores. Oar and paddle trips. May thru September. *River Rats, Inc.* P.O. Box 3231, Aspen, CO 81611 (303)925–7648. Rivers run: Arkansas, Colorado and Roaring Fork. Oar and paddle trips. May thru September. *Rocky Mountain Center for Experimental Learning*, P.O. Box 3536, Boulder, CO 80307 (303)442–7420. Rivers run: Colorado, Dolores, Arkansas, North Platte. Oar, paddle, kayak, and canoe trips. *Rocky Mountain Expeditions, Inc.*, P.O. Box CC, Buena Vista, CO 81211 (303)395–8466. River run: Arkansas. Oar and paddle trips. May thru September. *Rocky Mountain River Expeditions* P.O. Box 1394, Denver, CO 80201 (303)289–5959. Rivers run: Colorado, North Platte, Dolores, Arkansas. Paddle trips. April 15 thru September 15. *Roger Paris Kayak School, Inc.* (Colorado Rocky Mountain School), Carbondale, CO 81623 (303)963–2433 after April 1. Rivers run: Roaring Fork, Colorado, Crystal, Arkansas, Eagle. Kayak instruction and trips. *Snowmass Whitewater*, Box 5566 Snowmass Village, CO 81615 (303)923–2000, ext. 54. Rivers run: Arkansas, Roaring Fork, Colorado, Dolores. Oar, paddle, and individual inflatable kayak trips. May thru September. *Timber Travels, Inc.*, P.O. Box 344, Wheatridge, CO 80033 (303)420–6089. Rivers run: Colorado, Arkansas, North Platte, Roaring Fork. Oar, paddle, and canoe trips. May thru September. *Viking River Expeditions*, P.O. Box 383, Greeley, CO 80631 (303)351–6796. Rivers run: North Platte, Colorado. Oar and paddle trips. Memorial Day thru Labor Day. *Western Adventure Safaries, Inc.*, P.O. Box 1732, Grand Junction, CO 81501 (303)242–6621. Rivers run: Colorado, Dolores. Oar, paddle, and motor trips. April thru early October. *Whitewater Odyssey*, 957

E. 9th, Broomfield, CO 80020 (303)466–6545 or 423–6746. Rivers run: Arkansas, Colorado, Dolores, North Platte, Cache la Poudre. Oar and paddle trips. April thru September. *Wild Water West River Excursions*, 8240 Queen St., Arvada, CO 80005 (303)421–2102. Rivers run: Colorado, North Platte, Arkansas, Dolores, Cache la Poudre. Paddle and oar trips. May 1 thru August 15. *Wilderness Aware*, Box 401, Colorado Springs, CO 80901 (303)687–9662. Rivers run: Arkansas, Colorado, Dolores, North Platte, Cache la Poudre. Oar and paddle trips. April thru September. *Wilderness Sports, Ltd.*, P.O. Box 36, Bond, CO 80423 (303)926–3774. River run: Colorado. Paddle and some oar trips. Mid-May thru mid-September.

Highways & Maps

The free Colorado highway map *Colorful Colorado*, a shaded-relief map in full color, shows interstate, U.S., state, and county highways and roads, mileage between points, interchanges, points of interest, mountain passes, Continental Divide areas, ranger headquarters, roadside parks, campgrounds, national and state forests, national parks and monuments, government reservations, airports, streams, lakes, and reservoirs. The reverse side of the map tells motorists where to find such features as the Continental Divide, highest altitude, colleges and universities, museums, mineral hot springs, and national parks and monuments. A key to the points of interest marked on the map identifies them and groups them into such categories as state and national parks or recreational areas, national historic landmarks, state fishing and hatchery areas, and ski and winter sports areas. Colorado peaks and mountain passes are also listed in the map guide, and vicinity maps of Boulder, Denver, Colorado Springs, and Pueblo are included. The map may be ordered from: Colorado Marketing Section, 602 State Capitol Annex, Denver 80203.

Also free from the Marketing Section at the above address is the booklet *Colorado Top of the Nation Mini-Tours*. The booklet is a guide to 15 automobile circle tours through some of the most scenic and historic areas of the state.

The Marketing Section also publishes a free 50–page book, *Colorful Colorado Invites You*, which describes each of the tour areas in detail and provides a map of the region showing the location of points of interest, campgrounds, ghost towns, boat launches, roadside rests, historical markers, ski areas, and other recreational sites. The book describes the wildlife, geology, history, and recreational opportunities of different areas of the state. It also lists additional sources of information on travel throughout the state and includes a short article on how to take good color pictures. This publication may be ordered from the Marketing Section at the address given above.

If you plan to drive through Colorado, remember that road conditions change as quickly as the weather, especially at high altitudes. To find out the latest road conditions, call (303)630–1234 or (303)630–1515 for recorded reports. For specific information on highway and driving regulations, contact the Department of Highways, 4201 E. Arkansas Ave., Denver 80222.

Arapaho National Forest & The Breckenridge Ski Village

The Arapaho National Forest covers a million acres of public wilderness camping, fishing, alpine and cross-country skiing, a big-game hunting country along the Continental Divide in the area of the headwaters of the Colorado River. On the opposite side of the Great Divide, the historic Platte River flows along its long, shallow course towards the Atlantic. The forest is divided into three divisions, two small ones west of Loveland and a larger one south of these and west of Denver. The Rabbit Ears Range, part of the Continental Divide, forms the natural northern border of the forest. The mountains form the southernmost peaks of the North Park Range and run east from the end of this range to the boundaries of the Rocky Mountain National Park. The last portion of the range east of the Rocky Mountain National Park area is called the Never Summer Range, so named because of its perennially snowy peaks, which rise to heights of more than 12,000 feet.

The Gore Range-Eagles Nest Primitive Area takes in more than 61,000 acres of alpine fishing, camping, and hunting country in the Arapaho and White River national forests. Trails lead up into the craggy heights of Meridian Mountain and Climbers Lake (11,000 ft.); Eagles Nest Mountain (13,397 ft.); Mt. Powell (13,534 ft.); the alpine Boulder Lake; and the lake basins of Red Peak and Buffalo Mountain. The Gore Range Trail runs for 50 miles along the east slope of the range, winding past crystal lakes and turbulent streams. This rugged, roadless area west of Dillon Reservoir is accessible only by foot and horse. Remember that arctic weather conditions exist above timberline; summer tempertaures can drop to below freezing within an hour, and sudden severe thunder and wind storms are common. Bring warm clothes, and adapt yourself to the thin air before you attempt a strenuous trip.

The southern portion of the forest encompasses the mountains of the Front Range, which run from Longs Peak on the north to Mt. Evans on the south. The 14,264-foot Mt. Evans has North America's highest paved highway, which runs through 14 miles of alpine tundra. This verdantly forested area is crossed by trout streams and dotted with campgrounds. Another area of the Continental Divide runs through the high-country meadows and forests of this region. Atop Arapaho Peak lies the Arapaho Glacier, a remnant of the great ice masses of the Pleistocene era which carved cirques and canyons into the craggy mountains. Nearby, the jagged peaks of Kiowa, Navajo, and Apache mountains surround a huge natural basin that holds the spectacular Isabelle Glacier. The glacier is accessible by trail from the campground at Brainard Lake at the foot of the Continental Divide; the climb provides a pleasant day trip.

VACATION/ LODGING GUIDE

Information Sources, Maps & Access

A full-color U.S. Forest Service *Arapaho National Forest Map* is available for 50¢, along with camping, fishing, hunting, and wilderness travel info from: Forest Supervisor, Arapaho National Forest, 1010 Tenth St., P.O. Box 692, Golden 80402 (303)234-4185. A black-and-white *Arapaho National Forest Travel Map* showing most of the same features (no recreation directories included) is available free from the same address. This map explains special restrictions on travel throughout the forest. Also available from the forest supervisor's office is a free booklet describing a self-guided auto tour through the Arapaho and Roosevelt national forests, *The Moffat Road*. The tour shows you the former "hill" route of the Moffat Railroad, which led a tortuous course up the mountains of the area and crossed the Continental Divide through Rollins Pass. The line was started in 1903 and finished in 1927.

Another free brochure from the supervisor's office is the guide to *Dillon Reservoir Recreation Area*. Built in 1964, the reservoir provides boating and camping opportunities. The brochure includes a map and description of the area.

The forest is accessible by way of State Rt. 72 running north from Interstate 70 or State Rt. 119 running west from Interstate 25. Accommodations, guides, and equipment rentals are available at Dillon, Golden, Granby, Grand Lake, Hot Sulphur Springs, Idaho Springs, and Kremmling.

Gateways & Accommodations

Central City

(Pop. 200; zip code 80427; area code 303.) One of Colorado's historic gold-rush era mountain towns, Central City was once known as the richest square mile on earth, or Gregory Gulch. The area attractions of this colorful old boom town on Colorado 119 include the famous Central City Opera House on Eureka St., the Victorian Tiller House Hotel on Eureka St., the Central City Story at the Armory, Bobtail Tunnel mine tour on burro-powered train 1 mile east of town at Black Hawk, the reconstructed Colorado Central Narrow Gauge Railway Tour on Colorado Hwy. 119, and the outdoor beer garden, wild game and fowl dinner, and Bavarian atmosphere of the Black Forest Inn at 260 Gregory St. (582–9971).

Denver

(Pop. 514,700; zip code, see below; area code 303.) Colorado's mile-high capital city is flanked on the west by the massive snowcapped Front Range of the Rockies and on the east by the Great Plains. Area attractions of this onetime silver-mining boom town include the Denver Museum of Natural History & Gates Planetarium in City Park (388–2031); Denver Zoo; Denver Art Museum at 100 W. 14 Ave. Parkway in Civic Center complex; State Capitol at E. Colfax Ave. & Sherman St.; Colorado Heritage Center at 1300 Broadway, with exhibits in the history of Colorado; Molly Brown House at 1340 Pennsylvania St., the Victorian home of a survivor of the *Titanic;* Forney Transportation Museum at 1416 Platte St., with hundreds of rare, antique cars, carriages, planes, trains; Denver city parks; Larimer Square, historic old city area with entertainment, dining, and shopping at the 1400 block of Larimer St. Popular downtown Denver restaurants include: *The Broker* in a remodeled bank at 821 17 St. (893–5065); *Cafe Promenade* at 1430 Larimer St. (893–2692); *Colorado Mine Co.* at 4490 E. Virginia Ave. (321–6555); *Leo's Place* in restored early 1900s building at 4 E. 16th St. and Broadway (861–2308); *Mario's* for good Italian dinners at 1747 Tremont Place opposite Brown Palace Hotel (825–4271); *Old Spaghetti Factory*, a popular family spot at 1215 18th St. (534–0537); *Quorum* at 233 E. Colfax Ave. and Grant St., elegant award-winning restaurant (861–8686); *Scotch 'N' Sirloin* for great steaks at 12th and Grant Sts.

(861–8551). Accommodations: (Airport area) *Denver Plaza Inn* (rates: $37 double), 142 excellent rooms, dining room, coffee shop, heated pool, sauna, tennis courts at 7201 E. 49th Ave., 80022 (287–7548); *Hilton Airport Inn* (rates: $53 double), 202 excellent rooms, Henrici's Restaurant, coffee shop, heated pool, at 4411 Peoria, 80239 (373–5730); *Holiday Inn—Airport* (rates: $36 double), 302 excellent rooms, dining room, cocktail lounge, heated pool, at 4040 Quebec St., 80218 (321–6666); *Sheraton Inn—Airport* (rates: $43–46 double), 199 excellent rooms, dining room, cocktail lounge, heated indoor pool, at 3535 Quebec St., 80207 (333–7711). (Downtown area) *Best Western Spa Motor Inn* (rates: $26–29 double), 70 rooms and family units, dining room, coffee shop, heated pool, at 930 Valley Hwy., 80204 (292–0220); *Brown Palace Hotel* (rates: $53–70 double), a world-renowned hotel with 500 superb rooms and family suites, 4 dining rooms including the Palace Arms Restaurant (825–3111), coffee shop, since 1892 at 321 17th St., 80202 (825–3111); *Denver Hilton* (rates: $49–66 double), 860 outstanding rooms, dining room, coffee shop, heated pool, at 16th St. and Court Place, 80202 (893–3333); *Holiday Inn Denver* (rates: $44 double), 396 excellent rooms and family units, dining room, cocktail lounge, heated pool, at 1450 Glenarm Pl., 80202 (573–1450); *Ramada Inn* (rates: $34 double), 125 rooms, dining room, cocktail lounge, heated pool, at 1150 E. Colfax, 80218 (831–7700). (Denver area north) *Holiday Inn—North* (rates: $36–41 double), 152 excellent rooms and family units, dining room, cocktail lounge, heated pool, at 4849 Bannock, 80216 (292–9500). (Denver area south) *Holiday Inn—South* (rates: $37 double), 255 excellent rooms, 2 dining rooms, coffee shop, heated pool, at 1475 S. Colorado Blvd., 80222 (757–7731); *Holiday Inn—Southeast* (rates: $39 double), 213 excellent rooms, dining room, coffee shop, cocktail lounge, heated indoor pool, off I–25 Exit 89 at 9009 E. Arapahoe, Englewood 80110 (770–1421); *Howard Johnson's South Motor Lodge* (rates: $39–46 double), 186 excellent rooms, restaurant, coffee shop, heated pool, playground, at 6300 E. Hampden Ave., 80222, off I–25 Exit 91 (758–2211); *Rodeway Inn—Greenwood Village* (rates: $38 double), 200 excellent rooms, dining room, coffee shop, cocktail lounge, heated pool, at 5111 S. Valley Hwy., Greenwood Village 80110 (771–6911); *Writers Manor Hotel & Henrici's Tudor Crown Restaurant* (rates: $50 double), 350 outstanding rooms and suites, superb Old World dining, coffee shop, cocktail lounge, heated pools, racquet club, indoor jogging track, airport limo service, at 1730 S. Colorado Blvd., 80222 (756–8877). (Denver area west) *Holiday Inn—West* (rates: $37–41 double), 197 rooms, dining room, coffee shop, cocktail lounge, heated indoor pool, at 14707 Colfax Ave., Golden 80401 (279–7611); *Howard Johnson's West Motor Lodge* (rates: $36–42 double), 95 excellent rooms, restaurant, coffee shop, heated pool, next to Rocky Mountain Lake at 4765 Federal Blvd., 80211, off I–25 Exit 70 (433–8441); *Ramada Inn—Foothills* (rates: $32 double), 152 excellent rooms, restaurant, coffee shop, heated pool, at 11595 W. 6th Ave., Lakewood 80215 (238–7751); *Ramada Inn I–70 West* (rates: $33.75 double), 137 excellent rooms, dining room, cocktail lounge, heated pool, at 101011–70 Service Rd. N. off I–70 Exit 65 (422–7200).

Dillon

(Pop. 200; zip code 80435; area code 303.) A popular, modern gateway to Arapaho National Forest vacation areas, Dillon Reservoir, and the Keystone-Arapaho Basin Ski Area and Copper Mountain Ski Area (which see). Area restaurants include the *Snake River Saloon* 6 miles east of town on U.S. Hwy. 6 (468–2788) and *La France*, downtown across from Lake Dillon in alpine location with superb French provincial cuisine (468–6111). Area accommodations: *Best Western Ptarmigan Lodge* (rates: $31 double), 22 rooms and family units, next to Lake Dillon in scenic location (468–2341); *Holiday Inn at Lake Dillon* (rates: $36.75 double), 218 excellent rooms and family units, restaurant, heated indoor pool, sauna, tennis courts, near Lake Dillon off I–70 Exit 38 (668–5000); *Ramada Silverthorne at Lake Dillon* (rates: $29–31 double), 158 excellent rooms and family units, dining room, cocktail lounge, heated indoor pool, off I–70 Exit 39 in Silverthorne 80498 (468–6200).

Georgetown Village

(Pop. 500; zip code 80444; area code 303.) This historic 19th-century mining town in the scenic Loveland Valley area of the Arapaho National Forest is the site of the famous Hotel de Paris, built in 1875 and visited by many notables, including Jay Gould. This gilded, ornate hotel, the most famous in Colorado during 1880s and 1890s, was owned and operated by the infamous Louis du Puy. Area attractions include the Hotel de Paris Museum at 409 6th St., Georgetown Loop Railroad Historic Mining Tour ½ mile west of town on U.S. Hwy. 6, Bownan-White House at 901 Rose St., and Hamie House at 3rd and Argentine Sts., once one of Colorado territory's most luxurious mansions. Accommodations: *Best Western Lodge at Georgetown* (rates: $28–30 double), 55 excellent rooms, dining room, cocktail lounge, at 1600 Argentine St. (569–3211).

Granby

(Pop. 600; zip code 80446; area code 303.) A popular gateway to the Winter Park Ski Area and the Shadow Mountain National Recreation Area on U.S. 40. Accommodations: *Broken Arrow Motel* (rates: $16 double), 12 rooms, 1 mile west of town on U.S. 40 (887–3532); *Trail Riders Motel* (rates: $16–18 double), 11 rooms and family units, on U.S. 40 (887–3738).

Hot Sulphur Springs

(Pop. 200; zip code 80451; area code 303.) A popular forest gateway on U.S. 40 at the mouth of Byers Canyon. Accommodations: *Canyon Motel* (rates: $18–24 double), 12 rooms and restaurant, on U.S. 40 (725–3395).

Idaho Springs

(Pop. 2,000; zip code 80452; area code 303.) A popular summer gateway in the heart of mining country. Area attractions include the world's longest mining tunnel, the 6.2–mile-long Moffat Tunnel; Colorado School of Mines guided mine tours; and the highest mountain road in the United States, along Colorado Hwys. 130 and 5 to Mt. Evans. Accommodations: *Argo Motor Inn* (rates: $24–32 double), 16 excellent rooms and family units, some with fireplaces, housekeeping units, in rustic alpine design, off Interstate 70 Exit 51 (567–4473).

Winter Park

(Pop. 100; zip code 80482; area code 303.) On the western slope of Berthoud Pass in the Arapaho National Forest is this popular summer and winter gateway to the Arapaho mountain country and the Winter Park and Ski Idlewild alpine and Nordic ski areas. Several excellent guest ranches are nestled in the surrounding high-country valleys. Accommodations: *Best Western High Country Inn* (rates: $27–35 double, modified American plan), 60 excellent rooms and family units, dining room, heated indoor pool, sauna, adjacent to the Winter Park Ski area and Arapaho National Forest, in town on U.S. Hwy. 40 (726–5566); *Brookside Inn* (rates: $18 double; $56 double, modified American plan), 12 rustic lodge accommodations and family units, on U.S. 40, 2 miles west of Winter Park (726–5944); *Olympia Motor Lodge—A Friendship Inn* (rates: $18–24 double), 15 rooms and family units, 2½ miles west of Winter Park Ski Area on U.S. Hwy. 40 (726–5539); *Winter Haven Lodge* (rates: $22 double; $522 weekly, double, modified American plan during ski season), 22 rustic alpine rooms in Hideaway Park Village, 2 miles west of Winter Park Ski Area (726–5353).

Lodges, Guest Ranches & Ski Centers

★★★*Arapaho Valley Ranch* is a beautiful family ranch resort nestled in the Arapaho Valley on the west slope of the Continental Divide at an elevation of 8,300 feet in some of Colorado's most spectacular scenery, surrounded by the Arapaho National Forest and only 3 miles from the south boundary of Rocky Mountain National Park. The South Fork of the Colorado River flows through the ranch and joins Lake Granby—Colorado's second-largest body of water—on the ranch proper. Ranch activities include fishing, trail rides, hiking and backpacking in the surrounding alpine country of the Arapaho Forest and Rocky Mountain National Park, and auto tours. Lake Granby and Monarch Lake hold rainbow, brown, and lake trout and kokanee salmon. The surrounding high-country lakes and streams offer fishing for native cutthroats. Ranch-based activities include hayrides, cookouts, songfests, square dances, Little Indian Lake stocked with rainbow trout and boats, acres and acres for children to play in with no poisonous plants or snakes, movies, horseshoes, volley ball, and swimming. Accommodations consist of American-plan, spacious lodge rooms and housekeeping cabins. Family-style meals are served in the rustic main lodge dining room. This mountain ranch also offers free children's supervision, a heated swimming pool, and a wading pool. Daily American-plan rates (with horses) are $30 per person daily. For additional information and rates, contact: Arapaho Valley Ranch, P.O. Box 142 Granby, CO 80446 (303)887–3495.

★★★*Bar Lazy J Guest Ranch*, on the Colorado River near Rocky Mountain National Park, is a full-service family resort surrounded by handsomely landscaped grounds. Activities include fishing for German and brown trout in the Colorado or in Williams Fork Lake, cookouts, boating, hiking the Arapaho National Forest, swimming in a 40–foot outdoor pool, and a fully supervised program for children. Bar Lazy J has a string of fine saddle horses for scenic trail rides plus competent wranglers to offer instruction and guide your wilderness outings. Accommodations are in warm and comfortable guest cabins with all modern amenities that sleep 2–8 persons in each. The river is just a short walk from your doorstep. The main lodge houses a timbered dining room with a great roaring fire where home-cooked specialties are served family-style, perhaps preceded by a cocktail in the spacious lounge or on the riverfront porch. Evening activities run the gamut from billiards and Ping-Pong to square dancing. Weekly rates, including lodgings, 3 meals a day, horseback riding, daily maid service, and all recreational facilities, are $265 per adult, $210 for children 4–9 years old, and $95 for children under. Daily rates, not including horseback riding, are also available. For additional details write: Bar Lazy J Guest Ranch, Parshall, CO 80468 (303)725–3437.

★★★★*Beaver Village Ski Chalet and Guest Ranch*, tucked away at the foot of Berthoud Pass and surrounded by million-acre Arapaho National Forest, offers a perfect setting for year-round vacations. In winter there's free shuttle service to the nearby slopes of Winter Park with its 770 acres of fine ski terrain, superb trails, ski school, and other facilities. If ski touring is your sport, several trails start right at the lodge and lead to quiet, secluded spots. The lodge carries a full line of rentals for skiers. Après-ski amenities include a sauna and whirlpool baths, the Whiskey Barrel cocktail lounge, ski movies, and hot punch get-togethers. Summer activities run the gamut from horseback riding (with free lessons for beginners) to raft trips on the Colorado River and trout fishing in the Fraser River or Beaver Village's privately stocked lake. Other possibilities include tennis, swimming in the outdoor heated pool, hiking in the national forest, and overnight pack trips. Special supervised recreational programs are available for children 4–12 years old. The Beaver Village Dining Room prides itself on superlative, varied menus, everything from blueberry pancakes to prime ribs. Accommodations are available in beautifully furnished lodge rooms and suites, or in 1–, 2–, and 3–bedroom apartments with private balconies, mossrock fireplaces, full kitchens, queen-size beds, and full private baths. Weekly summer package rates, including meals, horses, lodging, and all amenities, are approximately $280–340 per person, double occupancy for standard and deluxe lodge rooms; $450 per person, double occupancy, for condominiums. Early-season and children's discounts are available, also reduced per-person rates for groups of 3–6 adults. Winter rates, including 5 days' lodging, breakfast and dinner daily, and shuttle service to Winter Park, are $163–182 per person, double occupancy. Package rates for longer stays are available. For full information and rates write: Beaver Village, P.O. Box 43, Winter Park, CO 80482 (303)726–5741.

★★★★*Breckenridge Ski Village & Touring Center* is located 70 miles west of Denver high in the Rockies of the Arapaho National Forest. The ski center and the historic gold-rush boom town of Breckenridge, with its Victorian wood-front buildings and boardwalks, is a nationally famous, full-service resort area. The ski area along Peak 8 and Peak 9 of the Ten Mile Range, the first great skiing discovery in Colorado, is amazingly varied, with slopes, trails, bowls, and glades and a 2,213–foot vertical drop. Breckenridge Trails range from a 2½–mile beginners' trail to the steepest face in Colorado, with 50 other runs in between. Mountain facilities include a superb lift complex, 56 miles of downhill runs, Peak 9 Restaurant, and 2 full-service base areas, including rentals and qualified nursery staffs. The renowned Breckenridge Ski School, with up to 110 instructors, offers GLM and nursery and children's classes, through advanced, racing, and deep-powder technique. The Ski Touring School & Mountain Guide Services offers cross-country instruction and backcountry guided tours along trails that meander past odd mines and cabins dating back to the early 1800s. Downtown Breckenridge, with its colorful Old West gold-rush buildings, offers an amazing variety of lodges, shops, restaurants, and entertainment—all with an authentic western atmosphere. The colorful, informal restaurants—from Andreas Pleasure Place & Bordello Bar, High Tortilla, the Miner's Camp, Ore Bucket, and H. P. Cassidy's Sports Emporium

& Eatery to the Whale's Tail—offer a wide variety of good food, from omelettes and haute cuisine to Mexican, continental, Oriental, and western country, as well as entertainment, dancing, and live music. Free shuttle bus service connects resorts during daytime hours. In-town shuttle runs within Breckenridge free of charge. For detailed information on the town and ski center, contact: Breckenridge Ski Corporation, P.O. Box 1058, Breckenridge, CO 80424 (303)453–2368. A *Trail Map & Skiers Guide* is available free upon request. Lodging in Breckenridge ranges from dorms to luxurious alpine lodges, Victorian hotels, and condominiums, listed below.

Asgard Haus offers deluxe studio and 2–6–bedroom condominium units with fireplaces, kitchens, and underground parking. Daily rates: $35–75. Contact SCI Mgmt. Co., 120 N. Main (303)453–2288.

Blue River condominiums offer 1–8–bedroom units with shuttle bus service, fireplaces, kitchens, and TV in rooms. Daily rates: $60–75. Contact: Blue River Condominiums, 580 Colorado Hwy. 9 (303)453–2260.

Breckenridge Inn, a Best Western ski lodge with rooms and rustic 2–bedroom chalets, kitchens, heated swimming pool, tennis courts. Daily rates (double): $20–32. Write: 600 S. Ridge St. (303)453–2333.

Christiana condominiums offer 1–8–bedroom luxury units with fireplaces, kitchens, laundry facilities, Jacuzzi, swimming pool, and TV. Daily rates: $80–120. Contact: Romero Corp., 100 Ski Hill Rd. (303)453–6065.

Claimjumper offers 2–3–bedroom condominium units with fireplaces, kitchens, pool, sauna, and TV. Daily rates: $90–135. Contact: High Country Escape, 100 Village Rd. (303)453–1434.

Claude Martin Lodge offers dormitory and lodge units with continental breakfast, and lounge with fireplace. Daily rates: $10–48 per person. Contact: Claude's Lodge, 0087 Summit Co. Rd. 11 (303)453–2420.

Crofutt's Nap-Sack Lodge offers economy bunk-style accommodations, with continental breakfast and lounge with fireplace. Daily rates: $10 per person. Write: 200 Ski Hill Rd. (303)453–2460.

Fireside Inn offers excellent rooms with shuttle bus service, game room, lounge with fireplace, sauna, and modified American plan. Daily rates: $22–44 per person. Write: 212 Wellington (303)453–6456.

High Country Lodge offers both dormitory and rustic lodge rooms with continental breakfast, game room, lounge with fireplace, and laundry facilities. Daily rates: $8–40 per person. Contact: 5064 Summit Co. Rd. 3 (303)453–2577.

Mother Lode offers deluxe condominium accommodations with studio and 1–3–bedroom units, with fireplaces, kitchens, laundry facilities, swimming pool, sauna, and TV. Daily rates: $40–100. Contact: High Country Escape, 100 Village Rd. (303)453–1434.

Ramada Inn at Silverthorne offers excellent rooms and atmosphere with shuttle bus service, continental breakfast, game room, lounge with fireplace, laundry facilities, Jacuzzi, heated swimming pool, and sauna. Daily rates: $29–60. Write: 220 Tanglewood Lane, Silverthorne (303)468–6200.

Ski & Racquet Club offers deluxe studio and 1–3–bedroom condominium units with fireplaces, game room, kitchens, lounge with fireplace, laundry facilities, heated pool, and sauna. Daily

rates: $55–90. Contact: High Country Escapes, 100 Village Rd. (303)453–1434.

Shangri-La Inn offers good rooms with dining facilities and cocktail lounge. Daily rates: $28–42. Contact: 9277 Colorado Hwy. 9 (303)453–2225.

Skiwatch offers deluxe 1–3–bedroom condominium apartments with fireplaces, game room, kitchens, laundry facilities, sauna, and underground parking. Daily rates: $100–120. Contact: SCI Mgmt. Co., 120 N. Main St. (303)453–2288.

Summit Inn offers good rooms with dining facilities and cocktail lounge. Daily rates: $22–32. Write: 0165 Summit Co. Rd. 6 (303)453–2900.

The Lift offers good lodge rooms and deluxe condominium units with Jacuzzi, heated pool, and laundry facilities. Daily lodge rates: $28–35. Write: SCI Mgmt. Co., 120 N. Main St. (303)453–2288.

For additional listings contact the Breckenridge Resort Assoc., P.O. Box 1909, Breckenridge, CO 80424 (303)453–2918.

★★★★*C Lazy U Ranch* is a handsome, year-round guest and working ranch located high in the Rockies near the headwaters of the Colorado River. In winter the ranch offers free shuttle transportation to the nearby Winter Park-Mary Jane ski complex, second-largest in Colorado, plus excellent private or group lessons, equipment rentals, and 12–15 miles of groomed, marked trails throughout the C Lazy U's 5,000–acre spread. Competent skiers on the ranch staff will help beginners master the basics of cross-country towing. The more daring are welcome to blaze their own trails across the quiet countryside. Other cold-weather activities include ice-skating, horse-drawn sleigh rides, sledding, tubing, outdoor ski picnics around a roaring fire, or a variety of indoor pleasures, such as relaxing in the sauna, card games, movies, and ski clinics. In summer there's horseback riding (each guest is assigned a horse for his exclusive use) through beautiful and varied mountain scenery, along with instruction for first-time and beginning riders. Stream and lake fishing right on the property, swimming in a heated pool, tennis, skeet shooting, raft trips, and cookouts are other favorite ranch activities. Special supervised programs for children and teenagers, including riding and group activities, are also available. Accommodations are in attractive lodge rooms or in 2– and 3–room suites, many of which feature fireplaces. All-inclusive weekly summer rates: $340–420 per person, depending on type of lodgings and season. Winter rates, between January 2 and March 31, average $250–275 per person weekly. Christmas and New Year's week rates are higher. Children's discounts and daily rates are available. The above rates include all meals, lodging, horseback riding, tennis, fishing, sauna, and all activities except skeet shooting, raft trips, and golf. For additional details write: C Lazy U Ranch, Granby, CO 80446 (303)887–3344.

★★★★*Copper Mountain Village & Touring Center* is a sprawling summer and winter resort complex 75 miles from Denver at the eastern approach to Vail Pass, surrounded by a million acres of U.S. Forest Service Land. Named for a mine at its 12,400–foot summit, Copper Mountain offers superlative skiing on over 50 miles of powder and packed powder trails which follow the original contour of the mountain and challenge all levels of ability. A unique covered chair ("the Bubble") combines with 7 other double chairs and 2 surface lifts to provide an uphill capacity of 10,500 skiers per hour. Other facilities include a comprehensive ski school with special instruction for children, a full-service day lodge, regularly scheduled Nastar races, and complete ski rentals. Ice-skating on the village pond, cross-country skiing, moonlight tours, and sleigh rides are among Copper Mountain's other cold-weather pleasures. During the spring and summer months, the Copper Mountain Racquet Club moves into full swing with 6 championship courts and a variety of teaching aids to sharpen your game. A challenging golf course dotted with numerous lakes and bunkers weaves its way through the center of the village. Horseback riding, boating and sailing on Lake Dillon, hiking, fishing, white-water rafting, and bicycling are all popular in season. Summer is also the time for concerts, when the Colorado Philharmonic performs during the Copper Mountain Music Festival. Accommodations at the village are in 15 striking contemporary condominiums with a large range of luxuries, including fireplaces, full kitchens, sheltered parking, saunas, and heated pools. Convenient walkways connect the condominiums with nearby restaurants and entertainment spots, such as the Midnight Sun, with its 2 disco floors, movie house, and après-ski specials. Five different restaurants serve everything from tacos and delicatessen sandwiches to appetizing *haute cuisine*. Other facilities include a children's play center and nursery, riding stables, a scenic chair-lift ride, and wilderness outfitting services. A wide variety of vacation packages are offered, beginning as low as $110–120 per person (off-season, winter), for 5 nights of lodging and a 4–day lift ticket. For a complete rate schedule and information on facilities write: Copper Mountain, P.O. Box 1, Copper Mountain, CO 80443 (303)668–2882.

★★★★*Copper Mountain Ski Touring Center* has a network of nearly 25 miles of marked and regularly maintained cross-country trails originating at the base of the Copper Mountain alpine area and extending along the rolling hills from the top of Vail Pass to Copper Mountain. The backcountry behind the trail network, a magnificent untracked wilderness, is considered some of Colorado's finest touring terrain. In addition to regularly scheduled full-day tours, Copper Mountain has a staff of 20 certified instructors and private or group lessons for both adults and children in all aspects of ski touring. There are also moonlight tours, including a picnic supper around an open campfire, 2–day backcountry touring seminars, and overnight trips with lodgings in snow caves or tents and seminars on winter camping. Special annual events include a combination downhill and cross-country race on touring skis and a giant slalom race, also on cross-country skis. For complete details and rates write: Copper Mountain Ski Touring Center, P.O. Box 1, Copper Mountain, CO 80443 (303)668–2882.

★★★*Devil's Thumb Ranch & Cross-Country Ski Center* is a large working and guest ranch on the west slope of the Rockies, bordering the Arapaho National Forest. In winter the ranch is a cross-country ski center, with 37 miles of groomed trails. The ranch is the official Rocky Mountain training site for the U.S.A. Cross-Country Ski Team. The Devil's Thumb staff, directed by Dick Taylor, former U.S. Olympic team captain, includes training athletes and former national team members. There are many national races held here each season, but there are also lessons and trails here for beginning skiers. There is a completely equipped ski shop with rental and retail equipment, group and private lessons, and half-day, full-day, and moonlight tours each day. Winter rates include lodging, free use of the cross-country trails, breakfast and dinner, sauna and Jacuzzi, and free transportation to Winter Park. In summer the trails are used for horseback riding and the running program. Also, there is fly-fishing on streams and beaver ponds used exclusively by ranch guests. Summer rates include 3 meals per day, fishing privileges, participation in the running program, and transportation to off-the-ranch activities. A weekly package includes a steak ride and a breakfast ride. There are also 2–hour, 3–hour, and all-day rides by reservation daily. Rates: $23–45 per person per night, depending on type of

room and number of persons occupying the room. The ranch offers cabins and lodge and dorm rooms for families, couples, and groups. Meals are served in the rustic main lodge dining room, looking across the Ranch Creek Valley meadows to the peaks of the Great Divide. Contact: Devil's Thumb Ranch, Box 125, Fraser, CO 80442 (303)728–8298 or 8155.

★★★*Idlewild Ski Area and Lodge* is surrounded by fine downhill and cross-country terrain near the challenging slopes of famous Winter Park. Base facilities include a cafeteria, cocktail lounge, dining room, nursery, deck porch, heated pool, and day-care ski-school program for children 4–8. Idlewild has developed a reputation as one of the best learning areas in the country, with expert instruction in GLM (direct parallel) skiing and the American teaching method. Advanced skiers will appreciate the convenient shuttle to Winter Park, just a few minutes away. Other amenities include a rental shop, sleigh rides, a paneled lounge with a fireplace, and après-ski activities. All 29 rooms at the lodge are fully carpeted with private baths. Rates average $34 per person daily, double occupancy, or $220 per person weekly. Per-person rates are lower for 3 or 4 to a room, and children are offered discounts according to age. Prices include lodging, 2 meals a day, shuttle service to Winter Park, and use of lodge facilities exclusive of lift tickets and instruction. Ski packages are available. Idlewild is open all summer long and offers a full spectrum of wilderness recreation, including horseback riding, tennis, and river rafting. For more information write: Ski Idlewild & Idlewild Lodge, Box 3, Winter Park, CO 80482 (303)726–5562.

★★★★*Keystone Mountain/Arapaho Basin Ski Area and Vacation Lodges* offer superlative winter sports and accommodations on 2 great mountains. Undulating, well-groomed Keystone Mountain is ideal for beginning and intermediate skiers; Arapaho Basin has above-timberline powder and steep terrain, with bowls of deep-powder fluff and challenging roller-coaster runs, for experts and hot-doggers, plus a ski season that extends right up to June. All told, there are 14 lifts, 560 acres of snow, and runs for every level of ability. Nearby Breckenridge and Copper mountains double your skiing terrain and allow you to try out 4 mountains (one per day) on a single lift ticket. Keystone also has a fine ski school offering instruction in both American teaching and graduated-length methods, from beginning to free style, under the expert guidance of professional instructors. Other amenities include a children's center staffed by trained personnel, 15 fine restaurants and night spots, specialty shops, indoor tennis, a dozen pools and saunas, and a figure-skating center. The *Keystone Lodge*, with its adjoining conference center (for groups to 700), offers superb mountain views, an intimate cocktail lounge, a steakhouse, continental dining room, and a handsome *brasserie* for family dining. All deluxe hotel rooms are fully carpeted, with TV, private baths, and sumptuous decor. Rates: $40–60 daily, double occupancy. There are also plush condominiums, beautifully furnished and carpeted, with fully equipped kitchens, one or more private baths, and a spacious living room/entertainment area. TV and telephones with 24–hour switchboard service are included, as are linens and maid service. Rates: $45–145 daily for 2–6 guests. Keystone also offers a variety of ski packages, including learn-to-ski vacations, ski weeks, and midweek ski breaks. For full information write: Keystone Resort Assoc., Box 38, Keystone, CO 80435 (303)468–2316.

★★*Lake Dillon Condotel*, located in the heart of Colorado's premier ski country on the sprawling Dillon Reservoir, offers modern housekeeping condominiums with 1–2 bedrooms plus 30 exceptionally roomy private bedrooms with queen-size beds and baths. Less than an hour's drive away is the Vail ski area; 5–15–minute drives take you to Loveland, Arapaho, Keystone, Copper Mountain, and Breckenridge ski slopes. Summer activities in the Lake Dillon area include fishing, sailing, swimming, hiking, mountain climbing, tennis, and golf. A continental spa, recreation room, playground, and spectacular views provide additional pleasures. Condominium rates: $35–45 double occupancy per night for a minimum stay of 2 nights; $70–90 for 4 guests. For complete information write: Lake Dillon Condotel, P.O. Box 308, Dillon, CO 80435 (303)468–2409.

★★★*Sitzmark Ski Lodge and Guest Ranch* offers year-round vacation accommodations and outdoor recreation. Summer activities include horseback riding and hiking through the Arapaho National Forest, swimming in a large heated pool, excellent lake and stream fishing, float trips on the Colorado River, camping, and backcountry trips. During the winter months, the nearby Winter Park and Mary Jane ski areas offer 51 ski trails, 14 lifts, rentals, a ski school, and cafeteria

cum warming house. There's also superb cross-country skiing in the national forest and, back at the lodge, a Finnish sauna, cheerful pub, and handsome dining room for unwinding after a day on the slopes. Year-round accommodations are in pleasantly furnished cabin and lodge rooms, deluxe lodge rooms, and secluded chalets. Summer rates per adult are $180–280 weekly, depending on type of accommodations and number of guests to a room, and include 3 meals a day, horseback riding and instruction, lunch rides, private fishing, steak fries, and use of lodge facilities. Winter rates per adult are $140–280 weekly, including lodging and private bath (except for dorm accommodations), breakfast and dinner, free transportation to Winter Park, ski storage, sauna, and movies. Year-round children's rates are scaled according to age. For full information write: (summer) Sitzmark Guest Ranch, Box 65 S7, Winter Park, CO 80482; (winter) Sitzmark Ski Lodge, Box 1239 W8, Hideaway Park, CO 80450. Phone year-round: (303)726–5453 (Winter Park) or (303)255–9148 (Denver).

Snow Mountain Ranch—YMCA of the Rockies is set on 2,500 high-country acres in the Rocky Mountain National Park area with year-round accommodations and activities including backpacking, fishing, horseback riding, cross-country ski touring, and hiking in the Grand Lake, Shadow Mountain, Winter Park, and Lake Granby backcountry areas. Ranch accommodations range from private rooms in the rustic Aspenbrook, Silver Sage, and Blue Ridge lodges to fully modern 2–, 3–, 4–, and 6–bedroom housekeeping cabins, each with a fireplace. A ski rental shop is conveniently located on the grounds. Daily (5–day) housekeeping cabin rates range from $35 (2 bedrooms) to $75 (5 bedrooms). Daily lodge rates (double) are $21. Snow Mountain Ranch is only 75 miles from Denver on Interstate 70 and U.S. Highway 40. Buses, trains, and airplanes are available out of Denver to Granby, 7 miles from the ranch. Shuttle transportation is available from Granby to Snow Mountain upon request. Contact: (summer) Box 558, Granby, CO 80446 (303)887–3332; (winter) 25 E. 16th Ave., Denver, CO 80202 (303)861–2593.

★★*Snowshoe Guest Ranch* is located south of Steamboat Springs near the Arapaho National Forest. This year-round family vacation ranch offers horseback-riding trips through open range and the meadows and wooded slopes of the Arapaho Forest, fishing in area streams and highcountry ponds for rainbow, brown, and cutthroat trout, archery, hiking, backpacking, nature trails and wildlife photography, hunting for deer and elk, and cross-country skiing. The rustic mountain lodge and cabins accommodate up to 30 guests. There is a double bed in each lodge bedroom and two doubles in each of the cabin units. Each cabin unit has a fireplace. The ranch offers home-cooked family-style meals, cookouts, and campfires in an informal western tradition. American-plan daily rates for cabin accommodations with 2 double beds is $75, or $395 weekly. American-plan lodge rates with double bed and private bath is $40, or $195 weekly. For additional info, contact: Snowshoe Guest Ranch, Kremmling, CO 80459 (303)724–3596.

★★★*Sun Valley Guest Ranch*, built on the site of a 1916 homestead, is located just across the Colorado River from the west gate of Rocky Mountain National Park. Horseback riding, the most popular activity at Sun Valley Ranch, runs the gamut from short trail rides to 5–day wilderness pack trips. The ranch raises and shows Appaloosa horses, so many of the saddle-string horses you'll be riding are home-bred mounts. There are also nearby streams and a private lake for fishing, a heated pool, breakfast rides, and other activities. Three generous western-style meals daily are served in the main lodge, which also houses a recreation room and lounge area. Accommodations are in comfortable and picturesque lodgepole pine cabins with full modern baths and daily maid service. Weekly rates, including all meals, lodging, scheduled ranch activities, and all riding except pack trips, are $225 per person (double occupancy), or $35 daily. Children's rates are scaled according to age. The ranch is open year-round for a variety of seasonal activities such as big-game

hunting, fall color tours, and winter sports. For more information write: Sun Valley Guest Ranch, Box 470, Grand Lake, CO 80447 (303)627–3670.

★★★*Tally Ho Ranch*, near the famed Winter Park and Idlewild ski areas, encompasses some 360 beautiful acres adjacent to the Arapaho National Forest. From November through April, there's superb downhill sport at Winter Park, 15 minutes away, with free transportation provided between the lodge and the slopes. Cross-country skiing begins right at Tally Ho's doorstep and extends over miles of trails and open terrain. Since this is a working ranch specializing in Clydesdale and Suding horses, there's superlative horseback touring during the warm weather months. Other activities include fishing in 2 streams and a small lake, swimming in the heated pool, golf, and evening entertainment. Accommodations are in spacious, handsomely furnished bedrooms, many with fireplaces, and all with wall-to-wall carpeting and private baths. The main lodge building is furnished in antique pine and houses a large, comfortable lounge with a dance floor, card room, bar with fireplace, and dining room overlooking the mountains and meadows. Ski-season package rates for 5–7 days are $200–273 per person, double occupancy, including lodgings, ski tickets, breakfast, and dinner. For more information and a complete list of rates (specify season), write: Tally Ho Ranch, Box 51, Winter Park, CO 80482 (303)726–5958.

Winter Park Ski Area, surrounded by the unspoiled expanse of the Arapaho National Forest, is one of Colorado's finest and most comprehensive winter sports meccas. Winter Park Mountain alone has 34 trails and over 420 acres of skiable terrain. Add the challenging new Mary Jane system, with its 18 trails and 350 acres, and you have a vast interconnected network of 52 separate trails and 4 mountain faces forming the rugged brow of the Continental Divide. There are steep drops for the expert skier, wide bowls for intermediates, and gentle slopes for the beginner. A strategic chair-lift system—13 in all, plus a new triple chair—moves skiers around the area at a combined rate of 15,750 per hour. A single ticket works for all lifts. The Winter Park area also encompasses fine restaurants and day lodges, a rental and repair shop, numerous sport shops, snow-making facilities, and a superb ice-skating/health-club complex. The Winter Park Ski School has a professional staff of 150 instructors, private and class lessons, "graduated kid method" programs for children, and a fine free-style and racing program. Winter Park is a popular summer vacation retreat, too, with excellent terrain and facilities for tennis, fishing, backpacking, horseback riding, sailing, and river rafting. For information and an area directory, write: Winter Park Resort Assoc., P.O. Box 5A, Winter Park, CO 80482 (303)726–5588.

Travel Services

Rocky Mountain Outfitters, Inc., are backpacking and ski-touring specialists offering instruction, rentals, tours, and guided trips. Daily ski tours in the Arapaho National Forest, 2–hour moonlight tours, and winter camping trips are offered in season. During the summer months, backpacking and mountaineering trips are sponsored for both families and individuals. Complete rental equipment for ski touring and backpacking, as well as brand-name sales at fair prices. The main year-round store is located on Main St. in Granby; a winter shop is operated at Beaver Ski Chalet in Winter Park. For information write: Rocky Mountain Outfitters, Inc., P.O. Box 574, Granby, CO 80446 (303)887–3777.

Dinosaur National Monument

The spectacular Dinosaur National Monument takes in an area of

about 330 square miles of rugged and scenic wilderness in the eastern Uinta Mountains. Paved roads lead into the area from Monument Headquarters at Dinosaur, Colo., and from Jensen, Utah, near the famous quarry. John Wesley Powell saw "reptilian remains" in the monument area in 1871, but it was Earl Douglass, of Pittsburgh's Carnegie Museum, who found the "Dinosaur Ledge" quarry in 1909, when he discovered the tail bones of a *Brontosaurus*. The scenery of the monument is dominated by the towering limestone and shale canyons of the Green and Yampa rivers. Both rivers flow placidly through broad green valleys before plunging headlong through, not around, the mountains into their respective canyons. The major features of the Green River Wildlands in the monument include the awesome Canyon of Lodore (where Powell lost one of his boats, the *No-Name*, at Disaster Falls), Hills Half Mile, Steamboat Rock, the fierce Whirlpool Canyon, the verdant meadows of Island and Rainbow parks, Moonshine Rapids, and the wild roller-coaster rapids and eddies of Split Mountain Canyon.

Fossil displays are located at the monument headquarters and information center at the national monument entrance and at the Dinosaur Quarry Visitor Center on Utah Hwy. 149, 7 miles north of Jensen, UT. The visitor centers and Split Mountain area are open year-round. No lodgings are available, except for campgrounds at Split Mountain Gorge and Green River near the visitor center in Utah and at the Echo and Lodore Park areas in Colorado.

Information Sources, Maps & Access

For detailed information and a free *Dinosaur National Monument Map/Brochure*, write: Superintendent, Dinosaur National Monument, Dinosaur, CO 81610 (303)374–2216. A beautiful, full-color 30–by–15 inch *U.S. Geological Survey Dinosaur National Monument Shaded-Relief Map* ($2) may be ordered from: Distribution Branch, U.S. Geological Survey, Federal Center, Denver, CO 80225. The national monument is located 88 miles west of Craig, Colorado, on U.S. Hwy. 40, then north on the monument road for 31 miles.

Grand Mesa National Forest

The Grand Mesa National Forest encompasses 368,418 acres of glacier-carved canyon country, carpeted with evergreen forests and wild-flower meadows. The forest is named for Grand Mesa, the nation's largest table-topped mountain, rising some 10,000 feet above the confluence of the Colorado and Gunnison rivers at Grand Junction. This vast mesa, the largest in the country, offers cross-country skiing, backpacking and wild-country fishing for rainbow, brown, cutthroat, and brook trout in its more than 300 gin-clear alpine lakes, including Cottonwood, Mesa, Island, Eggleston, Big Battlement, Ward, and Griffeth, and camping along the Land o' Lakes Trail. For those who prefer a more accessible retreat, many of the turquoise cirques near the mesa rims are easily reached by car. Gravel-surfaced roads provide access to much of the lake area, and two paved roads cross the mesa. Those who prefer the solitude of wilderness travel should try the many remote lakes accessible only by four-wheel drive, horseback, or foot. More than 4,000 mule deer and 200 elk are taken each year by big-game hunters in the forest. Black bear also inhabit the mesa country.

Information Sources, Maps & Access

Detailed information and a full-color *Grand Mesa National Forest Map* (50¢) may be obtained from: Supervisor, Grand Mesa National Forest, P.O. Box 138, Delta, CO 81416 (303)874–7691.

The Grand Mesa National Forest and lake country is reached from Grand Junction via Interstate Highway 70 and U.S. Highway 50 and Colorado Highways 65, 92, and 133. Lodging, meals, guides, supplies, and outfitters are available at Grand Junction, Rifle, Grand Mesa, Molina, Collbran, Plateau City, and Bowie.

Gateways & Accommodations

Grand Junction

(Pop. 20,200; zip code 81501; area code 303.) The seat of Mesa County was once known at Ute, then West Denver, and finally was named for its location at the junction of the Gunnison and Colorado (formerly known as the Grand) rivers. Area attractions include the Colorado National Monument, a fascinating 28–square-mile area 4 miles west of Grand Junction of sheer-walled canyons, pinnacles, and towering monoliths reached via Colorado Hwy. 340 and the spectacular Rim Rock Drive; Powderhorn Ski Area; Lands End at the western end of Grand Mesa National Forest, reached via U.S. Hwy. 50, which offers a spectacular view of western Colorado; and Grand Junction Historical Museum and Institute of Western Colorado at 4th & Ute Sts. Area Accommodations: *Best Western Bar X Motel* (rates: $34 double), 78 excellent rooms and family units, restaurant, heated pool, airport service, at 1600 North Ave. off U.S. 6 and I–70, Exits 5 and 8 (243–1311); *Holiday Inn* (rates: $35 double), 210 excellent rooms and family units, dining room, coffee shop, cocktail lounge, heated pool, at 755 Horizon Drive, off I–70 Exit 7 (243–6790); *Howard Johnson's Motor Lodge*, (rates: $34–39 double), 100 excellent rooms, restaurant, coffee shop, heated pool, at 750 Horizon Drive off I–70 Exit 7 (243–5150); *Ramada Inn Roadside Hotel*, (rates: $36 double), 142 excellent rooms, dining room, coffee shop, heated pool, airport service, at 718 Horizon Drive off I–70 Exit 7 (243–5080).

Lodges, Guest Ranches & Ski Centers

★★*Grand Mesa Lodge* overlooks Island Lake in the Grand Mesa National Forest and offers comfortable housekeeping cabins and motel rooms. In addition to well-stocked Island Lake, there are more than 200 other good trout lakes on Grand Mesa, some of them accessible only on foot or horseback. Others are easily reached by driving through incomparable forest scenery. The lodge has boat rentals on Island Lake and a tackle and grocery shop. For hikers, there are several fine trails leaving the highway near the lodge. Two easy paths lead to Lake View Point and the edge of the mesa for spectacular views of the surrounding high country. Accommodations range from rustic, but modern and convenient, fishing cabins to new housekeeping cottages (refrigerators, gas heat, hot water, cooking facilities), and fully carpeted motel rooms with picture windows overlooking the lake and mountains. A coffee shop and dining room serve appetizing home-cooked fare. Rates: $18–40 daily. For additional information write: Grand Mesa Lodge, Star Route, Box 205, Cedaredge, CO 81413 (303)856–3211.

★★★*Mesa Lakes Resort* is located on the Grand Mesa—the largest flat-top mountain in the world, with elevations varying between 10,000 and 11,000 feet—surrounded by the lakes, streams, and alpine meadows of the Grand Mesa National Forest. Mesa Lakes Resort lies nestled among a group of 7 mountain lakes situated high above the Grand Valley of the Colorado River. The resort offers outstanding high-country fishing, backpacking, hunting, and cross-country skiing. Powderhorn, a national alpine ski area, is only 10 minutes away on the north slope of the Grand Mesa. Mesa Lakes Resort accommodations consist of 25 rustic cabins with modern conveniences and 1–6 beds. Each cabin contains a fireplace, kitchen, and dining and bathroom facilities. Regular rates for the cabins (meals not included) range from $17.50 to $52.50 per night. All overnight stays include free firewood and shuttle service to Powderhorn Ski Area. The resort dining room, noted for its fine food and service, overlooks beautiful Beaver Lake in the cabin area. The resort also maintains several types of boats and a large string of horses for pack trips along the Grand Mesa backcountry trails. Mesa Lakes Resort is the center for cross-country skiing activities on the Grand Mesa. Hot meals and drinks and plenty of parking are available 7 days a week. Some of the many cross-country trails start at the lodge. A practical selection of hats, socks, sunglasses, and ski wax are in stock, courtesy of Lewis & Clark, Ltd., Grand Junction. Terry Paulson, a leading Colorado cross-country ski racer, is available for informal skiing, touring, and trail advice. Additionally, the menu includes a box lunch for those who desire to picnic on the snow. Cross-country ski rentals and lessons are available at Lewis & Clark Ltd., Board & Buckle Co., and Marmot Mountain Works Ltd. in Grand Junction. The lessons are given in the Mesa Lakes Resort area. For additional information, contact: Mesa Lakes Resort, Mesa, CO 81643 (303) 268–5467.

★★★*Powderhorn Lodge & Ski Area*, nestled in a broad bowl on the northern slopes of Grand Mesa, is just a short 40–mile drive from western Colorado's largest city, Grand Junction. Accessibility and family-organized prices have made the Powderhorn area a popular ski mecca, without long lift lines or slope jam-ups. Wide, open, and uncrowded trails are tailored to every level of ability; 2 double chair-lifts and a Poma lift have a combined capacity of close to

2,500 skiers per hour. There are also miles of cross-country trails and open stretches in Grand Mesa National Forest. The Powderhorn Lodge, located less than 100 feet from the ski area, offers fine accommodations and entertainment throughout the season. Amenities include a restaurant/cocktail lounge, daily maid service, sauna, courtesy car, and conference and meeting room facilities. Daily rates, including private ski lockers and use of sauna: $33 double occupancy; $67 for family suites; and $12 for dorm rooms. Special winter packages covering 5–7 nights of lodging and 4–6 days of skiing plus transportation to and from the lodge are also available. For details write: Powderhorn Lodge, P.O. Box 150, Mesa, CO 81643 (303)268–5410.

★★*Trail's End Ranch*, located just north of Collbran in the Plateau Valley, is a family-owned working and guest ranch. Appaloosa and quarter horses are on hand for trail rides through the adjoining national forest and other scenic areas. A riding arena at the ranch will help you learn various skills or practice gymkhana events. Guided trips can be arranged to favorite spots on Grand Mesa and around the Vega Dam for excellent trout fishing, plus there's a stocked pond right on the ranch. In the fall, deer hunting is available on the ranch's own property during the big-game season. Other activities include fish fries beside the lake, barbecues, hayrides, hiking, rodeos, archery, and trapshooting. Rustic log guest cabins have private baths, carpeting, and comfortable furnishings. There's a large lounge area for evening activities, and a dining room where everything from Southern fried chicken to Mexican food is served family-style. Per-person weekly rates are $245, including all meals, lodging, horseback riding, and ranch activities. Children's rates are on a sliding scale determined by age. Season runs from Memorial Day weekend through Labor Day. For more information write: Trail's End Ranch, Collbran, CO 81624 (303)487–3338.

Gunnison National Forest & The Black Canyon

This famous fishing, big-game hunting, and wilderness camping area embraces 1,773,589 acres on the western slopes of the Rockies. The forest is bounded on the north by the peaks of the Elk Range, on the east and south by the Continental Divide, and on the west by Uncompahgre Valley. The forest was named for Capt. John W. Gunnison, who explored this area in 1853 in search of a route for the proposed transcontinental railroad. The swift, deep-flowing Gunnison is one of the nation's top trout streams for trophy rainbows and browns up to 10 pounds. The once-free-flowing middle portion of the Gunnison (before it flows through the Black Canyon) has been dammed to form the Blue Mesa, Morrow Point, and Crystal reservoirs, which form the Curecanti National Recreation Area. Twenty-mile-long Blue Mesa Lake offers good early-season fishing for kokanee salmon and rainbow, brown, and lake trout. Visitor information centers are located at Elk Creek and Cimarron.

The West Elk Wild Area of the forest covers 62,000 acres of rugged canyons, high mountain meadows, dense forests, and fantastic rock formations. Elevations here range from 8,000 to 12,920 feet. Mountains of the West Elk Wild Area include the Beckwith Mountains, the West Elk Range, and the Anthracite Range. Wilderness fly-fishermen will find cutthroat trout in the remote alpine lakes and feeder streams.

The eroding forces of wind, water, and glaciers have sculpted the Black Canyon of the Gunnison River out of the mountains of central Colorado. The Black Canyon of the Gunnison National Monument includes 10 miles of the most scenic portion of the 50–mile canyon. Sheer walls rise 3,000 feet at their highest point, forming the deepest gorge in Colorado, which narrows in places to a mere 10 feet. Near the center of the monument, erosion has created a fantastic display of spires, pinnacles, and knobs of rock along the 2,400–foot walls. Here the gorge opens to a width of 150–300 feet, revealing its colorful crystalline walls. Granite, gneiss, and schists glint in the sun in an array of color ranging from white to red, black, and blue. The canyon is at its most beautiful when the autumn reds and yellows of scrub oak, mountain mahogany, aspens, and willows flash amidst the green of pine and spruce. Elk, bear, and an occasional mountain lion range the canyon rims; beaver, muskrat, and mink live along the river. The deep-flowing, boulder-studded pools of the Black Canyon stretch of the Gunnison hold trophy rainbows.

The river that courses through the canyon was named for Capt. John W. Gunnison, who explored the river in 1853 but was forced to turn back when he reached the dark depths of the canyon.

Information Sources, Maps & Access

For detailed information and a full-color *Gunnison National Forest Map* (50¢) and a free *West Elk Wild Area* map/brochure, write: Supervisor, Gunnison National Forest, 216 N. Colorado, Gunnison, CO 81230 (303)641–0471.

State Rt. 133 runs south from Interstate 70 to the forest area. The forest is also accessible by taking State Highway 789 south from Interstate 70 near Grand Junction to Delta, then picking up State Highway 92. Ranger station offices are located at Gunnison and Paonia. Lodging, guides, supplies, and outfitters are available at the towns of Cimarron, Gunnison, Almont, Crested Butte, Marble, Tincup, Paonia, Crawford, Maher, and Aspen.

For detailed information and a free *Black Canyon of the Gunnison* map and brochure, write: Superintendent, Box 1648, Montrose 81401 (303)249–9661. A special 23–by-30–inch U.S. Geological Survey map, *Black Canyon of the Gunnison National Monument, Colorado*, is available for $2 from: Distribution Section, U.S. Geological Survey, Federal Center, Denver 80225. The map, on a scale of 2,000 feet to 1 inch, is available in either a contour or a shaded-relief edition. The Black Canyon is reached via U.S. 50 and Colorado Hwy. 344, 14 miles northeast of Montrose.

Gateways & Accommodations

(See "Uncompahgre National Forest" for additional gateway listings under "Montrose.")

Crested Butte

(Pop. 400; zip code 81224; area code 303.) See listing under "Lodges & Guest Ranches."

Gunnison

(Pop. 4,600; zip code 81230; area code 303.) The town is a historic gateway to the vast recreation lands of the Gunnison National Forest and the trout pools and riffles of the famed Gunnison River. Area attractions include Curecanti National Recreation Area, old mining towns, and the Gunnison Pioneer Museum on U.S. Hwy. 50 (641–9963). Accommodations: *Best Western Tomichi Village* (rates: $32–34 double), 48 excellent rooms and family units, restaurant, cocktail lounge, heated pool, 1 mile east of town on U.S. Hwy. 50 (641–1131).

Lodges, Guest Ranches & Ski Centers

★★★★*Almont Resort*, midway between Gunnison and Crested Butte, offers 26 modern, roomy cabins which still preserve the flavor of the resort's late-19th-century origins. Many of the early buildings—including a cabin built by Teddy Roosevelt—are still in use, though all have been brought up to date and feature private baths, individual heating, twin or double beds, and daily maid service. European and American plans are available, with excellent meals served in the main dining room and an inviting cocktail lounge for winding down after a day in the outdoors. Among the most popular activities here are skiing the 35 runs at Crested Butte, rainbow trout fishing in nearby streams and lakes, guided fall hunting trips, horseback riding, and hiking through western Colorado's spectacular countryside. Cabin rates: $22–28 daily for 2 people (both 1 and 2 bedrooms available; American-plan rates: $44 daily for 2 guests. For complete information write: Almont Resort, Bar 47 Ranch, Almont, CO 81210 (303)641–1009.

★★*Cement Creek Ranch*, located in a hidden valley at 9,000–foot altitudes, is a small wilderness hideaway surrounded by Gunnison National Forest. Fishing for trout in the cold, clear waters of Cement Creek, horseback riding through groves of Engelmann spruce and aspen, and swimming in a natural, warm, spring-fed pool are favorite activities here. There are also numerous hiking trails, old mines and ghost towns, and 13,300–foot Italian Mountain, all waiting to be explored on day or overnight trips. Accommodations are in 8 pine-paneled housekeeping cabins with fully modern kitchens and baths. All linens, cooking and eating utensils, and towels are supplied. Rates: $20–36 per day, depending on cabin size and number of guests in each. Season runs from June 1 through early November, so hunters can enjoy the ranch as a base of operations for fall elk and deer seasons. For full details write: Cement Creek Ranch, Crested Butte, CO 81224 (303)349–5541.

★★★★*Crested Butte Mountain Ski Village*, situated in west-central Colorado, offers deluxe alpine accommodations and excellent downhill and cross-country skiing. Crested Butte is nationally recognized for its high-country ski touring. Helicopter service is available for alpine and Nordic trips to untouched wilderness locations. The 35 spectacular downhill runs are designed for every kind of skier. The trail system lets beginners ski on one part of the mountain, experts on another. The area is noted for its uncrowded slopes and lifts, which were designed to handle more skiers than the accommodations. The mountain offers wide, sweeping, sunny bowls with plenty of steep drops and grades in a picturesque alpine setting. Jokerville and North Face are both nationally famous expert slopes, with 55–60% gradients. Mountain men regularly pack the intermediate and beginner runs. Many slopes, however, are left untouched for deep-powder enthusiasts. The ski village, within walking distance of the lifts, offers lodges, condominiums, inns, restaurants, night spots, shops, swimming pools, ski instruction, a deli and health club. Crested Butte's famous ski program, headed by Robel Straubhaar, is staffed by 50 instructors. Cross-country lessons and guided tours are available through the Crested Butte Nordic Program. Down the road from the ski village is the old Victorian boom town of Crested Butte—designated a National Historic District by Congress—with its historic wood-front stores, gourmet restaurants, shops, night spots, arts, and crafts. Regular bus service operates between the town, ski area, and the Gunnison and Crested Butte airports.

Many of Crested Butte's original Victorian buildings still stand: the Old City Hall (1884), Elk Mountain House (1881), the Protestant Church (1883), Old Rock Schoolhouse (1883), now a museum, and the railroad depot (1881). There are colorful shops galore—the Mule

Skinner, Water Wheel, Glacier Lily, the Company Store, Eagle Nest Studio, and Zaccharia Zyyp & Co., and many more. The town boasts some of the best restaurants in the West, such as Le Bosquet for French cuisine, Elk Mountain Lodge for home-style western cooking, the Slogan Bar with its Victorian decor complete with ceiling fans, and Soupçon for country food and atmosphere. At the ski village, the Red Lady Lounge offers dancing and entertainment.

Crested Butte Accommodations are available at the following lodges and chalets (rates are based on double occupancy for 7 nights during the regular season—Jan.-Mar.): *Crested Butte Lodge* (rates: $202–209), at ski village, with dining room, fireplace in lobby, daily maid service, sauna, suites available; *Elk Mountain Lodge* (rates: $139), in town with cocktail lounge, dining room, fireplace in lobby, maid service, pets allowed; *Forest Queen Hotel* (rates: $145), in town with breakfast, cocktail lounge, fireplace, maid service; *Nordic Inn* (rates: $210), at ski village with continental breakfast, fireplace, lobby, maid service, sauna, pets allowed; *One Bucket Lodge* (rates: $147–165), in town with children's rates, continental breakfast, fireplace, maid service, sauna, whirpool; *Poverty Gulch* (rates: $139–195), in town with dining room, fireplace, family room, maid service; *Silverlode Inn* (rates: $199–223), at ski village with cocktail lounge, dining room, fireplace, game room, maid service, sauna; *Ski Crest Lodge* (rates: $195–202), at ski village, with cocktail lounge, dining room, fireplace, game room, maid service, pool, and sauna; *Alpine Chalet Rentals* (rates: $297–594), at ski village, with fireplace, kitchen, laundry facilities, telephones in rooms, 2–6–bedroom chalets; *Rocky Mountain Chalet Rentals* (rates: $332–367), at ski village with children's rates, fireplaces, lobbies, telephones in rooms, 2–4–bedroom homes.

For detailed rates, condominium rentals, lodging reservations, and flight bookings on Frontier Airlines and Aspen Airways from Denver, contact: Crested Butte Central Reservations, Box 1149, Crested Butte, CO 81224 (303)349–6601.

★★★*Harmel's Ranch Resort*, a family guest ranch surrounded by the Gunnison National Forest, is located at the confluence of Spring Creek and the Taylor River on 300 acres of trees, meadows, and streams. Horseback riding, wilderness pack trips, fishing the renowned streams of Gunnison County, white-water float trips, hayrides, jeep trips, and forest picnics are some of the most popular activities at the ranch. There's also a heated swimming pool, plus a recreation lounge for indoor games and movies. American-plan accommodations are available in fully carpeted lodge rooms and deluxe 1–2–bedroom suites with private baths, fine views, and separate dressing rooms. Individual and housekeeping cottages, scattered among tall pines beside the river, have fully equipped modern kitchens, all linens and utensils, comfortable furnishings, automatic hot water, and electric heating. The lodge dining room offers excellent, hearty meals at reasonable rates. Modified American-plan rates, including 2 meals daily, maid service, and many ranch activities (except horseback riding, jeep and float trips) are $50–57 daily for 2; $66–88 daily for 3; and $82–104 for 4. European-plan cabin rates: $26–40 daily for 2–4 guests. Evening-meal plans and special weekly rates are also available. For a complete schedule of rates and descriptive information write: Harmel's Ranch Resort, Box 944, Gunnison, CO 81230 (303)641–1740.

★★*Lost Canyon Resort*, on the renowned Gunnison River, offers a full gamut of wilderness pleasures: fall hunting for elk, deer, and bear; fishing the Gunnison and nearby lakes for trout and kokanee salmon; jeep trips and horseback riding through breathtaking high-mountain country; and a vast winter playground just 20 miles north at

the Crested Butte Ski Area. Accommodations are available in completely modern apartment-type units ($22 double), individual log cabins ($24 double), or in large log cabins with 3 double beds in each ($30). All are equipped for housekeeping with private baths and kitchens with gas ranges and electric refrigerators, dishes, cookware, plus all linens and blankets. For complete information write: Lost Canyon Resort, Box 26, Gunnison, CO 81230.

★★*Pioneer Lodge*, situated at base of 12,000–foot Cement Mountain in Gunnison National Forest, is a small resort composed of picturesque log cabins spaced far apart and surrounded by towering pines. Cement Creek, just 50 yards from your doorstep, affords some excellent fishing, and there are several other streams within hiking or driving distance waiting to be explored. Crested Butte, famous for superlative skiing, is only 9 miles away. Housekeeping cabins are all furnished with refrigerators, gas ranges, private baths, and all dishes and linens. Rates: $20–28 per day for 2 people, depending on the size of the cabin. For more information write: Pioneer Lodge, Crested Butte, CO 81224 (303)349–5517.

★★*Rocky River Resort* is located right on the banks of the Gunnison River approximately 7 miles north of Gunnison. In addition to ⅓ mile of privately owned river frontage, perfect for fishing, there are 3 major reservoirs and numerous mountain lakes and beaver ponds within easy driving distance. Hiking, big-game hunting, horseback riding, boating, swimming, and waterskiing are all available in the Gunnison area. The resort offers both new cabins and log cabins from two old resorts that are no longer in existence. The original homesteaders' cabin, built in 1892, is still in use. Many cabins overlook the river, and all are fully furnished for housekeeping with blankets, bed linen, cooking utensils, dishes, etc. You bring only your personal gear and clothing. For complete rates and information write: Rocky River Resort, Rt. 3, Box 14, Gunnison, CO 81230 (303)641–0174.

★★*The Six J's Guest Resort* is located at 8,500–foot attitudes in the premier fishing and big-game country of Colorado's Gunnison County. There are 16 single and double housekeeping cabins, a large clubhouse and restaurant, children's playgrounds, a private lake stocked with fat rainbows, and a good trout stream right at your cabin door. Deer hunting is usually good within walking distance from the resort, though the big bucks and elks favor higher altitudes, accessible by 4–wheel drive. Big-game season starts the third Saturday in October and lasts for 2–3 weeks. Horseback riding and hiking the beautiful mountain terrain are popular activities spring through fall. Cabins are fully furnished with complete kitchens, good foam beds, showers, etc. A grocery store on the premises stocks both fresh and frozen foods, or you can take your meals in the Six J's Restaurant. For information and rates write: The Six J's Guest Resort, Powderhorn, CO 81243 (303)641–0220.

Wuanita Hot Springs Ranch offers 80 acres of prime horseback-riding country surrounded by national forest and summer grazing land. This handsome guest ranch offers miles of scenic trails, jeep trips to old mining towns, fishing for trout on private streams and lakes, and some of the most breathtaking scenery in the West. Natural hot springs supply clear, pure hot water for the lodge and year-round swimming pool. In the fall, hunting trips for elk and deer are sponsored. Winter activities include sledding and cross-country skiing with special bus service to nearby Monarch and Crested Butte Winter Sports Area. Accommodations in 2–room paneled lodge units, each with a private bath, are $30 per day or $190 per week, all-inclusive. Families and groups are especially welcome. For further details write: Wuanita Hot Springs Ranch, Rt. 2, Box 56, Gunnison, CO 81230.

Travel Services

Pimatise Kayaking offers weekly beginning clinics (day or evening)

and concentrated weekend clinics in the art and sport of kayaking, using a swimming pool, lake, and the Taylor River as classrooms. Students begin in the pool with instruction in the Eskimo Roll. Flatwater skills on the lake are refined by exercises using slalom gates. The final class takes place on the river, using a high brace to gain awareness of actual water conditions. Instruction is limited to small groups (3 students maximum on all river classes), and the latest equipment is employed to polish your skills. Beginning clinic tuition is $65 per person for 5 sessions. Pimatise (the name derives from the Knisteneaux Indian word for "life") also offers intermediate and advanced instruction on the Taylor River or in the swimming pool to perfect your roll. The half-day rate is $15. Private lessons are available at $15 per hour. For more information write: Pimatise Kayaking, Box 532, Crested Butte, CO 81224 (303)349–5210 or (303)349–6595.

Pike National Forest

This 1,105,000–acre forest is dominated by the towering grandeur of famous Pikes Peak (14,110 ft.). In 1803, Lt. Zebulon M. Pike first saw the majestic mountain of central Colorado that now bears his name. He estimated its height at 18,000 feet and described it as "so remarkable as to be known to all savage nations for hundreds of miles around, to be spoken of with admiration by the Spaniards of New Mexico, and to be the bounds of their travels northwest." In 1820, Dr. Edwin James, botanist and historian, made the first recorded ascent of the mountain. During the gold rush of 1859, thousands of Conestoga wagons crossed the plains bearing the motto "Pikes Peak or Bust!" on their sides. The grand mountain was the gateway to gold country.

Some of the state's finest elk, deer, mountain sheep, antelope, and bear habitat is found in the Pikes Peak region and the surrounding mountains. Wild-flower meadows share the lower elevations of these mountains with forest floors of blueberry shrubs, bluebells, purple monkshood, and yellow butterweed. Nearer the timberline grow forget-me-nots, mountain pinks, and alpine gentian. Hundreds of miles of forest roads and trails weave through the forest and provide access to the headwaters of the Platte and Arkansas rivers, South Platte River, Rampart Range, Tarryall Mountains, Mosquito Range, Kenosha Mountains, Pigmatite Points, Devil's Head, and the scenic Windy Ridge-Bristlecone Pine Botanical Area, the Lost Creek Scenic Area, and the Abyss Lake Scenic Area.

Florissant Fossil Beds National Monument is situated near the forest boundary off U.S. 24, 2 miles south of Florissant on County Rd. 1. This red sandstone petrified forest, first discovered by gold prospectors, contains huge fossil trees, also stumps similar to the giant sequoias in California. A collection of Florissant insect fossils are on display at the University of Colorado Museum (see "Boulder").

Information Sources, Maps & Access

A U.S. Forest Service *Pike National Forest Map* is available for 50¢ from: Pike National Forest, Carpenters Hall, 403 Cascade Ave., P.O. Box 2380, Colorado Springs 80901 (303)636–1602. Free from the same source is a *Pike National Forest Travel Map*, which shows most of the same features as the official service map in black and white and describes travel regulations and restrictions in effect throughout the forest. The office also distributes a free brochure, *Pikes Peak*, describing the history, surrounding topography, and flora and fauna of this outstanding feature. The forest, which includes all of the life zones found in Colorado, supports a rich variety of bird life. A *Checklist of Birds* includes 261 species that inhabit the forest or migrate through it. This list is available free from the Forest Office (address above). A beautiful shaded-relief map, *Pikes Peak & Vicinity* (also available in a topographic edition), 32 by 32 inches, is available from the Distribution Branch, U.S. Geological Survey Federal Survey, Denver 80225 for $2. On the reverse side of the map is the geologic story of Pikes Peak and the adjacent area. If you plan to drive through this area, write to the Forest Supervisor's Office (above) for a free copy of *The Short Line Gold Camp Auto Tour*, a guide to a car tour that includes such sites as the Silver Cascades, the precarious railroad switchbacks that early locomotives followed over the mountains of the gold country, and such famous boom towns as Cripple Creek, where the discovery of the precious metal marked the beginning of the 1859 gold rush.

The forest is accessible by U.S. Highway 185 south from Denver, U.S. Highway 24 from Colorado Springs, or State Highway 9 north from Route 50, which runs west from Pueblo. Lodging, guides, supplies, and outfitters are available at the towns of Woodland Park, Manitou Springs, Monument, Shamballa, Colorado Springs, Westcreek, Deckers, Lake George, Estabrook, Buffalo Creek, South Platte, and Tarryall.

Gateways & Accommodations

Colorado Springs—Gateway to Pikes Peak

(Pop. 135,100; zip code, see below; area code 303.) This famous resort area at the base of Pikes Peak is named for nearby springs and its historic predecessor, Colorado City. Area attractions include the fantastic rock formations at the Garden of the Gods; Ute Trail Monument; Air Force Academy, 12 miles north of town on I–25; Buffalo Bill Wax Museum at 400 W. Manitou Ave.; scenic Serpentine Drive to Cave of Winds off U.S. 24; Pioneers' Museum at the Old Courthouse at 215 S. Tejon St.; Mt. Manitou Scenic Railway at 515 Ruxton Ave.; Broadmoor-Cheyenne Mountain Highway; Cheyenne Mountain Zoological Park; Pikes Peak Ghost Town 2 miles west of town at 400 S. 21st St.; May Natural History Museum on Colorado Hwy. 115, 8 miles southwest of town at Golden Eagle Ranch; Flying W Ranch—an Old West working cattle and horse ranch at 6100 Wilson Rd. (598–4000); Manitou Cliff Dwellings Museum west of town on U.S. Hwy. 24 bypass; North American Air Defense Command tours at Peterson Air Force Base Visitors Center on U.S. 24; and superb dining at the *Briarhurst Manor Inn* at 404 Manitou Ave. (685–5061) and the rustic *Red Cloud Inn* in an alpine setting on U.S. Hwy. 24 in Cascade opposite Pike's Peak Road Turn-off (684–9915). Accommodations: *Anters Plaza Hotel* (rates: $41–49 double), 276 outstanding rooms and family units, rooftop heated pool, dining room, coffee shop, cocktail lounge, downtown at Chase Stone Center on Pikes Peak Ave. 80903 (473–5600); *Best Western Four Seasons Motor Inn* (rates: $43–50 double), 308 superb rooms and family loft units, dining room, coffee shop, cocktail lounge, 2 heated pools, tennis courts, off I–25 Exit 57 at 28865 S. Circle Drive, 80930 (576–5900); *Best Western Inn at Woodmoor* (rates: $30–32 double), 103 excellent rooms and family units, dining room, coffee shop, heated pool on Woodmoor Lake, off I–25 Exit 73 in Monument 80132 (481–2213); *Best Western Palmer House* (rates: $34 double), 150 excellent rooms, dining room, cocktail lounge, heated pool, north on I–25 Exit 64 at Fillmore St., 80907 (636–5201); *Hilton Inn* (rates: $41–49 double), 126 outstanding rooms and family units, restaurant, cocktail lounge, heated pool, north off I–25 Exit 65 at 505 Popes Bluff Trail (598–7656); *Holiday Inn—Central* (rates: $37–38 double), 207 excellent rooms and family units, dining room, coffee shop, cocktail lounge, heated pool, downtown at 8th and Cimmaron Sts. 80905 (473–5530); *Holiday Inn—North* (rates: $37–38 double), 220 excellent rooms and family units, dining room, coffee shop, indoor heated pool,

sauna off I–25 Exit 64 at 3125 Sinton Road, 80907 (633–5541); *Howard Johnson's Motor Lodge* (rates: $32–39 double), 64 excellent rooms, restaurant, coffee shop, heated pool, north on I–25, Exit 65, at 4610 Rusina Road, 80707 (598–1700); *Ramada Airport Inn* (rates: $34–38 double), 154 excellent rooms, dining room, cocktail lounge, heated pool at Garden of the Gods Road and I–25 (596–7660); *Sheraton Motor Inn* (rates: $36.50 double), 104 excellent rooms and family units, dining room, cocktail lounge, heated pool, at 8110 N. Academy Blvd. 80918 (598–5770).

Cripple Creek

(Pop. 400: zip code 80813; area code 303.) This town at base of Mt. Pisgah was once a rough-and-ready gold-rush boom town that produced up to $25 million worth of gold in a single year. Many celebrities were associated with the town, including Lowell Thomas and Jack Dempsey, who once worked in the mines and won a long, bloody fight for a $50 purse. Area attractions include the Cripple Creek District Museum on Colorado Hwy. 67; the Old Homestead at 253 E. Myers Ave., once the town's red light district; Cripple Creek Industries Mollie Kathleen mine tour north of town on Hwy. 67; and the old rural mining towns of Elkton and Victor, south of Cripple Creek off Colorado Hwy. 67. Accommodations: *Imperial Hotel & Dining Room* (rates: $17–22 double), 30 rooms, authentic turn-of-the-century Victorian decor, dining, Gold Bar Room Summer Theatre, at 123 N. 3rd St. on Hwy. 67 (689–2922).

Lodges & Guest Ranches

★★★★*The Broadmoor Hotel and Ski Resort* encompasses a 5,000–acre complex with fine facilities for a broad spectrum of activities—golf on three 18–hole championship courses, tennis on 16 all-weather courts, ice skating, swimming, horseback riding, boating, fishing, and scenic tours of the beautiful Pikes Peak region. Ski facilities include 2 shops serviced by a double chair-lift, an expert ski school, and an inviting day lodge at the base of Cheyenne Mountain. The main slope at Broadmoor is ½ mile long with a 600–foot vertical drop; the bottom half is groomed for beginning to intermediate skiers, the top half is designed for experienced enthusiasts. A steeper side trail, 2,000 feet long and strictly for experts, departs from the main slope at the top and reenters at the halfway point. Snow-making machines and night skiing on floodlit slopes are additional attractions. Back at the hotel and recreation complex, a 5–minute drive away, there are 9 dining and beverage areas, ranging from the elegant Edwardian Penrose Room to the intimate Golden Bee Pub. Each restaurant has its own unusual touches, such as the live orchestra at luncheon and dinner in the glassed-in garden Terrace Room or the pewter and crystal table service at Charles Court. In addition there are lively spots for nightly entertainment, a movie theater, saunas and a steambath, shops and boutiques, convention facilities, guided tours of the Colorado Springs area, and all the other amenities characteristic of a world-famous resort. Accommodations are in handsome twin rooms ($45 daily, double occupancy), parlor suites (from $85 daily), double rooms ($55–85 daily), and deluxe suites (rates quoted on request). For more information write: The Broadmoor, Colorado Springs, CO 80901 (303)634–7711.

★★*Deckers Resort* has rustic housekeeping cabins on the South Fork of the South Platte River in the heart of Pike National Forest. Fishing is good here year-round for famous Colorado mountain trout; you can purchase licenses and gear in Deckers' fully stocked bait and tackle shop. Other attractions include hunting in season, nearby mineral springs, and the superb mountain scenery of Pike National Forest. Cabins are fully equipped with kitchens and basic eating and cooking utensils. Rates: $20 per night for 2 people, $28 per night for 4. Also on the premises, Deckers Restaurant offers a complete menu of fine foods and liquors in pleasant surroundings overlooking the South Platte River. This quiet backroads resort is only 52 miles southwest of Denver and 43 miles northwest of Colorado Springs. For additional information write: Deckers Resort, Route 2, Box 87, Sedalia, CO 80135 (303)647–2332.

★★★★*The Hearthstone Inn*, a handsome Victorian-style hotel in the heart of Colorado Springs, has been restored to mint condition and features 14 guest rooms with antique furnishings, excellent personalized service, and a wealth of extras—hand-stitched quilts, old-fashioned breakfasts, and a solid oak staircase—that give the inn its period charm. Every room has a private bath, except two rooms on the third floor which share a bath, and though the plumbing is fully modern, most have antique marble lavatories. Many of the inn's windows offer views of Pikes Peak in the distance; just behind the mansion is a rambling city park. City bus service is available to Colorado Springs' many fine restaurants, local museums, and other attractions. There's also a knowledgeable innkeeper on hand to help you plan visits to such Colorado milestones as the Garden of the Gods, Cripple Creek Gold-Mining District, Cheyenne Mountain Zoo, Cave of the Winds, and other Rocky Mountain landmarks. Rates range from $25 (double occupancy) for a "hideaway" gable room to $55 (double occupancy) for the deluxe Victorian suite. All rates include a hearty breakfast. For a complete description and history of the inn write: Hearthstone Inn, 506 North Cascade Ave., Colorado Springs, CO 80903 (303)473–4413.

★★★★*JVL Lost Valley Ranch* is a superb year-round family vacation and working cattle and horse ranch that has been in operation since 1883. Tucked away in the high country of the Pike National Forest, the ranch offers outstanding family accommodations and 28,000 acres of mountain meadows, forests, lakes, streams, and canyons for high-country trail rides, fishing, cross-country skiing, and hiking. Ranch facilities include the ranch house, trading post, tack room, Hay Loft Opera House, Rodeo Arena, trap shooting area, Chapel in the Pines, swimming pool, and tennis courts. Lost Valley accommodations consist of 26 modern, comfortably appointed cabins which contain a total of 44 guest rooms. Each cabin has a living room, and most contain fireplaces. An added feature is the absence of TV or phones in the cabins. The ranch prides itself in western cooking at its finest, served family-style in the rustic main lodge dining room. The complete American-plan price includes 3 meals daily, luxurious western accommodations, horseback riding, tennis courts, fishing in our own trout stream, swimming pool in the fall and spring, and all other activities except trapshooting and pack trips. Daily rates: $28–32 per person. A full 7–day week costs $196–224 per person. Special rates available for children 10 years of age and under. The Lost Valley Ranch wagon will meet your plane in either Colorado Springs or Denver. For additional information, contact: Robert Foster, General Manager, JVL Lost Valley Ranch, Deckers Rt. 2, Sedalia, CO 80135 (303)647–2311.

★★★★*Tumbling River Ranch* is located high in the heart of the Rockies about 50 miles southwest of Denver, surrounded by the Pike National Forest with its millions of acres of unspoiled country, alpine meadows, mountain lakes, and streams. The snowcapped peaks of the Continental Divide are within riding distance to the west, and Mt. Evans—with the world's highest auto roads—is to the east. Pikes Peak can be seen from the ranch. Ranch wildlife includes elk, deer, bear, mountain goats, beaver, and a large band of bighorn sheep, which can often be seen from the dining room of the main ranch house. The ranch is located along about 5 miles of Geneva Creek (the Tumbling River). The accommodations are in two clusters—the Upper Ranch and the Lower Ranch—which are about a half-mile apart (a very pleasant walk along the creek). The original homestead cabin, built around the turn of the century, is still the favorite of many old guests. The Upper Ranch House and the Lower Ranch Pueblo were both built during the 1920s and reflect a rustic quality that can no longer be duplicated. An early mayor of Denver built the Upper Ranch House as his mountain home, and it still retains the original warmth and charm. It contains 5 guest bedrooms (each with its own fireplace and bath), the dining room for the upper ranch, a large living room with huge stone fireplace and superb view, and a lounge (B.Y.O.). Also at the upper ranch are half a dozen cabins (typically with two separate units that can be opened to adjoin). Each unit has a private bath and fireplace. In addition, there is a heated pool, sauna, game room with Ping-Pong, pool, etc., office owners' homes, corral, trading post, and a pond stocked with trout. The Lower Ranch Pueblo is truly a showplace. It was built by the daughter of Adloph Coors as her mountain home. Indians from Taos were used in the construction and the carving of decorative beams. The Spanish-Indian decor is extraordinary. The Pueblo has 7 guest bedrooms, each with a fireplace, as well as a dining room, living room with huge fireplace, game room, and lounge. The old homestead cabin is just across Three Mile Creek from the Pueblo. The ranch takes great pride in its home-cooked meals, breads, and pastries. Typical dinners feature steak, turkey, ham, prime rib, trout, or barbecued ribs, and there are also excellent cookouts, lunches, and dinners. Twenty miles to the north of the ranch is historic old Georgetown, which a century ago became known as the Silver Queen, the silver-mining capital of the Rockies. Its old homes and stores are extremely well preserved for visitors to enjoy. The main ranch is at 9,200 feet, far too high for poisonous snakes or hay fever plants. Summer activities include hiking, fishing, backpacking, and trail rides in the surrounding high country. Winter activities include cross-country skiing and downhill skiing at the nearby Geneva Ski Basin. Geneva has two double chair-lifts, two Poma lifts, and 20 runs. Waiting time for getting on the slope is minimal. There are ample trails for beginning, intermediate, and advanced skiers. Runs include both wooded trails and open-slope skiing. And Geneva uses its modern snow-making equipment to insure that skiing surfaces are always ready for skiers. The ski area prides itself in the quality of its ski instruction. The Geneva Ski School offers classes for beginning, intermediate, and advanced skiers, and even for little children in the Nursery Ski School. There are separate slopes for each level of skiing expertise. Also available at Geneva is a nursery for the small fries and a fine rental shop, cafeteria, lounge, and shop. You may contact Geneva Basin directly by calling (303)789–1426 or by writing to them at Post Office Box 65, Grant, CO 80448. Tumbling River American-plan summer rates, which include lodging, meals, horses with wranglers, jeep trips, children's counselors, fishing, heated pool, sauna, and evening activities, are $275 weekly per person, double occupancy. Winter rates, which include lodging, breakfast, dinner, shuttle to and from Geneva Ski Basin, ice skating, sledding, and use of all ranch facilities, are $30 per person per day on holidays and weekends and $25 on weekdays. Special rates available for children under 12. For additional information, contact: Tumbling River Ranch, Grant, CO 80448 (303)838–5981.

Travel Services

Black Forest Glider Port, 30 minutes from downtown Colorado Springs, specializes in glider instruction, with lessons ranging from a 20–minute introductory flight ($20) to 27–flight soaring courses ($495) which will prepare you for high-performance sailplanes. Individual instruction begins at $12 per hour. Sailplane rentals, airplane tow, and hangar facilities are also available. Campsites and accommodations in the Lennie Inn Motel. Write: Black Forest Glider Port, 9990 Gliderport Road, Colorado Springs, CO 80908 (303) 495–4144.

Colorado Youth Soaring Camp, operated by Black Forest Glider Port, offers soaring instructions and backpacking for young people 14–18 years of age. Instruction is given by professional, FAA-licensed flight instructors, and is custom designed for each student, depending on experience. Excellent soaring conditions exist along the magnificent front range of the Rockies, and only the finest training sailplanes are used. Daily ground-school sessions complement the in-flight instruction. Backpacking trips explore the Sangre de Cristo Range and the Lost Creek Area of the Pike National Forest. Trips are supervised by Backcountry Adventures, a Colorado Springs-based group backed by many years of experience in wilderness skills. Inclusive fee for 10–day soaring adventures is $760; for 10 days of soaring and 4 days of backcountry camping, the inclusive fee is $870. Write: Colorado Youth Soaring Camp, c/o Black Forest Glider Port, 9990 Gliderport Road, Colorado Springs, CO 80908.

Rio Grande National Forest

This 1.8–million-acre reserve of scenic high-country forest lies along the eastern slope of the Continental Divide, embracing portions of the spectacular San Juan and Sangre de Cristo mountains. This is the region of the headwaters of the historic Rio Grande del Norte, the "Great River of the North," whose famous trophy rainbow and brown trout waters plunge through the rugged Upper Rio Grande

Wild Area. Between the 14,000–foot heights of the ranges, the fertile San Luis Valley of southern Colorado stretches for a hundred miles. The Alamosa, Conejos, and Rio Grande rivers flow easterly to the valley where they form the Rio Grande del Norte. The "Great River of the North" makes an oxbow bend in the valley and heads south to New Mexico, where it begins a long journey to the Gulf of Mexico far beyond. The San Juan Mountains in the western portion of the forest had their beginnings some 60 million years ago with a great outpouring of molten lava from beneath the earth. Later, faulting raised the mountains higher. Streams falling from great heights carved deep canyons. Today the mountain slopes are covered with fir, blue and Engelmann spruce, and aspen. In autumn the aspen flashes gold amid the green. Cottonwood groves border the river, and ponderosa pine grows in the drier areas. The scenic 58,014–acre Upper Rio Grande Wild Area includes the Rio Grande Reservoir, Vallecito Trail, Ute Creek, Simpson Mountain, Rio Grande Pyramid, and Weminuche Pass. Big game includes elk, mule deer, black bear, bobcat, mountain lion, and a few bighorn sheep.

The forest has hundreds of miles of remote wilderness trails for hiking, backpacking, horseback riding, and pack trips. One of the most exciting backcountry areas of the forest is the famous La Garita Wilderness lying astride the Continental Divide, the natural barrier between the Rio Grande National Forest and Gunnison National Forest to the northwest. The wilderness encompasses some 49,000 acres of alpine meadows, rushing streams, and towering peaks. The mountains rise to the heights of San Luis and Stewart peaks, over 14,000 feet in elevation. Glaciers have carved steep talus slopes and formed rocky deposits in the craggy heights where bear, coyote, and mountain lion roam. In the summer, elk, deer, and mountain sheep range the heights; ptarmigan, blue grouse, and coney also inhabit the slopes. Beaver dams are found along the snow-fed streams, whose waters hold native cutthroat and Eastern brook trout.

Information Sources, Maps & Access

Detailed information, a full-color *Rio Grande National Forest Map* (50¢), and the free *La Garita Wilderness Map/Brochure* and *Guide to High-Country Auto Tours in the Rio Grande National Forest* may be obtained from: Supervisor, Rio Grande National Forest, 1803 W. Hwy. 160, Monte Vista, CO 81144 (303)852–3801.

The auto tour guide covers three car tours which begin in the San Luis Valley between the two major sections of the Rio Grande National Forest, swing up into the mountains surrounding the valley in different directions, and swing back down again into another part of the 100–mile valley. Areas visited include the San Juan and Sangre de Cristo mountains and the headwaters of the Conejos, Alamosa, and Rio Grande rivers.

The forest is reached via U.S. Highways 50, 160, 84, and 285 and via Colorado Highways 149 and 114. Lodging, guides, supplies, and outfitters are available at the towns of Del Norte, Monte Vista, Alamosa, La Garita, Saguache, Baxterville, Creede, and Wagon Wheel Gap.

Gateways & Accommodations

Alamosa—Gateway to Great Sand Dunes National Monument

(Pop. 7,000; zip code 81101; area code 303.) The town is located at the junction of U.S. 160 and 285 on the Rio Grande River. Area attractions include Pike's Stockade, a replica of a log stockade built by Zebulon Pike in 1807, 12 miles south of town off U.S. 285; and Fort Garland State Historical Monument, a restored army post, commanded by Kit Carson in 1866–67. The mysterious, colorful Great Sand Dunes National Monument with its shifting 700–foot-high ridges, disappearing rivers, Indian Springs water hole, and wild horses, is located in the San Luis Valley. The valley lies along the 10–mile base of the Sangre de Cristo Mountains. Scientists have unearthed Folsom spear points here dating back 10,000 years. The monument is 35 miles northeast of Alamosa via U.S. 160 and Colorado Hwy. 150. For information contact: Superintendent, Box 60, Alamosa 81101 (378–2312). For information on Great Sand Dunes jeep tours, contact: Box 1165, Alamosa (378–2222). Accommodations: *Best Western Alamosa Inn* (rates: $26–35 double), 143 excellent rooms and family units, restaurant, indoor heated pool, at 1919 Main St., 1 mile west of town on U.S. 160/285 (589–2567).

Antonito

(Pop. 1,100; zip code 81120; area code 303.) The town is situated on U.S. 285 just north of the New Mexico border. The narrow-gauge Cumbus & Toltec Scenic Railroad offers sight-seeing rides between Antonito and Chama, New Mexico. For reservations and information, contact: Box 668, Antonito (376–5483). Accommodations: *Narrow Gauge Railroad Inn* (rates: $24–27 double), 32 excellent rooms, restaurant on U.S. 285, 1 block south of the railroad depot (376–5441).

Del Norte

(Pop. 1,600; zip code 81132; area code 303.) A Rio Grande National Forest gateway with a district ranger office located on U.S. 160. Accommodations: *El Rancho Motel* (rates: $16 double), 16 rooms on U.S. 160 (657–3332).

Monte Vista

(Pop. 3,900; zip code 81144; area code 303.) On U.S. 160/285. Area attractions include Rio Grande River and Monte Vista National Wildlife Refuge. Accommodations: *Best Western Movie Manor Motel* (rates: $28–34 double), 37 rooms, restaurant, cocktail lounge, 2 miles west of town on U.S. 160 (852–5921).

Lodges & Guest Ranches

★★★*The Balloon Ranch* is an unusual and provocative enterprise: a full-service resort devoted to the art of ballooning. The ranch has its own 140–acre spread of wide-open spaces in the San Luis Valley, bordered by the Great Sand Dunes and Rio Grande National Park, where novice and seasoned aeronauts can indulge in long and leisurely flights under near-perfect weather and observation conditions. A special 2–day introductory package provides basic instruction in this incredible sport, or you can take advantage of private

lessons, complete certification courses, and hourly rides with a professional pilot. In addition to ballooning, the ranch offers a number of earthbound activities, such as fishing, river rafting, horseback riding, tennis, and Nordic and alpine skiing in season. The main lodge is decorated in handsome earth colors and features beamed ceilings, natural wood furnishings, a congenial dining room, and a big stone fireplace. A whirlpool and sauna are on hand for après-balloon relaxation. Single, double, and family guest rooms are available for an intimate total of 22 guests at a time. All rooms are fully carpeted and have good views of the countryside. Double-occupancy package rates, including lodging, all meals, 1 balloon ride, tennis, and basic ranch facilities, are $70 per person for 2 nights, 3 days; $130 per person for 4 nights, 5 days; and $210 per person for 7 nights, 8 days. For a complete rate schedule and further details write: The Balloon Ranch, Star Route, Box 41, Del Norte, CO 81132 (303)754–2533.

★★★*Boca Grande Inn & Resort* is a 150,000–acre working ranch located in the Sangre de Cristo mountains, bordered on the north by the Rio Grande National Forest and on the south by the Great Sand Dunes National Monument. The Boca Grande Inn and A-frame chalets offer comfortable, spacious accommodations and services. Ranch activities include horseback riding on trails in the mountains, meadows, and forests, golf, tennis, fishing in the private ranch lake and forest lakes and streams, and fall hunting trips for elk and deer in the national forest lands. Area attractions include the Great Sand Dunes and the partially restored Independence Gold Mine, from which $50 million in gold was mined in its 1880 boom. Boca Grande is located just off Colorado Highway 17 near Crestone. For rates and info, contact: P.O. Box 126, Crestone, CO 81131 (303)256–4311.

★★*Broadacres Guest Ranch* is an intimate resort high in the Rockies offering 12 comfortable, river-view cottages. The famous Rio Grande runs for miles through the ranch and provides excellent fishing for stocked rainbows and German browns. There are also 2 fine lakes heavily stocked with Eastern brookies, rainbows, and natives. Horseback trips are available direct from the ranch to the top of Table Mountain, where one of Colorado's highest table lakes boasts fine angling for Yellowstone natives. Other trails explore the streams and mountain meadows around Miners, Rat, and Shallow creeks. Gentle saddle horses and picnic grounds are perfect for family excursions. All cottages are well equipped for housekeeping with dishes, pots, pans, linens, etc. Rates vary from $12 to $65 daily dependent on the size of the cottages and number of guests. For more information write: Broadacres Guest Ranch, Creede, CO 81130.

★★★*Hamilton's Rainbow Trout Lodges & Dude Ranch,* located in the Conejos River Canyon of south-central Colorado's San Juan Mountains, occupies a lush and beautiful site surrounded by the Rio Grande National Forest. There are over 50 miles of stocked trout streams along the Conejos, Elk Creek, and their tributaries, plus a generous handful of jewellike mountain lakes, some within walking distance of the lodge. Opportunities for horseback trips abound, and the lodge offers complete pack trip equipage, including experienced guides and skillful cooks to attend the chores and horses. Other activities at Hamilton's include swimming in the big outdoor pool, tennis, volleyball, and a full spectrum of evening entertainments. Modern aspen cabins have pine paneling, open fireplaces, a minimum of 2 bedrooms, and attractive furnishings. Daily rates of $70 for 2 include 3 meals a day, lodging, horseback riding, and other activities. For full information write: (before June 1) Rainbow Trout Lodges, 32453 Upper Bear Creek Road, Evergreen, CO (303)674–7149); (after June 1) Antonito, CO 81120 (303)376–5659.

Rocky Mountain National Park

This famous fishing, backpacking, and camping preserve lies in a spectacular setting of high peaks and mountain valleys, forests, and alpine tundra along the central Front Range stretch of the Continental Divide. Here, nestled among the high peaks, lies Grand Lake, the state's largest natural body of water and the headwaters of the mighty Colorado River. Huge glaciers have carved gulches, canyons, and hundreds of cirques into the mountains. At the time our country declared its independence, this area formed part of New Spain's northern frontier and was inhabited by Hopi Indians. It was not until 1860 that Joel Estes, the first known American settler of the area, arrived here. (He later moved his family out of the area, after two or three other families followed him, complaining of too many people.) The beauty of the region soon became famous. The Rocky Mountain National Park was created in 1915. More than 300 miles of trails lead through such remote sections of the park as the Wild Basin Area, a mountain valley with a spectacular variety of lakes, waterfalls, and icy mountain streams; Tahosa Valley; Bear Lake country in the heart of the park; Glacier Gorge and Loch Vale in the famous Longs Peak area; the glacial lakes of Moraine Park and Odessa Gorge; the distant Mummy Range; the rock formations of Lumpy Ridge; and the trout waters of the North Fork Big Thompson River.

The popular Shadow Mountain National Recreation Area borders the southwest portion of the park. Lake Granby and Shadow Mountain Lake are man-made reservoirs in this area which fill portions of the Colorado River valley. The area is open to boating, fishing, and hunting. Deer, coyote, bobcat, red fox, yellowbelly marmot, chipmunk, badger, pine squirrel, ground squirrel, and beaver inhabit the region. Rainbow, lake, and brown trout and kokanee salmon are taken in the two major lakes.

Information Sources, Maps & Access

Vacation travel information, a free *Rocky Mountain National Park Map/Brochure*, a free *Shadow Mountain NRA Map/Brochure*, and free pamphlets may be obtained from: Superintendent, Rocky Mountain National Park, Estes Park, CO 80517 (303)586–2371. A special U.S. Geological Survey *Rocky Mountain National Park Map* shows the park and adjacent areas on a scale of 1 mile to 1 inch. It is published in a 29– by 39–inch shaded-relief or contour edition for $2. The full-color U.S. Geological Survey *Denver Mountain Area*

Map (available for $2 in either a shaded-relief or a topographic edition) shows the eastern slope of the Front Range of the Rockies, including Rocky Mountain National Park and portions of the Arapaho, Roosevelt, and Routt national forests. Both maps may be ordered from: Distribution Branch, U.S. Geological Survey, Federal Center, Denver, CO 80225.

The park is accessible by State Highway 72 running northwest from Denver, or U.S. Highway 34 running west from Interstate 25 through Loveland. One of the most spectacular scenic auto routes in the nation is the Grand Loop Tour from Denver to Boulder, along the Longs Peak Route to Estes Park, through the park, over the Great Divide, along the Trail Ridge Road to Grand Lake and Idaho Springs. Within the park, Trail Ridge Road from Estes Park to Grand Lake traverses the crest of the Rockies and includes an awesome 4-mile section over 12,000 feet; Bear Lake Road along Glacier Creek to Bear Lake begins at the Beaver Meadows entrance.

Gateways & Accommodations

For additional gateway information and accommodations, see "Arapaho National Forest" and "Roosevelt National Forest."

Estes Park Village—Eastern Gateway to Rocky Mountain National Park

(Pop. 1,600; zip code 80517; area code 303.) This is the major gateway to the Rocky Mountain National Park and the famous Longs Peak area. Area attractions include the scenic Bear Lake and Trail Ridge roads, Aerial Tramway to the summit of Prospect Mountain, Ripley's Believe It or Not Museum at 145 Elkshorn Ave. on U.S. Hwy. 34, Hidden Valley Ski Area, Big Thompson Canyon east of town on U.S. 34, MacGregor Ranch & Pioneer Museum on Devil's Gulch Road ½ mile north of town, and scenic park tours. Area restaurants include the *Black Canyon* (586–4648), *National Park Village* (586–3183), and the famous *Old Plantation* (586–2800). Accommodations: *Aspen Lodge* (rates: $29–33 double), 23 excellent lodge rooms and family cottage units in scenic location below Longs Peak on Longs Peak Route (586–4241); *Estes Village Motor Inn* (rates: $32–38 double), 29 excellent rooms and family units, balconies with scenic view, heated pool, at 1040 Big Thompson Ave. (586–5338); *Fawn Valley Inn & Chalets* (rates: $26–40 double), 40 excellent family chalet kitchen units and rooms, with balconies, fireplaces, pool, on the beautiful Fall River, at 3700 Fall River Road, 1 mile from park entrance (586–2388); *Hobby Horse Motor Lodge* (rates: $28–38 double), 52 superb rooms and family units, heated pool, trout pond, adjacent to golf course, 1 mile east of town on U.S. Hwy. 34 at 800 Big Thompson Ave. (586–3336); *Holiday Inn* (rates: $36–38 double), 155 excellent rooms, dining room, coffee shop, heated indoor pool, sauna, at 101 S. St. Vrain Hwy. (586–2332); *Inn at Estes Park* (rates: $34–36 double), 147 superb rooms and family units, dining room, coffee shop, cocktail lounge, heated pool, sauna, at 1701 Big Thompson Ave., U.S. 34 (586–5363); *Lake Estes Best Western Motor Inn* (rates: $34–42 double), 58

outstanding rooms and family units, heated pool on U.S. 34 East (586–3386); *McGregor Mountain Lodge* (rates: $34 double), 19 excellent cottage units overlooking the Fall River Canyon, next to the park boundary west of town on U.S. 34 (586–3457); *Tyrol Motor Inn* (rates: $30–36 double), a beautiful alpine luxury inn, 54 spacious rooms with scenic views, adjacent to Edel Haus Restaurant, heated pool, sauna, east of town on U.S. 34 (586–3382); *Wind River Ranch* (rates: $440 weekly, American Plan), 20 rustic lodge rooms and family cottages on guest ranch, heated pool, trail rides and instruction, children's counselor, near base of Longs Peak, 7 miles south of town on Hwy. 7 (586–4212).

Grand Lake Village—Western Gateway to Rocky Mountain National Park

(Pop. 200; zip code 80447; area code 303.) The town is located on the northern shore of glacial Grand Lake, at the western end of scenic Trail Ridge Road. Grand Lake, the headwaters of the Colorado River, is the largest glacial lake in the state, believed by the Ute Indians to be a place of evil spirits. It was created aeons ago, when the valley of the Colorado was dammed by a moraine. Area attractions include National Park Service field trips and lectures, cross-country skiing, fishing, backpacking, boating, and the *Corner Cupboard Inn* for fine dining in a historic 19th-century building on Main St. (627–3813). During the summer, sailing regattas are held by the Grand Lake Yacht Club. Accommodations: *Baven Haven Lodge* (rates: $30–32 double), 23 excellent lodge rooms and cottages, spacious restaurant dining room, heated pool, beach, boats and outdoor activities, just south of Main St. (627–3381); *Driftwood Lodge* (rates: $20–28 double), 15 rooms and family units, overlooking Shadow Mountain Lake, heated pool, 3 miles south of the village on U.S. Hwy. 34 (627–3654); *Lemmon Lodge* (rates: $32–48 double), 20 rooms and family units on Grand Lake south of Main St. (627–3314).

Lodges & Guest Ranches

★★★*Indian Head Guest Ranch* is located in a quiet, secluded valley (7,800 feet) surrounded by the forests and lakes of Rocky Mountain National Park and Roosevelt National Forest. Your days here are filled with horseback rides over quiet mountain trails, hiking around majestic peaks, and fishing the many remote, well-stocked streams and lakes in the area. Creature comforts at the ranch include a heated swimming pool, excellent western cooking, and fully carpeted cabins with controlled central heating, tubs or showers, and stone fireplaces. Nearby Estes Park offers other pleasures, such as an 18–hole golf course, weekly rodeos and horse shows, movie houses, and a summer theater. Indian Head's season begins June 1. Guest accommodations are limited to 45 at a time. Double-occupancy rates for adults are $225 weekly ($34 daily) per person and include lodgings, all meals, riding, maid service, and use of ranch facilities. Children's rates are available. For more details write: Indian Head Ranch, P.O. Box 2260, Estes Park, CO 80517 (summer (303)586–5291; winter (303)586–5412).

★★★★*Lane Guest Ranch*, just under 70 miles from Denver, is located high in the mountains overlooking Rocky Mountain National Park and some of the most spectacular scenery in the West. Horseback riding, swimming, fishing for trout, and overnight pack trips are just a few of the activities offered. This is a small and secluded resort, accommodating 65 guests at a time in handsome rooms with carpeting, private baths, daily maid service, and huge picture windows surrounded by beautiful, naturally landscaped grounds. Superb meals are served in a poolside dining room with breakfast on a sunny patio. The climate—dry, clear, and temperate—is especially conducive to memorable vacations. Seven-night package plans, including accommodations, all dinners and breakfasts, entertainment, guides, horses, and overnight trips are $294 per person; children under 12, $154. Daily rates are $50 per person per day; $30 daily for children under 12. For full information write: Lane Guest Ranch, P.O. Box 1766 GO, Estes Park, CO 80517 (303)747–2493.

★★★★*Longs Peak Inn & Guest Ranch*, at the foot of the highest peak in Rocky Mountain Park, offers full-scale resort accommodations in an unspoiled setting only 65 miles northwest of Denver. Reliable, trail-wise horses are on hand for short and all-day trail rides to high-country meadows and lakes, for mouth-watering breakfast and lunch cookouts, or for overnight pack trips to a remote spot in the wilderness. Fishermen will find trout ponds right on the property, plus lakes and streams within walking or riding distance. There's also a large heated pool with a sun deck, a glass-walled dining room with gorgeous views, game rooms, a lounge with fireplace, and an intimate bar and lounge overlooking still more mountains. The surrounding area has many attractions, too: the bustling village of Estes Park, 2 excellent golf courses, Lake Estes, and the 405–square-mile wonderland of Rocky Mountain National Park. Accommodations are available for 80–90 guests at a time in either individual bedrooms with baths at the main lodge or in a nearby guest building. Adjoining bedroom units are available for families and groups. Rates vary from $26 to $29 per person daily (modified American plan), depending on size and location of rooms. Full American-plan

rates, weekly packages, and children's rates are available. For details write: Longs Peak Inn, Longs Peak Route, Estes Park, CO 80517 (summer (303)586–2110; winter (303)586–2639).

★★★*Machins Cottages in the Pines*, in Rocky Mountain National Park, are located at the foot of Eagle Cliff Mountain on the edge of Beaver Brook Valley. All 16 cottages occupy secluded settings shaded by tall pines on 14 private acres. There are radios, color televisions, completely equipped kitchens, and attractive furnishings in each cottage, and most have fireplaces. Cottages vary in size from large studio-type layouts with separate kitchen/dining areas ($150 per week) to spacious 3–bedroom cabins with picture windows, patios, and balconies ($325 per week). The village of Estes Park, a 10–minute drive away, offers shops, grocery stores, and laundromats. Also in the village are municipal golf courses, a swimming pool, and tennis courts. The area abounds in opportunities for horseback riding, wildlife photography, fishing, and other outdoor activities. For further information write: Machins Cottages in the Pines, P.O. Box 88, Estes Park, CO 80517 (303)586–4276.

★★★*Valhalla at Estes* offers 17 inviting cottages spaced well apart on 6 acres of pine-shaded grounds at the base of Eagle Cliff Mountain. The complex borders Rocky Mountain National Park and is just a brief walk away from the Big Thompson River and many good fishing lakes. If horseback riding is your sport, there are several fine stables within half a mile. Valhalla is open year-round, so guests can take advantage of the excellent ski facilities at Hidden Valley or snowshoe through the silent winter wilderness surrounding the cabins. Each of Valhalla's cottages is attractively furnished with fully equipped modern kitchens, at least one separate bedroom, tub/shower combination baths, wall-to-wall carpeting, and fireplaces with plenty of wood. All have black-and-white or color TV. Rates vary from $21 per day ($135 weekly) for a 1–bedroom cottage accommodating 5 guests to $45 per day ($290 weekly) for a spacious log cabin with 3 bedrooms, a Hollywood bed, and sofa bed. Also on the premises are volleyball and basketball courts, a library, recreation room, and heated wading pool. For additional information write: Valhalla at Estes, P.O. Box 1439, Estes Park, CO 80517.

★★*The Water Wheel*, just 1½ miles from Estes Park and 3 miles from the entrance to Rocky Mountain National Park, offers attractive log cabins, completely paneled, with interior balconies, a large living/dining area, 1 or 2 bedrooms, and handsome stone fireplaces. Cabins sleep 2–8 guests and vary in price from $20 daily for a small unit with a kitchenette to $37 daily for a 2–bedroom, balconied unit with sleeping space for 8. Cabins are fully furnished with linens, gas heat, showers, and cable color TV. Area activities include skiing at Hidden Valley (10 miles away), horseback riding at nearby stables, fishing on Fall River, and hiking. For further details write: The Water Wheel, Estes Park, CO 80517 (303)586–3100.

Travel Services

Rocky Mountain Ski Tours in Estes Park has been in operation since 1970 and is thus the oldest pure Nordic school in Colorado. Ski-touring instruction runs the gamut from 1–day classes covering any phase of touring to 3– and 5–day courses aimed at teaching all the basics and preparation for more strenuous touring. Regular day tours cover the spectacular trails in Rocky Mountain National Park and are accompanied by a guide-instructor to help you with minor problems of technique. Rocky Mountain Ski Tours also offers complete rentals for downhill and cross-country skiing, private classes in touring, and special programs in skills for instructors. "Senior Skis" is an adaptation of standard courses for older persons with special emphasis on individually paced instruction. For information write: Rocky Mountain Ski Tours, Box 413, Estes Park, CO 80517 (303)586–3553.

Roosevelt National Forest & The Rawah Wilderness

The Roosevelt National Forest encompasses 776,000 acres of top-ranked fishing, wilderness camping, and big-game-hunting country along the Continental Divide north and east of Rocky Mountain National Park. This is the region of the Laramie and Medicine Bow mountains arching down from Wyoming and the remote Mummy Range. The Laramie, St. Vrain, Boulder, and Cache la Poudre rivers flow through the evergreen and broadleaf forests of the mountain high country. The famous rainbow and brown trout waters of the Cache la Poudre rise in the Divide area at Poudre Lakes and roar through steep-walled canyons to the valleys of the High Plains. The name of the river derives from a tale of the Old West. In 1836 a group of French trappers were traveling by wagon through the rugged high country of the region, and a snowstorm overtook them. They were forced to lighten their wagon loads and cache their supplies, including a large amount of gunpowder, in the Rist Canyon area at the site of the present-day Early Trappers Monument. The name Cache la Poudre means "cache of powder." They recovered their hidden supplies the following spring. The canyon of the Cache la Poudre River is a popular vacationing area with good trout fishing.

The Brainard Lake Recreation Area in the forest is a popular gateway to the Indian Peaks backcountry. Glaciers carved these mountains about 100,000 years ago, creating their striking features. The Isabelle and Arapaho glaciers are remnants of these huge ice masses. Snowbeds lace the mountain crags, and glacial lakes fill the cirques left by the glaciation. The Indian Peaks area straddles the border between the Roosevelt and Arapaho national forests. About 55,000 acres of this area have been closed to motor vehicle travel and man-made developments and are being considered for inclusion in the National Wilderness System. Such trails as the Arapaho Pass, Arapaho Glacier, Devil's Thumb Pass, Kings Lake, High Lonesome, and Corona wind through the high country of these 12,000–foot peaks. Some of the trails are accessible from the Brainard Lake recreation area.

Another remote area, the Rawah Wilderness, encompasses some of the most beautiful backcountry in the forest. The wilderness area includes 27,000 acres of isolated alpine lakes, rocky peaks, evergreen forests, and abundant wildlife. Elevations in this majestic "island of wilderness" range from 9,500 to nearly 13,000 feet. Thick blankets of snow cover the area from November to June, providing water for the plains below. The area contains some beautiful wilderness stretches of the famed Laramie River, one of Colorado's top fly-fishing streams for rainbows and browns in the 5–7-pound class. The 26 high-country lakes of the wilderness area, including Camp, Rawah, Chambers, Twin Crater, and Island, and its many streams provide excellent fishing for rainbow, brook, native, Mackinaw, kokanee, and grayling. Mountain sheep, black bear, mule deer, and occasional elk roam the mountain heights. Other wildlife includes beaver, coyote, fox, mink, marten, rabbits, and squirrels. Mountain ptarmigan and grouse are the game birds of the area.

Information Sources, Maps & Access

Detailed vacation travel information and the full-color *Roosevelt National Forest Map* (50¢) and *Rawah Wilderness Map* (50¢) may be obtained from: Supervisor, Roosevelt National Forest, Fort Collins, CO 80521 (303)482–5155.

The forest is accessible by way of State Highway 119 west from Boulder or State Highway 7 leading west from Interstate 25. Lodg-

ing, guides, supplies, outfitters, and high-country packers are available at Fort Collins, Poudre Park, Owl Canyon, Rustic, Livermore, Virginia Dale, Red Feather Lakes, Logcabin, Loveland, Longmont, and Boulder.

The Roosevelt National Forest offers excellent ski mountaineering and tours. The Poudre and Redfeather Ranger Districts, 148 Remington St., Fort Collins 80521, offer a guide to winter wilderness travel in this area. This free guide, *Winter Backcountry Use Information—Ski Touring & Ski Mountaineering*, describes about 20 tours for cross-country skiers throughout the forest and in Rocky Mountain National Park.

Gateways & Accommodations

For additional gateway info and accommodations, see "Denver" under "Arapaho National Forest" and "Estes Park" under "Rocky Mountain National Park."

Boulder

(Pop. 66,900; zip code 80302; area code 303.) Colorado's major educational and scientific center is located in a beautiful valley under Flagstaff Mountain near the Flatirons. The city's water supply comes from the Arapaho Glacier on the east slope of the Continental Divide. Boulder is the headquarters of the Boulder Mountain Park System. Area attractions include the native sandstone and red tile buildings of the University of Colorado, University Museum and Fiske Planetarium, Pioneer Museum at Broadway and Arapaho Sts., National Center for Atmospheric Research at 1850 Table Mesa Drive, Flagstaff Scenic Highway, the Colorado Shakespeare Festival at the University of Colorado (July-August, 492–8181), and superb dining at the *Flagstaff House* on Flagstaff Road (442–4640) and the *Greenbriar* on Lefthand Canyon Road (442–9531). Accommodations: *Best Western Boulder Inn* (rates: $33–36 double), with 100 excellent rooms, restaurant, coffee shop, heated pool, sauna, at 770 28th St. near university campus (449–3800); *Best Western Golden Bluff Motor Lodge* (rates: $30 double), 75 excellent rooms and family units, coffee shop, heated pool, sauna, at 1725 28th St. (442–7450); *The Broker Inn* (rates: $41 double), 122 superb rooms and family units, dining room, coffee shop, heated indoor pool, sauna, at 555 30th St. at university campus (444–3330); *Hilton Harvest House Hotel* (rates: $44 double), 150 outstanding rooms and family units with fireplaces and kitchens, some with balconies, dining room, coffee shop, heated pool, tennis courts, at 1345 28th St. (443–3850); *Holiday Inn* (rates: $40–42 double), 113 excellent rooms, dining room, cocktail lounge, at 800 28th St. (443–3322); *Rodeway Inn* (rates: $32–35 double), 76 excellent rooms, dining room, cocktail lounge, heated pool, at 5397 Table Mesa Drive off Denver-Boulder Turnpike (U.S. 36) (499–4422).

Fort Collins

(Pop. 43,300; zip code 80521; area code 303.) This is the headquarters of the Roosevelt National Forest and a major industrial and cattle feed center on U.S. 287. Area attractions include the famous trout waters of the Cache La Poudre Canyon and the Rawah alpine lake country, Colorado State Forest Preserve, Horsetooth Reservoir, Colorado State University, Fort Collins Museum at 200 Mathews St., and 6 scenic auto circle tours, including the Red Feather Lakes & Deadman Lookout Tour, Buckhorn Valley Tour, Rist Canyon Tour, Ghost Tour, Stage Route Tour, Laramie River & the Rawahs Tour, and the Cache La Poudre Canyon Route, which goes through historic Indian country to Greyrock, a rustlers' hideout; old gold mines at Seven Mile Creek; Zimmerman Ranch; Virginia Dale, haunt of the Slade gang; and the Forks, an old stagecoach-era hotel. Accommodations: *Best Western Lamplighter* (rates: $28–40 double),

39 rooms, heated pool, at 1809 N. College Ave. (484–2764); *Best Western University Motor Inn* (rates: $26–32 double), 77 excellent rooms and family units, restaurant, heated pool, across from the university at 914 S. College Ave. (484–1984); *Fort Collins Best Western* (rates: $26–32 double), 35 rooms and family units, coffee shop, heated pool, at 2612 S. College Ave. (226–2600); *Ramada Inn* (rates: $26.75–40 double, 139 excellent rooms and family units, dining room, restaurant, coffee shop, heated pool, at 3709 E. Mulberry (493–7800).

Greeley

(Pop. 38,900; zip code 80631; area code 303.) This gateway to Roosevelt National Forest was founded by Nathan Meeker, the agricultural editor of Horace Greeley's New York *Tribune*. Area attractions of the farming and cattle center include the Meeker Home, built in 1870, at 1324 9th Ave.; and Fort Vasquez, a reconstructed fur-trading post, 17 miles south of town on U.S. Hwy. 85. Accommodations: *Best Western of Greeley* (rates: $26 double), 49 excellent rooms, dining room, cocktail lounge, heated pool, at 800 31st St. (353–2492); *Holiday Inn* (rates: $31–34 double), 100 excellent rooms, dining room, cocktail lounge, heated pool, at 609

8th Ave. (356–3000); *Ramada Inn* (rates: $28 double), 80 excellent rooms and family units, dining room, cocktail lounge, heated pool, at 330 W. Service Road on U.S. 85 (353–5900).

Longmont

(Pop. 23,200; zip code 80501; area code 303.) The city, on U.S. 287, is named after nearby Longs Peak to the west and is in the heart of Colorado's famous sugar beet country. Accommodations: *Best Western Longmont Lamplighter* (rates: $24–28 double), 54 excellent rooms and family units, heated pool, at 1642 N. Main St. (776–7620); *Centennial Inn* (rates: $28.50 double), 71 excellent rooms, dining room, cocktail lounge, heated indoor pool, at 3815 Hwy. 119 off I–25 Exit 118 (776–8700).

Loveland

(Pop. 16,200; zip code 80537; area code 303.) Known as the Sweetheart Town because of the popular tradition of using the post office to mail valentines, Loveland is on the U.S. 287 route to Estes Park and Rocky Mountain National Park. Accommodations: *Best Western Mile 254 Inn* (rates: $25–28 double), 33 rooms and family units, heated pool, at 2716 S.E. Frontage St. off I–25 Exit 123 (667–5202); *Coach House Best Western Motor Inn* (rates: $31.75 double), 63 excellent rooms, dining room, coffee shop, cocktail lounge, at 5542 E. U.S. Hwy. 34 (667–7810).

Lodges & Guest Ranches

★★★*Double J K Ranch*, located between Rocky Mountain National Park and the Roosevelt National Forest, was originally built as the Columbines Hotel and still retains much of its period charm in the form of bentwood chairs, stained-glass windows, polished wood floors, and big crackling fires. Today this family guest ranch offers horseback riding, hiking, sight-seeing, jeep tours, fishing in a stocked trout pond, and a full program of supervised children's activities so parents can get off on their own. Evenings are filled with square dancing, cookouts, hayrides, and even an occasional old-time melodrama staged by an obliging staff. Professional wranglers and surefooted saddle horses will cater to your riding needs and offer basic instruction for beginners. There's also a swimming pool, plus other recreational facilities such as pool and Ping-Pong tables, a spa, and volleyball courts. Accommodations are in attractive cabins (some have fireplaces) with full carpeting, private baths, and gas heat. Weekly rates, including meals, lodging, entertainment, all activities except horseback riding and jeep tours, and daily maid service, are $195 per person, double occupany, and $170 for each child 10 years of age or younger. For further information write: Double J K Ranch, Longs Peak Route, Estes Park, CO 80517 (303)586–2537.

★★*Glen Echo Resort* is located on the banks of the Cache la Poudre River at 7,200–foot elevations in the heart of the Roosevelt National Forest. Activities here include 50 miles of public stream fishing, hiking in the Rawah Wilderness Area, scenic drives, horseshoes, shuffleboard, and croquet. Several nearby lakes, including Red Feather lakes, also afford excellent fishing. Handsome, fully modern duplex cottages have carpeting, full baths, attractive kitchens, thermostatically controlled heat, all cooking and eating utensils, and linens ($23–28 daily, double occupancy). Rustic cabins have equally comfortable furnishings but share rest-room and shower facilities ($14–16 daily, double occupancy). Cabins will accommodate up to 6 guests in each, and are located on nicely landscaped grounds. The resort also has a pleasant restaurant and bar, a general store for groceries and fishing tackle, playgrounds, and several trailer spaces with service hookups and patios. For further details write: Glen Echo Resort, Poudre Canyon Drive, Hwy. 14, Fort Collins, CO 80521 (303)881–2208.

★★★*Lazy H Guest Ranch* sprawls along the eastern slopes of the Rocky Mountains in Roosevelt National Forest at an altitude of 8,300 feet. There are hundreds of miles of scenic trails over gentle

hills, meadows, and rugged mountains to explore on foot or horseback. Lazy H has been raising and training horses for years. An experienced staff of wranglers helps you select the mount best suited to your expertise, and all rides and overnight pack trips are accompanied by one of the staff. Other activities include swimming in the outdoor heated pool, hayrides, cookouts, trapshooting, and a full gamut of indoor evening diversions. None of the activities are regimented here; the pace is up to you. Accommodations are available in attractive lodge rooms and cabin suites with comfortable furnishings and private baths. Meals are served in a family-style dining room. Twice weekly, the lodge sponsors chuck-wagon breakfast rides with the first meal of the day served beside a mountain stream. On Fridays there's a gymkhana followed by a tasty barbecue. Other amenities include organized sight-seeing trips and a supervised children's program from 9 A.M. until after dinner each day except Sunday. Double-occupancy rates, including all meals, horseback riding, and ranch activities, are $200–225 per person weekly ($36–42 daily). Children's rates are scaled according to age. A $25 discount in weekly rates is available to nonriders. For further details write: Lazy H Guest Ranch, Allenspark, CO 80510 (303)747–2532.

★★★*Rawah Guest Ranch*, in the valley of the Big Laramie River, encompasses some 320 beautiful and unspoiled acres surrounded by the Roosevelt National Forest. Located at the trailhead of the Rawah Wilderness Area at 8,400–foot elevations, the ranch enjoys clear mountain air and mild summers. Horseback riding is the ranch specialty, with unlimited trails to explore and expert instructors to help you enjoy your time in the saddle. Fishing is another popular activity. The Big Laramie boasts some of Colorado's best brown-trout fishing, and other nearby streams and lakes abound in rainbows, cutthroat, and brookies. The Laramie's trout are not stocked, so be prepared for stream-bred fighters. There are no regimented activities at Rawah Ranch; you decide how to fill the day, whether it's an afternoon of loafing by the river or a visit to a local rodeo. A recreation room is on hand for rainy days or restless youngsters. Accommodations are available in attractive lodge bedrooms, in private guest cabins, or in the Little Ranch House with its 2 sets of living quarters separated by a granite wall in which fireplaces have been built. All rooms are fully modern, paneled, and handsomely furnished. The lodge building itself houses a sunny lounge and dining room where home-made ranch-style meals are the specialty. Rates vary from $185 to $230 per person weekly ($29–36 daily) and include all meals, horses, and maid service. For full details write: Rawah Guest Ranch, Glendevey, Colorado Route, Jelm, WY 82063; (307)435–5915.

★★★*Peaceful Valley Lodge & Guest Ranch*, in Lyons, Colorado, is, in the summer, a high-country guest ranch and in winter, a fine cross-country skiing resort. Situated in the heart of the Colorado Rockies Front Range, the ranch is located on 320 acres of beautiful pine and meadowland. Special features include a covered year-round swimming pool and an indoor riding hall. Horseback riding is very popular in addition to scout trips to mining towns and excellent trout fishing. Additional activities include overnight trips, either by four wheel drive cars or by horse, and special square dance vacation weeks June-August. The Swiss Chalet main house offers a warm fireplace and gathering area. Once a week during the summer months guests enjoy a combination horse show/rodeo that they may just enjoy or even participate in. Deluxe summer accommodations including all meals are priced at $287 per week per person. Discounts for children depend on age and vary from 15% to 50% off. Winter rates for late November until mid-April are approximately $30 less than those quoted above. Pets are not welcome. For further information call or write Peaceful Valley Lodge & Guest Ranch, Star Route, Lyons, Colorado 80540, (303)747–2582 or 747–2204.

★★★*Sylvan Dale Ranch* combines a working cattle and horse ranch with many luxury facilities of a full-service resort. Private guest cabins are set in a nicely landscaped grove shaded by stately trees, and have 1–3 bedrooms, private baths, wall-to-wall carpeting, and comfortable furnishings. The commodious central ranch building, overlooking the Big Thompson River, has a bright and cheerful dining room, fireside lounge, and meeting rooms for conventions. Activities center on the stable of dependable horses, with capable wranglers available to guide your trail rides and offer instruction. The ranch also has tennis courts, a large heated pool and sundeck, a recreation room, and courts for just about every imaginable competitive sport. Hayrides, overnight pack trips, square dancing, and fishing for trout in the Big Thompson are other favorite pastimes. Open year-round, the ranch accommodates 70 guests at a time or affiliated groups of up to 100. American-plan rates include all meals and recreation facilities: $180 weekly per person (double occupancy); $35 daily per person (double occupancy). Children's and triple-occupancy rates are available. Horseback riding is additional. For further details write: Sylvan Dale Ranch, 2939 North Country Road 31D, Loveland, CO 80537 (303)667–3915.

Routt National Forest & The Steamboat Ski Area

This 1,125,000–acre forest reserve is located in high country along the Continental Divide near Steamboat Springs. The forest was named for Col. John N. Routt, the last territorial and first state governor of Colorado. The famous deep-flowing trophy brown and rainbow trout waters of the North Platte River, a tributary of the Missouri and Mississippi, drain the North Park Region in the eastern portion of the forest. The wild Yampa, flowing toward the Green and Colorado rivers, drains the waters on the west. Atop the Great Divide lies the 72,472–acre Mt. Zirkel Wilderness. Elevations in the forest range from 7,000 to 13,000 feet. Remote high-country trails and forest roads provide access to the wilderness trout fishing and camping areas along the headwaters of the famed Encampment and Little Snake rivers, Big Creek Lakes Recreation Area, Williams Fork, Elkhead Mountains, and the remote tributaries and headwaters of the North Platte. The North Platte flows in sheer walled canyons through the wild Windy Hole, Narrow Falls, Cowpie, and Stovepipe rapids, surrounded by evergreen forests and meadows. The major tributaries of the North Platte—the Canadian, Michigan, and Illinois rivers—rise to the east of the forest high on the east slopes of the Medicine Bow and Never Summer ranges and offer some of the state's top-ranked rainbow and brown trout fishing.

U.S. Highway 40 now cuts through the forest mountains at the site of the historic Rabbit Ears Pass. The two rocky towers that mark the pass here became a landmark, first for the Indians, then for the explorers and Rocky Mountain trappers, and eventually for emigrants.

Information Sources, Maps & Access

For detailed vacation travel information and a full-color *Routt National Forest Map* (50¢) and *Mt. Zirkel Wilderness Map* (50¢), contact: Forest Supervisor, Routt National Forest, 137 10th St., Steamboat Springs, CO 80477 (303)879–1722.

U.S. 40, which runs from the Denver area northwest to the forest, U.S. 34 from Loveland, and State Highway 14 from Fort Collins provide access to the forest areas. Lodging, guides, supplies, outfitters, and packers are available at Craig and Steamboat Springs.

Gateways & Accommodations

Steamboat Springs

(Pop. 2,300; zip code 80477; area code 303.) This is a world-famous ski mecca and headquarters of the Routt National Forest. The surrounding alpine high country, once the home and hunting grounds of the Ute Indians, is the range of one of Colorado's largest Rocky Mountain elk herds. Area attractions include the hot mineral baths at Heart Springs Bathhouse, Fish Creek Falls off U.S. 40, Tread of Pioneers Museum at 5th and Oak Sts., the Steamboat Gondola over the Yampa River Valley, Summer Arts Festival at Stephens College (879–1060), and fine dining at the *Pine Grove Ranch Restaurant* in an early 1900s restored barn on U.S. 40 (879–1190) and the *Butcher Shop* (879–2484) on U.S. 40 at the ski area. Accommodations (see also "Lodges & Guest Ranches" below for additional listings): *Best Western Alpiner Motor Lodge* (rates: $32–34 double), 32 excellent rooms and family units, at 424 Lincoln Ave. on U.S. 40 (879–1430); *Best Western Ptarmigan Inn* (rates: $32–70 double), 31 superb alpine rooms, balconies, dining room, cocktail lounge, heated pool, sauna, at base of Mt. Werner in ski area (879–1730); *Larson's Subalpine Lodge*, (a *Friendship Inn*; rates: $24–38 double), 31 outstanding rooms, dining room, heated pool, sauna, at ski area on Columbine Drive (879–2600); *Rabbit Ears Motel* (rates: $22–34 double), 39 rooms just east of town on U.S. Hwy. 40 (879–1150); *Ramada Inn* (rates: $34–52 double), 117 excellent rooms and family units, dining room, cocktail lounge, heated indoor pool, sauna, tennis courts, 1 mile east of town on U.S. 40 (879–2900).

Lodges, Guest Ranches & Ski Centers

★★★*Bear Pole Ranch & Ski Lodge* is nestled in a broad, gently rolling valley known as Strawberry Park with over 50 miles of trails bordering the Routt National Forest. The ranch offers some of the best cross-country skiing in the nation, rustic lodging, and delicious home-cooked meals with western hospitality. The ranch, which is located only 15 minutes from the Steamboat Springs Ski Area, offers rustic mountain cabins and dormitory units, sauna, library, and guided moonlight, overnight, day, and advanced ski tours into Routt National Forest and Buffalo Pass along terrain of varying difficulty—open alpine meadows, streams, lakes, rolling hills, and forests. Breakfast and dinner are served buffet-style in the main lodge, constructed of hand-hewn logs. Hot, fresh-baked bread is a part of each evening menu. Equipment rentals and professional cross-country skiing instruction are available at the ranch. Ranch bus shuttle service is available to and from the Steamboat Springs Ski Area. During the summer, Bear Pole Ranch offers summer camp programs for young adults and wilderness adventure programs for older teenagers and family groups. American-plan winter rates (4 or more per cabin) range from $30 per day to $135 for 7 days. Special rates for children under 12. Dormitory rates range from $25 per day to $100 for 7 days. Special ski-touring package plans are available. For additional information, contact: Dr. & Mrs. Glenn Poulter, Bear Pole Ranch, Star Rte. 1, Steamboat Springs, CO 80477 (303)879–0576.

★★★*Glen Eden Ranch*, a year-round resort specializing in winter ski touring, is located near the historic town of Clark, 18 miles north of Steamboat Springs, and surrounded by the magnificent Routt National Forest. Groomed cross-country trails for novice to expert ski enthusiasts begin right at the lodge and extend over the smooth, gentle hills of the Elk River Valley deep into the national forest over miles of challenging mountain terrain and open meadows. For alpine skiing, the nearby Mt. Werner Ski Area has a gondola, 11 double chair-lifts, 53 trails, and a vertical drop of 3,600 feet. Other winter attractions of this fine resort include ice fishing, skating, sleigh rides, hot springs, and a winter carnival in Steamboat Springs. During the warm-weather months, the ranch offers horseback riding, trout fishing, river rafting, jeep tours, and hunting. Cabins have 2 bedrooms, with 1 queen-size and 2 twin beds, 2 modern baths, a living room with a queen-size hide-a-bed, fireplaces, a sun porch overlooking the Elk River, and a fully equipped kitchen with all utensils. A restaurant in the main lodge features tasty western cuisine and an extensive wine list; lighter fare and cocktails are served in a handsome fireside lounge. Every weekend there's country and western music and dancing in the big, open beam lounge overlooking the mountains. Nightly rates: $35–55 for 1–6 guests, including private cabins and daily maid service. A 10% discount is in effect for one-week and longer stays. For full details write: Glen Eden Ranch, P.O. Box 867, Clark, CO 80428 (303)879–3906.

★★★★*Steamboat Ski Area*, just outside Steamboat Springs and 157 miles northwest of Denver, boasts fine skiing for all levels of expertise on sprawling Mt. Werner, with 53 trails (33 miles in all) along its 3,600–foot vertical drop. The powder here is renowned as Colorado's lightest—325 inches annually of fluffy, dry snow ideal for professional racing, cross-country touring, and downhill thrills. About 50% of the trails are rated intermediate; the rest are evenly divided

between experts and beginners. Longest run is 2½ miles. A total of 15 lifts, including 11 double chairs and a 90–car gondola, offer a combined capacity of 14,700 skiers per hour, and long lift lines are extremely rare. The ski-school staff is headed by former Olympic champion Billy Kidd and staffed by an average of 100 professional instructors. The Steamboat Ski School's specialty is modified 6LM, and both private and class instruction are available for beginning through advanced skiers. Other facilities of Steamboat include two restaurants on the slopes (14 in the immediate vicinity), ice-skating rinks, sleigh rides, a ski-touring center, night skiing, equipment rentals, and a nursery for children 6 months to 7 years old. The season runs from about Dec. 2 through Apr. 15. For more information on skiing at Steamboat write: Steamboat Springs Chamber Resort Association, P.O. Box 717, Steamboat Springs, CO 80477 (303)879–0740.

The Holiday Inn of Steamboat Springs, with its natural wood and moss rock decor, reflects the area's rugged frontier charm on the outside. On the inside, large and modern soundproofed rooms provide comfortable accommodations with superb views of Mt. Werner. Just 5 minutes from downtown and the ski lifts, the Holiday Inn has all the conveniences right at your doorstep: restaurant, lounge with fireplace, cocktail lounge with live entertainment, saunas, a game room, and an outdoor heated pool. Free shuttle transportation is available to the ski area and airport. Daily rates per person: $30–40, single occupancy; $19–24, double occupancy. Ski packages, including lodgings and lift passes, are $90–180 for 4 nights, 3 days; $165–320 for 7 nights, 6 days. For additional information write: Holiday Inn, P.O. Box 1319, Steamboat Springs, CO 80477 (303)879–2250.

The Nordic Lodge, located 1½ miles from the slopes, offers a variety of attractive accommodations, ranging from deluxe rooms for couples to fine 2–bedroom units for families. All rooms have wall-to-wall carpeting, individual heat controls, color TV, full baths with tubs and showers, and direct-dial phones. On the premises are a heated pool, 2 saunas, and laundry facilities. Several fine restaurants are within easy walking distance. Other amenities include continental breakfast served in the lounge and free shuttle service to the slopes. Daily rates: $24–34 per person. Ski packages are $125–145 per person for 5 days, $163–191 per person for 7 days (excluding Christmas holidays). For more details write: Nordic Lodge, P.O. Box 70, Steamboat Springs, CO 80477 (303)879–0531.

Scandinavian Lodge, nestled right at the base of Mt. Werner, prides itself on a warm old-fashioned family atmosphere. Open year-round, the lodge has a unique Scandinavian atmosphere reflected in its timbered architecture, bright furnishings, and superb cuisine. Facilities on the premises include ski-touring trails, lessons and tours, a Nordic ski shop, a gymnasium and outdoor swimming pool, saunas, and a handsome dining room. From the lodge, guests can ski right to the Steamboat lifts. Rates: $20–48 per person daily, including 3 meals a day (holiday rates are 5% higher). Ski packages, including lodging, meals, and lift tickets, are $160–300 per person for 5 days and nights, $212–408 for 7 days and nights. For further information write: Scandinavian Lodge, Box 5040, Steamboat Village, CO 80499 (303)879–0517.

Steamboat Village Resort, at the base of Mt. Werner just a few steps from the gondola, is a beautiful and modern resort complex encompassing 80 hotel rooms and 22 hotel condominiums, plus 150 additional condominiums in three separate buildings. All are convenient to the slopes and to the resort's on-premise shops, restaurants, meeting rooms, saunas, and heated pool. Two popular night spots—The Hole in the Wall and the Sundance Room—feature name entertainment nightly. Day care and babysitting services are available. Daily rates: $52 for hotel rooms, $125 for a two bedroom condominium with a sleeping loft (low season rates available on request). Ski packages, including lifts and lodging, are $65–200 for four nights and three days; $95–210 for five nights, five days; $100–380 for seven nights, six days. For additional details, write: Steamboat Village Resort, P.O. Box ZZ, Steamboat Springs, CO 80477; phone: (303)879–2220 (in Colorado); (800)525–2501 (toll-free outside Colorado).

Storm Meadows Condominium/Townhouse Resort has a complete range of fully furnished, luxury accommodations right at the base of Mt. Werner. Each unit has a wood-burning fireplace, sun balcony, color TV, and well-equipped modern kitchen. Condominiums and town houses are grouped around a top-rate restaurant and full-service athletic club, which offers handball, racquetball, year-round swimming, therapy pools, yoga and exercise classes, saunas, and steambaths. Other amenities include daily maid service, a laundry room, ski lockers, and convention facilities. Steamboat lifts are accessible on skis. Daily rates: $65–72 for a convertible 1–bedroom unit accommodating 4 people; $160–175 for a 4–bedroom town house with sleeping quarters for 6–10 guests (2–night minimum; rates do not include use of athletic club). Ski-package plans available on request. For more information write: Storm Meadows Resort, Box AAA, Steamboat Springs, CO 80477 (303)879–1035.

★★★*Vista Verde Ranch*, a long-established guest and working cattle ranch, occupies some 600 acres in a valley of its own surrounded by the Routt National Forest and Mt. Zirkel Wilderness Area. Guided pack trips through this magnificent high country are a ranch specialty. The area abounds in trout streams and lakes, readily sighted wildlife, and scenic trails such as the historic Wyoming Trail. Favorite winter activities include ski touring over miles of well-groomed trails (instruction available at the ranch) and ice fishing on nearby Steamboat Lake. Individual hand-hewn log guest cabins have fireplaces, handmade pine furniture, carpeting throughout, full kitchens, private baths, and 2–3 bedrooms. The spacious main lodge has a comfortable living room with a big stone fireplace, a candlelit dining room overlooking meadows and mountains, a recreation room, and library. Vista Verde is proud of its delicious family-style meals, homemade breads and pastries, and produce fresh from the garden. Summer rates are $210 per person weekly ($33 daily) and include all meals, lodgings, a steak-fry, breakfast ride, fishing, and all ranch activities, except riding instruction, horses, and pack trips. Children's rates are $190 per week for children under 6. For additional information write: Vista Verde Guest Ranch, Box 465, Steamboat Springs, CO 80477 (303)879–3858.

Travel Services

Adventure Bound, Inc., headquartered in Steamboat Springs, sponsors 2–4–day river-rafting expeditions on a number of Colorado's spectacular waterways, including the Yampa and Lodore rivers through precipitous canyons in Dinosaur National Monument; the Green River, following John Wesley Powell's epic 1869 exploration; the Colorado River through the narrow gorge of Westwater Canyon and Utah's rugged Cataract Canyon; and the Green River in the unspoiled reaches of southeastern Utah. Adventure Bound provides experienced guides, top-quality equipment, pontoon rafts of neoprene rubber, and all meals. You can rent a sleeping bag or bring your own. Rates average around $80 per person for a 2–day trip, $140 for 3 days, and $160 for 4 days. Family and group discounts are available. Adventure Bound also offers 1– and 2–day paddle-raft or float trips on the Upper Colorado and North Platte rivers. For complete information

write: Adventure Bound, Inc., 6179 South Adams Drive, Littleton, CO 80121 (303)771–3752.

San Isabel National Forest & The Spanish Peaks

This 1,106,000–acre reserve in southern Colorado encompasses some of the most spectacular mountain wilderness areas in the state, including the hundreds of alpine lakes and meadows, canyons, waterfalls, and dense forests within the beautiful peaks of the Sangre de Cristo Range, Spanish Peaks, Collegiate Peaks, and the Sawatch Range. The Spanish Peaks, among the most important landmarks of the West for the Indians and early Spanish and French explorers, lie in the southernmost sector of the forest. The peaks rise abruptly out of the Great Plains, their great dikes and ridges radiating out like the spokes of a wheel. These dikes were once intrusions of volcanic material into the overlying sediment. Erosion eventually wore away the softer sedimentary rocks, leaving the impressive morphology of the Spanish Peaks.

The northernmost sector of the San Isabel Forest encompasses the spectacular peaks of the Sawatch Range, crowned by Mt. Elbert (14,433 ft.), the second-highest mountain in the 48 contiguous states. Nearby Mt. Massive (14,421 ft.) rivals Elbert in height, as do 19 other peaks in the forest over 14,000 feet. Mt. Massive is named for its size; it actually encompasses seven peaks over 14,000 feet and 70,000 acres of alpine tundra above timberline. A trail to the summit of Mt. Massive wanders through alpine flower fields and near the remnants of an old glacier. Both Mt. Elbert and Mt. Massive can be climbed by persons with no technical experience, but good physical condition is a prerequisite for the trips.

Ski Cooper Winter Sports Area, 10 miles north of Leadville, has fine terrain for beginning and intermediate skiers at base elevations of 10,500 feet stretching to 11,700 feet at the summit. This is an ideal spot for family skiing, with wide and easily negotiated trails for even the youngest powder enthusiast, plus a professionally staffed day-care center for those too young to ski. A double chair-lift, Poma, and high-speed T-bar can accommodate over 1,800 skiers per hour with no overcrowding or long lift lines. The downhill area is surrounded by miles of touring terrain, including 5 groomed trails with a total length of 7 miles in the beautiful San Isabel National Forest. The Cooper ski school offers professional instruction for all ages; classes and private instruction in the American teaching method are available. There's also a full line of rentals at reasonable rates.

Information Sources, Maps & Access

For detailed vacation travel and recreation information, a full-color *San Isabel National Forest Map* (50¢), and the free *Spanish Peaks Area Map/Brochure*, write: Supervisor, San Isabel National Forest, P.O. Box 753, Pueblo, CO 81002 (303)544–5277.

The northern sector of the forest is accessible by way of U.S. 50 west from Pueblo. The southern portion may be reached by taking Interstate 25 south from Pueblo, then traveling west from it on State Highway 12. The Lake Isabel area and the Wet Mountains are accessible by taking Interstate 25 south from Pueblo, then traveling west on State Highway 165. The town of Leadville serves the northernmost portion of the forest as an outfitting and supply center. Numerous guides and dude ranches are located nearby. Salida and Westcliffe serve the Sangre de Cristo Mountains section of the forest in this capacity; to the east, Pueblo is the main outfitting center.

Gateways & Accommodations

Canon City

(Pop. 9,200; zip code 81212; area code 303.) Pronounced Canyon City, the city is located on U.S. 50 at the mouth of the Grand Canyon of the Arkansas River. This old Ute Indian camping ground was first explored by Zebulon Pike during his search for the headwaters of the Arkansas in 1806. Joaquin Miller, the poet, served as the town's mayor, judge, and minister during the gold-rush days and proposed changing the name to Oreodelphia but was overruled by the crusty miners because they were unable to write or pronounce the word. In 1868 the town was offered the choice of being the new

site of either the state prison or university. The miners, with their keen knowledge of nature, chose the former because they felt it would be better attended. Area attractions include the Royal Gorge, or Grand Canyon, with its sheer 1,000–foot walls, Canyon City Museum at 612 Royal Gorge Blvd., Royal Gorge Scenic Railway on Royal Gorge Road off U.S. 50, the 35–mile-long Phantom Canyon Hwy. (Colorado 67) to Cripple Creek, and the scenic 3–mile-long Skyline Drive 4 miles west of town on U.S. 50. Accommodations: *Best Western Royal Gorge Motel* (rates: $27–29 double), 68 excellent rooms, restaurant, cocktail lounge, heated pool, trout pond, east of town on U.S. 50 at 1925 Fremont Drive (275–3377); *Ramada Inn* (rates: $32.50–40 double), 104 excellent rooms and family units, restaurant, coffee shop, cocktail lounge, indoor and outdoor pool, sauna, east of town on U.S. 50 at Dazier Avenue (275–8676).

Leadville

(Pop. 4,300; zip code 80461; area code 303.) This historic gold- and silver-mining town situated near timberline in the upper Arkansas River Valley on the east slope of the Great Divide is flanked by some of Colorado's highest peaks, including Mt. Elbert and Mt. Massive. Often referred to as Cloud City, or "two miles high, but miles ahead," Leadville produced fortunes in gold and silver during the 1880s. Today the Leadville Mining District produces more than $90 million worth of molybdenum a year. Well-preserved examples of the town's wild and woolly past include the Tabor Cottage at 116 E. 5th St., Tabor Opera House Museum at 308 Harrison Ave., the House with the Eye at 124 W. 4th St., Matchless Mine on E. 7th St., the 1878 Healy House at 912 Harrison Ave., and the Dexter Cabin, built by one of Colorado's early millionaires. Maps of the 9–mile loop highway of the "Silver Kings" and jeep tour info are available from the Chamber of Commerce, Box 861. The Leadville National Fish Hatchery, built in 1887, is located 8 miles southwest of town on Colorado Hwy. 300. Accommodations: *Best Western Silver King Motor Inn* (rates: $29–33 double), 62 excellent rooms and family units, restaurant, cocktail lounge, sauna, north of town at 2020 N. Poplar (486–2610).

Pueblo

(Pop. 97,500; zip code, see below; area code 303.) The headquarters of the San Isabel National Forest, Pueblo is also the business and steel-manufacturing center of the great Arkansas Valley. It was settled and named by the black mountain man and trapper Jim Beckwourth, who built a trading post here in 1842. Area attractions include El Pueblo Museum at 905 S. Prairie Ave. and the Pueblo Metropolitan Museum at 419 W. 14th St. Accommodations: *Best Western Chilton Inn* (rates: $29–36 double), 160 excellent rooms, restaurant, cocktail lounge, heated pool, at 800 Hwy. 50W., Exit 43 (543–6820); *Best Western Town House Motel* (rates: $27–31 double), 88 rooms, restaurant, cocktail lounge, heated pool, at 8th St. and Santa Fe, 81004 (543–6530); *Holiday Inn* (rates: $29–33 double), 191 excellent rooms, dining room, cocktail lounge, heated pool, at 4001 N. Elizabeth off I–25 Exit 43 (543–8050); *Pueblo West Inn* (rates: $29 double), 80 superb rooms and suites, dining room, restaurant, cocktail lounge, heated pool, tennis courts, golf, riding, at 251 McCullock Blvd., off I–25 Exit 43 (547–2111).

Salida

(Pop. 4,400; zip code 81201; area code 303.) A popular Rocky Mountain gateway to the San Isabel National Forest high country, Salida was founded by the Denver & Rio Grande Railroad in 1880. Area attractions include the Monarch Ski Area; Mt. Shavano State Fish Hatchery, 2 miles west of town on Hwy. 291; Salida Museum; Ghost Town Jeep Tours, 5 miles west of town at the junction of U.S. 50 and 285 at 11150 Hwy. 50 (539–2144); Tenderfoot Scenic Drive west of town on Hwy. 291; and Arkansas River Float Trips, 5 miles west of town at U.S. 50 and 285 junction (539–3778). Accommodations: *Best Western Colorado Lodge* (rates: $23–25 double), 25 excellent rooms and family units, heated pool, at 352 W. Rainbow Blvd. on U.S. 50 (539–2514); *Monarch Ramada Inn* (rates: $30–32 double), 100 excellent rooms and family units, dining room, cocktail lounge, indoor heated pool, near the east base of Monarch Pass, 19 miles west of town on U.S. 50 (539–2581); *Red Wood Lodge* (rates: $24–26 double), 19 excellent rooms and guest cottages, heated pool, west of town at 7310 U.S. Hwy. 50 (539–2528); *Western Holdiay Friendship Inn* (rates: $25–28 double), 35 excellent rooms and family units, heated pool, at 545 Rainbow Blvd. on U.S. 50 (539–2553).

Guest Ranches

★★★★*Don K Ranch* is a renowned family guest ranch located off Colorado Highway 96 via a 30–mile drive through picturesque buttes and mesas of the high plains cattle country and spectacular Red Rock Canyon, whose colorful rock walls rise to 1,000 feet. The ranch complex—barns and corrals, bunkhouse, guest houses, an Olympic-sized pool, and huge western log lodge—is nested in a hidden valley at 6,000–feet elevation in the Sangre de Cristo Mountains of the San Isabel National Forest. Ranch facilities consist of a large log lodge with its western living room and lounge, 2 dining rooms, an Old West bar, native stone fireplaces, pine paneling, and spacious upstairs guest rooms. The lodge and barns are built of huge ponderosa pines sawed to shape in the ranch's own sawmill—which has been converted for square dancing and games. The rustic guest cottage units are fully carpeted and redwood-paneled, with colorful western and Indian decor, private tiled baths with tub-shower combination, and thermostatically controlled heat. The cabins have large windows with mountain and forest views. Delicious home-cooked meals are served in the attractive lodge dining room. Ranch activities include trail riding, cookouts, swimming, rodeos, wildlife photography and nature hikes, and target shooting. Individual riding instruction is provided for children and adults at no charge. All-inclusive American-plan rates, which include cowboy guides and a children's counselor, are $47 per person in the guest cottage and $41 per person in the main lodge. There is a 20% discount for children occupying a room with 2 parents. Contact: Don K Ranch, 2677 S. Sileam Road, Pueblo, CO 81005 (303)784–6600.

San Juan National Forest & Mesa Verde National Park

This 1,866,000–acre tract embraces some of the finest wilderness camping, skiing, fishing, and hunting areas in the Rocky Mountain region, including the alpine lakes and meadows, canyons, cascades, and spruce, pine, and fir forests of the Weminuche Wilderness, Needle Mountains, and San Juan Mountains. The forest's rugged interior wildlands are the last refuge of the few remaining Colorado grizzlies. Golden, rainbow, brook, brown, and cutthroat trout grow to record size in the wild Animas River and in such lakes as crystal-clear Vallecito, Lemon, and Williams Creek. Vallecito Reservoir, with 22 miles of shoreline, is located in the heart of the forest and is nationally famous for its trophy rainbow and brown trout, northern pike, and kokanee salmon fishing. The Colorado record northern pike (30 lb. 1 oz.) and brown trout (24 lb. 10 oz.) were taken here.

The forest bears the marks of both man and nature. Unusual

geologic formations dot the high country, while abandoned mines recall the gold-rush days. The ruins of cliff dwellings inhabited thousands of years ago can also be seen here; after the cliff dwellers came the Utes, Navajos, and Apaches. The first white men to enter the area came with Juan Vásquez de Coronado in 1541. The next recorded expedition occurred over two centuries later, the journey of Escalante and Dominique to California. Prospectors entered the area in the 1860s. The last narrow-gauge passenger train in the country still makes the Durango-Silverton trip.

The Weminuche Wilderness, the largest wilderness area in Colorado encompasses 316,833 acres of the old San Juan and Upper Rio Grande primitive areas, much of it within the Needles. Some 250 miles of trails wind up through the high country, often gaining 5,000 feet in 4–5 miles. The Pine River Trail over Weminuche Pass was a route over the Great Divide used by the Weminuche Indians. Mt. Aeolus, Sunlight, and Wisdom peaks in this area reach heights of over 14,000 feet. At the lower elevations are Douglas fir, ponderosa pine, blue spruce, and aspen. Wild flowers carpet these slopes from spring till late autumn. At higher altitudes Engelmann spruce dominates the forests; alpine fir is also common. On the high alpine peaks, only hardy wild flowers and lichens grow. These high-country wild flowers are at their peak in mid-July.

Wildlife includes elk, mule deer, black bear, coyote, and bighorn sheep in the Ammarona Peak and Sheep Mountain areas. A few mountain lions range the rugged slopes. Birds of the area include the mountain ptarmigan and blue grouse. Hawks and eagles are often seen soaring among the craggy heights.

Outstanding features of the Weminuche Wilderness include Chicago Basin, the site of early mining interests; the 13,830–foot Rio Grande Pyramid, a mountain whose shape recalls the pyramids of Egypt; the Window, a natural gateway through a solid rock wall on a trail to Weminuche Pass; the Knife Edge, a huge wedge of volcanic rock that has been exposed by the forces of erosion; Emerald Lake, the site of several backcountry campgrounds; the Trinity Peaks, three mountains over 13,000 feet in the Grenadier Range; and hot springs on the West Fork of the San Juan River. There is no frost-free period here; temperatures fall as low as −30°F in the winter. Summer highs may reach 80°.

The prehistoric cliff dwellings and ruins of Mesa Verde National

Park lie to the south of the forest boundary on a majestic plateau rising abruptly out of semiarid land bordering the high country of the Continental Divide. Six mountain ranges in four states can be viewed from Park Point. The park includes 50,275 acres of canyon and mesa lands set aside for the preservation of its cliff dwellings and pueblos successively occupied by the prehistoric Basket Makers and the Pueblo Indians (A.D. 1000). The great drought between 1276 and 1299 is believed to have forced the Cliff Dwellers out of Mesa Verde. Their fate remains a mystery. Mesa Verde, Spanish for "green table," is a vast plateau reaching heights of up to 2,000 feet above Montezuma Valley. Year-round ranger-guided trips (weather permitting) are available to Spruce Tree House, in the canyon behind the museum, Cliff Palace on Ruins Road, Long and Step Houses on Wetherill Mesa, and Balcony House on Ruins Road. The Ruins Road Drive offers views of the ancient dwellings. Information is available at the Far View Visitor Center and Mesa Verde Museum at the park headquarters.

Information Sources, Maps & Access

For detailed vacation recreation information, a full-color *San Juan National Forest Map* (50¢), and the free *San Juan National Forest Booklet* and *Weminuche Wilderness Area Map Brochure*, write: Supervisor, San Juan National Forest, P.O. Box 341, Durango, CO 81301 (303)247–4874. Mesa Verde National Park information and a free *Mesa Verde National Park Map/Brochure* may be obtained by contacting: Superintendent, Mesa Verde National Park, CO 81330 (303)529–4465. A beautiful, full-color U.S. Geological Survey *Mesa Verde National Park Shaded-Relief Map* ($2) may be ordered from: Distribution Branch, U.S. Geological Survey, Federal Center, Denver, CO 80225.

The forest is reached from Cortez and Durango along U.S. Highway 160 and State Highway 145. U.S. Highway 550 runs north through the forest from New Mexico to Ouray, Montrose, Delta, and Grand Junction. Lodging, guides, supplies, outfitters, and packers are available at Cortez, Dolores, Durango, Pagosa Springs, Hermosa, Trimble, La Plata, Vallecito, Silverton, and Telluride.

Gateways & Accommodations

Cortez—Gateway to Mesa Verde National Park

(Pop. 6,000; zip code 81321; area code 303.) Cortez is in the famous "Four Corners" area of southwest Colorado (39 miles to the southwest is the Four Corners Monument on U.S. Hwy. 160, where you can stand in four states—Colorado, Arizona, New Mexico, and Utah—in one spot). Area attractions include the Four Corners Museum at 802 E. Montezuma St., the cliff dwellings and towers of the Indian ruins at Hovenweep National Monument off U.S. 666; and the Lowry Pueblo Ruins of the Anasazi Indians off U.S. 666. Accommodations: *Best Western Sands of Cortez* (rates: $26–30 double), 43 excellent rooms, heated indoor pool, ¼ mile east of town on U.S. 160 at 1000 E. Main St. (565–3761); *Best Western Turquoise Motel* (rates: $26–30 double), 46 excellent rooms and family units, heated pool, in town on U.S. 160 (565–3778); *Ramada Inn* (rates: $26–34 double), 79 excellent rooms and family units, coffee shop, on U.S. 160 at 666 S. Broadway (565–3773).

Durango—Gateway to the Silverton Historic Town

(Pop. 10,300; zip code 81301; area code 303.) The major gateway for tourists, skiers, fishermen, backpackers, and hunters heading into the spectacular high country of the San Juan National Forest, this historic Old West frontier town was founded by the Denver & Rio Grande Railroad. Area attractions include the historic Silverton Railroad, float trips on the Animas and Dolores rivers, Southern Ute Tourist Center, San Juan Tours to Mesa Verde National Park at 479 Main St. (247–9190), and the Purgatory Ski Area. Accommodations: *General Palmer House & the Palace Restaurant* (rates: $32–34 double), 35 superb rooms in a restored 19th–century hotel and 90's dining room near Rio Grande Narrow-Gauge Train Depot, at 567 Main St. (247–4747); *Holiday Inn* (rates: $38–42 double), 139 excellent units with dining room, cocktail lounge, heated pool, at 800 Camino Del Rio on U.S. 160 and 550 (247–5393); *Pino Nuche Motel* (rates: $22–24.72 double), 38 excellent rooms, dining room, heated pool, next to Indian Museum on Southern Ute Indian Reservation in the town of Ignacio (563–4531). *Ramada Inn* (rates: $34 double), 140 excellent rooms and family units with fireplaces and loft bedrooms, restaurant, heated pool, 4 miles north of town on U.S. Hwy. 550 and Colorado 789 (259–1010); *Silver Spur Motel & Restaurant* (rates: $28–30 double), 33 excellent rooms and family units, family dining facilities, coffee shop, heated pool at 3416 N. Main, 2 miles north of town on U.S. 550 and Colorado 789 (247–5552); *Strater Hotel & Opera House Restaurant* (rates: $24–32 double), 94 outstanding rooms and family units in 19th–century Victorian decor, superb dining, Diamond Circle Melodrama Theatre in summer, Gay 90's lounge, in town at 699 N. Main St., 2 blocks north of Rio Grande Narrow-Gauge Depot (247–4431).

Mesa Verde National Park

(Zip code 81330; area code 303) accommodations: *Far View Motor Lodge* (rates: $24–27 double), 100 excellent rooms and family units, dining room, cafe, off U.S. 160, 15 miles south of park entrance near the visitors center (529–4421).

Pagosa Springs

(Pop. 1,400; zip code 81147; area code 303.) This forest gateway named for its hot springs is on U.S. 160 near the Wolf Creek Pass Winter Sports Area. Accommodations: *Best Western Pagosa Lodge* (rates: $34–36 double), 60 excellent rooms and family units, dining room, cocktail lounge, heated indoor pool, cross-country ski trails, trail rides, fishing and boats, golf, tennis, located 3½ miles west of town on small lake on U.S. 160 (264–2271).

Lodges, Guest Ranches & Ski Centers

★★★*Ah! Wilderness Guest Ranch*, accessible only by single-gauge railroad from Silverton or Durango, boasts a beautiful setting on the Animas River in southwestern Colorado. Many of the daytime activities at the ranch are centered around the stable full of well-trained horses, with daily rides scheduled along 30 miles of well-marked trails that pass the gorgeous walls of the spectacular Animas Canyon. Other attractions include river fishing, a sauna, swimming tank, pack trips, and a full complement of activities for children. Cabins are comfortably furnished with large rooms and combination tub-shower baths. Delicious meals, including fresh produce from the ranch gardens, are served in attractive dining rooms. Rates begin at $200 per adult per week based on double occupancy (American plan) with discounts for children. For complete information write: Ah! Wilderness Guest Ranch, P.O. Box 997, Durango, CO 81301 (303)247–4121.

★★★★*Colorado Trails Ranch* encompasses a sizable complex of handsome Old West buildings and ultramodern cabins plus over 500 acres in the mountains bordering San Juan National Forest. Horseback riding is superlative here, thanks to expert instruction, surefooted horses, and the miles of beautiful trails on the ranch and in adjoining forest lands. Overnight pack trips, breakfast rides, and friendly saddle competitions are all on the weekly agenda. Other activities at the ranch include waterskiing on Vallecito Lake, tennis on professional courts, archery, trapshooting, and swimming in the heated outdoor

pool. Meals are served in a spruce-paneled, family-style gallery, and almost all recipes start from scratch under the skillful hands of a professional chef. Accommodations are available in old-fashioned country cabins, rustic on the outside and fully modern within (2 bedrooms: $1,055–1,450 per week); in contemporary alpine cabins for parties of 3–8 ($290–1,680 per week); or in handsome X-wing cabins with 2 bedrooms, 2 baths, wall-to-wall carpeting, and other amenities ($950–1,080 per week, or $360–595 per week for 1 bedroom). The above rates cover all meals, maid service, horses, and virtually all ranch activities and use of equipment. For more detailed information write: Colorado Trails Ranch, Box 848, Durango, CO 81301 (303)247–5055.

Purgatory Ski Resort in the mountains of the beautiful San Juan National Forest is one of the West's great ski areas, with a 10,550–foot mountain with a 1,600–foot vertical drop, 450 acres, 40 ski trails, lots of sun, and over 300 inches of snow per year. Set in the spectacular San Juan Mountains, half of Purgatory is devoted to intermediate skiers, and experts can ski the twisting Lower Hades, Styx, Catharsis, and powder-filled Dead Spike. Day services at Purgatory are readily available at the base of the mountain and at the Powderhouse at 10,300 feet. Services include the Purgatory Ski School headed by Fritz Tatzer and a staff of 50, and ski rental shops (cross-country equipment available) at Purgatory, Tamarron Resort (see below) and the new Purgatory Ski Shop in Durango. Other services include the Children's Playhouse, Sunday worship services on the mountain, and après-ski at the Mine Shaft Disco, Windom Peaks Lounge, and Le Canyon Gourmet restaurant at Tamarron Resort. The Old West boom town of Durango has the Assay Office Restaurant, Bar D Chuckwagon Suppers, the Cellar for Italian cuisine, the Palace Restaurant near the Narrow-Gauge Train Depot, and the Strater Hotel Opera House Restaurant. Accommodations at Purgatory and Durango are numerous and are geared to fit most budgets. Tamarron, 8 miles south of Purgatory, is a first-class deluxe resort. The Purgatory condominiums listed below offer easy access to the 4 double chair-lifts.

Angel-Haus offers lodge rooms and 1–, 2–, and 3–bedroom suites with color TV, ski lockers, sauna, fireplaces. Weekly regular season rates (double): $111 per person. Write: SSR, Box 348, Durango 81301 (303)247–8090.

Bakers Bridge Log Cabins offers rustic 2–bedroom units with kitchen, TV, fireplaces. Weekly regular season rates: $107–135 per person. Contact: Baker's Bridge Log Cabins, 13103 County Road 250, Durango 81301 (303)247–1374.

Brimstone offers lodge rooms, studios, and 1– and 2–bedroom suites with kitchens, ski lockers, fireplaces. Weekly regular season rates (2 to a room): $149 per person. Contact: Brimstone, P.O. Box 1031, Durango 81301 (303)247–9001.

East Rim offers studios with kitchens, ski lockers, and fireplaces. Weekly regular season rates: $131–189 per person. Contact: East Rim, SSR, 44 Shoel St., Durango 81301 (303)247–5528).

Whispering Pines offers 2–bedroom suites with kitchen, recreation room, snack area, color TV, ski lockers, restaurant, fireplaces. Weekly regular season rates: $114–156 per person. Contact: Whispering Pines, 34237 Hwy. 550, Durango 81301 (303)259–0954.

For additional information on the Purgatory Ski Resort and area lodges write: P.O. Box 666, Durango, CO 81301 (303)247–9000 or toll-free (800)525–5427.

★★*Safari Lodge*, located at the northeast end of Vallecito Lake, has modern log cabins (some with fireplaces) fully equipped for housekeeping with cooking facilities, plenty of hot water, refrigerators, linens, dishes, and double beds. Safari has its own corral of gentle, dependable horses which may be rented by the hour, half day, or day for trail rides in the beautiful San Juan Wilderness. Fishing is good in Vallecito Lake and the nearby Pinos River, or you can pack up to the upper lakes and streams of the wilderness. The lodge store supplies bait and licenses. Boats are available for rental with or without motors right at the lodge doorstep. Other activities include hunting on foot or horseback (Safari is right in the heart of deer country), hiking, and backpacking. Cabins vary in size from 1 room for 2 to a 3–bedroom unit with a large family room and 1½ baths. Rates: $18–30 daily. Weekly rates are also available. For full information write: Safari Lodge, Route 1, Bayfield, CO 81122 (303) 884–2482.

★★*Silver Streams Lodge and Cabins* are located near Vallecito Lake between the Florida and Pine rivers. Fishing is excellent in the lodge's own well-stocked trout pond or in beautiful Vallecito Lake, which holds the state fishing records for salmon and northern pike. Miles of mountain streams in the surrounding backcountry also provide unparalleled wilderness angling. There's good hunting in fall, when the entire countryside bursts into gorgeous color. Several riding corrals nearby will help you saddle up for horseback trips, or you can take to the mountains on foot over several trails. Silver Streams' cabins have 1–2 bedrooms and are fully equipped for housekeeping with complete kitchen facilities, private baths, all linens, and wood-burning fireplaces. The main lodge has a nice

fireside lounge and restaurant specializing in steaks and fresh local trout. Rates: $20–23 daily for 1–bedroom cabins, $30–37 for standard 2–bedroom cabins, and $39–48 daily for large 2–bedroom cabins with 3 double beds. The longer your stay, the lower the daily rate. Large cabins will accommodate up to 10 guests (rollaways and/or hide-a-beds are in each unit). For further information write: Silver Streams Lodge, Rt. 1, Bayfield, CO 81122 (303)884–2770. In winter write: Lou Blodgett, 4917 W. 17th St., Lubbock, TX 79416 (806)795–4936.

★★★★*Tall Timber* is a new luxury mountain resort in the heart of the 1 million-acre San Juan National Forest. Tall Timber is accessible only by the Silverton, the last regularly scheduled narrow-gauge railroad in the United States. Traveling toward the resort, the Silverton passes 1,000–foot-deep canyons cut by the Animas River, narrow granite ledges, and dense evergreen forests. The lodge offers outstanding fishing in the wild Animas River for trophy rainbow and brown trout, hiking, backpacking and trail rides in the surrounding high-country wilderness, and a chance to explore old mine sites, lost trails, and abandoned railroad spurs. Situated on a high alpine meadow, Tall Timber offers a fully heated pool, tennis courts, therapeutic hot spa, and beautiful, deluxe condominium apartments, called Timber Hearths or Timber Suites, each with its own massive fireplace. Each hearth has 2 bedrooms upstairs, and each suite has 1 bedroom upstairs. The master bedrooms have an inside balcony from which you can watch the last glowing embers of the evening's fire. All units have thermostatically controlled electric heat and private bars. Tall Timber offers continental cuisine with American-style service. The gardens provide fresh vegetables. Homemade breads and pastries make mealtime a highlight. Tall Timber's reputation for superb meals is unequaled. American-plan rates (double occupancy) for 1– or 2–bedroom suites: $295 per week or $60 daily. For additional information, contact: Tall Timber, SSR Box 90, Durango, CO 81301 (303)247–1412 unit 13.

★★★★*Tamarron* is a spectacular alpine resort set on 630 acres in the

San Juan National Forest. Within minutes is historic Durango, where the narrow-gauge railway starts its climb over the canyons of the Animas River past half-deserted mining towns to old Silverton. And west of Durango, you can explore the ancient Mesa Verde National Park cliff dwellings. The sports facilities at Tamarron include an indoor-outdoor heated swimming pool, horseback trails and stables, mountain trout streams, wild-river rafting on the Animas, tennis courts set amidst towering pines beneath a weatherproof dome, and a mountain-climbing school. In winter you can skate, hunt, or ski on Tamarron's own slopes or at the nearby Purgatory Ski Village with its nationally famous slopes and trails. Accommodations are in the elegant, timbered Tamarron Inn with scenic views or in a secluded condominium apartment. Luxurious inn rooms for 2 have a kitchenette and 2 queen-sized beds. Suites for 2 have a bedroom-living room, dressing area, and kitchen. Suites for 2 are available with a balcony. Suites for 4 have a living room, loft bedroom reached by spiral stairs, fireplace, sleeping area, full kitchen, and foyer. Suites for 6 have 3 baths, kitchen, fireplace, oversized living room, and balcony, plus a connection to separate bedroom-living room. Tamarron is 18 miles north of Durango. Fly Frontier Airlines to Durango from Denver and Albuquerque. Or drive via Route 550 and the Navajo Trail, Highway 160. Bus service from principal cities also available. For additional information and rates, contact: Tamarron, P.O. Box 3131, Durango, CO 81301 toll-free (800)525–5420.

★★★*Wilderness Trails Ranch* is a family vacation ranch in secluded Pine River Valley in the heart of the San Juan National Forest adjacent to the high-country meadows, lakes, streams and 14,000–foot peaks of the vast Weminuche Wilderness Area. Ranch activities include trail riding, hiking, fishing, trapshooting, cookouts, square dancing, rodeos, sailing on nearby Vallecito Lake, and wilderness pack trips. Ranch accommodations consist of rustic 2–5–bedroom log cabins situated among pines, spruce, and aspen. The cabins are large, clean, and comfortable, and each has a private bath. Meals are served family-style in the log-beamed dining room, with its rustic lounge and stone fireplace. Children are fully supervised by trained counselors during riding or playing. The ranch wranglers are skilled at both riding and horsemanship instruction. Area attractions include the weekly melodrama at the Diamond Circle Theatre in Durango, the historic Durango-Silverton Narrow-Gauge Railroad, and Mesa Verde National Park. Daily American-plan rates (double occupancy): $42 per person, with special children's rates. For additional information, contact: Wilderness Trails Ranch, Rt. 1 Box B, Bayfield, CO 81122 (303)884–2581. In winter call (303)247–0722.

Travel Services & the Durango—Silverton Railroad

Animas River Float Trips at Durango are offered by Colorado Rivers. These 1–day river trips offer both scenic and white-water adventure. Above town the river meanders slowly through the scenic Animas Valley. On the tree-lined banks you will often observe deer, beaver, muskrat, and many varieties of native birds as well as old homesteads and mining ruins. White-water excitement starts when the river changes character. It starts a plunge that loses 500 feet of elevation in 25 miles. Starting in Durango the river, in a series of riffles, rapids, swift stretches, and calm pools, resumes its rush to join the San Juan and Colorado. The scenery is unspoiled. Splashing water heightens the participant's preception. A lunch stop to dry out after the best of the rapids provides time to relax. Full-day trips cost $25 per guest; half-day trips are $15 for 2 guests. The firm also outfits trips on the San Juan River in southwestern Utah.These 2–6–day trips are outstanding in their archaeologic, geologic, and scenic interest. The San Juan is a Grand Canyon-quality river trip without

the huge white-water rapids often associated with such a trip. The Dolores River in Colorado is accessible in May and early June for adventurous veterans of other river experiences. Both 3– and 6–day tours are offered. Contact: Colorado Rivers Tours, P.O. Box 1386, Durango 81301 (303)259–0708.

The Durango-Silverton Railroad, a registered historic landmark, is the nation's last remaining regularly scheduled narrow-gauge (3 ft.) railroad, established in 1882 as a branch of the Denver & Rio Grande to serve the old Silverton mining camp. The spectacular 45–mile scenic route from Durango to Silverton passes through the San Juan National Forest high country and the Animas River Canyon, past towering cliffs and waterfalls, over trestles, and through mountain passes. The historic frontier mining center of Silverton at 9,000–feet elevation in the San Juan mining district, with its silver-boom Grand Imperial Hotel, false-front Old West buildings and gold-domed courthouse, produced as much as $2 million worth of silver annually during the early 1900s. The train departs daily at 8:30 A.M. and returns at 5:30 P.M. from May 28 to Oct. 1 from the Narrow Gauge Depot in the pioneer business district of Durango adjacent to the historic General Palmer House. For reservations, contact: Passenger Agent, Rio Grande Depot, Durango 81301 (303)247–2733.

Uncompahgre National Forest & The Telluride National Historic District

The remote alpine wilderness areas of the Uncompahgre National Forest located in southwest Colorado are renowned for their trout fishing, camping, and big-game hunting. The northern section of this million-acre forest reserve lies along the crests and slopes of the rolling, mesalike Uncompahgre Plateau; the southern portion embraces the rugged northern slopes of the San Juan Mountains. Sharp, rugged canyons cut through the Uncompahgre Plateau tableland and into the pinyon-juniper hills below. In the fall, quaking aspen groves flash gold against the evergreens. The Ute who once roamed the area believed the aspen once refused homage to the Great Spirit, who decreed thereafter that its leaves should tremble whenever it was looked upon.

The San Juan Mountains portion of the forest encompasses high rocky peaks, their slopes slit by deep, narrow canyons in some places and covered by alpine grasslands elsewhere. Snowcaps on the high summits feed plunging streams culminating in breathtaking waterfalls. Among the major mountains of this area are Uncompahgre Peak (14,309 ft.), Mt. Sneffels (14,150 ft.), and Wetterhorn Peak (14,017 ft.). A variety of trails wind through this remote high-country area, the land of the Uncompahgre Wilderness. Jeeps may be helpful in getting to some trailheads, but motorized vehicles are not permitted in the wilderness area. Camping is somewhat unrestricted in this backcountry; check with a ranger on wilderness travel regulations and restrictions.

Ute Indians called the areas north of Ouray *Uncompahgre*, meaning "Red Water Springs." Spanish explorers entered the area in 1777, and Rocky Mountain fur trappers worked their lines here during the 1830s and 1840s. The discovery of gold gave birth to the area's first settlement, Mineral Point, in 1873. By the 1880s many settlers had arrived. The towns of Lake City, Ouray, and Telluride had populations of several thousand people, and smaller settlements, such as Sherman, Capitol City, Red Mountain, Ironton, Alta, and Mineral Point, dotted the mountain valleys. All of the smaller settlements are now ghost towns.

Information Sources, Maps & Access

A full-color U.S. Forest Service *Uncompahgre National Forest Map* showing all man-made and natural features is available for 50¢, along with fishing, hunting, camping, and wilderness travel information from: Forest Supervisor, Post Office Bldg., Box 138, Delta 81416 (303)874–7691. A recreation site directory with the map lists the map locations, elevations, and facilities of all Forest Service recreation sites. A *Travel Map of the Uncompahgre National Forest* is available free from the same source. It shows most of the same features, but in black and white. It also describes and illustrates travel restrictions and regulations in effect throughout the forest.

To reach the forest, take State Route 146 south from Interstate 70 to State Route 141 and continue southwest to the forest border, or take State Route 789 south from Montrose on U.S. 50. Ouray, Telluride, Montrose, and Lake City are among the outfitting and supply centers in the area.

Gateways & Accommodations

Delta

(Pop. 3,700; zip code 81416; area code 303.) Accommodations: *Best Western Sundance Motor Inn* (rates: $25 double), 41 excellent rooms and family units, restaurant, cocktail lounge, heated pool, at 903 Main St. on U.S. Hwy 50 (874–9781).

Lake City—Gateway to the Powderhorn Primitive Area & Lake Fork Recreation Area

(Pop. 100; zip code 81235; area code 303.) The town is on Colorado Hwy. 149. Area attractions include the 137,000–acre Lake Fork Recreation Area with its old ghost towns, wilderness camping, hunting, and fishing areas, and Lake San Cristobal. The 40,400–acre Powderhorn Primitive Area, managed by the Bureau of Land Management, embraces a vast expanse of tundra at 12,000–feet elevation and forests of spruce, fir, and pine on the Cannibal and Calf Creek plateaus southwest of Gunnison. The rugged mountains of the region yielded fortunes in gold and silver during the 1890s, making the area Colorado's richest of the day. Among the famous mines of the area were the Headlight, the Old Lott, and the Anaconda. The wide, chill stretches of Cannibal Plateau recall a grisly episode from the days of the Old West. A party of prospectors from Utah reached the nearby home of Ouray, chief of the Ute, who warned the men to wait for the spring before challenging the tundra. Six men, including Alfred Packer, pushed on in spite of the chief's advice. Packer turned up at a white settlement 6 weeks later, claiming that his companions had deserted him in the wilds, leaving him to forage for roots and hunt small game to survive. The story seemed suspicious, as Packer's first request was for whiskey, not food. He appeared in

another settlement several days later with a good deal of money, which he spent drinking and gambling. An Indian arrived at one of the towns with strips of flesh from human bodies he had found along the prospectors' trail, and Packer was arrested. In the spring a photographer from *Harpers Weekly* discovered the bodies of Packer's companions, their skulls crushed. Local authorities arrested Packer and chained him to a rock to await trial, because there was no jail. He escaped. He was recaptured in Wyoming 10 years later, tried and convicted of murder and cannibalism, and sentenced to hang. But he won the right to a new trial on a technicality and was sentenced instead to 40 years in prison for manslaughter. He was granted parole a few years later and died a free man in Denver in 1906. In spite of its gruesome history and formidable backcountry wilderness, this area is a top-ranked hunting area. Alpine lakes dot the high reaches, providing good wilderness fishing. The Utes once hunted these high plateaus where mule deer, black bear, and coyote roam. A part of the area serves as wintering grounds for Rocky Mountain elk. Beaver dams dot the streams of the region, which offer excellent trout fishing. Bald eagles soar above the chilly plateaus. This remote area is accessible by way of State Highway 149, which runs southeast from Gunnison.

Montrose

(Pop. 6,500; zip code 81401; area code 303.) The major gateway to the Uncompahgre National Forest recreation areas, this mining and agricultural center is located west of the Curecanti National Recreation Area, formed by three reservoirs on the Gunnison River: Blue Mesa, Narrow Point, and Crystal. Area attractions include the Ute Indian Museum 4 miles south of town on U.S. Hwy. 550. Accommodations: *Best Western Red Arrow Motel* (rates: $32–44 double), 49 excellent rooms, restaurant, cocktail lounge, at 2830 W. U.S. Hwy. 160 (249–9641); *Black Canyon Motel* (rates: $25–28 double), 40 excellent rooms and family units, heated pool 1 mile east of town on U.S. 50 (249–3495); *San Juan Inn* (rates: $24–26 double), 23 rooms 1 mile south of town on U.S. 550 (249–6644).

Ouray

(Pop. 700; zip code 81427; area code 303.) This historic mining town surrounded by the beautiful San Juan Mountains on the scenic Million Dollar Highway (550) (named for the gold-bearing gravel with which it was paved) was named for a great Ute Indian chief. The town is nestled in a pear-shaped valley. It was founded in 1875, when rich silver lodes were discovered in the surrounding mountains. Area attractions include scenic jeep tours of the surrounding high country, old gold-rush ghost towns, and mines offered by San Juan Scenic Jeep Tours, 512 Main St. (325–4444); Box Canyon Falls on U.S. 550; Daisy Placer Diggins 2 miles north of town on U.S. Hwy. 550 with guided tours and displays of area mining history; the 1876 Gourmet Restaurant in an old 19th–century hotel at 118 7th Avenue (325–4213). Four-wheel drive rentals are available from Switzerland of America (325–4484). Accommodations: *Best Western Twin Peaks Motel* (rates: $26–28 double), 48 excellent rooms at 125 3rd Ave., on road to Box Canyon Falls (325–4427); *Box Canyon Motel* (rates: $20–29 double), 22 excellent rooms and family units, at 1st St. and 3rd Ave. at entrance to Box Canyon Falls (325–4551); *Bright Diamond Motel—Friendship Inn* (rates: $22–25 double), 22 excellent rooms and family units, at 201 6th Ave. (325–4938); *Ouray Chalet Motel* (rates $20–26 double), 30 excellent rooms and family units, on U.S. 550 and Colorado Hwy. 789 (325–4331).

Telluride

(Pop. 600; zip code 81435; area code 303.) See under "Lodges" below.

Lodges & Ski Resorts

★★*The Golconda Resort*, 60 miles southwest of Gunnison, is located on the shores of sprawling Lake San Cristobal, Colorado's largest natural lake. In addition to 10 motel rooms with excellent views of the lake, the Golconda offers 3– and 4–room housekeeping apartments and several modern log housekeeping cabins with fireplaces and 1 or 2 bedrooms. Rates vary from $18 per person for motel units to $36 for a 4–room apartment accommodating 6 people. Off-season discounts are available. Activities at the Golconda Resort include boating and water sports on Lake San Cristobal, cross-country skiing (equipment rentals at the lodge), hiking the Uncompahgre, fishing in Big Blue Creek, and hunting in season. The resort also offers free "mountain life" classes with guided hikes, ghost town tours, mushroom hunts, and nature trips. Attached to the lodge is a restaurant serving 3 meals a day, plus barbecues during the summer season. For details write: The Golconda Resort, Box 95, Lake City, CO 81235 (303)944–2256.

★★★★*Telluride Ski Center & Nordic Backcountry*, one of the nation's great downhill and cross-country ski areas, is located in the San Juan Mountains in the heart of the vast Uncompahgre National Forest at the end of an 18–mile serpentine box canyon formed by the San Miguel River. The ski center and historic boom town of Telluride—a national historic district—are surrounded on three sides by 13,000–foot peaks, which are ribboned by Ingram and Bridal Veil Falls. This valley was held sacred by the Utes, who referred to the San Juans as the Shining Mountains. The Utes refused the white man access through the canyon "door," but the miners, determined in their search for gold and silver, came over the top from the east by mule train across the 13,000–foot ridges—and were handsomely rewarded for their fortitude. Millions of dollars in precious metals have been extracted from Telluride environs since the 1870s, and today the Idarado mine is one of the most active in Colorado, with 500 miles of tunnels—more than enough to reach from Los Angeles to San Francisco.

During the height of Colorado's gold rush, Telluride boasted a population of 5,000 and sported 50 bars, gaming houses, and bordellos. It was here that William Jennings Bryan gave his "Cross of Gold" speech, and here also that Butch Cassidy, tempted by boom-town banking wealth, made his first unauthorized bank withdrawal.

The Telluride Ski Area, one of a handful of North American ski meccas with over 3,000 vertical feet, lies just a few blocks from the heart of the town of Telluride. The Telluride Ski Area offers the skier 40 miles of trails, including the "best beginner's area in the U.S.," miles of intermediate trails, and the heart-stopping Plunge and Spiral Stairs, the longest, steepest run in Colorado, over 3,000 feet of vertical and a 2½–mile rise.

During the summer, Telluride offers a wide variety of activities, from sight-seeing to backpacking camping, jeep tours, trout fishing in the high alpine lakes and streams, horseback riding, hunting, kayaking, tennis, mountaineering, bicycling, and much more, including the Telluride Bluegrass Festival, Chamber Music Festival, Film Festival, Jazz Festival, Hang Glider Invitational over Telluride Valley, and tours to the Mesa Verde National Park cliff dwellings. The Telluride Historical Museum contains a trove of Old West history.

Telluride's storybook main street dates back to the silver boom of the 1880s. Its Victorian architecture has been restored in dozens of colorful shops and eateries, including the *Chez Pierre* an old mining warehouse that has been transformed into a charming French restaurant with what has been described as the "best French cooking

between New York and San Francisco"; the *Floradora Saloon*; the *Flour Garden*, a perfect little place for breakfast; *Hole in the Wall* for great pizza; the *Ice House* for seafood; the *Iron Ladle* for breakfast, lunch, or dinner; and the *Silverjack Mining Co.* for lunch and dinner. All framed by the San Juan Mountains with Mt. Ballard, Mt. Palmyra, and Mt. Telluride rising 13,500 feet around the village.

The Telluride Ski Area has 6 high-speed double chair-lifts to get you where you're going easily and quickly. The town's bedroom capacity of 700 and the mountain's uphill capacity of 2,400 per hour make for uncrowded, hassle-free skiing, even during holidays.

The ski area also has a modern ski school, the ski center at Telluride, and a nursery for parents with children. The area is one of the nation's great cross-country ski-touring areas, offering top instruction and guided tours in the San Juan Mountains. The 2–day cross-country trip to the remote alta, where you'll spend the night in a rustic chalet, is one of the area's top attractions. This tour costs $30 per person per night and includes all meals, a sauna and Jacuzzi. For info write: Telluride Ski Touring, Box 672, Ophir, CO 81426, or call Paradise Trips (303)728–4316.

Full-service accommodations at Telluride are available at the following lodges, inns, and hotels. Package rates listed below are based on 5 nights' lodging and 4 days' lift tickets during the regular ski season (Jan.-Apr.) at double occupancy.

Brown Homestead, located ¾ mile west of town, offers 2– and 3–bedroom condominium units, fully furnished and equipped. Patios and sundecks allow you to enjoy the spectacular views and sunny location. Daily maid service, wood-burning fireplaces, completely equipped kitchens with dishwashers, beautiful furnishings. Eight condominium units, maximum occupancy 54. Rates: 1–bedroom, $105–141. Contact: P.O. Box 858, Telluride 81435 (303) 728–3777.

Bushwhacker Inn, located in the center of town, just around the corner from the Court House. Originally constructed as a church, the Bushwhacker has been completely remodeled into a European-style hostelry. It offers accommodations for 82 persons in its 24 units: some have private baths, and there are large bathroom/sauna facilities for those without. Amenities include TV lounge, lobby with fireplace, and a bar-restaurant, the Pastimes Saloon. Rates: $88. Contact: P.O. Box 176, Telluride 81435 (303)728–3383.

Dahl Haus, built in 1899 as a boardinghouse for Telluride's hardrock miners, today is a charming guest house. It offers antique furnishings, modern conveniences, and old-fashioned warmth and hospitality. In the open parlor is a working player piano, perfect for snowy evenings. Proprietress Sherry Campbell-Breuer serves up homemade goodies from her adjacent China Moon Bun Factory for continental breakfast. Eight units with a maximum capacity of 20. Rates: $97. Contact: P.O. Box 695, Telluride 81435 (303)728–9915.

Last Dollar Condominiums overlook the ski area, the town of Telluride, and Colorado's most spectacular peaks. Each first-class 2–bedroom, 1½–bath condominium has its own private sun deck, Jacuzzi, shower, fireplace, dishwasher, and washer-dryer. Experience the earliest sunrise and latest sunset in the area. Centrally located on the main highway 2 miles from Prospect Meadows Ski Base and 3½ miles from Coonskin base. It's an easy 5–minute drive to downtown Telluride. Four units, maximum capacity 32. Rates: $99–117. Contact: P.O. Box 181, Telluride, CO 81435 (303)728–3330.

Manitou Lodge, nestled against the ski mountain, overlooks the San Miguel River and is only a 2–minute walk from the heart of town. The lodge has 11 attractive rooms, each with a spectacular view, wall hangings, private bathroom, clock-radio, and refrigerator. Most rooms are on two levels with balconies on the river; some have fireplaces and bathtubs. There are a fireplace lounge with a fully equipped kitchen and a Jacuzzi for your enjoyment. The Manitou is located on Fir Street at the river, across from the skating rink and favorite cross-country trails. Maximum capacity 50. Rates: $106–121. Contact: P.O. Box 722, Telluride 81435.

New Sheridan Hotel, located on historic Main St., is where William Jennings Bryan gave his famous "Cross of Gold" speech in 1902. Lillian Gish and Sarah Bernhardt were honored guests at the Sheridan Hotel and gave dramatic performances at the adjacent Opera House. Renovated in 1977, the New Sheridan offers first-class accommodations and services, including room service, luxurious bathrooms, 24–hour switchboard, and accommodations ranging from single rooms to luxury suites. The Sheridan has 31 rooms, with a maximum capacity of 112. Rates: $108–166. Contact: P.O. Box 980, Telluride, CO 81435 (303)728–4351.

Telluride Lodge, located at the base of the Coonskin Lift on Highway 145, is Telluride's largest lodging facility, with a maximum capacity of 360. It offers accommodations ranging from standard hotel rooms with private bath to 3–bedroom luxury condominiums, complete with wood-burning fireplaces, sun decks, completely equipped all-electric kitchens with dishwasher-disposals, mud rooms, sliding glass doors, and ultramodern decor. Other amenities include a year-round heated outdoor swimming pool, Jacuzzi, saunas, bar-

restaurant, ski shop, meeting rooms, and doctor's office. Rates: $114–161. Contact: P.O. Box 127, Telluride 81435 (303)728–3831.

Tomboy Inn, located just across the highway from the Coonskin Lift, features standard motel rooms or deluxe, handsomely furnished condo units with fully equipped kitchens, wood-burning fireplaces, direct-dial phones, carpeting, and individually controlled electric heat. Owner-managers Pat and Bucky Schuler are natives of Telluride and will see to it that your stay is pleasant and comfortable. Relax in the lobby with color TV and fireplace, or enjoy a sauna. During the winter there's continental breakfast. There are 39 units with a maximum capacity of 120. Rates: $116–166. Contact: P.O. Box 325, Telluride 81435 (303)728–3831.

Victorian Inn, built in 1976, is one of Telluride's newest lodging facilities and is located just 3 blocks from the Coonskin Lift on Pacific St. It is owned and operated by Frank and Katy Scheer and features a large lobby-lounge, balconies, carpeted rooms with private baths, sauna and therapy pool, and close-in parking. The Scheers strive to provide old-fashioned hospitality and comfort, and the beautiful parlor stove in the lobby provides a cozy place for an evening's chat. Choose from standard units, studios, or the cottage. The Victorian offers 20 units with a maximum capacity of 68. Rates: $111. Contact: P.O. Box 217, Telluride, CO 81435 (303)728–3684.

Telluride is only 127 miles south of Grand Junction, serviced by United and Frontier airlines (Western Airlines on Saturdays), and only 62 miles south of Montrose, serviced daily by Frontier and Aspen airways with convenient connections from Denver. Rental cars and limousine service are also available on a regular basis.

White River National Forest & The Aspen/Vail Ski Villages

This 1,960,000–acre forest located northwest of Glenwood Springs embraces some of the nation's finest alpine and Nordic ski areas, backpacking trails, and the renowned White River, a fine summer stream for rainbow, brown, and brook trout. Hundreds of miles of hiking trails and forest roads wind through this spectacular high-country region to such areas as Eagle River, Hanging Lake, Bridal Veil Falls, Elk Range, Flattops Primitive Area, Sawatch Range, Gore Range-Eagles Nest Primitive Area, Roaring Fork, Ten-mile Range, and the Maroon Bells-Snowmass Wilderness. The forest is an excellent elk and mule deer range.

The Flattops Primitive Area lies within the 400 square miles of the White River Plateau, about 20 miles north of Glenwood Springs and 30 miles southwest of Steamboat Springs. The plateau, a lava-capped dome bordered by rimrock, is most prominent at the "Devil's Causeway," a ridge between the drainages of the East Fork of the Williams Fork River and the North Fork of the White River. The forces of time and nature have carved deep canyons far into the plateau. This superb green wilderness is a land of violent contrasts, with steep cliffs, sparkling blue lakes, jagged rocks, snowcapped peaks, meadows, and densely timbered valleys. A bark beetle infestation in the 1940s left 68,000 acres of spruce devastated, but spruce and alpine fir are beginning to regenerate the forest. If you travel through this area, be aware of the dangers of falling trees and the path obstructions they create.

About 160 miles of trails wind through the wilderness; from them experienced cross-country hikers can explore untracked valleys and plateaus and more than 30 fishing lakes, including Wall, Marvine, Big Fish, Island, Muskrat, Twin, Sable, and the renowned trophy trout waters of Trappers Lake. Half of the area's 100 miles of streams also offer good to excellent fishing for native cutthroat, rainbow, and Eastern brook trout. One of the most beautiful wilderness camping areas is the Lost Lakes Peaks, located due north of Trappers Lake.

The Flattops are a top-ranked hunting area for elk, mule deer, and black bear. Blue grouse, white-tailed ptarmigan, and snowshoe rabbits are the area's small game animals. Bobcats, coyotes, badgers, foxes, beavers, martens, minks, mountain lions, and a variety of smaller animals inhabit the wilderness.

The Maroon Bells-Snowmass Wilderness Area of the White River National Forest encompasses 66,380 acres of the central Elk Range, including some of the most breathtaking landscapes in all of Colorado. Peaks such as Capitol, Snowmass, Maroon Bells, Castle, and Pyramid range from 12,000 to 14,259 feet. Plunging streams and fine, large alpine lakes grace the heights of formidable, often richly colored peaks, unmarred by old mining claims. Much of the wilderness is above timberline, where small clumps of trees cling to the precipitous valley walls. Through these canyon valleys flow Snowmass, Maroon, Geneva, and Conundrum creeks. Below timberline, groves of aspen are interspersed with Engelmann spruce and subalpine fir. Wild flowers carpet these lower stretches and bloom prolifically on the tundra as well. Forget-me-nots, alpine lilies, alpine phlox, moss campion, and Indian paintbrush are just a few of them.

Almost 130 miles of trails wind through the wilderness, providing access to the spectacular lake and mountain scenery and alpine camping and fishing at Capitol, Avalanche, Willow, Geneva, and Snowmass lakes. The relatively inaccessible Pierre Lakes provide good trout fishing for those who wish to make the long hike.

The White River National Forest shares the Eagles Nest Wilderness amidst the Gore Range with neighboring Arapaho National Forest. Trails in this remote area lead into the areas of Meridian Mountain and Climbers Lake (11,000 ft.), Eagles Nest Mountain (13,397 ft.), Mt. Powell (13,534 ft.), and the alpine Boulder Lake.

Information Sources, Maps & Access

For detailed information, backcountry permits, and a full-color *White River National Forest Map* (50¢) and a free *Flattops Primitive Area Map* and *Maroon Bells-Snowmass Wilderness Map*, write:

Supervisor, White River National Forest, Old Federal Bldg., P.O. Box 948, Glenwood Springs, CO 81601 (303)945–6582.

The forest is easily accessible from Interstate 70, which runs between two of its major districts. Colorado Route 82 dips south of Interstate 70 and enters the forest near Aspen. Aspen, Yampa, Glenwood Springs, Trapper, and Leadville provide overnight accommodations and outfitting, guide, packhorse, and supply services.

Gateways & Accommodations

Aspen Village

(Pop. 2,400; zip code 81611; area code 303.) A world-famous skiing and summer recreation and cultural center high in the Rockies of the White Mountain National Forest, this historic silver-mining town produced up to $6 million a year at the close of the 19th century from area mines such as Smuggler, Molly Gibson, and Montezuma. Area attractions include the Aspen-Snowmass ski areas, Institute for Humanistic Studies, Aspen Historical Society Museum at 620 W. Bleeker St., area trout streams and hiking trails, scenic drives to Independence Pass and the marble quarries, Aspen Music Festival, and the famous *Copper Kettle Restaurant* in a remodeled old mine in a scenic location with gourmet international cuisine at 535 E. Deam Ave. (925–3151). For ski conditions call (303)222–0671. Accommodations (see also "Aspen-Snowmass Ski Area" for listings of inns and lodges): *Best Western Aspenalt Lodge* (rates: $38 double), 34 excellent rooms with scenic views in some, 17 miles northwest of Aspen on Colorado 82 (927–3191); *Holiday Inn* (rates: $42–46 dou-

ble), 120 excellent rooms and alpine lodge-style accommodations, dining room, coffee shop, heated pool, sauna, airport service, on Colorado 82 at base of Buttermilk Ski Area (925–1500); *Mountain Chalet—Snowmass* (rates: $34–50 double), 64 superb lodge rooms, with complete breakfast, fireplaces, heated pool, tennis, at Snowmass Village on Lower Village Road (923–3900); *Stonebridge Inn—Snowmass* (rates: $44–54 double), 97 outstanding rooms and suites, coffee shop, heated pool, sauna, in Snowmass Village (923–2420).

Glenwood Springs

(Pop. 4,100; zip code 81601; area code 303.) Long famous for its hot springs, the town is the major gateway to the White River National Forest and the Aspen-Snowmass and Vail ski areas. The town is the burial place of the notorious gunman Doc Holliday. Glenwood is situated off Interstate 70 at the confluence of the Colorado and Roaring Fork rivers, flanked on the north by the 10,000–foot Flattops and on the south by the Roaring Fork Valley. Area attractions include the Sunlight Ski Area hot spring pools off I–70 Exit 24, scenic drives to Bridal Veil Falls and the wilderness high country, and the fine food and Old West atmosphere of the *Buffalo Valley Inn* (945–5297). Accommodations: *Best Western Antlers Motel* (rates: $36.50 double), 53 excellent rooms and family units, heated pool, at 305 Laurel St., off I–70 Exit 24 (945–8535); *Best Western Caravan Motel* (rates: $31–38 double), 53 excellent rooms and family units, heated pool, at 1826 Grand Ave. (945–7451); *Hotel Denver* (rates: $22–39 double), 86 excellent rooms, dining room, coffee shop, cocktail lounge, at 7th and Cooper Sts., opposite railroad station (945–6565); *Glenwood Hot Springs Lodge* (rates: $31 double), 71 excellent rooms and family units, restaurant, athletic club, year-round hot spring pool, at 401 N. River Road, in center of town on Colorado River (945–6571); *Holiday Inn* (rates: $43.75–47.75 double), 81 superb rooms, restaurant, cocktail lounge, heated pool, steambaths, 2 miles west of town off I–70 Exit 23 (945–8551).

Vail Village

(Pop. 500; zip code 81657; area code 303.) The town is a spectacular alpine village ski area and summer gateway to the lakes, streams, and high country of the White River National Forest. Village restaurants include the *Clock Tower Inn* (476–5306), *Red Lion Inn* (476–5740) and *Tyrolean Inn* (476–2204). Accommodations (for additional listings see "Lodges & Guest Ranches" below): *Best Western Vailglo Lodge* (rates: $36–49 double), 34 alpine lodge rooms and family units with balconies, heated pool, at Lionshead Ski Area (476–5506); *Enzian Lodge* (rates: $44–65 double), 52 outstanding alpine chalet rooms, dining room, heated pool, at Lionshead Ski Area (476–2050); *The Crest Resort Hotel* (rates: $34–58 double), 147 superb lodge rooms and suites with fireplaces, balconies, dining room, coffee shop, cocktail lounge, at Lionshead Ski Area (476–2180); *The Lodge at Vail* (rates: $38–60 double), 400 outstanding alpine lodge rooms and deluxe apartments, dining room, restaurant, heated pool, sauna, at 174 E. Gore Creek Drive off I–70 Exit 35 (476–5011); *Mark Resort & Tennis Club* (rates: $48–50 double), 74 outstanding rooms and suites with balconies, dining room, cocktail lounge, heated pool, sauna, tennis courts, and instruction at Lionshead Ski Area (476–4444); *Ram's Horn Lodge* (rates: $31–50 double), 30 excellent alpine rooms, heated pool, in center of village (476–5646); *Sitzmark Lodge & Left Bank Restaurant* (rates: $26–58 double), 35 superb alpine rooms and dining, in village near ski lifts (476–5001).

Lodges, Guest Ranches & Ski Centers

★★★★*The Aspen/Snowmass Ski Area*, indisputably America's largest downhill ski mecca, comprises some 300 miles of trails, 37 lifts, and 4

mountains: Aspen, the Aspen Highlands, Buttermilk Mountain, and Snowmass. Aspen, Snowmass, and the Highlands are primarily for intermediate and advanced skiers, with challenging trails and runs of 3–3½ miles. Gentle Buttermilk, at 9,800–foot elevations, has fine trails for beginners and intermediate powder buffs. Skiing starts 4 blocks from Aspen's Main St. and continues 2 miles out of town in the Highlands, which boasts the longest (3,800–foot) vertical drop in Colorado. Just down the road are Buttermilk and Snowmass, the country's first architecturally planned ski village, where luxurious condominiums offer delightful year-round accommodations a short walk from ski lifts, golf courses, swimming pools, and a country club. Bigger than the other three mountains combined, Snowmass is a paradise for intermediate skiers and a popular family vacation area because of its supervised children's programs.

There are ski school and rental equipment facilities on every mountain, along with over 300 professional instructors who teach everything from basic GLM and ATM to racing and powder techniques. For nightlife and après-ski excitement, the bustling town of Aspen boasts music, dancing, movies, and more than 100 restaurants serving everything from burgers to *coq au vin*.

The Aspen area is a summer wonderland, too. Hiking and horseback riding through flower-carpeted mountain meadows, fishing the trout-filled lakes and streams, kayaking and white-water rafting on the Colorado River, jeep tours, and weekly rodeos are just some of the possibilities for vacation-minded visitors to Aspen-Snowmass. The two-month, world-famous Aspen Music Festival and the professional Ballet West attract music lovers and dance aficionados to the area every July and August. Many of the resorts and guest ranches that cater to skiers in the winter also offer fine summer activities.

Weekly package rates for the Aspen-Snowmass lodges listed below (7 nights' lodging): $126–341 for lodge rooms (double occupancy); $185–329 for a condominium studio; $199–411 for 2 in a 1–bedroom condominium; and $129–197 per person in dorm rooms. For detailed information, rates, and reservations for the lodges and condominiums listed below, contact: Aspen Reservations, Inc., P.O. Box 1188, Aspen, CO 81611 (303)925–4000).

Aspen Lodging:

Applejack Inn, 35 rooms, family-operated lodge on Main St. near skiers' shuttle, indoor pool and TV in every room. Continental breakfast.

Aspen Châteaux Company, a variety of standard to deluxe units. Fully equipped condominiums within walking distance of Little Nell lift and downtown Aspen. All have TV and most have fireplaces. Pool, sauna, whirlpool, and conference and party facilities available.

Aspen Châteaux Condominium Rentals, a selection of standard to deluxe condominium units. Management representatives for various apartments and houses around the Aspen area. Most units have fireplaces and TV and some have river balconies and sun decks. Houses often located slightly out of town, so transportation may be necessary. Pool, sauna, and whirlpool, conference and party facilities available.

Aspen Inn, 39 rooms and 21 apartments, located at the base of Aspen Mountain, 2 blocks from the town mall and Aspen Mountain lifts. Complete recreation facilities and restaurant, bar with entertainment, 24–hour switchboard, pool and sauna.

Aspen Manor, 22 rooms, convenient location in downtown Aspen near Aspen Mountain lifts and free skier shuttle stop. Comfortable rooms, all with color TV and phone. Pool, sauna, and whirlpool available. Continental breakfast included.

Aspen Properties. Property management representatives for a variety of condominium units and houses. All are fully furnished and located throughout the Aspen area. Many have TV, fireplaces, and private phones.

Aspen Silverglo Condominiums, 23 apartments located at the east end of Aspen, 3 blocks from Little Nell lift. Accommodations range from studio to 5–bedroom units, all fully furnished. Color TV and fireplace in every unit. Pool and sauna available for guests.

Aspen Square, 105 units ranging from studios to 2–bedroom condominiums, located in the center of town across from the Little Nell lift at Aspen Mountain. Heated pool, sauna, daily maid service. All units have fireplaces and color TV.

Bavarian Inn, 14 rooms and a few chalet apartments, located on west edge of town near a free shuttle stop. Clean, comfortable family-operated lodge. Restaurant serving breakfast. Heated pool.

Bell Mountain Lodge, 16 standard rooms and apartments. All units have private baths. Convenient downtown location 1 block from Aspen Mountain. Pool, courtesy transportation from airport, continental breakfast.

Boomerang, 19 rooms and 13 apartments located at the west end of town in a quiet setting. Units have private balcony or garden terrace. Telephone and TV in every unit. Sauna, lounge, heated pool, and whirlpool. Continental breakfast included.

Buckhorn Lodge, 9 economy rooms in small lodge conveniently located a few blocks from Aspen Mountain and within a short walking distance of center of town. Reasonable rates for the budget-minded guest. Color TV and radio in each room.

Chalet Lisi, 7 economy studios and 1–bedroom apartments located in a quiet residential area 3 blocks from town center. Small, friendly lodge. Sauna and laundry facilities on site. Baby-sitting service available.

Christiania, 15 standard rooms and several apartments located at west end of town near bus stop for skier shuttle. Full breakfast served to lodge guests in sunny lounge. Heated pool. TV and fireplace in several apartments.

Christmas Inn, 18 rooms, located a short distance from bus stop for skier shuttle. Sun deck and lounge have view of Aspen and ski area.

Continental Inn, 133 rooms and 21 studio apartments at the base of Aspen Mountain, Aspen's largest hotel, with complete recreation facilities, restaurant, bar with entertainment, 24–hour switchboard. Indoor and outdoor pools, large lobby.

Copper Horse, 14 economy rooms and dorm accommodations, most with shared baths, in restored Victorian house. Located on Main St. within walking distance of skier shuttle buses and downtown Aspen. Full complimentary breakfast served.

Crestahaus, 15 rooms in family-operated lodge located at east end of Aspen on hill overlooking town. Quiet surroundings, yet only minutes from center of town. Free shuttle bus stops next to lodge. Cozy lounge for guests with fireplace and TV. Private phone in every room. Continental breakfast.

Dolomite Villas, 9 condominiums. Large town houses, from 3 to 7 bedrooms, located on Aspen Mountain 2 blocks from center of town. Each has fully equipped kitchen, private sauna, fireplace,

laundry facilities, color TV, and private phone. Good views from decks and patios.

Dormer-Vous, 25 economy rooms, recently redecorated lodge with dorms and a few private rooms. Modern concrete building within walking distance of center of town, 2 blocks from Lift 1A. Lounge area for guests. Continental breakfast included.

Durant, 21 deluxe condominiums located at the base of Aspen Mountain just steps to lifts and town mall. All units have fireplaces and color TV and many have good views. Heated pool.

Fasching Haus, 26 units ranging from standard to deluxe. Condominiums have fireplaces and color TV. Studios to 5–bedroom units available. Located at the base of Aspen Mountain, 1 block from town. Conference rooms and recreation facilities on premises, including game room, pool, and sauna.

Fifth Avenue, 18 condominium units, 2– and 3–bedroom apartments, each individually decorated with spacious living room, fireplace, and private balcony. Pool, sauna, and laundry facilities available. Good location at base of Aspen Mountain.

Fireside, 20 rooms, quiet location at west end of Aspen. Warm, comfortable rooms and large lounge with panoramic view. Private heated pool and restaurant and bar on premises. Complimentary breakfast included.

The Gant, 140 deluxe 1–bedroom to 4–bedroom units at base of Aspen Mountain, 3 blocks east of Little Nell. Private balconies and fireplaces, heated pool, hot therapy baths, saunas, and dressing rooms. Recreation and conference center.

Gasthof Eberli, 11 rooms and a few apartments. Central location with warm family atmosphere. Pleasant lobby area with fireplace. Full breakfast included.

Glory Hole, 97 standard rooms. Completely rebuilt and redecorated lodge excellently located next to Little Nell lift. Offering 24–hour switchboard service, restaurant and bar on premises. Heated pool and whirlpool available for guests. All units have color cable TV.

Hearthstone House, 17 rooms. Attractive lodge situated within walking distance of lifts and mall. Afternoon tea served in large, sunny lounge, complete with library for guests. Full breakfast included.

Highlands Inn, 25 rooms. A complete resort facility with restaurant, bar, pool, sauna on premises. Located at the base of the Aspen Highlands Ski Area. Dorm rooms available.

Holiday House, 11 rooms and 8 studio and 1–bedroom apartments. Friendly lodge located just blocks from town mall and lifts. Bar, restaurant, pool, and sauna on premises.

Hotel Jerome, 30 rooms in historic hotel built during silver-mining days. Good central location on corner of Mill and Main. Rooms with or without bath, from single-occupancy rooms to quaint parlor accommodations. Restaurant, bar, and shops in hotel.

Innsbruck, 29 rooms in attractive Main St. lodge located across the street from free skier shuttle stop. Pool, sauna, and suites available. All rooms have color TV and private phone. Complimentary continental breakfast.

Le Clairvaux, 10 standard 2– and 3–bedroom condominiums. Located within walking distance of Little Nell lift, shops, and restaurants. All units have fireplace, TV, and private phone.

Limelite Lodge, 60 rooms in family-operated lodge centrally located. Mountain views from some rooms. Two swimming pools, whirlpool, and continental breakfast available for guests. Large, sunny lounge has mountain view. All units have telephone and color TV.

Little Red Ski Haus, 20 economy rooms in restored Victorian house converted to dormitory. Rooms with and without bath, 3 lounges, full complimentary breakfast. Located 3 blocks from center of town and lifts. Modest, quaint facility.

Maroon Creek, 11 studio to 3–bedroom apartments. Located at the base of Aspen Highlands Ski Area, 1½ miles from Aspen. Comfortable, attractive apartments, all fully furnished. Sauna.

Molly Gibson, 16 rooms in recently redecorated lodge with large fireplace lounge. All rooms have TV, radio, and phone. Many amenities, including heated pool, complimentary wine-tasting party, and continental breakfast. Some apartments.

North of Nell, 28 condominiums, including 1–, 2–, and 3–bedroom units near nightlife and next to Little Nell lift. All bedrooms and living areas look through sliding glass doors to private balconies with mountain views. TV and fireplace in every unit.

Nugget, 31 rooms, located on Main St. near skier shuttle stop. Choose twin, double, or king-size beds in newly remodeled motel accommodations. Spacious lounge has mountain view. Heated pool, full breakfast included.

Park Meadows, 14 standard apartments located adjacent to the Buttermilk ski area. Small studios and 1–bedroom apartments, completely furnished with full kitchens. Moderately priced family lodging. Sauna.

Plum Tree Inn, 48 standard rooms, located on Hwy. 82 west of Aspen and affiliated with the Pomegranate Inn. Color TV in every room and some units with fireplace and view. Restaurant, bar, and lounge on premises. Heated pool, sauna, and courtesy car.

Pomegranate Inn, 50 standard rooms, located adjacent to Buttermilk ski area, with restaurant and bar on premises. Heated pool, sauna, and courtesy car. All rooms have TV and private phones, and some fireplace rooms are available.

Prospector, 16 rooms and 2 apartments. Traditional lodge located downtown next to Wagner Park. Warm country home atmosphere with special lounge area where full complimentary breakfast is served.

St. Moritz, 15 rooms and 3 apartments. Many amenities available, including heated pool, sauna, TV in lounge. Town bus stops nearby. Attractive dorm rooms also available. Continental breakfast included.

Shadow Mountain, 20 two-bedroom apartments, complete with kitchens, sun decks, and good views. Excellent location overlooking town of Aspen and adjacent to Lift 1A at Aspen Mountain. Heated pool and elevator available for guests.

Smuggler, 33 rooms in economy motel located on Main St. within easy walking distance of town center. Accommodations range from moderate large rooms with 2 double beds to small units. Pool, continental breakfast.

Snowflake Lodge, 16 rooms and 18 apartments. Garden patio with heated pool, game room, lounge with color TV. Good location near town mall. Dorms available.

Snow Queen, 5 economy rooms, dorm accommodations in restored Victorian house located several blocks from downtown and lifts at Aspen Mountain. Small, modest facility.

Tyrolean, 8 economy kitchenette units with private phone in each unit. TV available for rent. Good Main St. location adjacent to free skier shuttle stops.

Vagabond, 12 rooms and a few modest apartments. Informal, relaxed lodge located 2 blocks from Little Nell lift, shops, and restaurants. Full breakfast served in sunny, pleasant lounge. Pool and sauna.

Vilcor, a variety of condominium units and houses. All apartments are fully furnished and equipped and all have fireplaces and telephones. Most houses are located slightly out of town, so some mode of transportation is advised.

Snowmass Village Lodging:

Aspen Châteaux Condominium Rentals, apartments located ½ mile from Snowmass Village mall area and within walking distance to Lift No. 6. Units are fully equipped and furnished and all have fireplaces. Pool, sauna, whirlpool, and recreation room on premises.

Crestwoods, standard to deluxe condominiums adjacent to Snowmass Village, with a beautiful view of mountains. All units have fireplaces and telephones. Pool, sauna, courtesy car available. Courteous and friendly staff ready to serve you.

Pokolodi/Inns at Snowmass, 73 rooms. One level below the Village Square, adjacent to the Recreation Center and the swimming pool. Ski to the lifts from most rooms. Pinata Restaurant on site.

Snowmass Village Property Management. Property managers for a variety of condominium units ranging from standard to deluxe in the Snowmass area. All apartments are fully furnished and are located throughout the village area. Most units have fireplace and phone. Pool and saunas available.

Timberline, standard to deluxe condominiums. Easy walk to the village of Snowmass. All units have telephones, fireplaces, and TV. Pool, sauna, and whirlpool also available.

Top of the Village, luxury condominium apartments located at the top of Snowmass Village. All units are fully equipped and furnished, and every apartment has a fireplace and telephone. Recreation facilities available, including pool, saunas, and whirlpool.

Woodbridge, located at base of the triple chair lift in Snowmass Resort. Two-bedroom and two-bedroom-plus-loft available. All units have fireplaces and color TV. Conference and meeting room facilities available for up to 400 people.

★★★*Ashcroft Ski Touring Center* offers 20 miles of mapped, marked, and maintained trails in the White River National Forest. The trails, professionally groomed with Scandinavian tracksetters, lead you into an unspoiled valley. Three different warming huts, potbellied stoves, complimentary bouillon, hot chocolate, tea, and coffee are all a part of a day's skiing at Ashcroft, a historic ghost town north of Aspen. A complete workshop affords expert service in waxing, ski repair, and rentals. A well-trained staff gives whatever help or advice a cross-country skier may require; and waxes, sun cream, glasses, film, and kindred amentities are at hand—including benches for the do-it-yourselfer. The Pine Creek Cookhouse lies halfway up the valley and is open for lunch or for special dinner tours. There are luncheon sittings at 12 and at 1:30 every day but Monday. The food (Swiss-Hungarian) is excellent and the Cookhouse is popular, so please phone reservations ahead and confirm at the King Cabin when you start out. Dinner tours start up the valley in the late afternoon, dine at the Cookhouse, and return by the light of miners' lamps. Ashcroft also offers guided day tours and overnights at the Kellog Woods Cabin (cost: $28 per person) and 2–day overnights at the Toplat Chalet, a private mountain hut near timberline at the gateway to Pearl Pass. In addition, they will guide you to Crested Butte, help find your way to remote wilderness huts, or plot your day's skiing at the Haydens, Star, or Cooper bowls (cost: $35 per day). For detailed info, rates, and maps, contact: Ashcroft Ski Touring, P.O. Box 1572, Aspen CO 81611 (303)925–1971).

★★★*Horseshoe Bend Guest Ranch*, overlooking Lake Nast in the White River National Forest, specializes in horseback riding through gorgeous mountain scenery and excellent fishing in lakes and streams surrounding the ranch, or in high-country wilderness waters accessible only on horseback. Raft trips on the Roaring Fork and Colorado rivers, backpacking, and overnight pack trips into the Upper Frying wilderness area are also offered. The lodge and ranch buildings are rustic on the outside, fully modern within, and surrounded by aspens, fir trees, and stately pines. Meals are served family-style in a handsome dining room and include a variety of tempting, home-cooked specialties. Some of the extras at Horseshoe Bend are scenic jeep tours, free riding lessons, and centrally heated cabins with lovely views. Rates range from $210 to $240 per person weekly for lodging and 3 meals daily (children under 10: $165–190 weekly). The ranch is also open during the fall and winter months for deer and elk hunting, cross-country skiing, and winter sports. For information write: Horseshoe Bend Guest Ranch, Meredith, CO 81642

(303)927–3570; (off-season) Box 92, Horseshoe Farm, Claremore, OK 74017 (918)341–9483.

★7 *Lakes Ranch*, a family-style, family-run operation, is situated at 8,250 feet adjoining the lakes, streams, and high-country ponds of the White River National Forest and Flattops Wilderness Area, 30 miles east of Meeker. Ranch activities include pack trips and trail rides, hunting, and fly-fishing on private ranch water, with trips to the nationally renowned White River and Flattops Wilderness lakes. The ranch has 9 rustic guest cabins with private baths. Breakfast and dinner are sit-down meals in the ranch lodge. American-plan rates: $50 per person, with reduced rates for children 5–16 years of age. For info, contact: 7 Lakes Ranch, Trappers Lake Rte., Box 25, Meeker, CO 81641 (303)878–4772.

★★*7–W Ranch*, a year-round family guest resort, is located high on a 9,000–foot mesa 35 miles northeast of Glenwood Springs in the heart of the White River National Forest. The ranch is surrounded by the 12,000–foot Flattops area—the largest primitive area in the state—much of which can be reached only on horseback. Short rides and overnight pack trips lead through quiet forest groves, past long stretches of grass, to breathtaking summits affording spectacular views of mountains, valleys, and canyons. Some of the best fishing in Colorado is in high mountain lakes well off the beaten track. Close to home, the lake next to 7–W's main lodge is well stocked for angling anytime. In the fall there's big-game hunting for elk and deer in the company of highly qualified guides. Snowmobiling across vast open meadows is popular during the winter months. Accommodations are in individual rustic cabins with comfortable beds and private baths. The main lodge houses a cozy lounge and dining room. For more information write: 7–W Ranch, Gypsum, CO 81637 (303)524–7328.

★★★★*Vail Ski Resort*, just 100 miles west of Denver, is the nation's largest integral winter complex, combining a big sprawling mountain, a total of 18 lifts, every type of ski terrain, and some 200 restaurants and shops. This famous winter retreat of presidents and celebrities offers the atmosphere of a European village in its delightful mix of alpine and contemporary architecture, narrow streets with gas lamps, and sidewalk cafes. The ski area itself covers 10 square miles of trails, including wide and gentle slopes for beginners, packed runs for the intermediate skier, and tough, steep runs for experts. The vertical drop is 3,050 feet, the longest run 5 miles. Two world-famous, south-facing snow bowls—Sun-Up and Sun-Down—attract powder lovers year after year. The Vail Ski School also enjoys a fine reputation for both downhill and cross-country instruction. Classes taught by seasoned professionals are scheduled every day, morning and afternoon, or you can sign up for private instruction by the hour or all day. In addition, there are special programs for children and teenagers, plus a children's mountain ("Peanut Peak") with its own kid-size Poma lift and schedule of supervised activities. Advanced skiers will appreciate the school's NASTAR race classes and intensive workshops in bump skiing, carving turns, and powder skiing. Other amenities of the Vail ski area include a day-care center for children 2–10 years old, free shuttle service from local lodges to the lifts, 5 restaurants right on the slopes, a complete line of ski rentals, and 163 miles of touring terrain for cross-country buffs. For more information write: Vail Resort Associates, Box 7, Vail, CO 81657 (303)476–1000. For ski school offerings write: Ski School at Vail, P.O. Box 819, Vail, CO 81657.

Antlers Condo-Hotel, at the edge of Gore Creek 200 yards from the gondola and chair lifts, is an ultramodern, 7–story structure with 70 individual rental apartments, each with its own balcony, fire-

place, cable TV, and fully equipped kitchen (refrigerator, electric range, disposal, dishwasher, and all cooking and eating utensils). Imaginative floor plans comfortably accommodate 4 guests in a 1–bedroom unit. Large 2–bedroom apartments with an upstairs loft provide ample sleeping quarters for 6–8 persons. Facilities on the premises include 2 saunas, a heated swimming pool, coin-operated laundry, and adequate parking space. Daily rates during the regular season: $70–75 for 2; $120 for 4; $5 per night for each additional person. Low-season rates and ski-week packages are available. For information write: The Antlers Condo-Hotel, P.O. Box 280, Vail, CO 81657 (303)476–2471.

Christiania at Vail occupies a choice location 100 yards from the lifts in the heart of Vail Village, just a few steps from fine shops and restaurants. Guests can ski right to their back door at the end of the day. The Christiania complex includes 3 condominium buildings and a wide choice of accommodations, from practical to elegant. In addition to nicely appointed hotel rooms with queen, king, or 2 double beds, there are fine apartments ranging in size from studios to 3 bedrooms. Other amenities: free continental breakfast, 2 saunas, a heated pool, color TV, and a meeting-recreation room. Daily rates: $30–50 double occupancy, low season; $40–60 per room high season (Dec. 21–Jan. 31). Ski-week packages, including accommodations and lift tickets, are $221–343 for 7 nights, depending on season and type of accommodations. For additional details write: Christiania at Vail, P.O. Box 758, Vail, CO 81657 (303)476–5641.

Holiday Inn of Vail, located in the village center midway between the gondola and chair lifts, offers a variety of guest accommodations, from standard lodge rooms with 2 double beds to sumptuous condominiums. Several meeting rooms are available for après-ski parties. A friendly lounge, with a crackling fire and Victorian antiques, also makes a fine place for relaxing after a day on the slopes. The Holiday Inn has 2 restaurants on the premises. The Gold Rush Dining Room serves 3 meals a day, beginning with a hearty skier's breakfast at 7 A.M. For more intimate dining there's the Fondue Stube with its tasty beef, cheese, and dessert fondues complimented by a selection of choice wines. An 1880s bar is also on hand for cocktails and nightly entertainment. On-premise facilities include a heated swimming pool, 2 saunas, and game rooms. Ski package rates are $137–239, including 7 nights' lodging and a 6–day lift pass. Daily rates on request. For further information write: Holiday Inn of Vail/Holiday House Condominiums, P.O. Box 35, Vail, CO 81657 (303)476–5631.

Kiandra/Talisman Lodge is a deluxe ski resort 2 blocks from the lifts, specializing in personalized service and first-class comfort. Accommodations range from lodge rooms to studios, luxurious penthouses, and condominium apartments. Complimentary coffee and the morning paper delivered to your door are indicative of the Kiandra's special touches. Facilities include 3 restaurants and lounges, 2 outdoor heated pools, saunas, a hot tub and whirlpool, and an exercise room. Daily rates: $22–32 per person, double occupancy. Ski-week packages, including accommodations and 6–day lift pass, are $211–302 per person. For more details write: Kiandra/Talisman Lodge, Box 1028, Vail, CO 81657 (303)476–5081. Outside Colorado, call toll-free (800)525–4200.

Lift House Lodge, located 40 feet from the Lion's Head Gondola, has 45 attractive studio condominiums with kitchens, 2 double beds, balconies, fireplaces, and color TV. Spectacular views of Vail Mountain and fine food are the specialties of the lodge's 2 restaurants. Other amenities: a therapeutic pool, ski shops, bank facilities. Daily rates per person: $25–38 single; $50–76 double. Ski-week packages are $118–170 (low and high season), including 7 nights' lodging and a 6–day lift pass. For more information write: Lift House Lodge, Box 1177, Vail, CO 81657 (303)476–2340.

Lions Head Lodge, near the gondola on Gore Creek, offers ultraluxurious accommodations with superb views of Vail Mountain and the Gore Range. Condominiums, ranging in size from 1 to 4 bedrooms, have lovely furnishings, fireplaces, and private balconies. The Lions Head Village is a townlike complex comprising saunas, a heated swimming pool, parking facilities, and a guest laundry. The ski area is just minutes from your door. Rates: $135–150 for a 2-bedroom condominium (up to 4 guests). Per-person ski packages: $320 including 7 nights' lodging and a 6–day lift ticket. For details write: Lions Head Area, Slifer and Co. Property Management, P.O. Box 1248, Vail, CO 81657 (303)476–2221.

Montaneros Condominiums, 50 yards from the gondola, has 1–3–bedroom condominiums with spacious aspen-paneled living rooms, fireplaces, color TV, fully equipped modern kitchens, and balconies facing the mountain. Restaurants and shops are within easy walking distance. Amenities include a big heated swimming pool, covered parking, saunas, daily maid service, laundry, and front desk and switchboard facilities. Daily rates: $60–85 for a 1–bedroom condominium, $95–120 for 2 bedrooms, $130–155 for 3 bedrooms. Holiday rates are about $15 higher. Ski-week packages (7 nights plus 6–day lift pass): $105–380 per person. For additional information write: Montaneros Condominiums, P.O. Box 459, Vail, CO 81657 (303)476–2491.

Mountain Haus at Vail offers first-class accommodations, operated on a hotel basis with a front desk and maid service, 150 yards from the ski area. A total of 75 units, including 1–, 2–, and 3–bedroom apartments, each with luxurious furnishings, a fully equipped all-electric kitchen, a dining area, fireplace, and a private bath for each bedroom. Located within the hotel are a restaurant and cocktail lounge, saunas, a heated pool, and a conference center with seating for 180 persons. Per-person daily rates: $26–31 double occupancy; $48–58 single occupancy. Ski-week packages, including lodging and lifts: $307 per person. For details write: Mountain Haus at Vail, P.O. Box 1748, Vail, CO 81657 (303)476–2434.

Westwind at Vail, situated 200 feet from the gondola and ski school, has lodge rooms and condominiums with private balconies, color TV, fireplaces, and complete kitchens. All the amenities of a fine hotel, including daily maid service, underground heated parking, and a full front desk operation, distinguish the Westwind from other local condominiums. Apartments range in size from 1 to 4 bedrooms, all beautifully decorated and comfortably furnished. Per-person daily rates: $18–20 double occupancy; $23–33 single. Ski packages are $93–185 for 4 nights' lodging, 3-day lift pass; $144–235 for 7 nights' lodging, 6-day lift pass. For full details write: Westwind at Vail, Box 427, Vail, CO 81657 (303)476–5031.

IDAHO

Introduction

The beautiful coniferous forests, wild rivers, snowcapped peaks, alpine meadows, deep mountain valleys, volcanic craters, and huge blue lakes of Idaho, the Gem State, lie entirely on the western watershed of the Northern Rocky Mountains. Within Idaho's 83,557 square miles are several of the nation's great fishing, hunting, and unspoiled wilderness camping areas: the eerie volcanic lava flows and cinder cones of the "Craters of the Moon" in the southern plain; the blue-ribbon trout waters of Henrys Fork of the Snake and Henrys Lake country in the Teton Basin; the rugged Selway-Bitterroot Wilderness along the northeastern Idaho-Montana boundary; the interior wildlands around the Salmon River (the historic "River of No Return") in the Chamberlain Basin of the vast Idaho Primitive Area, an area several times larger than Switzerland, bounded on the south by the snowcapped crags of the Sawtooth Mountains and Sun Valley; the famous elk-hunting ranges and wild rivers of the Clearwater country north of the Salmon River, traversed east and west by the ancient Nez Percé hunting trail, known as the Lolo Trail, which was traveled by the Lewis and Clark expedition; and the great lakes region of the sparsely settled Northern Panhandle, dominated by the deep, clear trophy lake and rainbow trout waters of Pend Oreille, Priest, Coeur d' Alene, and Spirit lakes, dense boreal forests, and the rugged peaks of the Selkirk Mountains. Lewis and Clark were followed by fur traders of the Hudson's Bay Company (based at Lake Pend Oreille) and the Missouri Fur Company (based on Henrys Fork of the Snake), as well as by successive waves of mountain men, gold prospectors, and homesteaders via the Oregon Trail.

Accommodations & Travel Information

For descriptions of Idaho's major guest ranches, lodges, ski resorts, motels and inns, see the "Idaho Vacation/Lodging Guide" which follows. For detailed information on all aspects of vacation travel in Idaho, contact the Division of Tourism & Industrial Development, Room 108, State Capitol Bldg., Boise, ID 83720 (208)384–2470.

Information & Services

Write to the Idaho Dept. of Fish & Game, P.O. Box 25, Boise 83707, for fishing and hunting seasons, regulations, special permits, *Wildlife Management Area Maps*, *Public Access Areas*, *Hunting Zone Maps*, and the useful, free guides *Hunting & Fishing in Idaho* and *Idaho Lakes & Reservoirs*, which provide detailed info, such as access, fish species present, campsites, and facilities for over 200 lakes, including Coeur d' Alene, Priest, Bear, Blackfoot, Hayden, Pend Oreille, and Spirit. The Dept. of Fish & Game also publishes an invaluable free guide, *Mountain Lakes of Idaho*, which contains detailed descriptions and access and fishing info for the Selkirk Mountains, Sleeping Deer area, Cabinet Mountains, Surveyors Ridge area, Five Lake Butte area, Selway Crags, Buffalo Hump area, Seven Devils area, Bighorn Crags, White Cloud Peaks, Cooper Basin, and Big Wood River headwaters.

Good highways and forest service roads provide automobile access to all parts of Idaho. Air service is available on a scheduled or a charter basis. Charter pilots are experienced and familiar with remote, backcountry airfields used as jumping-off points to the wilderness fishing and hunting areas. The state has about 180 licensed outfitters and 220 guides for fishing trips and big-game hunting in season. Hunters are not required by Idaho law to hire outfitters or guides, but they generally prove invaluable to non-residents. Some game management units lie partly or completely within federal wilderness or primitive areas. Motorized travel is prohibited within those areas, except for aircraft using established landing fields. Otherwise, travel is restricted to foot, horseback, boat, and float raft.

A number of Idaho guides and outfitters operate fly-in service for hunting, fishing, or float expeditions. Some air services provide transportation to the starting point of your wilderness trip, with pick-up service at your base camp. Among them are: *Flying W Ranch*, Rex E. Lanham, Rt. 2, Box 242, Emmett 83617 (hunting and fishing); *Mackay Bar Lodge*, Drawer F, Suite 1010, One Capital Center, Boise 83702 (hunting, fishing, and float trips); *Sulfur Creek Ranch*, Box 131, Boise 83707 (hunting, riding, and fishing); *Pinnacle Ranch*, c/o Marty and Dorothy Rust, P.O. Box 8003, Boise 83707 (hunting, fishing, riding, and rock-hounding); *Valley Flying Service*, Challis Municipal Airport, Box 156, Challis 83226 (hunting, fishing, ski touring); *Boise Air Service*, Boise Municipal Airport, Boise 83701 (back-country flying into all primitive areas); *Salmon Air Taxi*, P.O. Box 698, Salmon 83467 (hunting, boating, fishing); *Air Unlimited*, Box 656, Challis 83226 (hunting, fishing, float trips); *ACME Air Taxi*, Box 521, Salmon 83467 (hunting, fishing); *Gaige Aviation*, Boise Municipal Airport, Boise 83701 (flying to all backcountry fields); and *Teton Aviation*, Driggs 83422. Write to the individual outfitters and air services to find where they fly and what guide services and equipment they supply.

A free pamphlet, *Idaho Outfitters and Guides Association*, lists the names and addresses of members of the association and briefly describes their facilities and services. Many of these outfitters lead big game hunting, fishing, pack, or float trips. Some own guest ranches and lodges which provide supplies, accommodations, and other tourist services. Others lead wilderness training courses. Most of the guides and outfitters provide all basic equipment from the association at P.O. Box 95, Boise 83701.

A free *National Forest Ski Guide* describing Idaho's forest service ski touring areas—including the Lost Trail Ski Area in the Bitterroot National Forest and the Schweitzer and Chewelah basins in the Kaniksu National Forest—may be obtained by writing: U.S. Forest Service, Northern Region, Federal Bldg., Missoula, MT 59801. The Northern Region Office also publishes several useful, free booklets: *General Bibliography of Ski Touring Literature*, *Avalanche*, *Four Lines of Defense Against Hypothermia*, and *Winter Travel in the National Forests*.

The Idaho Recreation Guide, available from the Division of Tourism and Development for 50¢, lists and describes the public recreation sites, historic trails, national forests and parks, wilderness areas, and related recreational areas of the state. The guide has 22 full-color maps showing campgrounds and other recreational facilities accessible by road, trail, or boat. Send your order to: Tourism Division, State Capitol Building, Boise 83720.

If you plan to camp or hike in northern or southern Idaho, the free *National Forest Camp and Picnic Area Guides* for the northern and intermountain regions will be helpful. These directories list developed camp and picnic grounds, boat-launching sites, and beaches in the forests of northern and southern Idaho. The guides identify the facilities available at all the camp and recreation sites and give the access roads to them. For your copies, write: U.S. Forest Service, Northern Region Federal Building, Missoula, MT 59801, or Intermountain Region, 324 25th Street, Ogden, UT 84401.

There are seven national forests in southern Idaho, including the Caribou, Boise, Challis, Targhee, Sawtooth, Salmon, and Payette. The Forest Service provides a free directory to the recreation sites in these forests entitled, A *Guide to National Forest Recreation in Southern Idaho.* The directory lists all recreation sites in the forests, including campgrounds and picnic areas, and describes the available facilities, recreational opportunities (hunting, fishing, etc.), and special features nearby for each site. Small maps throughout the guide key the locations of these sites. For a copy, write: Forest Service, Intermountain Region (address above).

The Division of Tourism and Industrial Development publishes a comprehensive overview of the state's outdoor recreation opportunities in its *Idaho Parks and Outdoor Recreation Guide,* a map and guide brochure which lists and keys the state's campgrounds, parks, rivers, rock-hound areas, lakes, and other features. The guide lists campgrounds and recreation sites by region in state parks, national forests, and other public lands. Write: Division of Tourism and Industrial Development, State Capitol Building, Boise 83720. A listing of Bureau of Land Management recreation area campgrounds may be obtained by writing: B.L.M., Federal Bldg., 550 W. Fort Street, Boise 83720.

All of the major river systems in Idaho offer areas of good canoeing waters. These river systems, from north to south and east, include; the Kootenai, Pend Oreille, Spokane, Clearwater, Salmon, Weiser, Payette, Boise, Lost, Henrys Fork, Snake, Bruneau, Owyhee, Wood, Raft, and Bear. *Canoe Waters of Idaho,* a guide describing the areas of these rivers most suitable for canoeing, is available free from: Idaho Department of Fish and Game, P.O. Box 25, 600 South Walnut, Boise 83707.

Highways & Maps

A free full-color *Highway Map of Idaho* is published by the Idaho Department of Transportation, P.O. Box 7129, Boise 83707. The map shows highways and roads (including paved, improved, and unimproved roads), major geographical features, cities and towns, rest areas and interchanges, points of interest, winter sports areas, campsites, time zone lines, state parks and recreation areas, state monuments and historic sites, and historic trails, including the Lewis & Clark trail, Mullan Road, Lolo Trail, Nez Percé and Oregon trails, and Lander and Kettan roads. The map also lists the state parks and recreation areas and the facilities available at each, and gives camping fees and hunting and fishing license fees. A smaller, simplified map shows historic, geological, and recreational sites throughout the state.

VACATION/ LODGING GUIDE

Caribou-Cache National Forest

The Caribou-Cache National Forest lies on a high plateau along the Continental Divide in southeastern Idaho. Much of the old-growth timber has disappeared here to reveal rough mountainlands, once the hunting grounds of the Shoshone, Bannock, and Lemhi Indians. White settlers began to arrive in significant numbers in the 1850s. After decades of bloodshed, they pushed the Indians onto several reservations. But even after defeating the Indians, they found the business of scratching out an existence difficult; the land itself was inhospitable. Over the generations these people and their descendants upset the fragile ecology, overcutting the timber and depleting once-abundant game through uncontrolled hunting. Game management and conservation after the establishment of the national forest have helped the wildlife make an encouraging comeback.

The forest's 980,000 acres of mountains and valleys still encompass much backcountry wilderness. The forest has 20 developed camp and picnic areas, four summer home areas, four youth camps, and a winter sports area. One of the most popular recreation sites is Palisades Reservoir between Swan Valley, Idaho, and Alpine, Wyoming, where visitors boat, fish, camp, and hike.

Some of the region's best fishing is found in Bear Lake, with cutthroat and lake trout up to 25 pounds. North of Bear Lake the vast salt-grass marshes of the Dingle Swamp provide excellent shooting for mallards and Canada geese. Other productive waterfowl areas include Soda Springs, Grays Lake, America Falls Reservoir, and the Snake River. The Blackfoot Reservoir is a productive fishery; fishermen occasionally take trout in the 20–pound class.

Information Sources, Maps & Access

Vacation travel information and a full-color *Caribou-Cache National Forest Map* (50¢) may be obtained from the Supervisor, Caribou National Forest, 427 N. 6th Ave., Pocatello, ID 83201 (208)236–6700. The forest is accessible by way of U.S. 91, 191, and 30N. In addition to the forest's 21 camping areas, resort and motel accommodations are available in the nearby towns of Idaho Falls, Malad City, Montpelier, Pocatello, Soda Springs, and Swan Valley, Idaho, and Afton, Wyoming. The forest also has a winter sports area.

Gateways & Accommodations

Idaho Falls

(Pop. 37,000; zip code 83401; area code 208) is the major industrial and cultural center of the Upper Snake River Valley. The city, situated on Interstate 15, has a district office of the Caribou-Cache National Forest. Area attractions include the Intermountain Science Center at 1776 Science Center Dr., Idaho Falls of the Snake River, and the Lavas. Accommodations: *Best Western Stardust Motor Lodge* (rates: $23–25.75 double), with 253 superb rooms and family units, restaurant, coffeeshop, heated pool at 700 Lindsay Blvd. (522–2910); *Ramada Inn* (rates: $22–24 double), with 128 rooms and family units, restaurant, cocktail lounge, heated pool at 850 Lindsey Blvd. off 1-15 Lindsey Blvd. exit (523–6260).

Montpelier

(Pop. 2,600; zip code 83254; area code 208) is the major gateway to the Bear Lake Country of the Caribou-Cache National Forest. Area attractions include Minnetonka Cave off U.S. 89 and Bear Lake State Park, 20 miles south of town off U.S. 89. The town is situated at the junction of U.S. 89 and the Old Oregon Trail. A District Ranger's Office of the Caribou-Cache National Forest is located here. Accommodations: *Best Western Crest Motel* (rates: $26–30

double), with 53 excellent rooms and family units across from restaurant at 243 N. 4th St. on U.S. 30N and 39 (847–1782).

Pocatello

(Pop. 43,000; zip code 83201; area code 208) a major Intermountain transportation center, is situated on Interstate 15 in an area that was once part of the Fort Hall Indian Reservation. Area attractions include the Indian petroglyphs and a replica of old Fort Hall in Rosa Park—built in 1834 by the Hudson's Bay Co., Bannock County Historical Museum at Center St. and Garfield Ave., and a restored 19th Century Victorian Mansion known as Stanral House at 648 N. Garfield Rd. Accommodations: *Best Western Cotton Tree Inn* (rates: $32–37 double), with 99 excellent rooms and family units, restaurant, cocktail lounge, indoor heated pool, tennis court at 1415 Bench Rd. off I-15 Pocatello Creek Rd. exit (237–7650); *Holiday Inn* (rates: $30 double), with 206 rooms and family units, restaurant, dining room, cocktail lounge, heated pool at I-15 Exit 71 (237–1400).

Clearwater National Forest

The evergreen mantle of the Clearwater National Forest stretches westward from the high, snowcapped peaks of the Bitterroot Range along the Montana-Idaho border, covering 1,677,000 acres of canyon-furrowed mountain country. The forest shares the 1.2–million-acre Selway-Bitterroot Wilderness, the largest classified wilderness in the country, with three other national forests. The boulder-strewn wildwaters of the Clearwater Middle Fork, Lochsa, and Selway rivers plunge through the canyons of the forests; hot springs warm their snow-fed tributaries.

Hundreds of named peaks, buttes, streams, lakes, and campsites reveal the rich human history beneath the forest's cloak of wilderness. The Flathead Indians named the Lochsa River ("rough water"); the Nez Percé named the Selway ("smooth water") and Kooskia ("little river"). When Lewis and Clark arrived in the area, guided over the Lolo Trail by the Shoshone woman Sacajawea, about 6,000 Nez Percé Indians inhabited the region, drawing their physical and spiritual sustenance from the mountains. The tribe greeted the explorers as friends; they exchanged gifts with Lewis and Clark, gave feasts in their honor, and sent six of their chiefs to accompany the white men to the mouth of the Columbia River.

Information Sources, Maps & Access

For vacation travel and recreation information, a full-color *Clearwater National Forest Map* (50¢), and the free *Lewis & Clark Trail*

Map/Brochure and *Camp & Picnic Areas in the Clearwater Forest,* contact: Supervisor, Clearwater National Forest, Orofino, ID 83544 (208)476–4541. A full-color *Selway-Bitterroot Wilderness Map* (50¢) is also available from the supervisor's office. For additional information on the Lewis & Clark Trail and a free *Nez Percé National Historical Park Brochure,* write: Superintendent, Nez Percé National Historical Park, P.O. Box 93, Spalding, ID 83551.

The forest is reached via the paved two-lane Lewis and Clark Highway (U.S. 12). This all-weather highway cuts across the southern edge of the forest, crossing the Bitterroot Mountains at Lolo Pass (5,233 ft.), and parallels the route of the 1805–1806 Lewis and Clark expedition. Points of historical interest are marked along the highway by Forest Service signs. Numerous campsites are located along the highway. Lodging, supplies, guides, boat rentals, packers, and outfitters are located at Orofino, Kooskia, Bungalow, Canyon, Kelly Forks, Kamiah, and Powell, Idaho; and Missoula, Montana.

Recreation & Historic Areas

Clearwater National Wild & Scenic River

The renowned float-fishing and kayak waters of the Middle Fork of the Clearwater National Wild & Recreation River include the Middle Fork from Kooskia to Lowell, the wild Selway River from Lowell to Race Creek and from Paradise to the Magruder Ranger Station, and the Lochsa River from Lowell to the Powell Ranger Station—a total of 131 river miles. The Selway wild river segment flows for 54 miles from its headwaters to the Magruder Ranger Station and from the Paradise Guard Station to Race Creek. This wilderness river area is reached by trail and charter fly-in service in the Lowell and Smith Creek-Syringa areas. The 56,000–acre area provides top-ranked float-fishing for brown, cutthroat, rainbow, brook, and Dolly Varden trout and seasonal fishing for migratory salmon and steelhead. Access to the Middle Fork, Lochsa, and Selway is via U.S. Highway 12 from Kooskia. For detailed info on these scenic, wild, and often hazardous rivers, write: Lochsa Ranger District, Kooskia 83539.

Lewis & Clark Trail

The Idaho section of the historic Lolo Trail extends westward through the beautiful high-country wildlands of the Clearwater National Forest for about 90 miles, from 5,187–foot Lolo Pass over the Bitterroot Mountains to the village of Weippe, adjacent to the Nez Percé Indian Reservation located due east of Lewiston and the Snake

River. A dim trail through a primeval land, this east-west route follows the ancient Nez Perce hunting trail, traveled over the ages by the Nez Percé Indians from their homeland on the Columbia River through the Northern Rockies for 250 miles to the buffalo-hunting grounds of the Missouri River in the Deer Lodge Valley of Montana. In 1805, Lewis and Clark used the trail and pass to cross the rugged Bitterroot Range on their epic westward journey to the mouth of the Columbia River on the Pacific Ocean. The legendary Sacajawea (Indian for "boatpusher") led them through this wilderness on her own journey home from the Crows, who had stolen her many years earlier. On their return from the Pacific, Lewis and Clark retraced the path, living off the wild berries and game, including deer, crawfish, salmon, trout, and an occasional stray Indian horse.

The hostile Nez Percé, under Chief Joseph, traveled the Lolo Trail on their famous trek of 1877. Some 700 Indians with several thousand horses left their homeland by way of this trail, followed by Gen. O. O. Howard's army with artillery and supply trains. Today the Lewis and Clark Highway (U.S. 12) parallels the historic trail for about four miles west of the Montana line.

Nez Percé National Historical Park

The Nez Percé National Historical Park contains 23 historic sites, including the Lolo Trail, scattered over 12,000 square miles of northern Idaho. The major historical sites, shown on the free *Nez Percé National Historical Park* brochure (write to Superintendent's Office, above), include the Musselshell Meadow, one of the last active gathering spots of wild camas for the Indians; Weippe Prairie; Canoe Camp, where Lewis and Clark camped in the autumn of 1805 and built canoes and cached their supplies, and from where they headed down the Clearwater River to the Snake; the Pacific Fur Company Post, established in 1812; Lewis & Clark Long Camp, site

of the expedition's month-long encampment on the banks of the South Fork of the Clearwater River during the spring of 1806 on the homeward journey; and the Whitebird Battlefield, where the Nez Percé defeated one-third of General Howard's troops in the opening engagement of the Nez Percé War. There is a free guide to these areas, describing the locations, access, operating schedules, uphill facilities, maximum vertical drops, teaching facilities, lodging, and other services. It is available by writing to: Division of Tourism, Statehouse, Boise 83720.

Selway-Bitterroot Wilderness

A portion of the old Lewis & Clark Trail runs through the Selway-Bitterroot Wilderness. This rugged mountain territory straddling the Montana-Idaho border is the largest federally classified wilderness in the continental United States. It covers more than 1.25 million acres. The Selway (from the Nez Percé Indian word *Selwah*, meaning "smooth water"), Bitterroot, and Lochsa rivers wind through the Bitterroot Range here, at the lower elevations. In the higher reaches of the mountains, sparkling snow-fed lakes dot the wilderness in cirques carved by ancient glaciers.

Most of the trails follow stream bottoms at the lower elevations. Some of them were made by Indians who fished here for the abundant ocean-run salmon and steelhead trout before the first white men arrived. The spectacular scenery of the high country rewards those who make the effort of cross-country travel. The best season for visiting the high country is from mid-July through September, although cross-country ski touring is becoming popular in snow months. The lower elevations are snow-free from mid-March through November. The wilderness lies on both sides of the rugged Bitterroot Range, which forms the border between Idaho and northwest Montana and includes some of the toughest mountain terrain in the world, with thousands of high peaks, steep valleys, deep forests, and wild rivers. This is prime chinook country; salmon to 45 pounds are caught in the Selway, Clark Fork, Lochsa, and Middle and North forks of the Clearwater. Numerous trails lead to remote areas with such colorful names as Grizzly Saddle, Otter Butte, Sneakfoot Meadows, and Wahoo Pass. The hardy outdoorsman who is looking for a remote alpine fishing and big-game area should explore the scenic Selway Crags, located in the heart of the Clearwater River drainage between the Lochsa and Selway rivers. Access is by way of the Fenn Ranger Station above the mouth of the Selway, where a steep road winds its way up to the Big Fog Saddle. Old Indian trails at Big Fog lead into the lake basin area. Brook and cutthroat trout fishing is good in Old Man, Legend, Big Fog, Lone Creek, Florence, and Lizard Creek lakes. During the summer months the scenery is stunning; wildflowers and rose heather carpet the meadows and slopes. Be sure to check trail conditions with the District Forest Service Ranger on arrival. The wilderness has one of the country's largest elk herds, as well as moose, sheep, deer, and black bear.

Gateways & Accommodations

Lewiston

(Pop. 30,000; zip code 83501; area code 208) is a major jumping-off point for trips into the famous elk country of the Clearwater National Forest, to the Nez Percé National Historical Park in Spalding 15 miles east off U.S. 95, and along the scenic Lewis & Clark Highway. Lewiston was the first incorporated town in Idaho and the first capitol of Idaho Territory. It is situated at the confluence of the Snake and Clearwater rivers at the Idaho-Washington border. Scenic boat trips into Hells Canyon of the Snake River are provided by several Lewiston based outfitters; contact the Chamber of Commerce for a listing of licensed boat trip outfitters. Among the area attractions is the Luna House Museum at 3rd St. with free exhibits of Nez Percé Indian and pioneer artifacts (743–2535). Accommodations: *Best Western Tapadera Motor Inn* (rates: $24–30 double), with 80 excellent rooms and family units, cocktail lounge, heated pool next to restaurant on U.S. 12 at 1325 Main St. (746–3311); *Sacajawea Lodge* (rates: $21.63–23.69 double), with 97 excellent rooms and family units, steak and seafood dinners at the Helm Restaurant, heated pool on U.S. 12 at 1824 Main St. (746–1393).

Orofino

(Pop. 4,000; zip code 83544; area code 208) situated at huge Devorshak Reservoir on the North Fork of the Clearwater River, is a gateway to a great forest high country. The town, built in a canyon near the Lewis & Clark Canoe Camp Site of the Nez Percé Historical Park (three miles west of town on U.S. 12), is surrounded by mountains. Accommodations: *Konkolville Motel* (rates: $20 double), with 40 excellent rooms and family units next to restaurant, heated pool off U.S. 12 (476–5584).

Travel Services

For additional listings, see "Salmon River Country" in this section.

Coolwater Ranch offers guided packhorse, alpine fishing, and fall hunting trips in the Clearwater National Forest and Selway Bitterroot Wilderness. Contact Harry Vaughn, Coolwater Ranch, 1376 Walenta Dr., Moscow, ID 83843 (208)882–5367.

Muleshoe Wilderness Camp at the gateway to the Selway-Bitterroot Wilderness, is located at the scenic Elk Summit Road, which winds through the Clearwater National Forest to the Muleshoe base camp. Muleshoe is the sole officially designated licensed outfitter for 250 square miles of the Selway-Bitterroot Wilderness. The base camp has cabin accommodations and platform tents and offers fall hunting trips and wilderness pack and fishing trips for rainbow, brook, steelhead, cutthroat, and Dolly Varden trout in Hoodoo Creek, which runs through the center of the camp, and in the high-country lakes and rivers of the Selway-Bitterroot country. Camp services include pickup at the Missoula Airport. For information, literature, the *Muleshoe Hunting Bulletin*, and rates, write: Box 83, Harrison, ID 83833, (208)688–3422.

Snake River Outfitters offers guided and custom trips on the Snake and Salmon rivers as well as guided one-day boat trips in Hells Canyon for family groups as well as raft and jet boat combination trips. Four day trips in Hells Canyon cost $235 per person; three day trips on the Lower Salmon cost $165 per person. Contact: Snake River Outfitters, 811 Snake River Ave., Lewiston, ID 83501 (208)743–6276.

Coeur d' Alene National Forest

The fish and game areas of the 725,000–acre Coeur d'Alene National Forest are bounded by the Bitterroot Range on the Montana-Idaho border on the east, the St. Joe Mountains on the south, and the Purcell Trench on the west. The smaller Shoshone Range flanks the Bitterroots to the west, and beyond it lie the Coeur d'Alene Mountains, whose wooded foothills border the quicksilver waters of Coeur d'Alene Lake beyond the forest's western border.

Coeur d'Alene means "heart of an awl." Authorities believe the name is derived from a derogatory word used by the Indians who lived here to describe the Canadian trappers who entered the area in the early 1800s. The trappers responded by applying the term to the Indians themselves.

Beautiful Lake Coeur d'Alene is 30 miles long and has 104 miles of shoreline. The best fishing for kokanee salmon, Dolly Varden, cutthroat, and rainbow trout is at the south end of the lake along the west shore from Conkling Park to Windy Bay, and at the north end from Wolfe Lodge Bay to Arrow Point. Fishing is best in June and July.

The Coeur d'Alene River provides some of the best fly-fishing in the northern Panhandle for rainbows and cutthroats up to five pounds. Hayden Lake, on the western edge of the forest above Coeur d'Alene Lake, also has excellent spring and fall fishing for large rainbow and cutthroat. The lake yielded the Idaho state-record rainbow (19 lb.). Most trout caught in Hayden average between one and three pounds. Hayden, like Coeur d'Alene, is shored by evergreens and sheltered by mountains. It has two public access areas, one at Honeysuckle Beach on the west end and another at Sportsmans Park at the north end. Resort accommodations and boat rentals are available at the lake. Coeur d'Alene has about 30 points of access, and there are resort accommodations around the lake and at St. Maries and Coeur d'Alene. It is accessible by several roads from U.S. 95 on the west.

Blue fields of huckleberries cover the slopes of the Coeur d'Alene Mountains. Forests here are of Douglas fir, white and yellow pine, larch, cedar, western hemlock, Engelmann spruce, and lodgepole pine. Just west of Cataldo near the forest border is the Cataldo Mission, built in 1848 by Indians under leadership of Father Ravalli. The mission was abandoned in 1887 and fell into ruin, but citizens of area communities restored it in 1930. It holds two of the original Indian dye paintings that decorated the mission walls, one of heaven and the other of hell. The forest stretches to the north and east. Trails lead from McGee Ranger Station to Grizzly Ridge, McDonald Peak, Grassy Mountain, Lookout Peak, Cathedral Buttes, Elkhorn Peak, and McGee Peaks. Hundreds of mountain streams drain the forested hills, which harbor lynx, beaver, marten, bear, deer, and elk.

Information Sources, Maps & Access

For vacation travel and recreation information, a full-color *Coeur d'Alene National Forest Map* (50¢), and a free *Camp & Picnic Areas in Coeur d'Alene National Forest*, contact: Supervisor, Coeur d'Alene National Forest, Coeur d'Alene, ID 83814 (208)667–2561.

Major routes to the forest include Interstate 90 from Spokane, Washington, on the west and Missoula, Montana, on the east, and U.S. Highway 95 from Moscow on the south and Sandpoint on the north. Lodging, supplies, boat and equipment rentals, guides, and outfitters are available at Coeur d'Alene, Kellogg, Spirit Lake, Hayden, Twin Lakes, Rathdrum, Hauser, Chilco, Garwood, Hayden, Harrison, and Pinehurst.

Gateways & Accommodations

Coeur d'Alene

(Pop. 18,000; zip code 83814; area code 208) is a major gateway to the nationally famous recreation and vacation areas of Idaho's beautiful Panhandle lakes region. The town is a forest products center and headquarters of the Coeur d'Alene National Forest situated at the northern end of scenic Coeur d'Alene Lake. Guided tours of the Potlach Corporation sawmills are available free (664–8101). Cruises up Lake Coeur d'Alene are offered by the Finney Transportation Co. (664–2827) at the city dock and Wheeler's Marina, (664–8525). Coeur d'Alene stands on the site of a fort built by General Sherman in 1878 and abandoned in 1901. The old Fort Sherman Chapel stands at Hubbard St. and Woodland Dr. Accommodations: *Best Western North Shore Motor Hotel* (rates: $34.50–37.50 double), with 173 superb rooms and family units, fine dining in dining room and rooftop Cloud 9 Restaurant with stunning view of Lake Coeur d'Alene, marina, boats and motors, fishing, water sports, heated pool, on the lake on U.S. 10 business route in downtown (664–9241); *Holiday Inn* (rates: $30–35 double), with 124 excellent rooms, restaurant, cocktail lounge, heated poo! at junction of Interstate 90 and 95 (667–4661).

Guest Ranches

★★★★*Timber Ridge Ranch & Wilderness Camp* is a working stock and family guest ranch adjoining the magnificent Coeur d'Alene National Forest. Nearby Coeur d'Alene Lake, one of the most beautiful in the state, has a 107–mile shoreline punctuated by secluded bays and steep-sided inlets. Off to the south, the legendary St. Joe River winds its way through the very heart of the lake. The ranch has a fine corral of horses for trail rides through neighboring valleys and forests, plus a wide range of outdoor activities, including overnight pack trips, fishing, swimming, water skiing, hiking, supervised children's activities, hayrides, weekly rodeos—all the pleasures of a fine western guest ranch. In addition, the ranch maintains a remote wilderness camp at the gateway to the Selway-Bitterroot Wilderness, the perfect spot for pack trips and cabin-camping with all the comforts of home: electric lights, snug cabins, hot showers, and woodburning stoves. Accommodations at Timber Ridge Lodge are a welcome blend of luxurious comfort and Old West authenticity. Cabins built of native tamarack have lovely hand-made furnishings, barnboard panelling, woodburning stoves, private baths, and bright calico trimmings. There are also rustic guest rooms in the huge and handsome log lodge plus authentic teepees with central restrooms. Other amenities include a 24–foot pontoon boat for waterskiing and cruises, a fleet of rafts for whitewater adventures, a BYO bar, well stocked trout ponds, and excellent meals enhanced by fresh produce and home-cooked treats. Rates, including three meals a day, lodging, and all ranch activities, except pack trips: $300 weekly per person for cabins; $275 weekly per person for lodge rooms; and $225 weekly per person for teepees. Children's discounts and daily rates are available. Pack trips are $385 per person for seven days; cabin camping is $40 per person per day, all inclusive. For additional details, write: Timber Ridge Ranch, Box 83, Harrison, ID 83833 (208)689–3422 or 3315.

Craters Of The Moon National Monument

The eerie, blackened landscape of the Craters of the Moon National Monument bears testimony to a violent geologic past. Cinder cone-studded lava fields stretch across the face of south central Idaho; the monument itself is part of a 200,000–square-mile lava field stretching westward to the Columbia Plateau. The 83 square miles of the monument were formed less than 2,000 years ago, when lava boiling at 2,000° F poured from thousands of fissures in the earth. The lava floods destroyed all vegetation and left the land so barren that only a few of the hardiest plants could survive. Today, however, more than 200 plants are native to the area, including sagebrush, antelope bitterbrush, and mock orange. Wildflowers burst into bloom in the spring, lacing the blackened earth with magenta, yellow, and pink. Caves, natural bridges, terraces, and piles of stone add to the grotesquerie and unearthly splendor of the monument.

Sixty-eight square miles of the weird and fantastic formations of the Craters of the Moon are inaccessible by road—one of the four designated wilderness areas in the National Park System. This is true wilderness, cut only by three short trails (aside from deer trails). Maps and compasses are a necessity, as is a topographical map of the area (available at the visitor center). Permits are required. Bring your own water into this extremely dry area, and remember to wear sturdy shoes. In the summer, temperatures reach the 90s; in the winter they fall below zero.

The wilderness is never more beautiful than in the winter, when snow transforms the eerie shapes and carpets the rocky lava surface. Snowshoeing and cross-country skiing are among the best ways to experience this strange land.

There are no motel, hotel, or eating accommodations at the monument. The nearest towns are Arco (pop. 1,500), 18 miles to the east, and Carey (pop. 750), 24 miles to the west.

Information Sources, Maps & Access

For detailed information and a useful *Craters of the Moon Map/Brochure,* contact: National Park Service Office, Craters of the Moon National Monument, Arco, ID 83213 (208)527–3257 or 527–3207. A full-color U.S. Geological Survey *Craters of the Moon Topographic Map* ($2) may be ordered from: Distribution Branch, U.S. Geological Survey, Federal Center, Denver, CO 80225. The monument is reached via U.S. Highways 20, 26, & 93A, 20 miles southwest of Arco, Idaho.

Gateways & Accommodations

Arco

(Pop. 1,200; zip code 83213; area code 208) is the major gateway to Craters of the Moon National Monument, situated on the Big Lost River. Accommodations: *Lazy A Motel* (rates: $17–19 double), with 16 good rooms and family units near restaurant, just west of town on U.S. 20, 26, & 93A (527–8263).

Kaniksu National Forest & Lake Pend Oreille

Some of the most outstanding fishing waters in North America lie in this 1,600,000–acre preserve extending from western Montana across the northern Panhandle of Idaho into eastern Washington. Its northern boundary is formed by the province of British Columbia. The

entire region is well served by highways, Forest Service roads, and trails leading to such famous destinations as Pend Oreille Lake, the glaciers of 8,712–foot Snowshoe Peak, the Selkirk and Cabinet mountains wilderness areas, Clark Fork of the Snake River, Kootenai River, Myrtle Creek Game Preserve, Purcell Mountains, Priest Lake Area, and the Purcell Trench.

The beautiful evergreen-covered shores of 43–mile-long Pend Oreille Lake lie among the Selkirk Mountains. The Pend Oreille Indians once inhabited the surrounding country and the lands along the Clark Fork River. Young braves approaching maturity were sent into the mountains, where they were to stay till they dreamed of some animal, fish, or bird, which then became their "medicine." Each of the braves wore a tooth, claw, or feather from this creature to protect him from evil. The Indians held the islands of Warren, Cottage, Pearl, and Memaloose on Pend Oreille sacred, and used them as burial grounds. Instead of burying the dead, however, they suspended them from trees.

The lake is world-famous for its rainbow and Kamloops trout of up to 37 pounds and Dolly Varden trout up to the 32–pound world record. The months to fish the lakes are May and early June and October and November, when cooler temperatures bring the big fish to the surface. Pend Oreille also has good fishing for cutthroat, kokanee, perch, crappie, and largemouth bass.

Huckleberry, elderberry, and syringa cover the shores of the lake, which reaches depths of 1,800 feet. U.S. 10A runs along the north shore and western edge of the lake. The main public access areas on the lake are Garfield Bay, Sandpoint City Beach, Springy Point Camp Grounds, Bayview Public Dock, Blackwell Point Public Access, Pack River Bay Access Area, Sam Owens Recreation Area, Johnson Creek Recreation Area, and Morton Slough Access Area.

The Pend Oreille River flows for 28 miles downstream to the Washington border. The backwater and slough areas created by the Albeni Falls Dam provide some fine fishing for largemouth bass in the 1–6 pound class. Rainbows are taken upstream from the Priest River. Priest Lakes have good fishing for kokanee and Dolly Varden trout and are renowned for their large lake trout, or Mackinaw, up to 51 pounds. The kokanee salmon are vigorous fighters but have soft mouths, and a limber rod is recommended. Once caught, the salmon are delicious lightly smoked or kippered.

The main Priest Lake is about 19 miles long; Upper Lake, connected to the main lake by a two-mile river, is three miles long. The main lake is accessible by way of State Highway 57 from Priest River and U.S. 2, but the upper lake is accessible only by trail or water travel.

Resorts, cabins, and supplies are available at the main lake. Public access areas include: Coolin Public Access, Indian Creek State Park, and Kalispell Bay Recreation Area.

Dense pine and fir forests stretch out from the shores of the Priest Lakes, their verdant undergrowth challenging cross-country hikers. Smaller lakes and rarely fished streams lie throughout the surrounding country, which supports large populations of deer, bear, elk, and mountain goat. The free guide to *Nature Trails of the Priest Lake Ranger District* will help to identify some of the trees, plants, and shrubs along the Luby Bay, Hanna Flat, and other trails throughout the district. It may be obtained from: Supervisor, Kaniksu National Forest, Sandpoint 83864.

On the east of Priest Lake lies the southwest division of the Selkirk Mountains lakes area, drained by the Priest, Pack, and Kootenai rivers. Harrison, Brook, Standard, Two Mouth, and several beautiful high-country lakes offer good to excellent fishing for cutthroat and brook trout. They are accessible by way of the Myrtle, Snow, and Ruby Creek roads from the east, the Pack River road from the south, and roads from Priest Lake from the west. Climbers will be interested in the glacially formed Chimney Rock formation in this area, which rises vertically 200 feet above the surrounding terrain to an elevation of 7,136 feet. Climbing equipment is needed to scale the rock. A goat trail leads along the northern side of the formation to a narrow ledge extending a half mile eastward.

The southeast division of the Selkirk lakes area includes drainages east of the Selkirk Range and south to Pack River. Most of them may be reached by short hikes from the roads serving the area. Rainbow, cutthroat, and brook trout offer good to excellent fishing at Bloom, Bottleneck, Brook, Roman Nose, Snow, and a number of smaller lakes. For more detailed information on these and other alpine lakes, write to the Idaho Fish and Game Department (600 S. Walnut, Boise 83707) for the free 55–page *Mountain Lakes of Idaho* guide. The Selkirk Crest Special Management Area takes in 35,780 acres of this scenic, glaciated country. The area contains more than 20 lakes, including Myrtle, Pyramid, Ball, Two Mouth, and Beehive, nestled in the cirque basins. Trails in the area are where you find them, with a few trails maintained to a low standard.

Information Sources, Maps & Access

For detailed vacation travel information, a full-color *Kaniksu National Forest Map* (50¢) and the free *Selkirk Crest Map/Brochure* and *Camp & Picnic Areas* booklet, contact: Supervisor, Kaniksu National Forest, Sandpoint, ID 83864 (208)667–2561. Major routes to the forest include U.S. 95, 2, 195, and 10A and Washington Rt. 6.

Lodging, supplies, boat rentals, guides, and outfitters are available at Priest River, Sandpoint, Bonners Ferry, Old Town, Clark Fork, Eagle, Hope, Cabinet, Nordman, Meadow Creek, and Coolin.

Gateways & Accommodations

Bonners Ferry

(Pop. 4,000; zip code 83805; area code 208) on the Kootenai River, seat of Boundary County. Area attractions of this forest products and agricultural center, include the Moyie River and its falls and scenic drives along the Moyie River Canyon and Kootenai Canyon. Accommodations: *Deep Creek Motel* (rates: $21 double), with 13 good rooms and family units, restaurant, cocktails and heated pool seven miles south off Deep Creek exit of U.S. 2/95 (267–2373).

Lodges & Resorts

★★★*Elkins Tumlahee*, nestled in Reeder Bay on northern Idaho's beautiful Priest Lake, is a four-season family vacation resort with its own sprawling sand beach and swimming area and a complete marina with boats for fishing and water-skiing. The crystal clear waters of Priest Lake hold cutthroat, rainbow, mackinaw, and Dolly Varden trout plus kokanee salmon. In addition to the resort's own fine recreational facilities, there are nearby riding stables, tennis courts, and a golf course. Winter here is the time for snowmobiling, skiing, and the Pacific Coast Sled Dog Championships. There are 36 housekeeping cottages, most of which are on the lakefront, ranging in size from one-bedroom cabins to a two-story, six-bedroom cottage and in decor from rustic to ultra-modern. All have kitchens, private baths, linens, bedding, dishes and utensils. The spacious, main lodge houses a fine restaurant, cocktail lounge, grocery store, and gift shop. Across the way is a recreation room with indoor games. A weekly outdoor buffet, served in a pleasantly pastoral spot by the lake, has become a popular tradition at Elkins-Tumlahee. Rates: $25–80 daily for two to eight guests; $150–475 weekly. Off-season rates are lower. For a complete rate schedule and information, write: Elkins Tumlahee, Nordman, ID (208)443–2432.

★★★*Grandview Lodge & Resort* is a superb 4–season vacation center on Priest Lake in Idaho, just 90 miles north of Spokane, Washington. It is open daily Memorial Day through Labor Day and on weekends in the winter season. For summer fun, there is a heated swimming pool, a sandy beach on the clear lake, waterskiing or boating. Fishermen will find mackinaw trout, Dolly Varden, Kokanee salmon, and cutthroat trout in the 26,000 acre Priest Lake. In fact, the U.S. record lake trout and Kokanee were taken there. Marked hiking trails lead through patches of delicious wild huckleberries. And, in season there is mushroom hunting. The resort has launching and moorage facilities as well as boats and motors for rent. Boaters can motor out for a picnic on a secluded island or just tour the lake which lies 2,434 feet above sea level. The resort also runs seaplane tours, starting at their own seaplane ramp near the lodge. Summer temperatures average 75 degrees with the water in the 70s as well. In the winter there is a 3 to 5 foot snow on the ground at the lake and 10 feet in the mountains most of the season. Then guests can enjoy the hundreds of miles of groomed snowmobile trails around the lake and through the surrounding mountains. Cross-country skiing is also popular.The feature event of the winter season is the United States Pacific Coast Championship Sled Dog Races held in February at Priest Lake. Year-round, guests can enjoy dinner, cocktails and dancing in the Grandview Lodge with a view of the lake. Accommodations include condominiums, cottages and rooms in the lodge. Cottages & condos have fireplaces, and dishes and bedding are provided. The condo units have dishwashers and full baths. They are rented on a weekly basis with condos sleeping six ranging from $320 to $360 a week. Cottages sleep from six to ten and range from $170 to $340 a week, depending on size and location. Rooms in the lodge can be rented by the day and are $26 to $30 for one double bed and $30 to $34 for two double beds. For more information contact: Bob and Dorothy Benscoter, Grandview Lodge, Priest Lake, Nordman, ID 83848 (208)443–2433.

★★★*Hill's Resort*, on island-dotted Priest Lake in northern Idaho, is a rambling complex surrounded by tall evergreens and fronted by a long, sandy beach. Water sports—including swimming, sailing, canoeing, and water-skiing—are especially popular here, as are stream and lake fishing for rainbows, Dolly Varden, Kokanee, trophy Mackinaw trout, and cutthroat. Tennis courts, a nine-hole golf course, and a complete marina are all at your doorstep. Hill's Resort offers fully equipped, very attractive housekeeping cabins, most of which feature fireplaces, for $190–395 per week, depending on size and location, plus two- and three-bedroom luxurious condominiums ($345–375 weekly) with private balconies and panoramic views of the lake. There are also seven rooms in the lodge and two older, rustic cabins available by the day or week. Off-season discounts and daily rates are also available for all units. The main lodge has a handsome dining room, cocktail lounge, and well-stocked wine cellar. For further information, write: Hill's Resort, Route 5, Priest Lake, ID 83856 (208)443–2351.

St. Joe National Forest & Mallard-Larkins Pioneer Area

This beautiful 865,000–acre tract in north central Idaho embraces the St. Joe River (the highest navigable river in the world), St. Maries River, Potlatch River, Little North Fork of the Clearwater River, and the Mallard-Larkins Pioneer Area. These outstanding hunting, fishing, and backpacking areas are well served by a network of highways, forest service roads, and trails. Forests of lodgepole, fir, and spruce intermixed with hemlock and larch cover the rugged slopes, with an undergrowth of elder, syringa, dogwood, grape, heath, laurel, and huckleberry.

The river from which the forest takes its name flows down from the Bitterroot Mountains on the Montana border to the west. The St. Maries River flows northward through the forest to meet the St. Joe at the town of St. Maries. The Jesuit Father Pierre-Jean De Smet explored the lands of the lower St. Joe River in 1842 and named it the St. Maries. He founded the Sacred Heart Mission, which still stands in Desmet, and ministered to the Indians of the area.

The St. Joe River has more than 120 miles of free-flowing water whose foaming white waters and quiet fishing stretches attract canoers, kayakers, and rafters. At an elevation of 2,128 feet, tugboats can be seen towing large bails of logs to the mills at Coeur d'Alene. The scenery is outstanding, mostly in a primitive state, even though the river flows through somewhat populated areas. These tranquil waters lined with cottonwood trees give rise to the river's nickname, "the shadowy St. Joe." The lower six miles are on the "River through the Lakes," a unique phenomenon where the St. Joe River with its natural tree-lined levees meanders through Benewah, Round, Chatcolet, and Coeur d'Alene lakes. These levees are the summer home of the largest colony of osprey in North America. A trip from Heller Creek to Spruce Tree Campground runs through the furious white-waters of a 17–mile wilderness canyon; it makes a good two-day trip for experienced white-water kayakers. The quiet waters from St. Joe City to Coeur d'Alene Lake offer outstanding scenery and easy camping. The Gold Creek to Bluff Creek Bridge stretch challenges the most experienced white-water kayakers and canoers.

THE GREAT OUTDOORS ROAD ATLAS WESTERN UNITED STATES

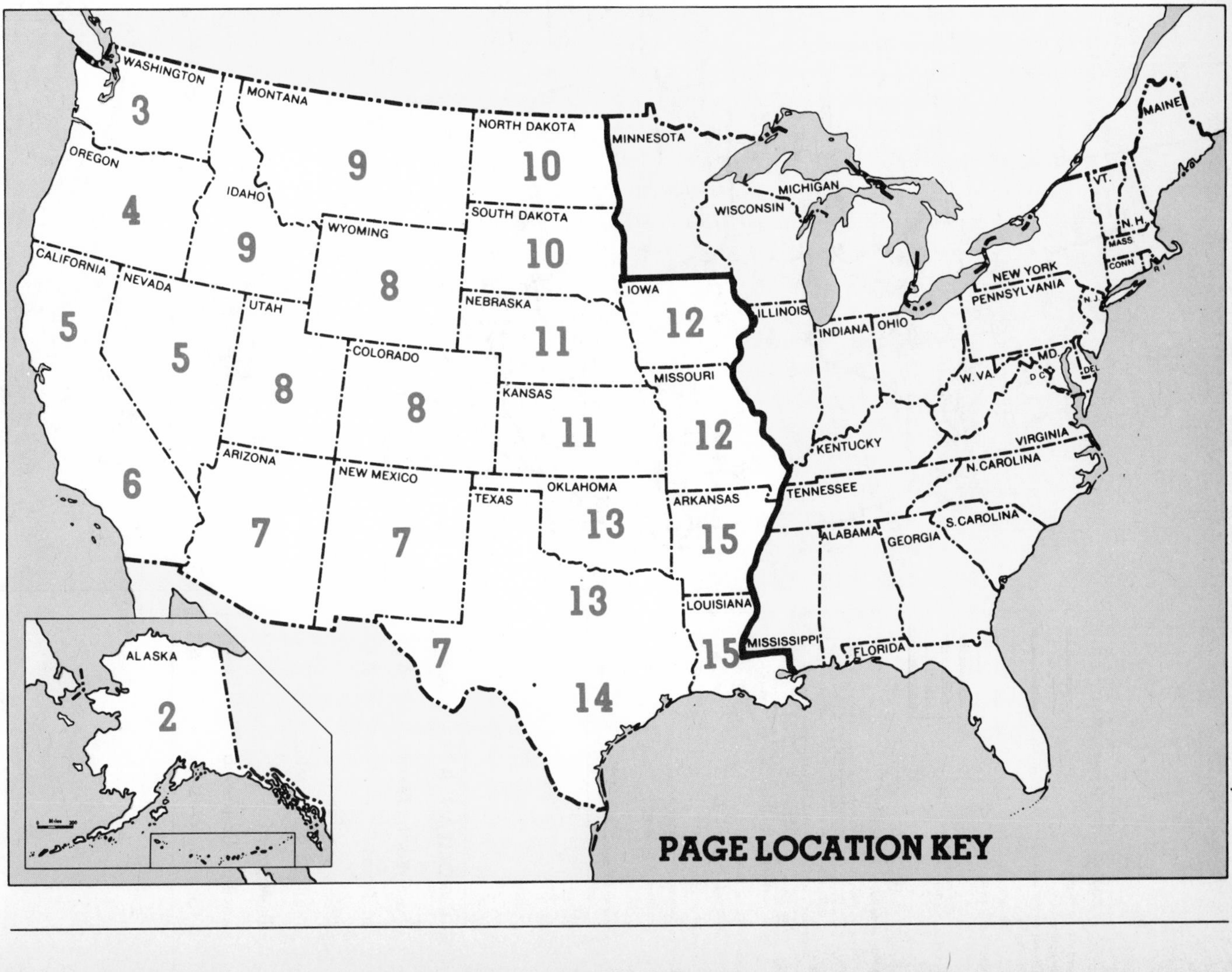

WASHINGTON 3
OREGON 4
CALIFORNIA 5 6
NEVADA 5
IDAHO 9
MONTANA 9
WYOMING 8
UTAH 8
COLORADO 8
ARIZONA 7
NEW MEXICO 7
NORTH DAKOTA 10
SOUTH DAKOTA 10
NEBRASKA 11
KANSAS 11
OKLAHOMA 13
TEXAS 13 7 14
MINNESOTA
IOWA 12
MISSOURI 12
ARKANSAS 15
LOUISIANA 15
ALASKA 2
WISCONSIN
MICHIGAN
ILLINOIS
INDIANA
OHIO
KENTUCKY
TENNESSEE
MISSISSIPPI
ALABAMA
GEORGIA
FLORIDA
S. CAROLINA
N. CAROLINA
VIRGINIA
W. VA.
MD.
D.C.
DEL.
N.J.
PENNSYLVANIA
NEW YORK
CONN.
R.I.
MASS.
VT.
N.H.
MAINE

PAGE LOCATION KEY

SYMBOLS USED IN THIS ATLAS

Limited Access Highways
National Parkways
Toll Roads and Interchanges
Major Highways
Other Important Roads
Mileage Between Dots

Selected Scenic Routes

Ferries

U.S. Interstate Route Numbers

Routes with odd numbers run north and south, the even-numbered routes east and west. Numbers progress lowest to highest from west to east and from south to north. Major routes have one- or two-digit numbers and the long, evenly spaced routes have numbers ending in 0 or 5.

Connecting full or partial circumferential routes around or in urban areas carry a three-digit number, using the main route number with an **even** number prefix. Radial and spur routes are also three-digits, using the main route number with an **odd** number prefix. For example: an auxiliary route to I–80 might be classified as I–180 or I–280.

Federal Route Numbers
State and Other Route Numbers
Trans-Canada Highway
Points of Interest, Recreation Areas
Major Commercial Airports
National Capitals
State and Provincial Capitals

METROPOLITAN AREA MAPS

WASHINGTON

Aberdeen-Hoquiam (A5)—Twin cities of the northwest; lighthouses, fishing fleet, canneries, lumber mill tours, beaches.
Bellingham (B3)—Gateway to Mount Baker Recreational Area; Public Museum (Indian and Eskimo displays); nearby: International Peace Arch at Canadian border.
Bremerton (B4, A1)—Naval shipyard and museum, tours of USS Missouri.
Deception Pass State Park (B4)—Narrow gorge, overhanging cliffs, foaming rapids.
Fort Simcoe Historical State Park (C5)—Preserved former frontier Army post.
Ginkgo Petrified Forest (C5)—Fossilized trees and logs, museum.
Grand Coulee Dam (D4)—World's largest concrete structure; National Recreation Area along Roosevelt Lake, water sports; nearby: 400-foot Dry Falls in Sun Lakes State Park.
Lake Chelan National Recreation Area (C4)—Picturesque glacial lake; water sports, alpine peaks.
Long Beach (A5)—Center of North Beach Peninsula coastal resort area, over 25 miles of continuous hard sand beach.
Longview (B6)—First planned city in Washington, beautiful Lake Sacajawea Park, lumber mill and aluminum plant tours; nearby: Mount St. Helens and Spirit Lake recreation areas.
Maryhill (C6-9 mi. south of Goldendale)—Replica of prehistoric Stonehenge ruin, Fine Arts Museum.
Mount Baker Recreation Area (B3)—Popular fishing, hunting and winter sports center.
Mount Rainier National Park (B5)—Highest point in Washington, greatest single-peak glacial system in United States; dense forests, sparkling lakes, ice caves, abundant wild plants and animals, Wonderland Trail.
North Cascades National Park (C3)—Spectacular alpine scenery, active glaciers.
Olympia (B5)—State Capitol, impressive Roman-Doric architecture of government buildings, State Capitol Museum, maritime "mothball" fleet, scenic drive.
Olympic National Park (A4)—Mountain wilderness, finest remnant of Pacific Northwest rain forests; active glaciers, alpine meadows, rare Roosevelt elk; coastal area of unspoiled beaches.
Richland (D5)—Atomic Energy Visitors' Center, displays, animated exhibits.
Ross Lake National Recreation Area (C3)—Popular vacation campground; boating, fishing, hunting.
San Juan Islands (B3)—Historic and vacation area; last place within territorial U.S. under British flag; sailing cruises, water sports.
Seattle (B4, A1)—Space Needle, Monorail, Science Center, Smith Tower, Pioneer Square, Fishermen's Terminal, Chinatown, Lake Washington Floating Bridges and Ship Canal, Chittenden Locks, Art Museum, Museum of History & Industry, Arboretum, Japanese Garden, Zoo, scenic drives, harbor cruises.
Spokane (E4)—Eastern Washington State Historical Museum, Duncan Gardens, Spokane Falls, Cliff Park, scenic city loop drive; nearby: Mt. Spokane State Park recreation area.
Tacoma (B5, A2)—Tallest totem pole in United States, Tacoma Narrows suspension bridge, Historical Society Museum, Point Defiance Park (Job Carr House, Old Fort Nisqually, Deep Sea Aquarium, Zoo), permanently moored submarine U.S.S. Cabezon, Tacoma smelter.
Vancouver (B6)—Oldest city in Washington; Fort Vancouver National Historic Site, U.S. Grant museum; nearby: Portland, Oregon, Columbia River gorges, Bonneville Dam.
Wenatchee (C4)—Apple Blossom festival, North Central Washington Museum (Indian relics); nearby: Rocky Reach Dam with underwater viewing gallery, Ohme Gardens.
Whitman Mission National Historic Site (D6)—Site of Indian Massacre; mission ruins, graveyard, museum.
Yakima (C5)—Fruit center; Produce Row, museum and historical exhibits; nearby: Indian rock paintings, Ahtanum Mission.

ALBERTA

Banff F1
Bellevue F2
Blairmore F2
Calgary F1
Coleman F2
Didsbury F1
High River F1
Pincher Creek F2

BRITISH COLUMBIA

Armstrong D2
Burnaby B3
Castlegar D3
Chilliwack B3
Cranbrook F3
Creston E3
Duncan A3
Fernie F2
Fruitvale E3
Golden E1
Grand Forks D3
Hope B3
Kamloops C2
Kelowna D2
Kimberley E2
Kinnaird E3
Ladysmith A3
Lake Cowichan A3
Langley B3
Lillooet B2
Merritt C2
Mission City B3
Nanaimo A3
Nelson E3
New Westminster B3
Oliver C3
Penticton C3
Port Alberni A3
Port Coquitlam B3
Port Moody B3
Princeton C3
Revelstoke D1
Rossland D3
Saanich A3
Salmon Arm D2
Sidney A3
Surrey B3
Trail E3
Vancouver A3
Vernon D2
Victoria A3
White Rock B3

IDAHO

Bonners Ferry E3
Coeur d'Alene E4
Cottonwood E6
Lewiston E5
Moscow E5
Priest River E4
Saint Maries E4
Sandpoint E4

OREGON

Beaverton B6
Enterprise E6
Forest Grove A6
Gresham B6
Heppner D6
Hermiston D6
Hillsboro B6
Hood River B6
La Grande D6
McMinnville A6
Milton-Freewater D6
Milwaukie B6
Molalla B6
Newberg B6
Oregon City B6
Pendleton D6
Pilot Rock D6
Portland B6
Saint Helens B6
Seaside A6
Sheridan A6
Tillamook A6
Union E6
Warrenton A5
Woodburn B6

WASHINGTON

Aberdeen A5
Anacortes B3
Arlington B4
Auburn B5, A2
Bellevue B4, A1
Bellingham B3
Blaine B3
Bothell B4, A1
Bremerton B4, A1
Buckley B5, B2
Camas B6
Cashmere C4
Castle Rock B5
Centralia B5
Chehalis B5
Chelan C4
Cheney E4
Chewelah E4
Clarkston E5
Cle Elum C5
Clyde Hill A1
Colfax E5
College Place D6
Colville D3
Coulee Dam D4
Davenport D4
Dayton D5
Des Moines A2
Edmonds B4, A1
Ellensburg C5
Elma A5
Enumclaw B5, B2
Ephrata D5
Everett B4
Ferndale B3
Fife A2
Fircrest A2
Goldendale C6
Grandview C5
Granger C5
Hoquiam A5
Issaquah B1
Kelso B6
Kennewick D6
Kent A2
Kirkland A1
Lacey B5
Leavenworth C4
Longview B6
Lynnwood A1
Marysville B4
Medical Lake E4
Medina A1
Millwood E4
Milton A2
Monroe B4, B1
Montesano A5
Moses Lake D5
Mount Vernon B4
Mountlake Terrace A1
Newport E4
Normandy Park A2
Oak Harbor B4
Okanogan C4
Olympia B5
Omak C4
Opportunity E4
Oroville D3
Othello D5
Pasco D5
Pomeroy E5
Port Angeles A3
Port Orchard B4, A1
Port Townsend B4
Poulsbo A1
Prosser C6
Pullman E5
Puyallup B5, A2
Quincy C5
Raymond A5
Renton B4, A2
Richland D5
Ritzville D5
Seattle B4, A1
Sedro Woolley B3
Shelton B5
Snohomish B4
Soap Lake D4
South Bend A5
Spokane E4
Steilacoom A2
Sumner A2
Sunnyside C5
Tacoma B5, A2
Toppenish C5
Tukwila A2
Tumwater B5
Union Gap C5
Vancouver B6
Walla Walla D6
Wapato C5
Washougal B6
Wenatchee C4
White Pass C5
White Salmon B6
Yakima C5

Map scale: 1 inch=58 miles

POINTS OF INTEREST

OREGON

Ashland (B5)—Annual summer Shakespeare festival, mineral springs.
Astoria (A1)—Unusual 125-foot Astoria Column with 7-foot spiral frieze portraying early history of Oregon Country, observation tower; Maritime Museum; nearby: Fort Clatsop National Memorial with restored Lewis and Clark stockade.
Baker (E3)—Former gold rush town, native gold exhibit; nearby: mineral springs, Anthony Lakes recreation area.
Bend (C3)—Center of scenic recreation area; nearby: Tumalo Falls, Century Drive, Lava River Caves, Newberry Crater, Pilot Butte, Cascade ski resorts.
Bonneville Dam (B2)—High-lift navigational locks, fish ladders, salmon pools.
Champoeg State Park (B2-outside Newberg)—Site of early Willamette River settlement, historical museum.
Columbia River Gorge (B2-east from Portland)—Scenic river drive, water-level and cliff-top roads, Multnomah Falls.
Condon-Day Fossil Beds State Park (D3)—Prehistoric fossil remains, ancient Indian pictographs in Picture Gorge.
Corvallis (B3)—Horner Museum with pioneer items and Indian artifacts.
Crater Lake National Park (B4)—Picturesque deep-blue lake in crater of extinct volcano, lake encircled by towering lava cliffs; Wizard Island symmetrical cinder cone, Phantom Ship lava formation, scenic Rim Drive.
Devil's Punch Bowl State Park (A3-8 mi. north of Newport)—Large bowl-shaped rock formation, cavern.
Eugene (B3)—Pioneer Museum, Oriental Art Museum; nearby: Cascade ski resorts.
Gold Beach (A5)—Famous steelhead trout and salmon fishing area, scenic tours on canyon-lined Rogue River.
Jacksonville (B5)—Early gold rush town, courthouse museum, stagecoach tour.
Malheur Cave (D4)—Grotto with glazed walls and ceiling, underground lake.
Mount Hood (B2)—Highest point in Oregon; recreation area, scenic Loop Highway.
Newport (A3)—Popular coastal resort center; nearby: Yaquina lighthouse, agate beaches.
Oregon Caves National Monument (A5)—Weird subterranean limestone formations.
Oregon Dunes (A3)—Fifty-mile stretch of towering sand mounds along coast.
Painted Hills State Park (C3)—Highly colored domes and ridges, plant fossils.
Pendleton (D2)—Famous annual Roundup and Indian pageant; nearby: Blue Mountains recreation areas.
Port Orford (A4)—Scenic seascapes, Battle Rock monument to pioneer-Indian battle; nearby: Prehistoric Gardens with life-size replicas of dinosaurs and other prehistoric animals.
Portland (B2)—"City of Roses" with test gardens and annual festival; Lambert Gardens, sunken gardens, rhododendron test gardens, Art Museum, Museum of Science & Industry, arboretum, zoo, scenic drive; nearby: colorful Lake Oswego, Fort Vancouver National Historic Site in Vancouver, Washington.
Salem (B2)—State Capitol, State Library, Bush House Art Museum; nearby: scenic Silver Falls State Park, Cascade ski resorts.
Sea Lion Caves (A3)—Underground cavern home for several hundred sea lions.
Seaside (A1)—Largest and oldest coastal resort; terminus of Lewis and Clark trail, monument.
Snake River Canyon (E2)—Hells Canyon, deepest gorge in North America, spectacular rugged terrain, upstream boat trips, scenic lookouts.
The Dalles (C2)—Old Fort Dalles Historical Museum, Celilo Indian Park, Winquatt Museum (Indian relics), The Dalles Dam.
Tillamook (A2)—Dairy center, tours of cheese factories, Pioneer Museum; nearby: scenic Cape Lookout and Oswald West State Parks.
Umpqua Lighthouse State Park (A4)—Highest sand dunes in United States, rhododendrons.
Upper Klamath Lake (B5)—Recreation area, white pelican preserve, bird refuge; nearby: Logging Museum at Collier Memorial State Park.
Wallowa Lake (E2)—Picturesque water sport recreation area, glacial deposits, Indian cemetery; nearby: Hat Point Lookout over Hells Canyon.

CALIFORNIA

Place	Key
Alturas	C 6
Anderson	B 6
Arcata	A 6
Blue Lake	A 6
Burney	B 6
Central Valley	B 6
Crescent City	A 5
Dorris	B 5
Dunsmuir	B 6
Eureka	A 6
Fortuna	A 6
McCloud	B 6
Mount Shasta	B 6
Redding	B 6
Rio Dell	A 6
Susanville	C 6
Tulelake	C 5
Weaverville	B 6
Weed	B 6
Yreka	B 5

IDAHO

Place	Key
Boise	F 4
Bovill	F 1
Cottonwood	E 1
Council	F 3
Craigmont	E 1
Deary	E 1
Elk River	F 1
Emmett	F 3
Fruitland	E 3
Glenns Ferry	F 4
Grangeville	F 2
Homedale	E 4
Horseshoe Bend	F 3
Idaho City	F 3
Kamiah	F 1
Kendrick	E 1
Kooskia	F 1
Lewiston	E 1
McCall	F 2
Moscow	E 1
Mountain Home	F 4
Nampa	F 4
New Meadows	F 2
Nezperce	F 1
Orofino	F 1
Parma	F 3
Payette	E 3
Pierce	F 1
Riggins	F 2
Wilder	E 4

OREGON

Place	Key
Albany	B 3
Altamont	B 5
Arlington	C 2
Ashland	B 5
Astoria	A 1
Baker	E 3
Bandon	A 4
Barnes	B 4
Bay City	A 2
Beaverton	B 2
Bend	C 3
Brookings	A 5
Burns	D 4
Canyon City	D 3
Canyonville	B 4
Carlton	B 2
Central Point	B 5
Chiloquin	B 5
Clatskanie	B 1
Condon	C 2
Coos Bay	A 4
Coquille	A 4
Corvallis	B 3
Eagle Point	B 5
Eastside	A 4
Elgin	E 2
Enterprise	E 2
Estacada	B 2
Eugene	B 3
Florence	A 3
Forest Grove	B 2
Fossil	C 2
Garibaldi	A 2
Gold Beach	A 5
Gold Hill	B 5
Grants Pass	A 5
Gresham	B 2
Halfway	E 2
Harrisburg	A 3
Heppner	D 2
Hermiston	D 2
Hillsboro	B 2
Hines	D 4
Hood River	C 2
Huntington	E 3
Jacksonville	B 5
Jefferson	B 3
John Day	D 3
Joseph	E 2
Keizer	B 2
Lakeview	C 5
Lebanon	B 3
Lincoln City	A 2
Madras	C 3
McMinnville	A 2
Medford	B 5
Merrill	B 5
Mill City	B 3
Milton-Freewater	D 2
Milwaukie	B 2
Molalla	B 2
Monmouth	A 3
Myrtle Creek	B 4
Myrtle Point	A 4
Newberg	B 2
Newport	A 3
North Bend	A 4
Nyssa	E 3
Oakland	B 4
Oakridge	B 3
Ontario	E 3
Oregon City	B 2
Pendleton	D 2
Philomath	A 3
Pilot Rock	D 2
Port Orford	A 4
Portland	B 2
Redmond	C 3
Reedsport	A 4
Riddle	A 4
Rockaway	A 2
Roseburg	B 4
Saint Helens	B 2
Salem	B 2
Scappoose	B 2
Seaside	A 1
Sheridan	A 2
Silverton	B 2
Sisters	C 3
Springfield	B 3
Stayton	B 3
Sutherlin	B 4
Sweet Home	B 3
The Dalles	C 2
Tillamook	A 2
Toledo	A 3
Union	E 2
Vale	E 3
Vernonia	B 2
Waldport	A 3
Wallowa	E 2
Warrenton	A 1
Weston	D 2
Willamina	A 2

WASHINGTON

Place	Key
Aberdeen	A 1
Asotin	E 1
Battle Ground	B 2
Benton City	D 1
Camas	B 2
Castle Rock	B 1
Centralia	B 1
Chehalis	B 1
Clarkston	E 1
Colfax	E 1
College Place	D 2
Connell	D 1
Cosmopolis	A 1
Dayton	E 1
Ellensburg	C 1
Elma	B 1
Goldendale	C 2
Grandview	D 1
Granger	C 1
Hoquiam	A 1
Kelso	B 1
Kennewick	D 1
Lacey	B 1
Lind	D 1
Longview	B 1
Morton	B 1
Moses Lake	D 1
Olympia	B 1
Othello	D 1
Palouse	E 1
Pasco	D 1
Pomeroy	E 1
Prosser	D 1
Pullman	E 1
Raymond	A 1
Richland	D 1
Ritzville	D 1
South Bend	A 1
Stevenson	B 2
Sunnyside	C 1
Tenino	B 1
Toppenish	C 1
Union Gap	C 1
Vancouver	B 2
Waitsburg	E 1
Walla Walla	D 1
Wapato	C 1
Warden	D 1
Washougal	B 2
West Richland	D 1
Westport	A 1
White Salmon	C 2

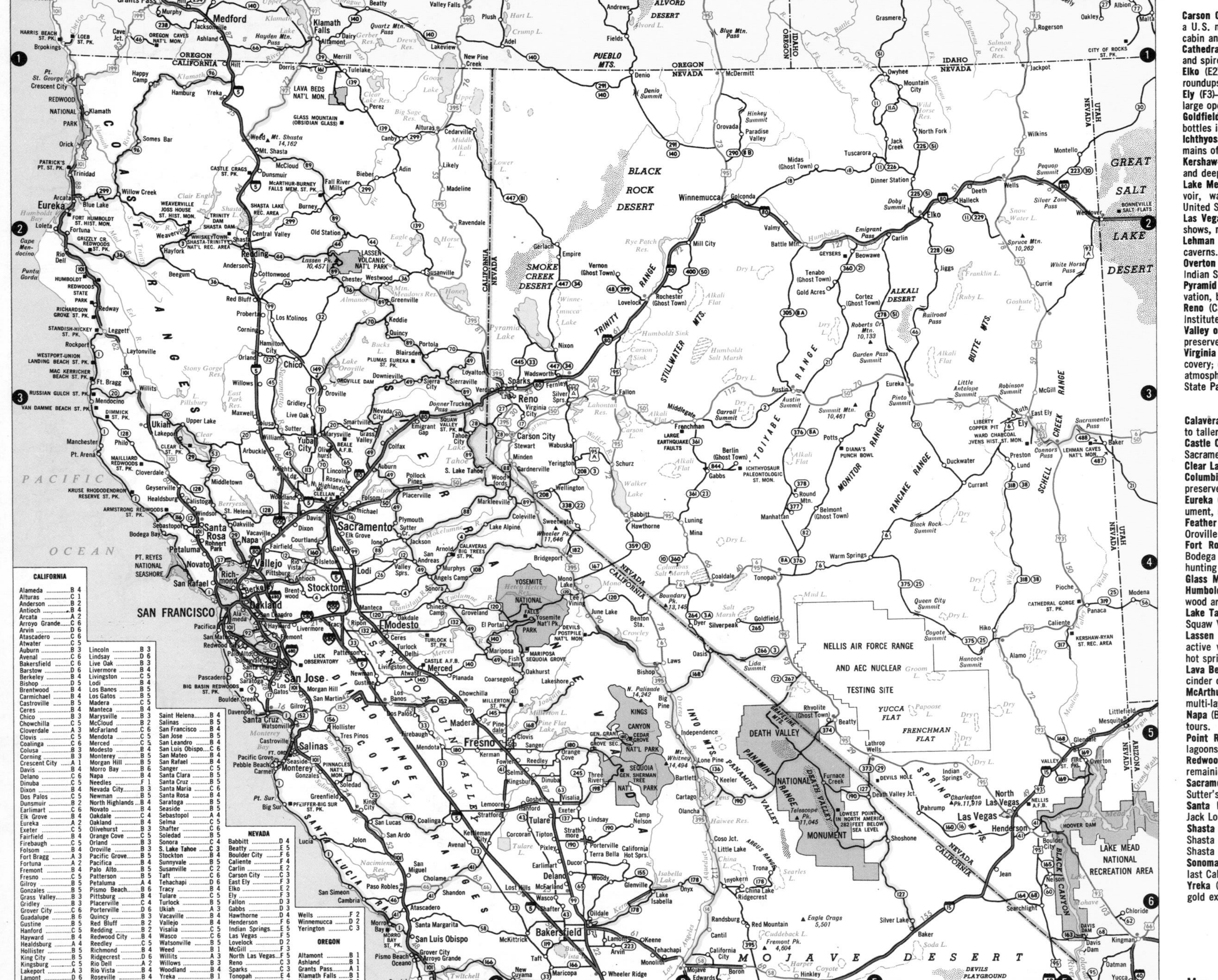

NEVADA

Carson City (C3)—State Capitol, Nevada State Museum (formerly a U.S. mint), historical exhibits; nearby: at Genoa, restored log cabin and stockade of first permanent settlement in Nevada.

Cathedral Gorge State Park (F4)—Colorful towering rock arches and spires formed from eroded cliffs.

Elko (E2)—Major cattle and sheep ranching center, stockyards, roundups; nearby: hot springs, fossil beds, ghost towns.

Ely (F3)—Mining center, mining and historical museum; nearby: large open-pit copper mine at Ruth.

Goldfield (D4)—Famous old mining camp; nearby: house made of bottles in ghost town of Rhyolite.

Ichthyosaur Paleontological State Monument (D3)—Fossilized remains of giant fish-lizard creatures.

Kershaw-Ryan State Recreation Area (F4)—Scenic colored cliffs and deep canyons.

Lake Mead National Recreation Area (F6)—Nation's largest reservoir, water sports, excursion trips; Hoover Dam highest in United States, conducted tours.

Las Vegas (F5)—Year-round desert resort city; gambling casinos, shows, nightclubs.

Lehman Caves National Monument (F3)—Honeycombed limestone caverns.

Overton (F5)—Lost City Museum with relics of ancient Pueblo Indian Settlement now submerged in Lake Mead.

Pyramid Lake (C3)—Picturesque mountain setting; Indian reservation, bird sanctuary.

Reno (C3)—Gambling casinos, mining museum, Desert Research Institute.

Valley of Fire State Park (F5)—Eroded red sandstone cliffs, well-preserved prehistoric stone drawings.

Virginia City (C3)—Site of Comstock Lode gold and silver discovery; old Opera House, church, saloons; old Western residential atmosphere; nearby: ruins of early frontier fort at Fort Churchill State Park.

NORTHERN CALIFORNIA
(North of San Francisco Bay Area)

Calaveras Big Trees State Park (C4)—Giant sequoia trees, related to taller coastal redwoods.

Castle Crags State Park (B2)—Towering granite rock spires along Sacramento River.

Clear Lake (A3)—Picturesque resort area.

Columbia Historic State Park (C4-5 mi. north of Sonora)—Well-preserved buildings of gold rush days; museum.

Eureka (A2)—Sport fishing centers; Fort Humboldt historic monument, redwood park.

Feather River (B3)—Scenic valley and canyon; site of new Oroville Dam.

Fort Ross State Historical Monument (A4-15 mi. northwest of Bodega Bay)—Restored stockade settlement of former Russian hunting and trading outpost.

Glass Mountain (B1)—Extensive deposit of black obsidian glass.

Humboldt Redwoods State Park (A2)—Center of vast coastal redwood area containing world's tallest trees.

Lake Tahoe (C3)—Scenic summer and winter resort area; nearby: Squaw Valley Olympic site, Donner Pass and monument.

Lassen Volcanic National Park (B2)—Lassen Peak (most recent active volcano in U.S. except for those in Alaska and Hawaii), hot springs, mud pools, steam vents.

Lava Beds National Monument (B1)—Unusual volcanic formations, cinder cones, lava caves; ancient Indian stone drawings.

McArthur-Burney Falls Memorial State Park (B2)—Outstanding multi-layered waterfall.

Napa (B4)—Center of Napa Valley wine-producing district; winery tours.

Point Reyes National Seashore (A4)—Recreation area, beaches, lagoons, sea lions, lighthouse.

Redwood National Park (A1)—Magnificent stands of timber; last remaining herd of native Roosevelt Elk.

Sacramento (B4)—State Capitol, scenic gardens, reconstructed Sutter's Fort, Indian and Pony Express museums.

Santa Rosa (A4)—Luther Burbank home and gardens; nearby: Jack London home and historical park.

Shasta Lake (B2)—Recreation area; Mt. Shasta (dormant volcano), Shasta Dam 602-feet high, caverns; nearby: gold rush towns of Shasta and Weaverville.

Sonoma (B4-10 mi. west of Napa)—Site of most northerly and last California mission; museum, old stone wine cellars.

Yreka (B1)—Center of Klamath River hunting and fishing area; gold exhibit.

Map scale: 1 inch=68 miles

ARIZONA

Place	Map key
Kingman	F 4
Yuma	F 6

CALIFORNIA

Place	Map key
Alameda	A 1,A 4
Albany	A 3
Alhambra	A 5
Alisal	A 2
Altadena	A 5
Anaheim	D 5,B 6
Antioch	A 1
Arcadia	B 5
Arroyo Grande	B 4
Arvin	C 4
Atascadero	B 3
Atwater	B 2
Avenal	B 3
Azusa	B 5
Bakersfield	C 4
Baldwin Park	B 5
Banning	E 5
Barstow	D 4
Beaumont	E 5
Bellflower	B 6
Belmont	A 4
Benicia	A 3
Berkeley	A 1,A 3
Beverly Hills	A 6
Bishop	D 2
Blythe	F 5
Brawley	F 6
Brea	B 6
Brentwood	A 1
Buena Park	B 6
Burbank	D 5,A 5
Burlingame	A 4
Calexico	F 6
Calipatria	F 5
Campbell	B 5
Carlsbad	D 5
Carpinteria	C 4
Carson	A 6
Castroville	A 2
Ceres	B 1
Chino	B 6
Chowchilla	B 2
Chula Vista	D 6
Claremont	B 5
Clovis	C 2
Coachella	E 5
Coalinga	B 3
Colton	C 6
Compton	A 6
Concord	A 3
Corcoran	C 3
Corona	D 5,C 6
Coronado	D 6
Costa Mesa	D 5
Covina	B 5
Culver City	A 6
Daly City	A 4
Danville	A 4
Davis	A 1
Del Mar	D 6
Delano	C 3
Diablo	B 4
Dinuba	C 2
Dixon	A 1
Dos Palos	B 2
Downey	D 5,B 6
Earlimart	C 3
El Cajon	E 6
El Centro	E 6
El Cerrito	A 3
El Monte	B 5
El Segundo	A 6
Elk Grove	B 1
Elsinore, L.	D 5,C 6
Encinitas	D 6
Escondido	D 5
Exeter	C 3
Fairfield	A 1
Fillmore	C 4
Firebaugh	B 2
Folsom	B 1
Fontana	C 5
Ford City	C 4
Fremont	A 1,B 4
Fresno	C 2
Fullerton	B 6
Garden Grove	B 6
Gardena	A 6
Gilroy	A 2
Glendale	D 5,A 5
Glendora	B 5
Gonzales	A 2
Grover City	B 4
Guadalupe	B 4
Gustine	B 2
Hanford	C 3
Hawthorne	A 6
Hayward	A 1,A 4
Hemet	E 5
Hermosa Beach	A 6
Hollister	B 2
Holtville	F 6
Huntington Beach	B 6
Huntington Park	A 6
Imperial	E 6
Imperial Beach	D 6
Indio	E 5
Inglewood	A 6
King City	B 3
Kingsburg	C 2
La Habra	B 6
La Mesa	D 6
La Puente	B 6
Lafayette	A 3
Laguna Beach	D 5
Lakewood	A 6
Lamont	C 4
Lancaster	D 4
Lemon Grove	E 6
Lemoore	C 3
Leucadia	D 6
Lindsay	C 3
Livermore	A 1
Livingston	B 2
Lodi	B 1
Lomita	A 6
Lompoc	B 4
Long Beach	D 5,A 6
Los Altos	A 5
Los Angeles	C 5,A 5
Los Banos	B 2
Los Gatos	A 2
Lynwood	A 6
Madera	B 2
Malibu	C 5,A 6
Manhattan Beach	A 6
Manteca	B 1
Martinez	A 3
McFarland	C 3
Meiners Oaks	C 4
Mendota	B 2
Menlo Park	A 4
Merced	B 2
Mill Valley	A 3
Millbrae	A 4
Milpitas	B 4
Mira Loma	C 6
Modesto	B 1
Monrovia	B 5
Montebello	B 6
Monterey	A 2
Monterey Park	B 6
Moorpark	C 4
Morgan Hill	A 2
Morro Bay	B 3
Mountain View	A 5
Napa	A 1
National City	D 6
Needles	F 4
Newark	A 4
Newhall	C 4
Newman	B 2
Newport Beach	D 5
Norco	C 6
Norwalk	D 5,B 6
Novato	A 1,A 3
Oakdale	B 1
Oakland	A 1,A 4
Oceanside	D 5
Oildale	C 3
Ojai	C 4
Ontario	D 5,B 6
Orange	B 6
Orange Cove	C 2
Oxnard	C 5
Pacific Grove	A 2
Pacifica	A 1,A 4
Palm Springs	E 5
Palmdale	D 4
Palo Alto	A 2,A 4
Palos Verdes Estates	A 6
Pasadena	D 5,A 5
Paso Robles	B 3
Patterson	B 2
Perris	D 5,C 6
Petaluma	A 1
Pico Rivera	B 6
Piedmont	A 4
Pinole	A 3
Pittsburg	A 1
Pleasant Hill	A 3
Pomona	D 5,B 6
Port Hueneme	C 5
Porterville	C 3
Ramona	E 6
Redlands	D 5
Redondo Beach	A 6
Redwood City	A 2,A 4
Reedley	C 2
Rialto	C 5
Richmond	A 1,A 3
Ridgecrest	D 3
Rio Vista	A 1
Riverside	D 5,C 6
Sacramento	B 1
Saint Helena	A 1
Salinas	A 2
San Anselmo	A 3
San Bernardino	D5,C 5
San Bruno	A 4
San Carlos	A 4
San Clemente	D 5
San Diego	D 6
San Fernando	A 5
San Francisco	A1,A 4
San Jacinto	D 5
San Jose	A 2,B 5
San Leandro	A 1,A 4
San Lorenzo	A 4
San Luis Obispo	B 4
San Mateo	A 1,A 4
San Pablo	A 3
San Rafael	A 1,A 3
Sanger	C 2
Santa Ana	D 5,B 6
Santa Barbara	C 4
Santa Clara	A 2,B 5
Santa Cruz	A 2
Santa Maria	B 4
Santa Monica	C 5,A 6
Santa Paula	C 4
Santa Rosa	A 1
Saratoga	A 2
Sausalito	A 3
Seal Beach	B 6
Seaside	A 2
Sebastopol	A 1
Selma	C 2
Shafter	C 3
Signal Hill	B 6
Simi Valley	C 4
Soledad	B 2
South Gate	A 6
South San Francisco	A 4
Stockton	B 1
Sunnyvale	A 2,A 5
Taft	C 4
Tehachapi	C 4
Temple City	B 5
Thousand Oaks	C 4
Torrance	C 5,A 6
Tracy	B 1
Tulare	C 3
Turlock	B 2
Union City	A 4
Upland	B 5
Vacaville	A 1
Vallejo	A 1,A 3
Ventura	C 4
Visalia	C 3
Vista	D 5
Walnut Creek	A 3
Wasco	C 3
Watsonville	A 2
West Covina	D 5,B 6
Westminster	B 6
Whittier	B 6
Woodlake	C 3
Woodland	A 1
Woodside	A 4

MEXICO

Place	Map key
Mexicali	F 6
San Luis	F 6
Tijuana	D 6

NEVADA

Place	Map key
Boulder City	F 3
Henderson	F 3
Las Vegas	F 3
North Las Vegas	F 3

POINTS OF INTEREST

CENTRAL and SOUTHERN CALIFORNIA

Channel Islands National Monument (C5)—Sea-lion rookery, nesting sea birds, fossil beds.

Death Valley National Monument (D3)—Extensive desert solitude, salt beds, borax deposits; lowest point in North America.

Devils Postpile National Monument (C2)—Symmetrical "fence post shaped" blue-gray basaltic rock columns.

Disneyland, Anaheim (B6)—Family amusement center; featuring Frontierland, Fantasyland, Adventureland, Tomorrowland; nearby: Knott's Berry Farm in Buena Vista.

Fresno (C2)—Center of San Joaquin Valley wine, raisin and fig region, winery tours.

Joshua Tree National Monument (E5)—Preserve of unusual Joshua trees, giant yuccas and other desert plants.

Kings Canyon National Park (C2)—Granite rock gorges, giant sequoia trees, large sugar pines; famous General Grant Tree.

Los Angeles (C5, A5)—Hollywood movie and TV studios, Civic Center, Exposition Park & Coliseum, Hollywood Bowl, Griffith Park (zoo and planetarium), Forest Lawn Memorial Park, Museum of Science & Industry, County Museum, Southwest Museum (Indian displays), Marine Museum, La Brea Tar Pits, Will Rogers ranch home, Olvera Street (Mexican market), Pueblo de Los Angeles Monument, San Fernando Mission; nearby: Malibu Beach, Rose Bowl, Mt. Wilson Observatory, Marineland of the Pacific, Signal Hill oil fields, Huntington Library & Art Gallery, San Gabriel Mission, Arboretum, Magic Mountain (theme park).

Monterey (A2)—Center of peninsula-resort area, former Spanish capital of California; Robert Louis Stevenson house, Presidio, Old Custom House, Fisherman's Wharf, homes of artists and writers; nearby: Carmel resort and artist colony, Pebble Beach, rare cypress trees, scenic Seventeen Mile Drive, Carmel and San Juan Bautista missions.

Muir Woods National Monument (A3)—Picturesque virgin stands of coastal redwood trees.

Oakland (A1, A4)—Public Museum, State Arboretum, art galleries, rose gardens, Jack London Square, Lake Merritt (salt lake); nearby: University of California main campus at Berkeley, scenic Mt. Diablo State Park.

Palm Springs (E5)—Fashionable desert resort, date gardens; palm tree filled canyon.

Palo Alto (A2, A4)—Stanford University's Art Gallery, Hoover Library and Memorial Church.

Palomar Observatory (D5)—World's largest telescope atop 6000-foot Palomar Mountain.

Pinnacles National Monument (B2)—Unusual spirelike volcanic rock formations; numerous caves.

San Diego (D6)—Major U.S. Naval Base, Balboa Park (Zoo, Natural History Museum, Museum of Man), Scripps Institute of Oceanography, Sea World underwater theater, San Diego mission, Star of India full-rigged iron ship, Serra historical museum, Old Globe Theater, Old Town with restored adobe buildings; nearby: Cabrillo National Monument, Silver Strand Beach, Mexican border town of Tijuana.

San Francisco (A1, A4)—Golden Gate Bridge, San Francisco-Oakland Bay Bridge, Fisherman's Wharf & Embarcadero, Chinatown, Telegraph Hill & Coit Tower, Civic Center (Opera House, Museum of Art, Auditorium), Golden Gate Park (Japanese Tea Garden, Academy of Sciences, arboretum, De Young Museum, planetarium, aquarium), Presidio Military Reservation, Nob Hill and Russian Hill cable cars, Maritime Museum, Cliff House & Seal Rocks, Wells Fargo Museum, Palace of the Legion of Honor, Mission Dolores.

San Jose (A2, B5)—Egyptian Museum, Winchester Mystery House; nearby: Santa Clara Mission, Lick Observatory, Big Basin Redwoods State Park.

San Juan Capistrano (D5-5 mi. north of San Clemente)—Famous mission; area noted for migrating swallows.

San Simeon (B3)—William Randolph Hearst's estate and famous collection of art treasures and antiques.

Santa Barbara (C4)—Spanish architecture, Mission Santa Barbara, County Court House, Art Museum, Museum of Natural History, Botanical Gardens; nearby: Danish settlement at Solvang, Santa Ynez Mission.

Santa Catalina (C5)—Island resort; marine gardens, seal rocks, tropical bird park.

Sequoia National Park (C3)—Groves of giant sequoia trees, forest museum; 3500-year-old General Sherman Tree; Mt. Whitney, highest point in California.

Yosemite National Park (C1)—Spectacular scenery; valleys, waterfalls, rock walls, domes, sequoia groves.

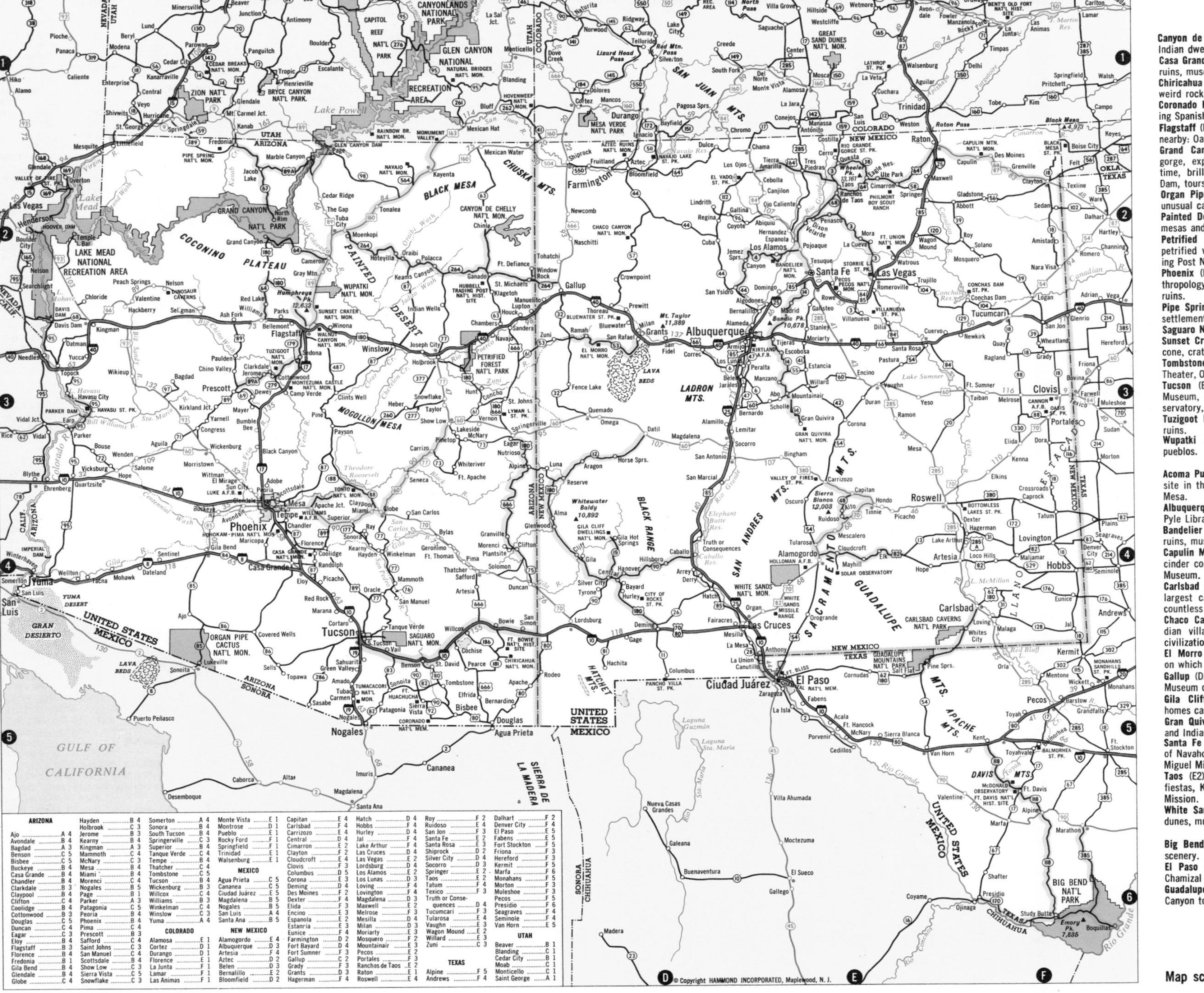

ARIZONA

Place	Key	Place	Key	Place	Key
Ajo	A 4	Hayden	B 4	Somerton	A 4
Avondale	B 4	Holbrook	C 3	Sonora	B 4
Bagdad	A 3	Jerome	B 3	South Tucson	B 4
Benson	C 5	Kearny	B 4	Springerville	C 3
Bisbee	C 5	Kingman	A 3	Superior	B 4
Buckeye	B 4	Mammoth	C 4	Tanque Verde	C 4
Casa Grande	B 4	McNary	C 3	Tempe	B 4
Chandler	B 4	Mesa	B 4	Thatcher	C 4
Clarkdale	B 3	Miami	B 4	Tombstone	C 5
Claypool	B 4	Morenci	C 4	Tucson	B 4
Clifton	C 4	Nogales	B 5	Wickenburg	B 3
Coolidge	B 4	Page	B 1	Willcox	C 4
Cottonwood	B 3	Parker	A 3	Williams	B 3
Douglas	C 5	Patagonia	C 5	Winkelman	C 4
Duncan	C 4	Peoria	B 4	Winslow	C 3
Eagar	C 3	Phoenix	B 4	Yuma	A 4
Eloy	B 4	Pima	C 4		
Flagstaff	B 3	Prescott	B 3		
Florence	B 4	Safford	C 4		
Fredonia	B 1	Saint Johns	C 3		
Gila Bend	B 4	San Manuel	C 4		
Glendale	B 4	Scottsdale	B 4		
Globe	C 4	Show Low	C 3		
		Sierra Vista	C 5		
		Snowflake	C 3		

COLORADO

Place	Key
Alamosa	E 1
Cortez	D 1
Durango	D 1
Florence	E 1
La Junta	F 1
Lamar	F 1
Las Animas	F 1
Monte Vista	E 1
Montrose	D 1
Pueblo	E 1
Rocky Ford	F 1
Springfield	F 1
Trinidad	E 1
Walsenburg	E 1

MEXICO

Place	Key
Agua Prieta	C 5
Cananea	C 5
Ciudad Juárez	E 5
Magdalena	B 5
Nogales	B 5
San Luis	A 4
Santa Ana	B 5

NEW MEXICO

Place	Key	Place	Key	Place	Key	Place	Key
Alamogordo	E 4	Capitan	E 4	Hatch	D 4	Roy	F 2
Albuquerque	D 3	Carlsbad	F 4	Hobbs	F 4	Ruidoso	E 4
Artesia	F 4	Carrizozo	E 4	Hurley	D 4	San Jon	F 3
Aztec	D 2	Central	D 4	Jal	F 4	Santa Fe	E 2
Belen	D 3	Cimarron	E 2	Lake Arthur	F 4	Santa Rosa	E 3
Bernalillo	E 2	Clayton	F 2	Las Cruces	D 4	Shiprock	D 2
Bloomfield	D 2	Cloudcroft	E 4	Las Vegas	E 2	Silver City	D 4
		Clovis	F 3	Lordsburg	D 4	Socorro	D 3
		Columbus	D 5	Los Alamos	E 2	Springer	E 2
		Corona	E 3	Los Lunas	D 3	Taos	E 2
		Deming	D 4	Loving	F 4	Tatum	F 4
		Des Moines	F 2	Lovington	F 4	Texico	F 3
		Dexter	F 4	Magdalena	D 3	Truth or Consequences	D 4
		Elida	F 3	Maxwell	E 2	Tucumcari	F 3
		Encino	E 3	Melrose	F 3	Tularosa	E 4
		Espanola	E 2	Mesilla	D 4	Vaughn	E 3
		Estancia	E 3	Milan	D 3	Wagon Mound	E 2
		Eunice	F 4	Moriarty	E 3	Willard	E 3
		Farmington	D 2	Mosquero	F 2	Zuni	C 3
		Fort Bayard	D 4	Mountainair	E 3		
		Fort Sumner	F 3	Pecos	E 2		
		Gallup	C 2	Portales	F 3		
		Grady	F 3	Ranchos de Taos	E 2		
		Grants	D 3	Raton	E 1		
		Hagerman	F 4	Roswell	E 4		

TEXAS

Place	Key
Alpine	F 5
Andrews	F 4
Dalhart	F 2
Denver City	F 4
El Paso	E 5
Fabens	E 5
Fort Stockton	F 5
Friona	F 3
Hereford	F 3
Kermit	F 5
Marfa	F 6
Monahans	F 5
Morton	F 3
Muleshoe	F 3
Pecos	F 5
Presidio	F 6
Seagraves	F 4
Seminole	F 4
Van Horn	E 5

UTAH

Place	Key
Beaver	B 1
Blanding	C 1
Cedar City	B 1
Moab	C 1
Monticello	C 1
Saint George	A 1

ARIZONA

Canyon de Chelly National Monument (C2)—Ruins of prehistoric Indian dwellings.
Casa Grande National Monument (B4)—Adobe tower ruins, village ruins, museum.
Chiricahua National Monument (C5)—Giant monoliths and other weird rock formations; nearby: Fort Bowie National Historic Site.
Coronado National Memorial (C5)—Scenic preserve commemorating Spanish exploration.
Flagstaff (B3)—Museum of Northern Arizona, Lowell Observatory; nearby: Oak Creek Canyon, Snow Bowl resort.
Grand Canyon National Park (B2)—Spectacular 217-mile long gorge, exposed rocks representing vast periods of geologic time, brilliant colors, staggering depths; nearby: Glen Canyon Dam, tours.
Organ Pipe Cactus National Monument (B4)—Natural display of unusual cactus.
Painted Desert (B2)—Extensive area of vividly colored plateaus, mesas and buttes.
Petrified Forest National Park (C3)—Large natural exhibit of petrified wood, Indian ruins, petroglyphs; nearby: Hubbell Trading Post National Historic Site.
Phoenix (B4)—State Capitol, Arizona Museum, Museum of Anthropology, Art Museum, Desert Botanical Gardens, Pueblo Grande ruins.
Pipe Spring National Monument (B2)—Ruins of Mormon pioneer settlement.
Saguaro National Monument (C4)—Forest of giant saguaro cacti.
Sunset Crater National Monument (B2)—Colorful volcanic cinder cone, crater, lava flows.
Tombstone (C5)—Health resort, former mining town, Bird Cage Theater, OK Corral, Boot Hill; nearby: Coronado National Memorial.
Tucson (B4)—Mission San Xavier del Bac, Historical Society Museum, restored Fort Lowell; nearby: Kitt Peak National Observatory, Arizona-Sonora Desert Museum.
Tuzigoot National Monument (B3)—Excavated prehistoric pueblo ruins.
Wupatki National Monument (B2)—Red sandstone prehistoric pueblos.

NEW MEXICO

Acoma Pueblo (D3-near San Fidel)—Oldest continuously inhabited site in the United States; nearby: 430-foot sandstone Enchanted Mesa.
Albuquerque (D3)—Old Town, Church of San Felipe de Neri, Ernie Pyle Library; nearby: pueblo ruins, Museum of the Old West.
Bandelier National Monument (E2)—Prehistoric Pueblo Indian ruins, museum.
Capulin Mountain National Monument (F2)—Symmetrical volcanic cinder cone, craters, lava flows; nearby: Fort Jordan Stockade & Museum.
Carlsbad Caverns National Park (E4)—Believed to be the world's largest cave, a series of connected underground caverns with countless magnificent and curious formations.
Chaco Canyon National Monument (D2)—Numerous ruins of Indian villages, represents highest point of prehistoric Pueblo civilization.
El Morro National Monument (D3)—Famous "Inscription Rock" on which are carved inscriptions by early explorers and settlers.
Gallup (D2)—Indian trade center, annual Intertribal Ceremonial, Museum of Indian Arts.
Gila Cliff Dwellings National Monument (D4)—Well-preserved homes carved in cliff face.
Gran Quivira National Monument (E3)—Ruins of Spanish mission and Indian house mounds.
Santa Fe (E2)—State Capitol, Palace of the Governors, Museum of Navaho Ceremonial Art, Museum of International Folk Art, San Miguel Mission, Cristo Rey Church.
Taos (E2)—Old Spanish town and art colony, annual religious fiestas, Kit Carson House, Art Museum, Taos Pueblo, St. Francis Mission.
White Sands National Monument (E4)—Glistening white gypsum dunes, museum.

WESTERN TEXAS

Big Bend National Park (F6)—Outstanding mountain and desert scenery.
El Paso (E5)—Christ Statue, Fort Bliss Replica, Sun Carnival, Chamizal National Memorial.
Guadalupe Mountains National Park (E5)—Rugged mountain and Canyon topography.

Map scale: 1 inch=87 miles

POINTS OF INTEREST

UTAH

Arches National Park (C5)—Eroded rock strata in forms of arches, windows, pinnacles and pedestals.
Bryce Canyon National Park (B5)—Giant horseshoe-shaped bowl, towering colorful eroded rock domes, spires, walls and terraces.
Canyonlands National Park (C5)—Variety of rock formations and erosion features, canyons, mesas, arches, pinnacles; nearby: scenic canyon panorama at Dead Horse Point State Park.
Capitol Reef National Park (B5)—Twenty-mile long uplifted cliffs with dome-shaped crown of white sandstone rock.
Dinosaur National Monument (C3)—Fossil remains of dinosaurs and other prehistoric animals; nearby: Flaming Gorge National Recreation Area.
Glen Canyon National Recreation Area (B5)—Expanding summer recreation area, water sports.
Golden Spike National Historic Site (A3)—Monument at completion point of first transcontinental railroad.
Natural Bridges National Monument (C5)—Three large erosion-carved sandstone bridges.
Rainbow Bridge National Monument (B6)—309-foot high symmetrical pink sandstone arch.
Salt Lake City (B3)—State Capitol, Mormon Tabernacle, Mormon Temple, Seagull Monument, Brigham Young Monument, Old Log House, Pioneer Memorial Museum, Zoo; nearby: buoyant Great Salt Lake.
Zion National Park (A5)—Outstanding multicolored canyon and mesa region, massive rock formations, natural amphitheater, scenic drive.

WYOMING

Casper (D2)—Center of oil region, refinery tours, Fort Caspar restoration, Pioneer Museum; nearby: Teapot Rock, Hell's Half Acre.
Cheyenne (E3)—State Capitol, State Museum, Hereford Ranch, Jim Baker Log Cabin.
Cody (C1)—Buffalo Bill Statue and Museum, Whitney Western Art Gallery, annual Wild West Show, dude ranches.
Fort Bridger (B3-30 mi. east of Evanston)—Restored fur-trade center and fort, museum.
Fort Laramie National Historic Site (E2)—Site of early fur-trading post, ruins and restorations of later military camp.
Grand Teton National Park (B1)—Impressive series of Rocky Mountain peaks, snow fields and valleys; scenic Jackson Hole, Jenny Lake Museum; nearby: Jackson Hole Museum, National Elk Refuge, winter sports area.
Thermopolis (C1)—World's largest mineral hot springs; nearby: scenic Wind River Canyon.
Yellowstone National Park (B1)—World's greatest geyser area, hot springs, mud pools, volcanic phenomena; spectacular canyon and waterfalls, wildlife sanctuary.

COLORADO

Aspen (D4)—Popular mountain resort and winter sports area, annual Summer Music Festival, sightseeing mountain chairlift; nearby: former gold mining town of Leadville.
Black Canyon of the Gunnison National Monument (D5)—Narrow deep sheer-walled canyon, black-colored granite and other ancient rock types.
Colorado National Monument (C4)—Steep-walled canyons, towering monoliths, weird sandstone formations.
Colorado Springs (E4)—Vacation and health resort, Pioneers' Museum, Fine Arts Center; nearby: Pikes Peak, Garden of the Gods, U.S. Air Force Academy, Mount Manitou Incline Railway, Broadmoor-Cheyenne Mountain Highway, Cheyenne Mountain Zoo.
Denver (E4)—State Capitol, Civic Center, State Historical Museum, Art Museum, U.S. Mint, Elitch's Gardens, Stockyards; nearby: Lookout Mountain, Red Rocks outdoor amphitheater, historic mining town of Central City, pioneer museums at Boulder, winter sports centers.
Great Sand Dunes National Monument (E5)—Among the largest and highest shifting dunes in the United States.
Mesa Verde National Park (C5)—Most notable and best preserved prehistoric cliff dwellings in the United States.
Rocky Mountain National Park (E3)—Impressive mountain area, glaciers, gorges, lakes, streams, forests, abundant wildlife; nearby: Estes Park resort, Shadow Mountain Recreation Area, Grand Lake, Big Thompson Canyon.
Royal Gorge (E5)—Deep rock gorge of red granite, incline railway, high suspension bridge.
Steamboat Springs (D3)—Famous ski resort, annual Winter Carnival, mineral hot springs.

ARIZONA
Fredonia .... A 6
Grand Canyon .... B 6
Page .... B 6

COLORADO
Akron .... F 4
Alamosa .... D 5
Antonito .... D 5
Arvada .... E 4
Aspen .... D 4
Aurora .... E 4
Berthoud .... E 4
Boulder .... E 4
Brighton .... E 4
Brush .... E 4
Buena Vista .... D 4
Burlington .... F 4
Center .... D 5
Cheyenne Wells .... F 4
Climax .... D 4
Colorado Springs .... E 4
Commerce City .... E 4
Cortez .... C 5
Craig .... D 3
Del Norte .... D 5
Delta .... D 5
Denver .... E 4
Durango .... D 5
Eaton .... E 3
Englewood .... E 4
Florence .... E 5
Fort Collins .... E 3
Fort Morgan .... E 4
Fountain .... E 5
Fowler .... E 5
Fruita .... C 4
Grand Junction .... C 4
Greeley .... E 3
Gunnison .... D 5
Holly .... F 5
Holyoke .... F 3
Idaho Springs .... E 4
Ivywild .... E 4
Julesburg .... F 3
La Junta .... F 5
Lakewood .... E 4
Lamar .... F 5
Las Animas .... F 5
Leadville .... D 4
Limon .... E 4
Littleton .... E 4
Longmont .... E 4
Loveland .... E 3
Meeker .... D 4
Monte Vista .... D 5
Ordway .... E 5
Pagosa Springs .... D 5
Paonia .... D 4
Pueblo .... E 5
Rangely .... C 4
Rifle .... D 4
Rocky Ford .... E 5
Salida .... D 5
Security .... E 4
Silverton .... D 5
Springfield .... F 5
Steamboat Sprs. .... D 3
Sterling .... F 3
Thornton .... E 4
Trinidad .... E 5
Uravan .... C 5
Walden .... D 3
Walsenburg .... E 5

IDAHO
American Falls .... A 2
Blackfoot .... B 2
Buhl .... A 2
Gooding .... A 2
Idaho Falls .... B 2
Jerome .... A 2
Montpelier .... B 2
Pocatello .... B 2
Preston .... B 2
Rexburg .... B 1
Rupert .... A 2
Saint Anthony .... B 1
Twin Falls .... A 2

KANSAS
Elkhart .... F 5

NEBRASKA
Alliance .... F 2
Chadron .... F 2
Gering .... E 3
Gordon .... F 2
Kimball .... E 3
Ogallala .... F 3
Scottsbluff .... E 2
Sidney .... F 3

NEVADA
Ely .... A 4
Glendale .... A 5
McGill .... A 4
Wells .... A 3

SOUTH DAKOTA
Hot Springs .... E 2
Lead .... E 1
Rapid City .... F 1
Spearfish .... E 1
Sturgis .... E 1

UTAH
American Fork .... B 3
Beaver .... A 5
Blanding .... C 5
Bountiful .... B 3
Brigham City .... B 3
Cedar City .... A 5
Clearfield .... B 3
Delta .... A 4
Ephraim .... B 4
Farmington .... B 3
Fillmore .... B 4
Helper .... B 4
Hurricane .... A 5
Hyrum .... B 3
Kanab .... A 5
Kearns .... B 3
Layton .... B 3
Lehi .... B 3
Logan .... B 3
Magna .... B 3
Manti .... B 4
Milford .... A 5
Moab .... C 5
Monticello .... C 5
Morgan .... B 3
Mount Pleasant .... B 4
Murray .... B 3
Nephi .... B 4
North Ogdén .... B 3
Panguitch .... B 5
Parowan .... A 5
Payson .... B 4
Price .... B 4
Provo .... B 4
Richfield .... B 4
Riverton .... B 3
Roosevelt .... C 4
Roy .... B 3
Saint George .... A 5
Salina .... B 4
Salt Lake City .... B 3
Santaquin .... B 4
Smithfield .... B 3
South Ogden .... B 3
South Salt Lake .... B 3
Spanish Fork .... B 4
Springville .... B 4

WYOMING
Afton .... B 2
Basin .... C 1
Buffalo .... D 1
Casper .... D 2
Cheyenne .... E 3
Cody .... C 1
Douglas .... E 2
Evanston .... B 3
Gillette .... E 1
Glenrock .... D 2
Green River .... C 3
Greybull .... D 1
Guernsey .... E 2
Hanna .... D 3
Jackson .... B 2
Kemmerer .... B 3
Lusk .... E 2
Mills .... D 2
Moorcroft .... E 1
Newcastle .... E 1
Pine Bluffs .... E 3
Pinedale .... C 2
Powell .... C 1
Rawlins .... D 3
Rock Springs .... C 3
Riverton .... C 2
Saratoga .... D 3
Sheridan .... D 1
Shoshoni .... D 2
Sinclair .... D 3
Sundance .... E 1
Thermopolis .... C 1
Torrington .... E 2
Upton .... E 1

IDAHO

American Falls (C6)—Lake recreation area; nearby: Massacre Rocks site of Indian raid.
Balanced Rock (B6)—40-foot mushroom-shaped sandstone formation.
Boise (A5)—State Capitol, Historical Museum, Art Gallery, Pioneer Village, Platt Gardens, annual Basque Festival; nearby: Bogus Basin ski center, Shafer Butte lookout.
Challis (B5)—Hot springs, Grand Canyon in Miniature.
City of Rocks State Park (B6)—Eroded rock formations resembling a small village.
Coeur d'Alene (A3)—Gateway to Idaho panhandle recreation areas (Coeur d'Alene Lake, Pend Oreille Lake, Priest Lake), boat tours; nearby: scenic Heyburn State Park, Cataldo Mission (oldest Idaho building).
Craters of the Moon National Monument (B5)—Volcanic phenomena, cones, craters, lava flows, caves, tunnels.
Hells Canyon (A4)—Deepest gorge in North America, spectacular rugged terrain.
Idaho Falls (C6)—Picturesque broad river falls, Sportsman's Island Park and museum, Latter Day Saints Temple, chinchilla ranch.
Kellogg (A3)—Largest lead and silver mines in United States, smelter and mine tours.
Lava Hot Springs (C6)—Popular health resort, mineral pools, natatoriums.
Lewiston (A4)—Snake River excursions, Luna House Indian museum, sawmill tours.
McCall (A5)—Center of Payette Lakes recreational area, winter sports, U.S. Forestry Service "Smokejumper" Center.
Pocatello (C6)—University Historical Museum, Ross Park (Indian pictographs); nearby: Fort Hall Monument, annual Indian dances, ski area.
Salmon (B4)—Wilderness recreation center; Salmon River boat rides, mountain pack trips; nearby: Sacajawea Monument, Old Fort Lemhi, Upper Gorge of Salmon River.
Shoshone Ice Caves (B6-18 mi. north of Shoshone)—Ice tunnel enclosed by lava formation.
Sun Valley (B5)—Famous year-round mountain resort, most sporting facilities, wilderness tours.
Twin Falls (B6)—212-foot Shoshone Falls, Snake River Bridge and Gorge; nearby: Thousand Springs, Magic Mountain ski area.

MONTANA

Big Hole National Battlefield (B4)—Site of 1877 battle with Nez Perce Indians, museum.
Billings (D4)—Black Otter Trail scenic drive, Boot Hill cemetery, Range Rider Monument; nearby: Pompey's Pillar sandstone rock formation.
Browning (C2)—Museum of the Plains Indian, annual Blackfeet Indian celebrations.
Butte (C4)—"Richest Hill on Earth" outstanding mining city, mine and smelter tours, mineral museum; nearby: Washoe Smelter's 585-foot smokestack in Anaconda.
Custer Battlefield National Monument (E4)—Site of famous "Battle of the Little Bighorn River," stone battlefield markers, Visitor Center with dioramas, artifacts; nearby: Bighorn Canyon National Recreation Area.
Flathead Lake (B3)—Year-round resort area, water sports; nearby: St. Ignatius Mission.
Glacier National Park (B2)—Rugged mountainous area straddling Continental Divide; glaciers, glacial lakes, dense forests, abundant wildflowers, Going-to-the-Sun Highway.
Great Falls (C3)—Giant Springs, Russell Art Gallery, metal refinery tours.
Helena (C4)—State Capitol, Art Gallery, Historical Museum, Last Chance train tour, St. Helena Cathedral; nearby: Gates of the Mountains gorge and wilderness, mineral springs.
Lewis and Clark Caverns State Park (C4-12 mi. west of Three Forks)—Largest limestone caverns in the Northwest; intricate passageways, jeep railroad and tram lift.
Missoula (B3)—Aerial Fire Depot "Smokejumper" School; nearby: National Bison Range, Bonner Lumber Mill, St. Mary's Mission.
Virginia City (C4)—Former capital of Montana territory, authentically restored gold rush town, Memorial Museum.

Map scale: 1 inch=83 miles

ALBERTA

Place	Key
Banff	B 1
Bellevue	B 2
Black Diamond	B 1
Bow Island	C 2
Brooks	C 1
Calgary	B 1
Canmore	B 1
Cardston	C 2
Claresholm	B 2
Coaldale	C 2
Coleman	B 2
Didsbury	B 1
Drumheller	C 1
Fort Macleod	B 2
Hanna	C 1
High River	B 1
Lethbridge	C 2
Longview	B 1
Magrath	C 2
Medicine Hat	D 2
Nanton	B 1
Okotoks	B 1
Olds	B 1
Pincher Creek	B 2
Raymond	C 2
Redcliff	C 2
Taber	C 2
Three Hills	C 1
Vulcan	C 1

BRITISH COLUMBIA

Place	Key
Cranbrook	B 2
Creston	A 2
Fernie	B 2
Golden	A 1
Grand Forks	A 2
Invermere	B1
Kimberley	B 2
Nakusp	A 1
Nelson	A 2
Revelstoke	A 1
Trail	A 2

IDAHO

Place	Key
Aberdeen	C 6
American Falls	C 6
Arco	B 5
Ashton	C 5
Blackfoot	C 6
Boise	A 5
Bonners Ferry	A 2
Buhl	B 6
Burley	B 6
Caldwell	A 5
Coeur d'Alene	A 3
Cottonwood	A 4
Emmett	A 5
Filer	B 6
Glenns Ferry	B 6
Gooding	B 6
Grangeville	A 4
Hailey	B 5
Idaho Falls	C 6
Jerome	B 6
Kamiah	A 4
Kellogg	A 3
Kimberly	B 6
Lewiston	A 4
Malad City	C 6
McCall	A 5
Montpelier	C 6
Moscow	A 4
Mountain Home	A 6
Nampa	A 5
Orofino	A 4
Payette	A 5
Pocatello	C 6
Preston	C 6
Priest River	A 3
Rexburg	C 5
Rigby	C 5
Rupert	B 6
Saint Anthony	C 5
Saint Maries	A 3
Salmon	B 4
Sandpoint	A 3
Shoshone	B 6
Soda Springs	C 6
Sun Valley	B 5
Twin Falls	B 6
Wallace	A 3
Weiser	A 5
Wendell	B 6

MONTANA

Place	Key
Anaconda	C 4
Baker	F 4
Belgrade	C 4
Big Timber	D 4
Billings	D 4
Boulder	C 4
Bozeman	C 4
Browning	C 2
Butte	C 4
Chester	C 2
Chinook	D 2
Choteau	C 3
Circle	E 3
Columbia Falls	B 3
Columbus	D 4
Conrad	C 3
Cut Bank	C 2
Deer Lodge	C 4
Dillon	C 4
East Helena	C 4
Eureka	B 2
Fairview	F 3
Forsyth	E 4
Fort Benton	D 3
Glasgow	E 3
Glendive	F 3
Great Falls	C 3
Hamilton	B 4
Hardin	E 4
Harlem	D 2
Harlowton	D 4
Havre	D 3
Helena	C 4
Kalispell	B 3
Laurel	D 4
Lewistown	D 3
Libby	B 3
Livingston	D 4
Malta	E 3
Miles City	E 4
Missoula	B 3
North Havre	D 2
Philipsburg	B 4
Plentywood	F 2
Polson	B 3
Poplar	F 3
Red Lodge	D 5
Ronan	B 3
Roundup	D 4
Scobey	E 2
Shelby	C 2
Sidney	F 3
Superior	B 3
Terry	F 3
Thompson Falls	B 3
Three Forks	C 4
Townsend	C 4
Walkerville	C 4
White Sulphur Springs	C 4
Whitefish	B 3
Wolf Point	E 3

NORTH DAKOTA

Place	Key
Beach	F 3
Belfield	F 3
Bowman	F 4
Crosby	F 2
Dickinson	F 3
Ray	F 2
Tioga	F 2
Watford City	F 3
Williston	F 3

OREGON

Place	Key
Baker	A 5
Enterprise	A 4
La Grande	A 4
Nyssa	A 5
Ontario	A 5
Vale	A 5

SASKATCHEWAN

Place	Key
Assiniboia	E 2
Estevan	F 2
Eston	D 1
Fort Qu'Appelle	F 1
Grenfell	F 1
Gull Lake	D 2
Herbert	E 1
Indian Head	F 1
Kindersley	D 1
Leader	D 1
Maple Creek	D 2
Melville	F 1
Moose Jaw	E 1
Outlook	E 1
Regina	F 1
Rosetown	D 1
Shaunavon	D 2
Swift Current	E 1
Watrous	E 1
Weyburn	F 2
Wolseley	F 1
Yorkton	F 1

SOUTH DAKOTA

Place	Key
Belle Fourche	F 5
Custer	F 5
Deadwood	F 5
Lead	F 5
Rapid City	F 5
Spearfish	F 5
Sturgis	F 5

WASHINGTON

Place	Key
Chewelah	A 3
Clarkston	A 4
Colfax	A 3
Colville	A 2
Newport	A 3
Pomeroy	A 4
Pullman	A 3
Ritzville	A 3
Spokane	A 3
Walla Walla	A 4

WYOMING

Place	Key
Afton	C 6
Basin	E 5
Buffalo	E 5
Cody	D 5
Gillette	F 5
Greybull	E 5
Jackson	C 6
Lovell	D 5
Newcastle	F 5
Powell	D 5
Sheridan	E 5
Upton	F 5
Worland	E 5

POINTS OF INTEREST

NORTH DAKOTA

Bismarck (B4)—"Skyscraper of the Prairies" State Capitol, Sakajawea Monument, State Historical Society Museum, Zoo.
Fort Abercrombie Historic Park (D4-at Abercrombie)—Reconstruction of first North Dakota federal fort, museum.
Fort Lincoln State Park (B4)—Rebuilt blockhouses and Mandan Indian village, museum; starting point for Custer's disastrous expedition to the Little Big Horn.
International Peace Garden (B2)—Formal gardens commemorating peace between the United States and Canada.
Lake Sakakawea (A3)—Recreation area, water sports.
Medora (A4)—Historic French-furnished 26-room Chateau de Mores, Rough Riders Hotel.
Theodore Roosevelt National Park (A3, A4)—Three-unit memorial in badland region of eroded domes, pyramids, buttes, canyons, petrified forest remnants, burning lignite coal vein.

SOUTH DAKOTA

Badlands National Park (A6)—Ruggedly eroded layered rock deposits with numerous prehistoric animal fossils, color-banded cliffs, canyons, buttes and pinnacles.
Black Hills (A5)—Scenic mountain and forest region, rock walls, spires, lakes, waterfalls; vacation area, Harney Peak, Wonderland and Crystal Caves.
Custer State Park (A6)—Highly picturesque section of Black Hills, Needles Highway, buffalo, deer and elk herds, Gordon Stockade; nearby: Crazy Horse Memorial.
Deadwood (A5)—Famous mining town, Adams Memorial Museum (pioneer exhibits), Mount Moriah Cemetery (graves of Wild Bill Hickok, and others), Broken Boot Gold Mine, Ghosts of Deadwood Gulch Wax Museum.
Jewel Cave National Monument (A6)—Limestone caverns, jewel-like calcite encrustations.
Lead (A5)—Tours of Homestake Mine (largest gold producer in Western Hemisphere); nearby: Terry Peak Lookout and Ski Area.
Mitchell (C6)—Corn Palace auditorium, annual Corn Palace Festival, Historical Museum.
Mount Rushmore National Memorial (A5)—Gigantic heads of George Washington, Thomas Jefferson, Abraham Lincoln and Theodore Roosevelt carved on mountain face.
Pierre (B5)—State Capitol, Soldiers and Sailors Memorial Hall; nearby: Lake Oahe recreation area.
Rapid City (A5)—Gateway to Black Hills region; Museum of Geology, Sioux Indian Museum, Dinosaur Park; nearby: Stave Church, Reptile Gardens, Horseless Carriage Museum, Rapid Creek Canyon, Stratosphere Bowl.
Sioux Falls (D6)—Pettigrew Museum (Indian and pioneer relics), Great Plains Zoo.
Spearfish (A5)—Scenic Spearfish Canyon, fish hatcheries, annual Black Hills Passion Play.
Wind Cave National Park (A6)—Limestone caverns with strong air currents, calcite crystal formations; nearby: Hot Springs health resort.
Yankton (C6)—Former capital of Dakota Territory, restored council chamber and museum.

KANSAS

Abilene (E4)—Eisenhower Museum, Library and Home, "Old Abilene" replica.
Coffeyville (F6)—Dalton Defenders Memorial Museum, Historical Museum.
Colby (C4)—Reconstructed sod buildings with interior furnishings, museum.
Council Grove (E4)—Kaw Mission, Hays Tavern, Last Chance Store, Cowboy Jail, Madonna of the Trail Monument, famous Council and Post Office Oak Trees.
Dodge City (C5)—Restored famous Front Street, Long Branch Saloon, Boot Hill Museum, Beeson Pioneer Museum; nearby: Fort Dodge, Dalton Gang Hideout and Museum.
Fort Larned National Historic Site (D5)—Well-preserved frontier fort, museum; nearby: Pawnee Rock landmark.
Fort Riley (E4)—Historical museum, restored territorial capitol.
Fort Scott (F5)—Carroll Plaza parade ground, Headquarters House, Fort Scott Museum, Fort Blair Civil War Blockhouse.
Garden City (C5)—Historical Museum, Zoo, large Buffalo Preserve.
Hanover (E4-13 mi. west of Marysville)—Old Pony Express Station Museum.
Hays (D4)—Kansas Frontier Historical Park, Natural History Library, Agricultural Experiment Station.
Hutchinson (D5)—Extensive salt deposits, tours of evaporating plants.
Kansas City (F4)—Intercity Viaduct, Art Gallery, Wyandot Indian Cemetery, Shawnee Mission, Wells Fargo Office, First Territorial Jail.
Lawrence (F4)—120-foot Bell Tower, Museum of Natural History, Art Museum, Entomological (insect) Museum.
Leavenworth (F4)—Fort Leavenworth Museum, first Territorial Governor's Residence.
Medicine Lodge (D6)—W.C.T.U. Shrine and Museum, Indian Stockade and Museum; nearby: scenic Gypsum Hills.
Osawatomie (F5)—John Brown Memorial State Park, log cabin, statue.
Salina (E4)—Indian Burial Pit, Smoky Hill Historical Museum, flour mill tours; nearby: weird eroded Rock City.
Scott County State Park (C5)—Important archaeological site, pueblo ruins; nearby: chalk bluffs and pyramids.
Topeka (F4)—State Capitol, Art Museum, State Historical Society Museum, Reinisch Rose and Rock Gardens, Zoo.
Wichita (E5)—"Cow Town" reconstruction, Historical Museum, Art Museum and Galleries, Friends Museum (pioneer and Indian relics), Beech Memorial Wind Tunnel.

NEBRASKA

Agate Fossil Beds National Monument (A2)—Fossilized mammal remains, Indian relics.
Chadron (B1)—Museum of the Fur Trade, reconstructed trading post.
Chimney Rock National Historic Site (A2)—500-foot red sandstone column landmark on the Oregon Trail.
Crawford (B1)—Fort Robinson Museum, Beef Cattle Research Station; nearby: Toadstool Park, arid badlands, fossil beds.
Fort Kearney Historical Park (D3-7 mi. south of Kearney)—Restored defense outpost on Oregon Trail.
Fort Niobrara National Wildlife Refuge (C1-near Valentine)—Museum, herds of longhorn cattle, buffalo, elk and smaller wildlife.
Hastings (D3)—House of Yesterday Pioneer Museum, Planetarium, Rainbow Fountain.
Homestead National Monument (E3)—Site of first claim under 1862 Homestead Act, typical homesteader log cabin, museum.
Lewis and Clark Lake (E1)—Popular vacation area, water sports, Gavins Point Dam.
Lincoln (E3)—State Capitol topped with 32-foot "The Sower" statue, Lincoln Monument, University of Nebraska State Museum (geology and early animal life), State Historical Society Museum, Art Gallery, William Jennings Bryan Home, Planetarium.
Minden (D3)—Pioneer Village including Indian fort, sod house, school house, general store, land office.
Nebraska City (E3)—Arbor Lodge State Historical Park (mansion, arboretum, historical exhibits).
North Platte (C3)—Buffalo Bill Cody's Home and Scouts Rest Ranch.
Omaha (E2)—Strategic Air Command Headquarters, Art Museum, Union Pacific Railroad Historical Museum, Mormon Cemetery and Monument, Zoo; nearby: Father Flanagan's Boys Town.
Scotts Bluff National Monument (A2)—800-foot landmark on the Oregon Trail, old wagon ruts, museum.

Map scale: 1 inch=68 miles

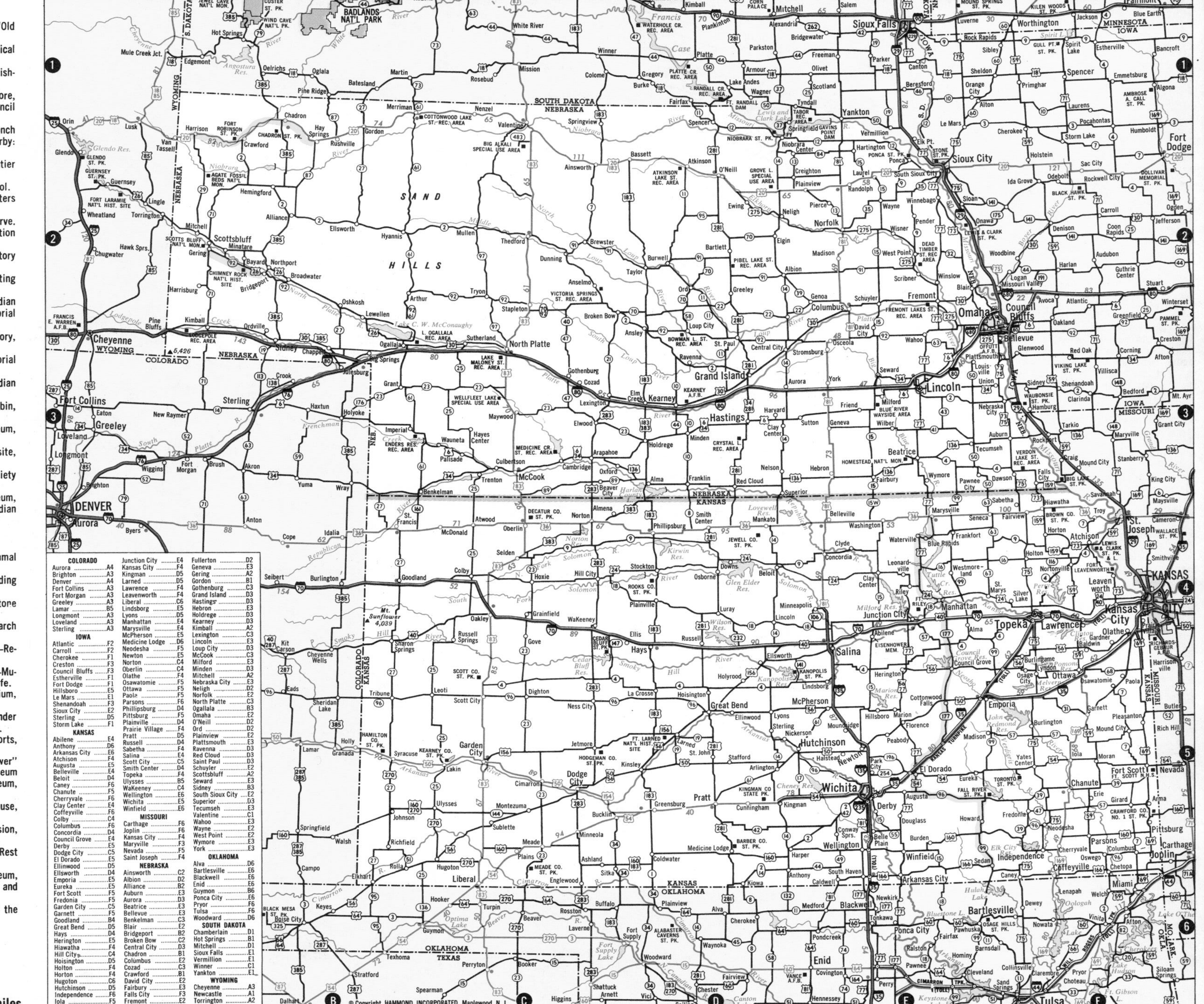

ILLINOIS

City	Grid
Alton	D 4
Aurora	E 2
Beardstown	D 3
Belleville	D 4
Belvidere	E 2
Benton	E 5
Bloomington	E 3
Cahokia	F 6
Cairo	E 6
Canton	D 3
Carbondale	E 5
Carmi	E 5
Centralia	E 4
Centreville	F 6
Champaign	E 3
Charleston	E 4
Chicago	E 2
Chicago Heights	E 2
Clinton	E 3
Collinsville	D 4
Danville	E 3
De Kalb	E 2
Decatur	E 3
Dixon	D 2
Du Quoin	E 5
East St. Louis	D 4, F 6
Edwardsville	D 4
Effingham	E 4
Elgin	E 2
Elmhurst	E 2
Evanston	E 2
Fairfield	E 5
Freeport	D 2
Galesburg	D 3
Geneva	E 2
Granite City	D 4, E 5
Harrisburg	E 5
Highland Park	E 2
Hoopeston	E 3
Jacksonville	D 4
Joliet	E 2
Kankakee	E 2
Kewanee	D 2
La Salle	E 2
Lake Forest	E 2
Lincoln	D 3
Litchfield	D 4
Macomb	D 3
Madison	F 5
Marion	E 5
Mattoon	E 4
Mendota	E 2
Metropolis	E 6
Moline	D 2
Monmouth	D 3
Morris	E 2
Mount Carmel	E 5
Mount Vernon	E 5
Murphysboro	D 5
Normal	E 3
North Chicago	E 2
Olney	E 4
Ottawa	E 2
Pana	E 4
Paris	E 4
Pekin	D 3
Peoria	D 3
Peru	D 2
Pontiac	E 3
Princeton	D 2
Quincy	C 3
Rantoul	E 3
Robinson	E 4
Rochelle	E 2
Rock Falls	D 2
Rock Island	D 2
Rockford	D 2
Salem	E 4
Springfield	D 4
Sterling	D 2
Streator	E 2
Taylorville	D 4
Urbana	E 3
Washington Park	F 6
Waukegan	E 2
West Frankfort	E 5
Windsor	E 4
Woodstock	E 2
Zion	E 1

IOWA

City	Grid
Algona	B 1
Ames	B 2
Atlantic	A 2
Bettendorf	D 2
Boone	B 2
Burlington	C 3
Carroll	A 2
Cedar Falls	C 1
Cedar Rapids	C 2
Centerville	B 3
Chariton	B 3
Charles City	C 1
Cherokee	A 1
Clarinda	A 3
Clear Lake	B 1
Clinton	D 2
Council Bluffs	A 2
Creston	B 3
Davenport	D 2
Decorah	C 1
Des Moines	B 2
Dubuque	D 1
Estherville	B 1
Fairfield	C 3
Fort Dodge	B 1
Fort Madison	C 3
Grinnell	C 2
Independence	C 1
Indianola	B 2
Iowa City	C 2
Iowa Falls	B 1
Keokuk	C 3
Knoxville	B 2
Le Mars	A 1
Maquoketa	D 2
Marion	C 2
Marshalltown	B 2
Mason City	B 1
Mount Pleasant	C 3
Muscatine	C 2
Newton	B 2
Oelwein	C 1
Oskaloosa	C 2
Ottumwa	C 3
Perry	B 2
Red Oak	A 3
Shenandoah	A 3
Sioux City	A 1
Spencer	A 1
Storm Lake	A 1
Washington	C 2
Waterloo	C 1
Waverly	C 1
Webster City	B 1
W. Des Moines	B 2

MISSOURI

City	Grid
Bellefontaine Neighbors	F 5
Berkeley	F 5
Boonville	C 4
Breckenridge Hills	E 5
Brentwood	E 6
Bridgeton	E 5
Brookfield	B 4
Cape Girardeau	D 5
Carthage	B 5
Caruthersville	D 6
Charleston	D 6
Chillicothe	B 3
Clayton	F 6
Clinton	B 5
Columbia	C 4
Crestwood	E 6
De Soto	D 5
Excelsior Springs	B 4
Farmington	D 5
Ferguson	F 5
Festus	D 5
Florissant	F 5
Fulton	C 4
Glendale	E 6
Hannibal	C 4
Independence	B 4
Jefferson City	C 4
Jennings	F 5
Joplin	B 6
Kansas City	B 4
Kennett	D 6
Kirksville	C 3
Kirkwood	E 6
Ladue	E 6
Lebanon	C 5
Liberty	B 4
Maplewood	F 6
Marshall	B 4
Maryville	A 3
Mexico	C 4
Moberly	C 4
Neosho	B 6
Nevada	B 5
Olivette	E 6
Overland	E 5
Pine Lawn	F 5
Poplar Bluff	D 6
Richmond Hts.	F 6
Rolla	C 5
Saint Ann	E 5
Saint Charles	D 4
Saint John	F 5
Saint Joseph	A 3
Saint Louis	D 4, F 6
Sedalia	B 4
Sikeston	D 6
Springfield	B 5
Trenton	B 3
University City	F 6
Warrensburg	B 4
Washington	D 4
Webster Groves	E 6
Wellston	F 6
West Plains	C 6

POINTS OF INTEREST

IOWA

Amana Colonies (C2-20 mi. southwest of Cedar Rapids)—Seven-village religious community organized on a corporate basis, manufacture of household goods, textiles and furniture.
Cedar Rapids (C2)—Location of one of world's largest cereal mills, scenic May's Island, Masonic Library.
Council Bluffs (A2)—Mormon Trail Memorial, Lewis & Clark Monument, Lincoln Monument, scenic Rainbow Drive.
Davenport (D2)—Municipal Art Gallery, Public Museum; nearby: scenic Wild Cat Den State Park with unusual rock formations.
Decorah (C1)—Norwegian-American Historical Museum; nearby: Clock Museum, Anton Dvorak Memorial, Ice Cave, restored Fort Atkinson.
Des Moines (B2)—State Capitol, Art Center, Historical Memorial & Art Building.
Dubuque (D1)—Old Shot Tower, Julien DuBuque Monument, Cable Railway, Zebulon Pike Lock & Dam; nearby: Crystal Lake Cave.
Effigy Mounds National Monument (C1)—Indian mounds in shapes of birds and animals.
Grotto of the Redemption (B1-13 mi. southwest of Algona)—City-block-large series of chambers built with numerous minerals, fossils, shells and ornate stones from all over the world.
Iowa City (C2)—Old Capitol, Natural Science Museum & Art Gallery; nearby: Herbert Hoover birthplace, library and tomb.
Keokuk (C3)—Mississippi River Museum, log schoolhouse replica, Keokuk Dam.
Maquoketa Caves State Park (D2)—Limestone caverns, balanced rock, natural bridge.
Sioux City (A1)—Floyd Monument, Grave of War Eagle, City Pioneer Museum, Art Center.

MISSOURI

George Washington Carver National Monument (B6)—Birthplace and Home of famous Negro Scientist and Educator.
Hannibal (C4)—Mark Twain Museum and Home, Becky Thatcher House, Tom Sawyer & Huckleberry Finn Statues, Mark Twain Cave; nearby: Mark Twain State Park (birthplace).
Independence (B4)—Harry S Truman Library and Museum, Old County Courthouse & Jail; nearby: Watkins Mill, rebuilt Fort Osage, Excelsior Springs health resort.
Jefferson City (C4)—State Capitol and Museum, Historical Society Museum; nearby: Churchill Memorial & Library in Fulton.
Kansas City (B4)—Liberty Memorial, Gallery of Art, Museum of Fine Arts, Historical Museum, Swope Park, Intercity Viaduct, Stockyards, Worlds of Fun (theme park).
Lake of the Ozarks (B5)—Highly developed recreation area, water sports.
St. Charles (D4)—Original State Capitol.
St. Joseph (A3)—Pony Express Stables, Jesse James House, Historical Museum.
St. Louis (D4, F6)—Jefferson National Expansion Memorial (Gateway Arch, Old Cathedral, Old Courthouse), Forest Park (Art Museum, Jefferson Memorial, Conservatory, Planetarium, Zoo), National Museum of Transport, Museum of Science and Natural History, Botanical Gardens, Library of Science and Technology, Grant's Farm; nearby: Jefferson Barracks Historical Park.
Springfield (B5)—Center of Ozark recreation areas, Art Museum; nearby: Wilson Creek Civil War Battlefield.

NORTHERN TEXAS

Amarillo (B3)—Center of Panhandle oil and gas region, Cattle Auction; nearby: Boys Ranch, Lake Meredith National Recreation Area, Alibates Flint Quarries National Monument, Pueblo ruins.
Canyon (B3)—Panhandle-Plains Historical Museum (prehistory, pioneer, Indian exhibits).
Dallas (E5)
Denison (E4)—Eisenhower Birthplace State Park; nearby: Denison Dam, Lake Texoma recreation areas.
Denton (D4)—North Texas State College Museum, D.A.R. Museum.
Fort Worth (D5)
Lubbock (B4)—West Texas Museum, Planetarium, Mackenzie State Park.
Palo Duro Canyon State Park (B3)—Colorful eroded canyon, pre-Pueblo ruins, miniature railroad, museum.
Texarkana (F4)—Dual municipality, divided between Texas and Arkansas, Jim Bowie statue; nearby: Red River Arsenal.

OKLAHOMA

Alabaster Caverns State Park (C2)—One of the world's largest gypsum caves, underground alabaster and onyx-like formations.
Anadarko (D3)—"Indian City" village re-creation, Southern Plains Indian Museum & Craft Center, Indian Hall of Fame, annual American Indian Exposition.
Ardmore (D4)—Headquarters for Lake Murray and Lake Texoma vacation areas; nearby: scenic Arbuckle Mountains and Turner Falls.
Bartlesville (E2)—Nellie Johnstone No. 1 (first commercial Oklahoma oil well), Price Tower; nearby: Woolaroc Museum (western relics), Oologah Reservoir recreation areas.
Black Mesa State Park (A2)—Unusual rock formations, dinosaur quarry.
Boiling Springs State Park (C2)—Pioneer water hole, springs bubble up through sand formations, vacation area.
Chickasaw National Recreation Area (E4)—Mineral springs, rolling hills, cascading streams, water sports.
Claremore (E2)—Health resort, Will Rogers Memorial, Davis Gun Collection.
Fort Gibson (E2)—Restored Old Fort Gibson and museum; nearby: Fort Gibson Reservoir recreation areas.
Guthrie (D2)—Former territorial capitol, Scottish Rite Temple.
Lake O' The Cherokees (F2)—Popular vacation and recreation area, world's longest multiple-arch dam.
Lake Texoma (E4)—Outstanding vacation and recreation area, water sports.
Lawton (D3)—U.S. Army Artillery & Missile Center Museum, General Sherman House.
McAlester (E3)—Indian Scottish Rite Consistory, Ohoyahoma Clubhouse Museum; nearby: Eufaula Reservoir recreation areas, Robbers Cave State Park.
Norman (D3)—University of Oklahoma Art Museum, Stovall Museum (Indian, Graeco-Roman, reptile displays).
Oklahoma City (D3)—State Capitol, Civic Center, Cowboy Hall of Fame, State Historical Society Building, Gerrer Art Center, Planetarium, Zoo, Stockyards, Frontier City Amusement Center.
Okmulgee (E3)—Old Creek Indian Council House & Museum.
Pawhuska (E2)—Osage Indian Tribal Museum.
Ponca City (D2)—Pioneer Woman State Monument & Museum, Indian Museum.
Quartz Mountain State Park (C3)—Rugged red granite hills, vacation area.
Sequoyah Home (F3-11 mi. northeast of Sallisaw)—Log Cabin home of Cherokee alphabet inventor and tribal statesman, museum.
Sequoyah State Park (E2)—Popular vacation area, water sports; formerly, a noted bandit hideout area.
Shawnee (D3)—St. Gregory Museum and Art Gallery.
Tahlequah (F2)—Courthouse (former Cherokee Capitol), Cherokee National Prison; nearby: Murrell Cherokee Home.
Tishomingo (E4)—Courthouse (former Chickasaw Capitol); nearby: unusual rock formations of Devil's Den.
Tulsa (E2)—Center of large oil region, Gilcrease Institute of American History & Art, Philbrook Art Center, Municipal Rose Gardens; nearby: Keystone Reservoir recreation areas.
Wichita Mountains Wildlife Refuge (C3-22 mi. northwest of Lawton)—Large herds of longhorn cattle, buffalo, elk, antelope, deer and other wildlife, panoramic view from nearby Mt. Scott.

Map scale: 1 inch=68 miles

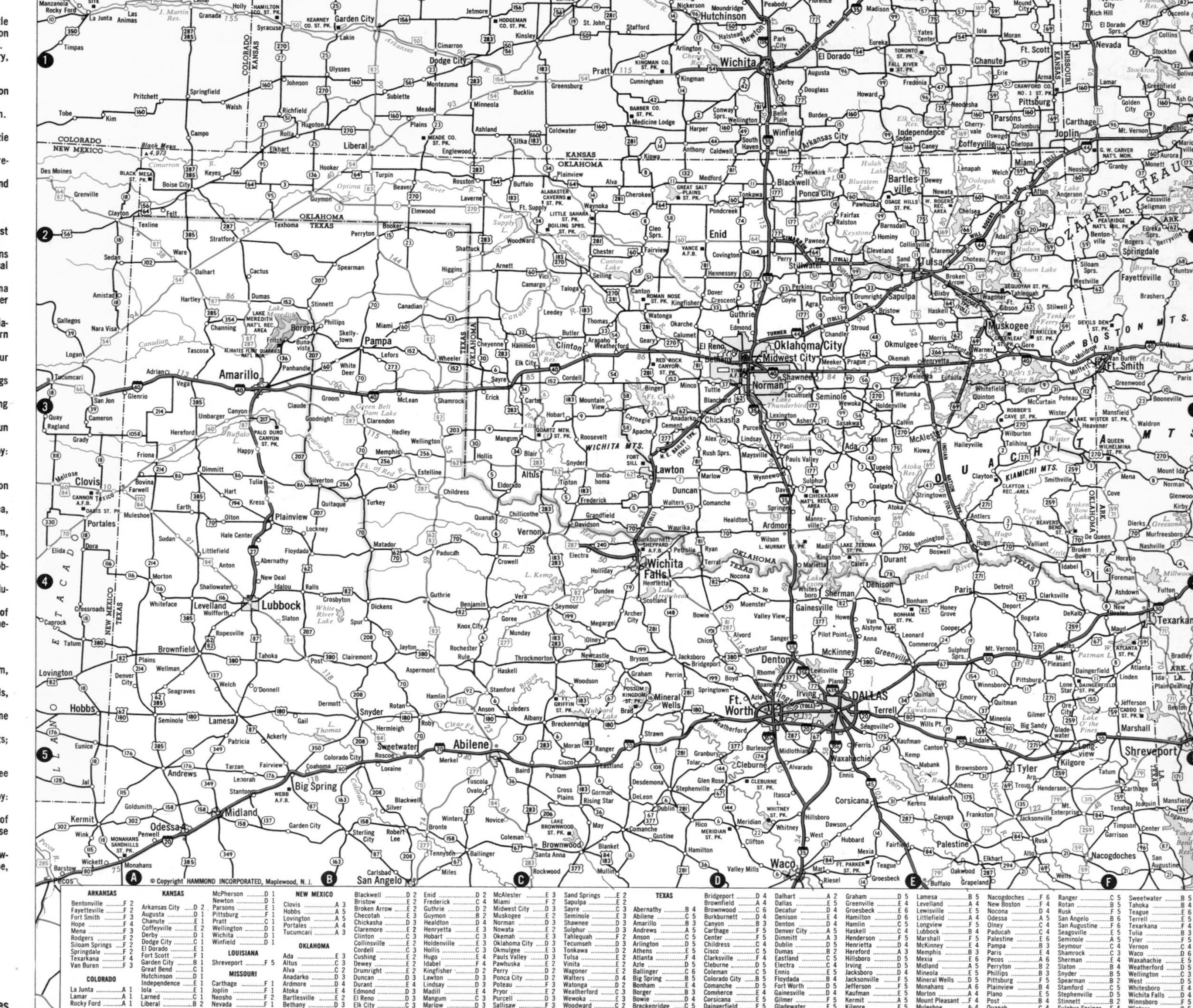

POINTS OF INTEREST

CENTRAL and SOUTHERN TEXAS

Aransas Wildlife Refuge (D4-15 mi. south of Tivoli)—Home of rare whooping crane and a variety of wild game birds.
Austin (D3)—State Capitol, Confederate Museum, Texas Memorial Museum, Ney Museum (sculpture), O. Henry Memorial Museum, Old French Legation, "Moonlight" Lamp Towers, Lake Austin cruises; nearby: L.B.J. Ranch near Johnson City, Longhorn Cavern State Park.
Bandera (C3)—Western displays at Frontier Times Museum.
Bastrop State Park (D3)—Isolated tract of forest known as the "Lost Pines of Texas."
Beaumont (F3)—Spindletop Monument commemorating first oil field, Temple to the Brave heroes' shrine.
Big Bend National Park (A3)
Brownsville (D6)—Fruit and vegetable center, resort area, historic Fort Brown; nearby: cathedral, fort and market place in Matamoros, Mexico.
Caverns of Sonora (B3-10 mi. west of Sonora)—Colorful multi-chambered underground cave.
Corpus Christi (D5)—Popular Gulf Coast resort area, northern entrance to Padre Island beaches.
Dallas (D1, F6)—Fair Park (Texas Hall of State, Cotton Bowl, Museum of Natural History, Museum of Fine Arts, Aquarium, Planetarium, Health & Science Museum, Garden Center, annual State Fair), Theater Center, Cotton Market, Zoo, Wax Museum, John Neely Bryan Cabin.
Fort Stockton (A2)—Ruins of adobe-walled Old Fort Stockton.
Fort Worth (D1, E6)—Civic Center (Will Rogers Memorial Coliseum, Memorial Tower, Art Center, Museum of Western Art, Children's Museum), Botanical Gardens, Zoo, Aquarium.
Fredericksburg (C3)—Vereins Kirche (1847 church replica); nearby: Balanced Rock, pink granite Enchanted Rock.
Galveston (F4)—Major port city and picturesque Gulf coastal resort.
Goliad (D4)—Chapel of Presidio La Bahia, Mission Espiritu Santo.
Houston (E3, E5)—Astrodome, Civic Center, Museum of Fine Arts, Contemporary Arts Museum, Museum of Natural History, Zoo, Port of Houston Observation Platform; nearby: NASA Space Center, 570-foot San Jacinto Monument, Battleship Texas.
Huntsville (E2)—Sam Houston Home and Memorial Museum, Steamboat House.
King Ranch (D5)—One of world's largest ranches, scientifically operated, visitor tours.
Langtry (A3)—Judge Roy Bean (saloon-courtroom) Museum.
Laredo (C5)—Gateway to Mexico, former capital of "The Republic of the Rio Grande," capitol building.
Meteor Crater (A2-near Odessa)—Ten-acre depression caused by a nickel-iron meteor.
Mineral Wells (D1)—Health resort; nearby: Possum Kingdom State Park vacation area.
Nacogdoches (F2)—Old Stone Fort Museum.
Padre Island National Seashore (D5)—Vacation playground, extensive beaches.
Port Arthur (F3)—Rainbow Bridge, annual oil festival.
San Angelo (B2)—Historic pioneer Fort Concho Museum, Art Gallery.
San Antonio (C3)—The Alamo, La Villita Spanish settlement, Spanish Governor's Palace, San Fernando Cathedral, Art Institute, Brackenridge Park (Natural History Museum, Zoo, Chinese and Sunken Gardens), San Antonio Missions National Historical Park; nearby: Cascade Caverns at Boerne.
San Marcos (D3)—Aquarena submarine theater, Wonder Cave; nearby: Sophienburg Memorial Museum.
Six Flags over Texas (E6-in Arlington)—Six section park depicting Texas history under Spain, France, Mexico, Republic of Texas, the Confederacy and the United States; amusements.
Stephen F. Austin State Park (E3)—Austin Statue, replica of Austin Home.
Tyler (E1)—20-acre Municipal Rose Gardens, annual Texas Rose Festival.
Waco (D2)—Browning Library; nearby: Marlin Mineral Wells, Old Fort Parker.

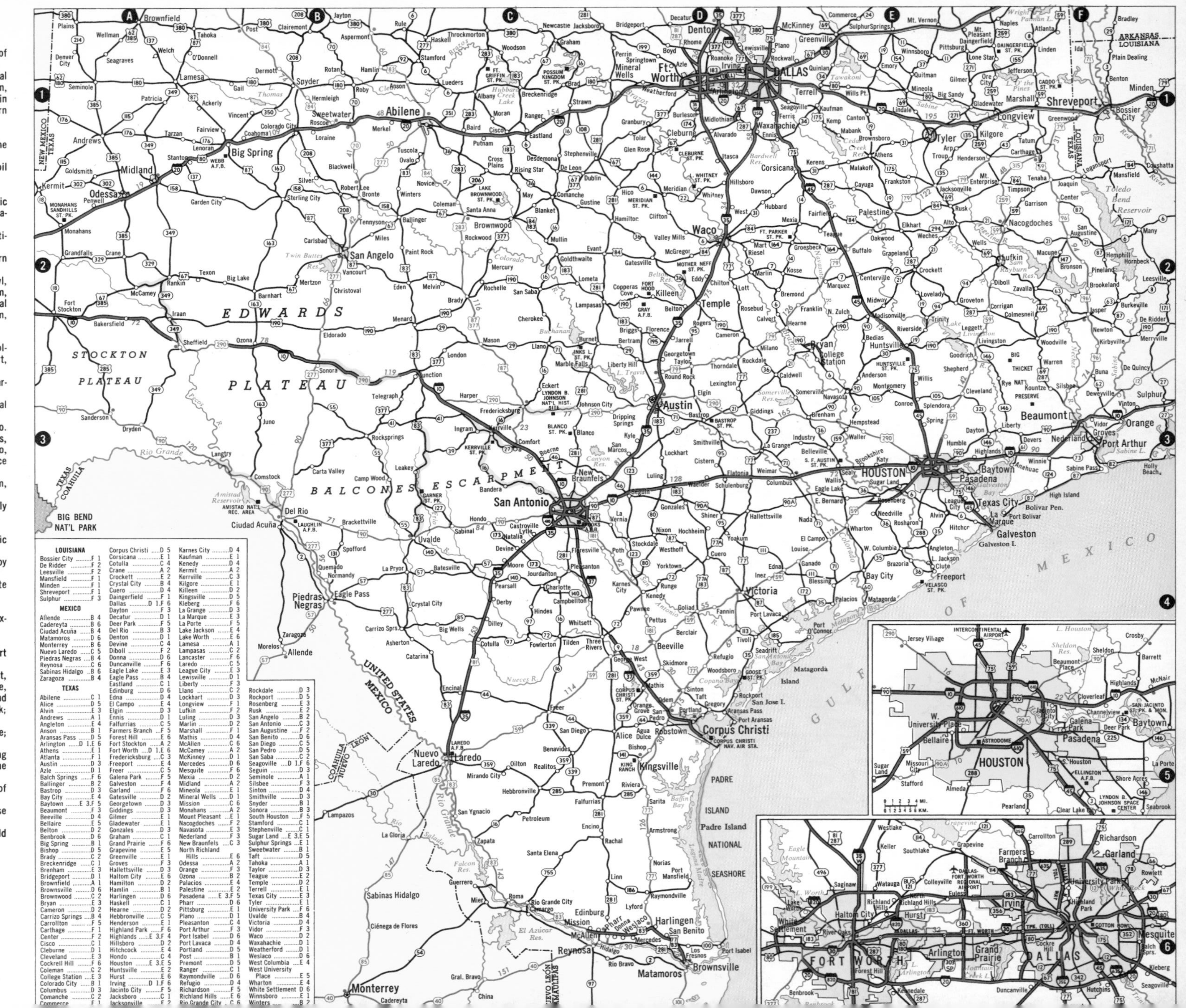

ARKANSAS

Eureka Springs (A1)—Health resort, Ozark Museum, Musical Museum, Carrie Nation's Home, Doll Museum; nearby: Pea Ridge National Military Park, Pivot Rock, Natural Bridge, Onyx Cave, Quigley's Castle, Wonderland Caverns.
Fayetteville (A2)—Mountain resort, mineral springs; nearby: Prairie Grove Battlefield Park.
Fort Smith (A2)—National Historic Site, original log fort, Old Commissary, museum, Judge Parker's Courthouse.
Hot Springs National Park (A3)—Health resort, bathhouses, museum, Quartz Crystal Cave.
Little Rock (B2)—State Capitol, restored Territorial Capitol, History Museum, Natural Sciences Museum, Art Museum, Stagecoach House, General MacArthur's Birthplace; nearby: prehistoric Indian mounds.

LOUISIANA

Baton Rouge (B5)—State Capitol, Old Arsenal Museum, Natural Science Museum, Art Museum, antebellum homes; nearby: Oakley, Audubon's plantation home.
Lafayette (B5)—Acadian settlement, old mansions; nearby: Morton Estate, Jungle Gardens, rock salt mines, Acadian House Museum.
New Orleans (C5)—Unique French Quarter, Absinthe House, Cabildo, state museum, Pirate's Alley, U.S. Customs House, Pharmacy Museum, Jazz Museum, Art Museum, Hibernia Tower, International Trade Mart, Audubon Park; nearby: Jean Lafitte National Historical Park, harbor boat cruises, Lake Ponchartrain, water sports.

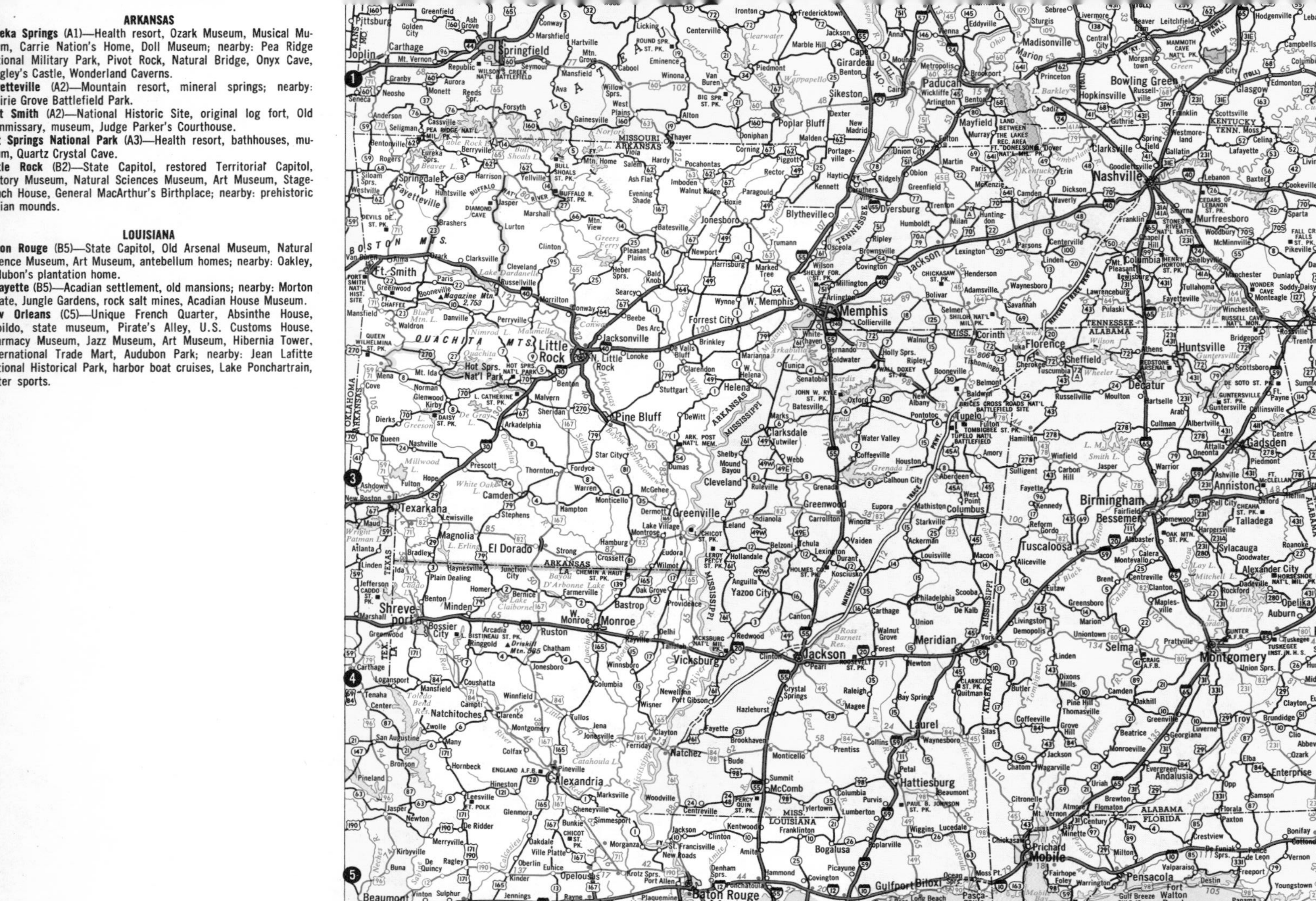

State	Place	Key
ALABAMA	Albertville	D 3
	Alexander City	E 3
	Andalusia	D 5
	Anniston	E 3
	Athens	D 2
	Atmore	D 5
	Attalla	E 3
	Auburn	E 4
	Bessemer	D 3
	Birmingham	D 3
	Chickasaw	D 5
	Cullman	D 3
	Decatur	D 3
	Dothan	E 5
	Enterprise	E 5
	Eufaula	E 4
	Fairfield	D 3
	Florence	D 2
	Fort Payne	E 3
	Gadsden	E 3
	Greenville	D 4
	Homewood	D 3
	Huntsville	D 2
	Jasper	D 3
	Mobile	D 5
	Montgomery	D 4
	Opelika	E 4
	Ozark	E 4
	Phenix City	E 4
	Prichard	D 5
	Russellville	D 3
	Selma	D 4
	Sheffield	D 2
	Sylacauga	D 3
	Talladega	E 3
	Troy	E 4
	Tuscaloosa	D 3
	Tuscumbia	D 2
ARKANSAS	Arkadelphia	A 3
	Benton	A 2
	Blytheville	C 2
	Camden	A 3
	Conway	B 2
	El Dorado	A 3
	Fayetteville	A 2
	Forrest City	B 2
	Fort Smith	A 2
	Helena	B 3
	Hope	A 3
	Hot Sprs. Nat'l Pk.	A 3
	Jacksonville	B 2
	Jonesboro	B 2
	Little Rock	B 2
	Magnolia	A 3
	Malvern	A 3
	Newport	B 2
	North Little Rock	B 2
	Paragould	B 2
	Pine Bluff	B 3
	Russellville	A 2
	Searcy	B 2
	Springdale	A 1
	Stuttgart	B 3
	Texarkana	A 3
	Van Buren	A 2
	Warren	B 3
	West Helena	B 3
	West Memphis	C 2
FLORIDA	Ft. Walton Beach	D 5
	Gainesville	F 5
	Panama City	E 5
	Pensacola	D 5
	Tallahassee	E 5
	Warrington	D 5
GEORGIA	Albany	E 4
	Americus	E 4
	Athens	F 3
	Atlanta	E 3
	Augusta	F 3
	Bainbridge	E 5
	Carrollton	E 3
	Cedartown	E 3
	College Park	E 3
	Columbus	E 4
	Cordele	F 4
	Dalton	E 2
	Decatur	E 3
	Dublin	F 4
	East Point	E 3
	Fitzgerald	F 4
	Gainesville	F 3
	Griffin	E 3
	La Grange	E 3
	Macon	F 4
	Marietta	E 3
	Milledgeville	F 3
	Moultrie	F 5
	Newnan	E 3
	North Atlanta	E 3
	Rome	E 3
	Smyrna	E 3
	Thomasville	F 5
	Tifton	F 4
	Valdosta	F 5
	Warner Robins	F 4
	Waycross	F 4
KENTUCKY	Bowling Green	D 1
	Glasgow	E 1
	Henderson	D 1
	Hopkinsville	D 1
	Madisonville	D 1
	Mayfield	C 1
	Middlesboro	E 1
	Owensboro	D 1
	Paducah	C 1
	Richmond	E 1
LOUISIANA	Abbeville	B 5
	Alexandria	A 5
	Bastrop	B 4
	Baton Rouge	B 5
	Bogalusa	C 5
	Bossier City	A 4
	Covington	C 5
	Crowley	A 5
	De Ridder	A 5
	Denham Springs	B 5
	Donaldsonville	B 5
	Eunice	A 5
	Franklin	B 5
	Gretna	C 5
	Hammond	B 5
	Houma	B 6
	Jennings	A 5
	Kenner	C 5
	Lafayette	B 5
	Lake Charles	A 5
	Mansfield	A 4
	Metairie	C 5
	Minden	A 4
	Monroe	B 4
	Morgan City	B 6
	Natchitoches	A 4
	New Iberia	B 5
	New Orleans	C 5
	Oakdale	A 5
	Opelousas	B 5
	Pineville	A 5
	Plaquemine	B 5
	Rayne	B 5
	Ruston	A 4
	Saint Martinville	B 5
	Shreveport	A 4
	Slidell	C 5
	Sulphur	A 5
	Tallulah	B 4
	Thibodaux	B 6
	Ville Platte	B 5
	West Monroe	B 4
	Westwego	C 5
	Winnfield	A 4
MISSISSIPPI	Aberdeen	C 3
	Amory	C 3
	Bay Saint Louis	C 5
	Biloxi	C 5
	Brookhaven	B 4
	Canton	C 4
	Clarksdale	B 3
	Cleveland	B 3
	Columbia	C 5
	Columbus	C 3
	Corinth	C 2
	Greenville	B 3
	Greenwood	C 3
	Grenada	C 3
	Gulfport	C 5
	Hattiesburg	C 5
	Holly Springs	C 2
	Indianola	B 3
	Jackson	C 4
	Kosciusko	C 3
	Laurel	C 4
	Leland	B 3
	Louisville	C 3
	McComb	B 5
	Meridian	C 4
	Moss Point	C 5
	Natchez	B 4
	New Albany	C 3
	Oxford	C 3
	Pascagoula	C 5
	Picayune	C 5
	Starkville	C 3
	Tupelo	C 3
	Vicksburg	B 4
	West Point	C 3
	Yazoo City	B 4
MISSOURI	Cape Girardeau	C 1
	Carthage	A 1
	Joplin	A 1
	Poplar Bluff	B 1
	Sikeston	C 1
	Springfield	A 1
TENNESSEE	Athens	E 2
	Bristol	F 1
	Chattanooga	E 2
	Clarksville	D 1
	Cleveland	E 2
	Columbia	D 2
	Cookeville	E 2
	Dyersburg	C 2
	Elizabethton	F 1
	Fayetteville	D 2
	Franklin	D 2
	Gallatin	D 1
	Greeneville	F 1
	Humboldt	C 2
	Jackson	C 2
	Johnson City	F 1
	Kingsport	F 1
	Knoxville	E 2
	Lawrenceburg	D 2
	Lebanon	D 2
	Lewisburg	D 2
	Maryville	F 2
	McMinnville	E 2
	Memphis	C 2
	Morristown	F 1
	Murfreesboro	D 2
	Nashville	D 2
	Newport	F 2
	Oak Ridge	E 2
	Paris	C 1
	Pulaski	D 2
	Shelbyville	D 2
	Springfield	D 1
	Tullahoma	D 2
	Union City	C 1
	Whitehaven	C 2
TEXAS	Beaumont	A 5
	Groves	A 5
	Marshall	A 4
	Orange	A 5
	Port Arthur	A 5
	Texarkana	A 3

Map scale: 1 inch=85 miles

The forest shares the 30,500–acre Mallard-Larkins Pioneer Area with the Clearwater National Forest. This area is a roadless subalpine wilderness on the high divide between the North and the Little North Fork of the Clearwater River. Lakes that fill the glacial cirques of the high country offer rainbow and cutthroat trout. Cutthroat average 10 inches in most lakes, but fish weighing several pounds have been taken from Heart Lake. During the early weeks of July, the ridge trail near Mallard, Heart, and Mud lakes passes through the best camping areas; mosquitoes are a problem at lower elevations. The area contains one of the state's largest bands of mountain goat and offers good hunting for mule deer, elk, bear, and moose. Many of the better lakes, including Crags, Larkins, Hero, and Heart, are lightly fished.

The forest is also the site of the Emerald Creek Garnet Area, where gem garnet deposits are found in alluvial deposits and the mica schist parent material. The garnets in the alluvial deposits are usually found in a sand and gravel stratum just above bedrock. They range in size from the tiniest particle to two inches in diameter, and include star garnets with 4– or 6–ray stars. Garnet sand, made up of small dodecahedron garnet crystals, is abundant throughout the area. A permit at a small cost allows visitors to hunt the crystals. Rubber boots, round-point shovels, buckets, and screens are needed for the rockhounding. For a free *Emerald Creek Garnet Area Map-Brochure* and more information on this region, write: District Ranger, St. Maries District, St. Maries 83861.

Information Sources, Maps & Access

For detailed vacation travel information, a full-color *St. Joe National Forest Map* (50¢) and the free publications, *Mallard-Larkins Pioneer Area, St. Joe River Float Trips, Winter Recreation, Camp & Picnic Areas,* contact: Supervisor, St. Joe National Forest, St. Maries, ID 83861 (208)245–2531. The St. Joe National Forest is accessible by way of U.S. 95A and Idaho 7, 8, and 43. There are dude ranches nearby and cabins available along the St. Joe River. Overnight accommodations, guide and outfitting services, supplies, and other services are available in the nearby towns of Avery, Clarkia, Moscow, Potlatch, and St. Maries.

Gateways & Accommodations

Moscow

(Pop. 15,000; zip code 83843; area code 208) is located in beautiful Paradise Valley on U.S. 95, is the home of Idaho State University. Of local interest is the Appaloosa Horse Museum on Pullman Hwy. (882–5578). Accommodations: *Mark IV Motor Inn* (rates: $22–24 double), with 87 excellent rooms and fine dining in the Mark IV Inn, with heated pool at 414 N. Main St. on U.S. 95 (882–7557).

St. Maries

(Pop. 2,500; zip code 83861; area code 208) is the headquarters of the St. Joe National Forest and the gateway to the St. Joe River Country. Area attractions include the St. Joe ghost town—once one of the wildest boom towns in the West, 12 miles east of town on St. Joe River Rd. and Heyburn State Park, 10 miles west of town on Idaho Hwy. 5. Accommodations: *Pines Motel* (rates: $20–22 double), with 49 good rooms and family units on Idaho 5 at 1117 Main St. (245–2545).

Lodges

★*St. Joe Lodge* is located in the St. Joe National Forest in a picturesque setting on the upper St. Joe River six miles by trail accessible only by horse or on foot. The lodge offers fishing for cutthroat and rainbow trout on the upper St. Joe and high mountain lakes; back country trail rides, camera trips, and backpacking in the alpine country of the upper St. Joe and Clearwater Divide, and Mallard-Larkins Pioneer Area. The lodge offers outstanding fall hunting for elk and deer. For rates and information, contact (summer): St. Joe Hunting & Fishing Lodge, c/o Red Ives Ranger Station, Avery, ID 83802; (winter) Hunters Rt., Springdale, WA 99173 (509)258–4226.

Salmon River Country

The Salmon, known to the Shoshone as *Tom-Agit-Pah,* or "big fish river," rises in the Sawtooth and Lemhi valleys of east central Idaho, fed by the snows of the majestic Sawtooth and Salmon River mountains in the south and the Clearwater and Bitterroot mountains in the north. It flows north through the great Chamberlain Basin to Salmon and west to Riggins, then north again to meet the Snake. The Salmon runs through a wilderness course of still, deep waters followed by frothing rapids and many 4–8–foot waterfalls, and a rock-ribbed canyon that is one-fifth of a mile deeper than the Grand Canyon, surpassed only by the awesome, sheer walls of the Snake River Canyon. The Salmon River Gorge is more than one mile deep for a distance of 180 miles. Rising at elevations of 8,000 feet, the Salmon cascades along its 425–mile-long course to an elevation of 905 feet at its mouth on the Snake, draining a high-country wilderness of 14,000 square miles in the Sawtooth, Challis, Salmon, Bitterroot, Nez Percé, and Payette national forests.

Information Sources, Maps & Access

For detailed vacation and recreation info, and U.S. Forest Service maps and brochures, contact the following Supervisors' Offices of the U.S. Forest Service: Salmon National Forest, Salmon, ID 83467 (208)756–2215 for the free *Middle Fork of the Salmon Map & Guide, Salmon-River of No Return Map & Guide, Lower Salmon River Map & Guide, Idaho Primitive Area Map & Guide, Bighorn Crags Map, Birds of the Salmon & Challis National Forests Guide,* and a full-color *Salmon National Forest Map* (50¢); Nez Perce National Forest, Grangeville, ID 83530 (208)983–1963 for a free *Hells Canyon-Seven Devils Area Map/Brochure* and a full-color *Nez Percé National Forest Map* (50¢); Payette National Forest, McCall, ID 83638 (208)634–2255 for a full-color *Payette National Forest Map;* Challis National Forest, Challis, ID 83226 (205)879–2285 for a free *Hiking Guide to Borah Peak* and a full-color *Challis National Forest Map* (50¢); Boise National Forest, 210 Main St., Boise, ID 83702 for a full-color *Boise National Forest Map* (50¢).

The Salmon National Forest is accessible by way of U.S. 93 and Idaho 28. More than 20 developed camping areas dot the forestlands; primitive camping is also available. Dude ranches serve the area, and overnight accommodations, guide and outfitting services, and supplies are available at the nearby towns of Leadore, Salmon, and North Fork. The Nez Percé National Forest can be reached by way of U.S. 95 and Idaho 9, 13, and 14. There are only two access roads to the Salmon River between Riggins and the end of the North Fork Road (a distance of about 80 miles). Both approach the river from the north. The Dixie Ranger Station road runs from Mackay Bar north to the junction with the Elk City-Dixie Road at Jack Mountain. Lodging, gear, boat rentals, guides, and outfitters are available at Kamiah, Kooskia, Grangeville, Lewiston, Lowell, Nezperce, Golden, Elk City, Dixie, and Red River Hot Springs.

The Payette National Forest is reached via U.S. Highway 95 and Idaho Highways 71 and 55. Lodging, supplies, boat rentals, guides, and outfitters are available at McCall, New Meadows, Tamarack, Council, Cambridge, Weiser, Yellowpine, Burgdorf, French Creek, Bear, Cuprum, Riggins, and Big Creek. The Challis National Forest has 52 camping areas and seven picnic sites. Resorts, hotels, cabins, dude ranches, and commercial guides and packers are available in and near the towns of Challis, Mackay, Salmon, and Stanley. The forest is accessible by way of U.S. 20, 93, and 92A. Boise National Forest can be reached by way of U.S. 20, 30, and 95 and Idaho 15, 17, 21, 52, and 68. The forest has 116 campsites, five picnic sites, and one swimming site and includes the Bogus Basin Winter Sports Area. Resorts, motels, and dude ranches offer overnight accommodations in the surrounding towns of Boise, Cascade, Emmett, Horseshoe Bend, Idaho City, and Mountain Home. Guide and outfitting services and boat rentals are also available in these towns.

Recreation Areas

Boise National Forest

This outstanding fishing, hunting, and wilderness camping area encompasses 2,639,000 acres bordered on the west by the Snake River along the Oregon border and includes the headwaters of the Boise, Payette, and Salmon rivers, the Sawtooth Wilderness, Cascade, Bull Creek Trail, Anderson Ranch, and Deadwood reservoirs, the beautiful snow-covered peaks of the Trinity Mountain Lakes Basin, and Seafoam Lakes Area.

Challis National Forest

The Challis National Forest, one of the finest backpacking, fishing, and big-game hunting areas in North America, takes in 2.4 million acres in the geographic center of Idaho. The forest, which includes parts of the Sawtooth and Idaho primitive areas, accessible only by foot, horse, or boat, is a top-ranked hunting area for deer, elk, mountain goat, bighorn sheep, antelope, and black bear. The Pahsimeroi Valley is the home of the state's largest herd of antelope. Waterfowl, upland game birds, hawks, and golden eagles are often sighted. The Lost River Range sweeps down through the forest area, crowned by Mount Borah (12,655 ft.), the highest peak in Idaho.

Parallel to this range on the east lies the Lemhi Range; on the west, the Salmon River Mountains; and below them, the alpine lakes of the White Cloud Peaks. The magnificent blue-spired ridges of the Sawtooth Mountains rise up further to the west. The headwaters of the Salmon River gather in the Stanley Basin among the shadows of these crags. The wildwaters of the Middle Fork of the Salmon flow northeast in the western portion of the forest along the southeast border of the Idaho Primitive Area. Primitive hiking and packhorse trails provide access to the remote alpine fishing, hunting, and wilderness camping areas in the Lost River Range, Sleeping Deer Area, and White Knob Mountains.

Idaho Primitive Area

The Idaho Primitive Area, lying partially within the Challis, Salmon, Payette, and Boise national forests, encompasses some 1,232,744 acres of the Chamberlain Basin in the geographic center of the state, bordered by the Middle Fork of the Salmon River to Rapid Creek on the south; the Bighorn Crags, Yellowjacket Range, and Sleeping Deer Mountain on the east; the main Salmon River on the north, and the western limit of the Marble, Monumental, Beaver, and Chamberlain creeks watersheds on the west. It is a majestic, wild area of rolling plateaus, high cliffs, alpine meadows, deep dark gorges, the beautiful high-country lakes of the Bighorn Crags, soaring 10,000–foot peaks, and almost everywhere forests. At the lower elevations grows western yellow pine; higher up are Engelmann spruce, limber pine, Douglas fir, and lodgepole pine. Hundreds of alpine lakes and streams offer excellent wilderness fishing, and hot springs bubble up here and there. Caves along the Big and Camas creeks and the Middle Fork of the Salmon bear the artwork of ancient inhabitants; brightly painted hieroglyphics, pictographs, and carved petroglyphs have withstood time and nature. Over 1,600 miles of wilderness trails wind through the Primitive Area, long famous for its outstanding big-game hunting for deer and elk, trout fishing, and wilderness camping to such destinations as the Bighorn Crags, Big Creek, Pistol Hot Springs, Phantom Meadow, Papoose Lakes, Rainbow Mountain, old mines and placer camps, cliff dwellings, and the Middle Fork of the Salmon River.

Middle Fork of the Salmon Wild & Scenic River

The Middle Fork of the Salmon joins the main Salmon about 20 miles west of Shaup. The Middle Fork pounds northward through steep-walled canyons from its source at the confluence of the Marsh and Bear Valley creeks through the 1¼–million-acre Idaho Primitive Area. It is this fork of the river that has been designated part of the National Wild and Scenic River System, preserved in its free-flowing state. The river flows through the Boise, Challis, Payette, and Salmon national forest sections of the Idaho Primitive Area before it meets the main Salmon. The rugged Bighorn Crags mountain range juts up near the confluence of the two rivers.

The mighty Middle Fork flows for 106 miles, plunging along its route through one of the deepest gorges in North America before joining the Salmon River. Near the junction of the Middle Fork and Salmon rivers loom the jagged peaks of the Bighorn Crags, one of the wildest and most rugged ranges in the Northwest. As in the main Salmon, deep-flowing pools dot the river between long stretches of dangerous rapids and falls. These scenic holding pools provide fishing for steelhead, cutthroat, rainbow, and Dolly Varden from spring

through fall. Nearly one-third of the chinook salmon spawning nests (locally called redds) in the Salmon River drainage are found in the Middle Fork and its tributaries. Float trips down the river often start at Dagger Falls, where a fish ladder assists salmon in the final stages of their spawning journey. July, August, and September are the best months for these trips; the highwater period from late May through June makes trips during these months hazardous. In the late summer when the water is low, landing fields downstream from Dagger Falls are the best starting points. If you lack knowledge of the river or experience at river running, hire the services of a licensed guide. Along the way are the rugged spires of the Bighorn Crags, Indian paintings and petroglyphs recalling a culture that existed 8,000 years ago, and the Sheepeater Hot Springs. Keep in mind that the Middle Fork Canyon is rattlesnake country. Numerous campsites are available along the Middle Fork, and many of them have spur trails leading out into the interior wilderness. Open flats along the river's edges and meadows in the high country provide natural campsites. For much of its distance, the Middle Fork is paralleled by a primitive trail. There are a number of small landing fields along the river for charter flights into the Idaho Primitive Area.

The Middle Fork of the Salmon River, called the "Impassable Canyon" on Colonel Bernard's map of 1879, includes most of the spawning grounds for the chinook salmon in the Salmon River system. It has special regulations for trout fishing, so if you plan to fish here, write for a copy of the regulations to: Idaho Department of Fish and Game, 600 S. Walnut St., Boise 83707.

Nez Percé National Forest & Hell's Canyon

The forest covers two million acres from north central Idaho to the state's western border with northern Oregon; it is bordered by the Salmon River in the south, the South and Middle forks of the Clearwater further north, and portions of the Lochsa and Selway in Selway-Bitterroot Wilderness. The Snake River Canyon forms a portion of its westernmost border. It encompasses the mountainlands beyond the Bitterroots to the west, including the Gospel and Clearwater mountains. The forest is dominated by the worldfamous rainbow and steelhead waters of the Clearwater River, which flows into the Snake River at Lewiston and forms one of the largest and most complex river systems in the northern Idaho fish and game country.

The 130,000–acre Hells Canyon-Seven Devils Scenic Area straddles the Snake River Canyon on the Idaho-Oregon border. Ninety-seven thousand of these acres lie within Idaho. This land is within the borders of the Nez Percé, Payette, and Wallowa-Whitman national forests. The Seven Devils Mountains of this area take their name from the legend of an Indian brave who became lost among the jagged peaks and encountered seven demons before he found his way back to his tribe. The volcanic mountain range reaches heights of over 8,000 feet. Hells Canyon cuts through the range to a depth of 7,900 feet from He Devil Peak; it is the deepest and narrowest gorge on the North American continent. In some areas the canyon walls are richly hued in red, orange, and yellow.

Much of the area is accessible only by river or trail. Many of the

trails lead up into the high country of the Devils, where you can see miles of Oregon, Washington, Idaho, and Montana stretching before you. The white waters of the Snake in this area are wild, comparable in volume and gradient with the Cataract, Marble, and Grand canyons of the Colorado or the Hells Half Mile-Disaster Falls rapids of the Green. Unless you are a highly skilled white-water runner, hire a licensed guide or outfitter to take you down the rapids, and let the area Forest Ranger know of your plans. Wild Sheep rapids and Granite Creek rapids are extremely dangerous for boating, and amateurs should remember that chances of resuming in case of upset are poor.

To the east, the wild fury of the Rapid National Wild River—a tributary of the Salmon—roars down from its headwaters in the Seven Devils Mountains through the wildlands of the Payette and Nez Percé national forests (for information on this violent stretch of water, write to the Supervisor's Office, Nez Percé National Forest).

Payette National Forest

The 2.3 million-acre Payette National Forest extends from the southern shores of the Salmon River through the vast wilderness of the Idaho Primitive Area and the Salmon Mountains. Major streams originating in the forest include the Weiser River, North Fork of the Payette, Big Creek, and most of the South Fork of the Salmon. The Hells Canyon of the Snake River forms a portion of the forest's western border. The forest's 154 fishing lakes and 1,530 miles of streams include outstanding trout and salmon waters. Glaciers formed many of its cirques and canyons.

Hundreds of remote alpine lakes dot the evergreen-clad slopes and meadows north of Payette Lake and McCall. These jewel-like lakes offer good wilderness fishing for brook, rainbow, and cutthroat trout. Mule deer, black bear, and elk range throughout the forests, and whitetail deer inhabit the Salmon River country. Bighorn sheep

roam the high country of the Idaho Primitive Area, and mountain goats range in the rugged country from McCall to the Middle Fork of the Salmon to the east. Cougar, beaver, fox, lynx, bobcat, marten, and muskrat are other forest furbearers. Game birds include Franklin, ruffed, and blue grouse and chukar partridge.

"River of No Return"

The tortuous waters of the Salmon River for an 80–mile stretch between the road's end west of North Fork and Riggins has been known as the "River of No Return" since it defeated Lewis and Clark in their search for a northwest passage to the Pacific. In the 79 miles from the end of the North Fork road to the end of the Riggins road, one-half mile upstream from the Wind River bridge, the Salmon drops a total of 969 feet, approximately 12 feet per mile. Peak flows occur from the middle of May to July 1. It is at its lowest in January and February, but these highs and lows are subject to seasonal changes. River crossings 100 years ago in the "No Return" stretch were made by swimming or by raft, cable crossing bridge, or ferry. Today you will find pack bridges at Horse Creek, Campbell Ferry (Trout Creek), Fivemile Trail (Mackay Bar) and Wind River (at the end of the road from Riggins). The ancient Nez Percé trail, used by the Indians during their travels east to hunt buffalo on the plains, crosses the Salmon near Campbell Ferry Bridge.

The first known attempt by white men to navigate the Salmon ended in tragedy when four Hudson's Bay Company trappers left Salmon in March 1832 to float down the river in a small boat made of hides. Two of the men were lost in the boiling white fury of the rapids; the other two managed to reach Fort Nez Percé 30 days later. About 1890 Henry Guleke and a man named Sanderland successfully ran the Salmon River Canyon and rapids in wooden flatboats steered by large sweeps. A new boat was built for each trip to float miners, prospectors, and trappers into this vast wilderness, and was dismantled at downstream destinations. The lumber from these flatboats was used to build many a Salmon River gold-mining camp. Unless you are skilled in white-water river running, hire a good guide if you plan to float the river. You should inform a Forest Ranger in the area of your plan to travel down the river, and follow the Idaho boating regulations. Information on the regulations is available from the Idaho Fish and Game Department, Boise 83707.

There are over 40 stretches of powerful brawling rapids on the main Salmon, including Ruby Rapids (3 miles of white water), Gun Barrel, Ranier, Salmon Falls, Bailey, Big and Little Mallard, Little Elk Horn, Johnson, Chittam, Five-Mile, Long Tom Creeks, and Pine Creek (considered the most hazardous by many), studded by huge boulders, jagged sawtooth rocks, sweepers, and numerous small chutes and cascades broken by quiet stretches of calm water and deep-flowing pools.

The first 30–40 miles of the Salmon, from its beginnings in the upper Sawtooth Valley, provide easy fishing from the shore or in float boats. Fishing this part of the river in the early morning mist, one is greeted by stunning vistas of the Sawtooth Mountains to the west and the famous White Cloud Peaks towering on the east. Fishermen start working the lower stretches for chinook in June, and as the runs grow larger, the anglers move upstream with the fish. The best fishing is usually in late June and July. Salmon eggs are the most effective bait, although large grass wobblers and spoons are also very productive.

Salmon National Forest & the Bighorn Crags

An outdoorsman's dream, this 1,768,000–acre tract located in east central Idaho was once the scene of the bloody Sheepeaters Indian War. Numerous trails, including the historic Nez Percé and Lewis and Clark trails, wind through the rugged wilderness along the Yellowjacket Mountains, Idaho Primitive Area, Lost River-Salmon River plains, Bitterroot Mountains, Salmon River Mountains, Beaverhead Mountains, and the Middle and North forks of the Salmon River. Elevations vary from 2,480 feet in the Salmon River Canyon to 11,350 feet at Big Peak near Leadore. The fishing is excellent in the Salmon and its tributaries for steelhead, cutthroat, Dolly Varden, and rainbow trout and chinook salmon. The forest encompasses portions of the Bighorn Crags area, a high mountain wilderness noted for its camping and big-game hunting for bighorn sheep, mountain goat, mule deer, and occasional elk and black bear. A special permit is needed when hunting sheep or goat. Elk and deer are included in the general license. Fishing is good for rainbow, cutthroat, and golden trout in the lake basins nestled beneath the high jagged peaks. The most productive lakes include Skyhigh, Ship Island, Big Clear, Glacier, Gooseneck, and Crater.

Salmon River Breaks Primitive Area

The upper Salmon has good fly-fishing from July on for Dolly Varden and brook trout. The middle stretch of the Salmon is popular for fall and spring steelhead fishing and for the chinook run in late April and May. For 180 miles of its course, the Salmon surges through treacherous V-shaped canyons and gorges. In the most rugged part of this wilderness, the 216,879–acre Salmon River Breaks Primitive Area borders the river on the north for 40 miles between Riggins and North Fork. On the south side of the river are the wilds of the Idaho Primitive Area. This area encompasses some very hazardous terrain that can be reached only by boats or rafts, and furnishes services for float trips popular during the steelhead runs.

Gateways & Accommodations

Boise

(Pop. 106,000; zip code, see below; area code 208) is the state capital and major business center of Idaho as well as the headquarters of the Boise National Forest. Founded as a gold-rush town during the 1800's, the city is situated on the Boise River at the upper end of Boise Valley, protected by great mountains on the north. Area attractions include the State Capitol, between Jefferson and State Sts., and the Boise City Zoo, State Historical Museum, and Boise Gallery of Arts all in Julia Davis Park at Capitol Blvd. and Myrtle St. Picturesque Idaho City, a historic gold rush ghost town and once the territorial capitol of Idaho and the Boise Basin and its ghost towns are located northeast of Boise on Idaho Hwy. 21. Accommodations: *Holiday Inn at Boise Airport* (rates: $35 double), with 265 excellent rooms, restaurant, cocktail lounge, heated outdoor and indoor pools, sauna, recreation center off I–80 Vista exit (344–8365). *Rodeway Inn*, (rates: $41–51 double), with 325 excellent rooms and family units with balconies, restaurant, coffeeshop, cocktail lounge, heated pool on Boise River at 29th & Chinden Blvd. off I–80 N. Garden City exit (343–1871); *Royal Inn* (rates: $32 double), with 100 excellent rooms, dining room, coffeeshop, heated pool, sauna off I–80 N. Curtis Rd. exit (376–2700); *Sheraton Downtown* (rates: $32 double), with 195 excellent rooms, restaurant, coffeeshop, cocktail lounge, heated pool at 1901 Main St. off I–80 Vista exit to city center (344–7691).

Challis

(Pop. 800; zip code 83226; area code 208) headquarters of the Challis National Forest, is a beautiful sub-alpine village on U.S. 93 surrounded by towering mountains in the heart of Salmon River country. The town is a popular jumping-off point for fishing, hunting and camping trips in the Idaho Primitive Area. Area attractions include the miniature Grand Canyon of the Salmon River, with

sheer walls reaching heights of up to 2,000 feet and the Upper Salmon River Gorge. Accommodations: *Holiday Lodge* (rates: $20–22 double), with 12 excellent motel rooms ¼ mile north of town on U.S. 93 (879–2259); *Village Inn* (rates: $20–22 double), with 22 excellent rooms and family units, restaurant on U.S. 93, ¼ mile south of town (879–2239).

Grangeville—Nez Percé National Forest Gateway

(Pop. 3,600; zip code 83530; area code 208) is a major fishing, hunting and camping gateway to the Nez Percé National Forest high country and the Idaho Primitive Area, located in one of the state's most beautiful valleys on U.S. 95 and the Clearwater River. Area attractions include White Bird, with its view of canyons and the Seven Devils Peaks to the west and the village of White Bird where the first battle of the Nez Percé Indian War was fought in 1877. Two district offices of the Nez Percé National Forest are based in Grangeville. Accommodations: *Monty's Motel* (rates: $20–22 double) with 14 good rooms and a heated pool at 700 W. Main St. (983–2500).

McCall—Payette National Forest Gateway

(Pop. 1,700; zip code 83638; area code 208) is the headquarters of the Payette National Forest located on lower Payette Lake. Several licensed outfitters headquartered here provide pack trips into the surrounding high country. Accommodations: *Shore Lodge*, (rates: $22–33 double), a rustic resort hotel built in 1948 with 100 excellent rooms and family units in scenic location on Payette Lake, heated pool, boats, swimming beach, fishing, tennis courts, trail rides and water sports, with lodge dining room and coffeeshop, one mile west of town on Idaho 15 (634–2244).

Mountain Home—Boise National Forest Gateway

(Pop. 6,400 zip code 83647; area code 208) located in the southwest portion of the state in the Boise-Owhyee Valley on Interstate 80N and jumping-off point for trips to the Bruneau wild & scenic river, Bruneau Dunes State Park, American Ranch Reservoir, and C.J. Strike Reservoir. Accommodations: *Hilander Motel* (rates: $21–23 double), with 33 excellent rooms and family units, restaurant, coffeeshop, on U.S. 30 and Air Base Rd. (587–3311); *Towne Center Motel* (rates: $23–25 double), with 31 excellent rooms and heated pool at 410 N. 2nd St. E. on U.S. 30 (587–3373).

Salmon—Gateway to the Idaho Primitive Area

(Pop. 2,900; zip code 83467; area code 208) flanked by the majestic Bitterroot and Salmon River Mountains. This historic Old West frontier town is a major gateway and starting point for trips down the Middle Fork of the Salmon River and into the vast alpine country of the Idaho Primitive Area. This picturesque village is nestled in the beautiful Salmon River Valley on U.S. 93 at the junction of the Salmon and Lemhi rivers. Area attractions include the Sacajawea Monument, wild river float trips, Island Park in the Salmon River, Lost Trail Winter Sports Area, and several area gold-rush ghost towns and the walls of old Fort Lemhi. For information on auto tours, contact the Chamber of Commerce. Local Indian and pioneer history displays may be viewed at the Salmon Museum on Main St. Accommodations: *Stagecoach Inn* (rates: $25–26 double), with 50 excellent rooms overlooking the Salmon River, free airport pickup, heated pool ¼ mile north of town on U.S. 93 (756–4251); *Wagons West* (rates: $20–24 double), with 52 good rooms and family units, restaurant overlooking the Salmon River, north of the Salmon River Bridge on U.S. 93 (756–4281).

Weiser—Gateway to Hells Canyon Recreation Area
(Pop. 4,100; zip code 83672; area code 208), named for an early German trapper, is located on U.S. 95 at the confluence of Snake and Weiser rivers near the Oregon border. The town is the site of a District Ranger's Office of the Payette National Forest and the principal gateway to the Hells Canyon-Seven Devils Mountain recreation area and the Oxbow, Brownlee, and Hells Canyon dams on the Snake River. A local attraction is the Historical Museum & National Fiddlers' Hall of Fame at 44 W. Commercial St. Accommodations: *Colonial Motel* (rates: $20–21 double), with 24 good rooms and family units at 251 E. Main St. (549–0150).

Guest Ranches & Lodges

★★★*Bogus Basin Ski Area & Lodges*, 16 miles north of Boise on the Bogus Basin Road, encompasses two big mountains, 1800 acres of superb ski terrain, 37 major runs, six double chairlifts, and a comprehensive ski school. Runs vary from gentle beginner and intermediate tree-lined trails to open powder bowls and steep, packed slopes for experts. Night skiing is especially spectacular here—numerous steady beacons reflected by crisp white powder transform the slopes into an enchanted mountain. You can ski 13 hours a day if you choose, or sleep late and still enjoy a full afternoon and evening in the basin. The ski school, with its staff of 50 certified instructors, offers a variety of class and private lessons plus a special four-day GLM "learn-to-ski week." Custom-tailored instruction is also available for advanced skiers who want to polish their skills or tackle new challenges. Other drawing cards at Bogus Basin are the two attractive day lodges, a nursery for young children, and a generous ski season beginning around Thanksgiving and continuing through mid-April.

The Pioneer Inn, Bogus Basin's new condominium guest facility, is located halfway up the mountain at the top of two chairlifts, so you can ski down the mountain first thing in the morning instead of waiting for a lift up. The inn has modern and comfortable accommodations for 200 guests and is accessible to all Bogus Basin facilities. For more information on the inn and ski area, write: Bogus Basin, 731 North 15th, Boise, ID 83702 (208)336–4500.

★★★*Indian Creek Guest Ranch* is a small and intimate ranch retreat bordering the spectacular Idaho Primitive Area and surrounded by Forest Service land. Because of its size, the ranch can tailor vacations around your preferences. Horseback rides along beautiful trails, fishing for rainbow trout, hiking, photography, visits to historic ghost towns, and jet-boat trips on the legendary Salmon River are some of the possibilities. Guest quarters are available in 3 attractive, pine-shaded cabins, each with comfortable furnishings and a private bath. The main ranch building houses a lounge and dining room where hearty, country-style meals are the specialty—prime ribs, steaks, chicken, home-baked breads, garden-fresh vegetables, and hand-cranked ice cream. Rates are $60 per person daily, including meals lodgings, guide service, tips, jeep rides, horses, and all ranch activities. For additional information, write: Indian Creek Guest Ranch, Star Route, Northfork, ID 83466 (Salmon Operator, ask for 24F–211).

★★★★*Mackay Bar Lodge & Stonebraker Ranch* offers a superb wilderness experience in the Salmon River backcountry of Idaho. The facilities include the Mackay Bar Lodge, the rustic Stonebraker Ranch, miles of wilderness in between, horses, mules, river rafts, a jet boat and all the equipment for making it in the wilderness. A trip to Mackay Bar could include a wild whitewater trip, pulling in a line with a steelhead or a rainbow fighting on the other end, or just picking wild flowers in a sunny alpine meadow. Mackay Bar Lodge is located 140 miles from Boise. It is reached via air charter from Boise to Sun Valley or by jet boat from the "End-of-the-Road" landing 26 miles up the Salmon River from Riggins, Idaho (a one hour trip). Of the two lodging houses, Mackay Bar Lodge is the most luxurious. It is at the confluence of the Main Salmon River and the South Fork of the Salmon River. It is half way between the comforts of home and the rustic simplicity of Stonebraker Ranch. Lodging includes the ultra-modern Ram House, a 3–level, 5–bath corporate retreat, rustic guest cabins, fully-furnished rental homes and lodge rooms. In the dining hall, as many as seventy people can dine in comfort. A typical meal is steak with Idaho spuds. Activities at the Mackay Bar Lodge include trail rides, hot tubs, backpacking, jet boating, tubing, exploring, fishing, visiting Indian caves, volley ball and meeting Buckskin Bob. Trout fishing is outstanding and guests can even pan for gold. The jagged canyons, winding rivers, lush green hills and valleys offer scenic beauty beyond compare. Rates include lodging, meals and use of ranch recreation facilities. Summer season is $75 per person per day and off season is $65. Private guest houses add $50 per house per day and the Ram House adds $100 per day. There are rates for children and for transportation to the lodge. The Stonebraker Ranch is in the Chamberlain Basin. Accommodations there include a ranch house, 2 log cabins of hand-hewn logs and four semi-permanent wood floor tents with heaters and cots. Real Salmon River country food is served family style and wine is free with dinner. At Stonebraker, guests can enjoy high-mountain lake and stream fishing, pack trips, trail rides, wilderness hikes, volley ball and croquet at no extra charge. Even camping gear is provided. Rates at the Stonebraker include meals and use of the recreational facilities and are $65 per person per day with lower rates for children under ten. But the best way to visit Mackay Bar is to sign up for one of the tours which lasts from three to seven days. The most inclusive is the Mixed Bag Trip which is touted as an Idaho wilderness smorgasbord. After a one-hour flight from Boise, guests are met in a buckboard and taken to Stonebraker Ranch in time for lunch. The afternoon can be spent fishing, riding or exploring. Early the next morning, the group saddles up for a pack trip on horseback down Chamberlain Creek. The evening is spent camping along the creek. By noon of the third day, they join a group of floaters on a white water trip already in progress. The next 2½ days are spent floating down the Main Salmon River in rubber rafts with time out for swimming, hiking and fishing. On the afternoon of the fifth day, they reach Mackay Bar Lodge. The final two days are spent there, jet boating, fishing, horseback riding or doing whatever the guest wants at no extra cost. The tour is seven days and nights with a maximum of eight persons on the trip. It is $700 per person including the flight from Boise, lodging, meals, equipment (except for a personal sleeping bag) and all mentioned activities. Tours start on various days from July through September. There is also a 3–day and night mini-mixed bag trip for $350 per person that includes a floating trip, a horseback pack trip and a stay at Stonebraker Ranch. For those whose real interest is the river, Mackay Bar has a "River of No Return" Main Salmon River trip that is five days and nights and is an excellent family vacation. The floaters occupy each rubber raft with a guide experienced in river running. There is also a one-man Tahiti inflatable boat for individuals who want to try out their whitewater skills. Four days and three nights are spent on the river, visiting sandy beaches, swimming and camping. On the afternoon of the fourth day, the group arrives at Mackay Bar Lodge where they can enjoy all the facilities including horseback riding, fishing, jet boating and exploring for the rest of the visit. This tour is $485 per person with starting dates from June through September. For the experienced whitewater enthusiast there is the Middle Fork tour with a rate of fall of over 22 feet per mile for one of the most exciting float trips in the country. Excellent fly-fishing adds to the trip. Six days and 5 nights are spent on the river

with freshly cooked western meals, rubber rafts, tents and experienced guides. This tour is $525 per person, and starts on various dates from June through September. For more information about Mackay Bar and their exciting wilderness vacations call or write: Mackay Bar, Corp., 3190 Airport Way, Boise, ID 83705 (208)344–1881.

★★★*Shepp Ranch* located at the confluence of the Main Salmon River and Crooked Creek, specializes in whitewater adventures, horseback trips and wilderness vacations. Owner/operator Jim Campbell came to Idaho to pursue a career in nuclear physics, but his interest in running rivers caused him to change directions. Shepp Ranch is in a remote area, 15 miles from the nearest roadhead. Cabins with comfortable furniture and fireplaces accommodate guests. Specialties include a hot tub, sauna and hearty western meals. Daily rates at the Ranch include all meals, lodging and use of horses, boats and guides. Groups of 14 or more can get exclusive use of the Ranch during their stay. The ranch is open from March through November. It is reached by charter plane from Boise. The Ranch also has several package tours. The Combination Ranch/Whitewater/Horseback tour is six days and five nights and includes roundtrip transportation from Boise, whitewater floats, horseback rides and jetboat trips. Trails take guests to old mining camps. Cost of the package from June 18 to Sept. 15 is $495 per person double occupancy and off-season is $395. There is a wildlife weekend including two days and a night, a jetboat trip on the Salmon River and an opportunity to enjoy Shepp Ranch. This weekend is $95 per person. The "River of No Return" Whitewater Float Trip includes camping out on the 90 mile stretch of the River and is $495 per person for six days and five nights with equipment provided. For details of all trips and more information write: Shepp Ranch, P.O. Box 3417, Boise, ID 83703 (208)343–7728.

★★*Torrey's Burnt Creek Inn* is located in the village of Clayton in the Challis National Forest on Idaho 75 near the northeast boundary of the Sawtooth National Recreation Area and the upper Salmon River. Lodging facilities are of rustic log and old western construction. Modern housekeeping units rent for $90 to $115 per week. Smaller modern and unmodern cabins rent from $50 to $85 per week. They are furnished with linens, bedding and a basic selection of kitchen utensils. Along with fishing and hunting, there is much to see and do in this area. There are several historic sites in the vicinity including ghost towns, a mining dredge, charcoal kilns, and two small museums for added interest. It is an excellent area for the amateur or student of geology. The natural scenic splendor provides a superb opportunity for the artist, photographer, or just to sit back and relax. For the explorer type, there are many miles of U.S. Forest Service trails to hike and ride or mountains to climb. The resort has a swimming pool and games such as badminton and horseshoes available for the guests. Horseback rides or pack trips into the back country lakes for fishing are available by reservation. Rubber boats are available for rafting the storied "River of No Return." The latter can be an exciting sport depending on how much white water you want to challenge. The Salmon River is open to most fishing the year around. Steelhead fishing starts in April and the spring run of the chinook salmon starts in June. Salmon fishing, the most popular fishing period on the river, continues until July 31. Thereafter, trout fishing is predominant. The latter part of September and October have provided some of the best trout fishing. As you have undoubtedly reasoned, this is a rugged scenic area with little sophistication and an area that limited numbers of our society have discovered. The original homesteaders, Mr. & Mrs. Torrey, made a start to serve the public as a hostelry and as a salmon fishing camp. Intervening years have changed things some but the basic premise is still to provide a place for guests to relax and enjoy this wonderful area. For additional information, contact: Val & Phil Johnson, Clayton, ID 83227 (208)838–2313.

Travel Services & Salmon River Float Trips

Guided float-trips, fishing, packhorse, and fall hunting trips in the Salmon River country and Idaho Primitive Area are offered by the following licensed outfitters, who are thoroughly familiar with the fascinating Indian, pioneer, and gold-rush history of the region, wildlife and woods lore and camp cooking.

Eldon Handy River Expeditions offers oar-powered float trips for up to 40 people on the main and Middle Fork of the Salmon River. Six day rates range from $360–395 with group discounts. Contact: Box 15, Jerome, ID 83338 (208)324–4339.

Frontier Expeditions, Inc. offers guided float trips on the main Salmon River with fishing, hearty meals, and overnight stops at China Bar Lodge during their regular four-day trips. Rates are $390 per person inclusive with special family rates. Contact: Box 839, North Fork, ID 83466 (208)865–2200.

Happy Hollow Camps offer guided float trips on the wild Middle Fork and main Salmon rivers and packhorse trips in the Salmon River Mountains. Overnight packhorse trips cost $35/person per day inclusive; float-trips cost $50/day per person. Contact: Box 694, Salmon, ID 83467 (208)756–3954.

Idaho Adventures offers a variety of wilderness and whitewater experiences on the state's three most famous rivers: the Snake, Salmon, and Middle Fork. Spring and fall steelhead fishing trips to a secluded riverside camp, six-day float trips through precipitous Hells Canyon, fall fishing along the Snake for smallmouth bass, spring photography tours, and one to three day float trips through beautiful valleys from April to September are just a few of the adventures sponsored by this firm. Idaho Adventures also maintains a white water rafting school plus guide and outfitting services for horseback, float, and camping trips. Rates for regularly scheduled six-day expeditions run from $415 to $450 and generally include air charter service from Lewiston or Boise to river put-in points, all meals en route, tents, life jackets, guides, and all necessary ground transportation. Fact sheets for each float trip, a detailed brochure, and other information may be obtained from Idaho Adventures, P.O. Box 834, Salmon, ID 83467 (208)756–2986.

Nez Percé Outfitters & Guides offers 3–5 day floatboat excursions down the Middle Fork of the Salmon River during July and August. In addition to shooting the rapids of this powerful stream, you'll have an opportunity to hike along old Indian trails, swim in sparkling clear pools, and fish for native cutthroat trout. All trips begin and end at Salmon. Transportation is provided to the embarkation point. Rates are $325 per person for three-day float trips, $425 per person for five-day trips. Nez Percé also sponsors guided pack-in camping trips in some of the most scenic areas of the Idaho wilderness, moving at a leisurely pace to high mountain lakes and streams where fishing is superb for native trout. Photographers and nature lovers will appreciate the abundance of wildlife: elk, deer, mountain goat, and bear. Seven-day guided camping trips are offered between mid-July and early September at rates of $45 per person per day. For complete information, write: Nez Percé Outfitters & Guides, Box 1454, Salmon, ID 83467 (208)756–3912.

Nicholson & Sons Float Trips, Inc. offer guided float trips on the Middle Fork of the Salmon for 106 miles with departure from the Salmon headwaters at Stanley. Six day rates are $395 per person, with family and group discounts. Contact: Roy L. Nicholson, Rt. 4, Twin Falls, ID 83301 (208)733–6139.

Norm & Bill Guth offer guided float trips on the Main and Middle Fork of the Salmon. The Guth's guided President Carter and his family on the Middle Fork in the summer of 1978. Rates are $375–400 per person. Custom guided trips available for fishermen. Contact: Box 705, Salmon, ID 83467 (208)756–3279.

Primitive Area Float Trips sponsors a broad spectrum of river trips on Idaho's superb network of wild and scenic waterways. There are 3–6 day fly-in excursions on the middle fork of the Salmon with a special emphasis on fly-fishing and photography; five-day rafting adventures through Hells Canyon of the Snake; an exciting four-day trip through the Selway Wilderness, with good trout fishing and turbulent whitewater over much of the distance; float trips through forested canyons of the Main Salmon River; and five-day excursions down the Owyhee River through southeastern Oregon's seldom visited, rugged wilderness. Exclusive trips may also be made on any of the above rivers using maneuverable McKenzie driftboats. Other options include combination raft and horseback trips, fly-out float trips, hunting/whitewater excursions for chukar partridge, spring and fall steelhead fishing and a deluxe 11–day journey along the middle fork and Main Salmon in central Idaho's vast wilderness. Rates vary according to the nature of the trip and group size: 3–day trips average $225 per person, 5–day trips are approximately $325 per person, and 11–day excursions are $465–525 per person. For complete details, write: Stanton C. Miller, P.O. Box 585, Salmon, ID 83467 (208)756–2319 or 756–3388.

Salmon River Lodge is located on the main river in the heart of the Salmon National Forest. The lodge offers the following vacation adventure trips: Salmon River Float trip, 5 days, $375 per person, includes first night at lodge and night's camping, guides, meals; combination float and pack trip, includes 4–day float down the Salmon, jetboat back, night at Salmon River Lodge, a 5–day pack trip, and another night at the lodge, $650 per person; Idaho Primitive Area pack trip, 7 days, includes 2 nights at the lodge and 5 days in the Primitive Area with guides, horses, and meals, $325 per person, custom trips for fishing available; Camera Safari includes lodging, meals, choice of one-day float, jetboat, or packhorse trip or a one-day car tour of Salmon country historic sites; Steelhead fishing trips in early spring or fall with lodging, meals, guides, and jetboat, $40 per person per day; fall guided hunting trips for elk, deer, black bear, bighorn sheep, cougar from $750–1,500 per person, 7–10 days. Lodge rates are $20 per day and include meals and jetboat trip across the Salmon to the lodge. Contact: P.O. Box 58, Salmon, ID 83467 (208)756–2646.

Rocky Mountain River Tours sponsors 6–day trips on the Middle Fork and Main Salmon rivers plus a 3–day adventure through Hells Canyon of the historic Snake River. The 108–mile whitewater raft trip down the Middle Fork of the Salmon takes you through rugged canyons and unspoiled scenery over 80 heart-stopping rapids. The Main Salmon is navigated via oar-powered boats through the second deepest gorge on the continent, between two designated primitive areas, with superlative trout fishing along the way. Spectacular rapids and towering, sheer granite walls make the Hell's Canyon trip a popular one, especially in spring, when mild weather and good fishing prevail. Rocky Mountain provides local round-trip transportation, guides, boats, and excellent meals served round a campfire. Rates are $225 per person for 3–day trips, $375–450 per person

for 6 days. For schedules and descriptions of all trips, write: Rocky Mountain River Tours, P.O. Box 693, Pocatello, ID 83201 (208)232–7064.

Wilderness River Outfitters & Trail Expeditions specializes in float trips on the Salmon, Owyhee, Snake, and Bruneau rivers. The 6–day, 5–night Salmon River expedition takes you through two of Idaho's most beautiful primitive areas, dramatic canyons, and spectacular alpine scenery. Trips down the Owyhee, 5–17 days in length, are characterized by fast-moving rapids, primitive desert scenery, and stretches of placid drifting water. Hells Canyon of the Snake is explored by both raft and on foot, with 4 days of backpacking through high peaks and rugged terrain to test your landlegs. The Jarbridge-Bruneau river trip is a one-guest-one-guide expedition along some of the best small stream whitewater in the country. Wilderness River Outfitters also offers 5–9 day backpacking adventures in Idaho's unspoiled back-country and winter ski touring trips through the Salmon River country. Rates are $325–415 per person for 4–day float trips; $325–1325 for Owyhee River expeditions; $425 per person for the backpacking-float trip excursion in Hells Canyon; $775 for the 5–day Bruneau River trip; and $280–300 per person for 5 days of guided backpacking or ski touring. For detailed information, write: Wilderness River Outfitters, P.O. Box 871, Salmon, ID 83467 (208)756–3959.

Wilderness Encounters, Inc. sponsors a variety of whitewater raft and combination raft/horseback trips along Idaho's most famous rivers, including a 90–mile stretch of the Main Salmon through the largest contiguous wilderness in the U.S.; 75–mile runs along the seldom-travelled Snake; and 36– or 85–mile Hells Canyon trips. Rates start at $245 for 3 days $365 for 6 days and include everything but your sleeping bag. Guides are top professionals with years of whitewater and trail experience. Wilderness Encounters also owns and operates the Shepp Ranch (which see), an old homestead built in the late 1880s on Indian trading grounds at the confluence of the Main Salmon River and Crooked Creek. Modern guest cabins are 15 miles from the nearest road and fully equipped with all the amenities. Daily activities are scheduled, with guided whitewater and horseback trips included in the weekly ($395 per person) rates. Groups of 12 or more can arrange for exclusive use of the ranch. For detailed information on river runs or the Shepp Ranch, write: Wilderness Encounters, Inc., P.O. Box 3417, Boise, ID 83703 (208)343–7728.

Wild Rivers West specializes in 3½–5½–day float trips down the wild Salmon River through the beautiful, rugged canyon country of the Idaho Primitive Area. You will travel in sturdy rubber rafts guided by skilled boatmen, with larger boats used to carry supplies and gear. Groups are limited to 4–12 people, so the emphasis is on personalized service and close involvement with the wilderness around you. Wild Rivers West supplies camping equipment, hearty meals cooked over an open fire, safety gear, and transportation between Salmon, Idaho, and put-in and take-out points. Rates are $315–335 per person for 3½ day trips, $340–365 for 4½–day trips, and $375–395 for 5½–day trips. Trips are scheduled from mid-June through early September. Wild Rivers West also offers one and two-day float trips on the Salmon, seasonal hunting trips for black bear and chukar partridge, and steelhead fishing excursions in late September and October. For more information, write: Wild Rivers West, Box 503, Salmon, ID 83467 (208)756–3572 or (208)865–2484.

Sawtooth National Forest & Sun Valley

The sharp-edged 10,000–foot peaks of this range dominate the 1,800,000 acres of the Sawtooth National Forest and Sawtooth Wilderness Area, one of the nation's most spectacular alpine backpacking, fishing, and cross-country skiing areas. The northern division of the forest in south central Idaho encompasses the Sawtooth National Recreation Area and the Sawtooth Wilderness, as well as the mountainlands of the famous Ketchum and Sun Valley area. The headwaters of the Middle and North Forks of the Boise, South Fork of the Payette, and the Salmon River gather among the jagged peaks of the Sawtooth Mountain Wilderness here, flanked by the White Cloud Peaks and the Boulder, Pioneer, and Smoky mountains. Most of the forest's southern division lies in southern Idaho, in the Cassia, Albion, Sublett, Black Pine, and Raft River mountains, cut by the tributaries of the Snake River. The major recreational facilities of the southern division are located at Rock Creek Canyon and Howell Canyon.

In the Sun Valley area to the southeast are the famous fly-fishing-only waters of spring-fed Silver Creek, a nationally renowned trophy rainbow fishery noted for its insect rich alkaline waters and abundant

growths of watercress, tules, bullrushes, and water lilies. The headwaters of Silver Creek are reached via the old Sun Valley Ranch lands. Bird life often seen throughout the forest includes marsh hawks, redtailed hawks, osprey, goshawks, sandhill cranes, and golden eagles.

Information Sources, Maps & Access

For detailed vacation, recreation, and wilderness travel information, a full-color *Sawtooth National Forest Map* (50¢) and the free *Sawtooth National Recreation Area & Wilderness Map/Brochure, White Cloud-Boulder Mountains Map/Brochure*, and a *Ketchum District Guide*, contact: Supervisor, Sawtooth National Forest, 1525 Addison Ave. E., Twin Falls, ID 83301 (208)733–3990 and the Sawtooth National Recreation Area Headquarters, Ketchum, ID 83340 (208)726–8291.

For detailed fishing, backpacking, cross-country skiing, float-trip, and hunting info in the Sun Valley area, write or call: *Sun Valley Sports Center*, Sun Valley Mall (208)622–4111 and *Dick Alf's Fly Shop*, Main St. (208)726–5282, both Sun Valley 83353.

The forest is accessible by way of U.S. 30N, 30S, and 93. It has 64 camping areas, eight winter sports areas, and nearby resort, dude ranch, hotel, motel, and cabin accommodations. Accommodations, supplies, and outfitting services are available at the nearby commu-

nities of Burley, Gooding, Sun Valley, Twin Falls, Ketchum, and Hailey.

Recreation Areas

Sawtooth National Recreation Area & Wilderness

The jagged Sawtooth Mountain peaks are the setting for the 216,383-acre national recreation area and wilderness of the same name, whose wildlands were sculpted by the great glaciers of long ago. Hundreds of alpine lakes were carved by them; as they melted, the torrential streams formed deep gorges in the mountain slopes. Deer, elk, mountain sheep, and mountain goats roam the high country and provide outstanding hunting. The glacial lakes clustered at the headwaters of the Middle Fork of the Boise, South Fork of the Payette, and Salmon River are a trout fisherman's paradise. The major lakes of the Sawtooth Range and Whitecloud Peaks region include Redfish, Pettit, Alturas, Stanley, Hell Roaring, Yellow Belly, and the spectacular Big Boulder and Boulder Chain lakes. Redfish is considered one of the world's most beautiful alpine moraine lakes. Most of the remote off-trail lakes provide fishing for Dolly Varden, rainbow, and brook trout, and Kokanee salmon—known locally as "redfish." The craggy Sawtooth peaks challenge the mountaineer. Atop the mountains, great snowbeds border wildflower meadows. This is the region of the Stanley Basin, where the mighty Salmon River is born. The brilliant yellows and blues of mountain buttercup and camas and dense evergreen stands cover the shores of Stanley Lake in summer; beyond them rise the great flanks of the Sawtooth Range.

The most popular entry points to the wilderness are the Pettit Lake Trail from Pettit Lake; Yellow Belly Trail; Hell Roaring Creek Trail; Redfish Creek Trail from Redfish Lake; and the Iron Creek Trail from Iron Creek Transfer Camp, all approaching the area from the east side of the Sawtooth Range. Most visitors enter the area in late July and August although most trails are easily accessible in June, early July, and September.

Sun Valley

This beautiful mountain and valley area was once among the homelands of the Northwest Indian tribes. White settlers entered the Wood River Valley after the last of the Indian wars in 1879. Boom towns arose in the 1880s after rich ores were discovered in the area. Towns like Ketchum and Hailey fell on hard times after the closing of the mines. Then in 1936 the Union Pacific Railroad chose the site of Sun Valley, just outside Ketchum, to create the famous ski resort that attracts some 200,000 people a year today. North of Ketchum are the wildlands of the Sawtooth National Forest, where Ernest Hemingway found inspiration for his work. A half mile past Sun Valley, a Hemingway memorial is inscribed: "Best of all he loved the fall/The leaves yellow on the cottonwoods/Leaves floating on the trout streams/And above the hills, the high blue windless skies/Now he will be a part of them forever."

Snow-fed streams, hot springs, lakes, and canyons lace the forest country. All of the area's streams and most of its lakes offer trout fishing. Brook trout are found in beaver ponds, and cutthroats in the high lakes. Rainbow are also common. Elk and deer range the southern slopes in Trail Creek, Warm Springs Creek, Deer Creek, and North Fork during the winter months. Ski touring, as well as downhill skiing, has been popular here since the 1930s, when the Pioneer Cabin was built as a ski-touring hut by Sun Valley. The landmark lies along the western edge of the Pioneer Mountains and offers brilliant mountain vistas.

White Cloud Peaks Backcountry

In the northern division, numerous trails and roads fan out into the

wilderness from the Sawtooth Valley, leading to such famous hunting and fishing areas as Boulder Mountain, Big Wood River, the Smoky Mountains, the Soldier Mountains, and the White Cloud Peaks. This outstanding big-game region was the former hunting grounds of the Shoshone and Sheepeater Indians. The hunting today, though not nearly as good as it was in the old days, is for elk, mule deer, mountain goat, bighorn sheep, antelope, and black bear. There is excellent rainbow trout fishing if you hike up to the lovely wilderness lakes basin located on the eastern slope of the Smoky Mountain Range.

The White Cloud Peaks and Boulder Mountains lie between the Salmon River on the north and west and the East Fork of the Salmon on the east. The Big Wood River borders the mountains on the south. The white limestone striations on the White Cloud Peaks give them their name, for they appear as summer clouds enshrouding the mountains. The Boulder Range is a rugged, bare mass of peaks and spires varying in elevation from 6,500 feet to almost 12,000 feet. More than a hundred alpine lakes dot the area, many of them formed in the cirques left by ancient glaciers. Clear mountain streams feed into the surrounding river systems. Elk and deer are plentiful throughout the area. At the higher altitudes among the rocky ledges and near the more remote lakes are mountain goats and bighorn sheep. Black bear and a few cougar also roam the area.

Gateways & Accommodations

Burley

(Pop. 8,200; zip code 83318; area code 208) in the heart of Idaho's famous potato, alfalfa, and sugar beet country, is the site of a District Ranger's Office of the Sawtooth National Forest and one of the world's largest potato flour mill plants. Area attractions include the strange, eroded rock formations of the Silent City of Rocks, which covers an area of 25 square miles. The area's rock walls—situated at the junction of two pioneer trails—bear the names and messages of thousands of early westward bound pioneers. Accommodations: *Best Western East Park Motel,* (rates: $20.50–22.50 double), with 14 excellent rooms on U.S. 30 at 507 E. Main St. (678–2241); *Ramada Inn* (rates: $24–26 double), with 130 excellent rooms and family units, restaurant, cocktail lounge, heated pool, two miles north of town on 1–80N (678–3501).

Ketchum—Gateway to Sun Valley & The Sawtooth Recreation Area

(Pop. 1,400; zip code 83340; area code 208) is located just south of the world-famous four-seasons resort and recreation center at Sun Valley (which see), nestled among the spectacular Boulder and Pioneer Mountains of the Sawtooth National Forest at 5,821 feet altitude. This mountain village is the site of two District Ranger Offices of the Sawtooth National Forest. Area Attractions include mountaineering, backpacking, alpine and nordic skiing, kayaking and trout fishing on Trail Creek, Silver Creek, Lake Creek, Warm Springs Creek, headwaters of the Lost River, East Fork of the Wood River, and the East Fork of the Salmon. Ketchum and Sun Valley are protected from the cold northern winds by the Sawtooth Mountains running east and west. Brilliant sunshine, frequent snowfalls and spectacular alpine scenery combine to make this area one of the nation's great winter sports meccas. Accommodations: *Alpen Rose* (rates: $49–69 double ski season), with 116 superb rooms and suites, dining room, cocktail lounge, heated pool at Saddle Rd., ½ mile north of town on Idaho 75 (726–4461). *Best Western Christiania Lodge* (rates: $34–36 double), with 38 excellent rooms and family units, heated pool, fireplaces just north of town on Sun Valley Rd. (726–3351); *Best Western Tyrolean Lodge* (rates: $30–35 double), with 42 alpine rooms and family units, fireplaces, heated pool south of town on Baldy Mountain Rd. (726–5336); *Heidelberg Inn* (rates: $36 double), with 30 excellent alpine rooms and family kitchen units, fireplaces, heated pool, north of town on Warm Springs Rd. (726–5361); *Tamarack Lodge* (rates: $27–45 double), with 25 ex-

cellent alpine rooms and family units, fireplaces, indoor heated pool just north of town on Sun Valley Rd. (726–3344).

Stanley—Gateway to the Sawtooth Recreation Area

(Pop. 100; zip code 83278; area code 208) is the headquarters and major entry point of the spectacular Sawtooth National Recreation area, nestled in the beautiful Stanley Basin, flanked on the west by the blue spires of the Sawtooth Range. Area attractions include the Redfish Lake Visitor's Center in the Sawtooth National Recreation Area off Idaho 75 at Big Redfish Lake with self-guiding trails, guided tours, campfire programs, and exhibits of the flora, wildlife, geology, and history of the area; Lady Face Falls; area gold-rush ghost towns; and the headwaters of the Salmon River. The area is one of the nation's finest alpine backpacking, fishing, mountaineering, and cross-country skiing areas. Accommodations (see "Lodges & Guest Ranches"): *Redwood Motel* (rates: $18 double), with 13 good rooms and family units on the Salmon River, 1½ miles north of the village on U.S. 93 (774–3431).

Twin Falls

(Pop. 25,000; zip code 83301; area code 208) is the major city in south-central Idaho's Magic Valley farm region. The city is located on Interstate 80N and has a District Ranger's Office of the Sawtooth National Forest. The major area attractions are the Snake River and Shoshone Falls, which cascades 212 feet and is known as the "Niagara of the West." Accommodations: *Best Western Apollo Motor Inn* (rates: $23–29 double), with 50 excellent rooms and family units, heated pool at 296 Addison Ave. W., north on U.S. 30 & 93 (733–2010); *Holiday Inn* (rates: $27–31 double), with 204 excellent rooms and family units, restaurant, cocktail lounge, heated pool, sauna two miles north of town on U.S. 93 at 1350 Blue Lakes Blvd. N. (733–0650).

Lodges, Guest Ranches & Ski Centers

★★★*Galena Lodge & Touring Center* is located in the Sawtooth National Recreation Area, 24 miles north of Sun Valley. The lodge offers gourmet cuisine and rustic mountain cabins located near the lodge for easy access to the trail system, or for more advanced skiers, tours of the Sawtooth Wilderness high country. The lodge offers guided cross-country day, moonlight, and overnight tours as well as ski tours of historical areas and powder terrain. USSA certified instructors and guides teach basic ski touring technique, advanced ski touring, free style powder skiing, telemark technique, and backpack skiing. Thunderpaws Express, a Siberian Husky sled team, is available by reservation for a memorable ride through the foothills of the Boulder Mountains. Galena Lodge is open daily at 9 A.M. to provide breakfasts, lunches and freshly baked sweets. For those who prefer dining on the trail, they will gladly prepare meals that travel well. Beverages include beer, wine, special hot drinks and freshly ground coffee. Evening dining at Galena is an experience unusual in the Ketchum-Sun Valley area. The setting is a hand crafted log lodge with kerosene lighting and warm fires, where groups of 10 or more may reserve for private dining. Cuisines include Scandinavian, Oriental, Middle Eastern, Italian and regional American. For rates, information and trail map, contact: Galena Lodge, Ketchum, ID 83340 (208)726–4010.

★★★*Idaho Rocky Mountain Ranch* is a 1,000–acre cattle and guest ranch surrounded by nearly a million acres of the Sawtooth National Recreation Area. The wild, beautiful Salmon River flows through the ranch lands. Float trips, riding, backpacking, hiking, and fishing are all available in the Sawtooth Recreation Area. The rustic ranch lodge and cabins were built in 1930 from timber on or near the ranch. All the log work was done by hand, and a forge was set up, and the wrought iron hardware and fixtures were fashioned on the site. Accommodations are in log cabins, each with a large stone fireplace, private bath and dressing rooms. Cabin rates (double) are $35 per day. Rooms in the main lodge with private bath are $28.50 (double) per day. Meals are served in the main lodge dining room. The ranch also has a private trout pond and nature hot water swimming pool. Contact: The Idaho Rocky Mountain Ranch, Stanley, ID 83278 (208)774–3544.

★★★*Mountain Village Lodge* offers comfortable, rustic rooms and fine food in the historic Old West town of Stanley, surrounded by the Sawtooth National Recreation Area. The Lodge features panoramic views of the Sawtooth Mountains and large, attractively decorated rooms. Hearty breakfasts, lunches and dinners are served in the Mountain Village Restaurant. Daily room rates (double) are $21. The Lodge provides free bus service to and from the Stanley airport as well as free sightseeing trips of the Sawtooth Recreation Area for guests. They also provide on request special package rates for Salmon River day float trips, cross-country skiing, and wilderness horseback trips in the Sawtooths. Contact: Mountain Village Lodge, Stanley, ID 83278 (208)774–3661.

★★★*Redfish Lake Lodge*, in the heart of the Sawtooth National Recreation Area, offers a variety of accommodations on the headwaters of the main fork of the Salmon River at beautiful Big Redfish Lake. Comfortable rooms in a rustic lodge, two-room cabins, or modern motel accommodations are available Memorial Day through October 15. There is also a fully-equipped Trailer Park with space by the day or week. Fishing for trout, salmon and kokanee or redfish, boating on Redfish Lake, horseback rides in the alpine-like Sawtooth wilderness area, hunting in season for elk, deer and goat, photography safaries, and swimming from a sandy white beach are some of the activities pursued at Redfish Lake Lodge. Lodge room rates are $15–24 double; cabins (2–6 persons) are $28–48. For additional information, write Redfish Lake Lodge, Stanley, Idaho 83278 (208)774–3536.

Sun Valley Ski Village & Summer Resort in the Sawtooth Mountains is one of the West's great year 'round vacation and outdoor recreation meccas. During winter season, Sun Valley is an alpine and cross-country skiers' paradise renowned for its miles of scenic high-country trails, deep powder snow, glistening slopes, mogul fields, and fan-shaped bowls. Dollar/Elkhorn Mountain offers 127 acres of groomed trails and runs for beginning and intermediate skiers; Baldy is the hellish one that rates with the finest mountains in the Alps, with a vertical drop of 3,380 feet and 923 acres of exciting runs and deep powder bowls. Sun Valley services include the sleigh ride out to Trail Creek Cabin, helicopter service and guides for backcountry alpine and nordic trips, a full-service Nordic Ski Center, indoor and outdoor ice skating, and the world-famous Sun Valley Ski School, with some 200 top-ranked instructors who offer the finest professional instruction available. The Sun Valley Nordic Center & Ski School offers one of the most advanced touring programs and instruction in the country, with over 100 miles of touring terrain open free to the public. Other services and facilities include a Play School for children, with hot lunches, ice skating and ski instruction; five restaurants on Dollar and Mt. Baldy; two glass-enclosed swimming pools; pedestrian mall with shops; and plenty of après-ski cocktail lounges, live entertainment, and discotheques, including dancing in the Duchin Room, the Boiler Room, Ram Bar and theatre and concerts in the Opera House. You can even take courses at the lively Sun Valley Arts & Humanities Center. No car is needed here. All your needs are within walking distance and free shuttle transportation is always available. Rustic, alpine resort accommodations are availa-

ble at the two mountain villages, Sun Valley and Elkhorn or the Ranch at Sun Valley. During the summer months Sun Valley offers tennis, golf, kayaking and raft trips on the Big Wood River, mountaineering, superb fly-fishing in alpine lakes and streams, horseback riding, swimming, ice skating, and pack trips in the Challis and Sawtooth national forests' high country. Four-season lodging and accommodations are available at the following Sun Valley resorts:

★★★★*Elkhorn Village Inn & Condominiums*, located one mile south of Ketchum on the high shoulder of Idaho's magnificent Sawtooth Range, is minutes away from Baldy Mountain and its 12 ski lifts via the Elkhorn Ski Shuttle. Elkhorn's triple chairlift serves Elkhorn/Dollar Mountain, just steps away from Elkhorn Village Inn. Cross-country skiing is popular on the foothills surrounding the village. Summer facilities and activities include the 18–hole Robert Trent championship golf course, year-'round ice-skating rink, olympic-sized swimming pool, and tournament-grade tennis courts. Year-round Youth Programs provide supervised activities for children three to eight. Vacation accommodations consist of spacious, attractive double rooms at the 146–room Elkhorn Village Inn or studios, 1, 2, 3, or 4 bedroom apartments in a fully-equipped condominium in Elkhorn Village, each with a kitchen and fireplace. Superb dining is available in Elkhorn's Chart House Restaurant, with cocktails and entertainment. No pets. Daily rates (double) range from $41–130 per person. For additional info, contact: P.O. Box 1067, Sun Valley 83353 (208)622–4511 or toll-free (800)635–9356.

★★★★*Sun Valley Lodge & Inn* built in 1936, is located in the Sawtooth Range one mile north of Ketchum off U.S. Highway 93. Accommodations consist of 500 superb lodge & inn rooms and one to four bedroom housekeeping condominiums in this resort complex. Dining and entertainment are available in the Lodge's elegant Duchin Room. Facilities and services include three heated Olympic-sized pools, sauna, golf course, ice skating rink, supervised children's program, fishing, ski instruction, tennis courts and instruction. Daily rates (double occupancy) range from $39–180/person. For additional info, contact: Sun Valley Lodge, Sun Valley, ID 83353 (208)622–4111.

Sun Valley is one of the West's most accessible resort areas, reached via U.S. Highway 93 at Ketchum and via Key Airlines from Salt Lake City and Boise to Hailey, just 20 minutes from Sun Valley Village. All Hailey arrivals are met by the Sun Valley Taxi-Limo (free) service. Car rentals, bus and limo service is available from the Sun Valley gateways of Boise, Salt Lake City, Twin Falls and Idaho Falls.

Travel Services & The Sawtooth Ski Hut System

Leonard Expeditions & Sawtooth Ski Hut System sponsors cross-country ski touring in the Sawtooth National Recreation Area, a region famous for its varied ski terrain and rugged beauty. Participants can test their skills on flat mountain meadows or 1500–foot powder bowls, and trips are paced (about 5 miles a day) for maximum enjoyment of the scenery with minimal stress to inexperienced skiers. Leonard Expeditions utilizes the unique Sawtooth system of ski huts for overnight touring. Two huts are located at each of the four sites originally scouted by guide Joe Leonard; one has bunk accommodations for eight guests, the other is a cookhouse with tables and chairs. All are comfortable shelters, with lanterns and woodstoves to take the chill off a wintry evening. You have a choice of all-inclusive ski tours (guides, excellent meals, and hut accommodations; $50 per person daily), "cook and carry" tours (you bring your own food, guides included; $25 per person per day), or use of huts without guide services, ($15 per person daily). Guided tent and

snow cave tours in remote stretches of the Sawtooth or White Cloud Mountains, personal guide service, private tours, and complete rentals are also available. For further information, write: Joe & Sheila Leonard, Leonard Expeditions, Box 98, Stanley, ID 83278.

Sun Valley Nordic Ski School & Touring Center is a complete facility for the cross-country buff offering everything from equipment rentals to overnight tours. The touring center is located just north of Ketchum and surrounded by both groomed and unmarked trails perfect for day tours. Sun Valley will give you maps, written instructions and advice on planning your trips. Most tours are geared to beginning and intermediate skiers. Some special offerings of this experienced firm include helicopter ski tours to the back country, a tour to the Devil's Bedstead Guest Ranch for lunch and a helicopter flight back, ridge skiing near Sun Valley, and night ski trips along a lighted course to the Trail Creek Cabin for dinner and dancing. Private lessons by appointment and regularly scheduled class lessons are available. Founder Leif Oldmark, a faculty member of the Sun Valley Health Institute, emphasizes a safe, easy method of cross-country skiing. "If you can walk," he promises, "you can cross-country ski." For more information, write: Sun Valley Nordic Ski Touring Center, Box 272, Sun Valley, ID 83353 (208)622–4111, ext. 2250 or 2251.

Snug Fly Fishing Service, headquartered in Elkhorn and Sun Valley, offers thorough instruction in the art of fly fishing and top-quality guide service on Idaho's renowned trout streams. According to Bill Mason, the firm's resident expert, the aim of the service "is to enhance the enjoyment of fly fishing while protecting the environment by instructing and advising the fisherman about equipment to be used, flies to be tied and waters to be sought according to the type of fishing he or she wants to pursue." Instruction in the above goals is offered through individual classes, half-day on-site seminars, and specific technique seminars. "Classroom" streams include Silver Creek, one of the finest trout streams in the country, and Big Wood River, a free-stone stream near the area's brown trout fishery. Guide services are available on a half- or full-day basis to these and other Sun Valley waters, with instruction offered right on the site. Half-day trips are $65; a full day is $85 for one or two fishermen. Rates include guide, lunch, and transportation. For information on both the Bill Mason Fly Fishing School and Snug's guide services, write: Snug Fly Fishing Service, Snug Company, P.O. Box 598, Sun Valley, ID 83353 (208)622–9305.

The Snug Company sponsors guided hikes and rock climbing adventures in the beautiful alpine wilderness surrounding Idaho's Sun Valley. Guided hikes in groups of two to ten persons ($17–20 per climber for day hikes) explore the little known backcountry and lead to mountain lakes, old mining towns, meadows, and other scenic areas. Overnight backpacking trips ($45–65 per person) are also available to some of the country's most beautiful valleys, rivers, and hidden alpine lakes. In addition the guide service offers a complete climbing school with professional instruction covering all aspects of the sport, from use of knots to rope handling to safety and technique. Basic through advanced courses are conducted at reasonable rates. For schedules and complete information, write: The Snug Company, P.O. Box 598, Sun Valley, ID 83353.

Snake River Birds of Prey Natural Area

The Snake River Birds of Prey Natural Area covers 31,000 acres of the Snake River Canyon surrounded by deserts and fields in southwestern Idaho. The canyon's pinnacles and rocky ledges attract more raptorial (meat-eating) birds than any other area of similar size in the country. Eagles, ospreys, falcons, owls, and hawks glide the canyons and hunt the fields. Of these magnificent birds, the golden eagle and the prairie falcon are the most abundant.

Near the river grow willow rushes and other water plants. Further away from the banks through the desert and fields, shrubs and grasses predominate. The birds of prey compete with coyotes and bobcats for the rodents and rabbits on which they feed. The golden eagles and great horned owls occupy the area year-round. Prairie falcons arrive late in February, after the owls and eagles have begun to nest. Most wintering raptors arrive earlier, in November or December. The American rough-legged hawk, which nests far to the north in Canada and Alaska, occupies this area in January, as do sparrow hawks, North American falcons, goshawks, bald eagles, and ospreys.

The birds of prey share their nesting grounds here with a variety of other wildlife, including mule deer, beaver, mink, waterfowl, and a variety of smaller birds. All of the raptors are completely protected under the Migratory Bird Treaty Act, the Bald Eagle Protection Act, and the Endangered Species Act. No discharging of firearms is allowed here between March 1 and August 31.

The communities of Boise, Nampa, Grand View, and Bruneau offer accommodations near the area. There are campsites at Bruneau Sand Dunes State Park and at the C.J. Strike Cove Site Recreation Area between Grand View and Bruneau. Summers here are hot,

often reaching to 100° or more. During the winter the temperatures rarely drop below zero.

Information Sources, Maps & Access

Although most visitors come to the area to see the birds, it is also used by hunters and fishermen. A free *Snake River Birds of Prey Natural Area Map* shows each of the species of the area in full color and describes them in detail. The map shows roads, power lines, historic trails, canyon rims, and springs. For the map brochure or other information about the area, write: Manager, Birds of Prey Natural Area, Boise District Office, Bureau of Land Management, U.S. Department of the Interior, 230 Collins Road, Boise 83702. The area is reached via Idaho 78 off Interstate 80.

Gateways & Accommodations

Nampa

(Pop. 25,000; zip code 83651; area code 208) in southwest Idaho, its the business center of Canyon County in the heart of the Treasure Valley farming region. Accommodations: *Best Western Desert Inn* (rates: $25.75–32 double), with 40 excellent rooms and family units, near restaurant, south of town on U.S. 30 (467–1161).

Targhee National Forest & The Henrys Lake Country

This 1,700,000–acre forest, famous for its fishing, backpacking, canoeing, hunting, and wilderness camping, forms a great semicircle around the headwaters of the Snake River near the western borders of Yellowstone and Grand Teton national parks. It encompasses the mountains and valleys north from the Grand Canyon of the Snake and the crest of the Teton peaks and west to the Little Lost River, and includes the nationally renowned trophy trout waters of Henrys Lake and Henrys Fork of the Snake—one of the great historic trout streams, considered by many to be the best dry-fly stream in the West. Henrys Fork is the largest spring-fed creek in the world. The forest extends north and south from the Continental Divide to the Upper Snake River Valley. Lodgepole pine dominates the densely wooded river region, intermixed with stands of alpine and Douglas fir and Engelmann spruce. The high-country slopes and meadows are resplendent with colorful wildflowers in late spring and summer.

The famous trout waters of Henrys Lake lie nestled at 6,500 feet elevation beneath the Red Rock, Reynolds, Targhee, and Boot Jack mountain passes, surrounded by evergreen forests. This mountain-fed lake is a vestige of the lakes of the Pliocene period, which then filled valleys throughout the region. When the ancient Indian tribes inhabited the lands of the forest, mysterious islands composed of a spongy grass-covered substance periodically rose and sank in the lake. According to legend, the Indians refused to explore these islands for many years before they decided to use them as burial grounds. The Indians believed that by the time the scaffolds erected for the dead sank, the souls of the dead Indians would be free from worldly cares. Over the years the burial grounds would sink and reappear

from the clear, warm spring-fed waters of the lake, bearing their haunting burden of the dead. Henrys Lake, which lies northwest of the headwaters of Henrys Fork at Big Springs, has excellent fishing for brook, cutthroat, and rainbow trout in the 5 to 15–pound class. The lake's warm spring-fed waters are rich in insect life and provide blue-ribbon fly-fishing for large cutthroats and brook trout. (Use dragonfly and shrimp nymph imitations.) Due south as the crow flies, Island Park Reservoir, at 6,300 feet, is an outstanding producer of big brook and hybrid trout and coho and kokanee salmon. Several Forest Service campgrounds dot the scenic shoreline of Island Park.

The Snake River System, perhaps the finest trout fishery in the Rocky Mountain region, is the area's foremost attraction. Henrys Fork, particularly the famous Railroad Ranch stretch, is famous for its big rainbows, cutthroats, and browns, with fish in the 10–12 pound class always a possibility. Below the Ashton Reservoir Dam, Henrys Fork annually yields 10–pounders to experienced fly fishermen. Nymphs, fished in September or early October, are the bill of fare for the lunker trout. The main Snake River is well known for its excellent smallmouth bass fishing, as well as for channel catfish, and sturgeon up to 400 pounds.

The Snake River is the most popular waterway in the forest for rafting, canoeing, and kayaking. The North Fork (Henrys Fork) of the Snake crosses the northeastern portion of the forest in a generally placid course with some white-water stretches. The South Fork of the Snake forms the border between Targhee and adjacent forests along the south and southeast. The canyon of the South Fork offers exciting white waters. Both forks of the river are floated by commercial outfitters and private parties. There are no fees, permits, or formal restrictions on use of the river by private parties. Before you set out on a float trip, however, contact experienced river runners in the area or a Forest Service Office to obtain current conditions and detailed information.

The Targhee is the home of Idaho's largest moose herd, and the state's largest antelope herd is found in and adjacent to the forest in the Birch Creek Area. A few protected silver-tip grizzlies and bighorn sheep inhabit the remote high-country areas. The Island Park area, including Henrys Fork of the Snake River, is one of the two most important wintering areas in the United States for the trumpeter swan.

Numerous wilderness trails lead to such scenic and interesting areas as Sawtell Peak (9,902 ft.) and the renowned Alaska Basin, characterized by its raw peaks, alpine lakes, and wildflower meadows. Access to the Alaska Basin is by trail from the Grand Teton National Park or from the end of the canyon road east of Driggs.

Although there are no formally classified wilderness areas within the forest, the quiet magnificence of the forest offers backpacking and hiking trips varying from short, easy treks to extended backpacking over steep, rugged trails challenging to the most experienced backpacker. The west slope of the Tetons provides spectacular back-country scenery.

Three ski areas with excellent skiing terrain and snow conditions serve the forest area—Kelly Canyon, Bear Gulch, and Grand Targhee. Cross-country skiing is gaining popularity, although there are no marked cross-country trails in the forest. Other winter activities include snowshoeing, sledding, and snowmobiling (trails available).

Camping areas dot the forest's mountain slopes, canyons, lakeshores, and riverbanks. The camping areas on the main highway to Yellowstone Park have better facilities and attractive settings, but they are usually filled to capacity by early evening in summer. More primitive and secluded camping areas lie within the forest interior. July, August, and September are the best camping months; June may bring a light snow.

Information Sources, Maps & Access

For detailed vacation travel, fishing, backpacking, and cross-country skiing information and a full-color *Targhee National Forest Map* (50¢), contact: Supervisor, Targhee National Forest, St. Anthony, ID 83445 (208)624–3151. The major routes to Targhee National Forest are U.S. Highways 191/20 and 26, Interstate 15, and Idaho Routes 47, 84, 31, 32, 33 and A2. Lodging, resorts, cabins, supplies, boat and canoe rentals, guides, packers, and outfitters are available at Island Park, Lake, Ashton, Drummond, Lamont, Felt, Tetonia, Driggs, St. Anthony, Rexburg, Swan Valley, Alpine, Idaho Falls, and Jackson, Wyoming.

Gateways & Accommodations

For additional listings, see "West Yellowstone, Montana."

Ashton—Gateway to Henrys Fork & Island Park

(Pop. 1,200; zip code 83420; area code 208) is a major jumping-off point for trips to Henrys Lake, Big Springs and Railroad Ranch section of the Henrys Fork, Bear Gulch Ski Basin, Falls River, and the Bechler River-Cascade Corner region of Yellowstone National Park (which see). Big Springs on the Henrys Fork of the Snake, the world's largest spring-fed river, has an average flow of 185 feet per second with a constant temperature of 52°. Big Springs is a refuge for giant rainbow trout, some up to 20 lbs. and more, which can be viewed from the Big Springs Bridge. Henrys Lake lies due northeast surrounded by the towering peaks of the Great Divide. Campgrounds are available at Henrys Lake State Park. Accommodations: *Four Seasons Motel* (rates: $17–21 double), with 13 good rooms and family units, just east of town at 112 E. Main St. (652–7769).

Blackfoot

(Pop. 8,700; zip code 83221; area code 208) is a southern gateway off Interstate 15 adjacent to the Fort Hall Indian Reservation. Area attractions include the Snake River and American Falls Reservoir. Accommodations: *Best Western Riverside Inn* (rates: $25–28 double), with 80 good rooms and family units, restaurant, cocktail lounge, off 1–15N Blackfoot exit (785–5000).

Driggs—Teton Basin Gateway

(Pop. 700; zip code 83422; area code 208) flanked on the east by the spectacular Teton Range, is the seat of Teton County and the business center of the Teton Basin—once known as Pierre's Hole, a famous rendezvous spot for mountain men and fur traders during the 1930's and 40's. The town has a District Ranger's Office of the Targhee National Forest. The Targhee Resort Ski Area is located on the west slope of the Tetons, 12 miles to the east of Driggs in Alta, WY (353–2308). Accommodations: *Best Western Teton West Motor Inn* (rates: $23–28 double), with 23 good rooms and family units on Idaho 33 at 476 N. Main St. (354–2363).

Rexburg

(Pop. 9,700; zip code 83440; area code 208) is the major farming and trade center in the Upper Snake River Valley north of Idaho Falls. Accommodations: *Best Western Fantastic Inn* (rates: $26–28 double), with 104 excellent rooms and family units, restaurant, coffeeshop, heated pool on U.S. 20 & 191 at 450 W. 4th St. (356–4646).

St. Anthony—Gateway to the Henrys Fork

(Pop. 3,000; zip code 83445; area code 208) is the headquarters of the Targhee National Forest and a major gateway to the Henrys Fork-Henrys Lake Country and the Bechler River Region of Yellowstone National Park. The old Fort Henry fur-trading post was located near here along the Henrys Fork. Accommodations: *Best Western Riverview Motel* (rates: $25–29 double), with 30 excellent rooms and family units, restaurant, in center of town on U.S. 20 and 191 (624–3711).

Lodges & Resorts

★★★★*Targhee Ski & Summer Resort*, situated high in the Teton Range one hour west of Jackson Hole, is one of the West's finest winter and summer resort areas. This year 'round resort offers wide open slopes for the novice and intermediate skier, with groomed and powder runs, and steep, deep powder for the experts. Activities include cross-country skiing and instruction on Teton Trails, summer ski racing camps, sleigh rides, camping, backpacking, soaring, photography, fishing and scenic flights over Grand Teton and Yellowstone national parks. The resort complex features lodge and condominium accommodations adjacent to the ski lifts, restaurant, outdoor heated pool, ski shop and school, cocktail lounge, movies, entertainment, ski rentals and repairs, and shuttle bus service between Jackson and Idaho Falls—the two major air gateways. Accommodations in the resort complex are available at:

Targhee Lodge, located at the ski resort within 30 yards of lifts, steak house, cafeteria, bar, and all resort facilities and services. Each of 15 rooms has twin queen beds and color TV.

Teewinot Lodge, located at the ski resort within 50 yards of lifts, steak house, cafeteria, bar, and all resort facilities and services. Each of 48 rooms has twin queen beds and color TV.

Sioux Lodge Apts, located at the ski resort within 50 yards of lifts, steak house, cafeteria, bar, and all resort facilities and services. Studio unit has a small sleeping room, living room, kitchenette, fireplace, TV. Studio with loft bedroom unit also has sleeping room, bunks, living room, kitchenette, fireplace, TV. Two bedroom unit has a bedroom and a sleeping room, living room, kitchenette, fireplace, TV.

Low season rates (based on double occupancy) range from $105–152 per person. Regular season rates (March-April, double) are $130–164 per person. For detailed information, contact: Targhee Ski & Summer Resort, Alta, WY via Driggs, ID 83422 (307)353–2304.

★★★*Teton Teepee*, a family-centered resort for the ski buff, is located five miles from Grand Targhee Ski Resort on the western side of the awesome Grand Tetons. The handsome lodge, located about 10 miles east of Driggs, Idaho, accommodates 92 guests, with a special dormitory for children. Nearby Grand Targhee Ski School offers expert instruction in powder skiing on acres of open terrain. Teton Teepee also features a free professional ski school. Gourmet western cooking and a full range of après-ski activities are additional attractions. Three, 5 and 7 day packages are available; prices include lodging, meals, transportation to and from the ski areas, lift passes and all lodge facilities. For rates and information, write: Melehes' Teton Teepee, Alta, Wyoming 83422 (307)353–8176.

Travel Services

Henrys Fork Anglers, Inc. located in Harriman State Park, is headquarters for varied fishing opportunities on 50 miles of the spring-fed Henrys Fork of the Snake River, Henrys Lake, and in the Yellowstone region. Everything from custom-tied flies and top-quality equipment to seasoned advice is available here, all expressly tailored to the western angling environment. The season begins with the late May salmon fly emergence that extends into Box Canyon in mid-June. By early June, extensive mayfly and caddis activity is underway; then dry fly and Hopper fishing continues throughout the remainder of the summer and into October. In addition to fine tackle and equipment, Henrys Fork Anglers offers expert guide service, backed by 25 years of know-how, on the Henrys Fork as well as on other famous lakes and streams in the Yellowstone Area. Either walk-wade or float fishing guided trips are available. Rates are $80 per day for one angler; $95 for two or three. For more information, write: Henrys Fork Anglers, Inc., Box 487, St. Anthony, ID 83445 (summer) (208)558–7525; winter (208)624–3595.

Red Baron, at Teton Peaks Airport in eastern Idaho, sponsors scenic glider rides over the Grand Tetons and Targhee Resort, as well as local, 20–minute glider rides—billed as "a great introduction to soaring." Glider rides are guided by experienced pilots who will be happy to demonstrate the controls and even let you handle them at your request. Red Baron also offers glider instruction and rentals, "soaring vacations" with visits to Grand Teton and Yellowstone National Parks, scenic flights in powered aircraft, commercial air charter, and flight instruction. Located 32 miles from Jackson and 74 miles from Idaho Falls. For details, write Red Baron, Teton Peaks Airport, Driggs, ID 83422 (208)354–8131.

Teton Expeditions offers a broad variety of outdoor adventures in the most scenic areas of the Idaho wilderness. White-water float trips of five to six days in length are offered along the Selway, Salmon, and Middle fork of the Salmon rivers, with challenging fishing along the way for rainbow, cutthroat, steelhead, and salmon. There are also one to two day river trips along the gentle Teton, turbulent Blackfoot, and north fork of the Snake rivers. Horseback pack trips are offered through the remote mountain valleys and lush forests of the Sawtooth Recreation Area, Big Horn Crags, Grand Tetons, and Idaho Primitive Area. Guides for these adventures are expert boatmen with a minimum of six years of river experience and extensive knowledge of the Idaho wilderness. Cost varies with the nature and length of your trip: 5–6 day river adventures are $325 per person; one-day float trips, $20 per person; and 5–day Teton trail rides, $220 per person. Teton Expeditions supplies all food, safety equipment, and most camping supplies. For full descriptions of each adventure, write: Teton Expeditions, Inc., 427 E. 13th St., Idaho Falls, ID 83401 (208)523–4981 or 523–3872.

Yellowstone National Park

See "Wyoming" chapter for detailed description.

Iowa

Introduction

Iowa's lakes, streams, woodlands, rolling uplands, bluffs, big river oxbows and floodplain sloughs, marshes, and crop fields offer a surprising diversity of outdoor recreation opportunities. The Hawkeye State lies wholly within the prairie region and contains 56,290 square miles bordered on the north by Minnesota; on the west by Nebraska and the Big Sioux and Missouri Rivers; on the east by Wisconsin, Illinois, and the Mississippi River; and on the south by Missouri.

Accommodations & Travel Information

For accommodations information in the Hawkeye state, contact Development Commission, 250 Jewett Bldg., Des Moines 50309 (515)281–3100 or the local Chamber of Commerce of the area you plan to visit. Some state park and recreation areas offer modern family cabins, each of which can house 4 persons with ease. Electricity, water, dishes, cooking utensils, refrigerator, and kitchen stove are included with each cabin; the renter must provide bedding, pillows, towels, and personal items. Reservations must be made through the park ranger; reservations for a minimum of a week are accepted. Cabins are rented for stays of less then 1 week on a first-come, first-served basis. The number of cabins available in each area is as follows: Backbone, 18; Lacey-Keosauqua, 6; Lake of Three Fires, 6; Lake Walleop, 12; Pine Lake, 4; Palisades-Kepler, 4; and Springbrook, 6. Palisades-Kepler has two cabins that can each accommodate 8. State park and recreation area camping sites are located in scenic areas throughout the state. For complete information on facilities of each state park or recreation area, consult the useful brochure *Iowa State Parks and Recreation Areas*, available free from: Conservation Commission, 300 4th St., Des Moines 50309 (515)281–5145. There is a convenient chart listing each recreation area, its mailing address, telephone number, highway location, and available facilities. The same information is also provided for the state forests. The areas are location-keyed to a map, and the brochure includes a chart describing the areas of the state preserve system. There is a section of rules and regulations, and information on reservations for the camping and recreational facilities.

Highways & Maps

The motorist traveling through Iowa should obtain a copy of the *Official Iowa Highway Map* which is distributed free by the State Highway Commission, 826 Lincoln Way, Ames 50010. The map shows all major roads and highways, both existing and proposed. It also indicates route markers that indicate different types of roads. Recreational facilities are also shown, such as state parks with and without camping, state and U.S. fish hatcheries, information centers, travel trailer disposal stations, scenic areas, and points of interest where local inquiry is advisable. A distance table showing mileage between major cities and towns is provided, and there is a chart showing state parks and recreation areas and the facilities provided in each.

Iowa Lakes, Streams & Recreation Areas

The 50 natural glacial lakes in northwest Iowa, known as the Iowa Great Lakes region, offer some of the best fishing in the central United States for smallmouth and largemouth bass, northern pike, channel catfish, white bass, yellow perch, walleye, crappie, and a few elusive muskellunge up to trophy weights in West Okoboji and Clear Lakes. The best fishing is found over the weed beds and brush piles and along the rocky shorelines, reefs, and sandbars in Spirit, East and West Okoboji, Clear, Storm, Silver, Trumbull, North Twin, Pine, Briggs Woods, Swan, Badger, Beeds, Arrowhead, Black Hawk, Crystal, Five Island, Upper and Lower Gar, and Little Spirit lakes. Beautiful Spirit Lake is a top-ranked walleye fishery with fish taken up to 14 pounds. For specific information on Iowa's Great Lake region, write: Spirit Lake Fish Hatchery, Spirit Lake 51360. The upland lakes and streams of northeast Iowa, known as "Little Switzerland," offer the state's top-ranked smallmouth bass and trout fishing. The Upper Iowa River, proposed for inclusion in the National Wild & Scenic River System, holds smallmouth bass up to 6 pounds, brown and rainbow trout, white bass, walleye, and channel catfish. The Upper Iowa flows past limestone bluffs, including the massive 200–foot Chimney Rocks, and several beautiful tributary trout streams such as Coldwater and Canoe Creeks. The Turkey and Big Wapsipinicon and Maquoketa rivers contain a wide variety of fish including smallmouth bass, northern pike, walleye, channel catfish, and crappie. The Elk Creek tributary of the Turkey River produced the state record 12–pound 14½ ounce brown trout. The farm ponds and lakes of the region—including Backbone, Fontana, Cedar Falls, Hendricks, Meyers, Hickory Hills, Sabula, and Sweet Marsh—hold largemouth bass, crappie, northern pike, and channel cats. The tailrace waters beneath the hydroelectric cams yield walleye, smallmouths, channel cats, and a few large northern pikes. The big impoundments and rivers of central and southern Iowa yield largemouth bass, northern pike, crappie, and large catfish. The 11,000–acre Rathbun Reservoir on the Chariton River, known as "Iowa's ocean," has been stocked with muskellunge and striped bass from South Carolina's Santee-Cooper Reservoir. Lake Geode consistently yields bunker largemouth bass in the 5–8 pound class. The big inland rivers yield northern pike, channel catfish, carp, walleye, and bullhead. The North Raccoon and scenic Middle Raccoon and Upper Des Moines and Iowa rivers yield smallmouth bass. Northern pike up to trophy weights are taken from the upper reaches of the Des Moines, Little Sioux, Winnebago, Iowa, Shell Rock, and Cedar rivers. The state's mighty boundary rivers, the Big Sioux and Missouri rivers on the west and the Mississippi on the east, with their numerous lakes, oxbows, sloughs, and backwaters, yield giant catfish, walleye, sauger, largemouth bass, and hordes of crappies and bluegills. The Hawkeye State ranks among the nation's leading pheasant, quail, and goose hunting states. It also offers excellent hunting for deer, squirrels, cottontails, and mallards. Some of the best pheasant shooting is found in the "Cash Grain" region of central Iowa. There are red fox, Hungarian partridge, raccoons, crows, jackrabbits, and a few coyotes and wild turkey in the eastern woodlands. Cornfield mallard shooting is popular late in the waterfowl season. Small crop fields, timbered creek bottoms, and brushy draws generally produce excellent hunting for upland game birds. The state's numerous rivers and streams provide excellent wood duck hunting early in the season. The Missouri River country is one of the nation's prime hunting areas for snow geese and rafts of mallards, teal, wood duck, widgeon, and gadwall. One of the most scenic hunting areas in the state is the White Pine Hollow Preserve in the extreme northwest corner of Dubuque County. It has been designated as a National Natural Landmark because of its virgin

VACATION/ LODGING GUIDE

stands of white pine, large cold-air slopes of Canada yew, and the rare monkshood. The White Pine Hollow has a stable population of whitetail deer and ruffed grouse as well as pheasants along the forest borders.

Information Sources, Maps & Access

The Iowa Conservation Commission publishes several free fishing and hunting guides, maps, and booklets, including *Iowa Fishing Regulations, Iowa Trout Maps, Iowa Mammals, Common Wildlife Tracks, Iowa Hunting & Trapping Laws, Public Hunting Areas, Upland Game Bird Hunting, Iowa Deer Hunting, Pheasant & Quail Distribution Maps, Deer Distribution Map, Red Rock Game Management Map, Bays Branch Public Hunting Area, Duck Point System Sheet, Lake Odessa Public Hunting Area, Iowa Woodland Flowers, Iowa Prairies, Simple Key to Iowa Trees, Yellow River Forest, Missouri River Spring Goose Migration, Stephens State Forest, Shimek State Forest, Boating Regulations*, and *Mississippi River Boating Facilities Guide*. The 31–page *Iowa Fishing Guide* (50¢) contains detailed descriptions of the state's major lakes, streams, and reservoirs as well as maps and charts. The Conservation Commission also publishes a free *Iowa Trout Fishing Guide*, which shows and lists all trout streams by county. The 35–page *Iowa Hunting Guide* (25¢) contains maps and indepth descriptions of the waterfowl flyways and the Big Sioux, Ingham High, Rice Lake, Upper Iowa, Ruthven, Big Marsh, Sweet Marsh, Missouri River, Blackhawk, Saylorville, Otter Creek, Maquoketa, Bays Branch, Red Rock, Coralville, Riverton, Mount Ayr, Rathbun, Wapello, and Odessa wildlife management units. The publications listed above and free maps of the *Big Sioux, Mount Ayr*, and *Otter Creek* wildlife management units may be ordered from: Conservation Commission, 300 4th St., Des Moines 50309. The following lake contour fishing maps showing depth and major hydrographic features may be purchased for $1 each by writing: Conservation Commission, Information and Education Section, 300 4th St., Des Moines 50309; *Clear Lake Depth Map, Storm Lake Depth Map, East Okoboji Depth Map, West Okoboji Depth Map, Spirit Lake Depth Map*, and *Rathbun Depth Map*. You can also obtain the following free: *Chartered Maps of Iowa Lakes, List of Artificial and Natural Lakes, Meandering Rivers, Rathbun Reservoir Recreation Map, Red Rock Recreation Map*, and *Guide to Iowa Great Lakes*. Small topo maps of the following lakes are available free upon request from the Iowa Conservation Commission (address above): Silver, East Okoboji, West Okoboji, Lost Island, Clear, Spirit, Five Island, Storm, North Twin, Upper and Lower Gar, Black Hawk, Meadow, Anita, Red Hawk, Ahquabi, Wapello, Geode, Little Spirit, Nine Eagles, Keomah, Iowa, Big Creek. The major auto routes serving the Hawkeye State include Interstate Highways 35, 80, and 29.

Lodges & Resorts

Iowa has a limited number of full-service vacation lodges and resorts. For detailed accommodations information, contact: Iowa Development Commission, 250 Jewett Bldg., Des Moines, IA 50309 (515)281–3100. For rates and reservations for Iowa's state park cabin system, contact: Conservation Commission, 300 4th St., Des Moines, IA 50309 (515)281–5145.

KANSAS

Introduction

The Sunflower State's rolling hills and grasslands, broad valleys, woodlands, and large impoundments boast some excellent hunting for deer, waterfowl, and upland game birds and fishing for largemouth bass, walleye, northern pike, transplanted striped bass up to 20 pounds and over, and giant catfish. Topographically the state is divided into three natural regions: the High Plains of the west, the Great Bend Prairie or Low Plains in the center of the state, and the beautiful Flint Hills region, or Bluestem Belt in the east, with its picturesque, rolling uplands interspersed with limestone bluffs. In the central region lie the Smoky Hills and Blue Hills uplands. South of the prairie region are the heavily eroded cliffs and terraces of the Cimarron Breaks, bordering the Cimarron River. The treeless High Plains were formed by the course of ancient streams that flowed eastward from the Rocky Mountains and deposited huge loads of gravel and debris. Major rivers include the great Missouri along the northeastern boundary, the Kansas and its tributaries, the Big Blue, Solomon, Republican, and Smoky Hill; the Neosho and its tributaries, the Cottonwood and Fall; and the Arkansas and its feeders, the Pawnee, Little Arkansas, Minnescah, Walnut, Rattlesnake, and Whitewater.

Accommodations & Travel Information

For information on hotels, motels, campsites, or whatever type of accommodation you are seeking, write to: Dept. of Economic Development, State Office Bldg., Topeka 66612 (913)296–3481 or to the local Chamber of Commerce where you plan to visit. Campers in Kansas should obtain a copy of the helpful free brochure *Camping & Campsites*, which lists and describes campsites, noting facilities available at each area, outstanding recreational activities, and the best approach by car. The exact location of each campsite is shown on a map that marks the highway routes leading to the areas. A handy chart showing federal lakes, recreation areas, and facilities is provided, and explicit auto route approaches are also given. A chart of state fishing lakes, state parks, and recreation areas is shown and details the facilities available at each area. A list of safety rest areas is provided, as well as rules and regulations governing forestry, fish and game, state parks, and motor vehicle information. You can write to: Dept. of Economic Development, State Office Bldg., Topeka 66612, for your copy. For fishing and hunting information, contact: Forestry, Fish & Game Commission, Box 1028, Pratt, KS 67124 (316)672–5911.

Highways & Maps

A free official *Kansas Highway Map* showing all major roads, highways, campgrounds, points of interest, and natural features may be obtained by writing: Dept. of Economic Development, State Office Bldg., Topeka 66612. The free map-guide *Frontier Trails of Kansas* may be obtained from the same address. This interesting publication shows and describes the state's historic exploration and pioneer routes, and the location of historic markers along major auto routes. The frontier trails described include the famous Chisholm Trail, named after Jesse Chisholm, an Indian trader who first marked it for his wagons—beginning in 1867 it became the major cattle trail to the Abilene stockyards; Lewis and Clark Trail, which traces the expedition's trail through Kansas to the mouth of the Kansas River and up the Missouri—the gateway to the northern Rockies and the Lolo Trail to the Columbia River and the Pacific Ocean; the Oregon Trail, which beginning in the early 1840s was known to westward-bound trappers as the Rocky Mountain Trail, to Mormons as the Great Salt Lake Trail, and to gold seekers as the California Trail; Pony Express Route, which carried mail overland from St. Joseph,

Missouri, to Sacramento, California, in 10 days, using a system of 9–to15–mile relays; and the Santa Fe Trail, which opened the great Southwest. The map-guide also shows and describes the state's major historic sites, including the beautiful Flint Hills and the last remaining expanses of native tall-grass prairies, which at one time covered 400,000 square miles of the United States; Dodge City, "Queen of the Cow Towns" and Boot Hill Cemetery; and the Pawnee Indian Village Museum at Republic.

Kansas Lakes, Streams & Wildlife Areas

Several lakes in the northeastern corner of the state provide excellent fishing for walleye, largemouth bass, crappie, and white bass including 6,930–acre Melvern Reservoir, on the Marais des Cygnes River south of Topeka; beautiful 12,600–acre Perry Reservoir on the Delaware River—one of the top channel catfish streams in the state; 4,000–acre Pomona Reservoir, with its submerged timber, coves, flats, and rocky bluffs; 15,800–acre Tuttle Creek Reservoir in the Big Blue River Valley—one of the nation's top crappie fisheries, with its jagged 112–mile shoreline outlined by dead timber and hidden coves, and the Deep Creek and Rocky Ford state fishing areas. In the southeast region of the state, fishermen will find crappie, white bass, largemouth bass, channel catfish, and a few striped bass in 4,400–acre Elk City Reservoir, with its 50 miles of shoreline ranging from steep, wooded slopes to rolling grasslands and big channel and flathead catfish, white bass, and crappie in 9,400–acre John Redmond Reservoir on the Neosho River, nestled in the scenic Fling Hills. The Fling Hills National Wildlife Refuge is located on the upper end of the lake. Other fishing lakes in the southeast include the Lake Crawford State Park, Marais des Cygnes Waterfowl Management Area, Neosho Waterfowl Management Area, strip-mine lakes scattered throughout Linn, Crawford, Bourbon, and Cherokee counties, and the Big Hill Lakes. In the north central portion of the state are the V-shaped 3,280 acres of Council Grove Reservoir, offering 27 miles of shoreline and fishing for white bass, catfish, crappie, and walleye—particularly below the dam in the outlet waters. The 3,550–acre Kanopolis Reservoir in the Smoky Hill River Valley, with its Indian rock carvings and fossils, holds huge schools of white bass and crappie, as well as walleye, flathead, and channel catfish. Other major fisheries in the north central area include Lovewell Reservoir; huge 16,187–acre Milford Reservoir on the Republican River—one of the state's top-ranked striped bass lakes, with a large population of white bass and crappie; beautiful 12,586–acre Waconda (Glen Elder) Reservoir on the Solomon River, featuring 100 miles of scenic shoreline and striped bass fishing; and 9,000–acre Wilson Reservoir, with its jagged 100–mile boulder-strewn shoreline and top-ranked crappie, white bass, walleye, largemouth bass, and striper fishing. In south central Kansas, the sprawling 9,500–acre Cheney Reservoir, 20 miles west of Wichita, home of the state record 33–pound 12–ounce striped bass, provides good fishing for largemouth bass, crappie, and channel catfish, in addition to trophy-sized stripers. The 2,600–acre Fall River Reservoir is noted for the large early spring migration of white bass up its Otter Creek and Fall River feeders. The 6,160–acre Marion Reservoir, with its 60 miles of shoreline nestled in the Cottonwood River Valley, holds a large variety of fish including walleye, white bass, crappie, largemouth bass, channel catfish, and a few blue catfish. Toronto Reservoir, which covers 2,800 acres in the Verdigris River Valley, produced the world record 5–pound 4–ounce white bass. In the High Plains of northwest Kansas lie the crystal-clear, trophy smallmouth bass waters of 6,869–acre Cedar Bluff Reservoir surrounded by jagged 50–mile shoreline. Kirwin Reservoir, which covers 5,080 acres in the Solomon River Valley, is noted for its early spring walleye migration and fishing for white bass, channel catfish, and crappie. The 2,187–acre Norton Reservoir with its 67–mile shoreline provides good fishing for trophy-sized smallmouth bass, crappie, northern pike, walleye, bluegill, and catfish. The 3,445–acre Webster Reservoir is noted for large numbers of big walleye. The major fishing areas in southwest Kansas include numerous state fishing lakes and the Cheyenne Bottoms Lake Meade State Park, Morton County Wildlife Area on the Cimarron Grasslands, and Lake Scott State Park.

The more than 304,000 acres of public hunting and game management lands in Kansas provide excellent uncrowded hunting in season for ducks, geese, doves, bobwhite quail, and pheasant. The Fling Hills country of eastern Kansas contains the largest single concentration of greater prairie chickens in the United States. Squirrel hunting is popular in the eastern regions and along the timbered streams in western Kansas. Other popular small-game species include cottontails, jackrabbits, and crows. Coyote range throughout the state. A growing whitetail deer herd is found along the state's woodland river valleys. The major state game management areas (GMA) include 7,958–acre Cheney GMA, 12,254–acre Cheyenne Bottoms Waterfowl Management Area, 11,834–acre Cedar Bluff GMA, 10,092–acre Fall River GMA, 25,100–acre Glen Elder GMA, 3,353–acre Lovewell GMA, 4,043–acre Kingman GMA, 3,000–acre Kingman Management Area, 15,660–acre Milford GMA, 2,016–acre Neosho Waterfowl Management Area, 4,757–acre Pratt Sandhills GMA, 5,979–acre Strip Pits Wildlife Management Area, and 13,000–acre Tuttle Creek GMA.

Information Sources, Maps & Access

A free 40–page guide, *Fishing in Kansas Lakes & Reservoirs*, may be obtained free upon request from: Forestry, Fish, & Game Commission, Box 1028, Pratt 67124. In addition, the commission publishes free *Kansas Fishing Regulations*, *Hunting Seasons & Regulations*, *Boat & Water Safety Laws*, and *Public Hunting in Kansas* brochures. The major auto routes serving Kansas are Interstate Highways 70, 35, and 135.

Lodges & Resorts

The Sunflower state has few full-service lodges and resorts. For detailed information on quality hotels, and motels, contact: Kansas Dept. of Economic Development, State Office Bldg., Topeka, KS 66612 (913)296–3481.

Introduction

Louisiana's pine and hardwood forests, rolling fields, lakes and reservoirs, beautiful moss-draped cypress bayous and meandering rivers, and the sun-drenched isles, lagoons, reefs, and flats of the Gulf Coast offshore waters offer some of the nation's finest trophy bass fishing, hunting, camping, and saltwater-fishing opportunities.

Accommodations & Travel Information

For information about vacation travel and accommodations in Louisiana, contact: Tourist Development Commission, P.O. Box 44291, Baton Rouge, LA 70804 or call (504)342–4890 for tourist information. The land of forests, rolling fields, scenic moss-hung cypress swamps, bayous, rivers, and lakes provides excellent opportunities for family vacations as well as primitive camping. A guide to all state-park camping areas is contained in the *Louisiana State Parks* brochure, available free upon request from the State Parks & Recreation Commission, P.O. Drawer 1111, Baton Rouge 70821. It also describes recreation facilities in all state-park areas. Free information about fees, facilities, and regulations may be obtained at the same address.

Highways & Maps

The state of Louisiana Dept. of Highways, Baton Rouge 70804, will send you a free *Louisiana State Highway Map*. It shows cities and towns, major and minor roads, route markers and population symbols, access points, mileage between major points, state parks, forests, wildlife preserves, rest areas, boat launching ramps, points of interest, ferries, airports, and campsites. It also includes an index of recreation sites and a mileage table. Close-up maps of New Orleans, Lafayette, Lake Charles, Monroe, Alexandria, Baton Rouge, and Shreveport are provided, as well as detailed close-ups of the Interstate highways entering these cities. A special feature is a chart of highway signs.

LOUISIANA

VACATION/ LODGING GUIDE

Louisiana's Forests, Lakes & Bayou Country

Louisiana's winding bayous, lakes, streams, coastal marches, forests, and rolling fields offer some superb fishing and hunting opportunities. The northern and central regions of the Bayou State are composed of gentle hills, pine forests, and thick pockets of cypress swamps, laced by bayous and dotted with lakes and sprawling reservoirs. Huge 250,000–acre Toledo Bend Reservoir—formed by damming the Sabine River along the Louisiana-Texas border—is the region's major body of water and offers some of the South's top fishing for big largemouth bass and crappie. Toledo Bend is also the state's top striped-bass fishery. The state record 25lb. 4oz. striper was taken here in 1976. Turkey Creek Lake and D'Arbonne Lake are among the most productive trophy bass and crappie lakes in the state. The latter lake also holds striped bass, stocked by the Wildlife and Fisheries Commission. Other top-ranked fishing waters in northern and central Louisiana include 13,500–acre Black Lake, and Chicot, Claiborne, Nantachie, and Vernon lakes. The shallow, cypress-studded backwater lakes and beautiful long, narrow oxbow lakes along the mighty Mississippi, known to the Indians as the "father of waters," provide good fishing for crappie, bream, bass, and catfish. The major fishing waters include the "flats" of False River Lake, noted for their spectacular bluegill fishing, and Bruin, St. John, Providence, and Concordia lakes. Some 850,000 acres of game-management areas in the northern and central regions provide good hunting in season for whitetail deer and small game.

Southern Louisiana has a varied terrain, which includes a region of bayous and swamps in the southeast, the 4–million-acre Atchafalaya Swamp, prairie country in the southwest, and pine forests laced by swift streams north of Lake Pontchartrain. The famous Atchafalaya Swamp (derived from the Choctaw Indian word meaning "long river") has good deer and duck hunting, canoe-camping, and fishing for trophy largemouth bass, crappie, and bream in Henderson, Catahoula, Grand, Dauterive, and Six-mile lakes and in Bayou Sorrel, Little Bayou Pigeon, Big Bayou Pigeon, the Upper Grand River, and in countless named and unnamed bayous to the west of the Atchafalaya River. Detailed topo maps are a must in this labyrinth of islands, bayous, and unmarked trails. The clear, fast-flowing streams of the bayous in the Florida parishes, located north of lakes Maurepas and Pontchartrain, provide good fishing for spotted bass, warmouth, rock bass, crappie, and catfish. Some excellent float fishing, using live bait such as shiners, night crawlers, crawfish, and crickets, or joined surface lures and Rapala-type lures, may be found in the Amite River, Bayou Sara, Bayou Lacombe, and the Blind, Natallany, Pearl, Pushepatapa, Tanipahoa, Tchefuncte, and Tickfaw rivers.

The coastal marshes of Louisiana provide superb duck and goose shooting, plus fishing in the brackish tidal inlets and bays for speckled trout, redfish, and flounder. The major inland coastal fishing areas include the Sabine, Lacassine, and Rockefeller wildlife refuges; Calcasieu Lake, noted for its superb speckled-trout fishing; and the Pointau-Chien, Salvador, Wiener, Biloxi, and Bohemia wildlife management areas in the southeast. The offshore waters of the Gulf of Mexico offer red snapper, cobia, bluefish, African pompano, dolphin, tarpon, amberjack, Spanish and hing mackerel, particularly around the oil-drilling platforms, which serve as a natural sanctuary for bait fish. Trophy billfish ride the "Loop" current each summer across the gulf. The major charter-boat centers for offshore fishing along the gulf shore are headquartered at Grand Isle, Empire, and Cameron.

The coastal lakes, grain fields, wooded swamps, marshes, and rivers of Louisiana form the major wintering area for ducks and geese east of the Rocky Mountains. Whitetail deer are found throughout the state, with the prime hunting grounds found in the hardwood deltas along the Mississippi and Atchafalaya rivers and in the central and northwest pine-woods areas. The greatest concentrations of wild turkey are found in the forested Florida parishes (counties) and northeast parishes along the Mississippi River. Bobwhite quail range throughout the state, with the best wing shooting found in the cutover pine woods in the south-central region. Louisiana is the major wintering area of the North American woodcock—also known as the "timberdoodle" or, locally, as the "bec." Woodcock range throughout the state, particularly in the forested areas with wet soils, where they probe with their long bills for earthworms. Other popular bird and game species include gray and fox squirrels, swamp and cottontail rabbits, and waterfowl. 595,000–acre forest reserve varies in terrain from dark, cathedral-like cypress swamps with hanging moss to the famous sandstone Kisatchie Hills. The forest—which encompasses the Cloud Crossing Recreation Area, Saline Lake, Kincaid Reservoir, Saline Bayou, and the Catahoula, Fort Polk, and Red Dirt game management areas in central Louisiana—provides excellent opportunities for fishing, hunting, canoeing, camping, and backpacking.

Information Sources, Maps & Access

For fishing and hunting information and regulations, write to the Wildlife and Fisheries Commission, 400 Royal St., New Orleans 70130. The commission publishes the following free fishing and hunting guides: a 39–page *Guide to Fishing in Louisiana*, a comprehensive illustrated guide to the major fishing areas and species; and a 67–page illustrated *Guide to Hunting in Louisiana*, which provides descriptions of game species and all state wildlife-management areas. The *Kisatchie National Forest Recreation Map*, available for 50¢ from the Forest Supervisor, Kisatchie National Forest, 2500 Shreveport Highway, Pineville 71360, shows major and minor roads, parish and state lines, landing fields, boat ramps, rest areas, points of interest, hunting camps, district ranger stations, lookout stations, campgrounds, and work centers. It also includes a recreation-site facilities index and a general description of the area. The forest is reached via U.S. highways 71, 165, 167, and 84, and Louisiana state highways 19, 21, and 28. Overnight accommodations, supplies, and equipment rentals are available at Alexandria, Leesville, Minden, and Winnfield. The forest is shown on the following U.S. Geological Survey 1:250,000–scale Topographic Maps: Alexandria, Lake Charles, and Shreveport. The major auto access routes serving the Bayou State are Interstate Highways 20, 30 and 10.

Lodges & Resorts

Louisiana has few full-service vacation lodges and resorts. For complete information on vacation accommodations in the Bayou State, contact: Tourist Development Commission, P.O. Box 44291, Baton Rouge, LA 70804 or call (504)342–4890 for tourist information.

MISSOURI

Introduction

The Show Me state's national and state forests, wildlife management areas, great lakes, and meandering, spring-fed Ozark float streams offer some of the best hiking, canoeing, hunting and fishing opportunities in the Central United States. This great state, once a frontier mecca and jumping-off place to the wilderness fur kingdom of the Upper Missouri River country and the Rocky Mountains, is divided into four natural regions; the glaciated plains located north of the Missouri River; the old plains located south of the Missouri River and west of the Ozark Highlands, the Missouri River Plains; and the south and central Ozark Highlands. Missouri has an area of 69,686 square miles, 19,000 miles of rivers, 718,000 acres of lakes, and 200 species of fish, including bass, walleye, muskellunge, northern pike, rainbow and brown trout, pan fish, and giant catfish.

Accommodations & Travel Services

The state's major vacation lodges and resorts are described in the "Vacation/Lodging Guide" which follows. For detailed information on all aspects of travel in the state, contact: Missouri Division of Tourism, P.O. Box 1055, Jefferson City, MO 65101 (314)751–4133.

Information & Services

For detailed information on all aspects of outdoor recreation and hunting and fishing regulations, contact: Information Section, Missouri Dept. of Conservation, P.O. Box 180, Jefferson City, MO 65101 (314)751–4115. The Missouri Department of Conservation publishes several free booklets and guides to the state's fish, game, flora, and wildlife: *Where to Fish, Where to Hunt, Wildlife Code of Missouri, Fishing Seasons & Limits, Show-Me Squirrel Hunting, How to Catch Fish, Deer Hunting in Missouri, Ducks at a Distance, Missouri Game Animals & Furbearers, Life History of Important Hook & Line Fishes in Missouri, Life History Chart of Missouri Mammals, Missouri Trees, Snakes & Facts About Them, Rare & Endangered Animals in Missouri, Rare & Endangered Fauna of Missouri.* Single copies may be ordered by writing: Dept. of Conservation, Information Section, P.O. Box 180, Jefferson City 65101. The department also publishes free map-guides to Missouri's state forests and wildlife management areas, which offer excellent opportunities for fishing, primitive camping, and hunting in season. Missouri offers many different kinds of camping facilities. Lakesides, forests, Ozark hills, and farmlands are all scenic settings for excellent campground services. *Camping in Missouri*, available free from: Division of Tourism, 308 E. High St., Jefferson City 65101, lists every campground owner or operated by the state or federal government as well as privately owned campgrounds. It tells you the name and address of each campground, access and routes, number of acres, number of trailer sites, tent sites, the basic fee, length of the season, and the time limit for guests. It also lists the available facilities and activities. An extra feature is a list of hiking and riding trails which indicates the name and location of the trail, and its length in miles. Hiking in Missouri can uncover many species. Twenty-six outstanding trails are listed in the 58–page booklet *Missouri Hiking Trails*, which can be ordered from: Dept. of Conservation, P.O. Box 180, Jefferson City 65101, for $1. It provides a clear black-and-white map for each trail, with a brief description of the area and a log. Among the trails described are the Whites Creek Trail, which runs through the heart of the Irish Wilderness Area in the Mark Twain National Forest; Monteau Wilderness Trail in the Rudolf Bennett Wildlife Area, which winds past the boyhood home of General Omar Bradley and an old Indian village and burial ground; Woodchuck Forest Trail, which winds past the boyhood home of General Omar Bradley and an old Indian village and burial

ground; Woodchuck Forest Trail, which winds along the Current National Scenic River past canebreak (bamboo) and giant bubbling springs; and the scenic Big Piney and Rock Pile Mountain wilderness trails. A useful 270–page guide, *Missouri Wildflowers*, may be obtained for $4 from the Dept. of Conservation (address above). This durable, pocket-size field guide to the wildflowers of Missouri includes description of almost 400 species, with 249 of them pictured in full color.

Highways & Maps

The *Official Missouri Highway Map*, published by the State Highway Commission, shows every major road in the state, indicating the width and number of lanes. It also features toll bridges and ferries, state patrol offices, caves, forest towers, hospitals, highway interchanges, frontier trails, points of interest and historical markers, airports, and roadside parks and rest areas. A population chart and a mileage chart are included, as well as an index of towns and villages. The reverse side of the map provides the traveler with detail maps of major cities. The city maps show parks, hospitals, universities, and airports along with main thoroughfares. There is also a state park index, which lists the recreational facilities offered in each of Missouri's 37 state parks. The map is free upon request by writing to Division of Tourism, 308 E. High St., Jefferson City 65101. The division also publishes a free full-color 43–page travelers' guide to the state, *Seven Ways to Get Away in Missouri*, which describes the seven major vacationlands: Pony Express, Mark Twain, Kansas City, Lake of the Ozarks, St. Louis, Big Springs, and Ozark Highlands regions.

Clark National Forest

This renowned canoe-camping, fishing, and hunting area embraces 800,000 acres along the Ozark Plateau in southern Missouri. The forest is a wild country of connecting ridges, rolling hills, deep hollows, clear, deep limestone streams, dense forests of oak, hickory, red cedar, and shortleaf pine, and caves and sinkholes. The major features of the forest include the famous smallmouth bass waters and canoe trails of the Current, Black, Gasconade, St. Francis, and Big Piney rivers, Lake Wappapello State Park, Clearwater Lake, Johnson Shut-ins State Park, and the Huzzah Wildlife Management Area. This is one of the finest wild turkey, deer, and upland game-bird hunting areas in the state.

VACATION/ LODGING GUIDE

The primitive 13,000–acre Bell Mountain Wilderness lies in the St. Francis Mountains within the Iron County Ranger District of the forest. The wilderness lies on the highest part of the Ozark Plateau and embraces the pools and falls of Shut-in Creek, numerous glades, deep gorges, and thick forests of oak, hickory, and red cedar. The wilderness is an outstanding scenic hiking, primitive camping, and hunting area.

Two of the state's finest hiking, camping, and hunting areas for deer, crow, squirrel, wild turkey, and upland game birds—the Deer Run and Indian Trails state forests—lie adjacent to the national forest boundaries. The scenic 13,255–acre Indian Trails State Forest lies adjacent to the western boundaries of the Clark National Forest, due east of the village of Salem. The major features of the area include Kiln Pond, Fishwater Creek, and the Meramec River. The 120,000–acre Deer Run State Forest—the largest state-owned forest reserve—lies between the Clark and Mark Twain national forests adjacent to Current River and Logan Creek.

Several of the state's outstanding float fishing streams for smallmouth bass and walleye flow through the rolling hills and woodlands of the forest including the Gasconade, Osage Fork, Little Piney, Black, St. Francis, and the renowned spring-fed Big Piney—considered by many to be the state's number one float fishing stream. The wild and unspoiled free-flowing stream, the largest tributary of the Gasconade River, flows through scenic pine forests and past spectacular limestone bluffs and hollows. Use of johnboats is restricted to the long, deep pools and eddies.

Information Sources, Maps & Access

The major man-made and natural features of the region including highways, roads, mines, ranger stations, recreation sites, trails, hunting camps, boat-launching and fishing access sites, and the Karkaghone Scenic Drive are shown on the full-color *Clark National Forest Map*, available for 50¢ from: Forest Supervisor, P.O. Box 937, Rolla 65401 (314)364–4621. The Forest Supervisor's office also publishes a free guide, *The Big Piney River*. A complete listing of float fishing outfitters and canoe rental services on the Gasconade, Big Piney, and Osage Fork is contained in the Missouri Float Fishing Outfitters Guide, available free upon request from: Division of Tourism, P.O. Box 1055, Jefferson City 65101. The forest is reached via U.S. Highways 60, 61, 66, and 67; Missouri Routes 8, 17, 21, 32, and 72. Overnight accommodations, supplies, guides, and boat rentals are available at Rolla, Fredericktown, Piedmont, Potosi, Ironton, Poplar Bluffs, Salem, and St. Louis.

Gateways & Accommodations

See "Mark Twain National Forest & Ozark National Waterways" entry which follows.

Mark Twain National Forest & Ozark Scenic Waterways

The four divisions of the famous 620,000–acre Mark Twain National Forest embrace the Ozark canoe trails along the Eleven Point and Current national scenic rivers surrounded by a wild backcountry of rolling hills, barren rock outcroppings, numerous sinkholes, limestone caves, and thick stands of oak and native shortleaf pine. The major features include Table Rock Reservoir—one of the state's best for lunker bass, trout, and walleye up to 17 pounds—Beaver Creek, Bull Shoals Lake, James and North Fork rivers, Roaring River State Park, Carman Springs Wildlife Refuge, Peck Ranch Wildlife Management Area, and the Irish Wilderness. The forest is one of the state's finest hunting regions for deer, waterfowl, wild turkey, and upland game birds.

Information Sources, Maps & Access

Vacation travel and recreation information, and a full-color *Mark Twain National Forest Map* (50¢) and the free *Hiking & Riding Trails Guide* and *Eleven Point National Scenic River Map/Brochure* may be obtained from: Supervisor, Mark Twain National Forest, Fairgrounds Rd., Box 937, Rolla, MO 65401 (314)364–4621. Detailed information on the Ozark National Scenic Waterways and a free *Ozark National Scenic Riverways Map/Brochure* may be obtained from the Superintendent, Ozark National Scenic Riverways, Van Buren, MO 63965 (314)323–4236. The beautifully produced, large-format *River Maps of the Current & Jacks Fork* is available for $2.75 (plus 50¢ postage) from: Ozark National Riverways Historical Assn., Van Buren 63965. A large *Lake of the Ozarks Contour Map* ($6) is available from: Structure Graphics, 917 Pyramid Dr., Valley Park, MO 63088. The forest is reached via U.S. Highways 60, 63, 66, and 160; Missouri Routes 5, 14, 39, 76, 87, 95, 125, 148, and 173. Overnight accommodations, supplies, guides, and canoe and johnboat rentals are available at West Plains, Willow Springs, Van Buren, Doniphan, Cassville, Ava, Willow Springs, Winona, Salem, Eminence, Alley Spring, Round Spring, Jadwin, Gladden, and Alton.

Recreation Areas

Eleven Point National Scenic River

The enchanting Eleven Point National Scenic River lies within the boundaries of the Winona and Doniphan Ranger districts of the forest. Starting at Thomasville, the river channel is narrow and easy to locate. Long stretches are separated by shallow riffles. Below Green Springs the volume of water increases as well as the speed and size of the rapids. The Eleven Point, which is fed by several of the most beautiful wild springs in the Ozarks, flows through the 17,880–acre Irish Wilderness—an unspoiled primitive camping and backpacking area marked by numerous caves and sinkholes, traversed by the Whites Creek hiking trail. The major features of the river include Posy, Roaring, Blowing and Graham Springs, Cane Bluff, Greer Spring, Graveyard Springs, Horseshoe Bend, Whites Creek, Boze Mill Springs, and The Narrows, McCormack Lake, Camp Five Pond, Greer Crossing and Buffalo Creek are national forest campgrounds located near the Eleven Point. Greer Crossing—a ford once used by the Osage Indians and horse-drawn wagons—is the focal point of activity on the river and the starting point for many float trips. Old Greer Mill, still standing on the hilltop south of the crossing, was powered by a unique cable system from a waterwheel in the spring.

Lake of the Ozarks

The famous Lake of the Ozarks in the central portion of the state to the northwest of Mark Twain National Forest, surrounded by colorful hills and bluffs of the forested northern Ozarks, has approximately 1,375 miles of shoreline, making it one of the largest man-made lakes in the world. Known as the "dragon lake" for its serpentine shape, this giant lake offers top-ranked fishing along its numerous cliffs, bays, hidden coves, and dead timber areas for lunker largemouth bass, striped bass, crappie, catfish, and the primitive paddlefish (known locally as spoonbill).

Ozark National Scenic Waterways

The famed smallmouth bass and walleye waters of the spring-fed, clear Ozark National Scenic Waterways—the deep-flowing Current and Jacks Fork rivers—are shown on the free map-brochure *Ozark National Scenic Riverways*, available from: Superintendent, Ozark National Scenic Riverways, Van Buren 63965. The map shows all campgrounds access points springs trails and unimproved roads along the rivers. The Current River, named *La Riviere Courante*—"The Running River"—by the French trappers who first explored the region from their base on the upper Great Lakes, flows through the ancient Ozark Hill country surrounded by giant springs, caves, and lush forests of oak, hickory, shortleaf pine, sycamore, sassafras,

blackgum, maple, and birch with a colorful understory of hawthorn, dogwood, bittersweet, redbud, and beautiful rose azalea, inhabited by deer, wild turkey, mink, bobcat, raccoon, opossum, gray and fox squirrels, osprey, owls, kingfish, green heron, and great blue heron. The Current is one of the state's top-ranked streams for walleye (known locally as "jack salmon") up to 20 pounds. The Current also produced the state record 14–pound 10–ounce brown trout. The major features along the Current include the trout springs in Montauk State Park, Medlock Spring and Cave, Welch Cave and Spring, the large sinkholes known as "Burr Oak Basin" and "The Sunkland" in the Akers Hieronymus Hollow, Rock House Cave, Bee Bluff, Paint Rock Bluff and Gravel Spring, Big Spring State Park, Bog Hollow, and Goose Lake—a pond in the river. The major features along the wild and scenic Jacks Fork River, a tributary of the Current, include the Prongs, Chimney Rock Cave, Jam Up Bluff and Cave, Ebb and Flow Springs, Bucks Hollow, Blue Spring, Sinking Branch, and Horse Hollow. The upper reaches of the Jacks Fork offer superb fly fishing for smallmouth bass. If you plan on floating the Current or Jacks Fork keep an eye out for root wads, obstructions caused by exposed roots and trunks of fallen trees. The major center of activity on the Jacks Fork is at Alley Spring; and at Akens, Pulite Spring, and Round and Big springs on the Current.

Gateways & Accommodations

Branson—Gateway to Bull Shoals & Table Rock Lakes

(Pop. 2,200; zip code 65616; area code 417) located on Lake Taneycomo, is a resort town with camps, hotels and boat docks lining the shaded lakeshore. Bull Shoals and Table Rock Lakes, nearby, offer excellent fishing and float trips. The area was made famous by the novel *The Shepherd of the Hills* and the cabin setting of the novel is now an attraction. Another attraction is Marvel Cave, one of the largest limestone caverns in Missouri, with 32 miles of passages. The total trip takes 9 hours, although there are plenty of attractions to be seen in less than that time, including an underground Grand Canyon and Lost River. Accommodations: (see "Lodges & Resorts" for additional listings): *Bentree Lodge* (rates: $29.50–35.50 by season), at Table Rak Lake with 44 family units and vacation homes, dining room, cocktail lounge, tennis on Indian Point Rd. (338–2218); *Crow's Nest Resort* (rates: $26 double in summer), with 14 excellent family units or at Table Rock Lake with swimming pool, dock, boats and motors on Indian Point Rd. (338–2524); *Holiday Inn* (rates: $33.50 double in season), with 220 excellent rooms and family units, restaurant, cocktail lounge, west of town on Missouri Highway 76 (334–5101); *White Wing Resort* (rates: $12–19

double in season), at Table Rock Lake with 12 good family units, swimming pool, dock, boats and motors in nice location on Indian Point Rd. (338–2318).

Lesterville & The Wilderness Lodge

(Pop. 250; zip code 63654; area code 314) is located directly on the Black River, with The Mark Twain National Forest on either side. The river is noted for its large and smallmouth bass, goggle-eye, and jack salmon. There is plenty of fishing and facilities for float trips. Nearby is a wild-turkey farm. Accommodations: *Wilderness Lodge* (rates: $36 double), with 27 excellent family rooms and cottages on the scenic Black River, restaurant, cocktails, with private beach, tennis, fishing, canoeing, float trips off Missouri 21 southeast of town (637–2295).

Osage Beach

(Pop. 1,100; zip code 65065; area code 314) is a tiny resort village located on the Lake of the Ozarks. Nearby is a fish hatchery which stocks the lake with bass and perch. There are good, manmade sandy beaches lining the lake. Attractions close by include: Indian Burial Cave, with a boat ride on an underground river and view of an underground waterfall; Gold Nugget Junction Theme Park, a replica of an 1890 frontier town offering rides, museums, and shops. Accommodations: *Best Western Lake Chateau Inn* (rates: $31–36 double in season), with 25 excellent rooms, restaurant, cocktail lounge, swimming pools, fishing dock, boats and motors on Lake of the Ozarks on US 54 (348–2791).

Poplar Bluff

(Pop. 17,000; zip code 63901; area code 314) is located on the outer fringe of the Ozark highlands, above the Black River. There is some good fishing in the area—on the Black River, the St. Francis River and the Current River. Lake Wappapello State Park offers 1854 acres for fishing, boating, swimming, camping, with cabins available. Duck hunting is also good in the area. Mark Twain National Forest is nearby. Accommodations: *Holiday Inn* (rates: $21–23.50 double), with 145 excellent rooms, restaurant, coffeeshop, cocktail lounge, swimming pool, three miles north of town on US 60, 67 (785–7711).

Rockaway Beach

(Pop. 200; zip code 65740; area code 417) located on the shore of Lake Taneycomo, is one of the most attractive of the southern Ozark villages. It is a fully equipped resort area with hotels, cabins and facilities for boating, fishing, hiking, riding, tennis, golf and waterskiing as well as other land and water sports. Boat docks and rentals are available. Accommodations: *Kenny's Court* (rates: $22 double), with 19 family housekeeping cottages on wooded grounds with heated pool and children's recreation area off 176 near the lake (561–4131); *Michel's Motor Lodge* (rates: $25.50 double), with 23 rooms and housekeeping cottages, heated swimming pool, children's play area off 176 near the lake (561–4135).

Rolla

(Pop. 13,000; zip code 65401; area code 314) a strategic center during the Civil War, it had its boom during the building of the St. Louis-San Francisco Railroad and is nicknamed "child of the railroad." Today, it is noted for its School of Mines—with the main attraction being the geological and mineral museums. The town is located in a beautifully scenic area with several miles of fishing streams. For recreation the Montauk State Park and Mark Twain National Forest offer fishing, hunting, camping, picnicking, swimming, and boating. Cabins and lodge facilities available. Accommodations: *Holiday Inn* (rates: $32 double), with 154 excellent rooms and family units, restaurant, cocktail lounge, swimming pool, kennel two miles west of town on Martin Spring Dr. (364–5200). *Howard Johnson's Motor Lodge* (rates: $27–35 double), with 80 excellent rooms, restaurant, cocktail lounge, heated pool, sauna, 1½ miles west of town at I-44 junction with Business Loop 66 (364–7111).

Springfield

(Pop. 146,000; zip code 65803; area code 417) located at the northern edge of the Ozark highlands, is near some of the most picturesque recreational areas in Missouri, and is its 4th largest city. There are many tourist accommodations in the city itself as well as many public parks for picnicking, swimming, golf, tennis, etc. Area attractions include Crystal Cave and Fantastic Caverns with their rock formations; the Exotic Animal Paradise; the National Battlefield dating from the Civil War and the Laura Ingalls Museum—writer of the "Little House" books. Accommodations: *Holiday Inn* (rates: $32 double), with 220 excellent rooms, restaurant, coffeeshop, cocktail lounge, swimming pool in nice location at 2700 North Glenstove Ave. (865–5511); *Howard Johnson's Motor Lodge* (rates: $31–38 double), with 320 excellent rooms, restaurant, cocktail lounge, heated swimming pool, sauna in scenic location at 2610 North Glenstone Ave. (866–6671).

Van Buren—Gateway to the Ozark National Waterways

(Pop. 700; zip code 63965; area code 314) located in a narrow valley directly on the Current River. The Current River is noted for its fighting smallmouth bass. There are many fishing and float trips available and accommodations. Nearby is Big Spring State Park with 4,416 wooded acres for camping picnicking, hiking, and fishing with cabins and lodges available. The park gets its name from the Big Spring—one of the largest in America—which surges from an immense basin at the bottom of a limestone cliff, drops from a ledge, rebounds from boulders, creating a spray that rushes off the river. There are more than 80,000 acres administered by the National Park Service along the Current and Jack Fork rivers. Clearwater Lake nearby also offers boating, swimming, waterskiing, camping, and fishing.

West Plains

(Pop. 7,000; zip code 65775; area code 417) is an agricultural and dairy center, noted for its auctions. An interesting attraction is the Joseph Aid Gun Collection containing several guns more than 100 years old. There are several motels and motor hotels in the area. Accommodations: *Ramada Inn*, (rates: $24–28 double), with 80

excellent rooms and family units, restaurant, coffeeshop, heated pool, one mile south of town at the junction of 63 and 160(256–8191).

Lodges & Resorts

★★*Arrowhead Lodge* is in the Ozarks and offers year-round family vacation accommodations. Their facilities include a heated swimming pool, children's playgrounds, boating, golf, fishing, hunting and horseback riding. There is also a fine restaurant and international gift shop on the premises. All rooms completely air-conditioned with telephones and TV. In season rates are $28–48 per night, double occupancy. The more expensive rooms have patios overlooking the lake. From October 1 to May 1 rates are reduced, ranging from $14–34. For more information, contact: Arrowhead Lodge, US Business Rte. 54, Lake Ozark, MO 65049 (314)365–2345.

★★★*Big Bear Resort at Lake of the Ozarks*, nestled on a quiet cove on wooded Horseshoe Bend, offers luxurious housekeeping suites, and swimming, boating, and fishing on the spectacular Lake of the Ozarks. Inboard, outboard motors, and pontoon craft are available for rent, and there are wide stretches of sandy beach and a heated pool for swimming. Nearby are the fantastic Ozark Caverns, Bridal Cave, Stark Caverns, aquariums, amusement parks, zoos, the Country Music Hall, Nashville Opery, and the J Bar H Rodeo. Family suites, with private bedrooms, bath, modern kitchens, and spacious living room/dining areas with fireplace are available for $60 per day for two couples, $80 for three couples, and $90 a day for four couples. Four bedroom penthouses are also available for $110 daily. For more information write: Jim Shackleford, Duck Head Road, Lake Ozark, MO 65049 (314)365–2115.

★★★*Eagle Rock Resort Motel at Table Rock Lake* with an area of 100 acres, is situated on top of a hill with a magnificent view of Mark Twain Forest. There is over one mile of waterfront on the Roaring River Arm of Table Rock Lake providing fine fishing for anglers including bass, catfish, walleye and crappie. At Roaring River Park and in Lake Trout anglers report very good trout catches. A complete marina service is less than a mile away. Ozark float-fishing trips on Kings and White Rivers can be arranged. Mark Twain Forest provides hunters with deer, turkey and quail. The resort has a swimming pool, boat launching ramp, a playground for children and parking for boat trailers. Nearby guests can visit Silver Dollar City, Caves, Shepherd of the Hills Farms and Theater, Christ of the Ozarks Passion Play, Beaver Lake Dam, Table Rock Dam and School of the Ozarks. Horseback riding, golf, restaurants and grocery stores are also nearby. Accommodations include guest rooms with or without kitchens. All have color TV, private screened porches, air-conditioning, bath and shower, and sound-proof walls. Meals are not included in rates, but free coffee is provided for rooms without kitchens and a cafe is ¼ mile away. The resort is family-oriented. Rates: bedroom without kitchens, $23 daily, $138 weekly; with two beds $26 daily, $156 weekly. For further information contact: Eagle Rock Resort motel, on Highway 86 and Table Rock Lake, Eagle Rock, MO 65641 (417)271–3222.

★★★*Fort Cook RV Park on Bull Shoals Lake* encompasses Theodosia Marina with a full range of services including, fishing boats; ski boats; paddle, row, and motorboats; motor rentals; outboard motor service; and a full range of fishing and boating paraphernalia. There are boat storage and parking areas and the Corps of Engineers provides a concrete boat launching ramp for public use. In addition to water sports, the park offers a wide variety of sports activities including hunting, day and night tennis, pool swimming, game room, basketball courts, a children's playground, beautiful scenery to explore and fine camping facilities. The Ozark area provides guests with many additional recreational and sightseeing opportunities. Accommodations at the resort include a two story motel unit with natural cedar exterior and lake views from each unit. There are also furnished two bedroom cottages designed for family use over an extended period of time. Meals, which are not included in rates, are available at the Lakeview Restaurant. Rates: Motel unit $14.50–26.50 depending on number of persons. For further information contact: Fort Cook RV Park, and Theodosia Marina Resort, at the Bridge on Highway 160, Theodosia, MO 65761 (417)273–4264 or 4444.

★★★*Kimberling Inn at Table Rock Lake* is nestled on the lake shore surrounded by the hills and forests of the Ozarks. The Inn features a large outdoor pool, private boat dock, two tennis courts and a children's playground. There is also a sauna and steam room, and this year Kimberling Inn will be adding a glass covered indoor heated swimming pool, and two brand new racquet ball courts. The pier, built out over the lake offers fine dining and two lounges, including a disco for evening entertainment. Each of the 100 rooms in the Kimberling Inn offer panoramic lake views. Summer rates, from May to October are $32.50 for two, and $37.50 for four persons. Winter rates are $19.50 for two, and $29.50 for four. For more information write: Kimberling Inn, Kimberling City, MO (417)739–4311.

★★★★*The Lodge of the Four Seasons* hugs the shores of the spectacular Lake of the Ozarks, offering luxurious accommodations, and superlative sports year round, to an ever changing background of the Ozark Hills. The Lodge has a complete health spa, three outdoor pools, horseback riding, and a large lakefront marina, with a complete variety of fishing craft and pleasure boats. The 18–hole championship golf course, and the 9–hole executive course offers challenge to any golfer, and there are also 6 tennis courts, many lighted for evening play. The lodge offers a variety of dining and evening entertainment, with an elegant continental dining room, a steakhouse, and casual deli. There are three lounges, with live entertainment, cocktails and dancing, Four Seasons Cinema, computer game room, bowling alley and a variety of gift shops. All contemporary guest rooms overlook the lake, and the terraced Japanese gardens. The Lodge of the Four Seasons offers a variety of holiday packages, anniversary, honeymoon, tennis and golf packages for three day/two nights from $104–239. For details write: The Lodge of the Four Seasons, Lake Road HH, Lake Ozark, MO 65049 (314)365–2381. Toll free numbers: in Missouri (800)392–3461, in Kansas, Ill., Okla., Neb., Ky., Ark., and Iowa (800)325–8611.

★★★*Long Creek Lodge on Table Rock Lake*, is reached by a scenic drive on Highway 65 from Springfield. Long Creek Lodge is new and modern, with 38 units which are air-conditioned and have all electric kitchenettes. Linens, cooking utensils and TVs are all furnished. The resort has two large swimming pools and a children's playground. The Long Creek Boat Dock has a launching ramp, boats and motors for rent, water skiing, scuba diving, bait and tackle. Fishing is excellent on Table Rock Lake with no closed season on bass, crappie, walleye, bluegill and trout. At the Boat Dock, there is the Long Creek Restaurant for days when guests don't want to cook in. A unit for two persons with no kitchen is $22 per day. A unit with two double beds and kitchen is $26 per day for two; one with separate bedroom, living and kitchen, with two double beds and a twin is $30 for two persons per day; and a large combination unit for groups up to 10 people is $48 for four people per day. There are rates for extra persons in a room. Lower rates and special discounts are in effect from September 5 through May 25. For information and reservations: Long Creek Lodge, Branson, MO 65616 (417)334–4684.

★★★*Millstone Lodge on the Lake of the Ozarks* features a full-service

marina accommodating power boats and sailboats. Lake of the Ozarks is in the center of the state, and the lodge and marina is on the north end of the large lake. Millstone has a heated pool, tennis courts, a playground for the children, a recreation room for indoor games and conversation and a general store. The marina also has a store carrying boating accessories. Millstone has a fine dining room with huge windows offering a breathtaking view of the Lake. Many Ozark favorites are served and on weekends they spread a buffet. After dinner, guests can relax in the lounge and enjoy live entertainment. Accommodations at the Lodge range from single rooms to three-bedroom suites with kitchenettes. All rooms have color TV and a telephone. Rates start at $22 in season and $18 off season for a room with one double bed. A lakefront apartment with living room, kitchen and two bedrooms and baths is $48 in season and $44 off season for up to four people. The most expensive room is the family suite with two bedrooms, each with two double beds, living room, kitchen and two baths for $66 in season and $58 off season. The season is May 25 through Sept. 3 and the Lodge is open from March 16 through November 3. Weekly rates are 10% discount for seven or more nights. For reservations and information on all the various accommodations, write Millstone Lodge, Route 1, Box 515, Gravois Mills, MO 65037 (314)372–5111.

★★★*Rock Lane Lodge* is located on the shore of Table Rock Lake, one of the most popular recreation spots in the state. Fine boating, water skiing, fishing, and canoeing can all be enjoyed from the lodge. The Lodge has a marina to equip anglers with boats, motors, professional guide service, and bait and tackle. The Lodge also has two swimming pools, sundecks, picnic areas, and astro putting green, tennis, a teen center, and a nature trail. The area offers a wide range of activities including music shows, museums, Shepherd of the Hills Farm, Silver Dollar City, and the natural beauty of Ozark mountain area. Accommodations at the lodge include rooms in the Rock Lane Lodge with air-conditioning, TV, and lake views. The "Top of the Rock" is a 40 room complex which was completed in 1974 offering the resort's most spacious luxurious rooms with private balconies, excellent lake views and color TV. Meals, which are not included in the rates, are available in the Rock Lane Lodge's dining room, which has a lovely view of Table Rock Lake. Gravel Bar cocktail lounge is the resort's gathering and dancing place. Rates: Rock Lane Lodge rooms for two $26–32. Top of the Rock accommodations for one, two, three or four $38–42. For further information contact: Rock Lane Lodge, Indian Point Road, Rt. 1, Box 640, Branson, MO 65616 (417)338–2211.

★★★★*Tan-Tar-A Resort at Lake of the Ozarks* dominates 75 acres of a wooded peninsula jutting into the lake, with over a mile of open shoreline, a 18–hole golf course, and a myriad of hiking and bridle paths meandering throughout the woods. Children will find their own special agenda of planned activities in the children's playhouse. Sailing and waterskiing instruction are offered at the Marina, and Tan-Tar-A has sailboats, sunfish, canoes, waterskis, speedboats and fishing boats to rent. Expert fishing guides will lead anglers to remote coves and fishing holes along the hundreds of miles of wooded shoreline in the Lake of the Ozarks. Scenic lake cruises are regularly scheduled for sightseers. In the winter, Tan-Tar-A opens an Alpine Ski Center with expert instruction and complete ski rentals. There is also a large skating arena, and a health club with an indoor pool, sauna, whirlpool baths, professional massage, jogging trails and indoor racquet ball courts. Other amenities include a billiard room with its own bar and grill, a bowling alley, entertainment center with games for all ages, five lounges, six fine restaurants, discos, boutiques, and a variety of unique shops. Deluxe rooms are fully carpeted, with color TV, and private balconies and patios providing magnificent views of the lake. Rates: $60–70 daily, single or double occupancy. Luxurious one and two bedroom private suites are also available, many with fireplaces, all with kitchenettes, and private patios and balconies with lake view. Rates are $100–120 for one-four persons in a one bedroom suite, and $140–160 for one-six persons in a two bedroom suite. For more information write: Marriott's Tan-Tar-A Resort, Osage Beach, MO 65065 (800)228–9290.

★★★*The Wheel House Inn on Lake of the Ozarks* is nestled in a quiet cove on the wooded Horseshoe bend. The Inn, completely constructed of native stone and cedar, has ¼ mile of sandy private beach for swimming, and a large heated outdoor pool. A modern electric lift takes guests to and from the pool and the lake edge. Private boat docking facilities are available for guests, and Wheel House Inn has a complete boat rental with ski boats, canoes, V-bottomed boats, and pontoon boats. In addition, there is also a Ships Store carrying fishing and boating supplies, and groceries. Each of the 34 modern units have wall-to-wall carpeting, TV and a magnificent view of the lake. Several units have kitchenettes, and deluxe apartments with kitchens, private bedrooms, and a living room/dining area are also available. Rates are $27 single occupancy and $35 single with kitchens, and $30 daily double occupancy. One-bedroom suites are $55 daily, and two-bedroom suites are $78 daily. For more information write: Wheel House Inn, Star Route HH, Box 234, Crow Road, Lake Ozark, MO 65049; (314)365–5306.

MONTANA

Introduction

Montana, the Treasure State, contains the magnificent high-country wilderness of the Northern Rockies in the west; the eastern two-thirds of the state is part of the Great Plains, dominated by the historic wildlands of the upper Missouri River and the huge Fort Peck Reservoir surrounded by the elongated Charles M. Russell National Wildlife Refuge, a 1–million-acre preserve bordering 180 miles of the river's course, inhabited by sharp-tailed grouse, pronghorn antelope, peregrine falcon, osprey, bald eagle, bison, elk, Canada goose, and black-footed ferret. The backbone of the Northern Rockies, broken by deep luxuriant valleys (locally called holes) and basins, stretches north from Yellowstone National Park to Glacier National Park and the Alberta boundary. The Great Divide follows a meandering route north and south, turning abruptly west along the crest of the Bitterroot Mountains into Idaho, which adjoins Montana on the west. Within Montana's 147,138 square miles are several of North America's legendary fishing, big-game hunting, and wilderness camping areas, including the blue-ribbon trout waters of the Big Hole, Madison, Yellowstone, Beaverhead, Gallatin, Flathead, Jefferson, and Big Blackfoot rivers; the scenic, lake-dotted high country of the Absaroka and Beartooth primitive areas; the grizzly habitat of the vast Bob Marshall Wilderness; the trophy trout waters of beautiful Flathead Lake, known as the Gem of the Rockies; the fabled big-game ranges of the Bearpaw, Mission, Cabinet, and Swan mountains; and the awesome scenic beauty of Glacier National Park, situated astride the crown of the Great Divide.

Accommodations & Travel Information

Montana's great wide open spaces and Rocky Mountain high country offer a number of choice vacation lodges, guest ranches, motels, hotels, and inns, which are described in the "Vacation/Lodging Guide." *Montana, Last of the Big Time Splendors*, a free booklet published by the Montana Dept. of Highways, describes the facilities and recreational opportunities at each campground, along with points of interest in each area. It also identifies good fishing areas, state and national parks and monuments, trails, and areas known for fly-in vacations, dude ranch vacations, backpacking, float trips, and skiing. Write: Montana Dept. of Highways, Advertising Unit, Helena 59601 (406)449–2492.

Information & Services

Nonresident big-game hunters and fishermen are well advised to hire the services of an experienced guide or wilderness outfitter. Their knowledge of the region will increase your enjoyment and chances of success tenfold. Be sure to plan your trip well in advance and write to the Montana Dept. of Fish & Game, Helena 59601 (406)449–2535, for detailed information about seasons, permits, and regulations, and for a free *Fisherman's Log*, *Fishing District Maps*, *Hunting Zone Maps*, *Popular Float Streams Guide*, and *Montana Hunting & Fishing Booklet*.

Montana Licensed Outfitters, a 31–page booklet provided free by the Dept. of Fish & Game, lists and describes all licensed outfitters in the state. The booklet gives the name, address, phone, hunt area, accommodations, and species hunted for each outfitter. A regional listing of the major outfitters and vacation guest ranches follows.

National Forest Camp and Picnic Areas in the Northern Region, a booklet published by the Forest Service, describes all campsites in Montana's national forests, giving access routes and naming attractions and facilities for each. For this free guide, write: Northern Region Office, U.S. Forest Service, Federal Building, Missoula 59801.

All the public lands of Montana, state fishing or boating access sites,

recreation and camp sites, highway rest areas, and ski areas are shown on a free map of the state published by the Bureau of Land Management. The map, on a scale of 20 miles to 1 inch, keys national forests and recreation areas, national parks, BLM lands, and lands administered by the Bureau of Sport Fisheries & Wildlife. The map also provides the names and addresses of other sources of information on outdoor recreation in the state.

Individual *BLM Quadrangle Maps* for 42 areas within the state are also available free from the bureau. These maps include Glacier, Blackfoot, Tiber, Fresno, Havre, Belknap, Bowdoin, Glasgow, Poplar, Muddy, Seeley, Sun River, Cascade, Highwood, Judith, Breaks, U.L. Bend, Haxby, Circle, Savage, Granite, Avon, Townsend Castles, Snowy, Roundup, Sinatra, Custer, Fallon, Big Hole, Dillon, Madison, Park, Beartooth, Pryor, Crow, Tongue, Powder, Box Elder, Red Rock, and Centennial. Both this series of maps, *National Resource Lands in Montana*, and the state map, *Montana BLM Recreation Map*, are available from: Bureau of Land Management, Montana State Office, 316 North 26th St., Billings 59101.

Highways & Maps

A free, comprehensive *Montana Official Highway Map* is distributed by the Montana Dept. of Highways, Helena 59601. The map includes descriptions of the history, geology, physical features, major regions, and recreational opportunities of the state. Montana state parks and monuments, historic sites, and points of interest are also indicated. All highways and roads, historic trails, airports, ski areas, campsites, rest areas, cities, and towns are keyed.

Two major trails cross through Montana on modern highways. The Old West Trail is a self-guiding automobile tour through five western states. Scenic and historic sites are marked with a Buffalo head symbol. In Montana the Old West Trail includes city circle tours of Billings, Butte, Fort Benton, Great Falls, and the Fort Peck area, and such sites as the Boothill Cemetery, historic riverboat landings, and museums of the Old West. The route through the state includes a tour of the mansion of a copper millionaire, the famous Big Sky of Montana resort, and a 14–mile round-trip river canyon excursion. A brochure called the *Old West Trail* is available free from: Old West Trail Foundation, P.O. Box 2554, 405 East Omaha St., Rapid City, SD 57701.

The Lewis and Clark Highway closely follows the route of Lewis and Clark between Lolo and Kooskia in 1805–1806. The highway winds through the beautiful Bitterroot Mountains. Campsites, hot springs, forests, and clear mountain springs dot the mountains along the historic route. A brochure describing the historic sites and recreational opportunities along the Lewis and Clark Highway is available free from: Northern Region Office, U.S. Forest Service, Missoula 59801. The brochure includes a map which marks camp and picnic areas, ranger stations, lookouts, and points of interest along the highway.

A leaflet distributed free by the Montana Dept. of Highways, Advertising Unit, Helena 59601, marks four scenic routes across the state between West Yellowstone and West Glacier. It describes the cities, lakes, rivers, forests, and mountains along these beautiful routes and places them in the context of the history of the state. Write to the Dept. of Highways and request *Montana between Glacier & Yellowstone National Parks*.

VACATION/ LODGING GUIDE

Beaverhead National Forest

Situated in southwestern Montana, this 2,195,166–acre reserve encompasses the rugged Beaverhead Mountains and some of the finest stretches of trout waters in the country, including the Madison, famous for its lunker browns and rainbows; Big Hole, called simply the Hole by early trappers and the Wisdom River by Lewis and Clark, which flows through a broad valley bottom and holds some giant rainbows and browns; and the mighty Jefferson River. Elevations in the forest range from 5,200 feet in the vicinity of Melrose east of Sheridan and Ennis Lake to 11,316 feet at Hilgard Peak in the Madison Range. From the lower elevations, where semidesert conditions prevail, lofty snow-covered mountains can be seen thrusting above the timberline, and although nearly 40 peaks exceed 10,000 feet, all of them can be climbed without special technical equipment. The Continental Divide Trail and many forest roads lead to the deep pools and riffles of the Beaverhead River; the challenging summits of the Snowcrest, Greenhorn, and Tobacco Root mountains; Schultz Lakes; Wade Lake; Echo Lake, nestled on the crest of the Madison-Gallatin Divide; the Pioneer Mountains; and Taylor Peaks.

Information Sources, Maps & Access

For detailed vacation travel, fishing, and camping information and a full-color *Beaverhead National Forest Map* (50¢) and *Anaconda-Pintlar Wilderness Map*, write: Supervisor, Beaverhead National Forest, Dillon, MT 59725 (406)683–2312. For a *Big Hole National Battlefield* map-brochure and information, write: Superintendent, P.O. Box 237, Wisdom, MT 59761. The Beaverhead National Forest is reached via U.S. Highways 287, 91, and 15 and Montana State Highways 287, 41, 257, 278, and 43. Supplies, guides, and outfitting services are available at Cameron, Alder, Virginia City, Norris, Nevada City, Pony, Dell, Lima, Jackson, Wisdom, Divide, Wise River, and Melrose.

Recreation & Historic Areas

Anaconda-Pintlar Wilderness

The 157,803–acre Anaconda-Pintlar Wilderness lies due east from the Selway-Bitterroot Wilderness astride the Continental Divide for 30 miles in the Anaconda Range of the Rocky Mountains. The rugged Anaconda Range is a true sierra, with spectacular cirques, U-shaped valleys, glacial moraines in the foothills, and turbulent streams that plunge down through alpine forests and steep canyons from the high-country meadows and lakes. The wilderness is laced by a network of hiking trails, including a 45–mile trail along the crest of the Great Divide, which provide access to the high peaks

and to the East Fork of the Bitterroot and its headwaters at Ripple, Kelly, and Hidden lakes, situated beneath Bitterroot Pass. The East Fork and its alpine headwaters hold cutthroat and rainbow of 4 pounds and over. From the Pintlar Peaks, named for Charles Pintlar, a pioneer trapper in the Big Hole country, the wilderness traveler can view the Mission Mountains to the northwest and the Bitterroot Range to the west. Pintlar Creek, a feeder of the Big Hole River, holds cutthroat, brook trout, and a few grayling. Sawed Cabin on Pintlar Creek was built by the fabled woodsman "Seven Dog" Johnson, who is said to have trapped mountain goats and packed them out of this high country to sell to zoos. The wilderness traveler in this remote area will pass through stands of alpine larch and pine and fields of mountain heather and wild flowers. One may see the tracks and signs of marten, mink, badger, cougar, and lynx. The Anaconda Range and the gentle slopes of the Sapphire Range, which adjoins the wilderness on the northwest, are inhabited by elk, moose, deer, and black bear.

Big Hole National Battlefield

This place commemorates the epic flight of the Nez Percé Indians from eastern Oregon during the summer of 1877 and their short-lived victory over U.S. Army forces in the Big Hole Valley of southeastern Montana. Led by the courageous Nez Percé leader, Chief Joseph, a band of 800 Indians, determined to resist displacement to a reservation, made the long and arduous journey from the tip of eastern Oregon through the Idaho Territory and over the Bitterroot Mountains into Montana Territory, stopping finally at Bear Paw Mountain just south of Canada. Although the Indians hoped to escape the army peaceably, they were forced to halt and face their pursuers nearly a dozen times, with often disastrous losses on both sides. In the Big Hole Valley, on August 9 and 10, the two forces met in one of the major battles of the Nez Percé Indian War. The Indians captured the enemy's howitzer, inflicted heavy casualties, and forced the army back across the Big Hole River. But two months later, broken in spirit and pursued by relentless troops, they were forced to surrender. The National Battlefield pays homage to the bravery of the Nez Percé and traces the history of the battle and the Indians' heroic flight against stupefying odds. A tour of this protected landmark covers the major confrontations, capture of the army howitzer, and retreat across the river. The visitor center offers an audiovisual program and exhibits, including the original cannon from the battle. The Big Hole National Battlefield is 12 miles west of Wisdom, Montana, on Highway 43. No camping or overnight facilities are provided in the park, but accommodations and campgrounds are available nearby.

Big Hole River Area

Flowing through the "Valley of 10,000 Stacks" into the Beaverhead from the north is the Big Hole River, named after the trapper's term for a large mountain valley. The Big Hole Battlefield, at the junction of Trail Creek and the North Fork of the Big Hole, marks the site of Chief Joseph's defeat of General Howard in 1877 during the flight of the Nez Percé's along the arduous Lolo Trail towards Canada. In the Big Hole Basin, the river flows through lush meadows dotted by thousands of haystacks. Men once traveled here from far and wide during the late hay harvest to earn a summer's pay in the vastness of the Old West. This historic blue-ribbon trout stream is one of the nation's truly great fly-fishing waters for trophy grayling and brook, rainbow, and brown trout, the latter up to 20 pounds. In late summer, wading the Big Hole is hazardous because moss covering the underwater rocks is thick and slippery; chain creepers or waders with felt soles are a must. The remote alpine lake headquarters of the Big Hole feeder streams on the Beaverhead Mountains, including Swamp, Big Lake, Miner, Hamby, Pioneer, and Darkhorse creeks, offer unsurpassed high-country fishing for grayling and cutthroat, brook, and rainbow trout, and hunting for moose, elk, deer, and black bear. The Jefferson, formed by the confluence of the Beaverhead and Big Hole, flows northeast for 70 miles, where it joins with the Madison and Gallatin at Three Forks, an ancient battleground of Crow and Blackfeet Indians, and marks the beginning of the mighty Missouri. Lewis and Clark named the Jefferson in honor of the great statesman responsible for the exploration and acquisition of the western United States.

Red Rock Lakes National Wildlife Refuge

Red Rock River rises high on the Continental Divide near the Henrys Lake area of the Targhee National Forest and flows through alpine meadows and precipitous gorges, plunging through Hell Roaring Creek canyon and the beautiful Alaska Basin, into Centennial Valley and the Red Rock Lakes National Wildlife Refuge, and winds westward through the Lima Reservoir, past the towns of Lima and Dell into the Clark Canyon Reservoir. The nesting areas in the 40,000–acre Red Rock Lakes National Wildlife Refuge, the single most important breeding grounds in the United States for the endangered trumpeter swan, are closed to fishing. The Red Rock from Dell to the Clark Canyon Reservoir is designated a red-ribbon trout stream and holds rainbow, cutthroat, and brown trout up to 7 pounds. Below Clark Canyon Dam, the Red Rock becomes the Beaverhead River.

Gateways & Accommodations

Dillon

(Pop. 4,500; zip code 59725; area code 406.) Headquarters of Beaverhead National Forest and seat of Beaverhead County, Dillon is set in the heart of the Beaverhead Valley ranch country. Area attractions include the old gold-rush ghost town of Bannack, one of Montana's oldest settlements and the first territorial capital, named after the Bannack Indians; Clark Canyon Reservoir State Recreation Area; and the Beaverhead County Museum with its fascinating displays of Indian artifacts and local pioneer and gold-rush history. Accommodations: *Best Western Royal Inn* (rates: $24–28 double), 49 excellent rooms and family suites, dining room, coffee shop, heated pool, at 650 N. Montana (683–4214); *Sundowner Motel* (rates: $21–24 double), 32 spacious rooms, at 500 N. Montana (683–2375).

Ennis

(Pop. 500; zip code 59729; area code 406.) Ennis is an old ranch town at the base of Fan Mountain on the famous Madison River, just south of Ennis Lake State Recreation Area. Ennis serves as a popular base camp for fishing and float trips on the Madison River. A national fish hatchery is located 12 miles south of town on U.S. Highway 287. Accommodations: *El Western Resort* (rates: $22–26 double), luxury rustic 1–4–bedroom log cabins and duplex cottages just south of town, on U.S. Hwy. 287 and the Madison River (682–4217); *Rainbow Valley Motel* (rates: $20–27 double), 18 deluxe rooms and family units in a scenic location, with heated pool, south of town on U.S. Hwy. 287 (682–4264).

Virginia City

(Pop. 100; zip code 59755; area code 406.) This colorful, historic gold-rush town due west of Ennis has been restored to recapture its rough 'n' ready Old West past. It was the first incorporated town in Montana, and after the discovery of gold in 1863 it became the second territorial capital as thousands of miners arrived to claim their share of the fabulous gold deposits at Alder Gulch, the richest placer deposit in the West. Alder Gulch, site of the Virginia City and Nevada City boom camps, produced some $300 million in gold during the height of the boom. During a seven-month period, 190 murders were committed by the notorious Plummer gang before they were run out of the territory. Some 21 road agents were hanged by vigilantes and buried in Boothill Cemetery. Today the restored buildings at Virginia City include the Wells Fargo Express Office, the Gilbert Brewery, the blacksmith shop, and the offices of the state's first newspaper. Area attractions include Nevada City, Boot Hill, the Virginia City Opera House, Watkin's Memorial Museum, the Bale of Hay Saloon, Tiffany windows in St. Paul's Episcopal Church, and the gold camp artifacts at the Thompson-Hickman Memorial Museum. Accommodations: *Fairweather Inn*, a restored gold rush hotel opposite the Wells Fargo Coffee House (rates: $19 double), 18 rooms on U.S. Hwy. 287 (843–5377); *Nevada City Hotel & Cabins* (rates: $19–25 double), 28 rooms in authentic gold rush log hotel and cabins, coffee shop, next to the Nevada City Music Hall on U.S. Hwy. 287 (843–5382).

Guest Ranches

★★★★*Canyon Creek Ranch & Guided Vacation Trips* is nestled at the base of 10,000–foot Sheriff Mountain high in the Pioneer Range of the Beaverhead National Forest. Ranch-operated trips provide access to some of the nation's top-ranked trout streams and alpine lakes country. Guided ranch trips include the June *Salmon Fly Hatch Float Trip* on Montana's blue-ribbon Big Hole River for big browns and rainbows. Only four trips are scheduled each year for this limited hatch. Guests spend four nights at the beautiful ranch, traveling to the river each morning and returning in the evening. Hearty breakfasts and dinners are served in the lodge. Lunches are usually eaten on the banks of the Big Hole, around a campfire, with fresh-caught fish as the main course. The *Canyon Creek Trout Fishing Trip* consists of wading, bank fishing, and floating several rivers, including the Big Hole and Beaverhead and wilderness streams for brown, rainbow, cutthroat, and brook trout. Fishermen stay in comfortable, modern log cabins, fully carpeted, with wood-burning fireplaces and private baths. Quality meals are enjoyed at the main lodge. The *Alpine Lakes Pack Trips* are taken in the Pioneer range of Beaverhead National Forest or in the 157,800–acre Anaconda-Pintlar Wilderness. A maximum of 10 persons are accommodated on each trip. Guests relax on their first and last nights at the main ranch and enjoy 8 nights and 7 days exploring the wilderness. Campsites are usually alongside one of several glacier lakes where fishing is good and wild flowers abound. The timberline meadows, slopes, and snowcapped peaks are inhabited by mule deer, elk, and mountain goat. During the fall, the ranch offers guided hunts for elk, mule deer, mountain goat, and sheep. Privacy, seclusion, and quality accommodations blend with the diversity of outdoor activities to make your trip a success. Lodging facilities are in four private log cabins. Each cabin is designed for four persons, with private bath, box-spring and innerspring mattresses, electric and propane lights, and a large wood-burning Franklin fireplace. All are fully carpeted and finished in authentic western decor. Porches are ideal for arm-chair relaxation or evening discussions. The rustic main lodge is the center of activity for delicious family-style meals and evening gatherings around the fireplace or on the porch. George and Sally Smith, your hosts, have 16 years of accommodating folks at Canyon Creek Ranch under their belts. General family activities for a 6–night and 5–day trip consist of a half-day float trip down the scenic Big Hole or Beaverhead River, where excellent fishing is enjoyed by novice and pro alike; an overnight pack trip to one of six pure alpine lakes uniquely beautiful and also offering big hard-fighting trout; a jeep trip to several mining ruins in the high country; and 8 hours of horseback riding in the alpine meadows above the ranch, where hundreds of wallflowers bloom the summer long. Many, many other family activities are also available. Guests arriving at Butte, Montana, via regularly scheduled airlines or private aircraft are met by Canyon Creek personnel and driven to the ranch, 54 miles southwest. Guests may drive directly to the ranch via the Trapper Creek Road, a half-hour trip out of Melrose up the canyon. For detailed information and rates, contact: Canyon Creek Ranch, Grand Domaine Retreats, 801 P Street, Lincoln, NE 68508 (402)477–9249.

★★★*Sundance Lodge* is a new year-round family resort in the Big Hole Valley on Highway 43 between Wise River and Wisdom, surrounded by the Beaverhead National Forest. The lodge is three miles from the Anaconda Pintlar Wilderness high country. Vacation activities include cross-country skiing, trout fishing, trail rides, float trips down the Big Hole River, fall hunting, sleigh rides, and hiking. Alpine skiers will enjoy the Deep Creek Ski Area, with its 1,000–foot vertical drop. Sundance offers rustic lodge facilities, large modern rooms, private baths, and electric heat. The lodge offers hearty western meals served family style in the dining room. Weekly American plan rates for lodge rooms are $160/person or $25/person per day. Weekly American plan rates for cabins with fireplaces are $195/person or $30/person per day. For additional information, contact: Sundance Lodge, Wise River, MT 59762 (406)689–2491.

Travel Services

Devers Brothers, Rt. 1, Box 27C, Dillon 59725, lead hunting and fishing expeditions throughout the state. Clinton C. Huth, *Wisdom Pack Station*, Wisdom 59761, leads hunting expeditions into Ravalli, Madison, Beaverhead, Silver Bow, Jefferson, Flathead, Gallatin, Deer Lodge, and Park counties, and fishing trips statewide. Accommodations include lodge, tent, and motel. Howard Keyes specializes in day trips statewide for hunting and fishing parties. Contact him through *Cottonwood Guide Service*, Rt. 2, Wilsall 59086. *Blue Sky Outfitters*, Rt. 1, Box 23, Dillon 59725, guides hunters and anglers in the renowned Big Hole and Beaverhead rivers country. *Jim Danskin* of Jim Danskin Tackle Shop, Box 276, West Yellowstone 59758, guides fly-fishermen on all rivers and lakes in Gallatin, Madison, and Yellowstone counties. *Will's Fly Fishing Center*, located across the border at P.O. Box 68, Island Park, ID 83429, guides fishermen along the Madison, Gallatin, Big Hole, and

Yellowstone rivers. The rustic *Sundance Lodge,* Wise River 59762, provides guided fishing and hunting in the Beaverhead National Forest and Anaconda-Pintlar Wilderness. The *Tobacco Root Guest Ranch,* Sheridan 59749, provides statewide guided fishing and big-game hunting trips. The rustic *Big Hole Lodge,* Wise River 59762, guides hunters and fishermen in the Beaverhead National Forest, Big Hole River area, and Anaconda-Pintlar Wilderness. *Angler's Paradise Lodge,* Melrose 59743, has guide service for hunters and fishermen along the Big Hole and Beaverhead rivers. *Reed Outfitting & Guide Service,* P.O. Box 645, Ennis 59729, operates in the Gallatin and Madison mountains. *Lakeview Ranch,* 2905 Harrison, Butte 59701, provides statewide fishing and hunting guide service. *Wise River Club,* Wise River 59762, offers fishing and hunting guide service throughout the Beaverhead National Forest. *Valley View Ranch,* Ennis 59729, guides big-game hunters and fishermen in the Beaverhead, Gallatin, and Yellowstone national park areas. Philip Wright of the *Complete Fly Fisher,* Box 105, Wise River 59762, guides anglers along the Big Hole, Madison, Beaverhead, Falls, Bitterroot, and Gallatin rivers. *Beaver Pond Sport Specialists,* 1700 West Main, Bozeman 59715, provides professional guide service and trips on the Big Hole, Beaverhead, Madison, Gallatin, and Yellowstone rivers.

Bitteroot National Forest

The Bitterroot National Forest encompasses 1.5 million acres of snowcapped peaks, alpine lakes and meadows, rushing mountain streams, and some of the most remote high-country wilderness in the West. The forest is located in west central Montana and takes in the rugged Anaconda-Pintlar Wilderness and a large portion of the vast Selway-Bitterroot Wilderness, which straddles the Montana-Idaho boundary along the crest of the Bitterroot Mountains. The Bitteroot River rises high in the alpine lakes of the wilderness along the western slope of the Continental Divide and meanders in a broad valley through the heart of the forest for 70 miles. The west and east branches of the Bitterroot meet at Conner, once known as the Place of Many Roads, where the long-gone trails of the Nez Percé and Salish crossed on their way east to the buffalo hunting grounds on the northern plains. A renowned float-fishing stream, the Bitterroot was named by the Salish Indians after the flower classified *Lewisin rediviva* by Meriwether Lewis in 1805 and found among the cottonwood stands that line the riverbanks. The Bitterroot holds large rainbow, brown, cutthroat, and brook trout. The rugged upper stretches of the river, including the West and East forks, provide top-ranked float-fishing for large rainbows. Its many oxbows and sloughs are fine shooting areas for duck and Canada goose. The Bitterroot high country and foothills are inhabited by mountain goat, deer, elk, and moose.

The Montana portion of the vast 1 million-acre Selway-Bitterroot Wilderness contains scores of sparkling blue alpine trout lakes at elevations ranging from 8,000 to 10,000 feet, which form the headwaters of the turbulent mountain tributaries that feed into the Bitterroot River. These high-country gems and the snow-fed mountain streams lie in the heart of elk and grizzly country and provide good fishing for rainbow, brook, and cutthroat trout. Access to the eastern slope of the range is by foot and packhorse trails, which are readily accessible from Highway 93 and the Nez Percé Trail road along the Selway River in Idaho.

The Indians made little use of this wilderness area. Their trails linking Idaho's Clearwater Valley with the Bitterroot Valley ran to the north and south, avoiding the rugged high country of the Bitterroot Divide. Their summer encampments were along the upper Selway (from the Nez Percé word *Selwah* meaning "smooth water"), lower Bear Creek, and Moose Creek areas, where they fished for salmon and steelhead and hunted the natural mineral licks for mule deer and elk. Wilderness campers in the area may see the remains of marten sets notched in trees and old line cabins built by trappers who once worked the area. The design of the marten set notches varied with the trapper, from a cathedral or rounded shape to a rectangular notch.

Information Sources, Maps & Access

For detailed information and a full-color *Bitterroot National Forest Map* (50¢) and *Selway-Bitterroot Wilderness Map* (50¢) write: Supervisor, Bitterroot National Forest, Hamilton, MT 59840 (406)363–3131. The Bitterroot National Forest is reached via U.S. Highways 93 and 10 and Montana State Highway 38. Supplies, guides, and outfitting services are available at Sula, Missoula, Hamilton, Darby, Conner, Woodside, Victor, Stevensville, Bonner, and Clinton.

Gateways & Accommodations

Hamilton

(Pop. 2,500; zip code 59840; area code 406.) This is the headquarters of the Bitterroot National Forest and the major business center of the Bitterroot Valley. Area attractions include the Big Hole National Battlefield, Painted Rocks State Recreation Area, St. Mary's Mission (the oldest church in the Pacific Northwest), Fort Owen State Monument, scenic drives and float trips on the Bitterroot River, and the Roaring Lion Restaurant on U.S. Highway 93. Accommodations: *Best Western Hamilton Motel* (rates: $30–32 double), 17 rooms and family units on U.S. Hwy. 93 (363–2142).

Guest Ranches

★★★★*Nez Perce Ranch* is one of the finest wilderness vacation ranches in the West. The ranch is located deep in the Bitteroot Mountains on the historic Nez Perce Trail followed by Lewis and Clark, surrounded by the scenic high country, tall pines and fir trees of the Bitteroot National Forest. The ranch lies adjacent to the vast Selway-Bitteroot Wilderness Area—the largest federally classified wilderness in the Continental United States. This delightful, Old West ranch, in one of the few unspoiled areas left in this country, is on the Nez Perce Fork of the Bitteroot River. The surrounding streams are a fly fishing paradise. While there are no planned recreational activities at the Ranch, guests enjoy wilderness fly-ins, hiking, float trips, horseback riding, birding, wildlife/fauna photography, cross-country skiing, rock hounding, mushrooming . . . and more. While no hunting is done on the Ranch, we offer quick access to over a million acres of forest—the Ranch is bordered on three sides by the Bitterroot National Forest. There are numerous logging roads a short drive from the Ranch providing quick access to areas otherwise difficult to reach. Game in the area consist of elk, deer, moose, mountain sheep and goats, bear and mountain lion. We can put you in contact with licensed and bonded outfitters if you desire their services or guide service on a daily basis. Located in deep pines on a ledge overlooking the beautiful Nez Perce Fork, each guest home offers complete and absolute privacy, comfort and good Western living. All guest homes are brand new, constructed of native logs, and kept sparkling clean. The floor plan includes a large family room complete with fireplace and open beam ceiling, efficiency kitchen—electric freezer/refrigerator combination and 30" electric stove, stainless steel sink and plenty of windows to make meal preparations as pleasant as possible. Baths are complete, including shower/tub facilities and independent heating system. The downstairs bedroom contains double bed, and the upstairs loft bedroom contains two double beds. A balcony overlooks the family room. Nez Perce Ranch guest homes are furnished in complete detail—all you need bring are personal items and groceries for meals you prefer to prepare. Pack a sleeping bag if your itinerary includes a pack trip or hike into a remote fishing spot. All meals are available daily served at the ranch Bunk House. Fine cuisine enjoyed in a relaxing and informal atmosphere. Meal costs are extra and are in the $20–25 range per person. Experience has proven that most families prefer breakfast in the privacy of their own home, lunching while fishing, hiking, etc., dining together in the evening at the Bunk House. Rates are $143.75 per person/ minimum weekly rate of $575.00 per home. A $200.00 deposit confirms reservations.

★★*Rainbow Wilderness Camp*, at Trapper Peak Ranch in the Bitterroot Valley, is especially tailored for young people 11–18 years of age who want to become better acquainted with the great outdoors in a true wilderness setting. Among the many activities offered during 4–week sessions are float trips on the exciting Salmon River, week-long seminars in wilderness survival skills, swimming, fishing, horseback pack trips, backpacking, and leisurely nature hikes. The ranch itself has excellent facilities, newly remodeled to insure high standards of comfort and safety. A highly experienced staff of counselors with extensive knowledge of the wilderness oversees all camp activities. The owners, Tom and Priscilla Drinville, have four teenagers of their own and have lived and worked with young people in Montana all their lives. Everything from basic horsemanship to building a log raft is taught with great patience and skill. Campers may choose a week of specific activities (backpacking, horseback trip, survival skills, Salmon River trip, or introductory week) at $197–272 for 7 days, or decide on a month-long stay covering all the above ($863 per camper). For detailed information write: Rainbow Wilderness Camp, Trapper Peak Ranch, P.O. Box 246, Darby, MT 59829 (406)821–3407.

★★*Trapper Peak Ranch and Indian Lake Outfitters*, in the Bitterroot Valley, offers professionally guided hunting and fishing trips in the magnificent Idaho-Montana wilderness. Hunts are sponsored fall through spring for the wide variety of game that abounds in the Selway-Bitterroot area: trophy elk, whitetail deer, mountain lion, bobcat, grizzly, mountain goat, and moose. During the summer, fishing and pack trips are scheduled to clear mountain streams and lakes teeming with rainbow, Dolly Varden, cutthroat, and brook trout. Trips operate from either comfortable wilderness base camps with roomy sleeping tents or bunkhouse-style quarters at the ranch. Wholesome and bounteous meals are served western-style at the ranch and base camps. You supply your personal gear, sleeping bag,

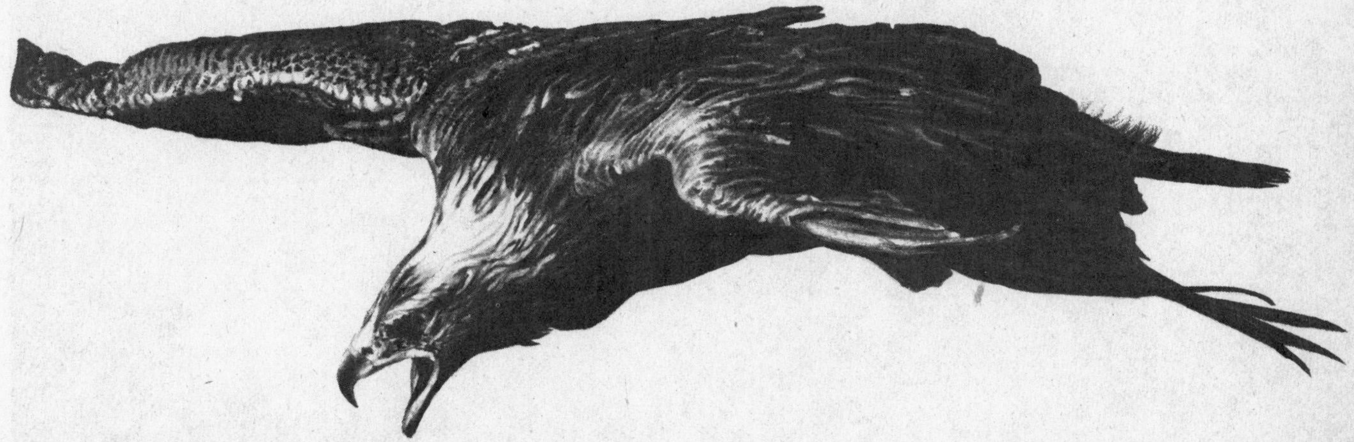

guns, fishing tackle, and saddle bags, if necessary; Indian Lake provides the rest. Transportation on the trips is by 4–wheel-drive vehicles, on horses, or on foot. All cleaning, skinning, and care of big game is provided for, including cold storage at the ranch. Length of trips varies from 7 to 10 days. Rates: $420 per person for 7 days of fishing; $900–1,750 per person for 7–day hunts, depending on the season and choice of game. For additional information write: Indian Lake Outfitters, Trapper Peak Ranch, P.O. Box 246, Darby, MT 59829 (406)821–3407 or (406)821–3665.

Travel Services

Bar 44 Outfitters, headquartered in Hamilton, Montana, sponsors guided hunting trips in the heart of the magnificent Selway-Bitterroot Wilderness. Hunts begin at Lost Horse Ranger Station with a full day's horseback ride through red cedar forests into the Idaho backcountry. After 32 miles you arrive at Bar 44's base camp, where good food, roomy tents with foam-padded beds and wood stoves, and 7–10 days of true wilderness hunting await you. Elk, deer, and bear are abundant in the Bar 44's 192,000–acre area, and expert guides assure the greatest possible hunter success. Guides will also care for your game until it reaches your point of departure, and make arrangements for coping, cutting, and wrapping. Bar 44 furnishes all equipment except saddle scabbard, gun, ammunition, sleeping bag, meat sacks, and personal gear. Hunting dates are from around mid-September through the third week in November. For complete details write: Bar 44 Outfitters, P.O. Box 493, Hamilton, MT 59840 (406)363–3522.

Custer National Forest & Beartooth Primitive Area

Divided into four major units scattered across the southern part of the state, Montana's share of the Custer National Forest covers nearly 1,100,000 acres of staggering mountain peaks, scenic lakes, glaciers, rushing waterfalls, and high plateaus. The stark granite outcroppings of the Beartooth Range dissolve into forested slopes in the east and then into rolling prairie in the Long Pines area of eastern Montana. Many plateaus in the forest, each extending over several square miles, exceed levels of 11,000 feet. The granddaddy of the Beartooth Mountains and Montana's highest mountain, Granite Peak (12,799 ft.), dominates the perpetual snowfields. Of the many lesser peaks, twenty-five tower above 12,000 feet. Exposed rock in the Beartooths, the oldest known in North America, is some 2.7 billion years old.

Information Sources, Maps & Access

For detailed vacation travel information, the full-color *Custer National Forest Map* (50¢), and the free *Beartooth High Lake Country Map*, contact: Supervisor, Custer National Forest, 2602 1st Ave. N., Billings, MT 59101 (406)657–6361. A free *Bighorn Canyon/Pryor Mountain Area Map & Guide* may be obtained by writing: National Park Service, P.O. Box 458, Fort Smith, MT 59035. The Custer National Forest is reached via U.S. Highways 212 and 310 and Montana State Highways 307, 397, 323, and 308. Supplies, guides, and outfitters are available at Ekalaka, Mill Iron, Fishtail, Roscoe, Red Lodge, Cooke City, Warren, Belfry, Ashland, and Birney. Ranger stations are at Ashland, Fort Howes, Red Lodge, Camp Crook (South Dakota), and Meyers Creek.

Recreation & Scenic Areas

Beartooth Primitive Area

Straddling the peaks of the Beartooth Range near the Wyoming border, the 230,000–acre Beartooth Primitive Area covers about half of the westernmost unit of Custer National Forest and spills over to the south into the Gallatin National Forest. Much of the wilderness area and surrounding forestland is above the timberline at 9,000 feet, and the country is rugged in the extreme, encompassing rock-strewn plateaus, high mountain peaks, steep canyons, glaciers, and some 300 mountain lakes which hold grayling and golden, brook, rainbow, and cutthroat trout. Near the western periphery of the primitive area flows the Stillwater River, a designated red-ribbon trout stream for browns, rainbows, and some brookies.

Custer Battlefield & Bighorn Canyon National Recreation Area

Between the Beartooth and Ashland divisions of the Custer National Forest lie the Crow and Northern Cheyenne Indian reservations, encompassing the Bighorn Lake and River, Rosebud and Bighorn mountains, and the Custer Battlefield National Monument. Just off U.S. 90, the Custer Monument and battlefield cemetery are reminders of that hot Sunday in June 1876 when the controversial Lt. Col. George A. Custer and 261 of his men met their death in an ill-fated encounter with Sioux and Cheyenne warriors. Most of the Bighorn country is the original home of Crow Indians, who called it the good country in recognition of the peaceful existence they led there. Winding through the Bighorn Mountains, the 3,000–foot-high rust-colored cliffs of the Bighorn Canyon tower above the river of the same name. River, mountains, and canyon all take their name from the bighorn, or Rocky Mountain, sheep native to the area.

Today, the Yellowtail Dam across the Bighorn River in Montana has created the 47–mile-long Bighorn Lake, the setting of the Bighorn Canyon National Recreation Area. This area of spectacular scenery is known as the land that time forgot. Tremendous geologic forces have metamorphosed once level layers of rock surrounding the basin into immense walls, or anticlines. The largest of these great arches is the Bighorn, which extends south from Yellowtail Dam to form the Bighorn Mountains. The river has cut deeply into the arch upstream of the dam, creating colorful cliffs rising almost one-half mile over the river, and exposing fossil-rich rocks up to 500 million years old.

Grasshopper Glacier

Another fascinating sight in Beartooth country is the Grasshopper Glacier, just north of Cooke City, named for the millions of ice-trapped insects lining the almost perpendicular face of this 80–foot cliff. Succeeding swarms of grasshoppers, chilled in passing over the glacier, fall each year and become embedded in the layers of black-flecked ice reaching depths of over 60 feet.

Gateways & Accommodations

Billings

(Pop. 61,600; zip code, see below; area code 406.) One of Montana's major manufacturing centers, Billings is on the west bank of the Yellowstone River. Area attractions include Boothill Cemetery, Chief Black Otter Trail Scenic Drive, the Yellowstone County Historical Museum, Indian caves, the Western Heritage Center, and the Range Rider of the Yellowstone Monument. Accommodations: *Best Western Northern Hotel* (rates: $26–27 double), 210 rooms and suites, Golden Belle Restaurant and Saloon, coffee shop, airport transportation service, downtown at 1st Ave. North and Broadway, 59103 (245–5121); *Best Western Ponderosa Inn* (rates: $29–31 double), 134 rooms and suites, restaurant, cocktail lounge, heated indoor pools, saunas, at 2511 1st Ave. North, 59104 (259–5511); *Dude Rancher Lodge* (rates: $21–24 double), 56 excellent rooms and suites, coffee shop, at 415 N. 29th St. off I-90 business loop, 59103 (259–5561); *Ramada Inn* (rates: $34 double), 253 excellent rooms and family units, dining facilities, cocktail lounge, heated pool, airport transportation service, 59104 (248–7151); *War Bonnet American Traveler Inn* (rates: $32–36 double), 102 superb rooms and suites, dining room, cocktail lounge, heated pool, airport service, at 2612 Belknap Ave., 59101 (248–7761).

Columbus

(Pop. 1,200; zip code 59018; area code 406.) The town was founded as a stage station on the historic Yellowstone Trail. Area attractions include the headwaters of the Stillwater River and the Absaroka Range. Accommodations: *Big Sky Motel* (rates: $18–20 double), 20 good rooms and family units, at Pike Ave. and Allen St. (322–4431).

Hardin

(Pop. 2,700; zip code 59034; area code 406.) Area attractions include Custer Battlefield and the Bighorn Canyon area. Accommodations: *American Inn* (rates: $25–27 double), 23 good rooms and family units, at 1324 Crawford Ave. (665–1870); *Western Motel—Friendship Inn* (rates: $25–27 double), 28 excellent rooms and family units, at 830 W. 3rd (665–2296).

Red Lodge—Gateway to Yellowstone Park

(Pop. 1,800; zip code 59068; area code 406.) Named after the Red Lodge clan of Indians who camped here long ago, the town is a spectacular tourist gateway to Yellowstone National Park and the Beartooth Mountains. Red Lodge is on the beautiful Beartooth Scenic Highway, which leads from the town through the alpine lakes of the Beartooth Plateau into Yellowstone Park to Cooke City. Area attractions include the Red Lodge Zoo, the Big Sky Historical Museum, the Red Lodge Mountain ski area in Custer National Forest, and the Sundance Recreation Area with its rustic alpine log chalet for dining off the Beartooth Highway. Accommodations: *Best Western Motor Lodge* (rates: $24–30 double), 14 rooms and family units, at 320 S. Broadway (446–1414); *Chateau Rouge* (rates: $28–32 double), 24 superb rustic rooms and family units with fireplaces and kitchens, on Beartooth Highway 212 (446–9975); *Rock Creek Mine Condominiums* (rates: $25–35 double), 38 rustic rooms and suites, Old Piney Dell Restaurant, in scenic Rock Creek area, cocktail lounge, skiing, fishing, tennis, horseback trails and riding on Beartooth Highway 212(446–1111); *Skyview Motel* (rates: $24–26 double), 15 rooms and family units, at 820 South Broadway, on Beartooth Highway 212(446–1510).

Guest Ranches

★★★★*Beartooth Ranch* occupies one of the most spectacular sites in Montana. Surrounded by the towering mountains of Custer National Forest, the ranch is bordered on the west by the 25,000–acre Beartooth Primitive Area, which extends all the way to Yellowstone Park. Trails through the primitive area allow you to explore snowy peaks, hidden valleys, rivers, glaciers, and trout-filled lakes. Beartooth maintains its own stable for day rides and longer pack trips in this awesome high country. Wrangling, rodeos, trail rides, and riding instruction are specialties of the ranch, but there's a host of other activities as well: fly-fishing for trout in the Stillwell River and other local streams, white-water rafting, scenic and fishing pack-trips, cookouts, square dances, and more. Accommodations are available in 12 spacious lodge rooms, all with bath and shower, and all facing Woodbine Falls across the river. Guest cabins, located in groves of shady trees, have private baths, living rooms, and fireplaces. Cabins vary in size to fit your family or group requirements. Daily maid service is included in the rates. All meals are served in a separate log and stone dining room, with an emphasis on home-made quality and freshness. For complete information write: Beartooth Ranch, Heart Four Bar, Nye, MT 59061 (406)327–4353 or (406)327–4304.

Travel Services

In the Beartooth High Country area *Boulder River Ranch*, McLeod 59052, leads big-game parties along the Boulder River drainage. *Big Horn Outfitters*, Route 1, Box 171, Joliet 59041, is a guide and outfitter for hunting and fishing expeditions in Park and Stillwater counties and the Gardiner and Jardine areas. *Beartooth Ranch*, Nye 59061, leads hunting and fishing trips in the Stillwater River, Slough Creek, and Lake Abundance Creek areas. Accommodations include cabins and tents. Florence Paulson of *Paintbrush Trails*, Box 902, Red Lodge 59068, specializes in day trips for hunting and fishing parties in the Custer National Forest. *Scott Brothers Outfitters*, 1925 Grand Ave., Billings 59102, lead day trips in the Yellowstone River area and in the Broadus and Powder River country. Edward Whaley of *Wilderness Outfitters and Guides*, Box 452, Hardin 59034, is a guide for hunting and fishing expeditions statewide. *Beartooth Plateau Outfitters*, Red Lodge 59068, guides fishermen by pack train in the high lakes country of Carbon and Stillwater counties. The 33 *Ranch*, McLeod 59052, guides hunters and fishermen in the Crazy Mountains and Custer National Forest. The *Hawley Mountain Guest Ranch*, Box 4, McLeod 59052, provides fishing and big-game hunting guides. *Rocky Mountain Outfitters*, Box 108, Roberts 59070, provide guided big-game hunting trips in Carbon, Stillwater, and Park counties.

Montana School of Fly-Fishing, located on the Stillwater River 36 miles northeast of Yellowstone National Park adjacent to the Beartooth Primitive Area, offers expert fly-fishing instruction, wilderness fishing expeditions, pack trips, and lodging at the Stillwater River Ranch. For info on rates, clothing, and pickup services at Billings, write: Montana School of Fly-Fishing, Nye 59061 (406)327–4365.

Yellowstone Wilderness Guides offers guided trips for backpacking, mountaineering, and cross-country skiing in the majestic Beartooth Primitive Area and Yellowstone National Park. For detailed information and rates, contact: Yellowstone Wilderness Guides, Red Lodge 59068 (406)446–2636.

Deerlodge National Forest & Lewis and Clark Caverns

This 1,357,500–acre reserve, astride the Continental Divide in southwestern Montana, takes its name from a curious natural landmark, an ash-colored mound shaped like a gigantic haystack which once sat in the middle of the valley at the head of Clarks Fork. On cold mornings, a column of steam would rise from its summit, like

plumes of smoke from a chimney. Closer inspection revealed that the mound was actually a boiling spring surrounded by a self-formed block of cement. Snake Indians called the object the White-Tailed Deer Lodge because deer, abundant in the nearby swamps, would come to lick the salt deposited on the mound's sides.

The forest is situated within the headwaters of the historic Jefferson and Clark Fork rivers, both renowned to fly-fishermen for brown and rainbow trout, and embraces a number of spectacular natural attractions, including the Tobacco Root and Highland mountains, Georgetown Lake, the Boulder River of the Jefferson, and Flint Creek Range. The Deerlodge area covers some of the richest mineral deposits in the state. Rock hounds and fortune hunters will find that the forest offers plenty of opportunities for pursuing their favorite pastimes. Panning for gold has frustrated many a modern-day prospector, but those who are willing to settle for brilliance instead of value will discover abundant deposits of fool's gold. Rubies have been found in Cottonwood and Upper Rock creeks in Granite County and in the Ruby River within Madison County. Placer gravels in the Tobacco Root and Ruby mountains hold garnets, and industrial-quality sapphires are found in the westernmost section of the Deerlodge.

Like many other regions of Montana, Deerlodge was once the scene of furious activity, when gold was suddenly discovered in the second half of the 19th century. The hopes and heartbreaks of that incredible era are spelled out by such names as Lost Dutchman, Miner's Gulch, Homestake Creek, Silver Hill, and Gold Creek. Abandoned mining towns, like Granite and Pioneer, are forlorn reminders of the boom towns that mushroomed overnight and then disappeared when the rush was over. Elkhorn, near the present-day town of Boulder, is another ghost settlement that prospered after 1872, when gold and silver were discovered in the area. Fourteen old saloons in this one tiny town, their walls riddled with bullet holes, testify to a hell-roaring past, when disputes were settled with fists or shotguns.

Less ominous and certainly more breathtaking is the Lewis and Clark Cavern, off U.S. 10 just southeast of the forest. The third-largest series of caves in the United States, Lewis and Clark Cavern is a succession of passageways and vaulted chambers studded with stalagmites and hung with a broken curtain of stalactites. Tortuous paths lead to the various recesses—the Cathedral Room, the Coffin, the Deepest Room, and the Lion's Den—where underground formations provide natural pillars, domes, spires, and colorful mosaics streaked with shades of golden brown and amber. The full tour

requires steady footing and an expert guide equipped with a miner's lamp.

Information Sources, Maps & Access

Detailed forest recreation information and a full-color *Deerlodge National Forest Map* (50¢) may be obtained by writing: Supervisor, Deerlodge National Forest, P.O. Box 400, Federal Building, Butte, MT 59701 (406)723–6561, ext. 2351. The Deerlodge National Forest is reached via U.S. Highways 10 and 91, Interstates 91 and 15, and Montana Highways 41, 287, 48, 274, 348, and 43. Supplies, information, outfitting services, and guides are available at Butte, Boulder, Twin Bridges, Whitehall, Jefferson City, Basin, Wickes, Deer Lodge, Elk Park, Divide, Warmsprings, Opportunity, Anaconda, Hall, and Philipsburg.

Gateways & Accommodations

Anaconda

(Pop. 9,800; zip code 59711; area code 406.) Base of the great Anaconda copper works, the city was first named Copperopolis in 1883. Area attractions include Georgetown Lake, Big Hole National Battlefield, Lost Creek State Park, and tours of the famous Anaconda plant and copper smelter. Accommodations: *Tradewind Motel* (rates: $20–24 double), 20 rooms and family units at 1600 E. Commercial (563–3428); *Vagabond Lodge* (rates: $20–22 double), 20 rooms at 1421 E. Park (563–5251).

Butte

(Pop. 23,400; zip code 59701; area code 406.) This is a famous mining center, originally settled in 1864 when two prospectors from Virginia City discovered placer gold in the Clarks Fork, known back then as Silver Bow Creek. Subsequently, Marcus Daly discovered one of the world's richest deposits of copper and in less than 20 years became the head of one of the world's most powerful mineral monopolies and a founder of Butte—known as "the richest hill on earth." Area attractions include the World Museum of Mining, Copper King Mansion (219 W. Granite St.), Lewis and Clark Caverns State Park, Berkley Pit Mine, and Lydia's Restaurant (on Highway 10 South) featuring Italian and American cuisine and a collection of modern metal art. Accommodations: *Best Western War Bonnet Inn* (rates: $33–37 double) 136 superb rooms, Apache Dining Room, coffee shop, cocktails, heated pool at 2100 Cornell Ave. (494–7800).

Deer Lodge

(Pop. 4,300; zip code 59722; area code 406.) The town, bisected by the Clark Fork, was an important stop on the old Mullan Wagon Road traveled by pioneers and miners on their way to the notorious Bearmouth mining camp. Area attractions include the Grant-Kohrs Ranch National Historic Site, one of the first ranches established in the Pacific Northwest. Area restaurants include 4B's off Interstate 90, Exit 184 (846–2620) and Scharf's Family Restaurant at 819 Main St. (846–3300).

Lodges

★★★*Fairmont Hot Springs Resort*, located at the foot of the beautiful Pintlar Mountains, is a 4–season family resort famous for its plush but informal accommodations. Guests have their choice of 4 indoor and outdoor swimming pools (2 are larger than Olympic size), all of them naturally heated by mineral springs. Other amenities include an 18–hole golf course and all-weather tennis courts. Horseback rides on trail-wise horses and hiking trips through the unspoiled Anaconda-Pintlar Wilderness are popular, too. The streams and lakes of the region promise fine trout fishing for the angler. In winter, nearby Discovery Basin has challenging ski slopes for all levels of ability, a double chair and pony lifts, cross-country trails, and a professional ski school. Ice-fishing on Georgetown Lake and snowmobiling are also favorite cold weather pursuits. Accommodations are in 190 deluxe rooms and suites, pleasantly furnished with private baths, TV, and single, double, or king-size beds. Dining facilities include a family restaurant, informal coffee shop, and cocktail lounge with dancing and live entertainment. Rates: $38–42 daily, double occupancy, $4 for extra person sharing room. For additional information, write: Fairmont Hot Springs Resort, Anaconda, MT 59711 (406)797–3241.

Travel Services

Sager Tours, which originate at the Fairmont Hot Springs Resort near Anaconda, offers sightseeing trips, 4–6 hours in length, to points of natural and historic interest in southwestern Montana. Some of the sights visited include the Lewis & Clark Caverns, Butte and the famous Berkley Pit, area ghost towns, and the historic Kohrs Ranch, an early Montana cattle ranch preserved in all details. Sager also offers fishing trips to Georgetown Lake (guide, equipment, boat and motor provided) and panning for sapphires in a local creek. Tour costs average $5–12 per person (minimum of 4 to a group), and in some cases include lunch. Longer tours up to 6 days are available; emphasis is on touring the old mining camps, rockhounding and geology, backpacking, fishing, or sightseeing. Write for details: Sager Tours, Fairmont Hot Springs Resort, 801 West 7th St., Anaconda, MT 59711 (406)563–7608.

Flathead National Forest

Named for the tepee-dwelling tribe that settled along the shores of Flathead Lake and in the Bitterroot Valley, this majestic forest reserve encompasses 2.5 million acres along the northern Rockies of northwestern Montana. Timbered mountains towering high above clear lakes, fast-flowing streams, and falls are the dominant features of this outstanding big-game hunting, wilderness fishing, and camping area. An excellent network of forest trails and roads winds through seemingly endless acres of larch, western white and yellow pine, Engelmann spruce, Douglas fir, and other virgin species that have escaped the chainsaw and ax, and provides access to the forest's superb fishing, hunting, and wilderness camping areas: Flathead Lake, Mission Mountains Primitive Area, Spotted Bear River, Jewel Basin, Swan River, Stillwater River, Bob Marshall Wilderness, Great Northern Mountains, and the north, south, and middle forks of the Flathead River, one of the country's great wild rivers, with superb fly-fishing for rainbow, cutthroat, and lunker Dolly Varden trout up to 20 pounds.

Information Sources, Maps & Access

For detailed vacation recreation information, a full-color *Flathead National Forest Map* (50¢), a *Bob Marshall Wilderness Map* (50¢), a *Mission Mountains Wilderness Map* (50¢), and the free *Guide to the Mission Mountains Wilderness* and *Hungry Horse Reservoir Recreation Area Map*, write: Supervisor, Flathead National Forest, 290 N. Main St., Kalispell, MT 59901 (406)755–5401. The Flathead National Forest is reached via U.S. Highways 2 and 93 and Montana State Highways 200, 40, 35, and 28. Outfitters, guides, supplies, and lodging are available at Kalispell, Polson, Whitefish, Columbia Falls, Hungry Horse, Coram, Martin City, Swan Lake, Creston, Bigfork, Somers, Kila, Marion, Elmo, Proctor, Arlee, St. Ignatius, Dixon, Perma, Ovando, Pablo, and Ronan.

Chinese Wall, near head of Moose Creek

Recreation Areas

Big Mountain Recreation Area & Hungry Horse Reservoir

The Flathead National Forest offers fine opportunities for boating and fishing on Tally, Swan, Whitefish, Lindbergh, Ashley, and Holland lakes. Eight miles north of Whitefish in the northern part of the forest is the Big Mountain Recreation Area, with ski trails for beginners and experts alike. Chalet and lodge accommodations, double chair lifts, T-bars, and rope tows are available. In the heart of the forest is the Hungry Horse Reservoir, surrounded by a key big-game range, beaches, campgrounds, and boat-launching ramps. Trolling for cutthroat trout is popular at the north end of the reservoir, and Dolly Varden are often caught along the southern end. The scenic Jewel Basin near the Bob Marshall Wilderness and due west of Hungry Horse Reservoir embraces exquisite gemlike lakes at the head of Graves and Aeneas creeks. The Jewel Basin wild country offers spectacular backpacking and wilderness camping opportunities among high-country crags and meadows.

Flathead Lake Area

Framed by the sheer-walled mountains of the Swan Range on the east and the Whitefish Range to the north, the Flathead Valley offers a haven in the midst of rocky peaks, and was called by the Indians "the park between the mountains." Entrance to the valley was a difficult and hazardous feat, and no permanent settlement in the area was accomplished until 1881. With the arrival of the Great Northern Railroad 10 years later, both lumbering and agriculture stimulated further growth and development. The valley is covered in part by the waters of Flathead Lake, just west of the national forest. One of the largest natural freshwater bodies within the continental United States, the lake is 28 miles long and 10 miles wide and is studded with tree-covered islands near its western shore. Just beyond the town of Dayton is a series of painted rocks, colored pictographs left by an early Indian artist. The lake offers fine fishing for trout, salmon, bass, and whitefish, as well as opportunities for swimming, boating, and waterskiing. Two campgrounds are located south of Woods Bay on the eastern shore.

Mission Mountains & Bob Marshall Wilderness

Two large sections of the Flathead have been set aside as roadless wilderness areas, the Mission Mountains Primitive Area in the Swan Lake Ranger District, and the Bob Marshall Wilderness, encompassing the Big Prairie Ranger Station and parts of other ranger districts. Trail systems in both areas permit backcountry travel on horseback, but no motorized vehicles or equipment are allowed. The 75,000 acres comprising the Mission Mountains Primitive Area offer a high-country retreat of seldom paralleled scenic beauty—rugged shining peaks, several small glaciers, alpine lakes, meadows, and clear cold streams.

To the east of the Mission Mountains, the Bob Marshall Wilderness lies along the Continental Divide for 60 miles within the Flathead and Lewis and Clark national forests. This vast, million-acre wildland is the summer range for three major elk herds and one of the last strongholds of native black-spotted cutthroat. The beauty of the rugged peaks and cold alpine lakes is heightened by the 12–mile-long escarpment known as the Chinese Wall, with its 1,000–foot vertical face through which there are only three passes. The terrain varies abruptly between 4,000–foot valleys and 9,000–foot cliffs. There is good fly-fishing for 3–pound rainbows and black-spotted cutthroat in the South Fork River, which rises on the western side of the Continental Divide and flows north into the Flathead, and in the tributaries that flow into it. There are also Dolly Varden—an occasional 20–pounder—and the ever present whitefish in the Big Salmon, Sunburst, Spotted Bear, and Lena rivers. The wilderness is famous for its elk, mule deer, whitetail deer, black and grizzly bear, and mountain goat; this is also the spring, summer, and fall range of the state's largest herd of bighorn sheep. Mountain goats are especially numerous along the cliffs of the Chinese Wall, and Shiras moose roam the Youngs, Basin, upper Middle Fork, and Danaher Creek valleys. Canada lynx, cougar, marten, coyote, and wolverine are present in the wilderness, although they are rarely seen.

National Bison Range

The National Bison Range, established in 1908 to save the great plains buffalo from extinction, covers 29 square miles south of Flathead Lake. The once vast herds of Buffalo, slaughtered at the turn of the century with the building of the Union Pacific Railroad, are now protected in this area of high grassy hills and stands of

ponderosa pine and groves of trembling aspen. The refuge is also inhabited by bighorn sheep, antelope, elk, whitetail deer, and Franklin and blue grouse. The area is easily reached via the Yellowstone-Glacier route, over U.S. Highway 93 to Ravalli and the junction with U.S. 10A. The refuge headquarters is at Moiese.

Gateways & Accommodations

Bigfork

(Pop. 4,500; zip code 59911; area code 406.) Bigfork is a popular tourist center on the eastern shore of the head of Flathead Lake near the mouth of the Swan River. Area attractions include the Woods Bay and Wayfarer recreation areas. Accommodations: *Holiday Resort Motel* (rates: $25–35 double), spacious, rustic rooms and family units, lake activities and cruises on Flathead Lake, on State Hwy. 35 (982–3482); *Timbers Motel* (rates: $26–29 double), 29 large, outstanding rooms and family units, heated pool, on State Hwy. 35 (837–6200).

Columbia Falls

(Pop. 2,700; zip code 59912; area code 406.) This is a gateway to the northern regions of Flathead National Forest and Glacier National Park. Accommodations: *Bad Rock Canyon Motel* (rates: $14–18 double), 9 rooms and family units, at 7075 U.S. Hwy. 2 (892–5969); *Cedar Lodge Motel* (rates: $16–18 double), 18 good rooms and family kitchen units, on State Hwy. 40 West (892–3274); *Mountain Shadows Motel* (rates: $16–20 double), 20 rooms and family units, restaurant, at the junction of U.S. Hwy. 2 and State Hwy. 40 (892–4333).

Kalispell

(Pop. 10,500; zip code 59901; area code 406.) Kalispell is the major vacation gateway to Flathead National Forest recreation areas and Glacier National Park to the northeast. The town, originally a fur-trading post of the Hudson's Bay Company, lies in beautiful Flathead Valley, flanked by the Whitefish Range on the north and the Swan Range on the east. Area attractions include Fort Kalispell, Hungry Horse Dam, the 23–room Conrad Mansion Historic Museum, and Ashley Lake and Bitterroot Lake state recreation areas on U.S. Highway 2. Flathead Lake lies just to the south. Accommodations: *Best Western Outlaw Inn & Hennessy's Restaurant* (rates: $32 double), outstanding rooms and dining, heated indoor pool, and saunas, on U.S. Hwy. 93 (755–6100); *Four Seasons Motor Inn* (rates: $24–28 double), 101 excellent rooms and suites, coffee shop, on U.S. Hwy. 93 (755–6123); *Red Lion Motor Inn & 4B's Black Angus Steak House* (rates: $33–38 double), 63 superb rooms and family units, dining, and cocktail lounge, at 1330 U.S. Hwy. 2 West (755–6700).

Whitefish

(Pop. 3,300; zip code 59937; area code 406.) On beautiful 7–mile long Whitefish Lake, the town is a popular tourist center and a Flathead National Forest and Glacier Park gateway. Area attractions include Hungry Horse Dam, Big Mountain Ski Area, and the Whitefish Lake State Recreation Area. Accommodations: *Alpinglow Inn* (rates: $25–48 double), 54 deluxe units in Ptarmigan Village on Big Mountain, with dining room, cocktail lounge, heated pool, saunas, near ski lifts (862–3511); *Bay Point Resort* (rates on request),

deluxe vacation units on beautiful Whitefish Lake with swimming pool, aqua sauna, boating, fishing, waterskiing, sailing, golf, skiing at Big Mountain, and quick access to Glacier Park, only 28 miles away, contact Vacations North, Box 1015 (862–2331 or 3302); *Mountain Holiday Motel* (rates: $28–30 double), 34 deluxe rooms and family units, heated pool, outdoor recreation, on U.S. Hwy. 93 (862–2548); *Ptarmigan Village* (rates: $35 double), 55 deluxe condominium units in a spectacular alpine setting on Big Mountain, overlooking Flathead Valley and Whitefish Lake, with touring trails, 21 miles of slopes, 2 tennis courts, golf, boating, fishing, hiking, and 2 heated pools with Jacuzzi and sauna (862–3594); *Viking Vacation Lodge* (rates: $32–35 double), 42 luxury rooms on Whitefish Lake with heated pool, sauna, dining room, cocktail lounge, coffee shop, rental ski equipment and fishing boats, courtesy bus service (862–3547).

Lodges & Guest Ranches

★★★*Flathead Lake Lodge Ranch* is a family vacation resort located on 2,000 acres surrounded by the Flathead National Forest wilderness. Ranch activities include horseback riding, rodeos, cookouts, canoeing, sailing, cruises of Flathead Lake, swimming in a heated pool, and tennis, as well as backpacking trips, packhorse trips, and fly-fishing in the Flathead River, Glacier National Park, and the National Bison Range. Accommodations are in spacious modern cottages and rooms in the massive, rustic log lodge. Daily rates include all activities (except for special guided packhorse, fishing, and backpacking trips and trap shooting). The lodge is reached via Hughes Air West and Frontier Airlines, with daily flights into Kalispell; by daily Amtrak train service into Whitefish; and by auto. The ranch provides transportation from Kalispell and Whitefish. For details & rates, contact: Flathead Lake Lodge, Bigfork, MT 59911 (406)837–4391.

★★*Montana Sports Ranch,* 80 miles northwest of Missoula, is situated in the Swan River valley and surrounded by the snowcapped peaks of the Swan and Mission mountain ranges. Sparkling lakes, trout-filled glacial creeks, hot springs, and thousands of acres of unspoiled wilderness guarantee rewarding vacations year-round. The ranch offers a full spectrum of seasonal activities: cross-country skiing in the Bob Marshall Wilderness, big-game hunting, pack trips and trail rides, camping, photography, fishing in mountain streams, plus tennis and swimming right on the ranch premises. A maximum of 36 guests can be accommodated at one time in comfortable, modern cabins. Family-style meals—corn-fed beef, fresh trout, garden vegetables, and home-baked breads—are served in the ranch dining room. Weekly rates: $175 per person (based on double occupancy), including all meals, lodging, horseback riding, and ranch facilities. Not included are alcoholic refreshments in the Western Lounge, personal gear, or overnight pack trips. For further information write: Montana Sports Ranch, Seeley Lake, MT 59868 (406)754–2351.

★★★★*Spotted Bear Ranch & Vacation Adventures* is a superb vacation ranch in the Flathead National Forest adjacent to the 950,000–acre Bob Marshall Wilderness Area. Glacier National Park lies due north. The surrounding high-country wildlands are inhabited by elk, deer, bear, eagles, wolverine, and coyote. Ranch activities include combination packhorse and float trips along the spectacular South Fork of the Flathead River and Big Salmon Lake area; packhorse trips in the Bob Marshall Wilderness along the granite faces of the Great Divide and the Chinese Wall; trout fishing in the South Fork of the Flathead, Spotted Bear Lake, Twin Creek, Bunker Creek, Trout Lake, and Sullivan Creek for cutthroat and Dolly Varden. There is also fall hunting for elk, mule deer, and mountain goat. Families enjoy 6 nights in a private log cabin that's fully carpeted and rustically appointed in western decor, with a breezy, screened back porch for great summer sleeping. Bathrooms have a tub or shower, and there's a Franklin fireplace. Families receive two half-day float trips on different segments of the scenic South Fork. Practiced raftsmen guide sturdy 13–foot inflatable rafts down this clear river past unforgettable scenery. Fishing, from raft or shore, is action-packed for cutthroat and Dolly Varden trout. Your guide is anxious to assist in any way he can and to pass along helpful information. Two half-day horseback excursions to beautiful backcountry spots are usually scheduled, and great lake fishing can be a part of these trips. Families have an opportunity to learn first hand the basic elements of horsemanship—haltering, saddling, and riding. An overnight camping trip on horseback is an alternative and can be a highlight adventure for youngsters. Facilities at the ranch consist of a main lodge and trophy room and 5 guest cabins. Meals are served family-style by the fireplace in the dining room. Grande Domain Retreats' "Standards of Service and Quality" assures that guests receive a consistent degree of excellence at Spotted Bear Ranch. The ranch is 50 miles south of Hungry Horse, Montana, or 20 air miles east of Kalispell. Guests may fly to Kalispell on regularly scheduled commercial airlines or drive directly to the ranch. Amtrak services Whitefish and East Glacier, where guests may also be met. An airstrip for light aircraft, maintained by the Forest Service, is 2 miles from the ranch. For rates and information, contact: Spotted Bear Ranch, Grande Domain Retreats, 801 P St., Lincoln, NE 68508 (402)477–9249.

★*Wilderness Ranch & Lodge* is located on the South Fork of the Flathead River in the Flathead National Forest, 55 miles from the village of Hungry Horse. The lodge offers guided pack trips into the Bob Marshall Wilderness for camping, photography, and fishing, as well as scenic float trips on the South Fork and trail rides along the Forest Service wilderness trails. The lodge also offers guided big-game hunting trips during the fall for elk, moose, black bear, mule deer, and mountain goats. Wilderness Lodge air service in a Cessna Skylane is available from the Forest Service Spotted Bear Airport, located ¾ mile north of the lodge and at Great Falls and Kalispell. Accommodations are in large, clean, comfortable cabins with showers and private bath. Meals are served family-style in the main dining room. American-plan rates: $30 per day per person. For additional information, contact: Wilderness Ranch & Lodge, Hungry Horse, MT 59919 (701)839–5353 in winter.

Travel Services & Ski Centers

Backpacking with Barrow, a wilderness camping guide service run by Shirley Barrow of Whitefish, offers guided trips during the summer to remote high-country areas of the spectacular Bob Marshall Wilderness with treks to Sunburst Lake, White River, and the

Chinese Wall. Distances are such that there is ample time during the 5–day backpack hike for fishing and wildlife photography. All the camp chores are done by the outfitter and guides, but you are welcome to help out if you would like to learn the basic skills of wilderness living. This wilderness trek is ideal for those with a special interest in bird-watching, fishing, flower and plant identification, photography, geology, and wildlife. The 5–day trip all-inclusive (you furnish your equipment) is $130 per person, with special discounts for family groups. Amtrak Rail services Whitefish from Seattle, Chicago, and intermediate points. Glacier Park International Airport (FCA) Hughes Airwest DC-9 daily service from Seattle and Spokane and connecting flights. Frontier Airlines daily 737 service from eastern and southern points. Rail and air arrivals can be met and picked up by private arrangements for a slight extra cost. Contact: Shirley M. Barrow, The Big Mountain, Box 1215, Whitefish, MT 59937 (406)862–3511.

Bear Creek Guest Ranch offers guided fishing, packhorse, cross-country skiing, and hunting trips in the Flathead National Forest and Bob Marshall Wilderness Area. Contact: Box 38, East Glacier, MT 59434.

★★*Rogers Guest Ranch* offers hunting and fishing trips in the Bob Marshall Wilderness Area, Swan Mountains, and Mission Range. Camp accommodations are in comfortable sleeping tents with cots and pads, heated by a wood stove. All meals are taken in the cook tent, where hearty, western-style fare is the specialty. Eight-day hunts for elk, grizzly bear, deer, and mountain goat cost $800 per person, including meals and lodging. Each hunter is furnished with a saddle horse, saddle, gun scabbard, saddlebags, and guide service. Hunts are scheduled between mid-September and the end of October. Fishing trips to Montana's premier streams and lakes are from 1 to 7 days at $50 per person per day. Family rates are available. The ranch makes all arrangements for transporting you from the Missoula airport to camp. For further information write: Rogers Guest Ranch, Box 107, Swan Lake, MT 59911.

Whitefish Nordic Ski Center is a full-service cross-country skiing facility offering certified instruction, a complete line of sales and rental equipment, and special guided tours ranging in length from a few hours to 3 days. Scenic overnight tours with an experienced guide take in the backcountry of Glacier National Park, or you can arrange for day and overnight trips through the wilderness area of your choice. Tents can be supplied by your guide. The more adventurous may want to try snow-cave camping. Special ski tours of the Whitefish Divide, 2 or 3 days in length, start at the top of Big Mountain via chair lift and offer both challenging cross-country and powder-bowl skiing with panoramic views of Glacier Park and the Canadian Rockies en route. A wood-heated tent hut and excellent meals provide welcome creature comforts after each day of skiing. Whitefish Center's ski school offers 2–hour morning and afternoon classes each day, 7 days a week, for all levels of ability. Group and private lessons, children's instruction, and survival clinics are all available. Touring rates: $7 per person for ½ day, $15 for a full day, $50 for 2 days and 1 night, and $70 for 3 days and 2 nights. Rates include meals and overnight lodging where applicable and all guiding service. For full details write: Whitefish Nordic Ski Center, 139 2nd Street, Whitefish, MT 59937 (406)862–5294.

Gallatin National Forest & The Yellowstone Country

The world-famous fishing, backpacking, ski touring, and big-game hunting area of the 1¾ million-acre Gallatin National Forest in the Rockies lies directly north of Yellowstone National Park, Wyoming, and encompasses a land of high peaks, wild rivers and crystal-clear lakes, brilliant green alpine meadows, and timbered hills. Elevations range from 4,000–foot valleys to 12,000–foot summits. Within Gallatin National Forest are the Gallatin, Jefferson, Madison, and Yellowstone rivers, the Spanish Peaks and Absaroka primitive areas, and the Beartooth Mountains. Above all, this is a prime backpacking and alpine trout-fishing region. Some of the more interesting areas are the Hyalite Range, with good hiking trails and climbing through scenic canyons, around lakes and waterfalls, and up 10,000–foot

peaks; the Boulder River high country, with its steep canyons, high peaks, and plateaus; the West Boulder River valley, a narrow canyon valley running parallel to the Absaroka Range; Mt. Cowen, a challenge to even the most experienced climbers; the Crazy Mountains, isolated to the east in the prairie, with peaks higher than 11,000 feet and deep canyons radiating out into the plains; Taylor and Hilgard peaks in the Madison Range; the Bridger Mountains, made up of 9,000–foot limestone peaks extending for 20 miles from Bozeman to Sixteen Mile Creek; Coffin Mountain in the Continental Divide, a good cross-country hiking area with old and not carefully maintained Indian trails; and Gallatin Petrified Forest, in the Tom Miner area; a popular spot for climbers and rock hounds.

The Yellowstone River, which flows through the forest, is a world-renowned trout river. The Yellowstone flows 104 miles through a blue-ribbon trout-fishing area and has pools 10–20 feet deep and riffles. The best time to fish the Yellowstone is September and October, for lunker rainbow, brown, and cutthroat trout, averaging 2–3 pounds.

The most famous river that flows through the forest, however, is the legendary Madison, one of the world's truly great trout streams. From its headwaters in Yellowstone Park, this officially designated blue-ribbon trout stream flows through Hebgen and Earthquake lakes in the Madison River Canyon Earthquake Geological Area formed by the 1959 earthquake, and on through Ennis Lake and the rugged Beartrap Canyon Primitive Area to its confluence with the Gallatin and Jefferson rivers at the head of the mighty Missouri. The 20–mile-long headwaters area of the Madison in Yellowstone is classic dry fly-fishing water; flowing lazily through lush alpine meadows and evergreen forests, its deep pools and warm thermal waters rich in insect life hold fat trophy brown trout, many 10–15 pounds. The wilderness fly-fisherman wading this stretch of the Madison will often see elk, mule deer, buffalo, geese, and an occasional trumpeter swan. The crystal-clear, placid water and sandy bottom with patches of moss and weeds here and there allow for leisurely wading and fishing. The Upper Madison between Earthquake and Ennis lakes is famous among fly-fishermen for its prolific June salmon fly hatch.

Information Sources, Maps & Access

For detailed vacation and recreation information, a full-color *Gallatin National Forest Map* (50¢), and free trail guides to the Spanish Peaks and Absaroka primitive areas, write: Supervisor, Gallatin National Forest, Box 130, Bozeman, MT 59715 (406)587–5271. The Gallatin National Forest is reached via U.S. Highways 191, 287, 10, and 89 and Montana State Highways 87, 293, 243, 298, and 339. Lodging, guides, supplies, and pack and outfitting services are available at Bozeman, West Yellowstone, Jardine, Gallatin Gateway, Livingston, Big Timber, and Clyde Park. Cooke City, once a prosperous mining settlement, lies nestled in an alpine setting along the scenic Beartooth Highway and serves as the center of outdoor recreation and jumping-off point for hikers, fishermen, hunters, skiers, and campers heading into Yellowstone National Park and the Absaroka and Beartooth mountains.

Recreation Areas

Absaroka Primitive Area

In the south of the forest along the Wyoming border is the 64,000–acre Absaroka Primitive Area, a majestic alpine trout-fishing and camping area. The terrain here varies from mountains near the head of Bull Creek to broad valleys created by Hellroaring and Slough creeks. Elevations range from 6,000 feet near Hellroaring Cabin to 10,218 feet at Roundhead Butte. Most of the Absaroka, however, is high plateau country with scattered meadows and deep valleys. Lodgepole pine, Engelmann spruce, and alpine fir grow in the moist basins, while whitebark pine covers the high ridges. The best way to reach the Absaroka Primitive Area is via packhorse on the trails from Jardine, Cooke City, Mill Creek, Passage Creek, or Lambert Creek, by the Stillwater Trail from Nye, or via trails originating in the south out of Yellowstone Park.

South of the forest lies the Yellowstone area, known to the Indians as the Land of the Evil Spirits and avoided by most of the local tribes, who feared the miraculous spouting geysers, hot springs, and bubbling "paint pots." (See chapter on Wyoming for a complete description of Yellowstone National Park lodging and services.)

Spanish Peaks Primitive Area

Just west of the Gallatin River within the forest is the 50,000–acre Spanish Peaks Primitive Area, named for Spanish beaver trappers killed by Crow Indians in 1836. Beaver still inhabit the area along with mule deer, moose, elk, bear, coyote, and bobcat. The foremost big-game attraction, however, is mountain sheep; the largest band in the whole area roams this roadless backcountry. A challenge to the hardiest hunter or angler, the area is extremely rugged, with elevations varying abruptly from 6,000 to 11,000 feet. Some of the noted peaks are Wilson and Blaze, the Table Mountains, and Indian Ridge. There are many icy streams and more than twenty cold, crystal-clear lakes, including Cascade, Chilled, and Spanish lakes and Hellroaring, Burnt, Asbestos, Deer, and Dudley creeks. In addition there are over 50 miles of trails within the Spanish Peaks, and the area is only 25 miles from Bozeman.

Gateways & Accommodations

Big Timber

(Pop. 1,600; zip code 59011; area code 406.) Seat of Sweet Grass County, Big Timber is named after the creek that flows into the Yellowstone opposite the town. Accommodations: *Fyre's C. M. Russell Lodge* (rates: $20–22 double), 42 comfortable rooms and rustic restaurant with stone fireplace, Box 670 (932–2145); *Lazy J Motel* (rates: $20–22 double), 15 very good rooms on U.S. Hwy. 10 (932–2125).

Bozeman

(Pop. 18,700; zip code 59715; area code 406.) Named after John M. Bozeman, who blazed the historic Bozeman Trail along which he guided the first train of immigrants from Wyoming into the Gallatin Valley in 1864, Bozeman's attractions include the Missouri River Headwaters State Park, the Gallatin Pioneers Museum, the Museum of the Rockies at Montana State University, the Bridger Bowl Ski Area, and the Madison Buffalo Jump State Monument. Accommodations: *Best Western City Center Motel* (rates: $26–29 double), 49 excellent rooms and family units, dining room, Black Angus Steak House, cocktail lounge, heated indoor pool, at 507 W. Main St. (587–3158); *Holiday Inn* (rates: $30 double), 182 excellent rooms and family units, dining facilities, cocktail bar, entertainment, indoor pool, sauna, 1 mile northwest of town off Interstate 90 (587–4561); *Ramada Inn* (rates: $28.50 double), 102 excellent rooms and family units, restaurant, cocktail lounge, heated indoor pool, free airport bus service, at 1325 N. 7th Ave. (587–5261).

Cooke City—Gateway to Yellowstone National Park

(Pop. 50; zip code 59020; area code 406.) On the scenic Beartooth Highway, this was once the receiving point for Buffalo Bill's Indian trade goods, shipped by boat up the Missouri and Yellowstone and then packed by horse and stage along the Beartooth Trail to Cody, Wyoming. The historic old gold-rush boom town today is a popular stopover on the way to Yellowstone Park. Accommodations: *Hoosier's Motel* (rates: $20–22 double), 11 excellent units, on U.S. Hwy. 212 (838–2241); *Mus Rest Friendship Inn Motel* (rates: $18–20), 11 motel units and family cottages, on U.S. Hwy. 212 (838–2272).

Gardiner—Gateway to Yellowstone National Park

(Pop. 500; zip code 59030; area code 406.) A year-round gateway and northern entrance to Yellowstone Park, the town is named for Johnston Gardiner, a trapper who explored the Yellowstone country in the 1830s. Accommodations: *Westernaire Motel* (rates: $19–22 double), 10 very good rooms with views of the Absaroka Range, on U.S. Hwy. 89 (848–7397).

Livingston—Gateway to Yellowstone National Park

(Pop. 6,900; zip code 59047; area code 406.) A famous Old West outfitting center and railroad and trade center on the Yellowstone River, the town was founded during the hectic boom days of the 1870s and 1880s. Area attractions include float-fishing trips on the Yellowstone, Dan Bailey's Fly Shop Fishing Wall of Fame, Emigrant Gulch, and old boom-town houses. Accommodations: *Best Western Yellowstone Motor Inn* (rates: $28–30 double), 100 superb rooms and suites, dining room, cocktail lounge, indoor heated pool, airport transportation, on South Park Road off Interstate 90 Exit 333 (222–6110); *Del Mar Motel—Friendship Inn* (rates: $24–26 double), 30 excellent rooms and suites, heated pool, on Interstate 90 business loop (222–3120); *Paradise Inn* (rates: $24–34 double), 43 outstanding rooms, dining room, coffee shop, cocktail lounge, indoor heated pool, at Exit 333—Yellowstone Park Road off Interstate 90 and Hwy. 89 (222–6320).

West Yellowstone—Gateway to Yellowstone National Park

(Pop. 800; zip code 59758; area code 406.) A famous western gateway and entrance to Yellowstone National Park, its attractions include the Madison River Canyon Earthquake Area and the West Yellowstone Museum (124 Yellowstone Ave.) with displays of area Indian history and wildlife, and Madison and Firehole river fishing trips (see Wyoming chapter). Accommodations: *Ambassador Motor Inn* (rates: $28–32 double), 52 superb rooms and suites, heated pool, airport transportation service and guided Nordic ski tours, at 315 Yellowstone Ave. (646–7365); *Best Western Desert Inn* (rates: $30–34 double), 58 excellent rooms and family units, heated pool at Madison and Firehole Aves. (646–7376); *Best Western Executive Inn* (rates: $32–36 double), 85 excellent rooms and family units, dining room and coffee shop, heated pool, at Dunraven and Gibbons Ave. (646–7681); *Best Western Weston's Lamplighter Motel* (rates: $26–28 double), 32 excellent rooms and heated pool, airport service (646–7373); *Big Western Pine—Friendship Inn & Rustlers Roost Restaurant* (rates: $20–38 double), 72 excellent rooms and suites, fine dining, heated pool, tennis, airport transportation service, at 234 Firehole Ave. (646–7622); *Three Bear Motor Lodge & Restaurant—A Friendship Inn* (rates: $24–28 double), 42 excellent rooms and family units, dining room, heated pool, at 217 Yellowstone Ave. (646–7353).

Lodges, Guest Ranches & Ski Centers

★★★★*Big Sky* is a sprawling four-season vacation complex dominated by towering Lone Mountain (11,200 ft.) and surrounded by some of the most beautiful country in Montana, including the Spanish Peaks Primitive Area and Beaverhead and Gallatin national forests. Just an hour's drive south, about 50 miles, is Yellowstone National Park. In winter, Big Sky has superlative skiing on 23 miles of groomed downhill trails on two ski mountains and 35 miles of cross-country trails winding through snowy forests and across alpine meadows. A 125–car gondola and double and triple chair lifts can accommodate 5,200 skiers an hour, so lift lines are seldom a problem. The Big Sky ski school offers a staff of professional instructors and classes for beginning, intermediate, and expert skiers. Beginners have their own special ski lift and cross-country trails. In warmer weather, backpackers and hikers take to the trails in the Spanish Peaks area or up Lone Mountain, fishermen try their luck in the west fork of the Gallatin River and several nearby lakes, and horseback enthusiasts saddle up for trail rides and pack trips into the wilderness. There are also tennis courts, a golf course, swimming pools, and accommodations to suit every taste and budget. Huntley Lodge, a handsome contemporary hotel and restaurant complex, has 204 rooms, a year-

round outdoor pool, saunas, whirlpool baths, and a full-service health club. A spacious lounge with a massive stone fireplace four stories high is the site of frequent parties and get-togethers. For dining, there's a fine, informal restaurant serving excellent international cuisine, plus a special *fondue stube* for lighter fare in relaxed surroundings. Chet's Bar is an old-time saloon with an authentic carved bar discovered by Chet Huntley in a local Montana town. Rooms range in size from standard ($40 daily, double occupancy) to deluxe suites ($50 daily, double occupancy) to self-contained spacious lofts ($60 daily, double occupancy). All have at least 2 queen-size beds, color TV, fine views, and direct-dial phones. The above are winter rates; summer prices are $10–15 lower. Children under 12 sharing a room with their parents are free. Big Sky also has 215 mountain villas—studios and 1–3–bedroom condominiums—all within easy walking distance of the gondola and chair lifts (winter rates: $55–90; $35–90 in summer). Facilities include fully electric kitchens, fireplaces, indoor swimming pools, saunas, heated garages, and elevators. In addition, the Mountain Hostel has 88 budget-priced rooms, each with a bath, and there's a separate summer guest ranch with cozy log cabins, a swimming pool, a family dining room, and riding stables. For full information on Big Sky's accommodations, special ski packages, and convention facilities, write: Big Sky of Montana, P.O. Box 1, Big Sky, MT 59716 (phone toll free (800)548–4486; in Montana, (800)332–4491).

★★★*Boulder River Ranch* sprawls along the main Boulder River, 28 miles south of Big Timber, in southwest Montana's magnificent Absaroka Range. The stretch of water flowing through the ranch domain has been rated one of the most productive trout streams in North America and is reserved for exclusive enjoyment of ranch guests on a fly-fishing-only basis. Aside from excellent and varied angling conditions, the ranch offers wonderful trail rides through some of Montana's most beautiful backcountry; swimming in natural pools; fall hunting for deer, bear, elk, and moose; jeep tours; float trips, and much more. This is a working guest ranch, owned and operated by the same family since 1918, so you will get a firsthand taste of western hospitality in an authentic environment. Guest capacity is limited to 35 at a time, with a special welcome extended to families. Cabins are rustic log structures, fully modern within and equipped for housekeeping. American-plan packages are available if you prefer to take your meals family-style in the main lodge. Weekly rates, including horses and use of ranch facilities: $210–230 per person per week on the American plan and $135–155 per person per week housekeeping. Special discounts for children and off-season rates are available. For complete details write: Boulder River Ranch, McLeod, MT 59052 (406)932–2226.

★★★*Bridger Mountain Lodge*, located at the base of the renowned Bridger Bowl Ski Area, is an authentic western homestead built from hand-hewn logs in the 1870s. Skiing is the big attraction here, with 25 miles of marked cross-country trails starting right at the door, superb downhill runs, a ski school, and excellent lift and T-bar facilities just 16 miles away. The lodge is in the process of expanding its facilities to take advantage of the fine hunting and fishing opportunities available in the fall and summer. Accommodations for approximately 40 guests are available in extra-large rooms with double beds and rustic log cabins for families and small groups. The lodge building houses a snug lounge with a big fieldstone fireplace, a library, and a pleasant dining room. There's also a convenient ski room for storage and an old-fashioned Finnish sauna. Daily rates, including full use of facilities, family-style breakfast and supper, and transportation to and from the Bozeman airport or railroad depot, are: $42 per person, single; $34 per person, double occupancy; and $26–28 per person for 3–4 guests sharing a room. A special 3–day package plan and children's rates are available. During off-season months, the lodge may be rented for business meetings, group functions, weddings, reunions, or as a retreat for special-interest clubs and affiliations. For more information write: Bridger Mountain Lodge, P.O. Box 374, Bozeman, MT 59715 (406)587–3088.

★★★*Chico Hot Springs Lodge* is located 30 miles from the north entrance to Yellowstone Park, just east of the Yellowstone River. Specialties of the lodge include swimming in Montana's largest mineral hot springs, horseback riding, trout fishing in the Yellowstone River or in a private trout lake, hiking, and cross-country skiing. Wilderness activities in the Absaroka and Beartooth mountains are guided by professional outfitters with an extensive knowledge of the region. The main lodge is a handsome, old-fashioned ranch house surrounded by tall trees and housing the family-style dining room and lounge. Lodge rooms are $16–21 daily, double occupancy. Newer motel units with private baths are $24 daily, double occupancy. Chico Hot Springs Lodge recently introduced a unique time-sharing plan for families interested in comfortable, rustic, and inexpensive vacations. One- and two-bedroom chalets in Paradise Valley, just north of the lodge, may be leased on a 20–year basis, at a minimum of one week per year, starting as low as $50 per week and with a 20–year option at the same rate. Chalets are fully furnished with old-fashioned fireplace stoves, kitchens, private saunas, washers, and dryers. All have spectacular views of the Absaroka Range. All time-share families are entitled to use lodge facilities and will automatically qualify as members of Resort Condominiums International, which offers the option of trading your vacation week at over 120 fine resorts around the world. For information on the lodge and/or time-sharing plan, write: Chico Hot Springs Lodge, Pray, MT 59065 (406)333–4411.

★★★★*Lazy K Bar Ranch*, a 20,000–acre working cattle and horse ranch operated since 1886 by the Van Cleve family, is located in the picturesque foothills of the Crazy Mountains in the Gallatin National Forest region, noted for its high plains, bull pine rims, and hundred-mile horizons. This superb working ranch offers hospitality to a limited number of guests who are looking for good food, riding, fishing, photography, bird-watching, hiking, rodeos, and overnight pack trips up along the numerous mountain trails to remote wilderness areas such as Hellroaring Creek and Lake, Half Moon Park, Blue Lake with its old miners' cabins, Glacier and Twin lakes, the Divide, Prospector's Cabin, and Campfire Lakes. Big Timber and Sweet Grass creeks and the beautiful alpine lakes hold brook, brown, rainbow, and cutthroat trout. The ranch's horse-breeding program, maintained since 1900, assures horses to suit each guest's ability and preference. Guest accommodations are in rustic log cabins located among the fir trees for privacy. Delicious well-balanced meals are served in the attractive ranch dining room. Lazy K Bar produces all its own pork, beef, milk, butter, and cheese, as well as many of its vegetables. Most of the breads and all of the pastries are baked at the ranch. An experienced ranch wrangler plans and supervises the activities and rides of younger children. Weekly ranch rates for cabin with bedroom, bath, and sitting room with fireplace or Franklin stove is $250 per person (double occupancy). Guest can be met at the Billings airport and at the Northern Pacific depot in Livingston. Contact: Paul Van Cleve III, Lazy K Bar Ranch, Big Timber, MT 59011 (406)537–4404.

★★★★*Lone Mountain Ranch* is one of the West's great family guest ranches, located in the Gallatin National Forest in a secluded setting along a clear mountain stream adjacent to the spectacular Spanish Peaks Primitive Area, halfway between Yellowstone and Bozeman. Activities in this alpine setting include trail rides and overnight pack trips into the Yellowstone, Gallatin National Forest, or Spanish Peaks backcountry; trout fishing in the high mountain lakes and in the nearby Gallatin, Madison, Firehole, Yellowstone, and Gibbon rivers; and guided cross-country ski tours during the winter months (see Yellowstone Nordic Skiing Adventures in "Travel Services" section below). Guided wilderness hikes are planned several times a week with emphasis on bird-watching and photography, tree and wildflower identification, wildlife photography, geology, Indian trails, and fly-fishing. Area attractions include Yellowstone Park, Quake Lake, Lewis and Clark Caverns, the ghost towns of Virginia City and Nevada City, the Playmill Theater in West Yellowstone,

fly-fishing and float trips down the Madison River, and kayaking on the Gallatin. Ranch accommodations are in rustic, modern log cabins with fireplaces, electric heat, baths, and showers close to the mountain stream that flows through the ranch. Cabins are cleaned daily. Delicious home-cooked meals are served in the ranch dining hall. The ranch serves homemade breads and desserts baked fresh daily. Weekly American-plan rates (double occupancy): $280–312. Contact: Lone Mountain Ranch, Box 145, Big Sky, MT 59716 (406)995–4644.

★★★★*Nine Quarter Circle Ranch* is an outstanding family vacation and horse ranch set among lodgepole pines overlooking broad grassy meadows on the east slope of the Rockies just 7 miles from the northwest corner of Yellowstone National Park. The ranch, established in 1892, is surrounded by the mountains, lakes, streams, and alpine meadows of the Gallatin National Forest. The ranch offers a wide variety of activities, including high-country trail rides, cookouts, rodeos, 2–day pack trips for teenagers, and some of the nation's top-ranked trout fishing for big rainbows and browns in Taylor Fork, which flows through the ranch, and in nearby Lightning, Buck, Wapiti, Snow Flake, and Indian creeks and the Gallatin and Madison rivers. Backpacking and trail-riding attractions on the ranch include the sunken forest, Marble and Snow Flake lakes, the Soap Saddle, the Paint Pots, the Taylor Cascades, the Petrified Forest, and vast expanses of primitive wildlife country. During the Indian summer days of September and early October, the ranch serves as a rustic base for the serious angler and offers easy access to the then uncrowded Yellowstone Park waters. Starting with the Labor Day weekend, the ranch cosponsors a series of 6–day fly-fishing schools with guided trips to the Yellowstone and high-country waters. Area sight-seeing attractions for family vacationers include Yellowstone Park, historic Virginia City, the Lewis and Clark Caverns, and the Madison Earthquake Area. Nine Quarter Circle accommodations consist of rustic, well-appointed log cabins with 1, 2, 3, or 4 bedrooms and private baths. Delicious meals are served family-style in the main lodge with its log-beamed walls and ceilings and massive stone fireplace in real western decor. Weekly rates (double): $273 each. The ranch is off Interstate 191. For additional information, contact: Nine Quarter Circle Ranch, Gallatin Gateway, MT 49730 (406)995–4276.

★★★*63 Ranch*, in Mission Creek Canyon 12 miles southwest of Livingston, is a working ranch with fine guest accommodations. Surrounded by breathtaking snow-crested mountains and peaceful valleys, the ranch is an ideal headquarters for horseback riding and hiking. Daily rides are scheduled through the region's many scenic areas, or you can saddle up for a leisurely pack trip to Yellowstone Park. Guests also have an opportunity to watch the cowboys at work and can join in for roundups and branding. Comfortably furnished guest cabins have single beds and private baths and are surrounded by tall trees for maximum privacy. Meals are taken in the cheerful dining room of the main ranch building, which also has a log-paneled lounge. Rates: $235–280 per person weekly, including use of saddle horses, riding instruction, accommodations with bath, and all ranch facilities. Pack trips are $45 per day. The daily rate for a stay of less than one week is $45 per person, including all the above. For more information write: Mrs. Paul E. Christensen, 63 Ranch, Livingston, MT 59047.

★★*Snowy Range Guest Ranch* occupies a spectacular secluded setting 35 miles south of Livingston, on 100 acres of deeded land, completely surrounded by the Gallatin National Forest and the 11,000–foot peaks of the Absaroka-Beartooth Wilderness Area. Clear mountain streams teeming with cutthroat trout border the property, and the blue-ribbon trout waters of the Yellowstone River are only a few miles away. Guided trail rides and pack trips explore the area's many trails and high mountain lakes. The ranch also offers float trips on the Yellowstone, guided fishing trips, and fall hunting trips for deer, moose, elk, and black bear (Snowy Range is a licensed outfitting and guide service). All housekeeping cabins are fully modern and well equipped, ranging in size from roomy 1–bedroom cabins with a kitchenette ($30 per night, $175 weekly) to large 2–bedroom cabins with accommodations for 6 guests ($50 per night, $300 weekly). You bring your own food, but all staples are provided. Hunting guests are offered American-plan rates, with meals served in the main lodge building ($700 per person weekly, including guide, horses, and pack service). Not included in summer housekeeping rates: horseback riding, float trips, guided fishing. Season runs from approximately June 15 to December 1; several cabins can be made available to winter sports enthusiasts. For more information write: Snowy Range Guest Ranch, Pray, MT 59065 (406)333–4457.

★★★*Watuck Lodge* is open year round, accessible in the winter months through Mammoth WY (the N. gate to Yellowstone Park). Accessible June through September by Highway 212 across Beartooth Pass at 11,000 foot elevation, right in the middle of one of N. America's largest wilderness areas. Offering 35 rooms (with baths) and an indoor heated pool, sunken lobby with fireplace. Fine dining in our Prospector dining room will accommodate up to 95 persons and the lounge boasts a 6 foot color TV and a view of the mountains, maybe even a moose or grizzly bear. Snowmobiling and cross-country skiing attract visitors in the winter, while fishing and exploring the wilderness keep summer tourists busy. Rates are $22–26 double. The lodge has a deluxe suite and rooms that accommodate up to 7 guests. Contact Watuck Lodge, Highway 212, Cooke City, MT 59020 (406)838–2251.

Travel & Cross-Country Skiing Service

For detailed information on stream conditions, hatches, and lodging in Montana's trophy trout country, write or call the angling specialists listed below, all of whom offer top-ranked professional guide service and float-fishing trips. The following firms are located in West Yellowstone (zip code 59757; area code 406): *Pat Barnes Tackle Shop* (Snake, Big Hole, Madison, Yellowstone), Box 296 (646–7564); *Bud Lilly's Trout Shop* (wading or McKenzie River driftboat trips on the Henrys Fork in Idaho and Madison, with custom trips in Yellowstone Park), Box 387 (646–7801); *Jim Danskin Tackle Shop* (Firehole, Madison, Yellowstone, Henrys Fork, Henrys Lake, Hebgen Lake), Box 276 (646–7663); *Bob Jacklin's Fly Shop* (Madison and Yellowstone Park waters), Box 604 (646–7336). Other area blue-ribbon guides include: *Beaver Pond Sport Specialists* (Big Hole, Beaverhead, Madison, Gallatin, Yellowstone, Upper Missouri), 1716 W. Main, Bozeman 59715 (406)587–4261; *Phil Wright's Complete Fly-Fisher* (Big Hole, Madison, Beaverhead Falls, Bitterroot, Gallatin), Box 105, Wise River 59762 (406)839–2243; *Will Godfrey's Fly-Fishing Center* (Henrys Fork, Henrys Lake, Yellowstone Park), Box 68, Island Park, ID 83429 (208)558–9960; *Henrys Fork Anglers, Inc.* (Henrys Fork, Henrys Lake, Firehole, Madison, Yellowstone, Spring Creek), Box 487, St. Anthony, ID 83445 (summer, (208)558–7525; winter, (208)624–3595.

Dan Bailey's Yellowstone Country Guide Service is available through the nationally famous Dan Bailey Flies & Tackle Shop for the Yellowstone, Madison, Gallatin, Boulder, Stillwater, Missouri, Big Hole, Smith, Beaverhead, Bitterroot, Clark's Fork of the Columbia, plus Rock Creek near Missoula and Big Spring Creek near Lewistown, and the famous Armstrong's and Nelson's spring creeks near

Livingston. Angling guide service may also be arranged for trips to the hundreds of beautiful alpine lakes which can be reached only by horse or on foot. For detailed information, rates, and a free catalog-brochure, write or call: Dan Bailey Flies & Tackle, 209 W. Park St., Livingston 59047 (406)222–1673.

Fenwick West Yellowstone Fly Fishing School. The Fenwick Corporation's nationally famous West Yellowstone school of fly-fishing is surrounded by the legendary trout waters of the Firehole, Snake, Madison, Gallatin, and Yellowstone rivers. You can choose a 3–day school that includes technique, development, and on-stream practice, or a 5–day school that adds a special guided water trip and a float trip. Special advanced schools, limited to fly-fishermen with previous experience, provide intensive instruction while you are actually fishing the fabled streams of West Yellowstone. The curriculum for all schools includes the art of fly-casting; types of fly line and rod and reel construction; insects and their life cycles; artificial fly construction, identification, choice of flies, and how to match the hatch; knots; leader construction and uses; how to read a stream, where the fish lie, and why they do so, and wading. Family accommodations are available at nearby motels, hotels, guest ranches, and U.S. Forest Service campgrounds. For free literature, rates, and info, write School Coordinator, Fenwick Fly Fishing Schools, P.O. Box 729, Westminster, CA 92683 (714)897–1066.

Yellowstone Nordic Skiing Adventures is one of the nation's finest cross-country skiing centers, based at Lone Mountain Ranch and Yellowstone National Park. Accommodations are in traditional, rustic log cabins with fireplaces at beautiful Lone Mountain Ranch and in cabins at Old Faithful in the spectacular Firehole River area in Yellowstone National Park. Accommodations are limited to 45 Nordic skiers. Lone Mountain Ranch Nordic Skiing Center is located 7 miles from the Big Sky alpine ski area, halfway between Bozeman and the west entrance to Yellowstone Park. The ranch buildings are scattered along a clear mountain stream in a secluded valley. Activities and services include mule-drawn sleigh rides, moonlit ski trips, rental skis, Nordic ski shop, certified instruction, guided all-day wilderness ski trips, a backcountry cabin, 35 miles of groomed trails, excellent snow conditions, varied terrain, and great food. Meals are served family-style in the ranch dining hall. All breads and desserts are baked fresh daily. The trails in this natural wildlife area—there are moose, coyote, pine marten, snowshoe hares, and mountain sheep—include the Yellow Mountain Trail; North Fork Trail, which begins at the ranch and follows the North Fork of the Gallatin River into the Spanish Peaks Primitive Area; Ridge Run Trail, along an abandoned logging road in Gallatin National Forest; Big Horn Pass Trail, which follows the Gallatin River toward its headwaters at Gallatin Lake; Fawn Pass Trail, which follows a Bannock Indian trail up Fan Creek and over the top of the Gallatin Range; Upper

Geyser Basin Trail, which starts at Old Faithful and winds through gentle terrain with numerous geysers, hot springs, and mud pots and close views of bison and elk; Mystic Falls Trail, which passes through rolling woodlands along the Firehole River to Mystic Falls; and Lone Star Geyser Trail, which begins at Old Faithful and climbs 500 feet to the Lone Star Geyser. On the Yellowstone Nordic trip to Yellowstone, a motor coach will pick you up at the ranch and take you through the beautiful snow-covered Gallatin Valley to West Yellowstone, Montana, where you will climb aboard a 10–passenger heated snow coach for your 30–mile trip to Old Faithful. The driver will stop wherever you wish, so you can take photographs of animals, geysers, hot springs, or the incomparable winter scenery. Be sure to take advantage of your driver's in-depth knowledge of Yellowstone. You will be staying in an individual cabin with bath at Old Faithful. Your meals will be served in the Snow Lodge dining room, only a short distance from your cabin. The large lobby with fireplace and a western bar are popular spots in the evening. If you happen to select a time when there is a full moon, be sure to take a moonlit ski trip. Geyser watching by moonlight is absolutely incredible. The trails in the Old Faithful area are marked and well broken, but ungroomed. There are trails to please every level of skier. Guides are available at Old Faithful, and they can add to your enjoyment by sharing with you their knowledge of the park's natural features. Yellowstone Nordic offers three basic guided tours: the Ranch Park Tour, which combines a snow coach ride into Old Faithful, lodging, meals, and skiing at Old Faithful, with a stay at Lone Mountain Ranch and skiing the 35 miles of groomed ranch trails (7 nights, $306 per adult, double occupancy); the Lone Mountain Tour (7 nights at the ranch, $248 per adult, double occupancy) with optional guided trips to Yellowstone, Spanish Peaks, and an overnight trip to a backcountry cabin; and the 2–night Mini Ranch Tour at Lone Mountain Ranch ($84 per adult, double occupancy). For additional info, contact: Yellowstone Nordic, Box 145, Big Sky, MT 59716 (406)995–4644.

Yellowstone Wilderness Guides, see "Wyoming" chapter under Yellowstone National Park for details.

Glacier National Park

This world-renowned family vacation, camping, hiking, and fishing area, often called the crown of the continent, lies astride the Great Divide of the Rocky Mountains in the northwest corner of Montana. The park encompasses more than 1,500 square miles of snowcapped peaks, sharp spires, deep green alpine valleys and meadows, and hundreds of azure lakes and glacial streams It stretches south from the Canadian boundary for 50 miles to the Flathead National Forest, and from the wild North Fork of the Flathead River east to the borders of the Blackfeet Indian Reservation. An intricate network of hiking and packhorse trails winds along ancient Indian and fur-trade routes through the wildlands of this mountain vastness, known to the Blackfeet as the backbone of the world, and provides access to the Continental Divide, which meanders from the Lewis Range to the Livingston Range, with numerous spurs, broken at intervals by the evergreen forests of lake-studded valleys; to Stoney Indian Peaks, named for the tribe of Stoney Indians who once inhabited the area near the headwaters of the Mokowania River; and to the ancient Grinnell and Sperry glaciers, beautiful Lake McDonald, known to the Indians as Sacred Dancing Lake, Swiftcurrent Valley, Logging and Kintla lakes, and hundreds of other remote backcountry fishing and camping areas.

Glacier's magnificent trails wind through the Rocky Mountain wildlands to more than 700 remote campsites and alpine lakes and streams that hold native cutthroat, lake trout, Dolly Varden, and arctic grayling. Arctic grayling, cutthroat, rainbow, and Dolly Varden are found in most of the lakes and streams in the Hudson Bay and Flathead River drainages. Glacier's wildlife includes the Rocky Mountain bighorn, mountain goat, moose, elk, silvertip grizzly, black bear, mule and whitetail deer, cougar, beaver, hoary marmot, lynx, river otter, wolverine, marten, pika, and other, smaller mammals. Birds of Glacier include great concentrations of bald eagles during the kokanee salmon spawning run in the Apgar region along McDonald Creek between the Middle Fork of the Flathead River and the foot of Lake McDonald, and osprey, water ouzel, ptarmigan, Clark's nutcracker, thrushes, and sparrows.

Nearly 1,000 species of plant life are found in Glacier country. On the arctic tundra of the windblown summits, there are only lichens,

moss, and the hardiest of alpine plants. In the valleys of the west slope of the Continental Divide are dense Pacific-type forests. The plains on the Atlantic watershed side of the Divide provide an expansive view of grassy, flower-covered meadows in startling contrast to the dark rugged wall of peaks in the distance.

All wilderness travelers who intend to have a fire or camp overnight must obtain a Backcountry Camping Permit, which can be obtained from any ranger or information center during the summer. Permits are issued on a first-come-first-served basis, and no earlier than 24 hours before departure time. In winter, and generally in late fall and early spring, permits may be obtained at Park Headquarters or at the St. Mary Ranger Station. Paved park roads provide access to eight of Glacier's campgrounds—Apgar, Avalanche Creek, Fish Creek, Many Glacier, Rising Sun, St. Mary, Two Medicine, and Sprague Creek. Primitive roadside campsites are located at Bowman Creek, Kintla Lake, Cut Bank, Logging Creek, and Quartz Creek.

The vast wildlands of the Blackfeet Indian Reservation, which stretch eastward from Glacier National Park, encompass several recreational sites and camps, including Chewing Blackbones, Lower Two Medicine, and Duck Lake campgrounds, historical sites, and the fascinating Museum of the Plains Indians.

Information Sources, Maps & Access

Complete vacation and recreation information and the maps and brochures *Glacier, Backcountry, Fish & Fishing in Glacier National Park, In Grizzly Country,* and *Ski Touring & Snowshoeing* may all be obtained free from: Superintendent's Office, Glacier National Park, West Glacier, MT 59936 (406)888–5441. A beautiful, full-color 36– by-42½–inch *Glacier National Park Topographic Map* ($2) may be ordered from: Distribution Branch, U.S. Geological Survey, Federal Center, Denver, CO 80225.

Glacier is on U.S. Highways 2 and 87, and near U.S. 91 and 93. Access to recreation areas within the park is provided by Going-to-the-Sun Road for 50 miles from West Glacier to St. Mary; by the Camas Creek Road, an 11–mile short route from Going-to-the-Sun Road near Apgar to Camas Entrance and the Forest Service North Fork Road and Polebridge; by North Fork Road, a narrow, primitive 43–mile road that parallels the North Fork of the Flathead from Going-to-the-Sun Road near Apgar to Kintla Lake; by U.S. Highway 2 for 55 miles from West Glacier to East Glacier Park; by the Blackfeet Highway, which parallels the Front Range of the Rockies from East Glacier Park north to Carway, Alberta: by Two Medicine Road for 12 miles from East Glacier Park to historic Two Medicine; by Many Glacier Road for 12 miles from Babb to Many Glacier; by Chief Mountain International Highway from Babb for 39 miles to Waterton, Lakes National Park, Alberta.

Gateways & Accommodations

Browning

(Pop. 1,700; zip code 59417; area code 406.) This is an eastern gateway to Glacier Park and the agency headquarters of the 1.5 million-acre Blackfeet Indian Reservation. Area attractions include the Museum of the Plains Indian & Craft Center and the Bob Scriver Museum of Montana Wildlife, both on U.S. Highway 2.

East Glacier

(Pop. 300; zip code 59434; area code 406.) This is the park's eastern gateway on U.S. Highway 2. Accommodations: *Jacobson's Scenic View Cottages* (rates: $16–18 double), 11 cabin units, on Hwy. 49 (226–4351); *Mountain Pine Motel* (rates: $22–23 double), 22 comfortable rooms, on Hwy. 49 (226–4551).

West Glacier

(Pop. 300; zip code 59936; area code 406.) This is the park's popular western gateway on U.S. Highway 2 on the Middle Fork of the Flathead River north of Hungry Horse and the Flathead National Forest. West Glacier is the administrative headquarters of the park. Accommodations: *Apgar Village Lodge* (rates: $22–26 double), cabin and motel accommodations, at Apgar Village and Lake McDonald (888–5484); *West Glacier Motel* (rates: $22–26 double), 18 good rooms and cafe, open May-Sept., on U.S. Hwy. 2 (888–9987).

Lodges & Mountain Chalets

★★★*Belton's Sperry & Granite Park Chalets,* operates two handsome, rustic lodges high in the mountains of Glacier Park, accessible only on foot or horseback over spectacular backcountry trails. Granite Park and Sperry Chalets were built about 1914 by Jim and Louis Hill of the Great Northern Railway, the prime developer of Glacier Park, as part of the hotel system in the park. Sperry Chalet is located on a broad alpine ledge on the west side of Gunsight Mountain

overlooking Lake McDonald and the Whitefish Range. Perched on a lava outcrop at the north end of the Garden Wall is Granite Park Chalet, with its equally impressive mountain panorama of the Lake McDonald Valley and the Livingston Range. Every effort has been made to preserve these splendid native rock buildings in their original, rugged state. Modern baths and kitchens have been installed, but private rooms are lit by candles or kerosene lamps and dining rooms glow under mantled lanterns. Overnight accommodations, including 3 meals daily, are $24 per person per day. Both chalets are truly a hiker's paradise. The main trail to Sperry is from the Lake McDonald Lodge parking lot. With an average hiking time of 4 hours, this 6.7 mile long, 3300 feet up, trail is a challenge to many hikers. However, the compensation of the beautiful vistas, the warm, friendly air of the chalet, and the camaraderie of others who "made it" make this trip an outstanding one. Mountain goats are almost daily visitors. Saddle horse trips to Sperry Chalet are available from the Lake McDonald Horse Barn. Trails to Granite Park include: the Garden Wall or "Hiline" trail from the Logan Pass parking lot (6646 feet), an easy 7.5–mile hike. This should be a leisurely, 4–hour trip to enjoy the many beautiful panoramic views, the rock formations, the colorful wildflowers, and the occasional glimpse of mountain sheep, goats and deer, afforded by this trail. The Swiftcurrent Pass trail from the Swiftcurrent Campground in the Many Glacier area (4930 feet) is a 7.9–mile hike up the Swiftcurrent Valley, with its many small lakes and flashing streams, over Swiftcurrent Pass (7185 feet) and down into Granite Park. The Loop Trail, from the Loop parking lot on Going-to-the-Sun Road (4297 feet) is not recommended for beginners when the weather is hot and dry, but this 4.5–mile trail with its spectacular, early-season wildflower display has few peers. For the truly venturesome, there is the Fifty Mountain trail from the Goat Haunt Ranger Station on the south end of Waterton Lake (24.5 miles). Saddle horse trips to Granite Park are available from Many Glacier, coming over Swiftcurrent Pass. For additional information, write: Belton Chalets, Inc., Box 188, West Glacier, MT 59936 (406)888–5511 May to Sept.

Glacier Park Lodge, at the eastern gateway to the park in East Glacier, Montana, has standard and luxury accommodations in 155 handsomely decorated rooms. Activities here run the gamut from golf on a spectacular 9–hole course to fishing in glacier-fed lakes. There's also a heated pool surrounded by the carefully tended gardens which brighten every corner of the lodge grounds. For the more adventurous, horseback rides are popular across neighboring valleys and up into the wooded foothills. Evenings offer live entertainment in the Medicine Lounge and occasional lectures by well-known naturalists. Rates: $28–32 (double occupancy) for standard rooms, $32–36 (double occupancy) for first-class accommodations. Open mid-June to mid-September.

Many Glacier Hotel, the largest in the park, with 191 rooms, is modeled along the lines of an alpine retreat and perched on the shores of Swiftcurrent Lake in the heart of Glacier. The hotel is renowned for its fine cuisine, inviting cocktail lounges, and wide variety of entertainment offered each evening. There are also interesting, illustrated talks by ranger-naturalists. Many Glacier Hotel is at the hub of Glacier activities. Rates are the same as for Glacier Park Lodge. The hotel is open from early June to mid-September.

Lake McDonald Lodge, on the shores of the park's largest glacial water basin, is surrounded by forestlands on the west side of the Continental Divide. The lodge is famous for its warm and tranquil atmosphere and country inn hospitality, right down to the rocking chairs on the front porch. The countryside around Lake McDonald is ideal for long or short hikes, or you can hire a horse and saddle up for tours along well-marked trails. The lake itself offers both fishing and boating. Lodge rooms are comfortably furnished with private baths, and many have spectacular views of the lake and mountains. Rates are the same as for Glacier Park Lodge. Private cabins are also available at $19–26 daily for 1–3 guests. Lake McDonald Lodge is open from early June to mid-September.

The Village Inn in Apgar Village is just a short drive from the park's west entrance. Every one of the ultramodern rooms has a beautiful view of snowcapped peaks and Lake McDonald, which fronts the inn for several hundred feet. There are units with kitchens for those who prefer housekeeping facilities, or you can enjoy the dining rooms at nearby Lake McDonald Lodge. Rates: $24–26 daily (double occupancy), $28–30 for efficiency (kitchen-bedroom) units, and $32–34 for 2–bedroom units. The inn is open from late May through mid-September.

The Rising Sun Motor Inn and Cabins is located 7 miles inside the park entrance from U.S. Highway 89, just off the scenic Going-to-the-Sun Road. Both motel units and cabins offer modern decor and superlative views of the mountains and sparkling St. Mary Lake. A restaurant on the premises serves fine food in relaxing surroundings. Rates: $24 daily for motel rooms (double occupancy), $18–22 daily for cabins (1–3 persons). The Rising Sun is open from early June through mid-September.

Swiftcurrent Motor Inn and Cabins, near the shores of Swiftcurrent Lake, offers 84 comfortable rooms in the center of Glacier National Park. A coffee shop on the premises offers a wide menu, from light snacks to a full dinner. There are dozens of mountain trails surrounding the inn, plus a complete camp store to supply you with everything needed for day trips and longer excursions. Rates: $24 daily for motel rooms (double occupancy), $12 daily for 1–bedroom cabins (no bath), and $15 daily for 2–bedroom cabins (no bath). Swiftcurrent is open from mid-June through early September.

Groceries and camping supplies for visitors to Glacier National Park are available at Lake McDonald, Rising Sun, Swiftcurrent, and Two Medicine. In the hotels, there is no lodging charge for children under 12 occupying a room with an adult. For more information on the above facilities, write: (May 15–Sept. 15) Glacier Park, Inc., East Glacier, MT 59434 (406)226–9311; (Sept. 15–May 15) Suite 7, 1735 E. Fort Lowell Road, Tucson, AZ 85719 (602)795–0377. In Montana, call toll-free (800)332–4114.

Travel Services

Izaak Walton Inn offers ski touring and guided overnight cross-country trips on 120 miles of marked trails in the Great Bear Wilderness area of Flathead National Forest and Glacier National Park. This rustic inn on U.S. Highway 2, 30 miles east of West Glacier, offers hearty meals and cocktails year-round. Contact: Izaak Walton Inn, Essex, MT 59916.

Rocky Mountain Outfitters, Inc., offers guided packhorse trips in the park from corrals at Apgar, Lake McDonald and Many Glacier. For information and rates, write: Rocky Mountain Outfitters, Inc., Box 39, Columbia Falls, MT 59912 (406)755–2442.

Helena National Forest

This 900,000–acre reserve, first explored by Lewis and Clark, embraces the beautiul Blackfoot River, the Elkhorn and Big Belt mountains, Baldy Lakes, the Lincoln backcountry, and the Gates of the Mountains and Scapegoat Wilderness areas. Within the forest, the waters of the historic Upper Missouri River and its many tributary creeks offer some of the finest big trout fishing in Montana. Seldom-fished stretches like Duck, Cottonwood, and Beaver creeks and Confederate Gulch offer fair to good catches of cutthroat, rainbow, brown, and brook trout, and most of them are easily reached by Forest Service roads. Canyon Ferry Reservoir, 7½ miles long and more than a mile wide, is popular with fishermen for rainbows, occasional browns, and a few walleye and yellow perch. Numerous recreation areas and campgrounds, boat ramps, and an inviting forest setting have made the lake a favorite focus for outdoor recreation. Park Lake, a jewel of a mountain lake just 8 miles southwest of Helena, offers a well-maintained campground and fishing for rainbows as well as an occasional grayling. Perhaps the most spectacular fishing along the entire length of the Missouri is at the base of Canyon Ferry Dam, where trophy-size rainbow and brown trout congregate when they find their journey upstream from the Hauser Reservoir blocked. Biggest catches are made from boats 14 feet long or larger in the middle of the Missouri's fast waters, but many fish are also taken at the shoreline.

Information Sources, Maps & Access

For detailed information, a full-color *Helena National Forest Map* (50¢) and *Scapegoat Wilderness Map* (50¢), and free *Gates of the Mountains Wilderness Map*, write: Supervisor, Helena National Forest, 616 Helena Ave., Helena, MT 59601 (406)449–5201. The Helena National Forest is reached via U.S. Highways 12, 91, and 287, Interstate 15, and Montana State Highway 200. Supplies, guides, and outfitting services can be found at Helena, East Helena, Lincoln, Blackfoot City, Avon, Wickes, Jefferson City, Clancy, York, Jimtown, Canyon Ferry, Whites City, Diamond City, Townsend, Hassell, and Radersburg.

Recreation Areas

Gates of the Mountains

One of the most spectacular sights within the forest is the Gates of the Mountains, discovered and named by Lewis and Clark in July of 1805, when they first entered the Missouri River canyon. "The most remarkable cliffs that we have yet seen," Captain Lewis wrote in his journal, "the cliffs rise from the water's edge on either side to the height of 1,200 feet." Southeast of the Gates of the Mountains lie the many ochre-tinted peaks of the Big Belt Range, including Willow, Sacajawea, Moors, Sawtooth, Middleman, and Needham, with elevations varying between 6,500 and 9,000 feet. The mountains take their name from a prominent encircling "belt" of limestone out-croppings. Another breathtaking canyon within the region, the Big Belt Canyon, is composed of lofty walls streaked with shades of green, red, and yellow, which vary from iridescent brilliance to subtle, shadowy tones, depending on the amount of sunlight. A popular drive within the forest along the scenic, 42–mile figure-eight route passes through the mountains and Helena's "canyon country," offering panoramic vistas of Trout Creek and Beaver Creek canyons. The side trip to Hogback Mountain (7,813 ft.) leads to a magnificent view of the Helena Valley and part of the Gates of the Mountains Wilderness.

Scapegoat Wilderness

In the northern reaches of the forest is the magnificent Scapegoat Wilderness, a 450,000–acre tract shared with Lewis and Clark and Lolo national forests. This huge tract straddles the Continental Divide and offers a landscape of incredible beauty, with limestone cliffs rising sharply against broad expanses of alpine meadows and numerous creeks and trails winding through dense forest growth. Stonewall Creek, skirting the base of Stonewall Mountain, has good fishing for cutthroat, brook, and brown trout, plus some Dolly Vardens. In the upper reaches of Copper Creek, followed for much of its length by a good jeep road, there is fair to good fishing in the

numerous beaver dams for cutthroat. Bighorn Lake, a remote backcountry cirque lake just below the Continental Divide, can be reached by an unmarked trail from the Bighorn Creek Trail and is reputedly excellent for whopper cutthroats and rainbows.

Other attractions within the Helena National Forest include the McDonald Pass Vista Point, Crow Creek Falls, Ophir Cave, and the rugged but scenic Hanging Valley Trail. In the winter, the forest offers recreational opportunities for skiers, snowmobilers, and snowshoers. There are two fine ski areas nearby: Grass Mountain, located on national forest land 23 miles east of Townsend, and the Belmont Ski Area, near Marysville, 25 miles northwest of Helena.

Gateways & Accommodations

Helena

(Pop. 22,700; zip code, see below; area code 406.) Helena is Montana's capital. It overlooks Prickly Pear Valley, named by Lt. William Clark, who painfully collected 17 cactus spines in his feet here while on his famous journey across the area. Helena's main street is built along the floor of Last Chance Gulch, site of the hell-roaring gold rush in 1864 that put the city, then known as Last Chance, on the map. In its heyday it was one of the richest cities in the country and boasted among its residents some 50 millionaires. In 1875 Helena became the capital of Montana Territory after a furious competition with the rival gold mecca, Virginia City. Area attractions include a train tour of Last Chance Gulch that departs from the Montana Historical Museum at 225 N. Roberts St., Pioneer Cabin at 208 S. Park Ave. (443–5837), Canyon Ferry State Recreation Area on Hwy. 284, rustic Frontier Town on U.S. Hwy. 12 (442–4560), the Victorian Governor's Mansion built in 1884, Benjamine H. Tatem House (440 S. Park) built in the 1860s, and the State Capitol Building, which houses Charles M. Russell's 12– by-25–foot painting *Lewis & Clark Meeting the Flatheads.* Restaurants include 4B's at 900 Last Chance Gulch (442–5275) and Black Sands, a popular family spot at 1225 Euclid on U.S. Hwy. 12 (442–3600). Accommodations: *Best Western Colonial Inn* (rates: $33 double), 121 outstanding rooms and family units, dining room, coffee shop, heated pool, cocktail lounge, sauna, at 2301 Colonial Drive (443–2100); *Best Western Jorgenson's Holiday Motel & Restaurant* (rates: $28–32 double), 102 superb rooms and family units, fine food in family restaurant, cocktail lounge, at 1720 11th Ave. (442–1770); *Helena Travelodge* (rates: $31.50–35.50 double), 70 excellent rooms and family units, dining room, cocktail lounge, airport service, at 22 N. Last Chance Gulch (443–2200).

Travel Services

K Lazy 3 Ranch, Outfitters & Guides offers summer pack trips and fall hunting trips into the breathtaking backcountry of the Bob Marshall and Lincoln Scapegoat wilderness areas. Sportsmen's camps are located in the heart of the big-game areas and are reached via a leisurely ride on reliable, gentle horses. The usual length of time for a successful hunt is 7–10 days, depending on weather conditions and experience. Hunting rates average $95 per person per day, all-inclusive, in a gruop of 4–8 hunters. Summer pack trips, with an emphasis on wilderness sight-seeing and fishing, are conducted to Scapegoat Mountain and the Bob Marshall Wilderness. Permanent

camps on high mountain lakes, such as Heart, Webb, Parker, and Twin, offer fine trout fishing. K Lazy 3 Ranch furnishes all accommodations for pack trips, plus horses, guides, individual sleeping tents, camp cots, food, and an expert cook. Another popular fishing and sight-seeing jaunt is a 4–day pack trip into the Bob Marshall Wilderness and a 4–day float trip out via the South Fork of the Flathead River. Rates for pack trips: $50 per person per day. For more details write: K Lazy 3 Ranch, Outfitters & Guides, Lincoln, MT 59639 (406)362–4258.

Kootenai National Forest & Cabinet Mountains Wilderness

This 1.8 million-acre tract is located in central northwest Montana and embraces the wilderness stretches of the Upper Kootenai River, the Salish Mountains, the Purcell Mountains, the Cabinet Mountains Wilderness, the Tobacco River, the Ten Lakes area, and the Yaak and Fisher rivers. The forest is named for the warlike Kootenai Indians, who were driven west of the Rockies by their archenemies, the Blackfeet, and settled in northwestern Montana and southeastern British Columbia. Renowned as great deer hunters and skillful tanners, the tribe very appropriately derives its name from the Indian word for "deer robes." Reminders of Kootenai domination in the area are found throughout the forest. Just south of Libby along the Kootenai River are the remains of ceremonial sweat baths used in Indian purification rites. The deep, swift Kootenai River, once a waterway favored by both Indians and fur traders, sweeps down from British Columbia and makes a 174–mile bend through Montana and Idaho around the Purcell Mountains before turning back toward Canada. A major tributary of the Columbia, the Kootenai, below Libby Dam, offers fishing for trophy-sized rainbow and cutthroat trout and white sturgeon up to 67 pounds. Most standard flies do the trick if the fish are taking, but spinners, spoons, and grasshoppers do well too. Unfortunately, all but the lower 38 miles of this once majestic emerald-green wild river have been impounded behind the U.S. Army Corps of Engineers' Libby Dam to form Lake Koocanusa.

Other features of the Kootenai National Forest include Kootenai Falls, a dramatic series of tumbling cascades that descend over 200 feet along the river east of Libby. David Thompson, the first white man to explore and map the Kootenai River, made the difficult portage around the falls in 1808 and called them the Lower Dalles. A trading post established by Thompson near the falls soon became a key stopover for trappers traveling the waterways of Montana. Many years later, between 1890 and 1902, steamboats plied the Kootenai between Jennings and Fort Steele in British Columbia. A short distance from the falls is the Kootenai Gorge, a narrow canyon through which the raging white water rushes with a deafening, ominous roar.

The Cabinet Mountains, just below the Purcell Range, were named by French-Canadian trappers who discovered boxlike openings resembling cabinets in the gorge of Clark Fork near the Montana-Idaho border. Between the Clark Fork and the Kootenai River lies the Cabinet Mountain Wilderness, a beautiful, lake-studded high-country reserve encompassing 94,272 acres within the Kaniksu and Kootenai national forests. The landscape here varies from high, snow-clad peaks to mountain lakes to timbered valleys, with elevations rising from 3,000 feet to 8,712 feet at the top of Snowshoe Peak.

Information Sources, Maps & Access

For vacation travel and recreation information and a full-color *Kootenai National Forest Map* (50¢) and *Cabinet Mountains Wilderness Map* (50¢), write: Supervisor, Kootenai National Forest, Libby, MT 59923 (406)293–6211.

The Kootenai National Forest is reached via U.S. Highways 2 and 93 and Montana State Highways 37 and 200. Lodging, supplies, guides, and outfitting services are available at Libby, Troy, Rexford, Eureka, Leonia, and Gateway. Ranger stations in the forest are at Troy, Libby, Raven, Eureka, Warland, Sylvanite, and Murphy Lake.

Gateways & Accommodations

Libby

(Pop. 3,300; zip code 59923; area code 406.) This logging and mining center, headquarters of the Kootenai National Forest on U.S. Highway 2, is surrounded by the Cabinet Mountains. Area attractions include the Robs Creek Scenic Area giant cedars south on Highway 56, Lake Koocanusa and the Libby Dam, and tours of the St. Regis Paper Co. sawmill and plywood plants (293–4141). Accommodations: *Caboose Motel* (rates: $21–23 double), 28 very good rooms, west of town on U.S. Hwy. 2 (293–6201); *Venture Best Western Motor Inn* (rates: $26–30 double), 50 superb rooms, dining room, on U.S. 2 west of town (293–7711).

Lewis & Clark National Forest & the Upper Missouri River

The Lewis & Clark National Forest lies in the heart of Missouri River country and is composed of two divisions: the 1 million-acre Rocky Mountain Division, encompassing the headwaters of the Sun, Teton, and Dearborn rivers high in the Sun River Game Preserve portion of the Bob Marshall Wilderness, and the 786,072–acre Jefferson Division, which encompasses the famed lands of the Big Snowy, Crazy Highwood, and Little Belt mountains and the renowned trout waters of Judith River, Big Spring Creek, and Smith River Canyon. The forest is a top-ranked big-game hunting area for antelope along the Musselshell River flatlands, for Rocky Mountain elk in the Little Belt and Castle mountains, and for deer, black bear, and grouse forestwide. The Missouri River, which forms a natural demarcation between the two forest divisions, was first explored by Lewis and Clark during their westward expedition of 1805. The party spent a month making a portage around the white fury of Great Falls, using a primitive cart along a well-traveled buffalo migration route. Lewis wrote on his return to the area the following year that "there were not less than 10,000 buffalo within a circle of two miles."

The 2,466–mile-long Missouri, believed to have been named for a tribe of Sioux living near the river and called the Emessourita, meaning "dwellers on the Big Muddy," forms a wild, untamed stretch, designated as a national wild and scenic river, between historic Fort Benton and the huge Fort Peck Reservoir. It flows through the rugged White Cliffs area of the Missouri River Breaks—between the Little Rockies and Bearpaw and Highwood mountains—with their spectacular, colorful eroded sandstone formations. A boat trip down to the "wild" Missouri passes through ancient Indian hunting grounds marked by tepee rings and *Pishkun*, or buffalo jumps, along the high cliffs and bluffs and historic landmarks that note the passing of the Hudson's Bay Company and North West Company, trappers, the Lewis and Clark expedition, Manuel Lisa and John Colter, and countless other explorers, fur traders, mountain men, and adventurers. A series of five boater campsites are situated at intervals on the Missouri between Virgelle and James Kipp State Recreation Area in Charlie Russell country at Coal Banks

Landing, Cow Island Landing, Judith Landing, Hole-in-the-Wall, and Slaughter River on the route of Lewis and Clark. Downstream from Fort Benton—once the major supply depot of the American Fur Company for camp traders in Montana, Idaho, and Canada and outfitting center for thousands of tenderfeet heading into the gold-rush country—are the faint remains of historic Fort McKenzie near the mouth of the Marias River, and Fort Cook, Fort Clagett, and Fort Chardon near the mouth of the Judith River. The Fort Benton Museum contains a reproduction of an early keel boat of the type used by Lewis and Clark during their arduous upstream exploration of the Missouri. Boaters on the "wild" river stretch may see golden eagles, pelicans, cliff swallows, elk, and bighorn sheep, described in *The Journals of Lewis & Clark 1804–1806 Expedition*. This stretch of the Missouri above Fort Peck Reservoir holds northern pike up to 20 pounds and prehistoric paddlefish. Fascinating *1893 Maps of the Missouri River* (6 sheets), with historical notes on the Missouri from the mouth of the Marias to Fort Peck Reservoir, may be obtained free upon request from: National Park Service, Rocky Mountain Region, P.O. Box 25287, Denver, CO 80225.

Information Sources, Maps & Access

Detailed information and a full-color *Lewis & Clark National Forest Map* (50¢) may be obtained by writing: Supervisor, Lewis & Clark National Forest, Box 871, Great Falls, MT 59401 (406)453–7678.

The major automobile routes to the Jefferson (eastern) Division of the forest are U.S. Highways 89, 12, and 87 and Interstate 90. Lodging, guides, supplies, boat rentals, and outfitters in the Jefferson Division are available at White Sulphur Springs, Harlowton, Thale, Neihart, Stanford, Monarch, Lewiston, and Great Falls. The Rocky Mountain (western) Division of the forest is reached via Interstate 15 and U.S. 287 and 89. Accommodations, supplies, guides, boat rentals, and outfitters are available at Cut Bank, Shelby, Conrad, Great Falls, Choteau, Augusta, Bowman's Corner, and Wolf Creek.

Gateways & Accommodations

Augusta

(Pop. 400; zip code 59410; area code 406.) The town is on U.S. 287 in the Sun River ranch country. Accommodations: *Wagon Wheel West Motel* (rates: $16–18 double), 13 rooms, on U.S. 287 (562–3295).

Choteau

(Pop. 1,600; zip code 59422; area code 406.) Choteau was once the headquarters for the great cattle ranches where herds grazed over vast tracts of north central Montana. Accommodations: *Western Star Motel* (rates: $16.50), 13 rooms, on U.S. Hwy. 89 at 426 Main St. (466–5777).

Fort Benton

(Pop. 1,900; zip code 59442; area code 406.) This is one of the oldest settlements in Montana. The post was a historic jumping-off point for the hordes of tenderfeet heading west for the Montana goldfields. Thousands of tons of supplies were shipped from the fort by ox team and pack train to the camp traders of the northwest. Exhibits of the early trading era and river steamers are housed at the Fort Benton Museum on Front St. Accommodations: *Fort Motel* (rates: $16 double), 11 rooms and family units, on U.S. Hwy. 87A at 1809 St. Charles St. (622–3312).

Great Falls

(Pop 60,100; zip code, see below; area code 406.) This thriving business center is on a bend of the Missouri River opposite the mouth of the Sun River, flanked by the Highwood and Big Belt mountains to the east and southeast, the Big Belt Mountains to the south, and the Rockies to the west. Area attractions include the Giant Springs, the state fish hatchery, and the Charles M. Russell Museum & Log Cabin Studios (12th St. and 4th Ave.) of the famous cowboy artist. Area restaurants include 4B's Black Angus Steak House at 3800 10th Ave. (761–4550) and the Village Inn south on Interstate 15 (866–3241). Accommodations: *Best Western Heritage Inn* (rates: $31 double), 253 excellent rooms and family units, heated indoor pool, saunas, cocktail lounge, room service, at 1700 Fox Farm Road (761–1900); *Best Western Ponderosa Inn* (rates: $29–31 double), 107 excellent rooms and family units, indoor heated pool, cocktail lounge, at 220 Central Ave. downtown (761–3410); *Holiday Inn* (rates: $31 double), 109 excellent rooms, coffee shop, cocktail lounge, heated pool, at 1411 10th Ave., 59405 (761–4600); *O'Haire Manor Motel* (rates: $23–27 double), 72 excellent rooms and suites, coffee shop, indoor heated pool, at 7th St. and 1st Ave., 59401 (454–2141).

Harlowton

(Pop. 1,400; zip code 59036; area code 406.) Overlooking the Musselshell River, Harlowton is the seat of Wheatland County. Accommodations: *Corral Motel* (rates: $18 double), 18 rooms, supper dining, east of town at the junction of U.S. Highways 12 and 191 (632–4331).

Lewistown

(Pop. 6,400; zip code 59457; area code 406.) This rich farming center in the Spring Creek valley lies at the geographic center of Montana. It was originally established in 1881 as a trading post on the old Carroll Trail between Helena and the mouth of the Musselshell River at Crow Island. Area attractions include famous Big Spring Creek, the Montana State Fish Hatchery at the head of Big Spring Creek on County Road 466, the Kendall and Gilt Edge gold-rush ghost town, the James Kipp State Recreation Area on U.S. Highway 191 on the Missouri River, and the ruins of Fort Maginnis. Accommodations: *Best Western Yogo Inn* (rates: $24–26 double), 84 superb rooms and suites, on 4 acres with gardens, dining room, Golden Spike Lounge, coffee shop, heated pool, at 211 E. Main St. (538–8721).

Guest Ranches

★★★*Korell's Circle Bar Guest Ranch*, bordered by the headwaters of the lovely Judith River, has fine family accommodations and all the activities you expect from a western-style vacation—trail rides into the canyons and forests of the adjoining Lewis & Clark National Forest, steak fries, great trout fishing right at your back door, jeep trips, and swimming in the ranch pool. There are gentle, mountain-trained horses to match every rider's ability and a friendly staff to offer pointers and guide your wilderness outings. Guest cabins are attractive log buildings, each completely different and spaced for maximum privacy. All have 1–2 bedrooms, hot and cold water, electricity, and gas heat. Some also feature fireplaces. Cookouts are served around an old-fashioned chuck wagon; all other meals are served in the pleasant, family-style dining room. There's also a lounge, a recreation room above the barn, and an athletic area with volleyball courts and a softball diamond. For full information and rates, write: Korell's Circle Bar Guest Ranch, Utica, MT 59452 (406)423–5454.

Travel Services

Missouri River Cruise Outfitters offers riverboat trips on 160 miles of the Missouri River—part of the designated Wild and Scenic River system—below Fort Benton, Montana. Guests follow the beautiful and historic route pioneered by Lewis and Clark on their 1805 expedition aboard the 32-foot-long *West Wind* riverboat, a comfort-

able craft with seating for 18 guests and ample storage for camping gear. Plenty of on-shore time is allowed for hiking to points of interest with guides well versed in the area's history. At night you pitch camp in a scenic spot and enjoy tasty meals prepared by the crew. The 2–5–day journeys are $45 per person per day, including food, camping equipment, and guides. Sleeping bags and air mattresses are not included, but may be rented for $5 per trip. Missouri River Outfitters also offers canoe rentals, trip-planning services, canoe outfitting, and special area maps. For additional information write: Bob Singer, Missouri River Outfitters, Box 1212, Fort Benton, MT 59442 (406)622–3295.

Lolo National Forest

This historic fishing, hunting, and camping region embraces 2 million acres of rugged high country surrounding Missoula and the Clark Fork of the Columbia and Blackfoot rivers in northwest Montana. The Clark Fork, once a major water trail for explorers and fur traders, bisects the forest, flowing from its headwaters in Deerlodge National Forest in a northwesterly direction past Bearmouth, Medicine Tree Hill, the mouths of Rock Creek and the Bigfoot River, through Hell Gate Canyon, Missoula, past the mouths of the St. Regis, Flathead, and Thompson rivers, and forms the Noxon Reservoir in Kaniksu National Forest before flowing into Idaho. The forest is laced by a network of logging roads and old Indian trails that wind through forests of pine, fir, hemlock, spruce, and quaking aspen, along rolling hills, and through the renowned big-game hunting and fishing country surrounding the Sapphire and John Long mountains, Garnet Range, the Bitterroot, Coeur D'Alene, and Cabinet mountains, Selley Lake, and along the Clark Fork, Blackfoot, Clearwater, Thompson and St. Regis rivers and the trophy trout waters of Rock Creek. The forest was once traversed by the old Kootenai Trail of the Salish Indians and traveled by David Thompson, Finan McDonald, Jacque Finley, and other fur traders of the North West Company in the early 1800s and by prospectors and pack trains during the boom days of the Coeur d'Alene and Kootenai mines in the 1860s. Within the forest is the site where, in 1805, Lewis and Clark set up the camp called Traveler's Rest on the Bitterroot River near the mouth of Lolo Creek.

Information Sources, Maps & Access

For detailed vacation travel and camping information and a full-color *Lolo National Forest Map*, write: Supervisor, Lolo National Forest, Bldg. 24, Fort Missoula, MT 59801 (406)329–3557.

The Lolo National Forest is reached via U.S. Highways 2, 12, and 10, Interstate 90, and Montana State Highway 200. Information, lodging, supplies, guides, and outfitters are available at Missoula, Ovando, Seeley Lake, Evaro, Hudson, Stark, Frenchtown, Alberton, Plains, Superior, Thompson Springs, Paradise, St. Regis, Greenough, Potomac, and Bonner. For a listing of outfitters for fishing, hunting, and wilderness pack trips in the Lolo National Forest, write: Dept. of Fish & Game, 490 Meridian Road, Kalispell 59901.

Gateways & Accommodations

Drummond

(Pop. 500; zip code 59832; area code 406.) On Interstate 90, Drummond was once the site of a trappers' camp. The Bearmouth Ghost Town, 14 miles west of town off Interstate 90, was once inhabited by the notorious Beartown Roughs and was the runner-up for the state capital. A million dollars in gold and silver was mined here in 1866 and 1867. Another area attraction is the Beavertail Hill Recreation Area. Accommodations: *Sky Motel* (rates: $17 double), 14 rooms and family units, on U.S. Hwy. 10 (288–3206); *Star Motel* (rates: $17 double), 10 rooms on U.S. Hwy. 10 (288–3272).

Missoula

(Pop. 29,500; zip code 59801; area code 406.) Missoula is the headquarters of the Lolo National Forest and the Regional U.S. Forest Service. This major Montana gateway and farming and business center is situated at the mouth of Hell Gate Canyon of the Clark Fork River, which cuts the city in two. Hell Gate, once an ideal spot for ambush by the Blackfeet, was named by French-Canadian trappers. The city is flanked on the south by the Bitterroot and Sapphire mountains. Area attractions include the U.S. Forest Service Smokejumpers Center, the University of Montana, and the following restaurants: *Club Château*, on Montana Hwy. 200 (728–9633); *The Depot* in the Old Northern Hotel, 201 W. Railroad St. (728–7007); *Heidelhaus*, 2620 Brooks St. (543–3200); and *Montana Mining Co.*, 1210 W. Broadway (543–6192). Accommodations: *Best Western Executive Motor Inn* (rates: $30–33 double), 51 rooms and suites, heated pool, at 201 E. Main St. (543–7221); *Holiday Inn* (rates: $36 double), 78 excellent rooms and family units, restaurant, coffee shop, heated pool, courtesy airport bus, at 1609 Broadway (543–7231); *Red Lion Motor Inn* (rates: $32–36 double), 76 superb rooms, dining room, restaurant, coffee shop, cocktail lounge, heated pool, at 700 W. Broadway (728–3300); *Red Lion Village Motor Inn* (rates: $31–43 double), 173 outstanding

rooms and family units, dining room, coffee shop, cocktail lounge, heated pool, at 100 Madison St. (728–3100).

Superior

(Pop. 1,000; zip code 59270; area code 406.) A onetime gold-mining town established in the 1870s, Superior is divided by the Clark Fork. Accommodations: *Big Sky Motel* (rates: $24 double), 24 excellent rooms, off Interstate 90, Exit 47 (822–4831).

Lodges & Guest Ranches

★★★*Double Arrow Ranch*, 3 miles from Seeley Lake on the edge of the Bob Marshall Wilderness, is a vacation dude resort offering a broad spectrum of outdoor activities: fishing for trout in the Clearwater River, horseback riding on winding ranch roads, wilderness pack trips, water skiing, swimming, and more. In the winter, cross-country and downhill skiing, snowshoeing, and tobogganing are popular. Surrounded by the magnificent high country of Lolo National Forest, Double Arrow offers modern, year-round accommodations in a comfortable lodge and cabins. For information and rates write: Double Arrow Ranch, Seeley Lake, MT 59868.

★★★*Hole-in-the-Wall Lodge*, a full-service guest ranch approximately 40 miles west of Missoula, specializes in spring black bear hunts, summer pack trips, and fall big-game hunts in both Montana and Idaho. A lovely trout stream winds right through the property, and adjacent streams, excellent for anglers, are within easy hiking or riding distance. The central lodge building houses a cocktail lounge, dining area, kitchen, and recreation area. New and modern duplex cottages have comfortable furnishings and nice views of the ranch and surrounding forest. Rates: $30 per person daily (double occupancy) or $22–25 per person for 3 or 4 to a cottage. Included are all meals, lodging, steak fries, and use of ranch facilities (no charge for daily horseback riding on stays of 4 days or more). Summer pack trips are $50 per person daily (minimum of 3 days), including meals, lodging, guides, rafts for lake fishing, and other necessary equipment. All-inclusive 5–day spring black bear hunts are $500 per person; fall hunting for elk and deer, $850 per person for 7 days. For additional details write: Hole-in-the-Wall Lodge, P.O. Box 86, Alberton, MT 59820 (406)728–5203, unit 7284.

★★★*Holland Lake Lodge*, at the southern gateway to the Bob Marshall Wilderness, specializes in year-round outdoor adventures, including customized family pack-in floating, fishing, and sight-seeing trips; guided and drop-camp hunting for grizzly, mountain goat, elk, deer, and other species; camping trips; and excursions on foot or horseback over more than 1,200 miles of trails in the surrounding backcountry.

Holland Lake Lodge's 7–10–day hunts operate from a base camp 20 miles into the wilderness, equipped with heated tents, cots, and a separate cook tent. Groups are limited to 6 hunters, with a guide for each 2 sportsmen. You can also arrange for a special trophy hunt at a separate spike camp with one guide for each hunter. The main lodge on Holland Lake has been recently renovated to provide cozy and comfortable accommodations in both lodge rooms and lakeside cottages, with or without kitchens. American-plan rates with accommodations in lodge rooms and 3 home-cooked, family-style meals daily: $30 per person per day. Cottage rentals are $30–43 daily for 4–7 persons. Hunts, summer fishing, and sight-seeing trips are additional. For more information write: Holland Lake Lodge, Seeley Lake, MT 59868 (406)754–2282.

★*Pine Shadows Resort*, located on Seeley Lake in the magnificent Seeley-Swan Valley, sponsors pack and float trips down the Blackfoot River, fishing expeditions in the Bob Marshall Wilderness, lake fishing and boating, waterskiing, and photography safaris in the surrounding wilderness. Winter attractions include hundreds of miles of well-marked cross-country ski trails, snowshoeing, and downhill skiing. Guided hunting and fishing trips are also offered. Accommodations in modern, lakeside cabins. For rates and information write: Pine Shadows Resort & Marina, Seeley Lake, MT 59868.

Travel Services

Double Arrow Outfitters, in Seeley Lake, sponsors summer pack trips for families or groups of 2 to 12 in the Bob Marshall Wilderness for riding, camping, photography, and fishing. Following marked trails and clear mountain streams, each group establishes base camps in secluded meadows. Each camp becomes a center of exploration for that immediate area. Double Arrow also conducts fall pack trips in the Bob Marshall area, specifically tailored for hunting elk, deer, black and grizzly bear, and goats. Guides, modern tents and camp equipment, and strong, agile packhorses are all provided. Write: Double Arrow Outfitters, Helen and C. B. Rich, Box 104, Seeley Lake, MT 59868.

★★★*White Tail Ranch*, a 1,400–acre packing and outfitting ranch in the Blackfoot Valley, has specialized in summer wilderness pack trips and big-game hunts since 1940. The ranch's location on the edge of the Bob Marshall Wilderness guarantees superlative 10–day all-inclusive pack trips, fishing expeditions to the area's finest trout waters, high-country tours of the rough terrain atop the Continental Divide, and drop-camp trophy hunts. White Tail Ranch maintains both a fully equipped fishing camp on Meadow Lake and a comfortable tent-camp for hunters at Danaher Valley in the heart of the Bob Marshall Wilderness. The attractive base lodge has 9 modern and semimodern cabins and a dining room for hearty buffet-style meals. Several nearby lakes are ideal for fishing and swimming. Horses, included in your rates, are available at all times for exploring the beautiful Montana countryside. A combination vacation of 4 days at the ranch and 3 days at the Meadow Lake Camp is $300 per person, including meals and equipment. Pack trips are $50 per person daily in groups of 4–8. Ten–day hunts from the Danaher Valley Camp are $1,200 per person (1 guide for each 2 hunters), and special 10–day trophy hunts are $2,000 per person. In winter the ranch offers wilderness ski touring with dogsleds at $35 daily per person. For additional information write: White Tail Ranch, Ovando, MT 59854 (406)793–6600.

Yellowstone National Park

See "Wyoming" chapter for detailed description.

NEBRASKA

Introduction

The Great Plains of Nebraska, which slope gently toward the Missouri River (the eastern boundary of the state), provide some of the nation's finest pheasant hunting and encompass the famous fishing and waterfowl hunting areas of the Sand Hills, the rugged Pine Ridge country, and the noted striped bass, walleye, and northern pike waters of McConaughy Reservoir. The broken tablelands in the westernmost portions of the Cornhusker State mark the eastern limit of the Rocky Mountain foothills.

Accommodations & Travel Services

Nebraska's major vacation accommodations are listed and described in the "Vacation/Lodging Guide" which follows. For detailed information on all aspects of travel in the state, contact: Nebraska Tourist Information, State Capitol, Box 94666, Lincoln, NE 65809 (402)471–3111. Be sure to request a free *Nebraska Travel Pack* and specific information about the area you plan to visit.

Information & Services

A number of free information publications of interest to Nebraska-bound anglers and hunters are available from: Game & Parks Commission, P.O. Box 30370, Lincoln 68503, including the 24–page *Boating Guide*; the 16–page booklet *Safe Boating*; the 16–page *Fishing Guide*, which contains fishing regulations, a full-color, 16–page *Fishing Nebraska Guide* to public fishing areas and species available; *Ice Fishing Guide, the Fishes of Nebraska* (98 pages, 50¢), which contains full-color plates, species information, and range maps; *Billfold Cards of Nebraska Hunting Seasons; Field Care of Big Game*; the 16–page *Hunting Guide; Where to Hunt in Nebraska*, a list of state and federal public hunting areas; the full-color, 16–page booklet *Crane River*, story of sandhill cranes and their annual spring sojourn on the Platte River; *Fremont Lakes Map-Guide*; the 16–page, full-color booklet *Outdoor Recreation in Nebraska; Two Rivers Recreation Area Map-Guide*; wildlife publications including *The Bobwhite Quail, Duck Identification Guide for Hunters, Facts About the Pheasant, Deer of Nebraska* (32 pages, full color), *Mourning Dove, The Ring-Necked Pheasant in Nebraska* (32 pages, full color); and the *"Your Wildlife Lands"* series—*The Panhandle, The Platte Valley*, and *The Sand Hills*, a valuable pocket-size guide, *Waterfowl Identification in the Central Flyway* (52 pages, 35¢), contains beautiful full-color plates of waterfowl species, showing winter and fall plumage, with brief descriptions.

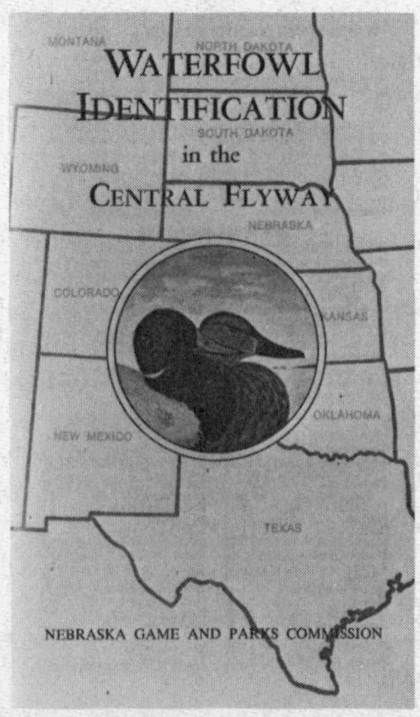

Nebraska's major state recreation and camping—areas including the 3,000 acres of wooded bluff lands of Indian Cove, Ponca and Niobrara state parks, and the Wildcat Hills Recreation Area with its herds of buffalo and elk—are described in the useful booklet *Nebraska Parklands*, available free from: Game & Parks Commission, P.O. Box 30370, Lincoln 68503. It describes and lists, in chart form, all the recreational facilities run by the commission, showing exactly what facilities are available in each area. It is lavishly illustrated with color photographs. Anyone planning on camping in Nebraska should send for the free brochure *Nebraska Camping Guide*, available free from the commission. This handy publication contains a chart listing all the state recreation areas, state parks, state wayside areas, state special use areas, and federal areas, showing facilities available in each area.

Rules and regulations governing the use of these areas are also noted in capsule form (area regulations; camping; fires, smoking; pets; fishing, hunting, and trapping; etc.). Nebraska's major canoe routes are described in the informative booklet *Canoeing in Nebraska*, available free from: Game & Parks Commission, P.O. Box 30370, Lincoln 68503. The canoe routes described include the winding Niobrara River, with its panoramic scenery and spring-fed tributaries, which hold rainbow and brown trout; the small (80–mile-long) Dismal River, which flows through the Sand Hills; Elkhorn River, one of the most overlooked canoe routes in the state; serene Calamus River in the Sand Hills country; the historic North Platte River, with its island-dotted channels; the Republican River and the 60–mile stretch of the great Missouri between Gavins Point Dam and Ponca; the Big Blue River, with its frequent logjams and thick vegetation; and the historic Platte River, known to the early pioneers as "too wet to plow, and too thick to drink."

Highways & Maps

A free *Official Nebraska Highway Map & Travel Guide* may be obtained by writing: Tourist Information Office, Dept. of Economic Development, State Capitol, Box 9466, Lincoln 65809. This useful full-color map shows all major highways and secondary roads, campgrounds and state recreation areas, airports, national forests and wildlife refuges, lakes and streams, waysides, historic sites, and points of interest. It also contains an inset map of the Great Platte River Road (Interstate 80), known to the Indians as the "Big Medicine Trail" and to the pioneers as the Oregon Trail.

Nebraska Lakes & Recreation Areas

The Cornhusker State's big open spaces, forests and rugged hill country, dotted by more than 3,300 lakes and slashed by 11,000 miles of streams, offer some surprisingly excellent fishing and hunting opportunities. Nebraska's Panhandle, the northwest corner of the state, offers fly-fishing and spin-casting for rainbow and brown trout and trolling for walleyes, and rainbows in the reservoirs, and is top-ranked for mule deer, antelope, wild turkey, and upland game birds in the Pine Ridge division of the Nebraska National Forest, Oglala National Grasslands, Crescent Lake National Wildlife Refuge, and state game lands and recreation areas. The shallow, natural lakes of the famous Sand Hills region hold some big northern pike, largemouth bass, and panfish. The Sand Hills country is inhabited by deer, antelope, grouse, pheasant, quail, dove, and waterfowl is found in the Valentine National Wildlife Refuge, Samuel R. McKelvie National Forest, Bessey division of the Nebraska National Forest, and state-managed game lands and recreation areas. The lakes and streams of the northeast, southwest, and southeast regions offer fishing for walleye, northern pike, bass, catfish, and panfish; their forests, grasslands, and wetlands provide excellent hunting for deer, upland game birds, waterfowl, and small game on state recreation areas such as the Dead Timber, Lewis and Clark Lake, and Branched Oak Lake recreation areas; state special use areas such as the Limestone Bluffs, Medicine Creek, Red Willow Reservoir, Cornhusker, and Iron Horse Trail areas; and on federal reservoir waterfowl areas such as Harvard Marsh, Macon Lakes, Killdeer Basin, Harlan County Reservoir, Clark Lagoon, and Atlanta Marsh.

VACATION/ LODGING GUIDE

Information Sources, Maps & Access

For detailed information on the areas described above, contact: Nebraska Tourist Information, State Capitol, Box 94666, Lincoln, NE 65809 (402)471-3111. If you plan a trip to the Pine Ridge Country, send for an informative map-guide *Recreation Guide Map—Nebraska Pine Ridge Area*. It contains a map of the entire area showing wooded areas, national parks, forest service lands, Game & Parks Commission lands, federal and state camping areas, roads and trails, lakes and reservoirs, rivers and streams, towns and villages, and boundaries. Historic trails are outlined (Laramie, Wyoming, to Fort Robinson, the Fort Robinson-Hat Creek Stage Road military telegraph line, Laramie Spottedtail, and Fort Robinson Road). Areas where hunting is prohibited are indicated. A sunrise/

sunset schedule is provided, as well as a chart showing recreation and wayside areas and the facilities available at each. The reverse side contains information on the history, recreation, wildlife, management, and plant life of the area. It is illustrated with attractive color photographs. A copy of this map-guide can be obtained free from: Game & Parks Commission, P.O. Box 30370, Lincoln 68503. Free maps of Nebraska's major lakes and reservoirs, including *Lewis and Clark Reservoir, Lake McConaughy, Harlan County Reservoir,* and *Crescent, Island,* and *Twin lakes,* are available from: Game & Parks Commission, P.O. Box 30370, Lincoln 68503. These maps show boat ramps, campgrounds, trailer spaces, river channels, deep water, and surface areas. The major auto access route serving the state is Interstate Highway 80.

Recreation Areas

Lake McConaughy and Lewis & Clark Reservoir

In the south are the trophy fishing waters of 35,000–acre Lake McConaughy—the state's largest body of water and top "big fish" lake. The bays, coves, and shoals along the 105–mile shoreline of "Big Mac," as the lake is known locally, yield northern pike to 25 pounds, walleye to 16 pounds, and hordes of white bass, rainbow trout, crappie, yellow perch, and striped bass, which grow to record weights on the large schools of threadfin shad. During May and August large schools of white bass drive the shad to the surface during feeding sprees, where they attract noisy flocks of diving, swooping gulls. Lake McConaughy has been stocked periodically with kokanee and coho salmon. Otter Creek, a feeder stream of Lake McConaughy, yields some big browns and lake-run rainbows. The North Platte River offers excellent fishing above Lake McConaughy for northern pike and channel catfish in spring and early summer. Red Willow Creek holds northern pike, largemouth and smallmouth bass, channel cats, crappie, and bluegill.

The northeast region of the state is dominated by the Missouri River and its Lewis and Clark Lake impoundment, which yields big walleye, sauger, channel catfish, crappie, white bass, and freshwater drum. The free-flowing, unchannelized stretch of the Missouri is the last of the "Big Muddy" that resembles its condition when traveled by Lewis and Clark in 1805. Here its shallow bars, undercut banks, and meandering channels yield walleye, catfish, sauger, white bass, and primitive paddlefish. The hundreds of farm ponds and sandpits scattered throughout the region hold largemouth bass, bluegill, and crappie.

Nebraska National Forest & The Sand Hills

This 225,000–acre reserve is scattered in several divisions throughout the famous Sand Hills region in northwestern Nebraska. The major features of this area include the North, Middle, and South Loup rivers, Valentine National Wildlife Refuge, the Niobrara, White, Upper Sanke, North Platte, and South Platte rivers, and McConaughy Reservoir, which offers the state's finest fishing for walleye and northern pike up to 27 pounds. The entire region provides the state's best hunting for pheasant, quail, sharptail and prairie grouse, wild turkey, waterfowl, mule and whitetail deer, antelope, and bobcat.

The Nebraska National Forest's Bessey district contains a completely man-made forest planted in 1902. A beautiful panoramic view rewards visitors at the Scott Lookout Tower. The Bessey recreation complex is located along the Middle Loup River 2 miles west of Halsey, and has excellent camping facilities. A large part of this area (about 16,000–acres) was destroyed by a major forest fire that swept through the area in 1965—there are still traces of the devastation. So far about 1,000 acres have been reforested. The fee-rich, shallow, weed-filled lakes of the famous Sand Hills region provide excellent fishing for big northern pike and largemouth bass, plus yellow perch, crappie, and bluegills. The renowned lake-dotted 71,516–acre Valentine National Wildlife Refuge offers fishing for the major species in Watts, Dewey, Ballards, Marsh, Duck, Rice, Clear, Pelican, and West Long lakes. Each year thousands upon thousands of mallards, pintails, and redheads nest in the refuge. The major Sand Hills lakes surrounding the refuge include Shell, Cottonwood, Round, Big Alkali, Long, Fish, Atkinson, Overton, Victoria Springs, Arnold, and Frye. The Merritt Reservoir on the Snake River offers excellent fishing for big rainbow trout, walleye, largemouth and smallmouth bass, crappie, bluegill, yellow perch, and white bass. Merritt produced the state record 18–pound 4–ounce muskellunge. The Snake River produced the state record 20–pound 1–ounce brown trout. The major Sand Hills brown trout tributaries of the Niobrara include Fairfield, Coon, Long Pine, Plum, and Schlagee creeks. The Dismal River west of Dunning also holds some big browns. The deep-flowing pools and sloughs of the Calamus River hold northern pike and channel catfish.

Pine Ridge Country & The Panhandle

The famous Pine Ridge fish and game lands, located in the distant northwestern corner of Nebraska's Panhandle, include the rugged Badlands, Pine Ridge, and High Plains. The Badlands and 4,000–foot-high Pine Ridge country were cut by ancient rivers and have been eroded by millennia of violent, sand-carrying winds. The area was the site of numerous Indian skirmishes: Buffalo Bill is said to have taken his first scalp here to avenge Custer's defeat at Little Bighorn. This unspoiled, pine-clad bluff country offers top-ranked hunting for wild Merriam's turkey, mule deer, pronghorn antelope, sharp-tailed grouse, and a few pheasant Brown and rainbow trout are found in Monroe, Sowbelly, Hat, and Soldier creeks and in the White River. Box Butte Reservoir holds northern pike, walleye, largemouth and smallmouth bass, white bass, and channel catfish. The streams of the Panhandle offer some of the state's top trout fishing. Brown and rainbow trout up to 5 pounds are taken from the North Platte during their early spring and late fall migrations up from Lake McConaughy. Some excellent backcountry fly fishing is found along tributaries of the North Platte such as Dry Sheep, Sheep, Spotted Tail, Pumpkin, Lodgepole, Wildhorse, Nine Mile, and Lawrence Fork Creeks. Lake Minatare, northeast of Scottsbluff, holds walleye, largemouth and smallmouth bass, rainbow trout, and channel catfish. The remote streams of the Pine Ridge and Niobrara valleys hold browns and rainbows. Most of the streams, including Monroe, Sowbelly, Hat, Soldier, Larabie, Chadron, Bordeaux, Beaver, and Pine creeks and the White and Niobrara rivers, flow through private ranchlands, and permission of the landowner is required. The major impoundments of the Panhandle—Whitney, Kimball, and Box Butte—hold northern pike, walleye, largemouth and smallmouth bass, white bass, and channel catfish. Island and Crane lakes in the Crescent Lake National Wildlife Refuge hold northern pike and largemouth bass.

Lodges & Guest Ranches

★★★*Chadron State Park* is located in the northwest part of the state at nearly 4,000 feet above sea level in the Pine Ridge country. It was established in 1921 and is the oldest State Park in Nebraska. On 840 acres, the Park has cabins, campsites and recreational facilities, open from May 15 through September 15, as well as during turkey, deer and antelope seasons. There is a swimming pool open in summer months with a fee of 75¢ for adults and 35¢ for children over six years of age. Guided horseback riding is available at $2 an hour and there are many scenic routes to drive or walk. Fishing and boating can be enjoyed on lagoon, and there is trout fishing in Chadron

Creek and nearby streams. The Park has playgrounds, picnic areas with fireplaces and restroom facilities, a store for picnic and camping supplies and a park headquarters building for information and assistance. Nine miles away is the town of Chadron, a college town, and nearby are the Museum of the Fur Trade (featuring Fur Trade Days in July), the reconstructed Bordeaux Trading Post and the Nebraska National Forest. Cabins at the State Park have two bedrooms and are equipped for housekeeping with four-burner stoves, refrigerators, utensils and tableware. Each of the 22 cabins has two double beds and cots are available for extra persons at $2 per night. Rates for large cabins are $16 a night or $14 a night for two or more nights; and $14 a night or $12 a night for two or more nights for the smaller cabins. Campsites are $1.50 per car per night, and the area has drinking water, restrooms, fireplaces and picnic tables. There are accommodations and special rates for groups of 60 or less. For more information and reservations write or call: Chadron State Park, Chadron, Nebraska 69337 (308)432–2036.

★★★*Fort Robinson State Park* is located 3 miles west of Crawford on Highway 20 in the Pine Ridge region. The original Fort Robinson was established on this site as a post Civil War Indian Agency protective post. It saw the last great gathering of the Sioux nation, was a prisoner-of-war camp and then a USDA research center, and is now the largest state park in Nebraska. There are nearly 24,000 acres of wide open country. Besides visiting the historic restored building of Fort Robinson, there is much to do at the Park. An Early Bird Wildlife Tour can start the day. Visitors gather at reveille and follow scenic roads to search for turkey, deer and other Pine Ridge wildlife. There is horseback riding on one or two hour trail rides starting at 7 A.M. and costing only $2 per hour. For those who don't want to get on a horse, but enjoy the Old West, there are stagecoach rides or rides in a buckboard surrey pulled by mules. For more modern tours of the Fort Complex, the wildlife areas and the Park, there is a tour train, jeep rides and air-conditioned vans for hire. Rather than buying souvenirs, visitors can learn to make their own leathercraft, lapidary or arts and crafts. Chadron State College students teach classes in the activities center, where there is also a game room. Guests can visit the 1874 Guardhouse where Crazy Horse met his death, the Trailside Museum of geologic and natural history with a 14–foot mammoth on display, the Fort Robinson Museum or the Visitor's Information center with recreational equipment, literature and event schedules. There is an indoor swimming pool enclosed by skylights and window-doors with a sundeck, wading pool, lockers and showers. Visitors can even bring their own horse and lodge it at the Equestrian Facilities. Three nights a week, there is a free Wild West Rodeo. Every night after sunset there is a one hour evening campfire slide and film program. Not to be missed is the Buffalo Stew Chuckwagon Cookout held nightly and costing only $2.50 for adults and $1.50 for children. Other evening entertainment is plays and melodramas at the Post Playhouse. Souvenirs, hot dogs, limited grocery supplies and snacks are sold at Sutler's Store, a rustic general store. Outdoor enthusiasts will enjoy hiking in the wilderness and trout fishing. The State Park is open from May 25 through November 18, as well as during turkey, antelope and deer hunting seasons. Accommodations take guests back in time. There are 24 rooms with private baths in the Lodge, which was a 1909 Enlisted Men's Barracks. A room with a double bed is $8 a night. The 1874–75 and 1887 Officers Quarters have become the Adobe housekeeping cabins with five to seven bedrooms rented at $30 to $52 a night. These may be rented by the floor with the ground floor including kitchen facilities and the second and third floors having bedrooms only. Adobe cabins also have housekeeping facilities with complete kitchens. Comanche Hall has sleeping rooms with community baths at $16 per night and two-room units with private baths at $16 per night. No reservations are accepted for Comanche Hall and rooms are rented on a first come, first served basis. For visitors who prefer to camp, there is a campgrounds with showers, grills, picnic tables, electrical hookups, water and a sump station. Rates are $1.50 per car per night or $2.00 with electrical hookups. For reservations and additional information contact: Superintendent, Fort Robinson State Park, P.O. Box 392, Crawford, NE 69339 (308)665–2660.

★★*Pine Hill Ranch* is a working guest ranch in the Pine Ridge of the Nebraska Panhandle. The ranch, over 1200 acres of open terrain, is ideal for trail rides and pack trips, and Pine Hill Ranch plans guest trips into the Black Hill, the Badlands, and other scenic places of historical interest. A clear spring-fed creek runs through the ranch property. Children can hunt the creek bed for fossils and Indian artifacts, join in the ranch chores or learn to milk a cow. Nearby fairs and rodeos liven the season. All meals are served family style in the pleasant dining room by hosts Alan and Kathy Harris. All horseback riding is included in the rates, overnight pack trips are $50 extra. A pioneer sod house, completely modernized for guest comfort, and two private guest rooms provide modern comfort with the rustic spirit of the open plains. Rates are $20 daily adults, and $120 weekly including meals. Children under 12 are $15 daily and $85 weekly. Hosts Alan and Kathy Harris will meet guests arriving by bus in Rushville and at nearby Chadron Airport. For details, write: Alan and Kathy Harris, Pine Hill Ranch Route 1, Rushville, NE 69360.

★★★★*Pine Ridge Sportsman's Lodge* is located in the famous wildlife-rich Pine Ridge country in the northwest corner of Nebraska. This superb, nationally renowned lodge offers outstanding accommodations, services, and hunting in season several thousand acres of beautiful bluff country—noted for its broad valleys, rugged buttes, and forests of ponderosa pine—for Merriam's wild turkey, pronghorn antelope, and mule deer. The new, two-story lodge, constructed of peeled, western cedar logs, is situated on Pine Bluff with a scenic view of Deadman Valley and historic Fort Robinson off in the distance. The lodge accommodates up to six guests in modern, fully carpeted rooms with private bath and shower, beamed ceilings, native stone fireplace, and authentic western decor. Delicious family-style meals are served in the main lodge dining room. For additional information and American Plan vacation package rates contact: Grande Domain Retreats, 801 "P" St., Lincoln, NE 68508 (402)477–9249.

★★★*Ponca State Park* is situated atop picturesque bluffs overlooking the Missouri River, with 836 acres of rolling hills and scenic forests. There is fine camping with paved camping pads and convenient showers and restrooms. Additional facilities include picnic tables, fireplaces, firewood, playground equipment and trailer dumping station. The Missouri River provides fishing and has a boat ramp. There are supervised trail rides through the park with qualified wranglers. Picnic areas have shelters, tables, fireplaces and wood, drinking water, restrooms, pop machines, and trails for hiking. The park also has an outdoor swimming pool. In addition to campsites, there are two-bedroom modern, air-conditioned housekeeping cabins. They have double beds, towels, bath with showers, large screened porches and kitchenettes with utensils and dishes. Rates: camping sites on first come, first served basis, $3 nightly. Group camping is $3 per night for up to 12 persons. Cabins, normally open from May 15–Sept. 15 are $16 for one night or $14 for two or more nights. Reservations accepted only for two or more nights. For further information contact: Ponca State Park, P.O. 486, NE 68770 (402)755–2284.

★★★*Rim Rock Ranch* is nestled in the Pine ridge of northwest Nebraska, bordered by the spectacular Fort Robinson State Park and the Nebraska National Forest. Fishermen will appreciate the myriad of mountain streams and lakes within easy reach; hiking trails explore the sheer sided canyons and towering buttes. Nearby Fort Robinson State Park offers trail rides throughout Sioux and Cheyenne country, stagecoach rides, wildlife and historic tours and a refreshing outdoor pool. Nearby are the mysterious canyons of the Badlands, the Blackhills, and Mt. Rushmore. Each private cabin is situated below the pine covered hills to provide maximum privacy and seclusion. All are comfortably furnished with queen-sized beds, private bath, fully-equipped, modern kitchens, and outdoor barbeques. Rates are $75 daily, and $450 weekly. Each reservation must be for a minimum of three days. For more information write: Rim Rock Ranch, Rt. 3, Box 30, Crawford, NE 69339 (308)665–2849.

NEVADA

Introduction

To the east of the Sierra Nevada lies the state of Nevada, with 110,540 square miles in the Great Basin, a rugged arid plateau broken by north-south mountain chains enclosed on the north by Oregon and Idaho and on the east by Utah and Arizona. The Sagebrush State, first explored by Spaniards and the fur traders Peter Skeene Ogden and Jedediah Smith, and the site of the famous Comstock Lode rush in 1859, contains several renowned outdoor recreation areas, including Lake Tahoe, Pyramid Lake, the Jarbidge Wilderness, Lake Mohave, and the Lake Mead National Recreation Area.

Accommodations & Travel Information

For information on accommodations and vacation travel in the Sagebrush State, contact: Travel & Tourism Div., Nevada Dept. of Economic Development, Carson City 89701 (702)885–4322. There is lots of room to roam on Nevada's expanse of land, and camping facilities are numerous. The *Guide to Bureau of Land Management* Campgrounds is available free from: Bureau of Land Management, Room 3008 Federal Bldg., 300 Booth St., Reno 89502. Free brochures are also available on the following outstanding camping areas. *Ruby Marsh Campground* is an excellent access spot for fishing, hunting, bird hunting, and mountain scenery in the colorful Ruby Valley. *Indian Creek Reservoir*, on the eastern slope of the Sierra Nevada, provides water sports and fishing among the pine forests. *Walker Lake Recreation Site* offers camping and fishing around the rocky, rugged terraces of Lake Walker. The *Curtz Lake Environmental Study Area* provides educational trails through forest and lake country, and the area is filled with small mammals and woodland birds. These areas are managed by the Bureau of Land Management, and free information can be obtained from the Carson City District, 801 North Plaza St., Carson City 89701. *Guide to BLM's Nevada Campgrounds*, free from the State Office of the BLM in Reno, is an index to all BLM-managed camping areas in the state. Additional camping information is available free from Travel and Tourism Division, Nevada Dept. of Economic Development, Carson City 89701.

Highways & Maps

The *Nevada State Highway Map*, available free from the Travel and Tourism Division, Nevada Dept. of Economic Development, Carson City 89701, shows all roads and highways, recreation areas, national forest land, towns, lakes and streams, airfields and railroads, and public lands.

Nevada Lakes, Forests & Recreation Areas

Nevada offers some of the best trout and bass fishing and hunting opportunities in the Far West. Lake Tahoe, nestled among the towering Sierras on the state's western boundary, is one of the West's premier trout waters. The lake is 21½ miles long and 12 miles wide and has a delightfully irregular rocky shoreline thickly forested with evergreens. With the peaks of the High Sierras in view above the trees, the lake is a brilliant blue-green, owing to its great depth—1,776 feet at one point. It is the tenth deepest lake in the world and the second clearest in the United States. The fishing in Tahoe was nearly destroyed near the turn of the century when hundreds of tons of the native Labontan cutthroat trout, also known as black spotted trout, were taken for commercial purposes and shipped to markets as far away as San Francisco. During the 1870s, the lake was stocked with Atlantic, king and silver salmon, rainbow, brown, golden, and mackinaw trout, and Great Lakes whitefish. Subsequent stockings of trout, including the native Labontan cutthroat, and kokanee salmon, beginning in 1949 have brought the fishing close to its former level of excellence. First recorded knowledge of the lake is in the report of Fremont's expeditions. When he was encamped at Pyramid Lake near the mouth of the Truckee River in 1844, Indians "made a drawing of the Truckee River, which they represented as issuing from another lake in the mountains three or four days distant, in a direction a little west of south; beyond which they drew a mountain, and farther still two rivers, on one side of which, the Indians said, "people like ourselves traveled." Fremont then crossed the Sierras over Carson Pass and saw Lake Tahoe, which he later called Mountain Lake. The name of the lake was changed many times, and finally the name Tahoe was put together from several Indian words. There are numerous camping spots and trails in this area. Among wildflowers are the snow plant, red and white heather, gentian, water lily, wild marigold. Indian paintbrush, pennyroyal, and primrose. Small trees include the ash laurel and holly; the larger trees include several varieties of pine, firs, alpine spruce, cedar, and tamarack. There is also a great variety of songbirds. The beautiful Truckee River, flowing out of Lake Tahoe, flows through a scenic wooded valley and holds rainbows and browns up to 15 pounds. Topaz Lake, on the California border, holds cutthroat, brown, and rainbow trout, as does 20–mile-long Walker Lake, which is fed by the East Walker River. Pyramid Lake is one of the West's outstanding rainbow and cutthroat trout fisheries. Some of the state's finest trout fishing is in the wilderness areas of the Humboldt River tributaries, rising high in the scenic Ruby, Jarbidge and Independence mountains in the northeast. These less-known lakes and streams offer wonderful opportunities for fishing and camping free from crowded conditions and misuses.

Many of the high-country lakes are situated amidst rugged and beautiful scenery and are accessible only by foot and horseback. The wilderness fisherman can enjoy roughing it for days in complete solitude. Along the crest of the Ruby Range, Snake Range, and Schell Creek Range lie hundreds of scenic alpine lakes and streams which hold cutthroat, eastern brook, brown, rainbow, and in the Jarbidge area, an occasional Dolly Varden. The Utah cutthroats found in a few of these high mountain streams are believed to be the only remaining populations of this pure trout strain in existence. The Independence-Mountain City area in the Humboldt National Forest contains a number of small mountain streams which provide often excellent fishing for wild cutthroat rainbow and brook trout. These include Jack Creek, the North Fork of the Humboldt River above the forest boundary, the East Fork of the Owyhee River, Bull

Run Creek, and the Bruneau River and its tributaries. Populations of native cutthroat are found in a number of streams in the Tuscarora Mountains and Independence Range. Some of the finest trout fishing in the region can be found on the following streams and creeks: Beaver, Bluejacket, Columbia, Gance, McDonald, Merritt, Snow, Trail, and Van Duzer. Several improved public campgrounds are found in the forest region. In the beautiful rugged Jarbidge Wilderness, the East Fork of the Jarbidge River and the headwaters of the Marys River provide fly-fishing for rainbows and Dolly Varden. Pan-sized trout are found in the O'Neil Basin in the headwaters of Canyon Creek, and in Wilson, Camp, and Sun creeks. The Salmon Falls River, which drains the basin, holds some lunker rainbow and cutthroat trout. In the extreme northeastern corner of the state, wild cutthroat are found in the seldom-fished Big Goose Creek and its Piney and Coon creek tributaries. A U.S. Forest Service campground is located on the West Fork of the Jarbidge. Wilderness fly-fishing for wild rainbow, cutthroat, and brook trout may be found in the scenic high-country lakes and streams of the Ruby Mountains in the Humboldt National Forest in northeastern Nevada. The South Fork of the Humboldt River and the Lamoille Creek are accessible by road. Hiking and pack trails provide access to the following streams and their alpine headwaters: Boulder, Pole Canyon, Secret, Long Canyon, Soldier, and North Feerlong creeks. The spring holes of the famed Ruby Marsh National Wildlife Refuge, located along the eastern slope of the range, hold some monster browns and rainbows in excess of 10 pounds. The largest fish caught to date was a 17–pound brown trout. Some 30,000 to 50,000 deer range through the Ruby and Butte mountains area, and deer weighing over 250 pounds have been reported. The Ruby Valley, crossed by the Fremont expedition in 1845, was once the home and hunting grounds of the Shoshone Indians. The Ruby Mountains were named for "rubies" (actually worthless garnets) found in an early gold pan. Favre Lake in the Ruby Range is one of the most scenic of the alpine lakes, and in the early morning it reflects surrounding peaks as though it were beveled grass. In the summer a meadow sloping down to the shore is frequented by grazing sheep. Lamoille Creek in the Ruby Mountains is a cold, clear, tumultuous stream that feeds from snow-covered peaks rising as high as 11,000 feet. Mountain mahogany and aspen blend into patches of pine and stunted willow, and a wide variety of wildflowers bloom on the stream's canyon floor.

In southern Nevada, the Colorado River and its impoundments, Lakes Mead and Mohave, a deep blue in their desert brown setting, attract thousands of anglers each year. Lake Mead began to fill in 1935 upon completion of Hoover Dam, and by 1941 had reached its maximum elevation along the 550–mile shoreline. By 1941 (when a 13 lb. 14 ounce largemouth was caught) the lake's bass-fishing reputation had spread across the nation. Lake Mohave, 67 miles long, is impounded by Hoover Dam and provides excellent fishing for rainbow trout, coho and hokanee salmon, and largemouth bass from Eldorado Landing to the south. The swift, frigid, crystal-clear tailrace waters below Hoover Dam yield lunker rainbows up to 21½ pounds. Nevada is an excellent mule deer hunting state and has limited hunting by permit only for antelope, elk, and bighorn sheep. The upland game bird hunting is for chukar partridge, quail, sage grouse, and mourning dove. The state has surprisingly good hunting for ducks and geese in its numerous marshlands and wildlife management area wetlands, particularly in the renowned Ruby Marshes in Elko County.

Located in the desert in western Nevada, northwest of Lake Tahoe, 30–mile-long Pyramid Lake is the remnant of a vast, ancient sea once 500 miles long and 300 miles wide. When Pyramid was first seen by Fremont in 1844, its waters teemed with giant Lahontan cutthroat trout, and it was the prize fishing grounds of the Paiute Indians. The world-record cutthroat (41 lb.) was caught here in 1925, and a 65 pound cutthroat was reportedly taken here at the turn of the century. Today, the lake once again is providing fishing for rainbows to 12 pounds and cutthroats. Pyramid Lake, the largest remnant of the ancient Lahontan Sea, is a sparkling blue body of water surrounded by colorful, deeply eroded hills. The lake, which has no outlet and is slowly receding from its former shoreline (marked by a white ribbon composed of the dead bodies of minute algae), is thought to have been named by Captain Fremont for the spectacular pyramid rising 475 feet above the surface just north of Anaho Island. Paiute Indian lore says the pyramid is the home of the lake spirit, which devours humans swimming in its waters. The surface of the lake is studded with tufa islands, including 248–acre Anaho Island near the southeastern shore, which contains the West's largest rookery of pelicans. North of Pyramid Island on the eastern shore is an unusual tufa formation known as the Squaw with a Basket. At the northern end of the lake is a cluster of sharp stone spires rising from the water known as the Needles. The Paiute tribal lands of the Pyramid Lake Indian Reservation surround the lake, and a tribal fishing permit is a necessity here.

Information Sources, Maps & Access

The Nevada Dept. of Fish & Game, P.O. Box 10678, Reno, NV 89510 (702)784–6214 publishes several useful information-packed fishing guides, which cost 25¢ each, and the free *Angler's Map of the Fishing Waters of Nevada*. The *Angler's Guide to Northeast Nevada* contains detailed area maps and descriptions of fishing in the Independence-Mountain City area, the Jarbidge-O'Neil area, and the Ruby Range. The *Angler's Guide to Eastern Nevada* contains maps and useful info about fishing in the Wayne E. Kirch Wildlife Management Area, Snake Range, Schell Creek Range, Illipah Creek-White River Area, Eureka County and Newark Valley, and Nye County. *The Angler's Guide to Lake Tahoe* and *The Angler's Guide to Lakes Mead, Mohave & The Colorado River* each contain a useful lake contour map and info about the fish species present and their feeding habits. Nevada *Fishing Seasons & Regulations, Deer Seasons and Regulations* (which contains a Mule Deer Hunting Map), and *Trophy Hunt Seasons & Regulations* (for elk, antelope, bighorn sheep, and mountain lion, which contains a Management Area Map) may be obtained by writing to the Department of Fish & Game. The department will provide big-game hunting guide and outfitter information upon request. *The Humboldt National Forest*

White Pine and Ely Ranger District Recreation Map, available for 50¢ from Ely District Ranger, P.O. Box 539, Ely 89301, shows all roads and trails, recreation areas, ranger stations, and lakes and streams. *The Humboldt National Forest—Ruby Division Map* is available for 50¢ from: Ruby Mountains Ranger District, Wells 89835. It shows all roads and trails, historic routes, ranger stations, recreation sites, and lakes and streams. *The Humboldt National Forest Map for the Humboldt and Santa Rosa Districts* is available for 50¢ from: Forest Supervisor, Humboldt National Forest, Elko 89801. It shows all roads and trails, recreation sites, lakes and streams, and ranger stations. The *Wheeler Peak Scenic Area Recreation Map* is available for 50¢ from: Ely Ranger District, P.O. Box 539, Ely 89301. It shows all roads and trails, ranger stations, lakes, and recreation sites. Write to the Forest Supervisor, Toiyabe National Forest, 111 N. Virginia St., Reno 89504, for detailed information on the forest Ranger Districts in the Central Nevada Division including the Tonopah Ranger District, P.O. Box 989, Tonopah 89040; Austin Ranger District, Austin 89310; and Fallon Ranger District, Fallon 89406. The *Toiyabe National Forest—Central Nevada Division Map* is available for 50¢ from the Forest Supervisor. It shows all roads and trails, recreation sites, ranger stations, and historic sites. The *Toiyabe National Forest—Las Vegas Ranger District Map* is available for 50¢ from: District Ranger, Las Vegas District, 1217 Bridger St., Las Vegas 89101. It shows all roads and trails, ranger stations, and recreation sites. The *Toiyabe National Forest—Carson Ranger District Map* is available for 50¢ from: District Ranger, 1536 South Carson St., Carson City 89701. It shows all roads and trails, recreation sites, ranger stations, landmarks, and boat ramps. See the "Arizona" chapter for detailed information about the Lake Mead National Recreation Area. The major auto access routes serving Nevada are Interstate 80 and U.S. Highways 50, 95, and 93.

Gateways & Accommodations

Boulder City—Gateway to Lake Mead National Recreation Area

(Pop. 5,200; zip code 89005; area code 702) is the major Nevada gateway to the Lake Mead National Recreation and Hoover Dam at 726 feet high. Guided tours of the dam via passenger elevators are offered daily, Memorial Day through Labor Day. Accommodations: *El Rancho Boulder Motel* (rates: $22–24 double) with 39 good rooms and family units, swimming pool on U.S. 93 at 725 Nevada Highway (293–1085); *Sands Motel* (rates: $18–22 double) with 25 good rooms and family units on US 93 at 809 Nevada Highway (293–2589).

Carson City—Gateway to the Toiyabe National Forest

(Pop. 28,000; zip code 89701; area code 702) named for Kit Carson, is located in Eagle Valley at the eastern slope of the Sierra Nevada. Area attractions include a District Ranger's Office of the Toiyabe National Forest, Bowers Mansion on US 395 built by one of the original comstock lode tycoons, and the Nevada State Museum in the old Mint Building. Accommodations: *Best Western City Center Motel* (rates: $29.40–31.50 double) with 89 good rooms, swimming pool, at 800 North Carson St. (882–5535); *Best Western Downtowner Motel* (rates: $27–29 double) with 34 good rooms at 801 North Carson St. (882–1333); *Hardman House Motor Inn* (rates: $28–30 double) with 62 excellent rooms and family units at 917 North Carson St. (882–7744); *Ormsby House* (rates: $32–35 double) with 202 superb rooms and family units, restaurant, coffee shop, swimming pool, at 600 South Carson St. (882–1890).

Crystal Bay—Gateway to Lake Tahoe

(Pop. 950; zip code 89402; area code 702) is a resort area and gateway to Lake Tahoe and the Ski Incline area (which see). Area attractions include the Ponderosa Ranch frontier town in Incline Village and the beautiful Lake Tahoe State Park. Accommodations: *Hyatt Lake Tahoe* (rates: $46–56 double) with 450 superb rooms and suites, restaurant, cocktail lounge, coffee shop, swimming pool and beach, sauna, tennis, golf, casino in Incline Village on Lakeshore Blvd. (831–1111); *Incline Motor Lodge* (rates: $33–37 double) with 32 good rooms and indoor swimming pool in Incline Village at 1003 Tahoe Blvd. (831–1052).

Elko—Gateway to the Humboldt National Forest & Wheeler Peak

(Pop. 7,600; zip code 89801; area code 702) is the headquarters of a vast cattle ranching area and a major gateway to the Ruby Mountains and Wheeler Peak Scenic Area in the Humboldt National Forest. The Northeastern Nevada Museum on 1–80 business route, houses collections of Indian and frontier artifacts. Accommodations: *Best Western Marquis Motor Inn* (rates: $34–40 double) with 49 excellent rooms and swimming pool at 736 Idaho St. on 1–80B (738–7261); *Best Western Thunderbird Motel* (rates: $35–38 double) with 70 excellent rooms and swimming pool at 345 Idaho St. (738–7115); *Holiday Inn* (rates: $32.75 double) with 115 excellent rooms, restaurant, coffee shop, cocktail lounge, kennel, and indoor pool at 3015 Idaho St., east on 1–80 (738–8425); *Red Lion Best Western Motor Inn* (rates: $38 double) with 71 excellent rooms and family units, restaurant, cocktail lounge, swimming pool, casino at 2050 Idaho St. east on 1–80 (738–8421).

Ely—Gateway to the Humboldt National Forest

(Pop. 8,000; zip code 89301; area code 702) is the commercial center of a sprawling mining and ranching area. Area attractions include the Hamilton Ghost Town, Cave Lake State Recreation Area, the huge Liberty Open Copper Pit Mine of the Kennecott Copper Co., and the Ward Charcoal Ovens Historic State Monument off US 93, built during the late 1800's mining boom. A District Ranger's Office of the Humboldt National Forest is located in town. Accommodations: *Copper Queen Motel* (rates: $25–27 double) with 24 good rooms, restaurant on US 93 at Avenue H (289–4884).

Las Vegas

(Pop. 160,000; zip code, see below; area code 702), Nevada's largest city, is a world famous gambling and entertainment center and gateway to the Lake Mead National Recreation Area. Area attractions include the strip of casinos and luxury hotels along Las Vegas Boulevard, Old Nevada Frontier Town on Blue Diamond Rd. in Red Rock Canyon, Red Rock Canyon Recreation Area, Valley of Fire State Park, and Mt. Charles Recreation Area in the Toiyabe National Forest. Scenic flights over Hoover Dam and the Grand Canyon may be booked at McCarran Airport. Accommodations: *Best Western Royal Las Vegas Motor Hotel* (rates: $34.50 double) with 237 excellent rooms, restaurant, coffee shop, cocktail lounge, casino, swimming pool at 5330 E. Craig Rd. 89110 (735–6117); *Holiday Inn Downtown* (rates: $41 double) with 418 excellent rooms, restaurant, cocktail lounge, swimming pool, casino, at 300 N. Main St. (385–1500).

Reno—Gateway to Lake Tahoe & Virginia City

(Pop. 82,000; zip code, see below; area code 702) the famous gambling and resort center known as "the biggest little city in the world." Reno, which boomed during the great Comstock Lode strike, is a popular gateway to the Lake Tahoe high country and ski areas. Area attractions include Pyramid Lake, Toiyabe National Forest, Mining Museum of the Mackay School of Mines at the University of Nevada, and Harolds Club which features collections of historic guns and rifles and old west artifacts. Accommodations: *Best Western Continental Lodge* (rates: $44 double) with 105 superb rooms, restaurant, cocktail lounge, swimming pool and landscaped gardens at 1885 S. Virginia St. 89509 (329–1001); *Best Western Daniel's Motor Lodge* (rates: $38 double) with 62 excellent spacious rooms at 375 N. Sierra St. 89501 (329–1351); *Holiday Inn Downtown* (rates: $38–41 double) with 300 excellent rooms, restaurant, coffee shop, cocktail lounge, swimming pool, casino at 1000 E. 6th St. 89502 (786–5151); *Holiday Inn-South* (rates: $36 double) with 156 good rooms, restaurant, cocktail lounge, swimming pool at 5851 S. Virginia St. 89509 (825–2940); *Nendel's Motor Lodge* (rates: $36 double) in Sparks with 224 good rooms and family units, restaurant, cocktail lounge, casino, swimming pool at 100 S. Sanford Way 89431 (358–6900).

Winnemucca—Gateway to Humboldt National Forest

(Pop. 3,600; zip code 89445; area code 702) is the commercial center of Humboldt County on the Humboldt River and Interstate 80. The town is a gateway to the Santa Rosa Mountains and the Charles Sheldon National Antelope Range in the northwest corner of the state. A District Ranger's Office of the Humboldt National Forest is based here. Accommodations: *Best Western Holiday Motel* (rates: $35–39 double) with 40 excellent rooms and swimming pool at W. Wennemucca Blvd., and Hanson St. (623–3684); *Best Western Winnemucca Motel* (rates: $39–43 double) with 68 excellent rooms, coffee shop, swimming pool at 741 W. Winnemucca Blvd. (623–2565).

Lodges, Ski Resorts & Guest Ranches

★★★★*Lake Mead Marina & Lodge* is the world's largest floating marina, covering over three acres afloat on Lake Mead near Boulder Dam. It has waterfront motel lodging, boat trips, fishing charters, water skiing, swimming, and dining afloat. The Lake Mead Lodge has 44 newly-remodeled rooms with air-conditioning and heat, plus the best views in southern Nevada. The dining room accommodates 250 people and there is a cocktail lounge and coffee shop. Visitors can rent a ski boat, complete with skiing equipment, gasoline and a licensed pilot. There are daily lake excursions on the *Echo IV*, charter fishing trips to catch bass in the world's largest man made lake, and boat tours to Boulder Dam. The warm waters of Lake Mead are inviting and the marina has a sand beach for fun in the sun. Lake Mead Marina has full service facilities for boats. There are complete boat launching facilities, 400 slips, 100 dry boat storage spaces, gasoline, oil, haul out facilities and a fully-stocked Ships Store. For reservations at the Lodge or more information about the Marina, write Lake Mead Marina and Lodge, Boulder City, NV 89005 (phone for the Marina (702)293–3484 and for the Lodge (702)293–2074).

★★★★*Incline Village* is a luxurious summer vacation and winter ski resort complex on the north shore of awesomely beautiful Lake Tahoe, 28 miles from Reno. The well-designed ski area offers a wide variety of downhill challenges, 21 runs altogether, plus 6 lifts, a mountaintop day lodge, a highly qualified ski school, beginners' areas, and a full line of rental equipment. The warm and handsome main lodge features a cafeteria, cocktail lounge, and complete ski shop. The incredible views of mountains, forests, and Lake Tahoe itself are complemented by a long and relatively mild ski season; snows generally come early and linger into spring. For warm weather pleasure, there are two fine golf courses, tennis courts, exclusive beaches, and unlimited opportunities for water sports. The Incline Village community encompasses shops, restaurants, casinos, cabarets, and condominiums and vacation homes. Accommodations are numerous and conveniently located, from resort hotel casinos to smaller family-owned motels. For information, write Incline Village Chamber of Commerce, P.O. Box 3207, Incline Village, NV 89450 (702)831–4440.

★★*Windybrush Ranch*, located in Smith Valley, Nevada, is on the east side of the high Sierra Mountains. From its windows snow can be seen year round. Wildlife in the area includes deer, coyotes, and an abundance of birds including quail, doves and pheasants. Hunting is not permitted. There is fishing in the Walker River which flows within walking distance and short-term fishing licenses are available for non-residents. Windybrush is a small family retreat from urban air and stress. Children, pets (from goldfish to horses), even infants are welcome here. Facilities include two double guest bedrooms in the ranch house as well as a family room that could be used by children for sleeping. Laundry facilities, hikes, picnics, game areas, lawn games, and reading material are all available. Rates include room, three meals per day with all the snacks you'd like, and total freedom of the ranch. Transportation to Topaz Lake for swimming, to local fishing areas, pick up at the local airport, and for local sight-seeing is furnished in the rate. The regular season (May through September) is on the American Plan at $96 per week for adults ($16 per day); children 6–12 with adult for $55 per week, ($9 per day); children under 6 are free. They also offer a rate for children 6–12 without adult at $120 per week or $18 per day. October-April rates are 10% less. For further information contact Margaret and Frank Parsons, Windybrush Ranch, Box 85, Smith, NV 89430 (702)465–2481.

NEW MEXICO

Introduction

New Mexico, the "Land of Enchantment," is bordered on the north by Colorado, on the east by Oklahoma and the panhandle plains of Texas, on the South by Mexico and Texas, and on the west by Arizona. Located on the eastern slope of the Great Divide, New Mexico contains several renowned fishing, hunting, and camping areas, including the trophy trout waters of the wild Rio Grande and Upper Pecos rivers, the beautiful snowcapped peaks and alpine meadows of the Sangre de Cristo Mountains—the southernmost extension of the Rocky Mountains—the canyonlands and ancient cliff dwellings of the remote Gila Wilderness, the trophy brown trout waters of the Chama and San Juan rivers, and the arctic tundra meadows of the scenic Wheeler Peak Wilderness and highcountry elk meadows of the beautiful San Pedro Parks Wilderness. New Mexico is the home of the historic Santa Fe Trail to Missouri and the notorious Lincoln County cattle war, starring Billy the Kid Bonney.

Accommodations & Travel Information

New Mexico's rustic ranch resorts, ski lodges, hotels, and inns, listed and described in the "Vacation/Lodging Guide," offer a full spectrum of outdoor recreation and activities in addition to accommodations and services. For specific information on all aspects of travel and outdoor recreation in the state, contact the Tourist Division, New Mexico Dept. of Development, 113 Washington Ave., Santa Fe, NM 87501 (505)827–5571.

Information & Services

Within the borders of New Mexico, the fifth largest state in the United States, lies some of the most varied topography in the country. Sagebrush, rimrock lands, sand deserts, prairie, and oak-scrub tracts contrast sharply with the soaring majesty of the Rocky Mountains, whose green, forested flanks rise to heights of over 13,000 feet. Much of this country is contained in the six national forests: Carson and Sante Fe in north-central New Mexico; Cibola, sprawling across the central and west-central part of the state; Lincoln, in the south; and Apache and its southern neighbor, ila, in the southwest corner. Much of the best trout fishing, big-game hunting, camping, canoeing, and hiking are located in these great land areas. Over one-half of New Mexico is publicly owned, including the national forests, state parks, one national park, Bureau of Land Management acreage, Game and Fish Department property, and National Grasslands. In addition, there is a vast amount of Indian reservation territory where fishing and hunting can be enjoyed on a fee basis. An excellent road network traverses the state, bringing the outdoors enthusiast to the edge of the wildest areas. Write to the State of New Mexico Department of Development, 113 Washington Ave., Sante Fe 87501, for the free booklets *Camping—Hunting—Fishing in New Mexico* and *New Mexico Fishing Waters*, which give an overview of the state's hunting and fishing opportunities, license information, and photographs of wildlife. Included also is a list by area of the campgrounds maintained by the state and federal governments and private owners, which provides information about capacity, facilities, location, altitude, and fees. A full-color map of the state and a map showing state-park locations complete this useful publication. Another helpful campground information source is the free map/brochure *New Mexico Outdoors*, published by the Department of Development, which breaks down camping areas by national forest, Indian reservation, wildlife refuge, etc., and expands on the facilities contained in the booklet mentioned above. A full-color map shows the national forests, Indian reservations, major river systems, important lakes, wildlife refuges, and campsites, and lists

state, federal, and Indian agencies that provide information for the sportsman, plus other useful material.

Write to the New Mexico Department of Game and Fish, State Capitol, Santa Fe 87503, for the free *New Mexico Fishing Information* folder, which gives the seasons' bag limits, general rules and regulations, Indian reservation laws, and new fishing developments. For boating ordinances, write for a free booklet, *New Mexico Boating Law*, produced by the New Mexico State Park and Recreation Commission, Box 1147, Santa Fe 87501. This publication also provides the various usage rules and conduct codes for the state's recreation areas and parks. A very useful free publication of the Department of Game and Fish is the map/brochure *Fishing Waters—Trout Waters, Warm Waters*. The full-color map shows the trout waters in blue and the warm-water-fish areas in red, and assigns a number to each of the important streams and lakes. The map alphabetically lists each major fishing place, gives its number and location on the map, describes the fish species present, and suggests where to fish. These areas are also cross-indexed by their watershed. This color-coded fishing guide should be obtained by anyone planning to fish in New Mexico. A free companion booklet, produced by the Department of Game and Fish, splits the state into 6 zones, and describes the fishing waters in each zone, again identifying them by number and map location on accompanying zone maps. Write to the Department of Game & Fish for the free *Hunting-Zone Maps* and for information on hunting rules and regulations pertaining to big-game species, upland game, and migratory birds.

Hundreds of campsites dot New Mexico's wide expanse, which ranges from the mystical desert mesas of the Navajo, Zuni, and Pueblo Indians to the mountains that sweep the state from north to south. In the southern part of the state, and at lower altitudes, the weather is mild year round. Be prepared for cool nights in the mountains. Campers will find accommodations in all areas of the state on state or federal lands. In some areas a fee is charged; in others, camping is free.

A booklet listing the state's campgrounds, *Camping—Hunting—Fishing in New Mexico*, is available free from the Department of Development (address above). The booklet describes the size, available facilities, and cost of the campgrounds.

Another map and camping guide, *New Mexico Outdoors*, may be helpful to use along with the booklet, and is available (also free) from the same place. While the booklet groups its campground listings by geographical area, this guide tells who administers them. In addition to the information given in the booklet, the guide lists special features of the campgrounds, such as wilderness access. The 25–page booklet *National Forest Camp & Picnic Grounds in Arizona & New Mexico* may be obtained free by writing: U.S. Forest Service, Southwest Region, Federal Bldg., Albuquerque 87101.

Those who seek the more remote reaches of the wild country will find them in the upper Pecos Wilderness of the southern Sangre de Cristo Mountains. Spectacular peaks ranging to over 13,000 feet rise from the area's main divides on the west and north. Gently sloping ridges and mesas separate the deep canyons that characterize the area. In the areas below the timberline, spruce, aspen, and meadows full of wildflowers carpet the earth. A *Trail Guide to the Geology of the Upper Pecos* describing fifteen trail logs for hiking and horseback riding in this area, may be ordered from the New Mexico Bureau of Mines and Mineral Resources, Publications Room, Socorro 87801, for $3.50. It includes a geology and trail map.

The Bureau of Mines also publishes the guide *Zuni-Cibola Trail* (see "Cibola National Forest") for $2.00. This guide summarizes the geologic features of the landscape on the trail, and describes archaeologic and recent events that have influenced the culture along it. The guide includes several trips out of Grant: lava flow to Zuni Mountains, across Continental Divide to El Morro National Monument, Ramah, and Zuni Pueblo. Also from the Bureau of Mines, *Mosaic of New Mexico's Scenery, Rocks and History* ($2.50), gives an overview of landscapes, flora and fauna, geology, recreation spots, and history.

The *Fenwick Corporation's New Mexico Fly Fishing School* is headquartered at Vermejo Park (which see), a 750–square-mile privately owned guest ranch and working cattle ranch with miles of streams and dozens of lakes that provide fly fishing for cutthroat, rainbow, brook, and a few golden trout. The school curriculum, open to beginners through advanced fly fishermen, includes intensive instruction in the art of fly casting, tackle, entomology, artificial flies, knots, fly presentation, stream lore, and wading. The school runs for three days during July, with special three-day advanced schools limited to fly fishermen with some previous experience. Family activities at this scenic wilderness-type resort include backpacking in the surrounding Rocky Mountain highcountry. For free literature, rates, and info: School Director, Fenwick Fly Fishing School, Vermejo Park, Drawer E, Raton 87740.

Southwest Safaris, based in Santa Fe, is the best-known wilderness outfitter in the state. The group specializes in taking people to the more remote areas of scenic beauty and historical interest in the southwestern United States. Southwest Safaris uses airplane travel to transport trip members from one area to another in order to allow the study of huge geological formations and widely separated Indian ruins, and to cut down traveling time. At the various points of interest, trip members are met by jeeps, horses, rafts, or cars. Tour members camp out during the spring, summer, and fall, but take lodging in the winter. All camping equipment is provided. Southwest Safaris' tours vary from one to twelve days, and include jaunts to Colorado, Utah, and Arizona, as well as New Mexico. The group also offers short air tours (one to four hours) covering Santa Fe, Taos, the Jemez Mountains, Sangre de Cristo Mountains, Rio Grande River, northeast Arizona, and southeast Utah. The seven-day "Southwest Safari" including lodging in Santa Fe before and after the trip is the most popular. The first flight includes the mesa, mountains, ruins, and great rivers of northwest New Mexico. A guided hiking tour of the famous cliff dwellings of the Anasazi Indians is a highlight of the day, along with a swim in Navajo Lake. The tour continues to Arizona, Colorado, and Utah by air, land, and water. Although the trips are scheduled for certain dates each year, private safaris are arranged all year by special request. On all tours, the pilot doubles as guide, conducting informal orientation sessions before flights and leading the explorations en route. For information on individual tours, write to P.O. Box 945, Santa Fe 87501 (505)988–4246.

A number of other groups lead wilderness tours throughout the state. For information about *Sierra Club* field trips and workshops, write to Bob Howard, 1522 Stanford NE, Albuquerque 87106. The *Wilderness Society* offers a "Way to the Wilderness Program," with guided backpack trips to the Pecos Wilderness. For details, write to the regional office, 4260 E. Evans Avenue, Denver CO 80222. *New Mexico Mountain Club* climbing-hiking school and trips are open to nonmembers by arrangement. To find out more about the trips, write to the club at Box 4151, Albuquerque 87106.

Commercial backpacking guides offering trips in New Mexico include *Base Camp Outdoor Supply Store*, 121 W. San Francisco, Santa Fe 87501; *Live! Wilderness Expeditions*, Box 157, Glenwood

88039; *Deep Creek Ranch*, Glenwood 88039; *Southwestern Expeditions for Youth*, Box 40451, Indianapolis, IN 46240; Wes Adams, *Wilderness Society Outfitter*, Star Route, Melrose 88124; *Wilderness Adventure*, Box 1259, Taos 87571; *Wilderness Experiences for Youth*, Box 12586, Albuquerque 87105; and *Wilderness and Wheels*, 1612 Brae Street, Santa Fe 87501. For mountain climbers, several mountain-climbing schools offer adventure, including *Realidad Ultima*, 1410 Cerro Gordo, Santa Fe 87501; and the *Natural High*, c/o 121 W. San Francisco, Santa Fe 87501. The *Bear Mountain Guest Ranch*, managed by Fred and Myra McCormick, Box 1163, Silver City 88061, offers commercial botany and birding workshops and hikes.

Commercial river guides operating float trips down New Mexico's wild rivers include *Get Down Rivers*, Doug Murphy, 9212 Bellehaven NE, Albuquerque 87112; *Live! Wilderness Expeditions*, Box 157, Glenwood 88039.

New Mexico offers excellent cross-country ski-touring opportunities on the hundreds upon hundreds of miles of old logging roads and hiking trails in the national forest lands and wilderness areas. Commercial ski-touring guides operating in the state include *Trail Adventures de Chama*, Box 86, Chama 87520 (summer address: 4839 Idlewilde Lane SE, Albuquerque 87108); *Base Camp Outdoor Supply Store*, 121 W. San Francisco, Santa Fe 87501; and *Wilderness Adventure*, Box 1259, Taos 87571.

Highways & Maps

An official road map of New Mexico is included in the free booklet *Camping—Hunting—Fishing in New Mexico*, available from the New Mexico Dept. of Development, 113 Washington Ave., Santa Fe 87501. The map shows the state's major geographical features, national forests, parks and monuments, Indian reservations, state parks, and points of interest. Complete campground listings for the state, and hunting and fishing information are also included in the booklet.

The U.S. Bureau of Land Management has published a free map and guide to *Public Lands in New Mexico*. The guide summarizes the major features of the 13,600,000 acres of public land in the state, and describes its most plentiful fish and game. It also lists regional offices where visitors can inquire about the boundaries of the public lands. The multicolor map, with a scale of 20 miles to the inch, marks public domain, national forests, Indian reservations, military reservations, land grants, wildlife refuges, and private lands. It also shows major highways, gravel roads, unimproved roads, parks and monuments, Indian pueblos, and points of interest. Write to: U.S. Bureau of Land Management, New Mexico State Office, P.O. Box 1449, Santa Fe 87501.

Carlsbad Caverns National Park

In 1901, Jim White, a cowboy, was attracted by a swarm of bats to an opening in the earth. He entered the opening and using oil smudges and string to mark his trail he went far down into the earth into the mysterious limestone world of the Carlsbad Caverns. White's discovery was followed by an expedition sponsored by National Geographic. In 1930, Congress declared the caverns a national park. Subsequent studies of the area showed evidence of ancient use of the caves. To date, more than 32 miles of the caverns have been explored and three different levels discovered, none of which have been completely explored. The caverns are inhabited by five different species of bats estimated at between 3 and 5–million in numbers.

Guided tours by park rangers descend through the rocky, dome-shaped entrance through Bat Cave to the Auditorium, a spacious cave noted for its acoustics, past formations suggesting ancient cliff ruins, past the Whale's Mouth and weird formations, stalagmites, obelisks, monoliths, pillars, huge dome-like vaults, down into the Green Lake Room, with its emerald pool and Frozen Water Falls formation to hanging forms of the King's Palace, 829 feet below the surface; to the Queen's Chamber, Totem Pole, Mirror Lake, 700–foot deep Bottomless Pit, Giant Domes, and Polar Regions.

A sweater and comfortable rubber-soled shoes are recommended for the three mile, 3½ hour tour of the caverns. A shorter 1¼ hour tour using the elevators, is available. The park is open year 'round. A visitor center and exhibit room is located near the park entrance. A day nursery and kennel service is available. Guided interpretive walks are available June-Labor Day. Lantern tours of a newly opened cave are available by reservation only (call 785–2233).

VACATION/ LODGING GUIDE

Information Sources, Maps & Access

For detailed park and tour information and a free *Carlsbad Caverns National Park* brochure, write: Administrative Offices, Carlsbad National Park, 3225 National Parks Hwy., Carlsbad, NM 88220 (505)785–2233. The Park is 27 miles southwest of Carlsbad on US 62 & 180 in the foothills of the Guadalupe Mountains.

Gateways & Accommodations

Carlsbad

(Pop. 21,000; zip code 88220; area code 505) is located in a 25,000–acre irrigated area that produces alfalfa, cotton and vegetable products. The area also produces 90% of the nation's potash. The town is the major gateway to Carlsbad Caverns National Park. Area attractions include the Living Desert State Park, northwest of town off US Hwy. 285; Lake Carlsbad Recreation Area; and the Carlsbad Museum in the town library at 102 S. Halagueno St. Accommodations: *Best Western Cavern Inn* (rates: $31–33 double), with 87 good rooms and family units, heated pool 20 miles south of city on US 62 at park entrance (785–2291); *Best Western Stevens Motel* (rates: $25–36 double), with 133 good rooms and family units, restaurant, cocktail lounge, heated pool, 1 mile south of town on US 180/62/285 at 1829 S. Canal St. (887–2851); *Holiday Inn*, (rates: $32–34 double), with 123 excellent rooms and family units, dining room, coffee shop, cocktail lounge, heated pool, three miles southwest of town on US 62/180 at 3706 National Parks Hwy. (887–2861); *Rodeway Inn*, (rates: $24–28 double), 107 excellent rooms and family units, restaurant, coffee shop, cocktail lounge, heated pool, sauna, 3½ miles southwest of town on US 62/180 at 3804 National Parks Hwy. (887–5535).

Carson National Forest & The Rio Grande

This great skiing, fishing and hunting region embraces 1,440,000 acres in northern New Mexico. Named after Kit Carson, the forest encompasses some of the most spectacular mountain areas in the Southwest, including the Sangre de Cristo Range an the 13,160–foot Wheeler Peak—the highest point in the Southwest. Big-game hunting is good throughout the region for elk, mule deer, antelope, black bear, Rocky Mountain bighorn sheep. The Jicarilla Apache Indian Reservation, a 758,000–acre wild area within the environs of the forest, is one of the state's top mule-deer hunting areas. Excellent mule-deer hunting is also found in the mountains and foot-hills near the Chama River, the Red River Canyon, and Eagle Nest Lake.

Information Sources, Maps & Access

For detailed vacation travel and recreation information and a full-color *Carson National Forest Map* (50¢) and a *Wheeler Peak Wilderness Map/Brochure,* write: Carson National Forest Supervisor, Box 558, Taos, NM 87571 (505)988–6327. A free *Rio Grande Gorge Map/Brochure* along with detailed info on the wild river section, campgrounds and fishing may be obtained from: Bureau of Land Management, New Mexico State Office, Box 1449, Santa Fe, NM 87501. Major routes to the Carson National Forest include U.S. Highway 64 off Interstate 25; U.S. 285 and state routes 38 and 3. Lodging, guides, supplies, and outfitters are located at Chama, Cimarron, Espanola, Farmington, Taos, and Tierra Amarilla.

Recreation & Scenic Areas

Rio Grande Indian Villages

The most famous of the Indian villages along the Rio Grande is the Taos pueblo, located just outside the boundaries of the forest. The Taos Indians have inhabited its two large five-storied structures for at least 800 years. The Indians farm their lands, raise cattle and horses, and work at jobs outside the pueblo, participating in the other cultures of the area while maintaining their own. The pueblo is entirely selfgoverning. An elected governor serves as civic head, while the *cacique* (priest) and the clan groups are still instrumental in the life of the pueblo. The ancestral religious ceremonies are still observed with traditional dances and songs.

Rio Grande National Wild River

The majestic Rio Grande, known to the Spanish conquistadors as the "Great River of the North" and from the legends of the Rocky Mountain trappers and early explorers as the "River of Ghosts," is one of the great wild rivers and one of the most productive natural trout fisheries in all the West. The river rises high in the mountain wilderness of Colorado's Rio Grande National Forest and flows through the weather-worn walls of the remote and rugged 70–mile Rio Grande Gorge in the Carson National Forest, where the river cuts southward into New Mexico and continues on its spectacular 2,200–mile journey to the sea. The champagne-like flows of frigid, crystal-clear water from gigantic clusters of huge springs produce the world-famous trout fishing found in the canyon country along this wild river. Trophy rainbows and hook-jawed browns up to 20 pounds lurk in the deep-flowing holes and feed on crayfish and other "hardshells" in the fast water and eddies that swirl around huge boulders. It also, surprisingly, holds northern pike that have drifted down into the Rio Grande Gorge from stockings made in Colorado.

The river flows from its Rocky Mountain headwaters through the San Luis Valley of southern Colorado, enters the great gorge some seven miles upstream from the New Mexico-Colorado border, and begins its tortuous 70–mile journey through the ancient layers of gray, black, salmon-pink, brown, and orange lichen-covered volcanic flows—reaching depths of 800 feet where an early lava flow crystallized into the black basalt now lining the bottom of the gorge—surrounded by colorful yellow bluffs, plains, and sagebrush-carpeted benchlands broken by fields and pastures. At the bottom of the gorge, the banks of the Rio Grande are covered by woodbine, stinging nettleweed, cockleburs, willows and waist-high grass, apache plume, the beautiful yucca, columbine, and benches of pinon, juniper, sagebrush, narrowleaf cottonwood, chamisa, and a few small oaks.

Wheeler Peak Wilderness

To the east, the snowcapped peaks of the Sangre de Cristo Range hold numerous alpine lake basins and small, rushing trout streams. One of the more famous lake basins is the Latir Lakes nestled below the towering Latir Peaks. Access to the Latir Lakes area is by trail. Twenty miles to the south, a cluster of alpine lakes forms the headwaters of the Red River and offers excellent trout fishing in a pure wilderness setting. Eagle Nest Lake, situated in the Merino Valley at an elevation of 8,400 feet, is another top trout-fishing lake. This famous wilderness hiking region, dominated by majestic Wheeler Peak, is located about 20 miles northeast of Taos. The tundra that covers Wheeler Peak and the other adjacent summits is rarely found in the Southwest. This region is infamous for sudden afternoon electrical storms. Make an early start and keep a watchful eye out for weather conditions. The plant life here varies from a tundralike subalpine turf to Engelmann spruce, cork-bark fir, and bristlecone pine. Four alpine lakes and several streams with access by trail lie within the boundaries of the wilderness and offer good trout fishing. Game species include mule deer, elk, bear, grouse, marmot, pike, and marten.

Gateways & Accommodations

Chama

(Pop. 900; zip code 87520; area code 505) at the junction of U.S. 64/84 and Hwy. 17 is a lumbering and trading center on the Chama River. The town is the terminus of the scenic *Cumbres & Toltec Narrow Gauge Railroad*, built in the 1880's, to Antonito, Colorado, through spectacular mountain country. For schedules and reservations call 756–2151. Accommodations: *Elk Horn Motor Lodge* (rates: $21–24 double), has 34 excellent rooms and family units two miles south of town on U.S. 84 on the Chama River with excellent fishing (756–2105).

Cimarron

(Pop. 900; zip code 87714; area code 505) is a historic frontier town divided into "New Town" and "Old Town" by the Cimarron River. The town was once part of the famous Maxwell Grant which covered 1,714,765 acres—a territory three times the size of Rhode Island which included the site of Raton, Vermejo Park and Ute Park. The Maxwell House, now in ruins, built in 1864 by Lucien Maxwell, a hunter and trapper who had accompanied General Fremont, housed a gambling room, dance hall, and billiards room. Maxwells, which stretched a city block, was the "cowboy capitol" of northern New Mexico and a principal stopover on the Santa Fe Trail visited by the likes of Kit Carson, Davy Crockett and Buffalo Bill Cody. Area attractions include the 137,493–acre Philmont Scout Ranch and Explorer Base and the Ernest T. Seton Memorial Library & Museum, both five miles south of town on Hwy. 21. Accommodations: *Best Western Kit Carson Inn* (rates: $22–26 double), with 38 good rooms, coffee shop, cocktail lounge on U.S. 64 (376–2288).

Espanola

(Pop. 4,500; zip code 87532; area code 505) is a farming products shipping point on the west bank of the Rio Grande on US 84. Accommodations: *Best Western Chamisa Inn* (rates: $34 double) with 51 excellent rooms, restaurant, cocktail lounge on New Mexico 68 at 920 N. Riverside Dr. (753–7291).

Farmington—Gateway to Aztec Ruins National Monument

(Pop. 29,000; zip code 87401; area code 505) is a historic frontier town, and busy commercial center at the confluence of the San Juan, Las Animas, and La Plata rivers. The Aztec Ruins National

Monument is 14 miles to the northeast at the town of Aztec. This E-shaped pueblo, one of the largest prehistoric Indian villages, once contained 500 rooms, built between 1110 and 1121 A.D. including the great kiva or ceremonial room. The monument contains a museum and offers interpretive program and self-guided tours. Other area attractions include Navajo Lake State Park, the fascinating Salmon Ruins built by the Pueblo Indians about 1100 A.D. 12 miles east of Farmington on Hwy. 17, and the Chaco Canyon National Monument on New Mexico Hwy. 57. Accommodations: *The Basin Lodge* (rates: $21 double), with 21 good motel rooms at 701 Airport Dr. (325–5061); *Best Western—The Inn* (rates: $35 double), with 124 excellent rooms and family units, dining room, coffee shop, indoor heated pool, sauna at 700 Scott Ave. (327–5221); *Enchantment Lodge of Aztec* (rates: $19–23 double), with 20 good motel rooms 1¼ mile west of Aztec on U.S. 550 (334–6143); *Holiday Inn of Farmington* (rates: $32 double), with 151 excellent rooms and family units, dining room, cocktail lounge, heated pool on U.S. 64 at 1000 E. Broadway (327–9811).

Questa

(Pop. 1,100; zip code 87556; area code 505) is a rustic old west town on the old Taos Trail on the north side of the Red River, flanked by the beautiful Sangre de Cristo Mountains on scenic New Mexico Hwy. 3. Accommodations: *Sangre de Cristo Motel* (rates: $22 double), with 14 comfortable rooms and family units, restaurant on Hwy. 3 at junction of Hwy. 38 (586–0300).

Raton

(Pop. 7,000; zip code 87740; area code 505) is a cattle-raising, coal-mining center at the foot of Raton Pass on the historic Santa Fe Trail. Area attractions include the Victorian decor and steak meals of *The Palace Restaurant* (445–3285) at 1st St. & Cook in an old 1890's hotel. Sugarite Canyon mountain park, and Capulin Mountain National Monument, 30 miles to the east via U.S. 64–87 and three miles north of Capulin on New Mexico 235. This 775–acre monument preserves one of the examples of a volcanic cinder cone in the nation, created 7–10,000 years ago. The monument mountain offers spectacular views. Due north of the monument on New Mexico 72 is the site of the old Crowfoot Ranch where Folsom point discoveries in 1926 provided evidence that prehistoric man was living here 10,000 years ago. Accommodations: *Holiday Inn* (rates: $30–34 double), with 87 excellent rooms and family units, dining room, coffee shop, cocktail lounge, indoor heated pool on U.S. 87 at junction of 1–25 (445–5555); *Melody Lane Motel* (rates: $28–32 double), with 34 excellent rooms and suites, restaurant, coffee shop, cocktail lounge at 136 Canyon Dr. ¼ mile north of town on 1–25 business loop (445–3655).

Red River

(Pop. 200; zip code 87558; area code 505) is a major recreation center and gateway to the Carson National Forest highcountry on New Mexico scenic Hwy. 38. Accommodations: *Alpine Lodge* (rates: $22–30 double), with 40 good rooms and family units, restaurant, cocktail lounge, ski shop at Red River on Hwy. 38 (754–2952); *Copper King Lodge* (rates: $22–30 double), with nine rooms and family units on the Red River (754–2965); *Golden Eagle Lodge* (rates: $22–30 double), with 21 rooms and family housekeeping units on New Mexico 150 (754–2227); *Red River Inn* (rates: $24 double), with 19 rooms and family units, restaurant, sauna, some fireplaces, in town on Hwy. 38 (754–2930).

Taos

(Pop. 2,500; zip code 87571; area code 505) is a colorful, historic adobe town built around a town square, the Plaza, the center of life in the village around which the first Spanish settlers built their homes. This incredibly beautiful Spanish and Indian art center, once the home of D.H. Lawrence, is on a plateau flanked by the snow-capped Sangre de Cristo Mountains. Taos is made up of three historic, distinct villages: the beautiful Spanish Town, known as Don Fernando de Taos with its historic plaza, once a fur-trading and trapping center and the hub of the old Navaho, Pecuris, Taos, Kiowa, and Santa Fe cattle trails and birthplace of the "Taos lightnin" whiskey used by the mountain men; The Indian Pueblo, known as San Geronimo de Taos, or Taos Pueblo, 2½ miles north of the plaza, with its adobe communal houses and old mission ruins; and the old Indian farming center, known as Ranchos de Taos, an old adobe village near the foothills of the Sangre de Cristo Mountains. Area attractions include the Kit Carson Home & Museum, ½ block east of the plaza; Taos Ski Valley (which see); D.H. Lawrence Ranch 20 miles north of town off New Mexico Hwy. 3 (776–2245); Mission of St. Francis of Assisi, a historic old southwest church four miles south of town on U.S. 64; and the colorful Taos craft shops, gallerys and restaurants. Accommodations (see "Taos Ski Valley" which follows): *Best Western Kachina Lodge & Motel* (rates: $30 double), with 122 excellent rooms and family units, restaurant, coffee shop, heated pool, ½ mile north of town on U.S. 64 and N. Pueblo Rd. (758–2275); *Holiday Inn de Taos* (rates: $33 double), with 101 excellent rooms and family units, dining room, coffee shop, cocktail lounge, heated pool, three miles south of town on New Mexico 68 (758–8611).

Lodges, Guest Ranches & Ski Centers

★★★*Angel Fire Ski Village & Summer Resort* is located in the Moreno Valley adjacent to the Carson National Forest in the Sangre de Cristo Range of the southern Rockies, 26 miles east of Taos. This four-season resort complex at 8,500 elevation offers outstanding

uncrowded alpine and ski touring terrain. Three chair lifts are in operation with 18 miles of trails in use. Near the entrance to Angel Fire, on New Mexico Highway 38, is the chair lift to the front slope (10,000–feet) which offers a spectacular panorama of Angel Fire, the Sangre de Cristo Mountains and Wheeler Peak Wilderness Area. The ski area includes a base lodge, ski rental shop, ski school and a mini A-frame warming hut near the top of the Back Basin slopes. Some skier's like to return from Back Basin to the village on the scenic 3½ mile Headin' Home Trail. During the summer months, Angel Fire offers golfing on a 9–hole scenic mountain course, tennis, sailing, fishing and packhorse trips into the surrounding high country wilderness. Nearby Eagle Nest Lake is considered to be one of the southwest's top trout and landlocked salmon lakes. Lodging facilities at Angel Fire are available at:

Angel Fire Chalets—Combines mountain ruggedness with contemporary design. Two and three bedroom units with fireplaces, beam ceilings, complete kitchen and laundry facilities. Rates on request.

Angel Fire Commons Condominiums—Elegant one, two and three bedroom condominiums each with its own "personality." Relax after a day on the slopes in the whirlpool and sauna. Units include fireplaces, up to three baths, complete kitchen facilities plus electric grill. Weekly rates (double) range from $83–177.

The Snowbird Condominiums—Studio units which sleep up to four include fireplace, color TV, kitchenette. Pool, game room and sauna are available to Snowbird guests. Weekly studio rates (double) range from $91–202.

The Starfire Lodge—Your choice of two bedroom, three bath condominium units with combination kitchen living/dining room plus three TVs and three phones. Or a single bedroom/bath with two queen size beds. Or a kitchen unit with a queen size foldout couch. A heated pool with bubble and a laundry center are available to Starfire guests. Weekly rates (double) range from $83–177.

The Wren Condominiums—One, two and three bedroom condominiums all featuring color TV, fireplace, fully equipped kitchens, living/dining areas and dramatic views of the mountain. Weekly rates (double) range from $91–202.

For additional info, contact: Angel Fire, Eagles Nest, NM 87718 (505)377–2301.

★★*Singing River Ranch*, secluded in Carson National Forest at an elevation of 8,000 feet on the banks of the Cabresto Stream, offers a leisurely stay in some of the most beautiful scenery in the world. The stream offers excellent trout fishing, and the environs attract hikers, rock hounds, horseback riders, and those just interested in a scenic drive. Ghost towns, museums, Indian Pueblos and historical points of interest are there for the sightseers. The Ranch has a heated swimming pool, paddle tennis court, a games room and recreational facilities for children. Housekeeping cabins, each with fully equipped kitchen facilities including utensils, dishes, linens and bedding run about $36 per day for two. For more information contact: Singing River Ranch, P.O. Box 245, Questa, New Mexico 87556 (505)586–0270.

★★★★*Taos Ski Valley* is an intimate alpine village nestled between the towering peaks of the Rocky Mountains with some of the nation's finest downhill skiing and alpine touring on Kachina Peak and the adjoining Wheeler Wilderness Area, which stretches south of the village boundaries with vast, enchanted snowfields. The Taos Ski Valley center offers beginner and intermediate slopes maintained nightly by a fleet of giant Pisten Bullies and Thiokols. Taos slopes are noted for their absence of ice, fog and white-outs. For the experts, an array of hidden powder bowes, glades, and chutes offer untouched powder snow protected from both wind and sun. The tree line is at 12,000 feet (twice that of the Alps). The Taos ski season starts the Saturday before Thanksgiving and extends to after Easter. Taos re-opens for late summer racing schools held in the sheltered bowls of Kachina or Stauffenburg regions in May or early June. Expert instruction is offered throughout the season by the nationally renowned Taos Valley Ski School. Ski equipment is available at the Taos Rental Shop. The Kinder Kafig offers a nursery school program designed for your child's vacation under professional supervision. First-class lodgings and restaurants are available at the ski village or in historic Taos, which is famous for its 700–year old adobe Pueblo, Millicent Rogers Museum, and its numerous art galleries and fine shops. Weekly accommodation rates listed below are quoted per person based on all-inclusive package plans (double occupancy). Write to the lodge, c/o Taos Ski Valley, NM 87571.

Hotel St. Bernard—Located at the base of Al's Run. Hotel, chalets, Alpenhof. Twenty-seven rooms. Superb French cuisine, discotheque, bar, heated covered swimming pool. 115 pillows. Rates: $400. Phone (505)776–2251.

Hotel Edelweiss—Small and intimate hotel located a few steps from St. Bernard with use of all St. Bernard facilities. Breakfast served in hotel, luncheon and dinner at St. Bernard. 65 pillows. Rates: $420. Phone (505)776–2301.

Hondo Lodge—Close to everything. 26 rooms with phones. Friendly atmosphere. Sauna, whirlpool, bar with entertainment. Southwestern decor. Large dining room serving haute cuisine. 60 pillows. Rates: $261. Phone (505)776–2277.

Innsbruck Lodge—Ski to and from the lodge. Fourteen rooms plus two small dorms. Austrian cuisine. Bar and restaurant, whirlpool, game and TV room. 44 pillows. Rates: $349. Phone (505)776–2277.

Kandahar Condominiums—Deluxe two bedroom/two bathroom apartments with fully-equipped kitchens, living area with fireplace and balcony. Ski to lifts. 128 pillows. Rates: $353. Phone (505)776–2226.

Rio Hondo Condominiums—AAA-approved luxury apartments located at the base of Strawberry Hill. Two bedrooms, living room with fireplace, dining area and fully-equipped kitchens, balcony, inside skiroom. Recreation lounge, jacuzzi, sauna, and laundry. 100 pillows. Rates: $361. Phone (505)776–2646.

Sierra Del Sol Condominiums—Luxury apartments just 70 yards from the lifts with fully-equipped kitchens, fireplaces, balconies, sauna, recreation lounge, and laundry facilities. Individual room or apartments. 215 pillows. Rates: $293. Phone (505)776–2981.

Thunderbird Lodge & Chalets—100 yards from lifts on the sunny side of the Valley. Twenty-four rooms in main lodge plus eight luxury rooms in two chalets. Saunas, whirlpool, lounge with live entertainment, outstanding French and Continental cuisine. 80 pillows. Rates: $385. Phone (505)776–2280.

Taos lodges near the mountains:

Abominable Snowmansion Ski Hostel—Friendly European-style skier's dorm. Spacious lodgeroom, game room and jacuzzi. Hearty family-style meals. Shuttle service available. 55 pillows. Rates: $235. Contact: Ron Stoney, Box 238, Arroyo Seco, NM 87514 (505)776–8298.

Hacienda De San Roberto—Deluxe accommodations in a de-

lightful mountain setting. Continental cuisine, bar, entertainment. Covered heated pool, jacuzzi and sauna. Complimentary transportation. 30 pillows. Rates: $396. Norm Seim, Box 449, El Prado, NM 87529 (505)776–2630.

Tennis Ranch of Taos—Condo-hotel with fireplaces in every room, indoor/outdoor tennis, sauna, jacuzzi, heated pool. Complimentary shuttle. Restaurant, cocktail lounge. 160 pillows. Rates: $395. Contact: Drawer BBB, Taos, NM 87571 (505)776–2211.

For additional information and a free *Taos Ski Trail and Village Map* contact: Taos Ski Valley, NM 87571 (505)776–2291.

★★★★*Vermejo Park Ranch* is one of the West's great, historic guest ranches and natural wildlife and outdoor recreation areas for trout fishing, hiking, photography, nature study, and horseback riding. Vermejo Park which has operated as both a guest and as one of the West's major cattle ranches since the early 1900's, encompasses 480,000 acres or 750 square miles of the famous 2–million acre Maxwell Land Grant of 1841. The Park is situated on the slopes of the Sangre de Cristo Mountains in northcentral New Mexico. This vast, unspoiled high country ranges from 6,000 to 13,000 feet and includes six life zones: Great Plains, Pinon-juniper, Ponderosa, Spruce-Fir, Krummholz and Alpine Tundra. Large herds of elk share the meadows and forests with deer, black bear, coyotes, mountain lion, and bobcats. Nesting and migratory birds range from the wild turkey, bald and golden eagles, to the smallest humming bird. The miles of high country and meadow streams, glacial and beaver lakes, accessible by jeep or backpacking, offer some of the nation's finest fly fishing for rainbow, cutthroat, brook, and golden trout. Trophy rainbow weighing over six pounds are taken each year from the lakes. Guided backpacking horseback trips into the wilderness of the high country and mountains at the 11,000 to 13,000 foot level are available along abandoned trails and seldom used ranch cattle trails into the high meadow and remote alpine lake areas. An experienced guide accompanies all trips and, like all ranch guides, is a college trained naturalist. Guest facilities designed to blend with the rustic mountain beauty of the Park are convenient to the lakes and streams. Guest facilities are centered around three lodges: Headquarters Lodge, at 7,500 feet with beautiful native stone buildings dating back to the early 1900's with accommodations for couples, families, and groups; Cresmer Lodge, located 12 miles west of Headquarters at 9,000 feet with two buildings and accommodations for up to 18 guests; Costilla Lodge at the foot of the Sangre de Cristo Range at an elevation of 10,000 feet with six spacious rooms for 12 guests. All lodges are equipped with a dining room and are fully staffed with cooks, waitresses, and maids. Daily American Plan summer rates (May through September) are $50 per person with special discounts for children under 15. Four-wheel drive ranch vehicles are available for rental. A remote, rustic family retreat is the Bernal Cabin with housekeeping facilities in the ponderosa pine and oak above Vernal Lake built in 1928 with ready access by four-wheel drive to all lakes, streams and the high country. This picturesque log cabin contains full windows on each side, with a view of the lake and mountains, large fireplace, two small bedrooms each with two beds and a large screened porch that runs the full width of the cabin, and a kitchen with RV-type facilities and a shower in the utility room. There is no "inside plumbing," only a Chick Sales, with no electricity. Propane lamps are provided. An ideal retreat for those who like to rough it in style. Boats are available at all locations at no charge. Bernal Cabin weekly family plan rates are $420; adult weekly rates (four guest minimum) are $700. For additional rates and info, contact: Vermejo Park, Drawer E, Raton, NM 87740 (505)445–3097 or 5028.

Trout Fishing
Hiking
Photography
Nature Study
Horsebacking

Cibola National Forest

This 1,660,630–acre forest lies south of Albuquerque in a region of great natural beauty where the Apache once roamed and hunted. Here the widely scattered ranges of the Datil, Gallina, Magdalena, Manzano, Sandia, San Mateo, Cebolleta, and Zuni mountains rise from the desert of central and western New Mexico. Big-game hunting is good throughout the mountainous backcountry for mule deer, bear, turkey, mountain lion, and Rocky Mountain bighorn sheep. Elk and antelope inhabit some areas of the forest.

Wilderness camping areas are plentiful in the rugged Sandia Mountains, particularly where they rise abruptly to 10,600 feet at the eastern edge of Albuquerque to form the 55,000–acre Sandia Recreation Area. The Sandia Crest Trail passes through the area, beginning at the terminus of Canyon Estates Road and extending north for 18 miles along the crest to North Sandia Creek. Many natural campsites can be found among the juniper, pine, and spruce-fir forests that cover the mountains to the timberline.

Elephant Butte Reservoir and Caballo Lake have good fishing for black and white bass, walleye, and channel catfish, along with some fine fishing for large rainbow trout in the cold tailrace waters beneath the Elephant Butte and Caballo Dams. Bluewater and McGaffey lakes are also good trout waters.

The 57,200–acre Bosque del Apache National Wildlife Refuge lies above Elephant Butte Reservoir and preserves the river bottomlands along the Rio Grande. This "Apache Forest" of Rio Grande cottonwoods provides a sanctuary for ducks, geese, sandhill cranes, and quail. Most of the refuge beyond the river bottomlands is sparsely covered dry desert lands.

Nearby the forest are Indian pueblos, prehistoric ruins, ice caves, and lava flows. Windmills mark infrequent habitations. This is old prospecting country, a land of long-lost mines. The area is open to recreational use all year, although the high-country winter is severe. Sandia Peak Ski Area attracts downhillers.

Information Sources, Maps & Access

For detailed vacation travel and recreation information and a full-color *Cibola National Forest Map* (50¢) write: Supervisor, Cibola National Forest, Box 1826, Albuquerque, NM 87103, (505)281–3304. The forest is reached by spur routes 142, 52, 78, and 107 off Interstate 400 and U.S. Highway 60. Lodging, guides, supplies, and outfitters are available at Albuquerque, Datil, Grants, Gallup, Magdalena, Mountainair, and Socorro.

Gateways & Accommodations

Albuquerque

(Pop. 302,000; zip code, see below; area code 505) is New Mexico's largest city founded in 1706 on the Rio Bravo del Norte (fierce river of the north) as the Rio Grande was then known. The Old Town section of Albuquerque, with its colorful shops, art and craft galleries, forms the historic core of the city. Area attractions include scenic auto drives along the Turquoise Trail to Sandia Crest in Cibola National Forest; Sandia Peak Ski Area; Sandia Frontierstown, 11 miles northeast on New Mexico 14N, a replica of an 1890's town; Rio Grande Zoo at 903 10th St. S.W., in Rio Grande Park; Sandia Atomic Museum on Main St. of Kirtland Airforce Base Bldg. 358, off 1–40, 7½ miles southeast of town; Sandia Peak Aerial Tramway, with restaurants and nature trail five miles northeast of city off 1–25 and Tramway Rd. (298–8518); Indian Petroglyph State Park nine miles west of town on Atrisco Road; Indian Pueblo Cultural Center at Menaul Blvd. & 12th St. N.W.; Museum of Albuquerque on Yale Blvd. S.W.; and the University of New Mexico on Central Ave. Accommodations: *Airport Marina Hotel* (rates: $46 double), with 266 luxury rooms and suites, restaurant, cocktail lounge, heated pool, tennis court at 2910 Yale Blvd. SE at International Airport (843–7000); *Best Western Four Seasons Motor Inn* (rates: $46 double), with two heated pools, tennis court, sauna at 2500 Carlisle Blvd. NE 87110 (265–1211); *Best Western White Winrock Motor Hotel* (rates: $29–35 double), with 175 excellent rooms and family units, restaurant, coffee shop, cocktail lounge, heated pool off 1–40, exit 162 at 18 Winrock Center (883–5252); *Holiday Inn-Midtown* (rates: $37–41 double), with 300 excellent rooms and family units, restaurants, coffee shop, heated pool, cocktail lounge at 2020 Menaul Blvd. NE 87107 (345–3511); *Howard Johnson's East* (rates: $26–30 double), with 152 excellent rooms and family units, restaurant, coffee shop, heated pool, 9½ miles east off 1–40, Subank Blvd. Exit at 15 Hotel Circle 87112 (296–4852); *Howard Johnson's-Midtown* (rates: $34–36 double), with 103 excellent rooms and family units, restaurant, coffee shop, heated pool at 1–25 and Lomas Blvd. 87102 (243–5693); *Rio Grande Motel—Old Town* (rates: $27 double), with 172 excellent rooms and family units, restaurant, coffee shop, cocktail lounge, heated pool off 1–40 Rio Grande Exit (843–9500); *Sheraton Old Town Inn* (rates: $46–48 double), with 187 excellent rooms and family units, restaurants, cocktail lounge, heated pool, tennis court off 1–40 Rio Grande Blvd. Exit (843–6300).

Gallup

(Pop. 16,000; zip code 87301; area code 505) a major gateway on Interstate 40, flanked on the north by the Navajo Indian Reservation and on the south by the Zuni Reservation. Area attractions include the El Morro National Monument, Museum of Indian Arts & Crafts at 103 W. 66th Avenue, McGaffey Recreation Area in Cibola National Forest, and the famous Zuni Pueblo, 41 miles south of Gallup on New Mexico Hwy. 53. This large village of red sandstone houses, located on the north side of the Zuni River, was one of Coronado's "Seven Cities of Cibola" which he believed to be built of gold. The historic mission church with its massive front towers, has been restored. The best time to visit the pueblo is in November or early December during the Shalako Dance, a festival during which the gods enter the village to bless the new houses. During August, Indian Ceremonial Dances take place at Red Rocks State Park, five miles east of Gallup. Accommodations: *Best Western Royal Holiday Motor Hotel* (rates: $21 double), with 50 excellent rooms and family units, heated pool at 1903 W. U.S. Hwy. 66 (863–9595); *Travelodge of Gallup* (rates: $26–30 double), 99 excellent rooms, restaurants, coffee shop, heated pool, sauna at 2003 W. U.S. Hwy. 66 (863–9385).

Grants

(Pop. 9,000; zip code 87020; area code 505) a Cibola National Forest District Ranger Office site and a major producer of uranium ore on Interstate 40. Area attractions include the Laguna Pueblo, 33 miles east of town off 1–40 and the Zuni-Cibola Trail, a scenic auto route along New Mexico Hwy. 53 to the Ice Caves, Bandera Crater, El Morro National Monument and the Zuni Pueblo. Accommodations: *Holiday Inn of Grants* (rates: $29 double), with 159 excellent rooms and family units, restaurant, cocktail lounge, heated pool at junction of 1–40 & U.S. 66 (287–4426).

Santa Rosa

(Pop. 2,500; zip code 88435; area code 505) an eastern gateway on 1–40 and the Pecos River. Area attractions include the State Fish Hatchery off 1–40, two miles south of town and the Fort Summer State Monument 45 miles south of town on U.S. Hwy. 84. Accommodations: *Best Western Adobe Inn* (rates: $26 double), 59 excellent rooms, heated pool at junction of 1–40, Exit 275 (472–3446); *Holiday Inn*, (rates: $30–32 double), with 100 excellent rooms and family units, restaurant, dining room, heated pool on Will Rogers Dr. at junction of 1–40 (472–5411).

Socorro

(Pop. 5,850; zip code 87801; area code 505) during the 1880's, this Rio Grande Valley town was a booming silver-mining center with 44 saloons lining its streets and served as a supply point for 200 wagon trains serving the mines. The restored Old San Miguel Mission, built in 1628, is at 403 El Camino Real. Accommodations: *Best Western Golden Manor Motel* (rates: $20–22 double), with 39 excellent rooms, restaurant, heated pool at 507 N. California St. on U.S. 60 (835–0230); *El Rio Motel* (rates: $17–21 double), with 45 good rooms and family units, restaurant, cocktail lounge, heated pool at 400 California St. N.E. (835–0510).

Tucumcari

(Pop. 7,100; zip code 88401; area code 505) an eastern New Mexico gateway on Interstate 40 and farming and cattle center. Area attractions include Ute Lake, Conchas Lake and the Tucumcari Historical Museum at 316 S. Adams St. Accommodations: *Best Western Pow Wow Inn* (rates: $32.50–34.50 double), 75 excellent rooms and luxury family units, restaurant, cocktail lounge, heated pool, one mile west of town on 1–40 (461–0500); *Ramada Inn* (rates: $26–32 double), with 61 good rooms, restaurant, cocktail lounge, heated pool on U.S. 66 at junction of U.S. 54 (461–3140).

Lodges

★★*Conchas Lodge* is a 38–room modern resort on the south shore of Conchas Lake, surrounded by working ranches, spectacular mesas, and ancient ghost towns. The 15–square mile lake offers ideal fishing for largemouth bass, channel catfish, walleyes, bluegill, and crappie. A nearby marina carries a complete line of tackle and boat rentals for both fishing and water skiing. Swimming, hunting in season, hiking, skin diving, and golf are other activities pursued by

guests of the lodge. Facilities include a swimming pool, spacious lounge, and restaurant with panoramic views of the lake. All rooms are air-conditioned, with double beds and private baths. Rates vary from $22 per day for two guests to $34 for four. For further information, write: Conchas del Sur, Ltd., P.O. Box 1045, Conchas Dam, NM 88416 (505)868–2988.

Gila National Forest & Cliff Dwellings Area

This vast 2,694,471–acre forest encompasses some of the most primitive wilderness areas in the Southwest. The forest, located in southwestern New Mexico, is a land of steep mountains, rough canyons, mesas, river channels, and flood plains. The Continental Divide snakes through this awesome canyon country for about 150 miles, with elevations ranging from 4,500 to 11,000 feet. Forest roads and trails provide access to the remote hunting, fishing, and camping areas in the Big Burro Mountains, Mogollon Mountains, Diablo Mountains, Black Range Primitive Area, Gila Wilderness, and the Tularosa Mountains.

The deep and sinuous gorges of the Gila River country were set aside as the Gila Wilderness in 1924 as a tribute to the forester Aldo Leopold; it was the country's first roadless wilderness. The 429,506–acre wilderness and the surrounding 135,978–acre Gila Primitive Area embrace the Mogollon and Diablo mountains. The deep canyons of the Gila River dissect the region, which is surrounded by a jumbled terrain of rocky spires and broad pine-covered flats, rolling hills, and grassy beaches. The outermost boundaries lie in the desert foothills, but the area itself reaches upward through juniper woodland to ponderosa pine and on to spruce-fir forests interspersed with meadows and stands of aspen.

The finest trout fishing in the forest is found in the interior of the Gila Wilderness. The middle and west forks of the Gila River and Mogollon Creek offer fair to good fishing for rainbows and browns. Trout are also found in Roberts, Snow, and Wall lakes, about 10 miles south of the Beaverhead Ranger Station. Big-game hunting is good throughout the forest for mule deer, Sonoran whitetail deer (or "fantailed" deer), bighorn sheep, antelope, and javelina.

Most of the main trails are well maintained and easy to follow. Trails following the river bottoms are occasionally flooded by flash storms or spring runoff. Flooding frequently affects the trails along the west fork, middle fork, and main Gila River. There are numerous crossings, but you should be prepared to get wet. Light canvas shoes are recommended. The trails starting on the south and west side of the Gila Wilderness and in the Gila Cliff Dwellings Area begin at low elevation and climb steadily uphill.

In the Willow Creek-Snow Lake area the trail heads are at high elevation, eliminating the necessity of long climbs out of deep valleys. Be alert for rattlesnakes. Use a walking stick to poke ahead of you where overhanging vegetation covers your view of the trail.

Man has lived in the Gila country for 10,000 years. The ancient Gila Cliff Dwellings are situated deep in the canyons, accessible only by foot or horseback, and are preserved as a national monument. Members of the Mogollon culture built the cliff dwellings and occupied them until about A.D. 1300, when they abandoned their home for unknown reasons. Spanish explorers entered the area in the early 1500s and gave the country its name, after a Yuma Indian word meaning "running saltwater." Still later, such historical characters as Geronimo, Billy the Kid, and Butch Cassidy were associated with the Gila.

The Black Range Primitive Area encompasses 169,356 acres of rugged, rocky canyons, forested peaks, old burns, and remote streams due east of the Gila Wilderness. Several primitive trails wind through the remote interior wilderness camping areas and provide access to the Continental Divide, Diamond Creek, Granite Peak, Reeds Peak, and the headwaters of the Members River. The Black Range was used by the infamous Chief Geronimo as a hideout. The rare Gila trout is found in a few of the remote streams.

Information Sources, Maps & Access

For detailed vacation travel and recreation information and a full-color *Gila National Forest Map* (50¢) contact: Supervisor, Gila National Forest, 301 W. College Ave., Silver City, NM 88061 (505)388–1986. The Gila National Forest is reached by spur routes 90, 180, and 61 off Interstate Highway 10 and by state routes 90 and 52 off Interstate 25. Lodging, supplies, guides, packers, and outfitters are available at Glenwood, Reserve, Silver City, Truth or Consequences, Luna, Quemado, and Lordsburg.

Gateways & Accommodations

Silver City

(Pop. 8,500; zip code 88061; area code 505) is the headquarters gateway to the Gila National Forest and the Gila Cliff Dwellings at the junction of U.S. 180 and New Mexico 90. This historic gold and silver mining town occupies a scenic location in the foothills of the Pinos Alta Range, an extension of the Mogollon Mountains. Area attractions include the Silver City Museum at 312 W. Broadway, tours of the Phelps Dodge open pit copper mine (538–5331), Kennecott

Copper Corp. Santa Rita Copper Mine & Museum, 14 miles east of town on State Hwy. 90. Accommodations: *Copper Manor Motel* (rates: $22–26 double), with 65 good rooms, 1 mile northeast of town on U.S. 180 at 710 Silver Heights Blvd. (538–5392).

Truth or Consequences

(Pop. 4,600; zip code 87901; area code 505) is a health resort, formerly known as Hot Springs, and a trading center for the surrounding cattle ranches, mining and farming areas. Area attractions include Elephant Butte Reservoir, Caballo Lake, Geronimo Springs Museum at 325 Main St., and the Black Range Mountains. Accommodations: *Ace Lodge* (rates: $16 double), with 38 good rooms and family units, heated pool north of town at 1014 N. Date St. (894–2151); *Red Haven Motel* (rates: $14–19 double), with 10 good rooms at 605 Date St. on I–25 & U.S. 85 (894–6112).

Lodges & Guest Ranches

★★★*Bear Mountain Guest Ranch*, nestled in a forest of pinons and junipers at 6000–foot altitudes in the Pinos Altos Mountains, commands 160 quiet, unspoiled acres adjoining the Gila National Forest. Accommodations are available in two modern guest cottages with kitchens, plus rooms and suites in the handsome, hacienda-style main house. Activities include day tours of the area's many outstanding sights such as the prehistoric Gila Cliff Dwellings, numerous ghost towns, Indian ruins, and verdant state parks. Birdwatchers will appreciate host Myra McCormick's forays into the vast areas around Silver City in search of rare and beautiful species. Special plant-identification workshops, wildflower tours, and nature photography field classes are also on Bear Mountain's annual agenda. There's even a walking tour of elegant Victorian mansions in Silver City. If fishing's your sport, there are nearby lakes and streams, including the forks of the Gila River, in which to test your skills. Delicious family style meals are served in the commodious main house with its rambling sun porches and white-washed walls. American plan rates average $30 daily for one; $42 daily for two; housekeeping rates are $40 daily for a four-bedroom cottage (one-four guests) and $21 daily for a one-bedroom cottage. Special rates are available for retired persons and members of conservation clubs. For more information, write: Bear Mountain Guest Ranch, P.O. Box 1163, Silver City, NM 88061 (505)538–2538.

★★★*Elephant Butte Resort*, just outside Elephant Butte Lake State Park, has 48 attractive modern rooms, comfortably furnished, with air conditioning, private baths, and color TV. The resort complex includes a freshwater pool and sundeck, tennis courts, a marina, and golf course. There's also a 52–foot luxury yacht available for private parties and cruises around rock-rimmed Elephant Butte Lake. The nearby marina has a full line of boat rentals for sailing, water-skiing, and fishing. Hunting is good in season for big game, quail, dove, and an occasional pheasant. Also on the premises are a fine restaurant and cocktail lounge. Rates are $20–27 (double occupancy) for standard rooms and $35–50 for deluxe suites. For more information, write: Elephant Butte Resort, P.O. Box E, Elephant Butte, NM 87935 (505)744–5431.

Lincoln National Forest

This million-acre forest embraces the lofty Capitan, Guadalupe, Sacramento, and White Mountains in southern New Mexico. The forest contains the finest mule-deer range in the state and offers alpine and nordic skiing, backpacking and trout fishing in the beautiful high country lakes and streams in the scenic Cloudcroft and Riudoso areas. Wild turkey are found throughout the timbered areas of the forest. Upland game birds include Gambel and scaled quail on the forest fringes, and mourning dove, chukar partridge, and band-tailed pigeon.

The White Mountains Wilderness rises abruptly from the Tularosa Basin, starting from 6,000 feet and reaching an altitude of 11,400 feet, crossing five different life zones, and encompassing 31,171 acres of high-country meadows and mixed conifer forests. Primitive trails provide access to Big Bear Canyon, Nogal Peak, Church Mountain, Thra River, and Bonito Creek. Big-game species in the wilderness include mule deer, black bear, a few elk, and wild boar. There is fair trout fishing in several high-country lakes and streams. Winter activities include cross-country skiing and snowshoeing.

The Capitan Mountains, located due east of the White Mountains Wilderness, were the birthplace of Smokey Bear, discovered by firefighters after a 17,000–acre forest fire in 1950.

Information Sources, Maps & Access

For a *Lincoln National Forest Map* (50¢) and information on camping and trails, contact: Supervisor, Lincoln National Forest, Lincoln, NM 88338. The Lincoln National Forest is reached by U.S. highways 82, 70, 54, and 380. Accommodations, guides, supplies, and outfitters are located at Alamogordo, Artesia, Capitan, Carlsbad, Cloudcroft, Roswell, and Ruidoso.

Gateways & Accommodations

Alamogordo—Gateway to White Sands National Monument

(Pop. 23,000; zip code 88310; area code 505) is a popular tourist gateway to the Lincoln National Forest, Mescalero Apache Indian Reservation and the White Sands National Monument. Other area attractions include the International Space Hall of Fame at Indian Wells and Scenic Drive and the rock carvings at the Three Rivers Petroglyph Site, north off U.S. 54 at Three Rivers. The 146,535–acre White Sands National Monument is located 15 miles southwest of Alamogordo on U.S. 82 and 70 in the Tularosa Basin. The area is covered with gleaming white gypsum sands and calk-white dunes and drifts that rise up to 50 feet above the valley floor. Within the monument is an old lake bed that is believed to be devoid of life. Unusual species of plants, some with roots more than 40–feet long and plants that create their own nitrogen supply are found here. During the intense summer heat, some areas have been known to turn into plaster of paris. The history and geology of the area is

shown in displays, slides and exhibits at the Monument Visitor Center. Guided walks are conducted during the summer. For additional information, contact: Superintendent, Box 458, Alamogordo. Accommodations: *Best Western Desert Aire Motor Hotel* (rates: $24–27 double), with 96 good rooms, restaurant, coffee shop, large heated pool and sundeck, south at 1021 S. White Sands Blvd. (437–2110); *Holiday Inn* (rates: $29–36 double), with 104 excellent rooms and family units, restaurant, coffee shop, cocktail lounge, heated pool at 1401 S. White Sands Blvd. (437–7100); *Satellite Inn* (rates: $18–20 double), with 104 excellent rooms and family units, restaurant, coffee shop, cocktail lounge, heated pool at 1401 S. White Sands Blvd. (437–8454).

Cloudcroft—Gateway to the Cloudcroft Ski Area

(Pop. 500; zip code 88317; area code 505) is a popular four-season recreation center nestled at the crest of the beautiful Sacramento Mountains and the site of the nation's highest golf course. The village, situated due south of the Mescalero Apache Indian Reservation, is surrounded by the alpine lakes, forests and meadows of the Lincoln National Forest. The area is a popular summer art center. The Ski Cloudcroft Area is located 2½ miles east of the village on U.S. 82 and offers exciting slopes, ski school and rentals, retaurant and cafeteria (682–2587). Accommodations: *Aspen Motel* (rates: $22 double), with 16 good rooms, coffee shop east of town on U.S. 82 & New Mexico 83 (682–2526); *Cloud Country Lodge & Golden Spike Restaurant* (rates: $22–39 double), with 50 excellent rooms and family units, rustic dining, swimming pool at the junction of U.S. 82 and New Mexico 24 (622–2932).

Roswell

(Pop. 40,000; zip code 88201; area code 505) a one-time plains trading post, is a modern, attractive city on U.S. 285 and the Rio Hondo River. Area attractions include Bottomless Lake State Park, Bitter Lake National Wildlife Refuge, and the Roswell Museum & Art Center, noted for its exhibits of southwest artists, science and technology at 100 W. 11th St. (622–4700). Accommodations: *Best Western Roswell Inn* (rates: $29–33 double), with 123 excellent rooms, restaurant, coffee shop, heated pool at 1815 N. Main St. (623–4920); *Ramada Inn* (rates: $30 double), with 63 good rooms and family units, steak house, coffee shop, heated pool at 1310 N. Main St. (623–4021); *Sally Port Best Western Inn* (rates: $35 double), with 124 superb rooms and family units, restaurant, coffee shop, indoor heated pool, tennis court, sauna at 2000 N. Main St. (622–6430).

Ruidoso

(Pop. 2,200; zip code 88345; area code 505) is one of the Southwest's most popular four-season recreation centers, set high in the beautiful Sierra Blanca Mountains of the Lincoln National Forest. Area attractions include horseracing at Ruidoso Downs; Sierra Blanca Ski Area, with restaurant, ski school and rentals, gondola 16 miles northwest of the village on Hwy. 37 in the Lincoln National Forest (336–4356); White Oaks Ghost Mining Town; fine dining at the Silver Dollar Steak House in an Old West building (1892) 30 miles east of town on U.S. 70 (653–4425); Old Lincoln County Courthouse State Monument, with exhibits on the famous Lincoln County War, Billy the Kid, and dioramas on the Mescalero Apache, pueblo ruins, cave dwellings and ruins. The courthouse once contained the

Murphy-Dolan store, site of the famous shootout between the deputy's men and Billy the Kid and 19 followers during the Lincoln County War, which was ended by Gen. Lew Wallace, author of Ben Hur. For area info, contact: Chamber of Commerce, Box 698 (257–7395). Accommodations: *Best Western Swiss Chalet Inn* (rates: $36–45 double), with 80 excellent rooms and family units, restaurant in scenic location four miles north of village on New Mexico 37 (336–4392); *High Country Lodge* (rates: $35–55 double), with 32 superb family duplex kitchen cottages with two bedrooms each, fireplaces, heated indoor pool, tennis court, hiking trails, trout lake, guides five miles north of the village on New Mexico 37 (336–4321).

Resorts

★★★★*The Inn of the Mountain Gods*, owned and operated by the Mescalero Apache tribe, is a sprawling luxury resort in south-central New Mexico just outside the town of Ruidoso. The inn is situated on the banks of Lake Mescalero and surrounded by 460,000 acres of forest land, lakes, and streams. For summer recreation, there are six all-weather tennis courts, and 18–hole championship golf course, a heated outdoor pool, and a stable of horses for trail rides through the pine-blanketed Sacramento Mountains. Boating and fishing on the trout-stocked lake, are also popular, and in addition there are numerous other nearby lakes and streams, most of them open for fishing all year round. Hunters annually find game during the hunting seasons, including mule and whitetail deer, bear, and elk. The winter months provide excellent skiing conditions at Sierra Blanca, one of the Southwest's finest ski areas, just 40 minutes away. Facilities include 22 slopes, seven lifts, a fine day lodge, equipment rentals, and professional instruction. The inn itself is a striking contemporary structure, designed to complement its natural surroundings. Each of the 134 guest rooms, including six suites, overlooks the clear blue waters of Lake Mescalero. All have attractive furnishings, private baths, and balconies with sweeping views of the resort grounds and hills beyond. The lodge houses dining areas, cocktail lounges, meeting rooms, a disco club, and a handsome lobby with a three-story copper-sheathed fireplace. In the summer, the inn's own activities are rounded out by horse racing at nearby Ruidoso Downs. For rates and further information, write: Inn of the Mountain Gods, Mescalero, NM 88340 (505)257–5141.

Santa Fe National Forest

The Santa Fe National Forest is a majestic mountainland richly covered with pine, aspen, fir, and wildflower meadows. The forest, located in northern New Mexico, offers some of the finest fishing, hunting, and wilderness camping in the Southwest. Within the forest's bounds lies the Pecos Wilderness, where the 13,101–foot Truchas Peak shares winter snows with other lofty mountaintops and the San Pedro Parks wilderness. The wilderness headwaters of Pecos River contain forests of aspen, pine, fir, and spruce. Sloping gradually southward, the forest's Pecos Division is some 50 miles long and 25 miles wide. It includes the popular Santa Fe Ski Basin on the west, and farther south, historic Glorieta Pass and the old Santa Fe Trail. Hundreds of alpine lakes, beaver ponds, and wild streams, such as Spirit, Baldy, Truchas, Encantada, Ruth, North Fork, the Upper Pecos, and Mora rivers, have fishing for native cutthroat, rainbow, and brown trout.

The forest has the finest Rocky Mountain elk and mule deer range in the state. Other species here include black bear, mountain lion, bobcat, coyote, weasel, badger, raccoon, marten, mink, bald and golden eagles, and muskrat. Game birds are geese, ducks, dusky grouse, wild turkey, quail, and band-tailed pigeon. The major game areas lie in the interior of the forest among the Jemez, San Pedro, and Sangre de Cristo mountains, and along the Rio Grande and Guadalupe rivers.

Information Sources, Maps & Access

For detailed fishing, camping, backpacking and wilderness permit info, and a full-color *Santa Fe National Forest Map* (50¢) and free *Visitor's Guide to the Pecos Wilderness* and *Visitor's Guide to the San Pedro Parks Wilderness*, contact: Supervisor, Santa Fe National Forest, Santa Fe 87501 (505)827–2312. The Santa Fe National Forest is reached by Interstate 25, U.S. Highway 84, and state routes 63, 475, 76, 283, 266, 94, 3, 38, and 121. Lodging, guides, supplies, packers, and outfitters are available at Cuba, Espanola, Las Vegas, Los Alamos, Pecos, and Santa Fe.

Recreation Areas

Pecos Wilderness

The rugged 167,416–acre Pecos Wilderness encompasses the headwaters of the Pecos River at the southern end of the Sangre de Cristo Mountains in the Carson and Santa Fe national forests. The Upper Pecos, a scenic white-water river, drains a huge horseshoe-shaped basin with streams radiating out on either side, and has good fishing for wild rainbow, cutthroat, and brown trout. The wilderness encompasses magnificent forests of aspen, pine, fir, and spruce to the timberline of the high mountains. They are crowned by the 13,101–foot Truchas Peak. Elsewhere in the wilderness, deep canyons slice gently sloping ridges and mesas. Eagles are often sighted among the treeless peaks, while elk, black bear, mule deer, grouse, and turkey populate the meadows of the lower elevations. The wilderness is a top-ranked fall hunting area. Beaver dams are a common sight in the high country, and a few mountain lions, bobcats, bighorn sheep, marten, mink, and muskrat inhabit the area.

San Pedro Parks Wilderness

The San Pedro Parks, a beautiful backpacking paradise, covers 41,132 acres along the San Pedro Mountains in the western part of the Santa Fe National Forest. The wilderness is a land of gently rolling grass parks and boggy meadows interspersed among dense stands of spruce and mixed conifers at an elevation of 10,000 feet. Clear streams meander through the meadows of brilliant wildflowers and beaver ponds. For the hunter who enjoys a pack trip, the beautiful meadows and parks offer some of the finest elk and trophy mule deer opportunities in the state, as well as blue grouse, turkey, squirrel, wild turkey, and black bear. Backpackers should be prepared for showers in July and August. Daytime temperatures in the summer are often in the seventies, but nights vary from cool to cold. Snowfall usually begins in November. The wilderness is open to skiing and snowshoeing.

Gateways & Accommodations

Las Vegas

(Pop. 14,000; zip code 87701; area code 505) a farming and ranching center on Interstate 25 flanked on the west by the Santa Fe National Forest. Las Vegas was once a rough 'n' ready frontier stopover on the old Santa Fe Trail to Denver infested by one of the worst gang of cut-throats in the west, including Billy the Kid, Jack-knife Jack, Soapy Smith, Flyspeck Sam, Pock-marked Kid, Pownee Bill and sundry others. Area attractions include Fort Union National Monument and the Rough Riders' Memorial & City Museum in the Municipal Bldg. at 720 Grand Ave. Accommodations: *Best Western Town House Motel* (rates: $22–24 double), with 42 excellent rooms and family units at 1215 N. Grand Ave. (425–6717).

Los Alamos

(Pop. 16,000; zip code 87544; area code 505) was originally the site of the Los Alamos Ranch School for Boys on the remote Pajarito Plateau where secret research for the first atomic bomb was conducted during World War II. Area attractions include the county Historical Museum at the Fuller Lodge Cultural Center and the Bradbury Science Hall with exhibits on the history of nuclear energy research and lasers on Diamond Dr., south of Los Alamos Canyon Bridge. Accommodations: *Los Alamos Inn* (rates: $28–31 double), with 106 good rooms, dining room, cocktail lounge, heated pool on New Mexico Hwy. 4 at 2201 Trinity Dr. (662–7211).

Santa Fe

(Pop. 44,000; zip code 87501; area code 505) is the oldest capital city in the United States, founded in 1609, and one of the most picturesque. It has been a capitol for more than 300 years and the flags of four nations have flown over its historic Palace of the Governors. Santa Fe, a major vacation and tourism center, is nestled in a valley flanked by the snow capped peaks of the Sangre de Cristo Mountains on the east, Sandia Mountains on the south and the Jemey Range on the west. The Royal City, as it is known, with its ancient narrow streets and colorful adobe houses, has long been a magnet for travelers. For the Spanish, it was the terminus of El Camino Real, the Royal Highway. The historic plaza, a colorful old square, was the terminus of the Santa Fe Trail. Santa Fe attractions include scenic drives in the historic Pecos River Country, Ranchos de Taos, Bandelier National Monument, and Pecos National Monument; Cathedral of St. Francis of Assisi, built in 1869 by Archbishop Lamy, the "Bishop Latour" in Willa Cather's novel *Death comes to the Archbishop*; the adobe Palace of the Governors on the north side of the Plaza that is believed to have stood since 1609; La Fonda Hotel, historic meeting place of trappers, pioneers and frontiersmen known as the "inn at the end of the trail"; San Miguel Mission, the oldest church in the U.S. still in use at Old Santa Fe Trail & De Vargas St.; State Capitol; Museum of Navajo Ceremonial Art two miles southeast of town on Camino Lijo; and float trips along the Rio Grande. Accommodations: *Best Western Inn at Loretto*, (rates: $48–54 double), with 138 excellent rooms and family units, restaurant, cocktail lounge, heated pool, sauna at 211 Old Santa Fe Trail (988–5531); *Best Western Lamplighter Motel* (rates: $32–36 double), 63 rooms and family units, restaurant, indoor heated pool three miles southwest of town at 2405 Cerrillos Rd. (471–8000); *Garrett's Desert Inn* (rates: $39–43 double), with 82 excellent rooms and suites, restaurant, cocktail lounge, heated pool at 311 Old Santa Fe Trail (982–1851); *Hilton Inn of Santa Fe* (rates: $49–60 double), with 151 excellent rooms and suites, dining room, cocktail lounge, heated pool three blocks west of the Plaza at 100 Sandoral (988–2811); *Holiday Inn* (rates: $36–39 double), with 83 excellent rooms and family units, dining room, cocktail lounge, heated pool, 3½ miles southwest of town on U.S. Hwy. 85 at 2900 Cerrillos Rd. (471–8072); *Inn of the Governors* (rates: $42–44 double), with 81 good rooms, dining room, cocktail lounge, heated pool at Don Gaspar & Alameda Sts. (982–4333); *La Fonda Hotel* (rates: $44 double), with 165 excellent rooms and suites with fireplaces, dining room, coffee shop, cocktail lounge, heated pool on the historic Plaza at 100 E. San Francisco St. (982–5511); *Sheraton Inn of Santa Fe* (rates: $49 double), with 108 excellent rooms and suites, dining room, coffee shop, cocktail lounge, heated pool, airport service 1½ miles northwest of town at 750 N. Saint Francis St. off U.S. Hwys. 64, 84, & 285 (982–5591).

Lodges & Guest Ranches

★★★*The Bishop's Lodge* is a deluxe Santa Fe ranch resort situated on 800 acres in the foothills of the Sangre de Cristo Mountains. Once the private retreat of Archbishop Lamy, immortalized in Willa Cather's novel, *Death Comes to the Archbishop*, the lodge derives its name from the small chapel he built on a hillside just above the lodge, over a century ago. This deluxe family ranch resort, which combines the tradition of the Old West with modern services and elegance, offers a wide variety of ranch-based recreation, including trail rides along the mountain trails of the adjacent Santa Fe National Forest, swimming in an olympic-size pool, tennis on a complex of tournament-grade courts, automatic trap and skeet range, and trout fishing in high country streams and ponds. Lodge accom-

modations consist of attractive spacious guest rooms in New Mexican ranch decor with baths. Many have fireplaces and beamed ceilings. American and international gourmet cuisine is served in the beautiful main dining room. A special summer season program is designed for children 4–12 years old. Under the direction of trained counselor's the children will enjoy riding, swimming, lawn games, picnics, fishing, and lots of clean fresh air. The ranch Club XVI is designed for teenagers as a meeting place for table tennis, outdoor sports, and parties. All-inclusive rates are $40–60 (double occupancy). For additional information, contact: The Bishop's Lodge, P.O. Box 2367, Santa Fe, NM 87501 (505)983–6377.

★★★*Bar X Bar Ranch* is a rustic resort set among thousands of acres in the Santa Fe National Forest high country, valleys and mountain streams 25 miles east of Santa Fe. It is designed as a sportsmen's club, catering especially to fishermen and hunters. The fishing is excellent, with 33 alpine lakes and four streams to fish, plus fishing in the ranch-owned trout hatchery, which is the oldest private hatchery in the state. Hunters can bag turkey, mule deer, bear, grouse and elk right on the Ranch, and the Bar X Bar will arrange hunting expeditions. Guests can also explore the beautiful country and fascinating scenery here in the heart of the Santa Fe National Forest, visiting flower-filled meadows and forests of spruce, pine, aspen and fir. In the winter, there are the snow and ice sports to be enjoyed, including skiing, skating and snowmobiling. Horses are available nearby for $3.00 to $5.00 per hour and jeep tours of the high country can be arranged. There is a daily fee for trout fishing in the hatchery waters of $20 per person for up to a 5 lb. limit or $40 per family for 10 lb. Accommodations are in large rooms in the lodge where there is a dining room, or in cabins equipped with housekeeping facilities. Small cabins accommodating two to four persons rent for $35 per day or $210 per week and larger cabins for six to eight people are $50 per day and $300 per week. For information and accommodations, write or call: Honey-Boy Haven, Inc. Bar X Bar Ranch, P.O. Drawer #2, Pecos, NM 87552 (505)757–8500.

★★★*Los Pinos Ranch* is a small and unique summer guest ranch, in the heart of the Sangre de Cristo range of the Rocky Mountains, 45 miles from Santa Fe. It's located in "the most interesting 50 mile square in America," near quaint and historic Santa Fe, the artist colony of Taos, and Indian Pueblos and ruins all within a few hours drive. Los Pinos is situated near the headwaters of the Pecos River, at an elevation of 8500 feet, surrounded on every side by lofty peaks rising to an elevation of 13,000 feet and over. The average summer temperature is 76 degrees at noon, and 40 degrees at night. Horseback riding and hiking are the chief forms of recreation at Los Pinos—trails wind through dense spruce, pine and quaking aspen forests, carpeted with wild flowers—and the Rocky Mountain ponies are sure footed and gentle but spirited enough to interest the experienced rider. Guides are available and pack trips can be arranged. There are no poisonous snakes or insects or mosquitos, but there are herds of elk, mule deer, wild turkey and grouse. The sparkling streams with their deep pools, swift riffles and tiny hidden lakes make the Upper Pecos a tempting spot for the trout fisherman. Guests may fish on the premises. Ranch life is informal. Private cabins offer an atmosphere of relaxation with space for up to 14 guests. Food is the important highlight—with plenty of milk and cream, and all the fresh fruits, vegetables, meats and poultry that the nearby western markets can afford. Baking is done on the premises and lunch is served outdoors or can be packed for the trail. Dinner is served by candle light and an open fire. Water, absolutely pure, comes from the mountain stream. Bring warm, comfortable, sport clothing. The ranch is open from June 1–Oct. 1 and rates, on the American Plan, are $168 per person per week. (Children slightly lower.) Los Pinos has been a guest ranch for over 50 years, your hosts the McSweeneys and the Shoemakers can be reached at (505)757–6213 or by writing Los Pinos, Cowles (until Oct. 1) or Box 8, Rt. 3, Tererro, NM 87573. Their winter address is (until May 30) Craig Road, Morristown, NJ 07960 (201)538–0700.

★★★★*Rancho Encantado*, "the enchanted ranch," is an adobe palace surrounded by exquisitely landscaped gardens and the magnificent Sangre de Cristo and Jemey mountains in New Mexico's legendary chapparal country. Past guests of the ranch include a long list of movie luminaries and visiting royalty, as well as an appreciative clientele that returns year after year. The accommodations reflect the elegance of the aristocratic old Southwest—hand painted tiles, handsome Indian rugs, spanking white walls, and beamed roofs. Each room has its own distinctive furnishings and decorations, from colorful wall hangings to Victorian sofas. The dining room, which prides itself on native specialties, has justly received numerous accolades for both traditional southwestern fare and tasty international cuisine, including fresh seafood flown in from the Pacific coast each day. Activities range from guided trail rides to swimming in the pool and tennis on pro courts. The ranch also makes a fine starting point for ski trips, hunting, and sightseeing in some of New Mexico's most spectacular countryside. There are a total of sixty rooms and suites available—in the main lodge, cottages, and Casa Pinon guest house—and reservations are recommended well in advance. Double occupancy European plan rates are $66 daily for a large room in the lodge; $92 daily for elegant two-room suites with fireplaces; $84 daily for kitchenette units, and $114 daily for luxury suites. For additional information, write: Rancho Encantado, Route 4, Box C, Santa Fe, NM 87501 (505)982–3537.

★★★*Tres Lagunas* is a beautiful, full-service family resort located high in the Pecos Wilderness Area less than an hour's drive from Santa Fe. Fishermen will appreciate the three fully-stocked lakes and mile-long stretch of the upper Pecos River for secluded fly-casting. A stable of fine horses, miles of wilderness trails, and experienced wranglers cater to horseback riders. There are also quiet mountain trails for hiking and exploring, and organized pack trips with expert guides in the fall for hunting the deer and elk that roam the upper meadows of the Pecos Wilderness. Amenities at Tres Lagunas include a handsome lodge with an attractive lounge and dining room overlooking a waterfall, superb family-style meals, a heated swimming pool, and a well-stocked cocktail lounge. Spotlessly clean single and double guest cabins have private baths, dressing rooms, and fireplaces. American plan rates: $43 per person daily (double occupancy) in lodge rooms, $145 daily for four persons in two-bedroom cabins; $50 per person daily (double occupancy) in deluxe cabins. Horseback riding is extra. Children's rates are available. Rates include three meals per day and a limit of five trout daily from Tres Lagunas' private lakes. For full details, write: Tres Lagunas Guest Ranch, Route 2 Box 100, Pecos, NM 87552 (505)757–6194.

NORTH DAKOTA

Introduction

Several famous fishing, hunting, camping, and family vacation areas are set amid the grasslands and short grass steppes of North Dakota's big, wide-open spaces. North Dakota, the Flickertail State, first explored by Pierre La Verendrye, who in 1738 crossed the Assiniboine River in Canada to the Missouri River, searching for a "river to the west," contains the noted fish and big-game country of the Upper Missouri and its great impoundments—the Garrison and Oahe reservoirs, which provide some of the nation's finest fishing for big northern pike and walleye—and the scenic lakes and woodlands of the Turtle Mountain country in the northernmost reaches of the state.

Accommodations & Travel Information

For detailed information on all aspects of travel in North Dakota, contact: Travel Director, Highway Dept., State Capitol, Bismarck, ND 58505 or phone (1–800)472–2100 between 8:00 A.M. and 5:00 P.M. toll free, May through October 1.

Information & Services

A free complete *North Dakota Fishing Waters* guide may be obtained from: Game & Fish Dept., 2121 Lovett Ave., Bismarck 58505. The department also publishes a free *Game & Fish Management Areas* guide, *Game Management Area Maps*, *Fishing and Hunting Regulations*, and a *Map of North Dakota's Fishing Waters.* A helpful source of information on campgrounds and recreation areas is the free 32–page booklet *Rough Rider Guide to North Dakota.* Charts are provided, listing campgrounds and state parks and showing exactly what facilities are available in each area. There is also information on trailer regulations and traveling with pets. The booklet can be obtained by writing Game & Fish Dept. 2121 Lovett Ave., Bismarck 58505. Another helpful publication is a free brochure available from the State Park Service, Fort Lincoln State Park, Rte. 2, Box 139, Mandan 58554, entitled *North Dakota State Parks.* It describes briefly each state park, giving the reader an idea of the type of country, and extent of facilities available. A chart of parks and their facilities is also provided; the brochure is attractively illustrated with full-color photographs.

Highways & Maps

To help you get where you are going the *North Dakota Official Highway Map* is an essential tool. You can get your copy free from: Highway Dept., State Capitol Grounds, Bismarck 58505. The map shows all roads and highways, boundaries, railroads, and route markers. It also shows the locations of national parks, state parks, rest areas, airports, the Lewis and Clark Trail, Explorers Highroad, game preserves, fish hatcheries, ski areas, the Old West Trail, and other points of interest. There is a location index for the state's principal cities, towns, and villages as well as a chart for computing mileage distances between points shown on the map. A handy summary of traffic regulations and a list of radio stations are also provided.

VACATION/ LODGING GUIDE

North Dakota Lakes & Recreation Areas

The Sioux State offers a variety of outdoor recreation and vacation opportunities, including some of the nation's top northern pike and walleye fishing waters, as well as hunting in season for deer, upland game birds, and rafts of waterfowl. North Dakota is a transitional state separating the Great Lakes country of Minnesota on the east from Montana's Upper Missouri River plains and towering Rocky Mountain high country on the west. Its flat to gently rolling prairie lands, characterized by sloughs and thousands of small ponds or potholes, which form one of the most important waterfowl areas in the United States, are joined on the north by Canada's Prairie Provinces—Manitoba and Saskatchewan—and on the south by South Dakota. Major hunting and fishing areas include the huge Oahe and Sakakawea Reservoirs on the Missouri River and the Badlands surrounding the Little Missouri in the western half of the state; the Central Lakes country; the scenic Turtle Mountains in the north, and the Red River of the North and Bois de Sioux rivers, which form the eastern boundary.

Information Sources, Maps & Access

For information sources and maps, see the North Dakota Introduction under "Accommodations & Travel Services." The state is served by Interstate Highways 94 and 29.

Recreation & Scenic Areas

Custer National Forest

This million-acre reserve embraces the rugged hill country and Little Missouri grasslands of western North Dakota. The major features of this area include the Badlands of the Little Missouri, Knife, Heart, Green, Missouri, and Cannonball river, Garrison Reservoir, and Theodore Roosevelt National Memorial Park. The Badlands are a fantastic array of buttes and mesas in which layers of brick-red scoria and gray, blue, and yellow clays are exposed. Among them is 3,468–foot Black Butte, the state's highest point. The Garrison Reservoir offers some of the state's finest fishing for giant walleye and northern pike. This is a top-ranking hunting region for whitetail deer, antelope, big whitetail jacks, snowshoe hare, upland game birds, wild turkey, and waterfowl.

Fort Union Trading Post National Historic Site

On their epic 1805 journey to the Pacific, the Lewis and Clark expedition spent the winter at the small Mandan Indian village of cottonwood log huts known as Fort Mandan at the mouth of the Knife River on the Upper Missouri River. It was during this fierce North Dakota winter, with its mixture of arctic gales and long windless cold spells that produce sun dogs (the "false suns"—haloes around the moon), that Lewis and Clark hired Sacajawea of the Snake Nation, their famous squaw guide known to the Indians as "Boat Pusher," and learned of the Great Falls of the Missouri and the Rocky Mountain headwaters beyond. With the arrival of spring, the expedition traveled up the Missouri in wooden keelboats on their historic journey west that was to open the Rocky Mountain fur country and the lands beyond to the traders of John Jacob Astor's American Fur Company. In the summer of 1828 Kenneth McKenzie—head of the American Fur Company's Upper Missouri Outfit, known as the "King of the Missouri"—dispatched the keelboat *Otter* from the Mandans to the mouth of the Yellowstone to establish Fort Union for the Assiniboine fur trade. Soon a string of trading posts along the Upper Missouri, served by the steamboats of the American Fur Company—such as the *Yellowstone*, known to the Indians as

"the big medicine canoe with eyes"—brought immense wealth to the New York financiers and helped secure the westward course of the American empire. In 1865, with the decline of the American buffalo robe market, Fort Union was sold to the Northwestern Fur Company and in a few years was abandoned and dismantled by the army. Today Fort Union is being reconstructed as a national historic site. Travelers can reach the site via U.S. 2 and County Road 4 from Williston, which is 25 miles to the southwest.

Great Lakes of the Missouri

The state's premier fishing is found along the vast 200–mile-long course of Lake Sakakawea (also known as Garrison Reservoir), with its numerous bays and coves. Lake Sakakawea offers some of the nation's top-ranked fishing for northern pike up to 30 pounds and over, as well as walleye, sauger, crappie, white bass, rainbow trout, coho salmon, goldeye, and channel catfish. Boat ramps, tackle, cabins, and campgrounds are available at most of the major fishing areas along the lake's twisting, snakelike shoreline, such as Whitetail, Bear Den, White Earth, McKenzie, Charging Eagle, Nishu, and Little Missouri bays. The frigid tailrace waters below Garrison Dam yield large rainbow trout, sauger, walleye, pike, and channel cats. A few rainbows and browns are taken upstream from the mouth of the Yellowstone at the top of Lake Sakakawea just east of the Montana boundary. To the south lies the state's second great Missouri River impoundment, Lake Oahe, which straddles the boundary of the two Dakotas. The Oahe Reservoir is another top-ranked trophy northern pike and walleye fishery. The reservoir's major fishing areas are at the Oahe Game Management Area backwaters, Huffard-Fort Rice areas, and Badger, Cannonball, Porcupine, Battle, Beaver, Red Horse, and Cattail bays. Other North Dakota walleye and northern pike waters include Lake Tshida, Long Lake National Wildlife Refuge, Lake Ashtabula—famed for its giant northern pike—Jim Lake, Spiritwood Lake, Arrowwood Lake National Wildlife Refuge, Sully's Hill National Game Preserve & Devils Lake Country, Lake Darling-Upper Souris National Wildlife Refuge, Buffalo Lodge Lake, J. Clark Salyer Refuge on the Souris River, the Turtle Mountain Indian Reservation lakes, the Red River, and the Sheyenne, Heart, Cedar, Cannonball, and James rivers. Spiritwood Lake is another top-ranked smallmouth bass and muskellunge fishery. Gravel Lake in the Wapoka Game Refuge area of the Turtle Mountains produced the state record 40–pound tiger muskellunge. The scenic lakes of the Turtle Mountains in the northern prairie region yield walleye, pike, smallmouth bass, and trout. North Dakota offers sharptail grouse and duck hunting in the grasslands and pothole country.

Theodore Roosevelt National Memorial Park

Theodore Roosevelt National Memorial Park honors the former president and his interest in national conservation of our natural resources. Its 70,436 acres take in the Badlands, which include the site of Roosevelt's Elkhorn Ranch in western North Dakota. Major features include petrified forests, deep canyons, rolling prairies, and the Little Missouri River. Wildlife includes bighorn sheep, bison, and antelope. The Badlands straddle the final 320 kilometers (200 miles) of the Little Missouri River and span its valley for 8 to 48 kilometers (5 to 30 miles). Moving waters carved out this valley, one of many that have cut into ancient preglacial plains. The park is open year round, but the best time to visit is from May through October (during the winter, portions of the park road may be closed because of snow). The park offers interpretive programs and an extensive system of backcountry trails for those who wish to leave their vehicles at one of the roadside pullouts to explore the Badlands on foot. The marking and mapping of trails in the north and south units is not completed, visitors are advised to obtain directions from a park ranger before setting out. The Caprock, Coulee, and Squaw Creek trails are open, marked, self-guiding trails. Hikers are not restricted to the existing trails and are invited to explore at their leisure. The weather here is prone to extremes: proper clothing, head protection against the sun, and good boots are essential.

Turtle Mountains

The Wakopa Game Management area in the beautiful Turtle Mountains of north central North Dakota is a top fishing and canoeing area. Its 5,178 acres consist mainly of tree-covered rolling hills with a heavy sprinkling of natural lakes and potholes. Aspen, birch, oak, and wild fruits are among the common trees and shrubs of the area. It is currently being developed by the Game & Fish Department as a semiwilderness area. The natural habitat—wooded hills, grassy meadows, lakes, and marshes—makes the area ideal for fishing and canoeing. Lake Upsilon is good for pike, and trout fishing is excellent in Gravel Lake. Rainbows up to 5½ pounds have been taken here. The WGMA has two marked canoe trails. You can put in along the highway into Laird Lake and follow the trail 1½ miles into Hooker Lake with a ¼ mile portage. Those desiring a longer trip can put in at the public boat ramp on Lake Upsilon and canoe through Upper Walker Lake and make a short portage into the channel leading to Laird Lake, then continue through Rames and Island lakes and a short portage into Hooker Lake. This trail is 4 miles long and is clearly marked with signs. A free informative brochure on the area can be obtained by writing: Game & Fish Dept., 2121 Lowett Ave., Bismarck 58505.

Lodges & Resorts

North Dakota has few full-service vacation lodges and resorts. For detailed accommodations information, contact: Travel Director, North Dakota Highway Dept., State Capitol, Bismark, ND 58505 (1–800) 472–2100 toll free between May and October.

OKLAHOMA

Introduction

Oklahoma, the "Sooner State," which joins New Mexico on its western boundary, has a surprisingly varied terrain, dotted by numerous sparkling blue lakes formed by impounding its major rivers: in the northeast, the Ozarks sprawl into the state from neighboring Arkansas; in the southeast are the famed game lands and wild areas of the Kiamichi and Quachita mountains slashed by high-country streams; to the west are the Prairie Plains and bottomlands along the Red River and the Arbuckle Mountains and Wichita Range to the southwest; in the central and northwest regions are the Redbed Plains and High Plains. Oklahoma's major fishing, hunting, and camping areas include the renowned trout waters of the Illinois River with its numerous falls and deep pools; the trophy bass waters of huge Lake Texoma and Lake Tenkiller, nestled among the Cookson Hills; the fabled goose-hunting lands surrounding Great Salt Plains Lake; the oak and pine forest game lands of the Tiak National Forest; and the rugged trails of the Wichita Mountains Wildlife Refuge.

Accommodations & Travel Information

Oklahoma's major vacation lodges and resorts are described in the "Vacation/Lodging Guide" which follows. For detailed information on all aspects of travel in the 'Sooner' state, contact the Oklahoma Dept. of Tourism & Recreation, Tourist Information, 504 Will Rogers Bldg., Oklahoma City, OK 73105 (405)521–2464.

Information & Services

Oklahoma fishing and hunting regulations may be obtained from the Dept. of Wildlife Conservation, 1801 North Lincoln Blvd., P.O. Box 53465, Oklahoma City 73160. The department also publishes the following free guides, available from the address listed above: *Crow Shooting on Fort Cobb Public Hunting Area*; *Sport Fish of Oklahoma*; *Fish Facts*; *Floating the Illinois*; *McCurtin County Wilderness Area*; *Oklahoma Game Birds*; *Oklahoma Mammals*; *Rio Grande Turkey Management*; *Trout Fishing in Oklahoma*; and free maps of the Canton, Choctaw, Fort Gibson, and Lexington public hunting areas. The handy full-color booklet *Fishes of Oklahoma* may be obtained from the department for 50¢. The Dept. of Wildlife Conservation also publishes *Public Lands of Oklahoma* (35¢), an extremely useful large-format booklet that contains maps and descriptions of all public hunting lands in the state. There are many facilities available in Oklahoma's comprehensive system of campgrounds. *Oklahoma Campers Guide* lists all major areas and towns in the state, and the camping facilities convenient to each. It may be obtained free by writing to the Oklahoma Dept. of Tourism & Recreation, 504 Will Rogers Bldg., Oklahoma City 73105.

Public Recreation Areas of Oklahoma, available free from Dept. of Wildlife Conservation, 1801 North Lincoln, Oklahoma City 73105, lists major public recreation areas in the state, and which services are provided. A complete description of state-park facilities is provided in *Oklahoma State Parks*, which profiles 30 parks and lists state lodges and recreation areas. Information is available free from the Oklahoma Dept. of Tourism & Recreation, 504 Will Rogers Bldg., Oklahoma City 73105. The same office will also provide free information on hiking opportunities in state parks. The most popular areas are the Ouachita National Forest and the Charon Gardens Wilderness in the Wichita Mountains Wildlife Refuge. Abandoned logging trails and tall, cool forests are the attractions in the Ouachita National Forest, which is dotted with clear lakes and streams. More rugged challenges are offered by the Charon Gardens Wilderness area, which was once used as a religious site by the Comanche

Indians. Hikers must cope with near-vertical rock walls; and deer, elk, and buffalo are common. Oklahoma is a melting pot of Indian cultures, with 35 tribes inhabiting the state. Complete information about events and important sites is given in *Oklahoma and the Indian*, a free map/guide available from Oklahoma Indian Affairs Commission, 4010 Lincoln Blvd., Oklahoma City 73105.

Highways & Maps

Oklahoma's transportation system provides easy access to all recreation areas. The free *Oklahoma State Highway Map*, available from the Oklahoma State Highway Commission, shows all major roads and highways, towns and settlements, lakes and streams, national forest land, airfields and railroads, and recreation sites. *Oklahoma Tours* is a free brochure that lists several different possible road tours of the state, with descriptions of various scenic attractions and points of interest. It is available from the Tourism Promotion Division, Oklahoma Tourism & Recreation Dept., 504 Will Rogers Bldg., Oklahoma City 73105.

VACATION/ LODGING GUIDE

Oklahoma's Great Lakes & Recreation Areas

Oklahoma's great lake impoundments, with over 2 million surface acres of water, and mountainous plateau country provide some good fishing and hunting opportunities. The Grand Lake of the Cherokees, located on the Grand River in the northeastern corner of the state, is the state's largest body of water, with close to 1,000 miles of shoreline, and offers excellent fishing for largemouth bass and crappies. Rainbow trout, an exotic fish in Oklahoma, are caught in the cold, turbulent tailrace waters below Tenkiller Reservoir and in the 12–mile stretch of the Illinois below Tenkiller Dam. The waters of the lower Illinois are drawn from the bottom of Lake Tenkiller, which maintains a constant temperature of 60° throughout the year. When the river's water level begins to rise during generation of the hydroelectric dam, the big rainbows often go on a feeding binge, and fly fishermen often land hookjawed lunkers. Once the river has risen, float fishermen in canoes or johnboats have the advantage. Another rainbow trout fishery has been established on the beautiful spring-fed clear-running Blue River in southeast Oklahoma on the Blue River Public Hunting and Fishing Area. The Blue's numerous falls, deep pools, boulders, and small islands provide excellent trout habitat. The current state record 10 lb. 4 oz. rainbow was caught in the Illinois River in June 1966. Largemouth bass is the number-one sport fish in Oklahoma and is present in nearly every lake and stream, along with schools of white bass, channel catfish, and bluegills. The record largemouth in the state is 11 lbs. 5 oz. The average size is one and a half to four pounds in weight. The smallmouth bass is restricted to the cool, swift-flowing mountain streams of eastern Oklahoma, namely, the Mountain Fork River and the tributaries of the Grand and Illinois rivers. Oklahoma smallmouths seldom exceed two pounds. Walleye have been well established in the state as a result of an intensive stocking program that began during the spring of 1961 in the state's outstanding system of reservoirs. Large flathead catfish up to 66 pounds and channel cats are found in the large lakes and rivers. Big blue catfish up to 50 pounds are found in the lakes and rivers of southern Oklahoma, especially in the Red River system.

Information Sources, Maps & Access

For detailed vacation travel and recreation information, and the free publications—*Oklahoma Lakes, Public Recreation Areas of Oklahoma*, contact: Oklahoma Dept. of Tourism & Recreation, 504 Will Rogers Bldg., Oklahoma City 73105 (405)521–2464. For the free publications, *Wichita Mountains Wildlife Refuge Map/Brochure* and *Refuge Regulations*, as well as detailed information, contact: Refuge Manager, P.O. Box 448, Cache, OK 73527. For a free *Chickasaw National Recreation Area Map/Brochure* and information, contact: Chickasaw National Recreation Area, Sulphur, OK 73086 (405)622–3163. The major auto routes serving the state are Interstate Highways 35, 40, and 44.

Recreation Areas

Chickasaw National Recreation Area

This popular national recreation area is located in the south-central portion of the state off Interstate Highway 35. Its two divisions encompass the former Platt National Park and Arbuckle National Recreation Area. The Travertine District, formerly Platt National Park, takes in 912 acres that include the famous mineral springs, woodlands, streams and nature trails. The Travertine District Nature center offers wildlife exhibits and guided park ranger nature walks and summer programs. The Arbuckle Lake District embraces 2,350

acres and offers a variety of water sports, camping, hunting in season, and excellent fishing for bass, northern pike, crappie, walleye, and channel catfish. Overnight accommodations are available in Sulphur, where the recreation area headquarters and Visitor Center is located.

Great Lakes & Reservoirs

The major lakes and reservoirs, which include more shoreline than the Atlantic and Pacific coast, include Lake Texoma, a superb fishery for striped bass up to 40 pounds; 42,000–acre Robert S. Kerr Lake, a top-ranked fishing and waterfowl hunting area, with peak populations of ducks and geese numbering well over 50,000; long, winding 26,300–acre Keystone Reservoir, another fine striped-bass fishery nestled among scenic rolling hills; the renowned largemouth and smallmouth bass, and walleye waters of beautiful 12,500–acre Lake Tenkiller, nestled among the historic Cookson Hills, once a retreat for outlaw gangs and the former hunting grounds of the Cherokee Indians; the bass and walleye waters of beautiful Lake Wister, the gateway to the "Kiamichi Country" and Ouachita National Forest in southeastern Oklahoma; the prolific trophy largemouth-bass waters of Spavinaw and Eucha lakes in the east; the northern pike waters of Lake Corl Etling, nestled in the primitive reaches of "Black Mesa" country; scenic Broken Bow Reservoir, in the foothills of the Ouachita Mountains, with its 180–mile pine–fringed shoreline and island-dotted smallmouth- and largemouth-bass waters; the fabled goose-hunting lands surrounding Great Salt Plains Lake in northwestern Oklahoma; Oologah Lake, named for a famous Cherokee chief, meaning "Dark Cloud," adjacent to the birthplace of humorist Will Rogers; the trophy "big bass" waters of beautiful 12,000–acre Lake Hudson—site of the state's first trading post, established in 1796; beautiful Greenleaf Lake in the verdant Cookson Hills; and the clear, deep waters of 2,349–acre Arbuckle Lake, nestled amid the rugged outcroppings of the Arbuckle Mountains, with good fishing for bass and northern pike. The state's warm-water and trout-fishing opportunities are illustrated by the state's record fish.

Hunting & Wildlife Areas

Although much of the state's land is privately owned, there are some 500,000 acres of public hunting areas managed for wildlife and hunting by the Department of Wildlife Conservation, as well as national grasslands and 250,000 acres of the Ouachita National Forest, which sprawls across the border from Arkansas. These public hunting lands provide excellent cover for whitetail deer and upland game birds. Whitetails are found throughout the state, with the best hunting in the cypress swamps and conifer forests of the southeast. Other big-game species include a small number of antelope in the Panhandle and a small herd of Rocky Mountain elk in the Wichita Mountains National Wildlife Refuge. Hunting for both species is by special permit only. Small game animals include cottontails, jackrabbits, and gray squirrels in the oak and hickory forests of the east, and fox squirrels along the rivers and forest ravines of the west. The Fort Cobb Public Hunting Area has the largest winter crow roost in North America, numbering some ten million birds. The state also offers some of the best hunting in the country for coyotes, bobcats, and raccoons. There are eleven wildlife species known to exist in Oklahoma that are considered endangered. Loss of habitat, pesticide poisoning, certain forestry practices, and illegal shooting are the major causes of a threat that could mean the end of several species. Among them is the red wolf, which has been forced out of its range in southeastern Oklahoma. The red wolf is usually larger than the coyote, sometimes weighing up to 80 pounds. Despite its name, the red wolf is a combination of black, buff, and gray, and is often mistaken for a coyote. The southern bald eagle is another endangered species. This magnificent bird of prey is a junior cousin of the bird that is our national emblem. It is dark brown or gray in its early life, but its head and tail turn distinctly white later on. Despite its tremendous soaring ability, superb vision, and impressive size, it has been the victim of just about all of man's destructive intrusions.

Wichita Mountains National Wildlife Refuge

The Wichita Mountain Range comprises 61,480 acres, extending northwest and lying largely within Comanche country. The rounded summits of its granite peaks average 650 to 700 feet in height. Classed among the older mountains in the United States, they are interesting both geologically and scenically, and have attracted many thousands of Oklahomans, as well as tourists from other states. Until the middle of the nineteenth century, the only inhabitants of this area were Indians. The onetime presence here of a tribe of Wichita Indians has been substantiated, and remains of other tribal lodges have been found. President Theodore Roosevelt first proclaimed this area a wildlife preserve. Thanks to his initial efforts, the region is now a haven for buffalo. Other wildlife preserved in the refuge include elk, white-tailed deer, Texas longhorns, wild turkeys, and various birds. The buffalo herd in Wichita Mountains Wildlife Refuge now numbers about a thousand head. Old records reveal that "Black Dog," a bull of the original herd, lived to achieve the reputation as the largest buffalo, with an estimated weight of 2,800 pounds. The heaviest weights of bulls now on the range are in the 1,600– to 2,000–pound class. These big animals are not often seen by the public, as they tend to range apart from the rest of the herd. Every effort has been made to keep the herd in as natural condition as possible. The dozen refuge lakes that are open for fishing are stocked with bass, sunfish, crappie, and channel catfish. Included in the Wichita Refuge are nearly 8,900 acres of wilderness—land as wild as ever, little touched by the hand of man. The Charon Gardens Wilderness Area of 5,000 acres and the North Mountains Wilderness Area of 3,900 acres encompass some of the most rugged landscape in Wichitas. A two-hour hike will take you into the center of the Charon Gardens Wilderness, but the going is rugged and you should be in good physical condition before trying the more broken sections. There are no marked trails or drinking water. The North Mountain area is designated as a research area. It is reserved for research studies and is not open to the public.

Lodges & Resorts

★★★★*Arrowhead Resort* overlooks the spectacular Lake Eufaula in southeastern Oklahoma. On the lake there is a heated fishing dock, boat rentals, waterskiing, and swimming. Tennis courts, an 18–hole championship golf course, hiking trails and bicycle paths cover the open lawns and surrounding woods. The Lodge, built of native stone and timber, has 106 rooms, and 104 private cabins with kitchens. Double rooms are $25–37. Cottages accommodating two are $33 daily, and those accommodating four are $41 daily. Arrowhead Resort also has camping facilities with hookups for trailers, cookout shelters, archery, badminton, shuffleboard, horseshoe pits, and a childrens playground. For more information write: Oklahoma Resorts, 500 Will Rogers Building, Oklahoma City, OK 73105 (405)521–2464.

★★★*Fountainhead Resort* is a strikingly modern resort complex, with one side of the building curving above a landscaped lawn leading to the water's edge on 102,000–acre Lake Eufaula in the central part of the state. Lake Eufaula, one of the largest man-made lakes in the world, is considered one of the nation's top lakes for bass fishing,

and is the site of two national bass fishing tournaments. Other species include crappie and catfish. There is a full marina on the lake providing a guide service; fishing boat, pontoon boat, canoe, paddle boat and motor rentals; boat repairs and docking. Sailing, waterskiing (with boat rentals available) and swimming are also popular lake activities. The resort has an 18–hole golf course, with pro shop; camping and picnic areas; pool swimming; horseback riding; hiking; bicycles; hayrides; tennis; archery; shuffleboard; and miniature golf. Children can enjoy the resort's playgrounds and petting zoo. The resort's area has a full range of offerings including fine Italian cuisine at the outlying community of Kreb; Robber's Cave State Park in Wilburton; The Five Civilized Tribe Museum and Camp Gruber Public Hunting Area in Muskogee, and the McAlester Prison Rodeo in Prague. Accommodations at the resort include hotel rooms with park or lake balcony views; and cottages with kitchenettes. The resort operates on the European Plan, but a grocery store is for those with kitchenettes and gourmet buffets and Western cookouts are popular. Rates: Rooms: $22–41 nightly. Cottages $33 nightly. For further information contact: Fountainhead Resort, Checotah, OK 75740 toll free (800)522–8565.

★★★★*Lake Texoma Resort* is nestled on the shores of the spectacular 93,000–acre Lake Texoma, surrounded by 2,000 acres of unspoiled woodland. The lake holds big bass, crappie, channel catfish and blue catfish. Lake Texoma Marina rents fishing boats, ski boats, pleasure boats, and pontoon craft on an hourly, daily, or weekly basis. Hiking trails and bridle paths meander through unspoiled woods and over windy bluffs, with a spectacular view of the lake and surrounding countryside. Lake Texoma stables has a fine selection of horses, and hayrides and moonlight rides liven the week. There is also a challenging 18–hole golf course, and miniature golf, picnic areas, shuffleboard courts, and several hard-surface tennis courts. Lake Texoma Resort offers spacious lodge rooms, deluxe cottages, campgrounds, a grocery store, laundromat, and specialty bait and tackle shops. The lakeside dining room offers generous country-style meals with such specialties as country fried chicken, and fresh catfish. Autumn brings hunters to the area, lured by the white-tail deer, bobtail quail, cottontail rabbits, geese and ducks in the vast 50,000–acre preserve bordering Lake Texoma. Lodge rates are $18–21 for singles, and $25–37 double occupancy, depending on the season. Deluxe cottages accommodating up to eight persons have two bedrooms, a spacious living room dining area, with fireplace, color TV's, air-conditioning and private bath. Rates are $45 daily. Duplex cottages, accommodating four, are $33. Guests reserving the cottages are requested to bring their own cooking utensils. For more information write: Oklahoma Resorts, 500 Will Rogers Building, Oklahoma City, Ok 73105 (405)521–2464.

★★★★*Quartz Mountain Resort* nestled in a valley by Lake Altus in the foothills of the Wichita Mountains, offers boating, fishing, water skiing on the lake, hiking, horsebackriding, and biking in the surrounding countryside. The resort has a challenging golf course, several tennis courts, and badminton, archery, shuffleboard, horseshoes and ping pong on the lawns. The Lodge has 44 guest rooms, and 16 private cottages with kitchens. Double rooms are $27–34 Sunday through Wednesday, and $24–31 Thursday through Saturday. Cottages accommodating four are $28, and those accommodating six are $32. There are also private and group campsites available, a gift shop, and cookout shelters. For more information write: Oklahoma Resorts, 500 Will Rogers Building, Oklahoma City, Oklahoma 73105 (405)521–2464.

★★★★*Shangri-La at Grand Lake O' the Cherokees* is an incredible vacation complex on the tip of Monkey Island, a peninsula jutting out into the 59,000–acre lake. It is an hour and a half northeast of Tulsa, 177 miles from Kansas City, and 278 miles from Dallas. Guests can also fly in by private plane to the new million-dollar Golden Falcon Airpark, three miles from Shangri-La. Recreation facilities are outstanding. There are 27 holes of golf. The initial 7,000–yard, 18–hole course has been cited by *Golf Digest* as one of the top five courses in Oklahoma. There is also a driving range, putting green, well-equipped pro shop, carts for rent, lockers, showers and a "nine Plus" snack bar. PGA professionals will arrange lessons, clinics and tournaments. For tennis there are eight cushioned Plexipave courts—four indoor and four outdoor with lighting for night play. There is a tennis pro shop; showers, lockers, saunas and whirlpool baths especially for tennis players; lessons; clinics and tournaments. Proper tennis attire is required. In the recreational complex, there is also a bowling alley, game room, bicycle rental shop and a snack bar. After golf or tennis, guests may want to relax at the Tahitian Health Spas. There are separate spas for men and women, with exercise equipment, stream, massage, sauna and whirlpool. An outdoor pool is open in season and an indoor pool is located inside the Tahitian Terrace. The Marina is protected by a large breakwater and has more than 100 covered slips. There is water skiing, fishing boats and cruisers for rent, pontoon boats with a pilot and fishing guide service. The service dock is fully equipped. A Game Room has pool tables, electronic games and pinball machines. There is volleyball on the south lawn, and water volleyball in the indoor pool. In bad weather, golfers can still hit a few balls on the indoor putting course or using the indoor golf driving net. Shangri-La even has its own "mass transit" system. Guests can ride around the lodge area in the Golden Eagle Express, specially designed tram-buggies. For a Western atmosphere, there is the Hogan, a Navajo-design pavilion with a barbeque, cook-out or baron of beef served around a huge fireplace with western entertainment. For a tropical mood, choose the Tahitian Terrace, a relaxing lounge area with tropical plants, palm trees, flowing streams, rustic bridges and South Seas background music. At night there is a Hawaiian luau. Or for an elegant evening, there is the Golden Eagle with a gourmet dinner and the nostalgic big-band sound of a 12–piece orchestra for listening or dancing. A casual meal can be enjoyed in the Angus Dining Room, featuring prime rib. Shangri-La has several shops, a beauty salon and barber shop and babysitters. Guests can schedule cruises from Shangri-La marina to Har-Ber Village, a reconstructed pioneer village. The Shangri-La Aqua-Home can take up to 40 passengers on day or evening lake cruises. Guests are accommodated in 306 units including the Main Lodge, Golden Oaks Lodge, a townhouse complex and condominiums. Room rates in the Main Lodge and Golden Oaks are double occupancy, European Plan. Room in the Main Lodge are $44/day in summer and $34 off season Junior suites are $60 in summer and $50 off season. The Shangri-La Country estates is a 34–room townhouse complex with a private swimming pool and tennis courts. Suites have kitchens and living rooms and are $65 for two persons summer season and $55 off season; and $65 for two persons summer season and $55 off season; and $85 for four persons summer season and $75 off season. Privately owned condominiums are also available for daily, weekly and monthly rentals. These range from one- to three-bedroom units. There are also special golf, tennis and vacation packages. For further information write: Shangri-La, Route 3, Affon, OK 74331 (908)257–4204.

Introduction

The Beaver State's alpine lakes, forests, mountains, and wild rivers are bordered on the north by the Columbia River and Washington, on the east by Idaho and the great canyons of the Snake River, on the south by California and the Siskiyou Mountains, and on the west by the rugged, wave-cut bluffs and wild sand dunes of the Pacific, rimmed by towering coastal forests of cedar, pine, spruce, and hemlock, with an understory of laurel, sweet gale and rhododendron, beautiful red-barked madronas, watery sphagnum bogs, and tangled thickets of the spiny devil's club. Oregon contains 96,981 square miles of varied topography, including several of the nation's outstanding fishing, hunting, backpacking, and wilderness camping areas, such as the historic steelhead and trophy trout waters of the Rogue National Wild River and the fabled Deschutes, or "River of Falls"; the spectacular Eagle Cap Wilderness in the rugged Wallowa Mountains; the haunting wonders of Crater Lake National Park, formed by the wrecking in prehistoric times of ancient 14,000–foot Mount Mazanna; the picturesque high country of the Sky Lakes wilderness and the headwaters of the Rogue; the Blue Mountains and Wenaha backcountry—the "Island of Shoshone"; the classic blue-ribbon fly-fishing waters of the North Branch of the Umpqua and Metolius rivers; the fabled waterfowl shooting areas and camas prairies of Malheur and Klamath lakes, the wild McKenzie River; and the spectacular "black forests" and wilderness areas of the High Cascades—culminating at 11,245–foot Mt. Hood, the state's highest peak—carpeted along the alpine meadows and forest floors with sorrel, orchids, Indian pipe, the blood-red snow plant, and the rare moccasin flower. The towering virgin forests of the Beaver State were first explored by the fur traders of John Jacob Astor's Pacific Fur Company and the Hudson's Bay Company, who ruled the territory from 1821 under John McLoughlin at Fort Vancouver—"the Father of Oregon." The year 1842 saw the beginning of the great migration of pioneers over the Oregon Trail—known to the Indians as the "Great Road of the Whitetops" (covered wagons).

OREGON

Accommodations & Travel Information

Oregon offers a wide variety of hunting and fishing and family vacation accommodations, ranging from remote wilderness camps and cabins to deluxe ranch vacation resorts. The state's major lodges, guest ranches, ski resorts, inns, and motels are described in the "Vacation/Lodging Guide" which follows. For detailed information on all aspects of travel in the Beaver State contact: Oregon Travel Information, State Highway Bldg., Salem 97310 (503)378–6309.

Information & Services

For detailed information about fishing and hunting regulations, seasons, wildlife code, and permits, write: Information Branch, Oregon Dept. of Fish & Wildlife, 1634 S.W. Alder St., P.O. Box 3503, Portland 97208. The Fish & Wildlife Dept. publishes several maps and guides of use to the fisherman and hunter, including the free guides *Fishing in Oregon, Hunting in Oregon, To Catch a Steelhead, A Guide to Salmon & Steelhead Hatcheries*, and *Lakes of Oregon's National Forest Series*; the free leaflets *Upland Game Birds, Salmon of Oregon, Mammals of Prey, Big Game, Trout of Oregon, Warm-Water Lakes with Public Access, Oregon's Furbearers, Pond & Diving Ducks, Geese of Oregon, Warm-Water Game Fish, Hawks, Rock, Surf & Bay Fishes, Owls, Long-Legged Wading Birds*, and *Shore Birds of Oregon*; and the free *Oregon Wildlife* magazine, published monthly. The free *Oregon Game Management Unit Map* shows and describes all Big Game Management Units.

Oregon is one of the best places in the country for camping, thanks to the wealth of forestland, scenic shoreline, cold, clear rivers and lakes, and the towering mountain peaks. The state park system is outstanding, offering 238 parks and recreation areas, many of them dotting the coastline. Almost all of Oregon's state parks offer campsites with drinking water and firewood. The county and private park systems add to this network of campgrounds. Boating and fishing are available, and many extra facilities can often be found. *Oregon Parks*, a free map guide available from the Oregon State Highway Division, Travel Information Section, Salem 97310, gives a complete index of parks and facilities, as well as a basic set of rules and regulations. It also features a large map of the state, showing all state, national, county, and private parks and other points of interest. *The Pacific Northwest National Forest Campground Directory*, available free from the U.S. Forest Service-Pacific Northwest Region, 319 W. Pine St., P.O. Box 3623, Portland 97208, lists each national forest in the state and gives complete information on facilities.

There are many guides, packers, and outfitters in this ruggedly beautiful state. Fishing and hunting services are available in every part of the state, and they provide instructions and equipment for all types of river, lake, and ocean fishing, as well as for camping and big-game hunting. The *Oregon Guides and Packers Directory*, free from P.O. Box 722, Lake Oswego 97034, lists guides and packers by regional area, stating which rivers, lakes, or land areas they service. The many wilderness sports opportunities available in Oregon's national forests are serviced by several outfitters, listed by forest in *Resorts & Packers on the National Forests*, free from the U.S. Forest Service, Pacific Northwest Region, 319 S.W. Pine St., P.O. Box 3623, Portland 97208. It tells the name and address of each operator, the services provided, season of use, and things to do, and includes a map of Oregon showing national forest land, resorts, park and saddle stock, and highways and towns.

The Oregon stretch of the Pacific Crest National Scenic Trail begins at the Columbia Gorge above Bonneville Dam. From the time it climbs out of the Columbia River gorge, it follows the Cascades at altitudes from 4,000 to 7,100 feet through Oregon for 420 miles. It winds southward high on the flanks of Mount Hood, past Mount Jefferson, Three-Fingered Jack, and Mount Washington. After passing the Belknap lava area and the Three Sisters, the trail goes through a beautiful lake region, including Waldo, Odell, Crescent, and Diamond lakes. Further south it traverses Crater Lake National Park, along the uppermost crest to Fourmile Lake on the side of Mt. McLoughlin, and then across Lake of the Woods Highway 140 into California near the southern end of the Cascade Range.

The useful *Pacific Crest National Scenic Trail Map & Trail Log* is available free from the Pacific Northwest Region Office, P.O. Box 3623, Portland 97208. It provides a complete trail log, history and description of the trail, and nine separate area maps that show national forest boundaries, roads, the trail route, mileage, trail shelters, campsites, improved campgrounds, horse feed, ranger stations, forest service stations, lookout stations, and airstrips. The eminently useful *Pacific Crest Trail Volume 2: Oregon & Washington* ($5.95, 287 pages) published by Wilderness Press, 2440 Bancroft Way, Berkeley, CA 94704, is a superbly accurate guide to the Oregon section of the trail; it contains 140 two-color topographic maps.

Leisure Outfitters, Inc., offers a wide range of guided wilderness trips, including an Olympic Range headwaters expedition and coast range excursions, and runs a Goat Rocks Wilderness trail camp, a high-country trail camp in the Oregon Cascades, a Rogue River trail camp, a father-son camp, Wilderness Academy for Scouts, and a backcountry pack camp in the Umatilla National Forest, with trail riding, nature photography, and deer and elk hunting camps in the ancient hunting grounds of the Umatilla, Cayuse, Walla Walla, and Nez Percé Indians. They also offer geological expeditions and explorations with a base at the Oregon Museum of Science & Industry Lon Hancock Science Camp. Leisure Outfitters offers spring bear-hunting expeditions, a High Cascades hunt, a primitive weapons hunt, and riverboat elk-hunting and steelhead-fishing trips, and operates wilderness buck and elk hunting drop camps, spike camps, and trophy camps. Summer fly-fishing instruction is offered on the McKenzie, the Santiam, High Cascades lakes, and coastal streams. There are guided wild and scenic river-raft trips on the Rogue, Deschutes, Minam, Grand Ronde, and Owyhee rivers. Write for detailed information and catalog (which includes a wide mail-order

selection of unusual, hard-to-find gear) to: Leisure Outfitters, P.O. Box 7144, Salem 97303 (503)364–5532.

Lute Jerstad Adventures offers several unusual high-country horsepack, camping, and fishing trips. The *Imnaha River High Country Horsepack Trip* takes you through the heart of the Eagle Cap Wilderness. The major features of this excursion, which departs from historic Indian Crossing on the main Imnaha River, include camping along the South Fork, with side trips to Deadman Point and Boner Flats, up to the North Fork of the Imnaha to the Tenderfoot Basin, over Tenderfoot Pass, and down the east fork of the Wallowa River to the head of Wallowa Lake and Aneroid Lake. Wildlife includes deer, elk, bear, and mountain goat. Hikes can be taken to rims to 9,500–feet elevation with breathtaking views of this vast alpine country. The *Washboard Trail Wilderness Trip* combines high-lakes fishing for cutthroat and eastern brook trout with a horsepack trip on one of the most spectacular horseback trails in North America. The Washboard Trail is cut into a rim at 7,600 feet, and 3,000 feet below runs the wild Minam River. The trip starts at the end of Bear Creek Road out of Wallowa and passes through the rugged Granite Prong country to Bear Lake and the remote Sturgill Basin in the Eagle Cap Wilderness. The great grass meadows of the Sturgill Basin were a summer hunting camp for the Nez Percé Indians and are now a high-country summer range for elk. The final camp is near the historic Stanley Guard Station, an old V-notched log cabin built and manned as a ranger station in 1908, and one of the few original stations still standing. The *Minam River and High Lakes* horsepack and fishing trip offers fly-fishing for native rainbow trout along the Lostine River to Minam Lake, nestled high in the Eagle Cap Wilderness at 7,400–feet elevation. The major features along this route include the Big Burn; West Minam Meadows, a wild-flower sanctuary of great beauty and solitude; Green Lake, renowned for large, fat brook trout; and the famous Bowman Trail. Guided wild and scenic river trips are on the Deschutes, John Day, Owyhee, and Grande Ronde rivers. Write to Lute Jerstad Adventures, P.O. Box 19527, Portland 97219 (503)244–4364), for detailed info and their free *Adventures Catalog*.

Wilderness Pack Trips, P.O. Box 71, Rogue River 97537, offers guided base camp and drop pack trips into the Oregon Cascades and Klamath Mountain country of the Rogue River, Siskiyou, and Umpqua national forests.

Several other outfitters offer statewide wilderness white-water and fishing trips. *Don L. Henry*, Box 7144, Salem 97303, provides statewide steelhead, salmon, and trout fishing, elk hunting, and scenic trips, as well as educational and recreational expeditions. *Dean Helfrich Guide Service Pacific Northwest Fishing & Camping Trips* provides packaged excursions down the Rogue and Owyhee rivers and Idaho's Middle Fork Salmon River; write: 2722 Harvest Lane, Springfield 97477. *Whitewater Guide Trips, Inc.*, 12120 S.W. Douglas, Portland 97225, offers guided excursions and salmon, steelhead, and trout fishing trips on Hells Canyon of the Snake and the Deschutes, John Day, McKenzie, Grande Ronde, and coastal streams, and operates scenic fishing and youth camps. *Wilderness Water Ways*, 33 Canyon Lake Dr., Port Costa, CA 94569, offers guided white-water raft trips on the Rogue, Illinois, and Klamath rivers.

River Trips Unlimited, c/o Irv Urie, 1810 Corona Ave., Medford 97501, offers a blend of rugged white-water travel and luxurious accommodations. All of the trips are completely planned and outfitted, with time out for fishing and swimming. Meals and lodgings are in comfortable rustic cabins. *Brigg's Guide Service*, 2750 Cloverlawn Drive, Grants Pass 97526, services the mighty Rogue River. They will provide rafts or kayaks and furnish cabins and meals. *Jerry's Rogue River Jet Boats and Wild River Trips* offers round-trip excursions from Gold Beach up to Agness or Paradise Bar. The boat pilots point out historic and natural sights along the way. Inflatable kayaks are the main feature of *Orange Torpedo Trips*, P.O. Box 1111, Grants Pass 97526. They equip river trips for the Rogue and the Deschutes. All services, including meals and transportation, are provided, and trips last 1–3 days. Experienced guides accompany all parties, and many of the first-timers are beginners. *Court's White Water Trips* provide excursion jet boats from Gold Beach to Clay Hill Rapids or Paradise Bar. Guides explain the sights along the river. Write to them at Box 1045, Gold Beach 97444. *The Hells Canyon Navigation Co.*, Box 145, Oxbow 97840, provides both jet boat and float trips down the Snake River. Hells Canyon provides a wide variety of wildlife and scenic beauty, and drop-off fishing trips are available in the summer.

Highways & Maps

The Oregon highway system is among the best in the nation. What began as primitive Indian and pioneer trails developed into a streamlined, fast-moving system that takes care not to mar the beauty of the country. Some of Oregon's highways are panoramic as well as functional, fitting themselves easily into their magnificent surroundings. U.S. 101 travels down the 400 miles of coastline. From your car, you can see the broad, sandy beaches, rugged headlands, interesting rock formations, picturesque lighthouses, and varied wild flowers. Beachcombers can look for driftwood and sea shells or take time out to fish or dig for clams. Interstate 80N (or the alternate upper-level Scenic Highway) follows the sweeping course of the Columbia River. Huge dams, rushing waterfalls, and lofty cliffs and mountains vie for your attention. The Hood River valley is famous for apples and pears, and numerous state parks provide recreation areas. Spectacular views of the Columbia Gorge are one of the highlights of this scenic highway.

The free *Official Highway Map of Oregon* is available from the Oregon Dept. of Transportation, State Highway Division, Salem 97308. It shows all major and minor roads, population markers, points of interest, state parks, rest areas, airports, lighthouses, fish hatcheries, winter sports areas, and national forest lands.

Fremont National Forest & Gearhart Mountain Wilderness

The Fremont National Forest encompasses 1,194,000 acres in south-central Oregon on the east slope of the Cascade Range. The forest, named after Capt. John C. Frémont, who along with Kit Carson, the guide and frontiersman, led one of the first exploration parties through southern Oregon, is divided into two distinct sections: one area encompasses the Warner Mountains from Abert Rim to the California border; the other encompasses the mountains between Lakeview and Klamath Falls, bordered by the Deschutes Forest on the north, the Winema Forest on the west, and California on the south. Numerous forest roads and trails provide access to interior areas. The Abert Rim, along the east side of Lake Abert, is the largest and most exposed geologic fault in North America, rising nearly 2,500 feet above the lake, with a 640-foot vertical lava cliff at the topmost part. When Frémont saw Abert Lake in 1843, during his search for the mythical Buena Ventura River that was supposed to flow from Klamath Lake into San Francisco Bay, it was 50 square miles of water. In years when rainfall has been below normal, however, it has been completely dry.

Gearhart Mountain Wilderness contains some of the oldest volcanic domes in western Lake County. Gearhart Mountain, at 8,364 feet, is the highest and oldest. After the original volcanic material cooled and moistened, glaciers carved out a large amphitheater known as the Head of Dairy Creek. Today, its impressive headwalls tower over a primitive camping area of mountain meadows and springs. More than 20 miles of trails provides access to such areas. Three miles from the southeast entrance to Trail 100 lies the Dome, with its massively eroded cliffs 300 feet high stretching westward from the 7,380–foot dome for almost a mile. A half mile from the same trailhead are the stark sentinellike hoodoos (columns of rock in fantastic shapes) of the Palisades. Nearby, the Sprague River flows for about 90 miles, much of it through the Klamath Indian Reservation, and offers good fishing for rainbows to 3 pounds and browns. The Chewaucan River is the largest and finest trout stream in the forest. The river rises in the mountains northwest of Lakeview and flows in a northerly direction for about 50 miles into the Chewaucan Marsh. The Chewaucan offers superb dry fly-fishing for native rainbows. To the south, on the California-Oregon border, large, shallow Goose Lake is an excellent waterfowl-shooting area.

VACATION/ LODGING GUIDE

Information Sources, Maps & Access

The full-color *Fremont National Forest Map*, available for 50¢ from the Forest Supervisor, P.O. Box 551, Lakeview 97630 (503)947–2151, shows forest roads, trails, boating sites, ranger stations, campgrounds, and points of interest, including the Warner Canyon Ski Area, Slide Mountain Geologic Area, and Mitchell Recreation Area. For detailed fishing, hunting, and wilderness camping information and a free *Gearhart Wilderness Map*, write to the Forest Supervisor.

Fremont National Forest is reached by U.S. Highway 395 and Oregon Highways 140 and 31. Lodging, supplies, fishing, and big-game hunting guides and outfitters are located at Bly, Lakeview, Valley Falls, Paisley, Summer Lake, and Silver Lake.

Gateways & Accommodations

Lakeview

(Pop. 2,700; zip code 97630; area code 503.) The town is the hub of a beautiful area popular with hunters, fishermen, vacationers, and rock hounds, who often unearth a variety of stones and Indian artifacts. The region was once a vast grazing area and the site of treacherous range wars between sheep raisers and cattlemen. The strife ended when the government established the Fremont National Forest, which surrounds Lakeview, and opened the disputed grazing lands to homesteaders. Area attractions include Abert Rim, north of town along U.S. Hwy. 395, the highest fault scarp in North America; Old Perpetual Geyser, 3 miles north; the Hart Mountain National Wildlife Refuge, 35 miles northeast on unpaved road, a 24,000–acre preserve for pronghorn antelope, sage hen, and bighorn sheep; and the Schminck Memorial Museum, in town at 128 South E St., containing Indian artifacts and displays of early pioneer life. A district ranger's office of the Fremont National Forest is located in Lakeview. Accommodations: *Best Western Skyline Motor Lodge* (rates: $24 double), 28 fine rooms, color TV, restaurant adjacent, open year-round, at 414 N. G St., junction of U.S. 395 and Oregon State Hwy. 140 (947–2194); *Lakeview Lodge Motel* (rates: $20–22 double), 40 rooms, 10 two–room units, 3 with kitchens, color TV, restaurant nearby, at 301 N. G St., ½ block south of junction of U.S. 395 and Oregon State Hwy. 140 (947–2181).

High Cascades— Crater Lake National Park

The many geological wonders of Crater Lake National Park are located along the northwestern boundary of Winema National Forest. The park embraces 160,290 acres of the southern Cascade Range. Crater Lake lies inside the great pit, or Caldera, created by the collapse of the Mt. Mazama volcano in prehistoric times. This ancient volcano is one in a north-south chain of huge cones built during the last few million years along the crest of the Cascade Range, stretching about 600 miles from Lasser Peak in California northward to Mt. Garibaldi, near Vancouver, British Columbia. Other prominent volcanoes in the chain include Mounts Shasta, Jefferson, Hood, Saint Helens, Adams, Rainier, and Baker. According to geologists, Mt. Mazama once had an elevation of 14,000 feet. The upper portion of the mountain caved inward and left a craterlike rim rising to 2,000 feet. Today, the lake lies at 6,239 feet above sea level, is 4 miles wide and 6 miles long, and is the deepest body of fresh water in the United States, reaching depths in some places of nearly 2,000 feet. Crater Lake was discovered on June 12, 1853, by John Wesley Hillman, a young prospector and member of a party in search of a rumored "Lost Cabin Mine." Hillman named it Deep Blue Lake. Sixteen years later, it was changed to its present name. Multicolored rock walls 500 to 2,000 feet high surround the blue waters. The lake has never been known to freeze, and although it has no visible outlet, its waters are fresh. The Pacific Crest Trail passes around the western slope of the mountain, and short trails lead up and along the rim. Throughout most of the year, the area is covered by a deep blanket of snow. With the arrival of summer, the deep greens of the coniferous forests are patched with the brilliant meadow displays of phlox, monkeyflower, Indian paintbrush, lupine, and aster. Black bear, coyote, elk, bald and golden eagle, water ouzel, and mule and whitetail deer inhabit the wilderness.

Fishing is fair at best for rainbows, Dolly Varden, and cutthroat trout in the lake. If you intend to fish in the lake, the best places are the shallows, such as those around Wizard Island. Boats are available for hire at the landing below Rim Village at the southwest side of the lake. Camping facilities in the park are located at Mazama Campground (198 sites), Rim Village (54 sites), Lost Creek (12 sites), and the primitive Pinnacles campground.

Information Sources, Maps & Access

The major features of the park, including Mt. Mazama, Eagle Crags, Wizard Island, the haunting Phantom Ship, Palisades, and the Pumice Desert, are shown on the beautiful full-color *Crater Lake National Park Topographic Map* ($2) published by the U.S. Geological Survey. This map, which is also available in a shaded-relief edition, shows lake depth contours, the scenic Rim Drive, Crater Lake Lodge, and wilderness trails, including the Pacific Crest National Scenic Trail. The reverse side of the map contains a detailed geological history of the park and fascinating maps and charts showing the floor of Crater Lake, distribution of pumice deposits, and a geologic map of the lake and Mt. Mazama.

Fishing, backcountry camping, trail information, and copies of the Crater Lake National Park U.S. Geological Survey map may be obtained by writing: Superintendent, Crater Lake National Park, P.O. Box 7, Crater Lake 97604 (503)594–2211.

Several useful guidebooks to the park are available from the Crater Lake Natural History Association, Crater Lake 97604; *Along Crater Lake Roads*, Rukle, $1; *Ancient Tribes of the Klamath Country*, Howe, $5.95; *Birds of Crater Lake*, Farner, $2,50; *Crater Lake National Park*, Spring, $2.95; *Crater Lake: Story of its Origin*, Williams, $2; *Wildlife and Plants of the Cascades*, Yocum and Brown, $4.95. *Exploring Crater Lake Country* by Ruth Kirk, $4.95, is an excellent guide to the park's ancient geologic history, forests, wild flowers, wildlife, the Klamath Indians, settlement days and the Modoc War, the Rim Drive, boating, hikes, and trips beyond the park's boundaries.

The park is reached via Oregon 62 off U.S. 97 and via Oregon 62 off Interstate 5.

Lodges

★★★*Crater Lake Lodge* is a sprawling, old-fashioned inn overlooking Oregon's spectacular Crater lake and surrounded by natural parkland. The handsome shingle and stone lodge boasts 80 attractive rooms, a spacious lobby, big fireplace, rustic cocktail bar, and main dining room. A separate building houses a cafeteria and formal dining room with beautiful views of the lake. Also available in the summer are sleeping cottages ($14 per day double) and fully equipped Ponderosa cottages ($23 per day double). Rates for lodge rooms are $24–27 per day, double occupancy. Many rooms overlook the lake. Popular activities at the lodge include hiking along the park's system of marked trails, launch tours of the lake to Wizard Island, and auto tours along the Rim Drive, a 33–mile route circling the Caldera's edge. Evenings are filled with programs by National Park Service naturalists and special entertainments given by the lodge crew. For more information write: Crater Lake Lodge, Crater Lake, OR 97604 (503)594–2511.

High Cascades—Deschutes National Forest

The 1,588,000–acre Deschutes National Forest is located on the eastern slope of the southern Cascades in one of the great fishing regions of the Pacific Northwest and encompasses the headwaters of the Metolius and Deschutes rivers. Within this great forest rises Newberry Crater, an extinct volcano with cinder cores, boiling sulfur springs, fields of yellow and black and red obsidian glass, and blue mountain lakes. The name Deschutes derives from the fur-trading era, when the river was known as *Rivière des Chutes*, meaning "river of falls."

Information Sources, Maps & Access

The major features of the forest, including forest roads, trails, campgrounds, ranger stations, and portions of the Mt. Jefferson, Three Sisters, Mt. Washington, and Diamond Peak wilderness areas, are shown on the *Deschutes National Forest Map*, available for 50¢ from: Forest Supervisor, 211 Northeast Revere, Bend 97701 (503)382–6922. The full-color *Three Sisters Wilderness Map*, showing all topographic features, forest service trails, shelters, campsites, ranger stations, woodlands, and the Pacific Crest National Scenic Trail, may also be obtained for 50¢ by writing to the forest supervisor's office. For detailed hunting, fishing, and wilderness camping info write: Sisters Ranger Station, Sisters 97759. The full-color *Diamond Peak Wilderness Map* (50¢) and trail, mountain climbing, wilderness camping, fishing, and hunting information may be obtained by writing: District Ranger, Crescent Ranger Station, Crescent 97733. For additional information about fishing and hunting, campgrounds, and wilderness permits and trails, and for the free publications *Deschutes National Forest Fishing Directory* and *Hunting in the Deschutes National Forest*, write to the supervisor's office (address above). The fishing directory contains useful info about the forest's alpine fly-fishing lakes, big-water lakes, rivers and streams, and reservoirs, including location, route of access, elevation, size, depth, and fish species present.

The Deschutes National Forest is reached via U.S. Highways 20 and 97 and Oregon Highways 31, 51, 58, 126, 22, and 242. The Diamond Peak Wilderness can be reached from the Willamette Valley or central Oregon via the Willamette Highway (58) or forest roads. The Three Sisters Wilderness is accessible by the Willamette Highway, Oregon Highway 126, and forest roads. Lodging, supplies, guides, and wilderness outfitting service are available at Crescent, Crescent Lake, La Pine, Sunriver, Bend, Redmond, and Sisters.

Recreation Areas

Diamond Peak Wilderness

The Diamond Peak Wilderness area embraces 35,400 acres astride the Cascade Crest in the southwestern portion of the forest, due west of scenic Odell and Crescent lakes. The major features of the wilderness include Summit Lake, the Calapooya Mountains, and the Pacific Crest, Crater Butte, Diamond Peak, Bear Mountain, and Fawn Lake trails. Diamond Peak, elevation 8,744 feet, is considered one of Oregon's ten major peaks by mountain climbers. Climbers should always travel in organized groups, fully equipped and under the leadership of competent and experienced guides.

Three Sisters Wilderness

The Three Sisters Wilderness is a vast, 196,708–acre preserve located astride the High Cascades in the Willamette and Deschutes national forests about 45 miles due east of Eugene. The popular South Sister nestles a crystal clear lake in a crater at 10,200 feet. The Three Sisters have fourteen glaciers on their slopes, including the massive 1½–mile-wide and ¾–mile-long Collier Glacier, the largest in Oregon. If you think you are seeing smoke clouds at the high elevations, they are most likely pulverized rock blown off the glaciers by the strong winds. Numerous trails lead into the interior camping areas near the Husband (7,520 ft.), Broken Top (9,165 ft.), Wife (7,045 ft.), and Little Brother (7,822 ft.), passing through lava fields, glaciers, meadows, high forests of fir and mountain hemlock, and along the shores of hundreds of mountain lakes and ponds. The trail network contains over 50 miles of the Pacific Crest Trail.

For the alpine fisherman, three chains of lakes lie off the western slope of the wilderness: Mink Lake Basin, the Horse Lake group, and the Sisters Mirror group. Mink Lake is the largest—350 acres of water lying at 6,000–feet elevation near the headwaters of the McKenzie River.

Pacific Crest Trail

A network of over 400 miles of trails leads off to the remote interior areas, including the Pacific Crest Trail as it winds past Mt. Jefferson, Three-Fingered Jack, and Mt. Washington, through the Belknap lava fields, and on past the Three Sisters into the alpine lake country. The Deschutes River, a renowned canoe route and one of the most famous trout streams in the region, rises in the lava lakes and flows south for 85 miles through Crane Prairie and Wickiup reservoirs. The upper Deschutes has some excellent fly-fishing for good-sized rainbows and browns. In some areas the river flows through private ranches, and permission should be obtained.

Gateways & Accommodations

Bend

(Pop. 13,700; zip code 97701; area code 503.) A gateway to the Deschutes National Forest, this attractive town of well-planned streets and wooded parks is surrounded by some of the state's finest natural recreation areas. A graceful curve of the Deschutes River—from which the town takes its name—sweeps through the heart of Bend. The Cascade Lakes Highway, a scenic 76–mile drive, runs southwest from Bend through the national forest, past Elk Lake and the Crane Prairie Reservoir, to Pringle Falls. There are three fine state parks within a 12–mile radius, including Lava River Caves State Park (south of Bend on U.S. Hwy. 97) with its mile-long lava tunnel. The Mt. Bachelor Ski Area, 22 miles southwest on the Cascade Lakes Highway, has excellent ski facilities and incredible views of area lakes and the Cascade Range. Two district ranger's offices of the national forest are located in Bend. Accommodations: *Best Western Entrada Lodge* (rates: $30 double), 19 excellent rooms with queen-sized beds and color TV, on quiet wooded grounds, heated pool, sauna, putting green, ski package plans available, 4 miles west of Bend on Century Drive, Box 975 (382–4080); *Red Lion Motel* (rates: $29–40 double), 75 excellent rooms with oversize beds, heated pool, restaurant adjacent, at 849 N.E. 3rd St., ½ mile east of town on U.S. Hwy. 97 (382–8384); *Riverhouse Motor Inn* (rates: $28–30 double), 93 excellent rooms with oversize beds, balconies or patios, scenic riverfront location, heated pool, saunas, whirlpool, restaurant and cocktail lounge, at 3075 N.W. Hwy. 97, 1 mile north of Bend (389–3111); *Thunderbird Motel* (rates: $28–35 double), 76 superlative rooms with color TV and oversize beds, 3 two–room units, heated pool, saunas, restaurant adjacent, at 1415 N.E. 3rd St., ½ mile east of town on U.S. Hwy. 20 (382–7011).

Crescent

(Pop. 900; zip code 97733; area code 503.) The site of an old stagecoach station, Crescent is surrounded by Deschutes National Forest. A district ranger's office is located here. Accommodations: *Woodsman Motel* (rates: $20–22 double), 13 rooms with queen-size beds, on the Deschutes River, color TV, playground, kitchen unit, restaurant adjacent, on U.S. Hwy. 97, 10 miles north of Oregon State Hwy. 58 junction (433–2710).

Redmond

(Pop. 3,700; zip code 97756; area code 503.) The town lies almost midway between the Ochoco and Willamette national forests. Just a few miles south on U.S. 97 is the Deschutes National Forest; a district ranger's office is located in town. Local points of interest include Petersen's Rock Gardens, 7 miles south off U.S. 97 (open daily); Smith Rock State Park, 7 miles northeast of town off U.S. 97, 605 acres with colorful cliffs above the Crooked River; and Clive Falls State Park, 4 miles west on U.S. 126, on the banks of the Deschutes River. Accommodations: *86 Corral Motel* (rates: $23–25 double), 36 comfortable rooms, many with queen-size beds, color TV, 2 two-room units, restaurant adjacent, at 517 W. Birch Ave., ¼ mile north of town on U.S. 97 (548–4591); *Village Squire Motel* (rates: $22–25 double), 24 air-conditioned rooms, color TV, near city park and pool, free airport transportation, at 629 S. 5th St., 1 block south on U.S. 97 (548–2105).

Sisters

(Pop. 500; zip code 97759; area code 503.) Gateway to the Deschutes National Forest, Sisters is named for the snowcapped Three Sisters Mountains just south of town. Accommodations: *Sisters Motor Lodge* (rates $16–18 double), 9 rooms, 3 with kitchens, excellent views, restaurant nearby, 2 blocks west at junction of Hwys. 126 and 20 (549–2551).

Lodges, Resorts & Ski Centers

Blue Lake Resort, in Deschutes National Forest, is perched on the shores of a gemlike body of water surrounded by towering evergreens. The resort's riding stables and pack station offer guided day trips in nearby wilderness preserves, pack trips, and short, guided scenic rides, such as the 1–hour tour around spectacular Blue Lake Crater Rim. For the fisherman, there are fighting rainbow trout just a short paddle from your doorstep. In wintertime the resort provides a snug base for cross-country and downhill skiers. In addition to many miles of marked and unmarked trails in the area, the Hoodoo Ski Bowl is just 11 miles away. Accommodations range from simple sleeping quarters with bath to 2–bedroom apartments for 6 or more guests. All units have picture windows with fine views, and most feature kitchens, fireplaces, and patios or decks facing Blue Lake and the mountains. Rates: $18–26 daily, double occupancy. Resort facilities also include a restaurant and a well-stocked grocery and tackle store. For more details write: Blue Lake Resort, Star Route, Sisters, OR 97759 (503)595–6671.

Cultus Lake Resort is located in the heart of the Deschutes National Forest and surrounded by untouched, primitive areas laced by streams and studded with beautiful lakes. Right at the lodge doorstep is 1,200–acre Cultus Lake, famous for its rainbow trout and giant Mackinaw, up to 36 inches. Swimming and boating are excellent too. A nearby marina offers motorboat and canoe rentals. The lodge boasts its own fine strip of sandy beach, plus a flower-bordered deck perfect for sunbathing. The handsome, pine-paneled cabins have large fireplaces, modern plumbing, and picture windows. The central lodge building features a good restaurant, bar, coffee shop, and grocery and tackle shop. Daily rates: $20–22 for 2, $31 for 4. Additional guests in each cabin are $2 per person daily. The resort is open from mid-May to mid-October. For more information write: Cultus Lake Resort, Box 262, Bend, OR 97701 (503)977–3903; in winter (503)382–2494.

Mt. Bachelor Ski Area & Lodges. Surrounded by the wintry wilderness of the Deschutes National Forest, the Mt. Bachelor ski area is one of Oregon's finest cross-country and downhill ski meccas, offering trails for every level of expertise, open slopes, groomed bowls; average crisp day temperatures of 26°; fabulous spring skiing with a 16–foot average snowpack. There's a full complement of services to make your ski vacation more enjoyable: an excellent ski school with group and private classes, 7 chair lifts, 2 ski and rental shops, a day-care center, 3 fine day lodges boasting a variety of restaurants, and a

recreational race program for intermediate, advanced, and expert skiers. There's also a separate Nordic Sports Center with its own lodge, sports shop, rental service, special tours, and instructional facilities. Groomed cross-country trails include touring trails and a separate training and race course. All trails are machine-packed, double-tracked, well signed, and patrolled daily. Touring buffs will also appreciate the untracked slopes and trails of the national forest, a quiet alpine paradise ringed by the snow-blanketed mountains of the Sisters Wilderness. The entire area is served by a number of fine motor inns and lodges, including the following.

★★★*The Riverhouse Motor Inn* is located on the beautiful Deschutes River, convenient to downtown Bend, and offers 93 modern guest rooms with king, queen, and water beds. A restaurant and lounge offer fine dining and entertainment. Facilities include a 24–hour Sambo's pancake house, ski wax room, saunas, barber shop, beauty shop, and shuttle service to the ski bus. Packages include one ski lesson per person and a book of discount tickets. Midweek, 3–night rates: $64 per person. Standard 4– and 6–night package rates: $86 and $125 per person (lodging only, based on double occupancy).

★★★*The Cascade Lodge*, on Highway 27 in Bend, has 29 nicely appointed, large, quiet rooms with queen-size beds, color TV, phones, and free first-run movies in rooms. Handsomely landscaped grounds encompass a big swimming pool and professional putting green. Several choice restaurants are in the immediate vicinity. Midweek 3–day package rates: $58 per person. Standard 4– and 6–day rates: $78 and $115 per person (rates are double occupancy and include one free ski lesson and a book of discount tickets).

Bend Riverside, located near the city park and the Deschutes River, has 190 modern units, 100 of which have kitchens and fireplaces. All accommodations have private baths and color TV. Facilities include a covered swimming pool, tennis courts, sauna, and Jacuzzi. Fine restaurants are within walking distance. Midweek 3–day package rates: $64 per person. Standard 4– and 6–day and night rates: $85 and $125 per person (including one ski lesson and discount ticket book, based on double occupancy).

★★★*Mt. Bachelor Village*, bordering the Deschutes River on Century Drive, has 80 modern, completely furnished ski houses with kitchenettes. Other facilities include a heated pool, sauna, and tennis courts. Three Sisters Wilderness and Cascade Lakes are just a short drive away. Midweek 3–day package rates: $71 per person. Standard 4– and 6–day packages: $93 and $154 per person (based on double occupancy and including one free ski lesson, discount ticket book, and free continental breakfast).

★★*The Westward Ho Motel*, on Highway 97, has 54 well-equipped 1– and 2–room units with color TV, phones, radio, shower or combination baths. Also on the premises are a heated pool and Jacuzzi. The motel is surrounded by a fine variety of restaurants. Midweek 3–day package rates: $55 per person. Standard 4– and

6–day package rates: $74 and $105 per person (based on double occupancy and including one free ski lesson and a discount ticket book).

For more information on individual lodgings, additional packages and summer and nightly rates, write: Tour Marketing, 1123 S.W. Washington, Portland, OR 97205 (503)223–7355. For detailed literature on the Mt. Bachelor area, ski facilities, and listings of ski lodges, write: Mt. Bachelor, P.O. Box 828, Bend, OR 97701 (503)382–8334.

★★*Odell Lake Resort*, in the high lake country of Oregon's Cascades, offers fully equipped housekeeping cabins, lodge rooms, a full-fledged marina with rental boats and motors, tackle shop, and attractive restaurant. The lodge itself is surrounded by towering pine trees and perched on the edge of 6–mile-long Odell Lake, which offers great fishing in season for 25–40–pound Mackinaws, big rainbows, Dolly Varden, and Atlantic and blueback salmon. Boats are available for the excellent fly-fishing on nearby Davis and Gold lakes. Rates: $14–15 per day double occupancy for lodge rooms; $17–44 per day for housekeeping cabins with accommodations for 2–8 persons. For further information write: Odell Lake Resort, P.O. Box 72, Crescent Lake, OR 97425 (503)433–2540.

★★*Paulina Lake Resort*, a year-round family resort in Deschutes National Forest, has superb fishing for kokanee salmon and rainbow trout in 1,300–acre Paulina Lake, which also boasts good angling for big German brown trout (the state record—35½ lbs.—was taken from this lake). Hiking is another favorite pastime; there are trails around the lake, to the summit of 8,000–foot Paulina Peak, and through the national forest. In winter the resort offers snowmobiling and cross-country skiing over miles of challenging trails and across untrammeled open meadows. Accommodations are in rustic log cabins with completely equipped kitchens and full bath facilities. Several have fireplaces, covered porches, and pleasant views of the lake. Rates: $20–35 daily for 2–4 guests; larger cabins accommodate up to 8 guests ($2 extra for each additional person over 4). Paulina Lake Resort also has tent-cabins equipped with wood cookstoves, 2 double beds, and communal rest rooms. You must bring your own linens, dishes, pots, and pans ($10–12 daily for 4 guests). Resort facilities include a well-stocked general store, fine restaurant, and complete line of boat rentals. For additional information write: Paulina Lake Resort, P.O. Box 7, La Pine, OR 97739 (503)536–2246.

★★★★*Sun River Lodge & Ski Touring Center*, located 15 miles south of Bend, is flanked by the peaks of the Cascade Range on the west and the Paulina Range on the east. The alpine lakes, meadows, streams, and trails of the sprawling Deschutes National Forest surround Sun River on three sides. This superb Pacific Northwest year-round lodge and resort complex offers outstanding fishing for brook, rainbow, and brown trout up to trophy weights in the wild and scenic Deschutes River, which borders Sun River for 8½ miles, and in the hundreds of high-country lakes of the Cascade Range; skiing at nearby Mt. Bachelor, with daily transportation on the Sun River Ski Bus; cross-country ski touring along the 200 miles of high country in the Deschutes Forest with guided tours to Broken Top Volcano; trail riding from the Sun River stables; tennis on 14 paved courts (rental equipment available); swimming in heated Olympic-size pool and connecting diving pool; boating, hiking, backpacking; and golf on the Sun River 18–hole championship golf course, with PGA professional instruction and rentals. Sun River Lodge accommodations consist of spacious, attractive 1–bedroom units, housekeeping suites, 1–3–bedroom lodge condominiums constructed of natural wood and stone with fireplaces, and family-sized suites with kitchens, spacious living and dining areas, and loft bedrooms. Lodge dining facilities include the elegant Sun River Dining Room; the Potter's Wheel for breakfasts, lunches, and informal dinners; Owl's Nest Lounge, with a towering fireplace, live music, and dancing; the Wagon Wheel outdoor barbecue; Tree House Pizza Parlor, the Deli, and the Dough Factory, for Old World pastries and coffee. Daily rates (double occupancy): $42–65. Outdoor playground, movies, and baby-sitting services available for children. Sun River also offers one of the best private airports in the United States. Hughes Airwest offers daily jet flights to Redmond (33 miles north of Sun River) from Portland, Los Angeles, and San Francisco. Ground transportation to the lodge is available. The lodge is reached by auto via U.S. Highway 97. Contact: Sun River Lodge, Sun River, OR 97701 (503)593–1246.

★★★★*The Inn of the Seventh Mountain*, the nearest lodge to the Mt. Bachelor ski area in central Oregon, is a luxurious vacation complex offering a wide variety of accommodations and creature comforts. The surrounding wilderness of Deschutes National Forest and Mt. Bachelor itself provide superlative downhill and cross-country skiing. The inn has its own ski clinic, a full line of rental equipment, and year-round skating rink, plus a heated pool and saunas for unwinding after a day on the slopes. In the spring there's tennis, too, while Mt. Bachelor skiing continues through Memorial Day. Accommodations range from standard lodge rooms with queen-size beds and deluxe rooms with private balconies to self-contained studio units and 1– or 2–bedroom family suites, with fireplaces, full kitchens, color TV, private baths, and balconies. Nightly rates: $30 (double occupancy) for lodge rooms, $40 (double occupancy) for studios, and $60–112 for 1–3–bedroom suites. Midweek and comprehensive ski packages are also available. An extra attraction of the inn is the restaurant and lounge, open all day and evening, serving excellent food in handsome surroundings. Nightly entertainment, including free movies, is featured in the lounge. For additional information write: The Inn of the Seventh Mountain, P.O. Box 1207, Bend, OR 97701 (503)382–8711 or toll-free in Oregon (800)452–6810.

Travel Services

Deschutes Guide Service, Inc., offers state-licensed guides for 1–2–day float trips on Oregon's beautiful Deschutes River. One-day expeditions explore the river from Warm Springs to Trout Creek (2 people per boat, $60 each); 2–day trips follow the Deschutes from Trout Creek to Maupin (2 people per boat, $190 each). Summer and fall steelhead fishing and day-long jet boat trips on the lower river from Macks Canyon to Kloan are also available. Food and shelter are provided on all overnight trips. For additional details write: Deschutes Guide Service, Inc., South Main St., Madras, OR 97741.

High Cascades—Mt. Hood National Forest

The Mt. Hood National Forest, with a total of 1,118,000 acres, sweeps in a vast panorama of snowcapped peaks and evergreen forests, rivers and lakes and cascades, from the banks of the Columbia River almost to the white bulk of Mt. Jefferson, more than 100 miles south of the forest's northern boundary. Mt. Hood, the monarch of Oregon's High Cascades, towers over lesser mountains as it casts its long shadow across dense forests, deep ravines, alpine meadows, and lakes that reflect its splendor in their cold, tranquil depth. The headwaters of five rivers—Bull Run, Sandy, Clackamas, Hood, and White—are in the forest, and countless swift small trout streams race down the high-country slopes.

The forest encompasses some of Oregon's finest camping, fishing, and hunting areas. Hundreds of miles of forest roads and trails lead to interior areas such as the Fish Creek Divide, Firecamp Area, Jefferson Park, Olallie Meadows, Bull Run Lake, Salmon River, Columbia Gorge, and the Mt. Hood Wilderness.

The Pacific Crest Trail (also known as the Oregon Skyline Trail) winds south through the forest from the Columbia Gorge Work Center near Cascade Locks, past Wahtum Lake, and over Lolo Pass, and then skirts the west side of Mt. Hood to Timberline Lodge. From here it passes Bird Butte, Little Crater, and Timothy lakes as it meanders south and west between the forest and the Warm Springs Indian Reservation. The trail continues on through the high lake country and enters the Mt. Jefferson Wilderness at Breitenbush Lake, from where it winds southward into the Willamette National Forest.

The scenic Mt. Hood Wilderness, one of Oregon's most popular recreation areas, encompasses 14,160 acres of fragrant pine forests, alpine lakes, meadows, and wild streams, in the Zigzag Ranger District of the forest. The wilderness is dominated by the perpetually snowcapped peak of 11,245–foot Mt. Hood, the state's highest mountain. North of Crater Rock, numerous mountain fissures still emit steam and hydrogen sulfide gas. On clear and windless days, these gas emissions, or fumaroles, are visible from as far away as Portland. Numerous glaciers, such as the Zigzag, White River, Newton Clark, Eliot, Coe, Ladd, and Reid glaciers, cling to its precipitous slopes. Below Mt. Hood's towering bulk, numerous trails lead through alpine and forested areas to such points as Crater Rock, Devils Kitchen, the Chimney, Cooper Spur, Langille Crags, Mississippi Head, Hot Rocks, Pinnacle Ridge, and Vista Ridge. The Timberline

Trail is a relatively 37.6–mile route that weaves clear around Mt. Hood. Several stone shelters with corrugated iron roofs unique to the wilderness were built during the construction of the Timberline Trail by the Civilian Conservation Corps over 30 years ago.

The large, 300,000–acre Warm Springs Indian Reservation lies adjacent to the eastern boundary of the national forest. The remote backcountry of the reservation contains some interesting fishing waters. On the western boundary, the High Cascade lakes of the Mill Creek area, north of the Mt. Jefferson Wilderness, lie clustered in a circle around Olallie Butte (7,215 ft.). These lakes provide good fishing for rainbow, native cutthroat, and brook trout. Access to the high lakes area is by trail and unpaved roads. Fishing permits are required and are available from the Office of the Confederated Tribes of the Warm Springs Reservation, Warm Springs 97761. Lake Simtustus, formed by the damming of the Deschutes River above Warm Springs, is located along the eastern edge of the reservation and has good fishing for rainbows, Dolly Varden, and an occasional Deschutes River steelhead passing through the lake. Lake Billy Chinook, just north of Lake Simtustus, is in the form of three huge sprawling arms, formed by the damming of the Crooked, Metolius, and Deschutes rivers.

The famed Metolius River, one of Oregon's classic dry fly streams, heads in the springs on the east slope of the High Cascades under the lee of Three-Fingered Jack and flows along the southern boundary of the reservation. Fishing is most productive along the upper fly-fishing-only stretches for rainbows and an occasional lunker Dolly Varden. Sections of the lower stream are inaccessible along the canyon in the Metolius Breaks area.

Information Sources, Maps & Access

For vacation travel and recreation information, a full-color *Mt. Hood National Forest Map* (50¢), *Mt. Hood Wilderness Topographic Map* (50¢), and a *Forest Trails of the Columbia Gorge Map* (50¢), contact: Supervisor, Mt. Hood National Forest, P.O. Box 16040, Portland, OR 97216 (503)667–0511.

Mt. Hood National Forest and the Columbia Gorge area are reached via scenic Interstate 80N, U.S. Highway 26, and Oregon Highways 224 and 35. Lodging, supplies, guides, and outfitting services are available at Government Camp, Rhododendron, Zigzag, Mt. Hood, Bull Run, Cascade Locks, Eagle Creek, Estacada, Hood River, Odell, Dee, Bonneville, Bridal Veil, Multnomah Falls, and The Dalles.

Gateways & Accommodations

The Dalles

(Pop. 10,400; zip code 97058; area code 503.) This city was named by French voyageurs of the Hudson's Bay Company, who noted a resemblance between the basalt-lined channels of the Columbia River and the flagstones (*les dalles*) of their native village streets. The channels, as well as the falls and rapids which once made the river above the Dalles unnavigable, have been submerged under backwater of the Columbia River dams. The Dalles Dam, a major link in the development of the river, is located at the eastern edge of town. Train tours of the fish ladder, power-house, and locks are offered daily mid-May to mid-September between 10 A.M. and 5 P.M. Other points of interest include the Fort Dalles Museum at 15th and Garrison Sts., containing rare and unusual exhibits of pioneer life, and St. Peters Landmark, a red brick Gothic church with a 146–foot steeple and a wooden Madonna carved from the keel of a ship. The Dalles is a key outfitting point for Mt. Hood National Forest. Accommodations: *Portage Inn* (rates: $27–29 double), 78 excellent rooms and suites, oversize beds, some balconies, color TV, heated pool, free airport pickup, dining room and cocktail lounge, at 3223 N.E. Frontage Road, 2½ miles east of town at the junction of Interstate 80N and U.S. 197 (298–5502); *Tillicum Motor Inn* (rates: $19–21 double), 85 fine rooms, 18 with kitchens, color TV, heated pool, 24–hour restaurant, free airport pickup, at 2114 W. Sixth St., off Interstate 80N, exits 82 and 83 (298–5161).

Hood River

(Pop. 4,000; zip code 97031; area code 503.) This gateway to Mt. Hood National Forest is a quiet and attractive town laid out on steep terraces along the Columbia River between Hood River and Indian Creek gorges. Mt. Hood, Oregon's highest peak at 11,245 feet, is visible from all parts of the town and reached via the Loop Highway circling the eastern shoulder of the mountain, 18 miles south of town off Oregon State Hwy. 35. Just south of town is Panorama Point, which offers fine views of the Hood River valley. Accommodations: *Hood River Inn* (rates: $32–34 double), 64 excellent air-conditioned rooms, 32 with private patios overlooking the Columbia River, heated pool, deck, playground, restaurant, cocktail lounge, in Hood River Village, ½ mile northeast of town (386–2200); *Meredith Motel* (rates: $18–24 double), 21 air-conditioned rooms with views of the Columbia River, color TV, free coffee in rooms, at 4300 Westcliff Drive, 1½ miles west of town, just off Interstate 80, Exit 62 (386–1515).

Portland—Gateway to the Columbia Gorge & Mt. Hood

(Pop. 382,600; zip code, see below; area code 503.) The Beaver State's largest city and commercial center, Portland occupies both banks of the Willamette River near its mouth on the Columbia and is flanked on the east and north by the snowcapped peaks of Mt. St. Helens, Mt. Adams, and Mt. Hood and the scenic Columbia River gorge. This attractive, modern city, often referred to as the City of Roses, is the headquarters of the Mt. Hood National Forest and a popular gateway to the spectacular High Cascade wilderness fishing, hunting, camping, and skiing areas. Area attractions include the scenic Columbia River Highway and Mt. Hood Loop Highway; Portland City Park system, including Forest Park, a 7,000–acre wilderness park minutes from the city center; Washington Park Zoo,

west on Canyon Road; Pendleton Woolen Mills tours at 10505 S.E. 17th St., 6 miles south of Portland in Milwaukee (654–0444); and the Western Forestry Center with exhibits at 4033 S.W. Canyon Road. Accommodations: (Airport) *Sheraton Inn—Portland Airport* (rates: $45 double), 217 excellent rooms and suites, Northwoods restaurant, coffee shop, cocktail lounge, heated pool, adjacent to Portland International Airport (288–7171). (Downtown area) *Benson Hotel* (rates: $44–64 double), 330 outstanding rooms and suites, London Grill and Trader Vic's restaurants, cocktail lounges, at 309 S.W. Broadway at Oak, 97205 (228–9611); *Holiday Inn* (rates $32.75 double), 184 excellent rooms and suites, restaurant, cocktail lounge, at 10 N. Weidler St., 97227 (234–9881); *Portland Hilton Hotel* (rates: $54–76 double), 460 excellent rooms and suites, Canlis' Restaurant, coffee shop, cocktail lounges, heated pool, sauna, at 921 S.W. 6th Ave. (226–1611); *Portland Motor Hotel* (rates: $36 double), superb rooms, restaurant, coffee shop, cocktail lounge, heated pool, at 1414 S.W. 6th Ave. downtown, off 1–5 City Center Route (221–1611); *Ramada Inn* (rates: $31–32 double), 100 excellent rooms and family units, restaurant, coffee shop, cocktail lounge, heated pool, 9 miles south off 1–15, Tualatin Exit, at 7125 S.W. Nyberg Road, 97062 (638–4141); *Red Lion Motor Inn* (rates: $41–47 double), 240 outstanding rooms and suites, restaurant, dining room, cocktail lounge, heated pool, at 310 S.W. Lincoln, 97201, off 1–5, 4th Ave. Exit (221–0450); *Sheraton Hotel* (rates: $40–47 double), 300 excellent rooms and suites, dining room, Islands of Kon-Tiki Restaurant, coffee shop, cocktail lounge, heated pool, at 1000 N.E. Multnomah St., 97232, off 1–80N, Coliseum-Lloyd Center Exit (288–6111).

Lodges & Resorts

★★*Ford's Metolius River Cottages*, located on one of Oregon's premier fly-fishing streams, are within easy hiking or driving distance of the area's impressive forests and mountain lakes. Cottages range in size from deluxe sleeping rooms to spacious 2–bedroom cabins and all are fully equipped for housekeeping with a few extras thrown in: electric skillets, coffee makers, and toasters. Within the Metolius River area there are many opportunities for water sports, lake fishing, and horseback riding. Cottage rates vary from $19 per day (2 persons) for 1–room units to $29 per day (1–4 persons) for the big Log House. Season runs from April 20 to October 25. For further details write: Ford's Metolius River Cottages, Camp Sherman, OR 97730 (503)595–6290.

★★★★*Kah-Nee-Ta Vacation Resort* is located in a lush valley laced by the crystal waters of the Warm Springs River just 114 miles from Portland. The surrounding 630,000 acres—a wilderness of strange rock formations, canyons, and caves—are owned by the Confederated Tribes of the Warm Springs Reservation. In keeping with native atmosphere, the resort complex offers huge tepees for family camping in addition to luxurious lodge accommodations and 1– or 2–bedroom cottages. Resort facilities include an enormous swimming pool, mineral baths, a handsome restaurant and snack bar, an 18–hole golf course 1 mile away, convention facilities, and opportunities for horseback riding and tennis. Guest rooms in the lodge have attractive furnishings, private decks, dressing areas, and color TV. Daily summer rates: $35–65 (double occupancy) for cottages; $15 per day for tepees. For more information write: Kah-Nee-Ta Vacation Resort, Warm Springs, OR 97761 (503)553–1112; toll-free inside Oregon (800)452–1138.

★★★★*Timberline Lodge*, a fabulous stone alpine chalet situated at a base elevation of 6,000 feet on the south side of Mt. Hood, is the Northwest's premier ski resort, offering deluxe accommodations and outstanding year-round alpine and cross-country skiing. During the High Cascade summer Timberline offers skiing, mountaineering,

tennis, and golf at Bowman's Mt. Hood Golf Resort. Summer temperatures on Mt. Hood vary from below freezing to 90°. Be prepared for extremes when planning long hikes, skiing, or climbing. At the Timberline Ski Complex, the new Palmer Snow Field 1¼–mile double chair-lift, with a vertical rise of 1,700 feet, offers some of the most spectacular and exhilarating skiing anywhere in the world. The Timberline Ski School, directed by Bud Nash, offers expert instruction by experienced professionals. The lodge also offers intermediate through advanced ski touring in Mt. Hood National Forest. The trails in the government camp area at a base elevation of 4,000 feet offer plenty of scenic terrain for the beginner and intermediate skier. Nordic instruction is available through the ski school. Timberline accommodations range from rustic chalet rooms—with bunk rooms, sink, and hall bathroom—to spacious deluxe fireplace rooms, with wood-paneled walls, hand-hooked rugs, and alpine decor. Daily rates (double occupancy): $18–55. Delightful dining and continental cuisine is available at the Cascade Dining Room or the informal, cafeteria-style Ski Deli. Timberline also has a supervised children's playroom for toddlers from 2 to 8. Skiing and mountaineering rentals are available at the ski shop. For additional information and a free 6–page brochure describing the Timberline Trail system, contact: Timberline Lodge, Government Camp, OR 97028 (503)272–3311.

High Cascades—Willamette National Forest

The wilderness camping, fishing, and hunting areas of the 1.6 million-acre Willamette National Forest stretch for 110 miles along the western slope of the Cascade Range in northwest Oregon between the Mt. Hood National Forest on the north and the Umpqua National Forest on the south. The Willamette, the largest of Oregon's national forests, embraces several of the highest peaks in the cascades; Mt. Jefferson, Mt. Washington, and Three-Fingered Jack tower above luxuriant growths of Douglas fir. The world-famous trout and steelhead waters of the McKenzie, Santiam, Calapooya, and Blue rivers rise among the forest's highlands, and, with their tributaries, spread a network of scenic waterways throughout the entire region.

Information Sources, Maps & Access

The full-color U.S. Forest Service *Willamette National Forest Map* shows all forest service trails, Pacific Crest National Scenic Trail, logging roads, recreation and boat-launching sites, campgrounds, and major features, including the Quaking Aspen Swamp Botanical Area, Rebel Rock Geological Area, Lamb Butte Scenic Areas, the Willamette and McKenzie rivers, and the Three Sisters, Diamond Peak, Mt. Jefferson, and Mt. Washington wilderness areas. This map may be obtained for 50¢ along with the free 56–page booklet *The Forest by Road & Highway: A Motorist's Guide to the Willamette Trails—A Hiker's Guide*, by writing: Supervisor, Willamette National Forest, P.O. Box 1272, Eugene 97401 (503)687–6533. The full-color *Mt. Washington Wilderness Topographic Map* (50¢), *Mt. Jefferson Wilderness Topographic Map* (50¢), and the free *McKenzie River Trail Guide* and *Waldo Lake Recreation Area Map* may also be ordered direct from the forest supervisor's office.

The Willamette National Forest and wilderness areas are reached via U.S. Highways 20 and 97, Oregon Highways 22, 126, and 242, and forest roads. Lodging, supplies, wilderness outfitters, and guide service are available at McKenzie Bridge, Blue River, Rainbow, Vida, Sisters, Oakridge, Sweet Home, and Eugene.

Recreation Areas

McKenzie Wild & Scenic River

From its headwaters in Clear Lake in the Three Sisters Wilderness, the famed McKenzie River, a former haunt of Zane Grey and one of the nation's historic trout streams, flows southeast through beautiful forest for 60 miles to its mouth just north of Eugene. The upper stretches of the river have some spectacular white water and excellent fishing for cutthroats and the native McKenzie rainbows, known as redsides. No one should attempt to float the treacherous upper stretches without the services of a licensed guide. For information write to the *Mackenzie Guide Association*, Vida 97488. Several forest camps and state park campgrounds are located along the upper stretches of the river. The McKenzie's Clear Lake headwaters lie in a depression 2,000 feet deep, and were formed by the damming of the old Santiam Valley by the great McKenzie lava flow. Fed by giant springs, the lake is the coldest in the Cascades and is of such crystal clearness that rocks can be easily seen on the bottom at depths of 40 feet.

Mt. Jefferson Wilderness

The Mt. Jefferson Wilderness, a famous mountaineering and camping area, encompasses 99,600 acres of volcanic plateau country in the Deschutes, Mt. Hood, and Willamette national forests. Mt. Jefferson (10,495 ft.) was named by Lewis and Clark in 1806 in honor of Thomas Jefferson. Both Mt. Jefferson and the adjacent Three-Fingered Jack, an eroded volcanic cone at 7,841 feet, provide challenges to the experienced climber on their spirelike peaks. Mt. Jefferson has five major glaciers and massive rock outcroppings and talus slopes. At the lower elevations, dense conifer forests of mountain hemlock and subalpine, silver, and noble fir cover the deposits of pumice and glacial debris. Glacial erosion has formed many U-shaped valleys, alpine meadows, lakes, and streams.

Mt. Washington Wilderness & the Belknap Crater

The 46,655–acre Mt. Washington Wilderness is located along the crest of the Oregon Cascades adjoining the Three Sisters Wilderness in the Willamette and Deschutes national forests. A desolate, remote country of great beauty, the area is dominated by 7,802–foot Mt. Washington, which rises sharply above the lava-strewn plains. Mt. Washington is a vivid example of a dissected volcano whose ancient ice flows denuded the summit, leaving only the most resistant lava

fillings. The area adjacent to Mt. Washington has experienced more recent volcanic activity than any other part of the Cascade Range. The lava sheet surrounding the Belknap Cones, commonly referred to as a black wilderness, is one of the largest in the United States. Belknap Crater, located near the center of the McKenzie lava field, is a cinder and ash cone built up to an elevation of 6,872 feet. The volcanoes of the Northwest, including those in the Mt. Washington area at McKenzie Pass, are part of the "circle of fire" that rims the Pacific Ocean. Seventy million years ago Oregon was covered by a shallow sea dotted with volcanic islands. As the sea gradually withdrew, the continent emerged in the form of volcanic eruptions, which spread vast flows of basaltic lava over eastern Oregon about 15 million years ago. The High Cascade peaks are less than 10 million years old, and the eruptions have continued almost to modern times. When hiking in the wilderness, don't attempt to walk on the lava flows, for the footholds are unstable and the rock is extremely sharp.

Pacific Crest Trail

Hundreds of miles of high-country trails and remote logging roads provide the wilderness traveler with access to such renowned hunting, fishing, and hiking areas as the Three Sisters Wilderness, Mt. Jefferson and Mt. Washington wilderness areas, and the Diamond Peak Wilderness; they pass through high mountain forests of alpine fir and hemlock and along steep ridges, glaciers, lava flows, rocky summits, and hundreds of mountain lakes and ponds. The Pacific Crest Trail enters the north part of the forest from the Wapinitia Pass area, winding south through the huckleberry fields of Olallie Meadows and on along the rough mountain terrain, to Breitenbush Lake Camp, Pamelia Lake, Minto and Santiam passes, McKenzie Pass, Sunshine Campsite, Horse Lake Forest Station, and beautiful lake country, with numerous spur trails leading off to Irish, Taylor, Waldo, Lily, Cultus, and Maiden lakes.

Gateways & Accommodations

Eugene

(Pop. 76,300; zip code, see below; area code 503.) Headquarters of the Willamette National Forest and home of the University of Oregon, Eugene is flanked on the east by the lakes, peaks, and meadows of the High Cascades and on the west by the Coast Range. It is a major jumping-off place for trips up into the High Cascade wilderness areas. Area attractions include the Lane County Pioneer Museum at 740 13th Ave. W.; Natural History Museum at the University of Oregon; Butler Museum of American Indian Art at 1155 W. 1st St., and fine dining at the Coburg Inn, a gas-lit dining room in a restored Victorian house built in 1877, 5 miles north of Eugene off 1–5, Coburg Exit, at 209 Willamette St. (484–0633). Accommodations: *Best Western New Oregon Motel* (rates: $28.50–30.50 double), 73 excellent rooms and family units, next to restaurant, heated pool, at 1655 Franklin Blvd. (683–3669); *Black Angus Motel—A Friendship Inn* (rates: $19–21 double), 114 excellent rooms and family units, restaurant, cocktail lounge, heated pool, at 2121 Franklin Blvd., 97403, 1½ miles south of town on Oregon 99 (342–1243); *Holiday Inn* (rates: $34 double), 148 excellent rooms, restaurant, coffee shop, cocktail lounge, indoor heated pool, sauna, 1 mile northeast of town at 225 Coburg Rd., 97401 (342–5181); *Thunderbird Red Lion Motor Inn* (rates $30–33 double), 138 excellent rooms, restaurant, coffee shop, cocktail lounge, heated pool, at 205 Coburg Road, 9740, 1 mile northeast of town at 1–105 and Coburg Road junction (342–5201); *Valley River Inn* (rates: $34–47 double), 259 superb rooms and family units, restaurant, cocktail

lounge, heated pool overlooking the Willamette River, on Valley River Center Way off 1–5, Santa Clara exit (687–0123).

McKenzie Bridge

(Pop. 100; zip code 97401; area code 503.) This gateway to the Willamette National Forest straddles the clear, spring-fed McKenzie River, long a favorite with fishermen. Area attractions include Cougar Dam and Lake, a 6–mile-long reservoir, with campgrounds, picnic areas, swimming, fishing, and waterskiing; and Blue River Dam and Lake in the Willamette National Forest, with fishing, boating, picnicking, and campgrounds. Accommodations: *Log Cabin Inn* (rates: $18 double), 8 rustic cabins, 2 with housekeeping facilities, with porches and fireplaces, fishing, restaurant, off U.S. Hwy. 126 near the river (822–3446); *Sleepy Hollow Motel* (rates: $19–21 double), 14 air-conditioned rooms with oversize beds, open May-October at 54791 McKenzie Hwy., off Oregon State Hwy. 126, in Blue River 97413 (822–3805).

Salem

(Pop. 68,300; zip code, see below; area code 503.) Oregon's capital and third-largest city is located in the Willamette Valley on Interstate 5. Area attractions include Bush Pasture Park and Bush Park Museum at 600 Mission St.; the State Capitol Bldg.; the Enchanted Forest, a family entertainment area featuring famous children's story characters, including Alice in Wonderland, Snow White and a haunted house, 7 miles south of Salem off 1–5 in Turner (363–3060). Accommodations: *Holiday Inn* (rates: $31.50 double), 110 excellent rooms, restaurant, cocktail lounge, heated pool, at 745 Commercial St. off 1–5, Mission St. Exit (363–2451); *Salem Inn* (rates: $23 double), 66 excellent rooms, restaurant, heated pool, west off 1–5, Market St. Exit, at 1855 Hawthorne St. NE, 97301 (581–9410).

High Cascades— Winema National Forest

Winema National Forest encompasses 909,000 acres among the snowcapped peaks, valleys, and mountain lakes of the beautiful southern Oregon Cascades. This region, one of Oregon's finest wilderness camping, fishing, and hunting areas, is named after the Indian wife of the trapper Frank Riddle, and means "woman of the brave heart," in honor of Winema's valient efforts during the Modoc Indian War of 1873 to save the lives of many pioneers. Today, more than half of the forest consists of former tribal lands of the Klamath Indians, located in Klamath County. Recorded history in the Klamath Basin began with the explorations of Hudson's Bay Company fur trader Peter Ogden in 1826.

The Pacific Crest Trail enters the forest as it winds its way south from Crater Lake National Park, passing along Fourmile Lake and Devils Peak (where the hiker may encounter summer snowdrifts) and traversing the Oregon Desert for 10 miles. Numerous spur trails provide access to remote streams, alpine lakes, peaks, and primitive campgrounds. Trail elevations range from 4,000 to 7,000 feet. South of the forest boundary, the trail passes through private lands, and it is not as well maintained or marked. The last leg of the trail passes Lake of the Woods, with campgrounds and excellent fishing, and heads for Copco Lake, about 2 miles south of the Oregon-California border.

Mountain Lakes Wilderness embraces 23,071 acres in the southern part of Winema National Forest and is renowned for its beautiful alpine lakes and timbered shorelines surrounded by high mountains. The area lies about 40 miles south of Crater Lake in a large glacial basin around which are eight prominent peaks, including Crater Lake is in a large glacial basin around which are eight prominent peaks, including Crater Mountain (7,785 ft.), Greylock Mountain (7,747 ft.), Aspen Butte (8,208 ft.), and Whiteface Peak (7,706 ft.). A loop-trail system leads up through a forest of pine and fir to the lakes.

Some of the finest waterfowl shooting in the Northwest is found in the area around the Upper Klamath Lake Refuge, which includes the Klamath Marsh, Williamson River, Agency Lake, and Klamath River. Upper Klamath Lake is Oregon's largest natural freshwater lake, fed by the drainage from the High Cascades around Crater Lake. It forms the headwaters of the Klamath River. The Williamson River, with its headwaters in the Klamath Forest National Wildlife Refuge, was once one of the nation's great trout streams, holding rainbows up to 15 and 20 pounds. Unfortunately, the Williamson has declined in recent years because of heavy fishing pressure and easy access. Agency Lake, near the north end of Upper Klamath Lake, is a large shallow marsh area famous for its teeming waterfowl and spring fishing for giant rainbows up to 12, 14, and 20 pounds, that pass through the lake to spawn in the Wood and Seven Mile rivers.

Information Sources, Maps & Access

For detailed information and a full-color *Winema National Forest Map* (50¢) and *Mountain Lakes Wilderness Map* (50¢) contact: Supervisor, Winema National Forest, P.O. Box 1390, Klamath Falls, OR 97601.

Winema National Forest and Crater Lake are reached via Interstate Highway 97 and Oregon Highways 62, 232, 138, and 58. Lodging,

supplies, guides, and outfitting service are available at Klamath Falls, Chiloquin, Beaver Marsh, Sprague River, Diamond Lake, and Chemult.

Gateways & Accommodations

Klamath Falls

(Pop. 15,800; zip code 97601; area code 503.) A popular outfitting center for visitors to Crater Lake National Park, the Winema National Forest, the Tomahawk Ski Bowl, and the area's numerous fishing lakes, the city is named for the Klamath Indian tribe and a series of rapids on the Link River (there are no falls in town). Area attractions include the Klamath County Museum at 1451 Main St., housing numerous exhibits of local history and geology; Upper Klamath Lake, just north of town and bordered for 28 miles by U.S. Hwy. 97, the largest body of fresh water in Oregon; the Klamath Basin National Wildlife Refuge, 15 miles south off U.S. 97, a 22,800–acre preserve for migratory waterfowl; and the Favell Museum of Western Art and Indian Artifacts, at 125 W. Main St., containing displays of contemporary western artists, a miniature firearms collection, pioneer relics, and Indian artifacts. Nearby lakes and rivers support small populations of rare white pelicans. Klamath Falls is headquarters for the Winema National Forest; a district ranger's office is located here. Accommodations: *Budget Host Inn* (rates: $21–24 double), 48 good rooms, heated pool, color TV, nearby restaurant, at 11 Main St., on U.S. 97 (882–4494); *Cimarron Motel* (rates: $18–23 double), 164 excellent rooms, many with queen-size beds, color TV, swimming pool, restaurant and bar, at 3060 S. 6th St., 1½ miles east of town on Oregon State Hwy. 140 (882–4601); *Klamath Falls Travelodge* (rates: $29 double), 48 fine rooms, many with queen-size beds, color TV, restaurant opposite, at 124 N. 2nd St. at Main, 3 blocks south on U.S. 97 (882–7741); *Molatare's Motel* (rates: $21–23 double), 98 comfortable rooms, color TV, heated pool, restaurant and cocktail lounge, at 100 Main St., on U.S. 97 (882–4666); *Thunderbird Motel* (rates: $28–32 double), 108 excellent and spacious rooms, some 2–room units, oversize beds, color TV, heated pool, free airport pickup, 24–hour restaurant adjacent, at 3612 S. 6th St., 2½ miles southeast of town on Oregon State Hwy. 140 (882–8864).

Lodges & Guest Ranches

★★*Rocky Point Resort*, located 28 miles northwest of Klamath Falls on Oregon's largest freshwater lake, offers good to excellent fishing for large rainbows, brown trout, and perch. Upper Klamath Lake is also situated on the Pacific flyway for ducks and geese and promises fine waterfowl hunting in season. Since the resort is bordered by a game refuge, your chances of seeing and photographing the regional wildlife are especially good. Modern, all-electric housekeeping cabins have 1 ($20 per night) and 2 bedrooms ($35 per night) with hide-a-beds in the living rooms. The coffee shop and dining room overlooking Pelican Bay specialize in good food at reasonable prices. Rocky Point's marina offers moorage and boat, motor, and canoe rentals. There's also a small grocery store with necessary staples. For information write: Rocky Point Resort, Harriman Road, Box 92, Klamath Falls, OR 97601 (503)356–2287.

★★★★*Take It Easy Ranch Resort* is located in the beautiful Wood River valley of the Winema National Forest, 8 miles from the south entrance of Crater Lake National Park. The ranch, which is set among unspoiled high country of alpine wild-flower meadows, mountains, and tall evergreens, caters to the fisherman, waterfowl hunter, and family vacationer. The three crystal-clear ranch streams and nearby high-country lakes and wilderness rivers offer outstanding fishing for rainbow, brown, and brook trout up to trophy weights. The ranch is on the main Pacific flyway and stopover for millions of ducks and geese (mostly mallards, pintails, Canadian geese, and some wood and canvasback ducks and speckled and lesser Canadian geese). There are also miles of backcountry horseback trails on both the ranch and national forest lands. Some of the attractions in the area for side trips include Crater Lake National Park, Collier State Park with its logging museum, Lava Beds National Monument, Fort Klamath Museum, and the Upper Klamath Lake Wildlife Refuge. Ranch facilities include new, well-appointed cabins and a rustic natural log main lodge with a dining room, huge stone fireplace, and lounge. Delicious meals are served family-style, including cookouts and on occasion picnic lunches. Daily American-plan rates: $44–48 per person all-inclusive. The ranch is reached via auto off Oregon Highway 62 on the way to Crater Lake, Commercial Air Service, Amtrak, Greyhound into Klamath Falls. For additional information, contact: Take It Easy Ranch, P.O. Box 408, Fort Klamath, OR 97626 (503)381–2328.

Malheur National Forest & Wildlife Refuge

The Malheur National Forest, an outstanding hunting, fishing, and wilderness camping region, encompasses 1,470,000 acres in the southwestern portion of the Blue Mountains and contains the headwaters of the Malheur, Silvies, and John Day rivers. Mule deer and Rocky Mountain elk range from the craggy peaks of the Strawberry Mountains to the sagebrush flats of the Oregon desert.

The famous Malheur Lake National Wildlife Refuge and the adjacent marsh areas are prime country for mallards, pintails, and Canada, crackling, snow, and white-fronted geese. Malheur Lake and the nearby alkaline waters of Harney Lake were discovered in 1826 by Peter Skene Ogden. Early settlers named them the Bitter Lakes. In 1908 the area was set aside by Pres. Theodore Roosevelt as a game and bird refuge. The Malheur River and its tributaries also have good shooting areas. Malheur Lake is an excellent trout fishery with limit catches, and fish to 4 and 5 pounds are not unusual. The upper stretches of the Middle Fork of the Malheur River, with headwaters in the Strawberry Mountain Wilderness, provide good fishing for rainbow trout.

The Strawberry Mountain Wilderness lies along a high east-west divide south of the John Day River, with Slide Mountain on the east and craggy Canyon Mountain on the west. In the interior, numerous trails lead to Strawberry Mountain (9,044 ft.), Strawberry Lake, Pine Creek Mountain, Indian Creek Butte, and Rabbit Ears. There are five lakes in the area, and fishing is fair in some for brook and rainbow trout. Mud Lake, though it has no fish, is of interest as an "aquatic pasture" in its final stages, getting shallower and shallower each year as it fills with mineral deposits. Access is limited by snowpack during all seasons except summer, when wild flowers and bushes cover the meadows and hillsides, and the trails lead through open forests of pine and fir. The wilderness derives its name, as do the mountain and lake, from a creek along which there is an abundance of wild strawberries, located at the northwest corner of the Canyon Creek area.

The rugged, massive bulk of Steens Mountain lies to the east of the Malheur Refuge and dominates the landscape for 50 miles, rising nearly a mile above the surrounding plateau. Steens Mountain is actually a range with snow-covered crests, slopes clothed with sparse grounds of juniper and sagebrush, and cataracts pouring through small canyons to the lowlands. The Steens is a top-ranked hunting area for mule deer and antelope. The range was named for Maj.

Enock Steen, head of a cavalry expedition that in 1860 drove a band of Snake Indians to the summit and then annihilated them.

The famous Hart Mountain National Antelope Range lies westward of Steens Mountain. The refuge contains about 200,000 acres of rugged mountain and plateau country, dominated by the Warner Mountains. The refuge contains the largest herd of antelope in the United States.

Information Sources, Maps & Access

For detailed information and a full-color *Malheur National Forest Map* (50¢) and a *Strawberry Mountain Wilderness Map & Trail Log* (50¢), write: Supervisor, Malheur National Forest, John Day, OR 97845 (503)575–1731.

The Malheur National Forest and Strawberry Mountain Wilderness are reached via U.S. Highways 20, 26, and 395 and Oregon Highway 7. Lodging, supplies, guides and outfitters are located at John Day, Canyon City, Silvies, Prairie City, Long Creek, Mt. Vernon, and Burns. Malheur National Wildlife Refuge is reached via state highways 78 and 205 and U.S. Highway 20. The Steens Mountain country is reached by all-weather roads off Oregon Highway 78. The Hart Mountain National Antelope Range is reached by unimproved roads off U.S. Highway 395 and Oregon Highway 140.

Gateways & Accommodations

Burns

(Pop. 3,300; zip code 97720; area code 503.) Named for the Scottish poet Robert Burns, this town was once the capital of the old cattle empire and still serves a trading area larger than some eastern states. The area is a favorite jumping-off point for rock hounds and visitors to the Malheur National Forest. A district ranger's office is located here. The Malheur National Wildlife Refuge, 32 miles southeast of town, encompasses 181,000 acres and supports some 220 species of waterfowl, birds, and deer (museum and observation pond open daily; phone 493–2323 for information). Accommodations: *Best Western Ponderosa Motel* (rates: $24–28 double), 52 fine air-conditioned rooms, 5 two-room units, color TV, heated pool, tennis courts, at 577 W. Monroe, ½ mile west of town on U.S. Hwy. 20 (573–2047); *Silver Spur Motel* (rates: $22–26 double), 26 comfortable rooms, color TV, free coffee, at 789 N. Broadway, 7 blocks north off junction of U.S. 395 and 20 (573–2077).

John Day

(Pop. 1,600; zip code 97845; area code 503.) Headquarters of the Malheur National Forest, John Day was named for a scout of the 1811 Astor overland expedition. Area attractions include the Herman and Eliza Oliver Historical Museum, 2 miles south of town on U.S. 395, comprising exhibits of Gold Rush days and the Joaquin Miller Cabin (closed Nov.-Mar.; open daily 9 A.M.–3 P.M. the rest of the year), and the John Day Fossil Beds National Monument, 41 miles west of town on U.S. Hwy. 26, containing fossil beds more than 30 million years old. The monument covers 14,400 acres in three noncontiguous units; information centers and exhibits are at the monument headquarters in John Day (420 W. Main St.) and the former Cant Ranch in the Sheep Rock Unit, 8 miles northwest of Dayville on Oregon State Hwy. 19. Accommodations: *Dreamers Lodge* (rates: $22–24 double), 23 fine rooms, nearby restaurant, color TV, free coffee in rooms, free golf privileges, in town at 144 N. Canyon Blvd. (575–0526); *Western Motel* (rates: $20–22 double), 14 rooms, some with oversize beds, TV, free coffee in rooms, free golf privileges, at 731 W. Main St. (575–1821).

Ochoco National Forest

Ochoco National Forest, a popular hunting, fishing, and camping area, encompasses 845,855 acres of the Ochoco Mountain foothills and the Crooked River grasslands located at the western end of the Blue Mountains in the geographic center of Oregon. The first explorers in this area were Peter Skene Ogden and his party of Hudson's Bay Company trappers in 1825. The best fishing in the forest is found in the Crooked River in the deep cold pools beneath the Prineville Reservoir Dam for rainbows around 3 pounds and an occasional fish up to 8 pounds. The Crooked River, a large tributary of the Deschutes River, heads in the Ochoco Mountains and flows west through the Prineville Reservoir and on into Billy Chinook Lake adjacent to the Warm Springs Indian Reservation. There is also fair to good early-season trout fishing in the Monks, Wolf, Ochoco, Emigrant, Rock, and Silver creeks. The Prineville Reservoir, bordered by range land, canyon areas, bluffs, and picturesque rock formations, is a steady producer of 8–12-inch rainbows.

Information Sources, Maps & Access

The major features of the region are shown on the *Ochoco National Forest Map*, available for 50¢ from: Forest Supervisor's Office, P.O. Box 490, Prineville 97754 (503)447–6247. This full-color map shows campgrounds, boat ramps, horse facilities, trails and logging roads, ranger stations, and rock-hound areas. The forest is a top rock-hound area and is shown and described on the *Central Oregon Rockhound Guide Map*, available free from the supervisor's office. Additional wilderness travel, fishing, hunting, and camping information may be obtained by writing to the forest supervisor.

Ochoco National Forest is reached via U.S. Highways 26, 395, and 20. Lodging, supplies, fishing and big-game hunting guides, and outfitters are available at Burns, Riley, Silvies, John Day, Mt. Vernon, Paulina, Prineville, and Dayville.

Gateways & Accommodations

Prineville

(Pop. 4,100; zip code 97754; area code 503.) This gateway to the Ochoco National Forest was named for its first settler, Barney Prine, who built the town's original log structures—a store, hotel, saloon, and blacksmith shop sharing a single roof—all in one day. The area around Prineville was the site of many heated confrontations between cattlemen and sheep raisers during the range wars of the 1870s. Today Prineville is an outfitting center for hunters, fishermen, vacation travelers, and rock hounds. Extensive agate beds are found

near here. There are two district rangers' offices of the Ochoco National Forest in town. Accommodations: *Best Western Ochoco Inn* (rates: $22–25 double), 34 comfortable rooms with queen-size beds, color TV, restaurant and cocktail lounge, golf privileges, at 123 E. 3rd St., off U.S. Hwy. 26 (447–6231); *Rustlers Roost* (rates: $20–23 double), 20 fine rooms, 10 with kitchens, attractive Old West decor, color TV, restaurant nearby, golf privileges, at 960 W. 3rd St., ½ mile west of town at junction of U.S. 26 and Oregon State Hwy. 126 (447–4185).

Oregon Coast—Siuslaw National Forest & the Oregon Dunes

The Siuslaw National Forest, with a total area of 620,000 acres, stretches along the Pacific Coast from Coos Bay north almost to Tillamook, and inland to the slopes of the Cascade Range. Broken into many portions, the forest embraces many of Oregon's most famous beach resorts and is characterized by its dense stands of Sitka spruce, hemlock, cedar, and Douglas fir, its mountains, and its large coastal salmon and steelhead streams and wild, log-strewn, and rocky headland beaches. The name Siuslaw was taken from a small tribe of Yakim Indians who lived along the coast; it means "faraway waters." This is top elk, black bear, and steelhead country. Remote forest roads and trails lead to the best hunting and fishing areas, such as the Mill Creek Divide, Elos Prairie, Cascade Head, Mt. Hebo, Marys Peak, and Tahenitch Lake.

The far-flung sand dunes, lakes, forests, and ocean beaches of the Oregon Dunes National Recreation Area extend for 40 miles along the Pacific Ocean from the Siuslaw River on the north to the Coos River on the south. At the widest point, the area extends inland approximately 2½ miles. The Oregon Dunes are the most extensive, spectacular dune landscape on the Pacific coast. The dunes are accessible in a few places, such as Cleawox Lake, Sitcoos, Winchester Bay, and Horsefall Beach. These and other access points are shown on the *Oregon Dunes National Recreation Area Map-Brochure*, available free from: Superintendent's Office, Reedsport, 97467. This map also shows campgrounds, recreation sites, trails, and boat ramps. When traveling across the open sand, hikers should be aware that rain, dense fog, and wind may erase footprints and cause you to lose your way. The forest growth bordering the dunes is dense and lush, and spotting your trail back to your point of origin can be extremely difficult.

The 9,000–acre Cascade Head Scenic Research Area, established in 1974, and the surrounding experimental Cascade Forest are on the Hebo Range District and embrace the 1,600–foot Cascade Head and the beautiful Salmon River estuary. Sea Lion Point, south of Yachats, is the only known mainland sea lion rookery in the world. The Sea Lion Caves, located far below the Oregon Coast Highway 101, are inhabited during the winter by a herd of about 300 sea lions. The herd is ruled by an old bull whose throne is the center rock in the main cavern, a chamber 1,500 feet long and colored green, pink,

and pale yellow. These huge Steller's sea lions found along the Oregon coast were named by Dr. Steller, a German scientist with the Russian expedition headed by the explorer Bering in 1741. During the summer months, they live on rocky islands off the coast of Alaska. They generally leave for the Oregon shore about the first of September.

The Fort Clatsop National Memorial, 4½ miles southwest of Astoria, marks the westernmost point of the territory explored by Meriwether Lewis and William Clark on their historic journey of 1804–1806. It was here that the Lewis and Clark party made camp for the winter on December 8, 1805, felling logs and constructing rude huts around an open square. In his journals, Clark recorded the meager festivities of that first Christmas in the Pacific Northwest: "I rcved. a present of Capt. L. of a fleece hosrie [hosiery] Shirt Draws and Socks, a pr. Mockersons of white weazils tails of the Indian woman, & some black root of the Indians. . . . The day proved showery wet and disagreeable . . . our Dinner concisted of pore Elk, so much spoiled that we eate it thro' mear necessity." The fort is named for the Clatsop Indians, who were regular and sometimes troublesome visitors. The party left Fort Clatsop and headed back east in late March of 1806. On the day of departure, Clark summed up their winter experience: "we . . . have lived as we had any right to expect, and we can say that we were never one day without three meals of some kind a day either pore Elk meat or roots. . . ." The National Memorial includes a reconstruction of the original log fort and a visitor center and museum with audiovisual programs recreating the history of the expedition. There are also replicas of the equipment and clothing of the original party. The Visitor Center is open daily from 8 A.M. to 8 P.M. mid-June to Labor Day, and from 8 A.M. to 5 P.M. the rest of the year. Admission is free.

Information Sources, Maps & Access

Additional information and a full-color *Siuslaw National Forest Map* (50¢) may be obtained from: Supervisor, Siuslaw National Forest, P.O. Box 1148, Corvallis, OR 97330 (503)575–4480. An *Oregon Dunes National Recreation Area Map/Brochure* and information may be obtained by contacting: Superintendent, Oregon Dunes National Recreation Area, Reedsport, OR 97467 (503)271–3611.

The major recreation areas of the Siuslaw National Forest are reached by auto along the incredibly scenic Oregon Coast Highway 101 and connecting state highways 38, 126, 34, 18, and 22 and U.S. Highway 20. Lodging, supplies, guides, and outfitting services are available at Florence, Reedsport, Yachats, Waldport, Newport, Corvallis, Lincoln City, Pacific City, Tillamook, Hebo, Cloverdale, Beaver, Toledo, Tidewater, Swisshome, Minerva, Cushman, Sitcoos, and Coos Bay.

Gateways & Accommodations

Astoria—Gateway to Fort Clatsop National Memorial

(Pop. 10,200; zip code 97103; area code 503.) The city was named for John Jacob Astor, whose partners sailed around Cape Horn in 1810 and chose the site of the present-day town for a key fur-trading post. The post was located within a few miles of Fort Clatsop, the winter quarters of Lewis and Clark in 1805. Astoria's proximity to both the mouth of the Columbia River and the Pacific made it a popular stopover for missionaries, explorers, and settlers. Today the town attracts fishermen all summer long, and is a popular gateway to Pacific beaches. Points of interest include the Astoria Column on Coxcomb Hill 700 feet above the river, erected to commemorate the first settlement (open daily 8 A.M. to 10 P.M. June 1–Sept. 30; observation platform at top of 125–foot tower); the Clatsop County Historical Museum, at 441 8th St., with exhibits housed in an old Victorian Mansion (open daily 10 A.M.–5 P.M. May 1–Oct. 1; Tuesday thru Sunday, 12 P.M.–5 P.M. the rest of the year); Fort Clatsop National Memorial, 4½ miles southwest of town on U.S. Hwy. 101A, a replica of the log fort built by Lewis and Clark and living history program; Columbia River Maritime Museum, at 16th and Exchange Sts., with interesting memorabilia of the river and Pacific Northwest, including the lightship *Columbia*, active at the turn of the century (open daily May-October; Tuesday-Sunday the rest of the year); Fort Stevens State Park, 10 miles northwest of town, encompassing the wreck of the *Peter Iredale* at Columbia Beach (open year-round). Accommodations: *Crest Motel* (rates: $22–33 double), 24 excellent rooms on attractive grounds overlooking the Columbia River, color TV, at 5366 Leif Ericson Drive, 2 miles east of town on U.S. 30 (325–3141); *Astoria Dunes Motel* (rates: $30–35 double), 41 fine rooms, color TV, some oversize beds, free coffee in rooms, at 288 W. Marine Drive, ¾ mile west of town on U.S. Hwy. 30 (325–7111); *Thunderbird Motor Inn* (rates: $37–42 double), 124 excellent rooms, some with oversize beds and balconies, fine views of the Astoria Marina, color TV, seafood restaurant and cocktail lounge, at 400 Industry St., 1 block north of U.S. Hwy. 30, just west of bridge (325–7373).

Coos Bay

(Pop. 13,500; zip code 97420; area code 503.) This is a major forest-products and salmon-fishing center on Oregon Coast Highway 101. Area attractions include the salmon-fishing charters at the Charleston Boat Basin and the Gold and Silver Falls State Park in the Coast Range. Accommodations: *Best Western Holiday Motel* (rates: $28–30 double), 68 excellent rooms next to restaurant, on U.S. 101 at 411 N. Bayshore Drive (269–5111); *Thunderbird Motor Inn* (rates: $30–36 double), 112 excellent rooms and family units, restaurant, cocktail lounge, heated pool, on U.S. 101 at 1313 N. Bayshore Drive (267–4141).

Corvallis

(Pop. 35,200; zip code 97330; area code 503.) Situated on the west bank of the Willamette River just below the confluence with Marys River, Corvallis derives its name from the Latin term for "heart of the valley." Home of Oregon State University, the city is the hub of a large agricultural and lumber region, framed on the west by the Coast Range and on the east by the sharp crests of the Cascade Mountains. Headquarters for the Siuslaw National Forest are located here. Area attractions include Mary's Peak, highest peak in the Coast Range, 16 miles west on Oregon State Hwy. 34, and the Horner Museum in Gill Coliseum of O.S.U., containing Indian artifacts and relics of pioneer days. Best bet in local restaurants is the Gables (752–3364) at 1121 N.W. 9th St., specializing in prime ribs and seafood served in an Old English atmosphere. Accommodations: *Best Western Country Kitchen Motel* (rates: $24–30 double), 34 comfortable rooms, 3 two-room units, color TV, heated pool, dining room, bar, and coffee shop, at 800 N. 9th St. (753–7326); *Nendel's Inn* (rates: $27.50–29.50 double), 120 excellent rooms and family suites, 19 with kitchens, queen-size beds, color TV, airport pickup, dining room, cocktail lounge, at 1550 N.W. 9th St. (753–9151).

Florence

(Pop. 2,200; zip code 97439; area code 503.) Florence lies just north of an extensive area of wooded lakes and high sand dunes encompassed within the Jessie M. Honeyman State Park, which also boasts an excellent beach and acres upon acres of wild rhododendrons. By far the most popular area attraction is the Sea Lion Caves, 11 miles north on U.S. Hwy. 101, where visitors can observe sea lions in natural caverns carved by the pounding of the ocean. Half-hour tours are offered from dawn till dusk via special elevators (for more information, phone 547–3415). Accommodations: *Driftwood Shores Surfside Resort Inn* (rates: $28–38 double), 136 excellent rooms and 1–3–bedroom units with balconies overlooking the ocean, 88 housekeeping units, color TV, heated indoor pool, saunas, private beach, restaurant, cocktail lounge, at 88416 First Ave., 4 miles north of town, just west of U.S. 101 (997–8263): *Le Château Motel* (rates: $26–30 double), 48 excellent rooms, some with oversize beds, color TV, heated pool, recreation room, putting green, restaurant and bar opposite, at 1084 Coast Hwy. (Box 98), near U.S. 101, just north of junction with Oregon State Hwy. 126 (997–3481).

Lincoln City

(Pop. 4,200; zip code 97367; area code 503.) A popular coastal gateway and summer resort center on the Oregon Coastal Highway 101. Accommodations: *Coho Inn* (rates: $24–36 double), 50 rooms and family units overlooking ocean, with balconies and fireplaces, at 1635 NW Harbor St. (994-3684); *Inn at Spanish Head* (rates: $40–52 double), 130 excellent rooms and family suites overlooking ocean, with balconies, restaurant, cocktail lounge, heated pool, saunas, ocean beach, in scenic setting, at 4009 S. U.S. 101 (996–2161); *International Dunes Ocean Front Resort* (rates: $39.50–43.50 double), 189 excellent rooms and family units, with ocean view, restaurant, coffee shop, heated pool, cocktail lounge, ocean beach, west off U.S. 101 (994–3655); *Neskowin Lodge* (rates: $27.50–36 double), 75 excellent rooms and family units with ocean view, restaurant, cocktail lounge, indoor pool, sauna, in scenic location 10 miles

north of town on U.S. 101 (392–3191); *Sailor Jack's Oceanfront Motel* (rates: $25–33.60 double), 41 rooms and family units with fireplaces, sauna, and ocean beach, at 1035 N. Harbor (994–3696).

Newport

(Pop. 5,200; zip code 97365; area code 503.) A turn-of-the-century fishing village and resort center in a scenic setting at the mouth of the Yaquina River. Area attractions include: Undersea Gardens at 267 SW Bay Blvd.; the 19th-century two-masted schooner *Sara*, a marine sailing museum with exhibits and tours at 325 SW Bay Blvd.; Royal Pacific Wax Museum (265–2062) at 550 SW Coast Highway; and the Yaquina Bay Lighthouse, built in 1871, in Yaquina Bay State Park. Accommodations: *Best Western Windjammer Ocean Front Motel* (rates: $28–38 double), 72 excellent rooms and family units, next to restaurant, with fireplaces and beach, at 744 SW Elizabeth St. (265–8853); *Embarcadero Marina Resort* (rates: $48–65 double), 210 superb rooms and family apartments with fireplaces and balconies overlooking beautiful Yaquina Bay, fine restaurant, cocktail lounge, indoor pool and saunas, private marina with excellent fishing, clamming, and crabbing, boat charters and rentals, off U.S. 101 at 1000 SE Bay Blvd. (265–8521); *Inn at Otter Crest* (rates: $38–73 double), 246 excellent rooms and family housekeeping units, suites, with fireplaces, balconies with ocean view, restaurant, cocktail lounge, heated pool, swimming beach, tennis court, 9 miles north of Newport west on U.S. 101, Otter Rock Exit (765–2111); *Little Creek Cove Motel* (rates: $36–46 double), 25 family units with kitchens, fireplaces, balconies, off U.S. 101 at 3641 NW Ocean View Dr. (265–8587).

North Bend

(Pop. 8,600; zip code 97459; area code 503.) A forest products and fishing center on Oregon Coast Highway 101. Area attractions include the Coos-Curry Historical Museum in Simpson Park. Accommodations: *Pony Village Motor Lodge* (rates: $26–30 double), 94 excellent rooms and family units, restaurant, cocktail lounge, at Pony Village Shopping Center (756–3191).

Reedsport

(Pop. 4,000; zip code 97467; area code 503.) The town lies at the edge of the Oregon Dunes National Recreation Area, a scenic 40–mile stretch of coastal sand dunes and forest growth between North Bend and Florence. Umpqua Lighthouse State Park, 5 miles south of town off U.S. Hwy. 101, encompasses 500–foot sand dunes, the highest in the United States. Accommodations: *Tropicana Motel* (rates: $22–27 double), 41 rooms, some with oversize beds, small heated pool, restaurant adjacent, at 1593 Highway Ave., ½ mile south of town via U.S. 101 (271–3671); *Western Hills Motel* (rates: $22–28 double), 21 comfortable units, 4 with kitchens, small heated pool, color TV, at 1821 Winchester Ave., in town off U.S. 101 (271–2149).

Tillamook

(Pop. 4,000; zip code 97141; area code 503.) A popular Oregon Coast Highway gateway. Area attractions include the Three Capes Road scenic route, Three Arch Rocks National Wildlife Refuge, and the Pioneer Museum at 2nd St. and Pacific Ave. (842–4553). Accommodations: *Best Western Mar-Clair Motel* (rates: $26–30 double), 47 rooms and family units, restaurant, heated pool, at 11 Main on U.S. 101 (842–7571); *El Rey Sands Motel* (rates: $22–26 double), 22 rooms and family units, restaurant, on U.S. 101 at 815 Main (842–7511).

Waldport

(Pop. 700; zip code 97394; area code 503.) This small community on the south shore of Alsea Bay is popular with fresh- and saltwater fishermen. Crabbing, clamming, and boating are other summer activities pursued off the sandy beaches and rugged coastline on either side of the bay. There are two district rangers' offices of the Siuslaw National Forest in town. Accommodations: *Alsea Manor*,

(rates: $16–20 double), 16 comfortable rooms, color TV, 1 block from the beach, restaurant opposite, in town on U.S. 101, (563–3249); *Bayshore Inn,* (rates: $22–28 double), 92 excellent rooms, color TV, boat ramp, fishing, heated pool, dining room, cocktail lounge, recreation room, at 500 Bayshore Drive just north of Alsea Bridge (563–3202); *Deane's Oceanside Lodge* (rates: $17–22), 20 rooms and family suites, 5 with kitchens, beachfront location, at 8800 Hwy. 101, 5 miles south of town (547–3321).

Yachats

(Pop. 400; zip code 97498; area code 503.) The village takes its name from an Indian phrase meaning "at the foot of the mountain." The town is bordered on the east by the Siuslaw National Forest and on the west by a rocky shoreline and fine sand beach. Cape Perpetua, part of the national forest, 3 miles south of Yachats via U.S. 101, offers excellent views of the coast, nature trails, and interpretive displays of the area's history. Accommodations: *Adobe Motel* (rates: $33–36 double), 38 attractive rooms, 3 with kitchens, some with fireplaces and oversize beds, good views of the ocean, recreation room, restaurant, bar, ½ mile north of town via U.S. 101 (547–3141); *Fireside Motel* (rates: $25–36 double), 17 comfortable rooms, some with ocean views, color TV, restaurant nearby, 1 mile north via U.S. 101, Star Rte. N (547–3636).

Lodges & Resorts

★★★★*Salishan Lodge,* at Gleneden Beach on the Pacific coast, is a sprawling resort of striking contemporary design, bordered by the blue waters of an evergreen-rimmed inlet and surrounded by handsomely landscaped grounds. Facilities are many and excellent: a beautiful oceanside 18–hole golf course, outdoor and indoor tennis courts, separate well-equipped gyms for men and women, a hydrotherapy pool, and a large indoor pool. Other recreational possibilities include hiking the trails of a 750–acre forest preserve, beachcombing for driftwood on 3 miles of secluded and wild beach, and deep-sea fishing just a few minutes away. The informally elegant Gourmet Room has received numerous accolades for its superb continental and American cuisine. During the summer a separate restaurant offers candlelit dining and dancing. Also on hand are a cocktail lounge and coffee shop. The Salishan has 150 guest rooms, each with fireplace, balcony, soundproofing, oversize beds, color TV, individual temperature control, and sheltered parking right at your door. Covered walkways connect all buildings of the lodge complex. For additional information write: Salishan Lodge, Gleneden Beach, OR 97388 (503)764–2371.

Rogue River National Forest & Sky Lakes Wilderness

The famous 621,005–acre national forest is dominated by the historic Rogue River and the Klamath and Siskiyou mountains in southwestern Oregon. The major features of the forest are shown on the full-color *Rogue River National Forest Map* (50¢), including forest service recreation sites, boating facilities, primitive lodging roads and trails, campsites, Pacific Crest National Scenic Trail, ranger stations, horse facilities, points of interest such as the Blue Ledge Mine, Mammoth Sugar Pine, National Bridge, and Dutchman's Peak Lookout. Rogue River trails such as Beaver Meadows Trail, Frenchman Camp Trail, Hummingbird Meadow Trail, Red Blanket Trail, and numerous others, plus forest roads, provide access through the dense sugar pine and Douglas fir forests to the spectacular Rogue River Gorge, Fish Lake, Mount McLoughlin (9,497 ft.), and the Seven Lakes Basin in the Sky Lakes Wilderness.

Information Sources & Access

For additional information and a full-color *Rogue River National Forest Map* (50¢) and a *Sky Lake's User's Topographic Map* (50¢), contact: Supervisor, Rogue River National Forest, P.O. Box 520, Medford, OR 97501 (503)779–2351. For detailed information on the Rogue Wild & Scenic River and river permits, trail conditions, and camping, and the free *Rogue National Wild & Scenic River Map* and free *Rogue River Trails* booklet, contact: Bureau of Land Management, 310 W. Sixth St., Medford, OR 97051 (503)779–2351. For additional information write: *Rogue River Guides Association*, P.O. Box 792, Medford 97501, for free listing of over 70 members. Guided high-country packhorse trips in the Rogue River National Forest and Sky Lakes Wilderness and in the Umpqua and Siskiyou national forests are provided by *Wilderness Pack Trips*, P.O. Box 71, Rogue River 97537; they offer moving, base camp, and drop trips.

The forest and Sky Lakes Wilderness area are reached via Interstate Highway 5 and Oregon Highways 140, 230, 227, as well as the scenic Crater Lake Highway (62). Lodging, supplies, guides, and outfitting service are available at Medford, Grants Pass, Eagle Point, Butte Falls, Trail, Shady Cove, Union Creek, Rogue River, Gold Hill, and Ashland.

Recreation Areas

Rogue National Wild & Scenic River

The Rogue, equally famous today for its wild-river boating as it is for its salmon and steelhead fishing, begins high in the Cascades near Crater Lake in Seven Lakes Basin, where it is a cold, clear stream, and carves its way west through the coastal mountains for 200 miles to the Pacific. The Rogue, named by early French fur trappers *la Rivière aux Coquins*, "the River of the Rogues," after the warlike Indians in the area (another version has it that they named it *Rouge*, or "Red," for the color it takes on during flooding), is commonly divided into three sections by fishermen and boaters: Upper, Middle, and Lower. The upper river extends from below Grants Pass upstream through the Valley of the Rogue past Shady Grove, Needle Rock, and Cascade Gorge, through the Rogue River National Forest past Rogue River Camp, Union Creek Resort, and Minnehaha Camp to its High Cascade headwaters. The twisting Upper Rogue is a top-ranked trout stream with some healthy runs of summer and winter steelheads and Chinook salmon, particularly in the famed Pierce Riffle below Savage Rapids Dam and in the Leaning Tree Riffle. Points of interest along the upper river include the scenic Mill Creek Falls, the Natural Bridge, and Rogue River Gorge. Several U.S. Forest Service campgrounds are located at strategic points along the upper river, surrounded by cool forests of Douglas fir, sugar pine, ponderosa pine, white fir, and white pine.

The wild river wilderness of the Middle Rogue flows from Grants Pass to Brushy Bar through the picturesque Hellgate and Mule creek canyons, past towering cliffs and timbered slopes, and through rocky chutes, rapids, riffles, and deep pools. From Grants Pass to Hellgate Canyon, the Rogue is an easy 19–mile stretch of water with small, regular waves, clear passages, even riffles, and sandbars. The 13–mile stretch from Hellgate Canyon to Grave Creek has numerous rocks, eddies, and irregular waves, with clear but narrow passages. At Grave Creek the Rogue enters its 26–mile-long wilderness stretch, with a dizzying succession of long violent rapids, powerful and irregular waves, dangerous rocks, and swirling eddies. After the 6–foot drop at Grave Creek Falls is Rainie Falls, a vertical 10–foot drop requiring portaging or lining. The remaining stretch of the wild river, which brawls and spumes through Mule Creek Canyon, is a boiling white-water roller coaster with strange, violent crosscurrents and sudden eddies, surrounded by incredibly steep and extremely narrow canyon walls, in some places 50 feet high and only 15 feet across. Commercially guided float trips begin at several boating sites between Grants Pass and Grave Creek. There are trips of 3–8 days' duration. Some make overnight stops at commercial lodges along the river, while others camp out at public recreation sites. Be sure to write to: Supervisor's Office, Bureau of Land Management, Medford 97501, for regulations and boating permit information.

Rogue River Trail & Historic Sites

The wild Middle Rogue is paralleled by the Rogue River Trail from Grave Creek to Illahe. The trail is strictly for hikers and backpackers; it is closed to motorized vehicles, horses, and pack animals. The trail is well constructed and has moderate grades. If reasonable precautions are taken, the hike is comparatively safe, although hikers should always be wary of slides or washouts. Early summer and fall is the best time to hike the trail. Later in the season, temperatures are higher, but morning and evening hiking avoids midday heat.

Hikers normally take about 5 days for the entire distance. This allows time to stop and enjoy the scenery and to study the geology, plants, and wildlife along the way. A road reaches the river at Marial for those who want a shorter trip. Several primitive campsites are located along the trail, but facilities are limited.

The trail follows the most exciting part of the river. Grave Creek, the starting point, was named for the death of a young girl who was passing through with her family in 1846. The Indians dug up her body, stripped it of its clothing, and hung it over the branches of a tree as a mute, terrible warning to the white invaders. The beginning of the trail is very rocky. Old cabin sites and unusual rock formations occupy the banks, and hikers can stop to watch boats being lowered down treacherous Rainie Falls. After Tyee Rapids, a primitive campsite appears at Russian Creek. Tyee Bas was once a famous gold diggings. In the early days, some 300 Chinese took a million dollars in gold dust here. Deer and other wildlife stop to feed here, and interesting animal tracks can be detected in the soft sand. Bronco Creek, a few miles later, was originally named Jackass Creek in 1855 because of the loss of a pack mule as some men were trying to evade a band of Indians. Battle Bar is named after the skirmish that occurred during the Rogue River Indian War of 1855–56. Winkle Bar, a mile downstream from Battle Bar, is a stretch of rolling water named for pioneer prospector William Winkle and is the site of Zane Grey's famous summer steelhead fishing camp. The Rogue River Ranch, at Mile 23, is managed by the Bureau of Land Management and provides emergency aid. The first white man to settle in the area built a cabin just a short distance downriver from here, in 1880.

Downriver from Mule Creek, you can overlook the famous Coffee Pot, a churning whirlpool of crosscurrents. Brushy Bar was the site of a large gold-mining operation around the turn of the century. In 1905 a fire burned all summer long, and the resultant vegetation was, for a time, low brush, hence the bar's name. Flora Dell Creek offers a trailside pool which is perfect for a restful swim. The trail ends at the site of a historical Indian burial ground. Trenches, once built in the forest as fortification against the Indians, are still intact.

The observant wilderness traveler along the remote stretches of the Rogue may see great blue herons with their 6–foot wingspread, common mergansers, belted kingfishers, water ouzels, cliff swallows and their mud-walled nests, ospreys, bald eagles, pileated woodpeckers, blue and ruffed grouse, California quail, and waterfowl. Rogue River country is also inhabited by black-tailed deer, Roosevelt elk, black bear, otter, raccoon, and rattlesnakes.

Sky Lakes Wilderness & Pacific Crest Trail

To the east of the Rogue, the majestic Sky Lakes Wilderness and Rogue River Headwaters area lie along the Cascades for 27 miles, from Crater Lake south to the Lake of the Woods. This beautiful backcountry is a land of lofty peaks, blue lakes, and timbered slopes with elevations ranging from 3,800 feet in the canyon of the Middle Fork of the Rogue River to a lofty 9,497 feet at Mt. McLoughlin. The Pacific Crest Trail follows the backbone for about 35 miles, with numerous spur trails leading off to the Devils Peak area, Wizard Lake, Pelican Butte (8,036 ft.), and Squaw, Fourmile, Badger, and Wolf lakes, Blue Canyon Basin, Sky Lakes Basin, and Mudjekeewis Mountain. Be sure to carry food and water supplies, since there are no supply stores from Fourmile Lake to Crater Lake.

Gateways & Accommodations

Ashland

(Pop. 12,300; zip code 97520; area code 503.) Bordered on three

sides by the Rogue River National Forest, Ashland lies at the southernmost end of the Rogue River valley on the banks of Bear Creek. When pioneers first traversed the towering Siskiyou Mountains south of Ashland, they were rewarded by the sight of a vast green expanse of valley, and many decided to go no farther. The town was named in 1852 for the birthplace of Henry Clay at Ashland, Virginia. The Oregon Shakespeare Festival, one of the oldest on the continent, takes place in a replica of London's Fortune Theatre in Lethis Park each summer from mid-June to mid-September (write: Shakespeare, P.O. Box 158, or phone 482–2111). Other area attractions include the Mt. Ashland Ski Area, 10 miles south on Interstate 5, then 8 miles west on local road (482–4606), and Emigrant Lake, 6 miles southeast of town, which offers fishing and water sports in season. Accommodations: *Best Western Bard's Inn* (rates: $30–47 double), 32 fine air-conditioned rooms, some with queen-size beds, heated swimming pool, restaurant, open all year, near Shakespeare Theatre at 132 N. Main St. (482–0049); *Knight's Inn Motel* (rates: $19–23 double), 32 air-conditioned rooms, heated pool, restaurant adjacent, at 2359 Highway 66, 1 mile south of town (482–5111); *Timbers Motel* (rates: $23–26 double), 28 rooms, 2 with kitchens, heated pool, restaurant adjacent, at 1450 Ashland St. (482–4242).

Grants Pass

See "Siskiyou National Forest" for details on this Rogue River gateway.

Jacksonville

(Pop. 1,600; zip code 97530; area code 503.) One of the best-preserved pioneer towns in the Pacific Northwest, Jacksonville was founded during the gold rush of 1851–52 and prospered until the strike dwindled in the 1920s. More than 51 buildings, parks, exhibits, and cemeteries give a lively picture of what life was like in an early mining town. Among the more interesting landmarks and area attractions are the Beekman House, at 352 E. California St., the home of a wealthy 19th-century businessman; the Jacksonville Museum, housed in the Old Country Courthouse at 206 N. 5th St., containing an extensive display of early pioneer and Indian artifacts; and Pioneer Village, at 725 N. 5th St. on Oregon State Hwy. 238, a collection of authentic century-old buildings, furnished in period style, plus horse-drawn machinery, wagons, buggies, and displays of mining equipment. A good spot for dining is the *Jacksonville Inn Dinner House* (899–1900), at 175 E. California St. The restaurant is housed in a restored building from the gold rush days and specializes in prime ribs, homemade pastries, and fresh salmon in season. The inn also offers 8 air-conditioned hotel rooms at $23 double.

Medford

(Pop. 28,500; zip code 97501; area code 503.) Headquarters for the Rogue River National Forest, Medford lies in the heart of the Rogue River valley, surrounded by the steep walls of the Cascade and Siskiyou mountain ranges. Endless orchards both within and outside of the city give Medford a lovely, parklike air, especially in spring when apple and pear trees burst into bloom. A mild climate year-round is conducive to outdoor activities, and the area abounds in recreational attractions: 150 stocked streams and 17 lakes within an 80–mile radius, state parks, and the vast expanse of the Rogue River National Forest, a few miles to the north and south of town. The best bet in local restaurants is *Mon Desir Dining Inn*, at 4615 Hamrick Road in Central Point, offering fine cuisine and excellent service in a restored mansion complete with antiques, crackling fires, and a handsome garden (664–6661). Accommodations: *Best Western Thunderbird Lodge* (rates: $30–33 double), 120 excellent rooms and suites, color TV, oversize beds, heated pool, 24–hour restaurant, cocktail lounge, free airport pickup, at 1015 S. Riverside Ave., ½ mile south of town on Oregon State Hwy. 99 (773–8266); *Holiday Inn* (rates: $33–35 double), 168 excellent rooms and suites, color TV, indoor pool, wading pool, putting green, recreation room, dining room, cocktail lounge, free airport transportation, at 2300 Crater Lake Hwy., 2 miles north of town on Oregon State Hwy. 62, Exit 30 (779–3141); *Red Lion Motor Inn* (rates: $32–35 double), 190 superlative rooms, with private patios and balconies, color TV, 2 heated pools, dining room, cocktail lounge, coffee shop, free airport pickup, at 200 N. Riverside Ave. on Oregon State Hwy. 99 (779–5811); *Rodeway Inn* (rates: $29–33.60 double), 128 excellent rooms, 1 housekeeping apartment, color TV, heated pool, restaurant and cocktail lounge adjacent, free airport pickup, at 1150 E. Barnett Road, 1 block east of Interstate 5, Barnett Road Exit (779–5085).

Lodges & Resorts

★★*Fish Lake Resort*, in southern Oregon's Rogue River National Forest, is just 1½ miles from the famous Pacific Crest Trail and offers close access to Mt. McLoughlin for interested climbers. Fish Lake has fine trout fishing for both eastern brookees and rainbows and a 10–mph speed limit, which makes it ideal for sailboats and canoes. Other activities at the resort include deer and bear hunting in season, waterskiing on nearby Lake of the Woods, and fishing the many lakes and streams in the immediate area. Cottages are either on the lakefront or nestled among stately trees, and all have comfortable furnishings, fully equipped kitchens, eating and cooking utensils, and linens. One-bedroom cottages (4 people) are $18–20 per day. Also on the premises are a grocery store, tackle shop, game room, cafe, and gas station. Boat rentals, firewood, and ice are all available. Open year-round. For full details write: Fish Lake Resort, P.O. Box 40, Medford, OR 97501.

★★★★*Morrison's Lodge*, on the banks of the Rogue River 16 miles from Grants Pass, has been in operation for over 30 years and offers both housekeeping cottages and American-plan accommodations. Originally built for fall and winter steelheading, the lodge has expanded in recent years to include a host of other activities, such as

swimming in the river and capacious outdoor pool, 1–4–day float trips on the Rogue, tennis, hiking, and visiting the area's famous sights: Oregon Caves, Crater Lake, Lake Selmac, and the Shakespeare Festival at Ashland. Spacious, handsome housekeeping units have 2 bedrooms, a living and dining area, kitchen, bath, all linens and utensils, and a carport. All are surrounded by shady pines, are air-conditioned for summer, and feature big fireplaces for spring and fall. Morrison's also sponsors special jet boat trips over 50 miles of exciting white water and offers guides for both fishing and river-rafting. American-plan rates: $45 per person per day ($25 off-season); housekeeping cottages start at $32 per day for 2 persons, with a maximum of 5 at $40 per day. For complete rates and information write: Morrison's Lodge, 8500 Galice Roads, Merlin, OR 97532 (503)476–3825 or 476–3027.

★★*Union Creek Resort* is located in the Rogue River National Forest, 56 miles north of Medford on the Crater Lake Highway (62), adjacent to the famous Rogue River Gorge. The lodge offers fishing and hunting in season, backpacking and hiking trails, and cross-country skiing in the Rogue River high country and at Crater Lake National Park, 23 miles to the east. Ski groups can be accommodated in the lodge from October to May, with the use of kitchen and recreation and fireplace room. Special rates are available. Accommodations consist of lodge rooms, rustic sleeping cabins with private showers and baths, and fully equipped housekeeping cabins with 1 and 2 bedrooms. Lodge room rates are $13–16 per day double; sleeping cabins $15.50–17.50 per day; and housekeeping cabins $18–21 per day. The lodge has a fully equipped tackle shop and grocery store. Beckies' Cafe, noted for its homemade pies and bread, is just across the street. For additional information, contact: Union Creek Resort, Prospect, OR 97536 (503)560–3565.

★★★*Weasku Inn*, on southern Oregon's legendary Rogue River 6 miles from Grants Pass, offers great fishing in season for Chinook salmon, trout, and steelhead. Other attractions are 1–3–day river trips through magnificent scenery along the wild Rogue, waterskiing on Savage Rapids Lake, boating, picnicking, and sight-seeing. Comfortable private cabins, some with housekeeping facilities, are shaded by lofty fir and pine trees. Hearty, home-style meals are the specialty of Weasku Inn's attractive Calico Room in the main lodge, which also houses a wet bar (B.Y.O.), big stone fireplace, and congenial lodge. Housekeeping rates: $30–35 per day for 2 ($20 off season); regular rates: $25 per day for 2. White-water trips, guides, and meals are additional. For further details write: Weasku Inn, 5560 Rogue River Highway, Grants Pass, OR 97526 (503)479–2455.

Travel Services

Court's White Water Trips offers day and overnight journeys along a scenic stretch of the Rogue River via custom-designed, 10–18–passenger jet boats. Trips begin at Gold Beach in southwestern Oregon and progress past the town of Agness through a spectacular roadless wilderness, churning rapids, and the 1,500–foot vertical walls of Paradise Canyon in the heart of Rogue River country. The day trip includes a stop for lunch at the rustic Barbarian Lodge at Clay Hill Rapids, a wilderness retreat with modern amenities in a lovely riverside setting. Overnight guests spend the afternoon and following morning at the lodge, which offers swimming, fishing for steelhead, hiking the Rogue River trail, or loafing in the sun on a sandy beach. You may stay longer if you choose, Court's jet boats will return you to Gold Beach any day of the week. Pilots for the white-water trips are professional boatmen, licensed by the U.S. Coast Guard and experienced in the ways of the river. Trips are tailored to the participants' interests and may include stops for wildlife photography or time out to learn the history and geology of the Rogue from your guide. For further information and rates write: Court's White Water Trips, Box 1045, Gold Beach, OR 97444 (503)247–6504.

Rogue River Raft Trips are sponsored through Morrison's Lodge (see above), which maintains a complete outfitting center for white-water rafting on the fabulous Rogue. Trips of 3–4 days explore the Oregon wilderness over thrilling rapids and riffles, past Rainie Falls, Tyee Rapids, Zane Grey's cabin, Devil's Staircase, and other Rogue River milestones. You have the choice of either lodge trips with overnight accommodations at inviting inns and lodges along the way, or camping trips with all equipment provided plus a guide to oversee camp chores and cooking. Some variations on the above are availa-

ble, plus opportunities for 1–2–day trips and fall fishing for steelhead with accommodations at Morrison's Lodge, which provides the origin for all raft adventures. Rates for 3–day lodge trips are $175–195 per person; for 4 days of camping, $185–205 per person, depending on the number of persons to a party. Guides, meals, equipment, lodging, and sturdy inflatable rafts are all included. Lodge trips are scheduled between approximately May 1 and September 30, camping trips between May 1 and September 1. For additional information on Rogue River rafting write: Morrison's Lodge, 8500 Galice Road, Merlin, OR 97532 (503)476–3825.

Sundance Expeditions, one of the West's biggest and most comprehensive kayak schools, offers both intensive instruction in river techniques and exciting white-water runs on the Illinois and Rogue rivers. The Rogue and Klamath rivers are the "classrooms" for Sundance's 5– and 10–day kayak programs, which include day-long river outings with expert instruction in paddling skills, dry and wet exits, basic strokes, ferrying, eddy turns, and other techniques. The course culminates in a 3–day expedition on the wild lower Rogue. Accommodations for participants are provided in the Sundance Riverhouse, a comfortable lodge bordering the designated "wild and scenic" section of the Rogue. Here you will find a sauna for tired muscles, laundry facilities, a lounge, and fine meals served on a deck overlooking the river. Rates: $225 per person for 5 days; $425 for 10 days. Sundance also offers a 4–day white-water run on the Illinois River through the rugged terrain of the Kalmiopsis Wilderness Area, 4 days of rafting on the Rogue downstream through Rainee Falls, fall steelhead fishing expeditions, and charter trips tailored to your specifications. The Illinois and Rogus river trips are $200 and $210 per person, respectively. Meals, life jackets, boats, guides, and other relevant equipment are included. For more details write: Sundance Expeditions, 14894 Galice Road, Merlin, OR 97532 (503)479–8505.

Siskiyou National Forest & The Oregon Caves

The Siskiyou National Forest, an outstanding fishing, hunting, and wilderness camping region, takes in 1,158,420 acres in the southwestern corner of Oregon, with a small extension into California. The forest encompasses a major portion of the rugged Siskiyou Mountains, joining the Cascade Range to the east and the Coast Range to the northeast. *Siskiyou* is the Indian word for a bobtailed horse. In 1828 Alexander McLeod, a Hudson's Bay trapper, was heading a party in the mountains and got lost in a snowstorm. The group suffered severe privations and lost several horses, among them the bobtailed racehorse belonging to McLeod. The mountain pass where they were became known thereafter as "the pass of the Siskiyou," a name that was later given to the entire range.

Numerous forest roads and trails wind through the backcountry to such areas as the Kalmiopsis Wilderness, Big Craggies, Coquille Falls, Vulcan lake, Chetco Divide, Rogue River Canyon, and Elk River. The Illinois River Trail provides stunning views of the river canyon. The scenic Chetco River, flowing for 50 miles through a thick forest of myrtlewood trees, has good fishing for cutthroat, rainbow, and steelhead, and in its lower stretches are Chinook and coho salmon. The 36–mile-long Sixes River is one of southern Oregon's best producers of steelhead. The Illinois River, a large tributary of the lower Rogue, is renowned for its tremendous autumn run of half-pound steelhead and Chinook and coho salmon.

The unusual, 76,900–acre Kalmiopsis Wilderness is located in the Siskiyou Mountains in the central portion of the forest. A harsh, brushy area of low-elevation canyons, the wilderness contains the headwaters of the Chetco River, over 12 species of conifers, including the rare Brewer, or weeping, spruce, and the rare *Kalmiopsis leachiana*, a member of the heath family found only in the Chetco and Illinois river basins. This is a true primitive camping area, with a few shelters and old cabins left over from the early gold-mining days. The trails are in fairly good condition, but tend to be steep and very rocky.

The Oregon Caves National Monument, 20 miles east of Cave Junction via Oregon State Hwy. 46, encompasses a natural labyrinth of subterranean corridors, chambers and passageways, carved by the drip and flow of water deep inside Mt. Elijah. Called the Marble Halls of Oregon by frontier poet Joaquin Miller, the various chambers bear such evocative names as Paradise Lost, the Queen's Organ, and Dante's Inferno. Stalactites, pillars, limestone canopies, and fantastic rock formations line the twisting passageways and many galleries of this famous cavern. Colored lights pierce through arched vaults at intervals, giving the marble walls a prismatic translucence. Guided tours of the national monument are strenuous and recommended only for those in good physical condition. Rubber footgear and coveralls may be rented from the concessioner when moisture in the caves is heavy. Tours are offered daily at scheduled intervals; the monument is closed during bad weather. For information on area accommodations, see Cave Junction below.

Information Sources, Maps & Access

For additional information and a full-color *Siskiyou National Forest Map* (50¢) and the *Kalmiopsis Wilderness Topographic Map* (50¢), which includes the Big Craggies Botanical Area, contact: Supervisor,

Siskiyou National Forest, P.O. Box 440, Grants Pass, OR 97526 (503)479–5301. For an Oregon Caves National Monument brochure and information, contact: Superintendent, Oregon Caves National Monument, Cave Junction, OR 97523.

The Siskiyou National Forest is reached via U.S. Highway 199 and the scenic Oregon Coast Highway 101. Lodging, supplies, guide service, and outfitters are available at Brookings, Pistol River, Gold Beach, Port Orford, Powers, Galice, Selma, Grants Pass, Cave Junction, and Elk Creek.

Gateways & Accommodations

Brookings

(Pop. 2,700; zip code 97415; area code 503.) On the Pacific Coast just north of the California border, Brookings is a commercial and sportfishing center. A district ranger's Office of the Siskiyou National Forest is located here. East of town on U.S. 101 is Azalea State Park, 36 acres of wild and beautiful azaleas, some blooming twice a year. The Palmer Butte Overlook Scenic Drive, east of Brookings, extends for 10 miles and rises to an elevation of 2,000 feet for sweeping views of the ocean and Coast Range Mountains. Accommodations: *Best Western Brookings Inn* (rates: $28–32 double), 41 excellent rooms with color TV and queen-size beds, restaurant, open all year, at 1143 Chetco Ave., ¼ mile north of town on U.S. 101 (469–2173); *Brookings Thunderbird Motel* (rates: $23.50–26.50 double), 42 fine rooms, oversize beds, color TV, 2 efficiency apartments, carports, restaurant opposite, open all year, at 1144 Chetco Ave., ¼ mile north on U.S. 101 (469–2141).

Cave Junction

(Pop. 400; zip code 97523; area code 503.) This gateway to the Siskiyou National Forest is so named because it lies along the route leading to the Oregon Caves National Monument, 20 miles east of town on Oregon State Hwy. 46. Other area attractions include the Kerbyville Museum, 2 miles north on U.S. 199, built in the early 1870s and furnished in period style (open daily May-October; by appointment rest of the year, 592–2076), and Woodland Deer Park, 1½ miles south on U.S. 199, a wildlife park with over 200 animals on a 4-acre preserve (592–3802). There are two district rangers' offices of the Siskiyou National Forest in Cave Junction. Accommodations: *Junction Inn* (rates: $24–26 double), 60 excellent rooms, some with oversize beds, color TV, heated pool, playground, restaurant, family rates available, at 406 S. Redwood Highway, at junction of U.S. 199 and Oregon State Hwy. 46 (592–3106).

Gold Beach

(Pop. 1,600; zip code 97444; area code 503.) On the edge of the Siskiyou National Forest, this town takes its name from the profitable placer mining that was carried on in the 1850s at the sandy mouth of the Rogue River. Today the town and its beaches attract fishermen for the excellent surf casting and Rogue River steelhead fishing. Gold Beach is also the starting point for float and jet-boat trips along the Rogue. A few miles south of town is Cape Sebastian State Park, a group of open and forested park units covering 1,100 acres. The landmark promontory, which rises 700 feet above the water, was named by Captain Vizcaino in 1603. Trails lead to view points commanding sweeping views of the Pacific. Accommodations: *Best Western Inn of the Beachcomber* (rates: $38–40 double), 32 excellent rooms, with oversize beds and ocean views, beachfront location, color TV, heated indoor pool, saunas, restaurant opposite, at 125 S. Ellensburg, ½ mile south of town on U.S. 101 (247–6691); *Ireland's Rustic Lodges* (rates: $25–34 double), 8 charming cottages, some with fireplaces, ocean views, and kitchens, on beautifully landscaped grounds, private beach, open year-round, at 1120 S. Ellensburg, 1 mile south of town on U.S. 101 (247–7718); *Jot's Resort* (rates: $32–38 double), 75 fine rooms with queen-size beds and balconies overlooking the river, 25 efficiency units, 11 two-room units, heated pool, marina, fishing, boat trips, restaurant and cocktail lounge open all year, off the north end of the Rogue River Bridge (247–6676); *Tu Tu Tun Lodge* (rates: $47 double), 16 excellent rooms with patios and balconies overlooking the Rogue, handsome resort building, heated pool, boat dock and ramp, fishing, boat trips, recreation room, library, dining room, cocktail lounge, on N. Bank Road, 7 miles east of U.S. 101 (247–6664); *Western Village* (rates: $29–32 double), 25 comfortable rooms, 1 kitchen unit, some with queen-size beds and ocean views, restaurant opposite, at 975 Ellensburg, ½ mile south of town on U.S. 101 (247–6611).

Grants Pass

(Pop. 12,500; zip code 97526; area code 503.) Located on the banks of the Rogue River, the city was once a regular stop on the old California Stage route. Enthusiastic road builders gave the town its name when news reached them of General Grant's capture of Vicksburg in 1863. A district ranger's office of the Siskiyou National Forest is located here. Area attractions include the Oregon Caves National Monument, Rogue River boat trips, and excursions to Hellgate Canyon, which originate at the Riverside Motel on the north bank of the river. Each summer, in late July or early August, gladiolus fields near Grants Pass burst into gorgeous bloom. Accommodations: *Best Western Riverside Motel* (rates: $25–34 double), 106 excellent rooms with sundecks and balconies overlooking the river, 1- and 2-bedroom units, 2 heated pools, whirlpool, free airport pickup, dining room, coffee shop, cocktail lounge, Hellgate Canyon excursions originate here, 971 S.E. 6th St., ½ mile south of town on Hwy. 99 (476–6873); *Colonial Motor Inn* (rates: $24–28 double), 61 comfortable rooms, color TV, heated pool, oversize beds, restaurant opposite, at 1889 N.E. 6th St., ¾ mile north on Hwy. 99 (479–8301); *Royal View Motor Inn* (rates: $32–38 double), 60 excellent air-conditioned rooms, with queen-size beds and private patios or balconies, color TV, free in-room movies, heated pool, restaurant and bar, at 110 N.E. Morgan Lane, 1 mile north of town on U.S. 199 (479–5381); *Shilo Inn* (rates: $25 double), 71 excellent rooms, color TV, heated pool, steam bath, sauna, restaurant adjacent, at 1880 N.W. 6th St., ½ mile north on Hwy. 99 (479–8391).

Lodges

For additional listings, see "Rogue River National Forest."

★★★*The Oregon Caves Château* offers modern convenience and a rustic style of architecture. The attractive structure rises 6 stories from the canyon floor, blending with the surrounding forest and moss-covered marble ledges. The lobby contains a huge double fireplace of rough marble and picture windows with mountain views. The rustic, wood-paneled dining room contains a mountain stream that winds its way across the room and on to the sea. Comfortable rooms have picturesque views and baths. Daily rates based on European plan for 1 or 2 guests: $19–22; cottage rooms with bath are available at $18 per day. Contact: Oregon Caves Château, P.O. Box 151, Grants Pass, OR 97526.

Umatilla National Forest & The Blue Mountains

The Umatilla National Forest encompasses the beautiful Blue Mountain Range, Oregon's oldest land, known to geologists as the Island of Shoshone, and one of the top mule deer and elk-hunting regions

in the United States. The forest takes in 1,400,000 acres in northeastern Oregon and extends in a northeasterly direction up into Washington. The forest and the Umatilla River take their name from an Indian word meaning "water rippling over sand." The forest region was first explored by members of the Lewis and Clark expedition during their trip down the Columbia River in 1805. The old Oregon Trail, used by countless pioneers, crossed the Blue Mountains from the Grande Ronde Valley to the Umatilla Valley. The forest was once the scene of several Indian battles, beginning with the Whitman Massacre in 1847. Several gold-boom ghost towns and caved-in mines are found scattered through the backcountry.

A particularly good elk and mule deer area consists of the fir, spruce, and pine forests of the 111,200–acre Wenaha Backcountry Area located along the crest of the northern Blue Mountains. This roadless area is characterized by rugged basaltic ridges and outcroppings separated by deep canyons and white-water streams. There is a goodly population of whitetail deer along the banks of the Wenaha River during the fall months. Numerous forest roads and over 900 miles of trails provide access to many backcountry areas such as the Jump-Off Joe area and the Vinegar Hill-Indian Rock area—a tough, remote wilderness located on the boundary of the Malheur and Umatilla national forests.

The forest's top-ranked trout streams include the Tucannon, Wenaha, Walla Walla, and North Fork John Day rivers. The scenic Grande Ronde runs through a deep gorge in the Blue Mountains and is a popular wildwater float trip between Rondowa and Troy in the Walla Walla Ranger District. The river is not difficult to navigate, but when the water is high and fast, experience is needed, and it is recommended that life preservers be worn at all times.

Information Sources, Maps & Access

The major features of the forest, the Wenaha backcountry, and the adjacent Umatilla Indian Reservation are shown on the *Umatilla National Forest Map*. This full-color map, which also shows forest roads and trails, horse-loading ramps, recreation sites, and campgrounds, may be obtained for 50¢ by writing to: Forest Supervisor's Office, Umatilla National Forest, 2517 S.W. Hailey, Pendleton 97801. For hunting, fishing, trail, and river information and the free publications *Umatilla Forest Facts* and *Trail Closure Map*, write to the supervisor's office.

The Umatilla National Forest and Wenaha backcountry are reached via Interstate 80N, U.S. Route 12, and Oregon Highways 204, 82, and 3 and Washington Highways 128 and 129. Lodging, supplies, guides, and outfitters are available at La Grande, Elgin, Wallowa, Minam, North Powder, Troy; and Walla Walla, Washington.

Gateways & Accommodations

La Grande

(Pop. 9,600; zip code 97850; area code 503.) Occupying a beautiful setting at the foot of the Blue Mountains near the western edge of the Grande Ronde Valley and spread out along a gentle slope on the south bank of the Grande Ronde River, the town is the home of Eastern Oregon State College and a gateway to vast outdoor recreation areas, including the Umatilla National Forest and Anthony Lakes Ski Area. The Mt. Emily scenic route, outside of Grande Ronde, winds through 10 miles of unspoiled scenery to the top of Mt. Emily, 3,000 feet above the valley. Accommodations: *Best Western Pony Soldier Motor Inn* (rates: $27–31 double), 151 excellent rooms, 3 with kitchens, many oversize beds and refrigerators, color TV, 2 swimming pools, sauna, whirlpool, restaurant adjacent, 1 mile east of town on Hwy. 83, east of Exit 261 off Interstate 80N (963–7195); *Royal Motor Inn* (rates: $21–22 double), 45 comfortable rooms, most with oversize beds, color TV, restaurant nearby, at 1510 Adams Ave. (963–4154).

Pendleton

(Pop. 13,200; zip code 97801; area code 503.) Located on the old Oregon Trail and divided into two unequal sections by the Umatilla River, Pendleton is a gateway to the Umatilla National Forest, Spout Springs Ski Area, and the Umatilla Indian Reservation. Each year the city hosts one of the West's most famous rodeos, the Pendleton Round-Up. Beginning in mid-September, this boisterous 4–day event includes the Westwood Ho parade of stagecoaches and prairie schooners, the Happy Canyon Indian Pageant, and rodeo competitions that attract contestants from all parts of the United States and Canada. Indian tribes from throughout the Pacific Northwest come to dance their native dances, re-create war scenes, and show off their elaborate finery. Visitors to the Round-Up should make reservations for lodgings well in advance. Accommodations: *Best Western Tapadera* (rates: $29–32 double), 47 fine air-conditioned rooms, many with queen-size beds, color TV, restaurant, cocktail lounge, at 105 S.E. Court Ave., 1 block south of town on U.S. 30 (276–3231); *Chaparral Motel* (rates: $23–26 double), 51 rooms and suites, 3 two-bedroom units with kitchens, color TV, balconies, oversize beds, restaurant adjacent, 620 Tutuilla Road, 1 mile west of town on Interstate 80N, Exit 209 (276–8654); *Imperial 400 Motel* (rates: $26–38 double), 52 excellent rooms and suites, color TV, oversize beds, heated pool, airport transportation, at 201 S.W. Court Ave., 1½ miles west of town on U.S. 30 (276–5252); *Indian Hills Motor Inn* (rates: $31–39 double), 100 spacious and attractive rooms, some with balconies and queen-size beds, 5 two-room units, heated pool, dining room, coffee shop, cocktail lounge, free airport pickup, at 300 Patawa Road, off Interstate 80N, Exit 210 (276–6111).

Guest Ranches

★★★*Bar M Ranch* is nestled in the magnificent Blue Mountains of northeastern Oregon on a lush stretch of wilderness adjoining Umatilla National Forest. The hand-hewn log ranch house, built in 1864 and used during the Civil War as a stagecoach station, gives a good idea of the unique rustic flavor of this resort. All of the cabins are surrounded by shady trees and spacious lawns. The lovely Umatilla River flows through the ranch grounds, and there are warm springs gushing from a nearby cliff—the same springs that supply the big ranch swimming pool with naturally warm water. Riding is a favorite activity here, with plenty of remote mountain lakes and meadows to explore over a growing network of trails. Fishing is good May through June for native and introduced trout in the Umatilla. All meals are served family-style in the ranch house and include a sumptuous menu of homemade specialties: freshly baked breads and pies, and vegetables and berries right from the garden. American-plan rates: $195–220 per person weekly, including all meals, horseback riding, lodgings, and use of ranch facilities. Special children's and family rates are available. For more information write: Baker's Bar M Ranch, Route 1, Adams, OR 97810 (503)566–3381.

Umpqua National Forest

The Umpqua National Forest, covering a total area of 984,000 acres, lies mainly within Douglas County in southeastern Oregon. The forest is named for the Umpqua Indians, who once fished its rivers and hunted in the great pine woods and high country. The renowned fly-fishing waters of the North and South Umpqua rivers, formed by tributaries in the Cascade and Calapooya mountains, flow through majestic evergreen forests and rugged wilderness valleys and

unite to form the main Umpqua, which cuts through the Coast Mountains, the lower reaches forming a wide estuary. The world-famous steelhead trout waters of the North Umpqua, which have lured famous fly-fishermen such as Zane Grey and Herbert Hoover, rise in beautiful Diamond Lake, flow through the Umpqua National Forest, and join the main Umpqua below Roseburg. The scenic, swift-flowing North Umpqua is a difficult stream to wade, and the hardy steelheader must be able to handle a long line. The river is well served by excellent fishing camps. Lemolo Lake, located near the Diamond Lake headwaters on the North Umpqua, holds large brown trout up to 15 pounds, plus rainbows and kokanee salmon. Good campgrounds are located at Lemolo Falls and at Kelsay Valley. Beautiful Diamond Lake, which reflects the snowcapped summit of Mt. Bailey on its placid surface and looks across undulating forested hills at Mt. Thielsen, is famous for its trophy rainbow trout. The scenic South Umpqua rises in Fish Lake high in the Cascades near Crater Lake and flows down through Umpqua National Forest to its confluence with the main Umpqua at Roseburg. This is a top-ranked salmon and steelhead stream. Numerous forest service campsites are located along its upper stretches.

The historic Bohemia Mining District covers about 225 square miles of mountainous country heavily timbered with old fir, spruce, and hemlock. Turbulent mountain streams, deep gorges, wooded scarps, and jagged peaks make this a region of great natural beauty. The district was named for "Bohemia" Johnson, who discovered gold-bearing quartz here in 1863.

Information Sources, Maps & Access

Additional information, a full-color *Umpqua National Forest Map* (50¢), the free *Tour of the Golden Past* (a guide to the old Bohemia Mining District), and *Umpqua National Forest Guide, Pacific Crest National Scenic Trail Map*, and *Douglas County Parks Map/Guide* may be obtained by writing: Forest Supervisor, Umpqua National Forest, P.O. Box 1008, Roseburg 97470 (503)672–6601.

The Umpqua National Forest is reached by Oregon Highways 227, 230, 138, and 62. Lodging, supplies, fishing and hunting guides, and outfitters are located at Tiller, Roseburg, Diamond Lake, Union Creek, Clearwater, Steamboat, Myrtle Creek, and Canyonville.

Gateways & Accommodations

Cottage Grove

(Pop. 6,000; zip code 97424; area code 503.) This gateway to the Umpqua National Forest is divided into eastern and western sections by the Coast Fork of the Willamette River. A district ranger's office is located here. Points of interest include the Cottage Grove Dam and Reservoir, 6 miles south on Highway 99; the Dorena Dam and Reservoir, 5 miles east on an unnumbered road; the Cottage Grove Historical Museum, at Birch Ave. and H St.; a 19th-century church containing displays of local historical interest; and the Steam Excursion Train, at the Village Green Motor Hotel, which offers a 2–hour round-trip excursion through the scenic Row River valley (daily during the summer, on weekends and holidays the rest of the year; phone 942–3368). Accommodations: *Village Green Motor Hotel* (rates: $36–39 double), 100 superlative rooms and 2– or 3–bedroom suites with fireplaces, elegant decor, oversize beds, luxury facilities, on beautifully landscaped grounds, large swimming pool and wading pool, putting green, tennis courts, golf privileges, airstrip adjacent, excellent restaurant, cocktail lounge, coffee shop, dancing and entertainment, 1½ miles east of town off Cottage Grove Exit on Interstate 5, Box 277 (942–2491).

Roseburg

(Pop. 14,500; zip code 97470; area code 503.) This city is situated along a curve of the Umpqua River among steep, forested hills which surround the city on all sides. One of these, Mt. Nebo, was supposedly a stepping-stone for the legendary giant Paul Bunyan and Babe the Blue Ox, his loyal companion. Roseburg is headquarters for the Umpqua National Forest. A scenic drive via Oregon State Highway 138 leads from Roseburg through magnificent forest stands along the Umpqua River to Diamond Lake. Other area attractions include the Douglas County Museum, at the local fairgrounds off Interstate 5, containing memorabilia of pioneer days (daily 8:30 A.M.–5 P.M.); and Wildlife Safari, 5 miles south via Interstate 5, a drive-through park where African and Asian animals wander freely in natural surroundings (open daily, 9 A.M. till dusk). Accommodations: *Best Western Douglas Inn* (rates: $21–26 double), 46 air-conditioned rooms, color TV, restaurant opposite, at 511 S.E. Stephens St., 2 blocks west of town via Hwy. 99 (673–6625); *Best Western Thunderbird Inn* (rates: $23–26.50 double), 54 comfortable units, 6 with kitchens, oversize beds, color TV, heated pool, restaurant opposite, at 427 N.W. Garden Valley Blvd., 1 mile north of town via Interstate 5, Exit 125 (673–5561); *Holiday Motel* (rates: $28.50–32.50 double), 40 excellent rooms, color TV, heated pool, nearby restaurant, at 444 S.E. Oak Ave., in town, take Exit 124 off

Interstate 5 (672–4457); *Ponderosa Inn* (rates: $24–29 double), 60 attractive air-conditioned rooms, with oversize beds, color TV, swimming pool, dining room, cocktail lounge, 10 miles north of town at junction of Interstate 5 and Hwy. 138 (459–2236).

Lodges & Resorts

★★*Diamond Lake Resort* is a four-season family resort on the shores of one of Oregon's prettiest mountain-rimmed lakes, high in the white-capped Cascades 18 miles north of Crater Lake. Summer activities include fishing for rainbow trout, boating, horseback riding, swimming, and scenic boat trips around Diamond Lake. When snow hits the ground, there's cross-country skiing over huge expanses of virgin terrain. Diamond Lake Resort has access to 200 miles of marked snowmobile trails and a special 16–passenger heated sleigh pulled by a Sno-Cat. There is also ice-skating at the nearby marina. Accommodations are in motel-type sleeping units ($18–20 daily), fully equipped, deluxe housekeeping cottages ($24 daily), and handsome lakeshore cabins with room for up to 6 guests in each ($26–28 daily). The main lodge building houses a lounge and recreation room, a restaurant and dining room, and several double guest rooms with bath. Boat and motor rentals, riding horses, protected moorage, stores and service stations, and snowmobile rentals are available. For more information write: Diamond Lake Resort, Diamond Lake, OR 97731 (503)793–3333.

★★★*The Steamboat Inn* is a small, select fishing resort located 38 miles east of Roseburg on Maple Ridge Point beside the famed steelhead waters of the North Umpqua River. The inn prides itself on both fine fishing and superlative dining. The fisherman's dinner, a mouth-watering tradition since the 1930s, begins with a light aperitif and continues through skillfully prepared soups, hors d'oeuvres, entrees, and dessert, complemented by a good selection of wines. Streamside picnic dinners and lunches at the Steamboat Inn are equally memorable. Accommodations are in 6 fully modern, attractive guest cabins in beautiful wilderness surroundings. There's also a full selection of fishing gear tailored to meet the demands of the North Umpqua's fighting steelhead. Cabins are usually reserved a year in advance for July and August, so plan ahead. Rates are $25 per night, double occupancy; meals run about the same per day. If your idea of a first-class vacation combines rewarding fishing with gourmet fare, this is the place. For information write: Steamboat Inn, Box 36, Toketee Route, Idleyld Park, OR 97447 (503)498–2411 or 496–3495.

Wallowa-Whitman National Forest

The Wallowa-Whitman National Forest encompasses 2,238,000 acres of big-game hunting, fishing, and wilderness camping country in northeastern Oregon. *Wallowa* is a Nez Percé Indian word referring to the tripods placed in rivers to hold a pole lattice structure for catching salmon and trout. The Wallowa River valley, known as the Valley of the Winding Waters, was the home of the elder Chief Joseph and his son Joseph of the Wallowa Nez Percé. The young Joseph is famous for his brilliant leadership in the Nez Percé War in 1877. The Whitman portion of the forest was named in honor of Dr. Marcus Whitman, who led a missionary party in 1836 from Missouri to Fort Walla Walla on the Columbia River. His group was among the first to traverse the Oregon Trail. The forest ranges from the gentle Blue Mountains and the rugged Wallowa Mountains down to the spectacular canyon country of the mighty Snake River on the border with Idaho. The short, snow-tipped Wallowa Mountain range thrusts up a mass of marble and granite reaching heights of 9,000 feet in an area covering less than 350 square miles. In their isolation, the Wallowas form an imposing sight. From their slopes flow a number of streams that have cut deep, rock-walled canyons. To the east is the broken Imnaha River basin, the spectacular Hills Canyon of the Snake, and the lofty, snowcapped peaks of the Seven Devils Range.

Information Sources, Maps & Access

For additional information, permits, and the full-color *Wallowa-Whitman National Forest Map* (50¢) and *Eagle Cap Wilderness Topographic Map* (50¢), contact: Supervisor, Wallowa-Whitman National Forest, P.O. Box 907, Baker, OR 97814 (503)523–6391. For detailed information and maps on Hells Canyon and Snake National Wild & Scenic River, write: Hells Canyon National Recreation Area, P.O. Box 907, Baker, OR 97814.

The Wallowa-Whitman National Forest is reached via Oregon Highways 7, 237, 86, 203, 244, 204, 82, and 3 and Interstate Highway 80N. Lodging, supplies, guides, and outfitting services are available at Baker, Union, La Grande, Minam, Lostine, Imnaha, Lewis, Homestead, Halfway, Cornucopia, Medical Springs, North Powder, and Elgin.

Recreation Areas

Eagle Cap Wilderness

The majestic Eagle Cap Wilderness embraces 293,476 acres in the heart of the Wallowa Mountains. The massive Eagle Cap is the central peak, forming the hub of many streams and over 50 lakes that lie at the foot of its precipitous slopes or in the high mountain basins. The rugged granite and limestone peaks are nearly devoid of timber, and where there is soil present, whitebark pines cling to the ridges. The rough topography is broken by many deep canyons, towered over by some of the highest peaks in eastern Oregon, with Sacajawea, at 10,033 feet, the highest. Other peaks popular with mountaineers include the Matterhorn—whose white limestone peak is in vivid contrast to the reddish-brown color of the adjoining rock formations—Pete's Point, Brown Mountain, Aneroid Mountain, and Eagle Cap. When climbing these peaks, exercise caution at all times. At the lower elevations, primitive trails, including the spectacular Washboard Trail, lead through forests of pine, firs, and Englemann spruce and through meadows ablaze with colorful buttercups, lupine, fleabane, and fawnlily to such wild areas as Swamp Basin, Hurwal Divide, Big Sheep Basin, Lake Basin, Lostine River, Hurricane Divide, Minam River, and the Imnaha Divide.

The world's entire population of rare Wallowa gray-crowned rosy finch (*Leucosticte tephrocotis wallowa*) nests only in such selected areas of the wilderness as Pete's Point, Jewett Lake, and Glacier Lake near Eagle Cap Mountain. These birds, first discovered in 1923, prefer a habitat of snowfields, rocks, and meadow patches.

Snake National Wild & Scenic River

Hells Canyon of the Snake River is the deepest canyon in North America. Its steep walls rise on the Oregon side to 7,000 feet at Bear Mountain, with the Seven Devils Range of Idaho forming a majestic backdrop towering to 9,000 feet. The Snake National Wild & Scenic River has some of the finest smallmouth bass fishing to be found anywhere, with bronzesides to 5 pounds and over quite common. Good-sized rainbows are found at the mouths of feeder streams. The Snake also holds some giant sturgeon, and channel catfish up to 20 pounds. About the only way to fish the Snake effectively is by boat, floating down from below the rapids at Eagle Bar. Access is generally by horse trail or jet-powered boat from Homestead. The major features along the Oregon-Idaho wild and scenic stretch of the Snake include the Wild Sheep, Granite, China, High Range, Wolf Creek, Zigzag, and Frenchy rapids.

Gateways & Accommodations

Baker

(Pop. 9,400; zip code 97814; area code 503.) Located on the upper reaches of the Powder River, Baker is a gateway to the Hells Canyon National Recreation Area and Wallowa-Whitman National Forest. A district ranger's office is located here. Within a few hours' drive are numerous ghost towns, relics of the area's gold-rush days. For information, contact the Chamber of Commerce, Box 69 (523–5855). Accommodations: *Best Western Sunridge Inn* (rates: $26–28 double), 105 excellent rooms and suites, oversize beds, balconies, heated

pool, restaurant, cocktail lounge, at 1 Sunridge Lane, off Interstate 80N at City Center Exit (523–6444); *Hereford Motel* (rates: $18–19 double), 42 fine rooms, most with oversize beds, color TV, heated pool, sauna, at 134 Bridge St., 2 blocks east of town on U.S. Hwy. 30 (523–4457); *Royal Motor Inn* (rates: $19.50–22 double), 36 rooms and suites, color TV, heated pool, at 2205 Broadway (523–6324).

Joseph

(Pop. 800; zip code 97846; area code 503.) This town in the remote wilderness of northeastern Oregon bears the name of two famous Nez Percé chieftains, father and son, who held sway over this valley, their hereditary home, until 1877. The younger Chief Joseph refused to be herded onto a reservation and led his people on a long and arduous trek eastward before surrendering to the U.S. Army just south of the Canadian border in Montana. A monument at the north end of Wallowa Lake commemorates this courageous leader. Joseph is an outfitting center for the many area lakes, resorts, and Hells Canyon National Recreation Area. Accommodations: *Indian Lodge Motel* (rates: $23 double), 15 comfortable rooms, color TV, at-door parking, nearby restaurant, on Hwy. 82 (432–2651); *Ponderosa Motel* (rates: $19–21 double), 25 air-conditioned rooms, color TV, free coffee, nearby restaurant, at 102 S.E. Greenwood St. in Enterprise 97828, 7 miles north on Hwy. 82 (426–3186).

Ontario

(Pop. 6,500; zip code 97914; area code 503.) Ontario is a trading center for the eastern border counties of Oregon and gateway to a vast wilderness of lakes and rivers, rolling rangeland, canyons and mountains. The area is a rock hound's paradise; semiprecious stones, petrified wood, marine fossils, and quartz crystals abound. The Chamber of Commerce, at 125 S. Oregon St., carries maps showing the best locations for different types of stones. Southwest of town is Owyhee Lake, accessible via Oregon Hwy. 201, framed by spectacular red-colored cliffs along its eastern shore. Nearby are precipitous, multihued tributary canyons and Succor Creek Canyon, where numerous traces of Indian civilization have been found. Accommodations: *Best Western Holiday Motor Inn* (rates: $20–22 double), 74 air-conditioned rooms, many with oversize beds, 24–hour restaurant, bar, heated pool, at 615 E. Idaho Ave., off Interstate 80N, Exit 376 (889–9188); *Best Western Tapadera* (rates: $24–28 double), 100 excellent rooms and suites, with oversize beds, color TV, balconies, heated pool, sauna, 24–hour restaurant, cocktail lounge, free airport pickup, at 725 Tapadera Ave., off Interstate 80N, Exit 376 (889–8621).

Lodges

★*Boulder Park Lodge—Gateway to the Eagle Cap Wilderness* is located high in the Wallowa-Whitman National Forest on the southern edge of the Eagle Cap Wilderness. This wilderness outpost offers rustic log housekeeping cabins, dining room, and guided pack trips into the Eagle Cap Wilderness and the Minam River country. This spectacular wilderness area, with its alpine meadows and lakes, offers excellent fishing for big rainbows, backpacking, and hunting in season for elk and deer. The lodge accommodations consist of large 2– or 3–bedroom log cabins and modern 1–room log cabins. Boulder Park is located 42 miles northeast of Baker, Oregon. For rates and info, contact: P.O. Box 417, La Grande, OR 97850. No phone.

Travel Services

Eagle Cap Pack Station, Oregon's largest riding and packhorse station, offers expertly guided fishing, camping, photography, and elk-hunting trips in season in the spectacular Eagle Cap Wilderness and Hells Canyon areas. For rates and info, contact: Eagle Cap Pack Station, P.O. Box 416, Joseph, OR 97846 (503)432–4145.

Hells Canyon Guide Service offers professionally guided wild and scenic float trips down the Hells Canyon of the Snake River with custom fishing trips in season for smallmouth bass up to trophy weights and steelhead. For rates and info, contact: P.O. Box 165, Oxbow, OR 97840 (503)785–3305.

Snake River Packers & Outfitters offers wilderness float trips in the Hells Canyon National Recreation Area of the Snake River as well as custom-guided steelhead fishing trips and fall elk-hunting trips in the Eagle Cap high country. Contact: Snake River Packers & Outfitters, Enterprise, OR 97828 (503)426–3307.

SOUTH DAKOTA

Introduction

South Dakota contains the remote trophy trout waters and rugged big-game ranges of the Black Hills National Forest and the Badlands, with their fantastic pinnacles of rainbow-hued sandstone in the westernmost portion of the state, extending to the Bear Lodge Mountains in Wyoming; the nationally famous great northern pike and walleye waters of the great lakes of the Missouri, Lake Kampeska, and the hauntingly named Enemy Swim Lake Country. The Sunshine State, explored by Lewis and Clark during their 1805 expedition up the Missouri, and the home of Sacajawea, Sitting Bull, and Crazy Horse, was the site of the great Dakota Gold Boom and the 1890 massacre of Indian families at Wounded Knee.

Accommodations & Travel Services

Listings and descriptions of the state's major vacation accommodations are found in the "Vacation/Lodging Guide" which follows. For detailed information on all aspects of travel in the state, contact: South Dakota Tourism Development, Pierre, SD 57501 (605)773–3301. Request their free annual *South Dakota Vacation Guide.*

Information & Services

Several publications of use to South Dakota-bound anglers and hunters may be obtained free from: Information & Education Branch, Dept. of Game, Fish, & Parks, State Office Bldg. 1, Pierre 57501, including the 35–page *South Dakota Angler's Almanac*, a guide to the state's public fishing waters; *South Dakota Fishing Guide*, which contains regulations, seasons, and limits. *South Dakota Guide to State Public Shooting Areas & Federal Waterfowl Production Areas; Know Your South Dakota Fishes; Nonresident Fall Hunting*; and the *South Dakota Hunting Guide*, which includes regulations, seasons, and special permit information. Anyone planning to camp in South Dakota should send for an informative *Directory of Campgrounds in South Dakota*, available free from: South Dakota Campground Owners Assn., 1035 Lawrence St., Belle Fourche 57717. The brochure contains descriptions of the association's member campgrounds, listing facilities and phone numbers, and including a map so that you can see where each campground is. It is best to check with the campground in question before setting out, to determine what the current rates are and to get information on rules and regulations.

Highways & Maps

In order to be sure of taking the most direct highway route to your destination in South Dakota, write for the free *South Dakota Official Highway Map* to: Dept. of Economics & Tourism Development, Pierre 57501. The map shows all roads and highways, national forests, parks and monuments, Indian reservations, national grasslands areas, roadside rest areas, airports, railroads, and other points of interest. A location index of cities and towns is provided. The reverse side of the map indicates a number of scenic and recreational attractions that would make enjoyable family excursions. Inserts detail Rapid City, Sioux Falls, and Aberdeen. Along the highways of South Dakota there are various Tipi Rest Areas. These areas, characterized by a distinctive, 56–foot-high steel and concrete tipi framework, provide rest rooms and tourist information centers. The buildings themselves are fashioned after the sod houses and dugouts that dotted the prairies during pioneering days.

South Dakota Lakes & Recreation Areas

Few people are aware that South Dakota's great lakes and the wide open spaces of its vast rolling grasslands and rugged hill country offer some of the finest fishing and hunting in the United States. The Sunflower State, also long known as the pheasant capital of the world, is divided into two parts by the Missouri River, which flows through the middle of the state from north to south. The eastern half of the state holds rich glacial farmlands and, in the northeast, hundreds of natural blue lakes carved out by the receding glacial ice cap. Rising from the great plains to the west of the Missouri are the rugged Badlands and Black Hills, crowned by 7,242–foot Harney Peak, the highest point in the state and the highest point in the nation east of the Rocky Mountains.

Information Sources, Maps & Access

A useful full-color *Map of the Great Lakes of South Dakota* contains a Lake Oahe Area Map and Lake Sharpe Area Map, a facilities chart, and shows all principal highways, secondary roads, elevations, boat ramps, parks and recreation area campgrounds, historical sites, airports, Indian Reservation lands, and rangelands. It describes historical sites and points of interest, including the ancient Arikara Indian fortress and village predating Columbus; Fort George, established as a trading post of the Missouri Fur Company in 1819; Little Eagle, where Sitting Bull was killed at his cabin on Grand River in 1890; and Fort Manuel, established as a trading post in 1812 by Manuel Lisa and the purported grave-site of Sacajawea. (More than 80 historic sites lie beneath the waters of Lake Oahe, including Lewis and Clark campsites, Indian missions, trading posts, and Indian villages. For information, write: South Dakota Historical Society, Pierre 57501.) The map of the great lakes may be obtained free by writing: Information & Education Branch, Dept. of Game, Fish, & Parks, State Office Bldg. 1, Pierre 57501. This department also publishes a free pamphlet on the *Missouri River Waterfowl Refuges*, renowned for their mallard and Canada geese. A free *Map of the Northeastern Lake Region* may be obtained by writing: Northeastern Lake Region, P.O. Box 783, Watertown 57201. Useful *Lake Contour Maps* which show water depth, bottom composition, dams, and contours, are available free upon request for most major South Dakota lakes including famous Enemy Swim, Punished Woman, Pelican, Poinsett, Kampeska, Kampeska Gravel Pits, Waubay, Nine Mile, Bear Butte, East Vermilion, Blue Dog, Red Iron, and Cottonwood, to name a few. Write to: Information & Education Branch, Dept. of Game, Fish & Parks, State Office Bldg. 1, Pierre 57501, for a free map listing. For detailed information on the Black Hills and a full-color *Black Hills National Forest Map* (50¢), contact: Supervisor, Black Hills National Forest, P.O. Box 792, Custer, SD 57730 (605)673–2251. For detailed information and maps of both the Badlands and Black Hills, contact: Black Hills Badlands & Lakes Association, Sturgie, SD 57785 (605)347–3646). For detailed information on the Badlands National Monument and a free *Badlands Map/Brochure*, contact: Superintendent, Badlands National Monument, Interiro, SD 57750 (605)433–5364. Visitors to this area should obtain a copy of the *U.S. Geological Survey Map of Badlands National Monument and Vicinity* ($2), showing the Badlands National Monument and adjacent areas and contours, roads, cities, towns, borders, campgrounds, streams, lakes, and ponds. The size is 48 × 24 inches, scale, 1:62,500. It may be ordered direct from: Distribution Branch, U.S. Geological Survey, Federal Center, Denver, CO 80225. The major auto access routes serving the Sunflower State are Interstate Highways 29 and 90.

VACATION/ LODGING GUIDE

Recreation & Scenic Areas

The Badlands

South Dakota's haunting Badlands—known to the Indians as *Mako Sica* and to the early French explorers as *Mauvaises Terres*, both meaning literally, "Bad Land"—were described by General George A. Custer as "a part of hell with the fire burned out." The Badlands lie just east and north of the Black Hills, dominated by the Badlands Wall: a range of grasslands, roded multicolored peaks of gray, tan, buff, olive, deep rose, and cream. It is a barren country of ghostly peaks, lofty pinnacles, terraces, and cathedral-like spires which rise above eroded, rounded domes, with washed-out gaps forming natural windows. The Fossil Trail winds through an ancient region once roamed by giant saber-toothed tigers, dog-sized camels, titanotheres, and hyracodons. Historic Big Foot Pass lies in the heart of the Badlands. It was through this opening that Indian Chief Big Foot, with his hand of 400 warriors, eluded the U.S. Cavalry. After his escape from the Badlands, Big Foot and his braves met their gruesome fate at the Battle of Wounded Knee—the last conflict between the whites and the Indians and the culmination of the Messiah War.

Black Hills National Forest

This 1,223,000–acre preserve, whose name is a direct translation of the Sioux term *Paha Sapa*, is in the wildlands of western South Dakota and extends into the Bear Lodge Mountains region of Wyoming. This jumbled region of ponderosa pine forests, rushing streams, deep canyons, and cascades is a top-ranking deer and elk hunting area. Fly fishing is good for brook, brown, and rainbow trout up to 4 and 5 pounds in Spring, Spearfish, Beaver, Elk, Redwater, and Box Elder creeks and in Cox's Creek and Mirror lakes. Forest roads provide access to the Taylor Divide, Belle Fourche River and National Wildlife Refuge, Elk Mountains, Mount Rushmore, Pactola Lake, Cheyenne River, and the Angostura Reservoir—one of the state's finest lakes for walleye, northern pike, and black bass to 6 pounds. When white men first discovered gold in the hills, they proceeded to invade this sacred land of the Sioux, first by force, then by treaty. Remains of old mining towns can still be seen.

Great Lakes of the Missouri

When Lewis and Clark traveled up the Missouri in the early 19th century it was a wild river, a challenge to conquer. Today it has been tamed by four large dams—Oahe, Big Bend, Fort Randall, and Gavins Point—built by the U.S. Army Corps of Engineers, creating deep blue-water lakes. There is a 2,300–mile shoreline extending along the prairie grassland in the shadow of rising bluffs. Anglers can find isolation and year-round trophy fishing in this wilderness paradise. The Missouri River and its great lakes claim 20 South Dakota fishing records, including a 35–pound 8–ounce northern pike, a 113–pound paddlefish, and a 7–pound 7–ounce suager. There are outstanding facilities for boating, hunting, camping, exploring, and hiking. Lake Oahe, impounded by the Oahe Dam above Pierre, is one of the nation's top-ranked northern pike and walleye fisheries. The reservoir impounds 370,000 surface acres and winds for 230 miles from Pierre to Bismarck, North Dakota. Lake Sharpe to the south is impounded by Big Bend Dam at Fort Thompson. The lake stretches for 80 miles along prairie bluffs and grassy lowlands. Further south lie Fort Randall Dam, which impounds Lake Francis Case, and Lewis and Clark Lake. All of the great lakes hold trophy-sized walleye, northern pike, white bass, channel catfish, and white and black crappie. The cold, tailrace waters below the dams offer outstanding fishing for sauger (known locally as "sandpike"), walleye, catfish, paddlefish, and sturgeon. There are boat-launching sites at major fishing access areas along the great lakes. Fishing supplies, equipment, and boat rentals are available at the major outfitting centers located along the lakes.

Northeastern Lake Country

The beautiful gravel-bottomed, forest-fringed lakes of the northeast lake region provide some of the state's finest fishing for walleye and trophy northern pike. Here, amid the state's greatest concentration of natural lakes, are the legendary waters of Enemy Swim, Blue Dog, Kampeska, and Buffalo lakes. The region's major lakes include 4,820–acre Lake Kampeska; 2,800–acre Lake Pelican; 1,502–acre Blue Dog Lake; 2,150–acre Enemy Swim Lake; the famed 5,000 acres of North and South Waubay lakes; 2,300–acre Rush Lake; 1,161–acre Round Lake; 1,146–acre Lake Alice; 365–acre Lake Cochrane; 7,866–acre Lake Poinsett, the state's largest natural lake; the 2,200 acres of North and South Buffalo lakes; 1,700–acre Roy Lake; 21,280–acre Big Stone Lake, straddling the South Dakota-Minnesota boundary; and the 2,480 acres of North and South Drywood lakes. Rainbow trout are caught in the Kampeska Trout Ponds and Amsden Lake. The scenic mixed hardwood and evergreen forests of the northeast lake country are slashed by several swift-flowing streams and rivers: the Big Sioux River holds northern pike, walleye, and panfish; Gary Creek yields brook trout; the South Fork of the Yellowbank River holds brook trout; and Sieche Hollow holds some big brown and rainbow trout.

Lodges & Resorts

South Dakota, like most of the Great Plains states, has a limited number of full-service vacation lodges and resorts. For accommodations information, contact: South Dakota Tourism Development, Pierre, SD 57501 (605)773–3301.

TEXAS

Introduction

Texas, the largest of the contiguous states, containing 265,986 square miles, offers some excellent fishing and hunting opportunities in the forestlands and sagebrush flats, mountain and canyon country, and 6,000 square miles of freshwater lakes and streams, plus scores of tidal bays and 624 miles of shoreline along the Gulf of Mexico.

Accommodations & Travel Information

Descriptions of Lone Star State's major guest ranches, lodges, and resorts are found in the "Vacation/Lodging Guide" which follows. For detailed vacation travel information, contact: Division of Travel & Information, Dept. of Highways & Public Transportation, Austin, TX 78701 (512)475-3661.

Information & Services

Fishing and hunting seasons, size limits, bag and possession limits and special regulations are contained in the free publications *Texas Hunting Guide* and *Texas Fishing Guide*, available from the Texas Parks & Wildlife Dept., John H. Reagan Bldg., Austin 78701. The hundreds of campgrounds in this wide and varied state provide excellent facilities and access to natural areas. *Texas Public Campgrounds*, available free from the Travel & Information Division, State Dept. of Highways & Public Transportation, P.O. Box 5064, Austin 78763, lists and describes all the public camping areas in the state. *Texas—A Land of Contrasts*, a free and enormously useful 205–page book with many color illustrations, lists local, state, and federal campgrounds as well as complete information on virtually every recreational facility and service in the state. It is available free from the same office, and it includes maps of every region in the state, information on trails, state parks, forest lands, hunting and fishing, rocks, minerals, flowers, birds, special events, tourist bureaus, and weather. The pine forests of Texas are covered with a network of trails. They offer scenic beauty as well as glimpses of wildlife, forest plants and vegetation, wild flowers, and birds. Along the state's trails, you may discover a bird sanctuary or such small animals as raccoons, minks, squirrels, muskrats, foxes, and rabbits. Relics of Indian life and lore are present, as well as mute remains of pioneer history. There are several recreation areas, and good fishing in the lakes and streams. *Ride the Texas Forest Trail*, a list and description of Texas trails, is available free from the Texas Highway Dept., Austin 78701. It includes an overall map indicating highways, towns, and farms.

Highways & Maps

The free *Texas Official Highway Travel Map* is available from the State Dept. of Highways & Public Transportation, Travel & Information Division, P.O. Box 5064, Austin 78763. It shows all highways and roads, towns, lakes and rivers, and tourist bureaus. Detailed folders are available from the State Dept. of Highways & Public Transportation for the following vacation travel trails—great circle loops of from 500 to 700 miles along hard-surfaced byways off the beaten path of fast-moving freeways and Interstate routes: *Pecos Trail, Plains Trail, Mountain Trail, Lakes Trail, Independence Trail, Tropical Trail, Brazos Trail, Hill Country Trail, Forts Trail*, and the *Texas Forest Trail*. A detailed guide to the highways and byways, scenic and recreation attractions, and just about everything you need to know about travel in the Lone Star State, including weather information, is contained in the giant 205–page *Texas—A Land of Contrasts* travel guide, available free upon request from the Travel & Information Division (address above).

Texas Forests, Lakes & National Parks

The Lone Star State is rimmed on the north by the Red River, on the east by the Sabine, and on the west and south by the historic Rio Grande, all of which contain a series of large impoundments. The scenic green-canopied Piney Woods and Big Thicket region of East Texas offers some of the state's finest whitetail deer, wild turkey, and upland game-bird hunting and trophy largemouth-bass fishing in the Southwest. Here are the vast, fragrant pine forests of the Angelina, Davy Crockett, Sabine, and Sam Houston national forest lands, and the lunker-bass waters of famous Lake Caddo and Lake o' the Pines, Livingston, Palestine, Sam Rayburn, Wright Patman, and Toledo Bend reservoirs, set among scenic, rolling forestlands. Huge 32,700–acre Caddo Lake, which straddles the Texas-Louisiana border, is renowned for its trophy bass and primeval beauty—fringed by dense moss-covered forests. Caddo, believed to have been created by the great New Madrid earthquake of 1811, has a confusing maze of channels, 42 miles of which have been marked as "boat roads" by the state. To the west, in the "Gateway" region between the rolling prairies and the Brazos Valley, are the bass waters: 33,750–acre Cedar Creek Lake, one of the most popular in north-central Texas; Eagle Mountain Lake, noted for its huge schools of white bass, and Granbury Lake on the Brazos River, Grapevine Lake, and Lewisville, Lavcon, and Palestine lakes. Some of the state's best bass fishing is found here in huge 89,000–acre Lake Texoma; in 36,700–acre Lake Tawakoni, with its more than 5 miles of submerged timber and countless coves and inlets; and in the clear blue waters of 15,760–acre Lake Whitney, with its towering cliffs and sheltered coves and inlets. The woodlands and glades of the Brazos River Valley to the south, named Brazos de Dios, the "Arms of God," by the Spanish, provide good hunting for deer and wild turkey, and bass fishing in Mexia, Somerville, Waco, and Stillhouse Hollow lakes.

The "Ranch and Hill" country to the west provides fishing for rainbow and brown trout on the Guadalupe River below the Canyon Lake Dam, and for trophy bass in the submerged brush areas of the upper reaches of 22,050–acre Corpus Christi Lake. Scenic 19,800–acre Possum Kingdom Lake, in the rolling prairie country to the north, is a popular bass-fishing and hunting area. Greenbelt Lake, on the Salt Fork of the Red River, is known as the "northern pike capital of Texas," and produced the state-record 18 lb. 2 oz. northern.

To the west of the rolling prairie country are the arid flatlands of the Texas High Plains, the wetlands of the Buffalo Lake National Wildlife Refuge, and the beautiful blue waters of Lake Meredith and the Sanford Recreation Area, set among the colorful buttes and cliffs of the Canadian River Valley. To the south is the rugged Pecos River Country, home of Pecos Bill, legendary king of the cowboys, and Judge Roy Bean—the "Law West of the Pecos." The clear blue waters of the huge 67,000–acre Amistad Reservoir—a joint project of the United States and Mexico and a national recreation area—impounds the waters of the Rio Grande just below its confluence with the Devils River. The numerous coves and inlets of the great lake—which extends for 74 miles up the Rio Grande, 13 miles up the Pecos River, and 25 miles up the Devils River, surrounded by rugged wild lands—provides top-ranked fishing for trophy largemouth bass. For detailed information about fishing, regulations, accommodations, fishing guide service, and marinas, write: Amistad National Recreation Area, Del Rio 78840.

To the west lie the lofty mountains and spectacular canyons of the "Big Bend" Country of the Rio Grande and the rugged Guadalupe Mountains. The 708,221–acre Big Bend National Park encompasses the wild country of spectacular canyons, bluffs, stark desert, and

VACATION/ LODGING GUIDE

mountains bordered on three sides by the "Big Bend" of the Rio Grande—the international boundary between Mexico and the United States—known to the Spanish conquistadors as the "Great River of the North" and to the early pioneers as the haunting "River of Ghosts." This rugged wilderness, once the home and hunting grounds of the Comanche Indians, is inhabited by mule deer, javelina, mountain lion, pronghorn antelope, gray fox, and bobcat. The rugged Chisos Mountains—the Apache word for "ghostly"—with their red, yellow, blue, and purple slopes, dominate the landscape north of the "Big Bend." The major features along the Rio Grande as it flows through the park include the awesome Mariscal Canyon; the Break—where the canyon walls recede from the river for a distance of one-fourth mile; the short but scenic San Vicente and Hot Springs canyons; and Boquillas Canyon. Old Comanche trails, petroglyphs, dugouts, and numerous caves are located along the dark, shadowed floors of the canyon. Guadalupe Mountains National Park, once the home and hunting grounds of the Apache, established in 1972, preserves 77,518 acres of desert wilderness dominated by El Capitan, surrounded by deep canyons, towering cliffs, high parklike valleys, ghostly white salt flats, countless caverns, and spectacular mountain vistas in northwest Texas, just south of the New Mexico line. The mountain slopes are covered with Texas madrona, Douglas fir, limber pine, aspen, and ponderosa pine, and are inhabited by mule deer, elk, bobcats, coyote, and a few mountain lions. Access to the interior is limited to hiking and wilderness camping. Only experienced, well-equipped backpackers should enter the rugged backcountry. A small, primitive campground is at the Pinery, near Pine Springs on U.S. 62/180.

The near-tropic region to the east, along the Gulf of Mexico, encompasses the famed trophy bass and catfish waters of the huge 78,340–acre Falcon Reservoir, straddling the U.S.-Mexico boundary, and the renowned saltwater fishing centers at South Padre Island, Aransas Pass, Corpus Christi, and the Padre Island National Seashore. During the early 1900s, the Mustang Island area was one of the world's great tarpon centers, but it has rapidly declined over the years. The renowned saltwater fishing meccas along the Gulf of Mexico on Texas' 624–mile east coast provide fishing for tuna, marlin, sailfish, pompano, snook, king and Spanish mackerel, wahoo, speckled trout, flounder, grouper, jewfish, red snapper, sheepshead, drum, bluefish, southern kingfish and several varieties of sharks. The coastline teems with gulls, egrets, pelicans, and roseate spoonbills, plus a few rare whooping cranes that winter at the Aransas National Wildlife Refuge.

Texas is thought by many to be the nation's number one deer state. Whitetails are found throughout the state, but are hunted most successfully in the hill country, where they are found in greater numbers than anywhere else in the United States. Mule deer and pronghorn antelope are found in the rugged western portions of the state, along with javelina and wild boar. Game birds include huge

numbers of ducks and geese, which winter in the state, as well as wild turkey, mourning and white-winged doves, pheasant, prairie chickens, sandhill cranes, and several types of quail. Unfortunately, most of the hunting lands in Texas are privately owned, requiring permission from the landowner before entering or hunting, or the payment of a "lease" or fee.

National forestlands in Texas include the Angelina, Davy Crockett, Sam Houston, and Sabine national forests, located in the "Piney Woods" region in eleven East Texas counties, with a combined total of 658,023 acres. The Angelina National Forest, the smallest, with 154,139 acres, is a great pine forest and game preserve bordered in part by the Angelina River, Shawnee Creek, and Ayish Bayou, all of which offer good float fishing. Camping facilities, boat-launching sites, and hiking trails are located at Boykin Springs, Letney, Townsend, Harvey, Caney Creek, Sandy Creek, and Bouton Lake recreation areas. Huge, 113,410–acre Sam Rayburn Lake, with a 560–mile shoreline, is the largest lake in the state, with vast areas of flooded timber providing prime trophy bass habitat. The Sabine National Forest lies adjacent to the Louisiana border, and covers 183,843 acres on the Toledo Bend Reservoir—one of the nation's finest trophy bass fisheries. Forest Service campgrounds along Toledo Bend include Indian Mounds, Willow Oak, Ragtown, and the Lakeview primitive camping area. The scenic Davy Crockett National Forest encompasses 161,556 acres in Houston and Trinity counties and contains the Neches Bluff, Ratcliff Lake, and Kickapoo recreation areas. Sam Houston National Forest encompasses 158,235 acres and contains a portion of the vast two-million-acre Big Thicket National Biological Reserve—a wild, junglelike region of tangled, often impenetrable pine and hardwood forests, vines, shrubs, creepers, rare ferns (some over 6 feet tall), orchids, and remote ponds bordered by wild flags, white and red lilies, and cattails.

Information Sources, Maps & Access

For detailed outdoor recreation information contact the Texas Division of Travel & Information, Austin 78701 (512)475–3661 and the Texas Parks Wildlife Dept., John H. Reagan Bldg., Austin 78701 (512)475–4888. The *National Forests in Texas Recreation Map*, available for 50¢ from the Forest Supervisor, Box 969, Lufkin 75401, shows all roads and trails, streams, lakes, campgrounds, ranger stations, trail shelters, boat ramps, and points of interest. These East Texas National Forests are reached via Interstate 90, 10, and 45; state highways 21, 7, 150, 87, 147, 13, and 94; and U.S. highways 96, 287, and 59. Accommodations, supplies, and services are available at Houston, Conroe, Lufkin, Center, Huntsville, and San Augustine. The forests are shown on the following U.S. Geological Survey 1:250,000–scale Overview Maps: Angelina N.F., Davy Crockett N.F., Sabine N.F., Palestine, Sam Houston N.F., Beaumont. These maps are available for $2 each from: U.S. Geological Survey, Federal Center, Denver, CO 80225. Write to Big Bend National Park 79834 (915)477–2251 for complete information on canyons, the Rio Grande, hiking, float trips, camping, fishing, rules and regulations, safety, and use of horses and vehicles. The *Big Bend Map/Guide*, available free, provides a contour map and description of the park, and indicates services, facilities, roads, trails, and campgrounds. Big Bend National Park is reached via U.S. 90, 385, 80, and 67, Interstate Highway 10, and Texas State Highway 118 and Texas Ranch Road 170—the Camino Real. For detailed information on Guadalupe Mountains National Park contact: Superintendent, Guadalupe National Park, 3225 National Parks Hwy., Carlsbad, NM 88220. The major Interstate auto routes that serve the Lone Star State are: 40, 27, 20 and 10.

Lodges, Resorts & Guest Ranches

★★★*Amistad Lodge* is located in the desert countryside near huge Lake Amistad, ten miles from Del Rio and just 13 miles from Cuidad Acuna, Mexico. Lake Amistad attracts many visitors who come to boat and fish. Amistad Lodge accommodates boaters by offering free parking for trailered boats of guests. For anglers, there is an outdoor room designed for fish cleaning. The lodge also has licensed fishing and hunting guides available. There is a private pool with a patio for sunbathing. In the spring, the area is bright with cactus blooms. Delicious meals are served in the Amistad Lodge Restaurant, which is one of the most popular restaurants in the area among the locals. Six nights a week, there is live entertainment for listening and dancing pleasure. The Lodge has 40 bedrooms and kitchenette units. All have air-conditioning, TV and carpeting. Large bedrooms are $22/single and $26/double per day. One-bedroom suites are $30 and two-bedroom suites are $56. For information or reservations, write Larry and Ann Scruggs, Amistad Lodge, P.O. Box 1209, Del Rio, TX 78840 (512)775–8591.

★★★★*Channel View*, luxurious condominiums on the sparkling Aransas Channel overlooking the Gulf of Mexico, offers day or night fishing from a lighted pier, private boat marina, swimming in a fresh water pool set in a tropical garden, and 1, 2, 3, and 4–bedroom condominiums with fully equipped modern kitchens, color TV's, spacious living room dining areas, and private sundecks. Summer rates extend from March 1 to September 30, and are daily $60 for a one-bedroom apartment, $75/two-bedroom, $85/three-bedroom, $85 for two-bedroom units facing the channel, and $165 daily for deluxe penthouses. Winter rates are daily, $40/one-bedroom, $50/two-bedroom, $60/three-bedroom, $60/two-bedroom with channel view, and $100 daily for deluxe penthouses. For more information write: The Channel View, P.O. Box 776, Port Aransas, TX 78373 (713)749–6156.

★★★*Chisos Mountain Lodge at Big Bend National Park* is located along the Rio Grande in an area offering dramatic scenic contrasts. Imposing canyons, colorful arroyos, flowering deserts and expansive plains blend together in the old frontier atmosphere of the area along the Rio Grande, where the Sierra del Carmen and Fronteriza ranges of Mexico dominate the landscape to the south. Travel to the mile-high Chisos Mountains, spend a day on an outing to the Santa Elena and Boquillas Canyons or follow trails in Big Bend National Park to view the stark, striking panoramas of the area. Guests can take short scenic trail rides, visit "The Window"; or an all-day escorted ride to spectacular South Rim. Experienced guides, fine saddle horses and lunches are available. There are hiking trails in South Rim and the Lost Mine Peak trail to impressive Casa Grande. Fine campgrounds are administered by the National Park Service located in the Chisos Mountains, Rio Grande Village and at Cottonwood. Trailer sites with electric and water hookups are located at the Rio Grande Village Camp store and at Panther Junction Service Station. The Chisos Mountain Lodge is situated 5,400 feet above sea level, offering a magnificent view. Each motel-type room has two double beds, bath, shower, air-conditioning and heating. Also available are frame cottages, designed for comfort, at minimum rates, with adjacent central buildings with rest rooms and showers. Meals, not included in rates, are available in the lodge dining room and coffee shop. Rates: Chisos Mountains Lodge motel units: $28 double occupancy; separate rates for frame cottage units. For further information contact: National Park Concessions, Inc., Big Bend National Park, TX 79834 (915)477–2291.

★★★*Circle R Ranch*, nestled in a broad rolling valley by the Medina River, boasts the finest selection of horses in five counties,

and has professional cowboy guides to lead trail rides over 550 acres of sprawling ranch terrain and the surrounding hills. The ranch has a lighted rodeo arena, a western ghost town, square dance halls, and a large restaurant serving generous country-style meals and Texas barbeque. There is swimming and fishing on the Medina River, boats to rent, a large pool, golf driving range, tennis, archery, rifle range, and trap shooting. All rustic cabins have fireplaces, and are modernly air-conditioned, with tile baths. There is also a roomy bunkhouse. In the evenings, country western dance combos play poolside, there is a juke box in the cozy B.Y.O. bar, and square dances, hayrides to the river, and Texas style cookouts highlight each week. Cottages must be reserved for a minimum of two days. Rates are $45 daily single occupancy, and $40 double occupancy, including meals. Weekly rates are $292 single occupancy, and $260 double occupancy. Circle R has its own private landing strip and refueling facilities. For more information write: Circle R Ranch, Box 1376, TX 78055 (512)589–2324.

★★★*Dixie Dude Ranch* is a small family guest ranch nestled in a broad open valley in the Texas Hill country. The rugged hills and broad plateaus are ideal for riding. Experienced wranglers will select suitable mounts for guests from their fine selection of horses, many bred and trained at the ranch. There is also a large outdoor pool and a children's pool, where poolside parties are given in the evening with patio dancing. Dixie Dude Ranch specializes in generous country style cooking, southern fried chicken and Texas barbeque are among the ranch favorites. In the evenings, guests gather in the Round-up Room for cocktails, roast marshmallows on an open fire, play bingo, bumper pool, and cards in the lounge, or watch TV by the stone hearth. Spacious lodge rooms and private cottages all have air-conditioning, and TV. Rates include lodging, daily riding and swimming, and three hearty country style meals. Rates are daily $30 per person double occupancy, and $33 for singles. Weekly rates are $205 per person double occupancy, and $225 for singles. For more information write: Mrs. D.H. Cromwell, Bandera, TX 78003 (512)796–4481.

★★★*Fin and Feather Lodge at Toledo Bend Lake* on sheltered Housen Bay on Toledo Bend Lake offers outstanding fishing for bream, striped bass, black bass, white perch, and catfish. Fishermen can cast from the lakeshore, the lighted pier, or rent a boat from the marina. Expert fishing guides show anglers the best spots in the secluded coves and bays of sprawling Toledo Bend. The Fin and Feather staff will clean, fillet and freeze your catch, or serve it to you that night for dinner. The dining room overlooking the lake serves a special fisherman's breakfast at dawn, as well as a leisurely breakfast for late risers. Fresh seafood specialties, such as stuffed crab, fresh catfish, and shrimp are a part of each evening menu. There are also moonlight cruises, sailing and water skiing on the lake, and a large outdoor pool. The lodge has spacious air-conditioned rooms, and family housekeeping units, complete with kitchens. Campsites and trailer sites are available, with water and electric hookups. The tackle shop sells groceries, sportswear, hot sandwiches, cold beer, and complete line of bait. For details write: The Fin & Feather Lodge, P.O. Box 810, Hemphill, TX 75948 (713)579–3368.

★★★*Flying L Resort and Country Club* is a year round-resort located in the Texas Hills, one of the most scenic ateas of the state. The resort has horseback riding and bridle paths leading through towering oaks and shallow streams. There are lighted tennis courts, and an 18–hole championship golf course, which provides a challenge for both amateurs and serious pros. There's an Olympic size swimming pool with cabanas and a snack bar, as well as facilities for volleyball, badminton, shuffleboard, ping pong and horseshoes. The Flying L has a full service airport with a 3,200 foot paved and lighted runway. Accommodations are private modern suites. Gourmet dinners are served in the resort's beautiful clubhouse. There are facilities for conventions, groups, receptions and tournaments. Rates: Suites $27–42/daily. Meals are not included in rates. Holiday rates available. For further information contact: The Flying L Resort and Country Club, P.O. Box 98, Bandera, TX 78003 (512)796–3721.

★★★*Indian Lodge*, is nestled in a deep canyon in the center of Davis Mountain State park in southwestern Texas. The whitewashed walls of Pueblo design perfectly complement the broad sloping mountains that rise in all directions to elevations of 5,000 feet. Nearby, is the historic Fort Davis, the McDonald Observatory, and the 75–mile scenic drives through the Davis Mountain Range. The park has picnic sites, camp sites, and trailer hookups. Hiking trails wind over the Davis Range, widening into panoramic vistas looking west towards Mexico. Throughout the summer, there is an interpretive nature program and evening campfires. Indian Lodge is fully air-conditioned, and has a heated outdoor pool, and delicious home-cooked meals served with mountain hospitality. Rates are $16 daily for singles, and $18 for a double room. Deluxe suites are $23. For more information write: Indian Lodge, P.O. Box 786, Fort Davis, TX 79734 (915)426–3254.

★★★*Island Retreat*, on the golden stretches of Mustang Island, in the Gulf of Mexico, offers miles of sand beach, swimming in the pounding Gulf surf or a large outdoor pool. Modern motel rooms, some with kitchenette and deluxe apartments with private patio or balcony border the beach. Summer rates (May 1 to September 30) are $31 for two persons in a motel room, $35 for four. Motel rooms with kitchens, $37. One bedroom apartments are $50 for four, two bedroom apartments will accommodate six for $59, three bedroom apartments are $68.50 for eight. Luxurious penthouses accommodate eight and are $85. Summer reservations must be made for a minimum of three nights. Winter rates, from October to April are $20 for two in a motel room, $22 for four. Motel rooms with kitchens, $25 for four. One bedroom apartments, $27 for four, two bedroom apartments, $30, three bedrooms, $36, and penthouses, $59 for eight. For more information write: Island Retreat, P.O. Box 637, Port Aransas, TX 78373 (512)749–6222.

★★★★*Lakeway World of Tennis Resort* is a year-round resort on Lake Travis, specializing in tennis vacations, but also offering golf and other outdoor recreation. The Resort is 20 miles northwest of Austin, just three hours drive from Dallas or Houston and one hour from San Antonio. There are 33 tennis courts located throughout the resort. A clinic program, developed in cooperation with the World Championship Tennis training schools in the U.S. and Europe, features high caliber instructors such as Billy Freer who ranked #1 in South Africa, competed at Wimbledon and in the U.S. Open and has been teaching for 10 years. There are also children's clinics in the summer, weekend mini-clinics and other tennis packages. After a workout on the court, guests can take a dip in nothing less than a racquet shaped swimming pool. Lakeway has much to offer the golfer as well. There are 27 holes with 9 more under construction, featuring lush fairways and white sand bunkers. Instruction is available. Since Lakeway is a Texas resort, they have not neglected the western recreation. They have a brand new Equestrian Center with scenic trails winding through the hills, and horses available for rent. The resort's location on 65–mile, deep, clear Lake Travis makes it a natural for water sports including fishing, boating, sailing and water-skiing. A full-service Marina fills the needs of boaters, providing launching ramps for private boats, as well as a variety of craft for rent. Hikers and joggers will enjoy the wilderness trails

where they are apt to meet a wild turkey or a family of deer. In the evening the El Lago Dining room offers fine cuisine and a beautiful view of Lake Travis and the hills. After dinner, there is dancing and live entertainment in the Yacht Club lounge. Guests can stay at the Lakeway Inn which has 145 rooms, each with a private patio or balcony. There are also townhouses with full kitchens, large bedrooms and private baths that can accommodate two or more couples and are convenient to the tennis. There are also cottages with two bedrooms, two baths and a kitchen. Rates vary, depending on the package chosen. For room only on the European Plan a room for two starts at $60, with junior suites including fireplace at $70 a day, and cottages at $100 a day. Other fees when not on a package are $10 for trail rides, $5 a day for tennis, $15 for 18 holes of golf and $9 an hour for a 10–foot sailboat. For complete information on all packages and accommodations write: Lakeway World of Tennis Resort, 101 Lakeway Drive, Austin, TX 78734 (512)261–6600 or toll free (800)252–9222.

★★★★*Lost Valley Resort Ranch* is situated in the Texas Hill Country, just 45 minutes northwest of San Antonio on State Highway 16. It is also conveniently accessible by private plane, because guests can land at the 3,800–foot paved Purple Sage air strip owned by Continental Oil Company. Lost Valley has its own golf course on the gently rolling land, with fairways among stately live oak trees. Weather permits year-round playing, and there is a club house and pro shop with golf carts and clubs for rent, as well as five regulation tennis courts and a large swimming pool. Anglers will enjoy fishing the streams on the ranch property, as well as hooking catfish and bass in nearby Medina Lake. The 25–mile-long lake also has water-skiing, sail boating, and motor boating. Lost Valley Resort Ranch uses the trail horses owned by Lost Valley Downs—Texas' largest horse racing facility for thoroughbred and quarterhorse races. Trail rides are supervised by experienced wranglers. The American Plan at the Ranch is all inclusive. At no additional charge it includes lodging, three meals a day, golf privileges all day, a daily horseback ride, use of swimming pool, tennis, shuffleboard, horseshoes, volleyball, badminton, fishing and hiking trails. Meals can be enjoyed in the resort's restaurant. Or, for a change, guests can enjoy a steak fry under the stars or a sunrise breakfast after an early morning trail ride. A room with two double beds in $38 per day per person double occupancy. The weekly rate is 10% less. There are also family units with two adjoining rooms that will sleep up to eight people. The first two occupants pay the regular rate, each additional occupant is $32. Children under 6 are $16 and infants under 2 are $8 a day. All accommodations are air-conditioned, carpeted and equipped with telephones. No service charge is added and tipping is not expected.

For information and reservations, contact: Lost Valley Resort Ranch, P.O. Box 857, Bandera, TX 78003 (512)796–3716.

★★★*Mayan Dude Ranch*, in the Texas Hill Country northwest of San Antonio, offers western fun, outdoor recreation, and nightly entertainment. Dress is casual and there are many planned activities for families and individuals. The Mayan has its own large string of horses, with temperaments to fit a range of riding experience. Even guests who have never been in the saddle before, will be riders before the week is over. A morning and an afternoon ride is planned each day with experienced guides. Every other day or so, guests can ride horseback to the cowboy breakfasts served on the open range along the banks of the Medina River. Other mornings, guests ride to the breakfast on a hay wagon. The ranch has a huge 75 by 35 foot pool, fed by two sparkling mountain streams. There is hiking, hunting for fossils and arrowheads, two tennis courts, shuffleboard, volleyball, fishing, and much more. Meals are served in their dining room with a view of miles of hill country. There are also barbeques, steak fries, Mexican cuisine feasts, and old fashioned fish fries. The Ranch has its own ghost town, wild west shows, saloon floor shows with can-can girls, and square dances. The weekly activity schedule lists some kind of fun and entertainment for every evening. And the Mayan Room Cocktail Lounge is open until midnight. The only phone is in the office, so guests can really get away from it all. There are frontier museums, craft shops and a golf course nearby. There are two types of accommodations. Guests can live in "Fort Mayan" in unique western fort units with a hitchin' post for horses, two adjoining bedrooms, rough cedar interiors and a private patio. There are also Western native rock cottages with one and two bedrooms. All types of rooms have custom-built western furniture with air-conditioning and heat. Some have fireplaces for cool nights. Daily rate is $38 to $40 and includes everything—lodging, meals, horseback riding, and all facilities and entertainments. The resort is family owned and operated and hosts are Grace, Judy and Don Hicks. For more information write to them at Mayan Dude Ranch, Bandera, TX 78003 (512)796–3312.

★★★*Miramar Resort Motel at Padre Island* offers luxury accommodations on the south end of this wild and beautiful island. Padre Island is a year-round resort area, with warm winter sunshine, as well as cool summer breezes. The Resort has a freshwater swimming pool and a private beach. There are four golf courses within 45 minutes drive and Mexico is just 30 minutes away with bull fights, shopping, and evening entertainment. Padre Island has public boat ramps for visitors to launch their crafts. For those without boats, charter services and boats for rent are available. The Miramar accommodations include pool or Gulf of Mexico views from rooms, suites and villas. All units are soundproof with air-conditioning, color television and telephones. Most units also have kitchens, fully equipped with standard-sized appliances and all utensils. Deluxe bedrooms with two double beds are $30 per day in summer and 28 per day in winter. Gulf-front bedrooms with kitchen, four single beds and bath is $38 per day in summer and $30 per day in winter. The villas are individual two-room cottages with bedroom, living room, kitchen and bath. They are about a block from the pool and beach and rent for $38/summer and $25/winter. There are also poolside and gulf-front suites, an executive suite sleeping six, large 15 × 30 bedrooms with kitchens and suites with two baths. For more information write: Miramar Resort Motel, Box 2100, South Padre Island, TX 78578 (512)943–2691.

★★★★*Sea Gun Resort Hotel at Aransas National Wildlife Refuge*, is a year-round resort on the edge of the Lamar Peninsula, favored by naturalists and birdwatchers drawn to the saltflats, bays, and marshes of the Texas Gulf coast by the abundant wildlife: deer, wild turkey, javelin, and over 400 species of waterfowl and song birds. Sea Gun borders the spectacular 47,000–acre Aransas National Wildlife Refuge, the winter home of the near-extinct Whooping Cranes, who migrate 2,500 miles here from their summer home in Canada, near the Arctic Circle. Sea Gun Resort has complete facilities for field expeditions, and offers regular trips into the wildlife sanctuary and the remoter islands on its 65′ vessel, the "Whooping Crane." In addition, Sea Gun Resort has a complete marina, swimming pool, lighted fishing pier, and tennis, golf, cycling, and hunting in season. The dining room is open for three meals daily and offers sumptuous buffets each Sunday. Picnic lunches will be prepared for fishing parties. Poolside hotel rooms are available, and there are one and two bedroom cottages some with kitchens available. Hotel rooms are $20 daily single occupancy, and $25 daily for two-four people. Hotel rooms with kitchenettes are $27 single occupancy, and $32 double occupancy. One bedroom cottages are $36 for one-three people, two bedroom cottages are $55–60. Plush suites, with two bedrooms, two baths, bar, and kitchens are $80. For more information write: Sea Gun Resort Hotel, Route 1, Box 85, Rockport, TX 78382 (512)729–2341.

★★*7–A Ranch Resort & Pioneer Town* revives wild west adventure on the banks of the Blanco River near Wimberley, Texas. Gay 90's musicals, world famous medicine shows and melodramas play on the stage of the Opera house. An old-fashioned ice cream parlor, print shop, livery, penny arcade, gift shops and the Pioneer Museum of Western Art line the streets. The Pioneer Town and Pacific Railroad leaves the quaint station for scenic rides through the surrounding hill country. In addition there is an outdoor pool, fishing in the river, horseback riding, and hearty country-style meals and sumpuous buffets at the Silver Spoon Cafe. All of the private one and two bedroom cabins are air-conditioned, and have screened-in porches, complete kitchenettes, and can accommodate two-eight persons. Rates vary according to the number of people, from $20–40 daily, and $120–230 weekly. The Indian and Cowboy Lodges with 10 bedrooms each accommodate up to 50 persons. Each lodge has a large, central kitchen, and living rooms with stone fireplaces. Daily rates for two in the lodge without kitchens is $22 daily and $110 weekly. These lodges may be reserved for conferences, family reunions, and group seminars. For more information write: 7–A Ranch Resort Rt. 1, Box 259, Wimberly, TX 78676 (512)847–2517.

★★★*South Padre Marina* condominiums border the waterfront on South Padre Island, surrounded by Laguna Madre, and the Gulf of Mexico. Each condominium has a private boat dock, with full marina services. Deep sea fishing ventures may be chartered, and there is a large pool, two hard-surface tennis courts, and sailing, swimming, and surfing in the warm Gulf waters. South Padre Island is minutes away from the spectacular Rio Grande Valley, and the delightful shops and restaurants of Old Mexico. The luxurious condominiums have plush wall-to-wall carpeting, complete kitchens, and one, two and three bedroom/bath combinations. Summer rates are $60 daily for a one bedroom, $360 weekly. Two bedroom units are $85 daily and $510 weekly. Three bedroom condominiums are $100 daily, and $600 weekly. For more information write: South Padre Marina, P.O. Box 2308, South Padre Island, TX 78597 (512)943–1385 or 943–5419.

★★★*Tejas Village at Lake O' the Pines* is a rustic retreat located high on a hilltop among tall pines noted for its quiet, restful atmosphere. The largest marina on the lake is a feature of the resort and offers everything to accommodate anglers and water sport enthusiasts. Facilities include a bait house, tackle shop, and boat stalls and barge

stalls are available. The resort has a pool close to all units and many quiet wooded areas for strolling. Accommodations include motel rooms, housekeeping units, and private cottages. All housekeeping cottages feature electric kitchens, dining, living and bedroom areas with baths. Linens, dishes and cooking utensils are provided. All units have maid service and air-conditioning. Meals, not included in rates, are available at the resort's restaurant at reasonable prices, and a grocery store is located at the marina. Rates: Motel rooms double occupancy $19–35; housekeeping units in Pine Cove Facing Lake, double occupancy $35–39, housekeeping units for four $48–52. Private cottages are available at some times and rates can be obtained from the Lodge. For further information contact: Tejas Village, Route 1, Jefferson, TX 75657 (214)777–2460.

★★★★*Woodcreek Resort* is the result of the dream of Lawrence Clayton Smith, who first visited this Hill Country 25 years ago and began to plan for a luxurious resort. He purchased the ranch in 1971 and spent the next eight years transforming it into a luxurious resort community. Cypress Creek and the Blanco River wander through the property and all the accommodations are along the Creek. There are lighted Lakold tennis courts, with lessons available and a well-stocked Tennis Shop. The resort has two championship 18–hole golf courses, a pro shop, lockers, rentals carts and rental clubs. For guests who want to get in shape there is Health Club complete with saunas, a whirlpool, a swimming pool, an exercise room with Universal gym equipment, indoor air-conditioned handball and racquetball courts, a steam room and locker rooms. There is bass fishing and perch fishing along Cypress Creek and Lawryl Lake, and at Canyon Lake just minutes away. A mini-marina has sailboats, paddleboats and canoes for rent, but motor boats are not allowed in Woodcreek to preserve the quiet and natural environment. Visitors who want to camp out will find elaborate camping facilities near the Health Spa on Cypress Creek. Weekend hayrides, daily trailrides through the scenic hills, and rental bicycles add to the outdoor fun. Children will find hours of amusement in the Children's Arcade. Waiters and waitresses in period costumes serve in the Westworld Restaurant and the Old Waterhole. Guests can enjoy eating in eleven different settings including a jail, an old-time bank, a General Store, a Teepee or a flashy saloon. Weather permitting, there is dancing to live music outdoors in the Beer Garden. Besides all the fun and relaxation right at the resort, there are many things to see within an easy drive of the Resort. Pioneer Town, an authentic reproduction of a western town, complete with melodramas and Gay Nineties show, is just five minutes away; Aquarena Springs in San Marcos is 25 minutes away; and Wonder Cave, opened in 1908, is nearby. Guests can also visit LBJ Ranch, the Texas Capital City of Austin, and the University of Texas. Accommodations at the Resort are in lodge rooms and luxury townhouses, with one, two or three bedrooms. Lodge or townhouse bedrooms are $35 per night, European Plan, double occupancy. A one-bedroom townhouse is $55 per night, two-bedroom is $90 per night and three-bedroom is $125 per night. There are also special townhouses at the health spa and golf course available for $45 to $115 per night. For further information and reservations: Woodcreek Resort, #1 Woodcreek Drive, Wimberley, TX 78676 (512)847–2221.

★★★*World of Resorts Inn* is part of a 5,500–acre leisure community on Lake Travis, 16 miles from Austin. This bi-level ultra-modern hotel has many recreational facilities, plus guests at the Inn can use the many facilities of the Lake Travis World of Resorts community. The community has three golf courses—LagoVista Country Club's 18–hole championship course, a 9–hole par 3 course and the new 18–hole World of Resorts Country Club Course. There are lighted tennis courts, five swimming pools, two Country Clubs and parks and picnic areas. There are two marinas. The Lago Vista Marina has a launching ramp on Lake Travis, a sheltered fishing well, fuel, a snack bar, boat docking facilities and slips for rent. Visitors can enjoy boating, water-skiing and fishing on the 65–mile-long Lake Travis—the largest of the chain of seven Highland Lakes. The Inn also has its own swimming pool; facilities for lawn games such as badminton, croquet and horseshoes; a restaurant and a cocktail lounge. Rooms at the Inn all have modern furnishings, shag carpeting and private balconies with spectacular views. There is color TV in each room and connecting rooms for families are available. Inn rooms are $28 to $32 a day double occupancy, European plan. One-bedroom suites with parlors are $49 and up, and two-bedroom suites are $73 and up. There are also condominiums and packages for tennis and golf. For information and reservations write: World of Resorts Inn, Box 826, Lago Vista, TX 78641 (512)267–1102.

★★★★*The Y.O. Ranch* is not a dude ranch, but a working ranch recently opened to the public on a limited basis. It was established in 1880 and is privately owned by the Schreiner family. There are 70,000 acres on which graze the largest herd of privately-owned quality registered Longhorn cattle in the world, as well as exotic game, collected from four continents. Guests of the ranch stay in restored historic log cabins. They are comfortably modern, but furnished with Old West antiques. There are also guest rooms around the central lodge with fireplaces and antique furnishings. Accommodations are $20 per person, half price for children 12 and under. This price does not include meals—but Miss Bertie's home cooking is both reasonable and delicious. They feature hot home-made bread, fresh meats and vegetables from the garden in season. Breakfast is $3.50, lunch and dinner are $6.50. Tours of the ranch are given Wednesday through Sunday from spring through fall by reservation only. Tours start at 1 P.M. and last one to two hours in the ranchs' vehicles. A full day's photographic safari is $125 which includes a guide and vehicle for as many as four persons. Guests also enjoy hiking on the ranch, but there are no horses available. Also, Richard and Dot Salmon of South Africa have started a Youth Outdoor Awareness camping program on Y.O. ranch. Children from all over the world can participate and details on this program and special adult programs are available. For information write: Charles Schreiner IV, Y.O. Ranch, Mountain Home, TX 78058 (512)640–3222.

UTAH

Introduction

Utah, once the home and hunting grounds of the Ute Indians, and long called Deseret, which in the *Book of Mormon* means "land of the working bee," encompasses Great Salt Lake, a remnant of the ancient Lake Bonneville, arid deserts, vast colorful canyonlands, and the Wasatch and Uinta ranges of the Rocky Mountains. The Beehive State is bordered on the north by Idaho, on the west by Nevada and the Great Basin, on the south by Arizona, and on the east by Wyoming and Idaho. It contains within its boundaries the world-record trout waters of Flaming Gorge Reservoir, the alpine lakes and elk meadows of the High Uinta Primitive Area, the Green River Wilderness and Dinosaur National Park, the beautiful Fishlake Hightops, the trophy bass and trout waters of Lake Powell National Recreation Area, and the awesome pink, yellow, red, white, and black cliffs of Canyonlands National Park and the Colorado River. The first Americans to explore the Utah territory were the mountain men and fur traders of the Rocky Mountain Fur Company, including the legendary Jim Bridger, who is credited with the discovery of Great Salt Lake. The most famous settlers were the Mormons, led by Brigham Young.

Accommodations & Travel Information

Descriptions of Utah's major vacation lodges, guest ranches, inns, motels, and hotels are contained in the "Vacation/Lodging Guide" which follows. For detailed information about all aspects of travel in the state, contact the Utah Travel Council, Council Hall, Capitol Hill, Salt Lake City, UT 84114, or phone (801)533–5681.
Insert photo 214 & 215

Information & Services

For detailed fishing and hunting information, contact the Utah Division of Wildlife Resources, 1596 W. North Temple, Salt Lake City 84116 (801)533–9333. For up-to-date info on fishing and hunting conditions, phone (801)532–2473.

Write also to the Division of Wildlife Resources for fish and game seasons and regulations, license and permit information, *Waterfowl Management Area* and *Deer Management Unit Maps*, and the useful 40–page *Utah Fishing and Hunting Guide* (50¢), *Waterfowl Hunting in Utah* (50¢), and *Utah Upland Game Birds* (50¢).

The 44–page booklet *Popular Utah Fishing Waters* is a must for anyone planning a fishing trip to the state. This useful guide contains detailed descriptions of the most productive fishing spots, with info

about access, lodging, and services. You can get a copy by sending 50¢ to the Division of Wildlife Resources.

Hundreds of camping sites dot Utah's vast outdoors. Several free guides are available to help you find them. The Utah Travel Council publishes two good booklet guides to campgrounds throughout the state, *A Guide to Utah's Camp and Picnic Areas* and *Utah's Part of the Earth Campground Directory*. Both guide list campgrounds in national parks, monuments, recreation areas, and forests; Bureau of Land Management campgrounds; and private campgrounds. They give the number of camping units at each site, the available facilities, and nearby recreational opportunities. The Bureau of Land Management publishes a leaflet listing and describing its recreation sites in the state, most of which are free. The publication, *BLM-Developed Recreation Sites in Utah*, gives location, size, and access for each of the campgrounds and describes the facilities at each one. A small map designates each site. For the Travel Council Guides, write: Utah Travel Council, Council Hall, Capitol Hill, Salt Lake City 84114. For the BLM publication, write: Bureau of Land Management, Utah State Office, P.O. Box 11505, Salt Lake City 84111.

Beautiful, professional scroll maps showing every bend, island, rapid, fall, campsite, and contour of the *Green River* ($4, showing Red Canyon, Canyon of Lodore, Whirlpool Canyon, Split Mountain Canyon, Desolation Canyon, and Gray Canyon); *Colorado River* ($3, Gore Canyon to Grand Junction); *Westwater Canyon* ($3); *Cataract Canyon* ($3); *Yampa River* ($2.50); *Dolores River* ($3.50); *San Juan River* ($2.25); *Lake Powell* ($5); and *Flaming Gorge* ($3) are available from Western Whitewater Co., Star Rt. 13, Heber City 84032. These maps, painstakingly produced by riverman Leslie Jones, include fascinating historical annotations, difficulty ratings, and river-running and scouting advice. Each scroll map comes with a transparent, watertight case.

Highways & Maps

The Utah Travel Council publishes a free full-color *Utah Highway Map* which shows geographical features, highways, roads, trails, cities and towns, national and state parks, forests, and recreation areas, campsites, and other points of interest. The map, on a scale of about 17.4 miles to 1 inch, is available from the council, Capitol Hill, Salt Lake City 84114.

The council also publishes a free guide for motoring tourists called *Utah! 24 Discovery Tours*. The guide, available from the council address above, outlines points of interest, routes, and seasonal events for tours through northern Utah, the eastern shore of Great Salt Lake, Wasatch Front Pioneer Trail, Salt Desert, Salt Lake City, Salt Lake Canyons, and many other tours throughout the state.

The regional *Utah Multipurpose Maps*, also available from the council, are another valuable resource for visitors to the state. This series of eight regional map/guides includes descriptions of many outdoor recreational centers and points of interest in each of the regions, which are keyed on the maps. The maps, on a scale of 4 inches to 1 mile, mark private land, Indian reservations, public lands, state lands, national parks and monuments, national forests, primitive areas, national recreation areas, military reservations, picnic areas, campsites, historical sites, view points, ruins, geological formations, rock-hounding areas, golf courses, boat-launch sites, marinas, ski areas, snowmobile trails, game reserves, and bird refuges. The map/guides also contain campground guides, which describe the size, location, and recreational opportunities at public campsites in each region.

Bryce Canyon National Park

The park is a series of deep crevasses in 12 huge natural amphitheaters, slicing down a thousand feet through many layers of pink and white limestone. Situated on an 8,000–9,000–foot plateau in southwestern Utah, the park encompasses hundreds of geological formations which range in appearance from the ruins of ancient temples to the form of men marching across the great plateau. Many trails wind throughout, and horses are available for riding trips. The park is 26 miles southeast of Panguitch on U.S. 89 and Utah Highway 12.

Twenty miles of roads follow the high plateau rim to many of the park's scenic wonders. The Bryce Canyon Visitor Center at headquarters contain exhibits on natural science, archaeology, and area history. During the summer, rangers conduct hikes and lectures daily and guide half-day horseback trips into Bryce Canyon.

Information Sources, Maps & Access

For detailed park information and a free *Bryce Canyon National Park Map/Brochure*, contact: Superintendant, Bryce Canyon National Park, UT 84717 (801)834–5322. A beautiful full-color U.S. Geological Survey *Bryce Canyon National Park Shaded-Relief Map* ($2, also available in a topographic edition) may be ordered from: Distribution Branch, U.S. Geological Survey, Federal Center, Denver, CO 80225.

VACATION/ LODGING GUIDE

Lodges & Inns

★★★*Bryce Canyon Lodge & Western Cabins* is located in the park a short distance from the visitor center. This stone and timber lodge with its western cabins, a national historic landmark, lies nestled among a ponderosa pine forest. Foot trails and auto routes provide quick access to the canyon rim—with its beautiful pastel-colored formations—from Fairyland View to Bryce Point. The lodge offers three types of rustic cabin accommodations: Frontier Cabins, with a double and single bed, carpeting, individual heating, and shower; Pioneer Cabins, close to the main lodge, each with 4 single beds, heating units, and shower; Western Cabins, at the canyon face, each with 2 double beds, carpeting and ornamental fireplaces, bathtub, shower, and telephone. Daily rates: $18–28. The lodge also offers fine dining facilities in a picturesque setting, native handicrafts, service station facilities, church services, and guided park tours by

open-air shuttle to Bryce Point and other scenic views. A camper store located ½ mile north of the lodge near Sunrise Point, sells food provisions and hiking and camping supplies. Accommodations and facilities are available from mid-May into October. Contact: TWA Services, Inc., 4045 S. Spencer St., Suite A–43, Las Vegas, NV 89109 (801)586–9476 or call toll-free (1–800)634–6951.

★★★*Bryce Canyon Pines* is located 6 miles from the park entrance east of the Red Canyon summit on Utah Highway 12. Motel facilities include 34 units ranging from good to deluxe, some with fireplaces, indoor heated pool, dining room, coffee shop, and Butch Cassidy/Red Canyon Trail rides. Write: Double Canyon Pines, Star Rte. 1, Panguitch, UT 84759 (801)834–5336.

★★★*Pink Cliffs Village* is a 38–unit Friendship Motor Inn, located 2 miles north of the park entrance at the junction of Utah Highways 22 and 12. Facilities include 2–room units, heated indoor pool, restaurant, coffee shop, pub, and airport shuttle service. Daily rates (double): $25.50. Contact: Pink Cliffs Village, Bryce Canyon, UT 84717 (801)834–5355.

★★★*Ruby's Inn—Best Western* offers 83 motor inn units 1 mile north of the park entrance on Utah Highway 12. Facilities include some 2–bedroom units and suites, heated pool, dining room, restaurant, and coffee shop. Ruby's also offers scenic helicopter flights, horseback rides, and tours. Daily rates (double): $30. Contact: Best Western Ruby's Inn, Bryce Canyon, UT 84764 (801)834–5341 or call toll-free (800)528–1234.

Cache National Forest

This 679,000–acre tract straddles the boundary between Utah and Idaho and extends from the Weber River on the south to Soda Springs on the north. The first white men to visit the region, in 1824, were American beaver trappers who *cached*, or hid, their furs in today's Cache Valley. The trappers used the area as their winter quarters to take advantage of the bison and other game in "Willow Valley," as they called it. Major features of the forest include the Bear River Range, Wellsville Range, Logan River, Dingle Swamp, and Bear Lake. The Bear River Range is a northern extension of the Wasatch Mountains. The Bear River rises southeast of the forest in the Uinta Mountains, circles around into Idaho, flows down along the western side of the Bear River Mountains, and empties into Great Salt Lake. Among the fine trout streams and lakes in the forest are Pineview Reservoir, White Pine and Deep lakes, and the Blacksmith Fork, well known for its brown trout. The Logan River, southwest of Bear Lake, has produced a record 27–pound brown trout. A good number of 10–20–pound browns are caught here each year. Big game in the forest includes elk, mule deer, and black bear. Many nongame species, including bobcat, cougar, mink, and fox, add to the beauty of the wildlife of the area.

Logan Canyon between Logan and Bear Lake on Highway 89 is a mile-deep chasm carved by the ceaseless force of the Logan River, named for Ephraim Logan, an early trapper. It is most spectacular in the fall, when the brilliant colors of changing leaves add to the hues of the canyon itself. Minnetonka Cave in St. Charles Canyon 8 miles west of St. Charles, Idaho, extends about 2,200 feet into the limestone mountain. Guided tours into its beautiful stalactite and stalagmite formations are conducted from June to September. At Hardware Ranch in Blacksmith Fork Canyon, a herd of elk is fed each winter. Boating and fishing are popular at Pineview Reservoir.

The forest is the site of the Beaver Mountain and Snow Basin winter sports areas.

Information Sources, Maps & Access

A full-color *Cache National Forest Map* (50¢) and detailed forest information may be obtained from: Supervisor, Cache National Forest, 427 N. Sixth Ave., Pocatello, ID 83201.

The forest is reached by Interstate 80N off Interstate 80, north of Coalville, or by driving north on Interstate 15 from Salt Lake City. Interstate 80N can also be taken south into the forest area from Idaho. Lodging, guides, supplies, and outfitters are available at Lewiston, Smithfield, Logan, Garden City, Laketown, Randolph, Woodruff, Huntsville, Devils Slide, Ogden, Wasatch, Paradise, and Brigham City.

Gateways & Accommodations

Brigham City—Gateway to Golden Spike National Historic Site

(Pop. 14,000; zip code 84302; area code 801.) The Golden Spike National Historic Site is located 32 miles west of the city off Interstate 80N and Interstate 15. This is the site where the storied golden spike joined the Union Pacific and Central Pacific railroads to form the nation's first transcontinental railway on May 10, 1869, at Promontory Point. During the summer, the visitor center offers living history programs reenacting the original ceremony as well as a self-guided auto tour. Accommodations: *Best Western Motel* (rates: $21–25 double), 17 rooms, at 505 N. Main St. (723–8584); *Red Baron—A Friendship Inn* (rates: $23 double), 30 rooms and family units, restaurant, heated pool, at 1167 S. Main St. (723–8511).

Garden City—Gateway to Bear Lake & Beaver Mountain Winter Sports Area

(Pop. 100; zip code 84028; area code 801.) The Bear Lake State Recreation Area is located 1 mile north of town on U.S. 89. Accommodations: *Sweetwater Park on Bear Lake* (rates: $45 double, summer; $28 double, winter), 256 superb resort hotel and apartment units with fireplaces and balconies, dining room and restaurant, cocktail lounge, marina with boats, canoes, sailboats, water sports, fishing, heated pool, sauna, beach, tennis courts, 5 miles south of town on Utah 30, with shuttle service to Beaver Mountain Winter Sports Area (946–3306).

Logan

(Pop. 22,300; zip code 84321; area code 801.) This thriving Mormon-founded city on U.S. 88/91 is the home of Utah State University. Accommodations: *Best Western Baugh Motel* (rates: $24–26 double), 77 excellent rooms, at 153 S. Main St. (752–5220).

Ogden

(Pop. 69,500; zip code, see below; area code 801.) Ogden is Utah's second-largest city and a major transportation center for the intermountain region. The Ogden area was once a major rendezvous for trappers and fur traders of the American Fur Co., the Hudson's Bay Co., and the Rocky Mountain Fur Co. The town, named for Peter Skene Ogden of the Hudson's Bay Co., was founded and planned by Bringham Young in 1849. Accommodations: *Best Western Moonlite Inn* (rates: $26–28 double), 70 excellent rooms and family units, restaurant, coffee shop, heated pool, at 1825 Washington Blvd. east off 1–15, 12th St. Exit (621–8350); *Holiday Inn* (rates: $35 double), 110 excellent rooms, restaurant, heated pool, kennel, at 3306 Washington Blvd. (399–5671); *Ramada Inn* (rates: $30.50 double), 148 excellent rooms and family units, restaurant, coffee shop, cocktail lounge, heated pool, at 2433 Adams Ave. (394–4503).

Capitol Reef National Park

This colorful national park with its archaeological remains, petrified forests, great rock temples and cliffs, and huge arches in blues, greens, reds, purples, and pinks, takes in 241,671 acres along the great Capitol Reef, which extends for about 65 miles from Lake Powell to Thousand Lake Mountain. The park is named for huge rock formations with white-capped domes resembling the nation's capitol. The major features of the park include the Fremont River Gorge, the Grand Wash, the Great Curtain, the red and gray pinnacles known as the Three Wise Owls and Capitol Gorge. The area north of the road from Cathedral Cliffs to Chimney Rock is rich in petrified and fossilized remains from the Age of Reptiles. Self-guiding foot trails and scenic drives wind through the park from the Capitol Reef Visitor Center, which offers an orientation program and natural history exhibits.

Information Sources, Maps & Access

For detailed park information and a free *Capitol Reef National Park Map/Brochure*, contact: Superintendent, Capitol Reef National Park, Torrey, UT 84775 (801)425–3871. Park roads are generally open year-round, the best season being April through October. The park visitor center offers lectures and natural history exhibits. The park is located 76 miles southeast of Richfield via Utah highways 119 and 24.

Lodges

★★*Rim Rock Motel* is located 2 miles west of the park on Utah Highway 24. Facilities include 20 rustic units with new, fully carpeted rooms, suites, and excellent dining room and restaurant. Rim Rock also offers horseback riding, tours of the park, and fishing and hunting guide service. Daily rates (double): $22–25. Contact: Rim Rock Motel, Torrey, UT 84775 (801)425–3843).

Colorado River Canyonlands Country

The silt-laden Colorado River, which rises near the Continental Divide in Rocky Mountain National Park, Colorado, flows through the awesome Upper Grand Canyon, where the face of the earth breaks away into a 3,000–foot chasm, offering perhaps the most sensational canyon panorama in Utah. At Dead Horse Point, south of Moab, the hiker is able to overlook 5,000 square miles of the red and rugged Colorado Plateau. This majestic view sweeps east to the La Sal Mountains, south to the Abajo Mountains, southwest to the Henry Mountains, west to the Aquarius Plateau, and down into a tremendous gorge, at the bottom of which, in a canyon within a canyon, the Colorado flows through a maze of buttes and mesas. Aeons ago, the Colorado was a wide, shallow stream flowing aimlessly across the flat and unscarred Colorado Plateau. As the surrounding land uplifted, the river cut deeper and deeper into the red sandstone. Today, the river roars between steplike walls some 3,000 feet below the surface of the plateau.

Near Moab is the famous Petroglyph of the Mastodon, known as the riddle of the Colorado. The mastodon is an ancient drawing chipped in red sandstone, measuring 42 inches from trunk to rump. The petroglyph was discovered in 1924, but little information regarding the strange carving was available until 1933, when Dr. Laurence M. Gould, a noted geologist-geographer on Byrd's first Antarctic expedition, visited and photographed it. The weathering of the sandstone in which the drawing is carved proves that it is very old, as does the fact that it is located 300 feet above the present riverbed—far above other petroglyphs of lesser age along the Colorado. If it is true that early man carved only images of what he actually saw, the petroglyph was carved at least 8,000 years ago, before the mastodon became extinct.

Information Sources, Maps & Access

The Exploration of the Colorado River and Its Canyons, the classic by John Wesley Powell ($3) may be obtained from Dover Publications, Inc., 180 Varick St., New York, NY 10014. *River Runners' Guide to the Canyons of the Green and Colorado River*, Vol. III, Marble Gorge and Gravel Canyon ($4), may be obtained from the Powell Society, 750 Vine St., Denver CO 80206. A complete listing of Colorado River guidebooks is contained in the free catalog *Books for River Runners*, available upon request from Westwater Books, Box 365, Boulder City, NV 89005. A full-color *Manti-La Sol National Forest Map* (50¢) and area information may be obtained from the Supervisor, Manti-La Sol National Forest, 350 E. Main St., Price, UT 84501. The Colorado River country and the forest divisions are

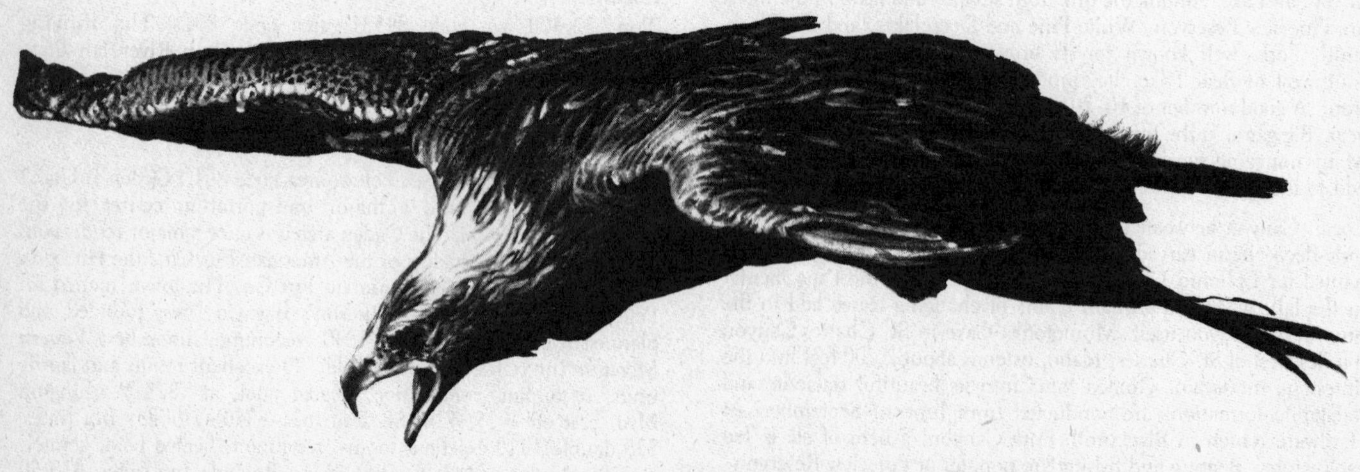

reached via Interstate 70 and U.S. 163 and Utah 128. For detailed vacation travel and recreation information and a free *Canyonlands & Arches National Park Map/Brochures*, contact: Superintendent, Canyonlands National Park, 446 S. Main St., Moab, UT 84532 (801)259–7165. The features of the park are shown on the beautiful, full-color *Canyonlands National Park & Vicinity Shaded-Relief Map* ($2) available from: Distribution Branch, U.S. Geological Survey, Federal Center, Denver, CO 80225.

Two useful guidebooks, *Canyon Country Scenic Tours* ($1.95) and *Canyon Country Hiking & Natural History* ($3.95) may be obtained from: Wasatch Publishers Inc., 4647 Idlewild Road, Salt Lake City 84117. The parks are reached via Interstate 70 and U.S. 163.

Recreation & Scenic Areas

Arches National Park

Arches National Park is sandwiched into a triangle of the Colorado River, Interstate 70, and U.S. 163 in the southeast corner of the state. The park was named for its many arches, the largest concentration of these natural wonders in the world, ranging from holes hardly large enough to crawl through to massive sandstone bridges. The arches were formed by wind, water, and frost erosion over thousands of years. Landscape Arch, with a span of 291 feet, is one of the world's largest natural arches. Foot trails lead to some of the park's most interesting features. The visitor center at the park entrance has guided tours and campfire talks by park rangers.

Canyonlands National Park

The great twisting blue forks formed by the confluence of the Green and Colorado rivers in the heart of the "Land of the Standing Rocks" are surrounded by a labyrinth of upheaved domes, red and orange cliffs, Indian ruins, deep red sandstone chasms, pinnacles, and needlelike spires of the awesome 337,258–acre Canyonlands National Park. The first trip through the Canyonlands on the Green and Colorado rivers was made by Denis Julien, a French trapper. He was followed by Major Powell's expedition in 1869 and the ill-fated Brown-Stanton expedition. The Green River flows through the deep, colorful Labyrinth and Stillwater canyons; surrounded by red buttes, spires, and mesas, this is the longest smooth-water stretch of the river. The major features of the Canyonlands include Butch Cassidy's Robber's Roost Canyon hideout on the Old Outlaw Trail, the roaring, foaming waters of Westwater Canyon, the Spur, Housethief Point, the ancient cliff dwellings at the Island in the Sky, the Grabens, Orange Cliffs, the Needles, Dead Horse State Park, and the twisting waters and islands of the Colorado River.

The park has three natural divisions: the Maze district along the western boundary of the park, which takes in the Maze and Horseshoe Canyon and the Land of Standing Rocks; the 111,000–acre Needles region with its colorful spires, meadows, and parks; and the Island in the Sky, in the northern region.

Manti-La Sal National Forest

The Manti-La Sal National Forest is divided into two portions. The La Sal division lies half a day's drive to the north of the main portion, the Manti. In both sections, the forest is a place of contrast. The orange, buff, and red sandstones of the cliffs and canyons stand out against the green patches of ponderosa pine, spruce, and fir. Abajo Peak, in the Manti Forest division, provides a sweeping panorama of the Colorado Plateau, broken eastward only by the San Miguel and La Plata mountains, southward by Black Mesa, westward by the Kaiparowits and Aquarius plateaus, and northward by the Book Cliffs.

Monument Valley Navajo Tribal Park

The park sprawls across the Utah-Arizona border, encompassing the wonders of Monument Valley, where maroon buttes and pinnacles soar upwards to 1,000 feet above the red desert floor. Jeep tours of the valley may be arranged at Goulding's Lodge & Trading Post, founded in the 1930s by Harry Goulding, known to the Navajos as Long Sheep. The park visitor center is situated off U.S. 163 and provides information on self-guided tours. The visitor center houses an Indian crafts and arts shop. Park entrance fee is $1.50.

Natural Bridges National Monument

The monument encompasses a 7,600–acre area of spectacular eroded rock formations, including three water-carved natural bridges and several ancient cliff-dweller villages of the Anasazi Indians. This fantastic plateau country 51 miles west of Blanding with its box-walled canyons, gorges, whorls, windows, and turrets is cut by the meandering loops of the San Juan and Colorado river tributaries. The 8–mile Bridge View Loop Drive and hiking trails provide access and views of the natural bridges and cliff dwellings in White and Armstrong canyons. A visitor center and museum are in the Monument Headquarters Building.

Gateways & Accommodations

Blanding—Gateway to Natural Bridges & Hovenweep National Monuments

(Pop. 2,300; zip code 84511; area code 801.) On U.S. 163, Blanding is a gateway to the Manti-La Sol National Forest and area monuments, including Hovenweep National Monument, Natural Bridges, and nearby Edge of the Cedars State Historical Monument, with its ancient Indian ruins, petroglyphs, and artifacts (587–2833 for information). Hovenweep National Monument consists of six clusters of ancient Indian cliff dwellings, pueblos, and towers dating from A.D. 1100–1300, believed to have been built by the same tribe responsible for the cliff dwellings found in Mesa Verde National Park. The monument is reached via U.S. 163 and Utah 262 from Blanding. Accommodations: *Best Western Gateway Motel* (rates: $17–25 double), 33 rooms and family units, on U.S. 163 (678–2278).

Bluff

(Pop. 300; zip code 84512; area code 801.) This historic Mormon pioneer town on U.S. 163 is a gateway to the Four Corners country and Mesa Verde National Park. Accommodations: *Recapture Lodge* (rates: $15–19 double), 12 rooms and family units, across from restaurant, with guided jeep tours of the surrounding Indian and canyon country and raft trips on the San Juan River, plus family guest accommodations in old 5–room pioneer house, on U.S. 163 (672–2281).

Green River

(Pop. 1,000; zip code 84525; area code 801.) On Interstate 70, the town is a major gateway to the Colorado River and Green River country. Accommodations: *Best Western River Terrace Motel* (rates: $27–30 double), 51 rooms and family units, heated pool, on the Green River (564–3401).

Mexican Hat

(Pop. 100; zip code 84531; area code 801.) Located on U.S. 163 and the San Juan River, the town is named for a nearby eroded rock formation resembling a gigantic Mexican sombrero in Monument Valley in the southeastern corner of the state. The Goosenecks State Reserve, overlooking the canyons of the San Juan River, is 9 miles to the northwest. Accommodations: *Goulding's Trading Post & Lodge* (rates: $28.69 double), 19 comfortable rooms, with scenic view of

Monument Valley, family-style meals served in dining room, jeep tours, at Goulding's Junction, 2 miles west of U.S. 163 (727–3231); *San Juan Motel—Friendship Inn* (rates: $21–24 double), 22 rooms and family units, restaurant, jeep tours of Monument Valley, on U.S. 163 in Mexican Hat (683–2220).

Moab—Gateway to Arches & Canyonlands National Parks

(Pop. 4,800; zip code 84532; area code 801.) Located in the awesome Colorado River Canyon country on U.S. 163 at the southern boundary of Arches National Park, this recreation and tourist center for southern Utah is the commercial center of a vast cattle and sheep region. Rafts and guides based here provide scenic white-water trips down the Colorado to Cataract Canyon. Scenic sight-seeing flights over Canyonlands and Arches national parks and Glen Canyon National Recreation Area are conducted by *Mustang Aviation—Canyonlands Air Service* (259–7781 or 259–8811), based at Canyonlands Field, 18 miles north of Moab on U.S. 163. Other area attractions include Manti-La Sal National Forest lands; Dead Horse Point State Park, with a visitor center, museum, camping and picnic grounds overlooking the Colorado River, 12 miles north of town on U.S. 163, then 22 miles southwest on Utah 279; Moab Museum at 118 E. Center St. with fascinating exhibits of natural and pioneer history. Accommodations: *Best Western Green Well Motel* (rates: $30–34 double), 41 excellent rooms and family units, restaurant, coffee shop, heated pool, at 105 S. Main St. on U.S. 163 (259–6151); *Moab Friendship Inn* (rates: $30–32 double), 35 excellent rooms and family units, at 168 N. Main St. on U.S. 163 (259–6147); *Moab Travelodge* (rates: $28–30 double), 56 excellent rooms and family units, restaurant, heated pool, at 550 S. Main St. on U.S. 163 (259–6171); *Ramada Inn* (rates: $32 double), 83 excellent rooms and family units, restaurant, heated pool, at 182 S. Main St. on U.S. 163 (259–7141).

Monticello

(Pop. 1,400; zip code 84535; area code 801.) Pronounced monti-SELL-o, the town is situated in the Abajo Mountains and is the seat of San Juan County. It serves as a district office of the Manti-La Sal National Forest and as a gateway to Canyonlands National Park. Accommodations: *Canyonlands Motor Lodge* (a Friendship Inn; rates: $21–25.50 double), 30 rooms, heated pool, at 389 N. Main St. on U.S. 163 (587–2266).

Price

(Pop. 6,200; zip code 84501; area code 801.) Price is the headquarters of the Manti-La Sal National Forest on U.S. 6/50 and was once a favorite haunt of Butch Cassidy and his Wild Bunch, who operated out of Browns Hole and Robbers Roost. Area attractions include the Prehistoric Museum of the College of Eastern Utah at City Hall, with intriguing exhibits of Indian culture, natural history, and fossils of a prehistoric dinosaur. Directions to the local dinosaur quarry, Indian dwellings, Robbers Roost, Devils Stewpots, Little Grand Canyon, and Price Canyon Recreation Area may be obtained here along with maps at the Chamber of Commerce office in the same building. Accommodations: *Best Western Green Well Motel* (rates: $24–34 double), 98 excellent rooms, restaurant, coffee shop, cocktail lounge, heated pool, at 655 E. Main St. on U.S. 6/50 & Utah 10 (637–3520); *Carriage House Inn* (rates: $23–27 double), 42 excellent, new rooms, dining room, coffee shop, at 590 E. Main St. on U.S. 6/50 (637–5660); *Crest Motel* (a Friendship Inn; rates: $18.50–21.50 double), 84 excellent rooms and family units, restaurant, at 649 E. Main on U.S. 6/50 (637–1432).

Travel Services

Canyonlands Tours, Inc., offers guided jeep tours of the awesome Colorado River country and Canyonlands National Park and the history-rich scenic areas of the Four Corners country. Day trips of the Canyonlands country cost $25 per person; 6–10-day tours and custom guided trips are also available. Contact: Canyonlands Tours, Inc., 180 S. 2nd East, Monticello, UT 84535 (801)587–2929.

Horsehead Pack Trips promise an "experience in living much the way the old-time cowboys did," with gear and supplies packed to a different wilderness camp each day. Scenic spots explored include the Maze and Angel Arch of Canyonlands National Park, ancient Indian dwellings, the hideout country of Butch Cassidy and his gang, awesome Grand Gulch with its Basketmaker and Pueblo Indian ruins, Blue Mountain, and colorful Woodenshoe Canyon. Trips range from 2 to 5 days, with ample time allowed for exploring, relaxing, and side trips. Rates for pack trips are $40 per person per day, including guide, wranglers if needed, saddle and pack horses, all meals, and all equipment except personal gear. Walking trips with pack stock and daily guided horseback riding into Canyonlands National Park or on Blue Mountain are also available. Participants receive basic horseback-riding lessons, if desired, and surefooted mounts that know this country well. The pace is kept slow, 8–10 miles a day on the average, so even beginners will find these trips easygoing and rewarding. For further information write: Horsehead Pack Trips, P.O. Box 374, Monticello, UT 84535 (801)587–2929.

Outlaw Trails, Inc., offer expertly guided wild and scenic river raft trips, jeep tours and packhorse trips in the Colorado River country and Canyonlands National Park, and combination river/jeep/pack trips. Jeep tours of the Canyonlands take in Butch Cassidy's hideout and ancient Indian petroglyphs. Pack trips follow the Old Outlaw Trail through Robbers Roost Canyon and Horsethief Canyon. For rates and info, contact: P.O. Box 336, Green River, UT 84525 (801)564–3593.

Tag-A-Long Tours offers expertly guided river-raft trips and jeep tours of the Canyonlands country with an emphasis on the local history, geology, and wildlife of the red rock canyon country. Special family rates. Contact: Tag-A-Long Tours, 452 N. Main St., Moab, UT 84532 call toll-free (800)453–3292.

Dixie National Forest—"Land of the Rainbow Canyons"

This 2 million-acre reserve straddles the Divide between the Great Basin and the Colorado River in southern Utah. The land varies from mountains of over 11,000 feet to broad mesas and rolling hills to steep-walled gorges. Many trails and forest roads wind through green high-country forests and amber hills along the Markagunt, Paunsaugunt, and Aquarius plateaus. The Aquarius Plateau, also known as Boulder Mountain, is one of the largest and highest timbered plateaus in America. It is dotted with hundreds of trout-bearing alpine lakes at altitudes of 10,000–11,000 feet. A 400–800-foot rim of lava rock around the edge of the plateau separates the lakes on the top from those just under the rim. Many of the remote wilderness lakes, surrounded by high alpine tundra meadows and beaver flows, have been aerially stocked with rainbow, brook, and cutthroat trout and a few grayling. The lakes are reached by foot or packhorse and provide excellent wilderness base camps.

Panguitch Lake, which fills a volcanic basin a mile long and three-quarters of a mile wide, has excellent fishing for rainbows and kokanee salmon. The wilderness hiker will find good fly-fishing along the parklike Duck Creek and Navajo and Aspen-Mirror lakes. The Escalante has good cutthroat, and the Santa Clara has some big rainbows and brown trout.

The forest meadows are carpeted with brilliant wild flowers, grass, shrubs, and trees during the warmer months. Before white men walked here, these lands were the home of the Paiute Indians and of a mysterious group archaeologists refer to as the Mesa Verde branch of the Anasazi culture. For protection from marauding tribes and the elements, the Mesa Verde people built cliff dwellings high on the canyon walls of the Colorado tributaries. The people vanished long before the white man arrived, but their dwellings are still visible from the road near Escalante.

The Cedar Breaks National Monument is located on the Markagunt Plateau in the southwesternmost portion of Dixie National Forest on Utah 143 near the famed Brian Head Ski Area at an elevation of 10,000 feet. Some 2,000 feet higher than Bryce Canyon, Cedar Breaks, known to the Indians as the circle of painted cliffs, takes 5,837 acres embracing a vast natural amphitheater ½ mile deep and 2 miles from rim to rim, painted like the wheel of a gigantic circus wagon. Cedar Breaks is surrounded by a cool high-country forest. Camp and picnic grounds are located near Point Supreme. A visitor center and museum are located 1 mile north of the south entrance.

Brian Head Ski Resort, a spectacular ski and winter sports area, is located due north of Cedar Breaks. It is dominated by the summit of Brian Head, the highest peak in southwestern Utah (11,299 ft.). This beautiful high-country alpine area offers excellent downhill and cross-country skiing, with 2 double chair-lifts, ski school and rentals, restaurant and children's nursery (phone 586–4636 for Brian Head information). The summit of Brian Head offers an awesome panorama of the Zion and Bryce canyon country and the Colorado River wildlands.

Information Sources, Maps & Access

The *Dixie National Forest Map* is available for 50¢ from: Forest Supervisor, Dixie National Forest, Cedar City 84720. The map, on a scale of 4 miles to 1 inch, marks roads and highways, trails, ranger stations, streams, and improved recreational areas. A chart gives the size and available facilities of the campgrounds within the forest. Two detailed trail guides describing flora and fauna, geological features, and other points of interest along the trails are also available from the above address. The guides *Bristlecone Pine Trail* and *Lost Hunter Trail* are free. The Forest Service also publishes a free guide to the flowers of the forest, *How to Know Wildflowers near Your Camp,* which is available at the same address.

The *Lakes of the Aquarius Plateau Guide*, available for 50¢ from the Utah Division of Wildlife Resources, 1596 W. North Temple, Salt Lake City 84116, describes access, lakes, and fish species present.

To reach the forest, drive east on State Rt. 14 from Cedar City or north on U.S. Highway 89 from Kanab, or dip south on U.S. 89 from Interstate 70 at Salina. Lodging, supplies, and guides are available at St. George, Enterprise, Cedar City, Panguitch, Escalante, Beaver, Boulder, Antimony, and Teasdale.

For a *Cedar Breaks National Monument Map/Brochure* and information, contact: Superintendent, Cedar Breaks National Monument, Box 749, 82 N. 100 East, Cedar City, UT 84720 (801)586–9451. The monument is reached via Interstate 15 and Utah 14 and 143.

Gateways & Accommodations

Cedar City—Gateway to Cedar Breaks & Brian Head

(Pop. 8,900; zip code 84720; area code 801.) On Interstate 15, this popular recreation and vacation center is flanked on the east and southwest by the alpine forests, lakes, and streams of the Dixie National Forest. Area attractions include the Iron Mission State Historical Monument, on Interstate 15, 1 mile north of town; Cedar Canyon Winter Sports Area on Utah 14; Old Iron Town on Utah 56, founded in 1851; the site of the Mountain Meadows Massacre of 1857, where a company of California-bound Arkansas emigrants were slaughtered by Paiute Indians and Mormons during the tensions of the "Utah War." Area accommodations: *Best Western El Rey Motel* (rates: $22–28 double), 52 excellent rooms and family units, restaurant, cocktail lounge, heated pool, sauna, at 80 S. Main St. (586–6518); *Best Western Town & Country Inn* (rates: $28–32 double), 104 excellent rooms and family units, restaurant, coffee shop, heated pool at 200 North Main St. (586–9911); *Chalet Village at Brian Head* (rates: $26–32 double), 82 alpine rooms and family units with fireplaces, winter sports, shuttle service at base of Brian Head summit, 8 miles north of Cedar Breaks National Monument Visitor Center on Utah 143 (586–6778); *Swiss Village—Best Western* (rates: $25–27 double), 30 excellent rooms, restaurant, in beautiful Parowan Valley north of Cedar City off 1–15, Parowan Exit at 580 N. Main St. (477–3391).

Hatch

(Pop. 100; zip code 84735; area code 801.) The town is a Dixie National Forest gateway due west of Bryce Canyon National Park on U.S. 89. Accommodations: *Best Western New Bryce Motel* (rates: $22–24 double), 20 excellent rooms and family units, restaurant, in town on U.S. 89 (735–4265).

Panguitch

(Pop. 1,300; zip code 84759; area code 801.) A major gateway to the famous trout waters of Panguitch Lake and the Dixie National Forest high country, Cedar Breaks National Monument, and Bryce Canyon National Park, Panguitch is located on U.S. 89 in the colorful Kaiparowits Plateau region. Scenic Utah Highway 12 passes through Bryce Canyon and the spectacular wilderness of the Kaiparowits and Aquarius plateaus for 121 miles to Boulder and the Anasazi Indian Village monument. Accommodations: *Bryce Way—Friendship Inn Motel & Restaurant* (rates: $21–22 double), 20 excellent rooms and family units, heated pool, at 429 N. Main St. on U.S. 89 (676–8881).

St. George—Gateway to Dixie National Forest & Zion National Park

(Pop. 7,100; zip code 84770; area code 801.) This Mormon town on Interstate 15 was founded in 1861. It is the site of a Mormon temple, the first to be built in the state and Brigham Young's winter home. Accommodations: *Four Seasons Motor Inn & Rafters Dining Room/Treehouse Coffee Shop* (rates: $26–28 double), 80 excellent rooms and family units, heated pool, sauna, airport service, at 747 E. St. George Blvd. on 1–15 Business Loop (673–4804); *Hilton St. George* (rates: $29–47 double), 100 superb new rooms and suites, restaurant, coffee shop, cocktail lounge, off 1–15 Bloomington Exit at 1450 Indian Hills Drive (628–0463); *Rodeway Inn & Sugar Loaf Cafe* (rates: $22–27 double), 50 excellent rooms and family units, dining, coffee shop, heated pool, at 260 E. St. George Blvd. off 1–15 Business Loop (673–6161); *St. George Downtown Travelodge* (rates: $24–28 double), 61 excellent rooms and family units, restaurant, coffee shop, heated pool, sauna, at 60 W. St. George Blvd. on 1–15 Business Loop (673–4666).

Lodges

★★*Meadeau View Lodge* in the Dixie National Forest has quiet and comfortable accommodations in a spacious, tree-shaded inn overlooking a beautiful meadow. Within easy driving distance are Zion and Bryce canyons, the north rim of the Grand Canyon, Lake Powell, and Cedar Breaks National Monument. Fishermen will find numerous streams and ponds in the area, most of them fine producers of rainbow, brown, and brook trout. The high forests and canyons offer superb hunting for deer in season and prime hiking terrain during the spring and summer months. Other popular activities are cross-country skiing, snowmobiling, and rock-hounding. The lodge has a comfortable lounge with a circular fireplace, a dining room overlooking the meadow, and a sheltered patio surrounded by tall aspen and pine trees. All rooms have twin, double, or queen-size beds, private baths, and pleasant views. Rates: $21–24 double. For further information write: Meadeau View Lodge, P.O. Box 356, Cedar City, UT 84720 (801)648–2495.

Fishlake National Forest

This 1.5 million-acre reserve is located in central Utah at the southern end of the Great Salt Lake Basin. It embraces three longitudinal strips of the High Utah Plateau, including part of the Wasatch, Aquarius, Sevier, and Tushar plateaus and all of the Fish Lake and Pavant plateaus. The forest is named after the beautiful Fish Lake, the state's largest natural freshwater lake, nestled beneath the Fish Lake Hightops. Glacial deposits formed the lake's basin and dammed its waters. Fish are unusually active in the icy waters of the 8,800–foot-high lake. Among them are lunker rainbow and Mackinaw trout ranging in size from 1 to 35 pounds.

The tops of the plateaus are generally small, either flat or rolling, and the sides slope gently to deep valleys carved by radiating canyons. The plateaus rise from 5,500–foot valleys to their 10,000–foot summits. Backpackers will find the mountain trails up to the Fish Lake Hightops challenging. They will also find good fishing in the lakes of the heavily wooded Aquarius Plateau. The top of this scenic tableland, with an area of 49 square miles, is crowned with dense stands of aspens and evergreens. The Aquarius is a remnant of a vast plateau that once extended each and south of the present-day Green and Colorado rivers, attaining, in prehistoric times, heights of nearly a mile above those of today. Here the wilderness traveler enters a land of wide, sage-silvered deserts, colossal mesas, pinnacles and spires that spring from the sand, and floorlike areas jumbled with vividly colored rocks. Other good fishing streams are the Beaver and Fremont rivers, and the Clear, Fish, Monroe, Salina, Gooseberry, and Seven Mile creeks, all of which hold rainbows and browns.

The forest is also known for its large herds of mule deer. Black bear and mountain lion roam the area, and a small herd of elk flourishes on the Fish Lake Plateau. Upland game includes sage, ruffled, and blue grouse. Limited numbers of waterfowl nest among the lakes and streams.

Information Sources, Maps & Access

A full-color *Fishlake National Forest Map* (50¢) and detailed forest information may be obtained from: Supervisor, Fishlake National Forest, Richfield, UT 84701.

The forest is easily accessible from the east by way of Interstate 70; from the south, take U.S. 91 and Interstate 15 north. Lodging, meals, supplies, guides, and outfitters are available at Beaver, Monroe, Richfield, Torrey, Salina, Redmond, Ephraim, and Gunnison.

Gateways & Accommodations

Beaver

(Pop. 1,500; zip code 84713; area code 801.) This former frontier boom-town on Interstate 15 is now a farming and cattle-raising center, flanked on the east by the Fishlake National Forest high country. Old Cove Fort, built by the Mormons with volcanic rock in 1867 for defense against Indian massacre, is off Interstate 15, 23 miles north of town. Accommodations: *Best Western Paice Motel* (rates: $25–26 double), 24 excellent rooms and family units, heated pool, off I–15, Beaver Exit at 161 S. Main St. (438–2438).

Fillmore

(Pop. 1,400; zip code 84631; area code 801.) This town on Interstate 15 is a Fishlake National Forest District Ranger Office site. Utah's first territorial capitol, converted into a museum, is located here at 50 W. Capitol Ave. Accommodations: *Best Western Paradise Inn* (rates: $24–25 double), 46 excellent rooms and family units, restaurant, coffee shop, heated pool, off I–15 at 800 N. Main St. (743–6895).

Richfield

(Pop. 4,500; zip code 84701; area code 801.) The town was settled by Brigham Young's followers. It is now headquarters of Fishlake National Forest, on U.S. 89. Area attractions include the Fishlake Hot Springs and Big Rock Candy Mountain, a lemon-colored hill, 25 miles south of town on U.S. 89. Accommodations: *Best Western Holiday Host* (rates: $28–30 double), 65 excellent rooms and family units, heated pool, at 145 S. Main St. on U.S. 89 (896–5481); *Rodeway Inn* (rates: $22–24 double), 50 good rooms and family units, restaurant, heated pool, at 69 S. Main St. on U.S. 89 (896–5491).

Flaming Gorge National Recreation Area

Flaming Gorge country has two distinct districts: a desert area across the border in Wyoming composed of small hills and shale badlands, and a mountainous area in Utah embracing canyons and forests. The Green River enters the Uinta Mountains of Utah through a brilliant red canyon, named Flaming Gorge by Maj. John Wesley Powell. In 1962 the Flaming Gorge Dam was built to impound the waters of the river. Today Flaming Gorge Lake extends 91 miles to the north and has fast become one of the world's most prolific producers of trophy, hook-jawed browns in the 10, 15, 20, and 30–plus pound class, metallic-flanked rainbows up to 18 pounds, cutthroat trout up to 10 pounds, and fast-growing trophy Mackinaw up to 20 pounds. The monster trout gorge themselves on the chubs and small rainbows that feed just below the surface of the lake. The most effective fishing method for the great browns is to slow-troll a Rapala Sinking Countdown plug (which resembles a wounded chub) at the base of the canyon walls on the cold deep Utah side of the lake; in the Goosenecks, Bear Canyon, Jarvie Canyon, Hideout Canyon, and Gold Point areas; and at the mouths of feeder streams and the ledges along the old Green River channel. Flaming Gorge recently produced the new world-record brown (the old record brown—39 lb. 8 oz.—taken in Scotland in 1866 was snag-hooked and recently declared ineligible for world-record status) and is reported to hold monster browns of 35–40 pounds.

The Green River continues through the Red Canyon below the dam. Here a family can enjoy a river trip in comparative safety. The first 12 miles below the dam, known as Utah's Blue-Ribbon Trout Stream, offer one of the best chances to catch trophy rainbow trout in the state. The lake and the stream below are very cold much of the year and are often whipped by strong winds, so upsets can be uncomfortable and sometimes dangerous. Be cautious. Because of these conditions, life preservers are required, as are extra paddles and a bail bucket. The Red Canyon Visitor Center on Utah 44 contains exhibits of area natural and pioneer history.

Browns Park, a long valley where the Green River wanders through

low hills, is an important wintering place for deer and elk. Here many species of waterfowl and animals benefit from enlarged nesting and forage areas. Hunting and fishing are allowed during specified seasons. Duck and goose hunting are particularly good, and ice fishing is popular on the lake during the winter.

As the Green River flows south from the Flaming Gorge area, it slices through the canyons of the Dinosaur National Monument. In this area the rapids become fast and furious, and only the highly skilled can challenge them. The Dinosaur National Monument superintendent requires you to obtain a permit or to travel this section of the river with a guide who holds such a permit.

Cedar Springs Marina, Inc. (801)889–3495, Dutch John, UT 84023, provides boat rentals, tackle, and lake tours. *Dutch John Service,* Dutch John, UT 84023, is located 3 miles below Flaming Gorge Dam and offers raft rentals for Red Canyon trips, pickup service, and fishing supplies.

Campgrounds with modern facilities are located at Bootleg, Lucerne Valley, Antelope Flat, and Buckboard Crossing.

Information Sources, Maps & Access

Detailed information and a free pamphlet on the Green River below the dam, *Three Faces of the Green River,* is available from: District Ranger, Flaming Gorge National Recreation Area, U.S. Forest Service, Dutch John, UT 84023 (801)789–5253.

A free brochure, *Flaming Gorge National Recreation Area,* available from the District Ranger, U.S. Forest Service, Box 157, Dutch John, UT 84023, describes all camping sites within the recreation area and their facilities. It also includes a color map of the area and a description of the recreation opportunities in the area.

Utah Highway 44 north from Vernal and Wyoming Highway 530 south from Green River provide access to the lake. Overnight accommodations are available at two lodges in the southern part of the recreation area.

For additional information, see "Uinta Mountains High Country."

Lodges

★*Flaming Gorge Lodge* offers motel-type accommodations in the Flaming Gorge Recreation Area of northeastern Utah and southern Wyoming. The reservoir impounded by the Flaming Gorge Dam offers 65 square miles of water surface ideal for boating, year-round fishing, and waterskiing. Marinas and concrete boat-launching ramps with fish-cleaning stations are located at various convenient points around the reservoir. Other recreational possibilities include floating the crystal-clear Green River, fall deer and elk hunting, exploring the Sheep Creek Geological Area, hiking, backpacking, and camping. The Flaming Gorge Lodge complex encompasses a general store, cafe, dining room, service station, raft rentals, and boat storage. Daily motel rates: $22–25 for two or three persons to a room ($30 and up for rooms with kitchenettes). Lower winter rates are in effect between November 1 and March 31. For more information on the recreation area and lodge, write: Flaming Gorge Lodge, Dutch John, UT 84023 (801)889–3773.

★*Red Canyon Lodge* is on the shore of one of the beautiful Greens Lakes, only one mile from the rim of the spectacular Red Canyon. This family resort offers housekeeping units, fishing, row-boating and a picturesque dining room. The cabins are nestled among the pines and are equipped with beds, table, chairs and small wood stoves for heating or cooking. There is no piped-in water except in bathrooms attached to some of the cabins. A central shower house provides all toilet facilities and hot water for cabins without bathrooms. The lodge furnishes bedding and linens, but no cooking utensils. There is a small recreation room in the main lodge, a general store and gas service. Rates for cabins, $9.50–11 for two per night. For information, contact: Red Canyon Lodge, Dutch John, UT 84023 (801)889–3715.

Glen Canyon National Recreation Area

The principal feature of the Glen Canyon National Recreation Area is Lake Powell, a body of water 186 miles long with 1,960 miles of canyon-indented shoreline. The lake was formed by the Glen Canyon Dam, built by the Bureau of Reclamation between 1956 and 1964 on the Colorado River in southern Utah. The rough canyon country of the Colorado Plateau has been known to various Indian tribes for 2,000 years. The name Glen Canyon was given to this area of the Colorado River by John Wesley Powell, who led explorations of the region in 1869 and 1871.

Today the lake is a recreation center for fishermen, boaters, and campers. Lake Powell provides easy access to the Rainbow Bridge National Monument, which contains the largest natural stone bridge in the world. At Bridge Canyon, a foot trail about ½ mile long leads to the natural bridge. Towering sandstone walls edge the river upstream from Lees Ferry, and the cold, clear channels of this area hold trophy trout. Canyons easily accessible by boat from Wahweap include Antelope, Navajo, Dungeon, Cathedral, Driftwood, and Cascade.

Throughout Lake Powell the fishing is good for rainbow trout, large-mouth bass, and kokanee salmon. Catches of trout and bass up to 10 pounds are common, particularly in the spectacular, steep-walled Lost Canyon area.

The Rainbow Bridge National Monument, a spectacular natural bridge 309 feet high with a span of 278 feet, is reached via a 1–day boat trip from Page, Arizona. Contact the Glen Canyon NRA superintendent for information (see below).

Information Sources, Maps & Access

Wahweap, just upstream from the dam, offers camping and boating facilities and supplies, including boat rentals and a campground with 178 sites for tents and trailers (no utility hookups). Other outfitting and supply centers include Page, Bullfrog, Lees Ferry, Halls Crossing, Hite, and Rainbow Bridge Floating Marina. For more information about the supplies and services at each of these communities and addresses of concessioners, write: Superintendent, Glen Canyon National Recreation Area, Box 1507, Page, AZ 86040 (602)645–2471, and ask for the free brochure *Glen Canyon Dam and National Recreation Area*. The brochure includes a map of the area on a scale of 4 miles to 1 inch which marks roads, trails, floating signs, and combination facilities, as well as major geological features.

A U.S. Geological Survey *Glen Canyon Recreation Area Topographic Map* on a scale of 1:250,000 is available for $2. This full-color map is 32 by 36 inches and shows natural and man-made features, including primitive roads, dams, and campgrounds. It may be ordered from: Distribution Branch, U.S. Geological Survey, Federal Center, Denver, CO 80225.

Glen Canyon is accessible by U.S. 89, which intersects east-west routes north and south of Glen Canyon. Page has bus service from Flagstaff, Ariz., and Salt Lake City, and scheduled flights from Phoenix and Grand Canyon, Ariz., and Salt Lake City. Roads of the area are always open, and the main waterways of the lake are open all winter.

Gateways & Accommodations

Kanab—Gateway to Glen Canyon, Bryce & Zion National Parks

(Pop. 1,400; zip code 84741; area code 801.) Kanab is a famous western movie-set location and the center of an extensive cattle and sheep-raising area. Zane Grey lived here in 1912 while writing *Riders of the Purple Sage*. Accommodations: *Best Western Red Hills Motel* (rates: $28–30 double), 55 excellent rooms, heated pool, across from restaurant, at 125 W. Center St. on U.S. 89 (644–2675); *Four Seasons Motor Inn—A Friendship Inn* (rates: $28–30 double), 41 rooms and family units, restaurant, heated pool, at 36 N. 300 West on U.S. 89 (644–2635).

Page, Arizona

(Pop. 1,400; zip code 86040; area code 602.) Page, on U.S. 89, is the headquarters of the Glen Canyon National Recreation Area. Charter air services offer daily sight-seeing flights over Lake Powell and the surrounding wildlands from 7 A.M. to 7 P.M. during the summer. Boat- and raft-trip services on Lake Powell and Glen Canyon are based at the John W. Powell Museum at 6 N. Seventh Ave., which has exhibits on area history, Indians, and geology. Accommodations: *Lake Powell Motel* (rates: $23–25 double), 24 rooms, restaurant, cocktail lounge, on U.S. 89, 4 miles north of Glen Canyon Dam (645–2477).

Resorts

★★★*Bullfrog Resort & Marina*, on the shore of brilliant blue-green Lake Powell, offers modern housekeeping and non-housekeeping accommodations overlooking Bullfrog Bay. Housekeeping units are fully equipped with up-to-date appliances and have 1 to 3 bedrooms ($26 per night for 2). Non-housekeeping units have queen or 2 double beds ($18–28 per night for 1 to 4 persons). The Bullfrog Marina offers house- and motorboat rentals, plus guided tours of Lake Powell's scenic marvels: Lost Eden Canyon, Indian ruins and "moki" steps, the restored Anasazi village at Defiance House, twisting

Escalante Canyon, and the Miner's Stairs, where early placer miners pickaxed a series of steps up the steep rock. Also on the premises are an attractive restaurant, grocery store, and rentals for waterskiing—one of Lake Powell's greatest delights. The climate is mild, with warm water, sunny days, and low humidity—even the winters are pleasant. Off-season rates between mid-October and mid-March (20% discount on all facilities). For information write: Bullfrog Resort & Marina, Lake Powell, Hanksville, UT 84734 (801)684–2233.

★★★*Wahweap Lodge and Marina* overlooks Lake Powell's spectacular Wahweap Bay and the imposing sand sculptures of Antelope Island. There are 125 comfortable modern rooms, a glass-walled Rainbow Room for dining, the Driftwood Lounge featuring nightly summer entertainment, a coffee shop, and big swimming pool. Rates: $24–31 daily (double occupancy). Guests have free use of the golf course and tennis courts at nearby Page Country Club. Boat tours of Lake Powell, including 1–day or longer cruises, are also sponsored through the lodge, which offers powerboat rentals for exploring the lake or waterskiing. An unusual and leisurely way to enjoy this magnificent lake is on board the family-sized, fully equipped houseboats available at Wahweap Marina. Houseboats are easy to navigate and come equipped with beds, heaters, refrigerators, 8–track tape decks, showers, and other amenities. For more details write: Wahweap Lodge and Marina, P.O. Box 1597, Page, AZ 86040 (602)645–2433.

Green River Country & Dinosaur National Monument

When Maj. John Wesley Powell passed through this area in 1869 on the first scientific explorations of the Green and Colorado rivers, he called it an area of "wildest desolation." Powell was not the first to run the Green since the upper river had been traveled by mountain men in search of beaver. Gen. William Ashley, father of the Rocky Mountain Fur Company, made the first recorded boat trip on the Green in 1825 in search of fur-trading sites. The Ashley expedition traveled in rawhide-covered canoes to the mouth of the Duchesne River. Today the tortuous canyons, frothing rapids, and deep flowing pools lure wild-river floaters and fishermen from across the nation.

The Green rises high in Wyoming's Bridger Wilderness and flows down the slopes of the Rockies, where it meanders across a long highland valley and enters Utah's Uinta Mountains through the brilliant Red Canyon, named Flaming Gorge by Major Powell. Before the Flaming Gorge Dam was built in 1962, the riverbed through the Uintas was little more than a sluiceway for glacial debris washing off the Wind River Range. The Green now flows for its first 18 miles in Red Canyon through Flaming Gorge Lake (one of the nation's top brown trout fishing areas) and for its second 12 miles through a stretch of frigid, deep, state-designated blue-ribbon rainbow and brown trout waters. Motors are not permitted on the 12–mile stretch between the dam and Red Creek. A riverside foot trail follows this part of the river. Most boating parties leave the river at Little Hole. At the lower end of Red Rock Canyon, below Little Hole, is Red Creek Rapids, a frothing mass of churning water and rocks. For detailed fishing and boating info on this stretch of the river, write: District Ranger, Flaming Gorge National Recreation Area, U.S. Forest Service, Dutch John, UT 84023.

The Green flows from Red Canyon through the low hills and wide river bottoms of Browns Park, a long, mountain-rimmed valley that straddles the Utah-Colorado boundary. Isolated by its mountain fastness, the area was a favorite winter retreat of the mountain men during the early 1800s and was named after the fur trader Baptiste Brown. Old cabins located not far from the river once provided refuge for the Wild Bunch led by Butch Cassidy. The roughness and ruggedness of the area, its proximity to three state lines, and its strategic position between Hole-in-the-Wall, Wyo., and Robber's Roost, Utah, made this area a gathering place unsurpassed for its number of unsavory characters. The valley is a major wintering range for deer and Rocky Mountain elk. The Browns Park National Wildlife Refuge embraces a part of the Colorado portion of the river. This meandering section of the Green holds trophy rainbows and browns in the 10–pound-and-over class and provides excellent duck and goose hunting. For the nitty-gritty on the Browns Park area of the Green, write: Bureau of Land Management, Vernal 84078; or Browns Park National Wildlife Refuge, Bureau of Sport Fisheries & Wildlife, P.O. Box 398, Vernal 84078.

The Green flows from the Browns Park area through the imposing Gates of Lodore into the spectacular Dinosaur National Monument, an area of about 330 square miles of rugged and scenic wilderness in the eastern Uinta Mountains. Paved roads lead into the area from Monument Headquarters at Dinosaur, Colo., and from Jensen, Utah, near the famous quarry. John Wesley Powell saw "reptilian remains" in the monument area in 1871, but it was Earl Douglass, of Pittsburgh's Carnegie Museum, who found the "Dinosaur Ledge" quarry in 1909, when he discovered the tail bones of a *Brontosaurus*. The scenery of the monument is dominated by the towering limestone and shale canyons of the Green and Yampa rivers. Both rivers flow placidly through broad green valleys before plunging headlong through, not around, the mountains into their respective canyons. The major features of the Green River Wildlands in the monument include the awesome Canyon of Lodore (where Powell lost one of his boats, the *No-Name*, at Disaster Falls), Hills Half Mile, Steamboat Rock, the fierce Whirlpool Canyon, the verdant meadows of Island and Rainbow parks, Moonshine Rapids, and the wild roller-coaster rapids and eddies of Split Mountain Canyon.

The Green River leaves the Split Mountain Canyon, meanders through the Uinta basin, flows through the large wooded islands and bottomlands of the Ouray National Wildlife Refuge, and enters the famous wildlands of Desolation Canyon, surrounded by the colorful Book Cliffs on the west and by the Uintah and Ouray Indian Reservation lands on the east. The refuge provides excellent opportunities to observe blue heron, ducks, geese, and beaver. The Green flows through the precipitous walls of Desolation and Gray canyons, forming numerous frothing white-water rapids, eddies, and crosscurrents, and winds on through the great Canyonlands to its junction with the Colorado River.

Information Sources, Maps & Access

A beautiful full-color 30–by–51–inch U.S. Geological Survey *Dinosaur National Monument Shaded-Relief Map* ($2), may be ordered from: Branch Distribution, U.S. Geological Survey, Federal Center, Denver, CO 80225. For detailed info on this section of the Green, and a free *Dinosaur National Monument* map and brochure, and river-running and backcountry travel permits write: Dinosaur National Monument, Box 101, Dinosaur, CO 81610 (303)374–2216. A *River Runners' Guide to Dinosaur National Monument and Vicinity* ($3.50 postpaid) may be obtained by writing: Dinosaur Nature Association, Box 127, Densen 84035.

For free information on outfitters offering guided trips on this section of the Green River, write: Bureau of Land Management, Box 11505, Salt Lake City 84111. The bureau also distributes private permit information. For info about *Ute Trails and Rivers*, a guide service for hunting, fishing, and rafting trips run by the Ute Indian Tribe, write: Ute Trails and Rivers, Fort Duchesne 84026.

Two detailed guides to the river in this area, entitled *Dinosaur River Guide* and *Desolation River Guide*, are available from Westwater Books, P.O. Box 365, Boulder City, NV 89005, at $4.95 each ($6.95 for a waterproofed edition). The guides include an in-depth map of the route of the river in the wilderness, including unimproved dirt roads, light-duty roads, medium-duty roads, heavy-duty roads, campgrounds, boat landings, and rapids. Facts about the history, geology, and wildlife of the area are also included. The following may also be obtained from Westwater at the address above: *The Wild Bunch at Robber's Roost* ($6.95), about Butch Cassidy and his gang, by Pearl Baker; *Dinosaur National Monument & Vicinity* ($3); *Desolation and Gray Canyons* ($3).

A free booklet, *Running the Green River from Sand Wash to Green River, Utah*, is available from: Bureau of Land Management, Utah State Office, Salt Lake City 84111. It includes an informative map of that section of the river, the Desolation Canyon. The map marks all major rapids and rates them in degree of difficulty. It also shows unimproved roads, jeep trails, hard-surfaced roads, and streams running into the river, as well as campsites and points of interest along the way. The booklet includes bits of history, archaeology, geology, and wildlife lore that will add to your river experience, and describes the most difficult rapids.

The Green River country is reached via U.S. 40, Utah 44, Interstate 70, and U.S. 163. For additional information, see "Flaming Gorge National Recreation Area," and "Colorado River Canyonlands Country" in this section.

Travel Services

Guided scenic and wild-water raft trips on the Green River are provided by the following professional trip outfitters: *Adventure River Expedition*, 4211 Mars Way, Salt Lake City, UT 84117 (801)278–1867; *Canyon Country River Adventures, Inc.*, 3580 Winesap Road, Salt Lake City, UT 84121 (801)943–1013; *Hatch River Expeditions*, 411 E. 2nd N., Vernal, UT 84078 (801)789–3813; *Holiday River Expeditions*, 519 Malibu Drive, Salt Lake City, UT 84107 (801)266–2087; *Tag-A-Long Tours*, 452 N. Main St., Moab, UT 84532 (801)453–3292; *World Wide River Expeditions, Inc.*, 445 E. Scott Ave., Salt Lake City, UT 84115 (801)467–6426.

Uinta Mountains High Country

The rugged Uinta Mountains run east-west (the largest such range in the United States) at elevations from 12,500 to 13,500 feet along the crest. They lie within both the Ashley and Wasatch national forests and contain some of the finest wilderness fishing, camping, and alpine and cross-country skiing areas within the state. The Ute and Paiute Indians hunted and fished for centuries in the part of the High Uinta Mountains that was incorporated into the Wasatch National Forest in 1906. The word *Wasatch*, meaning "high mountain pass," is taken from their language. Early in the 1800s, explorers and trappers followed the ancient Indian and game trails across the mountain passes to the Kamas Valley and into Salt Lake Basin. Following the exploration trails blazed by the legendary Kit Carson, Jedediah Smith, and Jim Bridger, wagon trains of pioneers and forty-niners took the trail from Wyoming over the Uinta and Wasatch ranges through the Salt Lake Valley to California. Hundreds of miles of trails and forest roads wind through the Uintas, following the old paths along the Whiterocks River, Big Bush Creek, Duchesne River, Blacks Fork and Lake Fork rivers, Sheep Creek Canyon, Spirit Lake, Chepeta Lake, and the Green River. Deep green meadows and pine forests cover the high country, where the hunting along the northern slopes is excellent for deer, bear, elk, and moose. Most mountain streams are muddy in the early season and are best suited to bait-fishing. Fly-fishermen come into their own later, when the water clears and drops. Many of the remote, "lost" alpine lakes and their feeder streams, reached only by backpacking cross-country, hold grayling and rainbow, brown, brook, and cutthroat trout up to trophy weights.

Although most of the trails are in good condition, backpackers and wilderness fishermen should be alert for bogs, wet fields, and mud holes. All of the larger rivers but the Yellowstone have bridges across them. Even in summer, temperatures can dip below freezing at night. In addition to good boots and long johns, rain gear is advisable, for thunderstorms are frequent and sudden during the summer.

Information Sources, Maps & Access

For detailed information on the High Uintas, a full-color *Wasatch National Forest Map* (50¢), and a free *High Uintas Primitive Area Map/Brochure*, contact: Supervisor, Wasatch National Forest, 125 State St., Salt Lake City, UT 84111 (801)524–5030. An invaluable guide for both fishermen and backpackers called *High Uinta Trails* ($3) may be ordered from: Wasatch Publishers, Inc., 4647 Idlewild Road, Salt Lake City, UT 84117. For a full-color *Ashley National Forest Map* (50¢) and forest information, contact: Supervisor, Ashley National Forest, Vernal, UT 84078 (801)789–0323.

The following series of guides to the remote wilderness high-country lakes are available for 50¢ each from the Utah Division of Wildlife Resources, 1596 W. North Temple, Salt Lake City, 84116; the *Lakes of the High Uintas Series*, which includes the following individual booklets: *Ashley Creek, Burnt Fork Creek, Sheep Creek—Carter Creek,* and *Whiterocks River Drainages; Weber, Provo, and Duchesne River Drainages; Rock Creek and Lake and Lake Fork River Drainages;* and *Yellowstone, Swift Creek, Dry Gulch, Uinta River Drainages*.

The Ashley National Forest and Green River country is reached by auto on U.S. Highway 40 and Utah Highways 44 and 330. Lodging, guides, supplies, and outfitters are available at the towns of Vernal, Whiterocks, Bridgeport, Dutch John, Duchesne, and Manila.

The Wasatch National Forest is reached by U.S. Highway 40, Utah Highway 44, and Wyoming Highway 414 from Lonetree. Lodging, supplies, guides, and outfitters are available at Vernal, Whiterocks, Holiday Park, Mountain Home, Defas Park, Ogden, Heber City, Brigham City, and Logan.

Recreation Areas

Ashley National Forest

Ashley National Forest covers 1,398,986 acres in northeastern Utah and southwestern Wyoming, ranging from the heights of the majestic Uintas to the brilliance of the Green River's Flaming Gorge. The forest is named after Gen. William H. Ashley, who led parties of fur traders into Utah territory in 1825. He traveled down the Green River, then circled the Uintas on his way to a rendezvous up Henrys Fork. The alpine lakes of the high country reflect the beauty of Utah's highest mountain, Kings Peak (13,528 ft.). Below the timberline lie 650,000 acres of virgin timber, including lodgepole and ponderosa pine, Engelmann spruce, and Douglas fir. The forest abounds in big game, especially mule deer and elk. Black bear, moose, and antelope also roam the slopes, and a few Rocky Mountain bighorn sheep can be found. Game birds of the high country include the sage, ruffed, and blue grouse. At lower elevations are the California quail and chukar partridge.

High Uinta Primitive Area

The Uinta Primitive Area was named after the Uintah Indians, a branch of the Ute tribe that once inhabited the area. The Uintahs hunted here before the coming of the white man, following the game up the mountains in summer, drying the meat, tanning the hides, and gathering and drying berries. Elevations range from about 8,000 feet in the lower canyons to 13,528 on Kings Peak. This relatively large wilderness tract (237,177 acres) is a scenic coniferous forest interspersed with cool mountain lakes. Rocks of the area include multicolored quartzites and shale, and their rich red contrasts with the green trees.

The scenic High Uintas Highland Trail runs in a general east-west direction along the crest of the mountains. A network of trails across the area, with the Highline Trail the trunk or main artery, provides access to Mirror Lake, Four Lake Basin, Rocky Sea Pass, Rainbow Lake, Rock Creek, Deadhorse Pass (perpetual cool winds blow over this high pass and the view from the summit is breathtaking), Red Knob Pass, North Star Lake, Chain Lakes, North Fork of the Uinta River, Gunsight Pass (from which the vast meadows of Henrys Fork drop off to the north), Henrys Fork Lake, Glass and Bear lakes, and Fish Lake and through dense timber and lush meadows to Henrys Fork Park, the eastern terminus of the Highline Trail. Somewhere in Upper Rock Creek Valley is reportedly one of the "lost" Caleb Rhodes gold mines. No one has ever been able to find a trace of the lode mine, but it is well established that Rhodes left a fortune when he died.

Wasatch National Forest

The Paiute and Ute Indians once lived in the mountains and semidesert valleys of this million-acre forest, and they gave it its name, which means "high mountain pass." The rugged, scenic country of the Uinta Mountains ranges from 4,000 feet to 13,528 feet at Kings Peak. The canyons of the Wasatch-Uinta region have echoed over the years to the passage of Indians, trappers, explorers, Pacific emigrants, Mormon pioneers, wagon freighters, California gold seekers, Pony Express riders, Overland Stage drivers, and travelers of every description. Hunting and fishing are excellent in this vast region dotted and laced by hundreds of lakes and streams, and grassy alpine meadows and tundra.

Gateways & Accommodations

Duchesne

(Pop. 1,100; zip code 84021; area code 801.) Duchesne is a gateway to Ashley National Forest and the High Uintas on U.S. 40. An Ashley National Forest district ranger's office is located here. Accommodations: *Ells Motel* (rates: $21–30 double), 30 rooms and family units, on U.S. 40 (738–2433).

Salt Lake City

(Pop. 175,900; zip code, see below; area code 801.) The capital city of Utah was founded by Mormon leader Brigham Young in 1847 as a New Zion, flanked by the beautiful mountains of the Wasatch Range on the east and by the glimmering waters and white salt beds of Great Salt Lake on the west. Before achieving its present status as the great intermountain business and cultural center, Salt Lake City was successively a fur-trading center, a religious enclave and site of the Utah War of 1857–58, a Pony Express post, and a railroad center. Area attractions include the shops, restaurants, and theaters of the Shopper's Mall, housed in an old trolley barn built by railroad magnate E. H. Harriman in 1908 on 7th St. East and 5th St. South; Hansen Planetarium (364–3611) at 15 S. State St.; Hogle Zoological Gardens at 2600 E. Sunnyside Ave.; Pioneer Monument State Park, where Brigham Young and his followers first entered Salt Lake Valley in 1847 at the mouth of Emigration Canyon; the famous

Mormon buildings in Temple Square; Great Salt Lake State Park, 17 miles west of the city on U.S. 40 and 1–80; the State Capitol at the top of State St.; Old City Hall and the Visitor Information Center of the Utah Travel Council at State St. and 2nd St. North; the Utah Museum of Natural History and Utah Museum of Fine Arts at the University of Utah, overlooking the city. Unique dining and atmosphere is available at *Print Shop Restaurant* on Arrow Press Sq., Bldg 1, 3rd floor at 165 S. West Temple (322–1013) and *The Royal Palace* in a historic church built in 1889 at 249 S. 400 St. (359–5000). Accommodations: *Best Western Little America Hotel* (rates: $38–52 double), 500 superb rooms and family units, dining room, cocktail lounge, restaurant, coffee shop, heated pool, in beautiful location downtown at 500 S. Main St., 84101, off 1–18 and 1–15, 6th St. Exit (363–6781); *Holiday Inn—Airport* (rates: $33 double), 196 excellent rooms, restaurant, coffee shop, heated pool, on U.S. 40 at 1659 W. North Temple, 84116 (533–9000); *Holiday Inn—Downtown* (rates: $38–43 double), 160 excellent rooms and family units, restaurant, cocktail lounge, heated pool, off 1–80 and 1–15, 6th St. Exit, at 230 W. 6th St., 84101 (532–7000); *Hotel Utah* (rates: $44–68 double), 560 superb rooms and elegant suites, rooftop dining, restaurant, coffee shop, downtown across from Mormon Temple Sq. at S. Temple and Main St., 84111 (531–1000); *Hotel Utah Motor Inn* (rates: $33–36 double), 156 excellent rooms and family units, restaurant, heated pool, on U.S. 40 across from Temple Sq., at 124 W. North Temple, 84110 (532–3100); *Ramada Inn* (rates: $34 double), 312 excellent rooms and family units, restaurant, coffee shop, cocktail lounge, heated pool, sauna, children's playground, on U.S. 89 at 999 S. Main St., 84111 (531–7200).

Vernal—Gateway to the High Uintas, Flaming Gorge National Recreation Area & Dinosaur National Monument

(Pop. 3,900; zip code 84078; area code 801.) Vernal is an Old West frontier town in a large green valley at the junction of U.S. 40 and Utah 44 to Flaming Gorge in the northeast corner of the state. During the 1890s the town was a favorite haunt of Butch Cassidy's Wild Bunch, who operated out of nearby Brown's Hole. Area attractions include the Green River and Dinosaur National Monument; Jones Hole National Fish Hatchery in a beautiful scenic area on Jones Hole Road off Utah 44 north; Ouray National Wildlife Refuge on Utah 88, 30 miles southwest of town; Utah Field House of Natural History at Natural History State Park at 235 East U.S. 40, with fascinating free exhibits on archaeology, fossils, and minerals of the region. Accommodations: *Antlers Motel—Friendship Inn* (rates: $28.50 double), 53 excellent rooms and family units, heated pool,

on U.S. 40 at 423 W. Main St. (789–1202); *Best Western Lamplighter Inn* (rates: $26–30 double), 60 excellent rooms and family units, restaurant, on U.S. 40 at 120 E. Main St. (789–0312); *Dinosaur Motel* (rates: $24–34 double), 50 excellent rooms and family units, the Skillet Restaurant, heated pool, at 251 E. Main St. on U.S. 40 next to Utah Field House of Natural History (789–2660).

Guest Ranches & Ski Centers

For additional listings, see "Flaming Gorge National Recreation Area" and "Green River Country & Dinosaur National Monument."

★★★★*Alta Ski Area*, located in Little Cottonwood Canyon 25 miles southeast of Salt Lake City, is blessed by ideal snow conditions and an unusually long season, from mid-November to May. An average winter temperature of 20–25 degrees, with less than 10% humidity, guarantees dry, feather-light powder over the area's sprawling terrain. There are dozens of well-packed runs—the longest is 3½ miles—plus unlimited unpacked trails for deep-powder aficionados. An efficient lift system comprising 6 double chairs and 4 rope tows keeps skiers moving at an average capacity of 5,600 per hour. The Alta Ski School, under the direction of racing champ Alf Engin, specializes in both American and deep-powder skiing technique. All 70 instructors at the school are certified professionals; both private and class lessons are available. Alta also offers a comprehensive ski-touring program, ranging from 1–hour trips for the novice to complete tours for the more advanced cross-country skier. Other conveniences include 2 mid-station restaurants, 4 ski shops, and full equipment rentals. For complete information on skiing at Alta, write: Alta Ski Lifts, Alta, UT 84070 (801)742–3333.

Alta Peruvian Lodge, right at the foot of the mountain, offers comfortable accommodations in nicely furnished dormitories and suites with spectacular views of the Alta Ski Area. A heated swimming pool at your doorstep, fine dining and cocktail facilities, and a recreation room provide après-ski relaxation. Also on the premises are a ski shop, liquor store, and ski rental/repair shop. Daily rates: $22 for dorms, $38 for 2–bedroom suites. Ski packages, including lodgings, lifts, and 2 meals per day: $90–150 for 3 days, $150–250 for 5 days, $200–340 for 7 days (rates based on double occupancy). For more details write: Alta Peruvian Lodge, Alta, UT 84070 (801)742–3000.

The Goldminer's Daughter is a handsome contemporary hotel a few steps from the lifts with accommodations ranging from dormitory rooms (4 twin beds and private bath) to larger rooms with king, queen, or 2 double beds. A small number of suites and kitchen units is also available. Facilities include a top-floor restaurant with panoramic mountain views, cocktail lounge, game room, sauna, cafe, and ski rental/repair shop. Daily rates: $24–35 per person, including breakfast and dinner. Ski packages are $95–125 for 3 days, $160–210 for 5 days, and $215–285 for 7 days. Lifts and 2 meals daily are included. For further information write: The Goldminer's Daughter, Alta, UT 84070 (801)742–2300.

Snowpine Lodge, located 200 yeards away from the lifts, boasts a friendly Alpine atmosphere and comfortable rooms with bunk beds and adjacent shower/washroom facilities. Although rooms are designed for quadruple occupancy, quarters for 2 can be arranged if available. An attractive fireside lounge and game room has a pool table, bar, and table games for evening enjoyment. Other amenities are a dining room, daily maid service, a ski shop, rentals and repairs, and a convenient rope tow to the lifts. Shuttle bus service is also available to the nearby Snowbird ski area. Rates: $20 per person daily. Ski packages, including lift passes and 2 meals a day, are $80 per person for 3 days, $130 for 5 days, and $170 for 7 days. For more information write: Snowpine Lodge, Alta, UT 84070 (801)742–3274.

★★★★*Park City Ski Area*, Utah's largest ski area, surrounds the site of a once booming silver-mining town, the weathered relics of which can still be seen off the ski trails and intermingled with modern additions in the town itself. The ski area has literally something for everyone. Novice skiers will find a special area served by 2 chair lifts; intermediates can enjoy mile upon mile of long, rambling runs through diverse terrain; and for advanced skiers, there's the Jupiter Bowl, containing every kind of steep terrain from wide-open spaces to narrow gullies and tree-lined chutes. The Jupiter Bowl receives about 30% more snow than the area's 300–inch annual average, so experts can enjoy plenty of deep-powder days. Additional pleasures include unlimited cross-country skiing on remote trails, night skiing on a 1¼–mile-long intermediate trail, and helicopter powder-ski trips to the Uinta Mountains (sponsored by Utah Powder Guides). For competitive spirits, there are NASTAR races every Wednesday and Saturday throughout Park City's long season (mid-November to early May). The Park City Ski School has excellent beginners' instruction in graduated length and American teaching methods. A staff of 100 instructors offers private and class sessions in parallel, racing, and powder-skiing techniques. Instruction is also available for children as young as 3 years. Other facilities and services are 9 double chair lifts, a triple chair, and a gondola, 3 day lodges, a nursery, and complete equipment rentals and repairs. The town of Park City is a thriving spot for restaurants and nightlife. There are more than 30 restaurants, an old-time melodrama theater, 16 bars and night spots, a racquet club with indoor tennis courts, and an arts center for film festivals, art classes, concerts, and exhibits. For information or self-guided tours of Park City's historical sites and area maps, contact: Chamber of Commerce at 509 Main St.

Park City has a full spectrum of lodging facilities, from a mid-mountain inn to plush town houses and condominiums. Accommodations range in size from economical dorm rooms to luxurious 4-bedroom apartments. For full information and rates write: Park City Ski Corp., P.O. Box 39–SD, Park City, UT 84060 (801)649–8266.

Edelweiss Haus (rates: $35–90 double), an alpine condominium hotel with 45 rooms and family housekeeping apartments with fireplaces, heated pool, sauna, at 1482 Empire Ave. (801)649–9342.

Mid-Mountain Lodge (rates: $24.50 per person American plan, ski package), offers the only on-mountain lodging in the Rockies, 100 rustic rooms, dining room, sauna and game room at 8,300–feet elevation, at the Park City gondola mid-station (801)649–8500 or 9950.

Park City Resort Condominiums (rates: $24.50–162.00 double), 175 superb alpine rooms and housekeeping apartments, dining room, restaurant, cocktail lounge, heated pool, sauna, full range of outdoor activities including tennis and golf, mine train trips, off 1–80, Park City Exit, at 1515 Park Ave. (801)649–8200.

Skiers Lodge (rates: $35 double), 18 excellent rooms and family units with fireplaces, at 1235 Norfolk Ave. (801)649–8800.

★★★★*Snowbird Village Ski & Summer Resort* is one of the West's great ski resorts, 31 miles from Salt Lake City by bus, limo, taxi, car, or helicopter. With an average snowfall of 450 inches a year, the resort offers outstanding skiing ranging from the gently rolling beginners' run in Gad Valley to the deep-powder expert runs up to 2½ miles such as Little Cloud, Johnson, and Peruvian Cirque and the Gadzooks and Bananas mogul fields. Lifts include 5 double chairs and a 125–passenger aerial tram with capacity for 6,600 skiers per hour. Snowbird has a vertical drop of 3,100 feet. Facilities and services include restaurants, entertainment, free guide service, cross-country skiing trails, helicopter skiing, ice skating, three enclosed and heated tennis courts, ski shops, instructors, ski rentals, shuttle bus service.

Snowbird's four luxurious lodges—*The Cliff, Iron Blosam, The Lodge at Snowbird* and *Turramurra*—are all within easy walking distance of one another, the Snowbird Center and the ski lifts. Each features a heated swimming pool, men's and women's saunas, ski lockers, laundry facilities, and valet parking. All Snowbird lodge guest rooms have private baths, color TV, floor-to-ceiling windows, balconies, and spectacular views of the surrounding mountains. Nightly rates from $53 for 2 persons, and in 5– or 7–night packages including chair-lift tickets. Packages with 7 nights' lodging and 5–day chair-lift ticket, from $226 per person, double occupancy.

During the summer Snowbird offers hiking, swimming, summer tram rides, tennis, dancing, and the University of Utah/Snowbird Summer Arts Institute with art and music courses, lectures, concerts, exhibits, and workshops.

American, Hughes Airwest, Frontier, United, Texas International, and Western airlines serve the Salt Lake International Airport. Transportation to Snowbird from the airport and Salt Lake City via regularly scheduled bus service (Utah Transit Authority), taxi, rental car, charter limousine, or helicopter. Shuttle service to Alta and Park City. Automobiles are not necessary in the Snowbird Village.

For information and reservations, contact: Snowbird Central Reservations, Snowbird, UT 84070 (801)742–2000.

★★*U-Bar Ranch—Gateway to the High Uintahs* specializes in packing, fishing, and hunting trips on the spectacular high country of the Uinta Mountains. Some of the best fishing in the West is available in the Uinta River, Beaver Dam, and the many streams linking the region's backcountry lakes, including Henry Fork Basin, Painter Basin, Kidney Lake Area, Fox and Island lakes, and Red Castle Lake. Pack trips organized and guided by U-Bar Ranch offer a chance to discover unspoiled lakes, explore remote canyons, and climb rugged mountain paths. In the fall, hunting is great for elk, deer, mountain lion, and bear. Ranch cabins, primitive but snug, are ideal as a base camp for your trips or for lodging before and after the excursion. Pack trips and guided hunts average $125 per person per day, including all equipment except personal gear. Horses, tents, and camping equipment may be rented on a per diem basis for unguided trips. For more information write: U-Bar Ranch, Box 254, Neola, UT (801)353–4121 spring through fall.

Travel Services

For additional listings, see "Flaming Gorge National Recreational Area" and "Green River Country & Dinosaur National Monument."

Piute Creek Outfitters, a small family-operated service, leads 2–10–day pack trips through beautiful mountain valleys and past spectacular peaks in the Wasatch National Forest. You will travel in a party of no more than 8 people, each riding a saddle horse, with usually one pack animal for each 2 persons. The longest day's ride is 5 hours. Frequent breaks for lunch, fishing, or exploring make for a pleasurable and relaxed trip, and gentle, trail-wise horses can be easily handled by even inexperienced riders. Piute Creek Outfitters supplies all necessary equipment, horses, tack, wranglers, guides, and an experienced camp cook to prepare tasty fare after a day on the trails. You are also provided with canvas tents for 2–8 people, warm sleeping bags with fresh cotton liners, ground pads, and a first-aid kit. The base camp is less than a 2–hour drive from Salt Lake City Airport. Transportation and accommodations prior to and after the trip may be arranged at additional cost. Rates: $50 per person for 2–day trips; $250 for 4 days; $360 for 6 days; $480 for 8 days; and $600 for a 10–day "exploratory" pack trip of Utah's high Uinta country. Piute Creek also sponsors 1–day steak rides to a lovely pond for a campfire feast. For more information write: Piute Creek Outfitters, Route 1A, Kamas, UT 84036 (801)783–4317.

Uinta National Forest & The Sundance Ski Area

This alpine mecca encompasses some of the state's finest alpine and nordic skiing, backpacking and scenic areas, including deep canyons with spectacular waterfalls, the Alpine Scenic Highway around Mt. Timpanogos and the Nebo Scenic Loop Road. The major features of this 780,000–acre forest include the Provo River, the Strawberry Reservoir area, the Sheeprock Mountains, and the Mount Nebo and Rayson Lake recreation areas.

The Timpanogos Cave National Monument is located on the steep north slope of 12,008–foot Mt. Timpanogos in the beautiful Wasatch Range. The monument on Utah 92, 7 miles east of American Fork, covers 250 acres in a canyon, reached by a mile-long switch-back trail and a ramp trail that climbs 1,200 feet up a sheer cliff-wall. Visitors to the cave should wear rubber-soled hiking shoes. Within the monument area are the cave, the canyon, Mt. Timpanogos, and a tiny glacier. The cave is actually three distinct caves connected by man-made tunnels and is half a mile long. The natural wonders of the caves include a hidden lake and fantastic formations that range across the color spectrum. The cave was reportedly first discovered in 1915 "by a group of Lehi people," who kept its location a secret and attempted to obtain a mining claim on the area from the Forest Service to develop it as a tourist attraction. A visitor center and museum are at the monument. The area is reached via the Alpine Scenic Loop Drive, which circles Mt. Timpanogos from the town of American Fork and provides access as well to American Fork Canyon and the Bridal Veil Falls.

The Sundance Ski Area, located in the heart of Utah's prime ski country just an hour's drive from Salt Lake City, offers uncrowded, relaxed skiing for those seeking an alternative to the resort scene. A series of gentle beginner slopes and longer intermediate runs provide a step-by-step introduction to skiing. There are also plenty of steep challenges for the expert on hundreds of acres of terrain high in the backcountry. The longest run is a little over 2½ miles, and lift lines are a rare occurrence. Two double chairs and a triple chair move skiers at a rate of 3,400 per hour. Instruction for all ages and all levels of ability is available through the Sundance Ski School, which has a staff of 45 instructors well versed in both graduated length and American teaching methods. An extra attraction of the area is floodlit night skiing till 10 P.M. 3 days a week. The Sundance Lodge has a lovely restaurant built around an 80–foot pine tree, specializing in tasty, affordable beef and seafood dishes. Other facilities include a snack bar, ski shop, rentals, general store, and banquet facilities. A limited number of mountain homes and guest cabins are available in the area and should be reserved well in advance. In addition, there are fine motel accommodations in Provo and Heber, 20 miles away. For information on Sundance and area lodgings, write: Sundance, PO Box 837, Provo, UT 84601 (801)225–4105; in Utah call toll-free (800)662–5901.

Information Sources, Maps & Access

A full-color *Uinta National Forest Map* (50¢) and area information may be obtained from: Supervisor, Uinta National Forest, 290 N. University Ave., Box 1428, Provo, UT 84601 (801)377–5780.

The forest is easily accessible by way of U.S. 15 south from Salt Lake City. Lodging, supplies, guides, and outfitters are available at Orem, Provo, Springville, Pleasant Grove, and Spanish Fork.

Gateways & Accommodations

Heber City

(Pop. 3,200; zip code 84032; area code 801.) This is a popular Uinta gateway. The Wasatch Mountain Railway, known locally as the "Heber Creeper," offers a 3½–hour scenic ride through the Provo River canyon to beautiful Bridal Veil Falls in the Wasatch Mountains. The railway depot is located at 100 N. 6 West St. (654–2621). Other area attractions include Wasatch Mountain State Park and the Utah State Fish Hatchery on Utah 113 near Midway. Accommodations: ***Best Western High Country Inn*** (rates: $24–26 double), 41 excellent rooms and family units, restaurant, coffee shop, on U.S. 40 at 1000 S. Main St. (654–0201); *Homestead Motel & Restaurant* (rates: $27–41 double), 43 superb rooms and family resort units, fine dining, and outdoor recreation, including riding and Nordic skiing, at 700 N. Homestead, 5 miles west off 1–80, Heber City Exit to U.S. 40, in Midway (654–1102).

Provo

(Pop. 53,100; zip code 84601; area code 801.) Named after a young trapper, Etienne Provot, who explored the area in 1825 for General Ashley of the American Fur Co. in St. Louis, this major industrial, business, and intermountain cultural center is on Interstate 15, bordered on the east by the peaks and alpine forests of the Wasatch Range and on the west by Utah Lake. The city is the home of Brigham Young University and the headquarters of the Uinta National Forest. Area attractions include the Pioneer Museum at 500 N. 500 West on U.S. 89, with its fascinating pioneer village (375–1822); Sundance Ski Area and Utah Lake State Park; and scenic alpine auto routes (contact the Tourist Bureau in the Pioneer Bldg. at 500 N. 500 West). Accommodations: *Best Western Columbian Motel* (rates: $24–26 double), 26 excellent rooms and family units, heated pool at 70 E. 300 South (373–8973); *Holiday Inn* (rates: $31 double), 78 excellent rooms, restaurant, heated pool, off 1–15, S. University Ave. Exit, at 1460 S. University Ave. (374–9750); *Rodeway Inn* (rates: $27–29 double), 115 excellent rooms and family units, restaurant, coffee shop, cocktail lounge, heated pool, at 1290 S. University Ave. off 1–15, S. University Ave. Exit (374–2500).

Zion National Park

Zion National Park lies deep in southwestern Utah, covering over 229 square miles of breathtaking canyon country. The park includes a huge main canyon and several side gorges sliced out of a high plateau by the ancient Virgin River, which follows the same meandering course today as it did millions of years ago when it was 5,000 feet above its present level. Colorful sheer rock walls create some of the most spectacular natural beauty of the southern Utah landscape. Some of the major formations include the Great White Throne, Angels Landing, Cathedral Mountain, and the Pulpit, all easily visible from the roadside. Horseback and foot trails also wind through this rocky wonderland.

Zion Museum, at the park visitor center, has exhibits of local wildlife and flora. About 65 miles of well-maintained trails provide access to the interior regions. Information on horseback trips is available at the Visitor Center Information Office. The spectacular Zion-Mt. Carmel Highway, connecting U.S. 89 and Interstate 15, traverses a portion of the peak, up an awesome series of switchbacks in Pine Creek Canyon through the 5,607–foot-long Zion Tunnel to Mt. Carmel.

Information Sources, Maps & Access

For detailed park information and a free *Zion National Park Map/Brochure*, contact: Superintendent, Zion National Park, Springdale, UT 84767 (801)772–3256. A beautiful full-color U.S. Geological Survey *Zion National Park Shaded-Relief Map* ($2, also available in a topographic edition) may be ordered from: Distribution Branch, U.S. Geological Survey, Federal Center, Denver, CO 80225. The park is reached via Utah Highway 15 off Interstate 15 or U.S. 89.

Lodging

★★*Zion Lodge* is located in the park on the floor of Zion Canyon beneath the towering canyon walls and the awesome Watchman, West Temple, Towers of the Virgin, Mountain of the Sun, and Three Patriarchs. A short walk from the lodge leads to the Virgin River and the Emerald Pools Trail. The lodge is reached via the Zion-Mt. Carmel Highway, which winds through a mile-long tunnel cut through solid stone and descends along a 3–mile series of switchbacks for 800 feet into the canyon to the Virgin River. Lodge accommodations consist of 3 types of rustic cabins: Frontier Cabins, with a double and single bed, carpeting, individual heating and shower; Pioneer Cabins, each with 4 single beds, heating units, and shower; and Western Cabins, which feature 2 double beds, carpeting, fireplaces, bath and shower, telephone, and western high-pitched roofs. Zion Lodge facilities and services include a dining room (box lunches available) with a magnificent view of the canyon, soda fountain, church services, native handicrafts, and guided tours by open-air shuttle to the Temple of Sinawava, Angels Landing, Great White Throne, and other view points. Daily lodge rates (double): $18–28. Contact: TVA Services, Inc., 4045 S. Spencer St., Suite A-43, Las Vegas, NV 89109 (801)772–3213 or call toll-free (1–800)634–6951.

Zion area inns and lodges located outside the park boundaries on Utah Highway 15 include:

★★*Best Western Driftwood Lodge*, located 2 miles south of the park entrance, with 21 motor inn units, heated pool, and restaurant in secluded location. Daily rates (double): $22–26. Contact: Box 98, Springdale, UT 84767 (801)772–3262.

★★*Bumbleberry Inn*, located ½ mile southwest of the park entrance on Highway 15, with 23 motor inn units, heated pool, restaurant. Daily rates (double): $22–26. Contact: Bumbleberry Inn, Springdale, UT 84767 (801)772–3224.

Pioneer Lodge, with 40 motor inn units, 1 mile south of the park entrance. Facilities include a restaurant and heated pool. Daily rates (double): $23–25.50. Contact: Box 116, Springdale, UT 84767 (801)772–3233.

Zion Park Motel, 12 modern units ½ mile south of the park entrance, with heated pool. Daily rates are $19–22 double. Contact: Box 365, Springdale, UT 84767 (801)772–3902.

WASHINGTON

Introduction

The state of Washington, bordered on the north by British Columbia and the island-dotted Juan de Fuca Strait, on the east by Idaho, on the south by Oregon, and on the west by the Pacific and the beautiful San Juan Islands and the southernmost reaches of the fabled Inside Passage, covers 68,192 square miles and embraces the historic steelhead and trout waters of the wild Skagit River, the classic fly-fishing waters of the North Fork Stittaguamish River, the great salmon-fishing grounds of Puget Sound, the "lost" lakes and ancient dry falls of the Grand Coulee country of the historic Columbia River, North Cascades National Park, Indian Heaven high country, the wild Olympic Peninsula—dominated by the massive glaciers and snowfields of the rugged Olympic Mountains, and the High Cascade alpine wilderness fish and game areas. The volcanic, snowcapped peaks of the Cascade Range, surrounded by fragrant coniferous forests, culminate at Mt. Rainier (14,410 ft.), Mt. Adams (12,307 ft.), Mt. Baker (10,750 ft.), and Glacier Peak (10,436 ft.). The incredibly scenic coastal areas of the Evergreen State were explored in 1778 by the legendary British explorer Captain Cook, followed by Captain George Vancouver, who discovered, explored, and named the Gulf of Georgia, the Hood Canal, Mt. Baker, and Mt. Rainier. The mouth of the historic Columbia River, the long-

sought "River of the West," an ancient Indian water trail traveled by successive waves of explorers, voyageurs, and settlers, was discovered in 1792 by Robert Gray of Boston, followed in 1805 by Lewis and Clark on their epic overland westward journey along the Missouri, Snake, and Columbia rivers. In 1810 David Thompson, explorer and geographer of the North West Company, built Spokane House near the Great Bend of the Columbia to exploit the vast untapped fur forests of the Pacific Northwest. The Washington Territory was later ruled by fur traders of the Hudson's Bay Company.

Accommodations & Travel Information

Washington's key lodges, resorts, hotels, motels, and inns are described in the "Vacation/Lodging Guide" Washington's *Olympic Peninsula Directory*, available free from Olympic Peninsula Travel Association, P.O. Box 625, Port Angeles 98362, contains a useful listing with descriptions of fishing, hunting, and vacation resorts, lodges and camps, marinas, commercial campgrounds, and steelhead float trip operators.

Information & Services

Information on the steelhead, trout, and warm-water fisheries in the Evergreen State is contained in the following informative, illustrated guides, available free upon request from: Department of Game, 600 N. Capitol Way, Olympia 98504 (206)753–5700: *Trout of Washington, Fishing & Hunting in Washington, Washington Steelheading,* and *Spiny-Rayed Fish of Washington*. The Department of Game also publishes a free *State Fishing Guide List* and fishing regulations booklets and information about public access, boat-launching sites, fly-fishing-only waters, and seasons. The color-coded *Columbia Basin Recreation Areas Map*, available free from the Department of Game, shows the famous big-game and waterfowl hunting areas, fishing waters, and camping areas of the Columbia Basin.

The *Washington Salmon Hatcheries Guide* contains a complete history of the state's salmon hatchery operations, including a description of natural and artificial salmon life cycles, distribution maps, and a list of the state's salmon hatcheries. The hatcheries guide and the useful publication *Tips for the Salmon Salt Water Angler*, which contains detailed descriptions of "mooching" methods and equipment and of types of herring bait used in Puget Sound, as well as a map of major salmon-fishing areas, may be obtained free from: Washington Dept. of Fisheries, Olympia 98504. The Dept. of Fisheries also publishes a free sportfishing regulation pamphlet giving fishing areas, an area map, the best fishing periods, tideland recreational areas for gathering shellfish, and freshwater areas for salmon, including the seasons.

For detailed information on licenses, permits, and season limits, and for the free *Washington Deer Hunting Areas Map*, color-coded *Wildlife Recreation Areas Map*, and *Game Management Unit Map*, write: State Game Dept. 600 N. Capitol Way, Olympia 98504 (206)753–5700.

The *Pacific Crest National Scenic Trail Map & Trail Log*, available free from: Regional Forester, P.O. Box 3623, Portland, OR 97208, contains a detailed trail log and maps of the Cascade Crest Trail, showing primitive and dirt roads, spur trails, connecting trails, campsites, improved campgrounds, trail shelters, horse feed, district ranger and forest service stations, lookout towers, and airstrips. The forest supervisors in charge of the four national forests through which the trail passes will give travelers information regarding packers and outfitters, but arrangements should be made well in advance for a National Park Service-U.S. Forest Service Joint-Use Wilderness Permit. If you plan on hiking the entire Pacific Crest Trail, write to: Cleveland National Forest, 3211 5th Ave., San Diego, CA 92103. Self-addressed food and supply packages should be mailed to the following Cascade Crest Trail post offices: Stevenson 98648; Mt. Rainier National Park 98397; Chelan 98816. For trail info in Manning Park, write to: Ranger, British Columbia Forest Service, Manning Park, B.C., Canada. For border-crossing info, write to: Canadian Government Office of Tourism, 150 Kent Street, Ottawa, Ontario, for the free booklet *Canada Border-Crossing Information*.

The *Oregon, Washington National Forest Campground Directory* contains a comprehensive listing and description of services and facilities of all U.S. Forest Service Campgrounds in the Gifford Pinchot, Mt. Baker, Snoqualmie, Olympic, Okanogan, and Wenatchee national forests. This eminently useful 96–page camper's bible contains a full-color *National Forests Map of the Pacific Northwest Region* as well as individual national forest maps showing highways, forest roads, forest headquarters and district ranger stations, campgrounds, and winter sports areas. It may be obtained free along with wilderness travel and camping permits from: U.S. Forest Service, Pacific Northwest Region, P.O. Box 3623, Portland, OR 97208. A comprehensive listing and description of campgrounds in North Cascades National Park, Ross Lake and Lake Chelan national recreation areas, and Olympic and Mt. Rainier national parks is contained in the free booklet *Camping in the National Park System*, available free from: National Park System, Pacific Northwest Regional Office, 931 Fourth & Pike Bldg., Seattle 98101. A listing of *Primitive Camping Areas* in the state may be obtained by writing: Dept. of Natural Resources, Public Lands Bldg., Olympia 98504. A useful 18–page *Washington State Parks Outdoor Recreation Guide*, which describes all state park and recreation area facilities and activities, is available free from: State Park & Recreation Commission, P.O. Box 1128, Olympia 98504.

Northwest Alpine Guide Service offers backpacking trips, nature study camps, mountain-climbing expeditions, and ski tours. Two-week backpacking trips cover 50 miles of the Brooks Range north slope through caribou migration routes to Barter Island. Other trips in the Brooks Range explore the granite spires of Arrigetch Peaks or the challenging Gates of the Arctic. An 8–day backpacking adventure is also offered in the mist-shrouded Queen Charlotte Islands off the coast of British Columbia. If ski towing's your preference, N.A.G.S. sponsors cross-country jaunts in the area around Batnuni Lake in British Columbia (8 days) and along hundreds of miles of different snow trails in Washington (2 days). The numerous mountains of Washington are ideal for 2– and 3–day climbs of varying levels of difficulty. From May through September you can participate in guided climbs up Mt. Baker, Mt. Thompson, Mt. St. Helens, Whitehorse and Glacier mountains, Mt. Olympus, and other peaks. Nature study camps in Alaska, the Northwest Territories, and Washington offer week-long experiments in wilderness living under the guidance of trained naturalists. Each location—such as the subarctic Carcajou Mountains, the Olympics and Cascades, and the Arctic National Wildlife Range—is selected to give you the opportunity to observe different types of communities and to learn about their interrelationships. In most cases, all food, local transportation, camping equipment, and guides are provided. Rates for N.A.G.S. programs average $575 for week-long nature camps, $1,000 for 2 weeks of backpacking in Alaska, $350 for 8–day ski tours, and $125 for 3–day climbs. For complete rates and information write: Northwest Alpine Guide Service, Inc., 1625 Ninth St., Seattle, WA 98101 (206)622–6074.

Highways & Maps

The Evergreen State's scenic and recreation routes, including Highways 123 and 410, which wind through Mt. Rainier National Park

and the Gifford Pinchot National Forest; Highway 2, which winds through Stevens Point at 4,061 feet in the High Cascades region of Snoqualmie National Forest; Highway 542, which runs through Mt. Baker National Forest to the Mt. Baker Wilderness; Highway 20 in the North Cascades and Okanogan and Colville national forests; and Highway 101 through the scenic coastal rain forests and mountains of Olympic National Forest and Park, are shown on the *Washington State Highway Map*, available free from: Dept. of Commerce & Economic Development, Travel Development Division, General Administration Bldg., Olympia 98504. The map shows all major state and federal highways, roads, population centers, state parks and campsites, highway rest areas, points of interest, ski areas, trout and salmon hatcheries, toll ferries, airports, national parks, and forests. In addition, it shows the route of the historic Lewis and Clark Trail of 1805, the Cariboo Trail of 1859–68 to the British Columbia goldfields, Old Stagecoach Road, the Colville Road of 1826–81, and Mullan Road, and the sites of fur-trading forts and Indian rock paintings.

The North Cascades Highway (20), thought by many to be the most scenic wilderness recreation route in the United States, winds for 88 miles through the North Cascades high country from Marblemount, the oldest settlement in the Mt. Baker region and once used as a supply base by prospectors; eastward through the foothills of the Cascades through the Mt. Baker National Forest and the North Cascades high country, paralleled on the north and south by the North Cascades National Park; past the town of Newhalem and the wild Skagit River, the town of Diablo and the beautiful blue-green waters of Diablo Lake (caused by the "rock flour," or fine sediment fed by glacial streams), Ross Lake National Recreation Area, which extends some 24 miles northward into Canada, the Pasayten Wilderness, and the incredibly scenic Washington Pass Overlook at 5,477 feet elevation; and again eastward through Okanogan National Forest, past the towns of Mazama, Winthrop, and Twisp to its junction with Highway 97 at Okanogan. Four miles east of Winthrop on Methow River Road is the North Cascades Smokejumper Base, home of the first airborne fire fighters in the Pacific Northwest. Harts Pass, the northernmost access point to the Pacific Crest Trail in Washington, is reached via a 20–mile side trip from Mazama. The road, built during the 1890 gold rush, is very narrow; trailers are not allowed beyond the 10–mile point. A small campground can be used as a base for hikes to Slate Peak and old gold mines in the Harts Pass Area. Slate Peak provides a 360° panorama that encompasses several hundred square miles of wilderness mountain scenery, from Mt. Baker on the west through the glaciated valleys and spruce and hemlock forests of the Pasayten Wilderness, to the sere eastern horizon, and south to the Glacier Peak Wilderness.

The *North Cascades Highway Map*, available free from: Mt. Baker National Forest, Bellingham 98225, shows the entire length of the highway, ranger stations, campgrounds, boating facilities, points of interest, mileage between points, wilderness areas, trails, national forests, parks, and recreation areas. In addition the map provides a detailed history of the region and describes the climate, vegetation, geology, and glaciers of the North Cascades. The highway is served by the Marble Creek, Mineral Park, Early Winters, Klipchuck, and Lone Fir U.S. Forest Service campgrounds and by the Goodell Creek and Colonial Creek National Park Service campgrounds. For additional information write or call: North Cascades National Park, Marblemount Ranger Station, Marblemount (206)873–4590; Mt. Baker National Forest, Baker River Ranger Station, Concrete (206)853–2851; or Okanogan National Forest, Winthrop Ranger Station, Winthrop (206)996–2266.

Washington State Ferries

Washington State Ferries, the largest mass-transit passenger-vehicle ferry system in the United States, provides regularly scheduled service across Puget Sound to the San Juan Islands and Whidbey, Vashon, and Bainbridge islands and the Kitsap Peninsula. The *Puget Sound & San Juan Islands Scenic Guide & Map*, available free along with rates, schedules, and travel information, from: Washington State Ferries, Seattle Ferry Terminal (Pier 52), Seattle 98104 (206)464–6400, contains a detailed map and descriptive information about the snow-fed rivers, mountain lakes, rain forests, and salmon-fishing meccas off Sekiu, Neah Bay, and La Push in the Olympic Peninsula and Hurricane Ridge area; the fjordlike Hood Canal, which stretches almost the entire length of the Olympic Mountain Range; the Kitsap Peninsula and Bainbridge Island; scenic Vashon Island and Tacoma; Saanich Peninsula and Victoria; the emerald-green maze of the scenic San Juan Islands; and picturesque Whidbey Island, the second-largest island in the contiguous United States.

Gifford Pinchot National Forest & Wilderness Areas

The 1,330,000–acre Gifford Pinchot National Forest (as big as Delaware) contains some of the most beautiful mountain wilderness in the United States. The forest is located in southwest Washington on the western slope of the Cascade Mountains and, to the south, borders the Columbia River gorge in rough, heavily timbered terrain (route of the 1805–1806 Lewis and Clark expedition). Numerous trails, including segments of the Cascade Crest Trail, lead to the high peaks, glaciers, and meadows of the Mt. St. Helens area, the Mt. Adams Wilderness, and the Goat Rocks Wilderness. Other backcountry trails lead to the Big Lava Beds, a 12,500–acre lava flow that issued from a cone with a 500–foot-wide crater; to Cougar Lake; to the Mt. Margaret area, a rugged alpine wilderness dotted with hundreds of small lakes; and to Indian Heaven Lakes, McClellan Meadows, Sawtooth Ridge, Shark Rock, and Silver Star Mountain.

Information Sources, Maps & Access

For detailed information and a full-color *Gifford Pinchot National Forest Map* (50¢), *Mount St. Helens-Spirit Lake Area Map* (50¢), *Goat Rocks Wilderness Map* (topographic, 50¢), and *Mount Adams Wilderness Map* (50¢), write: Supervisor, Gifford Pinchot National Forest, P.O. Box 449, Vancouver, WA 98660 (206)694–1586. Gifford Pinchot National Forest is reached by State Highways 141, 503, and 504 and U.S. Route 12. Lodging, supplies, outfitting, and guide service are available at Castle Rock, Morton, Stevenson, Vancouver, White Salmon, Randle, and Packwood.

Recreation Areas

Cougar Lakes Wilderness

Cougar Lakes Wilderness encompasses 127,000 acres adjacent to the eastern boundary of Mt. Rainier National Park in the Snoqualmie and Gifford Pinchot national forests. The wilderness is a summer range for elk and provides good rainbow and brook trout fishing in the American and Bumping rivers and Cougar and Bumping lakes. Access to the remote interior lakes and alpine meadows is by the Cascade Crest Trail over towering Chinook Pass and spur trails. One of the joys of high-country fishing in Washington and the Northwest lies in the fact that with a topographic map the angler can be his own explorer. You can discover lakes stocked years back by the

VACATION/ LODGING GUIDE

Dept. of Game and the original trail blazers with native and black-spotted Montana cutthroat trout, golden trout, Montana grayling, and rainbow and eastern brook trout. Keep in mind, though, that it takes a bit of study to find these seldom visited "lost" lakes.

Goat Rocks Wilderness

The famous Goat Rocks Wilderness encompasses 82,680 acres of rocky crags, meadows, glaciers, alpine lakes, and ridges, located high in the Cascades on the east flank of the great triangle formed by Mt. Rainier, Mt. Adams, and Mt. St. Helens, with elevations ranging from 3,000 feet at Glacier Lake to 8,201 feet on Mt. Curtis Gilbert. The wilderness derives its name from the bands of mountain goats that roam its high peaks. The Tieton and Klickitat rivers drain the eastern side of the area, and streams of the Cowlitz River system feed from the western side. The alpine central portion of the wilderness lies above timberline.

The wilderness has approximately 95 miles of trails leading from dense forests and valleys up through broad meadows, ridges, and fields of lupine, heather, and phlox on up into the arctic-alpine mountain zone with its barren rocky soils, rock-conglomerate slopes, snowfields, and glaciers. The Cascade Crest Trail winds through the heart of the wilderness, with many side trails leading off to such places as Old Snowy Mountain, Goat Ridge, Cispus Pass, Devil's Horns, Beargrass Butte, Angry Mountain, Snowgrass Flats, and Packwood Glacier. Wallput, Packwood, Goat, and Lost lakes, plus many other lakes in the area, provide good fishing for native cutthroat, brook, and rainbow trout. Access to the high lakes can be very difficult. For alpine enthusiasts, Goat Rocks is perfect for cross-country hiking and snowshoeing from White Pass to Hogback Mountain. Many of the trails are not free of snow until mid-August, and the weather is always unpredictable.

Indian Heaven Area

The Indian Race Track at the south end of the lake-dotted Indian Heaven wild country was the site of pony races many years ago when the Indians hunted and camped in the area. A groove some 2,000 feet long and 10 feet wide, worn by the ponies' hooves, is still plainly visible. A portion of the large Twin Buttes huckleberry fields is reserved for the exclusive use of Indians in accordance with an old treaty agreement. Other historic huckleberry fields are located on the north side of Mt. Adams, in the Nowich Butte-Bare Mountain area, in Mosquito Meadows, and on Hamilton Mountain.

Mt. Adams Wilderness

The bold, soaring summit of Mt. Adams, towering above a sea of dense forest, dominates 32,400–acre Mt. Adams Wilderness, located on the west slope of the High Cascades in the Gifford Pinchot Forest adjacent to the Yakima Indian Reservation. Mt. Adams, or Pah-To, according to Indian legends, at 12,307 feet, is second only to Mt. Rainier in height and bulk among Washington's peaks. The area is extremely rugged, having undergone successive volcanic convulsions. Mt. Adams was formed by volcanic eruptions of ash and cinder accompanied by flows of basaltic and andesitic lava. Its largest glaciers and most severe examples of erosion are found on the northern and eastern flanks, where prevailing storm paths have caused large accumulations of snow and ice. The arctic-alpine zone near Mt. Adams's summit includes many vents, blowholes, and caves. Hydrogen sulfide gas still issues from crevasses, and large deposits of sulfur cover the crater floor. The peak is adorned by the massive Mazama, Avalanche, White Salmon, and Klickitat glaciers, below which are lava crags and flows, alpine meadows, lakes, and forests of hemlock, pine, spruce, fir, and larch.

Numerous trails lead into the wilderness and join with the Round-the-Mountain Trail and the Cascade Crest Trail, which runs along the western side of the mountain and leads to Hellroaring Meadows, Lookinglass Lake, Bird Creek Meadows, Ridge of Wonders, and the Madcat Meadows. Hikers should detour to the north side of the mountain to gather some of the delicious wild blackberries and

huckleberries that grow along old burned-over areas. Fishing is generally poor, since the lakes are either too shallow or lack the necessary food to support a healthy fish population. Big-game hunting, however, is very good for mountain goat, elk, black bear, and blacktail deer. National forest campgrounds are located on the western side and near the southern boundary of the wilderness.

Mt. St. Helens-Spirit Lake Area

This renowned fishing, hunting, cross-country skiing, and wilderness camping area is located in the St. Helens Ranger District of the Gifford Pinchot National Forest. Spirit Lake, which holds rainbow trout up to 7 pounds and serves as a fall salmon migration route, lies in a primitive region of mountains and small alpine lakes, nearly 30 of which may be reached by trails that radiate from the Forest Service campgrounds. Spirit Lake's clear, cold waters reach depths of 1,300 feet, and its bottom is white pumice. In some places the bottom has yet to be found! Spirit Lake was named by the Indians of the region, who interpreted many sounds of the lake and forest as the haunting voices of departed spirits. One legend tells of an Indian brave who, seeking food for his starving tribe, trailed a giant bull elk to the lake, only to be led by the phantom to his death in the water. The Indians were said to believe that each year both of them appeared over the lake on a certain night. Other legends attribute the name to the legendary *Siatcoes*, outcasts from other tribes, to whom were attributed supernatural powers. Mt. St. Helens, one of the youngest volcanic peaks in the country, last erupted in 1842. To the Klickitat Indians, the mountain was known as *Tah-one-lat-clah*, meaning "Fire Mountain." Big game and wildlife in the high-country areas include Roosevelt elk, black bear, deer, beaver, cougar, bobcat, eagle, and ruffed and blue grouse. Spirit Lake Campground has 170 campsites, with facilities for auto and trailer camping. A public boat launching site is located at Duck Bay. The Kalama Spring Campground provides camping facilities on Mt. St. Helens' south side. Located due north of the Mt. St. Helens-Spirit Lake area is the Mt. Margaret backcountry, a backpacker's paradise of flower-studded alpine meadows and high mountain lakes separated by steep, rock-crested ridges.

Gateways & Accommodations

Naches

(Pop. 700; zip code 98937; area code 509.) On the route to Mt. Rainier National Park and White Pass Ski Area. Accommodations: *Game Ridge Motel* (rates: $11.50–16 double), 15 rooms and family units on Naches River, on Hwy. 12, 17 miles west of town (672–2212).

Packwood

(Pop. 800; zip code 98361; area code 206.) This is a major gateway on U.S. Highway 12 to Mt. Rainier National Park and the Goat Rocks Wilderness Area of the Gifford Pinchot National Forest. Accommodations: *Mountain View Lodge* (rates: $19 double), ½ mile east of town on Hwy. 12, 12 miles southwest of the Stevens Canyon entrance to Mt. Rainier National Park, 18 motel units, suites, and housekeeping cottages (494–5555).

Vancouver

(Pop. 42,500; zip code, see below; area code 206.) The city lies at the north mouth of the Columbia River. Area attractions include the Fort Vancouver National Historic Site; the Ulysses S. Grant Museum, with collections of military and Indian artifacts; Clark County Historical Museum; and Covington House, the oldest house in the state. Accommodations: *Ferryman's Inn Best Western* (rates: $27–29 double), 98 excellent rooms, heated pool, at 7901 NE 6th Ave. (574–2151); *Shilo Inn* (rates: $24–26 double), 66 rooms and suites, heated indoor pool, sauna adjacent to restaurant, courtesy airport transportation, at 13206 Hwy. 99 (473–0511); *Shilo Inn Downtown Vancouver* (rates: $28–30 double), 120 excellent rooms and suites, heated pool, and sauna adjacent to restaurant, at 401 E. 13th St. (696–0411); *Thunderbird Inn at the Quay* (rates: $33–34 double), beautiful riverview setting overlooking Columbia River and Interstate Bridge, 159 superb rooms and suites, restaurant, heated pool, and dock facilities, at the foot of Columbia St. (694–8341); *Vancouver Travelodge* (rates $27–30 double), 48 family motel units in downtown location, at 601 Broadway (693–3668).

Travel Services

Indian Creek Corral offers guided packhorse trips in the spectacular Goat Rocks Wilderness Area and along the Pacific Crest Trail, 2 to 14 days long, from July to September. For information and rates, contact: Indian Creek Corral, Star Route, Box 218, Naches, WA 98937.

Mt. Adams Wilderness Institute, in its ninth successful year of operation, offers a unique program of instruction in mountaineering techniques, wilderness travel, and alpine environment. It has earned a reputation as one of the outstanding schools of its kind in the United States. Headquartered at the Flying L Ranch near the Mt. Adams Wilderness Area along the eastern edge of the Gifford Pinchot National Forest, the institute offers 8–day or 12–day courses June through July. The goal is to provide a total mountain experience with intensive, individual instruction in all aspects of mountain travel, including snow and ice climbing, crevasse rescue, rappelling, glacier route-finding, wilderness navigation, and expedition planning; exposure to actual climbing situations under varying conditions and difficulty; backpacking and camping in remote alpine wilderness; and interpretation of the surrounding High Cascade environment—flowers, trees, geology, lava flows, glaciers, mountain weather patterns, and wildlife. The 12–day program features a "Round-the-Mountain" expedition (about 60 rugged miles), with base camps established in several locations. The 8–day trip takes you to the "Great East Side"—less backpacking but no less strenuous than the longer session. Actual climbing instruction is about the same on both courses. And

in either case, your trip culminates with an exciting climb to the summit (weather permitting), via Mazama Glacier and a high camp at 8,300 feet. The 8–day session costs $325; the 12–day session, $425 per person. Cost includes all food, gear, leadership, instruction, and transportation to and from Portland, Oregon. For additional information and literature, contact: Mt. Adams Wilderness Institute, Flying L Ranch, Glenwood, WA 98619 (509)364–3511 or (509)364–3488.

Mt. Baker-Snoqualmie National Forest

Mt. Baker National Forest encompasses 1,283,000 acres of spectacular mountains in the upper northwest corner of the state bordering on British Columbia. Mt. Baker was called *Kom Kulshan,* meaning "white and steep," by the aboriginal Lummi, Nooksack, and Skagit tribesmen. In 1792, thirteen years before the journey of Lewis and Clark, the English explorer Capt. George Vancouver named the great peak soaring above the shoreline of upper Puget Sound Mt. Baker in honor of his first lieutenant. The forest contains 40 percent the glacier-covered area in the United States, excluding Alaska, and has more than 200 lakes at least an acre in size. Several outstanding trout and steelhead streams flow through the area, including the Suiattle, Sauk, Nooksack, and Skagit, which is one of the state's top streams for trophy steelhead. The large Nooksack River, flowing in a loop through northern Whatcom County, was at one time one of the Northwest's best steelhead streams, but present-day pressure through Indian tribal fishing rights has drastically reduced the catch. The Sauk River, a major tributary of the Skagit, holds some big Dolly Varden and cutthroat trout and has a good run of large winter steelhead. Baker Lake has good early-season fishing for kokanee and rainbow and Dolly Varden trout. The Cascade Crest Trail winds from Harts Pass through the Pasayten and Glacier Peak wilderness areas. Hunting is good for deer and black bear.

The Snoqualmie National Forest preserves 1,211,901 acres of the majestic central Cascade Mountains, from Stevens Pass south to White Pass. Big-game hunting is good throughout the forest for elk, mule deer, black-tailed deer, black bear, and mountain goat. Renowned rivers such as the White, Skykomish, Snoqualmie, and Yakima flow through the forest and provide excellent fishing for steelhead, rainbow, brook, and cutthroat trout. Numerous trails pass

through deep forests of giant fir and hemlock, fields of heather and snow lily, and high mountain meadows to such end points as the Alpine Lakes Wilderness, Bumping Lake, Cougar Lakes, Commonwealth Basin, McClellan Butte, Dutch Millers Gap, Mt. Defiance, and the Tuscohatchie backcountry. The Cascade Crest Trail winds through the area from Cady Pass to Goat Rocks. The lovely roadless wilderness of the Alpine Lakes area contains over 700 lakes, most of which provide good fishing for the backpacker willing to tote along a fly rod. Bumping Lake offers good fishing for small kokanee and rainbow trout. Forest Service campgrounds near Bumping Lake are located at Cougar Flat, American River, and Cedar Springs. Access to the Cougar Lakes area is by trail from Swamp Lake. Flowing from its headwaters near Snoqualmie Pass (Snoqualmie means "moon people"), the lovely South Fork of the Snoqualmie River is famous for its excellent fishing, rapids, deep pools, and numerous waterfalls, including the 250–foot Twin Falls. Snow and Gem lakes, lying high in the mountains about 5 miles from Snoqualmie Pass, offer good fishing for cutthroats and rainbows.

Information Sources, Maps & Access

For detailed information, trail guides, and a full-color *Mt. Baker-Snoqualmie National Forest Map* (50¢) and a full-color *Glacier Peak Topographic Map* (50¢), write: Supervisor, Mt. Baker-Snoqualmie National Forest, Seattle, WA 98101 (206)442–5400. The Mt. Baker-Snoqualmie National Forest recreation areas and Glacier Peak Wilderness area are reached via scenic Washington Highways 9, 530, and 542, North Cascades Highway 20, U.S. Route 2, and Interstate 90. Lodging, supplies, and outfitting and guide service are available at Marblemount, Rockport, Concrete, Glacier, Mt. Baker, Sedro Woolley, Darrington, Monte Cristo, Granite Falls, Silverton, Gold Bar, Index, Skykomish, Snoqualmie, North Bend, Enumclaw, Roslyn, Cle Elum, Everett, Seattle, Tacoma, and Yakima.

Recreation Areas

Bald Eagle Natural Wildlife Area

The Skagit River Bald Eagle Natural Wildlife Area comprises more than 1,000 acres along a scenic stretch of the middle Skagit River between Rockport and the old logging town of Marblemount in northwestern Washington. This particular segment of key wooded bottomland and gravel bars is the winter gathering grounds for the largest known concentration of northern bald eagles anywhere on the west coast of the continental United States. Each winter 100 to 300 eagles come to the Skagit to feed on spawned-out salmon, which line the river banks from December to March. While the eagles depend upon spent salmon for their staple winter diet, the primary purpose of the natural area is to provide a wilderness buffer strip, or river corridor, for feeding bars, perch trees, and roost trees. The huge raptors, with wingspreads up to 7½ feet, require tall trees

for perching sites and gravel bars free from disturbance. Future plans of the State Game Dept. include camouflaged trails, a viewing tower, and blinds to allow public observance of the majestic birds.

Glacier Peak Wilderness

The majestic Glacier Peak Wilderness lies to the south of the North Cascades National Park, embracing the eastern and western slopes of the Cascades Range in Snoqualmie and Wenatchee national forests. This awesome 464,240–acre North Cascades wilderness area derives its name from Glacier Peak (10,436 ft.), the fourth-highest mountain in the state, with its more than 30 sister peaks and massive ice fields, Dome Peak, Spire Peak, and Sentinel Peak rising to 8,000 feet above the valleys. More than 90 glaciers lie within the area, giving rise to a number of rivers, including the Suiattle. To the northeast of the wilderness boundary are Stehekin River and Lake Chelan. The Stehekin, which flows into the head of Lake Chelan, is famous for its large rainbow and cutthroat trout. The Cascade Crest Trail is the major route through the wilderness, weaving its way north across mountain slopes, over passes, through alpine meadows, then west past Glacier Peak on along the Suiattle River, then eastward across Suiattle Pass and on down Agnes Creek to the Stehekin River. Connecting trails from both east and west provide opportunities for loop hikes and access to the Napeequa Valley, Entiat Glacier, Seven-Fingered Jack, Lyman Lake, Heather Ridge, Fourth of July Basin, the Seven Sisters, Mt. Le Conte, White Rock Lakes, Mt. Buckindy, and Hurricane Peak.

Gateways & Accommodations

Bellingham

(Pop. 39,400; zip code 98225; area code 206.) The city overlooks the San Juan Islands and Puget Sound. Area attractions include the Whatcom Museum of History and Art, scenic Chuckanut Drive, and the Mt. Baker Ski Area. Area accommodations: *Leopold Inn* (rates: $21–28 double), 180 excellent units and suites, heated pool, restaurant and cocktail lounge, downtown at 1224 Cornwall (733–3500); *Pony Soldier Motor Inn,* (rates: $24.50–28.50 double), 67 excellent units and heated pool next to restaurant, at 215 Samish Way (734–8830); *Scottish Motel* (rates: $22–24 double), 93 motel units, heated pool, and sauna near restaurant, at 506 Riverside Drive (384–4040).

Cle Elum

(Pop. 1,700; zip code 98922; area code 509.) Accommodations: *Cedars Motel* (rates: $19–20 double), 29 good units next to restaurant, at 1001 E. 1st St. (674–5535).

Everett

(Pop. 53,600; zip code, see below; area code 206.) A forest products and shipping center at the mouth of the Snohomish River, Everett is flanked on the west by the Olympic Mountains and on the east by the Cascade Range. Area attractions include Whidebey Island and Deception Pass State Park. Accommodations: *Holiday Inn*-Everett (rates: $34 double), 180 excellent rooms and suites, dining room and coffee shop, heated indoor pool, at 101 128th St., 98204 (337–0440); *Rodeway Inn* (rates: $27–31 double), 74 excellent units, dining room, cocktail lounge, heated pool, at 9325 South Broadway, 98204 (355–1570).

Seattle

(Pop. 530,800; zip code, see below; area code 206.) Area accommodations include: (Airport vicinity) *Seattle Airport Hilton* (rates: $50–66 double), 145 excellent rooms and suites, dining room, coffee shop, heated pool, sauna, courtesy transportation, at 17620 Pacific Hwy., 98188 (244–4800); *Holiday Inn of Sea-Tac* (rates: $42 double), 260 excellent units, dining facilities, coffee shop, heated pool, opposite Seattle-Tacoma International Airport, 98188 (248–1000). (Downtown Seattle area) *Best Western Continental Plaza* (rates: $33 double), 90 deluxe units, heated pool, restaurant, suites with view of surrounding mountains and Lake Union, ½ mile north of Seattle on Hwy. 99 at 2500 Aurora Ave. N., 98109 (284–1900); *Best Western Greenwood Inn* (rates: $37–39 double), 183 excellent units in downtown Bellevue, with dining room, cocktail lounge, heated pool, and deluxe suites, at 625 116th Ave. N.E., 98004 (455–9444); *Holiday Inn—East* (rates: $37 double), 180 superb units in downtown Bellevue, with balconies, Jonah and the Whale Restaurant, heated pool, at 11211 Main St., 98004 (455–5240); *Holiday Inn—Issaquah* (rates: $32 double), 100 excellent units, dining room, cocktail lounge, coffee shop, heated pool, sauna, off Interstate 90, Exit 15, at Lake Sammanish State Park, 1601 12th Ave. N.W., 98027 (392–6421); *Red Lion Inn at Sea-Tac* (rates: $53–63 double), 400 spectacular units, with heated pool, dining room, coffee shop, sauna, balconies, opposite Seattle-Tacoma International Airport at 18740 Pacific Hwy. S., 98188 (246–8600); *Sheraton Renton Inn* (rates: $42 double), 700 rooms and suites, dining room, coffee shop, cocktail lounge, heated pool, at 800 Rainier Ave. in Renton, 98055 (266–7700); *Seattle Hilton* (rates: $71–74 double), 240 excellent units in downtown location, with dining room, coffee shop, cocktail lounge, suites, at 6th Ave. & University St., 98101 (624–0500); *Travelodge by the Space Needle* (rates $34–38 double), 80 good units and heated pool, at 6th Ave. N., 98109 (623–2600).

Tacoma

(Pop. 154,600; zip code, see below; area code 206.) Accommodations: *Best Western Lakewood Motor Inn* (rates: $29 double), 78 units, Lakewood Terrace Restaurant, cocktail lounge, heated pool, at 6125 Motor Ave. S.W., 98499 (584–2212); *Best Western Sherwood Inn* (rates: $24–26 double), 121 excellent units, dining room, cocktail lounge, heated pool, at 8402 S. Hosmer St., 98444 (535–2800); *Holiday Inn* (rates: $35 double), 108 comfortable rooms, dining room, cocktail lounge, pool, at 3518 Pacific Hwy. E., 98424 (922–0550).

Yakima

(Pop. 45,600; zip code, see below; area code 509.) Accommodations: *Best Western Red Lion Motel* (rates: $25–29 double), 58 excellent rooms and family units, heated pool, near restaurant, 818 N. 1st St., 98901 (453–0391); *Holiday Inn* (rates: $30 double), 171 rooms and family units, dining facilities, cocktail lounge, pool, 9th St. and Yakima Ave., 98901 (452–6511); *Plaza Motor Inn* (rates: $29–32 double), 160 outstanding rooms and suites, dining room, coffee shop, heated pool, cocktail lounge, 7th St. and Yakima Ave., 98901 (248–5900); *Thunderbird Motor Inn* (rates: $30–39 double), 158 superb rooms and suites, dining room, coffee shop, cocktail lounge, 1507 N. 1st St., 98901 (248–7850).

Lodges & Ski Centers

★★★*Crystal Mountain Ski Area & Lodgings*, located 76 miles from Seattle in the Cascade Mountains of the Mt. Baker-Snoqualmie National Forest, offers challenges for every skiing ability, with over 4,500 acres of the finest terrain, from the gentle slopes of the Quicksilver Chairlift (C–4) to the challenging drop of Sunnyside under the Iceberg Ridge Chairlift (C–2). The top of Crystal Mountain stands at 6,830 feet to provide a vertical descent of 3,000 feet. This naturally offers a large variety of skiing from the summit to the valley floor below. This popular Cascade ski resort has 1 triple chair lift, 5 double chair lifts, 11 rope tows, and 1 T-bar providing uphill transportation.

Whether you are a beginning skier or an accomplished veteran, you will find the highly qualified Crystal Mountain Ski School staff courteous and skilled. For ski school rates and info, call (206)663–2365. A full line of ski rental equipment is available in the Crystal Mountain ski shop. The staff is always ready to help with equipment repairs and sundry items such as sunglasses and suntan lotion, and there is a complete ski shop where you will find the most up-to-date ski clothing and equipment. The resort opens in early November and runs into June. During July and August, scenic rides to the summit bring tourists and hikers face to face with nearby Mt. Rainier. At the top, the warm Summit House restaurant and bar offer skiers in winter and tourists in summer a cozy spot in which to relax and enjoy the 360–degree view of Cascade mountain peaks stretching from Mt. Hood in Oregon to the south, to Mt. Baker near the Canadian border to the north. The panoramic view includes well-known peaks such as Mt. Adams, Mt. St. Helens, and, on clear days, the Olympic Mountains west of Seattle. The village in the valley is located at an elevation of 4,400 feet. Conference facilities are available as well as overnight facilities, including two motels and many condominiums to accommodate as many as 1,100 guests. There are several restaurants, bars, and swimming pools and a general store.

Rustic accommodations are available at the following Crystal Mountain lodges: *Alpine Inn* (rates: $20–30 double with ski packages available), an excellent hotel with restaurant and Snorting Elk Center (206)663–2262; *Crystal Inn* (rates: $26–30 with private bath and shower), hotel accommodations with dining, lounge, and dancing (206)663–2330; *Crystal House* (rates: $22–30, ski packages), 24 spacious units and giant fireplace in the main lounge, 200 yards from the chair lifts (206)663–2236; *Silver Skis Chalet* (rates: $48–65), 60 modern apartment-style units surrounding a broad open courtyard, with heated pool, 1 or 2 bedrooms, kitchen, balcony, fireplace (206)663–2245; *Crystal Chalets* (rates: $48–65), an attractive 36-unit hillside condominium complete with kitchens, bedrooms, and fireplace (206)663–2311. For reservations and information, write the individual accommodations at Crystal Mountain, WA 98022, or call them directly.

★★★*Double K Mountain Ranch* is a small jewel of a lodge surrounded by the breathtaking high country of the Cascade Mountains. The flower-carpeted meadows, snowcapped volcanic cones, mountain lakes, and rushing streams offer year-round enjoyment for hikers, fishermen, cross-country skiers, and nature lovers. Swimming and boating are also actively pursued on nearby Bumping Lake. The ranch accommodates 16 guests at a time in 6 twin bedrooms, 1 double and 1 single room, and a rustic cabin for 2. There are two fully modern pine-paneled baths in the ranch house and a half-bath in the cabin (shower facilities at the ranch). Both the ranch house and cabin have stone fireplaces. In winter there is furnace heat. Home-cooked meals prepared over a wood stove will satisfy even the most discriminating appetite. Rates: $185 per person weekly, including room, meals, and transportation to and from Yakima. Aside from July and August, when reservations are by the week only, guests are welcome for shorter stays (2–night minimum) at $35 per night. For full details write: Double K Mountain Ranch, Goose Prairie, WA 98929.

★★★*Hidden Valley Ranch and Country Inn*, on the eastern slopes of the Cascade range, commands 2,500 acres of meadowlands and gently rolling hills in a broad valley traversed by meandering Swank Creek. The ranch is an operating spread raising horses, cattle and feed; a remuda of 40 horses varies from gentle mounts to show-off rodeo horses, so there's a mount for every level of expertise, plus expert instruction in Western riding. Other activities include swimming in the heated pool, hiking and nature walks, trail picnics, wildlife photography, tennis, and moonlight rides. In winter, Hidden Valley's terrain provides superlative ski touring in an uncrowded and unspoiled snowy wilderness. Professional guide service, moonlight treks, and ice skating are also available. Accommodations are in private rustic cabins with twin beds, electric heat, showers, and sleeping quarters for 2–10 guests. Family style meals, expertly prepared, are served in the attractive main ranch house. Fresh bread and vegetables, ranch-raised pork and beef, and a selection of choice wines round out a varied and delicious menu. Bar service is not available. Rates are approximately $240 per person weekly ($40 daily) including meals, lodging, scheduled trail rides (summer), and guide service for winter ski touring. European plan rates (lodging only) are available for guests who do not want to participate in the full schedule of ranch activities. For additional information write: Hidden Valley Ranch, Route 2 Box 111, Cle Elum, WA 98922 (509)674–2422.

★★★★*Snoqualmie Summit Ski Area & Lodge* offers more than 200 acres of open, groomed slopes, 8 chair lifts (2 of them triples), 9 rope tows, and 2 Poma lifts—all of which add up to some of the best learning and training terrain west of the Rockies. The Snoqualmie ski school specializes in small classes and private lessons for all levels of ability, and there is a special 25% discount on equipment for students interested in the Graduated Length Method (GLM). There are 5 restaurants in the immediate ski area, ranging from inexpensive cafeterias to the plush Continental Restaurant where you can enjoy steak and seafood while savoring beautiful views of the Cas-

cades. Friday and Saturday nights, the Slide-in Tavern offers disco dancing, pizza, beer, and wine. Accommodations at the attractive Snoqualmie Lodge are $14–$18, double occupancy, for rooms without bath; $22–$26, double occupancy, for a private room and bath; and $26–30, double occupancy, for large rooms with private baths and sleeping quarters for 6 ($3.50 for each additional person). The lower rates reflect Sunday-through-Thursday discounts. Other amenities include a baby-sitting service, lift discounts, a day lodge, regularly scheduled races, and a full line of equipment rentals. For more details write: Snoqualmie Summit, 3767 East John St., Seattle, WA 98112 (206)434–6161.

★★*Snowline Inn—Mt. Baker Ski Area* offers 29 rustic, alpine rooms and family units, with fireplaces and balconies on Washington Hwy. 542. Rates range from $21 to $45, double occupancy. Contact: Snowline Inn, Box 51, Glacier, WA 98244 (206)599–2788.

★★★*White Pass Ski Village,* 14 miles southeast of Mt. Rainier National Park, has comfortable, attractive condominium-type accommodations surrounded by some of the finest ski terrain in the Cascades. All trails—up to 1,500–foot vertical drops and 2 miles in length—are expertly groomed. There are lifts and slopes for every level of expertise. Condominiums are only 250 feet from the slopes, and each unit has a fully equipped kitchenette, private bath, and linens. Many have fireplaces. Additional attractions of this fine ski resort include a heated pool, lighted slopes for night skiing, an excellent restaurant, après-ski activities, ski instruction, complete rentals, and a cafeteria and pub. Rates: $31 (double occupancy) daily for a studio, $44–52 for lodgings accommodating up to 4. The above rates apply on high-season weekends; weekday prices are slightly lower. White Pass also offers special midweek ski packages and facilities for business meetings. The resort is open during the summer season, with lift service available to the Goat Rocks area. For more details write: White Pass Co., P.O. Box 354, Yakima, WA 98907.

Travel Services

REI Mountain Schools offer evening lectures, weekend field trips and month-long wilderness training courses in backpacking, snow and ice climbing, and rock climbing techniques in the Washington Cascades. Each course incorporates some training in first aid and mountain rescue, but REI's main goal is to equip students with the skills that make the wilderness exciting with a minimum of accidents born of ignorance, haste, and misuse of equipment. Backpacking students learn to choose the best and least expensive equipment for alpine travel, become familiar with light cooking equipment, trailside recipes, navigation, compass and map reading, and the art of walking, pacing and conditioning. Students are led through a variety of mountain walks, and complete several overnight backpacking trips. Intermediate backpacking focuses on orientation, wilderness ecology, mountain first aid, route selection and basic snow and ice climbing and rock climbing techniques, beginning with a cross-country trip and completing a more technical traverse in higher elevations. Rock climbing students learn the basics of belaying and rappelling, and the dynamic precision of hand and foot work that will enable them to complete an ascent in the Washington Pass area. Intermediate rock climbing students learn to lead a climb, and complete a multi-pitch ascent. Basic snow and ice courses cover crampon and ice ax techniques, and culminate with a climb of a glaciated peak. Intermediate students complete a difficult route on one of the major mountains in the breath-taking Cascade Range. For details, write: REI Mountain Schools, P.O. Box C88126, Seattle, Washington 98188.

Mount Rainier National Park

The glacier-studded peaks, alpine valleys, meadows, forests, and lakes of Mt. Rainier National Park encompass 235,000 acres of the High Cascades. Mt. Rainier (14,410 ft.), with its steep, unstable rock, heavily crevassed glaciers, and sudden devasting storms, is the highest peak in the Cascade Range and one of the supreme mountaineering challenges in North America.

Mt. Rainier and the ancient volcanoes of the Pacific Northwest are part of the "Circle of Fire" that rims the Pacific from Mt. Lassen to Alaska's Mt. Katmai with its eerie "ghost forests" and Valley of Ten Thousand Smokes. Seventy million years ago the Northwest was covered by a vast sea, which gradually receded. The continent emerged as awesome volcanic eruptions spread great flows of molten lava. The eruptions of the Cascade Range—less than 10 million years ago—have continued almost to modern times. Emissions of hydrogen sulfide gas and steaming fumaroles are common near the summits of several of the great peaks. If you are planning a trip through the High Cascade wilderness areas, be sure to wear sturdy hiking boots as protection against the sharp, cutting edges of the hardened lava flows. There are over 350 miles of trails within the park. The Wonderland Trail is the longest, circling Mt. Rainier for a distance of about 90 miles, crossing meadows, streams, mountain passes, and forested valleys, and reaching a maximum elevation of 6,500 feet at Pan Handle Gap. Other trails, including the Cascades Crest Trail, Nisqually Vista Loop, and Trail of the Shadows, lead to such backcountry places as Sunrise Point, Goat Island Mountain, Eagle Peak, Grove of the Patriarchs, Cowlitz Divide, Ohanapecosh Park, and the Elysian Fields.

For most of the year Mt. Rainier lies under a blanket of snow, and even as late as July there may be 8–foot drifts in the sheltered coves. As the days grow warmer in the early summer months, the meadows become a brilliant sea of lupine, Indian paintbrush, marigold, and fawn lily. Then as summer turns to fall, the forests and fields mellow with the deep reds of huckleberry, maple, and mountain ash. Climbing Mt. Rainier is a dangerous feat and should be attempted only by the experienced mountaineer.

Fishing in the park can also be challenging. Generally the clear lakes are small and not fertile enough to support a large fish population. Most of them lie at 4,000–6,000 feet and are not free of ice until July. Access to the lakes is by trail on foot or packhorse. A few of the

more promising lakes to test your skill are Golden, Deadwood, Bear Park, Mowich, Mystic, and Palisades.

Information Sources, Maps & Access

For detailed park information and a free *Mount Rainier National Park Map/Brochure,* write: Superintendent, Mt. Rainier National Park, Longmire, WA 98397. A full-color 22–by–26–inch *Mount Rainier National Park Topographic Map* ($2) may be obtained from: U.S. Geological Survey, Federal Center, Denver, CO 80225. The park is reached via U.S. Hwy. 12 and Washington Hwys. 123, 410, 7, 706, and 165. Please note that park roads are usually closed about November 1, after the first heavy snowfall, until early summer.

Lodges & Inns

★★*Gateway Inn* offers rustic guest cottages in a scenic location at the western park entrance on Highway 706. Cottages have fireplaces and showers or baths. Facilities include a good dining room and coffee shop. Daily rates are $18 double. Contact: Gateway Inn, Ashford, WA 98304 (206)569–2506.

★★*Mountain View Lodge Motel* offers lodge and cottage accommodations approximately 12 miles southwest of the Stevens Canyon entrance to the park on U.S. Highway 12. Facilities include a pool and a playground for children. Daily rates are $13–22 double. Contact: Mountain View Lodge Motel, Box 525, Packwood, WA 98361 (206)494–5555.

★★*National Park Inn,* a rustic hotel located in Longmire on the road to Paradise Valley, is operated on the European plan, with meal service in the dining room, a gift shop, a gas station, and limited camping supplies. The inn has 10 rooms and suites, with and without private baths. Daily rates: $15 double without bath; $23 double with bath; $30 for suite with 2 bedrooms and 1 bath. Contact: Mt. Rainier Hospitality Service, 4820 S. Washington, Tacoma, WA 98409 (206)475–6260.

★★★*Paradise Inn* is located within the park about 22 miles from the southwest entrance and 20 miles from the southeast entrance in a spectacular alpine setting with a view of Mt. Rainier. This historic mountain inn is a rustic hostelry with 100 guest rooms with views, stone fireplaces, log rafters, and handcrafted Indian rugs in the handsome lobby. The dining room, with its wooden beams and parquet floors, accommodates up to 200 guests with efficient and friendly service. Other facilities include a cocktail lounge and snack bar. From the inn, guests may explore some 300 miles of high-country trails, fish in remote alpine lakes and streams, and join backpacking and climbing trips to Mt. Rainier. Guided nature walks are provided by National Park rangers. Paradise Inn daily rates (1 or 2 persons, based on European plan) are: $17 for a room without bath; $23–29 for a room with private bath; $24–29 for twin beds with bath; $39 for a 2–bedroom suite with bath. Contact: Mt. Rainier Hospitality Service, 4820 S. Washington, Tacoma, WA 98409 (206)475–6260.

★★*The Lodge,* located near the Nisqually entrance to Mt. Rainier National Park, is a delightful rambling inn surrounded by 18 wooded acres. The cigar-store Indian standing out front, one arm raised in a welcoming salute, marks the site of the old stagecoach stopover on the long journey across the Cascades. The hospitality today is just as warm as it was back then, with comfortable lodgings in attractive guest rooms and cabins. Most of the rooms offer splendid forest and alpine views, and there is an abundance of woods and clearings. The staff conducts special classes in canoe safety and technique, plus guided trips on the wilderness waterways of Idaho, Oregon, Montana, Washington, and British Columbia. For more information write: The Lodge, P.O. Box 86, Ashford, WA 98304 (206)569–2312.

Travel Service

Rainier Mountaineering has a staff of highly skilled and experienced mountain guides who will teach you the very latest in climbing techniques. This renowned firm, owned and operated by Louis Whittaker and W. Gerald Lynch, offers 1–day climbing schools; 2–day summit climbs of Mt. Rainier ($75 per person, including bunk space, sleeping bag, breakfast and dinner at Camp Muir, and group equipment for the summit ascent); 5–day snow-and-ice-climbing seminars at the Paradise Guide House ($225 per person, including meals and mountain hut bunk space); 6–day expedition seminars on Mt. Rainier ($300 per person); and guided expeditions to Mt. McKinley in Alaska, to the Himalayas, and to Mexico and Peru. For people with prior climbing experience, professional guides are available for private trips. These trips provide an excellent opportunity for people who already know the techniques of mountaineering to gain experience on a more challenging route up Mt. Rainier or any other northwestern peak. Trips must be arranged at least one month in advance. You provide all equipment, food, and transportation. Fee: $75 per person per day. No routes through Camp Muir.

All participants must have completed the RMI Basic Snow Climbing School during the current season, for a conditioning evaluation and climbing review. For additional information, contact: Rainier Mountaineering Inc., 201 St. Helena, Tacoma, WA 98402 (206) 627–6242. Summer address (June 1–Sept. 15): Mt. Rainier National Park, Paradise, WA 98397 (206)569–2227.

North Cascades National Park & Recreation Areas

Washington North Cascades is one of the great alpine camping, hiking, fishing, and big-game hunting regions in North America. North Cascades National Park encompasses 1,053 square miles in the heart of the region. A majestic alpine wilderness area, the park embraces heavily forested valleys, deep glaciated canyons, snowfields, fjordlike lakes, jagged peaks, and more than 150 glaciers. The summits of Mt. Challenger, Three Fingers, Del Campo, Mt. Shuksan, the Picket Range Wilderness, and Eldorado Peaks Wilderness are composed of granitic gneiss, forming spires, horns, peaks, and ridges. More than 300 glaciers cling to these crags, and hundreds of lakes lie in the glacial cirques below. Numerous trails follow the long valley bottoms, leading through thick rain forests on the western slopes and through open sunlit woodlands to the east, winding out of the forests at 4,000–5,000 feet over high passes, through beautiful alpine meadows, and on up along the glaciers clinging to the high peaks. Many of the high trails have snow on them in July. High-water melt early in the season makes stream crossings particularly dangerous. Be sure to use extreme caution when crossing snow bridges.

Mountain goat, moose, elk, deer, black bear, a rare grizzly or two, wolverine, mountain beaver, and bald eagle range throughout the wilderness areas. Fishing is excellent in the hundreds of alpine lakes and streams for small cutthroat, rainbow, and brook trout, and in the large glacial rivers and lakes for steelhead and trout to lunker size. The remote wild Skagit River, originating in British Columbia's Cascade Range, once flowed through a mighty gorge emerging into the flatland of the Skagit Valley, which has since been dammed to form 24–mile-long Ross Lake. The Skagit, which flows on through the old logging-camp country of the Mt. Baker National Forest region, yields some 35,000 steelheads up to 20 pounds each winter. The fishing in Ross Lake is good for rainbows from 2 to 4 pounds and Dolly Varden up to 12 pounds. For much of its length this lake is walled by sheer granite peaks. Beautiful fjordlike Lake Chelan lies to the south. The largest lake in the state, it is over 52 miles long. Often referred to as the Jewel of the American Alps, Lake Chelan provides very good early-season fishing for kokanee, rainbow, cutthroat, and large Dolly Varden. One of the most popular streams on the east slope of the Cascades is the Methow River, flowing southeasterly through the Cascades to join the Columbia River at Pateros. The Methow and its leading tributaries, Early Winters Creek, Lost River, and Wolf Creek, provide fine fishing for rainbow and cutthroat trout. The large, clear Skykomish River is an excellent steelhead stream.

The 505,514–acre Pasayten Wilderness forms a virtually unbroken fortress of wild backcountry in the Okanogan and Mt. Baker national forests stretching along the boundary of the Ross Lake National Recreation Area. The wilderness was established in 1968 by the same congressional act that established the North Cascades National Park and Ross Lake and Lake Chelan national recreation areas. Most of what is now the Pasayten Wilderness was formerly included in the North Cascades Primitive Area. The wilderness is a primitive area of naked peaks composed of granite, marble, gneiss, and schist, ice-scoured basins, U-shaped valleys, waterfalls, rock-strewn slopes, and sheer cliffs, which provide a violent contrast to the open sunlit forests of spruce, fir, ponderosa pine, willows, birches, and groves of aspen and the vast meadows blanketed in the summer with Indian paintbrush, scarlet gilia, bluebells, violets, and yellow fireweed.

Information Sources, Maps & Access

For North Cascades National Park information and the following free maps and brochures, write to Park Superintendent's Office, 311 State St., Sedro Woolley, WA 98284 (206)855–1331: *North Cascades National Park Map/Brochure, Ross Lake & Lake Chelan National Recreation Areas Map/Brochure, North Cascades Main Trails & Backcountry Map, North Cascades Campgrounds, Hiking in the North Cascades, Geologic History of the North Cascades, Weather and Climate of the North Cascades, Ross Lake National Recreation Area,* and *Campgrounds, Lakes & Glaciers in the Stehekin Ranger District.*

A full-color, 30-by-40-inch *North Cascades Topographic Map* ($2) may be obtained from: U.S. Geological Survey, Federal Center, Denver, CO 80225. A full-color *Pasayten Wilderness Topographic Map* (50¢) may be obtained along with wilderness travel information from: Supervisor, Okanogan National Forest, Okanogan, WA 98840. The North Cascades National Park, Lake Chelan and Ross Lake national recreation areas, and Pasayten Wilderness are reached via forest access roads off Washington's North Cascades Highway 20. Lodging, supplies, outfitting, and guide service are available at the old frontier logging and mining centers of Mazama, Stehekin, Newhalem, Marblemount, and Sedro Wooley.

Gateways & Accommodations

Sedro Woolley

(Pop. 4,600; zip code 98284; area code 206.) A major lumbering town in the Skagit River valley on scenic Washington Highway 20, Sedro Woolley is the administrative headquarters and major gateway to North Cascades National Park. Area attractions include the scenic train ride in old Northern Pacific passenger cars on the Lake Whatcom Railway and the Mt. Baker ski area. Accommodations: *Skagit Motel* (rates: $20–26 double), 47 units and adjacent restaurant, on Hwy. 20 (206)856–6001.

Winthrop

(Pop. 400; zip code 98862; area code 509.) This eastern gateway is located in the heart of the North Cascades on Highway 20 and is surrounded by the Okanogan National Forest. Accommodations: *The Virginian Motel* (rates: $21.50–29.50 double), 11 units, cottages, and cafe ¾ mile east of town on Hwy. 20 (996–2535); *Winthrop Inn* (rates: $26–30 double), 30 units, 1 mile east of town on Hwy. 20 (996–2217). (See also Sun Mountain Lodge below.)

Lodges & Resorts

★★★*North Cascades Lodge* is a sprawling complex on Lake Chelan in the alpine setting of Washington's spectacular Cascades. Nearby are beautiful Rainbow Falls, the brawling Stehekin River, and a valley inhabited by generations of mountain people. Some of the activities at North Cascades Lodge include hiking the wilderness, river rafting, horseback riding, cross-country skiing, and snowshoeing. There are also boat tours of the lake and an abundance of photogenic wildlife. Excellent accommodations are available in completely furnished housekeeping units ($27–35 daily) or in lodge rooms ($24–42 daily). On the premises are a dining room, a grocery store, banquet facilities, and a public marina. If you stay at the lodge 8 days, North Cascades pays for your return flight to Chelan. Special packages available through the lodge give guests an opportunity to fish and explore Domke Lake on 1-day fly-in trips. For more details write: North Cascades Lodge, Stehekin, WA 98852 (509)662–3822.

★*Ross Lake Resort* specializes in superlative fishing for rainbow trout in the awesome setting of the North Cascades. The lake, with its near-vertical shoreline, is surrounded by rugged mountains and giant boulders and is reached via a scenic drive along the Skagit River northeast from the town of Newhalem. The resort itself is built on huge rafts with accommodations for 75 guests, plus 53 boats and 36 outboard motors. You must bring your own groceries and supplies, since there are no stores in the immediate area and the lodge maintains only limited emergency goods. Ice and refrigeration for fish are available. Modern housekeeping units for 4–5 people are equipped with all linens, electric or propane stoves, hot water, refrigerators, bathrooms, and a fireplace or gas heat. Rates: $23 daily for 1 or 2 guests; $27 for 3. There are also older units with 4–8 bunks and communal bath facilities. These rent for $12 daily for 2; $15 for 3. Boat and motor rentals are not included in the above rates. For more information write: Ross Lake Resort, Rockport, WA 98283 (206)7–4735, via Mt. Vernon operator in Newhalem.

★★★★*Sun Mountain Lodge* is a first-rate mountaintop wilderness resort situated near a grove of pine trees on a mesa high above the lush Methow Valley in northern Washington. Activities here include trail rides through an untouched wilderness of mountain meadows and quiet forests, hiking up Gardner Mountain, tennis, soaking in a special hot pool, fishing in nearby Patterson Lake, and, in winter, cross-country skiing over miles of well-groomed trails. Sun Mountain also maintains a comprehensive ski school offering instruction in all aspects of ski touring, from basic lessons to advanced backcountry technique. Five-day trips in the Pasayten Wilderness with dogsled support are offered in the early spring. Guest rooms are comfortable and spacious, with queen-size beds, convertible couches, sundecks or patios, and splendid views from every room. The main lodge has an excellent dining room, a handsome modern lounge area, a gift shop, meeting facilities, and a cocktail lounge for dancing and nightly entertainment. Rates: $44 daily (double occupancy) on weekends from April 1 through October 22; $34 daily (double occupancy) Sunday through Thursday. For additional information write: Sun Mountain Lodge, P.O. Box 1000, Winthrop, WA 98862 (509)996–2211; in Washington call toll-free (800)572–0493.

Travel Services

Cascade Corrals offers overnight guided packhorse and ski touring trips in North Cascades National Park, Lake Chelan National Recreation Area, and Glacier Peak Wilderness. For information and rates, contact: Cascade Corrals, Stehekin, WA 98852(509)663–1521.

Pacific Northwest Float Trips offers guided raft trips down wild North Cascade region rivers like the Skagit, which include wildlife study and exploration of abandoned cabins and ancient Indian burial grounds. Contact: Pacific Northwest Float Trips, 829 Waldron St., Sedro Woolley, WA 98284 (206)855–0535.

Okanogan-Colville National Forests & Coulee Dam National Recreation Area

The Okanogan National Forest is an outstanding fishing, hunting, and wilderness camping area, encompassing 1,521,000 acres of

lovely valleys, alpine meadows and lakes, towering mountain ranges, and glaciers in north-central Washington. *Okanogan* is the Indian word for rendezvous, and applies to the area in the flatlands of the Okanogan Valley where the Indian tribes of British Columbia and Washington gathered for their annual potlatch. Over 1,200 miles of trail, including the Cascades Crest Trail from Manning Park on the Canadian border to Harts Pass, wind through the wild backcountry to such places as Great Goat Wall, a Yosemite-like glacier wall rising 2,000 feet above the valley floor; Slate Peak (7,500 ft.); Tatoosh Buttes; Lost River Canyon; Lake of the Woods; and the Pasayten Wilderness.

The Colville National Forest takes in 944,000 acres of the Selkirk Mountain region in the northeastern corner of Washington, bordered on the north by British Columbia and on the east by Idaho. This forest region is known primarily for its excellent mule deer hunting, with trophy bucks up to 440 pounds. Adjacent to the forest are the wildlands of the Colville Indian Reservation and Spokane Indian Reservation north of Roosevelt Lake and the Spokane River. The Roosevelt Lake area provides good hunting for whitetail deer, mule deer, and black bear, and wing shooting for quail, chukar partridge, mourning dove, pheasant, Canada goose, and brant.

The Coulee Dam National Recreation Area encompasses Roosevelt Lake and a narrow strip of land adjacent to the lakeshore. Franklin D. Roosevelt Lake stretches behind the dam for 130 miles, almost to the Canadian border. A scenic highway follows the lake northeastward through the old fur-trading territory of the North West Company, rolling wheatlands, and evergreen forests, past Fort Spokane, the Spokane Indian Reservation, and the Huckleberry and Kettle River mountains, to Gifford Ferry. Another scenic drive follows the Sanpoil River north through the Colville Indian Reservation to the old gold-mining town of Republic, through the national forest, then east over Sherman Pass. North of Kettle Falls, scenic roads follow the Columbia and Kettle rivers into Canada. Roosevelt Lake is the water gateway to the scenic Arrow Lakes region of British Columbia. Boaters planning to visit Canada are advised to inquire about inspection procedures from a park ranger or the U.S. customs service before crossing the international boundary.

Dry Falls, located south of Banks Lake and west of Coulee City, is the skeleton of one of the most spectacular waterfalls in geological history, some 100 times more powerful than Niagara. It once roared over an 800-foot precipice near the Upper Coulee. Lenore Caves, located 10 miles south of Dry Falls near the north end of Lake Lenore, were once used by prehistoric man and are today accessible by trail.

Information Sources, Maps & Access

A full-color *Okanogan National Forest Map* (50¢), the free *Okanogan National Forest Fishing Directory* and *Forest Roads & Trail Guide*, and information, may be obtained from: Supervisor, Okanogan National Forest, P.O. Box 950, Okanogan, WA 98840 (509)422-2704. A *Colville National Forest Map* (50¢) may be obtained from: Supervisor, Colville National Forest, Colville, WA 99114 (509)684-5221. Detailed info and a free *Coulee Dam National Recreation Area Map/Brochure* may be obtained from: Superintendent, P.O. Box 37, Coulee Dam, WA 99116. Okanogan National Forest is reached via the North Cascades Highway 20, Washington State Highway 153, and U.S. Highway 97; lodging, supplies, wilderness outfitting, and guide service are available at Methow, Twisp, Winthrop, Mazama, Conconully, Okanogan, Tonasket, and Oroville. Colville National Forest is reached via Washington Highways 155, 20, 21, 25, and 31 and U.S. Highway 395; lodging, supplies, outfitting, and guide service are available at Republic, Kettle Falls, Northport, Metaline Falls, Marcus, Colville, Chewelah, Deer Park, Newport, and Spokane. Coulee Dam National Recreation Area is reached via State Highways 17, 155, and 21 and U.S. Highway 2.

Gateways & Accommodations

Coulee Dam

(Pop. 1,400; zip code 99116; area code 509.) Accommodations: *Coulee House Motel* (Rates: $20–29 double), 47 excellent rooms and family units, heated pool, overlooking Coulee Dam on Washington Hwy. 155 (633-1101); *Ponderosa Motel* (rates: $20–29 double), 34 rooms and family units with view of dam, on Washington Hwy. 155 at 10 Lincoln St. (633-2100).

Moses Lake

(Pop. 10,300; zip code 98837; area code 509.) This city is a major gateway to Coulee Dam, Moses Lake Recreation Area, and the Potholes wildlife and recreation areas. Accommodations: *Best Western Hallmark Inn* (rates: $32 double), 138 rooms and suites overlooking Moses Lake, dining room, cocktail lounge, tennis courts, heated pool, at 3000 Marina Drive (765–9211).

Newport

(Pop. 1,400; zip code 99156; area code 509.) The town is the gateway to Colville National Forest and the 49° North Ski Area. Accommodations: *Golden Spur Motel* (rates: $17–20 double), 20 rooms and family units, on U.S. Hwy. 2 (447–2823).

Omak

(Pop. 4,200; zip code 98841; area code 509.) Omak is the gateway to Okanogan National Forest and the Pasayten Wilderness Area. Accommodations: *Omak Travelodge* (rates: $25–28.50 double), 60 good rooms and family units, at 121 N. Main St. (826–0400).

Spokane

(Pop. 170,500; zip code, see below; area code 509.) Accommodations: *Best Western Tradewinds—Downtown* (rates: $28–30 double), 59 excellent units with balconies, heated pool, across from restaurant, at West 907 3rd Ave., 99204 (838–2091); *Holiday Inn Downtown* (rates: $31–33 double), 153 excellent rooms and family units, dining room, cocktail lounge, heated pool, airport service, at East 110 4th Ave., 99220 (838–6101); *Holiday Inn West* (rates: $31–35 double), 140 excellent rooms and family units, dining room, cocktail lounge, heated pool, at 4212 Sunset Hwy., 99204 (747–2021); *Jefferson House Motel* (rates: $26–28 double), 56 superb rooms and family kitchen units, heated pool, airport service, at West 1203 5th Ave., 99204 (624–4142); *Red Lion Motor Inn* (rates: $35–38 double), 159 outstanding units and suites in rustic setting, dining room, cocktails, coffee shop, heated pool, at North 1100 Sullivan Rd., 99220 (924–9000); *Ridpath Hotel* (rates: $26–39 double), 360 spacious rooms and suites, restaurant, rooftop dining, cocktail lounge, coffee shop, at West 515 Sprague Ave., 99210 (838–2711); *Sheraton Hotel* (rates: $32–47 double), 389 outstanding rooms and suites, dining room, 1881 Restaurant, cocktail lounge, coffee shop, heated pool, at North 322 Spokane Falls Court, 99220 (455–9600); *Travelodge River Inn* (rates: $31–42 double), 152 superb rooms and suites, dining room, cocktail lounge, heated pool, tennis courts, at North 700 Division St., 99202 (326–5577).

Olympic National Park & Forest

The famous rain forests, towering stands of ancient cedars and firs, rugged coastal shores, glacier-fed streams, and majestic mountains of the Olympic Peninsula offer some of the finest steelhead and trout fishing, wilderness camping, backpacking, and big-game hunting opportunities in the Northwest. The peninsula is bordered on the west by the Pacific Ocean, on the north by the Strait of Juan de Fuca, and on the east by the placid inland salmon waters of Puget Sound. The 622,000 acres of the Olympic National Forest encompass a major portion of the peninsula and contain some of the truly great steelhead streams of the Pacific Coast. The vast stretches of unsettled backcountry provide excellent habitat for deer, black bear, and Roosevelt elk. Numerous hiking trails and forest roads lead to Mt. Jupiter, Marmot Pass, Mildred Lake, Silver Lake, and Mt. Walker.

The great steelhead rivers of the Olympic Peninsula flow from their glacial headwaters in the pinnacles of the Olympic Range through

dense rain forests and valleys and wilderness meadowlands bright with wild columbine, dogtooth violets, and Indian pipes, forming numerous rapids, whirlpools, and deep holding pools along their course to the Pacific.

The national forest forms a semicircle around Olympic National Park, a 1,400–square-mile wilderness in the heart of the peninsula. The park encompasses lush rain forests of giant Sitka spruce and hemlock towering above forest floors covered with thick mats of sphagnum moss, glacier-studded mountains, alpine lakes and meadows, rocky beaches and headlands, and powerful glacial streams renowned for their steelhead and salmon spawning runs. The park is dominated by the massive Olympic Mountains, which reach their greatest height at the summit of 7,954–foot Mt. Olympus. Several other peaks tower above 7,000 feet, and the elevation of the ridges and crests lies between 5,000 and 7,000 feet. The Olympic Range contains over 60 glaciers; the three largest, White, Hob, and Humes, are over 2 miles in length. The western side of the Olympic Peninsula has the wettest climate in the United States, with annual precipitation exceeding 140 inches. Mt. Olympus and the high-elevation backcountry receive much more precipitation from snow. In contrast, the northeastern side of the peninsula has one of the driest climates on the Pacific Coast.

Park roads provide access to over 600 miles of trails that lead through rain forests dense with ferns to wide, gravelly valleys and such points as the Seven Lakes Basin, the Bailey Range Mountains, Mt. Tom, Marymere Falls, Hurricane Hill, Lake Crescent, Mt. Storm King, Pyramid Peak, Flapjack Lake, Mt. Blue, Moose Lake, and Gravel Lake. The 50–mile-long Pacific Coast area has excellent wilderness beach trails along rocky headlands, around tidal pools, and by massive piles of driftwood. Be sure to obtain a tide table before you start your beach trek. This is tough hiking country, known for its slippery rocks and dense brush; getting lost is all too easy if you wander off the trail. A tide table, maps, and compass are essential.

Backcountry use permits are required for trail or beach camping. They may be obtained from the ranger station in the area where your hike originates. Mountaineering parties are asked to register at the ranger station nearest their route and to show that they have standard climbing gear.

Information Sources, Maps & Access

For detailed information on Olympic National Park and a free *Olympic National Park Map/Brochure* and *Climbing Mount Olympus*

bulletin, write: Park Superintendent, 600 East Park Ave., Port Angeles, WA 98362 (206)452–9715. A full-color 33–by–47–inch *Olympic National Park Topographic Map* ($2, also available in a beautiful shaded-relief edition) may be obtained from: U.S. Geological Survey, Federal Center, Denver, CO 80225. A full-color *Olympic National Forest Map* (50¢) and the free *Quinault Rain Forest Guide* and information may be obtained from: Supervisor, Olympic National Forest, Olympia, WA 98501 (206)753–9534. The Olympic National Forest and National Park are accessible via scenic U.S. Highway 101, reached via Interstate 5 from Oregon. Lodging, supplies, outfitting, and guide service are available at the scenic logging and fishing centers of La Push, Ozette, Neah Bay, Sekiu, Clallam Bay, Joyce, Elwha, Dungeness, Discovery Bay, Quilcene, Staircase, Hoodsport, Grisdale, Quinault, Queets, Forks, Heart o' the Hills, Humptulips, Olympia, and Port Angeles.

Gateways & Accommodations

Forks

(Pop. 1,300; zip code 98331; area code 206.) A major gateway to Olympic National Forest and National Park in the northwest region of the peninsula. Accommodations: *Forks Motel* (rates: $17–23 double), 58 comfortable rooms and family units, swimming pool, on Washington Hwy. 101 (374–6243).

Olympia

(Pop. 23,000; zip code, see below; area code 206.) Accommodations: *Best Western Motor Lodge* (rates: $26–28 double), 106 outstanding rooms and family units, dining room, cocktail lounge, heated pool, in downtown location at 900 Capitol Way, 98501 (352–7200); *Carriage Inn* (rates: $23–25 double), 62 outstanding rooms, next to restaurant, heated pool, 1211 S. Quince, 98501 (943–4710); *Olympia Westwater Inn* (rates: $36–70 double), 198 superb rooms and suites, restaurant, cocktail lounge, heated pool, courtesy airport transportation, 2300 Evergreen Park Drive, 98602 (943–4000); *Tyee Motor Inn* (rates: $26–34 double), 153 superb rooms and suites, dining room, cocktail lounge, coffee shop, heated pool, at 500 Tyee Drive, 98502 (352–0511).

Port Angeles—Gateway to Olympic National Park

(Pop. 16,400; zip code 98362; area code 206.) Headquarters for Olympic National Park. Accommodations: *Best Western Red Lion Bayshore Inn* (rates: $30–38 double), 128 outstanding rooms overlooking Strait of Juan de Fuca, restaurant, cocktail lounge, heated pool, at 221 N. Lincoln St. (452–9215); *Friendship Inn-Aggie's Port Angeles Motor Inn* (rates: $26–50 double), 114 rooms and suites, restaurant, cocktail lounge, heated indoor pool, sauna, at 602 E. Front St. (457–0471).

Lodges & Resorts

★★★*Kalaloch Lodge* is situated on the extreme western edge of Olympic National Park overlooking the thunderous breakers and white sand beaches of the Pacific Ocean. There's a safe swimming area in a protected lagoon near the lodge, plus unlimited opportunities for beachcombing, clamming, and fishing. Favorite off-season activities include steelhead fishing and hunting. Kalaloch has comfortable, nicely appointed lodge rooms, some with ocean views ($26–30 double occupancy); modern cabins with full kitchens, bedding, gas heat, and private shower baths ($26–40 double occupancy; additional guests are $5 per person daily); and semimodern 1–room cabins with cold running water, gas heat, stoves, and communal washrooms ($10–11 double occupancy). The Sea Crest House, a new 2–story motel set among tall trees at the far end of the resort, offers spacious and quiet accommodations with large picture windows overlooking the Pacific, private baths, and attractive furnishings ($36–42 double occupancy). Also on the resort grounds are a fine restaurant, gift shop, grocery store, and cocktail lounge. For more information write: Kalaloch Lodge, Star Route 1, Box 1100, Forks, WA 98331 (206)962–2271.

★★★*Lake Crescent Lodge*, nestled among towering spruce and fir trees on the southern shore of Lake Crescent, has guest accommodations ranging from inexpensive lodge rooms and family cottages to handsomely appointed motel rooms. Most rooms feature superb views of the lake or lofty Storm King Mountain, which forms a backdrop to the lovely resort. The deep blue waters of Lake Crescent are ideal for boating and trout fishing; rowboats are available at the lodge, or you can launch your own craft from the public boat ramp at the nearby Storm King Visitor Center. Hiking is another favorite activity in Olympic National Park. There are over 600 miles of trails, including the Marymere Falls Nature Trail leading from the lodge to a splendid series of cascades. Guests at the lodge can take

advantage of superlative salmon fishing in the Juan de Fuca Strait, just a short drive away. Lodge facilities include an attractive dining room with an appetizing menu, a cocktail lounge, gift shop, and recreation room. Rates: $26–32 daily for motel rooms with private bath and lake or mountain views; $27–36 for 1–bedroom cottages with fireplace, private bath, and lake and mountain view; $16–20 for 1– and 2–room cottages with private baths and mountain view; and $14–17 for lodge rooms with communal bath facilities. Lake Crescent Lodge is 20 miles from Port Angeles on U.S. 101; cab service is available from Port Angeles to both Crescent Lake and Hurricane Ridge lodges.

Hurricane Ridge Lodge is reached via a spectacular 18–mile drive over Hurricane Ridge Road, which winds its way past lush forests and mighty peaks from Port Angeles. The lodge is intended for day use only, and is especially popular with skiers during the December-to-April ski season. Food and refreshments are served here throughout the day, and the view alone—wave upon wave of snow-clad Olympic Mountains—is well worth the trip. Also on hand are a gift shop with native handicrafts for sale, ski rentals, lockers, a rope tow, and a Poma lift service. The lodge is also open during the summer months, from Memorial Day to mid-September.

For more information on the above facilities, write: National Park Concessions, Inc., Star Route 1, Port Angeles, WA 98362 (206)928–3211.

★★*Lake Crescent Log Cabin Resort*, on the north shore of the lake, has comfortable cabins, motel rooms, and A-frame units to suit every taste and budget. Sunny rustic cabins on a plateau overlooking the lake have 1 or 2 rooms and sleeping quarters for up to 4 guests ($16–28 daily, no housekeeping). Cabins nestled among tall shade trees have fireplaces, kitchens, good views of the lake, and accommodations for up to 6 persons ($23–36 daily). All cabins are carpeted and equipped with electric heat, private baths, and comfortable double beds. A-frame and motel-style rooms are located along the lakeshore and feature spacious rooms for up to 4 guests in each ($28–30; some with cooking facilities). The main lodge has a big sunny dining room with panoramic windows overlooking the lake and mountains, a grocery and tackle store, a recreation room, and a coffee bar. The resort's marina offers boat launching, moorage, lake cruises, and a full line of rental craft. For more information write: Lake Crescent Log Cabin Resort, Route 1, Box 6540, Port Angeles, WA 98362 (206)928–3245.

★★★★*Lake Quinault Lodge*, in the heart of the Olympic Peninsula and Rain Forest, is a handsome, rambling resort framed by huge evergreens and fronted by the deep blue waters of Indian-owned Lake Quinault. The lodge building is over 50 years old and still bears all the earmarks of an era when lofty ceilings, big stone fireplaces, and spacious guest rooms were *de rigueur* in respectable resorts. Of the 56 rooms, many have been upgraded but still retain a

1920s flavor; others are in a modern annex featuring private baths, queen-sized beds, and fireplaces. Activities here run the gamut from swimming in a generous, heated indoor pool to fishing right from the dock or in boats for native trout to float trips down beautiful, glacier-fed rivers. The Olympic National Forest, of course, offers unlimited opportunities for hiking, climbing, hunting, and sightseeing. On the lodge premises are a spa and saunas, a period-furnished lounge, gourmet dining room, game room, cocktail lounge, and gift shop. A genuine paddle-wheel boat leaves the dock daily for excursions around the lake. Canoes and rowboats may also be rented at the dock for fishing and exploring. Room rates: $26 single; $30–40 double. Off-season discounts, convention rates, and package plans are available. For full details write: Lake Quinault Lodge, P.O. Box 7, Quinault, WA 98575 (206)288–2571.

★★*La Push Ocean Park* overlooks a driftwood-strewn beach on the Pacific just a few miles south of Ozette Lake in northwestern Washington. Motel units right on the beach have beautiful ocean views, electric kitchens, and private baths. There are also 9 fully equipped housekeeping cabins and several campers' cabins with wood stoves, cooking equipment, a double bed, and a sleeping-bag loft. Kicker and charter boats are available for steelhead and ocean salmon fishing, or you can try your skill at surf casting. Swimming, surfing, and beachcombing are also popular activities. Some vacationers come just for the spectacular winter storms off the northwest coast. Rates: $19–23 daily for motel rooms, $12–25 daily for cottages (1–room to 2–bedroom), and $13 daily for rustic campers' cabins. For additional details write: La Push Ocean Park, Box 67, La Push, WA 98350 (206)374–5267.

★★★*Rain Forest Resort* is located on the south shore of beautiful Lake Quinault on the edge of Olympic National Forest near the Quinault Indian Reservation. Many well-maintained trails lead from the resort through the lush splendor of the Olympic Rain Forest and out of the Quinault Valley to the wild slopes of Mt. Tom, Mt. Olympus, Mt. Carrie, and the Bailey Range. Area activities include boating on the lake and river, fishing for summer steelhead and Dolly Varden, and hunting for elk, deer, bear, and cougar. The lodge has its own marina and a half-mile of sandy beach. Accommodations are available in a fully modern motel with carpeting and wood paneling or in fully equipped lakeside housekeeping cottages with sleeping space for 2–6 guests. Double-occupancy rates: in motel rooms, $16–20 daily; in housekeeping cottages, $14–19 daily. Open year-round, the resort is conveniently close to the charming village of Quinault. For details write: Rain Forest Resort, Quinault, WA 98575 (206)288–2535.

Travel Services

Lost Mountain Ranch sponsors guided group pack trips of 2–10 days through the alpine meadows and valleys of Washington's beautiful Olympic Mountains. On all hiking and riding trips, you move at a leisurely pace with plenty of time for fishing, relaxing, and exploring. Some of the areas visited include the ridge tops, meadows, and hidden lakes of the Dungeness High Country; the Dose Meadows and Elwha River, renowned for its fishing; and an "autumn color trip" to the park's most gorgeous fall scenery. Five-day hiking trips begin at $175 per person and include camping, equipment, experienced guides, and hearty ranch-style meals. A 3–day riding trip, including all of the above plus a sure-footed saddle horse, averages $165 per person. Lost Mountain Ranch also offers daily and hourly riding by appointment and custom packing for hiking or cross-country trips. For full information write: Lost Mountain Ranch, Route 6, Box 920, Sequim, WA 98382 (206)683–4331.

Rivers Northwest offers guided float trips through the spectacular rain forest country in Olympic National Park and Forest along the Hoh, Queets, and Quinault rivers. For detailed information and rates, contact: Adventure Tours, 19415 Pacific Hwy. S., Suite 414, Seattle, WA 98188 (206)824–2192.

San Juan Islands & The Inside Passage

The beautiful San Juan Archipelago includes some 172 islands and several hundred tide-washed rocks clustered in the northern waters of Puget Sound and the southernmost area of the Strait of Georgia. The archipelago is part of a submerged mountain chain that rises above sea level to a maximum of 2,454 feet at Mt. Constitution and forms the southernmost extension of the famous Inside Passage, which winds through the scenic labyrinth of islands that stretches north from Seattle for 1,000 miles along the British Columbia coast to Alaska and the Alexander Archipelago in the Tongass National Forest. The waters surrounding the maze formed by the San Juan Islands and Anacortes, Lummi, and Bellingham islands provide top-ranked fishing for coho, chinook, and humpback salmon. The rocky, jagged shores of the islands, many of which, such as Goose, Dot, Hat, Flattop, and Saddle Bag, are named for their unusual shapes, are covered by wind-stunted evergreens, with dense woodlands stretching inland. The picturesque isles are inhabited by eagles, deer, and wild goats. Deer are often seen swimming across the narrow channels between the islands in search of new browse. Several evergreen-fringed lakes nestled on the islands hold trophy trout and bass. Spring-fed Sportsman's Lake on San Juan Island offers top-ranked fishing for lunker smallmouth bass. Cascade Lake on Orcas Island holds big cutthroat, rainbow, and brook trout and kokanee salmon. Salmon-fishing camps and boat-rental docks are located on the major islands.

Information Sources, Maps & Access

For travel information and maps, write: San Juan Islands Chamber of Commerce, P.O. Box 98, Friday Harbor, WA 98250 (206)378–4600. For information about the proposed San Juan Wilderness Area, write: Manager, Willapa National Wildlife Refuge, Ilwaco, WA 98624. Access to the islands is provided by Washington State Ferries (see Introduction).

Lodges & Resorts

Bartel's Resort on Orcas Island offers spacious rooms and housekeeping cottages with fireplaces, a dining room, coffee shop, heated pool, tennis, dock, boats, and motors. Rates: $28–29 double occupancy. Contact: Bartel's Resort, Route 1, Box 1040, Eastsound, WA 98245 (206)376–2242.

Islander Lopez Motor Inn on Lopez Island has 25 comfortable rooms and suites, a restaurant and cocktail lounge, heated pool, and marina on Fisherman Bay. Rates at this Flag Inn: $27–38 double occupancy. Contact: Islander Lopez, Lopez Island, WA 98261 (206)468–2233.

Rosario Resort on Orcas Island is set on the beautiful, historic Moran estate grounds on Puget Sound. The resort is a converted mansion with 72 rooms and suites and housekeeping units, with dining room, cocktails, coffee shop, heated pools, sauna, tennis courts, dock, boats and motors, and nature trails on grounds. Rates: $16–46 double occupancy. Contact: Rosario Resort, Eastsound, WA 98245 (206)376–2222.

Wenatchee National Forest & Alpine Lakes Recreation Area

The Wenatchee National Forest, renowned for its outstanding alpine camping, cross-country skiing, fishing, and big-game hunting areas, encompasses 1,602,000 acres along the eastern slope of the Cascades just south of North Cascades National Park. The Columbia River forms its boundary to the east. The sweeping forests, snowcapped peaks, and hundreds of alpine lakes, meadows, and streams of the Wenatchee embrace a major portion of the spectacular Alpine Lakes Wilderness and National Recreation Area and the remote Enchantment Wilderness.

Hundreds of miles of high-country trails provide access to the Chelan Mountains, Entiat Mountains, Stuart Range, Enchantment Lakes Basin, Glacier Peak Wilderness, Swauk Pass area, Wenatchee Mountains, Nason Ridge, Tumwater Meadows, and the Chiwaukum Mountains. The Cascades Crest Trail enters the region at Rainy Pass and winds past the North Cascades National Park boundary and the Glacier Peak Wilderness-Lake Chelan National Recreation Area. If you are traveling by packhorse, be sure to carry feed, since forage is scarce along the way. The trail follows Agnes Creek past Suiattle Pass and Glacier Peak Mines and heads for Fire Creek Pass, Sitkum Creek, and White and Cady passes, with high views of beautiful open meadows. Both water and campsites are scarce in this area. The trail continues on past Wenatchee Pass and Union Gap to Stevens Pass, where the Great Northern Railroad completed its first

Cascade crossing in 1893. The town of Skykomish, 16 miles to the west, is a good place to resupply. From here the trail passes through the heart of the High Cascade lake country to Snoqualmie Pass. The last portion of this trail is inaccessible by saddle horse (and is also very risky on foot). Those using horses must use the Snow Creek Trail. The trail leaves the Wenatchee Forest on its way to Blowout Mountain to the south.

The Alpine Lakes Wilderness straddles the crest of the Cascade Mountains in the Snoqualmie and Wenatchee national forests about 50 miles east of Seattle. The wilderness encompasses magnificent valleys, forests of Douglas fir and hemlock on the west slope and ponderosa pine on the east. Hundreds of remote blue lakes and tarns lie in basins gouged by Ice Age glaciers at elevations ranging from 2,500 feet in the heavily timbered Foss River valley to over 8,000 feet in the barren Chiwaukum Range. The major features within this 162,400–acre wildland include the Snoqualmie River headwaters; Big Snow and Summit Chief mountains; Dorothy, Waptus, Deep, and Marmot lakes; Cathedral Peaks; and the Cle Elum River. Hundreds of miles of wilderness trails provide access to the remote interior areas. The remote Enchantment Wilderness lies adjacent to the Alpine Lakes Area on the east. Known as the Lost World Plateau, the Enchantment Wilderness encompasses some 30,700 acres of jagged granite spires, glacially carved slopes, and scenic lake basins interspersed with lush green mountain meadows at elevations ranging from 3,000 feet to 9,470 feet at Mt. Stuart. The area is reached by an extremely steep and rugged trail from the Icicle River.

Information Sources, Maps & Access

Detailed information, free trail guides, backcountry travel information, and a full-color *Wenatchee National Forest Map* (50¢) may be obtained from: Supervisor's Office, Wenatchee National Forest, P.O. Box 811, Wenatchee, WA 98801. (509)662–4335. Wenatchee National Forest is reached via Interstate 90, U.S. Routes 2 and 97, and Washington Highways 209, 207, 150, 151, and 28. Lodging, supplies, guides, and wilderness outfitting service are available at Cashmere, Chelan, Cle Elum, Ellensburg, Leavenworth, and Wenatchee.

Gateways & Accommodations

Cashmere

(Pop. 2,000; zip code 98815; area code 509.) Accommodations: *Village Inn* (rates: $22–24 double), 22 comfortable rooms and family units in downtown location, 229 Cottage Ave. (782–3522).

Chelan

(Pop. 2,400; zip code 98816; area code 509.) Chelan lies at the lower end of beautiful, fjordlike Lake Chelan. Accommodations: *Campbells Lodge* (rates: $42–50 double), 90 beautiful lodge rooms and suites, with balconies, restaurant, heated pools overlooking Lake Chelan, in center of town on Hwy. 97 (682–2561); *Inn at Wapato Point* (rates: $48–58 double), 148 excellent rooms and suites, with fireplaces, restaurant, cocktails, tennis courts, heated pools, swimming beach and marina on the north shore of Lake Chelan, at Manson, 98831 (687–9511); *Spader Bay Resort* (rates: $37.50 double), 49 superb rooms and suites, with balconies and fireplaces, kitchen units, heated pool, swimming beach and dock, sauna overlooking Lake Chelan, on Washington Hwy. 150 (682–5818).

Ellensburg

(Pop. 13,600; zip code 98926; area code 509.) The city is the seat of Kittitas County. It was once known as Robber's Roost and is the site of the famous annual Ellensburg Rodeo. Accommodations: *Holiday Inn* (rates: $31.50–33.50 double), 108 excellent rooms and family units, dining room, coffee shop, cocktail lounge, heated indoor pool, 1700 Canyon Road (925–9801); *Regalodge* (rates: $19.50–21.50 double), 30 excellent rooms and family units, heated indoor pool, 300 W. 6th Ave. (925–3116).

Leavenworth

(Pop. 1,300; zip code 98826; area code 509.) Resembles a Bavarian alpine village and is the site of the National Fish Hatchery and Stevens Pass Ski Area. Accommodations: *Der Ritterhof Motor Inn* (rates: $25–27 double), 24 comfortable rooms and family units, with balconies, patios, and heated pool, on U.S. Hwy. 2 (548–5845).

Wenatchee

(Pop. 16,900; zip code 98801; area code 509.) Accommodations: *Chieftain Motel & Restaurant* (rates: $26–28 double), 90 superb rooms and suites, heated pool, 1005 N. Wenatchee Ave. (663–8141); *Holiday Lodge* (rates: $20–26 double), 60 excellent rooms, heated pool, 610 N. Wenatchee Ave. (663–8167); *Thunderbird Motor Inn* (rates: $29–32 double), 150 outstanding rooms and suites with balconies, dining room, cocktail lounge, coffee shop, heated pool, on U.S. Hwy. 2 at 1225 N. Wenatchee Ave. (663–0711).

Wyoming

Introduction

Wyoming's Central Rocky Mountains are one of North America's great trout-fishing, hunting, backpacking, and cross-country skiing areas. Its high-country names are those of a legendary outdoor paradise: the Trois Tetons, Jackson Lake, Wind River Range, Beartooth High Lakes country, Teton Wilderness, Bighorn Mountains, Jackson Hole, Bridger Wilderness and Pago Agie Primitive Area, Medicine Bow Mountains and the Snow Range, Yellowstone National Park, Cloud Peak Wilderness, Wapiti Valley, and the craggy volcanic peaks of the massive Absaroka Range. Thousands of miles of hiking and timberline pack trails and forest roads provide access to the blue-ribbon trout waters of the upper Snake and Yellowstone, the headwaters of the Green, the North and South forks of the Shoshone; to the Gros Ventre wildlands; to the renowned trophy trout waters of the Wind, North Platte, Madison, Gardiner, Bechler, Gallatin, and Bighorn rivers; and to remote wildlands dotted by thousands of sparkling blue lakes surrounded by jagged peaks, glaciers, fragrant spruce and pine forests, and lush alpine meadows alive with the brilliant rainbow colors of Indian paintbrush, mountain cranberry, bearberry, andromeda, rosy sedum, and cassiopeia, and inhabited by deer, mountain lion, black bear, upland game birds, wolves, a few grizzly, and the nation's largest population of bighorn sheep and Rocky Mountain elk.

The Rockies cover the western two-thirds of Wyoming's 97,914 square miles; the eastern third is Great Plains country. The wild Wyoming frontier was first visited by the French explorers and fur traders François and Louis Vérendrye; followed by the trapper John Colter, the legendary mountain men of the Rocky Mountain Fur Company and Amercan Fur Company, and successive waves of government hunters and surveyors, adventurers, pioneers, cattlemen, and sheepherders.

Accommodations & Travel Information

Wyoming offers some of the nation's finest vacation guest ranches, lodges, and inns, nestled in the wide valleys of the Rocky Mountain high country. In addition to rustic western accommodations, many of the ranches and lodges listed in the "Vacation/Lodging Guide" offer guided packhorse, fishing, cross-country skiing, hunting, and float trips. Detailed information on all aspects of vacation travel may be obtained by contacting: Wyoming Travel Commission, 2320 Capitol Ave., Cheyenne WY 82002 (307)777–7777.

Information & Sources

For the free *Wyoming Fishing Regulations* booklet, which includes a fishing district map and rules for the national parks and Indian

reservations, write: Wyoming Game & Fish Dept., Communications Branch, Cheyenne 82002. The free *Wyoming Stream Fishery Classification Map*, published by the Fish Division of the Game & Fish Commission, Cheyenne, shows and classifies all fishing streams in terms of scenic beauty, accessibility, and size of trout population. Wyoming's Class 1, blue-ribbon streams include the Snake, Green, and North Platte rivers and Sand Creek. The Game & Fish Dept. also offers a free booklet called *Wyoming Fishing Guide*, which describes the waters within each numbered zone, gives the fish species present, size, access, and facilities available, and pinpoints the various lakes and streams on a series of zone maps.

The Bureau of Land Management areas are located mainly in the plateau lands outside of the mountain areas and contain limitless opportunities for fishing and hunting. Write for the free BLM publication *Wildlife and Recreation on Public Lands in Wyoming* to: Bureau of Land Management, Department of the Interior, 2002 Capitol Ave., Cheyenne 82001. The BLM also produces a series of maps of the various tracts under its jurisdiction.

Wyoming owns or cooperatively administers numerous lands, including Wildlife Units and Public Hunting and Fishing Areas. Write for the free booklet *Public Hunting and Fishing on Wyoming Game and Fish Commission Areas* to: Wyoming Game & Fish Commission, Box 1589, Cheyenne 82001.

Write to the Wyoming Travel Commission, 2320 Capitol Ave., Cheyenne 82002, for the free map-brochure *Family Water Sports—Big Wyoming*. This publication lists 62 lakes and rivers and gives the fish species found in each, availability of boats, guides, and bait and tackle in each area, and acreage of lake or length of stream. Each "water hole" is numbered, and the number appears in its appropriate location on the map. Public fishing areas are marked on the map with an *F* and marinas with an *M*. Included in this publication are license details; waterskiing, canoeing, kayaking, and rafting information; a list of outfitters who conduct float-fishing trips on principal waters; a list of marinas; general national and state park details; and a list of national parks, national forests, and other recreation areas, outlining the various water sports and facilities offered.

The Wyoming Travel Commission publishes a free guide to camping throughout the state, *Camping Big Wyoming*. This comprehensive guide lists campgrounds throughout the state in national parks, forests, and recreation areas. It also lists commercial campgrounds throughout the state by county. The directory gives the name, location, and type of each campground, as well as the number of tent and trailer sites, open season, limit of stay, free facilities, activities, special attractions, and nearest town and supplies. It designates campgrounds administered by the Forest Service, National Park Service, Bureau of Land Management, Wyoming State Parks, Wyoming Game and Fish Commission, and Natrona County Parks Board. A map in the guide keys the location of each campground described and the counties, parks, and forests in which they are located.

Backpacking—Climbing Big Wyoming, a free brochure published by the Wyoming Travel Commission, outlines the major sources of information for backcountry travel throughout the state. The brochure lists several good reference books on backpacking and mountain climbing in Wyoming and tells where to order them. It also gives the addresses of information sources for fishing and hunting, state parks and historic sites, geology, rock-hounding, and topographical maps. It tells where to write for information on hiking and backpacking in national parks, national forests, national recreation areas, national monuments, and other public lands. Special camps, wilderness schools, and mountain-climbing schools are also described in the guide, and their addresses are listed. To order the brochure, write: Wyoming Travel Commission, 2320 Capitol Ave., Cheyenne 82002.

The free *Wyoming Hunting Guide* leaflet, produced by the Wyoming Game & Fish Dept., Cheyenne 82002, describes general laws, firearm codes, fee schedules, application schedules and details, general species information including small game, and other basic input. A companion free leaflet, *Issuance of Licenses and Special Permits*, gives the necessary instruction for submitting and ordering big-game licenses by species. The Big Game Orders for each species can be obtained free from the Game & Fish Dept.

Highways & Maps

Wyoming's highways wind through some of the most awesome country in the United States and make some of the remote regions accessible. The *Wyoming Official Highway Map* shows these roads on a shaded relief background. The map also clearly marks streams and lakes, cities and towns, highways and roads (multilane, paved, gravel, graded, and earth), roadside parks, county seats, railroads, commercial and municipal airports, ski areas, and historic trails. Short descriptions of points of interest and historical sites are given on the map. Vicinity maps of the larger cities are included, as is a mileage chart for distances between cities. The map is available free from: Wyoming Travel Commission, 2320 Capitol Ave., Cheyenne 82002.

For more detailed information on the areas through which you plan to travel, use the free Big Wyoming region maps available from the Travel Commission, including *Central Big Wyoming*, *Western Big Wyoming*, *Northern Big Wyoming*, and *Southern Big Wyoming*. Each area map shows highways, cities and towns, historical sites, major natural features and points of interest, lakes and rivers, and wildlife of the area. Included with each map are extensive descriptions of the areas within the region, as well as information on outstanding natural features (fishing waters, rock formations, scenic backcountry, hunting areas), national forests, history, and wildlife. The maps covering areas of many waterways include charts describing fishing holes, which list camping, lodging, and boating facilities, nearest towns, lengths of the streams, and species of fish indigenous to the streams. These guides also list the addresses of additional sources of information on recreation in the regions they cover. The maps are free from: Wyoming Travel Commission, Cheyenne 82002. A fascinating map-guide to the Old Oregon Trail and Auto Route, *The Guide to the Lander Cut-off Oregon Trail*, is available free from: Bureau of Land Management, Box 1828, 2120 Capitol Ave., Cheyenne 82001.

Bighorn National Forest

The Bighorn National Forest covers 1,115,125 acres in the heart of the Bighorn Mountains in north-central Wyoming. The range rises like a giant wall out of the Great Plains to snowy peaks ranging in height from 9,000 to almost 14,000 feet. The lower levels of this north-south range are carpeted with pine, fir, and spruce. Lakes dot the eastern slopes of the mountains, and many streams are born here. The glacier-covered Cloud Peak (13,165 ft.) is the highest mountain in the range.

Sioux, Crow, and Cheyenne Indians lived and hunted here before whites settled in the area. The region was the scene of many conflicts between the tribes and the ways of life they represented. But none of these conflicts approached the fury of those fought against white intruders. In December 1866, along the eastern slopes of the Bighorns, Red Cloud and Sioux Indians ambushed Capt. William Fetterman and 81 soldiers and civilians in the state's worst military disaster. On the Red Fork of the Powder River south of this area, the Cheyenne warriors led by Dull Knife made their last stand against General Mackenzie's bluecoats.

The entire Bighorn region is drained by major tributaries of the Yellowstone River, including the Tongue, Bighorn, and North Fork Powder rivers. The beautiful Cloud Peak lake area has some outstanding fishing for brown, rainbow, Rocky Mountain cutthroat, brook, and golden trout from 8 to 10 inches, with an occasional fish tipping the scale at 3 pounds. A few of the Cloud Peak lakes hold Mackinaw up to a whopping 35 pounds—not bad for wilderness mountain fishing. The Bighorn region is the range for one of the state's largest elk herds, and there are also a large number of bighorn sheep.

Information Sources, Maps & Access

For detailed vacation travel, fishing, camping, and backpacking information and a full-color *Bighorn National Forest Map* (50¢) and *Cloud Peak Wilderness Map* (50¢), contact: Supervisor, Bighorn National Forest, Columbus Bldg., Box 2046, Sheridan, WY 82801 (307)672-2457. The Bighorn National Forest is readily accessible from the east by taking Interstate 90 to U.S. 87 (with which it merges just north of Buffalo), then turning west onto U.S. 14 near Sheridan. U.S. 14 and 14A lead into the forest from Cody to the west. Lodging, meals, guides, outfitters, and supplies are available at Lovell, Greybull, Buffalo, Ten Sleep, Dayton, and Sheridan.

VACATION/ LODGING GUIDE

Recreation Areas

Cloud Peak Wilderness

The Cloud Peak Wilderness encompasses 93,880 acres of rugged wildlands, stretching for 27 miles along the backbone of the Bighorn Range. Elevations in the wilderness vary from 8,500 feet to 13,165 feet at the summit of Cloud Peak. At elevations reaching above 10,000 feet are 256 alpine lakes and 49 miles of streams. The present-day moose population in the Cloud Peak area and the Bighorns is the result of a 1942 transplanting from the mountains of western Wyoming. Moose were extremely scarce in the early days of the Wyoming territory, and they were rarely reported in the journals of the trappers and scouts. It was not until the early 1900s that they began to migrate into the territory in steadily increasing numbers.

Bighorn Canyon National Recreation Area & Pryor Wild Horse Range

The Bighorn Basin is a natural valley covering more than 13,000 square miles (over 8 million acres) in Big Horn, Park, Washakie, and Hot Springs counties of northwestern Wyoming. The bighorn

sheep of the Absaroka Mountains to the west and the Bighorns to the east gave the basin its name.

The Bighorn River bisects the valley. Along with its tributaries, the Shoshone and Greybull rivers, it provides top-ranked fishing for rainbow, brown, and cutthroat trout. The legendary John Colter was the first white man to pass through this country, by way of the Pryor Gap of the Bighorn Mountains in 1807, on the trek that led him to the discovery of the natural wonders now called Yellowstone National Park. Later in the year a trapping party led by Ezekiel Williams traveled up the Bighorn River through what was then Crow Indian country. Edward Rose, a member of the party, remained here to become the first known permanent white resident of the valley.

Today, the Yellowtail Dam across the Bighorn River in Montana has created the 47–mile-long Bighorn Lake, the setting of the Bighorn Canyon National Recreation Area. This area of spectacular scenery is known as the land that time forgot. Tremendous geologic forces have metamorphosed once level layers of rock surrounding the basin into immense walls, or anticlines. The largest of these great arches is the Bighorn, which extends south from Yellowtail Dam to form the Bighorn Mountains. The river has cut deeply into the arch upstream of the dam, creating colorful cliffs rising almost one-half mile over the river, and exposing fossil-rich rocks up to 500 million years old.

The mountains are carpeted with forests of lodgepole and timber pine, fir, and spruce. Dwarf juniper, mountain mahogany, sumac, chokecherry, buffalo berry, and sage cover the foothills. Black bear, mule deer, elk, grouse, chukar and Hungarian partridge, waterfowl, pheasant, rabbit, muskrat, beaver, and mink inhabit the area, and wild horses roam the slopes. The Bureau of Land Management has established the 31,000–acre Pryor Mountain Wild Horse Range to preserve the habitat of the more than 200 wild horses that live beyond the western boundaries of the recreation area. Access to the range is by four-wheel drive.

Activities in the recreation area include hunting, boating, fishing, camping, and hiking. Bighorn Lake has an excellent walleye population, with a bonus of trophy-sized rainbow and brown trout. Another fascinating attraction in the area is the mysterious Medicine Wheel, left here by a prehistoric Indian culture. It is a circle of flat white stones 245 feet in circumference with 28 spokes, the monument of a vanished culture and religion. Other nearby features include the geologic marvels of Sheep Mountain and the Devil's Kitchen area north of Greybull. Wilderness campers will enjoy the remote beauty of the Cloud Peak Wilderness in the Bighorn National Forest about 40 miles east of Greybull.

Gateways & Accommodations

Buffalo

(Pop. 3,400; zip code 82834; area code 307.) A major gateway to the Bighorn Mountains, Buffalo is the seat of Johnson County, founded in 1879 by the cattlemen, miners, and freighters who opened the Sioux country. Once known as the rustlers' capital, it was the focal point of the Johnson County Cattle War of 1892. The Dull Knife Battle, the last major battle of the Indian wars, was fought here. Area attractions in and near this colorful Old West town include the Jim Gatchell Memorial Museum (Main & Fort Sts.), with displays of the Johnson County Cattle War; the site of Fort Phil Kearny and the Fetterman Massacre of 1866; and guided tours of the area sponsored by the Chamber of Commerce (684–7094). Accommodations: *Best Western Cross Roads Inn* (rates: $28–32 double), 60 excellent rooms and family units, dining room, coffee shop, heated pool, 1 mile east of town on Interstate 90 (684–2256).

Greybull

(Pop. 2,000; zip code 82426; area code 307.) This major center of the Bighorn Basin is named after a legendary bull buffalo who roamed along the Greybull River for years, successfully eluding hunters. Area attractions include the Bighorn River and the Greybull Museum (325 Greybull Ave.). Accommodations: *Best Western Yellowstone* (rates: $26–36 double), 33 rooms and family units, swimming pool, putting green, at 247 Greybull Ave. (765–4456).

Lovel—Gateway to the Bighorn Canyon National Recreation Area

(Pop. 2,400; zip code 82431; area code 307.) Area attractions include the Bighorn Canyon area, the Pryor Wild Horse Range, the Indian Medicine Wheel on U.S. Alternate Route 14, and the Horseshoe Bend Recreation Area. Accommodations: *Friendship Inn Horseshoe Bend Motel* (rates: $19–23 double), 22 good rooms on U.S. 14A and 310 (548–2221).

Sheridan

(Pop. 10,900; zip code 82801; area code 307.) Named for General Philip Sheridan, this is northern Wyoming's largest town, located in the saucer-shaped Sheridan Valley, flanked on the west by the Bighorn Mountains and on the east by the rolling Powder River country. The Eaton Dude Ranch, the first real dude ranch in the West, was located nearby at Wolf Creek. It once encompassed 7,000

acres along the foothills of the snowcapped Bighorns. Area attractions include the Connor Battlefield Historical Site, the Bradford Brinton Memorial Ranch Museum on Wyoming 335, Trail End Historical Home & Museum (400 Clarendon St.), former home of U.S. Senator John B. Kendrick (1857–1933), and the historic *Sheridan Inn*, a national historic landmark, offering delicious steak, prime rib, and freshly baked pastries. This famous hotel, erected in 1892, was the Sheridan home of Buffalo Bill Cody. The Cody Transportation Company, operated by Buffalo Bill, consisted of elaborate barns and a livery stable at the rear of the inn, where guests' horses were kept. Area accommodations: *Best Western Sheridan Center Motor Inn* (rates: $28–32 double), 142 excellent rooms and family units, dining room, coffee shop, outdoor and indoor heated pools, sauna, at 609–612 N. Main St. (674–7421); *Trails End Motel* (rates: $20–38 double), 53 excellent rooms and family units, dining room, coffee shop, indoor heated pool, at 2115 N. Main St. (672–2477).

Ten Sleep

(Pop. 300; zip code 82442; area code 307.) A rustic Old West town in Ten Sleep Valley, it is flanked on the east by the blue-black peaks of the Bighorn Mountains, Powder River Pass, and Ten Sleep Canyon, and on the west by the vast Bighorn Basin. The town was once 10 days' travel by horse from Fort Laramie and the same distance from Yellowstone Park. Area accommodations: *Valley Motel* (rates: $19–21 double), 20 good rooms just east of town on U.S. Hwy. 16 (366–2321).

Thermopolis

(Pop. 3,100; zip code 82443; area code 307.) This was once a favorite stopover of Butch Cassidy's Hole-in-the-Wall Gang along the Outlaw Trail. The town, surrounded by the wildlands of the Bighorn Basin, is famous for its hot springs. Area attractions include the Wind River Indian Reservation, Hot Springs State Park on U.S. Hwy. 20, Wind River Canyon, Hot Springs County Pioneer Museum (7th St. and Broadway), Boysen Reservoir and Boysen State Park, and the Wedding of the Waters, where the Wind River forms the Bighorn River. Accommodations: *Best Western Moonlighter Motel* (rates: $31–35 double), 26 rooms and family units, swimming pool, at 600 Broadway (864–2321); *Holiday Inn* (rates: $35–39 double), 80 excellent rooms and family units, restaurant, cocktail lounge, swimming pool, in Hot Springs State Park (864–3131).

Worland

(Pop. 5,100; zip code 82401; area code 307.) A ranching and petroleum center on the Bighorn River, Worland is a major gateway to the Bighorn National Forest to the northeast. Accommodations: *Sun Valley Motel* (rates: $22–26 double), 24 rooms, at 500 N. 10th St. (347–4251); *Town House Motor Inn* (rates: $22–25 double), 23 rooms, heated pool, at 119 N. 10th St. (347–2426).

Lodges & Guest Ranches

★*Dear Haven Lodge* is located high in Bighorn National Forest at the gateway to the unspoiled Cloud Peak Primitive Area. Ten Sleep Creek, one of the finest trout streams in the state, flows by the lodge. The surrounding high country offers excellent fishing in the remote alpine lakes, backpacking, cross-country skiing, and hunting in season for elk and deer. Accommodations are in a fully carpeted 6–unit motel with private showers or in housekeeping cabins with wood-burning stoves or gas heat in the larger cabins. Daily rates: small cabin with a double bed is $9; large cabin with 2 double beds is $18. Motel rates for 1 or 2 persons are $20. For additional information, contact: Deer Haven Lodge, Big Horn Sports, Inc., P.O. Box 121, Ten Sleep, WY 82442 (307)366–2449.

★★★*H F Bar Ranch*, located at the foot of the rugged Bighorn Mountains, is a year-round working ranch offering excellent family and guest accommodations from June to October. A stable of 200 horses and expert wranglers insure the most suitable mount for each guest, from the beginners to expert riders, and the surrounding terrain is traversed by scenic trails perfect for short and long rides. There is good fishing in the 10 miles or more of well-stocked streams running through the ranch, plus many other streams and lakes accessible on foot or horseback. Other activities include pack trips, rodeos, swimming in a heated pool, square dances, and barbecues. Guest accommodations for approximately 90 guests are in private, tree-shaded cabins, each with a living room, open fireplace, 1–5 bedrooms, and 1 or 2 baths. A few single and double rooms are also available in the lovely main house. A professional kitchen staff assures the best in home cooking. Rates: $280 per person weekly, including lodgings, all meals, horseback riding, and use of ranch trips. Pack trips are $5 extra per person per day. A 10% discount is allowed for children under 12, nurses, or governesses. For further details write: H F Bar Ranch, Saddlestring, WY 82840 (307)684–2487.

Travel Services

Bighorn-Cloud Peak Guided Trips by packhorse for sight-seeing, fishing, and big-game hunting are offered by *Caribou Resort*, Buffalo 82834 (307)684–5464 and *North Piney Corral*, Box 395, Story 82842 (307)683–2946.

Black Hills National Forest & Devil's Tower National Monument

The rich game lands and blue-ribbon trout streams of the Black Hills National Forest were once the sacred land of the Sioux Indians, for whom the hills were the home of many spirits. The Indians often camped on the edge of the Black Hills, or *Paha Sapa*, which they named for the darkness of the timbered slopes. But they ventured into the sacred hills only when it was necessary to hunt and fish, gather medicinal herbs, or obtain lodgepoles. Vast herds of antelope and buffalo grazed the nearby plains, providing the tribe with plentiful meat and skins. When white men moved into the territory in the mid–1800s, the Sioux under Sitting Bull fought to hold them back. At first the government attempted to keep out the gold seekers who streamed into the region after the discovery of the precious metal on French Creek near what is now Custer, South Dakota. But by 1876 the Indians had relinquished the territory between the Platte and Powder rivers to the white men. Thousands of gold-hungry settlers streamed north from Cheyenne and Rawlins. Such historical characters as Wild Bill Hickok, Calamity Jane, and Buffalo Bill were among the many travelers between Cheyenne and Deadwood.

Today, a few deep ruts remain in the soil of the region to remind us of the rush, and arrowhead-strewn fields recall the battles that preceded it. The initial rush gave way to a steady flow of newcomers, who rode the newly built Union Pacific Railroad to their destination. The buffalo are gone now, and many of the antelope, but the Black Hills remain a region of great natural beauty rich in wildlife. The area supports mule deer and elk and the state's largest concentration of whitetail deer and wild turkey. Such streams as Sand Creek, Cold Springs Creek, Redwater Creek, Beaver Creek, and the Belle Fourche River, as well as Lake Cook, offer excellent trout fishing for trophy rainbow, brook, and brown trout. Hiking and camping are popular among the birch and oak-covered slopes, as is ski touring during the winter months. Famous Sand Creek in the Sundance area, a designated blue-ribbon stream, is fed by a giant spring and offers excellent fishing for trophy hook-jawed browns up to 12 pounds. There are 6 miles of public access as well as pay-as-you-go fishing on Belle Fourche Club lands.

Sundance is a town rich in history. It is located at the foot of Sundance Mountain, known to the Sioux as *Wi Wacippi Paha*, "Temple of the Sioux." Legend says that the Sundance Kid (Harry Longabaugh) earned his title here. Sundance, a member of Butch Cassidy's Hole-in-the-Wall Gang, left for remote portions of the state after killing a deputy sheriff near the town. The imposing Devil's Tower, 28 miles northwest of Sundance, is composed of a mass of rock columns 1,000 feet across at the bottom and 275 feet wide at the top. It looms 1,280 feet over the Belle Fourche River, rising to a height of 5,117 feet above sea level. The Indians called the tower *Mateo Tepee*, or "Bear Lodge," and give it an important role in their mythology. It later became a landmark for explorers, trappers, and pioneers. The fluted, polygonal columns were formed by the cooling and crystallization of molten rock. The tallest formation of its kind in the country, it was named a national monument by Pres. Theodore Roosevelt in 1906.

Information Sources, Maps & Access

For a full-color *Black Hills National Forest Map* and detailed vacation travel and recreation info, write: Bearlodge Ranger District, Black Hills National Forest, Sundance, WY 82729 (307)283–1361.

The Black Hills region is reached via Interstate 90. Devil's Tower is located 29 miles northwest of Sundance on Wyoming Hwy. 24. Lodging, food, and supplies are available at Sundance. A beautiful full-color *Devil's Tower Shaded-Relief Map* ($2) may be ordered from: Distribution Branch, U.S. Geological Survey, Federal Center, Denver, CO 80225.

Gateways & Accommodations

Sundance

(Pop. 1,100; zip code 82729; area code 307.) This is a historic Old West town, onetime haunt of Butch Cassidy and his Hole-in-the-Wall Gang. Area accommodations: *Arrowhead Motel* (rates: $22–26 double), 12 rooms, on U.S. Hwy. 14 at 214 Cleveland St. (283–3307); *Bear Lodge Motel* (rates: $22–26 double), 16 rooms and family units, on Interstate 90 business loop (283–1611); *Best Western Apache of the Black Hills* (rates: $31–33 double), 40 excellent rooms and family units, swimming pool, at 121 South 6th St. (283–2073).

Grand Teton National Park & Jackson Hole

Grand Teton National Park is one of the most spectacular vacation, cross-country skiing, fishing, and wilderness camping areas in North America, embracing the snowcapped peaks of the mighty Teton Range and the waters of the Jackson Hole of the Snake River. The park has more than 220 miles of remote trails passing through dense forests and high meadows to spectacular timberline summits and lake basins. The wide, crystal-clear, blue-ribbon trout waters of Wyoming's picturesque 100–mile portion of the Snake River—once known to the Shoshonean Snake Indians as *Yam-pah-pa*, for a plant with long pencillike roots that grew along its banks, and to the French-Canadian voyageurs who attempted its treacherous canyon as *la Maudite Rivière Enragée*, the "Accursed Mad River"—rise in the rugged volcanic high country along the west slope of the Great Divide on the Two Ocean Plateau in the Teton Wilderness just south of Yellowstone National Park. The headwaters of the Snake flow northerly into Yellowstone, receiving the waters of the Heart and Lewis rivers, and then flow southward out of the park due north of Jackson Lake to begin their long, turbulent westward journey to the Columbia River and the Pacific Ocean.

The Snake flows southward from Jackson Lake for 60 miles through Grand Teton National Park and its incredibly scenic valley known as Jackson Hole to its confluence with the Hoback River, beyond which it enters the treacherous Grand Canyon, with its roaring white water, whirlpools, and turbulent crosscurrents. Jackson Hole lies about 30 miles west of the Great Divide and the towering peaks of the Wind River Range and is one of the largest enclosed valleys in the Rocky Mountains. It varies in width from 6 to 12 miles for some 60 miles north to south, and covers an area of 400 square miles. This awesome, mountain-bound valley is girded on the west by the stunning gray crags, sheer canyons, and perennial snowfields of the Tetons, which rise abruptly from the broad, peaceful, cobble-strewn plain and sagebrush flats to form one of the most precipitous mountain fronts in North America, reaching to heights of 13,700 feet at the raw, jagged peaks of the historic Trois Tetons (or "Three Breasts," as they were known to the woman-starved French-Canadian fur traders), which were important landmarks to the trappers and explorers of the early 19th century; on the north by the Yellowstone Plateau; and on the east and south by the peaks of the Absaroka Mountains and Mount Leidy Highlands, the Gros Ventre Range, the Wind River Range, and the Hoback Range.

Today Jackson Hole is noted for its luxuriant hay meadows and sagebrush flats, ranches, a great variety and abundance of wildlife, and some of the best trout waters in the nation. Shiras moose are often seen feeding along the marshy shores of the lakes and streams and in the meadow wetlands. Mule deer and a few whitetails roam the backcountry, and thousands of Rocky Mountain elk leave the winter browsing grounds of the National Elk Refuge near the outfitting center of Jackson and move up into the high country of the Teton National Forest and Yellowstone National Park to the north and east. A few small herds summer on the slopes of the Tetons to the west. Antelope roam the aptly named Antelope Flats, and bighorn sheep frequent the crags and ridges of the Tetons and the Gros Ventre Range to the east. Beaver lodges and dams are commonly seen along the Snake, and extensive beaver flows border the remote shores of Jackson Lake. Several pairs of bald eagles nest along the Snake along with a great variety of birdlife common to the area, including sandhill cranes, trumpeter swans, red-tailed hawks, osprey, great blue herons, and white pelicans.

Information Sources, Maps & Access

Detailed vacation travel, skiing, fishing, and backpacking information and the free *Grand Teton National Park Map/Brochure* and free *Weather Information, Floating the Snake River, Free Information, Hiking & Backcountry Camping, Winter in the Tetons* brochures and campground info may be obtained by contacting: Superintendent, Grand Teton National Park, Moose WY 83012 (307)733–2880. A beautiful 34–by–50–inch full-color *U.S. Geological Survey Grand Teton National Park Shaded-Relief Map* (also available in topographic edition, please specify) may be obtained for $2.75 from: Distribution Branch, U.S. Geological Survey, Federal Center, Denver, CO 80225. A large, full-color 3–by–6–foot *Teton-Bridger National Forest Map* ($2) and *Teton Wilderness Map* (50¢) may be obtained from: Supervisor, Teton-Bridger National Forest, Jackson, WY 83001 (307)733–2752. The Jackson Hole Airport is served daily by Frontier Airlines with prop-jet flights from Denver, Salt Lake City, and Billings. Grand Teton National Park is reached via U.S. Highways 16, 14–20, 89, 191, 187, and 287. Teton National Forest and Wilderness is accessible from the south by way of U.S. 189–187 leading north from Interstate 80.

Recreation Areas

Jackson Hole Ski Area

The Jackson Hole Ski Area comprises a magnificent Alpine wonderland of mountains, deep powder bowls, long and steep pitches for experts, meticulously groomed runs for intermediate skiers, and gentle slopes for beginners. All told, there are six square miles of ski terrain and a vertical drop of 4,139 feet. An aerial tram, 4 double chair lifts, and a triple chair lift are also on hand to cut down on your waiting time. The Jackson Hole Ski School is staffed by 30 fully certified instructors and offers instruction in basic parallel skiing, racing, and deep powder techniques. Private and class lessons are available. Special instruction for groups may be arranged through the ski school director. There are three restaurants on the slopes, serving everything from crepes at the top of Rendezvous Mountain to moderately priced hot meals and sandwiches at the Valley Station Cafeteria. For information on accommodations in the Jackson Hole Ski Area, see Teton Village under "Lodges and Guest Ranches" below. For maps and information on ski facilities, write: Teton Village, P.O. Box M, Teton Village, Jackson Hole, WY 83025 (phone toll-free (800)443–6931).

National Elk Refuge

The National Elk Refuge, located in Jackson Hole at the foot of the Gros Ventre Mountains, was established in 1912 to provide a winter feeding area for the Jackson Hole herd of Rocky Mountain elk. In addition to its large winter elk population, the 37–square-mile refuge is inhabited by coyotes, mule deer, a few bighorn sheep in winter, badgers, beavers, sandhill cranes, waterfowl, and the endangered trumpeter swan, which was originally brought here from Montana's Red Rock National Wildlife Refuge to establish a breeding colony. The refuge is located just north of Jackson on U.S. 187.

Teton National Forest & Wilderness

The 1.7 million-acre Teton National Forest encompasses the Two Ocean and Thorofare plateaus and the headwaters of the Yellowstone River in the Teton Wilderness, and the majestic wildlands surrounding the pools and riffles of the Upper Gros Ventre River (pronounced "Grow Vaunt," a typically vivid French-Canadian voyageur's name, meaning "big belly," to describe the Indian sign language of passing both hands over the stomach to convey hunger, given to a local tribe of Arapahos).

About 20 years before the journey of Lewis and Clark, the French-Canadian voyageurs of the North West Company learned from the Mandan Indians in the Upper Missouri country of a distant river known as the *Mi-tsi-a-da-zi*, which they translated as *Rivière au Roche Jaune*, or "Yellow Rock," which described the coloring of the Grand Canyon of the river we know today as the Yellowstone. The waters of this world-famous blue-ribbon trout stream rise high in the heart of the Rockies on the east slope of the massive Absaroka Range at 12,165–foot Younts Peak in the remote, seldom traveled Thorofare Plateau country of the vast 563,000–acre Teton Wilderness. The wilderness is bordered on the north by the wildlands of the Yellowstone Plateau, on the west and south by the Snake River and Jackson Hole ranch country, and on the east by the Shoshone National Forest and the great wall of the Absaroka Mountains, so-called after the Crow Indians, who called themselves *Absarokee*, meaning "People of the Raven."

Gateways & Accommodations

Afton

(Pop. 1,300; zip code 83110; area code 307.) A popular gateway to the Greys River area of the Bridger National Forest, Afton lies south of Jackson and east of the Wind River Range on U.S. Hwy. 89 in Star Valley. Area attractions include the Divide Winter Sports Area, the arch on Main St. made of thousands of Elk antlers, and *Brog's Original Cheese Company* in the center of town, a one-of-a-kind

family restaurant and cheese factory (886–5763). Accommodations: *The Corral* (rates: $22–26 double), 15 very good log cabin family units, just north of town on U.S. Hwy. 89 (886–5424).

Alpine

(Pop. 100; zip code 83127; area code 307.) A popular outdoor center on the Snake River at the head of Palisades Reservoir on U.S. 26/89, south of Jackson. Accommodations: *Best Western Flying Saddle Lodge* (rates: $22–26 double), 35 rooms, family units, and rustic cabins, restaurant, swimming pool, cocktail lounge (654–2334).

Jackson—Gateway to Grand Teton & Yellowstone Parks

(Pop. 2,100; zip code 83001; area code 307.) The historic center of Jackson Hole country and the southern gateway to Grand Teton and Yellowstone national parks, this colorful, bustling Old West town with its wood storefronts and boardwalks is flanked on the west by the Teton Range and on the east by the Gros Ventre Range. Area attractions include the National Elk Refuge and National Fish Hatchery on U.S. 187, Jackson Hole Museum (101 N. Glenwood Ave.), Snow King Mountain and Jackson Hole Ski Area Aerial Tram (at Teton Village, 733–2291), Ross Berlin's Wildlife Museum (862 W. Broadway), the Wax Museum of Old Wyoming (Cache St., 733–3112), and scenic drives along U.S. 187 and Gros Ventre Road. Restaurants include the *Open Range* at 75 N. Cache St. (733–3544), the *Pioneer* at 680 E. Broadway (733–3596), and the *Silver Spur* at 55 N. Cache St. (733–3279). Numerous craft and book shops are located on the Jackson Village Square. Accommodations: *Best Western Executive Inn* (rates: $34–38 double), 59 rooms, at 125 N. Jackson Ave. (733–3143); *Best Western Parkway Hotel* (rates: $34–40 double), 39 rooms, at 125 N. Jackson Ave. (733–3143); *Elk Refuge Inn* (rates: $30–34 double), 22 comfortable rooms and family units, just north of town on U.S. 187 (733–3582); *Friendship Inn—Western Motel* (rates: $24–36 double), 32 rooms, heated pool, at 101 Glenwood St. (733–3291); *Hitching Post Lodge* (rates: $28–32 double), 17 rooms, outdoor chuck-wagon breakfast, heated pool, evening horseback rides, at 460 E. Broadway (733–2606); *Ramada Snow King Inn* (rates: $45–47 with balcony), a spectacular new alpine chalet-style inn with 202 spacious rooms and suites, all with picture window views of Jackson Hole and the Tetons, 40–foot-high native stone lobby with view of Snow King Mountain Ski Area, decorated with original Indian paintings, wood-beamed alpine dining room overlooking the mountain, coffee shop, rustic bar and lounge, at 400 Snow King Drive (733–5200) or (800)443–5890; *Ranch Inn* (rates: $26–36 double), 45 rooms and family units, at 45 E. Pearl St. (733–6363); *Wort Hotel* (rates: $33–39 double), a classic Old West hotel with 52 comfortable rooms, food and drinks at the colorful Silver Dollar Bar, in the center of town at Broadway and Glenwood (733–2190).

Kemmerer—Gateway to Fossil Butte National Monument

(Pop. 2,300; zip code 83101; area code 307.) A popular gateway on U.S. 189 to Grand Teton National Park and the Bridger-Teton National Forest. The Fossil Butte National Monument (11 miles west of town on U.S. 30) contains fossilized fish, alligators, and birds that lived in or around a great inland lake some 60 million years ago. Accommodations: *Best Western Fairview Motel* (rates: $26–28 double), 20 excellent rooms, at 1429 First West Ave. (877–3938); *Lazy U Motel* (rates: $20–24 double), 21 rooms, at 521 Corral Ave. (877–4428).

Lodges & Guest Ranches

★★★*Flagg Ranch Village* is a renowned summer and winter guest ranch resort located on the banks of the Snake River, ideally situated on the highway 2 miles south of Yellowstone National Park and 4 miles north of Grand Teton National Park. Jackson Hole is 50 miles south of the ranch. During the winter months, the highway is kept open only from the town to the Flagg Ranch, and all travel into Yellowstone is by over-the-snow transportation. Summer activities at the ranch include guided horseback trail and sight-seeing rides, evening hayrides and cookouts. The Flagg also offers a variety of raft float trips on the Snake River ranging from a white-water trip of 1 hour's duration to a 3–hour scenic float trip. Our river guides can also arrange for guided fishing trips to the high-country lakes, rivers, and streams that abound in the area. During the winter months the ranch is a popular jumping-off center for cross-country skiing tours along the Yellowstone trails. The ranch also has 40 new Arctic Cat snowmobiles available for rental along with the necessary clothing. Overnight accommodations range from the all-new 2–story 50–unit motel to 120 cabin units that are open for the summer season from May 15 through October 15. All rooms are twin doubles, and the rates are $32–36 a night. The Flagg is a complete resort facility with a coffee shop, restaurant, cocktail lounge, gift shop, grocery store, and gas station. Pickup service at the Jackson Hole airport is available. For additional info, contact: Flagg Ranch, P.O. Box 187, Moran, WY 83013, or call toll-free (800)443–2311 (outside Wyoming) or (307)733–4818.

★★★*Game Hill Ranch & Wilderness Outfitters*, located due south of the Gros Ventre Mountains in Hoback Basin, is a small, family-operated facility specializing in wilderness excursions. The Wind River Mountains, Jackson Hole, and Grand Teton and Yellowstone parks are within easy access from the ranch, and provide the setting for a broad range of backcountry adventure: horse pack trips, backpacking, camera safaris, fishing, river floating, and ski touring. Guided trips, 5–10 days in length, are made all the more pleasurable through well-planned campsites, simple but tasty food, excellent equipment, and expert guides. Groups are limited in size (maximum of 6) to encourage greater participation with minimal negative impact on the environment. The ranch, a year-round working enterprise, makes a comfortable and convenient hostelry for the start and finish of your trip. You'll get a pleasant taste of ranch life, cozy accommodations, and superb home cooking. Guests are welcome to stay a few extra days before or after their trip. Rates average $340 for a 7–day backpacking adventure; $430 for 7–day horse pack expeditions; and $480 for 7–day photography safaris. Ski touring is a ranch specialty. The country surrounding Game Hill offers a winter paradise for cross-country tours. All tours are led by qualified guides and based at the ranch, where snug lodgings await you after a day in the backcountry. Rates are $33 per person daily, $200 weekly, including guide, instruction, lodgings, and all meals. For more information write: Pete and Holly Cameron, Game Hill Ranch, Bondurant, WY 82922 (307)733–2015 or (307)733–3281.

★★★*Goose Wing Ranch*, 39 miles east of the town of Jackson Hole, is a four-season guest ranch offering a full gamut of wilderness activities. For horseback riders, there are morning and afternoon trail rides, all-day picnics, gentle mounts for beginners and children, and 3– or 4–day pack trips into the beautiful, remote headwaters of the proposed Gros Ventre Wilderness Area. Hikers will find unlimited trails and mountains to climb, and there is good fishing all around, in either the Gros Ventre River, which runs right by the lodge, or nearby streams and gemlike mountain lakes. Complete guide and outfitting services are available for big-game hunting in the heart of

Teton country. Both spring and fall hunts may be scheduled through the lodge. Winter sports include ski touring and snowmobiling through spectacular winter scenery. Snug, 1–room log guest cabins will sleep up to 4 people. Each cabin has its own heat, hot water, and combination tub-shower. Other amenities include a spacious lodge and dining area and a new swimming pool. American-plan rates: $35 daily per person in summer, $25 in winter. A 10% discount is available to families of 5 or more for a minimum of 7 days. Pack trips are $90 per person per day, all inclusive (minimum of 4 people per trip). For more information write: Goose Wing Ranch, Box 496, Jackson Hole, WY 83001 (307)733–2768.

Grand Teton National Park Lodges. There are three major visitor facilities within the incomparably beautiful wilderness surrounding the Grand Tetons, each offering its own particular atmosphere but all of them constructed to blend with the area's natural splendor.

★★★*Jackson Lake Lodge* is situated on a bluff overlooking the lake and is the most luxurious of the three. There are 42 guest rooms in the main lodge and 343 motel-type rooms grouped around this central building. Within the lodge are a lounge with a 60–foot picture window and huge fireplaces, the Stockade Bar with an Old West flavor, a coffee shop, and the Mural Room, where excellent meals are served in a very hospitable setting. Other facilities on the premises include a beauty shop, gift shop, card room, large heated swimming pool, riding horses, and a service station. Conferences are welcome during the months of June and September. Motor lodge rooms are $34–39 daily (single or double occupancy) or $53 daily for rooms with a panoramic view. Rooms in the main lodge run from $38 to $53 daily (single or double occupancy).

★★★*Jenny Lake Lodge*, on the border of an alpine meadow, is only a short walk from Jenny Lake, a sparkling body of water named for the wife of an early trapper. There are fine trout streams and miles of hiking or riding trails in the valley as well as acres of forests to explore. The lodge consists of 30 sturdy log cabins, comfortably furnished and surrounded by trees. The main lodge houses an inviting lodge and dining room with superb meals and service. Privacy, quiet, and solitude are the keynotes here, with cool nights to guarantee a sound sleep. Rates are modified American plan (including breakfast and dinner): $95 per day for 1 guest; $105 for 2; $140 for 3; and $230 for 4 persons per day.

★★*Colter Bay Village*, set in a wooded area near the shores of Jackson Lake, comprises 208 log cabins with accommodations for up to 6 persons in each. On Jackson Lake are a beach and full-service marina with a boat-launching ramp. Nearby are the National Park Service Amphitheatre, visitor center, and Indian Arts Museum. The village includes central showers, a launderette, tackle and sport shop, service station, general store, chuck wagon restaurant, and bar. Rooms with private baths are $18–31 per day (1 or 2 persons); with semiprivate baths, $13 per day; and 2 rooms with a connecting bath for 1–4 persons, $31–39 daily. Tent cabins are also available for $9–11 per day. Each spacious tent is constructed of canvas logs and features an outdoor grill, wood-burning stove, 2 double-decker bunks (without bedding), a table, and benches.

For more information on any or all of the above accommodations in Grand Teton National Park, write: Grand Teton Lodge Company, Moran, WY 83013 (307)543–2811.

★★★*Heart Six Guest Ranch*, just 3 miles east of the Grand Teton National Park entrance, occupies a scenic spot in the Buffalo River valley bordered by the distant jagged peaks of the Tetons. Some of the ranch activities are horseback riding on forested mountain trails, trout fishing in lakes and remote streams, and float trips down the evergreen-fringed Snake River. Weekly events include the Saturday night rodeo in Jackson (transportation provided) and a breakfast cookout prepared over an open fire. Special children's activities are supervised by an experienced director. The ranch is open during the winter months for ski touring on trails in the adjacent Teton wilderness. The main lodge, with its panoramic views of the Tetons, houses 2 dining rooms, a modern kitchen, and a large lounge where evening entertainment is offered. Guest cabins are rustic but comfortable, with carpeting, modern baths, and nice views of the surrounding countryside. Rates, including the above activities and 3 family-style meals per day, are $315 per person weekly ($280 for children under 12; no charge for children under 3). Also available to guests are 1–5–day wilderness pack trips; arrangements must be made in advance. Daily and group rates on request. For more information write: Heart Six Guest Ranch, Moran, WY 83013 (307)543–2477 or (307)733–6650.

★★★★*Lost Creek Ranch* boasts an incomparably beautiful location in Jackson Hole, bordered by the towering peaks of Grand Teton National Park and Teton National Forest. The awesome views from the ranch sundecks alone are worth the visit. Comfortable, attractive accommodations are in 2–bedroom cabins, many with 2 baths, a living room, fireplace, and private porch. The main lodge comprises a spacious lounge, a children's den, an adults' card room, and a handsome dining room opening onto a huge deck-porch. Guided pack trips are offered deep into the wilderness for a day of trout fishing or just to explore the miles of horseback and hiking trails. The lodge has its own fleet of rubber rafts for floating and fishing the Snake River, or you can take advantage of 2 powerboats for sightseeing and fishing. Other amenities include a private skeet-shooting range, swimming pool, tennis court, electric blankets, and fresh coffee brought to your room each morning. Rates average $50–100 per person daily (dependent on number of persons in your family or group and type of accommodations), including lodgings, all meals, your own horse, and use of the swimming pool and tennis courts. Guest accommodations are limited to 45, and reservations are recommended well in advance. The ranch is open from early June through late September. For further details write: Lost Creek Ranch, P.O. Box 45, Moose, WY 83012 (307)733–3435.

★★★*Moose Head Ranch*, a small select family guest ranch, run by the Mettler family, is one of the few privately owned ranches in Jackson Hole left entirely within the boundaries of Grand Teton National Park. From its location in the Snake River valley, this ideal family vacation spot offers sweeping vistas of the 13,000–foot peaks of the Teton Range. Grand Teton National Park surrounds the ranch

and offers miles of scenic drives, riding and hiking trails, fishing in the Snake River and high country ponds and lakes, as well as two museums dealing with the fur-trade era and the art of the Plains Indians. This magnificent wildlife area is a photographer's paradise for moose, elk, deer, coyote, buffalo, trumpeter swans, otter, beaver, sandhill cranes, and bald and golden eagles. Moose Head's string of over 50 horses is hand-picked for supervised rides in small groups twice daily along the miles of park trails and in nearby Teton National Forest. The rustic ranch lodge contains a dining room where delicious meals are served family-style, a game room, a lounge with large stone fireplaces, and a laundry (free to guests). A large picture window looks out on the trout ponds and the Snake River to the 13,000–foot summit of Grand Teton. Rustic, attractively appointed log guest cabins are scattered among the cottonwoods and pines. Designed for privacy and comfort, the cabins have private baths and showers, electric heating, and porches. Campfire cook-outs, great food, scenery, and hospitality are the hallmarks of this fine family vacation ranch. American-plan rates: $55 per person per day (double occupancy) with special rates for children 6 and under. Large cabins with 2 bedrooms, 2 baths, and living room for parties up to 3 persons are $200 per day. The regular $55–each rate applies for 4 or more persons. Contact: Moose Head Ranch, Moose, WY 83012 (307)733–3141. Before June 5th: The Mettlers, Rte. 7, Box 1362, Tallahassee, Fl 32303 (904)877–1431.

★★★*Signal Mountain Lodge*, on the shores of Jackson Lake in Grand Teton National Park, is an excellent family vacation complex surrounded by some of the most breathtaking scenery in the country. Fishing is the favorite activity here, either from cabin cruisers on the lake or via leisurely floats down the Snake River. The lake yields some sizable Mackinaw trout, 16 to 22 inches long, and there is always a chance of battling a big 30–pounder. Marina facilities, including boat-servicing docks, fishing licenses, bait, tackle, mooring buoys, and boat trailer parking, are available at 2 convenient locations. Cabin cruisers, guides, and tackle are all available for charter. Scenic float trips down the Snake are scheduled daily and offer a superb opportunity to explore the unspoiled wilderness of Jackson Hole. The lodge is also close enough to Yellowstone Park for day trips to outstanding points of interest. Guests have a selection of 78 rental units ranging from deluxe 2–room family housekeeping apartments accommodating up to 6 persons in comfort to 1– or 2–room log cabins sleeping 1–7 guests. All accommodations have modern baths, electric heat, handmade rustic furnishings, and carpeted bedrooms. A few deluxe log cabins have wood-burning fireplaces. The main lodge building houses a large guest lounge, a modern grocery store, a cocktail lounge, a gift shop, a coffee shop, and a lovely dining room overlooking the lofty Teton Range across the lake. Daily cabin rates, European plan, are approximately $25–45 for 1–7 persons. Mountain-view lakefront apartments are $25–55 daily for 2–6 guests. Newer family units average $55–65 daily for 2–6 guests. For additional information write: Signal Mountain Lodge, P.O. Box 50, Moran WY 83013 (307)543–2831.

★★*Spotted Horse Ranch* is situated on the banks of the scenic Hoback River at 6,000 feet elevation, surrounded by the forests and mountains of the Teton National Forest. Ranch activities include trout fishing in the Hoback, Snake or Green Rivers as well as in high country beaver ponds; hiking, trail rides, float trips, and cook-outs. The Grand Tetons and Yellowstone Park are within easy reach of the ranch. Ranch guest cabins are of log construction with fully modern conveniences. All cabins are cleaned daily. Three good western ranch-style meals are served daily in the ranch dining room, overlooking the beautiful Hoback River. The ranch is located 17 miles south of Jackson on U.S. 187–189. Weekly American plan rates which include all activities, cabins, meals, horses and float trips, are $325 per person, with special discounts for children 12 and under. Daily rates are $50 per person. Transportation is available to and from Jackson Hole Airport. For additional information, contact: Spotted Horse Ranch, Jackson Hole, WY 83001 (307)733–2097.

★★★★*Targhee Ski & Summer Resort*, see "Targhee National Forest & Henry's Lake Country" in the Idaho chapter.

Teton Village is a complex of lodges, restaurants, condominiums, and meeting facilities centrally located in Jackson Hole, just 12 miles from the town of Jackson and 1 mile south of the Grand Teton National Park boundary. Nestled at the base of 10,450–foot Rendezvous Peak, the site of a convenient aerial tramway, the village is a prime jumping-off spot for the countless year-round activities that have made Jackson Hole and the surrounding wilderness a favorite with vacationers.

★★★*Alpenhof*, the inn closest to Jackson Hole ski lifts, is a luxury hotel of 30 hickory-paneled rooms, many with balconies and spectacular views. All rooms have extra-long beds, private baths, and soundproofed walls for a good night's rest. Other amenities include a large sundeck, heated pool, sauna, and a game room with table tennis and billiards. An intimate fireside cocktail lounge and outstanding restaurant offer fine food, drink, and entertainment. For groups and business conventions, the Alpenhof has a large (36′ × 18′)

meeting room, a 3–room VIP suite with separate living room and wet bar, and a private dining room and lounge. Rates: $28–38 double occupancy.

★★★*Crystal Springs Inn*, a comfortable family hotel, is close to the central village shops, restaurants, and tramway. There are 26 rooms accommodating a total of 92 guests, a family lounge with a self-service bar and TV, and laundry facilities right on the premises. Duplex rooms have 4 twin beds—on the balcony, 2 on the living level—full private baths, wall-to-wall carpeting, and a secure ski and boot locker. Rates: $25 for 2 daily, $31 for 4.

★★★*The Hilton Inn* offers plush accommodations in 80 elegantly decorated rooms to suit your vacation needs or conference preferences. Many have 2 double beds and balconies; some feature spiral staircases, sleeping lofts, and fireplaces. Connecting rooms, suites, and kitchenettes are also available. The inn has an intimate first-class restaurant with superb views from its large picture windows, plus a family restaurant and attractive coffee shop for more informal dining. A heated swimming pool, tennis courts, ski lockers and ski room, a fireside lounge, on-premise wilderness outfitters, ample convention facilities, and a game room with color TV round out the amenities of the Hilton Inn. Winter guests can ski right to the lifts, less than 100 yards away. Rates: $32–60 daily, double occupancy.

★★★*The Hostel* provides economy lodging for winter skiers and summer travelers in a modified Tyrolean-style hotel. Each of the 65 identical rooms has a double bunk, 2 twin beds, all linens, carpeting, and a bath with shower. A large, cheerfully furnished open-beam basement has a game room, a lounge with a big fireplace, and 2 meeting rooms which can be shut off for privacy. There's also a child-care center where the kids will get special attention while you're on the slopes. The hostel is convenient to village stores and restaurants. A good bet for the money. Rates: $15 daily for 2, $18 for 3 or 4.

★★★*The Village Center*, just next to the aerial tram station, has been recently remodeled and offers 22 large and handsome rooms in a multileveled building of attractive contemporary design. Each room has a kitchenette, comfortable furnishings, and a private bath with shower and tub. The Village Center houses a restaurant with a reasonably priced menu, an art gallery, a congenial bar, and the village's only general store. A 13–by–18–foot meeting room is available for conventions. Rates: $31–52 daily, double occupancy.

★★★*Sojourner Inn*, the largest hotel in Teton Village, is at the end of the main drive, convenient to both ski lifts and riding stables. There are 98 rooms, including 4 suites, with bright modern furnishings and scenic-view balconies. Three different restaurants offer family-priced dining, casual fondue dinners, or fine gourmet fare. Nightly entertainment is featured in the cocktail lounge. In addition, the Sojourner has free movies on color TV, a game room, and a heated open-air swimming pool. Five meeting and banquet rooms cater to business conventions. Rates: $25–35 daily, double occupancy.

Teton Village also offers several condominium communities with apartments ranging in size from studio efficiencies to spacious 3–5–bedroom town houses with private saunas and balconies. All have kitchens and attractive furnishings; many feature luxurious extras such as patios, use of private tennis courts, game rooms, swimming pools, and fireplaces. Daily rates are between $12 per person and $105 for a family of 6. For information on any of the above Teton Village lodgings and special package plans, write: Teton Village Resort Association, Teton Village, WY 83025 (phone toll-free (800)443–6931; in Wyoming, (800)442–3900.

★★★★*Triangle X Ranch* is set on 1,500 acres in the beautiful Snake River valley at the foot of the Gros Ventre Mountains, just south of Yellowstone National Park. To the west, the ranch faces the Snake River and the entire Teton Range beyond. This working ranch in historic Jackson Hole offers outstanding accommodations, services, and a wide range of outdoor activities, including trail riding, pack trips into the Teton Wilderness, fishing and float trips down the Snake, photographic expeditions, backpacking, and guided fall hunts at the headwaters of the Yellowstone for elk and deer. Ranch accommodations consist of rustic 1–, 2–, and 3–bedroom log cabins with their own bathroom and shower. The cabins are attractive and comfortably furnished. Meals are served family-style in the handsome sun-porch dining room. Ranch rates: $225–335 per person per week, including all meals, riding equipment, guide services, and ranch activities—everything except pack trips, special car travel, and float trips. Pack-trip rates are $55 a day each for 4 or more in a party. Guests are not charged ranch rates while on a pack trip. The ranch is reached by Frontier Airlines to Jackson. The ranch will meet your bus or plane at Jackson or any of the Yellowstone Park entrances. The ranch car will also meet the Northern Pacific train at Gardiner, Montana. Highways 187 and 287 lead north to the ranch from East-West Highway 30. For details, contact: Triangle X Ranch, Jackson Hole, Moose, WY 83012 (307)733–2183.

★★★*Turpin Meadow Ranch* offers year-round wilderness activities in and around the incredibly beautiful country of Jackson Hole. For fishermen, the Buffalo River is just a stone's throw away, and there are countless miles of productive trout streams in the adjacent Teton high country. A stable full of hardy, dependable horses is on hand for trail rides and pack trips. In the fall, there is hunting in small groups of sportsmen for the big game that abound in this area. From late January through April, cross-country skiing and snowshoeing are popular in the rolling alpine meadows of Togwotee Mountain. The nearby town of Jackson offers a host of diversions in any season: restaurants, galleries, museums, rodeos, and live theater. Other amenities of the lodge include a handsome, log-paneled dining room and lounge and rustic guest cabins with 1 or 2 bedrooms each, fully modernized and simply but attractively furnished. Rates, including meals, horses, and all ranch facilities: $481–560 weekly for 2 guests; $676 weekly for 3. Children too young to ride are welcomed at half the standard rate. Extra-luxurious accommodations are also available in the Grizzley Cabin, which has a king-size bed, 2 double beds, 2 baths, a big living room, and a scenic location next to the

Buffalo River ($860–1,750 weekly for 2–6 guests). For further information write: Turpin Meadow Geust Ranch, P.O. Box 48, Moran, WY 83013 (307)543–2496.

Travel Services & Snake River Float Trips

Bar T Five Outfitters offers several excellent wilderness vacation trips in the magnificent country of Jackson Hole and the Teton wilderness. The 5–day Teton Prairie Schooner Holiday, the firm's most unusual offering, takes guests along the back roads of the Targhee National Forest in modern versions of the old pioneer-style Conestoga wagons, drawn by horses, of course, but equipped with durable rubber tires and padded seats. In every other respect, the wagons are authentic. In the evening the wagons form a traditional circle and make camp for the night. All meals are chuck wagon-style and served over an open fire. The wagon master and cowboy guides are expert horsemen and accompany the daily forays on horseback into the beautiful countryside surrounding each camp. Rates are $225 per person, including overnight accommodations at the beginning of the trip, transfer from airport to motel, all meals and camping gear, wagons, and horses. More traditional offerings of Bar T Five Outfitters include a vacation on horseback through the Teton wilderness, with float trips and superb fishing en route, and horseback holidays through the unspoiled wilderness of Jackson Hole and the Gros Ventre Mountains. Rates: $325 and $445 all-inclusive for the 5– and 7–day Jackson Hole adventures; $695 per person for 10–day horseback trips in the Tetons. For complete information write: Bar T Five Outfitters, Box 2140, Jackson, WY 83001 (307)733–5386.

Box K Wilderness Pack Trips are 7–10–day expeditions on horseback through the wide-open spaces of Wyoming's lush and primitive backcountry. Participants explore geysers and natural hot pools, seldom visited streams and lakes teeming with native trout, and mountain meadows frequented by abundant wildlife—elk, deer, trumpeter swans, osprey, and occasional bear. Accompanying each trip are an expert guide and skilled camp cook. You bring your own sleeping bag, air mattress, clothing, and fishing gear. Box K supplies the rest. Rates: $385–410 per person for 7 days, $490–515 for 10 days, $75 per person per day for trips less than 7 days and more than 3. Twice each summer Box K Ranch also sponsors a special Jackson Hole trail ride, 7 days of riding from a stationary base camp to a different area each day. Riding competitions, pit barbecues, songfests, and the companionship of riders from all over the country are all part of the fun. You may bring your own horse or ride one from the ranch corral. For more information write: Box K Ranch/Jackson Hole Trail Ride, Box 11, Moran, WY 83013 (307)543–2407.

Jackson Hole Mountain Guides provides a range of programs and guide service to accommodate all levels of experience and interest among the spectacular peaks of the Grand Tetons. The eight day camps are the Mountain Guides' most popular offering and a most effective and exciting learning program. The eight days are a mini-expedition among crystalline high mountain lakes and streams and among the peaks that you climb each day. The eight day camps are designed to help you gain the skills and resources of self-confidence to prepare you to independently pursue your mountaineering goals. You are presented with the "tools" of climbing in their most refined form. You master not only the series of problems and situations that they have created as a curriculum but you gain a total awareness of what alpinism and the alpine environment are all about. The highest pleasure of climbing grows out of this awareness. A major feature of a camp is that it is a climbing trip. You backpack in, and live in mountaineering tents—you live and breathe climbing. The camp formats include instruction in basic and intermediate climbing, mountain photography, and technical ice climbing. The eight day camps cost $550/person. Daily instruction in field seminars costs $25/person. The Jackson Hole Mountain Guides offer custom guide service for individuals and small groups at $100/person per day. For additional information contact: Jackson Hole Mountain Guides, Teton Valley, WY 83025 (307)733–4979.

Powderhound Ski Tours provide a unique introduction to the wilderness splendors of Jackson Hole country. Experienced guides will lead you on fully equipped cross-country ski tours in Grand Teton National Park or the Bridger-Teton National Forest. A variety of tours is offered, including a ½–day introductory tour over easy terrain with special instruction in basic cross-country technique (especially geared to beginners); full-day tours of 6–8 miles through the most scenic areas of the park; special wildlife and winter ecology day tours; advanced day trips over challenging terrain for more experienced skiers; and overnight or dinner ski tours with a hearty meal served in a snug igloo at the end of the day. All instructor-guides are experienced skiers and competent naturalists familiar with the Jackson Hole terrain. Rates for the above tours range from $12 for ½ day to $35 for overnight trips, including equipment, instruction, guides, and lunch or dinner. Private lessons and 3– or 7–day vacation ski tours are also available. For complete descriptions write: Powderhound Ski Tours, Box 286, Wilson, WY 83014 (307)733–2208.

Rivermeadows-Rocky Mountain Fishing Service is one of the nation's finest fishing guide outfits, located in the center of some of the finest trout streams in the West—the Snake, Green, Henry's Fork, and private spring creeks. Rivermeadows consists of two ranches, 1½ hours apart: The Crescent H. Ranch in Jackson Hole and the 3 Rivers Ranch in Ashton, Idaho. This unique, co-operative system, managed by Vern Bressler of Jackson Hole, offers great fishing from June through October. Guests may stay at either or both ranches. Rivermeadows offers complete, top-quality services, including rustic Western ranch accommodations, good meals, guides, pack trips, float trips, shooting, tennis, and fly fishing instruction. For complete details and rates, contact: Vern Bressler, Crescent H. Ranch, Box 347, Wilson, WY 83014 (307)733–3674.

Snake River Float Trips. Scenic float trips and custom guided float-fishing trips on the Snake River below Jackson Lake are provided by the following outfitters: *Barker-Ewing, Inc.*, Box 124, Jackson 83001 (307)733–3410; Dick Allen of *Fort Jackson Float Trips*, 310 W. Broadway, Jackson 83001 (307)733–2583; *Grand Teton Lodge Co.*, P.O. Box 250, Moran 83013 (307)543–2811; *Heart Six Guest Ranch*, Moran 83013 (307)543–2477; *Jack Dennis Sports*, Box 286, Jackson

83001 (307)733–3273; *Lewis & Clark Expeditors*, Box 720, Jackson 83001 (307)733–4022; *National Park Float Trips*, P.O. Box 411, Jackson 83001 (307)733–4325; *Osprey Float Trips*, Box 1903, Jackson 83001 (307)733–4486; *Parklands Whitewater Expeditions*, Wilson 83014 (307)733–6203; *Solitude Float Trips*, Box 112, Moose 83012 (307)733–2871; *Triangle X Ranch*, Box 120, Moose 83012 (307)733–2183.

Sundance Ski Tours, headquartered in Teton Village and Jackson, offers half- and full-day guided cross-country tours in scenic wilderness areas of Grand Teton National Park. Half-day tours over gentle terrain are especially geared to the novice, with instruction provided in use of equipment and basic techniques. Sundance offers advanced tours for the hardy, experienced skier, which cover at least 6–8 miles a day. The emphasis is on downhill technique, winter safety, and route finding. Lessons are available in all aspects of touring, from the fundamentals through racing technique. There's also a winter ecology tour stressing wildlife observations and the habits and habitats of local species such as trumpeter swans, bald eagles, and large game animals. Rates, including equipment, guides, and lunch (full-day tours): $12 per person for half a day, $24 per person for a full day, and $16 per person for 1½–2–hour lessons. A minimum of 4 persons is necessary for each tour. Group rates and discounts for skiers with their own equipment are available. For full information write: Sundance Ski Tours, c/o Wildernest, Box 528, Teton Village, WY 83025.

Medicine Bow National Forest & the Snowy Range

The Medicine Bow Forest covers 1,398,288 acres. Three of its four divisions lie within the arc made by the North Platte River here, and the fourth (the Hayden Division) lies west of the river. The Medicine Bow Range, known locally as the Snowy Range, borders the Medicine Bow Division of the forest; its slopes are carpeted by forests of lodgepole pine, fir, and aspen. Many streams course through this division of the forest. Hundreds of lakes lie among the mountains at higher elevations. These glacial lakes vary in size from potholes to basins of a hundred acres and yield a variety of trout.

This region is one of the state's top fishing and big-game hunting areas for mule deer, elk, and antelope. Foot trails lead to the high-altitude Snowy Range trout lakes, such as Telephone, Klondike, Lewis, Gap, Shelf, Meadow, and Arrowhead lakes. Brook trout are found in most of the lakes at 9,500 to 11,000 feet elevation, along with grayling, cutthroat, and California golden trout. A major portion of the Snowy Range lakes area is closed to all motor vehicles except snowmobiles. Nearby, the Big and Little Laramie rivers hold plenty of 10– to 12–inch brown and rainbow trout. The blue-ribbon waters of the North Platte and Encampment rivers flow through the Hayden region and provide some of the finest fishing in southern Wyoming. The lightly fished upper reaches of the North Platte hold some real lunkers; 3– to 4–pound rainbows and browns are common, and an occasional tackle-buster will run up to 18 pounds.

The largest of the four divisions is the Snowy Range area, where the peaks of the Medicine Bow Range are veiled in white year-round. The Snowy Range Division and the Sierra Madre area across the North Platte River to the west offer both highly developed recreation areas and more remote areas where horsepacking, backpacking, cross-country skiing, and hiking are popular. In the more remote areas the pathways are closed to use by motorized vehicles. Elk and mule deer are often seen in the mountain country. Other wildlife species include black bear, bobcat, mountain lion, and coyote. A myriad of mountain streams and lakes offer some of the best trout fishing in the West.

This area is full of the history of the Old West. The town of Centennial lies near the entrance to the forest on Wyoming 130 (open during summer only). The town grew up after the discovery of a quartz gold mine was made here in 1876, and was named in honor of the U.S. Centennial. A rich lode was found here, but unfortunately was lost, giving rise to the legend of the "Lost Centennial Lode."

Information Sources, Maps & Access

Vacation travel and outdoor recreation information and a full-color *Medicine Bow National Forest Map* (50¢), and free *Snowy Range Map* may be obtained from: Supervisor, Medicine Bow National Forest, 605 Skyline Drive, Laramie, WY 82070 (307)745–7308.

Major auto routes to the Medicine Bow National Forest are Interstate Highways 80 and 25. Numerous secondary and forest service roads provide access through the forest districts. Lodging, supplies, guides, and outfitters are available at Laramie, Albany, Woods Landing, Rawlins, Elk Mountain, Encampment, Medicine Bow, Casper, Douglas, and Cheyenne.

Gateways & Accommodations

Cheyenne

(Pop. 41,000; zip code 82001; area code 307.) Wyoming's attractive capital city is surrounded by the ranching country of the prairie and the Laramie Mountains. This popular Old West gateway was founded during the rough 'n' ready days of the building of the Union Pacific Railroad. Its reputation for lawlessness was such that it soon became known as Hell-on-Wheels. Area attractions include the famous Frontier Days celebration in late July, the State Capitol and State Museum, Curt Gowdy State Park on State Highway 210, and Holiday Park, which features an old Union Pacific steam locomotive and the Cheyenne Art Center (Morrie Ave. and 19 St.). Accommodations: *Best Western Hitching Post Inn & Restaurant* (rates: $40–66 double), 250 superb rooms and family units, excellent restaurant and coffee shop, 2 heated pools and health rooms, cocktail lounge, at 1600 W. Lincolnway (638–3301); *Best Western Holding's Little American Motor Inn* (rates: $36 double), 189 outstanding rooms and family units, attractive dining room, cocktail lounge, heated pool, just west of town at junction of Interstate 25 and 80 (634–2771); *Downtown Motor Inn* (rates: $39–49 double), 85 excellent rooms, dining room, coffee shop, at 1719 Central Ave. (634–1331); *Firebird Motel Restaurant & Pancake House* (a Friendship Inn; rates: $29–36 double), 49 excellent rooms, restaurant, at 1905 E. Lincolnway (632–5505).

Laramie

(Pop. 23,100; zip code 82070; area code 307.) Named after the legendary Jacques La Ramie, a fur trapper killed by Indians near the river that bears his name, this attractive Old West town sits on the east bank of the Laramie River at the southeastern edge of the Laramie Plains. Laramie is one of Wyoming's oldest towns and home of the University of Wyoming. The first area settlements were the road ranches built during the 1860s along the Overland Trail on the Laramie Plains. With the construction of the Union Pacific Railroad, Laramie became a hell-raising boom town notorious for its shoot-outs, brothels, and outlaws. The Laramie *Boomerang*, founded by western humorist Bill Nye in 1881, is still published today. Area attractions include great cattle ranches, the Laramie Plains Museum at 603 Ivinson Ave., the Western Historical Collection & Museum of Geology at the University of Wyoming, and the Medicine Bow Ski Area, 32 miles west of town on Wyoming Hwy. 130. Accommodations: *Best Western Gas Lite Motel* (rates: $25–29 double), 27 rooms and family units, swimming pool, at 930 N. 3rd St. (742–6616); *Downtown Motel—Friendship Inn* (rates: $24–26 double), 30 rooms, at 165 N. 3rd St. (742–6671); *Holiday Inn* (rates: $43–46 double), 100 excellent rooms and family units, dining room, coffee shop, heated pool, 1 mile south of town at the junction of 287, 30, and Interstate 80 (742–6611); *Ramada Inn* (rates: $38 double), 80 excellent rooms and family units, dining room, coffee shop, heated pool, at 1503 S. 3rd St. (742–3721).

Rawlins

(Pop. 7,900; zip code 82301; area code 307.) The major western gateway to the Medicine Bow National Forest on Interstate 80; this Old West town, which boomed with the construction of the Union Pacific Railroad, is named after Gen. John A. Rawlins. Area attractions include Carbon Count Museum (9th and Walnut Sts.) and Seminoe State Park. Accommodations: *Best Western Bel Air Inn* (rates: $30–32 double), 100 excellent rooms and family units, attractive restaurant, heated pool, sauna, at 23rd and Spruce Sts. (324–2737); *Cliff Motor Lodge* (rates: $24–26 double), 38 excellent units, at 1500 W. Spruce St. (324–3494); *Holiday Inn* (rates: $29–36 double), 100 excellent rooms and family units, dining room, heated pool, kennel, at 1801 E. Cedar St. (324–2783); *Ramada Inn* (rates: $36.75 double), 89 excellent rooms and family units, dining room, cocktail lounge, at 2222 E. Cedar St. (324–6615).

Lodges

★★★*Medicine Bow Lodge* offers rustic, year-round accommodations in mountain-style cabins in the high plains of the Platte Valley flanked by the beautiful Snowy Range Mountains, with their remote alpine lakes, mountain streams, and meadows and wildlife in the southeast corner of Wyoming 60 miles west of Laramie. The seldom explored lakes and streams of the Snowy Range offer often excellent fishing for rainbow, brown, golden, and cutthroat trout. This informal, friendly family vacation lodge offers trout fishing; hunting for mule deer, elk, and antelope; horseback riding; and cross-country skiing in winter. Pack trips and trail rides (with instruction available) are a lodge specialty. A ranch rodeo is featured for guests. Other ranch activities include trapshooting, hiking, float trips down the North Platte River, Indian artifact hunts, and visits to local mining ghost towns or the historical museum at Encampment. Two mountain-fed trout streams flow through the ranchlands. Three home-cooked meals are prepared daily and served in the main lodge dining room. Each of the log cabins accommodates 4–9 guests. The ranch provides round-trip transportation from Laramie, Saratoga, or Rawlins. American-plan rates (which include all ranch activities except for overnight pack trips and trap shooting): $194 per person weekly (double occupancy) or $37 per day (double). For additional info, contact: John and Teri Owens, Medicine Bow Lodge, P.O. Box 752, Saratoga, WY 82331 (307)326–5439.

Shoshone National Forest

This magnificent forest reserve encompasses 2,431,000 acres in north-central Wyoming and includes some of the finest fishing, hiking, and big-game hunting areas in the West. Shoshone was the first national forest in the United States, created by Pres. Benjamin Harrison in 1891. Elevations range from 4,600 feet near Cody to 13,785 feet at Gannett Peak, the highest mountain in Wyoming. It is the only national forest in the state in which elk, mule deer, whitetail deer, mountain sheep, mountain goats, antelope, moose, black bears, and grizzly bears share a common range. Bald eagles, golden eagles, wolves, coyotes, waterfowl, and songbirds also inhabit the forest. Its streams feed the Clarks Fork, Shoshone, Greybull, and Wind rivers of the Missouri River basin. The forest lies among the Wind River and Absaroka Mountain ranges, where vast areas of sheer rock, alpine meadows, and evergreen forests make up the varied and spectacular scenery.

Information Sources, Maps & Access

Two full-color *Shoshone National Forest Maps* (North and South)

are available for 60¢ each along with a free *Wapiti Valley Map/Brochure* and detailed travel information from: Supervisor, Shoshone National Forest, P.O. Box 961, Cody, WY 82414 (307)587–4297. A *Beartooth High Lakes Country Map* (50¢) and *Index of Lakes* (50¢) may be obtained from the same address.

The Shoshone National Forest and Wapiti Valley are reached via U.S. Highways 16, 28T, Alternate 14, 212, and 310. Wyoming routes 296, 120, and 290 also provide access to the forest. Lodging, meals, supplies, guides, and outfitters are available at Wapiti, Pahaska, Meeteetse, Sunshine, Dubois, and Cody. The Beartooth Lakes country services and facilities are available at Red Lodge and Cooke City, Montana.

The Beartooth Highway, between Red Lodge (Montana) and Yellowstone National Park, is considered one of the nation's most spectacular scenic routes and provides access to the High Lakes Plateau in the Shoshone National Forest. Trailheads located off the highway provide access to the remote lakes and high-country wilderness camping areas.

Recreation Areas

Beartooth High Lakes Plateau

The spectacular Beartooth High Lakes Plateau, once the summer hunting grounds of the Mountain Crow and Arapaho Indians, takes in the northernmost portion of the Shoshone National Forest, where it adjoins the 230,000–acre Beartooth Primitive Area in Montana's Custer National Forest on the north. This renowned wilderness fishing and backpacking area embraces a scenic high country of stark, barren crags, ochre-tinted peaks, and ancient rock outcroppings surrounding rolling, boulder-strewn, arcticlike tundra plateaus at 9,000 to 10,000 feet elevation, broken by deep canyons, finger ridges, meadows, and hundreds of remote, blue, rock-bound lakes inhabited by grayling and rainbow, brook, cutthroat, golden, and lake trout and fringed by gnarled, stunted conifers which provide striking examples of krummholz (a German word meaning "crooked wood").

North Absaroka Wilderness

The North Absaroka contains 353,103 acres along the northeastern border of Yellowstone Park. Alpine lakes dot the peaks of this region, which rise to heights of 12,000 feet; fishing varies from good to excellent. Glaciers cap many of the peaks; meadows and forests cover the lower slopes. The Copper Lakes of the Sunlight Basin area offer good fishing for cutthroat and the prized golden trout (up to 20 inches) early and late in the season.

Wapiti Valley

The Wapiti District, the largest of the five Shoshone National Forest districts, encompasses the beautiful Wapiti ("elk") Valley, so named for the elk which abound here, as well as 550,000 acres within the North and South Absaroka Mountains Wilderness. The Shoshone Indians, for whom the forest was named, once used this valley as part of their hunting grounds. The North Fork of the Shoshone River runs through the valley, separating the North Absaroka region from the 679,520 acres of the Washakie Wilderness.

Washakie Wilderness

The Washakie Wilderness, which borders Yellowstone National Park to the southeast, encompasses 679,520 acres of the southern Absaroka Mountains. Its barren, volcanic terrain, sparse forests, and rocky crags offer top-ranked hunting for elk, moose, deer, and black bear. These mountains, like the Yellowstone Plateau, were formed through the alternating flows of lava and buildups of ash beds. Erosion has stripped these mountains of some of their former grandeur; eventually, it will wear them to rubble. If you plan to hike in this high country, wear sturdy shoes, as the rocks are sharp and jagged. It is an eerie country, strewn with the remnants of former forests and plants, fossilized by the repeated lava flows. A few of the tree trunk remains still stand upright near the head of Frontier Creek, where they lived millions of years ago.

Gateways & Accommodations

(For additional gateway listings see "Wind River Range" in this section and "Red Lodge" under "Custer National Forest" in the "Vacation/Lodging Guide.")

Cody—Eastern Gateway to Yellowstone Park

(Pop. 5,200; zip code 82414; area code 307.) Gateway to Shoshone National Forest, the Wapiti Valley, and Yellowstone National Park, this historic frontier town on the North Fork of the Shoshone River at 4,980 feet elevation was founded by Buffalo Bill Cody. Area attractions include the Buffalo Bill Museum and Historical Center (Sheridan Ave. and 8th St.), which includes the Plains Indian Museum, Winchester Museum, and the Whitney Gallery of Western Art; Spirit Mountain Caverns; Buffalo Bill's Pahaska Tepee Hunting Lodge (where he guided the Crown Prince of Russia); Wapiti Ranger Station, the oldest in the nation; and Old Trail Town, a reconstruction of Old Cody (3 miles west of town on U.S. Hwy. 16), which includes a log cabin used as a hideout by Butch Cassidy, historic Plains Indian artifacts, and the grave of Jeremiah Johnson. Scenic sight-seeing flights of Yellowstone National Park, Wapiti Valley, Sunlight Basin and the Absaroka Range, and the Beartooth Plateau are available from: *Wapiti Air Service*, Northfork Star Route, Cody (587–5095). Cody restaurants include: the *Golden Eagle* at 1219 Sheridan Ave. (587–2571); *Green Gables* on U.S. Hwy. 16(587–4640); and *King's Castle* on Old Airport Road (587–2522). Area accommodations: *Best Western Sunset Motor Inn* (rates: $30–34 double), 65 excellent rooms and family units, heated pool, at 1601 8th St. (587–4265); *Best Western Sunrise Motor Inn* (rates: $27–30 double), 35 excellent rooms and family units, at 1407 8th St. (587–5566); *Bill Cody's Ranch Inn* (rates: $32–38 double), 10 cottages in scenic mountain valley operated by Bill and Barbara Cody, dining room, wilderness packhorse trips, float trips, rodeo, cross-country skiing, guided fishing and hunting trips, located 25 miles west of town off U.S. Hwy. 16 to Yellowstone (587–2097); *Blackwater Lodge* (rates: $22–28 double), 16 log cabins on the North Fork of the Shoshone River, dining room, trail rides, 16 miles east of Yellowstone Park entrance on U.S. Hwy. 16 (587–3709); *Colonial Inn* (rates: $24–32

double), 38 excellent rooms, heated pool, on U.S. Hwy. 16 (587–4208); *Goff Creek Lodge* (rates: $26–29 double), 14 rustic log cabins, dining room, fishing, trail rides, in scenic location 10 miles east of Yellowstone Park on U.S. Hwy. 16 (587–3753); *Holiday Inn* (rates: $46 double), 132 excellent rooms and family units, dining room, cocktail lounge, heated pool, in Buffalo Bill Village at 1701 Sheridan Ave. (587–5555); *Pahaska Tepee* (rates: $26–28 double), 48 log cabin units in Wapiti Valley, restaurant, historic lounge, once Buffalo Bill's hunting lodge, located 2 miles east of Yellowstone Park on U.S. Hwy. 16 (587–5536); *Shoshone Lodge* (rates: $24.72 double), 16 rustic log cabins, restaurant, alpine and Nordic skiing at Sleeping Mountain Winter Sports Area, fishing, trail rides, guided trips, rustic Old West lodge with fireplace in scenic location 4 miles east of Yellowstone on U.S. Hwy. 16 (587–4044); *Wapiti Valley Inn* (rates: $23–24 double), 20 comfortable log cabin family units, heated pool, dining room, coffee shop, cocktail lounge, on U.S. Hwy. 16, 18 miles west of Cody (587–3961).

Lodges & Guest Ranches

★★★*Absaroka Mountain Lodge* is located in the heart of the Shoshone National Forest 12 miles east of the eastern entrance to Yellowstone National Park off U.S. 14–16–20. The ranch-type main lodge and log guest cabins are nestled back among the evergreens and aspens near the mouth of Gunbarrel Creek. The guest cabins are of authentic western decor and range from one bed to family-sized units with private baths. The rustic log-paneled main lodge has a stone fireplace and lounge. The dining room at the lodge is renowned throughout the Yellowstone Country for its superb meals and colorful Old West atmosphere. The surrounding highcountry lakes, streams, and alpine meadows of the Absaroka Range are accessible from the lodge by foot trails or horseback. Daily rates (double occupancy): $24–27. Contact: Absaroka Mountain Lodge, Box 7, Cody, WY 82414 (307)587–3963.

★★★*Castle Rock Ranch* is located in the Shoshone National Forest in an area with a variety of scenery from snowcapped mountains, rolling prairie grasslands to lush timbered meadows along cold, sparkling rivers, streams, and lakes. Summer activities center around trail riding and excellent trout fishing. There are two miles of private rivers to fish for brown, cutthroats and rainbows. A short hike to Chukar Lake leads you to more cutthroat trout fishing. Horseback riders can choose a gentle or spirited horse from the ranch's string of 60. The horses are well-trained and mountain-wise and pack horses are suitable for all ages. Guests can mount up with the wranglers and push the cattle from range to pasture. Wilderness trips into the beautiful mountainous and rugged country of northwestern Wyoming are arranged by the ranch via foot or horseback. They are expertly managed and guests are accompanied by qualified guides, wranglers and cooks. The scenery and terrain make the area a haven for hikers, rock hounds and photography buffs. Castle Rock Ranch offers a variety of hunts for elk, mule deer, antelope, big horn sheep, moose and black bear. The nearby town of Cody provides attractions like the American West Historical Center, the Cody night Rodeo, Old Trail Town and the White Water River Float. There is a pool on the ranch's premises, a game room, cookouts and horseshoe games. Trips to Yellowstone National Park can be arranged after arrival. The ranch caters to a limited amount of guests to provide personal attention and true "western" hospitality. Cabins are rustic, but have all the modern conveniences. They all have baths, and a view of the mountains and are only a few steps from the river's edge. Rates include meals, horseback riding, fishing, entertainment and laundry. Rates: One room, double occupancy $38 per day. Other accommodations range from $34–50 a night depending on the type of accommodation and number of people. For further information contact: Castle Rock Ranch, Rt. 2, Southfork, Cody, Wyoming, 82414 (307)587–2076.

★★★*Crossed Sabres Ranch & Yellowstone Wilderness Guides* is a fine family guest resort surrounded by evergreen-blanketed mountains and located just nine miles east of Yellowstone Park in the Shoshone National Forest. Weekly activities include guided tours of the park, visits to local points of historical interest, rodeo nights, cookouts, and float trips down the Shoshone River. A full stable of dependable mounts attended by capable wranglers is on hand for trail rides anytime. An overnight pack trip is also included in your week's stay. For the angler, there are numerous streams and lakes within hiking or riding distance. The best fishing is in June, when hungry trout rise to the bait after ice-out. Accommodations are in comfortable, tree-shaded cabins with modern baths and heating. Weekly adult rates of $275 per person include lodgings, your own horse and tack, overnight pack trip, guided trail rides, float trips, all ranch entertainment, and 3 hearty meals a day. Children's rates are also available. For more information write: Crossed Sabres Ranch, Wapiti, WY 82450 (307)587–3750.

★★★*Elephant Head Lodge*, in the spectacular Wapiti Valley, lies deep within the Shoshone National Forest 11 miles from the east entrance to Yellowstone National Park. Situated at the trailhead leading to an enormous rock formation in the shape of an elephant's head, the lodge is within hiking or riding distance of many other awesome sights. Activities here include fishing the beautiful Shoshone River and nearby mountain streams, wilderness trail rides on horseback, big-game hunting in the fall, backpacking through Yellowstone Park, and river raft trips. Accommodations are in comfortably furnished mountain cabins with private baths and individually controlled heat. Home-cooked meals are served in the western atmosphere of the Elephant Head Dining Room. There's also a lounge with a crackling fire every evening, a rustic bar, and cable TV. Daily rates: $25–34 (single occupancy), $29–34 (double occupancy). For more details write: Elephant Head Lodge, Wapiti, WY 82450 (307)587–3980.

★★★*Grizzly Ranch*, in the rugged and colorful Wapiti Valley, is a fine family guest ranch located halfway between historic Cody and Yellowstone National Park. The surrounding hills and meadows offer ideal terrain for horseback riding, the favorite activity at Grizzly Ranch, and each guest is assigned his own horse and saddle and given as much instruction as necessary by expert wranglers. The more adventurous may want to pack-trip for 5–7 days into the high country of Yellowstone Park or through the primitive reaches of Teton and Shoshone national forests. Fishing is good, too, in the nearby Shoshone River and numerous canyon streams. Other activities include horseshoes, tennis, hiking, and rock-hounding. The ranch also makes a fine base for fall big-game hunts. The ranch house, containing a cozy lounge and dining room, and handsome log guest cabins are surrounded by tall trees and scattered along the banks of Half-Mile Creek. Views of the valley and ridge are superlative from any angle. Each cabin has modern furnishings and a private bath. Rates: $210–280 per person per week, including all meals, riding, and ranch activities, plus the Cody Night Rodeo and a river float trip. All-inclusive pack trips are $65 per person daily in groups of 2 or more. For full details write: Grizzly Ranch, North Fork Route, Cody, WY 82414 (307)587–3966.

★★★★*Rimrock Dude Ranch*, located midway between Cody and Yellowstone National Park, is nestled among tall stands of pine on the banks of Canyon Creek. Long or short trail rides on horses chosen to suit your abilities and preferences cover such scenic spots

as the Absaroka Range, Shoshone National Forest, neighboring canyons and high peaks, and sparkling mountain lakes. Overnight pack trips are also easily arranged, led by experienced guides and wranglers into the Mirror Plateau of Yellowstone Park, the Teton Wilderness, and Shoshone National Forest. The ranch is just 1 mile from the north fork of the Shoshone River, where rainbow and cutthroat trout await the hardy angler. Nearby Buffalo Bill Lake, with trout in the 3–4–pound category, offers fine boat fishing. There's also swimming in the Shoshone or in DeMaris Hot Springs, a warm sulfur pool once used as a health spa by Indian tribes. Or you can take a float trip down some rollicking white-water stretches of the Shoshone. The ranch has lovely guest cabins with private baths, comfortable western decor, stone fireplaces, maid service, and heating facilities for cool weather. Larger families will appreciate spacious cabin accommodations for up to 8 guests. Evening activities include indoor games, square dancing, and the nightly Cody Night Rodeo a short drive away. Three fine meals a day are served in the log-paneled dining room. Daily rates, including horse and tack for each guest, all meals, lodgings, float trips, all ranch activities except pack trips, and free transportation from Cody: $42 per person, single; $37 per person, double occupancy; $35 per person, triple; and $34 per person, 4 to a cabin. Additional guests in parties of 5 or more are $19 daily per person. For more details write: Rimrock Ranch, Cody, WY 82414 (307)587–3970.

★★★*Seven D Ranch* is an ideal family vacation ranch located 50 miles northwest of Cody in the remote and beautiful Sunlight Basin area of the Absaroka Mountains and the Shoshone National Forest. The ranch offers superb fishing in the surrounding alpine lakes and streams, trail rides with cookouts, mountain climbing, hunting for Indian artifacts, backpacking, trapshooting, and overnight packhorse trips into the spectacular Mirror Plateau region of Yellowstone National Park. The remote alpine lakes at 10,000 feet in the Sunlight area hold cutthroat and golden trout. A trained counselor provides special attention to children during their activities. Accommodations for guests and families are arranged in comfortable log cabins with 1–4 bedrooms and private baths. Excellent home-cooked meals with home-grown garden produce and dairy products are served in the rustic main lodge dining room. This outstanding family ranch has been in operation since 1959. Daily American-plan rates (double): $38 per day based on a one-week stay, including lodging, meals, horse and tack for each guest, experienced wranglers, all-day trail rides, fishing, square dances, and cookouts. Rates for full horse-pack trip for 7–12 days for 3–4 persons are $100 per person per day. Pack trips into remote high-country wilderness areas such as the Beartooth Plateau can be arranged with advance notice. Regularly scheduled flights on Northwest Orient, Western, and Frontier Airlines and Amtrak trains provide fast, convenient transportation to Billings, Montana. Frontier Airlines has flights daily to Cody, and ranch vehicles will meet your flight in Billings or Cody. For additional information, contact: John and Lynn Dominick, Seven D Ranch, Box 109, Cody, WY 82414 (307)587–2686 or (307)587–3997.

★★★*Siggins Triangle X Ranch* is located in the beautiful south fork of the Shoshone River valley, 38 miles southwest of Cody, surrounded by the towering volcanic Absaroka Mountains with elevations of 9,000–12,000 feet. In 1914 Ray and Elizabeth Siggins homesteaded the land, and in 1928 the ranch was established as a guest ranch for families. The ranch offers excellent family accommodations and horseback pack trips and backpacking trips in the Washakie Wilderness and Thorofare country of the Teton Wilderness at the headwaters of the Yellowstone River. Other ranch activities include breakfast rides, steak fries, cookouts, horse wrangling, swimming in the ranch pool, and tennis. During the fall, guided high-country hunting trips are available at ranch-operated Thorofare and Ishawoa Mesa base camps for elk, deer, and bighorn sheep. The surrounding alpine lakes and streams hold cutthroat, rainbow, brown, and brook trout. The Thorofare country, a part of the Teton Wilderness area and a summer feeding ground for large herds of elk, awards the photographer and wildlife enthusiast with a real opportunity to see the elk in their natural environment. Quite often deer are seen at lower elevations, and it is not uncommon to see bighorn sheep around timber line. Ranch accommodations consist of rustic 2– and 3–bedroom cabins with baths and the bunkhouse lodge with 1–, 2–, and 3–bedroom units with bath and living room. Ranch rates: $38 daily and $266 weekly per person, with reduced rates for children age 12 and younger. Children under age 5 are free. The ranch is ideally situated for side trips to Yellowstone Park, Old Trail Town, the Irma Hotel and the famous Cherrywood Bar, and the Buffalo Bill Historical Center, which includes the Whitney Gallery of Western Art, Buffalo Bill Museum, Plains Indian Museum, and Winchester Museum. The Cody Municipal Airport is served by Frontier Airlines. Ranch vehicles will meet your plane on request. For additional info contact: Stan and Lila Siggins, Siggins Triangle X Ranch, Cody, WY 82414 (307)587–2031.

★★★★*Valley Ranch*, located 40 miles southwest of Cody in a spectacular, scenic mountain valley of the Absaroka Range of the Wyoming Rockies, is one of the oldest and finest working guest ranches in the West, homesteaded in 1892. The ranch atmosphere is relaxed and easy going . . . with good food, fishing, trail riding, fossil hunting and backpacking—ideal for families. High mountain snow-capped peaks surround Valley, and the South Fork of the Shoshone River, a great trout stream, flows through two miles of the Ranch property. There is also excellent trout fishing in our Ranch Lake, fed by cold-water Spring Creek. Wildlife is abundant (deer, antelope, moose, elk, and various western birds). Family pack trips or fishing trips to the high country can be specially arranged in advance, tailored to the liking of the individual group. Trips are available to Yellowstone and Teton National parks, Cody Nite Rodeo, Buffalo Bill Museum, Plains Indian Museum, Winchester Museum, Whitney Gallery of Western Art, and Old Trail Town. Valley was homesteaded in 1892 by "Buckskin Jenny" and Jim McLaughlin, and established as one of the West's first guest ranches in 1915 by Larry Larom and Winn Brooks (of the famous Brooks Brothers store). For 63 years Valley Ranch has provided quality vacations to

those who seek that "very special place." Each of the authentically rustic cabins has a bathroom, comfortable beds, and cozy wood stove for cool summer nights. Delicious meals are served family-style in the Main Lodge Dining Room. They also have a piano and card room, ping-pong room, and pool room. The original sod-roof homestead cabins still provide picturesque subjects for artists and photographers, as does the old Spring House . . . and Valley spring water is pure and cold. At various times during the season, they have special art workshops (in oil painting, photography, stained glass, etc.). Valley is also a working ranch with horses and livestock as well as farming and ranching activities. You are welcome to join in to help with moving cattle, putting up hay, or wrangling horses. Weekly American plan ranch rates are $304 per person for one bedroom cabin (double occupancy) to $281 per person for a 2–bedroom cabin (5 person occupancy). Deluxe suites with special rates are available in the Brooks House and Little Waldorf. Family scenic and fishing pack trips are $79 per person per day. For additional information contact: Valley Ranch, South Fork Star Route, Cody, WY 82414 (307)587–4661.

Travel Services

High Country Outfitters offers guided overnight packhorse trips in the North Absaroka Wilderness Area and the Mirror Plateau region of Yellowstone National Park from July through September. Trips offer wilderness fishing and wildlife photography for moose, elk, mule deer, bald and golden eagles, and bighorn sheep. Contact: Box 941, Cody, WY 92414 (307)587–3071.

Shoshone River Float Trips down through the red rock canyon area of the Shoshone River are offered by Kit Cody and Glenn Rice. This is a popular family adventure. Contact: Shoshone River Float, Inc., Cody, WY 82414 (307)587–3535.

Wind River Range

This majestic 2¼ million-acre range is one of North America's most spectacular wilderness fishing and backpacking regions. It encompasses portions of the Bridger and Shoshone national forests, the Glacier and Popo Agie primitive areas, part of the Wind River Indian Reservation, the 383,400–acre Bridger Wilderness with its 800 miles of trout streams and 140 square miles of glaciers, the headwaters of the Wind and Green rivers, and some 4,000 granite-bound lakes surrounded by towering spires, barren crags, steep-walled valleys, and alpine meadows inhabited by Rocky Mountain elk, Shiras moose, bear, mule deer, and the nation's largest population of bighorn sheep.

One of the most rewarding and least publicized fishing and backpacking areas in the Wind River region is found in the Shoshone National Forest along the upper stretches of the Big Wind River and its remote wilderness tributaries and headwater lake basins on the east slope of "the Winds" in the Glacier Primitive Area and in the vast Washakie Wilderness—a consolidation of the old South Absaroka Wilderness and Stratified Primitive area, located north of the rustic outfitting center of Dubois, the hub for entry into the vast unpopularized wilderness region.

Information Sources, Maps & Access

A full-color *Shoshone National Forest Map—South Half* (50¢) showing the Wind River area and Glacier and Popo Agie primitive areas as well as detailed vacation travel and recreation information may be obtained from: Supervisor, Shoshone National Forest—Wind River Ranger District, Dubois, WY 82513 (307)455–2466. A full-color *Bridger National Forest Map* (50¢) and *Bridger Wilderness Map Set* (3 maps, $1.50) and detailed vacation and backcountry travel information may be obtained from: District Ranger's Office, Bridger National Forest, Pinedale, WY 82941 (307)367–4326.

The west slope of the Wind River Range and the Bridger Wilderness is reached via Wyoming 28 and U.S. 189 and 187 off Interstate 80. The east slope of the range is reached via Wyoming 28 off U.S. 187 and by U.S. 287 off Interstate 80.

Recreation Areas

Bridger Wilderness

The Bridger Wilderness, named for the yarn-spinning Rocky Mountain trapper and guide Jim Bridger and often referred to as the land of 1,000 lakes, stretches for more than 90 miles south of Gannett Peak along the west slope of the Wind River Range. Gannett Peak crowns the rugged beauty of this formidable wilderness, towering over the valleys of the Green and New Fork rivers, where freezing temperatures, severe electrical storms, and clouds of mosquitoes test the prowess of the fisherman and backpacker. A great deal of the wilderness is trailless and should be explored only by experienced cross-country travelers with topo maps and compass.

The extensive glacial gouging of the last Ice Age has left nearly 1,300 rock-bound lake basins and potholes that dot a benchlike high-country wilderness between 9,000 and 11,000 feet in elevation surrounded by barren tundralike meadows covered by jumbled rocks and glacial debris, jagged glacier-studded peaks, and deep picturesque mountain valleys with numerous cascades and waterfalls. The wilderness has hundreds upon hundreds of lakes clustered beneath the awesome crest of the Great Divide at the headwaters of the Green River, Clear Creek, East Fort River, Big Sandy River, and Trapper, Pole, Boulder, Pine, Halls, and Washakie creeks, which hold brook, rainbow, brown, and cutthroat trout up to trophy weights.

Glacier Primitive Area

Some of the region's finest wilderness fly-fishing and alpine backpacking country is found within the majestic 182,510–acre Glacier Primitive

Area, just south of Dubois along the east slope of the Wind River Range. This little-known, largely trailless area, first explored in 1833 by Captain Bonneville, the legendary fur trader and explorer, is dominated by the towering 13,000–foot peaks along the crest of the Great Divide, culminating at 13,785–foot Gannett Peak (the highest point in the state), flanked on its east face by the massive Bull Lake, Fremont, Dinwoody, Gannett, and Grasshopper glaciers. Beneath the crest of the Divide is an unfolding panorama of glistening blue lakes and torrential streams that twist through deep gorges and sheer cliff-walled valleys toward their confluences with the Wind River.

Popo Agie Primitive Area

The barren, windswept crags and spires, sawlike ridges, moonlike alpine meadows, and granite-bound lakes and turbulent streams of the rugged 70,000–acre Popo Agie Primitive Area, pronounced "Po-Poz'-ee-uh" from the Crow Indian word meaning "beginning of the waters," are located southwest of the old outfitting and supply center of Lander along the eastern slope of the southern peaks of the Wind River Range and offer some of the region's finest high-country wilderness fishing and backpacking opportunities. Legend has it that Butch Cassidy, who frequented Lander in the 1890s during his travels with his "Wild Bunch" from their Hole-in-the-Wall hideout in the Bighorns along the old Outlaw Trail, once cached $70,000 in this area of "the Winds."

Green River Rendezvous

The magnificent evergreen, aspen, and cottonwood-fringed headwaters of the Green and its upper valley beneath the towering green-gray, snowcapped peaks of the Wind River Range were the historic center of operations for the Rocky Mountain Fur Company. The first "Green River Rendezvous" was held here in 1824, organized by Thomas Fitzpatrick, known to the Indians as Broken Hand, Chief of the Mountain Men, and attended by the legendary fur traders and explorers Jedediah Smith, David Jackson, William Sublette, whose massive frame gave rise to his Indian name of Mountain Thunder, and the wily Jim Bridger. The colorful rendezvous, which replaced the fixed trading post and was a forerunner of the cattle roundup, continued as an annual event, attended by as many as a thousand trappers, mountain men, and Indians from across the West, until the end of the free trapping era in the 1840s.

Gateways & Accommodations

Dubois—Gateway to the Glacier & Washakie Wilderness

(Pop. 900; zip code 82513; area code 307.) A historic ranching town on the Wind River and U.S. Hwy. 26–287, Dubois is the major eastern gateway to the Glacier Primitive Area and Washakie Wilderness in the Shoshone National Forest. The nation's largest herd of bighorn sheep inhabits the peaks due north of town. Several guide outfitters and guest ranches offer fishing, hunting, and packhorse trips into the spectacular alpine high country. Area attractions include the state fish hatchery and wildlife exhibit 1 mile west of town. Accommodations: *Branding Iron Motel* (rates: $18–20 double), 22 rooms, west of town on Hwy. 26–287 (455–2446); *Pinnacle Motor Lodge* (rates: $20–22 double), 10 rooms, heated pool, in alpine setting west of town on 26–287 (455–2506); *Red Rock Ranch* (rates: $20–22 double), 16 rooms and family units, trail riding, fishing ¼ mile north of town (455–2337); *Trail's End Motel* (rates: $20–22 double), 22 rooms and family units ½ mile west of town on 26–287 (455–2540); *Wind River Ranch* (rates: $20–22 double), 16 rooms and family units, superb view of the Wind River Range, dining room, guided packhorse trips, fishing, 17 miles west of town on Hwy. 26–287 (455–2500).

Green River—Gateway to Flaming Gorge National Recreation Area (see Utah chapter)

(Pop. 4,200; zip code 82935; area code 307.) Situated at the top of Flaming Gorge Reservoir on Interstate 80. Accommodations: *Coachman Inn Motel* (a Friendship Inn; rates: $26–30 double), 17 rooms, at 470 E. Flaming Gorge Way (875–3681); *Western Motel* (rates: $30–34 double), 32 rooms, at 890 W. Flaming Gorge Way (875–2840).

Lander—Gateway to the Popo Agie Primitive Area

(Pop. 7,100; zip code 82520; area code 307.) Lander is just south of the vast Wind River Indian Reservation on U.S. Hwy. 287. Due east are the alpine lakes and streams of the Wind River Range. Area attractions include Sinks Canyon State Park, Grave of Sacajawea (Indian word for "boat pusher"), who guided Lewis and Clark on their epic journey to the Pacific (7 miles north of town on 287), South Pass gold-rush ghost town (approximately 32 miles south of town on State Hwy. 28, then 2½ miles west), and the Fremont County Pioneer Museum at 630 Lincoln St. Area accommodations: *Best Western Holiday Lodge* (rates: $26–31 double), 33 excellent rooms and family units, at junction of U.S. 287 and State Hwy. 789 (332–2511); *Miner's Delight Restaurant & Inn* (rates: $30 double), in the historic Atlantic City gold-rush ghost town, superb continental cuisine and rooms for dinner guests in old boom-town hotel (no children, except on Sundays), 30 miles southwest of Lander via State Hwy. 28 (call 332–3513 for directions).

Pinedale—Gateway to the Bridger Wilderness

(Pop. 900; zip code 82941; area code 307.) This is a thriving ranching center and jumping-off place for some of the nation's finest high-country fishing, backpacking, and big-game hunting areas. Area attractions include float-fishing trips on the Green River, Father DeSmet Monument, Bridger Wilderness, Pinedale Mountain Winter Sports Area, Gannett Peak at 13,804 feet, and the famous Green River Rendezvous, held the second Sunday of July, commemorating the historic rendezvous of mountain men and Indians at old Fort Bonneville. Accommodations: *Sun Dance Motel* (rates: $21–23 double), 18 comfortable rooms and family units, in the center of town on U.S. Hwy. 187 (367–4336).

Guest Ranches

★★★★*Bitterroot Ranch* is a small family guest ranch in a spectacular valley (7,500–foot altitude) bordered by the 2.4 million-acre Shoshone National Forest and the vast Wind River Indian Reservation. The sprawling ranch terrain and national forest are ideal for trail rides and pack trips; Bitterroot Ranch has a fine selection of well-trained, surefooted horses and ponies for all levels of riding expertise. Careful instruction is available for novices. Fishermen will appreciate the fine trout streams and mountain lakes within easy reach. The East Fork of the Wind River, which flows through ranch property for over a mile, affords good sport on a barbless hook. Owner and host Bayard Fox is an avid fly-fisherman who is always glad to show fellow anglers the local hot spots. In the fall, a small hunting camp in the adjoining forest, accessible only on horseback, is available for hunters. Children will find their own special agenda of activities and accommodations in kids' tepees, copied in sturdy canvas from the authentic Sioux design. Guest cabins, constructed of hand-hewn native logs, are comfortable, cheerfully decorated, and equipped with a modern bath and either electric heat or a wood stove. Several 2–family cabins convert to generous quarters for big families or groups of 8–10 persons. Most cabins are situated to provide maximum seclusion and splendid views of the river and mountains. The main lodge contains a pleasant dining room, kitchen, and a living

room with a piano and stone fireplace. There's also an adults-only sun porch and poolroom with B.Y.O. cocktail hours. Rates, including lodgings, all meals, and daily riding: $315 weekly per person, double occupancy; $315–385 weekly for singles; and $280 weekly for a 3rd or 4th person sharing cabin or tepee accommodations. Pack trips are $10 extra per day. Daily rates average $40–55 per person. For full details write: Bitterroot Ranch, Duncan Route, Dubois, WY 82513 (307)347–3257.

★★★*Highland Meadow Ranch* is located 16 miles northwest of Dubois at the foot of Rams Horn Peak at 8,200 feet elevation near the cutthroat trout waters of Du Noir River—a tributary of the Big Wind River. The surrounding high-country wilderness is an outstanding habitat for elk, bighorn sheep, mule deer and Yellowstone moose. The ranch specializes in expertly guided wilderness pack, fishing, and fall hunting trips high among the peaks, glaciers, streams and remote lakes. Near the main ranch building individual log cabins nestle in the quiet and seclusion of the forest. Recalling the days of the rugged Old West in appearance, the cabins are furnished in modern comfort and luxury. There's western hospitality, a corral of fine riding horses, good food and superb personal service. Summer American plan guest rates are $175/person per week and includes a modern cabin, meals, horses and scenic mountain jeep trips. Pack trip rates are $65/day per person for a party of four. Daily guest cabin rates are $20 for two. For additional information, contact: Highland Meadows Ranch, Dubois, WY 82513 (307)455–2401.

★★*Triangle C Ranch* is located on the Wind River in the Shoshone National Forest. The ranch offers outstanding hospitality and fishing on four miles of private trout waters, trail rides, hiking, and guided fall hunting trips in the Washakie Wilderness. The ranch owners, Jane and Ken Kidraigh, maintain a superb string of mountain horses and take out 3 guided trail rides each day. These scenic high-country rides offer the chance to see elk, mule deer, moose, coyotes, and eagles. They also offer guided pack trips into the surrounding wilderness as well as steak rides and breakfast rides. They will assist you in planning day trips to Grand Teton National Park and Yellowstone as well as float trips down the Snake River. Weekly American plan rates in the rustic guest cabins are $210/person and include 3 hearty family-style meals per day in the Old West ranch dining room and ranch activities—hayrides, trailrides, cookouts, day fishing trips. Overnight guests are welcome. Airport pickup is available from Jackson Hole. For additional information contact: Triangle C Ranch, Dubois, WY 82513 (307)455–2225.

Travel Services

Bridger Wilderness Outfitters offers guided 1–day and 10–day scenic pack trips for fishing, camping, and photography up into the alpine lake country of the Wind River Range. The 10–day group pack trip covers a 50–mile circle in some of the most beautiful areas of the Bridger Wilderness, with instruction in wood lore, western horsemanship, and packing. Everything is supplied except sleeping bags and personal effects. For rates and additional information on fall guided hunting trips, contact: Box 951, Pinedale, WY 82941 (307)367–2747.

Fall Creek Ranch offers guided packhorse and fishing trips in the Bridger Wilderness. Contact: Box 181, Pinedale, WY 82941 (307)367–4649.

Green River Outfitters, with headquarters at Wind River Sporting Goods in Pinedale, offers expertly guided float fishing trips on the famous upper Green and New Fork rivers for rainbow, brown, and brook trout and pack fishing trips to remote lakes and streams in the

heart of the Bridger Wilderness on the west slope of the Wind River Range. Guided river float trips and wilderness fishing trips for rainbow, cutthroat, brook and golden trout are $80/day per person including a hearty steak lunch. For additional information contact: Green River Outfitters, Box 727, Pinedale, WY 82941 (307)367–2416.

Green River Float-Fishing Trips and Bridger Wilderness pack fishing trips are also provided by *Len Benson*, Saratoga 82331 (from Big Piney area); *Robert F. Garrett*, Box 1433, Jackson 83001; *Joe Hicks*, Pinedale 82941; *Harold Lu*, Pinedale 82941; *Richard Miller*, Pinedale 82941; *Lane Pen Eyck*, Pinedale 82941; and *Triangle R Lodge*, Pinedale 82941.

Skinner Bros. Wilderness Pack Trips, in operation since the 1920s, offers first-rate guided packhorse trips and fall hunts in the spectacular Bridger Wilderness. Contact: Skinner Bros., Pinedale, WY 82941 (307)367–4675.

Yellowstone National Park

Yellowstone, our oldest and largest national park, contains within its 2 million acres some of the most spectacular and beautiful fishing, backpacking, and canoeing country in North America, including the headwaters and Black Canyon of the Yellowstone, the Lamar River

and Mirror Plateau region, the remote upper stretches of the Firehole River, the rugged highlands, falls, cascades, canyons, and hot springs of the Gardiner, Madison, and Gibbon rivers, and the Bechler River in the serene Cascade Corner. Few realize that in spite of all its visitors, more than 97% of the park remains in a wilderness state, much of it rarely seen by human eyes.

The Yellowstone region was known to the Indians as the Land of Evil Spirits and the Burning Mountain and was avoided by most of the local tribes, who feared the awesome spouting geysers, thermal springs, and boiling "paint pots." The early trappers reported that Indian guides consistently lost their bearings when they entered the region. The only tribe to live permanently in what is today national park land was the Sheepeaters, a peaceful, cliff-dwelling tribe who hunted the wild sheep of the area and fashioned obsidian arrowheads of such an intricate design that they were also known as the Arrow Makers. The Sheepeaters maintained that their ancestors had lived in the geyser country "from the beginning" and that a large number of their following had been destroyed by a cataclysmic upheaval near the Upper Geyser Basin. An ancient Indian trail, known as the Great Bannock Trail, often used by the early trappers and explorers of Yellowstone (and still visible in places), extended from Henry's Lake in Idaho across the Gallatin Range, eastward through the northern regions of the park, to the Shoshone River and Bighorn Basin.

Famous Yellowstone Lake, the sprawling "lake in the mountains," whose shape was compared by the early explorers to the gnarled hand of an old trapper, is surrounded by dense boreal forests and the high-country wildlands of the snowcapped Absaroka Mountains on the east and the Great Divide and Two Ocean Plateau to the west and south. Yellowstone is the largest lake in North America above 7,500 feet elevation, with a maximum depth of 300 feet and an average depth of 30 feet. Its icy waters, crystal-clear and transparent to great depths, are fed almost entirely by the springs and snowfields of the Absaroka Range. The surface of the lake once stood 160 feet higher than at present, covering an area to the southern base of Mt. Washburn, some 20 miles to the north, and its waters flowed into Heart Lake and the Snake River. The lake's southern outlet was dammed up by glacial ice, and its waters rushed over the eastern base of Mt. Washburn, carving a deep gorge into the lava beds and forming the Yellowstone River.

The clear waters of the lower Yellowstone flow in a northerly direction from Yellowstone Lake through the heavily used Canyon Village vacation area, where the river is paralleled by the Grand Loop Road, past numerous mud pots and hot springs to Upper and Lower falls, where it enters the dazzling shades of yellow, red, orange, brown, and purple of the Grand Canyon, bordered on the east by the wildlands and petrified forests of the Mirror Plateau and on the west by the Washburn Range. The Yellowstone flows down through its rugged 20–mile-long trailless chasm, which reaches a maximum width of 1,500 feet and a depth of 750 feet, past small geysers and hot pools set deep in the canyon floor and the deep, boulder-filled, seldom fished cutthroat pools at Threemile Hole and Sevenmile Hole (reached by a spur route off the Howard Eaton Trail) to the Narrows and it confluence with the Lamar River near Tower Falls. Below Tower Falls the Yellowstone flows through the dark-shaded walls of the Black Canyon into Montana near the park's north entrance at Gardiner.

Information Sources, Maps & Access

For detailed vacation travel and backcountry recreation in Yellowstone—the official park season is May 1 to October 31—and a free

Yellowstone National Park Map/Brochure, contact: Superintendent, Yellowstone National Park, WY 82190 (307)344-7381. A beautiful, full-color *U.S. Geological Survey Yellowstone National Park Shaded-Relief Map* 38 by 48 inches (also available in a topographic edition) is available for $2 from: Distribution Branch, U.S. Geological Survey, Federal Center, Denver, CO 80225. It shows roads and buildings, trails, campgrounds, streams, depth contours of Yellowstone Lake, intermittent streams, cascades and falls, geysers, hot springs, mud pots, springs, lakes and ponds, marshes, contours, and elevations.

Numerous private dude ranches and resorts offer accommodations in national forests bordering Yellowstone, and many of them lead pack trips, hunting trips, fishing expeditions, and ski-touring treks into the park area. For the addresses of these resorts and ranches, see also "Shoshone National Forest" and "Grand Teton National Park & Jackson Hole" in this section.

Yellowstone Park is reached from Idaho via U.S. Highway 191–20; from Montana via U.S. Highways 191, 89, and 212; in Wyoming along U.S. Highways 212, 287–89, and 14–20. Lodging, meals, guides, and supplies are available at West Yellowstone, Gardiner, Cooke City, and Mammoth Hot Springs in Montana; at Ashton, Idaho; and at Cody, Wapiti, Pahaska, Moran, Moose, and Jackson in Wyoming.

Most park roads are open during the official season. The northeast entrance from Red Lodge may be closed early, however, due to snow conditions; be sure to check with the park headquarters on road conditions during winter.

Gateways & Accommodations

For listings, see "Jackson" and "Cody" in this chapter; and "West Yellowstone," "Gardiner," "Cooke City," and "Red Lodge" in the Montana chapter.

Lodges, Inns & Hotels

Yellowstone Park Lodgings. Located through the park, at all major sight-seeing areas, are a variety of hotel and cabin facilities, ranging from economical cottages to luxurious rooms and cabins.

★★*Canyon Village,* the most centrally located of the Yellowstone facilities, is also the newest and biggest. Serviced by a shuttle car linking the cabins and guest service lodge, the village complex encompasses a steak house, dining room, cafeteria, cocktail lounge, gift shop, and travel and information center. Two types of cabins are available. Luxury cabins, located among the trees, are spacious and modern with contemporary furnishings and full baths. Standard cabins have carpeting, modern interiors, and shower baths, and are situated in a forest clearing. Canyon Village is a major motorcoach terminal for Yellowstone tours. Public transportation is also available to neighboring cities. Special activities in the area include wildlife tours of Hayden Valley and the Central Plateau, horseback rides along Cascade Creek, and conducted nature walks. The village is open from early June to early September. Rates: $36–42 for luxury cabins; $24–28 for standard cabins.

★★★*Lake Yellowstone Hotel,* nestled in a grove of lodgepole pines on the northwest shore of the lake, is a charming old inn with a big dining room overlooking the lake, a cocktail lounge, private hotel rooms, and cabins. There are 281 guest units in all, including deluxe, newly remodeled rooms with private baths; carpeted rooms without private baths; standard cabins located next to the hotel; and modern family cabins with communal shower facilities. This area is one of the major motorcoach terminals from which tours of the park leave daily. Public transportation is available from here to peripheral towns. Open early June to late September. Rates: $24–41 for hotel rooms with private bath; $17–21 for rooms with nearby bath; $24–28 for standard cabins; $21–25 for family cabins.

★★★*Mammoth Hot Springs,* located 5 miles from the north entrance to the park, offers both hotel rooms and cabin accommodations. Surrounding this hotel are active reminders of Yellowstone's ever shifting topography—terraces which change daily as travertine deposits create new formations and hot water mixed with carbon dioxide dissolves the old. The Terrace Room, a spacious dining facility, overlooks these fascinating formations. Also on the premises are a cocktail lounge, coffee shop, gift shop, and travel and information desk. Overnight accommodations are available in handsome lodge rooms with full private baths, rooms without baths, standard cabins with carpeting and private showers, or simple and comfortable budget-rate cabins with nearby shower facilities. Stables are located in the area for exploring the Mammoth countryside on horseback. There are also ranger-conducted walks and talks to help you get acquainted with the Yellowstone area. Mammoth Hot Springs is open early June to late September. Rates: $24–28 for hotel rooms with private bath; $17–21 for rooms without private bath; $24–28 for standard cabins; $14–17 for budget cabins.

★★★*Old Faithful Inn* is a large, handsome, log hotel situated near the famous geyser and just a short walk from the Upper Geyser Basin. There are 100 newly remodeled deluxe rooms with bath, 99 standard rooms with full private bath, and 155 carpeted rooms with rest rooms in the hall. The Old Faithful Dining Room offers fine food in pleasant surroundings. A snack shop for quick service is located nearby. Also on the premises are a cocktail lounge, gift shop, and beauty salon. Coach tours leave the hotel daily, or you can see the wonders of the firehole countryside on a twilight tour. The inn is open from early May to early October. Rates: $24–41 for hotel rooms with private bath; $17–24 for hotel rooms with bath nearby; $24–28 for standard cabins; $14–17 for budget cabins.

★★*Old Faithful Snow Lodge* has comfortably furnished, electrically heated cabins with rustic exteriors that complement their wooded setting. Standard cabins are fully modern within and feature wall-to-wall carpeting, writing desks, and baths with shower. Two-family cabins, ideal for large groups, offer a pair of sleeping rooms separated by a half-bath. Shower facilities are nearby. Budget cabins are simply furnished, with automatic heat and hot and cold water. For those who are willing to bring their own linens and towels, budget shelters offer heated comfort at minimal cost. The Old Faithful Snow Lodge has a coffee shop, tap room, and gift shop. Reasonably priced food and drink are available in the nearby cafeteria and Four Seasons Snack Shop. Rates: $24–28 for standard cabins; $23–27 for 2–family units; $14–20 for budget cabins; and $10–16 for budget shelters.

★★*Roosevelt Lodge* is located in a remote section of the park, surrounded by volcanic hills and glacial valleys. Nearby are the petrified forests of Specimen Ridge, the volcanic pinnacles of Tower Fall, and the ancient Bannock Indian Trail. Accommodations here are simple and rustic. "Rough Rider" cabins have old-fashioned pitchers and wash facilities, wood-burning stoves for heat, and a supply of logs. Bath facilities are available. Rustic shelters are furnished with wood stoves, a table, chairs, and bed. You supply your own linens, blankets, and towels. The big, centrally located lodge has a lounge for unwinding in the evenings and a dining room specializing in western-style food. Activities available in the area include horseback rides through rolling sage hills, stagecoach outings in an authentic Concord coach, and regularly scheduled cookouts with sizzling steaks served over an open fire. Roosevelt Lodge is open from early June through August. Rates: $13–19 for cabins; $9–12 for shelters.

All of the above rates are on a daily basis, and depend on the number of guests per unit within the guidelines quoted. For information on any of the above facilities, write: Yellowstone Park Company, Travel Dept., Yellowstone National Park, WY 82190.

Travel Services

Yellowstone Nordic and *Fenwick West Yellowstone Fly-Fishing School*, see "Montana" chapter under Gallatin National Forest for details.

Yellowstone Park Company Guided Trips include winter snowcoach expeditions, ski touring, snowmobiling, and camping. For detailed information and Yellowstone Lake boat and canoe rental info, contact: Yellowstone Park Company, Yellowstone National Park, WY 82190 (307)344–7311.

Yellowstone Park Fly-Fishing Service offers day-long guided fishing trips on the blue-ribbon waters of the Firehole, Madison, and Yellowstone rivers, plus other creeks, lakes, and streams within the national park. Your instructor-guide will help you find where the fish are biting, select the proper lures for attracting local trout, and demonstrate the most effective fly-fishing techniques. Private instruction costs $60 per person per day; group instruction is $45 per person per day. Rates include the services of an instructor-guide for a minimum of 8 hours and basic instruction in fly-fishing. Yellowstone Park Company will provide transportation throughout the day, if needed, at added coat. Half-day rates are also available. For additional information write: Fly-Fishing Service, Yellowstone Park Company, Yellowstone National Park, WY 82190 (307)344–7311.

Yellowstone Wilderness Guides offer expertly guided backpacking, cross-country skiing, and mountaineering trips in Yellowstone's Mirror Plateau Region, Cascade Corner and Pitchstone Plateau, Hellroaring Plateau, and the Gallatin Range. Yellowstone Wilderness Guides also offer trips in the spectacular high country of the Beartooth Mountains Wilderness Area and the North Absaroka Wilderness. For detailed information, schedules, and rates, contact: Yellowstone Wilderness Guides, P.O. Box 446, Red Lodge, MT 59068.

INDEX

NEBRASKA, 254–259

NEVADA, 260–264

NEW MEXICO, 265–280

NORTH DAKOTA, 281–283

OKLAHOMA, 284–288

OREGON, 289–324

ABOUT THE AUTHOR

VAL LANDI was born and raised in Ringwood, New Jersey. He is the author of the highly acclaimed Bantam *Great Outdoors Guide* and a contributor to several of the nation's leading magazines. Mr. Landi now divides his time between New York City and research trips throughout the United States and Canada for his forthcoming traveler's field guide and ecology series.

Everything You Need to Know to Plan an Outdoor Vacation in the U.S. and Canada

THE BANTAM GREAT OUTDOORS VACATION AND LODGING GUIDES
by Val Landi

These easy-to-use regional guides will help you plan every detail of your vacation—how to choose the best vacation spot for you and your family, how to get there, and where to stay when you arrive. Each lodge and resort is rated on the basis of accommodations, facilities, and the area's recreational attractions. The guides are beautifully illustrated with drawings and photos and each contains a detailed, full-color road map of the region.

Order these volumes today:

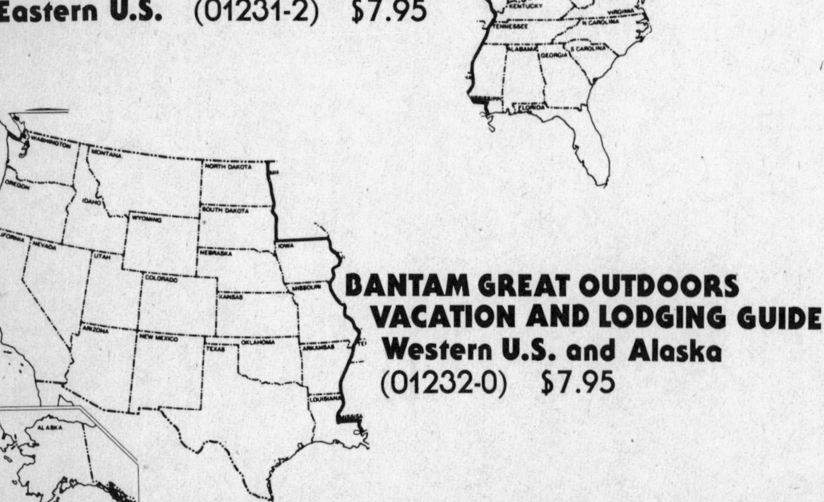

BANTAM GREAT OUTDOORS VACATION AND LODGING GUIDE: Eastern U.S. (01231-2) $7.95

BANTAM GREAT OUTDOORS VACATION AND LODGING GUIDE: Western U.S. and Alaska (01232-0) $7.95

BANTAM GREAT OUTDOORS VACATION AND LODGING GUIDE: Canada (01233-9) $7.95

Also available:
THE BANTAM GREAT OUTDOORS GUIDE TO THE UNITED STATES AND CANADA: The Complete Travel Encyclopedia and Wilderness Guide (01112-X) $12.95
The most comprehensive and authoritative guide to the American wilderness ever published is jammed with 20,000 entries on the history, geography, wildlife, dangers and delights of every notable outdoor area in every state and province in the U.S. and Canada. Beautifully illustrated, with a 16-page color atlas of relief maps of famous vacation areas. The perfect companion to the Vacation and Lodging Guides for planning your outdoor vacation.

To order: Send check or money order for $7.95 for each Vacation and Lodging Guide and $12.95 for each Great Outdoors Guide, plus $1.00 for postage and handling per book to:

Bantam Books
Dept. VL
414 East Golf Road
Des Plaines, Illinois 60016